Seventh Edition

Readings in Canadian History
PRE-CONFEDERATION

Seventh Edition

Readings in Canadian History
PRE-CONFEDERATION

R. DOUGLAS FRANCIS
University of Calgary

DONALD B. SMITH
University of Calgary

NELSON EDUCATION

NELSON / EDUCATION

Readings in Canadian History: Pre-Confederation
Seventh Edition

by R. Douglas Francis and Donald B. Smith

Associate Vice President, Editorial Director:
Evelyn Veitch

Executive Editor:
Anne Williams

Marketing Manager:
Lenore Taylor

Developmental Editor:
Linda Sparks

Permissions Coordinator:
Cindy Howard

Production Editor:
Lara Caplan

Copy Editor:
Karen Rolfe

Proofreader:
Kate Revington

Indexer:
Jin Tan

Production Coordinator:
Ferial Suleman

Design Director:
Ken Phipps

Cover Design:
Andrew Adams

Compositor:
Interactive Composition Corporation

Printer:
Webcom

Library and Archives Canada Cataloguing in Publication

Readings in Canadian history / [edited by] R. Douglas Francis, Donald B. Smith.—7th ed.

Includes bibliographical references and index.
Contents: [v. 1]. Pre-Confederation—[v. 2]. Post-Confederation.

ISBN 0-17-641536-X (v. 1).—
ISBN 0-17-641537-8 (v. 2.)

1. Canada—History—Textbooks.
I. Francis, R. D. (R. Douglas), 1944–
II. Smith, Donald B., 1946–

FC165.R42 2005   971
C2005-905052-7

For information about the photographs featured on the cover, see the Photo Credits (page 584).

CONTENTS

PREFACE ... ix

Topic One
The First Nations and European Contact ... 1

Article One
Children of Gluskap: Wabanaki Indians on the Eve of the European Invasion ... 4
Harold E.L. Prins

Article Two
The French Presence in Huronia: The Structure of Franco–Huron Relations in the First Half
of the Seventeenth Century ... 23
Bruce G. Trigger

Article Three
To See Ourselves as the Other's Other: Nlaka'pamux Contact Narratives ... 47
Wendy C. Wickwire

Topic Two
Women and the Fur Trade ... 61

Article Four
"Women in Between": Indian Women in Fur Trade Society in Western
Canada ... 64
Sylvia Van Kirk

Article Five
"A Most Important Chain of Connection": Marriage in the Hudson's
Bay Company ... 76
Heather Rollason Driscoll

Topic Three
Law and Society in New France ... 95

Article Six
Native Sovereignty and French Justice in Early Canada ... 98
John A. Dickinson

Article Seven
Violence, Marriage, and Family Honour: Aspects of the Legal Regulation of Marriage
in New France ... 112
André Lachance and Sylvie Savoie

Topic Four
Acadia ... 131

Article Eight
The Golden Age: Acadian Life, 1713–1748 ... 134
Naomi Griffiths

Article Nine
Imperial Transitions ... 145
Elizabeth Mancke

Topic Five
Disease as a Factor in Imperial Conflict ... 165

Article Ten
Biological Warfare in Eighteenth-Century North America: Beyond Jeffery Amherst ... 167
Elizabeth A. Fenn

Article Eleven
Microbes and Muskets: Smallpox and the Participation of the Amerindian Allies
of New France in the Seven Years' War ... 188
D. Peter MacLeod

Topic Six
The Conquest and Its Aftermath ... 203

Article Twelve
The Battle of Quebec: A Reappraisal ... 206
W.J. Eccles

Article Thirteen
A Change in Climate: The Conquest and the *Marchands* of Montreal ... 213
José Igartua

Article Fourteen
The Fall of New France ... 227
Allan Greer

Topic Seven
The Impact of the American Revolution on the Maritime Colonies ... 235

Article Fifteen
The American Revolution and Nova Scotia Reconsidered ... 238
George A. Rawlyk

Article Sixteen
The Family in Exile: Loyalist Social Values after the Revolution ... 248
Ann Gorman Condon

Topic Eight
Upper Canada and the War of 1812 ... 257

Article Seventeen
Reluctant Warriors: British North Americans and the War of 1812 ... 260
E. Jane Errington

Article Eighteen
His Majesty's Indian Allies: Native Peoples, the British Crown and the War of 1812 ... 268
Robert S. Allen

Article Nineteen
"Of Slender Frame and Delicate Appearance": The Placing of Laura Secord in the Narratives of Canadian Loyalist History ... 281
Cecilia Morgan

Topic Nine
The Rebellions of 1837 in the Canadas ... 295

Article Twenty
From Folklore to Revolution: Charivaris and the Lower Canadian Rebellion of 1837 ... 298
Allan Greer

Article Twenty-One
The Rebellion of 1837 in Upper Canada ... 313
Colin Read

Topic Ten
Social History of British North America ... 331

Article Twenty-Two
The Riddle of Peggy Mountain: Regulation of Irish Women's Sexuality on the Southern Avalon, 1750–1860 ... 334
Willeen Keough

Article Twenty-Three
The Feminization of Teaching in British North America and Canada 1845–1875 ... 360
Alison Prentice

Article Twenty-Four
Dry Patriotism: The Chiniquy Crusade ... 372
Jan Noel

Topic Eleven
Labour in British North America ... 385

Article Twenty-Five
Unfair Masters and Rascally Servants? Labour Relations among Bourgeois, Clerks, and Voyageurs in the Montréal Fur Trade, 1780–1821 ... 387
Carolyn Podruchny

Article Twenty-Six
Class Conflict on the Canals of Upper Canada in the 1840s ... 408
Ruth Bleasdale

Topic Twelve
Communities in British North America ... 431

Article Twenty-Seven
Gender Ideology and Black Women as Community-Builders in Ontario, 1850–70 ... 434
Shirley J. Yee

Article Twenty-Eight
The Orange Order and Social Violence in Mid-Nineteenth-Century Saint John ... 447
Scott W. See

Article Twenty-Nine
Reciprocal Work Bees and the Meaning of Neighbourhood ... 464
Catharine Anne Wilson

Topic Thirteen
Rupert's Land and the Red River Colony ... 487

Article Thirty
The Flock Divided: Factions and Feuds at Red River ... 490
Frits Pannekoek

Article Thirty-One
The Métis and Mixed-Bloods of Rupert's Land before 1870 ... 497
Irene M. Spry

Topic Fourteen
The Pacific Coast ... 515

Article Thirty-Two
Tracing the Fortunes of Five Founding Families of Victoria ... 518
Sylvia Van Kirk

Article Thirty-Three
Hardy Backwoodsmen, Wholesome Women, and Steady Families: Immigration and the
Construction of a White Society in Colonial British Columbia, 1849–1871 ... 537
Adele Perry

Topic Fifteen
Confederation ... 551

Article Thirty-Four
Confederation and Quebec ... 554
A.I. Silver

Article Thirty-Five
Confederation: The Untold Story ... 567
Paul Romney

CONTRIBUTORS ... 582

PHOTO CREDITS ... 584

INDEX ... 585

PREFACE

In this seventh edition of our two-volume *Readings in Canadian History*, as in previous editions, our concern has been to provide a collection of articles suitable for introductory Canadian history tutorials. This has meant selecting topics related to the major issues that are explored in such history courses, and providing valuable readings of a general nature. We have included articles that deal with the various regions of the country and, whenever possible, those that reflect new research interests among Canadian historians. Consequently, we have changed some of the readings. Unfortunately, because of space limitations, the addition of new articles meant that several worthwhile readings in the sixth edition had to be dropped. This new edition, however, will better meet the needs of introductory students in Canadian history today.

This volume includes two or three selections on each of fifteen topics, thereby affording instructors flexibility in choosing readings. Short introductions to each topic set the readings in a historical context and offer suggestions for further reading. We have also provided a series of questions in the introductions to each topic to guide students in their reading of the articles and as a basis for discussion in tutorials. It is our hope that this reader will contribute to increased discussion in tutorials, as well as complement course lectures and, where applicable, textbooks. In particular, *Readings in Canadian History* can be used effectively in conjunction with the textbooks *Origins: Canadian History to Confederation*, 5th ed. (Toronto: Thomson Nelson, 2004), and *Destinies: Canadian History since Confederation*, 5th ed. (Toronto: Thomson Nelson, 2004), both by R. Douglas Francis, Richard Jones, and Donald B. Smith. As a new feature for this edition, we have provided for each topic weblinks to primary sources on the World Wide Web. We have also provided suggestions of appropriate secondary sources.

Important reference works for students preparing essays and reports on different aspects of Canadian history include *Dictionary of Canadian Biography*, vols. 1–15, with additional volumes in preparation (Toronto: University of Toronto Press, 1966–); *Historical Atlas of Canada*, vols. 1–3 (Toronto: University of Toronto Press, 1987–1993); and the annotated bibliographical guides by M. Brook Taylor, ed., *Canadian History: A Reader's Guide*, vol. 1, "Beginnings to Confederation" (Toronto: University of Toronto Press, 1994); and Doug Owram, ed., *Canadian History: A Reader's Guide*, vol. 2, "Confederation to the Present" (Toronto: University of Toronto Press, 1994). *The Oxford Companion to Canadian History* (Don Mills, ON: Oxford University Press, 2004), edited by Gerry Hallowell, is also very useful.

ACKNOWLEDGMENTS

We wish to thank the following individuals who offered valuable suggestions for changes to the seventh edition of *Readings in Canadian History: Pre-Confederation*: Carolyn Podruchny of York University, Graham Broad of the University of Western Ontario, Paige Raibmon of the University of British Columbia, Jacqueline Gresko of Douglas College, Terry L. Chapman of Medicine Hat College, and Barbara Bessamore of the University College of the Fraser Valley.

In preparing past editions of the readers, we and the publisher sought advice from a number of Canadian historians. Their comments were generously given and greatly improved the original outlines of the collections. We would like to thank, in particular, Douglas Baldwin of Acadia University, Robert A. Campbell of Capilano College, Roger Hall of the University of Western Ontario, and Brent McIntosh, of the North Island College for their valuable reviews of the fifth edition. Thanks, too, for comments on earlier editions to Douglas Baldwin of Acadia University, Olive Dickason of the University of Alberta, Carol Wilton-Siegel of York University, John Eagle of the University of Alberta, Roger Hall of the University of Western Ontario, Hugh Johnston of Simon Fraser University, and Wendy Wallace and Paul Whyte of North Island College. Many other individuals made valuable suggestions; we are indebted to John Belshaw of the University of the Cariboo, Margaret Conrad of Acadia University, Beatrice Craig of the University of Ottawa, Chad Gaffield of the University of Ottawa, Marcel Martel of Glendon College — York University, Thomas Socknat of the University of Toronto, Robert Sweeny of Memorial University, Duncan McDowell of Carleton University, and Peter Ward of the University of British Columbia.

Heartfelt thanks also go to Anne Williams, Rebecca Rea, Linda Sparks, and Lara Caplan of Thomson Nelson, for their help and constant encouragement toward the completion of this seventh edition, and to Karen Rolfe, who copy edited the book. A special thanks goes to David Smith, who researched the World Wide Web for sources, particularly primary sources, appropriate for each topic. Finally, we wish to thank those Canadian historians who consented to let their writings be included in this reader. Their ideas and viewpoints will greatly enrich the study and appreciation of Canadian history among university and college students taking introductory courses in Canadian history.

Douglas Francis
Donald Smith
Department of History
University of Calgary

Topic One
The First Nations and European Contact

Captain Bulgar, Governor of Assiniboia and the Chiefs and Warriors of the
Chippewa Tribe of Red Lake. Watercolour by Peter Rindisbacher, 1823.
Gift-giving ceremonies accompanied First Nations negotiations with
Europeans as shown in this council in the Red River, 1823.

The Europeans who came to North America looked upon it as an empty continent, open for settlement. In reality, the First Nations claimed and inhabited almost every part of the "New World," from the Gulf of Mexico to the Arctic coast, from the Atlantic to the Pacific. At the time of European contact, more than 50 First Nations groups lived within the borders of what is now Canada.

In the pre-European period, there was neither a common designation for the country nor a common name for the native inhabitants. The First Nations owed their allegiance to their family, their band, their village, their community, and — in the case of several nations — their confederacy. But they had no concept of a pan-Indian identity. Each group spoke its own language and regarded its own members as "the people." This lack of a perceived common identity contributed to the First Nations' failure to resist the Europeans. Other factors included the reliance of some First Nations groups on European manufactured trade goods, the fur-trade rivalries, the colonial wars, and the catastrophic drop in population that resulted from exposure to European diseases.

Anthropologist Harald Prins in "Children of Gluskap: Wabanaki Indians on the Eve of the European Invasion," looks at the First Nations of what are now the Maritime provinces and northern New England. In "The French Presence in Huronia: The Structure of Franco–Huron Relations in the First Half of the Seventeenth Century," anthropologist Bruce Trigger traces the fortunes of the Hurons, one of the First Nations groups that came into the closest contact with French fur traders in the 17th century. Historian Wendy Wickwire examines accounts of the first meetings between the Nlaka'pamux, the Native people of what is now south-central British Columbia. The fur traders referred to the Nlaka'pamux, who speak a common language, as the "Thompsons," after the major river in their territory.

These three articles raise many important questions. How did the Wabanaki, for example, envision their world before European contact? What was their system of political organization on the eve of the newcomers' arrival? Why did the Hurons' contact with the French have such a dramatic effect on their society? What do the oral traditions of the Nlaka'pamux add to our understanding of the initial contact between the First Nations and the Europeans in what is now British Columbia?

Diamond Jenness's dated *Indians of Canada* (Ottawa: King's Printer, 1932; numerous editions since) must be supplemented by Olive Patricia Dickason, *Canada's First Nations: A History of Founding Peoples from Earliest Times*, 3rd ed. (Toronto: Oxford University Press, 2002); Paul Mogocsi, ed., *Aboriginal Peoples of Canada: A Short Introduction* (Toronto: University of Toronto Press, 2002); and Arthur J. Ray, *I Have Lived Here Since the World Began: An Illustrated History of Canada's Native People* (Toronto: Lester Publishing Limited, 1996 [rev. ed. 2005]). Alan D. McMillan and Eldon Yellowhorn have written a useful survey, *First Peoples in Canada* (Vancouver: Douglas and McIntyre, 2004). A good collection of articles on Canada's Native peoples, edited by R. Bruce Morrison and C. Roderick Wilson, is *Native Peoples: The Canadian Experience*, 3rd ed. (Don Mills, ON: Oxford University Press, 2004). Anthropologist Alice B. Kehoe provides an overview in her *North American Indians: A Comprehensive Account*, 2nd ed. (Englewood Cliffs, NJ: Prentice-Hall, 1992). Robert McGhee's *Ancient Canada* (Ottawa: Canadian Museum of Civilization, 1989) reviews what is currently known of Canada's First Nations and Inuit before the arrival of the Europeans.

A good introduction to the subject of early French–Aboriginal relations in the Americas remains Olive Patricia Dickason's *The Myth of the Savage and the Beginnings of French Colonialism in the Americas* (Edmonton: University of Alberta Press, 1984). Other useful introductions include Alfred G. Bailey's older study, *The Conflict of European and Eastern Algonkian Cultures, 1504–1700*, 2nd ed. (Toronto: University of Toronto Press, 1969 [1937]); the short booklet by

Bruce Trigger entitled *The Indians and the Heroic Age of New France*, Canadian Historical Association, Historical Booklet no. 30, rev. ed. (Ottawa: CHA, 1989), and his *Natives and Newcomers: Canada's "Heroic Age" Reconsidered* (Montreal/Kingston: McGill-Queen's University Press, 1985); and the first chapter, entitled "Native Peoples and the Beginnings of New France to 1650," in John A. Dickinson and Brian Young, *A Short History of Quebec*, 2nd ed. (Toronto: Copp Clark Pitman, 1993), pp. 2–26. For specific information on the Huron, see Conrad Heidenreich, *Huronia: A History and Geography of the Huron Indians, 1600–1650* (Toronto: McClelland and Stewart, 1971); and Bruce G. Trigger, *The Huron: Farmers of the North*, 2nd ed. (Fort Worth, TX: Holt, Rinehart and Winston, 1990). An interesting popular account of early First Nations–European contact is Robert McGhee's *Canada Rediscovered* (Ottawa: Canadian Museum of Civilization, 1991). Useful maps appear in R. Cole Harris, ed., *Historical Atlas of Canada*, vol. 1, *From the Beginning to 1800* (Toronto: University of Toronto Press, 1987).

Students interested in pursuing the subject further should consult Cornelius Jaenen, *Friend and Foe: Aspects of French–Amerindian Cultural Contact in the Sixteenth and Seventeenth Centuries* (Toronto: McClelland and Stewart, 1976); Bruce Trigger, *Natives and Newcomers: Canada's "Heroic Age" Reconsidered* (Montreal/Kingston: McGill-Queen's University Press, 1985); and Denys Delâge, *Bitter Feast: Amerindians and Europeans in the American Northeast, 1600–64*, translated from the French by Jane Brierley (Vancouver: University of British Columbia Press, 1993). A model study of ecological history in the early European contact period is William Cronon's *Changes in the Land: Indians, Colonists, and the Ecology of New England* (New York: Hill and Wang, 1983). For valuable secondary studies on early European–First Nations contact in what is now British Columbia see the bibliographical suggestions for Topic Fourteen: The Pacific Coast.

The Europeans' early attitudes to the question of Aboriginal sovereignty are reviewed in Brian Slattery's "French Claims in North America, 1500–59," *Canadian Historical Review* 59 (1978): 139–69, and W.J. Eccles's "Sovereignty-Association, 1500–1783," *Canadian Historical Review* 65 (1984): 475–510. Leslie C. Green and Olive Dickason review the ideology of the European occupation of the Americas in *The Law of Nations and the New World* (Edmonton: University of Alberta Press, 1989).

WEBLINKS

Canada's First Nations: European Contact
http://www.ucalgary.ca/applied_history/tutor/firstnations/contact.html

Contains European contact narratives from the perspective of Aboriginal peoples from each geographic region of Canada.

Canada Heirloom Series: Canada's Native Peoples
http://collections.ic.gc.ca/heirloom_series/volume2/volume2.htm

A detailed illustrated history of First Nations in Canada and their cultures.

Atlas of Canada: Aboriginal Peoples circa 1630, 1740, and 1823
http://atlas.gc.ca/site/english/maps/historical/aboriginalpeoples

Interactive maps detailing the changes in distribution of First Nations in Canada prior to the creation of Indian reserves.

Oneida Indian Nation — Culture & History
http://oneida-nation.net/historical.html

Describes the culture of the Oneida people and contains many pictures of their cultural artifacts.

Champlain Society
http://link.library.utoronto.ca/champlain/search.cfm?lang=eng

The digital collections of the Champlain Society contain numerous early primary source accounts of European contact with the First Nations, including Samuel de Champlain's voyages in New France. Browse the database by subject, and select for example, "Canada — Discovery and exploration," "New France — Discovery and exploration," or "Northwest, Canadian — History — Sources."

The Jesuit Relations
http://puffin.creighton.edu/jesuit/relations/

Translated and transcribed versions of *The Jesuit Relations and Allied Documents*, a very important source of knowledge of the history of New France and interactions between First Nations and emigrated settlers.

Article One

Children of Gluskap: Wabanaki Indians on the Eve of the European Invasion

Harald E.L. Prins

The native people of northern New England and the Maritime Provinces originally referred to their homeland as Ketakamigwa (the big land on the seacoast).[1] The area was thought of as the eastern part of a large island. This island was the earth as they knew it.[2] They referred to it as "top land," surrounded by the "great salt water." It was imagined as the center of a horizontally stratified universe, crowned by a sky-world where the spirits of the dead lived on as stars. Below was the netherworld, the realm of hostile spirits appearing in reptile form. A mysterious life force known as Ketchiniweskwe (great spirit) was thought to govern this universe.[3]

As inhabitants of the region where the skies first turn light in the morning, the native people of the northeastern coastal area were traditionally known as Wabanakiak (the people of the dawn).[4] They believed themselves to be the children of Gluskap, a primordial giant creature who came into being somewhere in the Northeast "when the world contained no other man, in flesh, but himself."[5] The meaning of his name is not certain and is sometimes translated as "good man," "the liar," or as "man out of nothing."[6]

Source: Reprinted from in *American Beginnings: Exploration, Culture, and Cartography in the Land of Norumbega*, edited by Emerson W. Baker, Edwin A. Churchill, Richard D'Abate, Kristine L. Jones, Victor A. Konrad, and Harald E.L. Prins by permission of the University of Nebraska Press. © 1994 by the University of Nebraska Press.

As Gluskap's children, the Wabanakis have been the inhabitants of Ketakamigwa ever since time began. Their descendents today include the people belonging to the Abenaki, Penobscot, Passamaquoddy, Maliseet, and Micmac tribes. Roaming through their homeland, the original Wabanakis became thoroughly familiar with all the natural features of the landscape, knowing the precise location of each river, lake, cape, and mountain. As hunters, fishers, and gatherers, they took regular stock of the available resources in their habitat and knew in great detail "what the supply of each resource was: deer, moose, beaver, fur-bearers, edible birds, berries, roots, trees, wild grasses. They knew the districts where each was to be found when wanted and, roughly, in what quantities."[7]

Of course, such ecological intimacy was possible only on the basis of a thorough geographic understanding of the immediate environment. But to what extent the Wabanakis' knowledge extended to territories beyond their tribal boundaries remains unclear.[8] It appears that they were familiar with territories as far south as the Hudson River, knew the area west until the St. Lawrence River, and could find their way north to Newfoundland, perhaps even beyond.

HISTORICAL ECOLOGY OF WABANAKI HABITAT

Until the end of the Ice Age about twelve thousand years ago, no human occupied the region now known as New England and the Maritime Provinces. However, when the glaciers retreated, small bands of Paleo-Indians moved into the tundras, preying on big game such as the mastodon, mammoth, musk-ox, and, most of all, large herds of grazing caribou. A few material remains, including flint spearpoints, knives, and scrapers have been found at their ancient camping places and kill sites at locations such as Debert, Munsungun, and Aziscohos lakes.[9] With climatic warming, the tundras of these Paleo-Indian hunting bands transformed gradually into a woodland habitat. The emerging woodlands represented a rich mosaic of tree stands with widely varying compositions. Environmental conditions initially favored white pine, followed by birch, oak, and hemlock. About five thousand years ago, a modern ecological system developed, with warm summers and cold winters marked by up to five months of snow-covered ground. Northern hardwoods such as maple, elm, ash, and beech appeared in the forests, followed later by spruce. Some of these trees, in particular the white pine, were enormous in dimension, measuring up to 5 feet in diameter and reaching more than 150 feet in height.

Broken by swamps, lakes, and ponds, these enormous territories have been drained by several major river systems since the end of the Ice Age. The 240-mile-long Penobscot, for example, collects water of 322 streams and 625 lakes and ponds, draining a total area of 7,760 square miles. The remainder of the territory is drained by the Restigouche, Miramichi, St. John, St. Croix, Kennebec, Androscoggin, Saco, and several other rivers.[10] Typical for this woodlands habitat, which became the homeland of the Wabanakis, is its thriving wildlife, traditionally its abundance of white-tailed deer along with moose and caribou. In addition, black bear, wolves, raccoons, red foxes, lynxes, bobcats, fishers, martens, otters, and skunks have long prospered here, as have rodents like beavers, muskrats, hares, and porcupines. Inland waters, at least seasonally, have formed the natural environment of fish such as salmon, trout, sturgeon, bass, smelt, and alewives; marine life at the coast includes not only an abundance of lobsters and shellfish (in particular, clams and oysters) but also sea mammals such as seals, porpoises, and whales (fig. 1.1). For thousands of years, multitudes of water birds have flocked to the area, again mostly seasonally — loons, ducks, cormorants, herons, geese, and swans. Pheasants, partridges, pigeons, grouse, and turkeys share in the bounty of the land along with hawks, majestic eagles, and birds of prey.

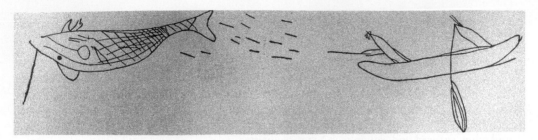

1.1. Micmac petroglyph at Kejimkujik Lake, depicting hunters lancing a large fish. In Garrick Mallery, "Picture-Writing of the American Indians," *Tenth Annual Report of the Bureau of Ethnology to the Secretary of the Smithsonian, 1888–1889*, 1893, p. 531.

The presence of the Wabanakis in this rich and expansive habitat affected not only the animals they hunted but also the landscape itself. Like many other native groups, the Wabanakis periodically burned the land to improve its natural productivity and aid in hunting. For instance, in the valley of the Penobscot River, "the ground is plaine, without Trees or Bushes, but full of long Grasse, like unto a pleasant meadow, which the Inhabitants doe burne once a yeere to have fresh feed for their Deere."[11]

THE ALNANBIAKS: THE REAL PEOPLE

The following description of the Wabanakis is an ethnohistorical composite, based on information winnowed from an array of archaeological, oral traditional, historical documentary, and ethnographic sources. As an assemblage, it reconstructs their culture as it existed when they first encountered Europeans on their shores. At this time, there may have been some thirty thousand Wabanakis living in northern New England and the Maritime Provinces.[12] They all spoke closely related languages or dialects belonging to the larger Algonquian family. Generally, these people referred to their own kinfolk as the Alnanbiaks, the Ulnooks, or some other term to express the idea of "real people" or "truly humans." These Wabanakis were divided into several major ethnic groups, also known as nations or tribes. Members of each particular ethnic group shared a territorial range and could be distinguished from the members of other groups primarily by a limited set of cultural features, including obvious identifications such as defined styles of dress and speech. The various Wabanaki groups maintained close relations, which allowed them to cope with mutual conflict resulting from intertribal competition for valued resources in their territories.[13]

In the early seventeenth century, French visitors to the region reported that the Wabanakis were divided into three such major groupings from northeast to southwest: the Souriquois, Etchemins, and Armouchiquois. Later these ethnonyms, as first recorded by Samuel de Champlain, were generally replaced by the terms Micmac, Maliseet-Passamaquoddy, Penobscot, and Abenaki (fig. 1.2). Although they were all linked to each other directly or indirectly by ties of kinship and friendship, they formed distinctive bands ranging in size from as few as fifty members to more than one thousand. These bands were formed primarily on the basis of voluntary association between related kin groups. Although individual status differences did exist, the social structure of these tribal communities was fundamentally egalitarian.

Accordingly, their political organization was based on democratic principles, and decisions concerning the commonweal were based on consensus among the members. Their chiefs, known as sagamores, were leaders who were recognized as first among equals. "They have

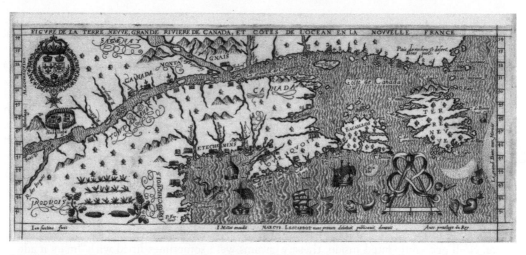

1.2. Extract from Marc Lescarbot, *Figure de la Terre Neuve, grand riviere de Canada, et côtes de l'ocean en la Nouvelle France,* in his *Histoire de la Nouvelle France,* 1609. Courtesy of Library and Archives Canada, NMC 97952.

Sagamores, that is, leaders in war; but their authority is most precarious. . . . . The Indians follow them through the persuasion of example or of custom, or of ties of kindred and alliance."[14] Responsible for the well-being and general security of their communities, these Wabanaki sagamores presided over the warriors. One such chieftain was Chief Mentaurmet, the sagamore of Nebamocago, the largest of three Wabanaki villages in the Sheepscot River valley. When a party of strangers arrived, Chief Mentaurmet received them, accompanied by "about forty powerful young men stationed around [his wigwam] like a bodyguard, each one with his shield, his bow and arrows upon the ground in front of him."[15]

Under leadership of these sagamores, the bands usually moved seasonally within their own districts, from their particular hunting areas to their favourite fishing, clamming, sealing, and fowling sites. Dispersing in small family groups during the fall, bands rejoined in the spring, usually near rapids or falls where they lived on the basis of an abundance of spawning fish. At these tribal gatherings, sometimes many hundreds of people assembled at one site, exchanging information, making new friendships, finding spouses for their children, and engaging in barter.

In charge of the collective pursuit of subsistence, allied sagamores made formal agreements with each other about territorial divisions within each tribal range. "These sagamies divide up the country and are nearly always arranged according to bays or rivers."[16] The territorial arrangements between the chieftains, each with his own following, enabled the kin groups to optimally exploit the ecological diversity of their allocated territory. These were usually situated along tributaries of the various rivers such as the Kennebec or Penobscot or in bays such as Passamaquoddy. This way, regional bands could carefully adjust their food-collecting strategies to the seasonal rhythms of resident game animals, fish runs, and plant growth cycles without running into conflict with their neighbors.[17]

MATERIAL CULTURE

As a Stone Age people, the Wabanakis tapped into the ever-shifting storehouse of nature for all their immediate supplies. Using primarily raw materials such as stone, bone, wood, and leather, they fabricated most of their own tools and weapons, including wooden bows and arrows, flint knives and scrapers, stone axes, bone fishhooks, long spears, and wooden clubs, as well as bark baskets, basswood fiber nets, rawhide snares, and traps. For example, bows were made of spruce or rock maple and were then polished with flaked stones or oyster shells and strung with moose sinew. Arrow shafts were made of white ash or young alders fitted with eagle feathers as flight-stabilizers and tipped with bone or flint points. Tribesmen fashioned lances from beech wood, equipping them with a sharply pointed moose bone, and crafted large cedar shields for protection.[18]

For winter travel, the Wabanakis used snowshoes made of white ash or beech, corded with leather thongs. To transport goods over the snow and ice, they used toboggans. As soon as the rivers became ice-free in the spring, they turned to their lightweight birch-bark canoes, which could seat as many as six or seven persons. Sometimes, these boats were made of spruce bark or even moose hide.[19] Especially on long-distance journeys, their seaborne craft were occasionally equipped with mast and sail, "which was . . . of bark but oftener of a well-dressed skin of a young Moose."[20]

Tree bark (white birch, as well as spruce) was used not only for the Wabanakis' canoes but also for covering their lodges. In addition to bark, they also used animal skins or woven mats as cover. Well accommodated inside, these wigwams were sometimes lined with "mats made of Rushes painted with several colours."[21] For added warmth, the Wabanakis used deerskins to line their winter quarters. Hemlock twigs or balsam fir needles usually covered the wigwam floor, on top of which were mats, hides, or soft sealskins, all spread around the central fireplace. In addition to the conical wigwam, which typically served as a one-family dwelling, the Wabanakis also built large communal or ceremonial lodges, sometimes measuring over one hundred feet long and thirty feet broad. The great wigwam at Nebamocago in the Sheepscot Valley, for example, could seat "fully eighty people"[22] (fig. 1.3).

Although the Wabanakis were familiar with pottery (since about three thousand years earlier), more popular were the many different types of birch-bark containers, which were "sowed with threads from Spruce [spruce] or white Cedar-roots, and garnished on the outside with flourisht works, and on the brims with glistering quills taken from the Porcupine, and dyed, some black, others red." They also made "dishes, spoons, trayes wrought very smooth and neatly out of the knots of wood, [and] baskets, bags, and matts woven with Sparke, bark of the Line-Tree [bass wood?] and Rushes of several kinds, dyed as before, some black, blew, red, yellow, [as well as] bags of Porcupine quills, woven and dyed also."[23]

TRADITIONAL HUNTERS, FISHERS, AND GATHERERS

Until the period of European contact in the sixteenth and early seventeenth centuries, the traditional Wabanaki mode of subsistence based on hunting, fishing, and gathering persisted in the territories east of the Kennebec River. In aboriginal northeastern North America, this river formed the northern boundary of an indigenous horticulture complex, which had originated in the highlands of Meso America some four thousand years ago.[24]

Beyond this ecological boundary, climatic conditions did not favor an indigenous Neolithic revolution. Accordingly, longstanding food-collecting strategies persisted among eastern Wabanaki groups identified as Etchemin (Maliseet-Passamaquoddy) and Souriquois (Micmac).[25] Early Europeans described them as "a nomadic people, living in the forest and scattered over wide spaces, as is natural for those who live by hunting and fishing only."[26] In the pursuit of game, in particular moose, deer, and caribou, Wabanaki tribesmen chased the animals with the help of packs of hunting dogs. Among others, bear, beaver, and otter were also favored targets. Moreover, especially during the summer months, the Wabanakis also hunted water fowl and other birds.

1.3. W.R. Herries, painting of a small Maliseet camp on the banks of a river, 1850s. Courtesy of Library and Archives Canada, C115891.

When they were on the coast, they searched for harbour seal and gray seal, which supplied them not only with soft hide but also with meat and oil. This oil was highly valued as grease for their hair and bodies and was also considered "a relish at all the feasts they make among themselves."[27] Sometimes, they also hunted whales or feasted on stranded whales.[28] During their stay on the coast, "when the weather does not permit going on the hunt," they went digging for clams at the muddy flats.[29] Other shellfish were also enjoyed, in particular lobster, "some being 20 pounds in weight." Surplus lobster caught during the summer months was dried and stored for winter food. Lobster meat was also good for bait, "when they goe a fishing for Basse or Codfish."[30]

In addition to traps or weirs, made of wooden stakes and placed in a shallow stream or small tidal bay, Wabanaki fishers used nets, hooks, and lines. Harpoons served to take porpoise and sturgeon, and special three-pronged fish spears enabled the Wabanakis to catch salmon, trout, and bass. Taking their canoes on the water at night, they lured the fish with torches of burning birch bark. This way, a man could spear up to two hundred fish during one trip.[31]

Adding to their diversified diet, the Wabanakis tapped the sweet sap of the maple tree and harvested greens, wild fruits, nuts, seeds, and last but not least, edible roots and tubers. On the basis of such intimate knowledge of nature, some Wabanakis became specialists in herbal medicine. Benefiting from the medicinal qualities inherent in certain roots, leaves, and bark, these Wabanakis brewed select teas or prepared poultices to be used as remedies.[32]

Among these hunters and gatherers, the burden of labor seems to have fallen disproportionately on the shoulders of native women. As one outside observer noted:

> Besides the onerous role of bearing and rearing the children, [women] also transport the game from where it has fallen; they are the hewers of wood and drawwers of water; they make and repair the household utensils; they prepare food; they skin the game and prepare the hides like fullers; they sew garments; they catch fish and gather shellfish for food; often they even hunt; they make the canoes . . . out of bark; they set up the tents wherever and whenever they stop for the night — in short, the men concern themselves with nothing but the more laborious hunting and the waging of war. For this reason almost everyone has several wives.[33]

Those Wabanakis who were migratory hunters, fishers, and gatherers moved every six weeks or so and could set up a village within hours. Among their favourite haunts was a site known to them as Kenduskeag, located on a tributary to the Penobscot (at Bangor). Drawn by the abundance of eel that could be taken here, a regional band of about three hundred members returned to this location each fall, setting up eighteen seasonal lodges and constructing fish weirs. Although there were other seasonal villages as large as Kenduskeag, most of these temporary villages were much smaller. On the shores of the Bay of Fundy, for example, one such Wabanaki encampment consisted of no more than eight wigwams.[34]

CORN PLANTERS IN SOUTHERN MAINE

Generally, the larger tribal communities existed in the region west of the Sheepscot. This area was inhabited by people originally named Armouchiquois (perhaps a derogative, meaning dogs) by their Souriquois neighbors.[35] In contrast to the eastern Wabanaki groups, who maintained a mode of subsistence based exclusively on hunting, fishing, and gathering, these Armouchiquois planted vegetable gardens. Having adopted the horticultural complex of tribes to the south shortly before the arrival of Europeans in the area (probably in the fifteenth century A.D.), these western Wabanaki groups grew hard flint corn, kidney beans, and squash, as well as tobacco, in their village gardens. Although precise estimates for the actual acreage under cultivation are unavailable, an average village with a population of four hundred "would have utilized between 330 and 580 acres of planting fields to insure subsistence maintenance over half a century."[36]

Using a technique called slash-and-burn, the Armouchiquois cleared fertile plains in river valleys. By stoking fires around the bases of standing trees, they burned the bark, thereby killing the trees. Later, they felled the dead trees with stone axes. As one tree toppled, it usually knocked down several others. Later, all this wood was removed by burning. Men cleared the land, and women took charge of the gardens. In May or early June, they planted the fields. With digging sticks, they made long rows of holes, about three feet apart. In each hole they put several corn and bean kernels. Several weeks later, they planted squash seeds in between the growing plants. As a result, the cornstalks became beanpoles, and the leaves of the squash vines smothered weeds. Once harvested, much of the corn was stored for the winter in large holes in the ground. Lined with dwarf-rush mats and covered with earth, each of these "barns" could hold some six to ten bushels. Meanwhile, the Armouchiquois continued to rely on traditional food-collecting strategies as well (fig. 1.4).[37]

In addition to the usual meals of roasted or boiled meat, fowl, fish and so forth, the corn-growing Armouchiquois feasted on thick corn chowder mixed with clams, fish, meat, or other ingredients. When they traveled, they preferred a simple fare of parched cornmeal mixed with water, known as *nocake*, their equivalent of fast food. Supplementing the corn, they also ate beans and a large variety of edible wild plants. Finally, in the summer, "when their corne [was] spent," squash was "their best bread."[38]

Clearly, horticulture not only permitted high population densities than in areas inhabited by migratory food collectors but also allowed for more permanent settlement patterns. Reluctant to leave their village gardens unprotected during periods of conflict, these Wabanaki corn growers had little alternative but to defend their settlements against hostile raiders. For instance, one fortified Armouchiquois village, located at the mouth of the Saco

1.4. Armouchiquois man and woman. The woman has an ear of corn and a squash; the man carries a quiver on his back and holds an arrow in one hand and a European knife in the other. Detail from Samuel de Champlain, *Carte Geographique de la Nouvelle France*, 1612. Courtesy of John Carter Brown Library at Brown University.

River, included "a large cabin surrounded by palisades made of large trees placed by the side of each other, in which they take refuge when their enemies make war upon them."[39]

REGIONAL TRADE NETWORKS

Although the Wabanaki bands were mostly self-sufficient communities, their highly mobile way of life enabled them to easily cross territorial boundaries. During periods of peace, for instance, periodic expeditions to neighboring villages took place. However, when intertribal relations turned hostile, the bands could strike against their enemies. Although foot travel was not uncommon, they mostly used their swift canoes, which made travel much faster and easier (fig. 1.5).[40]

Etchemin and Souriquois hunting groups living east of the Kennebec traded with the Armouchiquois from Saco and elsewhere, who supplied them with surplus produce from their gardens, "to wit, corn, tobacco, beans, and pumpkins [squash]."[41] On their long-distance trading journeys, Wabanaki tribesmen in general bartered such things as beautiful furs, strong moose-hide moccasins, dressed deerskins, and moose hides with the Narragansett and other southern neighbors. These trade goods were exchanged for luxuries such as wampum (blue and white beads made of quahog shell). Wampum was a specialty of the Narragansett of Rhode Island. "From hence they [neighboring tribes] have most of their curious Pendants & Bracelets; from hence they have their great stone-pipes, which will hold a quarter of an ounce of Tobacco . . . they make them of greene, & sometimes of black stone [with Imagerie upon them]. . . . Hence likewise our Indians had their pots wherein they used to seeth their victuals."[42]

1.5. Detail showing Micmac canoes from Jean-Baptiste Louis Franquelin, *Carte pour servir à l'éclaircissement du Papier Terrier de la Nouvelle-France*, [1678]. Original in Bibliothèque Nationale, 125-1-1. Reproduced from a photograph in Library and Archives Canada, NMC 17393.

PERSONAL APPEARANCES

Described as "of average stature . . . handsome and well-shaped,"[43] the Wabanakis were generally "betweene five or six foote high, straight bodied, strongly composed, smooth skinned [and] merry countenanced."[44] Their robust life-style and ordinarily protein-rich diet made them a healthy people. Moreover, they made regular use of sweat baths, followed by massage, and "afterwards rubbing the whole body with seal oil" or other animal fat in order to "stand heat and cold better." By greasing themselves, they were also protected against "mosquitos, [which then] do not sting so much in the bare parts."[45] According to one early European traveler to the region, "You do not encounter a big-bellied, hunchbacked, or deformed person among them: those who are leprous, gouty, affected with gravel, or insane, are unknown to them."[46]

Their personal fashions, including hairstyle and ornamentation, not only reflected individual taste but also served as cultural markers indicating social divisions based on ethnic affiliation, rank, age, gender, or marital status. Decorative devices, such as headdresses, could involve colorful arrangements with bird feathers, wampum, dyed porcupine quills, or moose hair.[47]

Among eastern Wabanaki groups, in particular the Souriquois and Etchemin, adult men typically tied "a knot of [their hair], with a leather lace, which they let hang down behind."[48] Sometimes, a few bird feathers were woven into these topknots. When a warrior died, his relatives "upon his head stuck many feathers," before his burial.[49] In contrast to the adult men, boys wore their hair "of full length." They tied it "in tufts on the two sides with cords of leather." Some of them had their hair "ornamented with coloured Porcupine quills."[50]

At times, these eastern Wabanakis differed from their corn-growing neighbors west of the Sheepscot, who were clearly recognizable by their distinct hairstyle. Typically, these Armouchiquois shaved "their hair far up on the head," leaving it very long at the back, which they combed and twisted "in various ways very neatly, intertwined with feathers which they attach[ed] to the head."[51] Farther south, in Massachusetts Bay, tribesmen commonly wore their hair "tied up hard and short like a horse taile, bound close with a fillet . . . whereon they prick[ed] feathers of fowls in a fashion of a crownet."[52]

Sagamores were sometimes distinguished by their own particular headgear. Their preroga-tive was a bird with an aggressive reputation, described as a "black hawk" (probably the eastern kingbird). Viewed as a symbol of their bravery, the dead bird's "dried body" was affixed to the topknot in their hair. Although most Wabanaki men plucked out their scant facial hair, some chieftains distinguished themselves by growing beards.[53]

Among the eastern Wabanakis, in particular the Souriquois, adult women generally wore their hair loose on their shoulders. However, those who were not yet married wore theirs "also full length, but tie[d] it behind with the same cords." They beautified themselves by making "ornamental pieces of the size of a foot or eight inches square, all embroidered with Porcupine quills of all colours." One visitor described the ornament: "It is made on a frame, of which the warp is threads of leather from unborn Moose, a very delicate sort; the quills of Porcupine form the woof which they pass through these threads. . . . All around they make a fringe of the same threads, which are also encircled with these Porcupine quills in a medley of colours. In this fringe they place wampum, white and violet."[54]

In addition to wearing wampum necklaces and bracelets, Wabanaki men as well as women also pierced their ears, often in several places. Special pendants "as formes of birds, beasts, and fishes, carved out of bone, shells, and stone" hung from their pierced ears, in which they sometimes also stuck "long feathers or hares' tails."[55]

As noted earlier, Wabanaki tribesmen also used paint to distinguish themselves. "When they goe to their warres, it is their custome to paint their faces with a diversitie of colours, some being all black as jet, some red, some halfe red and halfe black, some blacke and white, others spotted with diver kinds of colours, being all distinguished to their enemies, to make them more terrible to their foes."[56] For instance, whereas Etchemin tribesmen at Pemaquid painted "their bodies with black; their faces, some with red, some with black, and some with blue,"[57] Souriquois mariners on the southern Maine coast were reported to have had "their eyebrows painted white."[58]

The Wabanakis, as well as their southern neighbors, also marked their skin with red and black tattoos. Among the Souriquois, and probably among the other native groups as well, women tattooed the skin of their husbands or lovers. At the Massachusetts coast, for instance, tribesmen had "certaine round Impressions downe the outside of their armes and brestes, in forme of mullets [stars] or spur-rowels [and] bearing upon their cheeks certaine pourtraitures of beasts, as Beares, Deares, Mooses, Wolves, &c, some of fowls, as of Eagles, Hawkes, &c."[59] These designs probably represented their animal guardian spirits of family totems. The Wabanakis believed that wearing such tattoos endowed them with special spirit power.

Garments were made by the women, who dressed the hides by scraping them and rubbing them with sea-bird oil. Next, the women cut the supple leather and stitched the pieces together as robes, mantles, breechclouts, leggings, or moccasins. Finally, the leather was painted or "orna-mented with embroidery," using dyed moose hair or flattened porcupine quills. In addition to making a "lace-like pattern" or "broken chevrons," they also "studded [their clothing] with figures of animals," which were probably symbolic as well.[60] Small, funnel-sized copper objects, made of thin sheets rolled into form, were also used to embellish their clothing. Sometimes, the "leather buskins" of Wabanaki children were also decorated with these "little round pieces of red copper."[61]

During the warmer seasons, Wabanaki men usually donned a mantle made of smoothly dressed white moose hide or tanned deerskin, along with a soft leather breechclout, leggings, and moose-hide or sealskin moccasins. Usually, the moose-hide moccasins were made from old and greasy leather coats, which the women "embellish with dye & and edging of red and white Porcupine quills."[62] Occasionally, the men also wore coats made of wild goose or turkey feathers. When the weather turned cold, they were warmly dressed in thick fur robes made of beaver, otter, raccoon, or even bear skins. Black wolves were also highly valued; these furs were "esteemed a present for a prince" among the native peoples of the region.[63]

PLACE-NAMES: TURNING THE LANDSCAPE INTO A MAP

Native place-names in Wabanaki territories generally convey essential geographic information, describing the distinctive features of a locality such as its physical appearance, its specific dangers, or its precious resources. A name might, for instance, note where certain animals could be hunted, fish netted, or plants harvested. Specifically, *Shawokotec* (for Saco) referred to "the outlet of the river," *Pemaquid* signified "it is situated far out," *Machias* described "bad little falls," *Olamon* was the spot where "red ochre" for paint could be found, *Passamaquoddy* was attractive as "the place with plenty of Pollock," *Kenduskeag* was the "eel-weir place," and *Cobossecontee* (near Gardiner) was the place where "sturgeon could be found."[64]

Such place-names show how thoroughly familiar the Wabanakis were with the particular challenges and opportunities of their habitat. Ranging widely throughout northeastern North America, Wabanaki tribespeople depended dearly on such topographic marking points for their physical survival. Accumulating over hundreds, perhaps even thousands, of years, their individual experiences were committed to collective memory not only in the form of place-names but also in the form of tribal lore, tales, legends, songs, and, ultimately, myths. Thus embedded in their cultural fabric, place-names contain vital elements of ecological knowledge. Indeed, the purpose of place-names was "to turn the landscape into a map which, if studied carefully, literally gave a village's inhabitants the information they needed to sustain themselves."[65]

On their journeys, moving swiftly in their lightweight birch-bark canoes, the Wabanakis were guided by this knowledge. Place-names might indicate where to expect such difficulties as swift currents, dangerous rapids, and gravel bars or might suggest which fork to take or where to portage to a connecting travel route. Such information was crucial, especially when traveling for purposes of long-distance trade or raiding parties, but also during regular seasonal migrations. To this day, many place-names in New England and the Maritimes still contain elements of ancient Wabanaki toponyms.

Beyond the previously mentioned ecological toponyms, some place-names may derive from certain political realities in traditional Wabanaki society. For instance, early seventeenth-century European records reveal that Wabanaki tribesmen inhabiting the Maine coast in that period referred to the region from Cape Neddick to Schoodic Point (the end) as *Mawooshen* (also spelled *Moasson*).[66] Under this name, they apparently understood an area "fortie leagues in bredth, and fiftie in length, [comprising] nine rivers, [namely the] Quibiquesson, Pemaquid, Ramassoc, Apanawapeske, Apaumensek, Aponeg, Sagadehoc, Ashamahaga, Shawokotec."[67] Although we may always remain in the dark about the precise meaning of *Mawooshen*, it probably refers not to a stretch of land but to the confederacy of allied villages under a regional grand chief known as the Bashabes.

Other place-names make sense only in the context of native culture — place-names whose meanings are expressed in the context of the Wabanakis' particular worldview as recounted in myth. Traditional native storytellers attributed many topographic features in the landscape to the legendary activities of Gluskap, their culture-hero, who shaped the earth in a particular way so as to make it "a happy land for the people."[68] According to one story, rivers such as the Penobscot were formed when Gluskap killed the monster frog that had caused a world drought. The released waters streamed down the mountainsides toward the sea. Gluskap paddled along the coast in his canoe and entered all the rivers emptying into the ocean. "He inspected them. Wherever there were bad falls he lessened them so they would not be too dangerous for his descendants. He cleared the carrying places. Then he left his canoe upside down where it turned to stone [near Castine]. It may be seen there yet."[69]

In another legend, Gluskap beached his canoe on the eastern shore of Penobscot Bay and chased a moose up into the woods for a great distance.

> On the beach at the point mentioned is a rock about twenty-five feet long, shaped like an overturned canoe. The rocks leading from it bear footprints of Gluskap, which reappear frequently in the interior of the country according to some of the Indians who claim to have seen them. At another place farther down he killed the moose and cast its entrails across the water. There they still appear as streaks of white rock on the bottom of the bay at Cape Rosier. After cooking the moose he left his cooking pot overturned on the shore of Moosehead Lake and it is now to be seen as Kineo mountain on the eastern margin. . . . When the Indians find stones possessing natural shapes, resembling a face or a person, they sometimes keep them [saying]: "It looks like Gluskap, I guess he left his picture on it."[70]

NATIVE CARTOGRAPHY

Although there are no indications that the Wabanakis kept permanent cartographic collections, there is evidence that they made maps for temporary needs. If, for instance, a local scout encountered enemy tribesmen secretly roaming in the area, he would illustrate this for his kinsmen by scratching on a piece of bark a picture of the place, indicating the streams, points, and other landmarks. Sometimes, he would leave incisions in the bark of a tree near a stream, where his friends would follow by canoe, or place sticks on a trail, indicating that a message in picture writing, known as a *wikhegan,* was hidden nearby.[71]

Commenting on the use of such *wikhegan* among the Wabanakis inhabiting the Kennebec River area, a French missionary reported: "There [one of the tribesmen] took the bark of a tree, upon which with coal he drew [a picture of] the English around me, and one of them cutting off my head. (This is all the writing the Indians have, and they communicate among themselves by these sorts of drawings as understandingly as we do by our letters). He then put this kind of letter around a stick which he planted on the bank of the river, to give news to those passing by of what had happened to me" (see fig. 1.6).[72]

Wikhegan also served to depict regional maps. "They have much ingenuity in drawing upon bark a kind of map which marks exactly all the rivers and streams of a country of which they

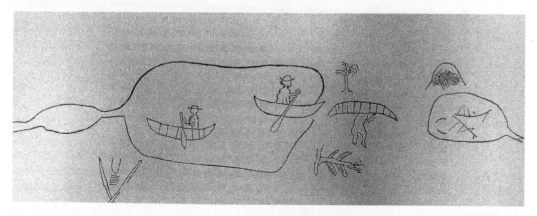

1.6. *Wikhegan* map on birch bark (ca. 1840) by Gabrien Acquin, a Maliseet describing his hunting trip. The *wikhegan* was left for his friend, who had gone down the river. From Mallery, "Picture-Writing of the American Indians," 336.

wish to make a representation. They mark all the places thereon exactly and so well that they make use of them successfully, and an Indian who possesses one makes long voyages without going astray" (see figs. 1.7 and 1.8).[73]

At certain points on the travel routes of the Wabanakis, tribespeople marked messages on rock ledges, which may have served as information centers. Traditionally such *wikhegan* could be found on the ledges of Hampden Narrows, which was therefore known as *Edalawikekhadimuk* (place where are markings). These marks probably indicated "the exact number of canoes going up and down the river."[74] Such markings also existed at Fort Point in Stockton Springs, a place the Wabanakis knew as *Aguahassidek* (stepping ashore). One of the traditional Penobscot tribal leaders recounted that "on their annual trip to salt water for the purpose of fishing," his ancestors "gave names to a number of places along the bay and river." Landing on the west bank of the river where it flows into Penobscot Bay, "they only stopped long enough to make the sign of their visit, showing which direction

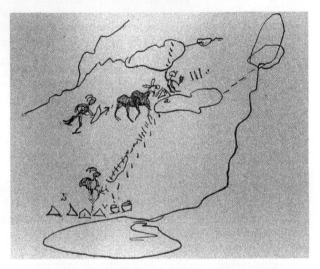

1.7. *Wikhegan* map on birch bark (ca. 1800) by Chief Selmo Soctomah, a Passamaquoddy Chief from Pleasant Point, describing a moose hunt. From Mallery, "Picture-Writing of the American Indians," 339.

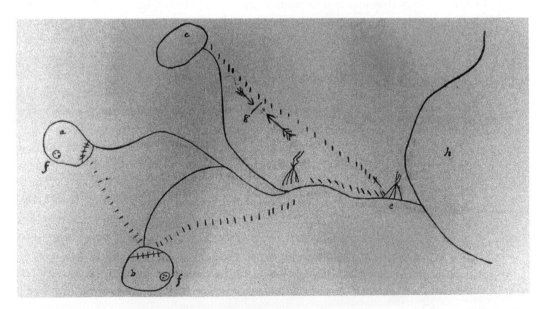

1.8. *Wikhegan* map on birch bark (ca. 1885) by Nicholas Francis, an old Penobscot hunter (from Old Town) representing a beaver trapping district near Moosehead Lake. From Mallery, "Picture-Writing of the American Indians," 338.

they were going, the number of their party and canoes, etc. On account of its being a marking place no one was ever allowed to mar or deface its outline by using it for a camping ground."[75]

Today, remarkable petroglyphs with canoes, birds, moose, humans, and other designs remain visible on a ledge at the west bank of the upper Kennebec River (Embden). Similar glyphs can still be seen on coastal rocks at Machias Bay (Birch Point). One mark at Machias appears to represent a native woman with sea-fowl on her head. One local Passamaquoddy hunter interpreted this symbol to mean "that squaw had smashed canoe, saved beaver-skin, walked on-half moon all over alone toward east, just same as heron wading alongshore." The hunter also noted that the three lines hammered out below the figure together resembled a bird track, or a trident, and represented the three rivers — the East, West, and Middle rivers of Machias — that merge not far above Birch Point (fig. 1.9).[76]

WENOOCH: WHO ARE THESE STRANGERS?

Thinking themselves to be the easternmost people on earth, the Wabanakis were unaware of Europeans until they sighted the first sailing ships in the early sixteenth century. Initially amazed to see bearded strangers landing on their shores, they "could not get over their wonder as they gazed at our customs, our clothing, our arms, our equipment," reported one of the early French visitors to the area.[77] Their original surprise is reflected in the Wabanaki name for the alien-looking invaders from across the ocean: *wenooch* (stranger), derived from their word for "who is that?" Other telling names, used by neighboring tribes, include "boat-men" (*mistek-oushou*), "coat-men" (*wautaconauog*), and "sword-men" or "knife-men" (*chauquaquock*).[78] New technologies, in particular steel knives, hatchets, copper kettles, glass beads, awls, mirrors, woolen cloth, and eventually firearms, were especially appreciated by the Wabanakis and could be had in exchange for wild animal pelts.

Despite their sometimes high regard for European innovations, the Wabanakis typically regarded the strangers "as physically inferior" and "found them ugly, especially because of their excessive hairiness."[79] According to one early European who lived among the Wabanakis: "[They]

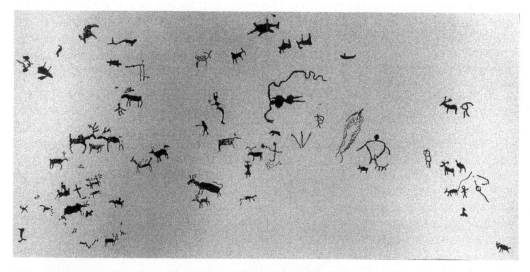

1.9. Petroglyphs at Birch Point, Machias Bay. From Mallery, "Picture-Writing of the American Indians," 1893, plate 12.

regard themselves as much richer than we are . . . Also they consider themselves more ingenious, [and] they conclude generally that they are superior to all Christians."[80] An eastern Wabanaki (Micmac) tribesman may have revealed the natives' typical attitude toward the Europeans who landed on their shores when he said: "You deceive yourself greatly if you think to persuade us that your country is better than ours. For if France, as you say, is a little terrestrial paradise, are you sensible to leave it?"[81]

Although no early Wabanaki maps on birch bark or other material are believed to have survived, some documentary records indicate native cartographic skills. A wonderful piece of evidence concerning native mapmaking skill is a reference in Captain Bartholomew Gosnold's account of his voyage to the Maine coast in 1602. Referring to a surprise encounter with a party of Souriquois traders at Cape Neddick, he reported, "One that seemed to be their commander . . . with a piece of chalk described the coast thereabouts, and could name Placentia [Plaisance] of the Newfoundland."[82]

Other early European records comment on the guiding skills of Wabanaki tribesmen living in the Pemaquid coastal region. Sir Ferdinando Gorges, for example, a well-known English entrepreneur who acquired colonial title over parts of Maine as its "Lord Proprietor," wrote that he understood the natives themselves to be "exact pilots for that coast [between Cape Cod and Cape Breton], having been accustomed to frequent the same, both as fishermen, and in passing along the shore to seek their enemies."[83]

During the same period, the French navigator Samuel de Champlain ran into some native mariners off Cape Ann, who offered him an accurate description of the region ahead. "I made them understand, as best as I could, that they should show me how the coast lay. After having depicted for them, with a piece of charcoal, the bay and the Island Cape, where we were, they represented for me, with the same crayon, another [Massachusetts] bay, which they showed as very large. They put six pebbles at equal distances, thus giving me to understand that each of these stood for as many chiefs and tribes. Then they represented within this bay a river [Merrimac] which we had passed, which extends very far."[84]

But, given the strategic potential of geographic intelligence, it is understandable that Wabanaki tribesmen became increasingly reluctant informants when strangers came to their lands requesting vital geographic information, such as the location of lakes, rivers, mountains, and other marking points in the landscape. This resentment became clear when an English surveyor requested their help on an expedition to the upper Penobscot and Moosehead Lake region in the 1760s. "The Indians are so jealous of their countrey being exposed by this survey," he wrote, "as made it impracticable for us to perform this work with acqurice."[85] When finally a few tribesmen were induced to serve as guides, they did so on condition that the foreigners take no notes and make no maps.[86]

Their request was not heeded. Soon, an abstract grid of meridians and parallels clamped the wilderness. Forced to yield to analytical cartographic representation, Ketakamigwa was no longer terra incognita to the strangers. Powerless to shield their homeland from European intruders, the Wabanakis may have recalled what their divine hero Gluskap told them as he climbed on the back of a giant whale to travel to an unknown island in the western seas: "I shall leave you and shall hearken no more to your calling, but shall wait the calling of the Great Spirit. Strange things shall happen, but those who bring about the changes will tell you all about them so you may understand them."[87] Indeed, the Wabanakis have come to understand the changes, and all too well. Yet, as Gluskap's children, they endure and "look for the end of their oppressions and troubles when he comes back."[88]

I thank Arthur Spiess and Emerson Baker, for their comments on an earlier draft of this paper, and especially my wife, Bunny McBride, for her skilful editorial hand.

NOTES

1. Sebastian Rasle, "A Dictionary of the Abenaki Language in North America, [1690–1722]," in John Pickering, ed., *Memoirs of the American Academy of Arts and Sciences*, n.s., 1 (1833): 533. In Rasle's dictionary, the word is spelled *ketakamig8*. According to the orthographic system used by Dr. Frank Siebert of Old Town, Maine, the "correct" Penobscot, eastern Abenaki form is *ktahkumik* —(big land). Siebert notes that the Penobscots used the term to refer to the mainland (Siebert, personal communication).

2. George Popham, Letter to King James I, December 13, 1607, *Collections of the Maine Historical Society* 5 (1857): 359–60. For the notion that the native peoples in New England thought of their land as part of a larger island, see among others Handrick Aupamut, *History of the Muhheadkunnuk Indians* (1790), in *Massachusetts Historical Society Collections* 9 (1804): 101; William Wood, *New England's Prospect* (Boston: Publications of the Prince Society, 1865), 2; Edward Winslow, "Winslow's Relation" (1624), in *Massachusetts Historical Society Collections*, 2d set., 9 (1832): 99.

3. Rasle, "Dictionary," 434; Frank G. Speck, "Penobscot Tales and Religious Beliefs," *Journal of American Folklore* 48 (1935); 4, 18–19. Dr. Frank Siebert suggests that the term *ketchiniweskwe* (great spirit) was invented by Roman Catholic missionaries. In Abenaki, the element *ni-wes* refers to dry seed (of corn), metaphorically expressing the idea of "spirit of life" (Siebert, personal communication).

4. Among others, see Joseph Laurent, *New Familiar Abenakis and English Dialogues, the First Ever Published on the Grammatical System by Jos. Laurent, Abenakies Chief* (Quebec: L. Brosseau, 1884), 46–47.

5. Nicolar, *Life and Traditions*, 7. Note that there are various spellings of the name Gluskap, including *Gloosk-ob, Koluskap,* and *Slooscap.*

6. There is no agreement on the precise etymology or meaning of the name Gluskap. See among others Nicolar, *Life and Traditions*, 12.

7. Frank G. Speck, "Aboriginal Conservators," *Bird-Lore* 40 (1938): 259.

8. Not surprisingly, a limited geographic understanding of territories beyond the immediate region is typical. Compare what Edmund Carpenter observed among the Inuit: "Aivilik men are keen geographers when describing their immediate surroundings. But once they venture to tell of the outer world, geography gives way to cosmography." Edmund Carpenter, Frederick Varley, and Roberty Flaherty, *Eskimo* (Toronto: University of Toronto Press, 1959), n.p.

9. For a brief review of Paleo-Indian remains in the region, see among others Arthur E. Spiess and Deborah B. Wilson, *Michaud: A Paleoindian Site in the New England-Maritimes Region*, Occasional Publications in Maine Archaeology 6 (Augusta, Maine Historical Preservation Commission and the Maine Archeological Society, 1987), 129–55.

10. David Sanger, *Discovering Maine's Archaeological Heritage* (Augusta: Maine Historical Preservation Commission, 1979), 20; Sanger, "Maritime Adaptations in the Gulf of Maine," *Archaeology of Eastern North America* 18 (1988): 84; and William Cronon, *Changes in the Land: Indians, Colonists, and the Ecology of New England* (New York: Hill and Wang, 1983), 27.

11. "The Description of the Country of Mawooshen," in Samuel Purchas, *Hakluytus Posthumus or Purchas His Pilgrimes, Contayning a History of the World, in Dea Voyages, and Lande-Travells, by Englishmen and Others*, 20 vols. (Glasgow: James MacLehose and Songs, 1906), 19:400. Perhaps forest burning also occurred among the eastern Wabanakis inhabiting Acadia (in particular Nova Scotia and New Brunswick); see Nicolas Denys, *The Description and Natural History of the Coasts of North America (Acadia)*, ed. and trans. William F. Ganong (Toronto: Champlain Society, 1908), 377. For evidence of this practice in Massachusetts, see Wood, *New England's Prospect*, 17; see also Cronon, *Changes*, 48–52, 181–82, and Thomas Morton, *The New English Canaan, or New Canaan: Containing an Abstract of New England Composed in Three Books* (Boston: Prince Society, 1883).

12. The precontact population estimates remain subject to debate. Pierre Biard, a French Jesuit missionary active among the eastern Wabakakis (1611–13), noted in his 1616 treatise *Relation de la Nouvelle France . . .* that natives informed him "that in the region of the great river [St. Lawrence], from Newfoundland to Choeacoet [Saco], there cannot be more than nine or ten thousand people." He added, "I believe it is the highest number" (Thwaires, *Jesuit Relations* 3:109–11). In this context it is important to note that Dean R. Snow, in *The Archaeology of New England* (New York: Academic Press, 1980), 33–34 (reiterated in Dean Snow and Kim M. Lansphear, "European Contact and Indian Depopulation in the Northeast: The Timing of the First Epidemics," *Ethnohistory* 35, [1988]: 22–2), erroneously assumes that these figures are "post-epidemic" with respect to Wabanakis in northern New England. Indeed, Biard's earlier estimates were even lower by about half (Thwaires, *Jesuit Relations* 2:73). The number of 30,000 presented here is nothing but an educated guess and is relatively low in comparison with other recent estimates for the region. For instance, Dean Snow calculated that there were about 10,000 western Wabanakis (including Penacooks), 11,900 Wabanakis from Saco to the Penobscot (Armouchiquois and Etchemins), and another 7,600 eastern Wabanakis (Etchemins) in the St. Croix and

St. John river areas. Farther east, he estimated the pre-epidemic number of Micmacs in the Maritimes at about 13,000 (Snow, *Archaeology,* 33–34). Snow's total population estimate for the groups here identified at eastern and western Wabanakis is 42,500. In this context, it is of interest to note that Snow's estimate for the Micmacs is substantially lower than the 35,000 recently suggested by Virginia Miller (who concluded that this was "not an unlikely minimum figure") in her article "Aboriginal Micmac Population: A Review of the Evidence," *Ethnohistory* 23(1976): 117–27. If Miller's figure had been taken into account, the total population for northern New England and the Maritimes would have been nearly 75,000.

13. The issue of ethnicity is problematical. For a more detailed discussion of Wabanaki ethnicity, see Harald Prins, *Tribulations of a Border Tribe: The Case of the Aroostook Band of Micmacs in Maine* (Ann Arbor: University Microfilms International, 1988), 152–202.

14. Biard, in Thwaites, *Jesuit Relations* 2:73.

15. "Description of the Country of Mawooshen," in Purchase, *Hakluytus Posthumus* 19:402–3. The orthography of Wabanaki names presents us with difficulties. For instance, Mentaurmet's name (as spelled by the English) was written as *Meteourmite* in Biard's 1612 letter (in Thwaites, *Jesuit Relations* 2:41).

16. Biard, in Thwaites, *Jesuit Relations* 3:89.

17. I am not suggesting that tribal territoriality among the Wabanaki ethnic groups conformed to what has been termed the "riverine model." See also Harald E.L. Prins, "Micmacs and Maliseets in the St. Lawrence River Valley," in W. Cowan, ed., *Actes du 17e Congres des Algonquinistes* (Ottawa: Carleton University, 1986), 264–78; Prins, *Tribulations,* 274–76.

18. This section on material culture draws on a variety of sources, including accounts by Biard, Morton, Wood, and Denys. Other important sources include Samuel de Champlain, *The Works of Samuel de Champlain,* ed. H.P. Biggar, 6 vols. (Toronto: Champlain Society, 1922–36); James Rosier, "A True Relation of the Most Prosperous Voyage Made This Present Yeare 1605, by Captain G. Weymouth, in the Discovery of the Land Virginia," in Henry D. Burrage, ed., *Rosier's Relation of Weymouth's Voyage to the Coast of Maine, 1605* (Portland: Gorges Society, 1887), 38–75; Marc Lescarbot, *The History of New France,* 3 vols. (Toronto: Champlain Society, 1907–14); John Josselyn, "An Account of Two Voyages to New England," *Massachusetts Historical Society Collections,* 2d ser., 3 (1833): 211–396.

19. Sebastien Rasle, Letter from Norridgewock (October 12, 1723), *Collections and Proceedings of the Maine Historical Society* 4 (1893): 267. According to Champlain (*Works* 2:15), "From Saco along the whole coast as far as Tadoussac [these birch bark canoes] are all alike." These Wabanaki hunting canoes, often no more than ten feet long, usually carries only about four to six individuals. Larger ocean-going canoes could measure more than twenty feet, carrying a fairly large number of people. Also note that Champlain (*Works* 1:338) observed that the wooden dugouts, not reported among the Wabanaki, were used south of Cape Ann, in Massachusetts and beyond.

20. Denys, *Description and Natural History,* 422; Morton, *New English Canaan,* 186.

21. Josselyn, "Account of Two Voyages," 297–98.

22. Rasle, Letter from Norridgewock, 266; Charles G. Willoughby, "Homes and Gardens of New England Indians," *American Anthropologist* 8 (1906); 116. The quote is from Biard, in Thwaites, *Jesuit Relations* 2:41.

23. Josselyn, "Account of Two Voyages," 307.

24. See among others Jesse D. Jennings, *Prehistory of North American* (Mountain View, Calif.: Mayfield Publishing Co., 1989), 258–60.

25. For general overview, see K.M. Bennett, "The Food Economy of the New England Indians," *Journal of Political Economy* 63 (1955): 269–97. See also Harald Prins, "Cornplanters at Meductic: Ethnic and Territorial Reconfigurations in Colonial Acadia," *Man in the Northeast* no. 44(1992): 55–72.

26. Biard, in Thwaites, *Jesuit Relations* 2:73.

27. Denys, *Description and Natural History,* 349.

28. Lescarbot, in Thwaites, *Jesuit Relations* 2:185. See also Rosier, who wrote that Wabanaki tribesmen on the central Maine coast hunted whales "with a multitude of their boats" (Rosier, "True Relations," 158).

29. Denys, *Description and Natural History,* 359, 171; see also Wood, *New England's Prospect,* 40, 75, 108.

30. Morton, *New English Canaan,* 39, 107, 226.

31. Denys, *Description and Natural History,* 435–37.

32. Ibid., 380, 381; Wood, *New England's Prospect,* 75; for wild rice gathering, see also Frank G. Speck, *Penobscot Man: The Life History of a Forest Tribe in Maine* (Philadelphia: University of Pennsylvania Press, 1940), 92. Frank G. Speck, "Medicine Practices on the North-eastern Algonquians," *International Congress of Americanists Proceedings* 19 (1915): 303–21.

33. Biard, in Thwaites, *Jesuit Relations* 2:77.

34. Thwaites, *Jesuit Relations* 2:49, 167, 249, 3:225. *Kenduskead* is sometimes also referred to as *Kedesquit*. See also Thwaites, *Jesuit Relations* 2:49, 3:225, and Snow, *Archaeology*, 33–47.

35. Based on Louis Paul (personal communication, 1985). Earlier, a Canadian missionary, J.A. Maurault, in *Histoire des Abenakis, depuis 1605 jusqu'à nos jours* (Sorel, Québec, Canada: L'Atelier Typographique de la Gazette de Sorel, 1866), suggested that the term referred to "land of the little dogs." See also Prins, *Tribulations*, 162.

36. Peter Thomas, "Contrastive Subsistence Strategies and Land Use as Factors for Understanding Indian-White Relations in New England," *Enthohistory* 23, (1976): 6–13, quotation on page 13; Howard S. Russell, *Indian New England before the Mayflower* (Hanover, N.H.: University Press of New England, 1980), 150–51; James Petersen (personal communication, 1989).

37. See among others Champlain, *Works* 1:327–30, 3:374–75; Lescarbot, *History of New France* 1:195; Wood, *New England's Prospect,* 106; Rasle, *Letter from Norridgewock*, 269; Morton, *New English Canaan*, 160; Russell, *Indian New England*, 168.

38. Wood, *New England's Prospect,* 75–77, quotation on page 75; Morton, *New English Canaan*, 205–21; Denys, *Description and Natural History,* 356–57.

39. Samuel de Champlain, *Voyages of Samuel de Champlain, 1604–1618,* ed. W.L. Grant (New York: Charles Scribner's Sons, 1907), 61–63.

40. Wood, *New England's Prospect,* 102.

41. Lescarbot, *History of New France* 2:324.

42. Wood, *New England's Prospect,* 69 (quotation), 79; Morton, *New English Canaan*, 201; B.F. De Costa, *Ancient Norumbega, or the Voyages of Simon Ferdinando and John Walker to the Perobscot River, 1579–1580* (Albany, N.Y.: Joel Munsell's Sons, 1890), 7. Regarding the intertribal trade in moose hides, it should be noted that similar networks existed in the St. Lawrence River valley, for example, where horticultural Hurons acquired hides from Montagnais hunters in exchange for surplus corn.

43. In Thwaites, *Jesuit Relations* 2:73, 3:75. For a good overview, see also Charles G. Willoughby, "Dress and Ornament of the New England Indians," *American Anthropologist* 7 (1905): 499–508.

44. Wood, *New England's Prospect,* 70.

45. Biard, in Thwaites, *Jesuit Relations* 3:117.

46. Ibid., 75.

47. For a good overview, see also Ruth H. Whitehead, "Every Thing They Make and Wear," unpublished manuscript, n.d., Provincial Museum of Nova Scotia, Halifax.

48. Lescarbot, *History of New France* 3:133–34.

49. Champlain, *Works* 1:444–45; generally, according to Lescarbot (*History of New France* 3:133), eastern Wabanaki groups such as the Micmacs did not fancy these decorative elements. However, when Jacques Cartier encountered tribespeople (who could have been Micmacs) in the Gulf of St. Lawrence in 1532, he described them as having topknots in which they wove "a few bird's feathers." In H.P. Biggar, *The Voyages of Jacques Cartier* (Ottawa: Public Archives of Canada, 1924), 22–23.

50. Denys, *Description and Natural History,* 414.

51. Champlain, *Voyages* (New York: Charles Scribner's Sons, 1907), 61–63; Lescarbot, *History of New France* 3:135.

52. John Breaton, "A Briefe and True Relation of the Discoverie of the North Part of Virginia . . . Made This Present Yeere 1602," in L.B. Wright, ed., *The Elizabethan's America: A Collection of Early Reports by Englishmen on the New World* (Cambridge: Harvard University Press, 1965), 143; Daniel Gookin, *Historical Collection of the Indians in New England,* in *Massachusetts Historical Society Collections,* 1st set., 1 (1806): 153; Wood, *New England's Prospect,* 71–72. The Wampanoags in southern Massachusetts were described as wearing "on their heads long hair to the shoulders, only cut before [and] some trussed up before with a feather, broad-wise, like a fan; another fox tail hanging out." William Bradford, cited in H.C. Porter, *The Inconsistent Savage: England and the North American Indian, 1500–1660* (London Duckworth, 1979), 429.

53. Morton, *New English Canaan*, 197; Wood, *New England's Prospect,* 31, 74. The Micmac chieftain Membertou was described as "bearded like a Frenchman" (Thwaites, *Jesuit Relations,* 2:23; see also Lescarbot, *History of New France* 3:140). Elsewhere, tribesmen were described a "thin-bearded," and some even sported false beards fashioned "of the hair of beasts" (Breton, in Forter, *Inconsistent Savage,* 414).

54. Denys, *Description and Natural History,* 414.

55. Wood, *New England's Prospect,* 84; see also Denys, *Description and Natural History* 414; J.P. Baxter, ed., *Documentary History of the State of Maine,* col. 10 (Portland: Maine Historical Society, 1920), 463.

56. Wood, *New England's Prospect,* 95.

57. Rosier, in Porter, *Inconsistent Savage,* 270; see also Josselyn, "Account of two Voyages," 297–98.

58. Breton, in Wright, *Elizabethan's America,* 137–38.

59. Abbe S. Maillard, *An Account of the Customs and Manners of the Micmakis and Maricheets Savage Nations, Now Dependent on the Government of Cape Breton* (London: S. Hooper and A. Morley, 1758), 55; Sieur N. de Dièreville, *Relation of the Voyage to Port Royal in Acadia or New France*, ed. J.C. Webster (Toronto: Champlain Society, 1933), 169–70. The quote is from Wood, *New England's Prospect*, 74.

60. The quotations are from Denys, *Descriptions and Natural History*, 407, 411; Biard, in Thwaites, *Jesuit Relations* 3:75; see also Wood, *New England's Prospect*, 101.

61. Rosier, "True Relation," 121. This red copper may have been mined locally, since the eastern Wabanakis were familiar with various mines on the coast of the Bay of Fundy. Early French explorers, including Champlain, refer to these mines (see also Thwaites, *Jesuit Relations* 3:296); a leather belt found at Merriconeag Sound, Maine, included some four hundred red copper pieces of varied size, attached to each other with soft leather strings (in *History Magazine* [1969]), 247.

62. Denys, *Description and Natural History*, 411; see also Wood, *New England's Prospect*, 108; Morton, *New English Canaan*, 201.

63. Denys, *Description and Natural History*, 370, 407, 411, 413; Wood, *New England's Prospect*, 73, 108; Morton, *New English Canaan*, 201, 207, 209, 210; see also Biard, in Thwaites, *Jesuit Relations* 3:75.

64. For the etymology of native place-names in Maine, see especially Fanny H. Eckstorm, *Indian Place Names of the Penobscot Valley and the Maine Coast* (1941; reprint, Orono: University of Maine at Orono Press, 1978).

65. Cronon, *Changes*, 65.

66. The meaning of *Mawooshen* remains unclear. Frank Siebert (personal communication, 1988) suggests that it refers to the Mousam River. In this context, it is of interest to note that Eckstorm (*Indian Place Names*, 101) "Discovered that many place names which Peboscot Indians could not translate were easily interpreted by Passamaquoddy and Micmac Indians." Recently, a Maliseet speaker, Louis Paul of Woodstock Reserve, New Brunswick, suggested that *mawooshen* refers to "a bunch of people walking or acting together"— *mawe* referring to a "coming together" of more than two people.

67. Captain George Popham, Letter to King James I (written from Fort St. George, December 13, 1607), in *Collections of the Maine Historical Society* 5(1857): 359–60. Samuel Purchas, *Purchas, His Pilgrimage, or Relations of the World and the Religions Observed in All Ages and Places Discovered, from the Creation unto This Present*, 3rd ed. (London: Printed by William Stansby for H. Fetherstone, 1617), 939–41.

68. Nicolar, *Life and Traditions*, 5.

69. Frank G. Speck, "Penobscot Tales," 42.

70. Speck, "Penobscot Tales," 42–45; see also Eckstorm, *Indian Place Names*, 200–201.

71. Among others, see Garrick Mallery, "Petroglyphs in North America," *Tenth Annual Report of the Bureau of Ethnology to the Secretary of the Smithsonian Institution, 1888–1889* (Washington, D.C.: Government Printing Office, 1893).

72. Rasle, Letter from Norridgewock, 300.

73. Chrestien Le Clercq, *New Relation of Gaspesia, with the Customs and Religion of the Gaspesian Indians*, trans. and ed. William F. Ganong (Toronto: Champlain Society, 1910), 136; see also Wilson D. Wallis and Ruth S. Wallis, *The Micmac Indians and Eastern Canada* (Minneapolis: University of Minnesota Press, 1955), 54–56.

74. See among others Mark Hedden, "Form of the Cosmos in the Body of the Chaman," *Maine Archaeological Society Bulletin 27* (Spring 1987): ii–iv; Marc Hedden, "Prehistoric Maine Petroglyphs" (a video-script), *Maine Archaeological Society Bulletin* 28(1988). The quotation is by Father Michael C.H. O'Brien, in Eckstorm, *Indian Place Names*, 66.

75. Joseph Nicolar, alias "Young Sebatis," in the *Old Town Herald* (1887?), reprinted in Eckstorm, *Indian Place Names*, 239–41; see also 65–66. Note that this place-name was originally spelled *Arquar-har-see-dek* by Nicolar.

76. In Malley, "Petroglyphs," 83. (Note than Birch Point is also referred to as Clarks Point.)

77. Lescarbot, *History of New France* 3:21.

78. *Wenooch*, also spelled *Waunnuxuh* or *a8enn8tsak*, is derived from *awaun-ewo* (who is that?) (plural *tsk*): Rasle, "Dictionary" 458; Trumbull, note 1 in Morton, "New English Canaan," 254; Roger William, *Key into the Language of the Indians of New England (1643)*, in *Massachusetts Historical Society Collections*, 1st ser., 3(1794): 89. When the eastern Wabanakis became more familiar with early Europeans on their coasts, they learned to communicate in pidgin with the strangers, referring to English as "Ingres," to the French generally as "Normans," to those from St. Malo as "Samaricois," and the Basques as "Bascua" (Biard, in Thwaites, *Jesuit Relations* 1:163).

79. Cornelius Jaenen, "Amerindian Views of French Culture in the Seventeenth Century," *Canadian Historical Review* 60 (1974): 271, 272; see also Biard, in Thwaites, *Jesuit Relations* 3:22, 75.

80. Biard, in Thwaites, *Jesuit Relations* 1:175; Francois Du Creux, *The History of Canada or New France*, ed. J.B. Conacher, 2 vols. (Toronto: Champlain Society, 1962), 1:160.

81. Cited in LeClerq, *New Relations*, 104.

82. Gabriel Archer, in *Massachusetts Historical Society Collections*, 3d ser., 8 (1843): 73–74.

83. Ferdinando Gorges, *A Briefe Narration of the Originall Undertakings of the Advancement of Plantations into the Parts of America, Especially Shewing the Beginning, Progress and Continuance of That of New England* (Boston: Publications of the Prince Society, 1890), 2:10.

84. [Samuel de Champlain], *The Voyages and Explorations of Samuel de Champlain, 1604–1616, Narrated by Himself, together with the Voyage of 1603*, trans. Annie N. Bourne, ed. Edward G. Bourne, 2 vols. (New York: Allerton Book Co., 1922), 1:106, 110.

85. Joseph Chadwick, "Survey of Routes to Canada, from Fort Pownal on the Penobscot to Quebec," manuscript, 1764, State Archives, Massachusetts State Library, Boston. Segments of this manuscript are cited in Eva L. Butler and Wendell D. Hadlock, "A Preliminary Survey of the Munsungan-Allagash Waterways," *Robert Abbe Museum Bulletin* 8 (1962): 17. Colonel Montresor, in *Maine Historical Society Collections 1* (1931): 354.

86. According to Butler and Hadlock, "[Chadwick] was allowed to keep no books and make no maps at the time, but later made a fairly accurate map and well documented account of his trip despite the difficulties he encountered" ("Preliminary Survey," 17).

87. Nicolar, *Life and Traditions*, 64.

88. Silas T. Rand, *Legends of the Micmacs* (1894; reprint, New York and London: Johnson Reprint Corp., 1971), 156.

Article Two

The French Presence in Huronia: The Structure of Franco–Huron Relations in the First Half of the Seventeenth Century

Bruce G. Trigger

Few studies of Canadian history in the first half of the seventeenth century credit sufficiently the decisive role played at that time by the country's Native peoples. The success of European colonizers, traders, and missionaries depended to a greater degree than most of them cared to admit on their ability to understand and accommodate themselves not only to Native customs but also to a network of political and economic relationships that was not of their own making. Traders and missionaries often were forced to treat Algonkians and Iroquoians as their equals and sometimes they had to acknowledge that the Indians had the upper hand. If the Europeans were astonished and revolted by many of the customs of these Indians (often, however, no more barbarous than their own), they also admired their political and economic sagacity.[1] Indeed, one Jesuit was of the opinion that the Huron were more intelligent than the rural inhabitants of his own country.[2] If the missionary or fur trader felt compelled to understand the customs of the Indians, the modern historian should feel no less obliged to do so.

In order to appreciate the role that the Indians played in the history of Canada in the first half of the seventeenth century, it is necessary to study their customs and behaviour and the things they valued. Because their way of life differed from that of the Europeans, the fur traders and missionaries who interacted with them frequently became amateur anthropologists, and some of them became very good ones. For some tribes the documentation amassed by these

Source: "The French Presence in Huronia: The Structure of Franco–Huron Relations in the First Half of the Seventeenth Century," *Canadian Historical Review* 49 (1968): 107–41. Reprinted by permission of University of Toronto Press Incorporated (www.utpjournals.com).

early contacts is extensive and of high quality. For no tribe is this truer than for the Huron.[3] From the detailed picture of Huronia that emerges from these studies, it is possible to ascertain the motives that prompted the behaviour of particular Indians, or groups of Indians, in a manner no less detailed than our explanations of those which governed the behaviour of their European contemporaries. I might add, parenthetically, that historians are not alone to blame for the failure to utilize anthropological insights in the study of early Canadian history. Iroquoian ethnologists and archaeologists have tended to avoid historical or historiographic problems. Only a few individuals, such as George T. Hunt, have attempted to work in the no man's land between history and anthropology.

Two explanations have been used by anthropologists and historians to justify the existing cleavage between their respective studies. One of these maintains that when the Europeans arrived in eastern North America, the Native tribes were engaged in a struggle, the origins and significance of which are lost in the mists of time and therefore wholly the concern of ethnohistorians. Because of this, there is no reason for the historian to try to work out in detail the causes of the conflicts and alliances that existed at that time.[4] Very often, however, the struggle between different groups is painted in crude, almost racist, terms (and in complete contradiction to the facts) as one between Algonkian- and Iroquoian-speaking peoples, the former being an indigenous population, mainly hunters, the latter a series of invading tribes growing corn and living in large villages. It should be noted that such a simplistic explanation of European history, even for the earliest periods, would now be laughed out of court by any competent historian. The alternative hypothesis suggests that European contact altered the life of the Indian, and above all the relationships among the different tribes, so quickly and completely that a knowledge of Aboriginal conditions is not necessary to understand events after 1600.[5] From an *a priori* point of view, this theory seems most unlikely. Old relationships have a habit of influencing events, even when economic and political conditions are being rapidly altered. Future studies must describe in detail how Aboriginal cultures were disrupted or altered by their contact with the Europeans, rather than assume that interaction between Indians and Europeans can be explained as a set of relationships that has little or no reference to the Native culture.

We will begin by considering developments in Huronia prior to the start of the fur trade.

THE HURON

When the Huron tribes were described for the first time in 1615,[6] they were living in the Penetanguishene Peninsula and the part of Simcoe County that runs along Matchedash Bay between Wasaga Beach and Lake Simcoe. The Huron probably numbered twenty to thirty thousand, and, according to the most reliable of the descriptions from the Jesuit missionaries,[7] they were divided into four tribes that formed a confederacy similar in its structure to the league of the Iroquois.[8] The Attignaouantan or Bear tribe, which included about half of the people in the confederacy, lived on the western extremity of Huronia. Next to them lived the Attingueenougnahak, or Cord tribe, and the Tahontaenrat or Deer tribe. Farthest east, near Lake Simcoe, were the Ahrendarrhonon or Rock nation. The Tionnontate, or Petun, who spoke the same language as the Huron and were very similar to them, inhabited the country west of Huronia near the Blue Mountain. The Petun, however, were not members of the Huron confederacy and prior to the arrival of the French, they and the Huron had been at war. Another Iroquoian confederacy, the Neutral, lived farther south between the Grand River and the Niagara frontier. Except for a few Algonkian bands that lived west of the Petun, there do not appear to have been any other Indians living in southern Ontario, except in the Ottawa Valley. The uninhabited portions of the province were the hunting territories of the Huron, Neutral, and Petun and also served as a buffer zone between these tribes and the Iroquois who lived south of Lake Ontario.

The Huron, like other Iroquoian tribes, grew corn, beans, and squash. These crops were planted and looked after by the women, who also gathered the firewood used for cooking and heating the houses. Contrary to popular notions, the men also made an important contribution to the tribal economy, inasmuch as it was they who cleared the fields for planting (no small task when only stone axes were available) and who caught the fish which were an important source of nutrition. Because of the high population density, the areas close to Huronia appear to have been depleted of game, and expeditions in search of deer had to travel far to the south and east.[9] In general, hunting appears to have been of little economic importance among the Huron.

Huron villages had up to several thousand inhabitants and the main ones were protected by palisades made of posts woven together with smaller branches. Inside large villages there were 50 or more longhouses, often 100 feet or more in length, made of bark attached to a light wooden frame. These houses were inhabited by eight to ten very closely related families. Families that traced themselves back to a common female ancestor formed a clan, which was a political unit having its own civil chief and war leader. Each tribe in turn was made up of a number of such clans and the clan leaders served on the tribal and confederal councils.[10]

The events that led to the formation of the Huron confederacy are not well understood. The Huron themselves said that it began around A.D. 1400, with the union of the Bear and Cord tribes, and grew thereafter through the addition of further lineages and tribes. Archaeologically it appears that, although one or more of the Huron tribes was indigenous to Simcoe County, other groups moved into historic Huronia from as far away as the Trent Valley, the Toronto region, and Huron and Grey counties to the west.[11] Two tribes, the Rock and the Deer, had been admitted to the confederacy not long before the arrival of the French.

Historians frequently have asserted that it was fear of the Iroquois that prompted the Huron to seek refuge in this remote and sheltered portion of Ontario.[12] While this may be why some groups moved into Huronia, it is clear that in prehistoric times the Huron outnumbered the Iroquois and probably were not at any military disadvantage. For this reason ethnologists have begun to seek other explanations to account for the heavy concentration of population in Huronia in historic times. An abundance of light, easily workable soil may be part of the answer. Since the Huron lacked the tools to work heavier soils, this advantage may have outweighed the tendency toward drought and the absence of certain trace minerals in the soil which now trouble farmers in that area.[13] Huronia also lay at the south end of the main canoe route that ran along the shores of Georgian Bay. North of there the soil was poor and the growing season short, so that none of the tribes depended on agriculture. They engaged mainly in hunting and fishing, and tribes from at least as far away as Lake Nipissing traded surplus skins, dried fish, and meat with the Huron in return for corn, which they ate in the winter when other food was scarce.[14]

As early as 1615 the French noted that Huronia was the centre of a well-developed system of trade. Hunt, however, seems to have seriously overestimated both the extent of this network and the degree to which the Huron were dependent on it.[15] The main trade appears to have been with the hunting peoples to the north, who happened to be Algonkian-speaking. The other Iroquoian tribes had economies similar to that of the Huron, so that with the exception of a few items, such as black squirrel skins, which came from the Neutral country, and tobacco from the Petun, trade with the other Iroquoian tribes was of little importance. Trade with the north, however, brought in supplies of dried meat, fish, skins, clothing, native copper, and "luxury items" such as charms, which were obtained in exchange for corn, tobacco, fishing nets, Indian hemp, wampum, and squirrel skins.[16] Although manufactured goods, as well as natural products, flowed in both directions, the most important item the Huron had for export undoubtedly was corn. In 1635 Father Le Jeune described Huronia as the "granary of most of the Algonkians."[17]

Whole bands of northerners spent the winters living outside Huron villages, trading furs and dried meat with their hosts in return for corn. The Huron assumed a dominant position in these trading relationships and the Jesuits record that when the Algonkians had dealings with them, they did so in the Huron language since the latter did not bother to learn Algonkian.[18] The social implications of such linguistic behaviour cannot be lost on anyone living in present-day Quebec. In the French accounts the Algonkians appear to have been better friends of the Rock tribe than they were of the Bear.[19]

Considerable quantities of European trade goods that are believed to date between 1550 and 1575 have been found in Seneca sites in New York State.[20] Since both archaeological and historical evidence suggests that there was contact between the Huron and the tribes that lived along the St. Lawrence River in the sixteenth century,[21] it is possible that trade goods were arriving in Huronia in limited quantities at this time as well. In any such trade the Algonkin [the Algonkian-speaking peoples of the Ottawa Valley] tribes along the Ottawa River would almost certainly have been intermediaries. It is thus necessary to consider the possibility that trade between the Huron and the northern Algonkians originally developed as a result of the Huron desire to obtain European trade goods.

There are a number of reasons for doubting that trade with the northern tribes had a recent origin. For one thing, the rules governing trade were exceedingly elaborate. A particular trade route was recognized as the property of the Huron tribe or family that had pioneered it, and other people were authorized to trade along this route only if they had obtained permission from the group to which it belonged.[22] Thus, since the Rock were the first Huron tribe to establish relations with the French on the St. Lawrence, they alone were entitled by Huron law to trade with them.[23] Because of the importance of this trade, however, the Rock soon "shared" it with the more numerous and influential Bear, and with the other tribes of Huronia.[24] The control of trade was vested in a small number of chiefs, and other men had to have their permission before they were allowed to engage in it.[25] An even more important indication of the antiquity of Huron contact with the north is the archaeological evidence of the Huron influence on the Native cultures of that region, which can be dated as early as A.D. 900 and is especially evident in pottery styles.[26] Taken together, these two lines of evidence provide considerable support for the hypothesis of an early trade.

In the historic period the Huron men left their villages to visit other tribes in the summers, while their women were working in the fields. Profit was not the only reason for undertaking long voyages. The Jesuits report that many travelled into distant regions to gamble or to see new sights — in short, for adventure. Trading expeditions, like war, were a challenge for young men.[27] Trading between different tribes was not always a safe and uncomplicated business and, for all they had to gain from trade during the historic period, the Huron frequently were hesitant to initiate trade with tribes of whom they had only slight acquaintance.

The dangers that beset intertribal contacts were largely products of another institution, as old, if not older than trade — the blood feud. If a man was slain by someone who was not his kinsman, his family, clan, or tribe (depending on how far removed the murderer was) felt obliged to avenge his death by slaying the killer or one of the killer's relatives. Such action could be averted only by reparations in the form of gifts paid by the group to which the murderer belonged to that of the murdered man. When an act of blood revenge actually was carried out, the injured group usually regarded it as a fresh injury; thus any killing, even an accidental one, might generate feuds that would go on for generations. This was especially true of intertribal feuds.[28]

The Huron and Five Nations had both suppressed blood feuds within their respective confederacies, but only with great difficulty. When quarrels arose between individuals from tribes not so united, they frequently gave rise to bloodshed and war. The chances of war were also increased because skill in raiding was a source of prestige for young men who therefore desired to pursue this activity.[29] If it were possible, prisoners captured in war were taken back to their captors' villages to be tortured to death, partly as an act of revenge, but also as a sacrifice to the sun or "god of war."[30] These three motives — revenge, individual prestige, and sacrifice — were common to all the Iroquoian-speaking peoples of the northeast and to many of their neighbours, and generated and sustained intertribal wars over long periods of time. Indeed, where no close political ties existed, such as those within the Huron confederacy, and where there were no mutually profitable trading relationships, war between tribes appears to have been the rule. The Huron were almost invariably at war with one or more of the Five Nations, and prior to the development of the fur trade (when they started to carry French goods to the south and west) they appear to have been at war with the Neutral and Petun as well.[31]

On the other hand, when a trading relationship developed between the Huron and some neighbouring tribe, every effort was made to control feuds that might lead to war between them. The payment that was made to settle a blood feud with the Algonkians was greater than that made to settle a feud inside the confederacy,[32] and the dearest payment on record was made to the French in 1648 to compensate them for a Jesuit *donné* murdered by some Huron chiefs.[33]

A second method of promoting stable relations between tribes that wished to be trading partners appears to have been the exchange of a few people both as a token of friendship and to assure each group that the other intended to behave properly. Very often, these hostages appear to have been children. Although this custom is never explicitly described by the early French writers, the evidence for its existence is clear-cut. A Huron, whose sons or nephews (sister's sons and therefore close relatives) were sent to the Jesuit seminary in Quebec, boasted that they were relatives of the French and for this reason hoped for preferential treatment when they went to trade on the St. Lawrence.[34] Others said they had "relatives" among the Neutral and Petun, and one man is reported as leaving his daughter with these relatives.[35] The priests and lay visitors who came to Huronia in early times were treated as kinsmen by the Huron, and families and individuals were anxious to have them live with them,[36] no doubt because the Huron regarded these visitors as pledges of good faith whose association with a particular family would establish good relations between that family and the French officials and traders downriver. The presentation of young children to Jacques Cartier at a number of villages along the St. Lawrence suggests, moreover, that this custom may have been an old one.[37]

The Huron thus not only traded with other tribes prior to the start of the fur trade, but also, in common with other tribes in the northeast, had developed a code or set of conventions that governed the manner in which this trade was conducted. Being a product of Indian culture, this code was designed to deal with specifically Indian problems. We will now turn to the French attempts to adapt themselves to the Native trading patterns after Champlain's first encounter with the Indians in 1608.

EARLY FRANCO–HURON RELATIONS

In 1608, the year Champlain established a trading post at Quebec, he was visited by the representatives of some Algonkin tribes from the Ottawa Valley, and, in order to win their respect for him as a warrior and to secure their goodwill, he agreed to accompany them the following year on a raid against their chief enemy, the Iroquois.[38] The regions to the north gave promise of more pelts and ones of better quality than did the Iroquois country to the south, and fighting with a tribe alongside its enemies was an effective way of confirming an alliance.[39] Thus Champlain's actions seem to have been almost inevitable. At the same time he probably also hoped to drive Iroquois raiders from the St. Lawrence Valley and to open the river as a valuable trade artery.[40]

When the Ottawa River Algonkin returned the next year, they were accompanied by a party of Huron warriors from the Rock tribe. In later times the Huron informed the Jesuits that they had first heard of the French from the Algonkians early in the seventeenth century, and as a result of this had decided to go downriver to meet these newcomers for themselves.[41] Very likely, Champlain's account and the Huron one refer to the same event. Some of the Ottawa River Algonkin, who were already probably in the habit of wintering in Huronia, may have tried to recruit Huron warriors for their forthcoming expedition against the Iroquois, and the Huron, prompted by curiosity and a desire for adventure, may have agreed to accompany them to Quebec.

Champlain was keenly interested at this time both in exploring the interior and in making contacts with the people who lived there. Learning the size of the Huron confederacy and their good relations with the hunting (and potentially trapping) peoples to the north, Champlain realized their importance for the development of the fur trade and set out to win their friendship. The Huron, on the contrary, were at first extremely hesitant in their dealings with the French,[42] in part because they had no treaty with them and also because they regarded the French as allies of the Algonkin, who might become hostile if they saw the Hurons trying to establish an independent relationship with them.

The ambiguity of the Huron position can be seen in the exchange of children that was arranged in 1610. At that time the Huron gave Champlain custody of a boy, who was to go to France with him, and in exchange they received a young Frenchman. When the Huron departed, however, the French boy (probably Étienne Brûlé) did not leave with them, but stayed with Iroquet, an Algonkin chief from the lower Ottawa.[43] Iroquet, however, seems to have been one of the Algonkin who was in the habit of wintering in Huronia. Thus a three-sided exchange seems to have been arranged in which the Huron laid the basis for a friendly relationship with the French, but one that was subordinate to, and dependent upon, their relationship with the Algonkin.

As trade with the French increased, the Huron began to appreciate French goods and to want more of them. Metal awls and needles were superior to Native bone ones, and iron arrowheads could penetrate the traditional shields and body armour of their enemies. Metal kettles were easier to cook in than clay pots and metal knives were much more efficient than stone ones. Clearing fields and cutting wood was easier when stone axes were replaced by iron hatchets. Luxury items, such as cloth and European beads, were soon sought after as well.[44]

The growing demand for these products in a population that numbered between twenty and thirty thousand no doubt made the Huron anxious to establish closer relations with the French, without, if possible, having to recognize the Ottawa River Algonkin as middlemen or to pay them tolls to pass through their lands.[45] Since the principal item that the French wanted was beaver pelts,[46] the Huron probably also began to expand their trade with the north at this time in order to secure these furs in larger quantities. In return for these furs, they carried not only corn and tobacco but also French trade goods to their northern trading partners. The tribes north of Lake Huron seem to have continued to trade exclusively with the Huron rather than seeking to obtain goods from the French. No doubt this was in part because Huronia was nearby and reaching it did not require a long and hazardous journey down the Ottawa River. Such a journey would have been time-consuming, if not impossible, for a small tribe. More importantly, however, they wanted corn for winter consumption, which the Huron, but not the French, were able to provide. Although there is no documentary evidence to support this suggestion, it seems likely that increasing supplies of corn permitted these hunters to devote more time to trapping and relieved them of some of their day-to-day worries about survival.[47] Thus the growth of the fur trade may have led the northern groups to concentrate on trapping and the Huron to devote more of their energy to producing agricultural surpluses to trade with the north.[48] On at least one occasion, the Huron were providing even the French at Quebec with needed supplies of food.[49] In the 1640s their close friends and trading partners, the Nipissing, were travelling as far north as James Bay each year in order to collect the furs which they passed on to the Huron.[50]

In spite of the Huron desire for French goods and their ability to gather furs from the interior, the development of direct trade between Huronia and the St. Lawrence required the formation of a partnership that was expressed in terms the Indian could understand. Without continual assurances of goodwill passing between Huron and French leaders and without the exchange of gifts and people, no Huron would have travelled to Quebec without fear and trepidation. Even after many years of trade, Hurons going to Quebec felt safer if they were travelling with a Frenchman whom they knew and who could be trusted to protect their interests while they were trading.[51] Champlain understood clearly that treaties of friendship were necessary for successful trading partnerships with the Indians. For this reason he had been willing to support the Algonkin and Montagnais in their wars with the Mohawk and, since it was impossible to be friendly with both sides, had maintained his alliance with these northern tribes in spite of Iroquois overtures for peace.[52] The cementing of a treaty with the various Huron tribes was clearly the main reason he visited Huronia in 1615, a visit made in the face of considerable opposition from the Ottawa River Algonkin.[53]

Quite properly in Huron eyes, Champlain spent most of his time in Huronia with the Rock tribe. This had been the first of the Huron tribes to contact him on the St. Lawrence and therefore had a special relationship with the French according to Huron law. When he accompanied a Huron war party on a traditional, and what appeared to him as an ill-fated, raid against the central Iroquois, Champlain was resorting to a now-familiar technique for winning the friendship of particular tribes.[54] What Champlain apparently still did not realize was that the aim of these expeditions was adventure and taking prisoners, rather than the destruction of enemy villages.[55] The Huron were undoubtedly far more pleased with the results of the expedition than Champlain was.

From 1615 on, a number of Frenchmen were living in Huronia; their main purpose in being there was to encourage the Huron to trade.[56] Many of these young men, like the coureurs de bois of later times, enjoyed their life among the Indians and, to the horror of the Catholic clergy, made love to Huron women and probably married them according to local custom. The rough and tumble ways of individuals like Étienne Brûlé endeared them to their Huron hosts and this, in turn, allowed them to inspire confidence in the Indians who came to trade. It has been suggested that the main reason these men remained in Huronia was to persuade the Huron to trade in New France rather than to take their furs south to the Dutch who had begun to trade in the Hudson Valley after 1609.[57] This explanation seems unlikely, however. Until 1629 most of the Dutch trade appears to have been confined to the Mahican.[58] Although the Dutch were apparently anxious to trade with the "French Indians" as early as 1633, the Mohawk were not willing to allow them to do so unless they were in some way able to profit from the trade themselves.[59] This the Huron, who had a long-standing feud with the Iroquois, were unwilling to let them do.

The main job of the early coureurs de bois appears to have been to live in Huronia as visible evidence of French goodwill and as exchanges for the Huron youths who were sent to live with the French.[60] In this capacity they were able to encourage the Indians to engage in trade. Each year some of them travelled downriver with the Huron to see that the Algonkin did not prevent the passage of their canoes or scare the Huron off with stories of disasters or plots against them in Quebec.[61] They also acted as interpreters for the Huron and aided them in their dealings with the traders.[62] Except for the years when the Mohawk blockaded the Ottawa

River, the Huron sent an annual "fleet" or series of fleets to Quebec bearing the furs they had collected.[63] It is unfortunate that the records do not supply more information on these fleets, particularly about who organized them and what was their tribal composition. The fleets left Huronia in the spring and returned several months later. When the St. Lawrence was blocked by the Iroquois, the Hurons made their way to Quebec over the smaller waterways that led through the Laurentians.[64]

The Recollet and Jesuit missionaries who worked in Huronia between 1615 and 1629 were accepted by the Huron as part of the Franco–Huron trading alliance and as individuals whose goodwill was potentially advantageous in dealing with the traders and authorities in Quebec. That they lacked interest except as shamans is evident from Gabriel Sagard's statement that it was hard to work among any tribe that was not engaged in trade (i.e., bound by the Franco–Huron alliance).[65] The priests appear to have restricted their missionary activities to caring for the needs of the French traders in Huronia and trying to make some converts among the Indians. Their preaching, as far as it was understood, did not appear to present a challenge or affront to the Huron way of life, although the customs of the priests were strange to the Indians, who found these men austere and far less appealing than the easy-going coureurs de bois.[66] For obvious reasons, relations between the priests and local traders were not good and Sagard claims that among other things the latter often refused to help the missionaries learn Native languages.[67] The most serious charge that the priests levelled at these traders was that their behaviour sowed confusion and doubt among the Huron and impeded the spread of the Christian faith among them.[68] These early experiences convinced the Jesuits that to run a mission in Huronia properly the priests must control those Europeans who were allowed to enter the country.

In the early part of the seventeenth century the colony of New France was nothing more than a trading post and its day-to-day existence depended upon securing an annual supply of furs.[69] Not understanding the long-standing hostility between the Huron and the Iroquois, the French were apprehensive of any move that seemed likely to divert furs from the St. Lawrence to the Hudson Valley. The French made peace with the Mohawk in 1624 and French traders did business with them, an arrangement that no doubt pleased the Mohawk as it made them for a time less dependent on the Dutch and therefore gave them more bargaining power in their dealings with Albany.[70] Nevertheless, the French became extremely alarmed about a peace treaty that the Huron negotiated with the Seneca in 1623. This appears to have been one of the periodic treaties that the Huron and Iroquois negotiated in order to get back members of their respective tribes who had been taken prisoner, but not yet killed, by the enemy.[71] As such, it was probably perfectly harmless to French interests. Nevertheless the situation was judged sufficiently serious for a delegation of eleven Frenchmen, including three clerics, to be sent to the Huron country.[72] Various writers have followed Jean Charlevoix in saying that this delegation was instructed to disrupt the new treaty. Charlevoix, however, wrote long after the event took place and is not an unbiased witness.[73] It seems more likely that the expedition had as its main purpose simply the reaffirming of the alliances made between Champlain and the various Huron chiefs in 1615. In actual fact the Huron probably had no thought of trading with the Iroquois at this time. To the chagrin of the Dutch, the Mohawk were firm in their refusal to allow the northern tribes to pass through their country to trade on the Hudson. The Huron undoubtedly felt that direct trade with the French, even if they were farther from Huronia than the Dutch,[74] was preferable to trade via the Mohawk with the Europeans in New York State.

The very great importance that the Huron attached to their trade with the French even at this time is shown by their efforts to prevent potential rivals, such as the Petun or Neutral, from concluding any sort of formal alliance with the French. Neither group seems to have constituted much of a threat, since the Petun had to pass through Huron territory in order to paddle north along the shore of Georgian Bay[75] and the Neutral, who do not seem to have had adequate boats, would have had to travel down the St. Lawrence River to Quebec — en route the Mohawk would have either stolen their furs or forced them to divert most of the trade to the south.[76] The Huron do not seem to have minded well-known coureurs de bois occasionally visiting the Neutral or other tribes with whom they traded, but when, on his visit to the Neutral in 1626, Father de La Roche Daillon proposed an alliance between them and the French, the Huron spread rumours about the French that brought an end to the proposed treaty.[77] The ease with which the Huron did this, and repeated the manoeuvre in 1640–41,[78] is an indication both of the insecurity that tribes felt in the absence of a proper treaty with foreigners and of the importance that the Huron placed on their privileged relationship with the French. These observations reinforce our conclusion that coureurs de bois did not live in Huronia simply to dissuade the Huron from going to trade with either the Mohawk or the Dutch, but instead were a vital link in the Franco–Huron alliance and necessary intermediaries between the Huron and the French fur traders in Quebec. Such were the services for which Brûlé received a hundred pistoles each year from his employers.[79]

Franco–Huron trade increased in the years prior to 1629. Undoubtedly the Huron were growing increasingly reliant on European goods, but it is unlikely that they were ever completely dependent on trade during this period. There is no evidence that the British occupation of Quebec led them to trade with New Holland or with the Iroquois. Several renegade Frenchmen, including Brûlé, remained in Huronia and probably encouraged the Huron to trade with the British.[80] It was during this period that Brûlé was murdered by the Huron living in Toanché. Since he was given a proper burial it is unlikely that he was tortured to death and eaten as Sagard reports.[81] More likely, he was killed in a brawl with the Huron among whom he lived. That he was killed during the British occupation of New France does not, however, seem to be without significance. Until the French withdrawal he had been protected not only by his popularity but more importantly by the Franco–Huron alliance. Once the French had departed, he was on his own.

THE JESUITS TAKE CONTROL

The Compagnie des Cent-Associés, which took effective control of the affairs of New France after the colony was retroceded to France in 1632, was different from earlier trading companies in that its members were more interested in missionary work than their predecessors had been. At this time the Society of Jesus also managed to obtain the de facto monopoly over missionary activities in New France that it was to hold for many years.[82] The Jesuits brought about a number of changes in policy with regard to Huronia. In particular, they were much more anxious to evangelize the Huron *as a people* than the Recollets had been.[83] As their prime goal they sought to lead the entire confederacy toward the Christian religion, rather than to convert individuals. Moreover, as a result of the strong influence they wielded at the French court, they were in a better position to command the support of officials and fur traders.[84] For the first while after they returned to the Huron country, the Jesuits continued many of the mission practices that had been current prior to 1629, such as sending Indian children to their seminary at Quebec.[85] As their knowledge of the Huron language and of the country improved (in both cases as a result of systematic study), they gradually began to modify their work along lines that were more in keeping with their general policy.[86]

A major bête noire of the missionaries prior to 1629 was the French traders who lived in Huronia and set a bad example for the Natives. In order to assure unity of purpose for their work, the duties that formerly had been carried out by these coureurs de bois were taken over by lay brothers, workmen, and *donnés* directly subject to Jesuit supervision.[87] Later accusations that the Jesuits were engaged in the fur trade seem to have sprung largely from this action. The oft-repeated claim that priests were vital to the fur trade in Huronia is obviously without foundation. The coureurs de bois, who had lived in Huronia for many years, not only had functioned effectively during this period without missionary support but also appear to have been substantially more popular and more effective in their dealings with the Huron than the priests had been. The Jesuits wished to be rid of this group principally to assure that the French living in Huronia would not be working at cross-purposes. The trading companies apparently were willing to allow the Jesuits to have their own way in this matter, but in return it was necessary that the laymen attached to the Jesuit mission discharge at least the most vital functions of organizing the annual trade which the coureurs de bois had done heretofore.[88] The reasons that the Jesuits had for wanting to be rid of the coureurs de bois were clearly religious, not economic.

The Jesuits' connections with the fur trade did not arise, however, simply from their desire to be rid of the coureurs de bois; they also depended on it not only to get into Huronia but also for their personal safety so long as they remained there. The Huron were obviously not at all interested in what the Jesuits had to teach, and on several occasions after 1634 they made it clear that they preferred the former coureurs de bois to the Jesuits and their assistants.[89] In 1633, and again in 1634, they offered a whole series of excuses, including the hostility of the Algonkin from Allumette Island, as reasons for not taking the Jesuits home with them.[90] Moreover, fearing revenge for the death of Brûlé, they were unwilling to allow their children to remain as seminarians at Quebec.[91] In 1634 Champlain made the official French position clear when he informed the Huron that he regarded the Jesuits' presence in their country as a vital part of a renewed Franco–Huron alliance, at the same time expressing the hope that they would someday agree to become Christians.[92] Since the Huron wanted to renew their former trading relationship with the French, they agreed to accept the priests as a token of this alliance. Henceforth they were bound by treaty to allow the Jesuits to live among them and to protect the priests from harm. The thought of having these individuals who were so respected by the French in Huronia and under their control must also have given the Huron confidence in their dealings with the French who remained in Quebec.

Although the Jesuits travelled to Huronia in 1635 in canoes that belonged to members of the Cord and Rock tribes, they were put ashore rather unceremoniously in the territory of the Bear tribe, where Brébeuf had worked previously and where Brûlé had been murdered.[93] It is not clear whether the Jesuits had wanted to go to this region or were left there by their Rock and Cord hosts who did not want to take them to their own villages. It is possible that the Bear, who were the most powerful of the Huron tribes, exerted their influence to have the Jesuits left among them. In this regard it is perhaps not without meaning that the Jesuits previously had discussed with the Indians the possibility of their settling in Ossossané, the chief town of the Bear nation.[94] Brébeuf was welcomed by the villagers of Ihonitiria, among whom he had lived before, and the Jesuits decided to settle in that village both because it was close to the canoe route to New France and also in order to persuade the villagers that they bore them no ill will for having murdered Brûlé. The latter, the Jesuits said, was regarded by the French as a traitor and debauched renegade.[95] Nevertheless, his murder haunted the Huron, and even some neighbouring tribes,[96] who feared that it might lead to war with the French. Such fears may have been responsible for the dispute that the Jesuits observed between certain villages of the Bear tribe shortly after their arrival in Huronia.[97]

It would appear that according to Native custom the Jesuits coming to Huronia had a right to expect they would receive free food and lodgings. This would have been in return for similar care given by the French to the young seminarists in Quebec.[98] In Huron eyes the latter had been exchanged as tokens of good faith in return for the Jesuits and their assistants.[99]

In fact, the Huron provided food and shelter for the Jesuits only rarely. The missionaries had to purchase or provide these things for themselves and found the Huron demanding payment of some sort for most of their services.[100]

For a time after their return to Huronia the Jesuits were the objects of friendly public interest and their presence and goodwill were sought after, in part because individual Hurons sought to obtain favours in Quebec through their commendation, in part because the services people performed for the Jesuits, and even attendance at religious instruction, were rewarded with presents of trade goods and tobacco. The latter, although a Native product, was scarce in Huronia at the time.[101] Since all of the priests (except perhaps Brébeuf) were struggling to learn the Huron language, most of the missionary activities during the first few years were confined to the Bear country. Only a few trips were made into more distant areas of Huronia.[102]

THE EPIDEMICS OF 1635 TO 1640

The first serious trial for the Jesuits, and for the Franco–Huron alliance, occurred between the years 1635 and 1640. An unspecified disease, either measles or smallpox, was present in Quebec the year the Jesuits returned to Huronia, and it followed the Huron fleet upriver. This was the beginning of a series of epidemics that swept away more than half the Huron population in the next six years.[103] These new maladies were especially fatal to children and old people. Because they were fatal to the latter group, many of the most skillful Huron leaders and craftsmen, as well as the people most familiar with Native religious lore, perished.[104] The loss of children may well have meant that the proportion of men of fighting age in the Huron population was below normal by the end of the next decade.

The Jesuits, who wished to save the souls of dying children, frequently baptized them, both with and without their parents' permission. The Huron, being unclear about the Jesuits' intention in doing this, observed that children tended to die soon after baptism and came to suspect that the Jesuits were practising a deadly form of witchcraft.[105] The rumour revived that the Jesuits had been sent to Huronia to seek revenge for Brûlé's murder,[106] a rumour which gained credence from pictures of the torments of hell that the Jesuits displayed in their chapel and from the ritual of the mass (which the Huron understood had something to do with eating a corpse).[107] According to Huron law, sorcerers could be killed without a trial, and in times of crisis extensive pogroms appear to have been unleashed against persons suspected of this crime.[108] Nevertheless, while individuals threatened to murder the Jesuits and on one occasion a council of the confederacy met to try the Jesuits on a charge of witchcraft,[109] none of the Frenchmen in Huronia was killed.

Although the majority of the people were frightened of the Jesuits and believed that they were working to destroy the country, their leaders repeatedly stressed that they could not afford to rupture the Franco–Huron alliance by killing the French priests.[110] One well-placed chief said that if the Huron did not go downriver to trade with the French for even two years, they would be lucky if they found themselves as well off as the [despised] Algonkians.[111] While this statement was a bit of rhetoric, it stresses the importance of the fur trade to the Huron at this time and their growing reliance on French trade goods. During the entire course of the epidemics only one village, apparently a small one, was willing to give up the use of trade goods, and hence presumably to sever relations with the French.[112] Instead, the Huron resorted to indirect means to persuade the Jesuits to leave Huronia *voluntarily*. Children were encouraged to annoy them, their religious objects were befouled, and occasionally they were personally threatened or mistreated.[113] The Jesuits noted, rather significantly, that these persecutions diminished before the annual trip downriver or after the return of a successful fleet.[114]

The French officials in Quebec were aware of the dangerous situation in which the Jesuits found themselves, but as long as feelings ran high in Huronia, these authorities could do no more than to try to spare them from the worst excesses of Huron anger. They did this by threatening to cut off trade if the Jesuits were killed.

By 1640 the serious epidemics in Huronia were over. That summer, the new governor of Canada, Charles Huault de Montmagny, took action to "punish" the Huron who came to Quebec for their bad treatment of the Jesuits.[115] It is not clear what form this punishment took, but it appears that in the course of his dealings with them he made it clear that he considered their bad treatment of the Jesuits had terminated the existing alliance. At the same time he offered to renew the alliance, but only on the clear understanding that the Jesuits would continue to live in Huronia and work there unmolested. This is the first time, to our knowledge, that French officials had injected a positive element of threat into their dealings with the Huron. Presumably, the great losses in manpower and skills that the Huron had suffered and their consequent increasing dependence on trade and French support made such action possible. The Huron were in good health and expecting an abundant harvest; hence, many of the anxieties that had plagued them in recent years were dispelled. Because of this they were once more in a good mood and, hence, under the protection of a renewed Franco–Huron alliance the Jesuits found themselves free not only to continue the mission work among them but also to intensify their efforts.[116]

Already during the final crisis of 1639, the Jesuits had decided to establish a permanent centre for their missionary work in the Huron area. This centre was foreseen as serving various functions. Not only would it provide a refuge in time of danger (such as they lacked in 1639), but it also would allow them to put up buildings of European design. It had not been economical to construct these in the Huron villages, which shifted their location about once every decade. The Jesuits' centre was thus designed to be a further example of European culture in the heart of Huronia, a focus from which new ideas could diffuse to the local population. Gradually, pigs, fowl, and young cattle were brought upriver from Quebec and European crops were grown in the fields nearby.[117] The residence of Ste Marie acquired a hospital and a burial ground and became a place where Christian Indians could come for spiritual retreats and assembly on feast days.[118] Being located apart from any one village, and near the geographical centre of the confederacy, it was better able, both from a political and a geographical point of view, to serve as a mission centre for all Huronia. (During the worst years of the epidemics the Jesuits had remained for the most part in the northwest corner of Huronia.) In 1639 the Jesuits also made a survey and census of the country prior to setting up a system of missions that would carry the Christian message to all of the Huron tribes and, as far as possible, to other tribes as well.[119]

The Jesuits had thus weathered a difficult period. It is clear that they had been allowed to enter Huronia and to continue there only because of the Franco–Huron alliance. That they were not killed or expelled from Huronia at the height of the epidemics is an indication of how dependent the Hurons were becoming on the fur trade and how much the alliance with the French meant to them. It also indicates that the Huron leaders were able to restrain their unruly followers in order to preserve good relations with New France.[120] Evidence of lingering malice towards the priests can be seen in the events that came to light on the visit of Fathers Brébeuf and Chaumonot to the Neutral country in the winter of 1640–41. There the priests learned that the Huron had offered the Neutral rich presents, if they would kill the missionaries.[121] In this way the Huron hoped to destroy two of the "sorcerers" who had been tormenting their nation, without endangering the French alliance. They also had other motives, however. The proposed murder, so long as it was not traced back to the Huron, would put the Neutral in a bad light and would prevent Brébeuf from pursuing any dealings with the Seneca. Although there is no evidence that Brébeuf planned to visit the Seneca, a rumour had spread that having failed to kill the Huron with witchcraft he now was seeking to turn their enemies loose upon them.[122]

A CRISIS IN HURON–IROQUOIS RELATIONS

If the year 1640 marked the end of the persecution of the Jesuits in Huronia, unknown to them and to their Huron hosts, it also marked the beginning of a crisis that was to destroy Huronia. Beaver had become rare in the Huron country and most of the skins they traded with the French came from neighbouring tribes to the north.[123] A similar decline in the beaver population of New York State seems to have reached a point of crisis by 1640. That year the number of pelts traded at Fort Orange is reported to have dropped sharply.[124] While it is possible that at least part of the decline was the result of clandestine traders cutting into official trade, most commentators agree that it was basically related to the exhaustion of the supply of beaver in the Iroquois' home territory.[125]

While this hypothesis is not well enough documented that it can be regarded as certain, it seems a useful one for explaining Iroquois behaviour during the next few years. There is little doubt that after 1640 the Iroquois were preoccupied with securing new sources of pelts. The main controversy concerning their relations with their neighbours during this period centres on whether they were seeking to obtain furs by forcing the Huron to share their trade with them[126] or were attacking their neighbours in order to secure new hunting territories. Although Trelease[127] supports the latter theory, the data he uses apply for the most part to a later period and come mainly from sources in New York State and New England. Contemporary Canadian evidence definitely seems to rule out his claims; indeed if his hypothesis were true, the events leading to the destruction of Huronia would make little sense at all.

Trelease's theory finds its main support in claims made by the Iroquois in the early part of the eighteenth century that they had conquered Ontario and adjacent regions as beaver hunting grounds. In the treaty of 1701, in which the Iroquois placed their "Beaver ground" under the protection of the King of England, the Iroquois said explicitly that they had driven the indigenous tribes from this area in order to hunt there.[128] Trelease errs, however, in assuming that the reasons the Iroquois gave for conquering this territory in 1701 were the same as those they actually had for doing so half a century earlier. There is no doubt that in 1701 the Iroquois (mainly the Seneca) were hunting beaver in Ontario, but since the Huron country was reported in the 1630s to be as hunted out as their own it is illogical to assume that they attacked this region in 1649 in order to secure more hunting territory. The Huron beaver supplies they sought to capture were those coming by trade from the north. Only after their attacks failed to capture the western fur trade and after Ontario was deserted for a time allowing the restoration of the local beaver population did the Iroquois begin to hunt there. Since they lacked historical records, it is not surprising that by 1701 the Iroquois believed the use that they were making of Ontario at the present time was the same reason they had for attacking the tribes there long before. The attacks the Iroquois launched against the Petun and Neutral, following their attack on the Huron, offer no opposition to this theory. Although these groups had not participated in the fur trade prior to 1649, there was considerable danger that with the Huron gone they would attempt to do so. Hence, their dispersal was also necessary.

Trelease's theory thus fails to provide an acceptable explanation of events in Canada in the middle of the seventeenth century. It seems much more likely that the Iroquois, and mainly the Mohawk, began by trying to force the Huron to trade with them and that only latterly, when their efforts in this direction were unsuccessful, did they decide to destroy the Huron (and their neighbours) as an intermediary group.

The Mohawk began to intimidate the Huron by harassing those travelling along the Ottawa River — a tactic that had the additional advantage of providing a supply of captured furs. In 1642 Iroquois raiders spread fear and terror throughout all of the Huron villages,[129] and in 1644 they succeeded in preventing contact between Quebec and Huronia.[130] The increasing number of guns that the Iroquois were acquiring from the Dutch, English, and Swedish colonies along the Atlantic seaboard gradually gave them military superiority over the Huron, among whom the French had limited and controlled the sale of guns.[131] In 1644 the French despatched more than twenty soldiers to Huronia to protect the Huron over the winter and assure the arrival of their furs in Quebec the next spring.[132] The Mohawk were also harassing the French in the St. Lawrence Valley, who were moved the next spring to discuss peace, both to assure their own safety and to reopen the river to trade. Although the subsequent treaty of 1645 was with the French, the Mohawk seem to have interpreted it as involving a commitment that in the future the Huron would trade with them as well as with the French.[133] The Huron, however, had no intention of doing this, and the French, who may not have perceived clearly what the Mohawk wanted, did not want to encourage them to divert trade. The main French reason for the treaty with the Mohawk was the short-term one of opening the river. The French had little to offer the Iroquois in return and refused to sell them guns, the one item they wanted.[134] When it became clear to the Mohawk that the Huron did not intend to trade with them, they renewed their attack on Huronia and on the Huron fleet.

THE DEVELOPMENT OF A CHRISTIAN FACTION

While this dangerous crisis in intertribal relations was boiling up, a situation was developing in Huronia that put a new strain on the Franco–Huron alliance.

Prior to 1640, most Christian converts were Hurons on the point of death, many of whom knew nothing about Christian theology but hoped that baptism would save their lives.[135] At one point during the epidemics a Huron version of the rite of baptism became part of a Native healing cult that was said to be inspired by a Native deity who had revealed himself as the real Jesus.[136] In these rites the sick were sprinkled with water as part of an orgiastic ceremony typical of traditional Huron healing rituals. After 1640, however, the Jesuits began to convert increasing numbers of people who were in good health. Many were men of importance, whose conversions made that of their families, friends, and tribesmen easier.[137] In order to prevent backsliding, the Jesuits at first made it a policy to baptize (except in cases of extreme ill health) only adults who had provided substantial proof of their devotion to Christianity and whose family life seemed to be stable.[138]

Many factors seem to have induced people to convert: some admired the bravery of the Jesuits, others wished to be able to follow a Christian friend to heaven, still others noted in their names a theological term that the Jesuits were using.[139]

Although economic motives were not the only ones involved in conversion, it is noteworthy that at least a few Huron became Christians to avoid participation in pagan feasts, which required them to give away considerable amounts of property in the form of presents and entertainment.[140] A far larger number of people hoped through conversion to receive preferential treatment in their dealings with traders and officials in New France.[141] In 1648, when only 15 percent of the Huron were Christian, half of the men in the Huron fleet were either converts or were preparing for baptism.[142] Those who traded with the French in Quebec not only were more exposed to French culture and to Christianity than were those who remained at home but also had more to gain from good relations with the French.

Commercial considerations may also explain why the Jesuits generally found it easier to convert men than women.

While stressing the practical economic motives that certainly motivated many conversions, personal and cultural factors should not be ignored. The Huron were increasingly dependent on French culture and in the eyes of many, but (as we shall see) certainly not all, of the Huron the priest was coming to replace the Native sorcerer as an object of awe and respect. This did not, however, lead the Huron to lose faith in themselves or in their culture, as it did in many other tribes.[143] Supported by the respect shown by the Jesuits for the Huron people and for much of their culture, many Huron converts appear to have been imbued with a sincere zeal to change and reform their own culture. No doubt the size of the Huron confederacy and its isolation from unsupervised contact with the Europeans did much to prevent the deterioration in self-confidence that is obvious among many weaker tribes. Had other circumstances not been adverse, I think it would have been possible for the Jesuits to have transformed Huronia successfully into a nation that was both Christian and Indian.

For a time the growing number of Huron converts posed no serious problems for the rest of society, although individual converts were frequently taunted and sometimes expelled from their longhouses with much resulting personal hardship.[144] (A woman who had been a member of a pagan healing society was threatened with death when after conversion she refused to perform in the society.[145]) Threats and assassination no doubt were the fate of other converts. The Jesuits and their assistants, however, were no longer attacked or molested in any way.[146] It appears that at least some headmen surrendered their political office on becoming Christians, since they felt that the obligation to participate in Huron festivals which these offices entailed was contrary to their new faith.[147] In this and in other ways the nascent Christian community avoided for a time the possibility of an open clash with the large pagan majority.

Gradually, however, a rift began. Some Christians refused, for example, to be buried in their tribal ossuaries, which in effect was to deny membership in their village or tribe.[148] They also refused to fight alongside pagans in the war parties but instead formed their own detachments, no doubt because of the religious implications of traditional Iroquoian warfare.[149] As the number of converts grew, men retained their political offices after conversion, but appointed deputies to handle the religious functions traditionally associated with them.[150] As the number of Christians who held these important offices continued to grow, the split between pagans and Christians became increasingly a political issue.

The Jesuits, for their part, now set as their immediate goal the Christianizing of an entire village.[151] Significantly the most promising town was Ossossané, where the Jesuits had been working for a long time. This town, belonging to the Bear tribe, was also the political centre of the Huron confederacy.[152] In 1648 they achieved their objective. By then the majority of people in Ossossané were converts. And that winter the chiefs of the village refused to allow the people who remained pagan to celebrate the traditional festivals, and they appointed a Jesuit as the chief headman of the village, with the right to act as a censor of public morals.[153]

THE PAGAN REACTION AND THE DESTRUCTION OF HURONIA

Although in 1645 such social revolutions were still several years in the future, many of the pagans had already begun to fear for the survival of their traditional customs and beliefs.[154] Undoubtedly a large number of these people were genuinely attached to the old ways and for this reason alone resented the growth of Christianity. It is also possible that many chiefs who wished to remain pagan began to fear a decline in their own influence as Christians began to play a stronger role in the life of the country. They probably resented the closer contacts that Christian chiefs had with the French and feared that these contacts would be used as a source of power. As a result of these fears and rivalries, pagan and Christian factions began to develop within the various tribes and villages throughout Huronia.[155]

Although the documentation in the Jesuit *Relations* is scanty, there appears to have been a considerable variation in attitude toward the Jesuits and Christianity among the different Huron tribes. The Bear, among whom the Jesuits had lived for the longest time and whose main town, Ossossané, had a large and rapidly growing Christian community, seem to have been the most pro-Christian and pro-French.[156] The Cord probably had much the same sort of attitude.[157] The Rock and Deer tribes, however, seem to have been considerably less friendly. The Jesuits report that the former tribe, being the easternmost, had suffered most from the attacks of the Iroquois and was therefore the most inclined to seek peace with their traditional enemies. The Rock were also described, however, as a tribe with a strong aversion to the faith, who never had been converted.[158] The Deer had a reputation among the Jesuits for being sorcerers,[159] and one assumes from this that they gave the missionaries a bad time. Both of these tribes joined the Iroquois of their own free will after the break-up of Huronia in 1649.[160] Despite this variation, however, there were people in all the Huron tribes who were starting to have misgivings about the future of Huronia and who resented the changes that the French alliance was bringing about.

After 1645 these sentiments seem to have led to the formation of a sizable anti-French party, which apparently found a certain amount of support everywhere in Huronia, except perhaps in Ossossané. This marked a new development in French–Huron relations, all previous opposition having been to the priests resident in Huronia rather than to the French in general. Supporters of this party seem to have reasoned that Christianity was a threat to Huronia, that Christianity flourished because the Jesuits were able to work there under the terms of the Franco–Huron alliance, and that the best way to save the country (and enhance the power of the pagan chiefs at the expense of their Christian rivals) was therefore to expel the Jesuits, break off the alliance, and begin trading with the Iroquois. In this way, not only would the traditional culture of Huronia be saved, but the attacks of the Iroquois, which had been growing in intensity,[161] could be brought to an end. Thus for the first time a respectable body of opinion in Huronia came to believe that an alliance with enemies who shared similar beliefs and culture was preferable to one with strangers seeking to change the Huron way of life. The threat that was facing the traditionalists made the thought of trading with their old enemies and rivals seem much less unpleasant than it had been a few years previously.

The first plan for a rapprochement with the Iroquois was well conceived and sought to exploit internal differences within the Iroquois confederacy for the Hurons' own advantage. Since the treaty of 1645 had failed to obtain the furs they wanted, the Mohawk were likely to be suspicious of, if not hostile to, further Huron blandishments. The Seneca likewise were unfriendly because of recent Huron attacks on them.[162] The Onondaga, however, had long enjoyed the position of being the chief tribe in the confederacy and were increasingly jealous of the Mohawk, who were exploiting their close contacts with the Dutch and the English in an effort to dominate the league.[163] It is therefore no surprise that it was through the Onondaga that the Huron attempted to make peace with the Iroquois.

The Jesuits did not record, and may not have known, the exact nature of the treaty that the Huron were trying to negotiate. The presence of a clause promising that the Huron would trade furs with the Iroquois is suggested by a remark, attributed to the Andaste or Susquehannock (who were allies of the Huron and sent ambassadors to the Onondaga to argue on their behalf), that such a treaty would promote the trade of all these tribes with one another.[164] It is also significant that among the Huron the Bear tribe was the one most opposed to this treaty.[165] The Jesuits said this was because the Bear had suffered less from Iroquois raids than had the other Huron tribes, but a second reason could be that the Christians, who were more numerous in this tribe than in the others, saw in these negotiations a clear threat to the Franco–Huron alliance and to their own power and well-being. Negotiations continued for some time, but were terminated in January 1648, when a party of Mohawk warriors slew a Huron embassy on its way to the chief Onondaga town to arrange the final terms of the treaty.[166] A distinguished Onondaga chief, who had remained in Huronia as a hostage, committed suicide when he learned what the Mohawk had done.[167]

There seems little reason to doubt the honesty of the Onondaga in these negotiations. The Mohawk probably attacked the Huron embassy because they were angry that negotiations were being conducted with the Onondaga rather than with them. The Mohawk may also have believed that the Huron were trying to deceive the Onondaga and that the only way of dealing with the Huron confederacy was to destroy it. In any case, the Mohawk managed to bring the first major political offensive of the anti-French faction in Huronia to an ignominious conclusion.

Even though this first effort had failed, at least some Huron apparently believed that a rapprochement with the Iroquois still was possible. Indeed, either because they were totally convinced of the necessity of appeasing the Iroquois or because of their extreme hatred of the Christians, a minority seems to have become convinced that a break with the French was a precondition for further negotiation. The group responsible for the next move was led by six, apparently distinguished, chiefs from three villages.[168] Unfortunately, these villages are unnamed. The chiefs decided to make a public issue of the question of a continued Franco–Huron alliance through the simple expedient of killing a Frenchman. They do not appear to have designated any particular victim, and their henchmen slew Jacques Douart, a *donné* whom they encountered not far from Ste Marie. Once Douart was slain, the conspirators issued a proclamation calling for the banishment from Huronia of the French and all of the Huron who insisted on remaining Christian.[169] An emergency council was convened (apparently from all over the country) and for several days these proposals were debated. On the one side were the Christians and those pagans who felt that the Franco–Huron alliance should continue; on the other the traditionalists who had stirred up the trouble and no doubt some other Hurons who hated neither Christianity nor the French, but who felt that a peace treaty with the Iroquois was important enough to be worth the termination of the French alliance. Among the latter must have been many refugees from the Rock tribe, which had been forced to abandon its villages as a result of Iroquois attacks only a short time before.[170] The pro-French party finally won the debate and the Jesuits in turn agreed to accept the traditional Huron compensation for a murder, in this case one hundred beaver skins.[171] The ritual presentation of this settlement made clear that it was designed to reaffirm and protect the Franco–Huron alliance, which the unprecedented actions of these chiefs had endangered. Thus ended what appears to have been the last attempt to rupture the Franco–Huron alliance.

During the summer of 1648 the Seneca attacked and destroyed the large town of St. Joseph. As the situation grew more serious, the Huron turned increasingly to the French for help and the number of conversions increased sharply.[172] As in 1644, a few French soldiers were sent to winter in Huronia. These soldiers, so long as they remained in Huronia, were believed sufficient to hold off the Iroquois, but they had been instructed to return to Quebec with the Huron fleet in the spring.[173] As the military situation in Huronia grew more desperate, the French in Quebec became increasingly anxious to profit as much as possible while they still could. In the summer of 1649, a party of over 30 coureurs de bois made a flying trip to Huronia and returned to Quebec bringing with them 5000 pounds of beaver.[174]

In the spring of 1649 the Iroquois unleashed the attack that resulted in the death of Fathers Lalemant and Brébeuf and brought about the dispersal of the Huron confederacy. Many factors contributed to the Iroquois victory, but their superior number of guns was undoubtedly the most important.[175] Hunt has suggested that the Huron were so given over to trading by 1649 that virtually all of their food was imported from the Neutral and Petun tribes and that the main factor in their defeat was therefore the cutting of their supply routes.[176] This suggestion is entirely without foundation. Agriculture was a woman's occupation and little affected by increasing trade. While men may have spent more time trading, the importation of iron axes made it easier to cut trees and hence there was no problem clearing the forests for agriculture. There are frequent references to the Huron as engaged in agricultural activities in the years prior to 1649, and one of the reasons the Iroquois returned to Huronia in the spring of 1650 was to prevent the planting of crops.[177] Driven from their homes and deprived of food, the Hurons scattered, and their trading monopoly came to an end. It is interesting that large numbers of Huron, particularly from the Rock and Deer tribes, migrated to the Iroquois country and settled there. The latter tribe settled en masse among the Seneca, where they lived in their own village and retained their separate customs for a long time.[178] Their tribal affiliations suggest that these refugees were for the most part traditionalists and probably among them were many of the people who had been the most hostile to the French during the last years of the Jesuit mission. This hostility explains how these groups were so easily adopted by the people who had destroyed their homeland.

For the Jesuits the destruction of Huronia was the end of their first dream of leading a nation to Christianity in the heart of the Canadian forest. At least once in the Relations they mentioned the work their colleagues were accomplishing in Paraguay and compared this work with their own.[179] The chance had been lost of converting a people to Christianity while allowing them to retain their language and those institutions and customs that were not incompatible with their new faith. Because they were writing for a patriotic French audience, the Jesuits have little to say about the constitutional status of the Huronia they wished to create. Nevertheless, it seems clear that what they aimed at was not so much a French colony as an Indian state, which under Jesuit leadership could blend the good things of Europe with those already in the Native culture. A Catholic Huronia would of necessity have been allied with France, the only Catholic power in eastern North America. Years later Louis de Buade de Frontenac probably came closer to a basic truth than he realized when he accused the Jesuits at Quebec of disloyalty because they kept the Indians apart from the French and taught them in their own language.[180]

The fur trade was the one means by which the Jesuits could gain admittance to Huronia and the only protection they had while working there. Ties with fur traders and government officials in Quebec were thus vital for the success of the Huron mission, but these ties do not seem to have prevented the Jesuits from seeking to serve the best interests of their Huron converts and Huronia at large — as they perceived these interests. To reverse the equation and say that the Jesuits were in Huronia mainly *for the purpose* of serving either the fur trade or the French government does not accord with anything we know about their activities.

In the short run the destruction of Huronia was a serious setback for New France. For a time the fur trade, on which the well-being of the colony depended, was cut to practically nothing. The Iroquois, on the other hand, seem to have achieved less than they hoped for from the destruction of Huronia. The western tribes soon became involved in a protracted war with the Erie,[181] and tribal jealousies rent the confederacy. As a result of these jealousies the four western tribes began to trade with the French to avoid travelling through Mohawk towns to reach the Dutch.[182] By 1654 the French were starting to put together the rudiments of a new trading network north of the Great Lakes.[183] The remnants of the Huron and Petun who had remained in this area, and more importantly the Ottawa, an Algonkian tribe, played a major role in pushing this trading network to the west in the years that followed.[184] As the population of New France increased, the young men of the colony, with or without official permission, joined in this trade. Thus the destruction of Huronia was neither a total nor a permanent disaster for New France and certainly it did not help to save North America for Protestantism and the Anglo-Saxons, as at least one eminent historian has suggested.[185]

A more serious question is what would have happened had the anti-French party in Huronia been successful. Had they been able to organize an effective resistance to the Huron Christians and conclude a treaty with the Iroquois, the trade from the north might have been diverted permanently from the St. Lawrence into the Hudson Valley. Had that happened (and as Sagard and Le Clercq indicate the people in Quebec knew it well[186]) the chances of the infant French colony surviving even for a short time would have been slim. Instead of the destruction of Huronia tipping the balance of power in favour of the English, its survival might well have led to a Huron–Iroquois alliance that would have resulted in the destruction of New France and the end of the French presence in North America.

NOTES

1. See, e.g., Samuel de Champlain's comment on the sagacity of the Indians in trade (H.P. Biggar, ed., *The Works of Samuel de Champlain* [6 vols.; Toronto, 1922–36], 2: 171), and Jean de Brébeuf, Gabriel Lalemant, and Francesco Bressani on the efficacy of Huron law (R.G. Thwaites, ed., *The Jesuit Relations and Allied Documents* [73 vols.; Cleveland, 1896–1901], 10: 215; 28: 49–51; 38: 277).

2. Thwaites, ed., *Relations* 18: 21. A similar statement is made by Paul Ragueneau (29: 281).

3. Invariably, however, these early witnesses of Indian culture were interested in rather limited aspects of Indian life and tended to interpret Indian culture in terms of their own. Because of this, a valid assessment of these early records requires a comparative knowledge of Indian culture in later times. The groundwork for our understanding of seventeenth-century Huron culture is thus the work of several generations of ethnologists and ethnohistorians in Canada and the United States. The best résumé of Huron culture is Elisabeth Tooker, *An Ethnography of the Huron Indians, 1615–1649* (Washington, 1964). For a shorter and less complete synopsis see W.V. Kinietz, *The Indians of the Western Great Lakes, 1615–1760* (Ann Arbor, 1940).

4. F. Parkman, *The Jesuits in North America in the Seventeenth Century* (Centenary Edition, Boston, 1927), 3, 4, 435, 436; G.E. Ellis, "Indians of North America," in J. Winsor, ed., *Narrative and Critical History of America* (8 vols.; Boston and New York, 1884–89), 1: 283.

5. G.T. Hunt, *The Wars of the Iroquois: A Study in Intertribal Relations* (Madison, 1940), 4, 19.

6. Biggar, ed., *Works of Champlain* 3: 49–51; 4: 238–44.

7. Thwaites, ed., *Relations* 16: 227.

8. L.H. Morgan, *League of the Ho-de-no-sau-nee, or Iroquois* (Rochester, 1851; reprinted New Haven, 1954). For a briefer description, see Morgan's *Houses and House-life of the Indian Aborigines* (Washington, 1881; reprinted with original pagination Chicago, 1965), 23–41.

9. Meat remained largely a festive dish, commonest in winter and spring (G.M. Wrong, ed., *Sagard's Long Journey to the Country of the Hurons* [Toronto, 1939], 82; Thwaites, ed., *Relations* 17: 141–43).

10. Thwaites, ed., *Relations* 16: 227–29. See also Elisabeth Tooker, "The Iroquois Defeat of the Huron: A Review of Causes," *Pennsylvania Archaeologist* 33 (1963): 115–23, especially 119, 120.

11. J.V. Wright, *The Ontario Iroquois Tradition* (Ottawa, 1966), 68–83. For information concerning the movements from the west I am indebted to a personal communication from Dr. Wright.

12. See, for example, D. Jenness, *The Indians of Canada* (5th ed.; Ottawa, 1960), 280.

13. B.G. Trigger, "The Historic Location of the Hurons," *Ontario History* 54 (1962): 137–48. For physiographic conditions, see L.J. Chapman and D.F. Putnam, *The Physiography of Southern Ontario* (2nd ed.; Toronto, 1966), 299–312.

14. Biggar, ed., *Works of Champlain* 3: 52, 53. On the importance of corn meal among the northern hunters see Wrong, ed., *Sagard's Long Journey,* 268.

15. Hunt, *Wars of the Iroquois,* 53–65.

16. For the reference to squirrel skins see Thwaites, ed., *Relations* 7: 13; to nets, 6: 309.

17. Thwaites, ed., *Relations* 8: 15.

18. Wrong, ed., *Sagard's Long Journey,* 86.

19. For a hostile statement about the Bear by the Algonkins, see Thwaites, ed., *Relations* 10: 145.

20. C.F. Wray and H.L. Schoff, "A Preliminary Report on the Seneca Sequence in Western New York State, 1550–1687," *Pennsylvania Archaeologist* 23 (1953): 53–63.

21. Colonel James F. Pendergast (personal communication) reports finding considerable evidence of Huron influence in late Iroquoian sites along the St. Lawrence River. These probably date from the sixteenth century or only a little earlier. For the historical evidence of contacts between the St. Lawrence Iroquoians and the interior of Ontario, see H.P. Biggar, ed., *The Voyages of Jacques Cartier* (Ottawa, 1924), 170–71, 200–202.

22. Thwaites, ed., *Relations* 10: 225.

23. Thwaites, ed., *Relations* 20: 19.

24. Thwaites, ed., *Relations* 20: 19. In 1640 Lalemant reported that the Rock still considered themselves the special allies of the French and were inclined to protect them. This attitude changed after the Jesuits became more active in the interior of Huronia.

25. Wrong, ed., *Sagard's Long Journey*, 99. Sagard says that a special council decided each year the number of men who could go out from each village. For more on the control of trade by old and influential men, see Thwaites, ed., *Relations* 14: 39.

26. J.V. Wright, "A Regional Examination of Ojibwa Culture History," *Anthropologica* N.S. 7 (1965): 189–227.

27. Thwaites, ed., *Relations* 5: 241.

28. The Huron claimed that their feud with the Iroquois had been going on 50 years prior to 1615 (Biggar, ed., *Works of Champlain* 5: 78).

29. Thwaites, ed., *Relations* 23: 91.

30. Wrong, ed., *Sagard's Long Journey*, 159–61. For comparative discussions of Iroquoian warfare see Nathaniel Knowles, "The Torture of Captives by the Indians of Eastern North America," *Proceedings of the American Philosophical Society* 82 (1940): 151–225; R.L. Rands and C.L. Riley, "Diffusion and Discontinuous Distribution," *American Anthropologist* 58 (1958): 274–97.

31. For the wars with the Petun, see Thwaites, ed., *Relations* 20: 43. Even at the time of Sagard's visit, there was a threat of war with the Neutral (Wrong, ed., *Sagard's Long Journey*, 151, 156, 157).

32. Thwaites, ed., *Relations* 33: 243.

33. Thwaites, ed., *Relations* 33: 239–49.

34. Thwaites, ed., *Relations* 13: 125. The Bear Tribe wanted the French to participate in their Feast of the Dead so that they could thereby claim them as relatives (10: 311).

35. Thwaites, ed., *Relations* 27: 25; 20: 59.

36. Chrétien Le Clercq, *First Establishment of the Faith in New France*, trans. J.G. Shea, 2 vols. (New York, 1881), 1: 97; Wrong, ed., *Sagard's Long Journey*, 71.

37. Biggar, ed., *Voyages of Cartier*, 132–3, 143. The custom of giving children to Cartier may have arisen, on the other hand, as a result of the Indians observing Cartier's predilection for kidnapping Indians. In 1534 he had seized the two sons of Donnaconna, the chief of Stadacona.

38. The fact that the Huron and Algonkians both were at war with the Five Nations naturally pitted the French against these latter tribes. Presumably Champlain's decision to side with the Huron and Algonkians was based on his conviction that it was impossible to maintain satisfactory relations with both sides, as well as on the economic factors mentioned in the text. For a discussion of the origins of the hostility between the Algonkians and Five Nations, see B.G. Trigger, "Trade and Tribal Warfare on the St. Lawrence in the Sixteenth Century," *Ethnohistory* 9 (1962): 240–56.

39. For Champlain's own comment on Indian expectations in this regard, see Biggar, ed., *Works of Champlain* 2: 70, 71, 110.

40. H.A. Innis, *The Fur Trade in Canada* (2nd ed.; Toronto, 1956), 23–26.

41. Thwaites, ed., *Relations* 15: 229. The first Huron chief to have dealings with the French was Atironta of the Rock tribe.

42. Biggar, ed., *Works of Champlain* 2: 188, 189, 193. For a more general reference see 2: 254.

43. Biggar, ed., *Works of Champlain* 2: 141; 4: 118, 119. This interpretation is reinforced by Champlain's statement that the boy was brought back by 200 Huron on June 13, 1611 (2: 186; 4: 136).

44. For comments on the Indians' desire for European manufactured goods, see Innis, *Fur Trade*, 16–19; Hunt, *Wars of the Iroquois*, 4, 5.

45. For examples of Algonkin harassment of Huron trade along the Ottawa River and various Algonkin attempts to imperil Franco–Huron relations (particularly by the Algonkin from Allumette Island) see Biggar, ed., *Works of Champlain* 5: 102; Wrong, ed., *Sagard's Long Journey*, 262; Thwaites, ed., *Relations* 5: 239; 7: 213; 8: 83, 99; 9: 271; 10: 77; 14: 53. The Montagnais also tried to intimidate the Huron, mainly to get free corn (Wrong, ed., *Sagard's Long Journey*, 265–68).

46. Innis, *Fur Trade*, 3–6, 11–15.

47. This is essentially the kind of relationship that existed between trading companies and Indian trappers in the north in more recent times.

48. Champlain reports that the Huron produced large food surpluses which he says were meant to carry them over years of poor crops (Biggar, ed., *Works of Champlain* 3: 155–56). At least a part of these surpluses was used for trade.

49. Le Clercq, *Establishment* 1: 298.

50. Thwaites, ed., *Relations* 35: 201. There is good evidence, however, that the Nipissing were travelling north even earlier (Biggar, ed., *Works of Champlain* 2: 255–56).

51. Le Clercq, *Establishment* 1: 211; Wrong, ed., *Sagard's Long Journey*, 244.

52. Biggar, ed., *Works of Champlain* 5: 73–80; Hunt, *Wars of the Iroquois*, 69.

53. The Huron had invited Champlain to visit their country as early as 1609 (Biggar, ed., *Works of Champlain* 2: 105). His attempt to travel up the Ottawa River in 1613 was brought to an end by the opposition of the Algonkin, among other things. Marcel Trudel (*Histoire de la Nouvelle-France*, vol. 2, *Le Comptoir, 1604–1627* [Montréal, 1966], 198–201) may be correct when he suggests that the Algonkin stirred up trouble between Champlain and Vignau in order to protect their trading interests in the interior.

54. Although Champlain visited all the major Huron villages, he returned repeatedly to Cahiague, a Rock village. He also spent more time there than anywhere else. Lalemant reports that in 1640 his reputation was still very much alive among the Rock (Thwaites, ed., *Relations* 20: 19).

55. Biggar, ed., *Works of Champlain* 3: 66, 69, 73; 4: 254–66; also Hunt, *Wars of the Iroquois*, 20.

56. Since most of the available data about this period was recorded by priests, we have little information about these men, and practically none from a friendly source. For what there is see, Biggar, ed., *Works of Champlain* 5: 101, 108, 129, 131, 132, 207; Le Clercq, *Establishment* 1: 205; Wrong, ed., *Sagard's Long Journey*, 194–95; Thwaites, ed., *Relations* 5: 133; 6: 83; 14: 17, 19; 18: 45; 20: 19; 25: 85.

57. A.W. Trelease, *Indian Affairs in Colonial New York: The Seventeenth Century* (Ithaca, 1960), 30.

58. Trelease, *Indian Affairs*, 46. Intermittent hostilities between the Mahican and Mohawk kept the latter from Fort Orange prior to the stunning defeat of the Mahican in 1628 or 1629 (48).

59. Trelease, *Indian Affairs*, 52–54; Thwaites, ed., *Relations* 8: 59–61; Hunt, *Wars of the Iroquois*, 34. In 1638 the Huron told the Jesuits that "Englishmen" had come as far as Montreal telling the Indians that the Jesuits were the cause of sickness in Huronia (and no doubt attempting to trade with them or divert trade to the south) (Thwaites, ed., *Relations* 15: 31.)

60. See, e.g., Biggar, ed., *Works of Champlain* 5: 101, 207.

61. Biggar, ed., *Works of Champlain* 5: 108. On the usefulness of having Frenchmen accompany the fleet see Wrong, ed., *Sagard's Long Journey*, 262. Sagard reports that in the 1620s the Iroquois refrained from attacking Huron flotillas when they knew Frenchmen were travelling with the Indians (261).

62. These were at least the functions that the Huron expected Frenchmen who had lived in Huronia would perform. The coureurs de bois are frequently referred to as interpreters (Biggar, ed., *Works of Champlain* 3: 168–72).

63. Wrong, ed., *Sagard's Long Journey*, 249–56.

64. This route apparently had been used in prehistoric times as well (Biggar, ed., *Voyages of Cartier*, 200–201, as interpreted by Innis, *Fur Trade*, 22).

65. Edwin Tross, ed., *Histoire du Canada et voyages que les Frères mineurs Recollets y ont faicts pour la conversion des infidèles depuis l'an 1615 . . .*, by G. Sagard (4 vols.; Paris, 1866), 1: 42. This statement refers to the visit Le Caron made with Champlain. On the Huron desire to have the priests act as go-betweens in their trade with the French, see Wrong, ed., *Sagard's Long Journey*, 244; Le Clercq, *Establishment* 1: 211.

66. The Indians often were reluctant to take missionaries back to Huronia with them (Thwaites, ed., *Relations* 4: 221). Some priests, however, became personally popular with the Huron. The popularity of Father Brébeuf during his initial stay in Huronia is evident from the welcome he received when he returned in 1634.

67. This claim appears in the *Dictionary of Canadian Biography*, vol. 1, *1000 to 1700* (Toronto, 1966), 133. It appears to be based on Sagard's comments on the behaviour of an interpreter named Nicolas Marsolet. Although Marsolet refused to teach the Montagnais language to the Recollets, he later agreed to instruct the Jesuits (Tross, ed., *Histoire du Canada* 2: 333).

68. It is perhaps significant that the main complaint was about the sexual behaviour of these men rather than the sale of alcohol to the Indians (cf. André Vachon, "L'Eau-de-vie dans la société indienne," Canadian Historical Association, *Report*, 1960, 22–32). Alcohol does not appear to have been a serious problem in Huronia, no doubt because the Huron did not at this time feel their culture threatened by European contacts. The Jesuits' distaste for these men is reiterated in the Jesuit Relations, particularly when they are compared with the *donnés* and other men who served in Huronia under Jesuit supervision after 1634. See Thwaites, ed., *Relations* 6: 83; 14: 19; 15: 85; 17: 45.

69. Trudel, *Histoire de la Nouvelle-France* 2: 405–34.

70. Trelease, *Indian Affairs*, 52; Hunt, *Wars of the Iroquois*, 69–70.

71. Thwaites, ed., *Relations* 33: 121.

72. Le Clercq, *Establishment* 1: 204; Tross, ed., *Histoire du Canada*.

73. There is nothing in Sagard or Le Clercq that implies that the priests were instructed to disrupt this treaty, as Hunt implies. Trudel (*Histoire de la Nouvelle-France* 2: 370) says that it was necessary to send Father Le Caron and the other Frenchmen to Huronia to prevent a commercial treaty between the Huron and the Iroquois. It is my opinion that the prospect of this treaty was a figment of the imagination of the French in Quebec and never a real possibility (see text below).

74. On the Mohawk refusal to let the French Indians pass through their country to trade with the Dutch see Trelease, *Indian Affairs*, 52–53; Hunt, *Wars of the Iroquois*, 34. Trudel's (*Histoire de la Nouvelle-France* 2: 364–66) suggestion that the Huron were about to trade with the Dutch and that the French who stayed in Huronia did so to prevent this seems unlikely in view of the traditional enmity between the Huron and the Iroquois. To reach Albany the latter would have had to travel through the tribal territory of the three eastern Iroquois tribes. Mohawk opposition to this seems to have effectively discouraged the Huron from attempting such trade.

75. Sagard says that the Huron did not permit other tribes to pass through their territory without special permission (Wrong, ed., *Sagard's Long Journey*, 99). The Jesuits say categorically that the Huron did not permit the Petun to trade with the French (Thwaites, ed., *Relations* 21: 177).

76. For a reference about canoes see Hunt, *Wars of the Iroquois*, 51.

77. Le Clercq, *Establishment* 1: 267. The Huron spread evil rumours about the Jesuits among the Petun when the Jesuits tried to do mission work there in 1640 (Thwaites, ed., *Relations* 20: 47–51).

78. Thwaites, ed., *Relations* 21: 207–15. At first the priests pretended to be traders. This pretence, however, failed.

79. Biggar, ed., *Works of Champlain* 5: 131.

80. The French later describe him as a traitor (Thwaites, ed., *Relations* 5: 241).

81. Tross, ed., *Histoire du Canada* 2: 431. For a description of his proposed reburial see Thwaites, ed., *Relations* 10: 307–309.

82. G. Lanctot, *A History of Canada*, vol. 1 (Toronto, 1963), 148–49.

83. It appears that one reason the Recollets received little support from the trading companies was that their policy of settling migratory Indians and of wanting Huron converts to settle in Quebec conflicted with the traders' own interests (Le Clercq, *Establishment* 1: 111).

84. The support of Governor Montmagny appears to have been particularly effective (Thwaites, ed., *Relations* 21: 143; 22: 309, 311).

85. Thwaites, ed., *Relations* 10: 33; 11: 97, 109, 111, 113; 13: 9; 14: 125 161, 231, 235, 255. On the discontinuation of the seminary, see 24: 103. During the first two years the Jesuits were back in Huronia they were struggling to orient themselves and to understand the nature of Huron society better. At first they tended to be rather patronizing. They gave advice on military matters (10: 53) and, failing to understand the nature of Huron politics, felt that their intervention was needed to mediate disputes among the different tribes (9: 273; 14: 17, 21). Later, when they realized how the Huron did things and that intervention was unnecessary, these efforts ceased.

86. One example is the decision to seek to baptize older men — and especially influential ones (Thwaites, ed., *Relations* 15: 109).

87. For Jesuit policy regarding lay assistants in Huronia, see Thwaites, ed., *Relations* 21: 293–303. See also 6: 81, 83; 15: 157; 17: 45; 20: 99; 25: 85; 27: 91.

88. Parkman, *Jesuits in North America*, 465–67. Concerning early charges of Jesuit participation in the fur trade and a declaration by the directors of the Company of New France concerning their innocence, see Thwaites, ed., *Relations* 25: 75.

89. Thwaites, ed., *Relations* 14: 17–19. For a clear statement that the Jesuits were aware that their presence in Huronia depended on the traders' ability to coerce the Huron to let them stay, see 34: 205. Soon after the Jesuits returned to Huronia, Brébeuf wrote that they won the esteem of the Indians by giving them arrowheads and helping them to defend their forts (34: 53). He hoped that the confidence won by these actions would permit the Jesuits eventually to "advance the glory of God."

90. The main reason seems to have been that the French had detained a Huron who was implicated in killing a Frenchman in Huronia (Thwaites, ed., *Relations* 6: 19). It is interesting to note that the Huron also made it clear they wanted Frenchmen with guns instead of, or at least alongside, the priests (7: 217).

91. Thwaites, ed., *Relations* 9: 287.

92. Thwaites, ed., *Relations* 7: 47. The officials in Quebec continued to exhort the Huron to become Christians (17: 171).
93. Thwaites, ed., *Relations* 8: 71, 91, 99.
94. That was in July 1633 (Thwaites, ed., *Relations* 5: 259). The people of Ossossané continued to press the Jesuits to move there.
95. Thwaites, ed., *Relations* 8: 99, 103–105. They also stayed at Ihonitiria because they felt it better to start work in a small village rather than a large and important one (8: 103). Ossossané was also unsatisfactory as its inhabitants were planning to relocate the village the next spring (8: 101).
96. Thwaites, ed., *Relations* 5: 239; 8: 99; 10: 309; 14: 99–103.
97. For an account of this dispute and the Jesuits' attempts to resolve it, see Thwaites, ed., *Relations* 10: 279–81, 307; 14: 21. No mention is made of the dispute after 1637, so presumably it was patched up. Brébeuf mentions elsewhere that, as a result of Brûlé's murder, other Huron were threatening the people of Toanché (the village where he was killed) with death (8: 99). The bad relations between Ossossané and the village of Ihonitiria (which was inhabited by Toanchéans) were exacerbated in 1633 when the latter became angry at the efforts of the chiefs of Ossossané to persuade all the Jesuits to settle in their village (5: 263).
98. Presents were also given to the Huron both as tokens of goodwill and to ensure the good treatment of the Jesuits.
99. For a discussion of the financial help the Jesuits expected to receive from the trading company see Thwaites, ed., *Relations* 6: 81–83. The financial support of the mission is discussed in Parkman, *Jesuits in North America*, 465–67.
100. Thwaites, ed., *Relations* 10: 249; 13: 141; 17: 95; 18: 19, 97.
101. Thwaites, ed., *Relations* 10: 301.
102. One of these trips was to visit the father of a young convert named Amantacha who lived at St. Joseph (Thwaites, ed., *Relations* 8: 139). A careful tabulation by [the author's research assistant] Miss [A. Elaine] Clark of the places the Jesuits mention visiting each year and the amount of attention given to each village in Huronia shows clearly that prior to 1640 their activities were confined to the Bear nation and particularly to the Penetang Peninsula. After that time their mission work spread into all parts of Huronia.
103. To less than twelve thousand.
104. Thwaites, ed., *Relations* 19: 123, 127; 8: 145–47. The high mortality rate among children is an overall impression gained from reading the Relations of the years 1636–40. It also corresponds with what is known about similar epidemics among other Indian groups.
105. Thwaites, ed., *Relations* 19: 223.
106. Thwaites, ed., *Relations* 14: 17, 53, 99–103.
107. Thwaites, ed., *Relations* 39: 129.
108. Thwaites, ed., *Relations* 19: 179.
109. Thwaites, ed., *Relations* 15: 59–67.
110. At all times the Huron leaders appear to have been convinced that killing a priest or one of their assistants would terminate the Franco–Huron alliance.
111. Thwaites, ed., *Relations* 13: 215, 217. For a French statement emphasizing the Huron dependence on trade goods see 32: 179 (1647–48).
112. Thwaites, ed., *Relations* 15: 21.
113. Thwaites, ed., *Relations* 15: 51.
114. Thwaites, ed., *Relations* 15: 55; 17: 115.
115. Thwaites, ed., *Relations* 21: 143; 22: 310.
116. Thwaites, ed., *Relations* 21: 131.
117. One heifer and a small cannon arrived in 1648 (Thwaites, ed., *Relations* 32: 99).
118. Thwaites, ed., *Relations* 26: 201.
119. Concerning the establishment of Ste Marie and the mission system see Thwaites, ed., *Relations* 19: 123–65.
120. There is a considerable amount of other evidence concerning the coercive power of Huron chiefs. See B.G. Trigger, "Order and Freedom in Huron Society," *Anthropologica* N.S. 5 (1963): 151–69.
121. Thwaites, ed., *Relations* 21: 213. About the same time the Huron were spreading bad reports concerning the Jesuits among the Petun (20: 54), with whom they had recently made a new treaty of friendship (20: 43). These rumours were spread by Huron traders.
122. Thwaites, ed., *Relations* 30: 75–77. So bitter was the Huron opposition to Brébeuf after he returned to Huronia that the Huron mission was compelled to send him down to Quebec until the situation quieted down (23: 35).

123. The Jesuit Relation of 1635 records that the beaver was already totally extinct in the Huron country and that all the skins they traded with the French were obtained elsewhere (Thwaites, ed., *Relations* 8: 57).
124. Trelease, *Indian Affairs*, 118–20; Hunt, *Wars of the Iroquois*, 32–34. For a later source see Jean Talon cited in Hunt, *Wars of the Iroquois*, 137.
125. Hunt, *Wars of the Iroquois*, 32–34; Trelease, *Indian Affairs*, 118.
126. This theory was first advanced by C.H. McIlwain in 1915. It was taken up in Innis, *Fur Trade*, 34–36, and Hunt, *Wars of the Iroquois*, 32–37, 74.
127. Trelease, *Indian Affairs*, 120.
128. E.B. O'Callaghan, ed., *Documents Relative to the Colonial History of the State of New York* . . . (15 vols.; Albany, 1853–87), 4: 908.
129. Thwaites, ed., *Relations* 23: 105.
130. Hunt, *Wars of the Iroquois*, 76.
131. Tooker, "Defeat of the Huron," 117–18.
132. Thwaites, ed., *Relations* 26: 71; 27: 89, 277. Brébeuf returned to Huronia at this time.
133. Hunt, *Wars of the Iroquois*, 77–78.
134. For the Iroquois desire to obtain French guns, see the evidence presented in Hunt, *Wars of the Iroquois*, 74.
135. Thwaites, ed., *Relations* 10: 13; 13: 171.
136. Thwaites, ed., *Relations* 20: 27–31.
137. Thwaites, ed., *Relations* 20: 225; 26: 275.
138. Thwaites, ed., *Relations* 15: 109. For the later relaxation of these requirements see 33: 145–47.
139. Thwaites, ed., *Relations* 19: 191.
140. Thwaites, ed., *Relations* 17: 111; 23: 129.
141. Concerning this preferential treatment see Thwaites, ed., *Relations* 20: 225, 227.
142. Thwaites, ed., *Relations* 32: 179.
143. Vachon, "L'Eau-de-vie."
144. Thwaites, ed., *Relations* 23: 67, 127; 26: 229. Pagan women also attempted to seduce Christian men to persuade them to give up their faith (30: 33). The Relation of 1643 mentions that some converts lived for six months at Quebec to avoid facing temptation in their homeland (24: 121).
145. Thwaites, ed., *Relations* 30: 23.
146. Thwaites, ed., *Relations* 21: 131.
147. Thwaites, ed., *Relations* 23: 185.
148. Thwaites, ed., *Relations* 23: 31.
149. For another reference to the Huron–pagan rift see Thwaites, ed., *Relations* 23: 267.
150. Thwaites, ed., *Relations* 28: 89. For other acts of Christian assertiveness around this time see 29: 263–69; 30: 63.
151. Thwaites, ed., *Relations* 25: 85.
152. Tross, ed., *Histoire du Canada* 1: 200; Thwaites, ed., *Relations* 5: 259.
153. Thwaites, ed., *Relations* 34: 105, 217.
154. For one incident see Thwaites, ed., *Relations* 30: 61–63. Various cults also arose that appear to have been aimed at organizing ideological resistance to Christianity. One was the cult of a forest monster (30: 27); the second was more explicitly anti-Christian (30: 29–31).
155. As one Huron put it, "I am more attached to the church than to my country or relatives" (Thwaites, ed., *Relations* 23: 137). The Jesuits also observed that it was hard to be a good Christian and a good Huron (28: 53).
156. Thwaites, ed., *Relations* 26: 217. The Jesuits had noted the special inclination of the Bear tribe to receive Christianity as early as 1636 (10: 31).
157. After the destruction of Huronia the Cord were very loyal to the French. They were the only Huron tribe that refused to leave Quebec to go and live with the Iroquois (Thwaites, ed., *Relations* 43: 191). Prior to 1640, the Cord were not at all friendly with the Jesuits (17: 59); their change in attitude seems to have come about soon after (21: 285; 23: 151; 26: 265).
158. Thwaites, ed., *Relations* 42: 73. Concerning their early desire for peace with the Iroquois see 33: 119–121.
159. Thwaites, ed., *Relations* 17: 89.
160. Thwaites, ed., *Relations* 36: 179. The Deer lived among the Seneca in their own village and on good terms with their hosts (44: 21). Many Rock people, including the Indians of Contarea, lived among the Onondaga (42: 73).
161. For evidence of incipient deterioration in morale and the beginning of the abandonment of Huronia in the face of Iroquois attack, see Thwaites, ed., *Relations* 30: 87; 33: 83–89.
162. Thwaites, ed., *Relations* 33: 125. Hunt (*Wars of the Iroquois*, 72) notes that in 1637 the Huron had broken a peace treaty with the Seneca.

163. Thwaites, ed., *Relations* 33: 71, 123.
164. Thwaites, ed., *Relations* 33: 131.
165. Thwaites, ed., *Relations* 33: 119–21.
166. Thwaites, ed., *Relations* 33: 125.
167. Thwaites, ed., *Relations* 33: 125–27. He probably did this through anger at his allies and to show the innocence of the Onondaga. He might also have committed suicide to avoid Huron vengeance directed against his person, but this would have been construed as an act of cowardice. It is unlikely that the Onondaga would have exposed an important chief to almost certain death had they not been negotiating in good faith.
168. Thwaites, ed., *Relations* 33: 229.
169. Thwaites, ed., *Relations* 33: 231.
170. Thwaites, ed., *Relations* 33: 81.
171. Thwaites, ed., *Relations* 33: 233–49.
172. Thwaites, ed., *Relations* 34: 227.
173. Thwaites, ed., *Relations* 34: 83.
174. Lanctot, *History of Canada* 1: 194, based on Thwaites, ed., *Relations* 34: 59–61.
175. Tooker, "Defeat of the Hurons," 117–18; Innis, *Fur Trade*, 35–36. For the effective use of firearms by the Iroquois see Thwaites, ed., *Relations* 22: 307. The Jesuits saw the danger of growing Iroquois firepower as early as 1642 (22: 307) but the French officials in Quebec never developed a policy to counteract it. The restiveness of the Huron pagans may be one reason why the French did not want too many guns in Huron hands, even if they were being sold only to Christians.
176. Hunt, *Wars of the Iroquois*, 59.
177. Thwaites, ed., *Relations* 35: 191.
178. Thwaites, ed., *Relations* 36: 179; 44: 21; 45: 243. Many of the Rock nation, particularly from Contarea, were later found living with the Onondaga (42: 73).
179. Thwaites, ed., *Relations* 12: 221. The work in Paraguay is also mentioned in 15: 127.
180. G. Lanctot, *A History of Canada* (Toronto, 1964), 1: 63.
181. Hunt, *Wars of the Iroquois*, 100–102.
182. Thwaites, ed., *Relations* 41: 201–203, and 44: 151; Hunt, *Wars of the Iroquois*, 99, 100.
183. Thwaites, ed., *Relations* 40: 215; Lanctot, *History of Canada* 1: 212–13. On the lack of furs in Montreal in 1652–53 see Thwaites, ed., *Relations* 40: 211.
184. Hunt, *Wars of the Iroquois*, 102–103.
185. Parkman, *Jesuits in North America*, 550–53.
186. Tross, ed., *Histoire du Canada* 3: 811; Le Clercq, *Establishment* 1: 204.

Article Three

To See Ourselves as the Other's Other: Nlaka'pamux Contact Narratives

Wendy C. Wickwire

The quincentenary of the 'discovery' of the Americas by Christopher Columbus has stimulated wide debate on the history of European contact. In December 1991 a chartered trawler carrying twelve Native people from British Columbia sailed out to meet the Spanish government-sponsored replicas of the *Nina*, *Pinta*, and *Santa Maria*, bound for San Juan, Puerto Rico, to commemorate Columbus's initial landing. The Natives' objective was to persuade the excursion's leader, Santiago Bolivar, a direct descendent of Columbus, to make a public apology on

Source: "To See Ourselves as the Other's Other: Nlaka'pamux Contact Narratives," *Canadian Historical Review*, 75, 1 (1994): 1–20. Reprinted with permission of University of Toronto Press Incorporated (www.utpjournals.com).

behalf of the Spanish government for the wrongs committed against them. The protesters estimated that 100 million or more deaths were inflicted on Native peoples from diseases introduced by Columbus and subsequent explorers.[1] In this encounter, something very basic was at stake: the history of colonial encounters from the point-of-view of First Nations' peoples.

This article examines accounts of the first meetings between Nlaka'pamux[2] and European explorers in the Fraser River canyon of south-central British Columbia in June 1808. Simon Fraser was the first non-Native to explore the area along the river that now bears his name. The leader of the North West Company crew consisting of nineteen voyageurs, two Indians, and two clerks, Fraser kept a journal to record his journey — to survey, as it were, the people he met and the terrain along the way. Fraser's journal has become the primary lens through which to view the initial interaction between the Nlaka'pamux and the first white explorers.

While Fraser recorded in writing his impressions of the 'Hacamaugh' (Nlaka'pamux) at 'Camchin'[3] (present-day Lytton) on 19 and 20 June, the Nlaka'pamux recorded their impressions of him. Unlike Fraser, however, the Nlaka'pamux transmitted their impressions orally, and the stories passed from one generation to the next. Anthropologist James Teit recorded some of these accounts almost a century ago. Still others survive as living oral accounts among contemporary Native elders. This article examines these early and more recent accounts in light of what they reveal about the Native oral/historical viewpoint.

THE PROBLEM OF 'HISTORY'

In the early years of this century, British Columbia was a haven for ethnographic research. Many of the names of those who worked here are well known — Franz Boas, Edward Sapir, Thomas McIlwraith, John Swanton, Marius Barbeau, Diamond Jenness, Charles Hill-Tout, James Teit. This was the era of 'total ethnography'— the assembling of complete descriptions of other societies or cultures.[4] Anthropologists believed that by recording everything and anything imaginable, from religious worldview to pictography, they could reconstruct an image of the pure and untarnished traditional culture. One of the essentials was 'folklore.' Hundreds of traditional stories were collected for publication in the early editions of the *Journal of American Folk-Lore* and the *Jesup Expedition* monographs.

Until recently, many readers have accepted these early texts at face value. Today, however, many are reading them with serious concerns about translation and representation. Critical theorist David Murray, in a recent study of speech, writing, and representation in North American Indian texts,[5] for example, asks what was recorded and why? What language was used in the recording? Who were the 'informants'? Why did they tell what they told? Most important to Murray is the position of the 'mediator' or 'interpreter.' He suggests that we look to this individual in order to better understand the 'stories' collected.

These are key questions in British Columbia where Franz Boas played a major role. Not only did Boas collect a mass of Native texts in British Columbia himself, but he also supervised the collection of hundreds of texts by others, among them James Teit. Between 1898 and 1917 Teit recorded oral narratives in south-central British Columbia. He sent these to Boas, who edited them in preparation for publication. Boas highlighted those that he believed to be the ancient ancestral stories and he downplayed stories about current events, personal experiences, and nineteenth-century epidemics, explorers, technology, and religious ideas. This bias in the early published ethnographic record is striking when one listens to Nlaka'pamux storytellers today and learns that stories about nineteenth-century events are well known.

Although this living history has been relatively ignored in British Columbia, it has been the focus of attention in other areas. In South and Central America, for example, anthropologists have been studying the history of contact as articulated by indigenous peoples with very positive results. Jonathon D. Hill has found that by shifting the focus away from 'what *really* happened' to the Natives' *own* historical consciousness (indeed, diversity thereof), he has come to appreciate other issues, such as 'how indigenous societies have experienced history, and the ongoing means by which they struggle to make sense out of complex, contradictory historical processes.'[6] Anthropologist Terence Turner has studied the interplay between myth and history which he finds 'complementary and mutually informing.'[7] This approach, explains Turner, tends to produce new images of Westerners and Western society — 'images formed by others during the process of Western expansion.' It also turns traditional anthropology on its head by placing ourselves, for a change, in the position of the 'other.'[8]

SIMON FRASER'S ACCOUNT, 1808

Fraser was much impressed with the inhabitants of Camchin and vicinity. At one village of 'about four hundred souls,' he observed that the people 'live among mountains, and enjoy pure air, seem cleanly inclined, and make use of wholesome food.' At his next stop, he was led to a camp where twelve hundred people were sitting in rows, waiting to see him and to shake his hand. The Indians fed the newcomers generously with 'salmon, berries, oil and roots in abundance,' as well as with the meat of six dogs.[9]

Fraser observed that people of Camchin attached some religious significance to his appearance. At the large ceremonial gathering there, for example, he noted that 'the Great Chief made a long harangue, in [the] course of which he pointed to the sun, to the four quarters of the world and then to us, and then he introduced his father, who was old and blind, [and who] . . . with some emotion often stretched out both his hands in order to feel ours.' After this event, Fraser noted that the Indians sang and danced all night long, while his crew-members watched with amusement. On his departure from Camchin, the Natives presented Fraser with 'berries, roots and oil in abundance.' He guessed that such gestures 'proceed[ed], perhaps, from an idea that we are superior beings, who are not to be overcome.'[10]

Fraser in turn presented one chief who had been particularly good to him with a gift: 'The Chief of [the] Camshins [sic] . . . is the greatest chief we have seen; he behaved towards us uncommonly well. I made him a present of a large silver broach which he immediately fixed on his head, and he was exceedingly well pleased with our attention.'[11] Fraser noted in his journal the Natives at Camchin had several 'European articles among them, a copper Tea Kettle, a brass camp kettle, and a strip of a common blanket, and cloathing such as the Cree women wear.'[12] These, he thought, came from settlements east of the Rockies.

On his return trip a month later, Fraser stopped again at Camchin but found the atmosphere there much changed. Not only did he feel ignored by the chief who had been so friendly towards him a month earlier, but he 'could perceive something unpleasant in their demeanour.' There was 'a disagreeable gloom' perhaps related to the fact that 'most of the children were really afflicted with some serious disorder which reduced them to skeletons.'[13]

NLAKA'PAMUX ACCOUNTS OF FRASER, CIRCA 1900

Much of what we know about the Nlaka'pamux comes from the writings of an early anthropologist, James Teit. Teit was an unusual man.[14] He had emigrated to Canada from the Shetland Islands in 1884, at the age of nineteen. When Franz Boas met him at Spence's Bridge, British Columbia, ten years later, he was living with his Nlaka'pamux wife, Lucy Antko, and was on very good terms with her people. Boas was so impressed with Teit's knowledge of the Nlaka'pamux language and culture that he engaged him right away to undertake ethnographic work. This marked the beginning of a life-long collaboration between the two men that led to the compilation of major ethnographies, collections of narratives and monographs on various subjects, including basketry and ethnobotany, much of which was edited by Boas.

Unlike many other anthropologists of the day, who entered Native communities as outsiders and who worked with one or two willing informants, Teit was an insider who consulted with a large number of individuals who were long-time friends, associates, and relatives through marriage. While he conducted his anthropological work, he simultaneously pursued other activities such as hunting and guiding, often in the company of Native people. From 1908 until his death in 1922, he played major roles in three native political organizations, The Interior Tribes of British Columbia, the Indian Rights Association, and The Allied Tribes of British Columbia.

Fortunately, Teit was interested in issues of the day as well as in issues of the past. Scattered throughout his collections of traditional folklore, for instance, are European legends, Bible stories, war stories, and accounts of noteworthy events of the 1800s.[15] In this latter category, there are also stories about the arrival of the first white explorers.

NATIVE PROPHECIES TELL OF STRANGE WHITE PEOPLE TO COME

According to Teit, there were among the Nlaka'pamux certain individuals, both male and female, who could predict the future. These prophets were much revered and travelled widely, telling people of things to come. Wherever they went, large numbers of people gathered to dance and sing, and especially to hear their messages. Although the dancing died out in 1858, the prophets lived on. Writing in 1900, Teit noted that 'in the last fifteen years, three prophets . . . have appeared among the tribe. One was a Fraser Valley prophet who travelled as far as Lytton; another was a woman from the Nicola Valley . . . and the last was an Okanagan woman who appeared in 1891.'[16] Stories of these and other prophets were still in circulation in 1915. Chief John Tetlenitsa of Spence's Bridge described a prophet who had lived in his community many years earlier. 'Present-day people,' he explained, 'believe his spirit really went over to France and that he foretold the advent of the Whites at an early date.'[17]

Teit described in detail the ritual associated with prophets' ceremonies,[18] and he recorded texts of several prophets' songs. These provide some insight into the Native perspective on initial encounters with whites. One prophet's song was said to have originated with a Spence's Bridge man named Kwalos. According to Tetlenitsa, Kwalos had been a dance chief, dreamer, and prophet who, 'before the first white people came to the county, had a series of dreams or visions which impressed him very much.' He had gathered the people together and told them about his dreams:

> He told how his spirit left his body and passed rapidly to the shores of a great lake in the far east where the clouds always hung low along the edge of the water. Here his spirit left the land and rolled along the clouds until it came to a land on the other side of the great lake. Here there were many strange people who spoke a language very different in sound from Indian languages. (He imitated the speaking of these people and what he said sounded very much like French.) [JAT] These people were very different from Indians and had many beautiful and wonderful things the Indians knew nothing of. They had light skins and different colours of hair and eyes and many kinds of fine clothes and ornaments.

Both the men and women dressed differently from Indians and their clothes were of peculiar patterns and materials. The women especially had very striking and beautiful dresses. These people were very numerous and did many strange things. They lived in many high houses made of stone. They had fires inside of stones (prob. stoves), and much smoke could be seen coming out of the stones (prob. chimneys). Their houses had mouths and eyes (prob. doors and windows) and around them were many open grassy lands and plots where there were many kinds of beautiful flowers and plants and grasses, some of which they used as food (prob. fields of grain, vegetables, etc. and flower gardens). Surrounding some of the houses were gorgeous flowers. Outside the houses were many rabbits (don't know what he meant by rabbits) and many goats (prob. sheep) from which the people obtained wool for clothes. Also there were animals somewhat like buffalo (prob. cattle) from which they drew milk, and the flesh of which they ate, and there were other animals somewhat like moose or deer (prob. horses) but without horns. All these animals were tame like dogs and mixed with the people. These white people had much music and singing, were very rich and seemed to be happy. In the dances, Kwalos prayed that the people he had seen would come over and enlighten the Indians and make them powerful, wise, rich and happy like themselves. He further stated that he believed these people would come to the Indians some time soon and then great changes would take place among the Indians — Kwalos used this song when he held dances in connection with his visions of the white man's land.[19]

Teit also recorded the prophecies of NokanekautkEn, alias Nelkwax, a dance chief of the Lytton division. Along with TcexawatEn of Ashcroft, NokanekautkEn had had visions in which he 'saw many things belonging to the whites . . . which none of the Indians had yet seen.'[20]

When one considers that European material goods had made their way to Camchin prior to Fraser's arrival, it is not surprising that stories and dreams of strange people east of the mountains also travelled to Camchin and other Native villages in British Columbia's southern interior prior to 1808.

The Sun Arrives

Teit recorded five Nlaka'pamux stories of first encounters with whites.[21] Two of these are especially interesting, because, unlike most stories, which are anonymous, the names of the storytellers are given. One was told by SEmalitsa, a woman from Styne Creek[22] near Lytton; and another was told by Waxtko, a woman from Spence's Bridge.[23] Names of the tellers of the remaining three stories are not mentioned.[24]

SEmalitsa's account of Fraser's arrival was based on a story her grandmother had told her about an event she had witnessed as a child:

My grandmother told me that when she was a young girl she was playing one day in the summer-time (about the time the service-berries get ripe) near the river-beach at the village of Strain,[25] when she saw two canoes, with red flags hoisted, come downstream. She ran and told her mother, and the people gathered to see the strange sight. Seeing so many people gathered, the canoes put ashore and several men came ashore. Each canoe carried a number of men (perhaps six or seven in each), and many of them wore strange dresses, and everything about them was strange. Some of the men looked like Indians, and others looked like what we call white men. Among them was a Shuswap chief who acted as interpreter. Our people were not afraid of the strangers, nor were they hostile to them. The strangers produced a large pipe, and had a ceremonial smoke with some of our men. After distributing a few presents, they boarded their canoes and went on to Lytton. They remained one or two days at Lytton, where they were presented with food of various kinds, and gave in exchange tobacco, beads, and knives. Runners from the river had come down about a day ahead of them along the east side of the Fraser River to Lytton. The Lytton chief ImentcutEn went up the east bank of the Fraser, and met them two or three miles above Lytton, and conducted them to his place with considerable ceremony. All the Lytton people were assembled to meet them, and before they left there they had many talks and smokes with the Indians. Next day a number of people who camped at Botani Valley came down to see them; and the news having reached up the Thompson as far as Spence's Bridge, some of the men from there also came down — those having horses, on horseback; and those having none, on foot. The Spence's Bridge chief ran on foot all the way, and arrived in time to see the strangers and to deliver a great speech, but some of his people arrived too late to see them. The Lytton chief at this time was also a great orator. The Spence's Bridge chief was presented with some kind of a metal or brass badge, and a hat worn by the leader of the strangers whom the Indians called 'the Sun.' He was called this because of some kind of shining emblem he wore on his hat or cap, which resembled the symbol of the Sun. The Indians applied names to most of the strangers, all taken from some feature of their appearance or from certain marks or emblems on their clothing.[26]

SEmalitsa's story was the only one to make reference to Fraser's second appearance at Lytton: 'Many people saw them again on their return journey, as they were again assembling on the rivers for salmon-fishing. Probably more people saw them when they came back than when they went down.'[27]

Teit published Waxtko's version of the Fraser story in 1917. Although Waxtko lived at Spence's Bridge, about twenty miles upstream from SEmalitsa's home, her story is very similar to SEmalitsa's:

When Kwolina'u.l[28] came to Lytton . . . [i]t was in midsummer. The berries were just ripe in the river-valley; and many of the tribe were assembled at Botani, digging roots and playing games. Some Thompson men, who had been up at La Fontaine on horseback, came back quickly with the news of the approach of these people. Tcexe'x was at Botani with others from Spence's Bridge. He hurried down to Lytton, and was there when the whites arrived. The chief of the latter we called 'Sun.' We did not know his name. Several chiefs made speeches to him, but Tcexe'x made the greatest speech.[29]

According to Waxtko, Tcexex's was her own relative. She described him as 'a prominent chief and a great orator . . . [and] an elderly man at the time when these whites came to Lytton.' Like SEmalitsa, Waxtko was told that Fraser had presented Tcexe'x with a silver broach:

This chief so pleased Sun, that he gave him a present of a large silver broach, or some other similar ornament, which he had on his person. On several occasions Tcexe'x used this attached to his hair in front, or on the front of his head. When I was a girl, I saw it worn by his sons. One of his sons inherited it; on his death his brother obtained it: and it was probably buried with the third brother who had it, as it disappeared about the time of his death. The last-named chief died at Lytton as an elderly man.[30]

Of the three remaining Simon Fraser stories, Teit noted that they were the 'mythological version[s]' of the capsizing of Fraser's canoe in Fraser River. In these three versions, Fraser and his crew are depicted as mythological figures who have returned. As the first teller noted:

Many years ago, but at a time long after Coyote had finished arranging things on earth, he appeared on Fraser River in company with Sun, Moon, Morning-Star, Kokwela, nmuipEm ('diver') and SkwiaxEnEmux ('arrow-armed person,' 'person with arrow arms or shoulders. . . .') This is the only time Coyote has appeared since the end of the mythological age.[31]

'Sun' here, as in both SEmalitsa's and Waxtko's accounts, is probably Fraser. In the second account, three heavenly bodies are mentioned — Sun, Moon, and Morning-Star, each of whom appeared briefly after the capsizing, but all of whom disappeared forever during the night.

According to a third version, there were two canoes, one of which carried seven heavenly bodies (sun, moon, morning-star, and others said to be stars); and the other carried seven Transformers — Coyote, NLikisEntem, Kokwela, Old-One, Ntcemka, SkwiaxEnEmux, and nmuipEm.

The first story describes in detail the canoe's capsizing:

> Continuing their journey, and when in the middle of the river, a short distance below Lytton, the Moon, who was steersman of the canoe, disappeared with it under water. The others came out of the water and sat down on a rock close above the river. Then Skwia'x'EnEmux ['arrow-armed person'] fired many lightning arrows,[32] and nmu'ipEm ['diver'] dived many times into the river.[33] The Sun sat still and smoked;[34] while Coyote, Kokwe'la, and Morning-Star danced. Coyote said, 'Moon will never come up again with the canoe;' but Sun said, 'Yes, in the evening he will appear.' Just after sunset, Moon appeared holding the canoe, and came ashore. All of them embarked, and, going down the river, were never seen again.[35]

In her account, SEmalitsa included a fragment of the capsizing which is very similar: 'After leaving Lytton, at some place close to Siska, one of their canoes was swamped in a rapid, and some of the men were saved with difficulty, after having been some time in the water.' She also commented on the merger of these explanations of the newcomers:

> Very many people thought they were the beings spoken of in tales of the mythological period, who had taken a notion to travel again over the earth; and they often wondered what object they had in view, and what results would follow. They believed their appearance foreboded some great change or events of prime importance to the Indians, but in what way they did not know.[36]

Accounts Compared

There are many common threads running through these early Native accounts. Most prominent is a figure called Sun, who appears with a crew of twelve to fourteen men from upstream in one or two birch-bark canoes. The two women's accounts coincide on the time of the newcomers' arrival, as well as the large ceremonial gathering held in Fraser's honour. Both also mention Fraser's gift of a metal broach to one of the chiefs, who accepted it with much pleasure. The capsizing of one or two canoes just downstream from Lytton is described in four of the five stories.

None of these Native accounts mentions hostility towards the newcomers. On the contrary, they depict a situation of warm exchange. Neither afraid or hostile, the Nlaka'pamux shared their food supplies liberally, smoked, and welcomed the newcomers with pomp and ceremony.

These early Native accounts also share points in common with Fraser's journal — for example, Fraser's arrival at Camchin in June; the silver broach which he gave to the Chief of the Camchins; the exchange of food for 'knife, awl and trinkets'; and the fact that Fraser's crew included 'Whites' as well as Indians. There is a particularly strong parallel between Fraser's and the Native accounts on the subject of the capsizing.

NLAKA'PAMUX ACCOUNTS OF FIRST NATIVE–WHITE ENCOUNTERS, 1981–91

Over the last several years, I have talked with Native elders in Spuzzum and Lytton about the portrayal in their accounts of the first encounters with whites. In Lytton, Louis Philips explained that his ancestors had been forewarned about the arrival of the whites:

> That old man at the Stein, they call him Lytton Dick. His Indian name is N-TEEH-low,[37] and he tell something that's going to happen maybe tomorrow or maybe next day. Long before it

happens . . . He used to tell the people, he'd tell the people, 'Not very long from now these peoples that's coming in here, from their country into our country . . . [they're] going to look different from what we are now and who we are. It's going to look different when those white people come here. Say they just look like us, only they're white . . . That old man, he's ahead of himself to tell all what's going to happen before it happens. . . .[38]

Louis's father had been told another story about the first whites to arrive at Lytton:

> [At the] Stein, there was a bunch of womens, old womens, young womens, out there picking 'CHA-kum,' and, hot day, they got sweating, and they go down to the river to take a bath in the river, and they see these boats coming, and the womens didn't know they were 'SHA-ma' or anything. They stay there on the beach taking a cold bath. This boat come and land. Simon Fraser had one of them old-fashioned shirts, starch in the front, and starch in the back, and that shine. Sunny day like this. And those women thought they seen Jesus Christ in person. And they all sit there naked. Never think, well, they pretty near naked all the time. And this white man come off the boat, and he look at the women sitting down on the beach. Looked at them. And they all thought they seen Jesus Christ. That starch, they shine. They thought they seen right through him. And he turn around the other way and the starch on his back shines. They thought they seen through him. They thought they seen Jesus Christ alive. He look at them all, sized them all up. And the young lady there, lift 'em up, stand 'em up, and rub 'em, and hug 'em. And after he got through, he got in a boat and he drift down. And these old womens, they all kneel down and pray, pray to the young woman that Shu-sha-klee[39] pick on. They thought, they tell this young woman, 'Ah, you must be a good woman. Jesus Christ come and rub you up and hug you. And us, we sit there and watch you.' Say, 'You must be a good woman.' They pray to this woman that Simon Fraser hug. They thought he was Jesus Christ. Old Yen-a-ma-ken. He's an old man at the Stein. I used to go there. My father was partly raised in the Stein, and he was one of them . . . Yen-a-ma-ken is my father's uncle. He used to tell that story when Simon Fraser first come through there. And that time, I was too small. I didn't know nothing.[40]

Phillips's story even contains details of an incident not reported in the earlier accounts which he would have been told (orally), but which the Jesup expedition and Teit did not hear and record. His account suggests that prophecies and stories of first encounters with whites may have been informed by long-distance travel.

> There was one guy, he used to disappear. Once time, three or four years before he come back. He goes way down south. He just go and keep on going. How far we went, he says there's no winter-time there. He said you could lay under a tree and sleep, wake up and go. He said the people around there are friendly just like our peoples here. They see a stranger, bring 'em in the house and feed you, bed you. And in the morning you go. He was the first one that seen it come true. I don't know how far he went. I don't how if he went to Mexico or where he went. But when he came back, he tell the others, he said, 'What he was telling us about, about what changes we're going to have,' he said, 'I seen some of it . . .' And when he comes back, maybe three or four years, as soon as they see him, they call up, maybe Boston Bar and Spence's Bridge, and Lytton. And get together and talk about it, what this man seen when he was away . . . There was some Indians they used to take off three or four years. They used to go a long ways. Never hear them talk about the north. They hear them talk about the south. No road, no trail. You just go through the brush. You just go by the shade of the tree. That's all the clock he's got. And he go so far and he come back. They say, 'How long you stay in one place?' 'Oh,' he says, 'I camp. They feed me, bed me. Look after me good. They look after me better than I look after myself, because I am a stranger' . . . He says, 'It's just like we do when we get a stranger here,' he says. We get a stranger here, always try to look after him. Indians is like that all over. Look after a stranger good. It's like that yet . . . White man is not like that. Some is like that, but some you got to give 'em money first before they do anything. That time when the white man came here, buckskin or dry fish was the biggest thing they can give.[41]

Nlaka'pamux elder Annie York of Spuzzum explained that her grandparents had told her that old chief Sh-PEENT-lum and his wife of Lytton had predicted the arrival of whites prior to their actual arrival:

> When Simon Fraser came down, the Lytton Indians were the first ones that knew them. They seen this man, the Lytton Indians seen this man coming down in the canoe with his party and Chief Sh-PEENT-lum soon spot it and he says, 'That's what my wife foretold. That man is coming to this area.' So he said to the Indians, 'You Indians must never touch him. You must never hurt him. See that white, what he got on his head?' He had a white handkerchief that tied around as a band. And he's the head man in the canoe. And when this Indian spotted him, Sh-PEENT-lum's servant, he camped down there somewhere on the other side of Siska. And that's where he forgot his axe, his little hatchet. But Sh-PEENT-lum said to his servants, 'You boys must make it. You must run after that canoe and you must catch up and give him his axe.'[42] And so they did. They caught up to him and gave him his axe. Sh-PEENT-lum told his men, these two boys, 'You must keep on going to Spuzzum. And send the word down there. But you must never hurt that man. That's the man of the sun. He's the son of the sun.'
>
> So these Indians came along and they came to Spuzzum and they spread the news all around. But our grandmother, our own grandmother, she was ten years old and they lived down there, on the other side of Spuzzum Creek, right at the mouth and there were several others. And Paul Yowla was there, and several others. And a special man came in a canoe. And when they see him, they knew who he was. That was the man that was foretold to come. They welcomed him.[43]

Like Louis's account, Annie's adds a whole level of detail not found in the earlier recorded accounts. This detail she learned orally from the account as it was told to her by those who had had it passed on to them by those who retold certain aspects that others did not. Annie continued:

> And when he came, this Indian came with dog, a little dog. And the Indians had fish boiled by their summer campfire, because it was in springtime. And they were boiling the fish. They offered him the fish, but he didn't want the fish. He kept pointing at the dog. And the Indians couldn't understand why he kept pointing at the dog. So they gave him the dog. What do you think they did? They killed the dog and ate it. That's what he had for his supper. The Indians didn't like that very much but the next morning they cooked the fish for them. And the chief came and then they had their pipe, the pipe that was always used. He flew his flag and he ordered all his tribe, 'You must meet this new man.' Because that was their traditional way of living. Pelok, he ordered all these people, 'You must never hurt this man. You must welcome him.' And so they did. And they stayed for a few days. And down there by the Cottonwood tree, there's a big cottonwood tree down there by Spuzzum Creek and that's where they camped, and our great grandmother was there and our grandmother was ten years old. She told us this story. There was a special woman, she's a relation of our grandmother, she was an entertainer, a singer. And she was asked to sing this special song when Simon Fraser was leaving. So they have a sort of special prayer that he must be safe in his voyage drifting down the Fraser River. Warned him . . . that's one of the waters that's very fierce . . . These people that was with Simon Fraser, they understand. When they was leaving, this woman sang this special song. And Simon Fraser, he was feeling so sad he has tears in his eyes when he was drifting away.[44]

Annie explained that Fraser's captain had forewarned the people not to touch any of the newcomers:

> Funny thing about that Simon Fraser's captain. The captain of Simon Fraser at Lytton warned these people not to touch them. 'If you do it, you're going to get some kind of disease, and it's going to clean you out.' And it did. Isn't that funny? . . . Sh-PEENT-lum says, 'That man

come from the sun. That's God's child to send here to be supervise us.' So he came to Spuzzum and he warned the people not to do it [touch him]. 'You're going to get sick if you do it.' It seems like this man used to get in trance and he can see everything, the way my grandaunt told it. I seen it today and I keep on seeing it.[45]

Sam Mitchell of Fountain (thirty miles upriver from Lytton) relayed another account of Fraser's encounter with some Lillooet Indians. This is, said Mitchell, a 'true story' about some people who came down the river 'a long time ago.' He had heard the story many times. This one had been told to Mitchell's father by an old Indian, 'Piyell,' who was two years old when this incident took place.

Some 'drifters,' Mitchell was told, beached their boat at a place well known for its rapids and asked some Indians there to help them carry it. The Indians helped with the portage. Although there were some who wanted to go after these 'white men' and steal their possessions, their leader told them, 'Don't bother them; they might be able to help us one day!' According to this version of the story, the leader of the drifters was a white man who had a tattoo of the sun on his forehead and a tattoo of the moon on his chest.[46]

ACCOUNTS COMPARED

There are many common threads in these stories. Fraser is strongly associated with the sun. For example, he is the 'man of the sun, son of sun' (Annie York) and he wears a tattoo of the sun on his forehead (Sam Mitchell). Although the shining metal broach of the turn of the century is absent in these contemporary stories, there is strong brightness or whiteness associated with Fraser that is similar to that of the shining broach — for example, the white handkerchief tied around the head (Annie York), and the white starched shirt which looked very bright in the summer sun (Louis Phillips). Just as the earlier Nlaka'pamux accounts attached religious significance to the appearance of newcomers, so too do the present-day accounts. In Phillips's account, Fraser was Jesus Christ; and in Annie York's account he was the son of the sun, God's son. The present-day stories, like their turn-of-the-century counterparts, also suggest that Fraser's arrival was no real surprise. Prophets and long-distance travellers had forewarned the people about strange people with guns who would come one day. At least two of the present-day accounts suggest that the chiefs advocated a policy of behaving peacefully towards Fraser and his crew.

The similarities between these oral accounts and Fraser's 1808 journal are also striking — for example, loss and return of what Fraser calls 'a piece of Iron.' York mentions this incident in her story, noting that the item returned was an axe (the current oral account here having the great degree of precision). Just as Fraser noted in his journal that at Spuzzum he was hospitably entertained 'with salmon, boiled and roasted,' Annie York mentions that when Fraser arrived there, the Indians were boiling salmon and that he was entertained by one of the women who sang for him. Fraser's observation that he was being treated as a 'superior being'[47] is confirmed in the contemporary accounts (York was told he was 'son of the sun' or the 'sun's son'; and Louis Phillips was told he was 'Jesus Christ'). Just as one Native account makes an association between the newcomers and disease (Annie York), Fraser's account suggests a link between the Natives' cold reception at Camchin on his return trip and disease among the children there.

One point of difference between the Native and non-Native accounts is the encounter between Fraser and a young woman at the mouth of the Stein River near Lytton. Fraser's journal (not surprisingly) makes no reference to such an incident.

SO WHAT DO THESE ACCOUNTS TELL US?

Contact history is largely a history based on written records by white explorers. In the flurry of ethnographic reporting that took place at the turn of the century in British Columbia under Franz Boas and others, the prehistoric past was given precedence over all else. Because of this emphasis, many Native people became known as people with a deep past but without a more recent past. As this article shows, however, prevailing ideas on this subject may well be more a reflection of non-Native preoccupations and interests than of the Native experience. Even my preliminary research suggests that Nlaka'pamux accounts of their initial encounters with whites *are* an important and reliable historical record. Not only is there a remarkable consistency with Fraser's account, but, on some points, such as Fraser's interaction with the Natives at the mouth of the Stein (Louis Phillips) and Spuzzum (Annie York), there is more detail in the Native accounts than in Fraser's journal.

These indigenous stories also reveal other important features of Native historiography. The naming of sources is important. For example, SEmalitsa attributed her story to her grandmother, who had witnessed the arrival of the first whites on her soil. Waxtko also named various individuals from her community who had seen and interacted with the first whites. Annie York attributed her story to her great-grandmother who, like, SEmalitsa's grandmother, had witnessed the arrival of Fraser at Spuzzum. Louis Phillips explained that old Yenamaken, his father's uncle, who lived at the Stein, had told his father the story of Fraser's arrival there. Sam Mitchell explained that he heard the story from his father, who had heard it told by an Indian named Piyell who was two years old when Fraser appeared. This 'oral footnoting' is richly contextual — in many ways far richer than our formal written accounts.

Foreknowledge is also an important component of the Native historical consciousness. According to many of these accounts, both past and present, Native people had heard about the first whites before they actually saw them via stories conveyed by long-distance travellers and via their prophets. There is even some suggestion that they knew how these strangers would look and behave. In some instances, many knew fairly precisely who the strangers were. What concerned them more than the precise identity of these people, however, were the changes they would bring with them.

These accounts have evolved over the course of almost two centuries of tellings. In doing so, they temper, and, today, they give us an open window on Fraser's often partial observations — for example, his comment that 'however kind savages may appear, I know that it is not in their nature to be sincere in their professions to strangers.'[48] Given the Native accounts, Fraser's view is distinctly one-sided. Despite the prophecies and the pervasive concern and uncertainty, nowhere was there evidence of malicious intent. Generosity and hospitality prevailed with all strangers; Simon Fraser was fêted as a God.

In fact, the society that is portrayed here is one in which there is no hostility, no stealing, a liberal sharing of food, and generous assistance provided along the difficult river. This confirms the ethnographic findings of James Teit almost a century later, that these were non-aggressive and friendly peoples.[49]

These Native accounts also provide a rare glimpse of how the first whites appeared to the Indians, from their style of dress to the organization of the canoe crews. Metal ornaments were a source of fascination — in particular, the metal broach Fraser wore on his head.

It is also revealing to contrast Fraser's 'factual' account with the Native 'contextual' account. To some Natives, Fraser and his crew could be explained according to their mythology. Fraser was not just another human being; he was the 'Sun' who had come from the east and was travelling to the west. Members of his crew included 'Moon,' 'Coyote,' and 'Old One,' among others. These 'people' had taken to travelling around again, as they had done in early times. Similar religious associations are present in current accounts. In York's account, Fraser was 'the son of the sun, God's sun'; in Phillips's, 'Jesus Christ.' In Mitchell's account he was someone who could one day help the people.

Finally, there are events chronicled in these Native historical accounts that are missing in Fraser's journal — for example, the story about a woman who is fondled by Fraser at the mouth of the Stein. Also new is the fear that the Indians would be 'cleaned out' by disease simply by touching the strangers.

In light of this Native history, perhaps the big question is what, ultimately, we are to make of the non-Native historical record based on the observations of a single male operating in an official capacity with a reputation at stake. In contrast, the Native accounts draw on a vastly larger tapestry of people that spans several generations. The story survives in oral memory to this day in Phillips's and in many others' minds. Here we have surely a wider, deeper 'history,' a history that does not rely on dead documents many steps removed, but on a collective memory traced directly to the many who were there. Here it is the written that is the more limited and problematic; the oral is the history that lives and is alive.

NOTES

This paper is dedicated to Annie York and Louis Phillips, two Nlaka'pamux elders who were both extremely knowledgeable local historians. Annie died on 19 August 1991 and Louis died on 2 June 1993.

1. Scott Simpson, *Vancouver Sun,* 10 Dec. 1991.
2. 'Nlaka'pamux' is the general term of identification used by the Native people of south-central British Columbia who speak a common language and who live in communities along the Fraser and Thompson rivers between Yale and Lillooet, between Lytton and Ashcroft, along the Nicola Valley between Spence's Bridge and Merritt, in the Nicola Valley to Quilchena, and in the lower reaches of the Coldwater Valley. Outsiders have called them by a variety of names, and it is these, more than their own terms of identification, by which they have become known. Simon Fraser, in 1808, called them the 'Hacamaugh' Indians. The Hudson's Bay traders called them 'Couteau' or Knife Indians. Later, in written records, they were referred to as the Thompson River Indians, after the major river in their territory. This latter term was eventually shortened to 'the Thompsons,' even though many of the people known as such lived nowhere near the Thompson River. Today, both within and outside the community, there is a revival of 'Nlaka'pamux,' their original term of self-identification.
3. W. Kaye Lamb, ed., *The Letters and Journals of Simon Fraser, 1806–1808* (Toronto 1960), 87–8.
4. George E. Marcus and Dick Cushman, 'Ethnographies as Texts,' *Annual Review of Anthropology* 1982, 35.
5. *Forked Tongues: Speech, Writing and Representation in North American Indian Texts* (Bloomington 1991).
6. 'Myth and History,' in Jonathan D. Hill, ed., *Rethinking History and Myth: Indigenous South American Perspectives on the Past* (Urbana 1988), 3.
7. Terence Turner, 'Ethno-Ethnohistory,' in *Rethinking History and Myth,* 237.
8. Ibid., 238. The title of this paper was drawn from a similar phrase used by Turner in his article, 'Ethno-Ethnohistory.'
9. Lamb, ed., *The Letters and Journals of Simon Fraser,* 86–7.
10. Ibid., 87–8.
11. Ibid., 95.
12. Ibid., 86–7.
13. Ibid., 119.
14. For more on the life and works of James Teit see Wendy Wickwire, 'Women in Ethnography: The Research of James A. Teit,' *Ethnohistory,* in press.
15. Folklore scholar Jarold Ramsey, who has studied North American Native narratives in some depth, notes that Bible-derived texts in print are best represented by the Salish-speaking peoples 'thanks to the tireless and open-minded transcribing of James Teit . . . at the turn-of-the-century.' *Reading the Fire: Essays in the Traditional Indian Literatures of the Far West* (Lincoln, 1983), 168.

16. James A. Teit, 'The Thompson Indians of British Columbia,' *Memoirs of the American Museum of Natural History,* vol. 1, pt 4 (New York 1900), 365–6.

17. Teit unpublished notes on 'Religious or praying dance song,' Catalogue no. VI.M. 51, Archives of the Canadian Museum of Civilization (CMC), Hull, Quebec.

18. Teit, 'The Thompson Indians,' 365–6.

19. Teit unpublished notes on song no. VI.M.51, CMC.

20. Teit, 'Religious or praying dance songs,' no. VI.M.102.

21. J.A. Teit, 'Mythology of the Thompson Indians,' *Memoirs of the American Museum of Natural History,* vol. 12, pt 2, (New York 1912), 414–16; James A. Teit et al., 'Folk-Tales of Salishan and Sahaptin Tribes,' *Memoirs of the American Folk-Lore Society,* vol. 11 (Lancaster, Penn. 1917), 64.

22. This is another spelling, used on several occasions by Teit. Today it is spelled 'Stein.' It is the name of the river that empties into the Fraser just above Lytton.

23. It is unusual in collections from this period to have the individual storytellers named. In the case of Waxtko, Teit noted that she was born around 1830 and died in 1912. Teit, 'Folk-Tales,' 64.

24. The absence of names, dates, and locations in the published collections stands in contrast to Teit's raw fieldnotes.

25. The more common spelling of this river today is 'Stein.'

26. Teit, 'Mythology of the Thompson Indians,' 415.

27. Ibid.

28. In a footnote, Teit notes that this word means 'birch-bark canoe,' and that it was a common name for Simon Fraser's party. Teit et al., 'Folk-Tales of Salishan and Sahaptin Tribes,' 64.

29. Ibid.

30. Ibid.

31. Teit, 'Mythology of the Thompson Indians,' 416.

32. This name may be related to the use of a gun. Fraser noted in his journal that at one place near Lytton, 'We fired several shots to shew the Indians the use of our guns. Some of them, through fear, dropped down at the report.' Lamb, ed., *The Letters and Journals of Simon Fraser,* 95.

33. The events of this story are similarly described in Fraser's journal. Ibid., 89–92. One of Fraser's canoes capsized shortly after leaving Lytton. Two men leapt off and got to shore. Meanwhile D'Alaire was swept three miles downstream to a point where he was able to crawl onto some rocks.

34. This fact in the Native account coincides closely with Fraser's comment in his journal that he was writing in his tent when the capsizing took place. Ibid., 90.

35. Teit, 'Mythology of the Thompson Indians,' 416.

36. Ibid., 415.

37. This transcription of Nlaka'pamux word and others throughout this paper are approximations only.

38. Excerpt from an audiotaped interview conducted by Wendy Wickwire with Louis Phillips in Lytton, 10 March 1991.

39. This is a common Native term used for Jesus Christ. Teit noted it also, spelling it as 'Suskule' and 'Susakre.' 'Mythology of the Thompson Indians,' 404.

40. Interview with Phillips.

41. Ibid.

42. This segment of Annie York's story is corroborated by Fraser's journal: 'Two Indians from our last encampment overtook us with a piece of Iron which we had forgotten there. We considered this as an extraordinary degree of honesty and attention.' *The Letters and Journals,* 39.

43. Segment of an audiotaped interview conducted by Imbert Orchard with Annie York in Spuzzum, BC, 1865. Copy given to Wendy Wickwire by Annie York, August 1981.

44. Ibid.

45. Segment of an audiotaped interview conducted by Wendy Wickwire with Annie York in Vancouver, 31 May 1985.

46. Randy Bouchard and Dorothy Kennedy, eds., 'Lillooet Stories,' *Sound Heritage,* 6, 1 (1977): 42–3.

47. Lamb, ed., *The Letter and Journals of Simon Fraser,* 88.

48. Ibid.

49. Teit, 'Thompson Indians,' 180–1.

Topic Two
Women and the Fur Trade

A First Nations woman wearing moccasins, leggings, and a Hudson's Bay blanket, and carrying a child in a cradleboard on a chest tumpline, with her family, York Factory, Hudson Bay.

French fur traders preceded the English within the boundaries of present-day Canada by nearly a century. In 1670, Charles II granted a royal charter to the "Company of Adventurers of England trading into Hudson Bay." The Hudson's Bay Company, as it became known, gained an exclusive monopoly, among English subjects, over the fur trade in "Rupert's Land"—all the territory whose rivers drained into Hudson Bay. Rupert's Land, named after Prince Rupert, the Hudson's Bay Company's first governor, comprised almost half of present-day Canada.

Prior to the Conquest in 1760, French traders operating out of Montreal opposed the Hudson's Bay Company's monopoly. Afterward, a new challenge arose, when British traders working out of Montreal allied with the French to form the North West Company. Only after the forced union of the two companies in 1821 did the Hudson's Bay Company have a practical monopoly of the northern fur trade, and only then did it truly enjoy the rights and privileges granted in 1670.

The Woodland First Nations welcomed the French and English traders with their iron manufactured goods — axes, knives, spears, and kettles. These durable items made hunting, cooking, and warfare easier and more efficient than had been the case when only stone, wood, and bone implements were available. As a result of the trade the Cree living near the Hudson's Bay Company's posts on Hudson and James Bays came to rely on the newcomers. An important consequence of the fur traders' arrival was the rise of a mixed-blood, or Métis, population, the result of intermarriage between the fur traders and Native women.

Until the 1970s historians of the fur trade generally ignored the role of the traders' wives. In her 1977 essay, "'Women in Between': Indian Women in Fur Trade Society in Western Canada," Sylvia Van Kirk redressed the balance and introduced them fully into her account. Recently Heather Rollason Driscoll has returned to the discussion in specific reference to the traders' selection of partners. Her essay, "'A Most Important Chain of Connection': Marriage in the Hudson's Bay Company," makes the discussion of women in the 19th-century fur trade more complex. What was the role of women in the early fur trade in Western Canada? Why did the taking of a First Nations wife decline in the early 19th century? To what extent did racial factors play a role in the fur traders' selection of a partner in the early and mid-19th century?

E.E. Rich has written the standard account of the Hudson's Bay Company and its rivals in *The Fur Trade and the Northwest to 1857* (Toronto: McClelland and Stewart, 1967). Also of interest is W.J. Eccles's "The Fur Trade and Eighteenth-Century Imperialism," *William and Mary Quarterly*, 3rd series, 40 (1983): 341–62. The first notable study of the fur trade is H.A. Innis, *The Fur Trade in Canada* (Toronto: University of Toronto Press, 1999 [1930]). A.J. Ray provides a more recent interpretation in his *Indians in the Fur Trade* (Toronto: University of Toronto Press, 1974). Daniel Francis has written a popular account of the personalities of the fur trade in Western Canada, *Battle for the West: Fur Traders and the Birth of Western Canada* (Edmonton: Hurtig, 1982). Three scholarly analyses that focus on the fur trade in a specific region include Daniel Francis and Toby Morantz's *Partners in Furs: A History of the Fur Trade in Eastern James Bay, 1600–1870* (Montreal/Kingston: McGill-Queen's University Press, 1983); Paul C. Thistle's *Indian–European Trade Relations in the Lower Saskatchewan River Region to 1840* (Winnipeg: University of Manitoba Press, 1986); and J.C. Yerbury's *The Subarctic Indians and the Fur Trade, 1680–1860* (Vancouver: University of British Columbia Press, 1986).

A survey of literature dealing with the First Nations' involvement in the fur trade is found in "The Indian and the Fur Trade: A Review of Recent Literature," by Jacqueline Peterson with John Afinson, *Manitoba History* 10 (1985): 10–18. Carolyn Gilman provides an excellent popular summary of the fur trade in the illustrated *Where Two Worlds Meet: The Great Lakes Fur Trade* (St. Paul: Minnesota Historical Society, 1982). For a short overview consult "The First

Businessmen: Indians and the Fur Trade" and "'A Mere Business of Fur Trading,' 1670–1821," two chapters in Michael Bliss's *Northern Enterprise: Five Centuries of Canadian Business* (Toronto: McClelland and Stewart, 1987), pp. 33–54, 79–108. Toby Morantz stresses the continuity of First Nations' culture throughout the early fur trade in "Old Texts, Old Questions: Another Look at the Issue of Continuity and the Early Fur-Trade Period," *Canadian Historical Review* 73 (1992): 166–93. For developments in the Great Lakes area, see Richard White, *The Middle Ground: Indians, Empires, and Republics in the Great Lakes Region, 1650–1815* (Cambridge, UK: Cambridge University Press, 1991).

Sylvia Van Kirk, in *"Many Tender Ties": Women in Fur-Trade Society, 1670–1870* (Winnipeg: Watson and Dwyer, 1980), and Jennifer S.H. Brown, in *Strangers in Blood: The Fur Trade Company Families in Indian Country* (Vancouver: University of British Columbia Press, 1980), provide accounts of women in the fur trade. Olive Patricia Dickason takes a pan-Canadian view of the rise of a mixed-blood population in her "From 'One Nation' in the Northwest to 'New Nation' in the Northwest: A Look at the Emergence of the Metis," *American Indian Culture and Research Journal* 6, 2 (1982): 1–21. Susan Sleeper-Smith has reviewed the lives of four Native women who married early French fur traders in the Great Lakes country, "Women, Kin, and Catholicism: New Perspectives on the Fur Trade," *Ethnohistory*, 47: 2 (Spring 2000): 423–51.

WEBLINKS

Champlain Society
http://link.library.utoronto.ca/champlain/search.cfm?lang=eng

The digital collections of the Champlain Society contain many European primary source accounts of the fur trade. Browse the database by subject, and select for example, "Fur trade — Canada," or "Hudson's Bay Company — Records and correspondence," or "North West Company — History."

Personal Histories of the Fur Trade
http://www.canadiana.org/hbc/sources/sources_e.html#autobio

A collection of many autobiographical accounts of life during the fur trade.

Hudson's Bay Company Heritage: Women
http://www.hbc.com/hbcheritage/history/people/women

Includes biographies of Thanadelthur and Isobel Gunn, prominent women in the history of the Hudson's Bay Company.

Country Wives and Other Fur Trade Women
http://collections.ic.gc.ca/tod/bios/cwives.htm

Biographies and descriptions of Aboriginal and European women in the fur trade. Contains a digitized copy of the Hudson's Bay Company's "Standing Rules and Regulations" on the subject of marriage.

Women of Aspenland
http://www.albertasource.ca/aspenland/eng/society/fur_trade_intermarriage.html

This page, which is part of a larger site, discusses intermarriage and mixed families during the fur trade in what is now Central Alberta.

Food and the Fur Trade
http://www.whiteoak.org/learning/food.htm

A detailed discussion of how the fur traders obtained and prepared provisions.

Aboriginal Women's Issues
http://www.canadiana.org/citm/specifique/abwomen_e.html

A detailed review of the many issues that Aboriginal women have faced, from the time of European contact to the present.

Article Four

"Women in Between": Indian Women in Fur Trade Society in Western Canada

Sylvia Van Kirk

In attempting to analyze the life of the Indian woman in fur trade society in western Canada, especially from her own point of view, one is immediately confronted by a challenging historiographical problem. Can the Indian woman's perspective be constructed from historical sources that were almost exclusively written by European men? Coming from a non-literate society, no Indian women have left us, for example, their views on the fur trade or their reasons for becoming traders' wives.[1] Yet if one amasses the sources available for fur trade social history, such as contemporary narratives, journals, correspondence, and wills, a surprisingly rich store of information on Indian women emerges. One must, of course, be wary of the traders' cultural and sexual bias, but then even modern anthropologists have difficulty maintaining complete objectivity. Furthermore, the fur traders had the advantage of knowing Indian women intimately — these women became their wives, the mothers of their children. Narratives such as that of Andrew Graham in the late eighteenth century and David Thompson in the nineteenth, both of whom had Native wives, comment perceptively on the implications of Indian–white social contact.[2] The key to constructing the Indian woman's perspective must lie in the kinds of questions applied to data;[3] regrettably the picture will not be complete, but it is hoped that a careful reading of the traders' observations can result in a useful and illuminating account of the Indian women's life in fur trade society.

The fur trade was based on the complex interaction between two different racial groups. On the one hand are the various Indian tribes, most importantly the Ojibway, the Cree, and the Chipewyan. These Indians may be designated the "host" group in that they remain within their traditional environment. On the other hand are the European traders, the "visiting" group, who enter the northwest by both the Hudson's Bay and St. Lawrence–Great Lakes routes. They are significantly different from the Indians in that they constitute only a small, all-male fragment of their own society. For a variety of factors to be discussed, this created a unique situation for the Indian women. They became the "women in between" two groups of

Source: "'Women in Between': Indian Women in Fur Trade Society in Western Canada," *Historical Papers* (1977): 30–47. Reprinted by permission of the author and the Canadian Historical Association.

males. Because of their sex, Indian women were able to become an integral part of fur trade society in a sense that Indian men never could. As country wives[4] of the traders, Indian women lived substantially different lives when they moved within the forts. Even within the tribes, women who acted as allies of the whites can also be observed; certain circumstances permitted individual women to gain positions of influence and act as "social brokers" between the two groups.

It is a major contention of this study that Indian women themselves were active agents in the development of Indian–white relations.[5] A major concern then must be to determine what motivated their actions. Some themes to be discussed are the extent to which the Indian woman was able to utilize her position as "woman in between" to increase her influence and status, and the extent to which the Indian woman valued the economic advantage brought by the traders. It must be emphasized, however, that Indian–white relations were by no means static during the fur trade period.[6] After assessing the positive and negative aspects of the Indian woman's life in fur trade society, the paper will conclude by discussing the reasons for the demise of her position.

I

Miscegenation was the basic social fact of the western Canadian fur trade. That this was so indicates active cooperation on both sides. From the male perspective, both white and Indian, the formation of marital alliances between Indian women and the traders had its advantages. The European traders had both social and economic reasons for taking Indian mates. Not only did they fill the sexual void created by the absence of white women,[7] but they performed such valuable economic tasks as making moccasins and netting snowshoes that they became an integral if unofficial part of the fur trade workforce.[8] The traders also realized that these alliances were useful in cementing trade ties; officers in both the Hudson's Bay and North West companies often married daughters of trading captains or chiefs.[9] From the Indian point of view, the marital alliance created a reciprocal social bond which served to consolidate his economic relationship with the trader. The exchange of women was common in Indian society, where it was viewed as "a reciprocal alliance and series of good offices . . . between the friends of both parties; each is ready to assist and protect the other."[10] It was not loose morality or even hospitality which prompted the Indians to be so generous with their offers of women. This was their way of drawing the traders into their kinship circle, and in return for giving the traders sexual and domestic rights to their women, the Indians expected equitable privileges such as free access to the posts and provisions.[11] It is evident that the traders often did not understand the Indian concept of these alliances and a flagrant violation of Indian sensibilities could lead to retaliation such as the Henley House massacre in 1755.[12]

But what of the women themselves? Were they just pawns in this exchange, passive, exploited victims? Fur trade sources do not support this view; there are numerous examples of Indian women actively seeking to become connected with the traders. According to an early Nor'Wester, Cree women considered it an honour to be selected as wives by the voyageurs, and any husband who refused to lend his wife would be subject to the general condemnation of the women.[13] Alexander Ross observed that Chinook women on the Pacific coast showed a preference for living with a white man. If deserted by one husband, they would return to their tribe in a state of widowhood to await the opportunity of marrying another fur trader.[14] Nor'Wester Daniel Harmon voiced the widely held opinion that most of the Indian women were "better pleased to remain with the White People than with their own Relations," while his contemporary George Nelson affirmed "some too would even desert to live with the white."[15] Although Alexander Henry the Younger may have exaggerated his difficulties in fending off young Indian women, his personal experiences underline the fact that the women often took the initiative. On one occasion when travelling with his brigade in the summer of 1800, Henry was confronted in his tent by a handsome woman, dressed in her best finery, who told him boldly that she had come to live with him as she did not care for her husband or any other Indian. But Henry, anxious to avoid this entanglement partly because it was not sanctioned by the husband, whom he knew to be insatiably jealous, forced the woman to return to her Indian partner.[16] A year or so later in the lower Red River district, the daughter of an Ojibway chief had more luck. Henry returned from New Year's festivities to find that "Liard's daughter" had taken possession of his room and "the devil could not have got her out."[17] This time, having become more acculturated to fur trade life, Henry acquiesced and "Liard's daughter" became his country wife. The trader, however, resisted his father-in-law's argument that he should also take his second daughter because all great men should have a plurality of wives.[18]

The fur traders also comment extensively on the assistance and loyalty of Indian women who remained within the tribes. An outstanding example is the young Chipewyan Thanadelthur, known to the traders as the "Slave Woman."[19] In the early eighteenth century, after being captured by the Cree, Thanadelthur managed to escape to York Factory. Her knowledge of Chipewyan made her valuable to the traders, and in 1715–16, she led an HBC [Hudson's Bay Company] expedition to establish peace between the Cree and the Chipewyan, a necessary prelude to the founding of Fort Churchill. Governor James Knight's journals give us a vivid picture of this woman, of whom he declared: "She was one of a Very high Spirit and of the Firmest Resolution that ever I see any Body in my Days."[20]

Post journals contain numerous references to Indian women warning the traders of impending treachery. In 1797, Charles Chaboillez, having been warned by an old woman that the Indians intended to pillage his post, was able to nip this intrigue in the bud.[21] George Nelson and one of his men escaped an attack by some Indians in 1805 only by being "clandestinely assisted by the women."[22] It appears that women were particularly instrumental in saving the lives of the whites among the turbulent tribes of the Lower Columbia.[23] One of the traders' most notable allies was the well-connected Chinook princess known as Lady Calpo, the wife of a Clatsop chief. In 1814, she helped restore peaceful relations after the Nor'Westers had suffered a raid on their canoes by giving them important information about Indian custom in settling disputes. Handsome rewards cemented her attachment to the traders with the result that Lady Calpo reputedly saved Fort George from several attacks by warning of the hostile plans of the Indians.[24]

The reasons for the Indian women's actions are hinted at in the traders' observations. It was the generally held opinion of the traders that the status of women in Indian society was deplorably low. As Nor'Wester Gabriel Franchère summed it up:

> Some Indian tribes think that women have no souls, but die altogether like the brutes; others assign them a different paradise from that of men, which indeed they might have reason to prefer . . . unless their relative condition were to be ameliorated in the next world.[25]

Whether as "social brokers" or as wives, Indian women attempted to manipulate their position as "women in between" to increase their influence and status. Certainly women such as Thanadelthur and Lady Calpo were able to work themselves into positions of real power. It is rather paradoxical that in Thanadelthur's case it was her escape from captivity that brought her into contact with the traders in the first place; if she had not been a woman, she would never have been carried off by the Cree as a prize of war. Once inside the HBC fort, she was able to use her position as the only Chipewyan to advantage by acting as guide and consultant to the governor. The protection and regard she was given by the whites enabled Thanadelthur to dictate to Indian men, both Cree and Chipewyan, in a manner they would not previously have tolerated. Anxious to promote the traders' interests, she assaulted an old Chipewyan on one occasion when he attempted to trade less than prime furs; she "ketcht him by the nose Push'd him backwards & call'd him fool and told him if they brought any but Such as they ware directed they would not be traded."[26] Thanadelthur did take a Chipewyan husband but was quite prepared to leave him if he would not accompany her on the arduous second journey she was planning to undertake for the governor.[27] It is possible that the role played by Thanadelthur and subsequent "slave women" in establishing trade relations with the whites may have enhanced the status of Chipewyan women. Nearly a century later, Alexander Mackenzie noted that, in spite of their burdensome existence, Chipewyan women possessed "a very considerable influence in the traffic with Europeans."[28]

Lady Calpo retained a position of influence for a long time. When Governor Simpson visited Fort George in 1824, he found she had to be treated with respect because she was "the best News Monger in the Parish"; from her he learned "More of the Scandal, Secrets and politics both of the out & inside of the Fort than from Any other source."[29] Significantly, Lady Calpo endeavoured to further improve her rank by arranging a marriage alliance between the governor and her carefully raised daughter. Although Simpson declared he wished "to keep clear of the Daughter," he succumbed in order "to continue on good terms with the Mother."[30] Many years later, a friend visiting the Columbia wrote to Simpson that Lady Calpo, that "'fast friend' of the Whites," was still thriving.[31]

As wives of the traders, Indian women could also manoeuvre themselves into positions of influence. In fact, a somewhat perturbed discussion emerges in fur trade literature over the excessive influence some Indian women exerted over their fur trader husbands. The young NWC [North West Company] clerk George Nelson appears to have spent long hours contemplating the insolvable perplexities of womankind. Nelson claimed that initially Cree women when married to whites were incredibly attentive and submissive, but this did not last long. Once they had gained a little footing, they knew well "how to take advantage & what use they ought to make of it."[32] On one of his first trips into the interior, Nelson was considerably annoyed by the shenanigans of the Indian wife of Brunet, one of his voyageurs. A jealous, headstrong woman, she completely dominated her husband by a mixture of "caresses, promises & menaces." Not only did this woman render her husband a most unreliable servant, but Nelson also caught her helping herself to the Company's rum. Brunet's wife, Nelson fumed, was as great "a vixen & hussy" as the tinsmith's wife at the marketplace in Montreal: "I now began to think that women were women not only in civilized countries but elsewhere also."[33]

Another fur trader observed a paradoxical situation among the Chipewyan women. In their own society, they seemed condemned to a most servile existence, but upon becoming wives of the French-Canadian voyageurs, they assumed "an importance to themselves and instead of serving as formerly they exact submission from the descendants of the Gauls."[34] One of the most remarkable examples of a Chipewyan wife rising to prominence was the case of Madam Lamallice, the wife of the brigade guide at the HBC post on Lake Athabasca. During the difficult winter of 1821–22, Madam Lamallice was accorded a favoured position because she was the post's only interpreter and possessed considerable influence with the Indians.[35] George Simpson, then experiencing his first winter in the Indian Country, felt obliged to give in to her demands for extra rations and preferred treatment in order to prevent her defection. He had observed that the Nor'Westers' strong position was partly due to the fact that "their Women are faithful to their cause and good Interpreters whereas we have but one in the Fort that can talk Chipewyan."[36] Madam Lamallice exploited her position to such an extent that she even defied fort regulations by carrying on a private trade in provisions.[37] A few years later on a trip to the Columbia, Governor Simpson was annoyed to discover that Chinook women when married to the whites often gained such an ascendancy "that they give law to their Lords."[38] In fact, he expressed general concern about the influence of these "petticoat politicians," whose demands were "more injurious to the Companys interests than I am well able to describe."[39] The governor deplored Chief Factor James Bird's management of Red River in the early 1820s because of his habit of discussing every matter "however trifling or important" with "his Copper Cold Mate," who then spread the news freely around the colony.[40] Too many of his officers, Simpson declared, tended to sacrifice business for private interests. Particular expense and delay were occasioned in providing transport for families. Simpson never forgave Chief Factor John Clarke for abandoning some of the goods destined for Athabasca in 1820 to make a light canoe for his Native wife and her servant.[41]

It is likely that Simpson's single-minded concern for business efficiency caused him to exaggerate the extent of the Indian women's influence. Nevertheless, they do seem to have attempted to take advantage of their unique position as women "in between" two groups of men. This fact is supported by the traders' observation that the choice of a husband, Indian or white, gave the Indian woman leverage to improve her lot. Now she could threaten to desert to the whites or vice versa if she felt she were not being well-treated:

> She has always enough of policy to insinuate how well off she was while living with the white people and in like manner when with the latter she drops some hints to the same purpose.[42]

Although Chipewyan women who had lived with the voyageurs had to resume their former domestic tasks when they returned to their own people, they reputedly evinced a greater spirit of independence.[43] Considerable prestige accrued to Chinook women who had lived with the traders; upon rejoining the tribes, they remained "very friendly" to the whites and "never fail to influence their connections to the same effect."[44]

From the Indian woman's point of view, material advantage was closely tied to the question of improved influence or status. The women within the tribes had a vested interest in promoting cordial relations with the whites. While George Nelson mused that it was a universal maternal instinct which prompted the women to try to prevent clashes between Indian and white,[45] they were more likely motivated by practical, economic considerations. If the traders were driven from the country, the Indian woman would lose the source of European goods, which had revolutionized her life just as much as if not more than that of the Indian man. It was much easier to boil water in a metal kettle than to have to laboriously heat it by means of dropping hot stones into a bark container. Cotton and woollen goods saved long hours of tanning hides. "Show them an awl or a strong needle," declared David Thompson, "and they will gladly give the finest Beaver or Wolf skin they have to purchase it."[46]

Furthermore, it can be argued that the tendency of the Indians to regard the fur trade post as a kind of welfare centre was of more relevance to the women than to the men. In times of scarcity, which were not infrequent in Indian society, the women were usually the first to suffer.[47] Whereas before they would often have perished, many now sought relief at the companies' posts. To cite but one of many examples: at Albany during the winter of 1706, Governor Beale gave shelter to three starving Cree women whose husband had sent them away as he could only provide for his two children.[48] The post was also a source of medical aid and succour. The story is told of a young Carrier woman in New Caledonia, who, having been severely beaten by her husband, managed to struggle to the nearest NWC post. Being nearly starved, she was slowly nursed back to health and allowed to remain at the post when it became apparent that her relatives had abandoned her.[49] The desire for European goods, coupled with the assistance to be found at the fur trade posts, helps to explain why Indian women often became devoted allies of the traders.

In becoming the actual wife of a fur trader, the Indian woman was offered even greater relief from the burdens of her traditional existence. In fact, marriage to a trader offered an alternative lifestyle. The fur traders themselves had no doubt that an Indian woman was much better off with a white man. The literature presents a dreary recital of their abhorrence of the degraded, slave-like position of the Indian women. The life of a Cree woman, declared Alexander Mackenzie, was "an uninterrupted success of toil and pain."[50] Nor'Wester Duncan McGillivray decided that the rather singular lack of affection evinced by Plains Indian women for their mates arose from the barbarous treatment the women received.[51] Although David Thompson found the Chipewyan a good people in many ways, he considered their attitudes toward women a disgrace; he had known Chipewyan women to kill female infants as "an act of kindness" to spare them the hardships they would have to face.[52]

The extent to which the fur traders' observations represent an accurate reflection of the actual status of Indian women in their own societies presents a complex dilemma which requires deeper investigation. The cultural and class biases of the traders are obvious. Their horror at the toilsome burdens imposed upon Indian women stems from their narrow, chivalrous view of women as the "frail, weaker sex." This is scarcely an appropriate description of Indian women, particularly the Chipewyan, who were acknowledged to be twice as strong as their male counterparts.[53] Furthermore, while the sharp sexual division of labour inflicted a burdensome role upon the women, their duties were essential and the women possessed considerable autonomy within their own sphere.[54] Some traders did think it curious that the women seemed to possess a degree of influence in spite of their degraded situation; indeed, some of the bolder ones occasionally succeeded in making themselves quite independent and "wore the breeches."[55]

A possible way of explaining the discrepancy between the women's perceived and actual status is suggested in a recent anthropological study of the Mundurucú of Amazonian Brazil. In this society, the authors discovered that while the official (male) ideology relegates women to an inferior, subservient position, in the reality of daily life, the women are able to assume considerable autonomy and influence.[56] Most significantly, however, Mundurucú women, in order to alleviate their onerous domestic duties, have actively championed the erosion of traditional village life and the concomitant blurring of economic sex roles which have come with the introduction of the rubber trade. According to the authors, the Mundurucú woman "has seen another way of life, and she has opted for it."[57]

This statement could well be applied to the Indian woman who was attracted to the easier life of the fur trade post. In the first place, she now became involved in a much more sedentary routine. With a stationary home, the Indian woman was no longer required to act as a beast of burden, hauling or carrying the accoutrements of camp from place to place. The traders often expressed astonishment and pity at the heavy loads which Indian women were obliged to transport.[58] In fur trade society, the unenviable role of carrier was assumed by the voyageur. The male servants at the fort were now responsible for providing firewood and water, although the women might help. In contrast to Indian practice, the women of the fort were not sent to fetch home the produce of the hunt.[59] The wife of an officer, benefiting from her husband's rank, enjoyed a privileged status. She herself was carried in and out of the canoe[60] and could expect to have all her baggage portaged by a voyageur. At Fond du Lac in 1804, when the wife of NWC bourgeois John Sayer decided to go on a sugar-making expedition, four men went with her to carry her baggage and provisions and later returned to fetch home her things.[61]

While the Indian woman performed a variety of valuable economic tasks around the post, her domestic duties were relatively lighter than they had traditionally been. Now her energies were concentrated on making moccasins and snowshoes. As one Nor'Wester declared, with the whites, Indian women could lead "a comparatively easy and free life" in contrast to the "servile slavish mode" of their own.[62] The prospect of superior comforts reputedly motivated some Spokan women to marry voyageurs.[63] The ready supply of both finery and trinkets which bourgeois and voyageurs were seen to lavish on their women may also have had an appeal.[64] Rival traders noted that luxury items such as lace, ribbons, rings, and vermilion, which "greatly gain the Love of the Women," were important in attracting the Indians to trade.[65] The private orders placed by HBC officers and servants in the 1790s and later include a wide range of cloth goods, shawls, gartering, earrings, and brooches for the women.[66] When taken by a trader, *à la façon du pays,* it became common for an Indian woman to go through a ritual performed by the other women of the fort; she was scoured of grease and paint and exchanged her Native garments for those of a more civilized fashion. At the NWC posts, wives were clothed in "Canadian fashion," which consisted of a shirt, short gown, petticoat, and leggings.[67]

The traders further thought that Indian women benefited by being freed from certain taboos and customs which they had to bear in Indian society. Among the Ojibway and other tribes, for example, the choicest part of an animal was always reserved for the men; death, it was believed, would come to any woman who dared to eat such sacred portions. The Nor'Westers paid little heed to such observances. As Duncan Cameron sarcastically wrote: "I have often seen several women living with the white men eat of those forbidden morsels without the least inconvenience."[68] The traders were also convinced that Indian women welcomed a monogamous as opposed to a polygamous state. Polygamy, several HBC officers observed, often gave rise to jealous and sometimes murderous quarrels.[69] It is possible, however, that the traders' own cultural abhorrence of polygamy[70] made them exaggerate the women's antipathy toward it. As a practical scheme for the sharing of heavy domestic tasks, polygamy may in fact have been welcomed by the women.

II

Thus far the advantages which the fur trade brought to Indian women have been emphasized in order to help explain Indian women's reactions to it. It would be erroneous, however, to paint the life of an Indian wife as idyllic. In spite of the traders' belief in the superior benefits they offered, there is evidence that fur trade life had an adverse effect on Indian women. Certainly, a deterioration in her position over time can be detected.

First there is the paradox that the supposedly superior material culture of the fur trade had a deleterious effect on Indian women. It was as if, mused Reverend John West, the first Anglican missionary, "the habits of civilized life" exerted an injurious influence over their general constitutions.[71] Apart from being more exposed to European diseases, the Indian wives of traders suffered more in childbirth than they had in the primitive state.[72] Dr. John Richardson, who accompanied the Franklin Expedition of the 1820s, noted that not only did Indian women now have children more frequently and for longer periods, but that they were more susceptible to the disorders and diseases connected with pregnancy and childbirth.[73] It was not uncommon for fur traders' wives to give birth to from eight to twelve children, whereas four children were the average in Cree society.[74]

The reasons for this dramatic rise in the birth rate deserve further investigation, but several reasons can be advanced. As recent medical research had suggested, the less fatiguing lifestyle and more regular diet offered the Indian wife could have resulted in greater fecundity.[75]

The daily ration for the women of the forts was four pounds of meat or fish (one-half that for the men);[76] when Governor Simpson jokingly remarked that the whitefish diet at Fort Chipewyan seemed conducive to procreation he may have hit upon a medical truth.[77] Furthermore, sexual activity in Indian society was circumscribed by a variety of taboos, and evidence suggests that Indian men regarded their European counterparts as very licentious.[78] Not only did Indian women now have sex more often, but the attitudes of European husbands also may have interfered with traditional modes of restricting family size. The practice of infanticide was, of course, condemned by the whites, but the Europeans may also have discouraged the traditional long nursing periods of from two to four years for each child.[79] In their view this custom resulted in the premature aging of the mothers,[80] but the fact that Indian children were born at intervals of approximately three years tends to support the recent theory that lactation depresses fertility.[81]

The cultural conflict resulting over the upbringing of the children must have caused the Indian women considerable anguish. An extreme example of the tragedy which could result related to the Chinook practice of head-flattening. In Chinook society, a flat forehead, achieved by strapping a board against the baby's head when in its cradle, was a mark of class; only slaves were not so distinguished. Thus it was only natural that a Chinook woman, though married to a fur trader, would desire to bind her baby's head, but white fathers found this custom abhorrent. The insistence of some fathers that their infants' heads not be flattened resulted in the mothers murdering their babies rather than have them suffer the ignominy of looking like slaves. Gradually European preference prevailed. When Governor Simpson visited the Columbia in the early 1820s, he reported that Chinook wives were abiding by their husbands' wishes and no cases of infanticide had been reported for some years.[82]

In Indian society, children were the virtual "property" of the women who were responsible for their upbringing;[83] in fur trade society, Indian women could find themselves divested of these rights. While the traders acknowledged that Indian women were devoted and affectionate mothers, this did not prevent them from exercising patriarchal authority, particularly in sending young children to Britain or Canada so that they might receive a "civilized" education.[84] It must have been nearly impossible to explain the rationale for such a decision to the Indian mothers; their grief at being separated from their children was compounded by the fact that the children, who were especially vulnerable to respiratory diseases, often died.[85]

It is difficult to know if the general treatment accorded Indian women by European traders met with the women's acceptance. How much significance should be attached to the views of outside observers in the early 1800s who did not think the Indian woman's status had been much improved? Some of the officers of the Franklin Expedition felt the fur traders had been corrupted by Indian attitudes toward women; Indian wives were not treated with "the tenderness and attention due to every female" because the Indians would despise the traders for such unmanly action.[86] The first missionaries were even stronger in denouncing fur trade marital relations. John West considered the traders' treatment of their women disgraceful: "They do not admit them as their companions, nor do they allow them to eat at their tables, but degrade them *merely* as slaves to their arbitrary inclinations."[87] Such statements invite skepticism because of the writers' limited contact with fur trade society, and, in the case of the missionaries, because of their avowedly hostile view of fur trade customs. Furthermore, the above statements project a European ideal about the way women should be treated, which, apart from being widely violated in their own society, would have had little relevance for Indian women. It is doubtful, for example, that the Indian women themselves would have viewed the fact that they did not come to table, a custom partly dictated by the quasi-military organization of the posts, as proof of their debased position.[88] The segregation of the sexes at meals was common in Indian society, but now, at least, the women did not have to suffice with the leftovers of the men.[89]

Nevertheless, there is evidence to suggest that Indian women were misused by the traders. In Indian society, women were accustomed to greater freedom of action with regard to marital relationships than the traders were prepared to accord them. It was quite within a woman's rights, for example, to institute a divorce if her marriage proved unsatisfactory.[90] In fur trade society, Indian women were more subject to arbitrary arrangements devised by the men. Upon retiring from the Indian Country, it became customary for a trader to place his country wife and family with another, a practice known as "turning off." Although there was often little they could do about it, a few cases were cited of women who tried to resist. At a post in the Peace River district in 1798, the Indian wife of an *engagé*, who was growing tired of wintering *en derouine*, absolutely rejected her husband's attempt to pass her to the man who agreed to take his place.[91] At Fort Chipewyan in 1800, the estranged wife of the voyageur Morin foiled the attempt of his bourgeois to find her a temporary "protector"; she stoutly refused three different prospects.[92] Indian women also did not take kindly to the long separations which fur trade life imposed on them and their European mates. Although the Indian wife of Chief Factor Joseph Colen was to receive every attention during his absence in England in the late 1790s, Colen's successor could not dissuade her from taking an Indian lover and leaving York Factory.[93]

Indian wives seem to have been particularly victimized during the violent days of the trade war, when rivals went so far as to debauch and intimidate each other's women. In 1819 at Pelican Lake, for example, HBC servant Deshau took furs from a NWC servant and raped his wife in retaliation for having had his own wife debauched by a Nor'Wester earlier in the season.[94] A notorious instance involved the Indian wife of HBC servant Andrew Kirkness at Isle à la Crosse in 1810–11. In the late summer, this woman in a fit of pique had deserted her husband and sought refuge at the Nor'Westers' post. She soon regretted her action, however, for she was kept a virtual prisoner by the Canadians, and all efforts of the HBC men to get her back failed. The upshot was that Kirkness himself deserted to the rival post, leaving the English in dire straits since he was their only fisherman. Kirkness was intimidated into remaining with the Nor'Westers until the spring with the threat that, should he try to leave, "every Canadian in the House would ravish his woman before his eyes." Eventually Kirkness was released, but only after his wife had been coerced into saying that she did not want to accompany him. As the HBC party were evacuating their post, the woman tried to escape but was forcibly dragged back by the Nor'Westers and ultimately became the "property" of an *engagé*.[95]

Such abusive tactics were also applied to the Indians. By the turn of the century, relations between the Indians and the Nor'Westers in particular showed a marked deterioration. In what seems to have been a classic case of "familiarity breeding contempt," the Nor'Westers now retained their mastery through coercion and brute force and frequently transgressed the bounds of Indian morality. An especially flagrant case was the Nor'Westers' exploitation of Chipewyan women at its posts in the Athabasca district. By the end of the eighteenth century, they had apparently built up a nefarious traffic in these women; the bourgeois did not scruple at seizing Chipewyan women by force, ostensibly in lieu of trade debts, and then selling them to the men for large sums.[96] The situation became so bad that the Chipewyan began leaving their women behind when they came to trade, and when Hudson's Bay traders appeared on Lake Athabasca in 1792, the Indians hoped to secure their support and drive out their rivals. The English, however, were too weak to offer any effective check to the Nor'Westers, who continued to assault both fathers and husbands if they tried to resist the seizure of their women. Since they were not powerful enough to mount an attack, the Chipewyan connived at the escape of their women during the summer months when most of the traders were away. Resentful of their treatment, many of the women welcomed the chance to slip back to their own people, so that the summer master at Fort Chipewyan was almost solely preoccupied with keeping watch over the *engagés* women.[97] By 1800 at least one voyageur had been killed by irate Chipewyan, and the bourgeois contemplated offering a reward for the hunting down of "any d—nd rascal" who caused a Frenchman's woman to desert.[98]

The Indians appear to have become openly contemptuous of the white man and his so-called morality. A northern tribe called the Beaver Indians took a particularly strong stand. At first they had welcomed the Canadians but, having rapidly lost respect for them, now forbade any intercourse between their women and the traders.[99] Elsewhere individual hunters boycotted the traders owing to the maltreatment of their women.[100] Sporadic reprisals became more frequent. Whereas Indian women had previously played a positive role as a liaison between Indian and white, they were now becoming an increasing source of friction between the two groups. Governor Simpson summed up the deteriorating situation:

> It is a lamentable fact that almost every difficulty we have had with Indians throughout the country may be traced to our interference with the Women of the Forts in short 9 murders out of 10 Committed on Whites by Indians have arisen through Women.[101]

Although there is little direct evidence available, it is possible that the Indian women themselves were becoming increasingly dissatisfied with their treatment from the whites. In spite of the initiative which the women have been seen to exercise in forming and terminating relationships with the traders, there were undoubtedly times when they were the unwilling objects of a transaction between Indians and white men. Certainly not all Indian women looked upon the whites as desirable husbands, a view that was probably reinforced with experience. George Nelson did observe in 1811 that there were some Indian women who showed "an extraordinary predilection" for their own people and could not be prevailed upon to live with the traders.[102]

The increasing hostility of the Indians, coupled with the fact that in well-established areas marriage alliances were no longer a significant factor in trade relations, led to a decline in the practice of taking an Indian wife. In fact, in 1806, the North West Company passed a ruling prohibiting any of its employees from taking a country wife from among the tribes.[103] One of the significant factors which changed the traders' attitudes toward Indian women, however, was that they were now no longer "women in between." By the turn of the century a sizable group of mixed-blood women had emerged and for social and economic reasons, fur traders preferred mixed-blood women as wives. In this way the Indian women lost their important place in fur trade society.[104]

The introduction of the Indian woman's perspective on Indian–white relations serves to underscore the tremendous complexity of intercultural contact. It is argued that Indian women saw definite advantages to be gained from the fur trade, and in their unique position as "women in between," they endeavoured to manipulate the situation to improve their existence. That the limits of their influence were certainly circumscribed, and that the ultimate benefits brought by the traders were questionable does not negate the fact that the Indian women played a much more active and important role in the fur trade than has previously been acknowledged.

NOTES

1. The lack of written Indian history is, of course, a general problem for the ethnohistorian. Indeed, all social scientists must rely heavily on the historical observations of the agents of white contact such as fur traders, explorers, and missionaries. Little seems to have been done to determine if the oral tradition of the Indians is a viable source of information on Indian–white relations in the fur trade period.

2. Glyndwr Williams, ed., *Andrew Graham's Observations on Hudson's Bay, 1769–91* (London: Hudson's Bay Record Society, vol. 27, 1969); Richard Glover, ed., *David Thompson's Narrative, 1784–1812* (Toronto: Champlain Society, vol. 40, 1962).

3. A fascinating study which indicates how the application of a different perspective to the same data can produce new insights is *Women of the Forest* by Yolanda and Robert Murphy (New York, 1974). Based on field work conducted twenty years earlier in Amazonian Brazil, the authors found that by looking at the life of the Mundurucú tribe from the woman's point of view, their understanding of the actual as opposed to the official functioning of that society was much enlarged.

4. Marriages between European traders and Indian women were contracted according to indigenous rites derived from the Indian custom. For a detailed explanation, see Sylvia Van Kirk, "'The Custom of the Country': An Examination of Fur Trade Marriage Practices," in L.H. Thomas, ed., *Essays in Western History* (Edmonton, 1976), 49–70.

5. See Murphy, *Women of the Forest,* ch. 6, for a useful comparison. Mundurucú women actively welcomed the social change brought about by the introduction of the rubber trade into their traditional economy.

6. An instructive study of the Indians' economic role in the fur trade is provided by Arthur Ray in *Indians in the Fur Trade* (Toronto, 1974). He shows that the Indian played a much more active, although changing, role in the dynamics of the fur trade than had previously been acknowledged.

7. HBC men were prohibited from bringing women to Hudson Bay. It was not until the early nineteenth century that the first white women came to the northwest.

8. In 1802 HBC men defended their practice of keeping Indian women in the posts by informing the London Committee that they were "Virtually your Honors Servants," HBC Arch., B.239/b/79, fos. 40d–41. For a discussion of the important economic role played by Native women in the fur trade, see Sylvia Van Kirk, "The Role of Women in the Fur Trade Society of the Canadian West, 1700–1850," unpublished Ph.D. thesis, University of London, 1975.

9. HBC Arch., Albany Journal, 24 Jan. 1771, B.3/a/63, f. 18d; "Connolly vs. Woolrich, Superior Court, 9 July 1867," *Lower Canada Jurist* 11: 234.

10. Charles Bishop, "The Henley House Massacres," *The Beaver* (Autumn 1976): 40.

11. Bishop, "The Henley House Massacres," 39. For a more technical look at the socioeconomic relationship between the Indians and the traders, see the discussion of "balanced reciprocity" in Marshall Sahlins, *Stone Age Economics* (Chicago, 1972), ch. 5.

12. In this instance the Indian captain Woudby attacked Henley House because the master was keeping two of his female relatives but denying him access to the post and its provisions.

13. Alexander Henry, *Travels and Adventures in Canada and the Indian Territories, 1760–1776,* ed. Jas. Bain (Boston, 1901), 248.

14. Alexander Ross, *The Fur Hunters of the Far West,* vol. 1 (London, 1855), 296–97.

15. W. Kaye Lamb, ed., *Sixteen Years in the Indian Country: The Journal of Daniel Williams Harmon, 1800–1816* (Toronto, 1957), 29; Toronto Public Library, George Nelson Papers, Journal 1810–11, 24 April 1811, 42.

16. Elliot Coues, ed., *New Light on the Early History of the Greater North West: The Manuscript Journals of Alexander Henry and David Thompson, 1799–1814* (Minneapolis, 1965), 71–73.

17. Coues, *New Light,* 163.

18. Coues, *New Light,* 211.

19. For a detailed account of the story of this woman, see Sylvia Van Kirk, "Thanadelthur," *The Beaver* (Spring 1974): 40–45.

20. Van Kirk, "Thanadelthur," 45.

21. Public Archives of Canada (P.A.C.), Masson Collection, Journal of Charles Chaboillez, 13 Dec. 1797, 24.

22. Nelson Papers, Journal and Reminiscences 1825–26, 66.

23. Ross, *Fur Hunters* 1: 296.

24. Coues, *New Light,* 793; Frederick Merk, ed., *Fur Trade and Empire: George Simpson's Journal, 1824–25* (Cambridge, MA, 1931), 104.

25. Gabriel Franchère, *Narrative of a Voyage to the Northwest Coast of America, 1811–14,* ed. R.G. Thwaites (Cleveland, OH, 1904), 327.

26. Van Kirk, "Thanadelthur," 44.

27. Van Kirk, "Thanadelthur," 45.

28. W. Kaye Lamb, ed., *The Journals and Letters of Sir Alexander Mackenzie* (Cambridge, Eng., 1970), 152.

29. Merk, *Fur Trade and Empire,* 104.

30. Merk, *Fur Trade and Empire,* 104–105.

31. HBC Arch., R. Crooks to G. Simpson, 15 March 1843, D. 5/8, f. 147.

32. Nelson Papers, Journal 1810–11, pp. 41–42.

33. Nelson Papers, Journal 1803–04, 10–28 *passim.*

34. Masson Collection, "An Account of the Chip[ewyan] Indians," 23.

35. E.E. Rich, ed., *Simpson's Athabasca Journal and Report, 1820–21* (London, H.B.R.S., vol. 1, 1938), 74.
36. Rich, *Athabasca Journal*, 231.
37. HBC Arch., Fort Chipewyan Journal 1820–21, B.39/a/16, fos. 6–21d. *passim*.
38. Merk, *Fur Trade and Empire*, 99.
39. Merk, *Fur Trade and Empire*, 11–12, 58.
40. HBC Arch., George Simpson's Journal, 1821–22, D.3/3, f.52.
41. Rich, *Athabasca Journal*, 23–24; see also Merk, *Fur Trade and Empire*, 131.
42. "Account of Chip[ewyan] Indians," 23–24.
43. "Account of Chip[ewyan] Indians," 23.
44. Ross, *Fur Hunters* 1: 297.
45. Nelson Papers, Journal and Reminiscences 1825–26, 66. Nelson claimed that around 1780 some Indian women had warned the Canadian pedlars of impending attack because in their "tender & affectionate breast (for women are lovely all the world over) still lurked compassion for the mothers of those destined to be sacrificed."
46. Glover, *Thompson's Narrative*, 45. Cf. with the Mundurucú women's desire for European goods, Murphy, *Women of the Forest*, 182.
47. Samuel Hearne, *A Journey to the Northern Ocean*, ed. Richard Glover (Toronto, 1958), 190.
48. HBC Arch., Albany Journal, 23 Feb. 1706, B.3/a/1, f. 28.
49. Ross Cox, *The Columbia River*, ed. Jane and Edgar Stewart (Norman, OK, 1957), 377.
50. Lamb, *Journals of Mackenzie*, 135.
51. A.S. Morton, *The Journal of Duncan McGillivray . . . at Fort George on the Saskatchewan, 1794–95* (Toronto, 1929), 60.
52. Glover, *Thompson's Narrative*, 106.
53. Hearne, *Journey to the Northern Ocean*, 35: "Women," declared the Chipewyan chief Matonabee, "were made for labour; one of them can carry, or haul, as much as two men can do."
54. There has been a trend in recent literature to exalt the Indian woman's status by pointing out that in spite of her labour she had more independence than the pioneer farm wife. See Nancy O. Lurie, "Indian Women: A Legacy of Freedom," *The American Way* 5 (April 1972): 28–35.
55. Morton, *McGillivray's Journal*, 34; L.R.F. Masson, *Les Bourgeois de la Compagnie du Nord-Ouest* 1: 256.
56. Murphy, *Women of the Forest*, 87, 112.
57. Murphy, *Women of the Forest*, 202.
58. Lamb, *Journals of Mackenzie*, 254; Glover, *Thompson's Narrative*, 125.
59. Masson Collection, Journal of John Thomson, 15 Oct. 1798, p. 10.
60. J.B. Tyrrell, *Journals of Samuel Hearne and Philip Turnor, 1774–92* (Toronto, Champlain Society, vol. 21, 1934), 252.
61. Michel Curot, "A Wisconsin Fur Trader's Journal, 1803–04," *Wisconsin Historical Collections* 20: 449, 453.
62. Nelson Papers, Journal 1810–11, 41: Reminiscences, Part 5, 225.
63. Cox, *Columbia River*, 148.
64. Coues, *New Light*, 914; Ross, *Fur Hunters* 2: 236.
65. Tyrrell, *Journals of Hearne and Turnor*, 273.
66. HBC Arch., Book of Servants Commissions, A.16/111 and 112 passim.
67. Lamb, *Sixteen Years*, 28–29.
68. Masson, *Les Bourgeois* 2: 263.
69. Hearne, *Journey to the Northern Ocean*, 80; Williams, *Graham's Observations*, 158.
70. Alexander Ross, *Adventures of the First Settlers on the Oregon or Columbia River* (London, 1849), 280–81; Glover, *Thompson's Narrative*, 251.
71. John West, *The Substance of a Journal during a residence at the Red River Colony, 1820–23* (London, 1827), 54.
72. The traders were astonished at the little concern shown for pregnancy and childbirth in Indian society; see, for example, Lamb, *Journals of Mackenzie*, 250, and Williams, *Graham's Observations*, 177.
73. John Franklin, *Narrative of a Journey to the Shores of the Polar Sea, 1819–22* (London, 1824), 86.
74. Franklin, *Narrative of a Journey*, 60. The Indian wives of Alexander Ross and Peter Fidler, for example, had thirteen and fourteen children, respectively.
75. Jennifer Brown, "A Demographic Transition in the Fur Trade Country," *Western Canadian Journal of Anthropology* 6, 1: 68.
76. Cox, *Columbia River*, 354.
77. J.S. Galbraith, *The Little Emperor* (Toronto, 1976), 68.
78. Nelson Papers, Reminiscences, Part 5, p. 155.

79. Brown, "A Demographic Transition," 67.
80. Margaret MacLeod, ed., *The Letters of Letitia Hargrave* (Toronto, Champlain Society, vol. 28, 1947), 94–95; Alexander Ross, *The Red River Settlement* (Minneapolis, 1957), 95, 192.
81. Brown, "A Demographic Transition," 65.
82. Merk, *Fur Trade and Empire*, 101.
83. Williams, *Graham's Observations*, 176, 178.
84. Ross, *Adventures on the Columbia*, 280; W.J. Healy, *Women of Red River* (Winnipeg, 1923), 163–66.
85. Lamb, *Sixteen Years*, 138, 186.
86. Franklin, *Narrative of a Journey*, 101, 106.
87. West, *Red River Journal*, 16.
88. Cox, *Columbia River*, 360.
89. Hearne, *Journey to the Northern Ocean*, 57.
90. Williams, *Graham's Observations*, 176.
91. Thomson's Journal, 19 Nov. 1798, p. 20.
92. Masson, *Les Bourgeois* 2: 384–85. We are not told whether she also escaped being sold when the brigades arrived in the spring as the bourgeois intended.
93. HBC Arch., York Journal, 2 Dec. 1798, B.239/a/103, f. 14d.
94. HBC Arch., Pelican Lake Journal, 18 Jan. 1819, D.158/a/1, f. 7d.
95. This account is derived from the Isle à la Crosse Journal, H.B.C. Arch., B.89/a/2, fos. 5–36d passim.
96. Tyrrell, *Journals of Hearne and Turnor*, 446n, 449.
97. Tyrrell, *Journals*, 449–50.
98. Masson, *Les Bourgeois* 2: 387–88.
99. Lamb, *Journals of Mackenzie*, 255; Rich, *Athabasca Journal*, 388.
100. Masson Collection, Journal of Ferdinand Wentzel, 13 Jan. 1805, p. 41.
101. Merk, *Fur Trade and Empire*, 127.
102. Nelson Papers, Journal 1810–11, 41–42.
103. W.S. Wallace, *Documents relating to the North West Company* (Toronto, Champlain Society, vol. 22, 1934), 211. This ruling was not enforced in outlying districts such as the Columbia. Even after the union in 1821, Governor Simpson continued to favour the formation of marital alliances in remote regions as the best way to secure friendly relations with the Indians. See Rich, *Athabasca Journal*, 392.
104. For a discussion of the role played by mixed-blood women in fur trade society, see Van Kirk, "Role of Women in Fur Trade Society."

Article Five

"A Most Important Chain of Connection": Marriage in the Hudson's Bay Company

Heather Rollason Driscoll

In 1830 George Simpson married his 18-year-old British cousin Frances and brought her to live with him in Rupert's Land. The news of their union spread quickly amongst George's fellow employees because it represented a break from a 150-year-old tradition. The cause of the sensation was not the fact that George had married nor was it Frances's age; rather, it was her place of birth.[1] George's employer, the fur trading enterprise known as Hudson's Bay Company

Source: "'A Most Important Chain of Connection': Marriage in the Hudson's Bay Company," in *From Rupert's Land to Canada: Essays in Honour of John E. Foster*, eds. Theodore Binnema, Gerhard J. Ens, and R.C. Macleod (Edmonton: University of Alberta Press, 2001): 81–107. Reprinted with permission of the publisher.

(HBC), had prohibited all employees from bringing British-born wives and daughters with them into fur trade country since 1684.

Scholars have interpreted the marriage of George and Frances as evidence of a significant shift in the state of social relations at fur trade posts. In their seminal studies of fur trade society Jennifer Brown and Sylvia Van Kirk noticed that over a number of generations traders' spousal preferences changed from Native to mixed-blood and finally to British-born women. In explaining the shifts, particularly the one associated with Frances's arrival, they focused upon racism as the chief causal factor. Sylvia Van Kirk proposed that "[w]ith the appearance of women of their own race, the fur traders began to exhibit prejudices toward native females which had previously been dormant."[2] Similarly Jennifer Brown suggested that traders found British-born women desirable because "[g]enetically, culturally, and in their social affiliations, they exhibited fewer Indian traits."[3] Based upon their work, other scholars have argued that racial prejudice increasingly determined traders' marriage partners. This thesis has been highly influential in the evolving canon of scholarship. More recently Veronica Strong-Boag described the significance of the arrival of British women to fur trade country in terms much stronger than ever used by Brown or Van Kirk:

> While early fur-trade society offered significant opportunities to native women, its long term heritage included a racism and sexism that would consign native and mixed-blood women to special victimization by male and white society well into the twentieth century.[4]

Unlike Brown or Van Kirk, Strong-Boag excludes all other elements contributing to the shift in marriage patterns.

Racism undoubtedly contributed to the shift, but as the dominant explanation it falls short. First, the appearance of these "dormant" racist beliefs coincides with economic events without which these racist notions would have taken hold. The economic situation characterizing the first two decades of the nineteenth century pushed the fur traders into new ways of thinking about their business; namely, it brought about the amalgamation of the rival HBC and North West Company (NWC), and the granting of permission for development of British-styled settlement within the heart of fur trade country. Both Brown and Van Kirk identify the joint influence of George Simpson and the Red River settlement (particularly the influx of clergy) as providing the environment in which racism could flourish.[5] It is assumed that Simpson's motive for marrying the British-born Frances instead of one of the women of Rupert's Land derived solely from his disdain for the latter. Yet there is evidence that his motive may have been multi-faceted. Furthermore, it is argued here that amalgamation of the HBC and NWC affected marriage practices in ways other than the need to standardize conduct between the two former companies. Brown and Van Kirk acknowledge that traders' views about who to marry changed after amalgamation, but overlook its role in these very same changes. Second, the impact of amalgamation and settlement upon marriage patterns can only be understood in the context of the fur traders' social milieu: a hybrid of British and Native practices and values. The marriage of George and Frances represents the product of all these events, beliefs and practices. It may be possible to identify the increasingly strong presence of racist beliefs associated with the choice of marriage partners around the time of the Simpson wedding, but this is best explained through the impact of changes to the business of the fur trade upon long established social practices in Rupert's Land.

This study represents a preliminary attempt to explore the relationships between an array of factors that affected a shift in marriage practices, and it focuses more on the social environment characteristic of the HBC than the NWC. A more thorough exploration of the primary sources is required to support these initial conclusions. By demonstrating the existence of parallel and persuasive explanations for the change in marriage patterns between the 1820s and

1840s, this paper may stimulate future research into this topic. To understand the chain of relationships that permitted George to wed Frances it is necessary to examine the first link in the chain: the HBC's use of British and Native marriage practices to further its business.

Analysis of the post managers' journals and minutes from meetings of company directors reveals similarities between the corporate structure of the HBC and the patriarchal household. The resemblance between the patterns of life on the Hudson Bay and British domestic life was not the result of an unconscious or accidental process; rather, right from the early stages of the company's existence, the London Committee intended its employees to recognize these similarities and behave accordingly.

From the moment of its incorporation in 1670, the HBC chose to model its field operations upon an idealized image of the patriarchal family.[6] The British style of patriarchal family consisted of a married couple, their children, and workers or servants. According to the ideal image of this family structure, the husband formally represented the head of the household, followed by the wife. Below them, in terms of social and economic status, came their children and then the household servants.[7] The status conveyed by marriage was key to differentiating the patriarch and his wife from the rest of the household. The act of marriage signalled a couple's economic independence from their previous households, for upon marrying it was expected that the couple would set up and finance their own household. Household servants entered a contract typically while in the state of bachelorhood and remained so until they were ready to leave the residence of their employer because it was assumed that marital obligations would compromise their loyalty to the household. In exchange for this demonstration of the servant's commitment to the patriarch's household, he or she received lodgings, clothing, and food; the servant could also apprentice a trade or benefit from the patriarch's business and social connections.[8] At the end of a period of service, the patriarch gave the servant a financial reward, similar to a dowry, that provided a measure of economic independence thereby aiding the former servant to establish his or her own household.[9] There are two observations of particular relevance to understanding the HBC's vision for the structure of trading post social relations. First, the head of the household was the only male supposed to be having sexual relations, let alone be married. Second, servants married only when they had achieved a measure of economic independence, typically occurring upon completion of an apprenticeship or contract of service.

The HBC's decision to use the patriarchal family as a model for organizing trading posts was not unprecedented; many institutions, including the British army and the merchant marine, had chosen to model their organizations upon this family style because of its familiarity to those working within the institution, its ability to enforce discipline over vast geographical distances, and the perception that it was a moral and humane method of controlling people.[10] Even the organizing interests of the Massachusetts Bay Company in the mid 1600s stipulated that:

> For the better accommodation of businesses, wee have devyded the servants belonging to the Company into severall families, as wee desire and intend they shall live together ... Our earnest is, that you take spetiall care, in settlinge these families, that the chiefe in the families (at least some of them) bee grounded in religion; whereby morning and evening famylie dutyes may bee duely performed, and a watchfull eye held overall in each famylie to by appointed thereto, that so disorders may be prevented, and ill weeds nipt before they take too great a head. It wilbe a business worthy your best endeavours to looke unto this in the beginninge.[11]

The HBC chose to institute this model because of a series of management problems specific to the company's activities.

According to the HBC's charter, the organization was to be run by a committee of seven elected investors, known as the London Committee, and overseen by an eighth investor known as the governor.[12] These persons met weekly in London to oversee the creation of company policy and direct activities at trading posts along the shores of Hudson Bay. With the body of the company employees working across the ocean, the committee needed a method to ensure employee loyalty, hard work, and deference. Yet the HBC's operational problems were greater than controlling employee activity and behaviour over great geographical distances; it also had to overcome limited communication between the body and head of the company. Ships travelled from London to Hudson Bay but once a year, arriving at the bay in August or September and departing soon thereafter. Thus the London Committee communicated with its post managers solely on an annual basis. From the time the ships left the bay until they returned the next year, post operations and employee behaviour were beyond the committee's direct control. Furthermore, the company was anxious to ensure maximum profitability and thus needed to prevent its employees from idling during the workday, keeping furs for private trade, or breaking their contracts to start independent businesses along the bay. The London Committee needed a method to enforce discipline and encourage activity in the environment of the trading post.

The company's management problems stood to be compounded by the characteristic worker recruited into service. In the early years of the company's existence, the London Committee hired the vast majority of employees from the London area. However, it began to look elsewhere, particularly for labourers, when London recruits used the competitive labour market in London to ask for higher wages. Beginning in 1702, the HBC contracted men from the village of Stromness in the Orkney Islands located north of mainland Scotland. The London Committee's decision to switch recruiting grounds to Scotland was logical for a variety of reasons. Orkneymen were reputed to be literate, amenable to harsh living conditions, and willing to work for lower wages than their London counterparts.[13] Stromness was a convenient recruitment centre as it was the last port of call to pick up supplies before company ships sailed across the ocean to Hudson Bay. As well, the Orkneys were home to a sizeable population of young poor men interested in new economic opportunities. Indeed, the majority of HBC recruits in the Orkneys came from the lower end of the economic scale.[14] The large difference in yearly wages between what one could earn in Orkney and in the HBC suggests a rational economic motivation for signing an overseas contract with the HBC; the most a ploughman could earn on Orkney was two to three pounds per year, whereas the HBC offered from six to 18 pounds for a labourer and from 20 to 36 pounds for a carpenter.[15] By the late eighteenth century, approximately three-quarters of all employees hired, or 416 out of 530, were Orcadian.[16] In other words, over 400 Orkney men, likely between the ages of 18 and 30, were in fur trade country at a time when they otherwise would have been apprentices or contracted to a household in Orkney.[17]

The company's directors hoped that employing the patriarchal family as the model for social relations at its trading posts would solve all of the problems posed by the circumstances of the bay. The problem of isolation could be minimized with a post patriarch who could watch over the men's activities on a daily basis. As most of the workers were at the fur trade posts when their peers were contracted into a household, they were familiar with the household concept and the patriarch was an authority figure. One of the main advantages for the HBC in using the patriarchal family as its model for post structure was that it limited employees' ability to rise up against the company or to quit it all together. By organizing employees in small "family" units, each employee was closely supervised by someone possessing a higher rank. Thus an employee's most important relationship was with a superior, not a peer. Furthermore, because there was a good distance between each trading post, an employee's working relationships were mostly with others at his post who filled very different positions; those who held ranks like his own most likely were scattered at other posts.

A more detailed analysis of the company's structure reveals that from the beginning the London Committee organized each post hierarchically, roughly mimicking the patriarchal household.[18] During the HBC's first years, the top position was that of governor who was responsible for overseeing the general affairs at all trading posts.[19] This governor's domain consisted of field operations and is to be distinguished from the governor of the company proper. Though the title "field governor" gradually disappeared as a distinct position in the early eighteenth century, it returned in the nineteenth century when the HBC underwent major structural changes. Significantly, the reappearance of this position coincides with other changes related to the appearance of Frances Simpson.

The factor, or chief factor as he was also called, was the patriarch of the trading post. It was to him that the London Committee sent their annual instructions. In turn, he was responsible for creating the yearly report on trading activities, employee behaviour and anything else he thought might interest his superiors. He set daily tasks for the servants and monitored supplies. As the head of the post, the factor had the privilege of leading the procession to welcome trading Natives and participating in the ceremonial smoking of the calumet. Besides ensuring a profitable trade, the chief factor filled the roles of patron, father-figure, and teacher to the employees below him.[20] He was responsible for the spiritual and physical welfare of the men at his post.[21]

Henry Sergeant, field governor and chief factor of York Fort beginning in 1683, wholeheartedly embraced his patriarchal role; at this time he was the only employee who brought his wife and a minister to fur trade country. Since the HBC structured the organization of employees at its trading posts based upon practices used in the navy and merchant marine, Mrs. Sergeant's presence seemed in line with the expectations associated with the role of a captain: the patriarch of a ship. Furthermore, as the company was still in the process of setting up its operations, the London Committee would have perceived positively any method of reinforcing the association of chief factor as post patriarch. Being the only man permitted to have his wife standing by his side certainly could have achieved this goal. Henry Sergeant's decision to bring the minister John French signified his patriarchal obligation to care for the spiritual sustenance of those under his watch and care.[22] That the HBC allowed him to bring the minister demonstrates again the company's determination to instill an image of its field leaders as patriarchs. Indeed, while the company soon altered its position on the presence of wives in fur trade country, it continued to support chief factors' role as caretakers of employee's souls.

Further evidence that the company's management of the posts reflected the patriarchal household exists in early directives from the London Committee to field governors and chief factors. When the committee appointed James Knight chief factor of Chichewan Fort in 1682, in light of his station they also gave him permission to bring along his brother, Richard, as his man-servant.[23] Like Sergeant's wife, Richard's presence would have helped to distinguish brother James's rank from the rest of the employees. Only the patriarch would have the company's permission for such a luxury.

The London Committee encouraged the men to take responsibility for the apprenticeship and training of their subordinates, thus mimicking the idealized patriarch's responsibilities toward his household servants. In 1710 the London Committee sent Chief Factor Henry Kelsey official encouragement for his attempt to educate York Fort's servants: "You doe well to Educate the men in Literature but Especially in the Language that in time wee may send them to Travell . . . We have sent you your dixonary Printed, that you may the Better Instruct the young Ladds with you, in ye Indian Langage."[24] Considering these examples, it seems clear that the HBC intended that the social structure of its trading posts and the behaviour of its employees resemble the patriarchal household. Further analysis of the organizational structure of the posts reinforces this conclusion.

Directly below the chief factor was the position of second who was apprenticed to the chief. Among other things, the second assisted in the keeping of the journals and account books. When the London Committee appointed William Grover as second at Churchill Fort in 1763, part of his new duties included learning a number of specialized trades. In a letter to Grover, the committee suggested that "at all convenient Seasons instruct Yourself in Mr Potts's method of keeping his Medicines and their particular Virtues . . . in case any Accident should happen when his ill state of health deprives you of his assistance."[25] Like the chief factor, the person selected for this position often had years of experience working in the fur trade. Grover had worked for the HBC in the fur trade for six years before receiving the appointment of second. Some of the larger posts had councils, akin to the arrangement between the head governor and the London Committee. The main part of the council consisted of the post's surgeon and writer, and if the post had any ships, its captains, and the second. These men constituted the immediate "family" of the symbolic patriarch.

The company referred to the remainder of the post's employees as "servants," who worked as tradesmen and labourers.[26] The company's directors expected servants to behave in similar ways to household servants, particularly in regard to the status of bachelorhood. Indeed, for many reasons the HBC preferred to hire bachelors over married men.[27] First, company officials believed that these men were more likely to stay in fur trade country for extended period and that they did not have conflicting sets of loyalties, as would be implied by the existence of a distant wife and children. Second, since the majority of HBC servants were brought up in an environment where the status of bachelorhood involved living in another's household, acting in deference to the head of the household, and maintaining one's single status until enough wages had been saved, it is likely that they carried such expectations into their employment at fur trade posts. As well, the company expected them to adhere to a working code of strict discipline and "to live virtuous, celibate lives" while in Rupert's Land.[28]

It is clear that the similarities between the structure of the HBC's trading posts and patriarchal household were deliberate and enduring. Yet there remains one large difference between the trading post and the household model. Company policy contained no sanctioned role for women at trading posts. Indeed, women's official absence led Jennifer Brown to contend that "[c]learly the company did not plan these posts to be households, for there were no women and children."[29] Originally the company did not have policies governing its employees' relationships with women; however 14 years into its existence the HBC revoked its flexible stance to forbid the presence of all women at trading posts.

When the London Committee prohibited women it acted in what it believed to be the best interests of the company. In 1684, one year after Henry Sergeant, his wife, her companion, and their daughter arrived in Rupert's Land, the HBC prohibited employees' wives and families from accompanying them.[30] No documentation survives explaining the company directors' rationale; however, it seems likely that the London Committee had decided there were less expensive methods to reinforce the authority of chief factors. Furthermore, the company was not a colonizing venture; its focus was on resource extraction, be it fish, furs, or minerals. The presence of women and children would have encouraged colonization and perhaps distracted chief factors' efforts from the company's primary goals. Most importantly, the HBC may not have wanted the added responsibility of ensuring the health and welfare of employees' families particularly in a place where Native people's actions were unpredictable and the environment could be harsh and unforgiving.

The ensuing experience of the Sergeant family reinforced the London Committee's conviction of the appropriateness of its policy. In part due to the new restrictions in 1687 they requested that Henry Sergeant and "the whole parcel of Women appertaineing to him" return to London.[31] Meanwhile the French engineered the capture of all the company's bayside posts. During the attack, Mrs. Sergeant's companion, Mrs. Maurice, was wounded. She was reunited with the rest of the family on Charlton Island where the French temporarily kept all HBC prisoners. As winter drew near the French then transferred their prisoners to the HBC's main post of Port Nelson since it was impossible to send them to England until the spring thaw. When that time arrived the Sergeant household sailed for London, never again to see the shores of Hudson Bay.[32] The departure of Mrs. Sergeant, her daughter, and Mrs. Maurice, signalled the last formal approval of British-born women's presence until Frances Simpson's arrival in 1830. In order to establish the possibility that reasons other than racism factored into the company's decision to revoke its policy on British-born women, it is necessary to look at its stance toward another group of women present at Hudson Bay.

When recruits signed their contracts with the HBC, their new work environment would be unlike anything they had encountered in Britain.[33] Rather than working in a trade shop or on a farm, these recruits would be entering the social milieu of the fur trading post.[34] While the patriarchal family served as the model for structuring relationships among the HBC employees, it did not govern the behaviour of the company's Native trading partners. Because the HBC depended upon Native peoples to trap, prepare, and transport the pelts to the trading post, and to provide the majority of fresh provisions for all HBC employees, Native peoples exerted considerable influence on post affairs. The presence of Native women in particular challenged the HBC's strict adherence to the patriarchal family as its operational model.

As with the prohibition of British-born women, the company's directors produced a similar conveyance pertaining to Native women. In 1682 the London Committee sent the following directive to field Governor John Nixon:

> We are very sensibly that the Indian Weoman resorting to our Factories are very prejudiciall to the Companies affaires, not only by being a meanes of our Servants often debauching themselves, but likewise by embeazling our goods and very much exhausting our Provisions, It is therefore our positive order that you lay strict Commands on every Cheife of each Factory upon forfeiture of Wages not to Suffer any woman to come within any of our factories, and that none of our Servants may plead ignorance, Wee doe hereby require, you to cause a writeing to bee affixed in Some publick place in every Factory intimateing our Commands herein, and the penalty in disobeying them: and if not withstanding all this, there shall be any refactory Persons that shall Presume to entertaine, any Weomon, let us have an account of them by the first Opertunity and we will not faile to send for them home fore wee cannot never Expect good Servises from such, whome neither the Lawes of God or Man can restraine from Wickedness.[35]

Apparently the London Committee believed that Native women not only were a drain on post provisions but a distraction to its employees. Directors may have also feared that unrestricted relations with Native women could jeopardize peaceful relations with Native traders and hunters. Indeed, in the early eighteenth century, employees at Churchill Fort learned that local Natives had killed French fur traders for mistreating Native women. These fears led chief factor James Knight to imprison Thomas Butler for "[a]gainst my Orders lyeing with a Woman of this Country to the Endanger of our Lives wch Sevll of the French was killd."[36] Clearly, the London Committee did not understand how their enterprise depended on Native women's work and therefore their policy, though understandable from a business perspective, was impracticable.

Native women occupied many roles in this trading post society; their skilled repertoire included serving as interpreters and diplomatists, preparing pelts, making clothing and snowshoes, transporting furs, and procuring food for the company's stores.[37] The Inuit woman Doll (as she was known in HBC correspondence) was a favoured interpreter who accompanied northern trading expeditions setting out from Churchill in the mid-eighteenth century. She was also responsible for negotiating a peace between the Inuit and the Chipewyan in the 1760s.[38] The HBC desired harmonious relations between different Native groups because it believed Native people would then concentrate on procuring furs rather than making war. Native women also represented the means to extend the company's trade.

When a fur trader formed an alliance with a Native woman, their union signalled more than an agreement between two individuals to co-habitate; it also symbolized the obligation of the trading post and the band toward one another. Typically, the band members hoped the alliance would gain them prestige amongst their own people and garner them preferential treatment during trade with the HBC, but they also believed the marriage committed the trader to provide them with assistance in times of need and protection in times of conflict. From the perspective of the HBC field operators, these alliances were valuable for similar reasons. A trader hoped the woman's male relatives would decide to hunt for the trading post in order to be near her, but primarily he wanted the band to bring their trappings exclusively to his post.[39] Thus, these unions represented an indispensable method of ensuring a continuing source of pelts.

The mentality of the household servant provides insight into HBC servants' perception of their relationships with Native peoples, particularly women, while residing in fur trade company. Company servants appeared to accept the association between the patriarchal household and their work with the HBC not only by their recognition of the hierarchical structure of company management, but also in regard to their contract with the company representing a stepping stone in being able to marry and establish their own household. William Thomson noted in his *History of Orkney* that eighteenth-century Orcadians tended to delay marriage until the couple possessed a reasonable degree of economic stability, often achieved by working as a servant or apprentice.[40] John Nicks found that the Orkney HBC servants mirrored their countrymen's behaviour by saving their wages until they could return home; thus, they tended "to view their work in the fur trade as a means to an end: a way of accumulating capital so that they might realize ambitions within their own society."[41] Many retired Orcadian employees bought farms or invested in businesses in their homeland. This mentality suggests that besides any sense of personal attachment to Native women, servants' perception of these relationships in the long-term was guided by economic rather than ethnocentric motives. For the most part, servants approached relationships with Native peoples in the context of work, particularly since they knew that upon completion of their contract(s) the company required them to leave Rupert's Land.

Herein lies one of the central conflicts between the HBC's operational model and the realities of the fur trade. According to the patriarchal model, only the head of the household should be having sex with women. However, as any employee who had worked for some time in the fur trade knew, ties with Native women were key to establishing good trading relations. The company's directors would have questioned the chief factor's morality if they thought he was "establishing good trading relations" with a Native woman from every band that came to the post. In turn his actions would not have been worthy of the rest of the employees' respect and deference, thereby decreasing his ability to govern effectively. As well, the company did not want its rank-and-file employees debauching themselves or, more importantly, having the opportunity to create another set of loyalties other than to the chief factor and the HBC. Remember that the HBC preferred to hire labourers of bachelor status because they had less reason to prematurely break their contracts. Because of official company policy, HBC records contain scanty and vague references to alliances between its employees and Native women, as post officers were reluctant to reveal that they were disobeying instructions in order to further trade.

While the London Committee maintained its position on forbidding Native women on post premises, it eventually came to accept, if only unofficially, the existence of alliances between traders and Native women. Chief Factor Andrew Graham commented on this contradiction between official policy and unofficial practice when he wrote reflectively in 1771 that "[t]he intercourse that is carried between the Indian ladies and the Englishmen is not allowed, but winked at."[42] In 1763 the London Committee sent surgeon John Potts the following directive:

> We observe with much Concern Venereal Complaints are not uncommon among our Servants at Prince of Wales's fort and that the same Disorder has made its appearance among the Indian Women there also. Which we think to be of the worst Consequence as the Natives already not sufficiently Numerous, may be greatly reduced by means thereof, if not prevented. Therefore we strongly enjoin you to use your utmost endeavours to Eradicate that Disease, in every object that shall present, who is affected therewith."[43]

The following year Potts received another letter on the subject: "We are glad you was able to effect the Cure of the two persons You mention and we rely on Your promised endeavours to eradicate the Veneral Distemper whenever it offers."[44] Obviously sexual relations between HBC traders and Native women existed in spite of any official company directives. Indeed, as Brown and Van Kirk have documented, by the end of the eighteenth century not only were these alliances common, but there was a growing population of mixed-blood children and future wives resulting from these unions.[45]

In the language of the fur trade, these alliances were known as country marriages, or *marriage à la façon du pays*. By definition, the union, symbolized by the exchange of words and gifts between a male fur trader and a Native or mixed-blood female, was an agreement to co-habitate for an unspecified period of time. Country marriages were usually temporary although some lasted until death or end of contract separated the couple. In economic terms, the marriage existed as long as the trader was stationed at the post where the woman's family traded; if either party moved or became displeased, the union dissolved. There was an unwritten code among traders that at the time of separation, or "turning off," the trader should assume some form of continuing responsibility for his former wife and any of their children.[46] Often when an HBC employee retired he attempted to ensure the continuing welfare of his country family, for when an employee chose not to renew his contract he had no choice but to leave fur trade country. This could be done by establishing accounts for them as Matthew Cocking did or by annuities established for them in a trader's will.[47] On the fourth of May in 1785 the London Committee recorded the payment of £10 in accordance with the will of Chief Factor Ferdinand Jacobs "being a Legacy left to his Daughter in Hudson's Bay."[48] Over time the London Committee appeared to accept, though still unofficially, the necessity of these marriages and the existence of an increasing number of families. Indeed, by 1808, the company's directors decided that schoolmaster should be sent to each major trading post for "the Religious and moral Education of the Children."[49]

As alluded to by the HBC's quiet acceptance of this practice, by the end of the eighteenth century significant social changes had occurred in the fur trade. These changes were rooted in the growth of economic competition between the HBC and its rivals coming out of the St. Lawrence River watershed. After the British takeover of New France in 1763, various groups of fur traders based in Montreal mounted a serious challenge to the HBC's hold on fur-producing territories west of Hudson Bay.[50] These traders travelled far inland, circumventing the HBC's posts, to seek out interested Native trappers and traders. In response to the aggressive trade strategy of these Canadian "pedlars" or "Nor'Westers," as they variously were called in the HBC correspondence, field officers such as Andrew Graham suggested that the HBC also open inland posts.[51] Prior to this point the HBC operated only seven posts, but with the opening of Cumberland House in 1774 the company commenced a program of rapid post construction and hiring to support their campaign in the North-West. Between 1774 and 1821 the HBC opened 242 new inland posts and increased the number of its employees from 200 to 900.[52] When the London Committee sanctioned this departure from its traditional coastal operations, and strove to match the Nor'Westers post for post, country marriages became all the more common amongst HBC men. The increased frequency of relations between Native women and traders was due to the inability of chief factors to supervise travelling inland servants and to the heightened importance associated with these marriages, in terms of creating loyal ties with families of Native trappers during a period of intensive competition.

Up to this point, mainly senior officers had entered into these unions. Labourers and tradesmen may have had liaisons with women outside post walls, but they could not enjoy the prestige and access to protection and privileges enjoyed by the post patriarch and his immediate family of officers.[53] However, when secondary officers and lower ranked men began to travel inland to winter with Native bands or to set up new posts, for the first time these men had something to offer to Natives. Now these lower ranked men were the ones leading Native traders back to the coastal posts or negotiating trades at the newer inland posts. Thus, marriage ceased to be a defining symbol of the post patriarch's authority as governing head of the trading post household.[54] Yet the HBC continued to rely upon the patriarchal household as its model for post organization and as a method to reinforce the chief factor's authority. Throughout the late eighteenth-century and into the nineteenth century, the company maintained its traditional management structure while it expanded its operations westward.

The HBC faced other challenges to ensuring its survival and profitability which in turn affected its stance on country marriages. The ongoing Napoleonic Wars carried serious repercussions for the HBC's ability to put pelts on the market. The company was unable to sell any furs between 1806 and 1809 because the war effectively shut the HBC out of European markets. In the meantime, HBC directors fretted over how they would continue to provide "supplies which were necessary for the Subsistence of Six Hundred European Servants their Wives and Children, dispersed over a vast and extended Field of the North American Continent."[55] Over the next couple of years the directors solved the problems faced by the HBC using a twofold approach. First, they acquired a loan from the Bank of England for £50 000 to help the company weather the war.[56] Second, the directors resolved to lessen the company's expenses, including the burden of supporting traders' families.

In 1810, Thomas Douglas, Lord Selkirk presented a radical proposal to the London Committee. He knew of the HBC's financial concerns and offered a means to alleviate some of these pressures by creating an agricultural colony within company territory. Though he intended to populate the colony with the poor from the Scottish Hebrides, there would also be room for retired HBC servants. His proposal was attractive to the committee because the families of HBC servants could farm land in the new colony and thus provide for themselves. The company had the option to acquire surplus food from the colony with the added benefit of saving transportation costs associated with shipping goods across the ocean. The colonists would also provide a protected market for company goods, a further financial boon. Although the directors initially rejected Selkirk's proposal, they eventually acquiesced particularly because of the potential financial relief presented by the colony. Committee member Charles MacLean argued if families could be removed from company territory to the colony, they would be able to shift funds formerly used for support of these families to hiring much needed men to compete with the Nor'Westers.[57] Thus on 11 June 1811 the London Committee gave its approval for the creation of the colony of Red River in the territory of Assiniboia.[58]

In 1821 the nearly disastrous competition between the HBC and the North West Company (NWC) led the two rivals to amalgamate into one company, still to be called the HBC. This act, more than anything else, created the environment in which George Simpson could break tradition by bringing Frances to fur trade country. Simpson, like many of his fellow fur traders, had intimate relations with Native women soon after his arrival to fur trade country. The combination of selected written descriptions by Simpson on his female relationships and then his move to bring his new wife Frances to Rupert's Land has persuaded scholars that Simpson's actions were governed by racial prejudice. But, when understood in the context of the immediate needs and the strategy of the HBC, and the practice of country marriages, it becomes apparent that other factors contributed to Simpson's decision to marry Frances and bring her to Rupert's Land.

George Simpson entered fur trade country in 1820 as a trader for the HBC. The very next year, the HBC appointed Simpson governor of the Northern Department. With only two seasons of experience George faced the challenge of overseeing the amalgamation of the rival companies. The former HBC and NWC used decidedly different management styles and corporate structures. They agreed to base the new organization upon the combination of the HBC's administrative and financial structure and the NWC's field expertise.[59] The directors aimed to streamline company operations, eradicate mismanagement and duplication, and rationalize the mechanics of trade.

With these goals in mind, Simpson worked over the next few years to standardize the prices of furs and reduce the number of employees, the wages of those who remained, and the HBC's financial commitment to the families of retired or departed traders. Simpson's report evaluating the management of the Columbia District contained the following suggestions:

> no question exists in my mind that by introducing economy and regularity with the necessary spirit of enterprise and a disregard to little domestic comforts it may be made a most productive branch of the Company's Trade . . . it must however be understood that to effect this change we have no petty coat politicians, that is, that Chief Facters and Chief Traders do not allow themselves be influenced by the Sapient councils of their *Squaws* or neglect their business merely to administer to their comforts and guard against certain innocent indiscretions which these frail brown ones are so apt to indulge in. The extent of evil arising from this source strangers can have no conception . . .[60]

One of Simpson's greatest management challenges involved establishing his authority and rank among approximately two-thirds of the officers in the new HBC, who had come from the old NWC and were used to a much less authoritarian system.[61]

During this time, George already had become involved with local women. In 1822 Simpson's first country-born daughter, Maria, was born and then baptized in February. Her mother, Betsy Sinclair, was the mixed-blood daughter of a chief factor and a Cree woman. Soon thereafter he terminated their brief relationship.[62] Just prior to departing on a lengthy tour of the company's territory, Simpson wrote to his good friend and fellow fur trader John George McTavish informing him to eradicate the traces of this last affair.

> My Family concerns I leave entirely to your kind management, if you can dispose of the Lady it will be satisfactory as she is an unnecessary & expensive appendage. I see no fun in keeping a Woman, without enjoying her charms which my present rambling Life does not enable me to do; but if she is unremarkable I have no wish that she should be a general accommodation shop to all the young bucks at the Factory and in addition to her own chastity a padlock may be useful.[63]

Caution is required in interpreting Simpson's words, for the intimate details of his relationship with Betsy are not known, nor does Betsy record her own perspective of the affair.

Using Simpson's attitudes toward women and marriage to symbolize and epitomize the changing trend in fur trade marriages and the status of Native, mixed-blood and British-born women is problematic for a number of reasons. First, Simpson's history of relationships with women is complex and ranges beyond those he had in fur trade country. He was an illegitimate child. As well, he fathered two daughters, not necessarily by the same woman, before he joined the HBC.[64] Thus, the scholarly belief that his behaviour toward his country-wives was guided by racism seems to be derived from scholars' predisposition to examine Simpson's life solely within the context of the fur trade. Second, Simpson's colourful and derogatory commentary in regard to his country wives, and the women born into fur trade country in general, can be found primarily within private letters to longtime male friends, such as John George McTavish. It is difficult to judge, from the letters alone, Simpson's frame of mind when he composed these words. Perhaps they were intended as banter, perhaps they were reflections of frustrating situations, or perhaps these words indeed represented his deepest beliefs about Native and mixed-blood women. Deciding which of these scenarios most aptly fits Simpson's true demeanor remains difficult.[65]

Significantly, Simpson's exit from the tryst coincides with his first concrete expression of concern regarding the connection between his interactions with women and his status in the company. The more persuasive rationale for Simpson's action is this connection to his status rather than Betsy's behaviour, particularly given her subsequent history with husband Robert Miles.[66] Several months after the christening of Maria, Simpson confided in another private letter to McTavish, that "I suspect my name will become notorious as the late Gov. in regard to plurality of wives."[67] In spite of his worries about Betsy, George apparently proceeded to become involved in a number of other relationships. He clearly expressed his concern about the effect specifically on his reputation in a subsequent letter to McTavish: "had I a good pimp in my suite I might have been inclined to deposit a little of my spawn, but have become so vastly tenacious of my reputation . . ."[68] Simpson's comment in the first cited letter to McTavish "I have no wish that she should be a general accommodation shop to all the young bucks at the Factory" also reflects his apprehension about the effect upon his reputation of Betsy's future behaviour with men from lower ranks. To be so involved would have created the intolerable state of placing the status-obsessed Simpson on the same level as these other men.

Simpson's anxiety about how his relationship with women could compromise his ability to command the respect of employees may have derived from his personality, but it also reveals the impact the HBC's corporate structure had on its employees' frame of mind. As the highest ranked man in the district, Simpson had to appear to those from lower positions as a model of decorum, discipline, and gentlemanly character. He had the added challenge of creating this persona in the unsettled environment of the recently amalgamated company. All of Simpson's trysts and entanglements with women had the potential to create a problematic working environment; not only could he lessen the social distance between himself and others by sharing the same woman, but he could also lose his employees' esteem or incur their anger depending on the details of the triangle.

As if to terminate the problems with employee relations associated with his connections to the women in fur trade country, in 1823 Simpson resolved to leave Rupert's Land in search of a British wife who could help create an aura of social propriety.[69] Given Simpson's complaints about his difficulty in maintaining a gentlemanly reputation, he likely believed his future wife would help distinguish and elevate him from the other employees. However, the trading post environment had changed from the time when Henry Sergeant had brought his wife to Rupert's Land as a method to reinforce his patriarchal authority, which meant that Simpson's marriage needed to be different.

Not only had the former HBC gradually, but unofficially, relaxed its prohibition on traders' involvement with Native and mixed-blood women, Nor'Westers had always been free to intermix with the women in fur trade country. The NWC did not use marriage as a method of instilling a sense of hierarchy and authority; rather, the Nor'Westers had relied upon marriage chiefly as a building block to establishing an ever expanding trade network. Thus if the HBC was to maintain the patriarchal household model as an effective method of reinforcing its post managers' authority, somehow it had to distinguish these officials from the rest of the employees. Because marriage had become so common, it seemed an unlikely device, but in fact it was one of the most striking tools at the company's disposal.

Meanwhile, the London Committee rejected Simpson's request to travel to London. Instead, Simpson continued to become involved with the women of fur trade country despite his concerns about such activities upon his ability to govern effectively. In 1823, the same year of Simpson's initial request for leave to London, he fathered a son. The identity of the mother has not survived in the documentary record. A few years later, and likely after a number of other relationships, he entered into a stable country marriage with Margaret Taylor, a mixed-blood woman.[70] While involved with Margaret, in 1826 Simpson attained the pinnacle of the HBC's field positions by becoming governor-in-chief of all the company's territory.[71] According to one of Simpson's biographers, John Galbraith, about this time Simpson consciously cultivated the pomp and splendour associated with his position of field governor, and he carefully designed his public appearances to emphasize his elevated status. For example, in 1827 Simpson hired Colin Fraser to play the bagpipes in the governor's canoe, particularly when the boat neared a trading post. The addition of Fraser to Simpson's crew helped to distinguish the arrival of the governor's boat from all the others.[72] Now, more than ever, he sought ways to demonstrate his elevated status.

The governor had not abandoned his quest in search of a British-born wife, in spite of the evidence that he shared an enduring and emotionally positive relationship with Margaret. Just as Margaret gave birth to their second child, Simpson left for London in August of 1829.[73] He was accompanied by his friend McTavish, and the chief purpose of their trip was to search for wives who could reflect their sense of their heightened position in the HBC. Both men achieved this goal. On 24 February 1830 Simpson and Frances were wed, and subsequently he brought her into fur trade country, as did McTavish with his new wife Catherine. The act of marriage to a British-born woman while under contract to the HBC itself was not a threat to the status quo of trading post life; a number of prominent HBC officers, such as Moses Norton, predated Simpson by having British wives while still working in Rupert's Land.[74] Rather, it was Simpson's decision to have Frances accompany him into fur trade country that upset the established pattern of marriages.

Evidence of a multi-faceted rationale for the marriages lies in the effect these two women had upon trading post society.[75] When Frances and Catherine arrived, all the wives of lower ranked employees were Native or of mixed-blood. In this way traders' changing marital preferences and the ethnicity of their wives appeared related, even though the documentary evidence indicates the reasons for the connection were based just as much in corporate strategy as any personal preference. Jennifer Brown contended that the impact on social relations at Moose Factory of Catherine McTavish's presence reinforced Chief Factor John McTavish's status, "[f]or the next four years, McTavish and his Aberdeenshire wife were the highest ranked residents at Moose, and like the Simpsons . . . , interposed new social barriers between themselves and the natives of the country."[76] Thus the need of highly ranked HBC officials to reinforce their status in this age of company reorganization appears to be directly related to the appearance of British-born wives in Rupert's Land.

Further evidence that business concerns shaped Simpson's attitude towards marriages to Native, mixed-blood and British-born women is revealed by his seemingly contradictory stances on whom traders should marry. While Simpson contravened the HBC's traditional ban on bringing British-born wives to Rupert's Land for himself, he simultaneously advocated that other traders continue to marry Native and mixed-blood women in the interests of the fur trade:

> the restrictions which the Honble. Committee have put on Matrimonial alliances and which I consider most baneful to the interests of the Company are tantamount to a prohibition of forming a most important chain of connection with the Natives, so we have solely to depend on the Indians who have no other feelings than those which interest and mercenary views create towards us; it is never matured to attachment and a price is only required to make those on whom our existence depends our inveterate Enemies.[77]

The only way to make sense of why Simpson encouraged some traders to marry British women while suggesting that others marry Native or mixed-blood women is to consider what distinguished these two groups of traders, and that factor was their rank. If Simpson's decision to abandon Margaret in favour of Frances was rooted in racism alone, he would not have continued to support country marriages of officers located in key fur-providing territories. He would have created policies requiring all HBC officials and servants to marry only British women; instead, Simpson encouraged just a few high-ranking friends to choose British wives. Considering the historic importance of women to the fur trade, and Simpson's ability to comprehend the workings of the fur trade in such a short time (as evidenced by his rapid promotion at such a crucial time), Simpson's actions are best explained in terms of business acumen.

British-born wives distinguished the post patriarch in ways that Native or mixed-blood women could not. They looked and behaved differently from the rest of the women in fur trade country, and their marital status was permanent and formally sanctioned by the church. All employees from lower ranks either had country marriages, which were perceived as temporary in nature and informal, or had British wives who were unable to join their husbands. Thus, while the post patriarch no longer was distinguished by marriage, he could at least be differentiated from the majority of married employees by the aura of contrast surrounding his wife.

When Chief Factor Colin Robertson attempted to have his mixed-blood country-wife, Therisa Chalifoux, befriend Frances Simpson, predictably George forbade the meeting between the two women: "Robertson brought his bit of Brown with him to the Settlement this Spring in hopes that she would pickup a few English manners before visiting the civilised world; but it would not do — I told him distinctly that the thing was impossible, which mortified him exceedingly."[78] Seen within the context of maintaining the position of post patriarch, George's words signify more than discrimination based on race. To maintain this new distinguishing feature of the fur trade patriarch, George could not afford to have his new British wife undermine her unique status by socializing with women married to anyone from a lower station in the company.

It is clear that the rationale for the marriage pattern of fur traders cannot be sufficiently explained by racial motives alone. If "shock waves"[79] were sent throughout fur trade country as a result of the appearance of British-born women at the fur trade posts, then the move by officers to differentiate themselves from those in the lower ranks had succeeded. By the time of amalgamation Native and mixed-blood women no longer helped to symbolize the patriarchal structure necessary to maintain authority and control in the HBC. There is enough evidence to suggest that officials' decision to bring their British-born wives to Rupert's Land was associated with a period of crisis in which it was necessary to create new ways of differentiating the head of a post from his inferiors.[80] Ideally employed as powerful, visible symbols in maintaining status differentiation, these marriages helped to reinforce the concept of the patriarchal family, which was implicit to the corporate structure of the HBC. As the company's age-old directives suggest, it had utilized the model of the patriarchal family as the chief method for instilling discipline and reinforcing employee ranks almost from the moment HBC traders arrived on the shores of Hudson Bay.

NOTES

1. Historians are unsure of the exact year of George Simpson's birth. He married at either age 38 or 43. See respectively Arthur Silver Morton, *Sir George Simpson, Overseas Governor of the Hudson's Bay Company, A pen picture of a man of action* (Binsfords-mort, 1944), 3; Frederick Merk, "Editor's Introduction," *Fur Trade and Empire: George Simpson's Journal*, rev. ed. (Cambridge, Mass: The Belknap Press of Harvard University Press, 1968), xliii.

2. Sylvia Van Kirk, *"Many Tender Ties": Women in Fur Trade Society in Western Canada, 1670–1870* (Winnipeg: Watson and Dwyer Publishing Ltd., 1980), 201.

3. Jennifer S.H. Brown, *Strangers in Blood: Fur Trade Families in Indian Country* (Vancouver and London: University of British Columbia Press,1980), xvi.

4. Veronica Strong-Boag, "Writing About Women," in John Schultz, ed., *Writing About Canada: A Handbook for Modern Canadian History* (Scarborough: Prentice-Hall Canada, Inc., 1990), 185. For other similar summaries of the significance of the arrival of British-born women see Brian Gallagher, "A Re-examination of Race, Class and Society in Red River," *Native Studies Review* 4 (1988): 38; Frits Pannekoek, "The Anglican Church and the Disintegration of Red River Society, 1818–1870," in Carl Berger and Ramsay Cook, eds., *The West and the Nation: Essays in Honour of W.L. Morton* (Toronto: McClelland and Stewart, 1976); Arthur J. Ray, "Reflections on Fur Trade Social History and Métis History in Canada," *American Indian Culture and Research Journal* 6, no. 2 (1982): 91–107.

5. Brown, *Strangers in Blood*, 214; Van Kirk, *"Many Tender Ties,"* 117, 119.

6. E.P. Thompson cautions historians when they use the terms like "patriarchal" to be aware of the difference between the "actual" and the "ideal." For example, he notes that between the mid-seventeenth century and well into the eighteenth century, the idea of patriarchy remained a popular choice as an effective management system; however, in actuality it was waning as a method of economic control over the labour force, primarily due to the increased geographic mobility of labourers. See E.P. Thompson, *Customs in Common* (London: Penguin Books, 1991), 37–38; see also Rosemary O'Day, *The Family and Family Relationships, 1500–1900: England, France, and the United States of America* (New York: St. Martin's Press, 1994), 24.

7. Readers interested in examining the scholarly debate surrounding the role and influence of this type of family structure upon society should begin by consulting the following sources: Peter Laslett, *Family Life and Illicit Love in Earlier Generations: Essays in Historical Sociology* (Cambridge: Cambridge University Press, 1977); Alan Macfarlane, *The Origins of English Individualism: The Family, Property and Social Transition* (New York: Cambridge University Press, 1978); Steven Mintz, *A Prison of Expectations: The Family in Victorian Culture* (New York: New York University Press, 1983). Though somewhat dated, this list forms the basis from which more recent debates have developed. For a more recent interpretation of this debate see Mary Abbott, *Family Ties: English Families, 1540–1920* (London and New York: Routledge, 1993).

8. According to Alan Macfarlane, the majority of marriages in England occurred after a contract or apprenticeship had been completed. Macfarlane claims that desirable female marriage partners were those who had access to economic stability either through personal wealth, or through a connection to the most influential person in the future husband's life, his patron. See Macfarlane, *The Origins of English Individualism*, 175; Laslett, *Family Life*, 217–19.

9. O'Day, *The Family and Family Relationships*, 175–76.

10. Gerhard Ens, "The Political Economy of the 'Private Trade' on the Hudson Bay: The Example of Moose Factory, 1741–1744," in Bruce G. Trigger, Toby Morantz, Louise Dechene, eds., *Le Castor Fait Tout: Selected Papers of the Fifth North American Fur Trade Conference, 1985* (Montreal: Lake St. Louis Historical Society, 1987): 387, 398; John E. Foster, "Trading-Post Social Organization," Lecture, History 663, University of Alberta, 17 March 1995.

11. *Massachusetts Records*, I, 397, as cited in O'Day, *The Family and Family Relationships*, 57. See ibid., 58, for other examples from American colonies.

12. The charter specifically states that "the said Governor and Company shall or may elect seaven of theire number in such forme as hereafter . . . shall bee called the Committee of the said Company . . ." See "Charter of the Hudson's Bay Company, 1670. The Royal Charter for incorporating The Hudson's Bay Company, A.D. 1670," *Charters, Statutes and Orders in Council relating to the Hudson's Bay Company* (London: Hudson's Bay Company, 1931). The first governor and committee were appointed.

13. Brown, *Strangers in Blood*, 24–25; Van Kirk, "*Many Tender Ties*," 11.

14. John Nicks, "Orkneymen in the Hudson's Bay Company," in Carol Judd and Arthur J. Ray, eds., *Old Trails and New Directions: Papers of the Third North American Fur Trade Conference, 1978* (Toronto: University of Toronto Press, 1980), 122. He suggests that these men joined the HBC with the hope of improving their economic and social status, either saving enough money to create a new position for themselves upon returning to the Orkneys or by working their way through the ranks of the HBC and returning with an already improved status.

15. J. Storer Clouston, *The Orkney Parishes: Containing the Statistical Account of Orkney, 1795–1798. Together with a General Introduction and Notice of each Parish* (Kirkwall: W.R. Mackintosh, The Orcadian Office, 1927), 112, 121. I realize that a ploughman and a carpenter may not be equivalent occupations; however, I could find information on yearly wages for only some occupations in Orkney and in the HBC. No identical occupations for both the HBC and the Orkney Islands were listed. As of 1811 the London Committee proposed that labourers be contracted for £18 per year for a three-year contract and £20 per year for a five-year contract. See HBCA, A.5/5 fo. 37.

16. Carol Judd, "'Mixt bands of Many Nations,': 1821–70," in Carol Judd and Arthur J. Ray, eds., *Old Trails and New Directions: Papers of the Third North American Fur Trade Conference, 1978* (Toronto: University of Toronto Press, 1980), 129; William P.L. Thomson, *History of Orkney* (Edinburgh: The Mercat Press, 1987), 218. For more information on the relationship between the Orkney Islands and the HBC see Nicks, "Orkneymen in the Hudson's Bay Company"; and *The Orkney Parishes: Containing the Statistical Account of Orkney*; Bruce S. Wilson, "The Orkneymen and the Hudson's Bay Company," in Patricia A. McCormack and R. Geoffrey Ironside, eds., *Proceedings of the Fort Vermillion Bicentennial Conference, September 23–25, 1988* (Edmonton: Boreal Institute for Northern Studies, 1990).

17. HBCA, A.5/5 fo. 31, 8 December 1810. The company contracted apprentices often around the age of 13 or 14 years.

18. Edith Burley's recently published version of her doctoral dissertation examines evidence of resistance by HBC employees to the company's authority. In the context of her study she similarly observes on the parallels between the ideal conception of the patriarchal family and the HBC's style of operations. See *Servants of the Honourable Company: Work, Discipline, and Conflict in the Hudson's Bay Company, 1770–1879* (Don Mills, Ontario: Oxford University Press, 1997), 2.

19. The HBC maintained five posts during the seventeenth century: Charles Fort, later known as Rupert, was built at the mouth of the Rupert River; Port Nelson, located at the mouth of the Nelson River, would become known as York Fort or Factory; Hayes Fort, later called Moose Factory, was found at the mouth of the Moose River; Severn Fort was positioned near the mouth of the Severn River; and Chichewan Fort, eventually known as Fort Albany, was stationed at the mouth of the Albany River. See Ernest Voohis, *Historic Forts and Trading Posts* (Ottawa: Department of the Interior, 1930), 4; and "Appendix A: Posts," *Copy-Book of Letters Outward, 1679–94*, edited by E.E. Rich, assisted by A.M. Johnson (Toronto: Champlain Society, 1948), 345–69.

20. Brown, *Strangers in Blood*, 33. On the same page she provided documentary evidence that traders perceived the chief factor in this light.

21. There are other examples of chief factors attending to the spiritual needs of their charges, but in all other cases the factors carry out the services themselves. Churchill Post Journal entries throughout the eighteenth century document the chief factor's performance of the ritual Sunday sermon. Chief factor Richard Norton of Churchill included weekly notices of his reading of prayers to the employees; see the entries dated 1 and 8 September 1723. HBCA, B.42/a/4 fos. 5, 6. Similarly chief factor Captain Anthony Beale wrote for his entry dated Sunday 20 August 1727 that he "read Prayers to According to the Liturgy of the Church of England:" see HBCA B.42/a/8 fo. 3. For other such entries in the latter part of the eighteenth century see HBCA, B.42/a/34 fo. 26d and B.42/a/42 fo. 1d. The London Committee's minute books from the latter part of the eighteenth century include orders for religious tracts they intended to distribute to the various chief factors for their men's use. See HBCA, A.1/46 fos. 21 and 87d, London Minute Book 1783–88.

22. Henry Sergeant's orders to depart for Hudson Bay are dated 24 January 1683. See "Appendix B: Biographies," *Letters Outward, 1679–94*, 388.

23. On Knight's appointment as chief factor see letter to Knight from the London Committee, 23 May 1682, *Letters Outward*, 51. On Knight's manservant see Ernest S. Dodge, "James Knight," *Dictionary of Canadian Biography*, Vol. 2 (Toronto: University of Toronto Press, 1969), 318.

24. Letter to Henry Kelsey at York, from the Governor and London Committee, 29 May 1710, Letterbook 603, 199, as cited in *The Kelsey Papers*, intro. by Arthur G. Doughty and Chester Martin (Ottawa: Public Archives of Canada and the Public Record Office of Northern Ireland, 1929), xxvii.

25. Regarding Grover's appointment to second at Churchill, see the letter to William Grover from the London Committee, 31 May 1763, HBCA, A.5/1 fos. 55, 108. For the reference to his new duties see the letter to Grover from the London Committee, 15 May 1765, HBCA, A.5/1 fos. 68, 135.

26. The company also hired boat crews, but as they were not necessarily permanent residents at the trading posts and therefore will not be included in this discussion.

27. Brown, *Strangers in Blood*, 10–11. Here Brown relates some of the difficulties encountered by the HBC when it employed married men and those with dependents.

28. Van Kirk, *"Many Tender Ties,"* 11.

29. Brown, *Strangers in Blood*, 20–22.

30. The daughter is first mentioned as a passenger aboard the HBC's yacht *Colleton* on the spring of 1786. Either the Sergeants brought her with them from England or she was born in Rupert's Land. See E.G.R. Taylor, "Introduction," *Letters Outward*, xxxiii. On the 1684 policy see Brown, *Strangers in Blood*, 11.

31. *Letters Outward*, 235, dated 3 June 1687.

32. *Letters Outward*, 390.

33. HBC contracts were for three-year periods, with the exception of apprentices who signed on for seven years. At the end of the contract the company and employee could negotiate another three-year renewal.

34. Foster, "Trading-Post Social Organization." Van Kirk describes trading post society as a combination of European and Native cultural elements, resulting in a "distinctive, self-perpetuating community," *"Many Tender Ties,"* 5.

35. Letter to Nixon from the London Committee, 15 May 1682, *Letters Outward*, 40–41.

36. HBCA, B.239/a/2 fo. 11, York Factory Post Journal 1715–16, 27 December 1715.

37. HBC trader and explorer Peter Fidler reported in a journal entry from 1790: "An Indian woman at a House is particularly useful in making shoes, cutting line, netting snow shoes, cleaning and stretching Beaver skins &c." As cited in *Journals of Samuel Hearne and Philip Turnor*, edited by J.B. Tyrrell (Toronto: Champlain Society, 1934), 327, footnote 6. For an in-depth examination of their varied roles and influences in the fur trade see Van Kirk, *"Many Tender Ties,"* specifically chapter three, "Your Honors Servants."

38. The first reference to Doll's use by the HBC as an interpreter occurs in Chief Factor Moses Norton's instructions to Captain Magnus Johnson, 17 July 1764. The letter directs Johnson to take the "Eskimo Woman Doll, who is sent with you as a Linguist." HBCA, A.11/14 fo. 1. On 14 September 1769 Doll died at Churchill Fort of an unnamed illness. Chief Factor Norton entered the following remark in the post journal to mark her passing: "the Death of the Woman I doubt will be a Loss to the Northern Trade with the Esquimaux as she has been of great Service on Assisting to make Peace between the Northern Indians and her Country People." HBCA, B.42/a/77, fo. 2d, Churchill Post Journal.

39. Daniel Harmon comments frequently in his journal about these alliances. Soon after he had entered the fur trade a Cree chief approached him: "who appeared very desirous that I should take one of his Daughters to remain with me . . . he wished to have his Daughter with the white people . . . I was sure that while I had the Daughter I should not only have the Fathers hunts but those of his relations also, of course [this] would be much in the favor of the Company & perhaps in the end of some advantage to me likewise." Though Harmon was a "Nor'Wester," his perception of alliances with Native women reflects the shared views of HBC traders. See *Sixteen Years in the Indian Country: The Journal of Daniel Williams Harmon*, edited by W. Kaye Lamb (Toronto: Macmillan, 1957), 62.

40. Thomson, *History of Orkney*, 220.

41. Nicks, 123.

42. Andrew Graham, *Observations on Hudson's Bay*, HBCA, E.2/7 fo. 24d; as cited in Van Kirk, *"Many Tender Ties,"* 41. Concerning this document, readers will be interested to note that there are 10 different volumes under the title of Graham's *Observations*. Some are in Graham's handwriting, others are not. There are substantive differences between the versions in terms of content and length. A detailed study comparing these versions has yet to be performed and may prove useful in revealing Graham's changing portrayal of Native peoples. In the meantime, interested readers are instructed to examine Glyndwr Williams's edited version of Graham's *Observations* for his understanding of this complex mass of manuscripts.

43. Letter to John Potts from the London Committee, 31 May 1763, HBCA, A.5/1 fo. 55, 108–9.

44. Letter to John Potts from the London Committee, 23 May 1764, HBCA, A.5/1 fo. 60, 118.

45. Brown, *Strangers in Blood,* 70; Van Kirk, *"Many Tender Ties,"* 45. Brown provides 15 documented examples of country marriages involving HBC employees; see *Strangers in Blood,* 52–58.

46. There is sufficient evidence that many Native and mixed-blood women did not act as victims of abandonment. Rather, they operated out of self-interest to ensure their own futures. When Joseph Colen left York Factory in 1798 for Britain, his former Cree wife and children re-allied themselves with another employee "who had long since been in the habits of her attention and Affection." See Brown, *Strangers in Blood,* 68. Consider the case of the Native woman Betsy who had a number of company employees as husbands. Throughout the course of her alliances she had saved 88 pounds, which allowed her a measure of financial security. She told British-born Letitia Hargrave that she would never marry again because the men would probably be after her money. See Letitia Hargrave to Mary MacTavish, 1 September 1840, *Letters,* 72; Van Kirk, *"Many Tender Ties,"* 89–90.

47. Van Kirk covers this topic in far greater details in chapter two, "Customs of the Country" of her *"Many Tender Ties."* See also John S. Galbraith, *The Little Emperor: Governor Simpson of the Hudson's Bay Company* (Toronto: Macmillan, 1976), 67.

48. The minutes from the London Committee's weekly meetings during the 1780s and 1790s include a few references to chief factors' provisions for their families after death. Jacob's wishes are recorded in HBCA, A.1/46 fo. 51d. Other similar references are contained in HBCA, A.1/46 fos. 89, 89d and A.1/47 fos. 36d, 92d and 113.

49. HBCA, A.5/5 fo. 14d, Letter to David Geddes from the London Committee, 30 March 1808.

50. During the late eighteenth century and early nineteenth century, the Nor'Westers formed a number of competing companies; however the rivalry with the larger HBC eventually drove them to form a coalition known as the North West Company. An introduction to the history of the various Montreal-based companies is contained within Gerald Friesen, *The Canadian Prairies: A History* (Toronto: University of Toronto Press, 1984); Harold A. Innis, *The Fur Trade in Canada* (Toronto: University of Toronto Press, 1930).

51. Glyndwr Williams, ed., "Appendix A," *Andrew Graham's Observations on Hudson's Bay 1767–1791*, Hudson's Bay Record Society, Vol. 27 (London: Hudson's Bay Record Society, 1969), 346–47.

52. Burley, *Servants of the Honourable Company,* 5. She also notes that during this same period the Nor'Wester organizations opened 342 posts. Most of the HBC and Nor'Wester posts lasted no longer than five years before being abandoned.

53. For example it was noted in the Churchill Post Journal that on the 14th of March 1724, "3 of our men gone over the River to the Hunters tent to lye there for 1 Night." The next morning they returned back to the post. Though it was not recorded why they spent just one night in the hunters' tent instead of in their regular lodgings, the existence of such events points to the opportunity for sexual relations with Native women. See HBCA, B.42/a/4 fo. 21.

54. Brown, *Strangers in Blood,* 51; Van Kirk, *"Many Tender Ties,"* 38, 45. There are two points to be made here. First, both authors agree that as marriage occurred with increased frequency throughout the ranks of the HBC, officers began to marry mixed-blood women in a similar frequency. This pattern of preference should not be surprising, if one considers the influence the patriarchal model had upon employees. These mixed-blood women were the daughters of post patriarchs. For employees seeking to rise in the ranks there was no better way to confirm one's "rightful place" in his immediate household than to be adopted into the patriarch's family by marriage to his daughter. Second, though not proven, it seems plausible that there would be a correlation between the increase of HBC posts and the number of country marriages. Interested readers should consult instead both Brown's *Strangers in Blood* and Van Kirk's *"Many Tender Ties,"* that contain extensive documentation of country marriages, though neither author correlates the frequency of marriage with the number of posts particularly since this was not their purpose. Perhaps future research in this area could sustain, or challenge, the argument for the economic and social motivations for these marriages in opposition to the argument reliant on ethnicity.

55. HBCA, A.1/49, fo. 93, letter from the London Committee to the Commissioners of the Royal Treasury, 21 December 1809. The full letter, including references to the impact of the Napoleonic Wars, consists of folios 91d–94d. Another reference to the effect of the war upon the HBC is located in HBCA, A.1/147, fo. 40d–41, London Committee Minute Books, dated 15 March 1809.

56. HBCA, A.1/49 fo. 102d, minutes from meeting of the London Committee, 20 September 1809.

57. HBCA, A.5/5 fos. 35–35d.

58. For the London Committee's discussion and Selkirk's original proposal, see HBCA, A.1/50 fos. 34–38.

59. Friesen, *The Canadian Prairies,* 83.

60. Merk, *Fur Trade and Empire*, 58.
61. Friesen, *The Canadian Prairies*, 84; Merk, *Fur Trade and Empire*, xlvi. For examples of how the Board of Governors and Simpson formulated the new policies examine the following references in *Journal of Occurrences in the Athabasca Department by George Simpson, 1820–1821, and Report*, edited by E.E. Rich, Vol. 1 (Toronto: The Champlain Society, 1938): on reduced wages see 2 February 1922, p. 306, 8 March 1822, p. 314, 16 July 1822, p. 339; on support for families see 2 February 1822, p. 311, 8 March 1822, pp. 314–15, 31 July 1822, p. 354. On the reduction of posts, Burley states that by 1821 the HBC operated 68 posts and the NWC ran 57. In the merged company the number of posts would be reduced to a total of 52. See Burley, *Servants of the Honourable Company*, 6. For a general discussion of the policies following amalgamation see Galbraith, *The Little Emperor*, 73–75; Morton, 64.
62. Galbraith, *The Little Emperor*, 60. Galbraith believes that the relationship between Betsy and George is better characterized as a brief fling than a country-marriage.
63. Private letter from Simpson to John George McTavish, 12 November 1822, as cited in *Minutes of Council Northern Department of Rupert Land, 1821–31*, edited by E.E. Rich and R.H. Fleming (Toronto: Champlain Society, 1940), 424.
64. See Galbraith, *The Little Emperor*, 68; Merk, *Fur Trade and Empire*, xliii.
65. Readers interested in Simpson's biography and in examining the various depictions of his character are advised to consult the following list: Merk, *Fur Trade and Empire*; Galbraith, *The Little Emperor*; *Journal of Occurrences in the Athabasca Department*; *Minutes of Council Northern Development of Rupert Land, 1821–31*; and Morton, *Sir George Simpson*.
66. Galbraith, *The Little Emperor*, 70.
67. Letter from Simpson to McTavish, 4 June 1822, as cited in *Minutes of Council*, 424.
68. Galbraith, *The Little Emperor*, 68.
69. Galbraith, *The Little Emperor*, 75.
70. See Galbraith, *The Little Emperor*, 95; Van Kirk, "*Many Tender Ties*," 161.
71. Merk, *Fur Trade and Empire*, xliv.
72. Galbraith, *The Little Emperor*, 95–96.
73. During Simpson's last tour of fur trade country before he left for England, he referred affectionately to Margaret as "my fair one." See Galbraith, *The Little Emperor*, 100. It is not known if Simpson forewarned Margaret of his intention to terminate their relationship.
74. Evidence that Norton was married to a British woman while still in the employ of the HBC is contained in HBC official correspondence to him. For example, see the letter to Moses Norton from the London Committee, 15 May 1760, HBCA, A.5/1 fo. 36. In this letter the committee informs Norton that they "have paid your Wife the Balance of your Account as you desired."
75. Galbraith, *The Little Emperor*, 102, 104.
76. Brown, *Strangers in Blood*, 133.
77. Simpson, 1821 Athabasca Report, *Journal of Occurrences*, 395–96.
78. HBCA, B.135/c/2, 15 Aug 1831; as cited in Brown, *Strangers in Blood*, 129–30.
79. Brown, *Strangers in Blood*, xv.
80. It has been necessary to focus upon the merger as a crisis in the new company's organization in order to illuminate the implications of policy changes on fur trade social relations. However, by highlighting a period as the turning point in social relations, it is easy to overlook long-term continuities. Part of this paper's argument hinges upon the assertion that the change in policy to allow British-born women at fur trade posts reflects the desire to maintain a long-term mode of operations. There are other continuities; for example, the percentage of officers married to mixed-blood women remained fairly stable (there was actually a small increase by three percent) well past the middle of the nineteenth century. See Gallagher, "A Re-examination of Race, Class and Society in Red River," 28–29, 31.

Topic Three

Law and Society in New France

A wood engraving of the Royal Arms of France, as taken from a gate in the city of Quebec by British troops in 1759.

The population of New France grew slowly, as the fur trade required only a small workforce. In the autumn of 1608, only 28 people lived at Quebec, and, more than 30 years later, the settler population of all of New France remained less than 300. With the establishment of direct royal government in 1663, however, the colony expanded.

Royal government helped the colony's growth in three specific ways. First, the Crown established an effective political system. Second, it dispatched a sizable military force, which contributed to the achievement of an effective truce with the Iroquois Confederacy, thereby securing twenty years of peaceful development for the colony. Third, the French government sponsored the immigration of several thousand settlers, men and women, who built a more diversified economy in New France. From 1663 to 1700, the colony's population grew from 2500 to 15000. By the late 17th century, the society of New France had taken on a definite form.

There are a number of excellent surveys of the society of New France. Louise Dechêne looks at Montreal in the late 17th century in *Habitants and Merchants in Seventeenth Century Montreal*, trans. Liana Vardi (Montreal/Kingston: McGill-Queen's University Press, 1992). In *The Beginnings of New France, 1524–1663* (Toronto: McClelland and Stewart, 1973), Marcel Trudel reviews several aspects of the society of New France in its early years. W.J. Eccles, in *Canada under Louis XIV, 1663–1701* (Toronto: McClelland and Stewart, 1964), and Dale Miquelon, in *New France, 1701–1744: "A Supplement to Europe"* (Toronto: McClelland and Stewart, 1987), examine later periods. Four valuable surveys of New France are Jacques Mathieu's *La Nouvelle-France: Les Français en Amérique du Nord, XVIe–XVIIIe siècle* (Sainte-Foy, PQ: Presses de l'Université Laval, 1991); Dale Miquelon, *The First Canada: To 1791* (Toronto: McGraw-Hill Ryerson, 1994); Allan Greer, *The People of New France* (Toronto: University of Toronto Press, 1997); and Peter N. Moogk, *La Nouvelle France: The Making of French Canada — A Cultural History* (East Lansing: Michigan State University Press, 2000).

What was the nature of this new North American society? In what respects, if any, did New France differ from France? In their essay, "Violence, Marriage, and Family Honour: Aspects of the Legal Regulation of Marriage in New France," André Lachance and Sylvie Savoie review the institution of marriage in early 18th-century New France. Did the frontier lead to greater freedom from the strict controls of the Church and State amongst married couples in New France? In "Native Sovereignty and French Justice in Early Canada," John Dickinson examines the legal controls the French had over First Nations communities in the St. Lawrence Valley. Did the French exercise judicial control over the First Nations in the Christian missions in the settled areas of New France?

Recently, several important studies on the history of women in New France have appeared. Chapter 2 in Alison Prentice et al., *Canadian Women: A History*, 2nd ed. (Toronto: Harcourt Brace, 1996), pp. 33–57, entitled "Women in the New World," and the opening chapter of Micheline Dumont et al., *Quebec Women: A History*, trans. R. Gannon and R. Gill (Toronto: Women's Press, 1987) survey the position of women in the French colony. Yves Landry provides a collective biography of the 770 female immigrants to New France between 1663 and 1673. An interesting article is Jan Noel's "New France. Les femmes favorisées," in R. Douglas Francis and Donald B. Smith, eds., *Readings in Canadian History: Pre-Confederation* (6th ed. Toronto: Nelson Thomson Learning, 2002), pp. 91–110. Allan Greer has written a biography of the late 17th-century Iroquois woman, Catherine Tekakwitha, who came to live in a mission station at Kahnawake near Montreal, *Mohawk Saint* (Don Mills, ON: Oxford University Press, 2005).

Other important studies of aspects of New France's society include Cornelius Jaenen's *The Role of the Church in New France* (Toronto: McGraw-Hill Ryerson, 1976), a review of an important institution in the colony, and W.J. Eccles's three volumes: *The Canadian Frontier,*

1534–1760 (New York: Holt Rinehart and Winston, 1969); *France in America*, rev. ed. (New York: Harper and Row, 1990); and *Essays on New France* (Toronto: Oxford University Press, 1987). A good summary of economic life in New France appears in "Doing Business in New France," a chapter in Michael Bliss's *Northern Enterprise: Five Centuries of Canadian Business* (Toronto: McClelland and Stewart, 1987), pp. 55–77. Peter Moogk's "*Les Petits Sauvages*: The Children of Eighteenth-Century New France," in *Childhood and Family in Canadian History*, ed. Joy Parr (Toronto: McClelland and Stewart, 1982), pp. 17–43, 192–95, deals with a subject that had previously been neglected in the literature. R. Cole Harris's *The Seigneurial System in Early Canada* (Madison: University of Wisconsin Press, 1966) provides a useful overview. Hubert Charbonneau et al., *The First French Canadians: Pioneers in the St. Lawrence Valley*, trans. Paola Colozzo (Newark: University of Delaware Press, 1993), provides an in-depth study of the population of New France.

For a first-hand account of New France in 1750, students should consult the English translation of Peter Kalm's *Travels in North America*, 2 vols. (New York: Dover Publications, 1964).

WEBLINKS

Virtual Museum of New France
http://www.vmnf.civilization.ca/vmnf/vmnfe.asp

A detailed site that describes New France, with a special focus on the education of children.

New France — Daily Life
http://northernblue.ca/hconline/chapters/3/3Fdailylife.php

A richly illustrated site about daily life in New France.

Early Censuses of Canada
http://estat.statcan.ca/Estat/data.htm

A searchable database of censuses taken in Canada from 1665 to 1871.

New France: New Horizons
http://www.champlain2004.org/html/exhibition.html

A virtual exhibit of New France containing over 300 digitized archival documents organized into topics such as Daily Life, Worship, and Survival.

Law in New France
http://www.canadiana.org/citm/themes/constitution/constitution3_e.html

A collection of digitized primary documents about the practice of government and law in New France.

A New France ABC
http://www.civilisations.ca/vmnf/avent/abc09-12/accu_cde.htm

Roughly two dozen objects used in daily life in New France are presented with information about their use and historical context.

Article Six

Native Sovereignty and French Justice in Early Canada

John A. Dickinson

As native territorial claims and the issue of self-government become increasingly important on the Canadian political agenda, questions of native sovereignty in historical context take on new meaning. The United States recognizes Indian nations as sovereign entities to whom the federal government is legally bound to carry out its 'trust responsibility.'[1] Canada has not followed this lead, and although some recent decisions — notably the Sparrow (1987) and Sioui (1990) cases — have been more generous in recognizing native claims,[2] aboriginal rights are never taken for granted. In recent Quebec cases, for example, the Crown has tried to prove that the Mohawks are not a distinct native people, but merely provincial citizens with the same rights before the courts as any others.[3] This paper focuses on both native and French reactions to differing concepts of authority and sovereignty in the St Lawrence Valley and the necessary accommodations that took place on both sides of the cultural divide before the fall of New France in 1760.

In Eastern Canada the situation is complex since France never made treaties with the populations on whose lands it established colonies. Historian William John Eccles has defined New France's relations with her native allies in peripheral regions as a form of sovereignty association and this term is equally applicable in the colony's core.[4] Unlike in other areas of North America where the initial period of 'non-directed cultural change'[5] did not long survive settlement, natives in the St Lawrence Valley and Upper State New York continued to control their destiny by playing off one imperial power against the other.

French imperial policy in the Americas did not recognize the existence of any native claims to the territory. By virtue of their cultural superiority, the French were masters of all lands they claimed through exploration. Natives were *Sauvages* who lived *sans foi et sans loi*— without any recognizable religious or civil institutions that would have made them equals of Europeans.[6] Before they obtained any rights they had to be 'humanized' by accepting Catholicism, when they became reputed French subjects,[7] and this legal friction was maintained throughout the French regime. Natives, however, considered themselves sovereign nations as the Seneca chief Cachouintioui made clear to Governor Roland-Michel Barrin de La Galissonière in 1748 when he stated that the Iroquois were happy to have the French and English settle among them to trade, but they had never ceded the lands that heaven had given them.[8] Two very different conceptions of authority and sovereignty were present in New France and came into conflict when deviance from accepted norms or problems of social control emerged.

NATIVE CONCEPTS OF SOVEREIGNTY AND AUTHORITY

Although native peoples did not have institutions that Europeans could easily recognize, they did possess effective mechanisms for social control within their communities and elaborate procedures for dealing with conflict with other groups. The historical record offers rich details on the mechanisms for resolving conflict with other communities, and the basic underlying concept

Source: John A. Dickinson, "Native Sovereignty and French Justice in Early Canada," *Essays in the History of Canadian Law, volume V. Crime and Criminal Justice,* eds. Jim Phillips, Tina Loo, and Susan Lewthwaite (Toronto: University of Toronto, 1994): 27–46. Reprinted with permission of the publisher.

was understood: members of the offending group would offer reparation payments to the victim's family. If reparations were not made, the victim's family could seek revenge, inviting further retaliation. As regards internal controls, it is unlikely that French observers fully comprehended the intricacies involved. As Simon Roberts has noted, all acephalous societies manage to maintain relatively ordered social lives without structures of authority. The inevitable disputes that arise are settled through a variety of mechanisms, including physical violence, channelling conflict into ritual, shaming, supernatural agencies, migration, the withdrawal of cooperation or ostracism, and mediation.[9] The amount of disruptive behaviour that could be tolerated was variable, but most native societies in the Northeast encouraged subdued, self-effacing conduct and avoided confrontation within the community. In some specific circumstances, such as in cases of treason or witchcraft, however, it seems that Huron councils could execute offenders. Despite these exceptions, the aim of native mechanisms for dispute resolution was not punishment, but the restoration of amicable relations.[10]

The most informative source on Huron concepts of authority is the *Jesuit Relations*. In 1636 Jean de Brébeuf noted that the Huron punished 'murderers, thieves, traitors, and sorcerers.'[11] The most striking feature of Huron custom to these European observers was that the community rather than the individual was held responsible: 'for the relatives of the deceased pursue not only him who has committed the murder, but address themselves to the whole village, which must give satisfaction for it, and furnish as soon as possible, for this purpose as many as sixty presents, the least of which must be the value of a new beaver robe.'[12] Murder was the most serious crime and required thirty presents for an adult male, forty for a woman, and even more for a member of another nation.[13] Wounds were 'healed' by the presentation of wampum or hatchets. Thieves could be dispossessed of all their belongings (although the Jesuits did not understand Huron concepts of property and might have misinterpreted what they observed). Sorcerers who poisoned people could be put to death immediately.[14] There are two recorded cases of Huron sorcerers being executed, a woman in 1637 and a man in 1640, at a time when Huron society was severely disrupted by the appearance of new European diseases.[15] An isolated case suggests that internal controls involved a more rigorous concept of authority. In 1677, a Mohawk chief named Annontaguelté executed a member of his hunting party near Lachine for stabbing a drunk Iroquois woman in the back. Governor Louis de Buade de Frontenac and Montreal judge Charles D'Ailleboust initiated judicial procedures against Annontaguelté charging him with murder. The accused retorted 'that he was not sorry for the death of the said Savage being his master and having the right to punish him for his misdeed but he was sorry that blood had been spilt on [French territory].[16] Executions of this sort might have been unusual, but this case stresses that natives considered that they alone were responsible for the resolution of internal conflicts.

The collective responsibility for deviance was a concept totally alien to the French. In French law the individual was responsible for his or her actions and had to bear the consequences. Punishment was personal and played out in elaborate public rituals aimed at impressing subjects with the power of the state and acting as a deterrent.[17] Native society also had an elaborate ritual to 'cover' or 'raise' the dead, but it did not seek to punish an individual. Rather it highlighted central features of native concepts of authority that relied on consensus and kin and community solidarity, rather than on coercive power.[18] The Jesuits had difficulty coming to terms with this concept of authority. Father Hierosme Lalemant wrote in 1646:

> I do not believe that there is any people on earth freer than they, and less able to allow the subjection of their wills to any power whatever,— so much so that Fathers here have no control over their children, or Captains over their subjects, or the Laws of the country over any of them, except in so far as each is pleased to submit to them. There is no punishment which is inflicted on the guilty . . . It is not because there are no Laws or punishments proportionate to the crimes, but it is not the guilty who suffer the penalty. It is the public that must make

amends for the offenses of individuals . . . the whole country assembles; and they come to an agreement respecting the number of presents to be given to the Tribe or relatives of him who has been killed, to stay the vengeance that they might take. The Captains urge their subjects to provide what is needed; no one is compelled to it, but those who are willing bring publicly what they wish to contribute; it seems as if they vied with one another according to the amount of their wealth, and as the desire for glory or appearing solicitous for the public welfare animate them on such occasions . . . This form of justice . . . is nevertheless a very mild proceeding, which leaves individuals in such a spirit of liberty that they never submit to any Laws and obey no other impulse than of their own will.[19]

The clash between different concepts of authority and individual as opposed to collective responsibility formed the basis of an ongoing struggle to find acceptable means of resolving interethnic conflict and violence in New France. Over time, both sides worked out a 'middle ground' that blended in the values and practices of the other culture to establish new conventions.[20]

THE EARLY YEARS

During the first quarter-century after the French established a trading post at Quebec in 1608, their inability to comprehend native customs[21] almost led to the sundering of the trade alliance. With never more than a few dozen traders wintering at Quebec,[22] the French were conscious of their vulnerability to native hostility. They were also completely dependent on native trading networks to supply them with furs, the sole economic incentive for colonization. Although Samuel de Champlain's participation in native warfare against the Iroquois and the desirability of access to trade goods put the alliance on a fairly sound footing, conflict between adventurous Frenchmen and independent natives was probably inevitable. The first incident occurred in 1616–17, when two Frenchmen were killed by Cherouny and another Montagnais in retaliation for a beating.[23] Although it is not known why the French beat the Montagnais, it is clear that, from the native viewpoint, reparations were called for to avoid revenge. The French insisted that the Montagnais hand over the culprits and explained that they were to be punished according to French law. The Montagnais withdrew to Three Rivers[24] and sent a delegation to offer reparations for the murders. Although the French traders were willing to accept native reparations because they were too few in number to resist an attack and feared disrupting the trading network, Recollet fathers Le Caron and Huet refused, arguing that a French life could not be sold for furs since this would be tantamount to licensing natives to kill Frenchmen at will.[25] It was finally decided to accept the presents and two hostages until Champlain arrived to settle the matter definitely. In no position to impose their concept of justice, the French refused to have further dealings with Cherouny until 1623, when he was granted an official pardon at Three Rivers. As a symbol of the pardon, Emery de Caen threw a sword in the St. Lawrence to bury the crime. This was interpreted by the natives as a sign of weakness, and the Hurons spent the winter joking that it only cost a dozen beaver pelts to kill a Frenchman.[26]

The French learned little from this incident and persisted in wanting to impose their law on natives.[27] Another similar incident occurred in October 1627, when Mahican Alic Ouche got into an argument with Quebec's baker. The Montagnais sought revenge and killed two sleeping Frenchmen.[28] Champlain ordered his men to be armed at all times and to shoot any Montagnais that approached them without permission. He demanded that the murderer be handed over to the French, but had to settle for three hostages, and it was only in May 1628 that the suspect was brought to Quebec by Montagnais chief La Forière, who asked for his pardon. Champlain refused and had the suspect imprisoned. Although he should have been executed according to French law, the prisoner was held until the following spring, when he was freed without receiving an official pardon.

French weakness in this incident alienated the Montagnais, who helped David Kirke's expedition capture Quebec in July 1629. By refusing to accommodate to native customs, Champlain elicited only contempt since he did not have the necessary force to impose French justice. French failure to compromise was again evident in three separate incidents in 1633.

When the French retook possession of Quebec, they learned of Etienne Brûlé's murder by the Huron. Fearing a murder accusation, some Huron were uneasy about returning to the St Lawrence to trade but Louis Amantacha, a Huron who had spent two years in France, reassured them that Brûlé's death was unimportant since the French considered him a traitor for having dealt with the English during the Kirke interlude.[29] Such a reaction must have been disconcerting to the natives, whose conceptions of community would have incited them to seek revenge.[30] During the trading fair at Quebec in July 1633, a Petite Nation Algonquin killed a Frenchman washing his clothes near Quebec. The Montagnais informed the French of the murderer's identity, and he was seized and imprisoned. The Huron, Petite Nation, and Kichespirini demanded his release, saying they feared that Jesuits travelling West would be killed by the accused's relatives. French authorities tried to save face, with Father Le Jeune interceding for the prisoner. The execution was put off until orders came from the King. The fate of the prisoner is unknown but, if he survived the winter at Quebec, he was probably released.[31] Once again the French were unable to impose their law, and their actions alienated some of their allies and prevented the Jesuits from reaching the Huron country in 1633. The Huron, remarked Father Le Jeune, 'see that the French will not accept presents as compensation for the murder of one of their countrymen; they fear that their young men may do some reckless deed, for they would have to give up, alive or dead, any one who might have committed murder, or else break with the French. This makes them uneasy.'[32] The final incident involved a French drummer boy who wounded a Nippissing with his drumstick. The Nippissings' reaction conformed to their cultural values: 'Behold, one of thy people has wounded one of ours; though knowest our custom well; give us presents for the wound.' The French refused to follow native custom and promised to punish the boy by whipping. This idea horrified the natives, who sought mercy, 'alleging that it was only a child, that he had no mind, that he did not know what he was doing.' One native threw his blanket over the boy, saying, 'Strike me, if thou wilt, but thou shalt not strike him.' The boy escaped punishment.[33] The application of French conceptions of law was again thwarted by the natives.

Inability to recognize the cultural values of the dominant group forced the French to retreat with loss of prestige.[34] Although much better armed, the French were heavily outnumbered and could not risk the trade alliance by imposing their concept of law on their allies. Champlain and the Jesuits were probably satisfied that they had not given in to native custom, but their disregard for proper methods of resolving violence brought contempt and threatened to undermine the alliance. In the years immediately following the eventful summer of 1633, there seems to have been little violence directed against the French.[35] The onslaught of smallpox and measles that decimated the native peoples from the Atlantic to the Great Lakes eroded native confidence, however, and the French started to emerge as powerful sorcerers who were not affected by disease. Fortunately, as settlement around Quebec increased, the Montagnais withdrew to the north and there was less day-to-day contact that could cause friction.

THE MURDER OF JACQUES DOUART

As the French became better acquainted with native customs, they began to realize that more could be gained through compromise than through confrontation. It is significant, however, that the first explicit recognition of native custom occurred in the Huron country, isolated from the centre of French administration. There had been a precedent, although the main European actors were probably unaware of it at the time. In 1623, Father Joseph Le Caron was threatened by a Huron with a club. The Recollets complained to the village chief, who held a council and convinced the community to give the priests a few bags of corn in reparation.[36] By the 1640s, the Jesuits had abandoned the original policy of complete assimilation and were willing to allow some native customs, and by the time of the murder of Jesuit *donné* Jacques Douart in 1648,[37] they were prepared to accept native concepts of conflict resolution. Indeed, wrote Father Ragueneau, '[i]t would be attempting the impossible, and even make matters still worse, instead of improving them, to try and proceed with Savages according to the method in which justice is administered in France, where he who is convicted of murder is put to death.'[38] This event offers the most detailed description of a traditional reparation ceremony.[39]

On 28 April 1648 six chiefs from three villages, who had always been hostile to Christianity, incited two brothers to murder the first Frenchman they met. They fell upon Jacques Douart in the woods near the Jesuit residence of Ste Marie and killed him with a hatchet blow to the head. The crime caused considerable turmoil among the Hurons since it threatened the French alliance at a time when the country was seriously threatened by Iroquois warfare. At the beginning of May, a general council decided that 'reparation should be made to [the Jesuits] in the name of the whole country.' The Huron presentation clearly demonstrated that the disruption of amicable relations rather than the murder of one individual by another was the main concern:

> A bolt from the Heavens has fallen in the midst of our land, and has rent it open; shouldst thou cease to sustain us, we would fall into the abyss . . . This country is now but a dried skeleton without flesh, without veins, without sinews, and without arteries,— like bones that hold together only by a very delicate thread. The blow that has fallen on the head of thy nephew, for whom we weep, has cut that bond . . . the wretched murderer thought that he was aiming at the head of a young Frenchman; and with the same blow he struck his country, and inflicted on it a mortal wound. The earth opened up to receive the blood of an innocent, and has left an abyss that is to swallow us up, since we are the guilty ones.
>
> . . . Thou alone can restore life to [the country]; it is for thee to collect all the scattered bones, for thee to close up the mouth of the abyss that seeks to swallow us.

Coached by Christian chiefs, the Jesuits presented the Huron with a small bundle of sticks to represent the presents they expected as atonement for this death.

When the presents had been collected from the different villages of the confederation, the reparation ceremony was held. The ceremony was divided into two distinct components: the *andaonhaan* designed 'to make peace, and to take away from their hearts all bitterness and desire for vengeance'; and the *andaerraehaan* that constituted the reparation.[40] The *andaonhaan* was made up of thirty-eight presents to calm the Jesuits, to erect a burial platform for the deceased, to reconstitute his body and to clothe him, to close the abyss that separated the Huron and the French, to appease the governor, and to make the Jesuits love the Huron and reopen their house to them. The *andaerraehaan* was composed of fifty presents.[41] Although Trigger states that this was the largest reparations payment ever recorded among the Huron,[42] it was not of unusual size. The *andaerraehaan* was standard for the murder of a stranger, but the *andaonhaan* was considerably larger than the nine presents enumerated by Brébeuf to settle internal disputes.[43] The size of the payment underlines the diplomatic importance of this ceremony, at which the Jesuits themselves reciprocated with a 3000-bead wampum[44] and other presents:

> to all the eight nations individually, to strengthen our alliance with them, to the whole country in common, to exhort them to remain united together . . . Another present of some

value was given to complain of the calumnies that were circulated against the Faith, and against the Christians, as if all the misfortunes that happen in these countries — such as war, famine, and disease — were brought here by the Faith . . . We also gave them some presents to console them for the loss they had recently suffered through the killing of some persons by the enemy. Finally we ended with a present which assured them the Monsieur the Governor and all the French . . . would have nothing but love for them, and would forget the murder, since they had made reparation for it.

There is no mention of reciprocation by the victims in any of the early documents, but the Jesuits, counselled by the Christian chiefs, were probably following custom when different nations were involved. A few gifts could console the family and restore village harmony, but many were required to renew an alliance, avoid general warfare, and maintain trading relations. Reciprocity was required to acknowledge the resumption of normal relations. This incident demonstrates not only the Jesuits' remarkable ability to adapt, but also the fact that the French now understood native custom and its diplomatic underpinnings.

If native custom provided a means of accommodation in the Huron country, it was not so acceptable to authorities in the St Lawrence valley. By the 1640s, Mohawk raids along the St Lawrence were the major threat, and violence against the French was almost always attributed to this common foe. It is possible that some unaccounted disappearances were caused by allies rather than the Iroquois, but no action was taken to discover the true murderer.[45] During the truce of 1653–60, murders committed by Iroquois at French settlements were considered crimes, not acts of war. More often than not, the Iroquois made reparation for Frenchmen who were killed. In 1656, Father Léonard Gareau was fatally wounded when the Algonquin convoy carrying him was attacked by Mohawks. His aggressors brought him alive to Montreal and 'offered two wretched little presents according to their custom. One was to show their regret for the accident that had happened, and the other to dry our tears and assuage our grief.'[46] After the murder of three Montreal men in 1658, an Oneida delegation presented Montreal governor de Maisonneuve with seven reparation presents to cover the dead.[47] Despite atoning for the crimes following native custom, both de Maisonneuve and Governor Louis D'Ailleboust considered that murder had to be punished. In November 1657, five Mohawks were taken by 'subtlety' at Three Rivers and sent to Quebec, where they were placed in irons.[48] The following year, an Onondaga hunting near Montreal and on friendly terms with the French was imprisoned by de Maisonneuve, seven Mohawk and five Oneida were captured by 'strategem' at Three Rivers, and three other Mohawks were taken when their canoe was wrecked near Quebec.[49] All but four of the prisoners had escaped or were released by the end of November, when a Mohawk delegation left Quebec carrying a wampum from the governor 'wiping away the blood at Three Rivers and Montreal.'[50] Although the French would have liked to punish the murderers, they had to bend to Iroquois custom and diplomacy to ensure the safety of French hostages in the Iroquois country.

REPRESSION OF VIOLENCE UNDER ROYAL GOVERNMENT

Iroquois warfare severely disrupted the trading networks of the French alliance after 1648. In the 1650s French *coureurs de bois* started ranging the West to collect furs and establish new networks less dependent on native middlemen. At the same time, the French population along the St Lawrence substantially increased, climbing from some 1250 in 1650 to about 7000 by 1670 and to over 15,000 by the turn of the century.[51] Although trade remained important, imperial politics gradually transformed New France into a 'military frontier' to impede British expansion. Native populations along the St Lawrence — especially in the Montreal area — were an essential link in French military strategy[52] and the importance of native warriors moulded official policy concerning mission communities.

The absolute monarchy of Louis XIV was more forceful in its desire to impose civilization on 'savagery.' After the Crown took control of the colony in 1663, French minister Jean-Baptiste Colbert instructed the intendant Jean Talon to induce the natives living near French settlements to abandon their customs and especially their language. Henceforth, official policy was clear: 'With one law and one master [French and natives] were to become a single nation with the same blood.'[53] The Jesuit policy of accommodation was discredited and Talon blamed the priests for not having 'civilized' the natives. He assured the minister that the missionaries would insist on total acculturation in the future, starting with language.[54] Although the Jesuits, and later the Sulpicians, gave lip service to royal commands, they realized that assimilation was impracticable.[55] Towards the end of the French regime, Father Degonner, unable to learn Mohawk, was considered useless and had to leave Sault St Louis.[56]

The effort to impose French customs and language was accompanied by a more determined policy to force the growing native populations[57] in the St Lawrence Valley to accept French law.[58] Whereas few natives lived close to French settlements prior to 1650, the establishment of a Huron village near Quebec in the 1650s and of two missions in the neighbourhood of Montreal after 1667 brought settled natives and the French into close contact. As early as April 1664, the Sovereign Council was faced with a case of rape committed by Robet Hache. Local native chiefs protested that they were not aware that this was a capital offence, and the council remitted the punishment. However, after obtaining the consent of six chiefs, it issued an edict subjecting natives to 'the penalties prescribed by French law for murder and rape.'[59] Despite this policy, virtually all native offenders received different treatment from whites.[60]

The available documentation reveals few crimes committed by natives that normally entailed corporal or capital punishment. In 1669, four Sokokis — 8rambech, Chipai8angan, 8ichanigan, and an unidentified woman — broke into Pierre Dupas' cabin on the Richelieu River and threatened the occupants, Dupas' servants, Etienne Clemenceau and Pierre du Pineau. The last-named killed Chipai8angan and 8ichanigan in self-defence. In the fracas, the woman was also killed, apparently by one of her countrymen. Sokoki chiefs, represented by Maanitou 8amet, asked that, in consideration of their alliance, the French pardon 8rambech since two of the aggressors were already dead. In consideration of public welfare and peace, the council suspended procedures against 8rambech and freed him.[61]

In 1684 a Huron from Lorette named Nicolas Tonaktouan, who had spent the previous six years in the West, berated the Sulpician missionary Joseph Mariet and threatened him with an axe. The Sulpician tried to claim that the Indian was sober, but Tonaktouan repeatedly said that he was drunk and remembered nothing of the incident. The Jesuit missionary from Sault St Louis interceded for Tonaktouan, 'for the good of the colony and to avoid the dangerous consequences a long trial and stern punishment might incur.' Threatening people in authority was considered a serious offence and deserved corporal punishment, yet Tonaktouan was merely banished from the Island of Montreal and fined 100 *livres*. While the fact that he was a stranger without close kin ties in Montreal explains why he was prosecuted, fear of alienating the Sault St Louis Iroquois probably explains the relative leniency of the sentence.[62]

Mariet was not the only Sulpician to be threatened by native people. René-Charles de Breslay was taken to task and shaken by the collar by two drunk Indians, a Nippissing named Pierre and an Iroquois named Tonnirata, in 1713. Despite the fact that de Breslay knew the aggressors, there was no prosecution.[63]

In the early eighteenth century, incidences of violence seem to have increased dramatically, natives killing both settlers and cattle,[64] but cases rarely came before the courts. In 1713, three Iroquois from Sault St Louis seriously injured Isaac Nafrechou, but after spending three weeks in prison, the case was dropped on the orders of Governor Philippe de Rigaud de Vaudreuil. Anxious to avoid conflict with the mission Indians, he accepted a reparation payment of thirty beaver skins.[65] In other known cases of assault causing bodily harm by mission Indians in the Montreal area, no legal procedures were initiated against the culprits and there is no record of reparations.[66] Indeed, when a man named Choret was severely beaten in Montreal in 1726, he was told by the local governor, de Longueuil, that his only recourse was against the Frenchman who had supplied the alcohol.[67]

Murder was equally difficult to deal with. There were four recorded cases of murder committed by natives against French settlers in the eighteenth century.[68] In 1719, two-year-old Pierre Gagnier of La Prairie was killed by H8ataki8isoé, a resident of Sault St Louis, who managed to return to the mission before he could be apprehended. The native council refused to surrender the suspect and complained that Jacques Détailly, who sold brandy to the natives, was responsible. Given firm native opposition, the case was never brought to court.[69] The Sault council's attitude was different a year later when an Iroquois murdered a Chateauguay woman, probably Michelle Garnier: 'The murderer was surrendered by his nation, condemned to have his head broken open and executed in front of the natives who thanked us.'[70] When Honoré Dany was killed by five Iroquois from the Sault in 1721 and his son-in-law seriously wounded, the Montreal royal court initiated proceedings against them. The royal judge, François-Marie Bouat, had the matter taken out of his hands by Governor Vaudreuil, who pardoned the accused after meeting with a delegation from the Sault. The Iroquois vigorously protested French intervention, stating that they would never allow their people to be imprisoned and that armed intervention would be required to take them from the village. With the further threat of leaving the colony should the governor insist on trying the accused, they promised to pay reparations to the widow.[71] The final case occurred in 1735 and involved an Attikamek, Pierre 8aononasquesche or Le Chevreuil, who killed a soldier working on Montreal's fortifications. He was arrested on the spot and thrown in jail. Two days later, a court martial sentenced him to death and he was executed by firing-squad in the presence of a Sulpician missionary and an interpreter.[72]

Nocturnal theft was also a capital offence in New France. In the only known case, the offender, Sieur Douville's Montagnais maidservant Marie, was hanged at Montreal in 1756.[73] By leaving her nation and integrating into French society, she had forfeited the protection of kin groups and native councils.[74]

All these cases involved capital punishment, yet only three natives were executed. In the 1720 case, it was the local native council that surrendered the criminal, and they seem to have been glad to be rid of an habitual troublemaker. In the cases of the Attikamek and Montagnais, both were far from home with no relatives to come to their defence. Neither the Attikamek nor the Montagnais were important military allies in the eighteenth century and their population was centred far from French settlements. When Iroquois who had the support of their council were involved, the French proceeded with caution so as not to endanger the fragile alliance. Native warriors — there were between 350 and 400 of them during this period[75]— were essential to the Montreal region's security.

Alcohol was at the root of all the murder cases and continued to be a major social problem throughout the French regime. As early as 1664, the Sovereign Council had ordered all settlers to apprehend drunk natives in order to learn the names of their suppliers.[76] This ordinance was followed by the arrest of Ta8iskaron and Anaka8abemat on 10 May. They were released two days later when they accused a soldier, Rouvray, of supplying drink.[77] Despite the severe penalties imposed by successive ordinances,[78] natives remained immune from prosecution for drunkenness. Disorder was rife in the streets of Montreal and in neighbouring settlements and regularly resulted in natives wounding or killing other natives. Even when the identities of the belligerents were known, however, royal justice dropped the investigation of native violence and concentrated on prosecuting the French alcohol suppliers.[79] French settlers seemed to be convinced that they could obtain no redress from the regular courts for misdemeanours committed by drunk natives.[80] And this conviction seems justified, since the courts freed intoxicated natives arrested in town as soon as they had identified their supplier.[81]

The authorities' continuing ambiguity regarding the status of natives before the law was never resolved. Although theoretically French subjects, there was little consensus as to whether they should be subject to regular royal courts. Governors supported their use as witnesses but claimed that they should have jurisdiction over them since the defence of the colony was at stake. Intendants tried to preserve their hegemony over the judicial field and even questioned their use as witnesses.[82] The court agreed with the unreliability of native witnesses, but ordered that they be called to prosecute French suppliers of alcohol since there was no other alternative.[83] Such prosecutions were numerous and, for a time, quite rewarding for the natives, who received half the fine.[84]

The fur trade also brought the natives into conflict with French concepts of sovereignty and authority. The Iroquois living in the mission communities of the St Lawrence maintained close kin and commercial ties with their fellow-countrymen living in what Europeans considered British colonies to the south. This 'illegal' trade has been discussed extensively in the historical literature[85] and was the subject of numerous ordinances throughout the eighteenth century.[86] The law was clear: no furs were to be taken to Albany or other English posts and no English stroud was to be brought to New France. Natives, however, continued to take furs to the English with little regard for French law, and an exasperated Governor Beauharnois went as far as to state in a 1741 letter that the Mohawks of Sault St Louis 'have English hearts' because of the trade and that the mission 'has become a sort of Republic.'[87] Given the refusal of the Iroquois to obey French law, authorities sought compromise, and the court agreed that Vaudreuil should allow natives to trade the product of their hunt in Albany and bring back English goods for their personal use.[88] If goods were seized by overzealous soldiers, disputes were to be settled by the governor, the intendant, and another judicial official rather than by the regular courts to avoid cumbersome procedure that threatened to alienate the natives.[89] There were occasional seizures of goods being carried by native peoples, but one must presume that they were acting as agents for French merchants in most of these cases.[90] More significant is a well-documented case in 1716 involving goods brought to Sault St Louis by Ontachogo.[91] In this case, Governor Ramezay ordered the Sieur de Chauvignerie to convince Ontachogo to give up eight pieces of stroud that he was storing for Montreal merchants. The envoy was to promise the Mohawk a third of the goods as a reward but to return empty-handed in case of opposition. Ontachogo surrendered six pieces of cloth but kept two as an advance on his reward and asked the authorities to write the Albany merchants and tell them that the goods had been seized so that they would not accuse him of theft.

French authorities realized that the native alliance was indispensable for the security of New France and that they could not afford to alienate the Iroquois. As regards French justice, the natives felt that they were outside the law. Native councils, as we have seen in the murder cases of Gagnier and Dany, successfully defended their people, blaming murder on alcohol and not the Indians. According to the natives, imprisonment could not be imposed by the French unless accepted by native councils. '[The Iroquois] consider that they are not subject to the laws and jurisdictions of the kingdom. Indeed, they told [Governor] Ramezay that their consent was required to imprison their people found drunk or carrying liquor, saying that we had no authority to put them in jail.'[92] The Crown was forced to recognize this situation: 'As to the natives' claim that we cannot imprison them without their consent and that they are not subject to the law of the land, this is a very delicate matter and must be dealt with carefully . . . We can hope to accustom them to military justice and then, little by little, they will get used to the same justice as the French settlers.'[93] This policy was never fulfilled. Any attempt at coercion was met with the threat that the mission communities would leave the country and join the English. Even towards the end of the French regime, action depended on concerting with native councils so as not to offend these valuable allies.[94] French authorities had to compromise with native tradition; accepting the concept that alcohol was responsible for crimes, and substituting reparation payments from the community for the corporal punishment of individuals, were major elements of this accommodation.

CONCLUSION

Although the state would have liked to treat the native population of Canada in the same way as its French subjects, it was never able to obtain this objective. Native alliances were vital for the protection of the colony and authorities could not risk alienating allies whose military prowess was indispensable for the defence of the settlements along the St Lawrence. These political considerations gave natives a relative immunity before the law since the French accepted that the maintenance of amicable relations was more important than the punishment of an individual.

This accommodation gave precedence to native mechanisms for conflict resolution involving different nations that were based on collective reparation payments to a victim's family. These mechanisms existed before the arrival of Europeans and continued to condition native responses to violence until the end of the French regime. Victims of violence had their wounds 'healed' or their corpses 'covered' with presents to ensure the resumption of amicable relations between communities. The French took almost half a century before they recognized the efficacy of native customs, but following the resolution of the Douart murder in 1648, reparations became an accepted means of meting out justice when natives were involved.

Missions were perceived as native territories controlled by the local population. They were havens where natives could find strong support from their communities, as was dramatically illustrated by the case of H8atak8isoé in 1719. Native councils refused state intervention in their internal affairs or interference with their people's freedom, as is illustrated by the claim that arrests could only be made with their consent. Regular courts could interrogate drunk natives and use their testimony to prosecute French liquor traders, but the natives were invariably set free as soon as they had identified their suppliers, regardless of the havoc they caused. Despite their reluctance to recognize native sovereignty, authorities were obliged to do so even if this was contrary to government policy. The instructions given to the Sieur de la Chauvignerie by Governor Ramezay not to use force to obtain contraband goods being stored at Sault St Louis is a good example. Unfortunately, documentation generated by the French administration tells little of how natives resolved conflict among themselves. There is clear evidence that natives were killed and injured by other natives during drunken brawls. Local councils probably had recourse to traditional mechanisms to maintain harmony within their communities, but violence, encouraged by alcohol abuse, was undoubtedly greater than in pre-contact times. The native councils' ready cooperation with colonial authorities to try and curb the sale of liquor is a reflection of the problems alcohol created and the degree to which they were willing to accommodate some external interference in their affairs. That native communities were able to overcome the disruptive effects of drunkenness is a tribute to the ongoing importance of native methods of mediation.

The Iroquois, Algonquin, and Abenaki mission communities were sorts of 'republics' that functioned independently of French authority. Their inhabitants were not subjects but allies who remained closely tied to the French through commercial and military bonds. A highly institutionalized legal system regulated French colonists, whereas a more informal concept of authority maintained ordered relations among natives. When interethnic conflict arose, native customs provided the most satisfactory means of restoring the alliance by recognizing the sovereignty of both parties.

NOTES

1. Christopher Vecsey 'The Issues Underlying Iroquois Land Claims' in Christopher Vecsey and William A. Starna, eds. *Iroquois Land Claims* (Syracuse: Syracuse University Press 1988) 3

2. Olive Patricia Dickason *Canada's First Nations: A History of Founding Peoples from Earliest Times* (Toronto: McClelland & Stewart 1992) 353–4

3. Marcel Trudel 'Rapport historique sur les Mohawks,' document submitted for the prosecution in *Quebec Ministry of Revenue v. Madeleine Meloche*

4. William John Eccles 'Sovereignty Association' in *Essays on New France* (New York: Oxford University Press 1988)

5. Robin Fisher sees natives as central forces in the historical process who adapted selectively to new forces and moulded them to serve their own ends in the initial period before being overwhelmed by major cultural change introduced by settlement: *Contact and Conflict: Indian-European Relations in British Columbia, 1774–1890* (Vancouver: University of British Columbia Press 1977) xi–xiv.

6. George F.G. Stanley 'The Policy of "Francisation" as Applied to the Indians during the Ancien Régime' *Revue d'histoire de l'Amérique française* 3 (1949) 334; Olive Patricia Dickason *The Myth of the Savage and the Beginnings of French Colonialism in the Americas* (Edmonton: University of Alberta Press 1984) 30 and Dickason *Canada's First Nations* 100, 108

7. Article 17 of the Charter of the Company of One Hundred Associates in 1627 recognized Indians who accepted Christianity as French subjects: Canada *Edits, ordonances royaux, déclarations et arrêts du Conseil d'Etat du Roi concernant le Canada* (Quebec: E.-R. Fréchette 1854) 1: 10. The same provisions can be found in article 34 of the Charter of the Compagnie des Indes occidentals in 1664: ibid. 1: 46.

8. Acte authentique des Six nations iroquoises sur leur indépendance (2 novembre 1748) *Rapport de l'Archiviste de la Province de Québec* (1921–2) facing p. 108

9. Simon Roberts *Order and Dispute: An Introduction to Legal Anthropology* (Harmondsworth: Penguin 1979) 12–13, 57–69

10. These mechanisms were analysed by Bruce G. Trigger 'Order and Freedom in Huron Society' *Anthropologica* 5 (1963) 151–69. Further research has validated their applicability to other Iroquoian and Algonquian societies in the Northeast and the Midwest: Richard White *The Middle Ground: Indians, Empires, and Republics in the Great Lakes Region, 1650–1815* (New York: Cambridge University Press 1991) 76. These mechanisms resemble those that Thomas Stone has characterized as 'forward-looking' whereby miners separated disputants or mediated between them to restore amicable relations: 'Atomistic Order and Frontier Violence: Miners and Whalemen in the Nineteenth Century Yukon' *Ethnology* 22 (1983) 327–39.

11. Reuben Gold Thwaites *The Jesuit Relations and Allied Documents* (New York: Pageant Book Company 1959) 10: 215 (hereafter *JR*). This statement is mostly confirmed by François-Joseph Le Mercier, who wrote, in 1637, that those who 'kill, rob, bewitch someone' were punished. Only traitors were not mentioned: *JR* 13: 210.

12. *JR* 10: 215. Ragueneau remarked in 1648: 'their justice is no doubt very efficacious for repressing evil, though in France it would be looked upon as injustice; for it is the public who make reparation for the offences of individuals, whether the criminal be known or remain hidden. In a word, it is the crime that is punished': *JR* 33: 233–5.

13. *JR* 33: 243

14. *JR* 10: 223–5

15. *JR* 14: 37–9; 19: 85–7

16. Archives nationales du Québec à Montréal (hereafter ANQM), Pièces judiciaires, 06 MT 1-1, box 42, 9 Aug. 1677. My thanks to Jan Grabowski for bringing this document to my attention.

17. Michel Foucault *Surveiller et punir: Naissance de la prison* (Paris: Gallimard 1975) passim

18. Recent studies stress that small-scale societies dependent on interdependence and strong interrelationships are reluctant to label offenders since labelling breaks social and economic bonds. Rather actions are labelled and, only after a gradual process involving evaluation of the disruptive effects of the action so that consensus can be achieved, is action taken. Once consensus is reached, however, punishment can be severe, including assassination. Douglas Raybeck 'Deviance, Labelling Theory, and the Concept of Scale' *Anthropologica* 33 (1991) 17–38.

19. JR 28: 49–51. A large part of this passage was rewritten almost verbatim in the 1648 *Relation* (33: 239–41). The translation of the second-last sentence is more felicitous and has been used here. On the absence of coercion see also *JR* 10: 233–5.

20. White *The Middle Ground* 52

21. Champlain, for example, was convinced that the natives had no legal code, and no form of punishment except revenge: Georges-Emile Giguère, ed. *Oeuvres de Champlain* (Montréal: Les Editions du Jour 1973) 2: 574

22. Marcel Trudel *Histoire de la Nouvelle-France* vol. 2: *Le comptoir, 1604–1627* (Montréal: Fides 1966) 486–50

23. Sources for this event are Giguère *Oeuvres de Champlain* 2: 610–14 and Gabriel Sagard *Histoire du Canada et voyage que les frères mineurs récollets y ont faicts pour la conversion des infidèles depuis l'an 1615* (Paris: Tross 1866) 1: 54–7. Although Sagard states that this murder occurred in April 1617, it is unlikely that several nations would have been gathered at Three Rivers at that time. Champlain indicates that it was towards the end of the summer of 1616, but necessarily after his departure on 20 July when the Huron and Algonquin would have been already heading home. The summer of 1617 is also a possibility since the bodies seem to have been discovered only in the spring of 1618. This incident is also discussed by Bruce G. Trigger 'Champlain Judged by His Indian Policy: A Different View of Early Canadian History' *Anthropologica* 13 (1971) 95–8.

24. According to Sagard's account, 800 natives threatened to cut all the Frenchmen's throats to prevent the French from avenging the deaths: *Histoire du Canada* 1: 54.

25. Ibid. 1: 56

26. Giguère *Oeuvres de Champlain* 3: 1047–9; Sagard *Histoire du Canada* I: 226.

27. Unhappy at the Huron reaction, Sagard remarked that when the French were stronger than the natives they would impose their will on them: *Histoire du Canada* 1: 227.

28. Sources are Giguère *Oeuvres de Champlain* 3: 1133–8, 1145–9, 1204–5; Sagard *Histoire du Canada* 3: 813–21. Trigger discusses this case in 'Champlain Judged by His Indian Policy' 98–100.

29. JR 5: 239–41

30. John Phillip Reid has emphasized the role of kin in retaliation in the far West: 'Principles of Vengeance: Fur Trappers, Indians, and Retaliation for Homicide in the Transboundary North American West' *Western Historical Quarterly* 24 (1993) 27. The Huron undoubtedly expected that Brûlé's kin would feel duty-bound to retaliate by killing the first Huron encountered.

31. JR 6: 7–17

32. JR 6: 19–21

33. JR 6: 219–21

34. Repeated violence directed against the French suggests that Reid is correct in concluding that failure to retaliate led to further aggression: 'Principles of Vengeance.'

35. That this violence was not more widespread is due to the importance of the trade alliance for the natives. The Jesuits in the Huron country were threatened because they were seen as witches responsible for the calamities befalling the nation, but the Huron could not afford to break the trade alliance: Bruce G. Trigger *The Children of Aataentsic: A History of the Huron People to 1660* (Montreal and London: McGill-Queen's University Press 1976) 2: 526–46.

36. Gabriel Sagard *Le grand voyage du pays des Hurons* ed. Marcel Trudel (Montréal: Hurtubise HMH 1976) 154–6

37. Accounts and different interpretations of this case can be found in Trigger *The Children of Aataentsic* 2: 744–50 and Lucien Campeau *La mission des jésuites chez les Hurons, 1634–1650* (Montréal: Bellarmin 1987) 272–8.

38. JR 33: 233–5

39. The account of these events is found in chapter 17 of the 1648 *Relation: JR* 33: 229–47.

40. Brébeuf, who undoubtedly witnessed a similar ceremony, describes the different parts: *JR* 10: 215–21.

41. As noted above, standard reparations seem to have been thirty presents for a man, forty for a woman, and fifty for a stranger, but the total could be as much as sixty. It is not clear, however, whether these figures refer only to the *andaerraehaan* or include the *andoanhaan*.

42. Trigger *The Children of Aataentsic* 2: 748

43. JR 10: 217

44. This was a very considerable amount, equal to three normal reparation presents.

45. John A. Dickinson 'La guerre iroquoise et la mortalité en Nouvelle-France, 1608–1666' *Revue d'histoire de l'Amérique française* 35 (1982) 34–5

46. *JR* 42: 237

47. *JR* 44: 193–5

48. *JR* 43: 169

49. *JR* 44: 95–7, 107, 111, 119

50. *JR* 44: 129

51. John A. Dickinson 'Les Amérindiens et les débuts de la Nouvelle-France; in Giovanni Dotoli and Luca Codignola, eds. *Canada ieri e oggi* (Bari: Schena editore 1986) 87–108

52. William John Eccles *The Canadian Frontier* (New York: Holt, Rinehart and Winston 1969) passim

53. Colbert to Talon, 5 Apr. 1667, *Rapport de l'Archiviste de la Province de Québec* (1930–1) 72

54. Talon to Colbert, 27 Oct. 1667, ibid. 84

55. Louise Tremblay 'La politique missionnaire des sulpiciens au XVIIe et au début du XVIIIe siècle' (M.A. thesis, Départment d'histoire, Université de Montréal 1981) 11–14, 61–70

56. *JR* 68: 225

57. John A. Dickinson and Jan Grabowski 'Les populations amérindiennes de la vallée laurentienne, 1608–1760' *Annales de démographie historique* (1993) 51–65.

58. Similar problems were encountered in the West, where violence against Frenchmen was frequent. In the single year 1684, thirty-nine Frenchmen were killed by allied Indians. Occasionally the French made a show of force and executed murderers, but more generally they pardoned them or accepted reparation payments: White *The Middle Ground* 75–93. Other examples of interracial violence are found on pages 107–8, 203–5, 229–32, 246–7. The situation deteriorated at the end of the French regime and Governor la Jonquière was forced to grant a general amnesty to all natives who had killed Frenchmen in the West to maintain the crumbling alliance: ibid. 209. Given its peculiar geopolitical situation, crimes in the West will not be dealt with here.

59. Canada *Edits, ordonances royaux, déclarations et arrêts* 2: 16–17. In 1674, drunkenness was to be punished by imprisonment and a fine of one moose hide: Pierre-Georges Roy *Ordonnances, commissions, etc., etc. des gouverneurs et intendants de la Nouvelle-France, 1639–1706* (Beauceville: L'Eclaireur 1924) 1: 163. Article XXX of the general police regulations of 11 May 1676 widened the scope to all crimes. Article XXIX stipulated that natives would be subject to corporal punishment for drunkenness: ibid. 2: 70. Later ordinances only prescribed imprisonment for drunkenness: ibid. 2: 38–40; Québec *Jugements et délibérations du Conseil Souverain* (Québec: A. Côté 1885) 4: 256–7. As Cornelius J. Jaenen has remarked, it is significant that natives were treated as a distinct group as well as being subject to general ordinances: 'The Meeting of French and Amerindians in the Seventeenth Century' *Revue de l'Université d'Ottawa* 43 (1973) 136.

60. There are only three known cases of natives being condemned for drunkenness in the Montreal district and all occurred in a twenty-one-month period between January 1688 and October 1689. A Mohawk named Anonchotte was probably sentenced to be flogged (there is no evidence that the sentence was carried out) and two others were fined ten *livres*: ANQM, Pièces judiciaries, passim.

61. Quebec *Jugements et deliberations du Conseil Souverain* 1: 570–2

62. Archives du Séminaire de Saint-Sulpice à Montréal (hereafter ASSSM), *Fonds Faillon*, FF 68–73. Tonaktouan did not obey the terms of the sentence since he was involved in a brawl four years later.

63. Ibid. FF 117

64. Archives nationales, Colonies, C11A, 43, 220–3, *Mémoire* from de Ramezay to Council, 1 Oct. 1721. With the signing of the Treaty of Montreal in 1701, the Iroquois threat was over, and this might have influenced French authorities in their efforts to deal with alcohol-related violence. However, the threat of English aggression against the colony was still present, making native military resources essential for security.

65. Ibid. 34, 23–6, Vaudreuil and Bégon to the minister 13 Nov. 1713

66. Jan Grabowski 'Searching for the Common Ground: Natives & French in Montreal, 1700–1730' (paper read at the French Colonial Historical Society Meeting, Montreal, 1992) 7.

67. Jan Grabowski 'Crime & Punishment: Sault-Saint-Louis, Lac des Deux-Montagnes and French Justice, 1713–1735' (paper read at a conference on native peoples and New France: Re-examining the Relationships, 1663–1763, McGill University, Montreal, 1992) 14.

68. Slaves, either Indian or Black, cannot be considered on the same footing as mission Indians since their legal status was different and, without family and kin connections within the colony, they had no one to defend them. Madame de Francheville's Black slave, Marie-Joseph-Angélique, was sentenced to death in 1734 for arson: Pierre-Georges Roy *Inventaire des jugements et délibérations du Conseil Supérieur de 1716 à 1760*

(Beauceville: L'Eclaireur 1932) 2: 147. Two Pawnee slaves were convicted by regular French courts in the 1750s. M. de Saint-Blin's slave, Constant, was put in the pillory and then banished for theft in 1757: ibid. 2: 203. Marie was hanged after stabbing her mistress in Three Rivers in 1759. The lower court sentence prescribed whipping, branding, and banishment, but, with the British occupying Quebec, the Superior Council sentenced her to death: ibid. 2: 213.

69. Grabowski 'Crime and Punishment' 10

70. ASSSM, L 581

71. ASSSM, HH 122

72. ANQM, Pièces judiciaires, box 132, 13 July 1735

73. Roy Inventaire 2: 202–3

74. By crossing the cultural divide separating Indians from Europeans, natives became outcasts in their own communities and could no longer count on the protection of their councils. Louis-Antoine de Bougainville mentions a Nippissing who was scorned by both native and Canadian society because he wore breeches and other French clothes, ate and slept like a Frenchman, and never went hunting or to war: Amédée Gosselin 'Le journal de M. de Bougainville' Rapport de l'Archiviste de la Province de Québec (1923–4) 271.

75. Dickinson and Grabowski 'Les populations amérindiennes' 57. During the 1720s there were only about 850 officers and men of the Troupes de la Marine for the whole colony. See, for example, Archives nationales, Colonies, C11A, 44: 26, Etat des troupes dans la colonie, 1721.

76. Quebec Jugements et délibérations du Conseil Souverain 1: 186, Ordinance of 25 Apr. 1664

77. Ibid. 1: 188–9

78. See note 59.

79. Grabowski 'Crime and Punishment' 6

80. In 1721, Marguerite Chorel declared that she was convinced that justice had nothing to do with natives but had she known the courts would act she would have complained to the judge: Grabowski 'Common Ground' 4–5.

81. Archives nationales, Colonies, C11A, 43: 220–3m Mémoire from de Ramezay to the Council, 1 Oct. 1721. In one case at least, the judge had to free a prisoner on the governor's orders before the interrogation: Grabowski 'Common Ground' 7.

82. The most dramatic example of this conflict is found in the joint letter of Governor Vaudreuil and Intendant Bégon to the minister, 5 Nov. 1713, Archives nationales, Colonies, C11A, 34: 23–6.

83. Ibid. C11B, 36: 28–9, Mémoire from the King to Vaudreuil and Bégon, 19 Mar. 1714

84. Grabowski 'Common Ground' 9–10. See also Roy Inventaires 2: 151, 165, 167, 170, 173, 202.

85. Jean Lunn 'The Illegal Fur Trade out of New France, 1713–1760' Canadian Historical Association Annual Report (1939) 61–76; Alice Jean Elizabeth Lunn Développement économique de la Nouvelle-France, 1713–1760 (Montréal: Les Presses de L'Université de Montréal 1986); Thomas Wien 'Selling Beaver Skins in North America and Europe, 1720–1760: The Uses of Fur-Trade Imperialism' Journal of the Canadian Historical Association n.s. 1 (1990) 293–317; Denys Delâge 'Les Iroquoiens chrétiens des "réductions," 1667–1760' Recherches amérindiennes au Québec 21 (1991) 65.

86. See, for example, Edict of 6 July 1709, Arrêt of 11 July 1718, Arrêt of 4 June 1719, Déclaration of 22 May 1718, Order of 14 May 1726: Canada Edits, ordonnances royaux, déclarations et arrêts 1: 320, 398, 401–2, 489, 505–6.

87. Edmund B. O'Callaghan, ed. Documents Relative to the Colonial History of New York State (Albany: Weed, Parsons 1856–87) 9: 1071

88. Archives nationales, Colonies, C11A, 43: 254–5, Vaudreuil and Bégon to the minister, 8 Oct. 1721

89. Ibid. 36: 411–12, Arrêt from the Conseil de Marine, 28 Apr. 1716

90. Only nine seizures of goods from natives were validated by the intendant: see Pierre-Georges Roy Inventaire de ordonnances des intendants de la Nouvelle-France (Beauceville: L'Eclaireur 1919) 1: 181, 229, 249, 267, 2sd; 2: 68, 75, 99, 130. In one of these cases some of the goods were returned to the native: ANQM, Pièces judiciaires, box 108, 28 Sept. 1724. Since natives had the right to transport personal effects, restitution followed. In 1740, for example, Governor Beauharnois informed the minister that three of the eleven pieces of stroud seized in 1738 had been given back to the natives because they had been purchased with the product of their hunt: Archives nationales, Colonies, C11A, 74: 4, Beauharnois to the minister, 28 Sept. 1740.

91. ASSSM, FF 194–200

92. Archives nationales, Colonies, C11A, 34: 23–6, Vaudreuil and Bégon to the minister, 5 Nov. 1713

93. Archives nationales, Colonies, C11B, 36: 28–9, Mémoire from the King to Vaudreuil and Bégon, 19 Mar. 1714

94. See, for example, the instructions given to the Marquis de la Jonquière in 1746; ibid. 83: 143, Mémoire from the King to La Jonquière, 1 Apr. 1746.

Article Seven

Violence, Marriage, and Family Honour: Aspects of the Legal Regulation of Marriage in New France

André Lachance and Sylvie Savoie

This essay falls within the framework of research into family life. For about thirty years now, researchers in Europe have been looking at the development of the family in terms of its composition and its educational, social, and economic functions. There have also been studies on contraception, sexual relations, and parent-child and husband-wife relationships. This essay is intended to shed light on some of these issues with regard to couples and families in New France.

Since the pioneer essays of Philippe Ariés, there have been important developments in the history of the family both in Europe and in North America. Although the leading research has been in demography, social and psychological studies are gradually beginning to make progress in this area as well.[1]

In Canada, works devoted to the history of the couple and the family are just beginning to appear. Monographs on the French regime have painted an idyllic picture of the pioneer family,[2] or studied the legal aspects of households,[3] but not many have focused on family attitudes or behaviour patterns. Only the studies in historical demography by Jacques Henripin and Hubert Charbonneau and the monographs by Marcel Trudel, Louise Dechêne, and John F. Bosher provide specific information on the Canadian family in the seventeenth and eighteenth centuries. Since the 1980s, however, historians and researchers in other disciplines have begun work in this new field, examining specific aspects of family life. Studies are now being done on childhood, midwives, fosterage, illegitimacy, family relationships, and matrimonial strategies which take into account the context of a new country and the influence of European traditions and habits.[4]

This essay deals with an area still largely ignored by Canadian historians: family violence and other family-related crime in seventeenth and eighteenth-century Canada. Research into this topic is hampered by the fact that in this period families went to great lengths to hide anything that might taint their honour. The code of silence played a major role in the concealment of 'family secrets' and hatreds and divisions within the family unit. Behind a façade of respectability family members hid all the things they were not supposed to talk about and tried to keep to themselves, such as abusive treatment of wives and children and disagreements between husbands and wives and parents and children. In the circumstances, it has been difficult to uncover evidence of these kinds of acts in the usual manner and, as a result, the realities of family life at that time are largely inaccessible to us. Fortunately, the judicial archives of the Prévôté de Québec, the royal jurisdictions of Montreal and Trois-Rivières, and the Superior Council of Quebec (Conseil supérieur de Québec) have records of both criminal proceedings and civil cases concerning applications for separation as to property and applications for separation as to bed and board and as to property, and these offer a glimpse of some of the realities of family life in that era. The picture is far from complete, of course, since it was only as a last resort, after trying every means of private redress, that a couple or a family would swallow its pride and expose its troubles in public by appealing to the courts. This essay is concerned with

Source: André Lachance and Sylvie Savoie, "Violence, Marriage, and Family Honour: Aspects of the Legal Regulation of Marriage in New France," in *Essays in the History of Canadian Law, volume V. Crime and Criminal Justice*, eds. Jim Phillips, Tina Loo, and Susan Lewthwaite (Toronto: University of Toronto, 1994): 143–173. Reprinted with permission of the publisher.

conflict, disorder, scandal, violence, and crime, in fact with everything that disturbed the 'normal' functioning of the family in New France.

We have searched both the civil and criminal archives of the royal tribunals of first instance of Quebec City, Montreal, and Trois-Rivières. The territorial jurisdiction of these courts of justice matched the administrative area of the government where the court was located. The tribunals of the first instance were known as 'royal jurisdictions' in Montreal and Trois-Rivières and as the Prévôté in Quebec City. Appeals from these courts were heard by the Quebec Superior Council. The council was the highest court in New France, and it had the power to make final decisions with sovereign authority in all civil and criminal cases. Theoretically it had territorial jurisdiction in all parts of New France, but since there were similar appellate courts in Louisiana (in New Orleans) and French Acadia (in Louisbourg), in practice it had jurisdiction only in Labrador, the royal posts, in Canada, in the Great Lakes Heartland, and in the area around the 'Western Sea.'[5]

Notarial deeds were also consulted with regard to separations.[6] In some cases, applications for separation as to property and the resulting financial arrangements were indeed found in the notarial archives.[7] One such case concerns Marie Josephe Aubuchon, who first entered into an amicable separation agreement drawn up by a notary although she later instituted legal proceedings in the jurisdiction of Montreal.[8] Catherine Frémont and her husband also agreed to a notarized separation as to property and as to bed and board.[9] Voluntary separations of this kind were theoretically not permitted and required confirmation by the courts to be valid, yet we were often unable to find any trace of such agreements in the records of the royal tribunals.[10] We also hoped to examine the archives of the Officialité de Québec, the ecclesiastical tribunal created by Msgr de Laval and officially recognized by the State in 1684. Unfortunately, the documents of this ecclesiastical court for the French regime seem to have disappeared.[11] Thus, our study is based mainly on the judicial records of the royal tribunals of first and last instance of Quebec, Montreal, and Trois-Rivières.

The geographical focus of our study is the St Lawrence valley. We have looked primarily at the first half of the eighteenth century, although we did use some data from the seventeenth century, and we have limited the subject-matter to couples and families. According to European and American as well as Canadian research, most families at that time consisted of a married couple and their children, sometimes a surviving grandparent, and in rare instances, an unmarried brother or sister. In Canada, the typical family was made up of a mother, a father, and four children. More complex families, such as those which included brothers and sisters of the spouses and/or elderly relatives, were far less common.[12] This study will examine the couple and the family with respect to acts which the society of that time considered breaches of the law, such as murder, physical abuse, verbal abuse, adultery, bigamy, and common law relationships.

THREATS TO MARRIAGE

But first, before studying family crimes, we must examine law and custom in regard to marriage in Canadian society in order to understand what was accepted and tolerated and what was not. In Canadian society, the married state was the norm for the majority of the adult population. Indeed, marriage was the very foundation of society and, as such, it was promoted in every possible way. The colonial government took various steps to foster marriage, offering such inducements as the 'royal gift' to encourage young people to marry early and to persuade soldiers of the Troupes de la Marine to wed local girls and establish families in the colony.[13] As a result, from the end of the seventeenth to the middle of the eighteenth century, the marriage rate remained fairly high.[14]

Marriage was strictly regulated by Church and State and governed by standards established by both canon and civil law. First and foremost, a religious marriage was a confirmation of a civil marriage. Without that sacrament, under the *ancient regime*, there was no marriage. Furthermore, such a union was indissoluble: 'the normal situation of husband and wife is to live together.'[15] Even when a secular court annulled the civil contract, the marriage sacrament remained intact. It was possible to have a marriage annulled, but only according to rules established by canon law.[16] While marriage remained a sacrament, it was seen increasingly as a contract influenced by the civil authorities.[17] Civil judges who 'in France during the seventeenth and eighteenth centuries challenged and reduced the jurisdiction of the Church in matrimonial matters' did so in the belief that marriage formed the basis of civil society.[18] The State began to assert and gradually to expand its jurisdiction over the institution of marriage.

In New France, every marriage created a new family unit which was regulated and organized in every detail according to 'custom,' regardless of the wishes of husband or wife.[19] The husband-wife partnership began not when the marriage contract was signed but when the marriage was solemnized in church.[20] Signing a marriage contract before a notary seems to have been a common custom throughout the colony.[21] Because of the influence of the *Coutume de Paris*, married couples lived in a community of property arrangement unless their marriage contract specified otherwise. The *Coutume de Paris*, officially imposed on the colony in 1664 with the creation of the West India Company, governed the organization of the family, the transfer of property, procedures for the recovery of debts, and landholdings.[22] The matrimonial regime of community property, which was the usual arrangement, included all moveables belonging to the husband and wife (furniture and moveable property) and immoveables acquired during the marriage (*acquêts*). Both spouses were liable for any moveable debts incurred by either of them prior to the marriage unless the marriage contract specified that each partner would pay any debts incurred prior to the marriage, in which case an inventory of property was to be drawn up. Private property (*biens propres*) — moveable property received from a parent, ground rent, immoveables owned on the day of marriage or subsequently acquired by succession or gift — did not enter into the community property. Private property remained within the family of the spouse who owned it.[23]

This type of matrimonial regime was characterized by the supremacy of the husband and the legal incapacity of the wife. 'The husband is lord of the moveable property and immoveable *acquests*,' wrote the jurist Ferrière in the eighteenth century.[24] The husband could dispose of, sell, 'give away or pledge the community property provided his actions were intended to be for their common good.'[25] The marital authority of the husband and the economic and legal subordination of the wife to her husband, even in domestic matters, determined how community property worked. The woman retained the status of a minor and had no legal capacity even after she reached the age of majority at twenty-five. According to Diderot's *Encyclopédie*, 'it is a husband's responsibility to defend the rights of his wife in legal proceedings.'[26] A married woman could not institute legal proceedings without her husband's permission or, in cases where he refused permission, leave from the court. She was not entitled to start a business without the consent of the person who administered the community property.[27] A married woman did not have the right to enter into contracts or other forms of legally binding obligations or to sell, dispose of, or mortgage her inheritance without the consent and permission of her husband. Even when her private property entered into the community, she had no rights over the property of that community until it was dissolved, which in most cases meant until her husband died. As long as the community survived, 'a woman's right was merely a right to protest, a potential or customary right, and the husband by whose work and industry the property was acquired was its master.'[28]

A wife's legal status was determined by the *Coutume de Paris*. However, in New France, where husbands were often absent in the Great Lakes Heartland working in the fur trade or on trips to France, it was not uncommon for a married woman to look after her family and manage the family estate on her own.[29] In such cases, a husband would give his wife the authority to manage their affairs before he left. As master of the community, the husband could, unilaterally, take any administrative action or dispose of any community-owned moveables as he saw fit.[30]

APPLICATIONS FOR SEPARATION

Although women were considered 'persons with no legal capacity,' a woman whose husband proved to be a poor manager or who ignored his family's physical well-being was permitted to institute proceedings for separation as to property and as to bed and board.[31] However, to do either, she needed her husband's permission or, failing that, leave from the court. In our examination of the archives of the Superior Council of Quebec, the royal tribunals of first instance of the Prévôté de Québec, and the royal jurisdictions of Trois-Rivières and Montreal, we found 163 applications for separation (Table 7.1). Although there may have been more — assuming some proceedings were settled before a notary — we believe the figure we have given here is fairly realistic. This procedure was not common in New France, but it did provide a way out of difficult emotional or economic situations for some women. Msgr Saint-Vallier, the second bishop of New France, wrote in the ritual for 1701 that 'although the Marriage bond cannot be broken, married persons may be separated as to living quarters, as to bed and as to property, but only on the basis of a judicial decision.'[32]

Thus, the law did offer women a right of protection. It was, however, a right women turned to only as a last resort, since the courts did not consent to separation until all other recourse had been exhausted. A woman could apply either for separation as to property only or for separation as to bed and board and as to property if her husband was not properly carrying out his role and obligations as master of the community property. In such circumstances, some women were able to limit the damage to the community property by separating. Once a woman was legally authorized to pursue her rights, she could file an application for separation as to property on grounds that the community property was being squandered, that her dowry was in jeopardy, or that her husband was insane. She could also file an application for separation as to bed and board, which always included separation as to property in any event, on grounds of cruelty and mistreatment, or physical abuse and threats, or on the grounds that her husband was

Table 7.1 Applications for Separation under the French Regime

Separations

Royal jurisdiction	Property only		Bed and board		Total
Montreal	57	(86.4%)	9	(13.6%)	66
Quebec (Prévôté)	44	(69.8%)	19	(30.2%)	63
Trois-Rivières	20	(100.0%)	0	—	20
Sovereign Council of Quebec	9	(64.3%)	5	(35.7%)	14
Total	130	(79.8%)	33	(20.2%)	163

insane and flew into 'rages,' that he had attempted to kill her or had threatened to kill her. Legal separation did not nullify the marriage, but it did permit spouses to cease living together.

Five types of separation were practised: informal separation, where the spouses lived apart without legal authorization; voluntary separation agreed to before a notary; separation by marriage contract, which affected only the property of the parties; separation as to property judicially obtained; and separation as to bed and board, where the marriage was not dissolved but the spouses were legally authorized to live apart.

How then did applying for and obtaining a separation affect a woman's legal status? According to Diderot, a separated woman was a woman 'who does not live with her husband or who is mistress of her property.'[33] A woman separated as to property could administer her property and institute legal proceedings without her husband's permission.[34] She did not, however, have the right to dispose of, sell, or mortgage that same property without either the husband's permission or leave from the court.[35] 'A separated woman,' according to the jurist Ferrière, 'cannot be made guardian of her property without such permission because it is a man's job, and for a woman to do it would be unseemly.'[36]

Furthermore, a woman who obtained a separation did not have full legal capacity. She continued to be subject to marital authority. She still required her husband's consent with respect to major decisions concerning her property, and she was merely allowed to administer her property, not to dispose of it as she saw fit. In reality, her administrative powers were limited — they extended only to her own property — and she often required her husband's agreement before she could act. The only appreciable advantage a woman gained by separation was that her husband could no longer dispose of her property and the revenues it generated with impunity. Since separation was considered a temporary arrangement, the intention was to 'protect the husband's prerogatives in case of reconciliation.'[37] If a reconciliation did take place, the responsibility of administering the community property reverted to the husband. According to attitudes of the time, allowing separated women to dispose of their property as they saw fit would be disadvantageous and even dangerous and could result in poor management or misuse of the property.[38]

Despite these legal obstacles, women did apply to the courts for separations. Who were they, and where did they come from? Clearly, most applicants lived within the royal jurisdictions of Montreal, Quebec, and Trois-Rivières. Although we have precise information on only 88 of the 163 applications (54 per cent), some major themes emerged from the data regarding applicants' place of residence (Table 7.2). The geographic distribution of applications (excluding those of undetermined location) indicates that 68 per cent originated in the cities

Table 7.2   Place of Residence of Couples Involved in Applications for Separation

Royal jurisdiction	Towns*		Outside the towns†		Total	
Montreal	23	(63.9%)	13	(36.1%)	36	(40.9%)
Quebec (Prévôté)	28	(82.4%)	6	(17.6%)	34	(38.6%)
Trois-Rivières	9	(50.0%)	9	(50.0%)	18	(20.5%)
Total	60	(68.2%)	28	(31.8%)	88	(100%)

*Montreal, Quebec, and Trois-Rivières
†Lachine, Boucherville, Rivière des Prairies, Beauport, Sainte-Foy, Batiscan, Maskinongé, etc.

of Quebec, Montreal, and Trois-Rivières, and 32 per cent in the neighbouring areas. Alain Lottin has noticed the same phenomenon, but only in the case of separation as to bed and board in the Officialité de Cambrai, 60 per cent of applications were filed by city dwellers.[39] Nancy F. Cott also found that most applications were filed by city dwellers, with three quarters of the applicants living in towns in Massachusetts and one quarter of them in Boston.[40] If we consider only the applications for separation as to bed and board brought before the royal jurisdictions, the applications came almost exclusively from the towns (nineteen from urban areas as opposed to one from outside the towns). It is as though living in an urban environment increased the grounds for separation.

Perhaps urban wives were more sensitive to abuse and could rely on greater support from their neighbours at separation hearings than women who lived in the country. It could be argued that a woman who lived in the city would be more likely to have neighbours who were familiar with her circumstances, because of the closer proximity of living quarters in urban environments. In some cases, witnesses at separation hearings testified that they were awakened at night by the sound of the husband beating his wife and the wife begging him to stop. According to A. Lottin, the crowded conditions and opportunities for escape available in cities gave rise to situations which led to separation. Also, people in rural areas tended to take longer to make up their minds about getting married than city people did.[41] Another possible explanation is that city dwellers were more familiar with separation procedures and, therefore, were more apt to separate. It should be noted that there were differences between urban and rural behaviour patterns due, from a demographic point of view, to geographic factors but also due to the fact that urban society was different and more diverse than rural society.[42]

WOMEN'S GRIEVANCES

The evidence submitted and the complaints filed by women enable us to analyse the conflicts between husbands and wives in qualitative terms. The grounds cited by applicants reveal why they sought separation as to bed and board or merely as to property. There were fixed limits to what a woman was prepared to tolerate in terms of divergent behaviour on the part of her husband. The charges alleged at separation hearings shed light on both the wife's grievances and the discord surrounding the couple's relationship.

The women's grievances reveal a real sense of anguish. Often, 'the poor supplicant is almost in despair, with no way of providing for her family's subsistence.'[43] Women applied for separation to avoid even greater misfortune. Generally, they acted before a complete collapse occurred, or before they became partially or totally insolvent. Some applicants, in particular those seeking separation as to bed and board, were attempting to escape from spousal violence and rage. Indeed, it was not unheard of for a judge, at the beginning of a hearing for separation as to bed and board, 'to prohibit [the husband], in clear and unequivocal terms, from physically abusing, disturbing or molesting [the supplicant] on pain of corporal punishment.'[44]

A woman seeking a separation as to property and a woman seeking a separation as to bed and board wanted more or less the same things. In both cases, the woman asked that her husband return with interest any sums she had brought into the marriage, that the property be seized, that an inventory be made, and that the property be divided. She also asked for compensation and that she be guaranteed payment of all amounts for which she had contracted jointly with her husband, that her personal belongings be restored to her, and that she receive support for herself and her children while awaiting dower. In the case of separation as to bed and board, the applicant also asked that she be allowed to live apart from her husband during the proceedings so as to avoid abuse and that her husband be prohibited from seeing her.

PRINCIPAL CATEGORIES OF COMPLAINT

At first glance, it would appear that the complaints and evidence follow a stereotype. They fall into three main categories: alcoholism, mistreatment (physical and verbal abuse), and family irresponsibility (inability of the husband to meet the needs of his family and his lack of involvement in family life). Such grounds were successfully raised in cases before the royal courts throughout the period studied. Were there other, undeclared reasons for marital incompatibility? Did the reasons cited by women come under valid grounds provided for under secular law? As grounds for separation as to property, the courts accepted squandering of property and insanity of the husband and, as grounds for separation as to bed and board and as to property, cruelty, and mistreatment, the fact that the husband was insane and flew into 'rages,' and physical abuse and threats. Although there may have been other underlying problems, the allegations in these categories — alcoholism, mistreatment, and family irresponsibility — were confirmed by witnesses who were, in many cases, neighbours of the couple. The charges were usually interrelated, especially in cases involving separating as to bed and board and as to property.

A plaintiff seeking a separation did not plead adultery as a cause. Secular law at that time was opposed to a woman pleading her husband's adultery.[45] In our research, we found only four references to 'other women.' In one such reference, a witness stated: 'I have known Mr. St-Aubin for about eleven years and for the past four or five years his behaviour has been rather disgraceful. He chases after women and he drinks.'[46]

In the case of alcohol, the law agreed with women that it disrupted family life, since habitual drinking usually meant spending time in bars, debauchery, and gambling. One witness testified that 'the said Ledoux is completely dissolute,' that he had very often seen him drunk, and that, moreover, he was not in his right mind and was going mad.[47] Another witness stated that on three or four occasions he had seen a man named Buisson (whose wife was seeking a separation) 'pass by his house fully clothed and return without his clothes or shoes on, and the rumour was that he sold his clothes in order to drink.'[48] The behaviour (misconduct) of a husband described as violent, disturbed, and given to excess was bound to interfere with the economic stability of the conjugal unit and lead to poverty and violence. How important was alcohol abuse compared to other grounds for complaints by women? Although alcoholism was not the main cause of separation, it was often the catalyst, since it usually resulted in family irresponsibility and cruelty. Alcohol is mentioned in 16.8 per cent of the cases (25 references). In one case, Etiennette Alton's husband asked her for money to buy wine. When she refused, he hit her with a stick to express his displeasure.[49]

Often, or, to be more precise, in 23.5 per cent of cases (35 references), women who applied for separation as to bed and board and as to property complained of being physically abused by their spouses. Marie Boucher said that her husband, Nicolas Vernet, severely abused her. Her evidence was supported by witnesses who stated that she had to leave her house at night to escape his beatings.[50] Women were not the only victims of male violence in families; children too were physically abused. One witness at a hearing said that he 'heard [people say] that when the said Buisson was drunk he would beat his wife and children so badly they had to leave the house,' adding that he 'saw them come out crying and complaining of their plight.'[51]

Under the *ancien régime*, a husband had a right, albeit limited, of correction over his wife. It was accepted that just as a father was entitled to discipline his children, a husband was entitled to inflict corporal punishment on his wife, since legally a woman was considered a child. However, the society of the time did impose some restrictions on the husband's right of correction. To begin with, the punishment had to be justified by the wife's behaviour, but even then, it could not go beyond certain limits. In general, husbands were allowed to hit their wives so long as they did not use sharp or blunt instruments or cause any injuries. Wife-battering was an art and men who did not want to be seen in a bad light by those around them were obliged to follow certain rules. They had to avoid hitting any sensitive area or vital organ, such as the head, breasts, or stomach; slaps, jabs, kicks, and punches on the backside were permissible provided they did not leave lasting marks.[52]

In the eighteenth century, the husband's customary right of correction over his wife gradually disappeared. In *Habitants et marchands de Montréal*, Louis Dechêne notes that there were no proceedings concerning spousal violence in the seventeenth century.[53] We found references to physical abuse in only nine of the applications for separation as to bed and board and as to property brought in the seventeenth century, but thirty-three such references in the applications brought in the eighteenth century. Moreover, the number of applications for separation as to bed and board and as to property more than tripled during that time. Does this mean that women and others in Canadian society were becoming less and less tolerant of abuse as the century progressed? While the figures seem to lead to that conclusion, the increase in both the population and the number of marriages during the eighteenth century should also be taken into account. Alain Lottin notes that in France, in the Officialité de Cambrai, separation as to bed and board was more common the second third of the eighteenth century (1737–74) than in the first third (1710–36).[54] Jean-Louise Flandrin confirms that wife-battering could no longer be justified as 'a duty to correct, which disappeared gradually' during the eighteenth century.[55] However, canon law continued to assert that 'a wife is subject to correction on the part of her husband.'[56] In Canada, society still appeared to tolerate limited use of that right. For example, the royal judges in Montreal were far from offended by the paradoxical explanation offered by two husbands as to why they had beaten their wives. One, whose wife was on trial for assault, said he had done it to show that 'he was opposed to all violence,'[57] while the other, whose wife was on trial for theft, claimed he had done it to cure her of stealing.[58]

Separation applications were brought by women from all social levels. However, women who applied for separation as to property only were not typical: they seem to have been better educated and more self-assertive than those who applied for separation as to bed and board. In many cases, they were women who looked after their husbands' business affairs when they were away or who were in business with their husbands. In general, as the wives of businessmen, merchants, or civil or military officers, they were members of the upper class. Most women who applied for separations as to bed and board, in contrast, were the wives of artisans and tradesmen and were therefore, as in France and New England at that time, regarded as members of the middle classes.[59] It should also be noted that separation as to bed and board was generally considered an extreme solution and, as indicated by the figures quoted above, it was fairly rare.

At hearings concerning separation as to bed and board, a husband accused by his wife of beating her defended himself by claiming his right of correction. In one case, a husband was indignant with his wife for complaining that he had struck her, saying that he 'reprimanded her only when she deserved it.'[60] In another case a husband pointed out that he had never abused his wife except 'when she made him lose his temper and drove him to it,' adding that although his wife appeared 'to have a few bruises today' on her face and body, it was 'not because he mistreated her,' since he had merely given her 'what she asked for — a slap across the face.'[61] Clearly then, in the eyes of husbands and society in general, the use of physical force could be justified on the grounds of the wife's conduct. For example, Françoise Duval, known as *Vinaigre*, stated that her husband 'beat her senseless' when he learned that she had prostituted herself with the skipper of a small boat in the port of Montreal.[62] Furthermore, if a woman who complained of physical abuse wanted to obtain a separation, she had to prove to the royal judges that her husband had indeed beaten her excessively. For example, Etiennette Alton had to produce a report signed by a surgeon as proof of 'the condition of the illness or injury' she claimed she suffered following abusive treatment at the hands of her husband.[63]

Limited violence was tolerated socially and did not lead to assault charges or to applications for separation as to bed and board on the grounds of abuse. However, neither wife nor society could continue to condone abuse that went beyond the permissible limits, as illustrated by the case of Françoise Petit-Boismorel. Françoise, who apparently did not wish to separate from her husband but rather to stop him from beating her, laid a complaint of assault before the royal jurisdiction of Montreal against her husband, the royal bailiff Antoine Puyperoux, Sieur de la Fosse. Fleury Deschambault, the judge before whom the couple appeared, settled the case by ordering temporary separation as to bed and board. However, some time later Françoise and Antoine resumed living together and he began beating her again. This time, Françoise's brother, Etienne, had to intervene forcefully to stop Puyperoux from hitting his sister, who, the bailiff claimed, had failed to arrange for firewood to be brought into the house.[64] We do not know how this case was resolved.

In cases of separation as to bed and board and as to property where mistreatment was alleged, witnesses who testified at hearings before royal judges confirmed the women's allegations. They stated that certain men were known to beat their wives and leave their children stark naked,[65] or that on several occasions they had seen the men lose their tempers and physically attack their wives, hitting them with sticks and kicking and punching them.[66] In the case of Jeanne Duplessis Faber, wife of Sieur Bailly de Baieuville, an officer in the Troupes de la Marine, the witnesses were Jean-Baptiste Petit, a Montreal carpenter, and his wife, who lived in the apartment next door to the Baieuvilles. They stated at the hearing that they had been awakened at night by noise from the Baieuville apartment and that, when they listened through the partition-wall, they could hear Madame Baieuville crying and carrying on and saying to her husband, 'Leave me alone, I beg you, you'll kill me, I'll scream." But Baieuville, jealous of the attention his wife had shown a visiting wig-maker, continued to beat her. She moaned and groaned and pleaded with him in a low voice, saying 'Leave me alone, please, I won't do it anymore. I'm sorry.' The Petits told the judge that the woman endured this abuse 'from eleven o'clock in the evening until about three or four o'clock the next morning.' They said that the following day they noticed she had 'scratches' on her face.[67]

When a man beat his wife at night to the point that her cries disturbed the neighbours, his violence towards her was regarded as serious enough to warrant intervention. Witnesses at hearings concerning applications for separation often described how they and others stepped in when the husband was beating his wife. In some cases, they managed to make him stop hitting her.[68] In other instances, the man continued to punch his wife and 'refused to listen to reason from neighbours or passers-by who witnessed the event.'[69] In addition, witnesses' statements were often tinged with indignation at the husband's disgraceful treatment of his wife and children. In their eyes, it seemed, there was no excuse for the husband's excessive physical abuse.

Family members also came to the aid of their daughters or sisters. Indeed, sometimes the father and/or brother of the victim took the initiative and became involved in the couple's quarrels. Such was the case of Marie-Renée Gauthier de Varennes, who had been abused for a number of years by her husband Timothée Sylvain, the King's doctor in Montreal. Her father, Pierre Gauthier de la Vérendrye, remonstrated with the husband a few times, but nothing came of it; Sylvain continued to beat his wife. Finally, Pierre Gauthier de la Vérendrye had had enough. With the help of his son, Gauthier de Varennes, he removed his daughter from the marital home and brought her back to live under the paternal roof. Ultimately, Marie-Renée was granted a separation as to bed and board by the royal court of the jurisdiction of Montreal.[70] Similarly, when Antoine Puyperoux, in the case mentioned above, beat his wife, Françoise Petit-Boismorel, her brother Etienne came to her aid.[71]

Clearly, married couples and their children did not live in isolation. In towns, they were constantly under observation, watched by people who lived in the same house, by their parents, by their neighbours, by the parish priest. They were continually aware of the image they projected, and they tried to appear dignified and honourable because their reputation and credibility in the community depended very much on how others saw them.[72] There was almost no privacy in the modern sense of the word. Their neighbours knew everything about them. They lived on the same street as people who might be called to give evidence about them. For instance, one witness was introduced as follows: 'For a year now he has been living in the aforementioned street practically opposite the house [of Marie-Madeleine Darragon and Julien Delière, dit Bonvouloir].[73] In the towns, there was often nothing more than a thin partition-wall separating the residence of the witness from the residence of the defendant. As Jean-Baptiste stated at the hearing mentioned above, his wife awakened him and told him to 'listen to that Sieur Baieuville beating his wife,' which he did, through the partition.[74] In another case, the witness worked in the shop adjoining the complainant's house.[75] Thus, a couple's relationship was subject to constant scrutiny by the community, so that when a husband behaved badly towards his wife, either because he mistreated her or because of excessive spending, the whole neighbourhood knew about it. According to one witness, 'what the supplicant alleges is only too well-known by the public,'[76] while another stated that several people had been witness to the couple's marital disputes.[77]

Spousal violence was of concern to the whole community. The conduct of a man who 'held his wife by the hair' was 'upsetting to the whole lower town,' according to testimony at a hearing for separation as to bed and board.[78] A dispute between husband and wife created a scandal and cast a shadow over the idealized picture of marriage which the elite hoped to promote. For example, one witness in a case testified: 'her husband beat her [his wife] every day without fail in full view of everyone — the more affluent people of the town were scandalized.'[79]

Every now and then spousal violence led one of the partners to commit murder. In 1751, Nicolas de Launay, dit Lacroix, who lived in Pointe-à-la Caille near Quebec City, killed his wife with an axe.[80] Marie-Josephe Ethier killed her husband in the same way, and then ran off with her lover.[81] In this last case, it appears the adulterer was behind the husband's murder. Unfortunately, the reason for the first murder is unknown. Except for one involuntary homicide where a husband killed his wife accidentally — his gun was 'at rest under his arm' when it accidentally discharged[82]— these were the only two cases of family-related murder we found.

Nearly one-third of husbands (30 per cent or 49 out of 163) whose wives applied for separation intervened during the legal proceedings. In cases of applications for separation as to bed and board and as to property or as to property only, attitudes varied. Some men refused to grant their wives permission to proceed, denied the facts presented in the complaint, as we have seen, or categorically refused and opposed the requested separation. Others reprimanded the witnesses. In the end, a few asked their wives to come back home, and the rest agreed to the separation.

Whether men did or did not agree to separations, their reactions described what they expected of their wives. A wife should not meddle in business matters without her husband's permission but should help him maintain and increase his property. A wife is obliged to behave according to her station and to abstain from foolish expenditures beyond her social class. One husband said he needed his wife with him 'in order to keep his expenses down.'[83] In addition, it is a wife's job 'to take good care of her family and to make sure her children are well brought up.'[84] The ideal wife was a virtuous woman whose behaviour was constant and beyond reproach. According to Msgr Laval, a woman should 'love her husband sincerely and affectionately, sharing all his concerns, both temporal and spiritual; always make an effort to win him over to God through her prayers, her good example, and other appropriate means; obey him, treat him with respect and gentleness, and be patient with him when he makes mistakes or is in a bad mood.'[85]

DECISIONS RENDERED

The decisions of the royal judges were influenced by the expectations of both wives and society and also by the role that women were traditionally expected to play. The number of decisions we were able to find (73 out of 163, or 45 per cent — see Table 7.3) is too small to enable us to confirm whether there was in fact a trend towards adopting more modern attitudes — for instance, making separations easier to obtain and reducing the level of toleration of violence and irresponsible behaviour on the part of the husband. Separation applications were denied in cases where the applicant failed to present enough evidence to prove the allegations against her husband or where the applicant's relatives were found to have been excessively involved in the disagreement. Of the fifty-one applications for separation as to property where the results are known, only one application was denied, but of the twenty-two applications for separation as to bed and board and as to property where the results are known, six (27.3 per cent) were not granted. The State, like the Church, seems to have been much more cautious about agreeing to separation as to bed and board. A. Lottin emphasizes that in-laws were 'if not the cause, [at least] the catalyst of conflicts which led to separation.'[86] In some cases, husband and wife agreed to stop the proceedings, rent a house, and resume living together away from their parents. Relatives and family solidarity clearly interfered with marital relationships. Women often went back to live with their parents to avoid mistreatment. When relatives became too deeply enmeshed in a couple's household they were liable to exacerbate disagreements between husbands and wives. In any case, that was the opinion of the public prosecutor and it is also what the documents tell us.

Separation applications were also denied in cases where a woman criticized her husband's behaviour in ways considered unacceptable. If a woman protested against her husband's attacks in an aggressive manner, verbally or otherwise, she was not granted a separation. For example, 'the wife of the said Lenclus was just as violent towards her husband as he was capable of behaving towards her.' The result was that 'the woman Lapierre was ordered to go back to her husband, and both parties were directed to live together amicably or face a prison sentence.'[87]

If a woman admitted abusing her husband, she no longer deserved permission to separate. The wife of one defendant 'was in an extraordinary rage, fuming and swearing like a sailor, saying every stupid thing imaginable against her husband and her children.'[88] A woman who did not devote herself to helping her husband manage 'the family finances' and who squandered the community property could be sure her separation application would be denied, as happened in the case of the wife of a certain Mr Demers. 'It is really too bad about Demers,' said a witness at the hearing. 'He was a decent man and things were going well for him until he married that women — he has been in financial trouble ever since.'[89]

Table 7.3   Results of Separation Hearings

Separation	As to property		As to bed and board		Total	
Granted	50	(38.5%)	16	(48.5%)	66	(40.5%)
Denied	1	(0.7%)	6	(18.2%)	7	(4.3%)
Unknown	79	(60.8%)	11	(33.3%)	90	(55.2%)
Total	130	(79.8%)	33	(20.2%)	163	(100%)

The prosecutor would dismiss an application from a wife who caused quarrels, who provoked the husband, or who behaved improperly. In one case, a witness said, 'the arguments were always started by Marie Vendezeque and she was the cause of all the unpleasantness in the household.'[90] In such cases, the applicant would be prohibited 'from leaving the house or going anywhere without her husband's permission.'[91] In many cases where separation as to bed and board and as to property was denied, the wife was ordered to 'go back and live with her husband, and he was directed to treat her as a good husband should.'[92] Thus, if a woman wanted to apply for a separation, her conduct had to be beyond reproach. If she had ever given her husband the slightest reason to mistreat her, her application would be denied. She had to show that she had been patient, that she had not retaliated when her husband abused her, and that she had always behaved properly regardless of the circumstances. Consequently, separations were granted only in cases where the evidence was irrefutable and the grounds were very serious.

Most of the time, when the courts granted a separation they did so in order to maintain the social and economic function of the marriage and the family; that is, their purpose was to protect the property necessary for the family's survival. Protecting the rights of the wife as a person was often incidental. The courts did not grant separations as to bed and board and as to property except in extreme cases, because 'the separation of spouses breaks up the estate, disrupts lines of descent, and weakens the social order.'[93]

ADULTERY

In this context, 'the obligations of a husband and wife were to live together in holy matrimony,' each with a role to play according to the example set by Joseph and the Blessed Virgin.[94] Anything that might endanger the union of man and wife and its corollary, the family, was severely punished. Adultery, for instance, was regarded as a threat to the unity of both the couple and the family and to its principal function, the perpetuation and preservation of the human race. In dealing with this offence, society adopted a double standard.[95] A woman was not entitled to lodge a complaint if her husband committed adultery. Legally, she was considered a minor and therefore had no right of recrimination against her husband who, in the eyes of the law, was her superior. A man, in contrast, was entitled to sue his wife for the same offence. A woman who was found guilty of the crime of adultery was usually ordered to apologize to her husband, in addition to being deprived of her dower. Generally, the judge allowed the cuckolded husband various options with respect to the physical punishment of his wife. He could have her put away in a convent at his expense, send her to live with her family, send her back to France if she was an immigrant, or simply take her back. A man was also entitled to apply for separation as to bed and board on the ground of adultery. Women, however, were prohibited under civil law from applying for separation on the ground of adultery alone. A woman's application would be allowed by the court only if she could cite other grounds such as those discussed above. In any case, women did not seek redress in the courts except as a last resort. A woman tended to tolerate her husband's bad behaviour for a long time before turning to the courts, because to expose her situation publicly was to admit her marriage was a failure. The lover of a woman found guilty of adultery was usually banished from the colony, fined, and ordered to pay damages and interest to the husband. In addition, the courts frequently required lovers to provide care and support for any children born as a result of such relationships. According to Sara Matthews Grieco, 'discrimination in favour of the husband in adultery cases was based, in particular, on the value attached to the chastity of women in a patriarchal society, where property circulated mainly in the hands of men' and women were considered 'property which declined in value when used by someone other than the legitimate owner.'[96]

In our study of the case law, we found eight cases of adultery in Canada in the seventeenth century (1650–99), but only one in the eighteenth. That trial involved Geneviève Maillet, her husband Pierre Roy, a sailor, and Pierre Sillon, known as Larochelle, also a sailor. As soon as he arrived in the colony, Pierre Sillon, aided and abetted by Geneviève Maillet, began passing himself off as Pierre Roy, Geneviève's husband. For a time, the pair succeeded in their subterfuge, living together openly and publicly for three months. However, when Sillon decided to go off on a fishing expedition without leaving any money behind for his mistress, who was pregnant with his child, the truth came out. Geneviève lost no time in coming before the intendant, Hocquart, claiming that 'her husband Pierre Roy known as Larochelle' had promised to pay her forty pounds out of his wages. When Pierre Sillon was pressed by the authorities to pay that sum, he admitted that although he and Geneviève Maillet had lived together as 'man and wife,' he was not her husband. The two lovers were tried for 'having abused the sanctity of marriage by living together publicly as husband and wife in an adulterous relationship.' They were found guilty. The court ordered Geneviève and Pierre to make an *amende honourable* in front of the 'main gates of the cathedral' and sentenced them both to be flogged 'in the usual public places and localities' in Quebec City. In addition, the court ordered that Madame Maillet be incarcerated in the Hôpital Général de Québec for three years. As for Pierre Sillon, he was banished from the colony for three years and ordered to take into his care — that is, 'feed, support and raise in the Catholic religion' at his expense — the child Geneviève was carrying.[97]

It should be pointed out, however, that there were probably numerous instances of adultery between voyageurs and Amerindians in the fur-trading areas. A white man travelling in the Great Lakes Heartland found it advisable in terms of survival to have an Amerindian woman at his side who could act as an interpreter and guide, prepare the skins, and so on. Voyageurs and traders often scandalized the missionaries by marrying 'according to the custom of the country,' that is, in accordance with Amerindian custom. An Amerindian common law wife, following her traditions, stayed in her marriage as long as her husband remained in the trading areas. When her white spouse returned to Canada's colony, she took the Métis children he had left behind and returned to live with her tribe.[98] The Canadian justice system never dealt with such cases of bigamy or adultery. Neither the justice system nor the colonial society of the time saw the Amerindians as a threat to the institution of the family, since the voyageurs usually came back to take care of their families in the colony.

Indeed, we found only one bigamy case in the eighteenth century. This is surprising in view of the fact that in the colony at that time it was extremely easy for a European to deceive the authorities into thinking he was free to marry. Being far away from his native country and not required, as he would have been in France, to produce papers regarding his civil status, an immigrant merely had to assert that he had not been married in France and, if necessary, to name a few witnesses currently in Canada who had known him in the mother country.[99] Although Robert-Lionel Séguin counted eight cases of bigamy in the seventeenth century, that number can be explained by the fact that the earlier period saw a greater influx of immigrants.[100]

The only bigamy case in the eighteenth century involved Jean-Julien Mainguy, dit Duplessis, who was originally from France. In 1726, in Charlesbourg, he married Marie-Josephe Valade, even though he was still bound to one Julienne Le Tessier, whom he had married in France in 1717 in a religious ceremony. Duplessis' Canadian wife had had three children by him by the time the bigamy was discovered and the marriage annulled.[101] There is no record of what became of the bigamist. Perhaps the reason why there were so few bigamy cases is that the men were far away from their mother country and the wives they had abandoned in France had no way of knowing where their husbands were.

Living in a consensual union was another crime which was seen as a possible threat to the institution of marriage in New France. Generally speaking, Canadian society was tolerant of common law relationships. It was understood that in most cases people lived in such relationships because the authorities, as a result of parental opposition, refused to give them permission to marry. Parents did not want their child to marry into a family which was socially inferior or did not have a good reputation. Robert-Lionel Séguin found six instances of couples living common law in the seventeenth century.[102] In the eighteenth century, we found only two. One case involved Jean-Baptiste Joubert and Geneviève Gendron. The parish priest at Sault-Saint-Louis would not marry them because of the opposition of Joubert's parents, who claimed that Geneviève was 'an immoral girl who had just given birth to a baby who was not their son's child' and that her family was disreputable too. Indeed, in 1734, one of Geneviève's sisters, Marie-Anne, had been sentenced to be hanged for the murder of her newborn child. Ultimately, in the face of the young couple's determination and their *mariage à la gaumine* at the parish church in Montreal in 1740,[103] the priest from Châteauguay married them on 18 January 1741.[104]

FAMILY REPUTATION AND FAMILY HONOUR

As the Joubert-Gendron case shows, a family's honour and reputation within its social circle was of paramount importance and had to be defended at all costs. According to Arlette Farge, under the *ancien régime* 'honour was considered as essential an asset as life itself and had to be defended by any means necessary.'[105] In New France, where this concept of honour was accepted as a given, it formed the basis of an entire social system which relied, in particular, on the social impact of reputation and public gossip.[106] Everyone was always judging everyone else. They divided each other into two groups — those who had a good name and were respected in the community and those who 'were not worth much,' such as the itinerant schoolteacher Jean-Baptiste Caron. Sent to New France by order of the king for smuggling salt, Caron was subsequently accused in the colony of stealing clothes.[107] In criminal trials, judges often questioned witnesses about the accused's reputation, and the witnesses answered by telling the court whether the person was or was not well thought of within his or her social circle. For example, in one case a witness testified that the accused was known as 'a very honest man' and that if he had been a 'good-for-nothing,' he (the witness) would not have had anything to do with him, while in another case a witness stated that the accused 'did not have a good reputation.'[108]

New France was basically an oral society, a place where the spoken word reigned supreme. People could measure their status, recognition, and esteem in the community by what others said about them. There was no question but that words were a powerful tool for regulating behaviour. 'Public gossip' defined a person's honour and reputation, creating perceptions which could only be overcome by the most overwhelming evidence. It was very difficult to convince people that men and women in their neighbourhood whom they had previously respected were disreputable, just as it was almost impossible to rehabilitate a bad reputation. The following is a case in point. In the Gouriaux, Duval, and Dumesnil families, both the men and the women had on several occasions been found guilty of stealing. In addition, the women were referred to as 'floozies [women of little virtue] who will sleep with anybody.' Those families were marked, and no other family would associate with them except for those of similar ill repute. It was said of the Gouriaux family at the time that its members were 'reputed to be guilty of all sorts of vices, including stealing and other shenanigans,' and that they 'have always had a bad reputation.'[109]

In such a climate, any comment that was offensive, defamatory, or even just evasive could have a disastrous effect on a person's reputation. Questioning the virginity or the sexual honesty of a woman was an attack both on the woman herself and on any man associated with her. Accordingly, the most common insult against a woman was the epithet 'whore' or any of its variations, such as 'tart,' 'hooker,' 'floozie,' or 'loose woman.'[110] A woman's honour was based essentially on sexuality (premarital virginity and conjugal fidelity) and on motherhood,[111] and one of the primary duties of the husband and father was to defend the honour and reputation of 'his' women and his family. For instance, Antoine Poudret Jr, a baker, took on the role of defender of female honour when he assaulted the master mason, Jean-Baptiste Payette known as St-Armour, for calling his wife a 'bloody whore.'[112] In some cases, fathers went to court to claim compensation when a daughter's virginity was called into question. In July 1714, Henry Delaunay, master wheelwright, appeared before Rouer D'Artigny, a judge at the Prévôté de Québec, to ask that the honour and reputation of his daughter Barbe be 'repaired' following statements made in public by Jean-Baptiste La Grange dit Toulouse, a domestic at the Hôtel-Dieu de Québec, to the effect that he had seen Barbe Delaunay with a man in a field 'in an indecent posture committing the crime of fornication.'[113] There were also assault cases where the whole family banded together to avenge the honour of the women of the clan, as in the case of Charles Leblanc of Côte St Michel near Montreal. Charles, his wife, and their two sons and two daughters all attacked the innkeeper Pierre Drouin, hitting him on the head with sticks, in revenge for his having insulted them by suggesting to one Joseph Roger, a lumberjack who was in love with one of Charles' daughters, Marie-Suzanne, that 'if he wanted to get her he should screw her.'[114]

The use of gossip to malign reputations and spread rumours was probably the most common form of self-regulation in Canada at that time. If a victim wanted to repair the damage to his reputation, he could always take matters into his own hands. There were more coercive forms of social control as well. One deterrent used to deal with flagrant breaches of established rules was, of course, to bring people before the courts. Another was the ritual of humiliation known as the charivari, where offenders were subjected to ridicule and mild forms of persecution. The charivari was a shrill musical parody organized by young people to show community disapproval in cases where a widow or widower remarried too soon following the death of a spouse or where there was too big an age difference between husband and wife. The cacophony of sound which characterized these raucous events echoed the social disorder which was being condemned. A group of young people would get together, go to the house of the newly married couple, and 'serenade' them with mockery and insults. The performance would be repeated every evening until the couple agreed to buy some peace and quiet by giving money, food, or drink to the 'musicians.' An event of this nature occurred in Montreal in December 1717, following the marriage in late November of Pierre Chartier, a forty-seven-year-old bachelor and merchant, to twenty-four-year-old Catherine Catin. A group of young men, resentful at having been done out of a young woman their age by an 'old geezer,' expressed their disapproval by holding a charivari near the merchant's house. The newlyweds refused to pay them, so the 'musicians' came back every evening for over a month to 'taunt' the couple, ultimately forcing their way into the house. This last incident so provoked the husband that he had the principal assailants charged with verbal and physical abuse.[115]

CONCLUSION

In conclusion, it is clear that the men and women of New France were bound by the Church, the State, and society. The Church and the State, who had the power to grant or refuse permission for couples to separate, exercised scrutiny and control over the lives of married couples. Both Church and State intended by their interventions (laws, instructions, regulations) to protect the stability of the couple and the family, at that time the natural environment in which individuals spent the most essential part of their lives. The community, in particular neighbours, also watched what was going on in peoples' homes. They saw to it that married couples conformed to prevailing social and religious values. When scandals erupted or people behaved in a disgraceful manner, neighbours intervened to help put straying couples back on the right path.

The influence of the *ancien régime* in New France led to a society where married couples and families were always watching each other. Scrutiny by neighbours and gossip elicited by inappropriate behaviour constituted a first line of defence against disorder. It is important also to remember that for the popular classes — labourers, artisans, shopkeepers, and the like — defending the honour of their families in conflicts involving such issues as assault, petty theft, and deception was not only a means of self-defence and assertion, but an opportunity for self-affirmation.[116] It was only when gossip proved ineffective that society turned to more elaborate forms of control. Generally, people saw the courts as a last resort and went to great lengths to avoid that recourse. Under the social system of New France in the seventeenth and eighteenth centuries, compromise and self-regulation were considered preferable to public punishment.

NOTES

1. P. Ariès *L'enfant et la vie familiale sous l'Ancien Régime* (Paris: Seuil 1973) and 'La famille, hier et aujourd'hui' *Contrepoint* 11 (1973) 89–97; A. Armengaud *La famille et l'enfant en France et en Angleterre du XVIe au XVIIe siècle: Aspects démographiques* (Paris: SEDES 1975); D. Blake Smith 'The Study of the Family in Early America: Trends, Problems and Prospects' *The Family in Early America* 34 (1982) 3–28; A. Colomp *La maison du père* (Paris: PUF 1983). See also the special issues of *Annales Economie Société Civilisation* (hereafter AESC) (1972) and of *Revue d'histoire de l'Amérique française* (hereafter RHAF) 39 (1985) on the family and society; T.K. Kareven 'The History of the Family as an Interdisciplinary Field' *Journal of Interdisciplinary History* 2 (1971) 399–414; J. Parr, ed. *Childhood and Family in Canadian History* (Toronto: McClelland and Stewart 1982).

2. G. Poulin *Problèmes de la famille canadienne-française* (Québec: PUL 1952) 9–27

3. J. Boucher and A. Morel *Livre du centenaire du Code civil: Le droit dans la vie familiale* 2 vols. (Montréal: PUM 1970)

4. J. Henripin *La population canadienne au début du XVIIIe siècle: Nuptialité, fécondité, mortalité infantile* (Paris: PUF 1954); H. Charbonneau *Vie et mort de nos ancêtres: Etude démographique* (Montréal: PUM 1975); M. Trudel *Montréal: La formation d'une société* (Montréal: Fides 1976) and *La Seigneurie des Cent-Associés* (Montréal: Fides 1983). The last devotes a chapter to the colonial family, describing its composition and structures in quantitative terms. Only L. Dechêne *Habitants et marchands de Montréal au XVIIe siècle* (Montréal and Paris: Plon 1974), after examining the composition of the households and the legal aspects which governed them, deals with the issue of family attitudes and behaviour patterns. J.F. Bosher 'The Family in New France' in R.D. Frances and D.B. Smith, eds. *Readings in Canadian History: Pre-Confederation* (Toronto: Holt, Rinehart and Winston 1986) 101–11 presents a general synthesis of this issue. The Collectif Clio *L'histoire des femmes au Québec depuis quatre siècles* (Montréal: Quinze 1982) also deals with the family from these perspectives, but puts more emphasis on the role of the woman within the family. The more recent research, which has grown out of the fertile ground provided by demography, anthropology, and sociology and which illustrates the interest generated by the family in New France since 1980, should also be mentioned. See M.-A. Cliché 'Fille-mères,' familles et société sous le régime français' *Histoire sociale — Social History* 21 (1988) 39–69 and 'L'infanticide dans la région de Québec, 1660–1969' *RHAF* 44 (1990) 31–59; D. Gauvreau 'Nuptialité et categories professionelles à Québec pendant le régime français' *Sociologie et société* 19 (1987) 25–35, and 'À propos de la mise en nourrice à Québec pendant le régime français' *RHAF* 41 (1987) 53–61; H. Laforce *Histoire de la sage-femme dans la région de Québec* (Québec: Institut québécois de recherché sur la culture 1985); J. Mathieu et al. 'Les alliances matrimoniales exogames dans le government de Québec, 1700–1760' *RHAF* 35 (1985) 3–32. We would also point out the many works in historical demography which have increased our knowledge about the family of that era: see especially H. Charbonneau et al. *Naissance d'une population: Les Français établis au Canada au XVIIe siècle* (Paris and Montréal: Presses universitaires de France and Presses de l'Université de Montréal 1987).

5. A. Lachance *Crimes et criminels en Nouvelle-France* (Montréal: Boréal 1984) 17–18.

6. We examined the court documents of the royal tribunals of Trois-Rivières, Québec, and Montréal from 1668 to 1760.

7. Although the notarial archives have not been examined in a systematic manner, research on separations before a notary enables us to assess the importance of this phenomenon.

8. National Archives of Quebec (hereafter ANQ), Montreal, Pièces judiciaires, 7 July 1740

9. ANQ, Montreal, Greffe du notaire Gervais Hodiesme, minute 3576, 3 July 1760

10. Diderot says that 'voluntary separations are not recognized' and that 'every separation as to property and as to bed and board or even just as to property . . . must be ordered by a court having full knowledge of the facts': *Encyclopédie* . . . 36 vols. (Geneva: Pellet 1777–9) vol. 8: 675 and 30: 827.

11. Nothing remains of the files of the Officialité du régime français. On the subject of the jurisdiction of the Officialité see A. Corvisier *Sources et méthodes en histoire sociale* (Paris: Société d'Enseignement supérieur 1980) and A. Lottin 'Vie et mort du couple; difficultés conjugales et divorces dans le nord de la France aux XVIIe et XVIIIe siècles *XVIIe siècle* 102–3 (1974) 59. The authors agree that the *officialités* gradually lost their jurisdiction over matrimonial cases, which were increasingly heard by secular judges in the eighteenth century. We do not know what happened in New France because of the lack of documents.

12. Dechêne *Habitants et marchands* 417

13. H. Charbonneau and Y. Landry 'La politique démographique en Nouvelle France' *Annales de démographie historique* (1979) 43–5

14. Collectif Clio *L'histoire des femmes au Québec depuis quatre siècles* (Montréal: Le Jour 1992) 91; Charbonneau *Vie et mort de nos ancêtres* 150–66.

15. A. Lottin *La désunion du couple sous l'Ancien Régime: L'exemple du Nord* (Paris: Editions Universitaires 1975) 24

16. Ibid. 137. The limited number of valid reasons (formal defect, lack of consent, bigamy, failure to reach puberty, impotence, non-consummation, and kinship) certainly limited the number of applications.

17. With respect to the trend towards marriage by contract rather than by sacrament, which was reinforced in the seventeenth and eighteenth centuries, see Armengaud *La famille et l'enfant* 22–8.

18. Lottin 'Vie et mort du couple' 59–60.

19. Y.-F. Zoltvany 'Esquisse de la coutume de Paris' *RHAF* 25 (1971) 368.

20. C. de Ferrière *Nouveau commentaire sur la coutume de la prévoté et vicomté de Paris* (Paris: Les Libraires associés 1770) 11.

21. Dechêne *Habitants et marchands* 418–19. According to Dechêne, signing a marriage contract was a 'normal procedure.' A high proportion of 'people who married had marriage contracts.'

22. Zoltvany 'Coutume de Paris' 365

23. Diderot, *Encyclopédie* 8: 671

24. C. de Ferrière *Dictionnaire de droit et de pratique* (Paris: Desaint 1762) 1: qrt. 225

25. De Ferrière, *Nouveau commentaire sur la coutume* 22

26. Diderot *Encyclopédie* 21: 73

27. De Ferrière *Dictionnaire de droit* 1: art. 16

28. F.-J. Cugnet *Traité abrégé des anciennes lois, coutumes et usages de la colonie du Canada* (Quebec: Brown 1775) 91.

29. Boucher and Morel *Le droit dans la vie familiale* 166

30. Diderot *Encyclopédie* 8: 674

31. Separation as to bed and board always included separation as to property. In this article, the expression 'separation as to bed and board' is used, rather than the more precise term 'separation as to bed and board and as to property,' in order to lighten the text.

32. *Rituel du diocèse de Québec publié par l'ordre de Saint-Vallier, évêque de Québec*, quoted in P.-A. Leclerc 'Le mariage sous le régime français' *RHAF* 13 (1959) 395

33. Diderot *Encyclopédie* 13: 865.

34. Ibid. 30: 827.

35. O. Martin *Histoire de la coutume de la prévôté et vicomté de Paris* 259

36. De Ferrière *Nouveau commentaire sur la coutume* 28

37. Ibid.

38. Ibid. 259.

39. Lottin *La désunion du couple* 114.

40. N.-F. Cott 'Eighteenth Century Family and Social Life Revealed in Massachusetts Divorce Records' *Journal of Social History* 10 (1976) 36

41. Lottin 'Vie et mort du couple' 67

42. L. Gadoury, Y. Landry, and H. Charbonneau 'Démographie différentielle en Nouvelle-France: Villes et campagnes' *RHAF* 38 (1985) 357–78

43. ANQ (Quebec), Pièces judiciaires et notariales [hereafter PJN], Nouvelle France [hereafter NF] 25, folio 110

44. ANQ, Quebec, Prévôté: registres, 1731

45. J. Portemer 'Réflexions sur les pouvoirs de la femme selon le droit français au XVIIe siècle' *XVIIe siècle* 144 (1984) 189–202

46. ANQ, Montreal, Pièces judiciaires, 25 May 1756
47. ANQ, Montreal, Pièces judiciaires, 15 Nov. 1741
48. Ibid. 17 July 1740
49. Ibid. 1691
50. Ibid. 25 Jan. 1757
51. Ibid. 7 July 1746
52. N. Castan 'Condition féminine et violence conjugale dans la société méridionale française au XVIIIe siècle' in *Le modèle familial européen: Normes, déviances, contrôle du pouvoir* (Rome: Ecole française de Rome 1986) 181
53. Dechêne *Habitants et marchands* 439
54. Lottin 'Vie et mort du couple' 65
55. J.-L. Flandrin *Familles, parenté, maison, sexualité dans l'ancienne société* (Paris: Hachette 1976) 127
56. Diderot *Encyclopédie* 21: 73
57. ANQ, Montreal, Pièces judiciaires, Affaire Gabriel Cordier, 4–15 Dec. 1744
58. Ibid., Affaire Antoine Laurent, 15 Jan.–21 Feb. 1734
59. Sylvie Savoie, 'Les couples en difficulté aux XVIIe et XVIIIe siècles: Les demandes de separation en Nouvelle-France' (MA thesis, University of Sherbrooke 1986), 42
60. ANQ, Quebec, Prévôté de Québec, Registre, 1735
61. ANQ, Quebec, PJN, 1012, 14 July 1734
62. ANQ, Montreal, Pièces judiciaires, 21 Feb.–10 Mar. 1756
63. Ibid. 1691.
64. Ibid. 2 Mar.–13 June 1714
65. Ibid.
66. Ibid. 8 July 1755
67. Ibid. 3 Dec. 1754
68. Ibid., Affaire Gendron, 1706
69. ANQ, Quebec, NF 25, PJN 961, 1733
70. ANQ, Montreal, Pièces judiciaires, 13 Jan.–25 Feb. 1738
71. Ibid. 1 Mar. 1716
72. A. Farge and M. Foucault *Le désordre des familles: Lettres de cachet des Archives de la Bastille* (Paris: Gallimard, Julliard 1982) 35
73. ANQ, Montreal, Pièces judiciaires, 1732
74. Ibid. 29 Nov. 1754
75. Ibid. 1732
76. Ibid. 7 July 1740
77. ANQ, Quebec, NF 25, PJN 961, 1733
78. ANQ, Montreal, Pièces judiciaires, 1714
79. Ibid. 7 July 1740
80. ANQ, Quebec, NF 11–37, Registre du Conseil supérieur de Québec, vol. 37, 122v–123v; NF 14–5, Pièces detaches du Conseil supérieur, 1730–60, no. 247
81. ANQ, Montreal, Pièces judiciaires, Affaire Marie-Josephe Ethier, 29 Oct. 1746–24 Mar. 1747
82. ANQ, Quebec, NF 25, PJN 928
83. Ibid., PJN, NF 25, f. 110
84. ANQ, Montreal, Pièces judiciaires, 1706
85. H. Têtu and C.-O. Gagnon *Mandements, lettres pastorales et circulaires des évêques de Québec* (Québec: Imprimerie A. Coté 1887) 1: 57
86. Lottin 'Vie et mort du couple' 73
87. ANQ, Quebec, PJN, NF 25, f. 961, 13 Aug. 1733
88. ANQ, Montreal, Pièces judiciaires, 1719
89. Ibid. 1719; separation as to bed and board denied
90. Ibid. 1692
91. ANQ, Quebec, Prévôté: registres, 1749
92. Diderot *Encyclopédie* 30: 828
93. L. Trenard 'Amour et mariage dans l'ancienne France' *L'information historique* 43 (1981) 80
94. J.-B. de la Croix de Chevrières de Saint-Vallier *Rituel du diocèse de Québec publié par l'ordre de Saint-Vallier, évêque de Québec* 296
95. For more on this subject see K. Thomas 'The Double Standard' *Journal of the History of Ideas* 20 (1959) 195–216

96. S.F. Matthews Grieco 'Corps, apparence et sexualité' in G. Duby and M. Perrot, eds. *Histoire des femmes en Occident, XVIe–XVIIIe siècles* (Paris: Plan 1991) 3: 91–2

97. Intendant Hocquart to the minister, 3 Oct. 1733, Archives Nationale de France, Colonies, C 11^A, vol. 60, f. 48–9, 117. See also *Jugements et délibérations du Conseil souverain* 3 Nov. 1668, Affaire Isabelle Alure, vol. 1, 528–30, and Affaire Marie Chauvet, 21 Jan. 1669, vol. 1, 540–2.

98. Collectif Clio *L'histoire des femmes* 101. See also S. Van Kirk 'The Custom of the Country: An Examination of Fur Trade Marriage Practices' in L.H. Thomas, ed. *Essays on Western History* (Edmonton: University of Alberta Press 1976).

99. For more on this subject see 'Le cahier des témoingages de liberté au mariage 1757–1763' in *Rapport des Archives de la province de Québec* (Québec: National Archives 1951–3).

100. See, for example, *Jugements et délibérations du Conseil souverain* vol. 1, 769–70, and vol. 2, 52–3, and R.L. Séguin *La vie libertine en Nouvelle-France au dix-septième siècle* (Montréal: Leméac 1972) 2: 505.

101. ANQ, Quebec, NF 2-21, Ordonnances de l'intendant Hocquart, 7 and 9 Mar. 1733, vol. 21, f. 29v–30v.

102. Séguin *La vie libertine* 2: 504–5.

103. 'Mariage à la gaumine' was a folk custom originally from France for young people who wished to marry without their parents' consent, or without a proper wedding. They would attend a regular church service and announce during the service that they regarded themselves as husband and wife. The clergy said the custom was based 'on a strict and illegitimate interpretation of the Papal ruling that marriage required the Church's blessing.' See J. Bosher, 'The Family in New France' in R.D. Francis and D.B. Smith, eds. *Readings in Canadian History: Pre-Confederation* (Toronto: Holt, Rinehart and Winston 1986) 105

104. ANQ, Montreal, Pièces judiciaires, Affaire Joubert-Gendron, 25 June–18 July 1740

105. A. Farge 'Familles: L'honneur et le secret' in Philippe Ariès and Georges Duby *L'histoire de la vie privée: De la Renaissance aux Lumières* (Paris: Seuil 1986) 3: 589.

106. On this subject see S.D. Amussen 'Féminin/Masculin: Le genre dans l'Angleterre de l'époque moderne' AESC 2 (1985) 269–87.

107. ANQ, Quebec, NG 25, PJN 1160

108. Ibid. NF 25, PJN 1655. See also PJN 1640 and ANQ, Montreal, Pièces judiciaires, 28 Oct.–5 Nov. 1722, 22 Dec. 1728–5 Jan. 1729, 14 May–7 June 1752; ANQ, Quebec, Procédures judiciaires, Matières criminelles, vol. 4, 40–9.

109. See, for example, ANQ, Montreal, Pièces judiciaires, 2 and 7 May 1731, 21 Feb.–10 Mar. 1756, 18 Feb.–1 June 1757, 23 Feb.–12 Mar. 1753; ANQ, Quebec, NF 25, PJN, 1736.

110. A. Lachance 'Une étude de mentalité: Les injures verbales au Canada au XVIIIe siècle (1712–1748)' RHAF 31 (1977) 233. See also P.N. Moogk '"Thieving Buggers" and "Stupid Sluts": Insults and Popular Culture in New France' *William and Mary Quarterly* 36 (1979) 524–47.

111. N. Castan 'La criminalité familiale dans le resort du Parlement de Toulouse, 1690–1730' in A. Abbiateci et al. *Crimes et criminalité en France, 17e–18e siècles* (Paris: A. Colin 1971) 106.

112. ANQ, Montreal, Pièces judiciaires, 1–3 Apr. 1727

113. ANQ, Quebec, NF 13-1, Matières de police, 1695–1755, 100 et seq.

114. ANQ, Montreal, Pièces judiciaires, 13 Feb.–12 Apr. 1736. See also 23–30 June 1729, 14–24 Sept. 1736, and 11 Sept. 1741–15 Sept. 1742.

115. ANQ, Montreal, Pièces judiciaires, 30 Dec. 1717 and 5 Feb. 1718. Pierre Chartier and Catherine Catin were married in Montreal on 27 November 1717: C. Tanguay *Dictionnaire généalogique des familles canadiennes* (Québec: Sénécal 1871) 3: 28. See also ANQ, Quebec, PJN 803, 1728. For more on the charivari see C. Karnoouh 'Le charivari ou l'hypothèse de la monogamie' in J. Le Goff and J.-C. Schmitt *Le Charivari* (Paris: Mouton 1981) 35 et seq. and R. Hardy 'Le charivari: Divulger et sanctionner la vie privée?' in M. Brunet and S. Gagnon, eds. *Discours et pratique de l'intime* (Québec: Institut québécois de recherché sur la culture 1993).

116. Farge 'Familles' 601.

Topic Four
Acadia

Acadians saltmarsh haying in the early 1700s. The reconstruction is by Azor Vienneau.

During the 15th century, Europe entered an age of expansion, marked by the development of overseas commerce and the establishment of colonies. The English, Portuguese, Basques, and French were among the earliest Europeans to harvest the rich Newfoundland fishery, and to travel to northeastern North America. They established a number of seasonal settlements on the Atlantic coast to prepare and dry their fish. The Basques, from what is now the border country on the Bay of Biscay between Spain and France, arrived in the 1520s and 1530s.

The French established their first permanent settlement on the Atlantic coast in 1604, naming it Acadia (later to become Nova Scotia). Its strategic location near the Gulf of St. Lawrence meant that England and France fought continually for its possession. The region changed hands frequently until 1713, when France ceded Acadia to England in the Treaty of Utrecht. For the next half-century, Britain ruled over the colony with its predominantly French-speaking and Roman Catholic population.

The Acadians sought to remain neutral in conflicts between England and France. Initially this was possible, but with the revival of hostility between France and England in 1755, Charles Lawrence, Nova Scotia's lieutenant governor, and his council at Halifax insisted that the Acadians take an unconditional oath of allegiance to the British Crown. When they refused, Lawrence expelled approximately 10 000 French Acadians. In "The Golden Age: Acadian Life, 1713–1748," Naomi Griffiths reviews Acadian society before the expulsion. Why were they so prosperous under the first four decades of British rule?

In her essay "Imperial Transitions," Elizabeth Mancke reviews British rule over the Acadians in the four decades from 1713 to the expulsion in 1755. How did England initially adjust to the presence of a dominant French Catholic population in the settled areas of Nova Scotia? Why did the English ultimately decide to expel the Acadians from Nova Scotia?

For an overview of European exploration in the North Atlantic, consult Samuel Eliot Morison, *The European Discovery of America: The Northern Voyages*, A.D. *500–1600* (New York: Oxford University Press, 1971), and Robert McGhee, *Canada Rediscovered* (Ottawa: Canadian Museum of Civilization, 1991). An illustrated account of the Norse and their arrival in northeastern North America is *The Vikings and Their Predecessors*, by Kate Gordon, with a contribution by Robert McGhee (Ottawa: National Museum of Man, 1981). Harold E.L. Prins reviews the history of the Mi'kmaq in *The Mi'kmaq: Resistance, Accommodation, and Cultural Survival* (Fort Worth, TX: Harcourt Brace, 1996). Ralph Pastore provides a good overview of the First Nations in "The Sixteenth Century: Aboriginal Peoples and European Contact," in *The Atlantic Region to Confederation: A History*, eds. Phillip A. Buckner and John Reid (Toronto: University of Toronto Press, 1994), pp. 22–39.

An abundant literature exists on the Acadians; in fact, by the end of the 19th century, 200 books and pamphlets had been written on the subject of the Acadian expulsion alone, many of them of a controversial and partisan nature. For an overview of the literature, see Jean Daigle, ed., *Acadia of the Maritimes: Thematic Studies from the Beginning to the Present* (Moncton: Université de Moncton Press, 1995). A short review of the historical debate appears in Thomas Garde Barnes's "Historiography of the Acadians' *Grand Dérangement* (1755)," *Québec Studies* 7 (1988): 74–86. Good introductions to Acadian society include Naomi Griffiths's *The Acadians: Creation of a People* (Toronto: McGraw-Hill Ryerson, 1973), her *The Contexts of Acadian History, 1686–1784* (Montreal/Kingston: McGill-Queen's University Press, 1992), and her recent study, *From Migrant to Acadian: A North American Border People, 1604–1755* (Montreal: McGill-Queen's, 2005). See as well J.B. Brebner's earlier *New England's Outpost: Acadia before the British Conquest of Canada* (New York: Columbia University Press, 1927); and Andrew H. Clark's *Acadia: The Geography of Early Nova Scotia to 1760* (Madison: University of Wisconsin Press, 1968).

For an account of life at Louisbourg, consult Christopher Moore's award-winning *Louisbourg Portraits: Five Dramatic True Tales of People Who Lived in an Eighteenth-Century Garrison Town* (Toronto: Macmillan, 1982). A.J.B. Johnston has written two books on the important French port: *Life and Religion at Louisbourg, 1713–1758* (Montreal/Kingston: McGill-Queen's University Press, 1996) and *Control and Order in French Colonial Louisbourg, 1713–1758* (East Lansing: Michigan State University Press, 2001). Terry Crowley provides a short history of this important port in *Louisbourg: Atlantic Fortress and Seaport,* Canadian Historical Association, Historical Booklet no. 48 (Ottawa: CHA, 1990).

Valuable maps of early Atlantic Canada appear in the *Historical Atlas of Canada,* vol. 1, *From the Beginning to 1800,* R. Cole Harris, ed. (Toronto: University of Toronto Press, 1987). For an overview of the 17th and 18th centuries, see Philip A. Buckner and John G. Reid, eds., *The Atlantic Region to Confederation: A History* (Toronto: University of Toronto Press, 1994).

WEBLINKS

Champlain Society
http://link.library.utoronto.ca/champlain/search.cfm?lang=eng

For primary sources on Acadia from the Champlain Society, browse the database by subject and select "Acadia."

Nova Scotia: 1749–1759
http://www.canadiana.org/citm/themes/constitution/constitution4_e.html

A collection of documents relating to the governing of Nova Scotia in the mid-18th century.

Maritime First Nation Treaties in Historical Perspective
http://www.ainc-inac.gc.ca/pr/trts/hti/Marit/index_e.html

A report by W.E. Daugherty assessing historical First Nation treaties in the Maritimes from 1686 to 1779.

Joseph Robineau de Villebon
http://www.ourroots.ca/e/toc.asp?id=6151

A digitized copy of a 1934 book containing letters, journals, and memoirs of Joseph Robineau de Villebon, a commandant in Acadia, 1690–1700.

The Acadians
http://www.cbc.ca/acadian/index.html

This CBC website describes the Acadian people, their history, and their position today.

Acadian Historical Village
http://www.virtualmuseum.ca/Exhibitions/Acadie/index_e.html

An online exhibit presenting the experience of life in a historical Acadian village.

Acadia Documents
http://www.canadiana.org/citm/themes/pioneers/pioneers2_e.html#acadia

A collection of documents relating to Acadians, including a 19th-century account of their expulsion.

Article Eight

The Golden Age: Acadian Life, 1713–1748

Naomi Griffiths

Until the 1950s Acadian history was most frequently written either as epic or as case study — as the drama of a people or as an example of the political and diplomatic struggles between great powers. The tragic nature of the deportation in 1755 seemed the obvious and fundamental starting point for all that the Acadians experienced since, and equally the culmination of everything that had occurred in their previous history. In the last 30 years, however, an ever-increasing number of scholarly works have been devoted to the examination of Acadian history from much more complex perspectives. These include attempts to analyze not merely 1755 as an event of major importance in the war between English and French for North America, but also works centred on Acadian language,[1] folklore,[2] geography,[3] sociology,[4] as well as on Acadian history as the history of a developing community.

Acadian studies have, in fact, come to an impressive maturity over the past 30 years. This maturity is magnificently documented in the work edited by Jean Daigle, *Les Acadiens des Maritimes,* where some twenty scholars present complex essays outlining the problems, the work done, and the work to be done in every area of Acadian studies from history to folklore, from political science to material culture.[5] The result of all this publication is, of course, the temptation, if not the necessity, for present scholars to look at past syntheses of Acadian history, to discover where the new information demands new theories, and to build, if not entirely new interpretations of the Acadian past, at least interpretations which are more richly decorated and more densely structured.

This challenge is as dangerous as it is irresistible, for the amount of material is considerable indeed. As a result, this paper is a cautious one. Its main aim is to paint Acadian life between 1713 and 1748 in such a way that the reader may sense the complex nature of the Acadian community during these years. This was the period to be remembered by the community in exile after 1755. All those over the age of ten or eleven in 1755 would have had some knowledge of these years. It was the time that would be recalled in exile and the time which would form the basis for the stories of past life as the Acadians once more established themselves in the Maritimes. It spanned the decades from the Treaty of Utrecht to that of Aix-la-Chapelle, during which years the lands on which the Acadians lived turned from being the border between two empires to the frontier between enemies.

The political geography of "Nova Scotia or Acadia," as the lands were called in the contemporary international treaties, had meant turmoil for its inhabitants from the outset of European colonization. As J.B. Brebner wrote, these lands were "the eastern outpost and flank for both French and English in North America." They made, in his words, a "continental cornice." Throughout the seventeenth century this cornice frequently changed hands between English and French. It became a true border for[,] whatever name it was given and whatever limits were claimed, it lay "inside the angle between the St. Lawrence route to French Canada and the northern route to New England which branched off from it south of Newfoundland."[6]

Source: Naomi Griffiths, "The Golden Age: Acadian Life, 1713–1748," *Histoire Sociale/Social History* 17, 33 (May 1984): 21–34. Reprinted by permission.

Those who settled there in the seventeenth century would quickly find their situation akin to that of such people as the Basques, caught between France and Spain; the Alsatians, moulded by French and German designs; and those who lived on the borders between England and Scotland or England and Wales.

It was the French who began the first permanent settlement in the area in 1604. Whatever the international designation of the colony over the next century, its non-Indian people would be called the Acadians. While predominantly French-speaking and Catholic, they were nevertheless a people who also absorbed English-speaking migrants such as the Melansons[7] and the Caisseys.[8] They also had a considerable knowledge of the Protestant religion, and it is very probable that some of the families who joined them from near Loudun in the 1630s were of the reform church.[9] By the end of the century the Acadians had known one lengthy and legitimate period of English rule, 1654–1668, as well as a number of much shorter periods of English control as a result of raids out of Massachusetts. By 1700 the Acadians were, as the detailed work of Professors Daigle and Reid has shown,[10] almost as accustomed to dealing with the officials of England as those of France. Thus the defeat of Subercase in 1710 and the subsequent transfer of the colony once more to English control by the Treaty of Utrecht was for the Acadians yet one more step in a complicated ritual, an exchange of control over them from France to England, something which had happened before and would most probably be reversed in the not too distant future.

This fundamental belief in the mutability of power, this dominant sense of the probability of alternate French and English control of the colony, became the cornerstone of Acadian politics during the years 1713 to 1748. It was the basis for the Acadian action over requests made by the English officials that they swear an oath of allegiance to the King of England. From the Acadian viewpoint, it would have been folly indeed to engage in any action which would bind them irrevocably to one Great Power when the other was still not only obviously in the neighbourhood, but even more obviously still interested in the future status of the colony and its inhabitants. Thus the Acadians built a policy compounded of delay and compromise. The oath to George I was first rejected outright; among other reasons they presented for the refusal, the Acadians of Minas remarked that "pendant que nos ancêtres ont étés sous la domination angloise on ne leur a jamais exigé de pareille Sermente."[11] [Editor's Translation: While our ancestors were under English rule they were never required to make a similar oath.] Later on, oaths were taken to George II, but in such circumstances as to enable the Acadians to believe that they had been granted the right to remain neutral. In fact, as Brebner pointed out, the practice of both English and French of referring to them from 1730 on as either "les français neutres" or "the Neutral French" indicates that this accommodation was generally tolerated, if not accepted, by those in power during these years.[12]

However it might have looked to outsiders, the question of neutrality was serious enough to the Acadians. It was in fact a consistent policy that was first enunciated in 1717 by the Acadians of Annapolis Royal and later adhered to by them, and others in time of war. On being asked for an oath of allegiance to George I, the Annapolis Royal Acadians refused, the reasons given being that matters of religious freedom were not yet clarified and danger from Indians, who were bound to disapprove friendship between Acadian and English, led to fears for Acadian security. Nevertheless, the response continued, "we are ready to take an oath that we will take up arms neither against his Britannic Majesty, nor against France, nor against any of their subjects or allies."[13] In 1744 when hostilities broke out between English and French in North America, Mascerene, then the lieutenant governor of the colony, wrote to his masters in London: "These latter [i.e., the French inhabitants] have given me assurances of their resolutions to keep in their fidelity to his Majesty."[14] Mascerene was convinced that had the

Acadians not remained neutral during the hostilities, the colony would have fallen to the French.[15] Certainly there is more than enough evidence to show the Acadian dislike of the war, including a most strongly worded letter from those of Grand-Pré to the French, pointing out forcibly that the village preferred peace to war, tranquillity and food to soldiers fighting across their farmlands.[16]

There is no doubt that between 1713 and 1748 the majority of the Acadians strove to live on their land truly as neutrals, giving loyalty to neither French nor English. This policy procured for their communities nearly 35 years of peace, but its final failure in 1755 has overshadowed its earlier success. It is worth emphasizing that it was a policy, not merely a series of inconsistent, unconnected reactions to the demands made by English and French. It was transmitted by delegates from the several Acadian communities to the English officials on a number of separate occasions and, as has been suggested, adhered to during a time of considerable pressure in the 1740s. It was a policy that produced peace and quiet for the Acadian communities, however catastrophic it finally proved to be. Its evolution and development gave the Acadians a knowledge of political action and a sense of their independent reality that would prove invaluable to them when they confronted the vicissitudes of the deportation.[17] Above all, it was the framework for the expansion and development of the Acadian communities between 1713 and 1748.

The demographic expansion of the Acadians during these years is commonplace in one sense; in another it is something acknowledged rather than fully understood. As Gysa Hynes wrote in 1973, "the rapid natural increase of the population of the Acadians during the period from 1650 to 1750 . . . has long been recognised, but no historian has explored the demography of Acadia before the Dispersion."[18] As a result, while it is generally agreed that the Acadian population probably doubled every twenty years between 1713 and the early 1750s without the aid of any considerable immigration, there has been little real analysis of this development.[19] Gisa Hynes's excellent article was a pioneer study relating above all to Port Royal/Annapolis Royal and has not been followed by much else. Enough raw material does exist, however, to outline the tantalizing landscape waiting to be fully explored, a demographic territory which differs significantly from contemporary Europe and also, in some considerable measure, from that of other colonial settlements in North America.

It is a debatable point whether the longevity of the Acadians or their fertility should receive most comment. At a time when only 50 percent of the population reached the age of 21 in France, 75 percent reached adulthood in Port Royal.[20] Further, while mortality did take its toll during the middle years, death coming through accident and injury rather than epidemic, old age was a common enough phenomenon. In fact at the time of the Treaty of Utrecht, when the French were making every effort to withdraw the Acadians from land ceded to the English and to establish them on Isle Royal (Cape Breton), one of the priests noted that the Acadians refused to go because

> It would be to expose us manifestly [they say] to die of hunger burthened as we are with large families, to quit the dwelling places and clearances from which we derive our usual subsistence, without any other resource, to take rough, new lands, from which the standing wood must be removed. One fourth of our population consists of aged persons, unfit for the labour of breaking up new lands, and who, with great exertion, are able to cultivate the cleared ground which supplied subsistence for them and their families.[21]

The presence of an older generation in the community meant a rich heritage of memories of past politics. Any Acadian over 42 in 1713 would have been born when the colony was controlled by the English, for the terms of the Treaty of Breda were not honoured by Temple until 10 January 1671. Any Acadian over 25 would have personal memories of the stormy raids by

New Englanders on their villages and of the French countermeasures. The reality of life on a border would be a commonplace for Acadian reminiscences in a community whose people lived long enough to remember.

If Acadians could see relatively long life as a possibility, they could also see life itself as abundant. From the travelling French surgeon-poet Dièreville to the almost equally travelling English official, Governor Philipps, the observations were the same. In 1699 the Frenchman wrote that "the swarming of Brats is a sight to behold."[22] The Englishman commented in 1730 on the Acadians' ability to increase and spread "themselves over the face of the province . . . like Noah's progeny."[23] Present-day research has confirmed the accuracy of these impressions. Gisa Hynes discovered in her analysis of Port Royal that four out of five marriages were complete, that is, "were not disrupted by the death of husband or wife before the onset of menopause."[24] In these marriages, if the women were under 20 on their wedding day, they had some ten or eleven children; those wedded between 20 and 24, nine children; and those married in their late 20s, seven or eight children.[25] For the population as a whole, it is probable that the average family in the colony had six or seven children.[26]

These bare statistical bones of Acadian family life can now be covered first with the skin of individual family genealogy and then clothed with the fabric of community life. As an example of the first, there is the life of Claude Landry, born in 1663, the youngest of some ten children of René Landry of Port Royal, who himself had arrived in the colony sometime in the 1640s from Loudun.[27] When he was about eighteen, Claude married Catherine Thibodeau, whose father had been an associate of Emmanuel LeBorgne and come to the colony from around Poitiers in the 1650s.[28] She was the fifth child in a family of sixteen, eleven of whom reached adulthood.[29] Catherine was apparently fifteen when married and bore her first child within the year. She had some ten children in all, eight of whom lived to maturity.

The young couple moved very early in their marriage to Grand-Pré, where they brought up their family and watched their children's children flourish. When Claude Landry died in 1747, aged 86, his grandchildren through the male line numbered 46 and his great-grandchildren, also through the male line, eleven. Claude's last child, a son, had been born in 1708; his first grandson was born in 1710. Between 1717 and 1747 there was only one year in which no birth is recorded for his sons, and it is not unlikely that one of Claude's two daughters might have had a child that year. The year 1735 saw the birth of the first great-grandchild within the male line.[30]

The growth of such extended families was supported by a healthy mixed economy, based upon farming, hunting, and fishing with enough trade, both legal and illegal, to make life interesting. In Grand-Pré the Landry family was part of the flourishing development which Mascerene had described in 1730 as "a platt of Meadow, which stretches near four leagues, part of which is damn'd [sic] in from the tide, and produced very good wheat and pease."[31] Westward this great marsh is edged by the massive presence of Cape Blomidon; the tides of the Bay of Fundy curve across its northern shore, and wooded uplands circumscribe its other boundaries. Between 1710, when the first grandson was born, and 1747, when Claude died, the population of the area grew from well under a thousand to something more than four thousand.[32] The community lived in houses scattered across the landscape, not grouped close together in a village. Charles Morris, who was commissioned by Governor Shirley of Massachusetts to make a survey of the Bay of Fundy area in 1747, reported that the dwellings were "low Houses fram'd of timber and their Chimney framed with the Building of wood and lined with Clay except the fireplace below."[33] Very often the houses sheltered a mixture of families, and the sheer work required to provide them necessities of life must have been considerable.[34]

The daily life of both men and women would be governed by the seasons, for the frame of the economy was what was grown and raised for food and clothing. Fishing, hunting, and trade could and did provide important additions to this base, but the standard of living of the majority of the Acadians depended on the produce of their landholdings. At the very least a household would possess a garden, and from the seventeenth century on travellers had noticed the variety and abundance of vegetables grown. Dièreville, whose evidence is of the close of the seventeenth century, remarked upon the wealth of cabbages and turnips,[35] and another report of the same period lists the gardens as including "choux, betteraves, oignons, carottes, cives, eschalottes, navets, panets et touttes sortes de salades."[36] Most families would have also an amount of land varying in size between that of a smallholding and a farm, depending on where the community was in the colony and what level of resources the family in question could command. A.H. Clark considered that the households of Grand-Pré and the surrounding area usually had five to ten acres of dyked and tilled farmland within the marsh, supplemented with an orchard situated on the upland slopes. Morris reported the marshlands to be "Naturally of a Fertile Soil . . . and . . . of so strong and lasting a Nature that their Crops are not Diminished in ten or twenty years Constant Tillage."[37] The crops sown included most of the grain crops common to western Europe: wheat, oats, rye, and barley, as well as peas, hemp, and flax. Writing in 1757, another traveller remarked on the abundance of fruit trees, apples, pears, "cherry and plumb trees," and noted that "finer flavoured apples and greater variety, cannot in any other country be produced."[38]

Working with the land, whether garden or farm, did not only imply digging and ploughing, weeding and gathering. There was also the care of livestock. Poultry was everywhere about, as much for feathers as for the eggs and meat. Down-filled mattresses and coverlets were a noted Acadian possession, and the export of feathers to Louisbourg a common item of trade.[39] Pigs rooting around the houses were so common that few surveyors interested in estimating Acadian wealth even bothered to count them. A number of observers, however, remarked on the Acadian liking for fat-back (le lard), which could be cooked with cabbage or fried and added to whatever vegetables were available.[40] Sheep were also numerous, raised for wool rather than for meat. Most households would also possess cows and a horse. The estimation of the total livestock in the colony varies widely since the Acadians, like most peasant populations, had no great wish to inform any official of the true extent of their possessions. Life must have been sustained at considerably more than bare subsistence, however, since extant records show that in the 1740s the Acadians, particularly those of Grand-Pré and of the Minas basin in general, were able to export cattle, sheep, pigs, and poultry to Louisbourg.[41] While the authorities at Annapolis Royal thundered against such trade, they also admitted that the Acadians were no worse than others, noting that "there is so great an illicit Trade carried on by the People of Massachusetts Bay and New Hampshire."[42] As has been suggested, the trade that existed was enough to make life for the Acadians interesting, and the goods imported included not only necessities such as "Spanish Iron, French Linnens, Sail Cloth Wollen cloths," but also "Rum, Molasses, Wine and Brandy."[43]

The sum of this evidence suggests an excellent standard of living among the Acadians, something which showed, of course, in the population increase of the first half of the eighteenth century. While there is little evidence of luxury, there is less of poverty. The staples of life, food, shelter, and clothing were abundant, even if the abundance was available only after hard work. Further, the absence of conspicuous consumption and the lack of development of towns and industry in no way meant an absence of specie. It is clear from the records of the deportation itself that Acadians took coinage with them into exile.[44] The Acadian community did not have the rate of economic growth that the New Englanders possessed, but it provided amply for the totality of individuals. Fishing and hunting added to the resources of the households. Charles Morris remarked that the population around Grand-Pré "had some shallops, in which they employed themselves in the catching of Fish just upon their Harbours, being out but a few days at a Time; This was rather for their Home Consumption than the foreign Market."[45] Clark remarked that the Acadians were "particularly interested in salmon, shad, gaspereau, and the like during their spring runs up the rivers and creeks."[46] As for hunting, it was less the meat that was immediately valued than the furs. Game was sought in order to sell it in Annapolis Royal,[47] but "avec les fourrures d'ours, de castor, de renard, de loutre, et de martre" [*Editor's Translation:* with the bear, beaver, fox, weasel and marten furs], they had material which gave them "non seulement le comfort, mais bien souvent de jolis vêtements."[48] [*Editor's Translation:* not only comfortable, but often attractive clothing.] Dièreville had also commented on the way in which the Acadians made shoes from sealskin and the hides of moose.[49]

Given the considerable work necessary to turn the resources of their environment into food and clothing for the family, it is extraordinary that the Acadians should have been criticized for being idle.[50] The tools they worked with were scarcely labour-saving devices and were basically of their own manufacture. Clark has listed the main implements available to them as "pickaxes, axes, hoes, sickles, scythes, flails, and wooden forks and rakes," as well, of course, as spades, essential for dike-building.[51] They were known as competent carpenters and joiners, and the census made by the French during the seventeenth century reported the existence of blacksmiths, locksmiths, and nailmakers among them.[52] Working basically in wood, the Acadians built their own houses, barns, and the occasional church, made their own furniture, including enclosed beds which must have provided considerable privacy in the crowded households, tables, chairs, chests, kegs, and barrels, as well as looms and spinning wheels.[53] There was a remarkably fluid, though not entirely egalitarian social structure. Considerable importance was attached to the actual possession of land, and the recognition of proper boundaries.[54]

Specie did not serve as a major regulator of the internal economy. The available evidence shows that it was rare indeed for Acadian communities to pay one another, except in kind, for goods and services rendered. The gold gained through trade, or through wages from French and English officials, was kept for trade and most reluctantly handed over for any other purposes, especially rents and taxes.[55] Labour relations among the Acadians tended to be either barter-based (perhaps two days' digging or ploughing in exchange for some quantity of seed grain), cooperative (three or four people engaged in quilt-making or fishing, the resultant produce being divided equitably), or communal (several households joined together to build another dwelling and ready to be reconvened for such a purpose whenever the occasion warranted). The social ambiance produced by such labour relations encouraged the development of a community where family connections were as important as the particular attainments of an individual. Marriage would be seen as the connection between kin rather than the limited engagement of two individuals of particular social status. As Dièreville remarked, to his considerable surprise social barriers seemed to have no part to play in the regulation of marriage.[56]

In sum, Acadian life between 1713 and 1748 centred around the demands and rewards of family and land, although this did not mean isolation from a wider environment. During these decades the care and nurture of children must have been the dominating factor in the lives of most Acadians, male or female. A child born every two or three years on average in individual families meant the arrival of a child almost every year in multi-family households. Even with the importation of some yard goods, the provision of clothes and coverings for the children demanded continuous thought and activity. Records emphasize the extent to which the Acadians were self-sufficient in this area. Dièreville remarked on the way in which they made their own outfits, including caps and stockings.[57] Raynal, writing for Diderot's *Encyclopaedia* with information supplemented by the memorials of those Acadians exiled to France, asserted that they depended for their daily clothing on "leur lin, leur chanvre, la toison de leurs brebis."[58] [*Editor's Translation:* their flax, hemp, and fleece from their sheep.] From diapers to shawls, from shirts to shifts, with considerable liking for mixing black with red for ornament, and binding their skirts with ribbons,[59] the Acadians spun, wove, knitted, and sewed their garments. Even with every economy between one generation and the next, even with children fully accustomed to hand-me-downs, the sheer number of bonnets and mittens, stockings and shoes, cloaks, coats, and trousers, shirts, blouses, and jackets that would be needed is difficult to envisage.

Organizing the clothing was probably as much a year-round occupation for the women as the provision of meals was their daily chore. Grains were usually ground at grist-mills rather than within each household, although there is a tradition that most families possessed pestles and mortars capable of making coarse flour for porridge.[60] Bread would be baked in each household and was considered by Isaac Deschamps to have been the staple of Acadian diets.[61] Linguistic studies by Massignon show that doughnuts and pancakes were also common. She discovered references to documents dated 1744 referring to *croxsignoles*, a form of doughnut, as part of the Acadian diet.[62] It is also probable that those who came to the community from Normandy and Ile-et-Vilaine brought with them a taste for buckwheat pancakes, something that was certainly common among Acadians in northern New Brunswick at the close of the eighteenth century.[63] There is a strange debate about whether the Acadians grew potatoes before 1755, since a number of popular guides such as the *Guide Bleu de Bretagne* refer to them introducing the vegetable to France.[64] Again, it is certainly true that the potato was a staple of Acadian diets by the opening of the nineteenth century,[65] but more evidence is needed before one can accept that it was a common food for the Acadians 50 years earlier. Milk was abundant[66] and the Acadians found in exile that they had been particularly fortunate in this respect.[67] Its plenteousness must have been a great help in coping with what was known as the *pourginés d'enfants*.[68]

This charming word for a numerous family invites consideration of the emotional climate in which families grew and developed. The evidence here is, at present, somewhat sketchy. The extent to which the Acadians cared for one another during their exile, seeking news of brothers and sisters as well as advertising for husbands and wives, suggests the importance of family relations.[69] As to the actual treatment of children during these decades, one has very few concrete details. It is possible that the reputation the Acadians had for long and faithful marriages was not coupled with a bitterness against those whose lives followed other patterns. One of the few cases relating to children that reached the English officials at Annapolis Royal between 1720 and 1739 was one where grandparents fought for the privilege of raising an illegitimate child.[70] The folklore research of Jean-Claude Dupont reveals a considerable amount about children's toys and games current in the nineteenth century, and it is probable that some of these, at least, were also part of Acadian life during the eighteenth century. Certainly the early mobile-rattle, a dried pig's bladder filled with peas and hung so an infant could bat it about and watch it swing, listening to its noise, which Dupont has reported for the nineteenth century, would have been a useful toy to have in the house in the eighteenth century.[71]

There were, of course, the usual arguments and quarrels among the Acadians, the kinds of disputes common to any group of people. The court records of Annapolis show not only debates over landholdings and boundaries, but also slander actions, particularly between women, and at least one appeal for aid to control a nagging wife.[72] But the tenor of life was undoubtedly rendered easier by the ready supply of necessities, a supply which might depend on continuous hard work but one that was available. There was no major shortage of food for the Acadians between 1713 and 1748; shelter was readily available; clothing was adequate; and, above all, there were no major epidemics. Even when plague did reach the colony, its ravages were confined, both in 1709 and 1751, almost exclusively to the garrisons.[73]

Quite how the Acadians escaped the general epidemics of the eighteenth century has yet to be fully determined. It is obvious from the mortality rates they suffered during the early years of exile that during the first half of the eighteenth century they had acquired no community levels of immunity to smallpox, yellow fever, or typhoid. When those diseases struck as the exiles reached Boston, Philadelphia, South Carolina, or the British seaports, a third or more of the Acadians died.[74] Yet the idea that this vulnerability developed because of the more or less complete isolation of the communities from outside contact is a theory which demands a great deal more examination. The Acadian tradition of trading-cum-smuggling which was established in the seventeenth century took at least some of the men regularly enough to Boston and probably to points south.[75] In the eighteenth century this activity was continued and Acadian connections with Louisbourg were also developed. The fact that between 1713 and 1748 no large body of immigrants came to the area has tended to overshadow both the trickle of newcomers to the settlements and the continuous nature of the relationships between this "continental cornice" and the wider world. The parish records of Grand-Pré examined by Clark show that of the 174 marriages for which detailed information is available almost exactly one-third involved partners either from elsewhere in the colony or from abroad, sixteen coming from France, eight from Quebec, and three from Cape Breton.[76] As for travellers, most of the settlements encountered them in the form of soldiers and traders as well as government and church officials. Given the normal rate of the spread of infections during these decades, it is extraordinary that no epidemics seem to have come to the settlements via contact with Boston or Quebec, Annapolis Royal, or Louisbourg.

If the life of the Acadian settlements was much more open to outside influences than has been generally thought, it was also much less controlled by religious devotion than has been generally supposed. There is no question that the Acadians cherished the Catholic faith. There is also no doubt that they were as much trouble to their priests as any other group of humanity might be. The immense political importance of the Catholic religion to the community has overshadowed questions about its social importance. Acadians' delight in litigation was not their only cross-grained trait. Quarrels that sprung up through their drinking were also matters that concerned their pastors. A report of the archdiocese of Quebec of 1742, which drew particular attention to this flaw, also inferred that bars (*cabarets*) were kept open not only on Sundays and feast-days, but also during the celebration of Mass.[77] This same report went on to condemn some of the Acadian communities that allowed men and women not only to dance together after sunset but even to sing "des chansons lascives [lewd songs]." The lack of detail in the report is frustrating: was the alcohol spruce beer? Cider? Rum? Were the cabarets found in the front room of the local smuggler, or did Grand-Pré have something close to a village hostelry? Was the dancing anything more than square-dancing? Was the music played on flutes, whistles, and triangles only? Or were there also violins? And the songs — which of the currently known folklore airs might they have been: "Le petit Capucin"? "Le chevalier de la Tour ronde"?

Considerably more work needs to be done in the relevant archives before the nature of Acadian beliefs before 1755 can be fully described. The document just cited suggests only that the Acadian interpretation of Catholicism before 1755 owed very little to Jansenism. This would be scarcely surprising. There is little indication, even with the present evidence, that the Acadians indulged in major projects of ostensible devotion, either public or private. There are no stone churches built by them before 1755 nor are there any records of vocations among them before that date, either to the priesthood or to the religious life. Religion among the Acadians seems to have been a matter of necessity but not a question of sainthood, an important and vital ingredient in life but not the sole shaping force of the social and cultural life of their communities.[78]

For, in sum, the life of the Acadians between 1713 and 1755 was above all the life of a people in fortunate circumstances, the very real foundation for the later myth of a "Golden Age."

The ravages of the Four Horsemen of the Apocalypse were remarkably absent, for famine, disease, and war barely touched the Acadians during these years. There was sufficient food for the growing families and apparently enough land for the growing population. One's nearest and dearest might have been as aggravating as one's kin can often be, but circumstances not only did not add the burdens of scarcity to emotional life but in fact provided a fair abundance of the necessities. Certainly the daily round for both men and women must have been exhaustingly busy; but work did have its obvious rewards and, for both sexes, it would be varied enough and carried out with companionship and sociability. While the season would often have imposed harsh demands for immediate labour, for seeds must be sown, crops gathered, fish caught and fuel cut as and when the weather dictates, the year's turning would also have brought its own festivities and holidays. Massignon's work suggests that the Acadians kept the twelve days of Christmas, the customs of Candelmas as well as the celebrations common to Easter.[79] The long winter evenings knew card-playing, dancing, and pipe-smoking, as well as storytelling and singsongs. The spring and summer months would see the celebrations of weddings and the most frequent new-births. Quarrels, scandals, politics, the visits of priests, the presence of Indians, people whose children occasionally married with the Acadians and who instructed the settlers in the use of local foods,[80] the presence of the English, now and again also marrying with the Acadians[81]— there is no doubt that Acadian life before 1755 was neither crisis-ridden nor lapped in the tranquillity of a backwater. It was instead a life of considerable distinctiveness. It was a life rich enough to provide the sustenance for a continuing Acadian identity, based not only upon a complex social and cultural life, but also upon the development of a coherent political stance, maintained throughout the settlements over a considerable period of years. It is not surprising that, fragmented in exile, the Acadians remembered these years and that this remembrance would be built into their future lives.

NOTES

1. For example, Geneviève Massignon, *Les Parlers français d'Acadie,* 2 vols. (Paris: C. Klincksieck, n.d.).

2. For example, Antonine Maillet, *Rabelais et les traditions populaires en Acadie* (Québec: Presses de l'université Laval, 1971); Anselme Chiasson, *Chéticamp, histoire et traditions acadiennes* (Moncton: Éditions des Aboiteaux, 1962); Catherine Jolicoeur, *Les plus belles légendes acadiennes* (Montréal: Stanké, 1981).

3. A.H. Clark, *Acadia: The Geography of Early Nova Scotia to 1760* (Madison: University of Wisconsin Press, 1968), and J.C. Vernex, *Les Acadiens* (Paris: Éditions Entente, 1979).

4. Jean-Paul Hautecoeur, *L'Acadie du Discours* (Québec: Presses de l'université Laval, 1976).

5. Jean Daigle, ed., *Les Acadiens des Maritimes: Études thématiques* (Moncton: Centre d'Études Acadiennes, 1980). See my review in *Histoire sociale/Social History* 16 (May 1983): 192–94.

6. J.B. Brebner, *New England's Outpost* (New York: Columbia University Press, 1927), 15–16.

7. While there has been considerable debate about whether this family had anglophone roots (for example, see Clark, *Acadia,* 101), there now seems no doubt of their origins. For details of their ancestry as recorded in declarations made by their descendants in Belle-Île-en-Mer after the deportation, see M.P. and N.P. Rieder, *The Acadians in France,* 3 vols. (Metairie, LA: M.P. & N. Rieder, 1972), 2, passim.

8. Bona Arsenault, *Histoire et Généalogie des Acadiens,* 2 vols. (Québec: Le Conseil de la vie française en Amérique, 1965), 2: 550.

9. This is suggested, in particular, in the reports of discussions with the second Mme La Tour, in Candide de Nantes, *Pages glorieuses de l'épopée Canadienne: une mission capucine en Acadie* (Montréal: Le Devoir, 1927), 150f.

10. Jean Daigle, "Nos amis les ennemis: Relations commerciales de l'Acadie avec le Massachusetts, 1670–1711" (Ph.D. dissertation, University of Maine, 1975); and John Reid, *Acadia, Maine and New Scotland: Marginal Colonies in the Seventeenth Century* (Toronto: University of Toronto Press, 1981).

11. This document, headed "answer of several French inhabitants, 10 February 1717," is printed in the *Collection de documents inédits sur le Canada et l'Amérique publiés par le Canada français,* 3 vols. (Québec: Le Canada français,

1888–90), 2: 171. The collection was published anonymously, but its editor is known to be the abbé Casgrain. The original of the document is in the Public Records Office, London (hereafter PRO), CO/NS 2, as part of the Nova Scotia government documents.

12. Brebner, *New England's Outpost*, 97.

13. T.B. Akins, ed., *Selections from the Public Documents of the Province of Nova Scotia* (Halifax, 1869), 15–16.

14. Mascerene to the Lords of Trade, 9 June 1744, printed in *Collection de Documents inédits* 2: 80.

15. This was also the opinion of the French officer in charge of the attack on Grand-Pré, Duvivier. He defended himself at his court-martial on the charge of failure, by protesting that Acadian neutrality had rendered his task impossible. Robert Rumilly, *Histoire des Acadiens*, 2 vols. (Montréal: Fides, 1955), 1: 304.

16. Letter from the inhabitants of Minas, Rivière aux Canards, and Piziquid to Duvivier and de Gannes, 13 October 1744, printed in Rumilly, *Histoire des Acadiens* 1: 304–5.

17. The full story of the Acadian years in exile remains to be told, but some indication of the strength of the community is given in Naomi Griffiths, "Acadians in Exile: The Experience of the Acadians in the British Seaports," *Acadiensis* 4 (Autumn 1974): 67–84.

18. Gisa I. Hynes, "Some Aspects of the Demography of Port Royal, 1650–1755," *Acadiensis* 3 (Autumn 1973): 7–8.

19. For a good overview of what is available, see Muriel K. Roy, "Peuplement et croissance démographique en Acadie," in Daigle, *Acadiens des Maritimes*, 135–208.

20. Hynes, "Demography of Port Royal," 10–11. In recent years scholarship about demography has been prolific. One of the most readable accounts of the French reality during the late seventeenth century is that of Pierre Goubert: "In 1969 the average expectation of life is something over seventy years. In 1661 it was probably under twenty-five. . . . Out of every hundred children born, twenty-five died before they were one year old, another twenty-five never reached twenty and a further twenty-five perished between the ages of twenty and forty-five. Only about ten ever made their sixties." Pierre Goubert, *Louis XIV and Twenty Million Frenchmen* (New York Random House, 1972), 21. On the demography of New England, see esp. James H. Cassedy, *Demography in Early America: Beginnings of the Statistical Mind, 1600–1800* (Cambridge, MA: Harvard University Press, 1969). Cassedy points out that the demographic scale was at first weighted toward mortality, but at a different time for each colony, "this precarious balance righted itself." The incidence of disease, malnutrition, and frontier warfare was demonstrably greater for New England than it was for Acadia. The conditions of life along the St. Lawrence were much closer to those along the Bay of Fundy. In the eighteenth century the population of Canada doubled every 30 years. In Acadia, however, the increase was even higher: it doubled every fifteen years between 1671 and 1714, and every twenty years between 1714 and 1755. Furthermore, migration was a minimal factor in Acadian demography after 1740. On Canada, see Jacques Henripin, *La population canadienne au début du XVIIIᵉ siècle* (Paris: Institut national d'études démographiques, 1954); on Acadia, see Roy, "Peuplement," 152.

21. Father Felix Pain to the governor of Isle Royale, September 1713, printed in Clark, *Acadia*, 187.

22. Sieur de Dièreville, *Relation of the Voyage to Port Royal in Acadia or New France*, ed. J.C. Webster (Toronto: Champlain Society, 1933), 93.

23. Public Archives of Canada (hereafter PAC), MG 11, CO 217, vol. 5, Phillipps to the Board of Trade, 2 September 1730 (PAC reel C-9120).

24. Hynes, "Demography of Port Royal," 10.

25. Hynes, "Demography of Port Royal," 10–11.

26. Clark, *Acadia*, 200f, arrived at somewhat different statistics, concluding that the average family size was closer to four or five.

27. Massignon, *Parlers français* 1: 45; Arsenault, *Généalogie* 1: 432, 433; 2: 666.

28. Arsenault, *Généalogie* 1: 518.

29. This calculation rests partly upon the assumption that the Acadians followed a common contemporary practice of using the name of a child that died for the next-born of the same sex.

30. Arsenault, *Généalogie* 1: 518; 2: 666, 667f.

31. PAC, MG 11, CO 217, vol. 2 (PAC reel C-9119).

32. These figures are my own estimations, based upon the work of Clark, *Acadia*, 216, and the overview by Roy, "Peuplement," 134–207.

33. "A Brief Survey of Nova Scotia" (MS in Library of the Royal Artillery Regiment, Woolwich, n.d.), 2: 25–26, cited in Clark, *Acadia*, 217.

34. There is considerable debate about the kin system of these households. Grandparents can only have lived in one home, and there is still debate on how siblings linked housekeeping arrangements.

35. Dièreville, *Relation*, 256.

36. PAC, MG 1, Series C 11 D, 3: 199–203, Villebon to the Minister, 27 October 1694.

37. Cited in Clark, *Acadia*, 237.

38. Captain John Knox, *An Historical Journal of the Campaigns in North America for the Years 1757, 1758, 1759 and 1760*, ed. A.B. Doughty, 3 vols. (Toronto, 1914–18), 1: 105.

39. PAC, AC 2B, 12, "Supplied from Acadia entering Louisbourg, 1740," printed in Clark, *Acadia*, 259.

40. L.U. Fontaine, *Voyage de Sieur de Dièreville en Acadia* (Québec, 1885), 56.

41. "Supplies from Acadia," in Clark, *Acadia*, 259; and "Report of custom collector Newton" (PAC, AC, NSA-26, 29–33), printed in A. Shortt, V.K. Johnston and F. Lanctot, eds. *Currency, Exchange and Finance in Nova Scotia, with Prefatory Documents, 1675–1758* (Ottawa, 1933), 223–24.

42. PAC, AC, NSA-26, 52, cited in Clark, *Acadia*, 258. See also the chart of Louisbourg trade on pp. 324–25.

43. PAC, AC, NSA-26, 51, cited in Clark, *Acadia*, 258.

44. For example, the Acadians sent to Maryland and South Carolina were able to purchase ships. See PAC, NS A/60, "Circular to the governors on the continent, July 1st, 1756, Halifax."

45. Morris, "A Brief Survey," 2: 4, quoted in Clark, *Acadia*, 244.

46. Quoted in Clark, *Acadia*, 246.

47. Fontaine, *Voyage*, 56.

48. Observations made by Moise de Les Derniers shortly after 1755 and printed in Casgrain, *Un pèlerinage au pays d'Évangéline* (Paris, 1889), App. III, 115.

49. Dièreville, *Relation*, 96.

50. It was Perrot who first commented upon this in 1686 (PAC, AC, C11D-2[1], 119, mémoires généraux); and many later observers, such as Dièreville and Phillipps, insinuated similar flaws.

51. Clark, *Acadia*, 232.

52. PAC, MG1, series C11D, 2: 96-106, report on Menneval, 10 September 1688.

53. R. Hale, "Journal of a Voyage to Nova Scotia Made in 1731 by Robert Hale of Beverley," *The Essex Institute Historical Collections* 42 (July 1906): 233.

54. Comments on the litigious nature of the Acadians span all regimes. See Clark, *Acadia*, 198, and Brebner, *New England Outpost*, 140.

55. In particular, note the trouble that Subercase faced collecting taxes, in Shortt et al., *Currency*, 16.

56. Dièreville, *Relation*, 93.

57. Dièreville, *Relation*, 96.

58. Guillaume Thomas François Raynal, *Histoire philosophique et politique des établissements et du commerce des Européens dans les deux Indes* (Paris, 1778), 6: 309.

59. Moise de les Derniers, cited in Casgrain, *Un pèlerinage*, 155.

60. Massignon, *Parlers français* 2: 548, 1316. The *bûche à pilon* is illustrated in Paul Doucet, *Vie de nos ancêtres en Acadie—l'alimentation* (Moncton: Éditions d'Acadie, 1980), 17.

61. Deschamps, cited in Clark, *Acadia*, 237.

62. Massignon, *Parlers français* 2: 550, 1320.

63. Massignon, *Parlers français* 2: 551, 1322; Ph.F. Bourgeois, *Vie de l'abbé François-Xavier LaFrance* (Montréal, 1925), 83.

64. *Les Guides Bleus de Bretagne* (Paris, 1967), 662.

65. Bourgeois, *Vie de l'abbé LaFrance*, 83.

66. Dièreville, *Relation*, 266, 110.

67. Records of the complaints of Acadians exiled to Brittany, described by Naomi Griffiths, "Petitions of Acadian Exiles, 1755–1785: A Neglected Source," *Histoire sociale—Social History* 11 (May 1978): 215–23.

68. Massignon, *Parlers français* 2: 648, 1702.

69. Griffiths, "Petitions of Acadian Exile," 218f.

70. A.M. MacMechan, ed., *Nova Scotia Archives*, vol. 3, *Original Minutes of H.M. Council at Annapolis Royal, 1720–1739* (Halifax, 1908), 112, 122.

71. Jean-Claude Dupont, *Héritage d'Acadie* (Québec: Leméac, 1977), 172, and *Histoire populaire de l'Acadie* (Montréal: Leméac, 1979).

72. MacMechan, *Nova Scotia Archives* 3: 3, 17.

73. W.P. Bell, *The "Foreign Protestants" and the Settlement of Nova Scotia: The History of a Piece of Arrested British Colonial Policy in the Eighteenth Century* (Toronto: University of Toronto Press, 1961), 44–45, 64–85, 328–35.

74. Griffiths, "Petitions of Acadian Exiles," 216f.

75. Jean Daigle, "Les Relations commerciales de l'Acadie avec le Massachusetts: le cas de Charles-Amador de Saint-Étienne de la Tour, 1695–1697," *Revue de l'Université de Moncton* 9 (1976): 353–61.

76. Clark, *Acadia*, 203–4.

77. Têtu et Gagnon, *Mandements, lettres pastorales et circulaires des évêques de Quebec, 1888*, 15–16, reprinted in E. de Grace, G. Desjardins, R.-A. Mallet, *Histoire d'Acadie par les Textes*, 4 fascicules (Fredericton: Ministère de l'éducation du Nouveau-Brunswick, 1976), 1 (1604–1760): 19.

78. A most interesting question which needs further investigation and which reinforces the theory of Acadian respect for, but not subservience to, the Catholic church, is the matter of dispensations for marriage between second cousins accorded at Annapolis Royal between 1727 and 1755, the usual reason for such dispensations being premarital pregnancy. Cf. Clark, *Acadia*, 203–4, passim.

79. Massignon, *Parlers français* 2: 691–99.

80. Not only fiddleheads but also *titines de souris (salicornia Europaia)* and *passe-pierre (saxifraga Virginiensis)*. See Massignon, *Parlers français* 1: 183.

81. Knox, *Historical Journal* 1: 94–96, quoted in A.G. Doughty, *The Acadian Exiles* (Toronto: Glasgow, Brook and Company, 1916), 40.

Article Nine

Imperial Transitions

Elizabeth Mancke

In 1713 Louis XIV, ostensibly at the request of the British government, released French Protestants who had been imprisoned on naval galleys. To match this French show of benevolence, Queen Anne sent a letter to Francis Nicholson, governor of Nova Scotia, informing him that Acadians who were 'willing to Continue our Subjects [were] to retain and Enjoy their said Lands and Tenements without any Lett or Molestation.' Those who chose to relocate into French territory could sell their property. Beyond showing herself to be as magnanimous a monarch as Louis XIV, Queen Anne's letter was a personal gesture to her new 'subjects' that symbolized Britain's sovereignty over Nova Scotia.[1]

Such displays of royal benevolence anticipated a complementary show of fealty from the recipients, in the case of the Acadians an oath of allegiance. As is well known, they demurred. By declining, Acadians implicitly, though whether willfully is unclear, challenged British sovereignty in Nova Scotia. The internationally negotiated transfer of Acadia from French to British sovereignty needed acceptance and legitimation on the ground by the Acadians, if not the natives as well. The absence of clear acceptance and legitimation raised a number of problems. If Acadians did not swear an oath of allegiance, could they still own their property as Queen Anne had promised, and practise Catholicism as stipulated in the Treaty of Utrecht? Were they entitled to the crown's protection? Did the refusal to swear the oath mean that Acadians did not acknowledge the territorial transfer of Acadia from France to Britain? How was the crown's responsibility to establish civilian government to be expressed if the local population refused the crown's sovereignty? Technically not subjects or denizens, were the Acadians to be treated as friendly aliens or enemy aliens? In short, how was civilian government to be established in Nova Scotia, and what kind of government would it be?

No colony in British America offered clear precedents. In all earlier British colonial ventures, the settlement of large numbers of English subjects meant that governmental authority

Source: Elizabeth Mancke, "Imperial Transitions," in *The 'Conquest' of Acadia, 1710: Imperial, Colonial and Aboriginal Constructions*, eds., John G. Reid, Maurice Basque, Elizabeth Mancke, Barry Moody, Geoffrey Plank, William Wicken (Toronto: University of Toronto Press, 2004): 178–202, 255–260. Reprinted with permission of the publisher.

and sovereignty were negotiated and legitimated within a common cultural matrix that included notions about law, property holding, governmental authority, the appropriate relations between the governed and their governors, and who was friend and who foe.[2] As well, these colonies developed creole colonial elites defined not just by their social and economic power, but also by political power. Even the conquered colonies of Jamaica and New York (with New Jersey carved off the latter) did not offer precedents. After the English conquest of Jamaica in 1655, most Spanish residents fled the island for Spanish territory, thereby obviating the problem of incorporating Spanish-speaking, Catholic residents into the English world.[3] In New York, conquered in 1664, most of the Dutch residents of the former colony of New Netherland had stayed; predominantly Protestants, most were naturalized by legislation or allowed resident status by executive patents.[4] In both Jamaica and New York, the arrival of English settlers soon consolidated English control.

In neither Jamaica nor New York did colonial officials suffer chronic fear that the Spanish or the Dutch would try to retake their former colonies. While Spain had other large colonies near Jamaica, in particular Cuba and Hispaniola, neither posed a threat of the magnitude that the French presence in Île Royale and Canada posed for Nova Scotia. New Netherland had been the only Dutch colony on mainland North America. After its loss, the Dutch evinced no serious interest in temperate climate colonies, concentrating their expansionist energies on colonies in tropical zones. Jamaica had no remaining native peoples, though it had a large maroon population living in the island's interior who challenged British control of the island through the eighteenth century.[5] New York had large numbers of natives, in particular the Houdenasaunee (Iroquois), and the English built on the trade and military alliances the Dutch had established. Nova Scotia's native peoples, by contrast, asserted their autonomy, intermittently resisted the British, and maintained diplomatic relations with the French.[6]

In Nova Scotia, none of the above characteristics existed. Political elites, as represented by metropolitan officials, had few ties to social and economic elites among the Acadians.[7] The dominant residential populations were Acadian and native. Acadians were Catholic and the natives at least nominally so, thus perpetuating ties to New France through the ministrations of French priests. While the British acknowledged native groups as self-governing, Acadians were to be within the pale of day-to-day British government. Yet under the English Test Act of 1673, their Catholicism made them ineligible to hold public office or sit on juries, even if they did swear an oath of allegiance. How was Nova Scotia to be governed when, by law, the majority of the European population could not participate in government? And if Acadians could not participate, who would? The near-absence of Protestant settlers in Nova Scotia before 1749 meant that under existing laws there were not enough people to establish the full apparatus of British government that had become conventional in other colonies: an assembly that would vote taxes to run the colony, county and/or town government for local administration, a land office and registry of deeds, and a judicial system.

New legislation on naval stores further complicated the recruitment of settlers for Nova Scotia, as well as reflected a piecemeal interest by the metropolitan government in the potential of new colonial resources. During the War of the Spanish Succession (1702–13), the Board of Trade persuaded Parliament to pass the Naval Stores Act (1705) to encourage the North American colonies to produce tar, pitch, rosin, turpentine, hemp, masts, yards, and bowsprits for use by the Royal Navy. To reserve the woods for naval stores, the legislation prohibited the cutting of 'Pitch, Pine, or Tar Trees,' under twelve inches in diameter on ungranted land, a clause which applied to land from New Jersey north. The 1691 charter of Massachusetts had already reserved trees over twenty-four inches in diameter for use as masts for the navy. Both the 1705 legislation and the Massachusetts charter were interpreted to extend to Nova Scotia, and thus land could not be granted to new settlers without being surveyed for naval stores. As written, the legislation implicitly required colonies to bear the cost of the surveys, and in Nova Scotia there simply was no money for such expenses.[8]

With its garrisoned, English-speaking, Protestant officials, and its dispersed native and French Catholic communities, Nova Scotia was not representative of early-eighteenth century British America. However, officials who governed Nova Scotia had the untenable charge 'to establish a form of Government consonant to that of the other Plantations in America.'[9] For nearly half a century, they struggled unsuccessfully to find the combination and sequence of conditions, short of deporting the Acadians, to pull the colony within the normative range of colonial governance. Their failure to craft and legitimate a new definition of colonial subject and an appropriate system of government that was acceptable in both Nova Scotia and Britain is testimony both to the profoundly English political and constitutional legacy of seventeenth-century colonial development and to how wrenching would be the accommodation of a more ethnically and constitutionally polyglot empire in the eighteenth century.[10]

In this sense, Nova Scotia's history is central to understanding the constitutional and political reconfiguration and redefinition of the British empire over the eighteenth century. The Acadians' refusal to swear an oath of allegiance after the Treaty of Utrecht made variable what had become normative and interdependent elements of British colonial governments. The maintenance of colonies depended on populations that acknowledged themselves subject to the British monarch, that staffed the civilian governments established on an English model, and that voted taxes to pay the expenses of running a colony. The absence of these three critical elements of colonial governments — a natural-born or naturalized subject population, a civilian government, and locally generated financial resources — stymied the men sent to govern Nova Scotia. Unable to act within established conventions, officials articulated a wide range of values about the fundamentals of colonial governance in order to explain why they were obliged to govern outside those norms. Their quandary makes the official record of post-conquest Nova Scotia an extended discussion about the nature of British colonial government.

Ironically, the severe limitations of Nova Scotia laid bare the skeleton of colonial governance that the success of other colonies obscured. Using the official record from 1710 to 1749, this chapter analyses what the political history of Nova Scotia can tell us about the nature of British colonial government in the early modern era. The chapter is divided into four sections: the first deals with the establishment of civilian government; the second considers the necessity of a civilian population of subjects; the third examines the problem of financing colonies; and the final section assesses the impact of shifting metropolitan policies after 1748. Within this analysis there are three important chronological periods. The first period, from 1710, the year of the conquest, to 1720, when Governor Richard Philipps arrived in the colony, was characterized by enormous ambiguity over the long-term status of the colony and its Acadian and native residents. The second period, 1720–30, saw the establishment of an executive council as the institutional cornerstone for the colony's civilian government. But as Philipps soon discovered, until the Acadians swore an oath of allegiance, the government would lack civilian subjects and thus the personnel to establish collateral institutions. In the late 1720s the Acadians swore qualified oaths of allegiance, giving the colony a civilian population of subjects, albeit Catholic and of suspect loyalty. In the third period, 1730–48, the colony's government began the process of surveying and registering Acadian lands and collecting quitrents, but it still could not call an assembly that could vote the taxes so necessary for financing colonies. The colony's financial straits ended in 1748 when Parliament appropriated monies to build Halifax as a north Atlantic naval port and new capital of Nova Scotia. Suddenly the colony had abundant financial resources, unprecedented both in the history of Nova Scotia and the history of British America, a shift, as it were, from colonial to imperial government.

Richard Philipps, appointed governor general of Nova Scotia in 1717, found upon his arrival in the colony in April 1720 that there 'has been hitherto no more than a Mock Government,' He recognized that without the Acadians swearing an oath of allegiance 'the British Government canot [sic] be said to be Established,' unless the government supplied resources to coax or coerce the Acadians into fidelity or to settle 'Natural born Subjects' in the colony.[11] The Acadians' unwillingness to swear an oath of allegiance compelled him to tell the Board of Trade that the effective extension of British sovereignty to Nova Scotia depended not just on the conquest and the subsequent Treaty of Utrecht, but also on the ongoing appearance and substance of a British presence in the colony. Quite simply, 'it is necessary that the Government at home exert itself a little and be at some extraordinary expence.' So appalled was Philipps at the state of the colony and the lack of resources for governing that he argued it would be better to give the territory back to the French than to 'be contented with the name only of Government.'[12]

Philipps's frustration, a decade after the 1710 conquest, is indicative of how incomprehensible conditions in Nova Scotia were from the perspective of the metropole. Much of the two years between the issuing of his original commission in 1717 and his arrival in Nova Scotia Philipps had spent in London negotiating with officials for instruction and powers that fitted the known problems of the colony. Since the conquest, metropolitan policy for governing this new acquisition was ill-defined. A garrison command under successive governors or their deputies had nominally governed the colony, and many of the concerns they communicated back to Britain dealt with the abysmal state of the finances for maintaining troops stationed at Annapolis Royal and the financial and psychological wounds sustained by everyone in the open antagonism that developed among the officers, especially between Francis Nicholson and Samuel Vetch.[13]

Various of Philipps's predecessors who had found themselves responsible for the colony had made hesitant moves to separate military and civilian governance, but like efforts to resolve other problems, their efforts fell victim to metropolitan indifference and internal squabbling. The winter after the conquest, four British army officers and two Acadians convened a court to adjudicate disputes.[14] After the Treaty of Utrecht, Thomas Caulfeild, lieutenant-governor under Nicholson and then Vetch, tried to establish courts suitable to the Acadians and the British, but Nicholson challenged his authority to do so. In reporting the incident to the Board of Trade, Caulfeild said that he had told Nicholson that as the highest civilian officer resident in the colony, he 'Should always endeavour to Cultivate as good an Understanding amongst the People as possible believing the same Essential for his Majesties Service.' Given the choice of establishing a court without a commission or holding 'myselfe blamable to Suffer Injustice to be done before Me without taking Notice thereof,' he chose the former.[15]

The decision of the French to build Louisbourg, combined with the death of Caulfeild in 1717, forced even indifferent metropolitan officials to acknowledge the colony's needs. The British crown formed a new regiment of foot, under the command of Colonel Richard Philipps, as a permanent part of His Majesty's land forces. Philipps was also appointed governor general of Nova Scotia, and his military commission would pay his gubernatorial salary. Philipps quickly recognized that his military commission did not include sufficient powers or instructions to manage Nova Scotia's known problems, much less its unknown ones. In particular, he was concerned that he have the authority to establish a civilian government. Staying in London until 1719, he negotiated with the Board of Trade and Board of Ordnance for more resources, power, and a new commission, without realizing how utterly inadequate these preparations would still be.[16]

The royal instructions to Philipps in 1719, and subsequent instructions drafted until 1749, included the injunction that until Nova Scotia's government was established the governor would receive 'a copy of the instructions given by his Majesty to the governor of Virginia, by which you will conduct yourself till his Majesty's further pleasure shall be known.'[17] John Bartlet Brebner labelled this government by analogy, which it was, but he overdrew the comparison to Virginia and underestimated the larger colonial context.[18] Since the Restoration, the Privy Council had slowly been regularizing and routinizing basic communications with colonies, and dispatches to one colony were often used as the template for instructions to other colonies.[19]

Similarities among colonies had emerged less from metropolitan design than from an English commitment to 'such devices as trial by jury, habeas corpus, due process of law, and representative government.'[20] An increasingly integrated British Atlantic economy depended on shared legal protections of property, thus encouraging compatible judicial systems throughout British America. Colonial charters, and then instructions to governors after many colonies were royalized, emphasized that no laws were to be passed that were inconsistent with English law. The Treasury expected colonies to be self-financing, and throughout the Americas this financial imperative encouraged the establishment of colonial assemblies, based on the model of the House of Commons and the principle that elected representatives should determine taxation.

By the end of the seventeenth century, from an imperial perspective, the problem with colonial governments lay not so much in their weaknesses, but stemmed rather from too much unchecked and undisciplined vitality and autonomy. Little in the 106 years between the founding of Virginia (1607) and the French cession of Acadia (1713) would lead metropolitan officials to believe that Nova Scotia would not develop a similarly vital government. And because much of metropolitan practice for governing far-flung territories had developed reactively rather than proactively, there was no bureaucratic practice of designing a colonial government.[21]

From within the colony, however, it was blindingly and frustratingly obvious that configuring Nova Scotia's government to the colonial standard would be a daunting, if not impossible, task. As Philipps noted, without people willing to acknowledge themselves subject to the British crown, the home government had to spend money to make manifest British sovereignty among a non-British people. If the merits of British government were not culturally internalized, as with natural-born subjects, or consciously accepted, as with naturalized subjects, then they had to be intentionally externalized, displayed, and made tangibly attractive. The presence of the governor general and the establishment of civilian government were two such manifestations. Philipps believed, perhaps arrogantly, that the Acadians were surprised to find that he, and not just a deputy, had come to Nova Scotia. Gauging the symbolism of leadership, the Acadians had concluded, he believed, that if the British did not send a high-ranking official to the colony, then they did not consider it important and they might well return the colony to the French.[22]

Philipps promptly set about to establish the foundation for a civilian government. He issued a proclamation to the Acadians reminding them of their duty to swear an oath of allegiance that would protect their rights to 'le libre Excercise de leur Religion,' as well as allow them 'de Droits et Privileges Civils comme S'ils estroint Anglois.'[23] On 25 April, his fifth day at Annapolis Royal, he convened a civilian council. Lacking a full complement of twelve Protestant civilians who could serve on the Council, he chose by rank three military officers.[24] A year later, on 11 April 1721, Philipps also constituted the Council as a 'Court of Judicature,' despite the absence of conditions necessary to establish courts 'according to the Lawes of Great Britain.' The Virginia instructions, however, did allow the governor and Council to sit as a court of justice, and given the large number of 'Memorialls, Petition[s], and Complaints' submitted to Philipps for his assessment, he thought it best to have them decided by the Council sitting in a judicial capacity.[25] Initially the Council planned court days for the first Tuesdays in May, August, November, and February, but in practice it heard cases throughout the year as they occurred. The Council secretaries never wrote separate minutes for executive and judicial business, and in many sittings the Council shifted back and forth between its two roles. Only by reading the text of the minutes can one discern distinctions in the Council's exercise of its two functions.

The seeming blending of executive and judicial functions was largely a consequence of limited personnel rather than a disregard of appropriate judicial procedure. In an analysis of Nova Scotia's justice system circa 1710–50, Thomas Barnes has argued persuasively that over time 'the council became less summary and more procedure-bound,' particularly after 1730, when the number of cases heard by the council increased. Lawrence Armstrong, who served as lieutenant-governor during most of the 1730s, and Paul Mascarene, who became Council president upon Armstrong's death in 1739, were staunch advocates of due process.[26] The rising number of civil cases in the 1730s prompted Armstrong to issue a memo to the Acadians that emphasized the injustice of attempts at 'Hurried' and 'Impatient' litigation that did not give people 'Due time to prepare and make Answer to Such Complaints & Petitions as have been often Lodged & Exhibited against them.' Haste also resulted in 'many frivolous and undigested Complaints' being brought to the Council. To curb the problems, Armstrong reinstated four terms in which the Council would sit as a court.[27]

The other major component of civilian government in early Nova Scotia was the system of Acadian deputies. On 29 April 1720 the Council, working beyond the letter of its instructions, voted to authorize the French inhabitants in the settlements on the Annapolis River to choose six deputies to represent their interests to the governor and Council. Within a few weeks the communities at Minas and Cobequid had also elected deputies.[28] While the system of deputies remained until the deportation of the Acadians beginning in 1755, their role in the government of Nova Scotia shifted considerably, especially after the oath taking in the late 1720s and 1730.[29]

In the early 1720s, the deputies had quasi-diplomatic functions. They were the spokespeople when the Acadians declined to swear an oath of allegiance in 1720. The Council consulted them for witnesses or evidence in both criminal and civil cases. During the hostilities between the natives and the British from 1722 until the signing of the peace treaty in 1725, the deputies were consulted about the presence of natives in their communities. Once peace obviated their quasi-diplomatic role, the importance of deputies temporarily declined. The Council contacted them very few times between 1725 and 1729 and their selection, or non-selection, became haphazard. On 21 November 1729, one day after arriving back in Annapolis Royal after an eight-year absence, Philipps notified the Council that he had appointed new deputies for the Annapolis River settlements and had increased their number from four to eight.[30] Philipps's unilateral decision to appoint deputies is indicative of how irregular their selection had become and how infrequently the Council had consulted them in the previous years. In 1732, after Philipps had returned to Britain and Lawrence Armstrong was the chief governing officer, the deputies complained that Philipps had appointed them rather than letting them be elected by the people they represented.[31]

One of the primary reasons for Philipps's 1729 return to Nova Scotia was to get the Acadians to swear an oath of allegiance, a new push that had been started in 1726 by Lawrence Armstrong after a five-year hiatus on the issue during which the peace had been negotiated with the natives. In Philipps's oath-taking negotiations with the Acadians, he promised them in the name of George II that their religious and property rights would be honoured, provided they surveyed and registered claims to the latter.[32] As he explained to the Board of Trade, the collection of quitrents would 'contribute towards the Support of Government.'[33] Informing the council on December 7, 1730, that he had obtained oaths from all the Acadians, he also noted that he had appointed Alexander Bourg, former procurator general under the French regime, as collector of rents. Philipps instructed him to report on 'what Homage and Duties they paid to the [French] Crown,' as the basis for establishing quitrents, one of the few instances of the British harkening back to practices of the French regime.[34]

The decision to survey and register Acadian lands and to charge quitrents generated a whole new set of administrative tasks that reinvigorated the role of the deputies, created new offices such as the farmers of rents, and fostered disputes over land boundaries that sent dozens of litigants to the Council for dispute resolution. It became common for deputies to ascertain the nature of land disagreements, to order inhabitants to make property lines, and to organize inhabitants to clear roads and keep dikes in good repair.[35] The enhanced importance of deputies to the administration of local government also brought about the regularization of their election. On 11 September 1732, the council decided, in consultation with lieutenant-governor Armstrong and the Annapolis River deputies, that annual elections for deputies would be held on 11 October, provided it was not a Sunday and 'then it Shall be on the Munday following.' Significantly, the chosen date commemorated the reduction of Port Royal.[36]

After Paul Mascarene became president of the council after the death of Armstrong in 1739, he wrote a memorial that codified the role of the deputies. They were to be men of property and good sense who had the interest of the community at heart. They had the power to consult among themselves and to convene meetings of the residents they represented. They were to monitor the maintenance of fences and the control of livestock, oversee the upkeep of bridges and roads, and find people to farm the king's rents.[37] In addition to the responsibilities of the deputies after 1730, the rent farmers were to record all land transactions, as well as wills and testaments, tasks associated with registrars of deeds and probate in other British colonies.

Administratively, most of the functions of local government common in British colonies had been institutionalized in Nova Scotia during the 1730s, largely through the office of the deputies, and they would remain critical to local administration until the deportation. Mascarene, in particular, described the nature of local government in Nova Scotia to the Board of Trade, noting that the needs of government were great enough to warrant allowing the Acadians to hold local offices.[38] Operational within the colony, the deputies had no legal standing under British law, which prohibited Catholics from holding public office, and virtually no acknowledgement outside the colony. Significantly, when the Acadians were deported, beginning in 1755, deputies who had faithfully served the British government were treated no differently from Acadians who had supported the French.

What is striking about Nova Scotia's early-eighteenth century record is how assiduously officials worked to create and maintain a government that honoured 'the rights of Englishmen,' including the minimization of military rule. The first four decades of British governance in Nova Scotia, despite the preponderance of members of the government with military commissions, is testimony to Jack Greene's argument that the single most defining characteristic of English, and then British, identity in the early modern Atlantic world was a commitment to English liberty.[39] If any place in seventeenth- or eighteenth-century British America had a government run on military principles, it would have been Nova Scotia, as some people at the time, and some historians, believed was true.[40] The chief pieces of evidence for this contention were the military officers and a government that deviated from other British colonial governments. Neither individually nor together do they make the case.[41]

First, we cannot assume that all men in the British army eschewed the English commitment to liberty. When outsiders charged that the officers stationed at Annapolis Royal were attempting to create a military government, ten of them protested that they served merely 'for want of other Brittish Subjects.' They acted 'with a due regard to the Liberty and Property of the Subject and the Peace and well being of his Majesty's Province,' and had 'never had any advantage or Salary.'[42] Men inclined to abuse their military power were likely to be checked, either by a superior officer or the council. After the death of lieutenant-governor Armstrong in 1739, the relationship between the civilian Council and the garrison command became a matter of contention. Alexander Cosby, lieutenant-colonel of the 40th regiment and Paul Mascarene's superior officer in the army, questioned the property of Mascarene, rather than he, serving as Council president. A Board of Trade ruling, however, had stated that in the absence of both the governor and lieutenant-governor, the most senior councillor would serve as council president, not the most senior military officer. Cosby tried to remove Mascarene from Annapolis Royal by ordering him to Canso to serve in the garrison there, but Mascarene refused to go. He reported to the Board of Trade that 'I am firmly persuaded if I had remov'd from hence, the Civil Government would have been of no use, and disorder would naturally have issued.' Despite endless slights from Cosby, Mascarene believed that he had preserved 'the good effects of the Civil Government administred . . . over the French Inhabitants of this Province.'[43]

In the settlement of Canso, inhabited largely by New Englanders engaged in the fishery, Governor Philipps had first appointed justices of the peace in 1720. In 1729, during his brief sojourn there, four residents petitioned Philipps to appoint a 'Civil Magistracy' that could sit in Canso and adjudicate 'the many Petty Differences & Cases which Daily Arise in this Fishery that Call for a determination too tedious & Triball to trouble Your Excellency with,' which he did.[44] In 1732 Edward How, one of Canso's justices of the peace, complained to Armstrong that Captain Christopher Aldridge, the highest-commanding officer at Canso, divested the 'Justices of the Peace and Civil Magistrates of all Authority.' Armstrong sent Aldridge a strong reprimand for having 'taken upon your Self the entire Management of the Civil as well as the Military affairs.' Apparently, Aldridge had told the angry JPs that he arrogated no more power than Philipps or Armstrong had as the chief authority in Annapolis. Armstrong corrected Aldridge's claim, noting that 'you assume a much Greater power than Either his Excellency or my self Ever pretended to and in making Either of us your precedent in such Respects; I must say . . . that you do us injustice.' Aldridge was not to conflate his military authority as the highest-ranking officer at Canso with his civilian authority as the president of the Council there, in which latter capacity he had to heed the advice and decisions of all civilian officers.[45]

Armstrong's strong defence of civilian government against usurpation by military men is ironic when framed against his pay. In 1728 or 1729, Armstrong petitioned the Board of Trade to receive a portion of Philipps's salary, based on the Virginia proviso that if the governor was not resident in the colony then the lieutenant-governor should receive a portion of the governor's salary. Armstrong pointed out that he, and not Philipps, had been serving as governor in Nova Scotia. The Board of Trade referred Armstrong's petition to the entire Privy Council, which concluded that it had no discretion over Philipps's salary. Virginia, which paid its governor from an export duty of two shillings per hogshead of tobacco, was the only mainland colony with a permanent revenue for the governor's salary, or the lieutenant-governor's in the former's absence. Philipps's salary, like the governors' salaries in Bermuda and South Carolina, came from the captaincy of an independent company of foot, and it was 'Founded on the Establishment of Your Majesty's Land Forces . . . and not within the Jurisdiction of Your Majesty's Privy Councill.'[46] Without an assembly to raise taxes for the governor or lieutenant-governor's salary, the men who served in Nova Scotia were entirely dependent on their military pay. Armstrong received some justice when in 1731 the British government ordered him to return to Nova Scotia with orders for Philipps's recall to answer charges that he had not paid the officers in his company. Upon resuming control of the government as lieutenant-governor, Armstrong would receive the governor's salary.[47]

The problem of how to pay officials of the crown serving in the colonies indicates that the appointment of men with military commissions to overseas postings had less to do with a desire to militarize the empire than a desire to run the empire parsimoniously. Commissioned officers had a salaried, bureaucratic relationship to the metropolitan government, whether they were stationed in London, Hanover, Gibraltar, or Annapolis Royal. Given the lack of Protestant subjects to serve in an assembly and vote taxes to pay a governor, and given an absence of metropolitan monies to pay a civilian to be governor, a British colonial government in early-eighteenth-century Nova Scotia would have been inconceivable without men who were also military officers. The ideological and pecuniary biases in favour of Protestant and self-financing overseas dependencies exaggerated the role of military men in Nova Scotia, and the men appointed to govern the colony understood the negative prejudice of that bias. Philipps, Armstrong, and Mascarene were all acutely aware that the perception that 'martial law prevails here' discouraged settlers from moving to the colony. Despite the hardships of a shortage of subjects, a monetary deficit, and some military officers who would have abused their power had they not been checked, the government of Nova Scotia from 1720 to 1749 was more civilian than military in its ethos and execution.[48]

The problems engendered by the Acadians' refusal to swear an oath of allegiance have generally been interpreted as ones of security; they were 'Snakes in [our] Bosoms,' to use Lawrence Armstrong's graphic phrase.[49] The problem was, however, more fundamental. The lack of subjects impeded the day-to-day governing of the colony, and in the minds of most British officials, civil governance was a symbiotic and dialectical relationship between the governed and their governors. So long as Acadians did not swear an oath of allegiance, and so long as they remained on Nova Scotian soil that could not be granted to Protestant settlers, a 'proper' civilian government with officials drawn from the local population could not be established. Land could not be granted or deeded. Taxes could not be assessed, except for minimal charges. The Navigation Acts made Acadian trade illegal. And, as Philipps noted, the presence of subjects in a colony legitimated claims of sovereignty in ways that treaties and soldiers could not.

The question was, who might become these Nova Scotian subjects? And how might they be cajoled or, if need be, coerced into this role? In the minds of British officials, two different groups were possible. The Acadians could swear an oath of allegiance, which, as noted above, did make possible the deeding of land. Legally they could not hold public office, but extra-legally, given the exigencies of the colony, they did. Protestants, either British or foreign, were preferable, because there were no legal bars on their participation in government. But they needed to be persuaded to move to the colony, and the legal and financial constraints on land grants needed to be removed. The Mi'kmaq and Wulstukwiuk were never mentioned as possible subjects for the purposes of establishing English-style civilian government. In the first instance, the British wished to achieve amity, in lieu of the open enmity, with them, with occasional and unresolved discussion about whether they were 'Friends or Subjects.'[50]

The terms of the Treaty of Utrecht, followed by Queen Anne's letter to Nicholson, obliged the British government to look first to the Acadians as potential subjects. Since the signing of the terms of capitulation in 1710, the British had made intermittent attempts to persuade the Acadians to swear an oath of allegiance. The Acadians, for their part, became adept equivocators, supported in some measure by the terms of the capitulation, their treaty rights, Queen Anne's letter, the weakness of colonial government, and the volatile geopolitics of the northeast. The first systematic attempt to persuade the Acadians to swear an oath of allegiance began in 1717, when John Doucett, the new lieutenant-governor under Richard Philipps, arrived in Nova Scotia. Doucett soon heard the range of Acadian explanations for why they would not swear an oath of allegiance. The foremost plea was that they were still considering relocating. Some Acadians thought they could move across the Bay of Fundy to the Passamaquoddy area 'where they Fancy themselves secure and that there no notice would be taken of them, tho it is still in his Majesty's Dominions.' Doucett, like other officials, looked on these protestations about moving with a jaundiced eye, noting that 'this has been their declaration every Winter for Five or Six Years Past so that wee do not give much Creditt to it.'[51]

Acadians also argued that if they swore an oath of allegiance to the British monarch, they would invite the wrath of the natives. This excuse elicited little sympathy; Doucett noted that if an Indian acts 'insolent in their Houses,' they do not hesitate to throw out the person. Doucett did not know of cases of Mi'kmaq taking revenge on Acadians.[52] On this matter, his scepticism was probably unfounded, given the ongoing tensions between the natives and the British that would not slacken until the mid-1720s. The British believed that the natives were tools of the French, and resisted understanding natives as agents independent of the French and negotiating their own issues. The Acadian response probably does represent their recognition of native autonomy, from the French government and from themselves, despite a long history of trade relations, intermarriage, and at times military alliances.

Rumours, reputedly started by the French priests, provided new rationales for procrastination. After the accession of George I in 1714, a priest working in Nova Scotia reputedly received a letter from France claiming that the 'Pretender was Again Landed in Scotland.' In response to the threat George I had 'sent for Ten thousand French' troops to drive back the Stuart pretender. Upon landing in England, the French troops 'all declared for the Pretender [and] . . . Establisht him on the Throne of Great Brittain.' In gratitude, he 'intended to give to the French, all they should ask,' which presumably included Acadia. Doucett rebutted this rumour, telling Peter Mellanson of Minas that 'King George . . . is, God be Praise'd, as firm & fixt in the Throne of Great Brittain as Ever Lewis the 14th was in the French Throne.'[53]

In recounting this story to the Board of Trade, Doucett hoped it would not find him 'impertinent,' but wanted to use the incident to ask it to find 'Some Method to Convince these People that their Priests are Fallible.' The story was not entirely far-fetched. Queen Anne had died in 1714, and there had been some uncertainty over her successor. But it was far-fetched that George I, a German prince, would ask the French for military support against the Stuart pretender they had been sheltering since the flight of James II in 1688.[54] A more plausible rumour was that the Acadian right to worship as Catholics and have French priests was a ploy by the British. Their priests reminded them that the British in Ireland did not allow Catholic priests and also dispossessed Catholic landowners of their real property. This rumour cast doubt on the promise of Queen Anne that the Catholic Acadians could continue to practise their religion and retain their property.

Both sides, Acadian and British, played a waiting game. For the Acadians, if the past were any measure, British governance might well be fleeting. In the first decade after the conquest, governors tried coercion, backed not by force, but by inflated rhetoric and a willingness to let British residents suffer a penalty worse than the one they meted on the Acadians. Nicholson, in his frustration with Acadian obstinacy, banned trade with them, which caused serious deprivation among the troops, who had few alternative sources for most food supplies.[55] Meanwhile the Acadians ate well and smuggled their surpluses to the French in Cape Breton. In the fall of 1717, Doucett, appealing to the Navigation Acts, banned Annapolis River Acadians from trading and fishing. He calculated that by spring and the start of the fishing season, these Acadians would abandon their obdurate position and would swear the oath of allegiance. They did not weaken. These threats depended on some ability to enforce them. With no government vessels to patrol the waters near Annapolis Royal, much less up the Bay of Fundy to Minas Basin or Cobequid, Doucett's pronouncements to the Acadians that it was

'Dangerous . . . to Triffle with so Great a Monarch [as George I],' were little more than bluster, and the Acadians surely understood as much.[56]

Richard Philipps's decision, pursuant to his arrival in April 1720, to have the Acadians elect deputies was to give him representatives with whom he could negotiate taking the oath of allegiance. By September, the Acadians had proved 'insolent' rather than compliant, obliging the Council to address the problem 'of the most effectuall way of setling this his Majestys Province.' It recommended telling the metropolitan government that 'more regular forces [be] sent over here to curb the Insolency's of the present french Inhabitants, and Indians,' a vain request until 1749. More reasonably and immediately, it decided that the five communities of Acadians be allowed to continue to elect deputies who would report to the governor and Council.[57]

Governor Philipps and the Council wrote the King on 27 September 1720 asking for guidance on how to proceed with the problem of making the Acadians subjects, noting that the French priests had told them that their allegiance to France was 'indissoluble,' an interpretation of the bonds of allegiance that was not inconsistent with some legal thought. After rehearsing the impunity with which the Acadians acted, largely because the King's authority scarcely extended beyond firing range of the fort, the governor and council asked for additional troops and matériel, as well as naval vessels for service in Nova Scotian waters.[58]

This letter, in the minds of the governor and council, shifted the responsibility for determining how to proceed in getting the Acadians to become British subjects to the King and his ministers. The following spring (1721) the Acadians living on the Annapolis River petitioned Philipps for permission to sow their fields or leave for Cape Breton. Philipps responded that he was extending the time allowed for them to submit to the British King, that he had written him, and until he had an answer the issue of the oath of allegiance was deferred. This deferral, unless he heard otherwise, protected their property rights.[59] In February 1723, after Philipps had returned to England, the Acadian deputies from Annapolis River presented Doucett with a memorial, along with Philipps's 1721 letter to them, requesting permission to plant their fields. Doucett and the Council determined that until they had further notice Philipps's decision stood, and they too would await a royal response.[60]

For the next three years, the issue of the Acadians swearing an oath of allegiance or leaving the colony was moot. The Board of Trade did not respond to Philipps's and the Council's 1720 letter. Peace in Europe, and especially amity with the French, had made the King's ministers complacent about colonial affairs. Relocating the Acadians posed as much of a problem for the British as it did a solution. After the signing of the Treaty of Utrecht, the French began resettling fishers from Placentia, Newfoundland, to Cape Breton. In 1717 they began the building of Louisbourg as a major administrative centre, commercial entrepôt, and naval base. The British recognized that the departure of seasoned French settlers to Cape Breton would be a gift to the French, who had a difficult time recruiting people to go to the colonies. Nova Scotian officials were also concerned that if the Acadians left the colony their lands would have to be quickly resettled and the dikes maintained so that the sea not reclaim its due.

Ongoing tensions with the natives also made peace the most pressing need in the colony, and the governor and Council dealt with little else in the early 1720s. Consequently, concern about an Acadian oath of allegiance receded. Only after 1725 did the question of establishing a civilian population of subjects re-emerge as a regular policy issue for the governor and Council, although by that time the reality of long-term Anglo-French peace muted the immediate security concerns that the Acadians had earlier posed. A new campaign to persuade them to swear an oath of allegiance began in 1725 with the appointment of Lawrence Armstrong as lieutenant-governor, who more generally attempted to implement policies that would bring the colony into greater conformity with practices of British colonial governance elsewhere.[61]

When Armstrong arrived back in Annapolis Royal, he began his efforts at getting the Acadians to swear an oath of allegiance with the people living along the Annapolis River. In the 1710s, the Acadians' two main concerns about swearing a British oath of allegiance had been whether they would relocate out of the colony and whether they would invite the retaliation of the natives; both issues had receded by 1726. Their new and persisting concern would be whether they would have to bear arms in future conflicts with the French or natives. Armstrong told them that as Catholics they were prohibited by law from military service so that the issue was irrelevant.[62] But the concern with military service was not so easily dismissed. Armstrong and the Council tried to circumvent the issue by having the Annapolis River Acadians swear an oath of allegiance with the exemption from military service noted in the margin of the French translation, neither part of the oath nor a formal addendum. The governor and council decided on this allowance as a device 'to gett them over by Degrees.'[63]

To administer an oath to the Acadians outside the Annapolis area, Armstrong commissioned Captain Joseph Bennett and Ensign Erasmus James Philipps to undertake the task. They reported back in the spring of 1727 that the Acadians had refused to swear the oath of allegiance. A priest, Joseph Ignace, told Philipps that the French and English were at peace and that 'the English Ought not to Trouble and Importune a Parcel of Inhabitants that would live quietly and pay the Taxes Justly required without takeing any Oath.' One Acadian, Baptist Veco, told Philipps that the people at Annapolis River were treated worse than before they had taken the oath, 'their Oxen being worked on the Kings Account Without being paid for them.'[64] The governor and council decided to write 'a Civil Letter' inviting 'them once more' to swear the oath of allegiance. When the Acadians declined the invitation to become subjects of the King of England, the governor and Council decided to bar trade up the bay, though the Annapolis River Acadians were exempted because of the oath they had sworn the previous fall.[65]

The death of George I and the accession of George II precipitated a second attempt in September 1727 to elicit an oath. Armstrong sent orders to the Annapolis River deputies to meet with him to consult on the matter. He discovered that the concessions he had made the previous year had not succeeded in winning them 'over by Degrees.' Rather they requested not just an exemption from military service but more priests besides, a presumption which briefly landed four deputies in jail and which prompted an extension of the trade ban to include them.[66] Armstrong and the Council hired a vessel for £100 and sent Ensign Robert Wroth and a detachment up the Bay of Fundy to proclaim the new king and ask the Acadians and natives to swear an oath of allegiance.[67] The Acadians found Wroth an obliging negotiator, who acceded in writing to their request for an exemption from military service. When he reported back to the Council, it found his concessions 'unwarrantable and dishonourable to His Majestys authority and Government and Consequently Null and Void.' At the same meeting, the Council voted that the Acadians' acknowledgement of George II's 'Title and Authority to and over this Province,' their qualifications notwithstanding, made them eligible for 'the Libertys and Privileges of English Subjects.' In particular, the trade ban that Armstrong had imposed on the Acadians would be lifted and trade between the Acadians and British was once again legal. It was yet another illustration of how difficult it was for the government to sustain any form of coercion.[68]

When Richard Philipps returned to Nova Scotia in 1729, he turned his hand to persuading the Acadians to swear an oath of allegiance that was not prejudiced by concessions. In May 1730 he informed the Council of the 'Submission of the Inhabitants of this Province,' save for 'about Seventeen of those of Chignictou who persist in their obstinacy in refusing to Conform to his Majestys Orders.'[69] Philipps might have made concessions to the Acadians to persuade them to swear an oath of allegiance, but there is no written record if he did. As governor he did not have to report in detail to the council, as had Robert Wroth, Joseph Bennett, and Erasmus James Philipps. The Acadians claimed he had made an oral promise that they would not have to bear arms, a contention that became a serious disagreement after 1749 with the establishment of Halifax and the appointment of a new colonial government.[70] During the 1730s and 1740s, however, officials in Nova Scotia treated the oaths as sufficient for beginning a more systematic, although still unconventional, development of British civilian government.

The lack of an oath had precluded much taxation of the Acadians, leaving the skeletal staff of British officials without funds to run the colony. From the conquest in 1710 to Parliament's 1748 decision to fund the building of Halifax, Nova Scotia's officials pleaded with London to finance the most basic needs of colonial government. The lack of a vessel to survey the coast, communicate with other communities, regulate trade, and protect the fishery meant that 'a Governor can be accountable for no more then [sic] the spott he happens to reside on.'[71] By the mid-1720s the ramparts at the fort at Annapolis Royal lay 'level with the Ground in Breaches sufficiently wide for fifty men to enter a breast.'[72] Without an assembly to vote taxes there was no way to raise money in an emergency 'tho' it were but a Shilling and its safety depended on it.'[73] The metropolitan government wanted British settlers in Nova Scotia, but before a governor could grant land the woods had to be surveyed 'for the Preservation of the Woods, which are necessary for the Service of the Royal Navy.'[74] Board of Trade missives that impressed upon Nova Scotia officials the need to preserve naval stores and to settle British subjects elicited responses that stated the obvious: without money to pay a surveyor, the land would remain unused by the navy and ungranted to British settlers.[75]

The unwillingness of the metropolitan government to fund the Nova Scotia government lent urgency to the swearing of an oath by the Acadians. Acadian acceptance of British subjecthood would allow some taxation and hopefully greater Acadian participation in government. Lawrence Armstrong recommended in 1728 that plans for persuading the Acadians to swear an oath of allegiance include posting a garrison on the isthmus. It would allow some oversight of communications between natives in the eastern and western portions of the colony and allow the regulation of the trade throughout the Bay of Fundy. A small garrison, Armstrong reckoned, would not cost more than £1000, 'which those Inhabitants (when subjected) are rich enough to make good.'[76] This infrastructure, however, required an initial investment by the metropolitan government, without which the revenues from the Acadians could not be collected.

Governor Philipps and his lieutenant-governors repeatedly enjoined the Board of Trade to invest in the colony's infrastructure, arguing that the enhanced collection of trade revenues would justify the expense. Among Philipps's initial critiques of Nova Scotia in 1720 was that New Englanders nearly monopolized the trade, but paid no impost towards the maintenance of the government. Upon returning to Nova Scotia in 1729, he recommended fortifying Canso and levying duties on the fish trade, which, he predicted, would generate a colonial revenue second only to the duties collected on the export of tobacco from Virginia, and would exceed the expense of fortifying Canso. The safety of the province, he reminded the Board of Trade, depended on continued peace with France, without which Annapolis Royal and Canso were extremely vulnerable. To recover those settlements if lost would be far more than the outlay for proper regulation and taxing of the fish trade.[77] Colonial officials cautioned the Board of Trade against putting too much emphasis on the collection of quitrents and not on the collection of duties from trade. Quitrents, they believed, would only generate limited revenues; rents collected in the 1730s produced between £10 and £15 annually.[78] Armstrong told the Board of Trade that a quitrent of a penny per acre per annum was too high for the quality of the land, particularly in comparison with neighbouring colonies, and would discourage British or foreign Protestant settlers from moving into the colony.[79]

Reports to Whitehall also emphasized how the financial weaknesses of Nova Scotia's government encouraged the violation of the crown's normal prerogative, particularly by New Englanders. In 1720, Philipps reported that New Englanders regularly took coal from the upper part of the Bay of Fundy, and he was powerless to regulate it in any way.[80] New England traders were frequently cited as agitators among the Acadians. Armstrong reported that William Gamble of Boston, formerly a lieutenant in the army, had told the Acadians not to take the oath of allegiance. In this instance, the issue seemed to have been a power struggle between Alexander Cosby and Armstrong, with Gamble telling the Acadians that Cosby would soon replace Armstrong as lieutenant-governor.[81] As Armstrong tried to explain to the Board of Trade, 'if His Majesty's British Subjects are Suffered to treat his Council with such Indignity and Contempt what can we expect from the French?'[82] The lack of financial resources meant that New Englanders, Acadians, and natives could flout with impunity the authority of the royal government sitting in Annapolis Royal.

Colonial officials believed that the underfunding of government kept the Acadians from swearing an oath of allegiance. Armstrong noted that the 'Lenity' of government encouraged Acadians to stall. Under his commission, he could inflict few penalties. He could prohibit them from fishing, but the Acadians were willing to bear the losses 'in hopes of some Speedy Revolution or Change of Government.'[83] In July 1727 Armstrong barred trade up the Bay of Fundy, on the basis that the Acadians were not subjects and therefore any trade with them was in violation of the Navigation Acts. His proclamation prohibited 'English' subjects from trading with the 'French,' which incensed New Englanders. Thomas Lechmere, Britain's surveyor general for North America, wrote the Board of Trade complaining about the prohibition and asking it to override Armstrong and reopen the trade.[84]

Lack of funds also jeopardized attempts to stabilize relations with natives. Beginning in the 1710s, officials in Nova Scotia repeatedly told the Board of Trade that gift-giving in negotiations with natives was not discretionary. John Doucett informed the Board of Trade in 1718 that gifts were necessary if the natives were to remain friends of the English. He believed that 'the Generality of the Indians would be Sway'd more by the benefitts they receive in this World then trust to all Benefitts their Priests can tell them they will receive in the [next].'[85] Philipps, in contrast, was 'convinced that a hundred thousand [pounds] will not buy them from the French Interest while their priests are among them.' Nevertheless, gift-giving could not be avoided and Philipps had spent £150 on sundry presents that he had distributed in his negotiations with the natives in 1720.[86] When finalizing treaties with the Natives in the mid-1720s, Doucett spent £300 of his own money on gifts.[87] Despite abundant evidence that could demonstrate that regular gift-giving was both important and cost-effective in establishing British–Native relations, it never became routinely funded.

From the perspective of Nova Scotia, Parliament's 1748 decision to fund the building of a northern American naval port on Chebucto Bay was almost too much government and too much money too late. The establishment of Halifax was only tangentially related to the colony's internal needs. Rather it spatially represented the convergence of a number of structural stresses in the empire that had been building over the eighteenth century and metropolitan strategies for handling them. The longstanding problems of Nova Scotia were subsumed under new imperial-level policy, but that meant that the solutions were not necessarily tailored to specific colony-level needs. At the end of the War of the Austrian Succession, Britain faced the problem of how to address the circumstances that had produced its desultory military performance in the war. Both the Ministry and Parliament believed that the Treaty of Aix-la-Chapelle (1748) had created a hiatus in fighting, rather than long-term peace, and it would be but a few years before unresolved problems in both Europe and the extra-European world would produce armed conflict. The British were already planning that in the next war territorial objectives would assume an importance that they had not had in the War of the Austrian Succession (1740–8) when commercial objectives had been paramount. Nova Scotia was just one of many points of territorial tension with other imperial powers: Canada, Rupert's Land, the trans-Appalachian West, Florida, the Caribbean, and Central America were all sites of actual or potential conflict. The building of Halifax was to prepare for hemisphere-wide conflict, a northern expansion of naval bases that stretched from Jamaica to Antigua to Bermuda to Nova Scotia.[88]

For nearly four decades, British officials in Nova Scotia had attempted to make the Board of Trade understand that the poor articulation between metropolitan policy and colonial conditions posed serious long-term problems and had to be rectified. Within the colony, officials recognized that resolving local problems would also resolve imperial problems. A better infrastructure would have allowed for the generation of more revenue and allowed a more systematic surveying of the land for both naval stores and grants to settlers. More government presence might have convinced the Acadians that the British were serious about keeping the colony. As well, it might have made Nova Scotia more attractive for British settlers. Colonial officials knew that the undetermined boundaries between France and British territory, whether on the west side of the Bay of Fundy or along the Canso Strait, would eventually become volatile if not addressed in peacetime. But as Richard Philipps told the Board of Trade in a 1730 communique, 'I am only the Watchman to call and Point out the danger, tis with Your Lordships to get it prevented.'[89]

The building of Halifax did not resolve the problem of the articulation between colonial needs and metropolitan policy, but in an immediate sense made the situation worse, particularly for the Acadians and natives. The escalation of Anglo-French competition privileged imperial needs at the expense of colonial needs. By shifting the seat of the government from Annapolis Royal to Halifax and appointing a new cohort of colonial officials, the metropolitan government eliminated, albeit unwittingly, the internal articulation between British officials, Acadians, and natives, both Mi'kmaq and Wulstukwiuk, that the old regime had crafted over the decades. In so doing, it destroyed an ambiguous but nonetheless shared past, and thus exacerbated the conflict between British officials, Acadians, and natives over the relationship between the past, present, and the future of Nova Scotia and their respective places in it.

The persistent endeavours by the French government to press its interest in Nova Scotia accelerated after 1748. Capitalizing on the ambiguity of the boundary between Nova Scotia and Canada, the French built Fort Beauséjour on the Isthmus of Chignecto. They encouraged—or forced, in some cases—Acadians to move across the Missaguash River, which the French had asserted was their eastern boundary. To resolve the dispute state-to-state the French and British convened a commission to determine the boundary, while in North America, British officials in Nova Scotia built Fort Lawrence just east of the Missaguash and stepped up their presence on the Acadians to swear an unqualified oath of allegiance. In the meantime, the Mi'kmaq protested the British decision to establish settlements and forts without consulting the people whose land it was. They attempted to resolve their differences through both face-to-face meetings with British officials and with attacks on new settlements in Chebucto Bay, Mahone Bay, and Minas Basin. British officials in Nova Scotia had little intention of negotiating with native people whom they deemed to be subjects in rebellion against the crown rather than autonomous nations. Instead, the governor accelerated tensions by authorizing attacks on the Mi'kmaq and offering bounties for their scalps.[90]

In 1755, British troops attacked and seized Fort Beauséjour and in its aftermath began deporting the Acadians, a policy that would continue until 1762. With an unprecedented deployment of soldiers and sailors, the British took Louisbourg in 1758 before moving down the St Lawrence River to defeat the French at Quebec (1759) and Montreal (1760). With the deportation of the Acadians and the defeat of the French at Louisbourg, British officials again recruited Protestant settlers for Nova Scotia. In October 1758, the governor of Nova Scotia, Charles Lawrence, issued a proclamation inviting New Englanders to move to the colony, a decision that further provoked the Mi'kmaq on whose lands these new settlers would plant themselves. When New England agents visited potential town sites they found themselves confronted by militant Mi'kmaq, whose objections delayed the arrival of settlers from 1759 to 1760 and forced the British into another round of treaty negotiations that allowed for settlements on the west side of peninsular Nova Scotia.

With the end of the Seven Years' War and the Treaty of Paris in 1763, the Anglo-French imperial struggle in North America came to an end. The problems of the British empire, however, did not. To some extent, the tortuous process of accommodation that had characterized Nova Scotia since the conquest of Port Royal had left a legacy of newly crafted methods for adapting to the multiethnic empire that now existed on an even larger scale and demanded constitutional accommodation.[91] This was seen in such specific contexts as the adoption of the exact wording of Philipps's 1719 instructions regarding British–native relations — hitherto unique to Nova Scotia, and renewed in instructions to all subsequent Nova Scotia governors until 1773 — to the new Province of Quebec. Quebec governors (and those of East Florida, West Florida, and, with alterations, Grenada) were now enjoined to maintain with native inhabitants 'a strict friendship and good correspondence, so that they may be induced by degrees not only to be good neighbors to our subjects but likewise themselves to become good subjects to us.'[92] More generally, the metropolitan government realized that in its new colonies it could not pretend that they would soon have a natural subject population, English institutions of government, and locally generated financial resources to fund the government. Rather, resources had to be provided to facilitate the transition to a more accommodating form of British government, a logic that eventually found explicit parliamentary expression in the Quebec Act of 1774.

Yet, in other contexts, the problem of weak articulation between metropolitan policy and North American conditions persisted. Again, this administrative disjunction was specifically seen in such situations as General Jeffery Amherst's ill-judged decision in 1760 to eliminate further gift-giving to First Nations, contributing directly to Pontiac's insurgency in 1763. More generally, this same disjunction led frustrated British officials in the Thirteen Colonies to attempt to use coercion to resolve problems. Civil war was the result, and it is well known that the second Treaty of Paris in 1783 left British North America a much smaller place. The experience of Nova Scotia during the four decades following the conquest of Port Royal was not enough to equip contemporaries to salvage very much of the First British Empire. In enabling historians to delineate the empire's difficulties more than two centuries too late, however, the Nova Scotia experience is just the right diagnostic.

NOTES

1. Queen Anne to Francis Nicholson, 1713, PRO, CO217/1, f. 95; and Brebner, *New England's Outpost*, 64–5.
2. Greene, 'Negotiated Authorities.'
3. Dunn, *Sugar and Slaves*, 152–3. A handful of Spaniards fled into the mountains and resisted the English conquest for five years before being driven out.
4. In the English system, the crown, or in the colonies the governor, could endenize aliens with a patent. Only Parliament could naturalize subjects; the rights of colonial assemblies to naturalize subjects was contested. See

Salmond, 'Citizenship and Allegiance,' 270–82; and Kettner, *The Development of American Citizenship,* 3–6, 30, 65–105.

5. Patterson, 'Slavery and Slave Revolts.'

6. See William Wicken, chapter 5 in *Essays in the History of Canadian Law,* vol. 5, ed. by Jim Phillips.

7. Maurice Basque, chapter 8 in *Essays in the History of Canadian Law,* vol. 5, ed. by Jim Phillips. Note exceptions, such as de Goutin.

8. Malone, *Pine Trees and Politics,* 10–27.

9. Paul Mascarene to Board of Trade, 16 August 1740, PRO, CO217/8 f. 72.

10. On the development of a distinctly English definition of seventeenth-century colonies in the Americas, see Canny, 'The Origins of Empire: An Introduction'; compare Griffiths, *The Contexts of Acadian History,* 39. For studies dealing with the increasingly polyglot nature of the empire, see Marshall, 'Empire and Authority in the Later Eighteenth Century'; Mancke, 'Another British America'; and Bowen, 'British Conceptions of Global Empire.'

11. Philipps to Board of Trade, 15 May 1727, PRO, CO217/4, ff. 373–4; Maxwell Sutherland, 'Richard Philipps,' DCB, III, 515–18.

12. Philipps to Board of Trade [1720], PRO, CO217/3, f. 104.

13. Bruce T. McCully, 'Francis Nicholson,' DCB, II, 96–8; and G.M. Waller, 'Samuel Vetch,' DCB, II, 650–2.

14. Brebner, *New England's Outpost,* 61.

15. Caulfeild to Board of Trade, 16 May 1716, in MacMechan, ed., *A Calendar of Two Letter-Books and One Commission-Book,* 38–9; Charles Bruce Fergusson, 'Thomas Caulfeild,' DCB, II, 122–3.

16. Maxwell Sutherland, 'Richard Philipps,' DCB, III, 515–18; *Journals of the House of Commons 1715–1751,* XVIII, 342, 483, 636; XIX, 11, 17, XXVI, 16.

17. 'Nova Scotia Governor to Follow Virginia Instructions,' in Labaree, ed., *Royal Instructions to British Colonial Governors,* I, 85.

18. Brebner, *New England's Outpost,* 73, 134, 138, 239. For an assessment see Barnes, '"The Dayly Cry for Justice,"' 14–16.

19. Labaree, ed., *Royal Instructions to British Colonial Governors,* vii–xvii.

20. Greene, 'Empire and Identity from the Glorious Revolution to the American Revolution,' 209.

21. Braddic, 'The English Government, War, Trade, and Settlement.'

22. Here, the English and French terms might have created some confusion, though one that Philipps worked to the best advantage he could with the Acadians and the Board of Trade. The governor general in New France was the top military official and resident of Quebec. Under him were governors in Trois-Rivières, Montreal, Île Royale, and Louisiana. The civilian counterpart to the governor general of New France was the intendant, with subordinates under him in each jurisdiction. In the British American colonies, each royal colony had a governor, with a lieutenant-governor who, in the absence of the governor, served in his stead. Only in some British colonies was there a governor general, that is, a military officer with a military command in addition to his civil commission as governor. André Vachon, 'The Administration of New France.'

23. Proclamation, 20 April 1720, PRO, CO217/3, f. 40. Author's translations: 'the free exercise of their religion;' and 'civil rights and privileges as if they were English.'

24. The highest-ranking civilian official in Nova Scotia, whether the governor, lieutenant-governor, or president of the Council, always had to justify the appointment of military officers to the Council. See, for example, Philipps to Board of Trade, 3 January 1729, PRO, CO217/5, ff. 190–6; Armstrong to Board of Trade, ibid., ff. 39–44; Mascarene to Board of Trade, 16 August 1740, PRO, CO217/8, f. 72; Mascarene to Board of Trade, 28 October 1742, ibid., ff. 177–8.

25. Council Minutes, 12 April 1721, in MacMechan, ed., *Original Minutes of His Majesty's Council at Annapolis Royal, 1720–1739,* 28–9.

26. Barnes, 'The Dayly Cry for Justice,' 18.

27. Armstrong, 'Proclamation to the Inhabitants of Nova Scotia,' in MacMechan, ed., *A Calendar of Two Letter-Books and One Commission-Book,* 177–8.

28. MacMechan, ed., *Original Minutes of His Majesty's Council at Annapolis Royal, 1720–1739,* 4; Philipps to Craggs, 26 May 1720, in MacMechan, ed., *A Calendar of Two Letter-Books and One Commission-Book,* 60.

29. The system of deputies is surprisingly underresearched. The standard scholarship treats the system as largely unchanging over the period c. 1710–55, which it was not. See Brebner, *New England's Outpost,* 149–52; and Griffiths, *The Contexts of Acadian History,* 41–5.

30. MacMechan, ed., *Original Minutes of His Majesty's Council at Annapolis Royal, 1720–1739,* 170.

31. Armstrong, 'Order for Choosing New Deputies,' 26 August 1732, in MacMechan, ed., *A Calendar of Two Letter-Books and One Commission-Book,* 190.

32. Minutes, 7 December 1730, in MacMechan, ed., *Original Minutes of His Majesty's Council at Annapolis Royal, 1720–1739*, 172–3; Minutes, August 1731, ibid., 188–9.

33. Philipps to Board of Trade, 25 November 1729, PRO, CO217/5, ff. 176–8.

34. Minutes, 7 December 1730, in MacMechan, ed., *Original Minutes of His Majesty's Council at Annapolis Royal, 1720–1739*, 173.

35. On the changing responsibilities of deputies from 1731 to 1740 see MacMechan, ed., *A Calendar of Two Letter-Books and One Commission-Book*, 187–247. On the appointment of rent farmers see ibid., 197, 212–13, 216–19, 226. On the increasing number of litigants, see Barnes, "'The Dayly Cry for Justice,"' 18–19.

36. Minutes, 11 September 1732, in MacMechan, ed., *Original Minutes of His Majesty's Council at Annapolis Royal, 1720–1739*, 255; and 'Order for the Election of Deputies,' 30 August 1733, 12 September 1734, and 14 September 1735, in MacMechan, ed., *A Calendar of Two Letter-Books and One Commission-Book*, 196, 200, 207–8. For whatever reason, the chosen date for commemorating the conquest did not conform to the actual anniversary.

37. Mémoire pour Monsieur [illegible], from Paul Mascarene, 27 May 1740, ibid., 241–2.

38. Mascarene to Board of Trade, 16 August 1740, PRO, CO217/8, f. 72.

39. Greene, 'Empire and Identity.'

40. Brebner, *New England's Outpost*, 137; Griffiths, *The Contexts of Acadian History*, 41; Barnes, '"Twelve Apostles" or a Dozen Traitors?'

41. See chapter 7 in *Essays in the History of Canadian Law*, vol. 5, ed. by Jim Phillips.

42. Council to Philipps, 10 June 1738, in MacMechan, ed., *A Calendar of Two Letter-Books and One Commission-Book*, 120–1.

43. Mascarene to Board of Trade, 28 October 1742, PRO, CO217/8, ff. 177–8; Maxwell Sutherland, 'Paul Mascarene,' DCB, III, 435–9.

44. MacMechan, ed., *A Calendar of Two Letter-Books and One Commission-Book*, 169; Petition of Joshua Peirce, Stephen Perkins, Elias Davis, and Thomas Kilby to Richard Philipps, 19 August 1729, PRO, CO217/5, f. 183.

45. Armstrong to Aldridge, 15 November 1732, PRO, CO217/7, ff. 6–6d; Armstrong to the Justices of the Peace at Canso, 15 November 1732, ibid., ff. 62–3.

46. Armstrong to Board of Trade, 24 November 1726, PRO, CO217/5, ff. 1–2; Extract of Instructions to Virginia, PRO, CO217/8, f. 184d; Court at St James, 10 March 1730, PRO, CO217/6, ff. 35–6; Labaree, *Royal Government in America*, 312–72; and Greene, *The Quest for Power*, 129–47.

47. MacMechan, ed., *A Calendar of Two Letter-Books and One Commission-Book*, 173–4.

48. Philipps to Secretary of State, 1721, ibid., 76; Armstrong to Aldridge, 15 November 1732, PRO, CO217/7, ff. 6–6d; and Mascarene to Board of Trade, 28 October 1742, PRO, CO217/8, ff. 177–8.

49. Armstrong to Board of Trade, 2 December 1725, PRO, CO217/4, f. 314.

50. Duke of Bedford to Board of Trade, 20 July 1749, PRO, CO217/9, f. 63.

51. Doucett to Board of Trade, 6 November 1717, PRO, CO217/2, ff. 175–6. For earlier attempts to have Acadians swear an oath of allegiance, see Brebner, *New England's Outpost*, 64, 75–6.

52. Doucett to Board of Trade, 6 November 1717, PRO, CO217/2, f. 175.

53. Doucett to Peter Mellanson, 5 December 1717, ibid., f. 197.

54. Doucett to Board of Trade, 6 November 1717, ibid., f. 176.

55. Caulfeild to Board of Trade, 1 November 1715, in MacMechan, ed., *A Calendar of Two Letter-Books and One Commission-Book*, 27; Caulfeild to Vetch [1715], ibid., 29.

56. Doucett to Board of Trade, 6 November 1717, PRO, CO217/2, f. 175.

57. Council Minutes, 24 September 1720, in MacMechan, ed., *Original Minutes of His Majesty's Council at Annapolis Royal, 1720–1739*, 15.

58. Philipps and Council to the King, 27 April 1720, PRO, CO217/3, f. 104; and MacMechan, ed., *A Calendar of Two Letter-Books and One Commission-Book*, 66–7.

59. Philipps to the Inhabitants at Annapolis River, 10 April 1721, ibid., 74.

60. Council Minutes, 11 February 1723, in MacMechan, ed., *Original Minutes of His Majesty's Council at Annapolis Royal, 1720–1739*, 43–4.

61. Maxwell Sutherland, 'Lawrence Armstrong,' DCB, II, 21–4.

62. Brebner, *New England's Outpost*, 88–9.

63. Minutes, 25 September 1726, in MacMechan, ed., *Original Minutes of His Majesty's Council at Annapolis Royal, 1720–1739*, 129–30.

64. Report of Erasmus James Philipps to Armstrong, 1727, PRO, CO217/5, ff. 31–2; Minutes, 23 May 1727, in MacMechan, ed., *Original Minutes of His Majesty's Council at Annapolis Royal, 1720–1739*, 144.

65. Minutes, 1 June 1727, ibid., 146; Minutes, 25 July 1727, ibid., 149–50.

66. Brebner, *New England's Outpost,* 89–91; and Sutherland, 'Lawrence Armstrong,' DCB, II, 23.

67. Minutes, 26–7 September 1727, in MacMechan, ed., *Original Minutes of His Majesty's Council at Annapolis Royal, 1720–1739,* 161–4; Instructions of Armstrong to Robert Wroth, PRO, CO217/5, ff. 49–50.

68. Minutes, 13 November 1727, in MacMechan, eds., *Original Minutes of His Majesty's Council at Annapolis Royal, 1720–1739,* 168.

69. Minutes, 16 May 1730, ibid., 171.

70. Brebner, *New England's Outpost,* 166–202.

71. Philipps to Board of Trade, 15 May 1727, PRO, CO217/4, ff. 373–4. For similar sentiments, see Report of Colonel Philipps on Newfoundland and Nova Scotia, 1718, PRO, CO217/2, ff. 171–2; Philipps to Board of Trade, 3 January 1719, PRO, CO217/3, f. 21; 'The State and Condition of His Majestys Province of Nova Scotia truely Represented,' 8 May 1728, PRO, CO217/5, ff. 17–18; David Dunbar to Board of Trade, PRO, CO217/8, ff. 107–8.

72. Philipps to Board of Trade, 15 May 1727, PRO, CO217/4, ff. 373–4.

73. 'The State and Condition of His Majestys province of Nova Scotia truely Represented,' 8 May 1728, PRO, CO217/5, ff. 17–18.

74. Report of Privy Council Committee, 15 February 1726, PRO, CO217/4, f. 324.

75. Philipps to Board of Trade, 3 January 1719, PRO, CO217/3, f. 21.

76. The State and Condition of His Majestys province of Nova Scotia truely Represented, 8 May 1728, PRO, CO217/5, ff. 17–18.

77. Philipps to Board of Trade, 2 October 1729, ibid., ff. 170–1; Philipps to Board of Trade, 2 September 1730, ibid., ff. 225–9.

78. Paul Mascarene to Board of Trade, 16 August 1740, PRO, CO217/8, f. 72. See also, 'Representation of the State of His Majesties Province of Nova Scotia,' 8 November 1745, in Fergusson, ed., *Minutes of His Majesty's Council at Annapolis Royal, 1736–1749,* 83.

79. Armstrong to Board of Trade, 20 November 1733, PRO, CO217/7 ff. 49–50.

80. Philipps to Board of Trade [1720], PRO, CO217/3, f. 104.

81. Armstrong to Board of Trade, 30 April 1727, PRO, CO217/5, ff. 28–30.

82. Armstrong to Board of Trade, 17 November 1727, ibid., f. 41.

83. Armstrong to Board of Trade, 9 July 1728, ibid., ff. 116–17.

84. Proclamation of Lt. Gov. Lawrence Armstrong, 29 July 1727, ibid., f. 71; and Thomas Lechmere to Board of Trade, 20 September 1727, ibid., f. 76.

85. Doucett to Board of Trade, 10 February 1718, PRO, CO217/2, f. 194.

86. Philipps to Board of Trade [1720], PRO, CO217/3, f. 119.

87. Doucett to Board of Trade, 16 August 1726, PRO, CO217/4, ff. 316–18.

88. Greene, '"A Posture of Hostility"'; Mancke, 'Negotiating an Empire.'

89. Philipps to Board of Trade, 2 September 1730, PRO, CO217/5, ff. 225–9.

90. Upton, *Micmacs and Colonists,* 48–60; and Paul, *We Were Not the Savages,* 86–148.

91. In recent years scholars have increasingly emphasized the multiethnic character of the North American colonies, particularly Pennsylvania, New York, New Jersey, and Delaware. But, as noted earlier, the cultural diversity in these colonies did not require serious political and constitutional adjustments on the scale of those required in early-eighteenth-century Nova Scotia and post-conquest Quebec. Indeed legal decisions have recognized that the Proclamation of 1763 and the Quebec Act of 1774 granted constitutional rights to *Canadiens* and First Nations in ways that are unparalleled in the constitutional history of the United States.

92. Labaree, ed., *Royal Instructions to British Colonial Governors,* II, 469, 478–9.

Topic Five

Disease as a Factor in Imperial Conflict

A reconstruction by the American artist Edwin Willard Deming
(1860–1942) of General Braddock's defeat by the French and their First
Nations allies at the Battle of Monongahela, 1755.

The Seven Years' War in Europe, which set France, Austria, Sweden, and a few small German states against Britain and Prussia, might well be viewed as the first "world war." Hostilities were waged from 1756 to 1763 over as large a portion of the world as in 1914–18. Britain engaged in naval campaigns against France (and later Spain) in the Atlantic, the Caribbean, the Mediterranean, and the Indian Ocean. Disease played a role in this world-wide conflict.

In North America, the struggle between Britain and France began in 1754 with a clash between French troops and Virginia militia in the Ohio country, the result of an attempt by the American colonists to expel the French from the area immediately west of the Allegheny Mountains. The following year, the British, under General Braddock, experienced a disastrous defeat at Monongahela (present-day Pittsburgh, Pennsylvania). In 1756, this North American struggle merged into the Seven Years' War. Until 1757, New France, although outnumbered in population twenty to one by the American colonies, held the upper hand.

The whole character of the war changed in 1758, when William Pitt became England's prime minister. Pitt regarded the North American campaign as a primary, not secondary, theatre of the war, and consequently redirected the emphasis of Britain's war effort to North America. The British fleet, with twice as many ships as its French counterpart, blockaded the French navy and kept it to its home ports, thus cutting off supplies and troop reinforcements to New France. Yet despite the extent of the British commitment, New France held out for another two years, until 1760. In her study, "Biological Warfare in Eighteenth-Century North America: Beyond Jeffery Amherst," Elizabeth A. Fenn examines the use of smallpox as a weapon in the final struggle between France and England for control of northeastern North America, and in the Revolutionary War between England and the Thirteen Colonies. What impact did smallpox have on the outcome of these conflicts? Peter MacLeod provides an insightful account of the First Nations' support for New France in his "Microbes and Muskets: Smallpox and the Participation of the Amerindian Allies of New France in the Seven Years' War." How did two smallpox epidemics that broke out during the war lead to a withdrawal of many First Nations allies of New France from the struggle?

For a review of the armed conflict between the French and English in the New World, consult I.K. Steele's *Guerillas and Grenadiers* (Toronto: The Ryerson Press, 1969) and his *Warpaths: Invasions of North America* (New York: Oxford University Press, 1994); also the important works by Fred Anderson, *The Crucible of War: The Seven Years' War and the Fate of Empire in British North America, 1754–1766* (New York: Vintage, 2000) and by William M. Fowler, Jr., *Empires at War: The Seven Years' War and the Struggle for North America, 1754–1763* (Vancouver: Douglas and McIntyre, 2005).

For an examination of New France's final years, see George F.G. Stanley's *New France: The Last Phase, 1744–1760* (Toronto: McClelland and Stewart, 1968); and Guy Frégault's *La Guerre de la conquête* (1955), translated by Margaret Cameron as *Canada: The War of the Conquest* (Toronto: Oxford University Press, 1969). C.P. Stacey's *Quebec, 1759: The Siege and the Battle* (Toronto: Macmillan, 1959; new edition, Toronto: Robin Brass Studio, 2002) examines that crucial year in the struggle. W.J. Eccles's "The French Forces in North America during the Seven Years' War" and C.P. Stacey's "The British Forces in North America during the Seven Years' War," in the *Dictionary of Canadian Biography*, vol. 3, *1741–1770*, pp. xv–xxiii and xxiv–xxx, respectively, review the military strengths of the two opponents. More is said of the French forces in Martin L. Nicolai, "A Different Kind of Courage: The French Military and the Canadian Irregular Soldier during the Seven Years' War," *Canadian Historical Review*, 70, 1 (1989): 53–75. Peter MacLeod has written an important study, *The Canadian Iroquois and the Seven Years' War* (Toronto: Dundurn Press, 1996).

WEBLINKS

Smallpox and Its Control in Canada
http://www.cmaj.ca/cgi/content/full/161/12/1543

An article by Dr. J. McIntyre and Dr. C.S. Houston in the *Canadian Medical Association Journal* (1999) about the history of smallpox in Canada.

The Seven Years' War
http://www.histori.ca/peace/page.do?pageID=335

Digitized letters, images, and maps about the Seven Years' War.

Louisbourg
http://www.ourroots.ca/e/toc.asp?id=4923

A digitized copy of a book published in 1760 that contains letters and memoirs of the islands of Île Royale (Cape Breton) and Saint John (Prince Edward Island). The book concludes with an account of the siege of Louisbourg.

Jeffery Amherst
http://www.biographi.ca/EN/ShowBio.asp?BioId=35854

The biography of Jeffery Amherst at the *Dictionary of Canadian Biography Online*.

World Health Organization: Smallpox
http://www.who.int/mediacentre/factsheets/smallpox/en/

Information about the historical significance and pathology of smallpox from the World Health Organization.

Article Ten

Biological Warfare in Eighteenth-Century North America: Beyond Jeffery Amherst

Elizabeth A. Fenn

Did he or didn't he? For generations, the Amherst–smallpox blanket episode has elicited animated debate both within and beyond academic circles. In books, journals, and now in Internet discussion groups, historians, folklorists, and laypeople have argued the nuances of the case. Some have contended that at General Jeffery Amherst's orders, British subordinates at Fort Pitt in 1763 did indeed infect local Indians with items taken from a nearby smallpox hospital. Others have argued that they did not, that the British lacked the knowledge, the ability, or the desire to do so. Still others have claimed that regardless of intent, the timing is wrong, that the Indians

Source: Elizabeth A. Fenn, "Biological Warfare in Eighteenth-Century North America: Beyond Jeffery Amherst," *The Journal of American History* 86, 4 (March 2000): 1552–1580. Published by permission of Elizabeth A. Fenn and *The Journal of American History*.

around Fort Pitt came down with smallpox well before the damning exchange of letters between Jeffery Amherst and his subordinate Henry Bouquet, and that in fact they were sick even before they received "two Blankets and an Handkerchief" out of the post's smallpox hospital. Finally, and perhaps predictably, a recent article has focused on the incident's genesis as a highly mutable cross-cultural legend that reflects deep anxieties about encounters with the "other."[1]

What follows is not an attempt to condemn or exonerate Jeffery Amherst. The man's documentary record speaks loudly enough regarding his character, if not regarding his ultimate culpability for the smallpox that struck Indians near Fort Pitt in 1763 and 1764. Nor is this essay an exhaustive accounting of all the accusations and incidents of biological warfare in late-eighteenth-century North America. It is, however, an attempt to broaden the debate and to place it in context.[2] Our preoccupation with Amherst has kept us from recognizing that accusations of what we now call biological warfare — the military use of smallpox in particular — arose frequently in eighteenth-century America. Native Americans, moreover, were not the only accusers. By the second half of the century, many of the combatants in America's wars of empire had the knowledge and technology to attempt biological warfare with the smallpox virus. Many also adhered to a code of ethics that did not constrain them from doing so. Seen in this light, the Amherst affair becomes not so much an aberration as part of a larger continuum in which accusations and discussions of biological warfare were common, and actual incidents may have occurred more frequently than scholars have previously acknowledged.

FORT PITT, 1763

The most famous "smallpox blanket" incident in American history took place in the midst of Pontiac's Rebellion in 1763. In May and June of that year, a loose confederation of tribes inspired by the Ottawa war leader Pontiac launched attacks on British-held posts throughout the Great Lakes and Midwest. On May 29, 1763, they began a siege of Fort Pitt, located in western Pennsylvania at the confluence of the Allegheny and Monongahela rivers. The officer in charge at Fort Pitt was the Swiss-born captain Simeon Ecuyer. On June 16, 1763, Ecuyer reported to Colonel Henry Bouquet at Philadelphia that the frontier outpost's situation had taken a turn for the worse. Local Indians had escalated the hostilities, burning nearby houses and attempting to lure Ecuyer into an engagement beyond the walls of the well-protected post, where traders and colonists, interlopers on Indian lands, had taken refuge. "We are so crowded in the fort that I fear disease," wrote Ecuyer, "for in spite of all my care I cannot keep the place as clean as I should like; moreover, the small pox is among us. For this reason I have had a hospital built under the bridge beyond musket-fire." Henry Bouquet, in a letter dated June 23, passed the news on to Jeffery Amherst, the British commander in chief, at New York. "Fort Pitt is in good State of Defence against all attempts from Savages," Bouquet reported, but "Unluckily the small Pox has broken out in the Garrison."[3] By June 16, then, from sources unknown, smallpox had established itself at Fort Pitt. It is likely that Amherst knew of the situation by the end of June.

But it was not Amherst, apparently, who first proposed the use of smallpox against the Delaware, Shawnee, and Mingo Indians surrounding Fort Pitt. Nor was it Amherst who executed the scheme. While the actual provenance of the plan remains unclear, a brief description of the deed itself appears in the diary of William Trent, a trader and land speculator with ties to the more prominent George Croghan. On June 23, the very day that Bouquet penned his letter to Amherst from Philadelphia, Trent reported that two Delaware dignitaries, Turtle's Heart and Mamaltree, visited Fort Pitt late at night and asked to speak with post officials. A conference took place the following day, June 24, in which the Indians urged the British to abandon the fort, and the British, for their part, refused. The parleys came up close, and the Indians asked for "a little Provisions and Liquor, to carry us Home." The British obliged their request. "Out of our regard to them," wrote William Trent, "we gave them two Blankets and an Handkerchief out of the Small Pox Hospital. I hope it will have the desired effect."[4] He does not mention who conceived the plan, and he likewise does not mention who carried it out, but Fort Pitt account books make it clear that the British military both sanctioned and paid for the deed. The records for June 1763 include this invoice submitted by Levy, Trent and Company:

> To Sundries got to Replace in kind those which were taken from people in the Hospital to Convey the Smallpox to the Indians Viz[t]:

2 Blankets	@20/	£2"	0"	0
1 Silk Handkerchief	10/			
& 1 linnen do:	3/6	0"	13"	6

Captain Ecuyer certified that the items "were had for the uses above mentioned," and Gen. Thomas Gage ultimately approved the invoice for payment, endorsing it with a comment and his signature.[5]

Had Jeffery Amherst known of these actions, he certainly would have approved. From the safety of his New York headquarters, he laid forth his own strategy for biological warfare in early July, prompted no doubt by Bouquet's letter of June 23 informing him that smallpox had broken out at the Monongahela post. In an undated memorandum that is apparently a postscript to a letter of July 7, 1763, Amherst proposed the following to Bouquet: "Could it not be contrived to Send the *Small Pox* among those Disaffected Tribes of Indians? We must, on this occasion, Use Every Stratagem in our power to Reduce them." Bouquet, now at Carlisle en route to Fort Pitt with reinforcements, replied on July 13, also in postscript: "I will try to inocculate the Indians by means of Blankets that may fall in their hands, taking care however not to get the disease myself." To this Amherst responded approvingly on July 16. "You will Do well to try to Innoculate the Indians by means of Blanketts, as well as to try Every other method that can serve to Extirpate this Execreble Race."[6] Unbeknownst to both Bouquet and his commander-in-chief, their subordinates at Fort Pitt had already conceived and executed the very plan proposed. If the garrison at Fort Pitt perpetrated a second, later act of biological warfare at Amherst's behest, the documents currently available make no mention of it.

What the documents do show, however, is that smallpox struck hard among the Indians around Fort Pitt in the spring and summer of 1763. On April 14, 1764, a man named Gershom Hicks arrived at the British post, having escaped from the Shawnee and Delaware Indians who had held him captive since May 1763. In a deposition taken the day of his arrival, Hicks reported "that the Small pox has been very general & raging amongst the Indians since last spring and that 30 or 40 Mingoes, as many Delawares and some Shawneese Died all of the Small pox since that time, that it still continues amongst them." Five months later, in September 1764, the epidemic continued to wreak havoc among the Shawnees. "Ye poor Rascals are Dieing very fast with ye small pox," reported Col. Andrew Lewis from Virginia's Blue Ridge Mountains; "they can make but Lettle Resistance and when Routed must parish in great Numbers by ye Disordere." Accounts of the plague continued to circulate as late as 1765, when Killibuck, a prominent Delaware leader, told the Indian agent William Johnson of the destruction it had wrought. "The Shawanes lost in three Months time 149 Men besides Women & Children by Sickness above a year ago," Killibuck reported: "also many of them dyed last Summer of the Small Pox, as did Several of their Nation." As the historian Michael McConnell has pointed out, it is possible and perhaps likely that the epidemic stemmed from multiple sources of infection. John M'Cullough, a fifteen-year-old captive among the Indians, reported that the disease took hold after an attack on some settlers sick with the smallpox along central Pennsylvania's Juniata River. The timing, however, is uncanny: the eruption of epidemic smallpox in the Ohio country coincided closely with the distribution of infected articles by individuals at Fort Pitt.[7] While blame for this outbreak cannot be placed squarely in the British camp, the circumstantial evidence is nevertheless suggestive.

Usually treated as an isolated anomaly, the Fort Pitt episode itself points to the possibility that biological warfare was not as rare as it might seem. It is conceivable, of course, that when Fort Pitt personnel gave infected articles to their Delaware visitors on June 24, 1763, they acted on some earlier communication from Amherst that does not survive today.[8] The sequence of events, however, makes it more likely that Amherst and Fort Pitt authorities conceived of the idea independently. In each case, the availability of contagious material (thanks to the smallpox epidemic at the post itself) seems to have triggered the plan of infection. Ecuyer reported the outbreak at Fort Pitt on June 16, and the attempt to communicate the disease took place eight days later. Amherst learned of the outbreak in Bouquet's letter of June 23, and the commander in chief proposed his own scheme on July 7. The fact that a single wartime outbreak could prompt two independent plans of contagion suggests that the Fort Pitt incident may not have been an anomaly. Evidence from other fields of battle indicates that in the minds of many, smallpox had an established, if irregular, place in late-eighteenth-century warfare.

WHY SMALLPOX?

As the twenty-first century begins, smallpox remains the only disease known that is appropriately discussed in the past tense. On May 8, 1980, the World Health Organization confirmed that after two thousand years of human suffering, smallpox had been eradicated from the world. A physical reminder of this triumph still appears in the mottled vaccination scar that most Americans born before 1971 bear on one upper arm. In 1971, the United States dropped smallpox from its routine immunization protocol, and unless they have travelled abroad, Americans born after that date have no such scar. Today, despite rumours of clandestine supplies of the virus, smallpox no longer poses an immediate public health threat.[9]

In the late eighteenth century, however, smallpox was the most fearsome disease known. In his characteristic prose, the British historian Thomas Macaulay later described it as "the most terrible of all the ministers of death." The charge of deliberate propagation of the disease was thus extremely serious, but it was also surprisingly common. In this regard, smallpox was unique among plagues, for it stands nearly alone in the annals of eighteenth-century biological warfare. This was the case in part because of the nature of smallpox itself and in part because of the world's rather extraordinary understanding of the illness even before Edward Jenner developed cowpox vaccination in 1796 and published his findings in 1798.[10]

Smallpox was caused by a virus called *Variola*.[11] For twelve days after infection occurred, the *Variola* virus circulated through the body while victims remained unaware that they incubated the disease. Then, usually on the twelfth day, influenza-like symptoms struck, typified by fever, headache, backache, vomiting, and, in some patients, a profound emotional despondency. Unless sufferers knew they had been exposed to smallpox, the diagnosis often did not become clear until day fifteen or sixteen, when the classic rash appeared.

The physical presentation of the rash served as a fairly accurate indicator of a patient's prognosis. If it turned inward and hemorrhaged beneath the skin, death was nearly inevitable and came quickly. This was rare, but it occurred most often among pregnant women. More typically, the characteristic pustules pushed through the skin surface, covering all of the body but concentrating most densely on the face and extremities, including the soles of the feet and palms of the hands. Some individuals developed confluent smallpox, in which the pustules ran together into one painful, oozing mass. Most of those unlucky sufferers died.[12] More frequently, however, the pustules remained discrete, and the disease pursued its course. The rash began drying out sometime in the third week. By the time a month had passed (four to five weeks after the initial infection occurred), most of the scabs had fallen off, leaving telltale scars behind to mark the patient as a survivor.

The consequences varied. Besides scarring and death, they could include blindness and bone deformity. For expecting mothers, smallpox usually resulted in premature termination of pregnancy. For children, there are indications that the disease may have stunted growth.[13] But for all smallpox survivors, the negative consequences of the disease had to be balanced against its ultimate reward — lifelong immunity. An individual who had lived through smallpox would never get the disease again.

Infection with *Variola* occurred by direct or indirect contact between human beings. There was no animal reservoir for smallpox. Nor was it transmitted by food, water, or a nonhuman vector such as the mosquito. Most often, *Variola* gained entrance to a potential victim through the respiratory tract, either by direct inhalation or by finger-borne contamination. Transmission could also occur through an open wound in the skin, but with the exception of deliberate cases of inoculation, this was relatively rare. In "naturally" acquired smallpox, respiratory tract contamination was far more common.[14]

Typically, infection took place when a sick person coughed or sneezed in the presence of a susceptible individual, especially during the first week of the rash when the mucous membranes of the mouth and throat were severely affected. Viral shedding was heaviest in such oropharyngeal secretions, but patients also released viable virus in urine, scabs, and the fluid of unhealed skin lesions. Scabs were probably the least infectious of these forms, because they buried the *Variola* virus in dried pustular matter. Far more contagious were desiccated droplets from skin lesions, nasal secretions, and saliva.[15]

The survival of viable virus in these dried-out bodily secretions meant that while face-to-face contact was the most common way of transmitting smallpox, it was certainly not the only way. Susceptible individuals might contract the disease by shaking out bedclothes, sweeping the floor, or doing anything else that caused viral particles to become airborne. Documented twentieth-century smallpox outbreaks have occurred among workers handling hospital laundry at a considerable distance from the hospital itself.[16] The implications for eighteenth-century studies are clear; the disease certainly could have spread by means of "two Blankets and an Handkerchief" from a smallpox hospital. And it could have spread by other means as well.

Eighteenth-century Americans, regardless of ethnic, social, or economic background, had never heard of a virus. In 1683, Anthony van Leeuwenhoek had observed bacteria, which he called "animalcules," through his microscope, but germ theory was barely nascent. Nevertheless, when it came to smallpox, hard experience had taught people important principles of both contagion and prevention. Because its features were so distinctive and because incidents of smallpox usually came after some kind of contact with a sick individual, the contagious nature of the disease was relatively easy to discern. This was not the case with infections such as typhus (usually transmitted by lice), bubonic plague (transmitted by fleas from rats), yellow fever (transmitted by mosquitoes), malaria (also transmitted by mosquitoes), cholera (transmitted by water), or even tuberculosis (which might remain latent for years).[17] Such diseases, obscure in their etiology, might well be attributed to swamp gases, moral turpitude, or astrological phenomena. But not smallpox.

"No condition of air &c can produce the small-pox," wrote Dr. William Douglass of Boston in 1722, "without some real communication of infection from a smallpox illness." Most eighteenth-century Americans familiar with the disease understood this; hence they implemented quarantine when smallpox struck. In 1721, when two men sick with smallpox turned up on a ship in Boston harbour, the town selectmen isolated them in a house marked by a red flag and then hired a nurse and posted guards to enforce the quarantine. Similarly, when smallpox broke out among the Creek Indians of Georgia and Alabama in 1748, unaffected members of the tribe followed the trader James Adair's advice "to cut off every kind of communication" with the infected towns. Near Charleston, South Carolina, in 1760, the governor ordered sentinels stationed outside the home of a woman who came down with smallpox. Eight years later, to control a particularly deadly outbreak, officials in Williamsburg, Virginia, imposed a three-week quarantine on anyone with symptoms of the disease.[18]

Even where legally imposed quarantine did not exist, susceptible Americans took pains to avoid contact with individuals and locales infected with the disease. In February 1763, a young Thomas Jefferson cancelled his plans to visit Williamsburg when he learned that the ailment had taken hold there. "The small pox is in town," he wrote to Dr. John Page, "so you may scratch out that sentence of my letter wherein I mentioned coming to Williamsburgh so soon." When the British evacuated Boston in March 1776, Abigail Adams could barely contain her eagerness to return to the city, but she checked herself because the troops had left rampant smallpox in their wake. "Do not you want to see Boston," she wrote to her husband John; "I am fearfull of the small pox, or I should have been in before this time." Three years later the pox struck the Moravian settlement of Salem, North Carolina. "This condition practically cut off all intercourse with Salem, and if people came or passed through they were afraid," noted one diarist.[19]

If people understood that contact with sick individuals could spread smallpox, they knew that contaminated objects could pass on the disease as well. In November 1775, when an overzealous revolutionary took "hospital stores consisting of blankets, sheets and shirts" from the British barracks in New York, the Provincial Congress ordered the items returned. "If we had sent the Blankets up to the [Continental] Army we might in all Probability have Poisoned the Northern Army by sending the small Pox among them," the Congress explained. Less than a year later, in April 1776, the Virginia Committee of Safety authorized the payment of £38.18.6 to Capt. James Grier, "the amot. of the valuation of sundry clothes belonging to his Company, burnt at Fredericksburg . . . to prevent the spreading of the Small pox with which it was Supposed they were infected." When a soldier died of smallpox in Richmond in 1781, the commissary supplied the African-American man who had nursed him with "a Jacket with sleeves, a pair of Breeches, a Shirt, and a pair of Stockings" in order "that his own may be destroyed."[20] Yet as the Fort Pitt incident shows, this valuable knowledge could serve two masters: while it helped people to control the disease, it also enabled them to spread it.

The same was true of inoculation, a powerful new weapon in the eighteenth-century anti-smallpox arsenal. In fact, inoculation was steeped in controversy precisely because it both controlled smallpox and contributed to its spread. Also called "variolation," inoculation had seen use for hundreds of years elsewhere in the world before Europeans learned of the procedure. Then, at virtually the same moment, in the four-year period from 1713 to 1717, Europeans around the globe latched onto the practice and sent word of it home. The timing was perhaps not coincidental, for smallpox had already begun a resurgence in Europe that would last through the rest of the century. Inoculation's two most famous popularizers were the Englishwoman Mary Wortley Montague and the American minister Cotton Mather. Montague learned of the practice in Constantinople, where her husband served as Britain's ambassador to Turkey. Mather learned of it in Boston from his slave Onesimus, one of thousands of Akan-speaking "Coromantee" slaves forcibly exported from Africa's Gold Coast to the colonies of the New World.[21]

The practice of inoculation was indeed remarkable, but modern readers must not confuse it with vaccination, the much safer procedure that Edward Jenner developed in 1796 utilizing the cowpox virus. Inoculation, by contrast, entailed deliberate infection with *Variola*. By implanting infectious smallpox material in an open wound, physicians learned that in most cases they could bring on a milder form of the disease than when the infection occurred "naturally." It is a phenomenon that eludes medical explanation to this day. The milder symptoms of inoculated smallpox cannot be explained simply by virtue of a cutaneous versus a respiratory route of infection. The Chinese had for centuries practised variolation by "insufflation"— blowing infectious scab material up the nostrils of the patient. The patient still came down with smallpox, and there was still great risk involved. But the case fatality rate of 0.5 to 2.0 percent from inoculated smallpox seemed enviable by comparison to the case fatality rate of 20 to 30 percent from the natural form of the illness.[22] In the end, survivors of inoculation won the same highly cherished prize as other smallpox survivors: lifelong immunity to the disease.

Effective though it was, inoculation came at a price. Inoculees did come down with smallpox, and like anyone else sick with the disease, they could pass it on to others in the "natural" way. In the absence of strict quarantine, inoculation was as likely to start an epidemic as to end one. Because the symptoms could be mild, inoculees often felt well enough to circulate in public, and they frequently did so, despite knowing the consequences for others might be fatal. Abigail Adams, for example, who had expressed her own fear of the contagion earlier, "attended publick worship constantly, except one day and a half" while she underwent inoculation in 1776. The Virginia outbreak of 1768 began when an inoculator allowed "some of his Patients to go abroad too soon," spreading the disease "in two or three Parts of the County."[23] Such incidents were by no means unusual and meant that inoculation was highly controversial if not banned outright in many of the English colonies.

OTHER ACCUSATIONS AND INCIDENTS

Eighteenth-century biological warfare is at best a slippery topic of inquiry. (The term "biological warfare" is itself anachronistic, but it remains well suited for describing what eighteenth-century Americans clearly viewed as a distinctive category of acts and allegations.) The long-standing debate over the Fort Pitt episode — easily the best-documented incident in the period — reveals how very treacherous the historical landscape can be. Even contemporaries could rarely prove culpability beyond refute in a suspicious outbreak of disease; for historians, the task is next to impossible. Accidents happened, and unintentional contagion was common, particularly in wartime. Moreover, in those rare cases where malicious intent was evident, as at Fort Pitt in 1763, the actual effectiveness of an attempt to spread smallpox remains impossible to ascertain: the possibility always exists that infection occurred by some "natural" route.

While all of this complicates the historian's task, it may nevertheless have enhanced smallpox's appeal as a weapon. For unlike rape, pillage, and other atrocities in which the intent and identity of the perpetrator could be made clear, the propagation of smallpox had the advantage of deniability. In the honour-bound world in which eighteenth-century military officials lived, this may well have been biological warfare's greatest attribute. It is possible, given the dearth of ironclad evidence, that biological warfare did not occur beyond the Fort Pitt incident. But another perspective also seems warranted, particularly when smallpox's deniability is taken into account: the shortage of conclusive documentation may simply indicate that perpetrators did not record their deeds.

The surviving evidence is rife with ambiguity. Some accusations served propaganda purposes in situations of social or military stress.[24] Others come from oral traditions, at times recorded long after the alleged incidents took place. Many allegations are unsubstantiated, and some are weakly substantiated at best. Nevertheless, the sheer weight of the evidence that follows points to the distinct possibility that eighteenth-century biological warfare was more common than historians have previously believed.

It may well have been Indians, not whites, who used the strategy first. In his voluminous *History and Description of New France*, Pierre-François-Xavier de Charlevoix recounts an Iroquois act of biological sabotage against the English during Queen Anne's War in the early 1700s. The English army, Charlevoix writes, "was encamped on the banks of a little river; the Iroquois, who spent almost all the time hunting, threw into it, just above the camp, all the skins of the animals they flayed, and the water was thus soon all corrupted." The army, Charlevoix continued, suspected nothing. Soldiers "continued to drink this water, and it carried off so many, that Father de Mareuil, and two officers . . . observing the graves where the dead were buried, estimated the number at over a thousand." This account is remarkable not only because it seems to be the only eighteenth-century American incident that did not involve smallpox but also because the perpetrators were Indians. In this regard, the fact that smallpox was *not* the weapon of choice is hardly surprising. Already decimated by repeated epidemics, American Indians everywhere more likely viewed smallpox as an enemy in its own right than as a weapon that might bring down their adversaries.[25] The years that followed would show how true this was.

Amherst aside, smallpox seemed to be everywhere during the Seven Years' War. D. Peter MacLeod has demonstrated elegantly how Indian participation in the conflict with the British waxed and waned according to their simultaneous struggle against smallpox. In 1755–56 and again in 1757–58, the disease wreaked havoc among the Indians allied with the French. After the Lake George campaign of 1757, the French-allied Potawatomis suffered greatly in a smallpox outbreak that they believed stemmed from deliberate infection by the British. In July 1767, the British Indian superintendent William Johnson interviewed a man named Cornelius Van Slyke, held prisoner among the Chippewas and the Potawatomis for four years. Van Slyke told Johnson the Potawatomis believed "that the great Number they lost of their People at & returning from Lake George in 1757, was owing to ye English poisoning the Rum, & giving them the Small Pox, for which they owe them an everlasting ill will." The innuendo here is that the infection was willful, and it is possible that biological warfare occurred. But it is far more likely that the source of the contagion that ravaged the Potawatomis was the famous attack (fictionalized in James Fenimore Cooper's *Last of the Mohicans*, 1826) on unarmed prisoners leaving Fort William Henry on August 10, 1757.[26] Many of those prisoners were sick with smallpox.

By the nineteenth century, intentional smallpox infection turned up regularly in Native American oral histories. The Ottawa Indians suffered from smallpox after the 1757 campaign, and their tradition held that the disease came from Montreal, ironically in the possession of the Indians' French allies at the time of the outbreak. "This smallpox," according to Andrew Blackbird's account, "was sold to them shut up in a showy tin box, with the strict injunction not to open the box on their way homeward." When they arrived at their village on the shores of Lake Michigan, the Indians opened the box only to find another box and then another inside. In the end, Blackbird says, the Ottawas "found nothing but mouldy particles in this last little box." Many inspected it, and shortly thereafter, smallpox broke out. According to the story, an enormous Ottawa village, extending for miles west of Mackinac, "was entirely depopulated and laid waste." It is unlikely that the French would have knowingly passed smallpox on to their Indian supporters at this crucial juncture in the Seven Years' War. But the accusation may well reflect a Native American perspective that since they had caught the disease while fighting for the French, the French were therefore responsible for the devastation it caused. Eager to retain and appease their Indian allies, French officials laid the blame for the epidemic in the British camp.[27] If further documentation for this alleged incident exists, it remains undiscovered. Nor is it clear how, if at all, this tradition might be linked to the Fort Pitt episode six years later.

Other accusations of deliberate contagion surfaced among the Ottawa Indians' Ojibwa neighbours. Around 1770, according to an Ojibwa account related by John J. Heagerty, traders at Mackinac infected visiting Indians with a contaminated flag presented to the Indians "as a token of friendship." After the homeward-bound Ojibwas unfurled the flag among friends at Fond du Lac on Lake Superior, smallpox broke out. Some three hundred reportedly died at Fond du Lac alone. Writing in 1928, Heagerty noted that the account still remained in circulation: "The Indians to this day are firmly of the opinion that the small-pox was, at this time, communicated through the articles presented to their brethren by the agent of the fur company at Mackinac." William Warren included another version of the same tradition in his *History of the Ojibway Nation* (1884), implying that it took place later, launching the region's devastating smallpox epidemic of 1780–82. It is worth noting that Warren, the son of an Ojibwa woman and a fur trader, discredits the account after he relates it, saying that the Ojibwas, Crees, and Assiniboines picked up the infection in a raid on a Hidatsa village on the upper Missouri.[28]

Not all accusations of biological warfare in this period came from Native Americans. In September 1757, vessels carrying some three hundred paroled British prisoners sailed from Quebec to Halifax, Nova Scotia. Some of the parolees were survivors of the massacre at Fort William Henry just over a month before. Some of them, moreover, were sick with smallpox. Four died in transit, and another twenty showed symptoms by the time they reached their destination. French motives in shipping the sick prisoners drew suspicion. "This was said," according to an unnamed accuser, "to have been an attempt to introduce the small-pox into Halifax, many men being ill of the disorder on their embarkation. Providence, however, frustrated this benevolent design."[29]

The next great conflict to shake the continent was the Revolutionary War. Once again, smallpox erupted repeatedly, and once again, those on the receiving end believed that the outbreaks were not all accidental. Allegations of biological warfare arose in the course of confrontations at Quebec, Boston, and Yorktown, as well as during the mobilization of the Earl of Dunmore's Ethiopian Regiment on the Chesapeake. At Boston, charges of deliberate smallpox propagation by the British cropped up even before the outbreak of hostilities at Lexington and Concord. "The [British] solders try all they can to spread the *smallpox*," wrote an unnamed Bostonian in January 1775. "One of their Officers inoculated his whole family without letting any person know it,— there was a man, his wife, and seven children, under the same roof, and not one of them ever had it." When the American siege of Boston began in April, the disease became epidemic among British soldiers and other residents of the city. "The small pox rages all over the Town," wrote George Washington from his headquarters in nearby Cambridge on December 14. "Such of the [British] Military as had it not before, are now under innoculation this I apprehend is a weapon of Defence, they Are useing against us."[30]

In fact, Washington already suspected that the British, in an effort to infect the vulnerable Continental Army, had inoculated some of the refugees leaving the city. On December 3, 1775, four deserters had arrived at the American headquarters "giving an account that several persons are to be sent out of *Boston*, this evening or to-morrow, that have been lately inoculated with the small-pox, with design, probably, to spread the infection, in order to distress us as much as possible." It was, according to Washington's aide-de-camp, an "unheard-of and diabolical scheme." Washington at first regarded the report with disbelief. "There is one part of the information that I Can hardly give Credit to," he wrote. "A Sailor Says that a number of these Comeing out have been inoculated, with deisgn of Spreading the Smallpox through this Country & Camp."[31]

A week later, however, as the pox erupted among the refugees, the American commander-in-chief changed his mind. In a letter to John Hancock on December 11, 1775, he explained his reappraisal: "The information I received that the enemy intended Spreading the Small pox amongst us, I coud not Suppose them Capable of — I now must give Some Credit to it, as it has made its appearance on Severall of those who Last Came out of Boston." The Americans controlled the outbreak through careful quarantine and disinfection of both refugees and their effects. In the aftermath, the *Boston Gazette* carried a sworn declaration from one refugee, a servant, saying that he had been inoculated and then, as the pustules broke out, ordered by his master to embark on a crowded vessel leaving the city. There he could not avoid communicating the infection to "A Number of said Passengers," as the boat's departure was delayed more than two weeks. According to another report, a Boston physician named Dr. Rand had admitted "that he had effectually given the distemper among those people" quitting the city.[32]

Both accusations and evidence of biological warfare dwindled as the siege of Boston continued in the opening months of 1776, but in March, as the British intent to evacuate the city became clear, American fears escalated once more. On March 13, watching British troops prepare to leave, Washington ordered "that neither Officer, nor soldier, presume to go into Boston" without his permission, "as the enemy with a malicious assiduity, have spread the infection of the smallpox through all parts of the town." That very evening the American commander received word "by a person just out of Boston, that our Enemies in that place, had laid several Schemes for communicating the infection of the small-pox, to the Continental Army, when they get into the town." Deliberate or not, smallpox exploded in Boston after the siege, infecting troops and civilians alike.[33]

Boston was not the only city besieged by American troops through the winter of 1775–76. At Quebec another siege was underway, and here again, smallpox emerged as a major player in military affairs. While the American efforts to keep the Continental Army free of smallpox were generally successful at Boston, they failed dismally at Quebec. Here the disease erupted almost immediately upon the Americans' arrival outside the walled city in late November and early December of 1775. What followed was one of the great disasters in American military history. An American attempt on the city failed in a blizzard on the night of December 31, and the army settled in for a miserable, snowbound siege that lasted until the first week of May 1776, when British reinforcements arrived. Riddled with smallpox, the Americans retreated, first to the town of Sorel, where the Richelieu River joins the Saint Lawrence, and then, in midsummer, southward to Ticonderoga and Crown Point. "Oh the Groans of the Sick," wrote one soldier during the retreat, "What they undergo I Cant Expres." At Crown Point, according to the physician Lewis Beebe, death became "a daily visitant in the Camps. But as Little regarded as the singing of birds."[34]

Many accused the British general, Sir Guy Carleton, of willfully infecting the American camp during the wintry siege of the Canadian city. In the deathbed diary he dictated in 1811, the Pennsylvania rifleman John Joseph Henry recalled that smallpox had been "introduced into our cantonments by the indecorous, yet fascinating arts of the enemy." The Continental Congress held hearings on the debacle even as the Northern Army still suffered from smallpox at Ticonderoga. Thomas Jefferson's abbreviated notes of the testimony reveal that several of the witnesses believed the epidemic was no accident. Capt. Hector McNeal, for example, said "the small pox was sent out of Quebeck by Carleton, inoculating the poor people at government expence for the purpose of giving it to our army." Likewise, according to another witness, it "was said but no proof that Carleton had sent it into the suburbs of St. Roc where some of our men were quartered." The testimony of a Dr. Coates reiterated the theme: "Was supposed Carlton sent out people with it," Jefferson noted in his shorthand. Jefferson, for one, found the testimony credible. "I have been informed by officers who were on the spit, and whom I believe myself," he wrote to the French historian François Soulés, "that this disorder was sent into our army designedly by the commanding officer in Quebec. It answered his purposes effectually."[35]

Smallpox was present at Quebec when the American army arrived, and it seems probable, as they mingled with habitants outside the city, that the troops would have picked up the *Variola* virus regardless of any actions on Carleton's part. "The small pox is all around us, and there is great danger of its spreading in the army," wrote the soldier Caleb Haskell on December 6, 1775, shortly after the siege began. "We have long had that disorder in town," observed a British officer on December 9, as the disease made its first appearance among the Americans. Carleton's humane treatment of the American smallpox victims taken prisoner when the siege ended would seem to undermine the argument that he deliberately infected the American lines.[36] Nevertheless, it remains possible. By providing a ready supply of inoculees and other contagious patients, the ongoing presence of smallpox in Quebec might in fact have made deliberate infection easier to disguise.

Meanwhile, farther south, more accusations of willful contagion surfaced in Virginia, where some eight hundred African-American refugees from slavery had rallied to the British cause in response to a promise of freedom from the colony's royal governor, John Murray, Earl of Dunmore. Written on November 7, 1775, and issued a week later, Dunmore's limited emancipation proclamation inspired African Americans and terrified the slaveholding revolutionaries who spearheaded the American revolt. By May 1776, however, smallpox had infested the governor's little band of freedom fighters in their precarious waterfront camp near Norfolk. Dunmore decided to move to a safe spot and inoculate his men. "His Lordship," according to a rumour in the *Virginia Gazette,* "before the departure of the fleet from Norfolk harbour, had two of those wretches inoculated and sent ashore, in order to spread the infection, but it was happily prevented."[37]

In the end, it was Dunmore's black regiment that suffered most from the disease, dwindling under its impact to 150 effective men and eventually withdrawing from Virginia entirely. "Had it not been for this horrid disorder," wrote Dunmore, "I should have had two thousand blacks; with whom I should have had no doubt of penetrating into the heart of this Colony." When the American rebels questioned one eyewitness to the ravages of smallpox and to Dunmore's final withdrawal, they broached the topic of biological warfare directly: "How long were they inocul[ated] & was it done to communicate it to the People on shore[?]" asked the interrogators. "By no means," was the vague response, "every one in the Fleet was inoculated, that had it not."[38]

A year later, in the spring of 1777, rumours of a Tory conspiracy to propagate smallpox swept the state of New Hampshire. "There are great numbers of people bound together by the most solemn oaths and imprecations to stand by each other and to destroy the persons who betray them," wrote Josiah Bartlett, one of the state's delegates to the Continental Congress; "besides ruining the paper currency it seems their design is, this Spring to spread the small pox through the country." Many patriots had expressed concern, he added: "we have reason to think most of the Tories in New England are in the plan." There is no further evidence that such a plan existed, although smallpox did erupt in Exeter in the spring of 1778.[39]

Additional accusations surfaced in 1781, as General Charles Cornwallis's southern campaign came to a close. The British retreat to Yorktown in many ways echoed Lord Dunmore's Virginia campaign five years earlier. Again, African-American slaves flocked to British lines seeking freedom from their revolutionary masters. And again smallpox cut them down, for African Americans, like all other Americans, were far more likely to be susceptible to the disease than were troops from Europe.[40]

As early as June 1781, American soldiers in Virginia suspected Cornwallis's army of using smallpox-infected blacks to propagate disease. "Here I must take notice of some vilany," wrote Josiah Atkins as his regiment pursued the British near Richmond. "Within these days past,

I have marched by 18 or 20 Negroes that lay dead by the way-side, putrifying with the small pox." Cornwallis, Atkins believed, had "inoculated 4 or 500 in order to spread smallpox thro' the country, & sent them out for that purpose." A Pennsylvania soldier, William Feltman, found a "negro man with the small-pox lying on the road side" on June 25, supposedly left by a British cavalry unit "in order to prevent the Virginia militia from pursuing them." By October, with surrender looming on the horizon, Cornwallis had become desperate. "The British," noted James Thacher in his diary, "have sent from Yorktown a large number of negroes, sick with the small pox, probably for the purpose of communicating the infection to our army." Writing three days after the capitulation, Robert Livingston hoped that reports of such conduct would sway Europeans to the American side. "In Virginia," he wrote, "they took the greatest pains to communicate the Small Pox to the Country; by exposing the dead bodies of those who had died with it, in the most frequented places." Benjamin Franklin later reiterated the charge in his "Retort Courteous."[41]

It may be tempting to dismiss such accusations as so much American hyperbole. But evidence indicates that in fact the British did exactly what the Americans charged. At Portsmouth, Virginia, in July 1781, General Alexander Leslie outlined his plan for biological warfare in a letter to Cornwallis. "Above 700 Negroes are come down the River in the Small Pox," he wrote. "I shall distribute them about the Rebell Plantations." Even if they pardoned their actions by saying they could no longer support so many camp followers, the fact that sick African Americans might communicate smallpox to the enemy could not have been lost on British commanders.[42]

BIOLOGICAL WEAPONS AND THE ETHICS OF WAR

As readers familiar with Hernán Cortés's smallpox-aided conquest of Mexico are no doubt aware, warfare and disease have historically come hand in hand. In many instances, accusations of biological sabotage have trailed close behind. One need only look to Thucydides' account of the plague of Athens, possibly the first description of smallpox on record, to find accusations that the unnamed pestilence arose from the malicious acts of a military foe. But late-eighteenth-century America differed from ancient Greece in a very important way: the technical knowledge required to carry out biological warfare was now commonplace. All that was needed was sufficient will and justification to perform the act. Today, in the post–Geneva Protocol era, many people find it hard to imagine an ethical construct that might affirm such behaviour.[43] But eighteenth-century rules of war left much more room for excess. While victims of smallpox found the deliberate transmission of the disease reprehensible, army personnel found sanction for such actions in customary codes of international and military conduct.

In the seventeenth and eighteenth centuries, many of the widely accepted rules of European warfare had seen codification in Hugo Grotius's *De jure belli ac pacis*, first published in 1625, and Emmerich de Vattel's *The Law of Nations*, published in 1758. Both works established theoretical protections in war for women and children and for the elderly and infirm. They addressed the issue of surrender, and they determined when soldiers should give "quarter" to their enemies. Beyond all this, they also included strictures against the use of poison weapons and "the poisoning of streams, springs, and wells." In an era before microbiology, in which deadly toxins and infectious microbes were hardly distinguishable, it is nearly inconceivable that either Grotius or Vattel would have excluded communicable disease from the general category of "poisons."[44] All of these rules applied, theoretically at least, to "civilized" nations engaged in what were termed "just" wars.

For our purposes, ironically, the most important corollary to these customarily determined rules was that in certain situations, they did not apply. Cases in point included not only "unjust" wars but also rebellions, wars against enemies who themselves violated the laws of war, and wars against "savage" or "heathen" people. Vattel used the Turks and Mongols as his example, but his general point is clear: "nations are justified in uniting together as a body with the object of punishing, and even exterminating, such savage people." An earlier formulation of this philosophy had allowed the English to pursue brutal policies in Ireland, on the grounds that the Irish were not just rebels but (despite their professed Christianity) barbarians as well. More than one historian has argued that Ireland provided the English with a convenient ideological precedent for their actions in the New World. And colonists did indeed justify their own savage conduct in New England's seventeenth-century wars by touting the "savagery" of the natives they brutalized.[45] In conflicts with "heathen" Indians, European rules of war gave licence to unfettered violence, complete annihilation, and yes, biological warfare.

Jeffery Amherst, for one, clearly adhered to this view. In 1763, during the summer of the Fort Pitt incident, Amherst stated his belief that total war against Native Americans was warranted. "Indeed," he wrote, "their Total Extirpation is scarce sufficient Attonement for the Bloody and Inhuman deeds they have Committed." Three weeks later he reiterated this opinion: "I shall only Say, that it Behoves the Whole Race of Indians to Beware . . . of Carrying Matters much farther against the English, or Daring to form Conspiracys, as the Consequence will most certainly Occasion measures to be taken, that, in the End will put a most Effectual Stop to *their very being*." Col. Henry Bouquet's sentiments mirrored those of his superior officer. It was Bouquet, after all, who was so enamoured of a proposal to hunt Indians with dogs. "As it is a pity to expose good men against them," he wrote, "I wish we could make use of the Spaniard's method, and hunt them with English Dogs, Supported by Rangers, and some Light Horse, and who would I think effectualy extirpate or remove that Vermine."[46] Brutality knew no bounds in wars with "savages," and in the view of these men, Native Americans clearly fit the bill.

Amherst and Bouquet were not alone. Backed by the force of both custom and law, many in the British military seem to have held similar beliefs. There is no evidence, for example, that the personnel who actually carried out the deed at Fort Pitt expressed any ethical qualms about their actions. Nor, apparently, did General Thomas Gage, who succeeded Amherst as commander-in-chief. It was Gage, in the end, who approved the reimbursement of Levy, Trent and Company for "Sundries got to Replace in kind those which were taken from people in the Hospital to Convey the Smallpox to the Indians" at Fort Pitt. The British general made it clear in an accompanying note that he had read the invoice closely, and his authorization of payment carried with it a tacit approval of the actions taken. Years later, during the siege of Boston, American officials feared Gage would himself try to "spread the small-pox" in the Patriot forces surrounding the city. "If it is In Genral Gages power I Expect he will Send ye Small pox Into ye Army," wrote Seth Pomeroy, who had become acquainted with Gage during the Seven Years' War; "but I hope In ye Infinight Mercy of God he will prevent It, as he hath don In Every atempt that he has made yet."[47]

By comparison to the British, the Spanish and French faced comparatively few charges of wielding smallpox against Native Americans in the eighteenth century. But here too, evidence indicates that European officials and colonists might have been receptive to the idea. An account from Baja California describes a 1763 epidemic that erupted when "a traveling Spaniard who had just recently recovered from smallpox presented a shred of cloth to a native." The vague wording, however, makes it unclear whether the infection was deliberate. In 1752, during the jockeying that preceded the Seven Years' War, smallpox made an appearance among several Canadian Indian tribes. Charles Le Moyne de Longueuil, the temporary governor of Canada, observed how useful it would be if the disease took hold among the Ohio tribes who had recently gone over to the English: "'Twere desirable that it should break out and spread, generally, throughout the localities inhabited by our rebels. It would be fully as good as an army."[48] Wishful thinking is a far cry from contemplating or proposing the deliberate dissemination of smallpox. But the governor's comment does indicate a mind-set that might have approved of such action.

Far more ambiguity surrounded the use of smallpox against Americans of European descent — the allegation that surfaced repeatedly during the Revolutionary War. Nothing captured these moral tensions so clearly as a little book titled *Military Collections and Remarks*, published in British-occupied New York in 1777. Written by a British officer named Robert Donkin, the book proposed a variety of strategies the British might use to gain the upper hand in the American conflict. Among them was biological warfare. In a footnote to a two-page section on the use of bows and arrows, Major Donkin made the following suggestion: "Dip arrows in matter of smallpox, and twang them at the American rebels, in order to inoculate them; This would sooner disband these stubborn, ignorant, enthusiastic savages, than any other compulsive measures. Such is their dread and fear of that disorder!"[49]

Such ideas may have been common in verbal banter, but they rarely made it into print. What happened next is therefore revealing, for it shows how controversial the topic of biological warfare was during the American Revolution: Donkin's provocative footnote survives in only three known copies of his book. In all others, it has been carefully excised. The person responsible for this act is unknown, as is the timing. But the fact that only three known copies survived intact seems to indicate that the excision took place close to the time of publication, before the volume was widely distributed.[50] Likely perpetrators include the author, the publisher, or an agent acting on behalf of British high command. Someone may well have found the suggestion morally offensive; or, in the battle for the "hearts and minds" of the American people, someone may have realized that explicit calls for biological warfare could only make enemies.

If the strategy was controversial, those who sought sanction for biological terror could nevertheless find it in customary codes of conduct. Donkin himself called the Americans "savages," and this alone countenanced the repudiation of behavioural constraints in war. The colonists, in fact, even cultivated a symbolic "Indian" identity in episodes such as the Boston Tea Party. But beyond this, the Americans were also "rebels." Sentiments regarding rebellion were changing, but popular insurrection, like savagery, could legitimate a war of unrestrained destruction — a war in which conventional strictures against biological warfare would not apply. Writing in 1758, Emmerich Vattel took a somewhat more moderate approach than Hugo Grotius had taken a century earlier. But there was no consensus on this among British officers. While some took a conciliatory stance early in the war, it appears that by 1779 a majority of British officers had become what one scholar has termed "hard-liners"— men who believed that "nothing but the Bayonet & Torch" could quell the colonial revolt. Included among them were men such as Banastre Tarleton, notorious for terrorizing the Carolina backcountry, and Charles Grey, famous for two nighttime bayonet attacks on sleeping American soldiers. In one of these attacks, Grey's men shouted "No Quarters to rebels" as they leapt upon their slumbering foes.[51]

If the mere fact of rebellion was grounds enough for such an attitude, the difficulties presented by long sieges and the Americans' unconventional fighting methods provided additional justification. In the view of many British soldiers, the Americans had themselves violated the rules of war many times over. Some took offence at the effective Patriot sniping during the retreat from Lexington. Others resented the withering musket fire at Bunker Hill, where General Gage's men believed "the Enemy Poisoned some of their Balls." Confronted by rebellion and frustrated by atrocities committed by a "savage" American enemy who often refused to face off head-to-head on the field of battle, British officers may well have believed the propagation of smallpox was justified and put this belief into practice, especially given the fact that the law of nations apparently permitted it. It is worth recalling that Jeffery Amherst, who had found biological warfare so unabashedly justifiable in 1763, was an extremely popular figure in England. According to the historian Robert Middlekauff, he was "probably the most admired military leader in the nation" during the era of the American Revolution.[52] That General Leslie and other British officers may have thought and acted as Amherst did should come as no surprise.

Predictably, accusations of willful smallpox infection subsided temporarily with the end of the Revolutionary War. They would resurface in the 1830s, when a terrible smallpox epidemic devastated Indians in the American West, striking many of the same tribes that had suffered under an equally deadly epidemic in the early 1780s. Fur traders circulating among Native Americans in the intervening years found that memories of the earlier outbreak were so strong that even the mere threat of willful infection could elicit compliance from uncooperative Indians.[53]

It is clear, however, that while Native Americans suffered most from smallpox, they were neither the only targets of its use on the battlefield nor the only ones who levelled the charge against others. The Fort Pitt incident, despite its notoriety, does not stand alone in the annals of early American history. Accusations of deliberate smallpox propagation arose frequently in times of war, and they appear to have had merit on at least one occasion — the Yorktown campaign — during the American Revolution. Elsewhere the evidence is often ambiguous. But it nevertheless indicates that the famous Fort Pitt incident was one in a string of episodes in which military officials in North America may have wielded *Variola* against their enemies. Justification for doing so could be found in codes of war that legitimated excesses even as they defined constraints. Biological warfare was therefore a reality in eighteenth-century North America, not a distant, abstract threat as it is today. Its use was aimed, as one patriot writer accusingly put it in the year of Yorktown, "at the ruin of a whole Country, involving the indiscriminate murder of Women and Children."[54]

NOTES

I am grateful to John Mack Faragher for suggesting that I write this article and for commenting on an early draft. Wayne Lee shared important references with me and helped me locate the essay in the field of military history. Members of the Michigan Colonial Studies Seminar and the Michigan History of Medicine and Health Colloquium provided helpful critiques of an earlier version, as did the Faculty and Graduate Student Seminar at the University of South Florida department of history. Further insights, references, and assistance came from Holly Brewer, Erika Bsumek, John Dann, Pat Galloway, Don Higginbotham, Margaret Humphreys, Paige Raibmon, Neal Salisbury, Mark Wheelis, and Peter Wood, as well as the editors and anonymous reviewers of the *Journal of American History*. Financial support came from the Charlotte W. Newcombe Foundation.

1. William Trent. "William Trent's Journal at Fort Pitt, 1763," ed. A.T. Volwiler, *Mississippi Valley Historical Review*, 11 (Dec. 1924): 400. For an excellent appraisal of the Fort Pitt episode that places it in the context of the larger and more complicated struggle for control of the Ohio Valley, see Michael N. McConnell, *A Country between: The Upper Ohio Valley and Its Peoples, 1724–1774* (Lincoln, 1992), 194–96. For an example of an Internet discussion devoted to biological warfare and smallpox, see the H-OIEAHC discussion log for April 1995, available at http://www.h-net.msu.edu/logs/. For the contention that the attempt at biological warfare was "unquestionably effective at Fort Pitt," see Francis Jennings, *Empire of Fortune: Crowns, Colonies, & Tribes in the Seven Years*

War in America (New York, 1990), 447–48, 447n26. On the issue of timing, see Bernhard Knollenberg, "General Amherst and Germ Warfare," *Mississippi Valley Historical Review* 41 (Dec. 1954): 489–94; Bernhard Knollenberg to editor, "Communications," *Mississippi Valley Historical Review* 41 (March 1955): 762; and Donald H. Kent, to editor, ibid., 762–63. For a cross-cultural analysis of the incident's place in a pantheon of other such "legends," see Adrienne Mayor, "The Nessus Shirt in the New World: Smallpox Blankets in History and Legend," *Journal of American Folklore* 108 (Winter 1995): 54–77.

2. A thorough appraisal of the use of biological warfare in the prescientific era can be found in Mark Wheelis, "Biological Warfare before 1914," in *Biological and Toxin Weapons: Research, Development, and Use from the Middle Ages to 1945,* ed. Erhard Geissler and John van Courtland Moon (Oxford, 1999), 8–34.

3. For a summary of the documentation of this incident, see Knollenberg, "General Amherst and Germ Warfare," 489–94; and Kent to editor, "Communications," 762–63. While my conclusions differ from Knollenberg's, much of the evidence consulted is the same. Simeon Ecuyer to Henry Bouquet, June 16, 1763 [translation], in *The Papers of Col. Henry Bouquet,* ed. Sylvester K. Stevens and Donald H. Kent (30 series, Harrisburg, 1940–1943), series 21649, part 1, p. 153. The series numbers cited here correspond to the Additional Manuscripts classification of the British Museum, London, where the original manuscripts are stored. These numbers are also printed in the published version of the papers. Because libraries holding the published *Papers of Col. Henry Bouquet* have bound them in a variety of configurations, I have cited the series number rather than the volume number to make the precise location of each reference clear. Bouquet to Jeffery Amherst, June 23, 1763, ibid, set. 21634, p. 196.

4. Alexander McKee gives the name of the second Delaware representative as "Maumaidtree." Alexander McKee, Report of Speeches of the Delaware Indians [addressed to George Croghan], Fort Pitt, June 24, 25, 1763, in *Papers of Col. Henry Bouquet,* ed. Stevens and Kent, ser 21655, p. 210; Trent, "William Trent's Journal at Fort Pitt," ed. Volwiler, 400.

5. Levy, Trent and Company: Account against the Crown, Aug. 13, 1763, in *Papers of Col. Henry Bouquet,* ed. Stevens and Kent, ser. 21654, pp. 218–19. While the account was submitted for payment in August, the items in it are all listed under the date "1763 June." As Mark Wheelis has pointed out, readers should note that William Trent refers to a single handkerchief in his journal, while the invoice is for two: one silk, one linen. Wheelis, "Biological Warfare before 1914," 23–73.

6. Memorandum by Sir Jeffery Amherst, [July 6, 1763], in *Papers of Col. Henry Bouquet,* ed. Stevens and Kent, ser. 21634, p. 161. (Stevens and Kent tentatively assign the undated document the date of May 4, 1763, but this is apparently an error.) Bouquet to Amherst, Aug. 11, 1763, ibid, 243; Bouquet to Amherst, July 13, 1763, in Jeffery Amherst, *Official Papers, 1740–1783* (microfilm, 202 reels, World Microfilms Publications, 1979), reel 32, frame 305. The published typescript of this last document deviates in important ways from the original. See Bouquet to Amherst, July 13, 1763, in *Papers of Col. Henry Bouquet,* ed. Stevens and Kent, ser. 21634, p. 214. For the July 16 letter, see Amherst to Bouquet, July 16, 1763, in Amherst, *Official Papers,* reel 33, frame 114. Here the deviations in the published typescript are insignificant. See Memorandum by Sir Jeffery Amherst, [July 16, 1763], in *Papers of Col. Henry Bouquet,* ed. Stevens and Kent, ser. 21634, p. 161. (Stevens and Kent tentatively assign the date of May 4, 1763, to this document as well, but this is incorrect.)

7. Deposition of Gershom Hicks, April 14, 1764, in *Papers of Col. Henry Bouquet,* ed. Stevens and Kent, ser. 21650, part 1, p. 102. Five days later, under pressure from Fort Pitt officials, Hicks recanted much of his testimony and deemphasized the Indians' martial intentions. He apparently made no reference to smallpox in his second deposition. William Grant, Re-Examination of Gershom Hicks, in *Papers of Col. Henry Bouquet,* ed. Stevens and Kent, ser. 21651, pp. 7–10. For more on Hicks, see Edward Ward to Sir William Johnson, May 2, 1764, in *The Papers of Sir William Johnson,* ed. Milton W. Hamilton (14 vols. Albany, 1921–1965), XI, 169–71. On the Virginia Indians, see Andrew Lewis to Bouquet, Sept. 10, 1764, in *Papers of Col. Henry Bouquet,* ed. Stevens and Kent, ser. 21650, part 2, p. 127. For Killibuck's account, see William Johnson, Journal of Indian Affairs, [Johnson Hall, March 1–3, 1765], in *Papers of Sir William Johnson,* ed. Hamilton, XI, 618. On the possibility of multiple sources of infection, see McConnell, *Country between,* 195–96. M'Cullough's report is in Archibald Loudon, ed., *A Selection of Some of the Most Interesting Narratives of Outrages, Committed by the Indians, in Their Wars, with the White People* (1808; 2 vols, New York, 1977), I, 331. Knollenberg has emphasized Gershon Hick's testimony that smallpox had ravaged the Indians "since last spring." He believes this means the disease was present among nearby tribes even before Fort Pitt personnel distributed the infected blankets on June 24. While it is possible that Knollenberg is right, he may also be investing too much precision into what Hicks intended as a general statement. Hicks had only been captured in May, and June might well be considered "spring" in the hills of western Pennsylvania. Knollenberg, "General Amherst and Germ Warfare," 494.

8. Such a communication might have been either written or oral in form. It is also possible that documents relating to such a plan were deliberately destroyed.

9. For the eradication certificate, see F. Fenner et al., *Smallpox and Its Eradication* (Geneva, 1988), frontispiece. On clandestine supplies, see "Virus in the Deep-Freeze?," *U.S. News & World Report*, Oct. 2, 1995, p. 17; Richard Preston, "The Bioweaponeers," *New Yorker*, March 9, 1998, pp. 62–65; and *New York Times*, June 13, 1999, pp. A1, A12. The United States announced on April 22, 1999, that it would not destroy its stores of the smallpox virus in large part because of the threat of bioterrorism: *New York Times*, April 23, 1999, p. A3. On the possibility that smallpox could be released in the course of archaeological excavations, see Joseph Kennedy, "The Archaeological Recovery of Smallpox Victims in Hawaii: Scientific Investigation or Public Health Threat?," *Perspective in Biology and Medicine* 37 (Summer 1994): 499–510; Peter Razzell, "Smallpox Extinction — a Note of Caution," *New Scientist*, July 1, 1976, p. 35; and W.B. Ewart, "Causes of Mortality in a Subarctic Settlement (York Factory, Man.) 1713–1946," *Canadian Medical Association Journal* 129 (Sept. 1983): 571–74.

10. Thomas Babington Macaulay, *The History of England from the Accession of James the Second*, ed. Charles Harding Firth (6 vols., London, 1914), V, 2468; Edward Jenner, *An Inquiry into the Causes and Effects of* Variolae Vaccinae *or Cow-Pox* (London, 1798).

11. Modern medical science has recognized two strains of the virus: *Variola major* and *Variola minor. Variola minor,* however, did not emerge until the closing years of the nineteenth century. Fenner et al., *Smallpox and Its Eradication,* 242–43.

12. Hemorrhagic smallpox, according to A. Ramachandra Rao's study of approximately 7000 cases of smallpox, occurred in only 2.4 percent of all cases; it was, however, notably more common among women, occurring in 22 percent of smallpox cases among pregnant women. Rao also reports that 62 percent of patients with confluent smallpox died. A. Ramachandra Rao, *Smallpox* (Bombay, 1972), 8, 126, 25.

13. Fenner et al., *Smallpox and Its Eradication,* 55; Hans-Joachim Voth and Timothy Leunig, "Did Smallpox Reduce Height? Stature and the Standard of Living in London, 1770–1873," *Economic History Review* 49, 3 (1996): 541–60.

14. Fenner et al., *Smallpox and Its Eradication,* 186–87, 1322–33.

15. Ibid., 182–87, and A.W. Downie et al., "The Recovery of Smallpox Virus from Patients and Their Environment in a Smallpox Hospital," *Bulletin of the World Health Organization* 33 (1965): 615–22.

16. Studies indicate that *Variola* virus in scabs "could retain infectivity at room temperature for years." Fenner et al., *Smallpox and Its Eradication,* 115–16, table 2.11. On laundry workers and the survival of smallpox in cotton and bedding, see Downie et al., "Recovery of Smallpox Virus," 622; C.O. Stalleybrass, *The Principles of Epidemiology and the Process of Infection* (London, 1931), cited in Fenner et al., *Smallpox and Its Eradication,* 194; Cyril William Dixon, *Smallpox* (London, 1962), 300–302, 419–21; and F.O. MacCullum and J.R. McDonald, "Survival of Variola Virus in Raw Cotton," *Bulletin of the World Health Organization* 16 (1957): 247–54.

17. On Anthony van Leeuwenhoek, see W. Barry Wood Jr., *From Miasmas to Molecules* (New York, 1961), 14–16. On the etiology of the diseases listed, see Bernard D. Davis et al., *Microbiology: Including Immunology and Genetics* (Hagerstown, 1973), 780, 803–4, 851–52, 904–8, 1379, 1384–87.

18. William Douglass to Cadwallader Colden, May 1, 1722, in "Letters from Dr. William Douglass to Dr. Cadwallader Colden of New York," ed. Jared Sparks, *Collections of the Massachusetts Historical Society* 32 (1854): 168. This episode led to one of the most famous smallpox epidemics in American history, culminating in the "inoculation controversy" and the fire-bombing of Cotton Mather's house. Ola Elizabeth Winslow, *A Destroying Angel: The Conquest of Smallpox in Colonial Boston* (Boston, 1974), 44–45. On the fire-bombing, see Cotton Mather, *The Diary of Cotton Mather*, ed. Worthington Chauncey Ford, *Collections of the Massachusetts Historical Society* 68 (1912): 657–58. On the Creek Indians, see James Adair, *Adair's History of the American Indians*, ed. Samuel Cole Williams (1930; New York, 1966), 364. On the Charleston outbreak, see Suzanne Krebsbach, "The Great Charlestown Smallpox Epidemic of 1760," *South Carolina Historical Magazine* 97 (Jan. 1996): 30–37. On Williamsburg, see Wyndham B. Blanton, *Medicine in Virginia in the Eighteenth Century* (Richmond, 1931), 285, 287; and John Duffy, *Epidemics in Colonial America* (Baton Rouge, 1953), 39.

19. Thomas Jefferson to John Page, Jan. 20, 1763, in *Papers of Thomas Jefferson*, ed. Julian P. Boyd (27 vols., Princeton, 1950–), I, 8; Abigail Adams to John Adams, March 31, 1776, in *The Book of Abigail and John: Selected Letters of the Adams Family, 1762–1784*, ed. L.H. Butterfield, Marc Friedlander, and Mary-Jo Kline (Cambridge, MA., 1975), 120; "From the Bagge MS. 1779," in *Records of the Moravians in North Carolina*, ed. Adelaide L. Fries (8 vols., Raleigh, 1922–1969), III, 1283.

20. New York Provincial Congress to J. Hancock, Nov. 2, 1775 (microfilm: microcopy 247, reel 81, item 67, vol. 1, p. 129), Papers of the Continental Congress, RG 360 (National Archives, Washington, DC); Virginia Committee of Safety, Proceedings of the Committee, April 30, 1776, in Robert L. Scribner and Brent Tarter, eds., *Revolutionary Virginia: The Road to Independence, a Documentary Record* (7 vols., Charlottesville, [1973]–1983), VI, 496; summary of letter from George Muter, March 8, 1781, in *Papers of Thomas Jefferson*, ed. Boyd, V, 96–97.

21. On the European acquisition of inoculation, see Donald R. Hopkins, *Princes and Peasants: Smallpox in History* (Chicago, 1983), 46–51. On the resurgence of smallpox in Europe, see Genevieve Miller, *The Adoption of Inoculation for Smallpox in England and France* (Philadelphia, 1957), 29–35. Mather's account of his interview with Onesimus can be found in George Lyman Kittredge, ed., "Lost Works of Cotton Mather," *Proceedings of the Massachusetts Historical Society* 45 (Feb. 1912): 422.

22. See Hopkins, *Princes and Peasants*, 109; and Fenner et al., *Smallpox and Its Eradication*, 165, 252–53, 268. For comparative case fatality rates, see ibid., 246.

23. Abigail Adams to John Adams, Aug. 5, 1776, in *Book of Abigail and John*, ed. Butterfield, Friedlander, and Kline, 150–51; William Nelson to John Norton, Feb. 27, 1768, in *John Norton & Sons, Merchants of London and Virginia: Being the Papers from Their Counting House for the Years 1750 to 1795*, ed. Frances Norton Mason (Richmond, 1937), 38.

24. The Jesuits faced many such allegations in seventeenth-century New France. See Reuben Gold Thwaites, ed., *The Jesuit Relations and Allied Documents: Travels and Explorations of the Jesuit Missionaries in New France, 1610–1791* (74 vols., Cleveland, 1896–1901), XI, 15, 39, XII, 85, 237, XIII, 215, XIV, 53, 103, XV, 19–35, XVI, 39, 53–55, XX, 28–31, 73, XXX, 227, XXXIX, 125–31.

25. Even the Aztecs may have tried to utilize such a strategy during the Spanish conquest from 1519 to 1521. Motecuhzoma reportedly asked his magicians to work "some charm" against the Spaniards that might "cause them to break out in sores" or even "cause them to fall sick, or die, or return to their own land." Ironically, it was the Aztecs, not the Spaniards, who succumbed en masse to smallpox. Miguel-Leon Portilla, ed., *The Broken Spears: The Aztec Account of the Conquest of Mexico* (Boston, 1966), 34. On Queen Anne's War, see Pierre-François-Xavier de Charlevoix, *History and General Description of New France*, ed. and trans. John Dawson Gilmary Shea (6 vols., New York, 1900), V, 221–22. For other incidents that *may* represent deliberate smallpox propagation on the part of Native Americans, see William Francis Butler, *The Great Lone Land: A Tale of Travel and Adventure in the North-West of America* (London, 1910), 367–72; and James G. McCurdy, *By Juan de Fuca's Strait: Pioneering along the Northwestern Edge of the Continent* (Portland, OR, 1937), 197.

26. D. Peter MacLeod, "Microbes and Muskets: Smallpox and the Participation of the Amerindian Allies of New France in the Seven Years' War," *Ethnohistory* 39 (Winter 1992): 42–64. On the epidemic among the Potawatomis, see ibid., 49; R. David Edmunds, *The Potawatomis: Keepers of the Fire* (Norman, 1978), 55–56; and James A. Clifton, *The Prairie People: Continuity and Change in Potawatomi Indian Culture, 1665–1965* (Lawrence, 1977), 102. The French, according to Cornelius Van Slyke, went to great lengths to convince the Indians "that in case they made peace with yᵉ English, they would soon repent it, as they [the British] would then come into their Villages, & thereby destroy em by poison, Small Pox & ca. Which the Informant says they believe as much as can be." William Johnson, "Examination of Cornelius Van Slyke," July 21, 1767, Native American History Collection (William L. Clements Library, Ann Arbor, MI). I would like to thank John Dann of the Clements Library for sharing this document with me. For a valuable appraisal of the Fort William affair, see Ian K. Steele, *Betrayals: Fort William & the "Massacre"* (New York, 1990).

27. Andrew J. Blackbird, *Complete Both Early and Late History of the Ottawa and Chippewa Indians of Michigan, a Grammar of Their Language, Personal and Family History of the Author* (Harbor Springs, MI, 1897), 2–3. Another vaguely worded accusation against the French can be found in a letter dated November 1681: we have forbidden the coming down of ninety Canoes belonging to Ottawas, heavily laden with peltries, through apprehensions of the small pox (*peste*), which was introduced among that people by well-known vagabonds (*libertins*), against whom the Governor was unwilling that information should be lodged." M. du Chesneau to M. de Seignelay, Quebec, Nov. 13, 1681, *Documents Relative to the Colonial History of the State of New-York: Procured in Holland, England, and France*, ed. Edmund Bailey O'Callaghan (15 vols., Albany, 1853–1887), IX, 154. On the French blaming the British, see MacLeod, "Microbes and Muskets," 50–51.

28. John J. Heagerty, *Four Centuries of Medical History in Canada* (2 vols., Toronto, 1928), I, 44–45. William Warren was a native-born Ojibwa speaker and interpreter who devoted much of his life to recording the tribe's history and lore. William W. Warren, *History of the Ojibway Nation* (1884; Minneapolis, 1957), 257–62.

29. Steele, *Betrayals*, 135–38; unattributed quotation in Heagerty, *Four Centuries of Medical History in Canada*, I, 42.

30. Extract of a letter from Boston, author unknown, *London Evening Post*, March 25–28, 1775, reprinted in Margaret W. Willard, ed., *Letters on the American Revolution, 1774–1776* (Boston, 1925), 57–58; George Washington to John Hancock, Dec. 14, 1775, in *The Papers of George Washington: Revolutionary War Series*, ed. W.W. Abbot and Dorothy Twohig (26 vols., Charlottesville, 1983–), II, 548.

31. Robert H. Harrison to Council of Massachusetts, Dec. 3, 1775, in *American Archives*, ed. Peter Force, 4th ser. (6 vols., Washington, 1837–1853), IV, 168; Washington to Hancock, Dec. 4, 1775, in *Papers of George Washington: Revolutionary War Series*, ed. Abbot and Twohig, II, 486.

32. Washington to Hancock, Dec. 11, 1775, in *Papers of George Washington: Revolutionary War Series*, ed. Abbot and Twohig, II, 533; Washington to Hancock, Nov. 28, 1775, ibid., 447; Samuel Bixby, "Diary of Samuel Bixby," *Proceedings of the Massachusetts Historical Society* 14 (March 1876): 297; Washington to James Otis St. [Mass. General Court], Dec. 10, 1775, in *Papers of George Washington: Revolutionary War Series*, ed. Abbot and Twohig, II, 526; John Morgan to Washington, Dec. 12, 1775, ibid., 541–42; Washington to Joseph Reed, Dec. 15, 1775, ibid., 553. On the servant refugee, see *Boston Gazette and Country Journal*, Feb. 12, 1776, p. 4. On Dr. Rand, see Ezekiel Price, "Diary of Ezekiel Price, 1775–1776," *Proceedings of the Massachusetts Historical Society*, 7 (Nov. 1863), 220.

33. George Washington, General Orders, March 13, 1776, in *Papers of George Washington: Revolutionary War Series*, ed. Abbot and Twohig, III. 458; Washington, General Orders, March 14, 1776, ibid., 466. "The Small pox prevails to such a degree in Boston," wrote Gen. Artemas Ward on July 4, "and so many of the soldiers got the disorder, that I apprehend the remainder of them must soon be inoculated." Inoculations began that very day. Artemas Ward to Washington, July 4, 1776, ibid., V, 210; James Thacher, A *Military Journal of the American Revolution* (Boston, 1823), 54; Whitfield J. Bell Jr., *John Morgan, Continental Doctor* (Philadelphia, 1965), 188; Price, "Diary of Ezekiel Price," 259.

34. Bayze Wells, "Journal of Bayze Wells of Farmington, May, 1775–February 1777," *Collections of the Connecticut Historical Society* 7 (1899): 267; and Lewis Beebe, "Journal of a Physician on the Expedition against Canada, 1776," *Pennsylvania Magazine of History and Biography* 59 (Oct. 1935): 337.

35. John Joseph Henry, "Campaign against Quebec," in *March to Quebec: Journals of the Members of Arnold's Expedition*, ed. Kenneth Roberts (New York, 1940), 374–75; Thomas Jefferson, "Notes of Witnesses' Testimony concerning the Canadian Campaign, July 1–27, 1776," in *Papers of Thomas Jefferson*, ed. Boyd, I, 435, 437, 447–48; Thomas Jefferson, "Comments on Soulés' *Histoire*, August 8, 1786," ibid., X, 373, 377n24. Other members of Congress were likewise convinced by the evidence. In 1777 full-scale inoculation of the Continental Army began, in part to address the troops' vulnerability to biological warfare. In May 1777, the Foreign Affairs Committee offered the following explanation: "Our troops have been under inoculation for the small pox with good success which purgation we hope will be the means of preserving them from fever in the summer, however it will frustrate one cannibal scheme of our enemies who have constantly fought us with that disease by introducing it among our troops." Foreign Affairs Committee to Commissioners in France, May 2, 1777 (reel 102, item 78, vol. 21, p. 99), Papers of the Continental Congress.

36. Caleb Haskell, "Diary at the Siege of Boston and on the March to Quebec," in *March to Quebec*, ed. Roberts, 482–83. The diarists Jacob Danford and Thomas Ainslie both stated that smallpox had "long raged in town." It should be noted that Danford's and Ainslie's diaries are suspiciously similar to one another as well as to the diary attributed to Hugh Finlay. Jacob Danford, "Journal of the Most Remarkable Occurrences in Quebec, by an Officer of the Garrison," *New-York Historical Society Collections*, 13 (1880), 181; Thomas Ainslie, *Canada Preserved: The Journal of Captain Thomas Ainslie*, ed. Sheldon S. Cohen (New York, 1968), 27; Hugh Finlay [?], "Journal of the Siege and Blockade of Quebec by the American Rebels, in Autumn 1775 and Winter 1776," *Literary and Historical Society of Quebec, Historical Documents* (no. 4, 1875), 5. American prisoners taken in the Americans' Dec. 31 attack on the city were granted permission to be inoculated in prison. See, for example, Francis Nichols, "Diary of Lieutenant Francis Nichols, of Colonel William Thompson's Battalion of Pennsylvania Riflemen, Jan. to Sept., 1776," *Pennsylvania Magazine of History and Biography* 20 (no. 4, 1896): 506; and John Topham, "The Journal of Captain John Topham, 1775–6," *Magazine of History* 13 (extra no. 50, 1866; reprint, Tarrytown, NY, 1916), 30, 38–39. When the Americans fled on May 6, 1776, many of the sick were left behind on the Plains of Abraham. Noting "that many of his Majesty's deluded subjects of the neighbouring provinces, labouring under wounds and diverse disorders," were "in great danger of perishing for want of proper assistance," Carleton ordered his men "to make diligent search for all such distressed persons, and afford them all necessary relief, and convey them to the general hospital, where proper care shall be taken of them." Carleton's orders are reprinted in Andrew Parke, *An Authentic Narrative of Facts Relating to the Exchange of Prisoners Taken at the Cedars* (London, 1777), 4–5.

37. The best account of Dunmore's Ethiopian Regiment remains Benjamin Quarles, *The Negro in the American Revolution* (Chapel Hill, 1961), 19–32. The accusation can be found in Dixon and Hunter's *Virginia Gazette*, June 15, 1776, quoted in *Naval Documents of the American Revolution*, ed. William Bell Clark, William James Morgan, and Michael J. Crawford (10 vols., Washington, DC, 1964–1996), V, 554. By another account, five of Dunmore's sailors deserted before the governor left Norfolk. "They inform me they have the smallpox," wrote William Woodford. The relation, if any, between these deserters and the rumours of willful propagation of smallpox at the same time is not clear. "Extract of a letter from Col. [William] Woodford to General [Andrew] Lewis, dated Norfolk, May 22," ibid., 209.

38. John Murray, Earl of Dunmore, to the Secretary of State, June 26, 1776, in George W. Williams, *History of the Negro Race in America from 1619–1800* (New York, 1885), 342, quoted in Gerald W. Mullin, *Flight and Rebellion: Slave Resistance in Eighteenth-Century Virginia* (New York, 1972), 132; "[James] Cunningham's Examination 18th July 1776," in *Naval Documents of the American Revolution*, ed. Clark, Morgan, and Crawford V, 1136. An unnamed "fever" also afflicted the men as they underwent inoculation on Gwynne's Island at the mouth of the Piankatank River: "Narrative of Captain Andrew Snape Hamond, [H.M.S. Roebuck, June 1 to June 30]," ibid., 840. Deserters from Dunmore's force did carry smallpox ashore. In July "a man that called himself a deserter from Lord Dunmore" broke out with smallpox a day after joining a Maryland militia regiment. While the documentation reveals no direct accusation of malfeasance, the innuendo is clearly there. "I have spoken to Dr. Browne, who had the care of the fellow, and he says he thinks he was inoculated," wrote Lieutenant Bennett Bracco. Bennett Bracco to Maryland Council of Safety, July 26, 1776, in *American Archives*, ed. Peter Force, 5th ser. (3 vols., Washington, 1837–1853), I, 592. On July 23, Maj. Thomas Price likewise informed the Maryland Council of Safety that the infection had reached his camp on St. George's Island. "We have several Deserters from the Enemy most of them in the small Pox," he wrote. Thomas Price to the Maryland Council of Safety, July 23, 1776, in *Naval Documents of the American Revolution*, ed. Clark, Morgan, and Crawford, V, 1193.

39. Josiah Bartlett to William Whipple, April 21, 1777, in *The Papers of Josiah Bartlett*, ed. Frank C. Mevers (Hanover, NH, 1979), 157–58. On Exeter, see Mary Bartlett to Josiah Bartlett, Mary 28, 2778, Box 1, Josiah Bartlett Papers, 1761–1794 (New Hampshire Historical Society, Concord, NH).

40. In London, smallpox had become endemic by this time. Moreover, in at least one rural area of England, the disease tended to appear in five-year cycles. Other rural areas were probably similar. British soldiers (and probably Hessians as well) were much more likely than Americans to have gone through smallpox in childhood. S.R. Duncan, Susan Scott, and C.J. Duncan, "The Dynamics of Smallpox Epidemics in Britain, 1550–1800," *Demography* 30 (Aug. 1993): 405–23.

41. Josiah Atkins, *The Diary of Josiah Atkins*, ed. Steven E. Kagle (New York, 1975), 32–33; William Feltman, *The Journal of Lt. William Feltman 1781–82* (1853; New York, 1969), 6; Thacher, *Military Journal of the American Revolution*, 337; Robert R. Livingston to Francis Dana, Oct. 22, 1781 (reel 102, item 78, vol. 21, p. 99), Papers of the Continental Congress. Franklin's accusation was direct: "Having the small-pox in their army while in that country, they inoculated some of the negroes they took as prisoners belonging to a number of plantations, and then let them escape, or sent them covered with the pock, to mix with and spread the disease among the others of their colour, as well as among the white country people; which occasioned a great mortality of both, and certainly did not contribute to the enabling debtors in making payment." Benjamin Franklin, "The Retort Courteous," in *Writings: Benjamin Franklin*, ed. J.A. Leo Lemay (New York, 1987), 1126–27.

42. Alexander Leslie to Charles Cornwallis, July 13, 1781 (microfilm: frames 280–81, reel 4), Cornwallis Papers, P.R.O. 30/11/6 (Public Record Office, London, Eng.). Johann Ewald, a Hessian soldier fighting for the British, felt that the loyal African Americans who absconded to the British were treated with great injustice when Cornwallis ordered them to leave camp: "I would just as soon forget to record a cruel happening. On the same day of the enemy assault, we drove back to the enemy all of our black friends, whom we had taken along to despoil the countryside. We had used them to good advantage and set them free, and now, with fear and trembling, they had to face the reward of their cruel masters." Johann Ewald, *Diary of the American War: A Hessian Journal*, ed. and trans. Joseph P. Tustin (New Haven, 1979), 335–36.

43. On Mexico, see Noble David Cook, *Born to Die: Disease and New World Conquest, 1492–1650* (New York, 1998), 211–14. On the plague of Athens, see Thucydides, *History of the Peloponnesian War*, 2.48. The Geneva Protocol went into effect in 1928, prohibiting biological warfare among nations signing the agreement. League of Nations, Treaty Series, "Protocol for the Prohibition of the Use in War of Asphyxiating, Poisonous, or Other Gases, and of Bacteriological Methods of Warfare," signed at Geneva, June 17, 1925, entered into force Feb. 8, 1928, *Publication of Treaties and International Engagements Registered with the Secretariat of the League*, 94 (no. 2138, 1929), 65–74.

44. Hugo Grotius, *De jure belli ac pacis libris tres*, ed. James Brown Scott, trans. Francis W. Kelsey (1646; 3 vols., New York, 1964), III, 734–36, 739–40; Emmerich de Vattel, *The Law of Nations: or, Principles of the Law of Nature; Applied to the Conduct and Affairs of Nations and Sovereigns* (1758; New York, 1964), 280, 282–83, 289; Barbara Donagan, "Atrocity, War Crime, and Treason in the English Civil War," *American Historical Review* 99 (Oct. 1994): 1149–51. Grotius and Vattel explicitly differentiated between poisoning an enemy's water supply and cutting it off completely. It was lawful, they said, to divert water flow or, in Vattel's words, to "cut it off at its source . . . in order to force the enemy to surrender." But poisoning the same water supply was forbidden. Vattal, *Law of Nations*, esp. 289; and Grotius, *De jure belli ac pacis*, 653.

45. Vattal, *Law of Nations*, 246. The Spanish friar Francisco de Vitoria had argued quite differently in the 1500s. "Even if the barbarians refuse to accept Christ as their lord, this does not justify making war on them or doing

them any hurt": Franciscus de Victoria [Francisco de Vitoria], *De Indis de ivre belli relaciones*, ed. Ernest Nys (1917; New York, 1964), 137–38. On Ireland, see Nicholas Canny, "The Ideology of English Colonization: From Ireland to America," *William and Mary Quarterly* 30 (Oct. 1973): 575–98; Barbara Donagan, "Codes and Conduct in the English Civil War," *Past and Present* (no. 118, Feb. 1988), 70–71; Donagan, "Atrocity, War Crime, and Treason in the English Civil War," 1139, 1148–49; and Howard Mumford Jones, "Origins of the Colonial Ideal in English," *Proceedings of the American Philosophical Society* 85 (Sept. 1942): 448–65. On New England, see Jill Lepore, *The Name of War: King Philip's War and the Origins of American Identity* (New York, 1998), 112; Ronald Dale Karr, "Why Should You Be So Furious?': The Violence of the Pequot War," *Journal of American History* 85 (Dec. 1998): 888–89, 899–909; and Adam J. Hirsch, "The Collision of Military Cultures in Seventeenth-Century New England," *Journal of American History* 74 (March 1988): 1187–1212.

46. Jeffery Amherst to George Croghan, Aug. 7, 1763, in Amherst, *Official Papers*, reel 30, frame 249; Amherst to William Johnson, Aug. 27, 1763, ibid., frame 257; Henry Bouquet to Amherst, July 13, 1763, ibid., reel 32, frame 305. For a published, typescript version of the last document, see *Papers of Col. Henry Bouquet*, ed. Stevens and Kent, ser. 21634, p. 216. For a full version of the proposal to use dogs, see ibid., ser. 21649, part 1, pp. 214–15.

47. Gage made the following note with his endorsement: "The Within Acc^t. not belonging to any particular Department, but the Articles ordered for the use of the Service, by the off. Comm^{dg}, Col°. Bouquet will order the Acc^t. to be discharged & place it in his Acc^t. of extraordinarys." Levy, Trent and Company: Account against the Crown, Aug. 13, 1763, in *Papers of Col. Henry Bouquet*, ed. Stevens and Kent, ser. 21654, pp. 218–19. The Reverend Thomas Allen has forewarned Pomeroy that Gage might deliberately spread smallpox. Seth Pomeroy to Asahel Pomeroy, May 13, 1775, in *The Journals and Papers of Seth Pomeroy, Sometime General in the Colonial Service*, ed. Louis Effingham de Forest (New Haven, 1926), 166; Thomas Allen to Seth Pomeroy, May 4, 1775, 167. On Pomeroy's familiarity with Gage, see John Richard Alden, *General Gage in America: Being Principally a History of His Role in the American Revolution* (Baton Rouge, 1948), 256.

48. Accusations that French Jesuits deliberately spread smallpox were quite common in the seventeenth century. (See note 24 above.) Jacob Baegert, *Observations in Lower California*, trans. M.M. Brandenberg (Berkeley, 1952), 77. For more on the California outbreak, see Robert H. Jackson, "Epidemic Disease and Population Decline in the Baja California Missions, 1697–1834," *Southern California Quarterly* 63 (Winter 1981): 316, 321. Charles Le Moyne, Baron de Longueuil, to Antoine Louis Rouillé, April 21, 1752, *Documents Relative to the Colonial History of the State of New-York*, ed. O'Callaghan, X, 249.

49. Robert Donkin, *Military Collections and Remarks* (New York, 1777), 190–91, insert.

50. Some copies of the book contain an engraved insert replicating the missing text. For an example of both the excision and the insert, see the copy of Donkin, *Military Collections and Remarks*, 190n., in the Clements Library, University of Michigan, Ann Arbor. I am grateful to John Dann of the Clements Library for bringing Donkin's book to my attention and for informing me of the recent discovery of a third intact copy.

51. On Indian-as-America symbolism, see Hugh Honour, *The New Golden Land: European Images of America from the Discoveries to the Present Time* (New York, 1975), 84–117, 138–60. See Vattel, *Law of Nations*, 336–37; and Grotius, *De jure belli ac pacis*, I, 139–63, II, 551. On views within the British military, see Stephen Conway, "'The Great Mischief Complain'd of': Reflections on the Misconduct of British Soldiers in the Revolutionary War," *William and Mary Quarterly* 47 (July 1990): 378–79; Stephen Conway, "To Subdue America: British Army Officers and the Conduct of the Revolutionary War," *William and Mary Quarterly* 43 (July 1986): 396–97; and Armstrong Starkey, "Paoli to Stony Point: Military Ethics and Weaponry during the American Revolution," *Journal of Military History* 58 (Jan. 1994): 18. The "Bayonet & Torch" quotation is from Patrick Campbell to Alexander Campbell, July 8, 1778, Campbell of Barcaldine Muniments, G.D. 170/1711/17, S.R.O., quoted in Conway, "To Subdue America," 392. On "hard-liners," see ibid., 404–5; and Conway, "'The Great Mischief Complain'd of,'" 370–90. On Banastre Tarleton and Charles Grey, see Harold E. Selesky, "Colonial America," in *The Laws of War: Constraints on Warfare in the Western World*, ed. Michael Howard, George J. Andreopoulos, and Mark R. Shulman (New Haven, 1994), 80–83.

52. Selesky, "Colonial America," 81–83. On the poisoned musket balls, see Thomas Sullivan, "The Common British Soldier — From the Journal of Thomas Sullivan, 49th Regiment of Foot," ed. S. Sydney Bradford, *Maryland Historical Magazine* 62 (Sept. 1967): 236. On Amherst, see Robert Middlekauff, *The Glorious Cause: The American Revolution, 1763–1789* (New York, 1982), 406.

53. In 1812 or 1813, when Indians around Astoria (at the mouth of the Columbia River) showed signs of hostility, the trader Duncan McDougall threatened to infect them with smallpox: "He assembled several of the chieftains, and showing them a small bottle, declared that it contained the small-pox; that although his force was weak in number, he was strong in medicine; and that in consequence of the treacherous cruelty of the northern Indians, he would open the bottle and send the small-pox among them. The chiefs strongly remonstrated against his

doing so. They told him that they and their relations were always friendly to the white people; that they would remain so; that if the small-pox was once let out, it would run like fire among the good people as well as among the bad; and that it was inconsistent with justice to punish friends for the crimes committed by enemies. Mr. McDougall appeared to be convinced by these reasons, and promised, that if the white people were not attacked or robbed for the future, the fatal bottle should not be uncorked." Ross Cox, *The Columbia River; or, Scenes and Adventures during a Residence of Six Years on the Western Side of the Rocky Mountains among Various Tribes of Indians Hitherto Unknown*, ed. Edgar I. Stewart and Jane R. Stewart (1831; Norman, 1957), 169–70.

54. Robert R. Livingston to Francis Dana, Oct. 22, 1781 (reel 102, item 78, vol. 21, p. 99). Papers of the Continental Congress.

Article Eleven

Microbes and Muskets: Smallpox and the Participation of the Amerindian Allies of New France in the Seven Years' War

D. Peter MacLeod

The arrival of Europeans created a new world[1] for the native peoples of North America. Postcontact Amerindians had no choice but to confront the challenge of life in a once-familiar habitat that was now infested with new groups of humans and the flora, fauna, and microbes that accompanied them. Two manifestations of the radically changed geopolitical and biological environments created by the newcomers to North America were epidemic disease and intra-European warfare.[2] In the mid-eighteenth century, the Amerindians of the Great Lakes (among others) faced both when a series of epidemics broke out during the Seven Years' War. Their response, at once pragmatic and informed, reveals something of Amerindian adjustment to the realities of life in postcontact North America, a process that remains in progress as the twentieth century draws to a close.

Following the establishment of European settlements in North America, Amerindians were frequently drawn into warfare between rival colonies. The issues at stake might or might not directly affect their concerns, but belligerent Europeans invariably attempted to involve their Amerindian allies in these conflicts.

Amerindian participation in warfare demanded decisions by groups and individuals regarding whether or not to go to war and the number of warriors that would actually fight. These decisions could be based upon factors ranging from cold calculations of geopolitical advantage to the desire for recreation and individual prestige.[3]

Throughout the Seven Years' War, the Amerindian allies of New France had to decide how to respond to annual invitations to go to war in the central theater on behalf of the French.[4] The details of their deliberations are unrecorded, but the results were manifested in a series of dramatic fluctuations in the numbers of Amerindians serving alongside the French in this

Source: D. Peter MacLeod, "Microbes and Muskets: Smallpox and the Participation of the Amerindian Allies of New France in the Seven Years' War," *Ethnohistory* 39:1 (Winter 1992). Copyright © 1992 by the American Society for Ethnohistory. All rights reserved. Reprinted by permission of the publisher.

theater, as individuals and groups elected to proffer or withhold their services. These variations correspond to smallpox epidemics. Sharp declines in the size of the Amerindian contingent in the central theater occurred immediately after outbreaks of the disease; when the epidemics had passed, their numbers in the field increased once more. Whatever positive factors impelled Amerindians to go to war in the 1750s, the numbers of warriors who actually took part in campaigns in the central theater between 1755 and 1759 were determined by the reactions of the allies to the flourishing and fading of the smallpox virus.[5]

The first official French contacts with the inhabitants of the New World in the 1530s were characterized by treachery and violence on the part of French adventurers, who quickly alienated the Amerindians. Nevertheless, in the first decades of the seventeenth century, a second wave of French expeditions established amicable and mutually profitable relations with the native people and began to form the concomitant military alliances that would endure until the British conquest. The Seven Years' War was the last, supreme test of the effectiveness of the Franco-Amerindian alliance system. With New France fighting for its very survival and heavily outnumbered in the field, both by Anglo-American colonials and by British regulars, the French relied to a considerable extent upon the manpower provided by their Amerindian allies to offset the imbalance. "Without them," conceded one French staff officer, who had no particular love for Amerindians, "the odds would be too unequal for us."[6] In the event, the alliance system rose to the challenge and proved capable of delivering a substantial force of Amerindian warriors to fight alongside the French regulars and Canadian militiamen.[7]

While the war in North America raged from Louisbourg in Acadia to Fort Duquesne on the Ohio, the most important region for the defense of New France was the central theater, which comprised the seigneurial tract of Canada, together with its approaches, and extended from eastern Lake Ontario to Quebec.[8] Rather than form raiding parties, like their counterparts in Acadia and the Ohio country, the bulk of the Amerindians serving in this sector were employed as auxiliaries to the French field army, filling an indispensable role as guides, scouts, skirmishers, and general purveyors of intimidation. They came primarily, but not exclusively, from the Canadian missions and the Pays d'en haut, and their numbers varied considerably from year to year.[9]

Reliable data on the mid-eighteenth century Amerindian population of New France do not exist. The Amerindians themselves did not keep statistics, and estimates made by Europeans vary greatly.[10] It is possible, however, to find in surviving French records an extensive series of reports on the Amerindians serving with the French. From these documents, one can assemble a fairly accurate account of the strength of the Amerindian element of the armed forces of French North America.

French officers were able to produce reliable records of Amerindian participation in the Seven Years' War, because the military activities of warriors serving in the central theater brought them into constant contact with the French for months at a time.[11] The allied contingents were far from being an undifferentiated mass. They served in tribal units, which were accompanied by commandants of western posts, missionaries, or interpreters, who knew the warriors as individuals and were thus able to make accurate reports on the size of the various groups. The fact that the French were supplying their allies with rations, equipment, clothing, and weapons, at great expense, made it necessary for French logisticians to keep track of Amerindian numbers. Finally, arrivals and departures in areas of operations were generally preceded and accompanied by ceremonies and conferences, which greatly facilitated the observation and recording of fluctuations in the magnitude of the Amerindian component of a French force.

In the central theater, the number of Amerindians serving with the French reached a peak each year with the assembly of a large body of warriors to accompany the French field army.[12] If the numbers of Amerindians attached to the French army in each calendar year are assembled,

Figure 11.1 Amerindian Warriors Serving with the French in the Central Theater, 1755–60

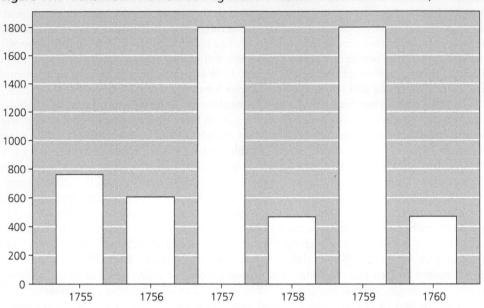

it is possible to produce a year-by-year graph of their participation in the war. One might expect this graph to resemble somewhat a bell curve, reflecting a steady increase in accordance with successive French victories during the early years of war, followed by a symmetrical decline thereafter. Conventional wisdom holds that Amerindians based their decisions on participation in the Seven Years' War primarily upon their perception of the likelihood of a French or British victory at a given time. This view is expressed concisely by George F. G. Stanley, who has written that "an Indian force was neither a steady nor reliable source of support as far as Canada was concerned; it rose and fell according to the military success or failure of French and Canadian arms."[13]

In fact, a graph of annual Amerindian participation in the central theater during the Seven Years' War takes the form of a jagged series of peaks and valleys that bear no consistent relation to political or military events (Fig. 11.1). The number of Amerindians serving with the French in the Laurentian valley twice declined, but each decline was followed by an equally striking increase. Furthermore, the number of warriors serving in the central theater peaked twice. In 1757, when French fortunes were at their height, this might have been expected, but an equal number of Amerindians fought in the 1759 campaign, when New France was on the brink of disaster.

If the changes in the number of warriors fighting in the central theater were not caused by Amerindian reactions to military events, neither were they the result of pressure exerted by the French in response to the changing demands of the war. For the French appear to have consistently attempted to recruit as many Amerindians as possible to serve with the field army, rather than first attempting to determine just how many warriors were really needed for a given campaign.[14] As their allies, moreover, the French could only offer warriors a chance to take part in a campaign. Whether or not they accepted was up to influential Amerindian leaders and individual warriors. The French were able neither to compel their allies to join them nor to turn away volunteers and order them to go home.

There were, however, forces at play in North America beyond the visible and political. Until the twentieth century, war and pestilence marched hand in hand, and what is a tragedy for humans is a splendid opportunity for the microscopic organisms that prey upon them. The conditions created by the outbreak of the Seven Years' War were particularly propitious for the flourishing of the tiny, brick-shaped virus known as variola major — smallpox. During every year of the war, more people than ever before were on the move in the North American interior. Every spring, thousands of Amerindians left their homes in the Canadian missions or the Pays d'en haut and traveled to the frontier zone that separated the rival colonies. There, they came into close contact for months at a time with thousands of European colonials or regulars as allies, opponents, or prisoners. Some of the Europeans, recruited from the disease-experienced populations of western Europe, where smallpox was endemic, were infected with that disease and unwittingly passed it on to the much more vulnerable colonials and Amerindians.[15]

An individual who had not acquired immunity through a previous attack of the disease courted death by simply approaching a smallpox victim. With every breath, sufferers expelled a cloud of minute water droplets, each alive with the virus, that could be inhaled by luckless passersby. Under some conditions, moreover, variola major could survive for a considerable length of time outside the human body; when worn or handled, the clothing and bedding of patients shed deadly, virus-bearing dust particles, an equally potent, if less common, source of respiratory infection. Victims suffered from a high fever, chills, nausea, headache, backache, and sometimes convulsions, delirium, or horrifying nightmares. The body became covered with flat, reddish spots that changed within days to pimples, then blisters, and finally scabbed pustules. Some victims died within days of the first appearance of the rash; others lingered in great pain for over weeks. Those who recovered were often scarred for life but henceforth immune to the disease.[16]

Prior to the introduction of vaccination as a defense against epidemic disease, death by disease was a greater risk for combatants than death on the field of battle. Once the war began and large number of reinforcements from the disease-experienced populations of Europe arrived, the question became not if, but when, an epidemic would break out, and how many would die.[17]

Immediately after the Seven Years' War began, the French turned to their Amerindian allies for assistance. In August 1755, a Franco-Amerindian army, which included 760 fighters from the Canadian missions, was deployed in the path of a British invasion on the Lake Champlain frontier.[18] Although the actual battle of Lake George ended in stalemate, this force managed to stop the British drive towards Canada. The French had scored a strategic victory by halting the British, but they were badly shaken by their tactical defeat. The governor general of New France, Pierre de Rigaud de Vaudreuil, contemplated making some effort to retrieve the situation, but "at that very instant the colony was afflicted with smallpox."[19] During the fall and winter of 1755–56, the disease "made astonishing ravages"[20] among Canadians, regulars, and the Amerindians who lived in the missions.[21] According to one French officer, whose account is confirmed by British intelligence reports, of three hundred warriors at the mission of Sault St. Louis, one hundred died in the epidemic.[22] It is likely that other tribes in the Laurentian valley suffered proportionately.

The outbreak of smallpox was one of the circumstances that compelled Vaudreuil to remain on the defensive in the fall of 1755.[23] As well, he found that as a result of the epidemic, he had "great difficulty in finding the men needed to crew the bateaux destined for the transport of provisions" and lacked the manpower to form raiding parties to harass the garrison of Fort Oswego,[24] which was an important part of his plan to reduce that fort in the following campaign.[25]

In 1756, the French confidently expected to augment the mission Amerindians fighting in the central theater with contingents from the western allies. By June, the French "were expecting momentarily at that post [Fort Niagara] a large number [of Amerindians] from the Pays d'en haut."[26] Smallpox, however, struck once more in the Laurentian valley and spread westward along French lines of communication to the interior, appearing first "at Niagara and subsequently at Fort Presqu'ile," the designated rendezvous for western Amerindians en route to the war zone.[27] In late June, "almost all of the natives from the Pays d'en haut had arrived there [at Fort Presqu'ile], but as soon as they were told that there was smallpox at Frontenac and Niagara, they did not wish to go further; most of them turned back."[28] A few days later, a further five hundred warriors arrived at that post, but no sooner had they disembarked than "all [of them] left . . . , having heard that there was smallpox in all of our forts." Only forty Menominees were willing to risk infection by continuing eastward.[29]

Rather than increasing with reinforcements from the west, the number of Amerindians serving in the central theater declined somewhat in 1756. In August, 260 took part in the successful siege of Fort Oswego on Lake Ontario, one of the two major British outposts on the frontier, while 300 more watched the Lake Champlain front.[30] After numerous arrivals and departures, this number remained at about 600 in mid-September, when all French forces were concentrated in the Lake Champlain area to resist an apprehended British invasion.[31]

By the spring of 1757, it appeared that both the medical and military situations had substantially improved. "Although the winter was very severe in the Pays d'en Haut, as well as at Montreal, there was almost no sickness."[32] A few cases of smallpox remained, but the epidemic had passed after spreading as far west as Fort Duquesne. The French were alarmed at the possibility that the disease would be communicated to the Ohio Amerindians and produce "a most unfortunate effect," but it ended there with the deaths of six Canadians.[33] The Ohio valley tribes had been struck by a serious smallpox epidemic in 1752, which may account for their apparent immunity five years later.[34] The capture of Oswego, moreover, "made an astonishing impact on the natives."[35] With French prestige enormously enhanced and one of Britain's two major frontier forts in ruins, "a large number of natives appeared full of enthusiasm for striking against the British during the next campaign."[36]

These predictions proved correct. In 1757, the number of Amerindian warriors in the central theater soared as eighteen hundred fighters from the Canadian missions and the Pays d'en haut flooded into the war zone.[37] The campaign, a complete success, resulted in the capture of Fort William Henry, on Lake George, a major British outpost on the frontier between Canada and New York. Following the victory, allied dispositions towards the French were reported to be uniformly positive. The commandant of Fort Niagara confidently predicted that in the next spring three thousand warriors would be passing through his post to fight for the French.[38]

Participation in the campaign of 1757, however, had brought the Amerindians from Canada and the west into contact with thousands of British and French regulars (including many recent arrivals from Europe), Canadian and Anglo-American militiamen, and Acadian refugees, some of whom were suffering from smallpox.[39] The Laurentian Amerindians, survivors of the 1755 epidemic, were largely immune to it. Those from the west were not. In the fall of 1757, word reached Canada of the outbreak of smallpox among the western allies, who had paid a terrible price for their support of the French. "All of these peoples, having descended for the siege of the fort [William Henry] . . . carried smallpox back with them to their country, where it made astonishing ravages."[40] Some of the allies, too ill to travel all the way home, wintered at Fort Niagara.[41] The rest returned to their villages in the interior, carrying the infection with them.

Very little information concerning the demographic impact of this epidemic exists. In the nineteenth century, it was remembered among the Ottawas of Michilimakinac as a catastrophe that virtually destroyed their community: "Every one taken with it [smallpox] was sure to die. Lodge after lodge was totally vacated . . . entire families being swept off with the ravages of this terrible disease. The whole coast of Arbor Croche, . . . where their principal village was situated, . . . was entirely depopulated and laid waste."[42] Most French accounts, however, confine themselves to laconic observations, for example, "At Michilimakinac many natives have died from smallpox."[43] A few sources are more specific. The Potawatomis were reported to have "perished almost completely during that epidemic."[44] Four years later, during a council at Green Bay, representatives of the Menominees informed the new British commandant that "they were very poor having lost Three Hundred warriors lately with the Small pox."[45] The exact losses from smallpox thus went largely unrecorded, but the epidemic was certainly disastrous for its victims, their families, and their bands and led to a general suspension of many normal activities. "These natives," noted a French officer, "almost ceased to hunt because of the malady" during the winter of 1757–58.[46]

Although they knew as little as the French of the existence of viruses, the Amerindians were well aware that they had been infected during their sojourn in the central theater. They had traditionally believed that illness was the result of misconduct towards humans or nonhumans that "offended the Master of Life."[47] But by the mid-eighteenth century, the link between European contact and epidemics was long established, and outbreaks of epidemic disease were frequently attributed to witchcraft performed by Europeans.[48] With regard to the provenance of the epidemic of 1757, an Ottawa narrative later recalled that

> the small-pox which they brought from Montreal during the French war with Great Britain . . . was sold to them shut up in a tin box . . . after they reached home they opened the box; but behold there was another tin box inside, smaller. They took it out and opened the second box, and behold, still there was another box inside of the second box, smaller yet. So they kept on this way till they came to a very small box, which was not more than an inch long; and when they opened the last one they found nothing but mouldy particles in this last little box. . . . They wondered very much what it was, and a great many closely inspected [the box and its contents] to try to find out what it meant. . . . pretty soon [there] bursts out a terrible sickness among them."[49]

Since the French had invited their allies to the area where they contracted smallpox, and Amerindian "custom in this situation is to say that the nation that invited them has given them an evil medicine,"[50] the French found themselves in an extremely awkward position. It quickly became apparent that Franco-Amerindian harmony in the Pays d'en haut was going to be one of the casualties of the epidemic.

If the tribes afflicted by the epidemic were peoples whose goodwill the French could ill afford to lose, they were also nations that would not lightly turn against the French. They had been allied to the French since the seventeenth century and had both traded profitably with Canadians and gone to war with them against the Iroquois, British, Fox, and Chickasaw, among others. French officers described the Menominee as "always very attached to French interests,"[51] the Potawatomi as the "the wisest and most obedient of all of the natives,"[52] and the Ottawa as having "always been attached to the French."[53] Their services as auxiliaries might be dispensed with, but their hostility would be fatal for the French presence in the west.

Heavily outnumbered by the Amerindians in the Pays d'en haut, where they occupied only a few scattered outposts, and with their military resources wholly committed to the struggle against the British, the French were in no position to begin a second war against their allies. For although Franco-Amerindian alliances were long-standing and cemented by mutual self-interest, they could be extremely fragile. The western allies contained a significant anti-French faction that had come close to unleashing a general war against the French during the War of the Austrian Succession a decade before, when supplies and trade goods were cut off as the result of wartime shortages. During the winter of 1757 and spring of 1758, it appeared as if general war was once again a serious possibility. As men, women, and children suffered and died "in all of the nations of the Pays d'en Haut"[54] and the allies reeled under the impact of the epidemic, resentment against the French began to rise and seek expression.[55]

In the winter of 1756, Amerindian war parties from the west had set out "every week" to raid the British. During the following year, with the Pays d'en haut in the grip of an epidemic, during "the entire winter there came only one party of natives, proof of their coolness"[56] towards the French. Formerly amicable allies began to turn against the French. In Detroit, "the Wyandot, always suspect and turbulent, are entertaining malign thoughts."[57] The Ottawas too "harbour evil intentions, the Potawatomis appear indisposed; in short, all of the nations are of the same inclination."[58] Worse, there were a number of outbreaks of violence against the French. The Menominees besieged Fort La Baye for three days, killed eleven Canadians, and made off with thirty thousand livres' worth of trade goods.[59] A party of Canadians wintering on the Wisconsin was attacked. Two men were killed, and one officer was taken prisoner.[60]

With their relationship with the western nations hanging by a thread, the French in desperation launched a diplomatic major offensive in the Pays d'en haut during the spring of 1758. Nearly one million livres' worth of trade goods was presented to the allies by the commandants of the western posts to "wipe away tears and cover the dead."[61] "Covering the dead" with gifts could be a gesture of respect and sympathy to the family and band of the deceased or compensation for a death for which the giver was responsible.[62] In the latter case, the presentation of gifts was at once an acknowledgement of culpability, a discharge of the obligations thus incurred, and a means to preserve the alliance by eliminating the necessity for blood revenge.

Furthermore, in a series of what must have been rather tense conferences at Michilimakinac, Detroit, and Toronto, the French attempted to lay the blame for the epidemic on the British. This claim was accepted by the pro-French faction among the allies;[63] over a century later Ottawa tradition continued to speak of the "wholesale murder of the Ottawas by this terrible disease sent by the British."[64]

In spite of the efforts of the French, the situation in the west remained tense throughout the year. While in August the Menominees handed over seven men who had taken part in the attack on La Baye, in October the commandant of Fort St. Joseph reported that the Potawatomis had been on the verge of killing a Canadian and were only dissuaded by news of the French victory at Carillon.[65] With the Amerindians of the west now "unwilling to go to war at our side,"[66] the men who joined the French in the campaign of 1758 came, for the most part, from the Canadian missions.[67] In July, after the Battle of Carillon, their number peaked at 470, a sizable reduction from the force mustered on Lake Champlain only a year before.[68]

Despite the victory at Carillon, the military situation of New France continued to deteriorate. In Acadia, Louisbourg had fallen. Fort Frontenac was destroyed in August, together with large quantities of supplies destined for the Amerindians of the Ohio and the Pays d'en haut.[69] In November, the French were forced to abandon Fort Duquesne, which was then occupied by the British.[70] With the French in the west suffering from a severe supply shortage, the western allies smoldering with resentment, and British armies preparing to close in on New France, it would not have been surprising to find the French fighting their last battles aided only by the Amerindians of the Canadian missions, or even alone.

While the epidemic of 1757 was a disaster for the afflicted Amerindians, its consequences for the French proved to be alarming but transient. By the end of 1758, the disease had run its course, and no further outbreaks were reported among the French or their allies. At the opening of the campaign of 1759, it was quickly apparent that French fortunes had made a remarkable recovery, at least as far as the adherence of the western allies was concerned.[71] In the spring, messages were dispatched to the missions and posts of Canada and the west, inviting Amerindians to come to Quebec to take part in the defense of New France.[72] Rather than hold back, the allies rallied to the French cause. From the west came "good news from [Forts] Michilimakinac, St. Joseph, Ouyatanon . . . [and] Detroit, great affection of the natives."[73] Nations that had seemed on the brink of war with New France a year before were once again sending contingents to fight alongside the French in the Laurentian valley in the penultimate campaign of the war.[74]

The Amerindians at Quebec during the siege of 1759 came from tribes as close as the Hurons of Lorette and as far away as the Dakota, who had fought in the Ohio valley for the French but had never sent warriors as far east as Canada.[75] Also making their Canadian debut were 162 Crees, who occupied so remote a place in the French trading network that they were "not armed with muskets (which they do not yet use)."[76] Between one thousand and twelve hundred Amerindians participated in the defense of Quebec.[77] Another three to four hundred fought on the Lake Champlain frontier,[78] while three hundred more awaited the British on the upper St. Lawrence.[79]

Even in 1760, when it was brutally apparent that all was lost for New France, numerous Amerindians continued to fight alongside the French. In the central theater, 270 fought at the Battle of Ste. Foye in April.[80] As late as the first week of September, days before the surrender of New France, there were still 474 Amerindians in the field.[81] With the remaining upcountry posts cut off from supplies from Canada, the war in the west had ground to a halt. Nevertheless, the commandant of Detroit reported that "all of the nations [of the Pays d'en haut] are willing to rally to the French," and, despite shortages of supplies, a few small parties of Amerindians continued to carry the war to the enemy.[82] On 28 November 1760, with the war finally lost, the Hurons, Weas, Potawatomis, and Ottawas of Detroit informed the departing French commandant, in the presence of British officers, that the French surrender did not apply to them and that "they would never recognize the King of England as their Father."[83]

On the surface, the Seven Years' War was a struggle between groups of humans to control the resources of North America. The British and French fought to dominate the continent, while Amerindians struggled to preserve their ancestral territories as best they could. As the humans fought among themselves, a fourth player appeared. An invisible, mindless, implacable enemy that struck down Briton, Frenchman, and Amerindian alike with impunity, variola major sought to survive and propagate at the expense of its involuntary human hosts. Smallpox imposed a rhythm of its own upon the intensity of Amerindian participation in the war in the central theater, as each outbreak was followed by a sharp drop in the number of Amerindians willing to fight for the French.

The importance of smallpox in determining the military behavior of Amerindians during the Seven Years' War should not, however, be overestimated. It was a negative, transient factor that affected the extent of their participation in the Seven Years' War but not their original decisions to form alliances with the French and to declare war on the British. Amerindians had undoubtedly made these commitments in accordance with their considered judgment as to where their best economic, political, and military interests lay. All other things being equal, the Amerindian allies of New France had for over a century generally been willing to respond favorably to French requests to join them in waging war in Acadia, the Laurentian valley, or the Pays d'en haut. During the Seven Years' War, however, their willingness was intermittently modified by the presence of the smallpox virus in the area of operations.

The impact of the smallpox epidemics manifested itself in different ways after the outbreaks of 1755 and 1757, as different groups of humans responded to the flourishing of the virus, and variously influenced the military behavior of the western allies and those from the Canadian reserves. The Laurentian Amerindians, perhaps reflecting closer ties with the French or propinquity to the war zone, were much more consistent purveyors of fighters to the central theater. Even in 1756, the disruptive effect of smallpox on their homes and families produced a modest decline in their numbers but did not prevent the mission Amerindians from fielding a fairly substantial contingent during the summer, which played an important role in the siege of Fort Oswego. Their response to the epidemics appears to have been quite similar to that of the Canadians with whom they shared the St. Lawrence valley. Losses from smallpox prevented neither the Canadians nor the Laurentian Amerindians from playing a part in the war, even as the epidemics were under way. Although their numbers varied from year to year, from a low of about 420 to a high of 820, the presence of a large body of fighters from the Canadian missions was a constant feature of the campaigns in the central theater. Whatever their success or failure as instruments of evangelization and acculturation, the Laurentian reserves proved their indispensable value as a reliable source of Amerindian military manpower during the Seven Years' War.

Although the tribes of the Pays d'en haut were afflicted only in 1757, their collective decisions were of crucial importance in determining the level of Amerindian support for the French, as measured by the number of armed men serving as auxiliaries with the field army. Regardless of French victories or defeats, despite the gradual choking off of supplies and steadily declining prospects for a French victory, it was smallpox that proved to be the key influence in decisions regarding the western allies' military participation between 1756 and 1759.

If the western allies, like the French, lacked precise knowledge of how diseases were transmitted, they certainly understood the danger of contagion, attempted to minimize the risk of infection by avoiding disease-stricken locations, and reacted with great resentment towards anyone who invited them into these areas. In 1756, their disinclination to risk contracting smallpox by serving in the central theater deprived the French of the services of well over five hundred fighters. On the other hand, it was the outbreak of smallpox in 1757 among the tribes of the west that disrupted their normal life, kindled widespread anger against the French, and induced the surviving western warriors to remain at home once more.

For most of the war, western Amerindian warriors in the central theater were most notable for their absence. Indeed, in only two years did the western allies make a significant contribution to the Franco-Amerindian force there. In 1755, 1756, 1758, and 1760, mission Amerindians constituted the bulk of the warriors fighting in the center. The great variations apparent in Figure 11.1 came from the infusion of western fighters into the theater, followed by their withdrawal.

Dramatic as they were, the impact of these fluctuations upon the actual course of the war was quite limited. The contribution of Amerindians to the French war effort varied not according to their numbers but according to the need for their particular abilities in a given campaign. So even a drastic decline in the number of Amerindians fighting on behalf of the French would not necessarily reduce the effectiveness of French military operations.[84] In 1756, during the siege of Oswego, the French found the 260 warriors on the scene quite sufficient to perform the various auxiliary functions required of them. Moreover, after the surrender, their number was small enough that they could easily be restrained from harassing the survivors of the garrison.[85] In contrast, in 1757, when the alliance system produced nearly 2,000 warriors to take part in the siege of Fort William Henry, there were far more Amerindians present than needed. When the fort was surrendered, it was impossible for the French to prevent their allies from killing or taking prisoner a number of members of the garrison and their dependents.[86]

A year later, when the number of Amerindians willing to serve in the central theater declined dramatically on account of the smallpox epidemic raging in the Pays d'en haut, a large body of Amerindians was neither present nor needed at the Battle of Carillon, a conventional engagement between armies of French and British regulars.[87] A substantial force of

Amerindians did arrive after the battle. But the local commander, the Marquis de Montcalm, failed to employ them in an aggressive campaign of harassment against the defeated British forces, as the governor general desired.[88] Under these conditions, increasing their number would have exacerbated French supply problems rather than harm the enemy. Finally, in 1759, the presence of thousands of Amerindian warriors in the field did not save the French. War in the central theater had come to be dominated by European regulars fighting conventional battles.

Though of limited significance to the outcome of the war, the fluctuations in the numbers of warriors in the central theater between 1755 and 1759 are of interest for what they reveal about the place of Amerindians in the geopolitical and biological context created by European contact and settlement. From the political perspective, that these variations resulted from outbreaks of smallpox is less significant than that they occurred at all. Although the tribes allied to New France were willing to declare war at its request, their actual participation changed considerably from year to year as their own priorities, policies, and inclinations dictated.[89] They respected neither the importunities of the French, who consistently sought to secure the services of as many of them as possible, nor French success or failure in battle. Amerindians retained their political independence and freedom of action; they were willing to assist the French in time of war, but only on their own terms.

Amerindians of the mid-eighteenth century would neither turn back the clock nor alter the environment produced by European contact. But they could and did develop ways and means of exploiting the opportunities afforded, and surviving the dangers posed, by the European presence. Although unaware of the existence of viruses, they knew that smallpox was extremely contagious and dangerous and behaved accordingly; they made considered decisions and took positive action. Their basing military and diplomatic decisions during the Seven Years' War on the incidence of the disease exemplifies the adaption, accommodation, and resistance that enabled Amerindians, and their culture, to endure the crushing impact of European contact and survive in North America.

NOTES

For their advice and encouragement I would like to thank Professor Cornelius J. Jaenen of the Department of History, University of Ottawa; Professor W. J. Eccles of the Department of History, University of Toronto; Dr. John Last of the School of Medicine/Epidemiology and Community Medicine, Faculty of Health Sciences, University of Ottawa; and the readers who evaluated this article in manuscript. I would also like to express my appreciation to Catherine Plewes, who produced the final drawing of the graph. All translations from the French are mine.

1. This expression is taken from James H. Merrell, "The Indians' New World: The Catawba Experience," *William and Mary Quarterly*, 3d ser., 41 (October 1984): 537.

2. Alfred W. Crosby, *Ecological Imperialism: The Biological Expansion of Europe, 900–1900* (Cambridge, 1986), passim; Crosby, *The Columbian Exchange: Biological and Cultural Consequences of 1492* (Westport, CT, 1972), 31–63; Henry F. Dobyns, *"Their Number Become Thinned": Native American Population Dynamics in Eastern North America* (Knoxville, TN, 1983), 8–32; Francis Jennings, *The Invasion of America: Indians, Colonialism, and the Cant of Conquest* (New York, 1975), 15–127; William H. McNeill, *Plagues and Peoples* (Garden City, NY, 1976), 61–65; Merrell, "The Indians' New World," 537–65; E. Wagner Stearn and Allen E. Stearn, *The Effect of Smallpox on the Destiny of the Amerindian* (Boston, 1954), 13–52.

3. Francis Jennings, *Empire of Fortune: Crowns, Colonies, and Tribes in the Seven Years War in America* (New York, 1988), 217–19, 261–62, 293–94, 371–74; James H. Merrell, " 'Their Very Bones Shall Fight': The Catawba-Iroquois Wars," in *Beyond the Covenant Chain: The Iroquois and Their Neighbors in Indian North America,*

1600–1800, ed. Daniel K. Richter and James H. Merrell (Syracuse, NY, 1987), 119–22, 132–33; Daniel K. Richter, "War and Culture: The Iroquois Experience," *William and Mary Quarterly,* 3d ser., 40 (October 1983): 528–59; Bruce G. Trigger, *The Children of Aataentsic: A History of the Huron People to 1660,* vol. 1 (Montreal, 1976), 51, 68–75, 103, 144–47.

4. *Allies* is used here to refer to those tribes with long-standing political and commercial relations with the French. They included, in the missions of the Laurentian valley, the Abenaki; Algonquin; Huron of Lorette; Iroquois of Lac des Deux Montagnes, La Présentation, and Sault St. Louis; and Nipissing; and in the west, the Ojibwa, Ottawa, Menominee, Mississauga, Potawatomi, and Wyandot. Other tribes were allied with the French, but these, together with the Micmac and Malecite of Acadia, were the most important. In the most detailed list of the Amerindians serving alongside the French army during the Seven Years' War, warriors from these tribes made up 92.5 percent of the warriors present. The remaining fighters were Delawares, Foxes, Iowas, Miamis, Oneidas, Sauks, and Winnebagos. See "L'armée du roy sur le Lac St. Sacrement," in Bougainville to d'Argenson, 9 August 1757, National Archives of Canada [hereafter NAC], Manuscript Group [hereafter MG] 4, microfilm reel F-721, France, Ministère de la Guerre [hereafter AG], A1, 3457, no. 121, fol. 3.

5. The descriptions of the epidemics that broke out between 1755 and 1757 are as complete as possible, but this article does not aspire to describe the epidemics themselves or their overall impact. Because of the limited quantity of evidence, it is not possible to describe the epidemic, only its impact upon the number of Amerindian warriors in the field in the central zone of operations, as recorded by French and Canadian officers.

6. Louis-Antoine de Bougainville, "Journal de l'expédition d'Amérique commencé en l'année 1756, le 15 mars," *Rapport de l'archiviste de la Province de Québec* [hereafter RAPQ], 1923–24: 313.

7. In 1757 and 1759, eighteen hundred Amerindian fighters were active in the Laurentian valley. Information from Acadia and the Ohio country is neither as complete nor as reliable as that concerning Amerindian military participation in the central theater. However, it would appear that the number of warriors active in the Ohio peaked at twenty-one hundred in 1756, and that the French estimated that they could count on the services of five to six hundred warriors in Acadia. Thus, in the mid-eighteenth century, the Franco-Amerindian alliance proved to be capable of delivering a maximum of about forty-five hundred warriors willing to fight alongside the French. See "Extrait des nouvelles en Canada, 1756," NAC, MG 1, microfilm reel C-2244, France, Archives des Colonies [hereafter AC], C11A, 100, fols. 447–48; Vaudreuil to Berryer, 5 October 1759, NAC, MG 1, microfilm reel F-391, AC, F3, 15, fol. 272; Bigot to Berryer, 15 October 1759, ibid., fol. 335; Vaudreuil to Berryer, 8 November 1759, ibid., fol. 360v; Henri-Raymond Casgrain, ed., *Journal du marquis de Montcalm durant ses campagnes au Canada de 1756 à 1760* (Quebec, 1895), 264–66, 331; Charles Nicolas Gabriel, *Le maréchal de camp Desandrouins, 1729–1792, guerre du Canada, 1756–1759, guerre de l'indépendance américaine 1780–1782* (Verdun, 1887), 278.

8. This was the French field army's area of operations during the Seven Years' War.

9. In the seventeenth and eighteenth centuries, a number of Amerindian communities were founded by the French in the St. Lawrence valley and populated with refugees from war, religious persecution, or Anglo-American expansion. These "reserves" formed a network of Amerindian enclaves on the periphery of the seigneurial tract of New France. See Cornelius J. Jaenen, *Friend and Foe: Aspects of French-Amerindian Cultural Contact in the Sixteen and Seventeenth Centuries* (Toronto, 1976), 160–61, 177–83.

10. One enumeration made in 1736 puts the number of warriors in the allied tribes at 16,323, while a second asserts that in 1764 there were 73,580. See Lawrence Henry Gipson, *The British Empire before the American Revolution,* vol. 5, *Zones of International Friction: The Great Lakes Frontier, Canada, the West Indies, India, 1748–1754* (New York, 1942), 39–40.

11. It would be interesting to compare variations in the numbers of Amerindians fighting in the central theater with those of their counterparts in the Ohio and Acadian areas. Adequate data for the entire 1755–60 period for the latter regions are not, however, available.

12. Other Amerindians served in war parties that raided deep into British North America, but their numbers on a given date were too small to affect seriously the following estimates. When French fortunes were at their height, during twenty days in May and June 1757, 49 warriors were observed passing through Fort Carillon, an average of about 2 per day. See Anne-Joseph-Hippolyte de Maurés de Malartic, *Journal des campagnes au Canada, de 1755 à 1760* (Dijon, 1890), 104–12. In fifty-six days during June, July, and August of that year, 260 warriors visited Fort Niagara en route to targets in the British colonies, an average of about 5 per day. See Anonymous, probably Pierre Pouchot, "Journal de Niagara, du mois de juin au mois d'août, 1757," in *Guerre du Canada: Relations et journaux de différentes expéditions faites durant les années 1755-56-57-58-59-60,* ed. Henri-Raymond Casgrain (Quebec, 1895), 90–114. While these figures may not be representative, they do give some idea of the relatively low intensity of the guerrilla war on the central front and of the limited numbers of Amerindians raiding at any one time.

13. George F.G. Stanley, "The Defence of Canada during the Seven Years' War: A Military Appreciation," in *Policy by Other Means: Essays in Honour of C.P. Stacey,* ed. Michael Cross and Robert Bothwell (Toronto, 1972), 67–68. Stanley has written extensively on Amerindian military affairs in the eighteenth and nineteenth centuries. See also Jennings, *Empire of Fortune,* 392, 401–2. This would have been very realistic behavior, and it is hardly likely that the Amerindian allies of New France, as rational actors, would have overlooked the military conjuncture when making decisions. Their perception of military events, the likely course of the war, and where their best interests lay, however, may very well have differed from that of historians who enjoy the benefit of hindsight and have ascribed this motivation to Amerindians.

14. In the fall of 1755, for example, "Mr. Vaudreuil has ordered all of the officers who command the northern posts to engage the largest possible number of natives to descend in the spring to Fort Presqu'ile from where he intends to have them advance to Oswego [in 1756]." See Jean-Guillaume-Charles de Plantavit de Lapause de Margon, "Mémoire et observations sur mon voyage en Canada," *RAPQ,* 1931–32: 23–24. For criticism of this policy, see Bougainville, "Journal," 238.

15. Although hard evidence is lacking, smallpox appears to have been significantly more prevalent in Europe in the eighteenth century than in previous centuries. See Donald R. Hopkins, *Princes and Peasants: Smallpox in History* (Chicago, 1983), 41.

16. Cyril William Dixon, *Smallpox* (London, 1962), 170–81, 296–312, 325–26; Hopkins, *Smallpox in History,* 3–9. This is meant to be only the most general description of how smallpox works. The actual impact of an epidemic varied according to the particular strain of the disease, the length of time since the last epidemic, density of population, and other factors. For the purposes of this article, the actual details of the medical effects of the epidemics are less important than the perceptions of the Amerindians and how these perceptions were reflected in their decisions and actions.

17. Although the scope of this article is limited to the impact of these epidemics on specific groups of North Americans, it should be noted that outbreaks of smallpox were not confined to the French and their allies. Divided by politics, ethnicity, and religion, the human inhabitants of the continent were united by biology. Political boundaries posed no obstacle to the spread of infectious disease, a continental phenomenon.

18. Dieskau to d'Argenson, 14 September 1755, NAC, MG 4, microfilm reel F-665, AG, A1, 3405, no. 80, fol. 1; "Relation depuis le depart des troupes de Quebec [*sic*] jusqu'au 30 du mois du 7bre, 1755," ibid., no. 106, fol. 4.

19. Vaudreuil to Machault, 8 June 1756, NAC, MG 1, microfilm reel F-390, AC, F3, 14, fol. 244.

20. Vaudreuil to Machault, 6 November 1756, NAC, MG 1, microfilm reel C-2400, AC, C11A, 101, fol. 155.

21. Vaudreuil to Machault, 25 September 1755, AC, F3, 14, fol. 157; Doreil to d'Argenson, 29 October 1755, AG, A1, 3405, no. 145, fol. 10.

22. "Relation de Mr. Leduchas capitaine au régiment de Languedoc Infantrie, à Mr. Lamy de Chatel," 15 July 1756, NAC, MG 4, microfilm reel F-666, AG, A1, 3417, no. 182, fol. 9; Williams to Johnson, March 1756, in *The Papers of Sir William Johnson,* ed. Almon W. Lauber, vol. 9 (New York, 1939), 412.

23. Vaudreuil to Machault, 8 June 1756, AC, F3, 14, fol. 244. It was not, however, decisive. See Vaudreuil to Machault, 25 September 1755, ibid., fol. 157. During the campaign of 1755, the French had planned to mobilize the Amerindians of Acadia, where the British had captured Forts Beauséjour and Gasperaux and were in the process of expelling the Acadians. This proved to be impossible, as "smallpox prevented the natives . . . from striking vigorously against the English." See Vaudreuil to Machault, 30 October 1755, AC, C11A, 100, fol. 160.

24. Vaudreuil to Machault, 8 June 1756, AC, F3, 14, fol. 244. Fort Oswego (or Chouaguen), on the southern shore of Lake Ontario, was one of the two major British posts on the Canada–New York frontier.

25. "Résumé des letters de M. de Vaudreuil des 2, 3, 4, 6, 7, et 8 février [1756]," AC, C11A, 101, fol. 498.

26. Doreil to d'Argenson, 18 June 1756, AG, A1, 3417, no. 166, fol. 9.

27. Vaudreuil to Machault, 8 August 1756, AC, C11A, 101, fol. 99; Vaudreuil to Machault, 15, June 1756, ibid., fol. 49.

28. Bougainville, "Journal," 207; Vaudreuil to Machault, 8 August 1756, AC, C11A, 101, fol. 99.

29. Bougainville, "Journal," 208–9.

30. Of the Amerindians who actually took part in the siege, twenty-three were Menominees and four Mississaugas. See Gaspard-Joseph Chaussegros de Léry, "Journal du siège du fort de Chouéguen, appurtenant aux Anglais, situé dans l'Amérique septentrionale par les 43 degrés, 45 minutes de latitude, pris par les Français le 14 août 1756," *RAPQ,* 1926–27: 403; Vaudreuil to Lévis, 18 August 1756, in *Lettres du marquis de Vaudreuil au chevalier de Lévis,* ed. Henri-Raymond Casgrain (Quebec, 1895), 30; Vaudreuil to Lévis, 22 August 1756, ibid., 32.

31. Malartic, *Journal,* 82; Bougainville, "Journal," 226.

32. Casgrain, *Journal du marquis de Montcalm,* 196.

33. Vaudreuil to Minister of Marine, 18 April 1757, AC, F3, 15, fol. 22.

34. Longueuil to Rouillé, 21 April 1752, in *Documents Relative to the Colonial History of the State of New York*, ed. Edmund B. O'Callaghan, vol. 10 (Albany, NY, 1858), 249.
35. Montcalm to Bourlamaque, 25 November 1756, in *Lettres de Bourlamaque du chevalier de Lévis*, ed. Henri-Raymond Casgrain (Québec, 1891), 137.
36. Bougainville, "Journal," 237.
37. "L'armée du roy sur le Lac St. Sacrament," in Bougainville to d'Argenson, 9 August 1757, AG, A1, 3457, no. 121, fol. 3.
38. Bougainville, "Journal," 313.
39. Jonathan Carver, *Travels through the Interior Parts of North-America, in the Years 1766, 1767, and 1768* (1778; reprint, *Carver's Travels through North America in the Years 1766, 1767, and 1768*, Toronto, 1974), 326; Robert Rogers, *Journals of Major Robert Rogers: Containing an Account of the several Excursions he made under the Generals who commanded upon the Continent of North America, during the late War* (London, 1765), 55n–56n; Casgrain, *Journal du marquis de Montcalm*, 225; Johnson to Wraxall, 17 July 1757, in *The Papers of Sir William Johnson*, ed. James Sullivan, vol. 2 (Albany, NY, 1922), 727; Pierre Pouchot, *Mémoires sur la dernière guerre de l'Amérique septentrionale, entre la France et l'Angleterre. Suivis d'observations, dont plusieurs sont relatives au théâtre actuel de la guerre, et de nouveaux détails sur les moeurs et les usages des sauvages, avec des cartes topographiques*, vol. 1 (Yverdon, 1781), 108.
40. Jean-Nicolas Desandrouins, "Recueil et journal des choses principales qui me sont arrivées, et de celles qui m'ont le plus frappées, depuis mon départ de France," in Gabriel, *Le maréchal de camp Desandrouins*, 135–36.
41. Bougainville, "Journal," 315.
42. Andrew J. Blackbird [Mackawdebenessy], *History of the Ottawa and Chippewa Indians of Michigan: A Grammar of Their Language, and Personal and Family History of the Author* (Ypsilanti, MI, 1887), 10. The "coast of Arbor Croche" (L'Arbre Croche) lay between what are now Cross Village and Harbor Springs, Michigan.
43. Malartic, *Journal*, 171. See also "Registre de la mission Saint-Ignace (église Ste.-Anne), Michilimakinac, 1695–1779," NAC, MG 8, microfilm reel C-2900, Archives paroissials, fols. 103–6.
44. Pouchot, *Mémoires* 1: 108.
45. James Gorrell, "A journall of Leuv t [*sic*] James Gorrell's Proceedings from the Day he took Post at Fort Edward Augustus (or La Bay) being the 12th October 1761 To the Present date Herof [14 June 1763]," in *The Papers of Sir William Johnson*, ed. Milton W. Hamilton, vol. 10 (Albany, NY, 1951), 702. A British trader recorded that "on the 10th of October [1766] we proceeded down the [Wisconsin] river, and the next day reached the first town of the Ottigaumies [Fox]. This town contained about fifty houses, but we found most of them deserted, on account of an epidemical disorder that had lately raged among them. The greater part of those who survived had retired into the woods, to avoid the contagion." See Carver, *Travels*, 48. Some bands may have suffered more than others. Overall, given that the numbers of Amerindians serving with the French forces in 1757 and 1759 were roughly equivalent, it is possible either that the demographic impact of the epidemic was quite limited or that the pool of available warriors was large enough for the Amerindians allied to the French to sustain significant losses and still field a substantial contingent.
46. Daine to Minister of War, 29 May 1758, NAC, MG 4, microfilm reel F-722, AG, A1, 3498, no. 87, fol. 2.
47. Peter Jones [Kahkewaquonaby], *History of the Ojebway Indians: With Especial Reference to Their Conversion to Christianity* (1861; reprint, Freeport, NY, 1970), 96. The epidemics that swept the Great Lakes region in the mid-seventeenth century were explained in the oral traditions of the Ojibwa of Lake Superior as the product of a time when "the evil spirit had found a strong foothold among them," and induced outbreaks of sorcery and murder that devastated their community. See William W. Warren, *History of the Ojibways, Based upon Traditions and Oral Statements* (1885; reprint, *History of the Ojibway Nation*, Minneapolis, 1970), 108–11. For a brief discussion of Amerindian views on disease, see William C. Sturtevant, "Animals and Disease in Indian Belief," in *Indians, Animals, and the Fur Trade: A Critique of Keepers of the Game*, ed. Shepard Krech III (Athens, GA, 1981), 182–85.
48. Jaenen, *Friend and Foe*, 100–103; Trigger, *The Children of Aataentsic* 2: 510, 534–38, 541–45, 589–96.
49. Blackbird, *The Ottawa and Chippewa Indians of Michigan*, 9–10. French reports of the actions of the western allies in 1756 and 1757 make it clear that these Amerindians held and acted both on empirical knowledge that to be present in a region where an epidemic was in progress could lead to infection and on the theory that epidemics were products of human sorcery.
50. Bougainville, "Journal," 316. See also Montcalm to Minister of War, 20 April 1758, AG, A1, 3498, no. 63, fol. 7; Bougainville, "Journal," 320; Casgrain, *Journal du marquis de Montcalm*, 350.
51. Bougainville, "Journal," 208.
52. Ibid., 275.
53. Ibid., 273.

54. Daine to Minister of War, 29 May 1758, AG, A1, 3498, no. 87, fol. 2.
55. Apart from the smallpox epidemic, which French sources identified as the primary cause of the Amerindians' anger, metropolitan officers alleged that this resentment was exacerbated by sharp trading practices, a failure to give the customary annual presents to Amerindians, and incompetence on the part of the commandants of the western posts. See Bougainville, "Journal," 320; Desandrouins, "Recueil et journal," 136; Casgrain, *Journal du marquis de Montcalm*, 350.
56. Bougainville, "Journal," 318.
57. Ibid., 322.
58. Ibid., 320. Edward P. Hamilton, ed. and trans., *Adventure in the Wilderness: The American Journals of Louis-Antoine de Bougainville, 1756–1760* (Norman, OK, 1964), 204, translates the "Ours" from the original as "Ottawa."
59. Malartic, *Journal*, 171–72; Casgrain, *Journal du marquis de Montcalm*, 350; "Journal de ce qui s'est passé dans les garnisons ou les camps qu'a occupé le regiment de Béarn depuis le 20 8bre 1757 jusqu'au 20 du même mois à 1758," NAC, MG 4, microfilm reel F-723, AG, A1, 3499, no. 191, fols. 11–12 (in fact the latter document ends not at 20 October 1758 but at 30 September 1758).
60. Daine to Minister of War, 29 May 1758, AG, A1, 3498, no. 87, fol. 2; Bougainville, "Journal," 320; Montcalm to Bourlamaque, 15 May 1758, in Casgrain, *Lettres de Bourlamaque*, 247.
61. Bougainville, "Journal," 316; Berryer to Bigot, 19 January 1759, NAC, MH 1, microfilm reel F-313, AC, B, 109, fol. 310. Given the rather creative accounting prevalent at the time, the amount charged to the Crown may not have been reflected in the value of the goods that the allies actually received, but the aid provided to the western nations seems nonetheless to have been substantial. See Bougainville, "Journal," 316; Montcalm to Minister of War, 20 April 1758, AG, A1, 3498, no. 63, fol. 7.
62. "The spirits of the slain are to be satisfied in one of two ways. The first is by spilling the blood of the nation by whom they fell; the other, by covering the bodies of the dead, and thus allaying the resentment of their relatives. This is done by making presents." Speech by Minweweh at Michilimakinac in 1761, as recorded by Alexander Henry in *Travels and Adventures in Canada and the Indian Territories between the Years 1760 and 1776* (1809; reprint, *Travels and Adventures in Canada*, Ann Arbor, MI, 1966), 44.
63. Montcalm to Minister of War, 20 April 1758, AG, A1, 3498, no. 63, fol. 7.
64. Blackbird, *The Ottawa and Chippewa Indians of Michigan*, 10.
65. Bougainville, "Journal," 355; Casgrain, *Journal du marquis de Montcalm*, 487.
66. Casgrain, *Journal du marquis de Montcalm*, 333–34.
67. The Amerindians of Canada and the Ohio valley were apparently unaffected by the epidemic. This is not surprising, given that both areas had been struck by smallpox within the last five years. See Casgrain, *Journal du marquis de Montcalm*, 329, 342; "Journal de ce qui s'est passé dans les garnisons ou les camps qu'a occupé le regiment de Béarn depuis le 20 8bre 1757 jusqu'au 20 du meme mois à 1758," AG, A1, 3499, no. 191, fols. 2–3, 11.
68. Casgrain, *Journal du marquis de Montcalm*, 408. French sources record the presence of "a dozen Ottawas" from Michilimakinac and forty-two Mississaugas in the central theater in 1758. See Bougainville, "Journal," 331; Malartic, *Journal*, 196; Casgrain, *Journal du marquis de Montcalm*, 433.
69. Vaudreuil to Berryer, 2 September 1758, NAC, MG 1, microfilm reel C-2401, AC, C11A, 103, fols. 180–81; "Mémoire," 15 November 1758, ibid., fols. 365–66.
70. Following the signing of the Easton Treaty in October and the withdrawal of the French from Fort Duquesne in November, many of the Amerindians of the upper Ohio withdrew from the war. See Jennings, *Empire of Fortune*, 369–414.
71. French sources, although explicit when reporting the refusal of Amerindians to participate in the war during outbreaks of smallpox, are less informative with regard to the reasons behind Amerindian willingness to return to the field in the years following epidemics.
72. Anonymous, "Mémoire du Canada," *RAPQ*, 1924–25: 154–55.
73. Montcalm to Bourlamaque, 15 March 1759, in Casgrain, *Lettres de Bourlamaque*, 291.
74. The news from the west at the outset of the campaign was equally positive. A delegation of Catawbas — clients of South Carolina — hitherto neutral, came to Michilimakinac to offer an alliance. See Malartic, *Journal*, 232; Montcalm to Bourlamaque, 15 March 1759, in Casgrain, *Lettres de Bourlamaque*, 311. A party of Delaware and Shawnee, both Ohio tribes that had signed the Easton Treaty, ambushed and turned back a British patrol on the Allegheny that was believed to be the vanguard of a British column en route to Fort Machault. See Montcalm to Bourlamaque, 12 May 1759, in Casgrain, *Lettres de Bourlamaque*, 311. And a Huron-Ottawa force conducted a major raid on British supply lines east of Fort Duquesne. See Casgrain, *Journal du marquis de Montcalm*, 517. These encouraging incidents were reflected in a renewed willingness on the part of the western allies to fight for the French. Apart from those employed as partisans in the western theater, about nine hundred Amerindians

joined in the relief expedition that marched from Fort Machault to attempt to raise the British siege of Fort Niagara. See Vaudreuil to Berryer, 30 October 1759, AC, F3, 15, fol. 348; Montcalm to Boulamaque, 31 March 1759, in Casgrain, *Lettres de Bourlamaque*, 367. Statistics from the west are fragmentary, but the highest recorded number of Amerindians fighting there was reached in 1756, when a little over two thousand were active in the Ohio country. See "Extraits des nouvelles en Canada, 1756," AC, C11A, 101, fols. 447–48. Of this body, seven hundred had been from the Ohio tribes, so the number fighting for the French was lower than but comparable to the numbers mustered in the west in previous years. Only thirty of the nine hundred mustered in 1759, however, actually took part in the engagement at La Belle Famille, where the French force was defeated. See Pouchot, *Mémoires* 2: 99. Note that these warriors, who took part in the fighting in the Pays d'en haut, are not included in the total of those active in the central theater.

75. Malartic, *Journal*, 251. The presence of a body of Dakota warriors in the Ohio valley in 1757 is noted in "JCB," *Voyage au Canada fait depuis l'an 1751 jusqu'en l'an 1761* (Paris, 1978), 117–18. Vaudreuil reported that the Amerindian contingent at the siege of Quebec was composed of "Abenakis and different nations of the Pays d'en haut." See Vaudreuil to Berryer, 5 October 1759, AC, F3, 15, fol. 272. In the central theater as a whole, other western tribes identified by name were the Mississauga and Iowa, in Malartic, *Journal*, 223, 251; Winnebago, in Bourlamaque to Vaudreuil, 5 September 1759, in Casgrain, *Lettres de Bourlamaque*, 35; Ottawa, in Desandrouins, "Recueil et journal," 307; Ottawa, Menominee, Ojibwa, and others, in Gabriel, *Le maréchal de camp Desandrouins*, 280; Miami, Potawatomi, Ojibwa, and Winnebago, in Anonymous, "Mémoire du Canada," *RAPQ*, 1924–25: 154–55; and Ojibwa and Ottawa, in Warren, *History of the Ojibways*, 195, 220.

76. Jean-Félix Rècher, *Journal du siège de Québec* (Québec, 1959), 43.

77. Vaudreuil to Berryer, 5 October 1759, AC, F3, 15, fol. 272; Bigot to Berryer, 15 October 1759, ibid., fol. 335v; "Journal des mouvemens [sic] qu'a fait le regt de Béarn [1759]," NAC, MG 4, microfilm reel F-724, AG, A1, 3540, no. 128, fols. 33–36.

78. Vaudreuil to Berryer, 8 November 1759, AC, F3, 15, fol. 360v, Gabriel, *Le maréchal de camp Desandrouins*, 278.

79. Casgrain, *Journal du marquis de Montcalm*, 501.

80. Jean-Guillaume-Charles de Plantavit de Lapause de Margon, "Relation des affaires du Canada depuis le 1er 10bre 1759 au . . . [21 May 1760]," *RAPQ*, 1933–34: 144; Henri-Raymond Casgrain, ed., *Journal des campagnes du chevalier de Lévis en Canada de 1756 à 1760* (Montréal, 1899), 257.

81. Roquemaure to Lévis, 212 August 1760, in *Lettres de divers particuliers au chevalier de Lévis*, ed. Henri-Raymond Casgrain (Québec, 1895), 124. They were not, however, considered entirely reliable. See postscript of 2 September, Bigot to Machault, 29 August 1760, NAC, MG 1, microfilm reel F-392, AC, F3, 16, fol. 115v. Other erstwhile allies hastened to make their peace with the British. Defections also occurred among the Canadians: "As the English armies advanced, the habitants deserted us." See Bernier to Accaron, 28 September 1760, NAC, microfilm reel C-2402, AC, C11A, vol. 105, fol. 394.

82. Bellestre to Berryer, 10 June 1762, AC, C11A, 105, fols. 606–8; Vaudreuil to Berryer, 24 June 1760, ibid., fols. 185–88; Vaudreuil to Berryer, 24 June 1760, ibid., fols. 189–92.

83. Bellestre to Berryer, 10 June 1762, AC, C11A, 105, fol. 606; "Conseil tenu le 28 Novembre 1760 au détroit en présence du sieur de Belestre [sic], capitaine des troupes détachées de la marine, commandant aud[it] poste par les Hurons, Outaonons, Poutewatamis, et Saulteux," ibid., fols. 609–15.

84. This did not prevent the French from attempting to enlist the largest possible number of warriors to join them in each campaign. See note 14.

85. Lapause de Margon, "Mémoire et observations," 34. Nonetheless, a few incidents occurred immediately after the surrender, before the French could place all of the prisoners under their protection.

86. Casgrain, *Journal du marquis de Montcalm*, 292–93.

87. Of a French force of 3,526, 15 were Amerindians. See Bougainville, "Journal," 337. Their role in the battle was marginal enough for Montcalm to describe himself as "without natives." See Casgrain, *Journal du marquis de Montcalm*, 401.

88. W. J. Eccles, "Montcalm, Louis-Joseph de, Marquis de Montcalm," in *Dictionary of Canadian Biography*, ed. Francess G. Halpenny, vol. 3, *1741 to 1770* (Toronto, 1974), 463.

89. The western allies were confronted, between 1755 and 1759, with two important phenomena, the Seven Years' War and a series of smallpox epidemics. During this period, the French wanted the Amerindians to react to the war in accordance with French priorities, by coming to the central theater to fight against the British whenever they asked them to. The Amerindians, however, acted according to their own agenda. They took part in the war when it suited their purposes. But when they found reasons to remain at home on account of the epidemics, they ignored French entreaties and shunned the central theater.

Topic Six

The Conquest and Its Aftermath

This engraving by Antoine Benoist, *A view of the Bishop's House with the Ruins, as they appear in Going up the Hill from the Lower to the Upper Town,* shows a view of Quebec after the British bombardment of 1759. It is based on a sketch by Richard Short.

Contrary to popular opinion New France did not fall as a result of its defeat in the Battle of the Plains of Abraham. The conquest of New France remained incomplete at the end of 1759, with the French in control of the St. Lawrence Valley apart from the area immediately around Quebec. Only in September 1760 did the French capitulate at Montreal. As W.J. Eccles points out in his provocative essay, "The Battle of Quebec: A Reappraisal," the fall of Quebec was in no respect inevitable. Why then did the British emerge victorious?

The Treaty of 1763 that ended the Seven Years' War confirmed the cession of New France to England. The British now faced again — as they had in Acadia from 1713 to 1755 — the difficult task of formulating a policy to govern a colony whose population differed in language, culture, and religion from their own. That policy, as outlined in the Proclamation of 1763, limited New France, now renamed the Province of Quebec, to the St. Lawrence Valley. It also aimed to transform the French colony into a British one through the establishment of British institutions and laws aimed at assimilating the French-Canadian population.

The policy failed, however. Very few English-speaking immigrants came to Quebec, preferring to settle in the warmer, more fertile Ohio Valley, amidst a familiar English-speaking population. Furthermore, James Murray and Guy Carleton, the first two governors of Quebec, sided with the French-speaking seigneurs against the aggressive, English-speaking merchants in the colony. Realizing that the colony was unlikely to become anglicized, Governor Carleton recommended reinstating French civil law, the seigneurial system of landholding, and the right of the Roman Catholic Church to collect the tithe. London accepted his proposals and, in the Quebec Act of 1774, reversed its earlier policy of 1763.

By that time, however, the basic economic structure of the colony had changed. The few English-speaking colonists who had settled in Quebec had taken a prominent role in the economic life of the colony. Although small in number, this Anglo-American commercial class had gained enormous influence — enough to secure the recall of James Murray, the first governor, in 1766. In terms of economic power, this group also commanded a majority of the investments in the fur trade by 1777. How had this tiny English-speaking group prospered so? Was it because of the return to France of the commercial class of New France, the superior abilities of the English-speaking merchants, or the favouritism practised by the British administrators? In "A Change in Climate: The Conquest and the Marchands of Montreal," José Igartua examines the rise of the English-speaking merchants in the fur trade. In "The Fall of New France," the epilogue to *The People of New France*, Allan Greer assesses the impact of the Conquest on Acadia, Canada, and the interior. What was the impact of the Conquest on the general population?

For a thorough discussion of the various interpretations of the Conquest, see Ramsay Cook's "The Historian and Nationalism," in *Canada and the French-Canadian Question* (Toronto: Macmillan, 1966), pp. 119–42, and his essay "Conquêtisme," in *The Maple Leaf Forever* (Toronto: Macmillan, 1971), pp. 99–113. Also of value is S. Dale Standen's "The Debate on the Social and Economic Consequences of the Conquest: A Summary," in R. Douglas Francis and Donald B. Smith, *Readings in Canadian History: Pre-Confederation*, 6th ed. (Toronto: Nelson Thomson Learning, 2002), pp. 203–210. For a short bibliography on the final years of the struggle for New France, 1759 and 1760, see the bibliography for Topic Five.

For an overview of the immediate post-Conquest period, see A.L. Burt's *The Old Province of Quebec*, 2 vols. (Toronto: McClelland and Stewart, 1968 [1933]); Pierre Tousignant's "The Integration of the Province of Quebec into the British Empire, 1763–91, Part 1: From the Royal Proclamation to the Quebec Act," in *Dictionary of Canadian Biography*, vol. 4, *1771–1800*, pp. ii–xlix; Hilda Neatby's *Quebec: The Revolutionary Age, 1760–1791* (Toronto: McClelland and Stewart, 1966); and Philip Lawson's *The Imperial Challenge: Quebec and Britain in the Age of the American Revolution* (Montreal/Kingston: McGill-Queen's University Press, 1989). Fernand Ouellet's *Histoire économique et sociale du Québec, 1760–1850* (Montréal: Fides, 1966), translated as *Economic and Social History of Quebec, 1760–1850* (Toronto: Macmillan, 1980), is an important study. A number of Ouellet's essays, edited and translated by Jacques A. Barbier, were published in the collection *Economy, Class, and Nation in Quebec: Interpretive Essays* (Toronto: Copp Clark Pitman, 1991). Michel Brunet presents an alternative view to Ouellet's in *Les Canadiens après la Conquête, 1759–1775* (Montréal: Fides, 1969).

Dale Miquelon's *Society and Conquest* (Toronto: Copp Clark, 1977) is a valuable collection on the effect of the Conquest on French-Canadian society; see also his *The First Canada: To 1791* (Toronto: McGraw-Hill Ryerson, 1994). An important local study is Allan Greer, *Peasant, Lord, and Merchant: Rural Society in Three Quebec Parishes, 1740–1840* (Toronto: University of Toronto Press, 1985). On the history of the early English-speaking population in the province of Quebec, see Ronald Rudin's *The Forgotten Quebecers: A History of English-Speaking Quebec, 1759–1980* (Québec: Institut québécois de la recherche sur la culture, 1985).

WEBLINKS

The Battle of the Plains of Abraham
http://www.champlain2004.org/html/11/14_e.html

Digitized primary-source documents relating to the Battle of the Plains of Abraham.

Rear-Admiral Charles Holmes
http://www.lib.uwaterloo.ca/discipline/SpecColl/archives/holmes/holmes.html#letter

A digitized copy of a letter written by Rear-Admiral Charles Holmes, third-in-command under Major-General James Wolfe, five days after the Battle of the Plains of Abraham.

Tactical Positions
http://www.masshist.org/maps/2739_Atlas_16/2739_Atlas_16.html#

A digitized, interactive version of a tactical map drawn in 1759 depicting British and French forces in the St. Lawrence River at the time of the Battle of the Plains of Abraham.

Louisbourg Grenadiers
http://www.militaryheritage.com/quebec1.htm

The transcribed account of a sergeant major in James Wolfe's forces, describing the months leading up to the Battle of the Plains of Abraham, the battle, and the days after it.

Wolfe & Montcalm
http://www.biographi.ca/EN/ShowBio.asp?BioId=35842
http://www.biographi.ca/EN/ShowBio.asp?BioId=35664

Biographies of Wolfe and Montcalm, leaders at the Battle of the Plains of Abraham, from the *Dictionary of Canadian Biography Online*.

The Treaty of Paris, 1763
http://www.canadiana.org/citm/_textpopups/constitution/doc26_e.html

A summary and digitized copy of the Treaty of Paris, 1763.

Article Twelve

The Battle of Quebec: A Reappraisal

W.J. Eccles

More nonsense has been written over the years about this momentous battle — the battle that changed the course of North American and European history — than about any other event in Canadian history. One has only to imagine what would likely have been the ultimate course of events had the French destroyed Wolfe's army on that day in mid-September 1759 to appreciate how significant an event it was.

The paper here reprinted was written to be read at a meeting of the French Colonial Historical Society. Having only twenty minutes allotted time, I had to make it brief. Nothing that further research has uncovered since it was written, however, has caused me to alter my interpretation of the event one iota. A considerably extended study of the battle will appear in a forthcoming work. This paper contains the gist of it.

The battle that took place on the Plains of Abraham on 13 September 1759 continues to exercise fascination for historians and romantics alike. Hardly a year goes by without another work appearing on some aspect of the epic struggle. Field Marshall Viscount Montgomery described it as 'one of the great battles of the world'.[1] He was right about that, but about little else concerning this particular event. General Douglas MacArthur is reputed to have stated that his famous 'end run' in Korea, effecting a landing far in the enemy's rear, was modelled on Wolfe's tactics. He obviously had not studied the terrain at Quebec or Wolfe's actual disposition of his army.

A common feature of most of the works on the battle is the bland acceptance of the stated, or unstated, premise that the outcome was a foregone conclusion. Yet with one notable exception the main actors in the 1759 drama, on both sides, did not regard an eventual British victory as assured; quite the contrary. In May, when an English assault on Quebec was anticipated, Captain Montgay of the Béarn regiment, the comte de Malartic, and the chevaliers de Lévis and de Montreuil, all expressed optimism that it would be beaten off.[2] In the second week of September the French were confident that the campaign was over, and that they had ended it with glory. The recent movements in the English camp were interpreted as preparations for their departure,[3] as indeed to some extent they were.[4]

After the event James Murray remarked in a letter to Amherst, 'the Fact is we were surprised into a victory which cost the Conquered very little indeed'.[5] And at Louisbourg, Thomas Ainslie wrote to his friend and mentor, Murray, 'I now congratulate you on your success at Quebec, a thing little expected by any here, and posterity will hardly give credit to it that such a handful of Men should carry so great a point against such numbers, and with such advantages, thank God you have escaped, it is a miracle that you have.'[6]

Wolfe himself admitted in a dispatch dated 2 September that he was not at all sanguine of success.[7] The defences of Quebec were far more formidable than he had anticipated. His attempts to take the city had failed, his assaults on the French lines had been beaten back with heavy losses. Much has been made of the desperate conditions in Quebec, then in ruins, and the shortage of supplies. On the English side, however, conditions were far worse. Their supply line extended down the treacherous St Lawrence to Halifax and then across the Atlantic to Portsmouth. By the end of August over a thousand men were in hospital, suffering from wounds, dysentery, and scurvy. In the hot weather the camps — plagued with flies, mosquitoes, and inadequate latrines — stank to high heaven.[8] Wolfe was not the only one to be taken ill.

Of the 8,500 troops who had left Louisbourg, nearly half were unfit for duty by the end of August. On the opposing side Montcalm had some fifteen to sixteen thousand men, less than four thousand of them regulars,[9] but the Canadian militia had shown that they were a fearsome adversary when properly used. In addition there were a thousand to twelve hundred Indian warriors in the French camp.[10] They were a psychological weapon of no small account. Desertion increased in the British ranks as the campaign dragged on. The reports of these deserters to their interrogators kept the French well informed of conditions in the enemy's camp. They also raised their confidence. The intendant Bigot remarked after one such interrogation, 'those types make everything look rosy.'[11] And Montcalm informed Lévis that several of these deserters had stated that the British now despaired of taking Quebec unless Amherst's army arrived to support them.[12]

The French, however, knew that Amherst would not appear before Quebec during the present campaign. The Abenaki of Saint-François had captured two British officers, with their Mohawk guides, bearing dispatches from Amherst to Wolfe informing him that he was waiting for word of the taking of Quebec before advancing, with his habitual speed of a glacier, farther north than Fort Saint-Frédéric on Lake Champlain.[13] In fact Amherst was manifestly convinced that Quebec would not fall. He devoted the entire summer to the construction, at enormous expense, of a massive fortification at Crown Point. That structure could patently serve no useful purpose were Quebec to be taken. Its function could only be to bar the Lake Champlain route to an army ascending the lake from Canada for an invasion of New York.

It was, therefore, in desperation that Wolfe ordered the devastation of the countryside around Quebec, some four thousand farms being put to the torch.[14] The bombardment of the city continued until only a handful of buildings were habitable.[15] Wolfe had decided that if Quebec could not be taken, then the usefulness of the colony to the enemy would be reduced to the minimum.[16] It made no sense whatsoever to destroy what it was intended to occupy and subsequently put to one's own use, particularly with winter fast approaching. This too gave the French rueful cause to be confident of the final outcome of the campaign.

The one person in the French camp who was convinced that the city would eventually fall to the British was, ironically, the commander in chief, the Marquis de Montcalm. All through the war he had been a chronic defeatist. Before the opening of each campaign he had declared vociferously that it would end badly and he sought to ensure that the blame would fall elsewhere than on him. On 24 February 1759 he wrote to Lévis, 'The colony is lost unless peace comes. I can see nothing that can save it.'[17] And on 9 August he wrote to the Chevalier Bourlamaque, 'I maintain that the colony is lost.'[18] He made his plans accordingly and what ensued was a self-fulfilling prophecy.

Montcalm's tactics stipulated that what remained of the French and Canadian regular troops after the inevitable debacle, but before the ensuring capitulation of the colony, would withdraw to Louisiana in a fleet of canoes by way of the Ottawa River, the Great Lakes, and the Mississippi. This move, he assured the minister in a mémoire sent to the court with Bougainville in 1758, would prevent the loss of a sizeable body of men and preserve the honour of French arms by a feat rivalling the retreat of the Ten Thousand that had immortalized the Greeks.[19] It was likely for this reason, later seen to have been a disastrous mistake, that he established his main supply base at Batiscan, 50 miles above Quebec.[20] On strategic grounds this made no sense, since it left Quebec vulnerable to an enemy landing across that vital supply line. On the other hand were the town to fall, as Montcalm anticipated, then the supplies would be there ready for a withdrawal to Montreal and the epic retreat to Louisiana.

When the British were known to be ascending the river, Montcalm drafted the terms to be submitted to them for the capitulation of Quebec and gave a copy to the town commandment, the Sieur de Ramezay.[21] He made careful preparations for defeat, but he conspicuously failed to prepare the town's outer defences. Relying on the opinion of his self-serving engineering officer, Major Pontleroy, who informed him that an enemy landing above Quebec could not hope to succeed and that the range across the river from Pointe Lévis was too far for cannon fire to be effective,[22] he did not fortify that vital point and made only the feeblest of attempts to dislodge the British when they landed and began constructing their batteries.

The British objective all through the campaign was to take Quebec, it being rightly assumed that once Quebec fell the French would be forced to surrender the entire colony. Attempts to take the town by manoeuvre on the left flank of the French lines had conspicuously failed, with heavy losses. Massive bombardment of the town had accomplished nothing except destruction of eighty per cent of the buildings. Attempts to cut the French supply line upriver had been beaten off. The only way the objective could be gained was somehow to force Montcalm to come out from behind his fortified lines to give battle in the open and then destroy his army. Wolfe admitted that he could not stay in the river beyond the end of September.[23] Vice-Admiral Saunders dared not risk a quarter of the Royal Navy's being caught in such dangerous waters by the onset of winter. On 5 September, Saunders wrote in a dispatch to the Admiralty, 'I shall very soon send home the great ships.'[24] By early September a protracted siege was out of the question. All that the French had to do was hold the enemy off for a matter of days.

Wolfe, frustrated at every turn, felt that he had to make one last desperate attempt to take Quebec before admitting defeat, abandoning the campaign, and sailing ignominiously back to England. He proposed another assault on the Beauport lines, but when he submitted his plans to his brigadiers they curtly rejected them. They pointed out that even were Montcalm to be defeated in an action there, he could still withdraw his army either into Quebec, or upriver to his supply depot then westward to Montreal, thereby necessitating another campaign the following year.[25] They proposed instead a landing well above Quebec, between the town and Montcalm's supply base at Batiscan. This, they pointed out, would force him to come out and give battle, and if defeated, then not only Quebec but the entire colony would have to capitulate.

Wolfe accepted the brigadiers' plan in principal, but made a change that nullified its main strategic aim and placed the British army in grave jeopardy. The road from Batiscan to Quebec forked some fifteen miles above the town. The northern branch road went through Ancienne-Lorette, five miles north of the Saint Lawrence, then proceeded across the Saint Charles river to join the Quebec-Charlesbourg road. Instead of landing above the fork, thereby severing all communication between Quebec and Batiscan, which was the essential feature of the brigadiers' plan, Wolfe chose to land at the Anse au Foulon, thereby leaving the vital northern road open. It was this road that the French army was to use, after the debacle, to make good its withdrawal to Saint Augustin and later to Montreal.

Much ink has been spilled over Montcalm's failure to strengthen his right flank, and the colossal good luck that allowed the British to scale the heights, virtually unopposed, and assemble their army on the Plains of Abraham. Blame for the event has been duly apportioned to certain individuals with varying degrees of regard for the evidence,[26] it being assumed that once Wolfe had gained that position what ensued was inevitable. C. P. Stacey has stated that since Wolfe was astride Quebec's supply line, which he clearly was not,[27] 'Nothing was left but for Montcalm to take the chance of a desperate stroke against an army far better than his own.'[28]

Stacey also opines that no matter how Montcalm had reacted to Wolfe's surprise landing, the French were doomed to defeat, 'so serious was the difference in military quality between the opposing forces'.[29] This assertion begs the question why it was that 3,500 troops of that same French army had been able to inflict such a crushing defeat on 15,000 British and American troops at Carillon the preceding year. Or why the chevalier de Lévis, again with that selfsame army, was able to defeat resoundingly the British under Murray on those same Plains of Abraham just seven months later.

What we have here is a classic case of the argument that because something happened, it *ipso facto* had to happen, was in fact virtually preordained. As the American novelist Mary McCarthy remarked about other battles in another war, 'a successful action is never examined in terms of what caused it, the result is seen as the cause.'[30] Anglophone historians are particularly prone to take this view since what the consequences of a French victory would have been are too mind-boggling to contemplate. Toronto, for example, might then today be a French-speaking city; and the Americans would have had to postpone their bid for independence.

If we strip ourselves of hindsight and examine closely the position of the British and French forces on the morning of 13 September, what do we actually find? Wolfe's army, numbering at most 4,500 men, extended in two lines from the edge of the cliff overlooking the Saint Lawrence to the wooded escarpment overlooking the Saint Charles river. To cover that front of some 1,300 yards the ranks had to be stretched thin. The files were over three feet apart, with a forty-yard interval between each of the battalions.[31] The soldiers had spent the previous day on the ships manoeuvring upriver or preparing to embark. At nine o'clock at night they had begun embarking in the landing craft. Five hours later the first of the three waves began slipping downstream with the tide towards the Anse au Foulon. They made their first landing in the final hours of darkness. The boats then returned to embark the next wave. By eight the entire force was on the heights, having had little or no sleep for the past twenty-four hours. They carried the usual hard rations and the only water they had was in their canteens. They had no tents or blankets, their only ammunition was that in their pouches. Two light field guns were brought up, but for one of them they had the wrong ammunition. They apparently had no doctors or surgeons with them.* This small army was ready for battle, provided it were to be fought within a few hours. Manoeuvre in that confined area, or a protracted assault on the town's fortifications, was out of the question. Time was not on their side.

One vital element that Wolfe had achieved, however, was surprise. Everything therefore depended on how Montcalm would react. Although he had been informed at dawn that the British had effected a landing, he refused to believe it. It was not until six-thirty, after receiving further frantic reports that the British were massed on the Plains, that he rode off to see for himself, then gave orders for the troops in the Beauport lines to be brought up at the double.[32]

The significance of this three-hour interval between Wolfe's arrival on the heights and Montcalm's appearance is that Wolfe was thereby afforded ample time, undisturbed, to survey the terrain and make his dispositions accordingly. The position that he chose and its relation to his objective, the destruction of the French army and the occupation of Quebec, therefore deserves critical examination.

It was axiomatic that an army, in the presence of an enemy, should seek to occupy the high ground. In this particular instance one would have expected Wolfe to occupy the heights of the Plains of Abraham, the broken ridge known as the Buttes à Neveu, which would have given

---

*When Vaudreuil learned that Wolfe had been wounded he wrote to Bougainville that he believed M. de Ramezay, commander of the Quebec garrison, had already sent two surgeons to the English general. Arthur G. Doughty and G. W. Parmalee, eds., *The Siege of Quebec and the Battle of the Plains of Abraham*, 6 vols. Quebec, 1901, vol. IV, 127; Vaudreuil à Bougainville, 13 Sept. 1759.

him a clear view of the town. Provided he could hold that commanding site, he could have brought up his heavy guns to batter a breach in Quebec's fortifications prior to an assault. Montcalm would not necessarily have brought his army out to give battle. He would still have had the option of keeping his main forces behind the town walls, relying on his own guns to disrupt the enemy's artillery emplacements[33] and using the Canadians — in conjunction with Bougainville's elite force ten miles upriver — to harass the British rear, with its precarious supply line. The obvious move for Wolfe to make under the circumstances was to occupy the commanding heights no matter how Montcalm reacted.

The astonishing thing is that Wolfe did *not* occupy those heights, despite the fact that nothing stood in his way. Inexplicably he drew up his little army on the low reverse slope, some six hundred paces from the crest of the ridge. From that position he could not see the walls of Quebec, or any part of the town.[34] Had he managed to bring up every gun in his massive armoury, not one of them could have ranged in on the walls of Quebec. If the French *quartier général* had racked their brains to devise a disposition of the enemy's forces best suited to their own purpose, they would have been hard pressed to come up with anything better than that position. If they had lured Wolfe into it, they could have expected plaudits from the shade of the Maréchal de Saxe. There Wolfe waited for Montcalm to come to him, while the Canadian militia spread along the brush-covered slopes on both his flanks and began inflicting casualties. In front of him, but out of sight, was the fortified town and the main French force. Ten miles to his rear was Bougainville with an elite force of 3,000 regulars and militia with some light cannon.[35] They could be expected to arrive on the scene at any moment. They would then have been across the British communication route and line of retreat to the Anse au Foulon. Wolfe had no reserves. Were he to fail to gain a crushing victory, retreat would have been extremely difficult, if not impossible. His army would have had to fight its way through Bougainville's force, then withdraw down the steep path to the beach and there wait for the tide to allow the boats to come in from the fleet to take them off. This would have been a lengthy operation, since it would have required three trips. It could hardly have been expected that the French would allow this withdrawal to go unharassed. Even if the first wave of boats managed to get away unscathed, the troops remaining on the beach would have been rendered all the more vulnerable. It is difficult to see how such a hastily improvised operation could have resulted in anything but surrender or slaughter. Wolfe and his men must have been aware of this as they stood there, waiting. Montcalm had that British army at his mercy.

All through the summer Montcalm had fought a defensive campaign, forcing Wolfe to come to him only to be beaten back with heavy losses. He had passed up obvious opportunities to launch limited attacks on the enemy's vulnerable position at Montmorency, and both officers and men had been sharply critical of his timidity.[36] He is reputed, on one occasion, to have rejected Lévis's urging to attack with the sage comment, 'Drive them thence and they will give us more trouble. So long as they stay there they cannot hurt us. Let them amuse themselves.'[37] All that Montcalm now had to do was to continue to employ that same Fabian strategy: seize the vacant high ground, bring up his guns, and wait for Wolfe to make a move. The longer he could delay an action the stronger became his position.

His contemporary defenders, and some historians, have sought to excuse his fatal decision to attack precipitately on the grounds that to have waited would have allowed the British to entrench themselves, thereby rendering an attack on their lines hopeless. Yet the British could have built the most formidable of entrenchments with the material available, logs and earth, and it would have availed them nothing. They would have dominated nothing more than the six hundred paces of terrain facing them. Guns on the commanding ridge would quickly have rent any such entrenchments asunder. Moreover, the British could sustain themselves on that site only for a matter of days, and only provided that they kept their supply line open. Water would have been a major problem. The Canadians and Indians, not to mention the French gunners, could have seen to it that they got precious little sleep. Moreover, the logs of the British ships state that on the 16th the weather broke. For the ensuing three days there were gale-force winds and heavy rain.[38]

There is just one point that needs to be made concerning the actual battle. Everyone remarks on Wolfe's thin red line of two ranks. What was really significant was that Montcalm chose not to advance in line but to attack in column. Captain John Knox, in his journal, states that the French attacked in three columns, two inclining to the right, opening fire obliquely as they advanced, at the extremities of the British line from 130 yards' distance.[39] Major Patrick MacKellar stated that when the French were within a hundred yards of the British line, 'it mov'd up regularly with a steady fire, and when within 20 or 30 yards of closing gave a General One,' which caused the French to turn and flee.[40] The British centre had not come under fire and it was its volleys, according to Knox, that broke the French charge.

In French military circles at this time a debate raged over the relative effectiveness of attack in column and attack in line. Eventually the proponents of attack in line gained the ascendancy. It came to be accepted that the column should be used to bring the army as close as possible to the enemy without coming under serious fire, then deeply into line by a variety of complex parade-ground manoeuvres ready for the attack. This allowed every man in the ranks to bring his musket to bear on the opposing force. To attack in column meant that only the front ranks could fire; those in the rear could merely take the places of those before them who fell, or else the columns had to change direction oblique to the enemy line, but even then only the outside file of one side of the column could use their muskets effectively. This is what occurred in Montcalm's attack, and with predictable results.

Some military thinkers in France, however, maintained that the shock effect of a charging column would break the line. It was also held that training and discipline were so poor in the French army that the line formation was too difficult to execute on the battlefield and maintain under fire. Moreover, it was believed that the French temperament, with its reckless but mercurial bravery, made attack in column something that only exceptionally well-trained and disciplined troops could withstand.[41]

The battle at Quebec on 13 September 1759 proved all the above points. The battle fought on the same ground the following year, between the same two armies, and again of equal numbers,[42] added further proof. This time it was the British commander, Brigadier-General James Murray, who obliged the enemy and marched out of the fortified town to give battle in the open. He massed his troops on the Buttes à Neveu, the same ground that Wolfe had allowed Montcalm to occupy undisputed. As C. P. Stacey succinctly puts it, 'This rise was an admirable position for a defensive battle, and with his numerous guns disposed in the intervals between his battalions Murray could expect to inflict a severe reverse on Lévis if the latter had the temerity to attack him'[43] Exactly the same, of course, had held true for Montcalm. Murray, however, repeated Montcalm's mistake. Fearing that Lévis would construct redoubts and be difficult to dislodge, he abandoned the high ground and launched an assault, hoping to strike them before they could form to receive the charge. In this he failed. Lévis got his battalions into line, repelled the British attack, then counter-attacked their flanks. The left flank was turned. A bayonet charge then broke the British line. They turned and fled, abandoning their guns. Murray came dangerously close to having his army destroyed.[44]

There was one signal difference between this battle and the previous one. This time both generals survived, which was perfectly normal for eighteenth-century warfare. The odd fact that in the 1759 battle both Wolfe and Montcalm received mortal wounds is a sure indication that there was something seriously wrong with the tactics they employed on that day. Yet regardless of how haphazard it all was, the outcome caused the history of North America to take a drastic turn with consequences that still plague us today. It gives one to think that perhaps the most overlooked determining factor in history has been stupidity.

NOTES

1. Field-Marshal Viscount Montgomery of Alamein, *A History of Warfare,* (London, 1968), 320.
2. Archives du Ministère de la Guerre, Vincennes. Series A1, vol. 3540, ff. 136–7, M. de Montgay à . . . Mtl., 17 mai 1759; ibid., f. 39, Malartic à . . . Mtl., 9 avril 1759; ibid., ff. 138–9; Lévis à . . . Mtl., 17 mai 1759; ibid., f. 115, Montreuil à Mgr . . . Mtl., 6 mai 1759.
3. Archives du Séminaire de Québec, Séminaire 7, no. 72C, Journal de l'Abbé Richer, 22 aoust.
4. Archives du Ministère de la Guerre, Vincennes, Series A1, vol. 3540, no. 103, Bigot au Ministre de la Guerre, Mtl., 15 oct 1759.
5. Public Archives of Canada, Murray papers, MG23, GII-1, vol. 1, 30, Murray to Amherst, Que., 19 May 1760.
6. Ibid., 8–9, Thos. Ainslie to James Murray, Louisbourg, 28 Oct. 1759.
7. C.P. Stacey, *Quebec 1759. The Siege and the Battle,* (Toronto, 1959), 184–91. The dispatch is here printed *in toto*.
8. Christopher Hibbert, *Wolfe at Quebec* (London, 1959), 104.
9. Archives du Ministère de la Guerre, Vincennes. Series A1, vol. 3540, f. 128, Journal de M. Malartic 1758–9; ibid., 149, Situation des huit Bataillons d'Infanterie françaises servant en Canada d'Après la Revue qui en a été faitte en Mai; *Rapport de l'Archiviste de la Province de Québec 1920–21,* 155, Journal du Siège de Québec, du 10 mai au 18 septembre 1759; Archives Nationales, Paris, Colonies, Series F3, Moreau de St Méry, vol. 15, f. 334, Bigot au Ministre, Qué., 15 oct. 1759.
10. Ibid.; H.-R. Casgrain, ed., *Collection des manuscripts du Maréchal de Lévis,* vol. VI, 214.
11. Ibid., vol. IX, 48–9.
12. Ibid., vol. VI, 183.
13. Archives Nationales, Paris, Colonies, Series C11A, vol. 104, f. 193, 1759 Journal tenu à l'armée; Casgrain, op. cit., vol. V, 41–2.
14. Archives du Ministère de la Guerre, Vincennes. Series A1, vol. 3574, f. 112, Evenemens du Canada depuis le Mois d'Octobre 1759 Jusqu'au mois de Septembre 1760; Casgrain, op. cit., vol. IX, 56.
15. Journal de M. Malartic 1758–9, loc. cit.; Casgrain, op. cit., vol. V, 349.
16. Public Archives of Canada, MG 23, GII-1, series 2–7, P. MacKellar's Short Account of the Expedition against Quebec, 20.
17. Casgrain, op. cit., vol. VI, 163.
18. Ibid., vol. V, 343.
19. Archives du Ministère de la Guerre, Vincennes. Series A1, vol. 3405, no. 217.
20. 1759 Journal tenu a l'armée, op. cit., f. 187.
21. Archives Nationales, Paris, Colonies. Series C11A, vol. 104, f. 332, Mémoire du Sieur de Ramezay.
22. Casgrain, op. cit., vol. IV, 96.
23. Stacey, op. cit., 102.
24. Sir Julian S. Corbett, *England in the Seven Years' War,* (London 1918), vol. I, 454, n. 1; Hibbert, op. cit., 126.
25. Stacey, op. cit., 97–8.
26. See in particular Stacey, op. cit., 162–78, 'Generalship at Quebec'.
27. Ibid., 154.
28. Ibid., 137.
29. Ibid., 154.
30. *New York Review of Books,* 25 Jan. 1973.
31. Capt. John Knox, *An Historical Journal of the Campaigns in North America,* (Champlain Society edition, Toronto, 1914–16), 99–101.
32. Stacey, op. cit., 135; Archives Nationales, Paris. Series F3, Moreau de St Méry, vol. 15, ff, 286–8, Vaudreuil au Ministre, Mtl., 5 oct. 1759; Archives du Ministère de la Guerre, Vincennes. Series A1, vol. 3540, no. 103, Bigot au Ministre, Mtl., 15 oct. 1759.

33. A great deal has been written on the weakness of the Quebec fortifications. Montcalm was scathing in his comments, but he always sought to make his situation appear far worse than it actually was. The engineering officer Pontleroy was equally critical, but he was not disinterested; he sought the post of chief engineer for the colony, claiming that such an appointment was needed since all the colony's forts would have to be rebuilt and he was the obvious man to do it. According to this, and Montcalm's rubric a fortified place that the French held was indefensible, but the moment the enemy occupied it, it became, *ipso facto,* impregnable. The other serving engineering officer in Canada, Desandrouins, a competent man of integrity, submitted a *mémoire* in 1778 on what forces would be required were the French to send an expedition to retake Quebec. He gave a good description of the fortifications, stated that they mounted 180 large guns, plus a large number of mortars, and made it plain that the fortifications of Quebec were indeed formidable. See Casgrain, op. cit., vol. IV, 322–4.

34. Francis Parkman, who went over the battlefield in 1879, noted in his *Montcalm and Wolfe* that, from the British line Quebec was hidden from sight by the Buttes à Neveu. He failed, however, to appreciate the military significance of the fact. Since his day the ridge has been reduced in height and levelled by the construction of buildings and, on the St Lawrence side, of a covered reservoir under what is today the battlefield park.

35. Archives Nationales, Paris, Colonies, Series F3, Moreau de St Méry, vol. 15, ff. 284–5, Vaudreuil au Ministre, Qué., 5 oct. 1759; ibid., ff. 337–40, Bigot au Ministre, Mtl., 15 oct. 1759.

36. Ibid., Series CIIA, vol. 104, ff. 168, 175–6, 179–80, 196, Journal tenu à l'Armée.

37. Corbett, op. cit., vol. I, 431.

38. William Charles Henry Wood ed., *The Logs of the Conquest of Canada,* (Champlain Society edition, Toronto, 1909), 315–16.

39. Knox Journal, op. cit., 99–101.

40. P. MacKellar, op. cit., 34.

41. Robert S. Quimby, *The Background to Napoleonic Warfare: The Theory of Military Tactics in Eighteenth Century France,* (New York, 1957).

42. G.F.G. Stanley, *New France, The Last Phase 1744–1760,* (Toronto, 1968), 248.

43. Stacey, op. cit., 164.

44. Stacey, op. cit., 245–9.

Article Thirteen

A Change in Climate: The Conquest and the *Marchands* of Montreal

José Igartua

When the British government issued the Royal Proclamation of 1763, it assumed that the promised establishment of "British institutions" in the "Province of Quebec" would be sufficient to entice American settlers to move north and overwhelm the indigenous French-speaking and Papist population. These were naive hopes. Until the outbreak of the American Revolution, British newcomers merely trickled into Quebec, leading Governor Carleton to prophesy in 1767 that "barring a catastrophe shocking to think of, this Country must, to the end of Time, be peopled by the Canadian Race."[1] But the British newcomers, few though they were, had to be reckoned with. By 1765 they were powerful enough to have Governor Murray recalled and by 1777 they would be strong enough to command the majority of investments in the fur trade.[2] Did their success stem from superior abilities? Did the British take advantage of the situation of submission and dependence into which the Canadians had been driven by the

Source: José Igartua, "A Change in Climate: The Conquest and the *Marchands* of Montreal," *Historical Papers* (1974): 115–34. Reprinted by permission of the author and the Canadian Historical Association.

Conquest? Did the newcomers gain their predominance from previous experience with the sort of political and economic conditions created in post-Conquest Quebec?

Historians of Quebec have chosen various ways to answer these questions. Francis Parkman was fond of exhibiting the superiority of the Anglo-Saxon race over the "French Celt."[3] More recently the studies of W.S. Wallace, E.E. Rich, and D.G. Creighton took similar, if less overt, positions.[4] One of the best students of the North West fur trade, Wayne E. Stevens, concluded: "The British merchants . . . were men of great enterprise and ability and they began gradually to crowd out the French traders who had been their predecessors in the field."[5]

The French-Canadian historian Fernand Ouellet attributed the rise of the British merchants to the weaknesses of the Canadian trading bourgeoisie: "Son attachement à la petite entreprise individuelle, sa réponse à la concentration, son goût du luxe de même que son attrait irrésistible pour les placements assurés étaient des principaux handicaps." [*Editor's Translation:* their attachment to small personal business, their response to concentration, their love of luxury, as well as their irresistible attraction to safe investments were the main drawbacks.] No evidence is given for this characterization and the author hastens to concede that before 1775 "le problème de la concentration ne se pose pas avec acuité" [*Editor's Translation:* the problem of concentration was not acute], but for him it is clear that the economic displacement of the Canadians resulted from their conservative, "ancien régime" frame of mind, bred into them by the clergy and the nobility.[6] Ouellet painted British merchants in a more flattering light as the agents of economic progress.[7]

Michel Brunet has depicted the commercial competition between the British newcomers and the Canadian merchants as an uneven contest between two national groups, one of which had been deprived of the nourishing blood of its metropolis while the other was being assiduously nurtured. For Brunet the normal and natural outcome of that inequality was the domination of the conqueror, a situation which he sees as prevailing to the present day.[8]

Dale B. Miquelon's study of one merchant family, the Babys, shed new light on the question of British penetration of Canadian trade. It outlined the growth of British investments in the fur trade and the increasing concentration of British capital. The author concluded:

> The French Canadians dominated the Canadian fur trade until the upheaval of the American Revolution. At that time they were overwhelmed by an influx of capital and trading personnel. English investment in the top ranks of investors jumped by 679% and was never significantly to decline. Even without explanations involving the difference between the French and English commercial mentalities, it is difficult to believe that any body of merchants could recover from an inundation of such size and swiftness.[9]

This conclusion had the obvious merit of staying out of the murky waters of psychological interpretations. But Miquelon's own evidence suggests that the "flood theory" is not sufficient to account for the Canadians' effacement; even before the inundation of 1775–83, British investment in the fur trade was growing more rapidly than Canadian. By 1772, to quote Miquelon, the "English [had] made more impressive increases in the size of their investments than [had] the French, and for the first time [had] larger average investments in all categories."[10]

It is difficult not to note the ascendancy of the British in the fur trade of Canada even before the American Revolution. The success of the British merchants, therefore, was rooted in something more than mere numbers. It was not simply the outcome of an ethnic struggle between two nationalities of a similar nature; it was not only the natural consequence of the Canadians' conservative frame of mind. It arose out of a more complex series of causes, some of them a product of the animosities between Canadians and British, others inherent to the differences in the socioeconomic structures of the French and British empires; together, they amounted to a radical transformation of the societal climate of the colony.

The aim of this paper is to gauge the impact of the Conquest upon a well-defined segment of that elusive group called the "bourgeoisie" of New France. It focuses on Montreal and its Canadian merchants. Montreal was the centre of the fur trade and its merchants managed it. Historians of New France have traditionally seen the fur trade as the most dynamic sector of the colony's economy; by implication it is generally believed that the fur trade provided the likeliest opportunities for getting rich quickly and maintaining a "bourgeois" standard of living.[11] It is not yet possible to evaluate the validity of this notion with any precision, for too little is known about other sectors of the economy which, in the eighteenth century at least, may have generated as much or more profit. Research on the merchants of Quebec should provide new information on the wealth to be made from the fisheries, from wholesale merchandising, and from trade with Louisbourg and the West Indies. But if one is concerned with the fate of Canadian merchants after the Conquest, one should examine the fate of men involved in the sector of the economy of Quebec which was the most dynamic *after* the Conquest, the fur trade. The paper examines the impact of the arrival of (relatively) large numbers of merchants on the Montreal mercantile community, the attitude of British officials towards the Canadians, and the changing political climate of the colony. It is suggested that it was the simultaneous conjunction of these changes to the "world" of the Montreal merchants, rather than the effect of any one of them, which doomed the Canadian merchants of Montreal.[12]

THE MONTREAL MERCHANTS AT THE END OF THE FRENCH REGIME

In 1752 a French Royal engineer passing through Montreal remarked that "la plupart des habitants y sont adonnés au commerce principalement à celui connu sous le nom des pays d'en haut."[13] [*Editor's Translation:* the majority of the inhabitants involved in commerce were active principally in the upper part of the region—the back country (west and north of Montreal).] It was only a slight exaggeration. By the last year of the French regime one could count over one hundred négociants, merchants, outfitters, traders, and shopkeepers in Montreal. The overwhelming majority of them had been in business for some years and would remain in business after the Conquest. Over half were outfitters for the fur trade at some time or other between 1750 and 1775; these men comprised the body of the merchant community of Montreal. Above them in wealth and stature stood a handful of import merchants who did a comfortable business of importing merchandise from France and selling it in Montreal to other merchants or directly to customers in their retail stores. Below the outfitters a motley group of independent fur traders, shopkeepers, and artisans managed to subsist without leaving more than a trace of their existence for posterity.[14]

The fur trade, as it was conducted by the merchants of Montreal before 1760, had little to do with the glamorous picture it sometimes calls to mind. For the outfitter who remained in Montreal, it was not physically a risky occupation; its management was fairly simple and the profits which it produced quite meagre. For the last years of the French regime the fur trade followed a three-tier system. Fort Frontenac (present-day Kingston) and Fort Niagara were King's posts; they were not lucrative and had to be subsidized to meet English competition. The trade of Detroit and Michilimackinac, as well as that of the posts to the southwest, was open to licencees whose numbers were limited. Some coureurs de bois (traders without a licence) also roamed in the area. The richest posts, Green Bay and the posts to the northwest past Sault Sainte-Marie, were monopolies leased by the Crown to merchants or military officers.[15] The export of beaver was undertaken by the French Compagnie des Indes, which had the monopoly of beaver sales on the home market. Other furs were on the open market.

The system worked tolerably well in peace time: there was a stable supply of furs, prices paid to the Indians had been set by custom, the prices paid by the Compagnie des Indes were regulated by the Crown, and the prices of trade goods imported from France were fairly steady. There was competition from the Americans at Albany and from the English on the Hudson Bay, to be sure, but it appeared to be a competition heavily influenced by military considerations and compliance with Indian customs.[16]

The system faltered in war time. Beaver shipments to France and the importation of trade goods became risky because of British naval power. Shipping and insurance costs raised the Canadian traders' overhead, but the Indians refused to have the increase passed on to them. This was the most obvious effect of war, but it also produced general economic and administrative dislocations which led H.A. Innis to conclude that it "seriously weakened the position of the French in the fur trade and contributed to the downfall of the French *régime* in Canada."[17]

Nevertheless, outside of wartime crises, the fur trade of New France was conducted with a fair dose of traditionalism. This traditionalism resulted from two concurrent impulses: Indian attitudes towards trade, which were untouched by the mechanism of supply and demand and by distinctions between commercial, military, political, or religious activities; and the mercantilist policies of France, which tried to control the supply of furs by limiting the number of traders and regulating beaver prices on the French market. While the fur trade structure of New France had an inherent tendency towards geographic expansion, as Innis argued, it also had to be oligopolistic in nature, if investments in Indian alliances, explorations, and military support were to be maximized. Open competition could not be allowed because it would lead to the collapse of the structure.[18]

It is not surprising, therefore, that most outfitters dabbled in the fur trade only occasionally. On the average, between 1750 and 1775, the Canadian merchants of Montreal invested in the trade only four times and signed up about eleven engagés each time, not quite enough to man two canoes. Few merchants outfitted fur trade ventures with any regularity and only six men hired an average of twelve or more engagés, more than twice before 1761 (see Table 13.1).

Table 13.1 Largest Canadian Fur Trade Outfitters in Montreal, 1750–1760

Name	Total No. of Years	Total No. of Hirings	Yearly Average
Charly, Louis Saint-Ange	6	85	14.1
Godet, Dominique	5	85	17.0
Léchelle, Jean	4	130	32.5
Lemoine Monière, Alexis	7	300	42.8
L'Huillier Chevalier, François	7	90	12.6
Trotier Desauniers, Thomas-Ignace "Dufy"	5	129	25.8

Source: "Répertoire des engagements pour l'ouest conservés dans les Archives judiciaires de Montréal," *Rapport de l'Archiviste de la province de Québec* (1930–31): 353–453; (1931–32): 242–365; (1932–33): 245–304.

Three of these were unquestionably wealthy: Louis Saint-Ange Charly, an import merchant who, unlike his colleagues, had a large stake in the fur trade, realized 100000 livres on his land holdings alone when he left the colony for France in 1764; Thomas-Ignace Trotier Desauniers "Dufy," who in a will drawn up in 1760 bequeathed 28000 livres to the Sulpicians; the illiterate Dominique Godet, who in a similar document of 1768 mentioned 5000 livres in cash in hand, land in three parishes in the vicinity of Montreal, "Batiment & Bateaux qui en dependent," around 5000 livres in active debts, and two black slaves.[19] Two other large outfitters left relatively few belongings at the time of their death: Alexis Lemoine Monière left less than 1000 livres, all of it in household goods, and François L'Huillier Chevalier just slightly more.[20] Little is known about the sixth man, Jean Léchelle.

If the fur trade made few wealthy men among those who invested heavily in it, it would be hard to argue that less considerable investors were more successful. It is not unreasonable to conclude that the fur trade was not very profitable for the overwhelming majority of outfitters and that it sustained only a very limited number of them each year. Yet the French had reduced costly competition to a minimum and had few worries about price fluctuations. How would Canadian outfitters fare under a different system?

THE ADVENT OF THE BRITISH MERCHANTS

With the arrival in Montreal of British traders, the workings of the fur trade were disrupted. At first, the licensing system was maintained and some areas were left to the exclusive trade of particular traders.[21] But from the very beginning the trade was said to be open to all who wanted to secure a licence, and the result could only be price competition. With individual traders going into the fur trade, the organization of the trade regressed. The previous division of labour between the Compagnie des Indes, the import merchants and outfitters, the traders, the voyageurs, and the engagés was abandoned and during the first years of British rule the individual trader filled all of the functions previously spread among many "specialists."

The story of Alexander Henry, one of the first British merchants to venture into the upper country, illustrates the new pattern of trade. A young man from New Jersey, Alexander Henry came to Canada in 1760 with General Amherst's troops.[22] With the fall of Montreal Henry saw the opening of a "new market" and became acquainted with the prospects of the fur trade. The following year, he set out for Michilimackinac with a Montreal outfitter, Étienne Campion, whom he called his "assistant," and who took charge of the routine aspects of the trip.[23] Henry wintered at Michilimackinac. There he was urged by the local inhabitants to go back to Detroit as soon as possible for they claimed to fear for his safety. Their fears were not without foundation, but Henry stayed on. His partner Campion reassured him: "the Canadian inhabitants of the fort were more hostile than the Indians, as being jealous of British traders, who . . . were penetrating into the country."[24] At least some of the Canadians resented the British traders from the outset and a few tried to use the Indians to frighten them away.[25]

Henry proceeded to Sault Sainte-Marie the following year. In the spring of 1763, he returned to Michilimackinac and witnessed the massacre of the British garrison during Pontiac's revolt.[26] He was eventually captured by the Indians and adopted into an Indian family with whom he lived, in the Indian style, until late June 1764. Undaunted, Henry set out for the fur trade again, exploring the Lake Superior area. He was on the Saskatchewan River in 1776, tapping fur resources which the French had seldom reached.[27] Finally he settled down in Montreal in 1781, and while he did join the North West Company after its formation, he seldom returned to the upper country himself.[28]

Henry was not the first British merchant to reach the upper country. Henry Bostwick had obtained a licence from General Gage before him in 1761,[29] and the traders Goddard and Solomons had followed Henry into Michilimackinac in 1761. By early 1763 there were at least two more British merchants in the area.[30] In Montreal alone there were close to 50 new merchants by 1765. Governor Murray's list of the Protestants in the district of Montreal gives the names, the origins, and the "former callings" of 45.[31] Over half of them came from England and Scotland and 20 percent were from Ireland. Only 13 percent came from the American colonies and an equal number came from various countries (Switzerland, Germany, France, Guernsey). In the proportion of more than three to one, the newcomers had been merchants in their "former calling." The others had been soldiers and clerks. Many of the newcomers were men of experience and enterprise. Among them were Isaac Todd, Thomas Walker, Lawrence Ermatinger, Richard Dobie, Edward Chinn, John Porteous, William Grant, Benjamin Frobisher, James Finlay, Alexander Paterson, Forrest Oakes, and the Jewish merchants Ezekiel and Levy Solomons, all of whom became substantial traders.[32]

The arrival of so many merchants could only mean one thing: strenuous competition in the fur trade. Competition ruthlessly drove out those with less secure financial resources or with no taste for sharp practices. Among the British as among the French, few resisted the pressures. The story of the trader Hamback is not untypical. Out on the Miami River in 1766 and 1767, he found that competition left him with few returns to make to his creditor William Edgar of Detroit. "I live the life of a downright exile," he complained, "no company but a Barrel of drunken infamous fugitives, and no other Comfort of Life."[33]

The Canadian merchants of Montreal had competition not only from British merchants in their town, but also from American merchants moving into Detroit and Michilimackinac. William Edgar, a New York merchant, was at Niagara in late 1761.[34] In 1763 he was established at Detroit, where he conducted a brisk trade supplying individual traders at Michilimackinac and in the southwest district.[35] From Schenectady, the partnership of Phyn and Ellice also carried on a profitable supply trade for the fur traders of the interior.[36]

Competition also came from the French on the Mississippi, who were trading in the Illinois country and the Lake Superior region. These French traders could all too easily link up with French-speaking traders from Canada, whose help, it was feared, they could enlist in subverting the Indians against British rule.[37] This always troubled Sir William Johnson, the Superintendent for Indian Affairs, who refused to abandon his suspicions of the French-speaking traders from Canada.

This many-sided competition produced a climate to which the Canadian merchants were not accustomed. The increased numbers of fur traders led to frictions with the Indians, smaller returns for some of the traders, and unsavoury trade practices.[38] Even the retail trade was affected. Merchants from England flooded the market at Quebec "with their manufactures, so much so that they are daily sold here at Vendue Twenty per Cent. below prime Cost."[39] In 1760 alone, the first year of British occupation, £60000 worth of trade goods had been brought into Canada.[40] From 1765 to 1768 the pages of the *Quebec Gazette* were filled with notices of auctions by merchants returning to England and disposing of their wares after unsuccessful attempts to establish themselves in the trade of the colony.[41]

By 1768 some thought the Canadians still had the advantage in the fur trade, even though there was "Competition" and a "strong jealousy" between Canadian and English. The Canadians' "long Connections with those Indians," wrote General Gage, "and their better Knowledge of their Language and Customs, must naturaly for a long time give the Canadians an Advantage over the English."[42] Sir William Johnson had expressed a similar opinion the previous year and had deplored the British merchants' tactics: "The English were compelled to make use of Low, Selfish Agents, French, or English as Factors, who at the Expence of honesty and sound policy, took care of themselves whatever became of their employers."[43]

Another observer, the Hudson's Bay Company trader at Moose Factory, complained of "Interlopers who will be more Destructive to our trade than the French was." The French had conducted a less aggressive trade: they "were in a manner Settled, their Trade fixed, their Standards moderate and Themselves under particular regulations and restrictions, which I doubt is not the Case now."[44] Competition was forcing the British merchants in Montreal into ruthless tactics, a development which upset the Hudson's Bay Company man and which would unsettle the Canadians.

The pattern of British domination of the fur trade began to emerge as early as 1767. Trading ventures out of Michilimackinac into the northwest were conducted by Canadians, but British merchants supplied the financial backing. The northwest expeditions demanded the lengthiest periods of capital outlay, lasting two or three years. British merchants, it seems, had better resources. Of the fifteen outfitters at Michilimackinac who sent canoes to the northwest in 1767, nine were British and six were Canadian; the total value of canoes outfitted by the British came to £10812.17 while the Canadians' canoes were worth only £3061.10. The British outfitters — most notably Alexander Henry, Isaac Todd, James McGill, Benjamin Frobisher, Forrest Oakes — invested on the average £1351.12 and the Canadians only £510.5. The average value of goods invested in each canoe stood at £415.17 for the British and £278.6 for the Canadians.[45] The Canadians' investment per canoe was only two-thirds that of the British and the Canadians were already outnumbered as outfitters in what would become the most important region of the fur trade.[46]

Open competition was not conducive to the expansion of the fur trade and an oligopolistic structure reminiscent of the French system soon reappeared as the only solution.[47] This led to the formation of the North West Company in the 1780s but already in 1775, those Montreal merchants who had extended their operations as far as the Saskatchewan felt the need for collaboration rather than competition. Again developments in the more remote frontiers of the fur trade foretold of events to occur later in the whole of the trade: the traders on the Saskatchewan were almost all of British origin.[48] The fur trade was returning to the structures developed by the French, but during the period of competition which followed the Conquest the Canadians were gradually crowded out. There was some irony in that. Why had the Canadians fared so badly?

THE ATTITUDE OF GOVERNMENT OFFICIALS

Much has been made of the natural sympathies of Murray and Carleton towards the Canadians and their antipathies towards the traders of their own nation. Yet for all their ideological inclinations there is no evidence that the governors turned their sentiments into policies of benevolence for Canadians in trade matters. Rather, it is easier to discover, among the lesser officials and some of the more important ones as well, an understandable patronizing of British rather than Canadian merchants. Colonial administrators may not have set a deliberate pattern of preference in favour of British merchants. But the Canadian merchants of Montreal, who put great store by official patronage, cared not whether the policy was deliberate or accidental; the result was the same.

Official preferences played against the Canadian traders in many ways. First, the lucrative trade of supplying the military posts was given to British and American merchants as a matter of course, and this occasion for profit was lost to the Canadians. Under the French regime some of the Montreal merchants, notably the Monières and the Gamelins, had profited from that trade.[49] Now it fell out of Canadian hands. This advantage did not shift to the sole favour of the British merchants of Quebec. New York and Pennsylvania traders were also awarded their share of the trade. The firms of Phyn, Ellice of Schenectady and Baynton, Wharton, and Morgan of Philadelphia received the lion's share of that business while the upper country was under the jurisdiction of Sir William Johnson.[50] But this was of little comfort to the Canadians.

Less tangible by-products of the British occupation of the former fur trading areas of New France are more difficult to assess than the loss of the supply trade; they were, however, quite real. One was the British military's attitude towards Canadians. The military were wary of French-speaking traders in Illinois and on the Mississippi. Although the French from Canada had been vanquished, French traders in the interior could still deal with France through New Orleans. No regulations, no boundaries could restrain French traders operating out of Louisiana from dealing with the Indians, and the Canadians who were confined to the posts protested against the advantage held by the French traders.[51] But who were these French traders? Did they not include Canadian coureurs de bois and wintering merchants? How could one really tell a French-speaking trader from Canada from a French-speaking trader out of New Orleans? Were not all of them suspect of exciting the Indians against the British, promising and perhaps hoping for France's return to America?[52] As late as 1768, when Indian discontent in the west threatened another uprising, General Gage failed to see any difference between French-speaking Canadians and the French from New Orleans:

> There is the greatest reason to suspect that the French are Endeavoring to engross the Trade, and that the Indians have acted thro' their Instigation, in the Murders they have committed, and the Resolutions we are told they have taken, to suffer no Englishman to trade with them. And in this they have rather been Assisted by the English Traders, who having no Consideration but that of a present gain, have thro' fear of exposing their own Persons, or hopes of obtaining greater influence with the Indians, continually employed French Commissarys or Agents, whom they have trusted with Goods for them to Sell at an Advanced price in the Indian Villages.[53]

Gage's suspicions of the French traders were nurtured by Sir William Johnson, who had to keep the Indians on peaceful terms with one another and with the British. It was part of Johnson's function, of course, to worry about possible uprisings and about subversive individuals. His job would be made easier if he could confine all traders to military posts where they could be kept under surveillance. But the traders had little concern for Sir William's preoccupations. If British traders were irresponsible in their desires of "present gain," the Canadian traders' vices were compounded by the uncertainty of their allegiance to the British Crown:

> Since the Reduction of that Country [Canada], we have seen so many Instances of their [the Canadian traders'] Perfidy false Stories & Ca. Interested Views in Trade that prudence forbids us to suffer them or any others to range at Will without being under the Inspection of the proper Officers agreeable to His Majesty's Appointment.[54]

Johnson's attitude spread to the officers under him, even though Carleton had found nothing reprehensible in the Canadians' behaviour.[55] Johnson's deputy, George Croghan, believed there was collusion between the French from Canada and the French from Louisiana.[56] In 1763 the commandant at Michilimackinac, Major Etherington, had displayed a similar mistrust of the Canadians.[57] Major Robert Rogers, a later commandant at Michilimackinac, checked the Canadians by trading on his own account.[58]

The British military's mistrust of the French traders from Canada was understandable. Before 1760, one of the major reasons for the American colonials' antagonism towards

New France had been the French ability to press the Indians into their service to terrorize the western fringes of American settlement. Thus there was a historical as well as a tactical basis for the military's attitude towards the Canadians. But British officers failed to recognize that not all Canadian traders were potential troublemakers and that there was indeed very little tangible evidence, as Carleton had reminded Johnson, of any mischief on their part. The military's attitude was directed as much by ethnic prejudice as by military necessity.

The Canadian traders could not fail to perceive this prejudice, and it dampened their spirits. Perhaps the military's attitude, as much as competition, forced the Canadians into partnerships with British merchants. (The express purpose of the bonds required for the fur trade was to ensure loyal conduct; what better token of loyalty could there be for a Canadian trader than a bond taken out in his name by a British partner?) The military's mistrust of the Canadian traders did not lessen with time. The advantage which this prejudice gave British traders would continue for some twenty years after the Conquest, as the American Revolution rekindled the military's fears of treasonable conduct by the Canadians.

Other patronage relationships between British military officials and British traders also deprived the Canadians of an equal chance in the competition for furs. It is hard to evaluate precisely the effect of such patronage; only glimpses of it may be caught. Late in 1763 a Philadelphia merchant who had lost heavily because of Pontiac's uprising wrote to William Edgar in Detroit that Croghan was in England where he was to "represent the Case of the Traders to his Majesty" and that General Amherst had "given us his faithful promise that he will do everything in his power in our behalf."[59] In 1765 Alexander Henry was granted the exclusive trade of Lake Superior by Major Howard, the military commandant at Michilimackinac. Nine years later Henry received the support of such patrons as the Duke of Gloucester, the consul of the Empress of Russia in England, and of Sir William Johnson in an ill-fated attempt to mine the iron ore of the Lake Superior area.[60]

These were obvious examples of patronage; other forms of cooperation were less visible. Another correspondent of William Edgar, Thomas Shipboy, asked Edgar to represent him in settling the affairs of a correspondent at Detroit and at Michilimackinac where, he added, "if you find any Difficulty in procuring his effects I dare say the Commanding officer will be of Service to you if you inform him in [sic] whose behalf you are acting."[61] Benjamin Frobisher also asked Edgar to "use your Interest with Capt. Robinson" to put a shipment of corn aboard the government vessel which sailed from Detroit to Michilimackinac.[62] Such shipping space was scarce and was only available through the courtesy of military officers or the ships' captains. Here again British traders put their social connections to good use. A last resort was sheer military force. Out on the Miami River, the trader Hamback saw "little hope of getting any thing from [Fort] St. Joseph at all, if I don't get protected, by the Commanding Officer, who might easily get those [Canadian] rascals fetch'd down to Detroit if He would."[63]

None of this patronage appears to have been available to Canadians. It is impossible to ascertain the degree to which military suspicions and patronage lessened the Canadians' chances in the fur trade. But more important, perhaps, than the actual loss of opportunities was the psychological handicap imposed upon the Canadians. What heart could they put in the game when the dice were so obviously loaded?

THE MERCHANTS' POLITICAL ACTIVITIES

The enmity between British merchants and the military, the merchants' growing agitation in favour of "British liberties," and their sentiments of political self-importance have been ably told by others and need not be retold here.[64] What needs to be underlined is that political agitation was unfamiliar to the Canadians. They had had no experience in these matters under French rule. Only on rare occasions during the pre-Conquest years had the Canadian merchants engaged in collective political representations; such representations were elicited by the governor or the intendant to obtain the merchants' advice on specific issues.[65] As French subjects, the Canadian merchants of Montreal had lacked the power to foster their economic interests through collective political action.

After 1760, the Canadian merchants would gradually lose their political innocence under the influence of the British merchants. During the 30 years which followed the Conquest they would make "l'apprentissage des libertés anglaises" and in 1792 they would take their place in the newly created legislative assembly more cognizant of the workings of the British constitution than the British had expected.[66] But that is beyond the concern here. In the years preceding the American Revolution the Montreal merchants were still looking for bearings. They showed their growing political awareness by following in the *Quebec Gazette* the political and constitutional debates which were rocking the British Empire. The merchants also began to voice their concerns in petitions and memorials to the authorities in the colony and in London.

The *Quebec Gazette* was the province's official gazette and its only newspaper before 1778. The paper published public notices for the Montreal district and occasional advertisements sent in by Montrealers as well as matters of concern to Quebec residents. It also made an effort to publish Canadian news of a general character. It closely followed the debates raging across the Atlantic over the *Stamp Act* and the general issues of colonial taxation. It reported on changes in the Imperial government and on contemporary political issues in England, notably the Wilkes affair.[67]

The pages of the *Gazette* also served on occasion as a forum for political discussion. In September 1765 a "Civis Canadiensis" declared his puzzlement at all the talk of "British liberties" and asked for enlightenment. The following year, a Quebec resident wrote a series of letters arguing that the colony should not be taxed.[68] In 1767, a debate arose on the British laws relating to bankruptcy and their applicability in Quebec.[69] Because of the pressures of Governor Carleton the *Gazette* stifled its reporting of controversial issues after 1770 and thereafter had little to print about American affairs.[70] In 1775 the *Gazette*'s political outpourings were directed against the American rebels and towards securing the loyalty of those Canadians who might be seduced by revolutionary propaganda.[71] The paper had become more conservative in its selection of the news but those Canadians who read the *Gazette* had been made familiar with the concepts of personal liberty, of "no taxation without representation," of the limited powers of the sovereign, and of the rights of the people. The *Gazette*'s readers most probably included the leading merchants of Montreal.

The *Gazette* was not the only instrument for the learning of British liberties. Anxious to give the appearance of a unanimous disposition among all merchants in Montreal, the British merchants often called on their Canadian confrères to add their names to various memorials and petitions dealing with the political and the economic state of the colony. The Canadian merchants who signed these petitions and memorials represented the top layer of the Canadian mercantile group in Montreal. Those who signed most often were the import merchants and the busy outfitters.

These Canadian merchants followed the political leadership of the British merchants. From 1763 to 1772 their petitions were either literal translations or paraphrased equivalents of petitions drafted by British merchants. It was only in December 1773 that they asserted views different from those of their British counterparts.[72] They petitioned the King that their "ancient laws, privileges, and customs" be restored, that the province be extended to its "former boundaries," that some Canadians be taken into the King's service, and that "the rights and privileges of citizens of England" be granted to all.[73]

The Canadians were becoming aware of their own position and were seeking to consolidate it against the attacks of the British element. The demand for the maintenance of the "ancient laws" was designed to counter British demands for British laws and representative institutions. The Canadians opposed the latter since, in their view, the colony was "not as yet in a condition to defray the expences of its own civil government, and consequently not in a condition to admit of a general assembly."[74] The demand for "a share of the civil and military employments under his majesty's government" came naturally to those who had lived under the French system of patronage. The Canadians had been accustomed to seek official patronage as the main avenue of upward mobility. The prospect of being denied such patronage was "frightful" to them, since they had little familiarity with alternate patterns of social promotion.[75]

In style as well as in content the Canadian merchants' petitions and memorials revealed differences in attitudes between Canadians and British. British memorials and petitions were rarely prefaced by more than the customary "Humbly showeth" and went directly to the point. In their own memorials and petitions, the Canadians first took "the liberty to prostrate themselves at the foot" of the royal throne and surrendered themselves to the "paternal care" of their sovereign. They often appealed to the wisdom, justice, and magnanimity of the king.[76] Their formal posture of meekness contrasted sharply with the self-assertion of the British. The Canadians' "Habits of Respect and Submission," as one British official put it,[77] may well have endeared them to Murray and Carleton, but those habits constituted a psychological obstacle against their making full use of their newfound "British liberties" to foster their own economic interest.

CONCLUSION

With the fall of Montreal to British arms in September 1760 something was irrevocably lost to the Canadian merchants of that city. More than the evil effects of the war or the postwar commercial readjustments, the most unsettling consequence of the Conquest was the disappearance of a familiar business climate. As New France passed into the British Empire, the Montreal outfitters were thrown into a new system of business competition, brought about by the very numbers of newly arrived merchants, unloading goods in the conquered French colony and going after its enticing fur trade. In opening up the trade of the colony to competition, the British presence transformed Canadian commercial practices. The change negated the Canadian merchants' initial advantage of experience in the fur trade and created a novel business climate around them.

Competition in trade, the new political regime, the Canadian merchants' inability to obtain the favours of the military, all these created a mood of uncertainty and pessimism among the Montreal merchants. The merchants could only conclude from what was happening around them that the new business climate of the post-Conquest period favoured British traders at their expense. They can be understood if they were not eager to adapt their ways to the new situation.

It may be argued, of course, that the changes which produced the new situation are subsumed under the notion of "Conquest" and that the previous pages only make more explicit the "decapitation" interpretation advanced by the historians of the "Montreal school."[78] It is true enough that the new business climate described here may not have been created after the Seven Years' War had Canada remained a French possession. But there is no guarantee that other changes would not have affected the Montreal merchants. During the last years of the French regime they had reaped few profits from the fur trade. After the Conquest they continued in the fur trade much on the same scale as before. The Montreal merchants were not "decapitated" by the Conquest; rather, they were faced in very short succession with a series of transformations in the socioeconomic structure of the colony to which they might have been able to adapt had these transformations been spread over a longer period of time.

This paper has attempted to show that the fate of the Canadian merchants of Montreal after the Conquest followed from the nature of trade before the Conquest and from the rate at which new circumstances required the merchants to alter their business behaviour. But it should be remembered that the decapitation hypothesis still remains to be tested in the area of the colony's economy which was most heavily dependent upon the control of the metropolis, the import-export trade of the Quebec merchants. Only a detailed examination of the role and the activities of the Quebec merchants, both before and after the Conquest, will fully put the decapitation hypothesis to the test.

NOTES

1. Public Archives of Canada [hereafter PAC], C.O. 42, vol. 27, f. 66, Carleton to Shelburne, Quebec, 25 November 1767; quoted in A.L. Burt, *The Old Province of Quebec*, 2 vols. (Toronto, 1968), 1:142.
2. See Burt, *Old Province*, vol. 1, ch. 6; Dale B. Miquelon, "The Baby Family in the Trade of Canada, 1750–1820" (Unpublished Master's thesis, Carleton University, 1966), 145–46.
3. Francis Parkman, *The Old Regime in Canada*, 27th ed. (Boston, 1892), ch. 21, especially 397–98.
4. W. Stewart Wallace, ed., *Documents Relating to the North West Company* (Toronto, 1934); Wallace, *The Pedlars from Quebec and Other Papers on the Nor'Westers* (Toronto, 1954); E.E. Rich, *The Fur Trade and the Northwest to 1857* (Toronto, 1967); Rich, *The History of the Hudson's Bay Company*, vol. 2 (London, 1959); D.G. Creighton, *The Empire of the St. Lawrence* (Toronto, 1956).
5. Wayne E. Stevens, *The Northwest Fur Trade, 1763–1800* (Urbana, IL, 1928), 25.
6. Fernand Ouellet, *Histoire économique et sociale du Québec, 1760–1850* (Montreal, 1966), 77.
7. Ouellet, *Histoire économique*, 104–6.
8. Michel Brunet, *Les Canadiens après la Conquête, 1759–1775* (Montreal, 1969), 173–74, 177–80.
9. Miquelon, "The Baby Family," 158.
10. Miquelon, "The Baby Family," 142.
11. The implication is unwarranted. A given economic sector can be dynamic and even produce the largest share of marketable commodities and still provide individual entrepreneurs with meagre profits. The macroeconomic level of analysis should not be confused with the microeconomic level. Jean Hamelin showed that only around 28 percent of the profits from the beaver trade remained in Canada. Since the Canadians had an assured market for beaver, one can wonder how much more profitable it was for them to deal in other peltries. See Hamelin, *Économie et Société en Nouvelle-France* (Quebec, 1960), 54–56.
12. The obvious economic explanation for the downfall of the Canadian merchants after the Conquest has to be dismissed. The liquidation of Canadian paper money by France hurt most of all those British merchants who bought it from Canadians for speculation. Canadian merchants had already compensated in part for the anticipated liquidation by raising prices during the last years of the Seven Years' War. Those Montreal merchants who had the greatest quantity of French paper were not driven out of business; on the contrary, the most prominent merchants were able to open accounts with British suppliers soon after the Conquest without too much difficulty. See José E. Igartua, "The Merchants and *Négociants* of Montreal, 1750–1775: A Study in Socio-Economic History" (Unpublished Ph.D. thesis, Michigan State University, 1974), ch. 6.
13. Franquet, *Voyages et mémoires sur le Canada en 1752–1753* (Toronto, 1968), 56.
14. For a more elaborate description of the size and the socioeconomic characteristics of the Montreal merchant community at this time, see Igartua, "The Merchants and *Négociants* of Montreal," ch. 2.
15. See H.A. Innis, *The Fur Trade in Canada*, rev. ed. (Toronto, 1956), 107–13.
16. See Abraham Rotstein, "Fur Trade and Empire: An Institutional Analysis" (Unpublished Ph.D. thesis, University of Toronto, 1967), 72.
17. Innis, *Fur Trade*, 117. For his discussion of the impact of war on the fur trade and on New France, see 114–18.
18. In theory, the French licensing system set up to restrict the trade remained in operation from its reestablishment in 1728 to the end of the French regime; only 25 *congés* were to be sold each year. In practice, military officers in the upper country could also acquire for a modest fee exclusive trade privileges for their particular area. With

some care, concluded one author, they could make an easy fortune. See Émile Salone, *La Colonisation de la Nouvelle-France* (Trois-Rivières, 1970), 390, 392–93. No clear official description of the licensing system was found for the period from 1750 to 1760, but the precise way in which the fur trade was restricted matters less than the fact of restriction.

19. On Charly see PAC, RG 4 B58, vol. 15, 19 September 1764, pass by Governor Murray to "Monsr. Louis Saint-Ange Charly [and his family] to London, in their way to France agreeable to the Treaty of Peace"; Archives Nationales du Québec à Montréal [formerly Archives judiciaires de Montréal; hereafter ANQ-M], Greffe de Pierre Panet, 16 août 1764, no. 2190. Trotier Desauniers "Dufy's" will is in ANQ-M, 29 juillet 1760, no. 1168, and Godet's will is in ANQ-M, 28 décembre 1768, no. 3140.

20. The inventory of Monière's estate is in ANQ-M, 28 décembre 1768, no. 3141; that of L'Huillier Chevalier's in ANQ-M, 15 [?] juin 1772, no. 3867.

21. See Alexander Henry, *Travels and Adventures in Canada* (Ann Arbor, University Microfilms, 1966), 191–92.

22. W.S. Wallace, *Documents Relating to the North West Company*, Appendix A ("A Biographical Dictionary of the Nor'Westers"), 456.

23. See Henry, *Travels*, 1–11, 34.

24. Henry, *Travels*, 39.

25. Henry, *Travels*, 50. Cf. the rosier picture by Creighton, *The Empire of the St. Lawrence*, 33.

26. Henry, *Travels*, 77–84. The Indians killed the British soldiers but ransomed the British traders, giving to each according to his profession.

27. Henry, *Travels*, 264–92.

28. See Wallace, *Documents*, 456; Milo M. Quaife, ed., *Alexander Henry's Travels and Adventures in the Years 1760–1776* (Chicago, 1921), xvi–xvii.

29. Henry, *Travels*, 11; Quaife, *Henry's Travels*, 12 n. 6.

30. Rich, *History of the Hudson's Bay Company*, 2: 9.

31. See PAC, C.O. 42, vol. 5, ff. 30–31, Murray's "List of Protestants in the District of Montreal," dated Quebec, 7 November 1765.

32. See Miquelon, "The Baby Family," 181–87.

33. PAC, MG 19 A1, 1, William Edgar Papers, 1: 97, F. Hamback to W. Edgar, 2 November 1766. See also 1: 95, Hamback to D. Edgar, 29 October 1766, and 1: 104–106, same to Edgar, 23 March 1767.

34. William Edgar Papers, 1: 12.

35. See William Edgar Papers, vols. 1 and 2.

36. R.H. Fleming, "Phyn, Ellice and Company of Schenectady," *Contributions to Canadian Economics* 4 (1932): 7–41.

37. See Marjorie G. Jackson, "The Beginnings of British Trade at Michilimackinac," *Minnesota History* 11 (September 1930): 252; C.W. Alvord and C.E. Carter, eds., *The New Regime, 1765–1767* (Collections of the Illinois State Historical Library, vol. 11), 300–301; Alvord and Carter, eds., *Trade and Politics, 1767–1769* (Collections of the Illinois State Historical Library, vol. 16), 382–453.

38. See "Extract of a Letter from Michilimackinac, to a Gentleman in this City, dated 30th June," in *Quebec Gazette*, 18 August 1768; see also Rich, *History of the Hudson's Bay Company* 2: 26: "The suspicions between the Pedlars [from Quebec], and their encouragements of the Indians to trick and defraud their trade rivals, especially by defaulting on payments of debt, were widespread and continuous."

39. *Quebec Gazette*, 7 January 1768.

40. Burt, *Old Province*, 1: 92.

41. The flooding of the Quebec market by British merchants was part of a larger invasion of the colonial trade in North America. See Mark Egnal and Joseph A. Ernst, "An Economic Interpretation of the American Revolution," *William and Mary Quarterly*, 3rd series, 29 (1972): 3–32.

42. Quoted in Alvord and Carter, eds., *Trade and Politics*, 288.

43. Alvord and Carter, eds., *Trade and Politics*, 38.

44. Quoted in E.E. Rich, *Montreal and the Fur Trade* (Montreal, 1966), 44.

45. These figures are somewhat distorted by the inclusion of a single large British investor, Alexander Henry, who outfitted seven canoes worth £3400 in all. See Charles E. Lart, ed., "Fur-Trade Returns, 1767," *Canadian Historical Review* 3 (December 1922): 351–58. The definition of the northwest as including Lake Huron, Lake Superior, and "the northwest by way of Lake Superior" given in Rich, *Montreal and the Fur Trade*, 36–37, was used in making these compilations. The French traders were "Deriviere," "Chenville," St. Clair, Laselle, "Guillaid [Guillet]," and "Outlass [Houtelas]."

46. See Rich, *Montreal and the Fur Trade*, 36–37.

47. Jackson, *Minnesota History*, 11: 268–69.

48. Rich, *History of the Hudson's Bay Company* 2: 68.
49. On the Monières, see Igartua, "The Merchants and *Négociants* of Montreal," ch. 2. On the Gamelins, see Antoine Champagne, *Les La Vérendrye et les postes de l'ouest* (Québec, 1968), passim.
50. See R.H. Fleming, *Contributions to Canadian Economics* 4: 13; on Baynton, Wharton and Morgan, see *The Papers of Sir William Johnson* [hereafter *Johnson Papers*], 14 vols. (Albany, 1921–1965), vols. 5, 6, 12, passim.
51. PAC, C.O. 42, vol. 2, ff. 277–80, petition of the "Merchants and Traders of Montreal" to Murray and the Council, Montreal, 20 February 1765; *Johnson Papers* 5: 807–15, memorial and petition of Detroit traders to Johnson, 22 November 1767; 12: 409–14, 1768 trade regulations with the merchants' objections.
52. See Alvord and Carter, eds., *The New Regime*, 118–19, and *Trade and Politics*, 39, 287; see also Stevens, *The Northwest Fur Trade*, 44.
53. *Johnson Papers*, 12: 517, Thomas Gage to Guy Johnson, New York, 29 May 1768.
54. *Johnson Papers* 5: 481. See also Alvord and Carter, eds., *The New Regime*, 118–19; *Johnson Papers* 5: 362; Alvord and Carter, eds., *Trade and Politics*, 39; *Johnson Papers* 5: 762–64; 12: 486–87; Stevens, *The Northwest Fur Trade*, 28.
55. PAC, C.O. 42, vol. 27, ff. 81–85, Carleton to Johnson, Quebec, 27 March 1767.
56. *Johnson Papers* 12: 372–75, Croghan to Johnson, 18 October 1767.
57. Henry, *Travels*, 71–72.
58. See PAC, C.O. 42, vol. 26, f. 13, Court of St. James, Conway [Secretary of State] to the Commandants of Detroit and Michilimackinac, 27 March 1766. See also Alvord and Carter, eds., *Trade and Politics*, 207–8, Gage to Shelburne, 12 March 1768; 239, Johnson to Gage, 8 April 1768; 375, Gage to Johnson, 14 August 1768; 378, Gage to Hillsborough, 17 August 1768; 384, Johnson to Gage, 24 August 1768; 599, Gage to Hillsborough, 9 September 1769. More than trading on his own account, Rogers was suspected of setting up an independent Illinois territory. He was eventually cleared. See "Robert Rogers," *Dictionary of American Biography*, vol. 16 (New York, 1935), 108–9, and *Johnson Papers*, vols. 5, 6, 12, 13, passim.
59. PAC, William Edgar Papers, 1: 43–44, Callender to Edgar n.p., 31 December 1763.
60. Henry, *Travels*, 191–92, 235.
61. PAC, William Edgar Papers, 1: 90, Thos. Shipboy to Rankin and Edgar, Albany, 21 August 1766.
62. William Edgar Papers, 1: 201, Benjamin Frobisher to Rankin and Edgar, Michilimackinac, 23 June 1769.
63. William Edgar Papers, 1: 104–106, F. Hamback to Edgar, 23 March 1767.
64. The most detailed account is given in Burt, *Old Province*, vol. 1, chs. 6 and 7. See also Creighton, *Empire of the St. Lawrence*, 40–48.
65. See for instance E.-Z. Massicotte, "La Bourse de Montréal sous le régime français," *The Canadian Antiquarian and Numismatic Journal*, 3rd series, 12 (1915): 26–32.
66. See Pierre Tousignant, "La Genèse et l'avènement de la Constitution de 1791" (Unpublished Ph.D. thesis, Université de Montréal, 1971).
67. See *Quebec Gazette*, 15 September 1766 and the issues from June to September 1768.
68. See *Quebec Gazette*, 26 September 1765. Tousignant, "La Genèse," pp. 21–39, points out the political significance of this letter.
69. See texts by "A MERCHANT" in the 10 and 17 December 1767 issues, and rebuttals in the 24 and 31 December 1767 and 7 and 21 January 1768 issues.
70. Tousignant, "La Genèse," 39.
71. See issues of 13 and 27 July, and 5 October 1775.
72. Canadian notables of Quebec broke with the "Old Subjects" earlier: a petition, thought to date from 1770 and signed by leading Canadians of that city, asked for the restoration of Canadian institutions. See Adam Shortt and Arthur G. Doughty, *Documents Relating to the Constitutional History of Canada*, 2nd. ed. (Ottawa, 1918) [hereafter *Docs. Const. Hist. Can.*], 1: 419–21.
73. The petition and the memorial are reproduced in *Docs. Const. Hist. Can.* 1:504–6, 508–10.
74. *Docs. Const. Hist. Can.* 1: 511. The British merchants of Montreal signed a counter-petition in January 1774, requesting the introduction of an assembly and of the laws of England. See 1: 501–502.
75. Recent historians have highlighted the influence of the military and civil administrations as sources of economic and social betterment in New France. See Guy Frégault, *Le XVIIIe siècle canadien* (Montréal, 1968), 382–84; W.J. Eccles, "The Social, Economic, and Political Significance of the Military Establishment in New France," *Canadian Historical Review* 52 (March 1971): 17–19; and Cameron Nish, *Les Bourgeois-Gentilshommes de la Nouvelle-France* (Montréal, 1968), passim.
76. See PAC, C.O. 42, vol. 24. ff. 72–73v.; ff. 95–95v; vol. 3, f. 262; *Docs. Const. Hist. Can.* 1: 504–508.
77. See *Docs. Const. Hist. Can.* 1: 504.

78. Maurice Séguin, of the History Department of the Université de Montréal, was the first to present a systematic interpretation of the Conquest as societal decapitation. His book, *L'Idée d'indépendance au Québec: Genèse et historique* (Trois-Rivières, 1968), which contains a summary of his thought, was published twenty years after its author first sketched out his thesis. Guy Frégault's *Histoire de la Nouvelle-France*, vol. 9, *La guerre de la Conquête, 1754–1760* (Montréal, 1955) is a masterful rendition of that conflict, cast as the *affrontement* of two civilizations. Michel Brunet, the most voluble of the "Montreal school" historians, has assumed the task of popularizing Séguin's thought. See Brunet, "La Conquête anglaise et la déchéance de la bourgeoisie canadienne (1760–1793)," in his *La Présence anglaise et les Canadiens* (Montréal, 1964), 48–112. Brunet developed the point further in *Les Canadiens après la Conquête*, vol. 1, *1759–1775* (Montréal, 1969). An abridged version of Brunet's position is provided in his *French Canada and the Early Decades of British Rule, 1760–1791* (Ottawa, 1963). For a review of French-Canadian historiography on the Conquest up to 1966, see Ramsay Cook, "Some French-Canadian Interpretations of the British Conquest: Une quatrième dominante de la pensée canadienne-française," Canadian Historical Association, *Historical Papers* (1966): 70–83.

Article Fourteen

The Fall of New France

Allan Greer

Built over the course of a century and a half, the French empire in North America suddenly collapsed between 1758 and 1760. The French had begun the Seven Years' War (on this continent, 1754–60) with a string of victories, coupled with devastating frontier raids mounted by Natives and French Canadians. But eventually Britain, urged on by the beleaguered Thirteen Colonies, decided on an all-out effort to crush French power in Canada. Though the conflict centred primarily on Europe (there it did actually last seven years, 1756–63) and involved clashes around the globe, Prime Minister William Pitt resolved to make the North American theatre a top priority. By the summer of 1758, some 42 000 British and colonial troops had been assembled, poised for the attack on New France. Just as significant, about one-quarter of the formidable British navy was deployed in the area, dominating the northwestern Atlantic so completely that supplies and reinforcements from France were effectively cut off. France and England had been squabbling in North America inconclusively for six decades, but now, quite suddenly, the balance of forces shifted dramatically against the French and, for the first time, the British could realistically aim, not simply at territorial gains and strategic advantages, but at total victory.

The naval blockade strangling trade into the St. Lawrence was devastating in its effects on both Canada and the *pays d'en haut*. In the Laurentian colony, its effects combined with an unfortunate series of short harvests to produce a shortage of almost all vital commodities, above all, food. At the same time, an unprecedented military build-up and the voracious appetite for supplies that it accompanied placed impossible demands on colonial supplies. Urban civilians were particularly hard hit and, in the winter of 1758–59 starvation became a serious threat. In Quebec City, it was said, "workers and artisans, ravaged by hunger, can no longer work; they are so weak they can hardly stand up." In an effort to relieve the cities and ensure supplies to

Source: Allan Greer, "The Fall of New France," *The People of New France* (Toronto: University of Toronto Press, 1997), pp. 109–21. Reprinted by permission of the publisher.

the military, squadrons of soldiers were sent into the countryside to requisition grain at the point of a gun. Meanwhile, in the *pays d'en haut*, post commanders lacked the gifts and trade goods needed to play the role of a proper "father." Moreover, the French, under the pressures of intensifying war, had been taking a high-handed approach with the Indian nations of the Great Lakes and the Ohio country, effectively abandoning the cultural compromises underpinning the "middle ground," and alienating their allies. Thus, when the British appeared on the horizon with substantial forces, most Native groups made peace with the invaders, in part in order to rid the country of the now-hated French. These defections opened the way to the British, who soon captured Detroit and the other western posts.

Meanwhile, Canada was under attack by two major armies of invasion, one of them making its laborious way up the heavily defended corridor leading north via Lake Champlain to Montreal, the other taking a seaborne route by way of the Gulf of St. Lawrence. This latter, amphibious, assault entailed a costly but successful siege of Louisbourg in 1758, followed by the siege of the hitherto impregnable defences of Quebec. Week after week in the summer of 1759, British batteries bombarded the capital without mercy, while raiding parties burned villages all up and down the St. Lawrence in defiance of then-current rules of civilized warfare. Finally, a decisive engagement on the Plains of Abraham delivered Quebec to the English. This battle, so widely known today because of its dramatic qualities, was really only one episode in a much larger campaign. Historians have pointed out that it was, in fact, a very near thing, which, with a little luck on their side, the French might well have won. But even so, would a different outcome on the Plains of Abraham have kept Canada French? Not likely. The British investment in the reduction of New France was simply overwhelming. Not one, but three armies were pressing into the colony, from the west and the south, as well as the east, and in the summer of 1760 they all bore down on the last French stronghold of Montreal. Its fate more or less sealed two years earlier, Canada was, on 9 September, finally surrendered to the invaders.

England was definitely on a winning streak in the later part of the Seven Years' War. Its European ally, Prussia, emerged victorious in central Europe, and Britain itself captured French possessions around the world: slaving stations on the coast of Africa, colonial establishments in India, and precious sugar islands in the West Indies. Then Spain entered the war on France's side, and the English promptly took Havana and Manila. In the complicated diplomatic arrangements which concluded the war (1763), Britain acquired title strictly within the realm of European imperial pretensions, of course — to most of North America. France retained fishing rights on the coast of Newfoundland, but Île Royale was annexed to Nova Scotia, and Canada was recognized as a British province. Louisiana, which had been largely untouched by the fighting, was divided: the western part, including New Orleans, went to Spain, while Britain acquired the eastern part along with formerly Spanish Florida.

And where are the people of New France in this geopolitical story of conquest and defeat? Did the social configurations sketched out in earlier sections of this book [*The People of New France*] play any part in provoking war? Nineteenth-century historians sometimes suggested that a fight to the finish between the French and the English in North America was somehow the product of essential differences in the two nationalities which led to the formation of fundamentally incompatible colonial societies, and vestiges of that view can still be found in modern interpretations. Equally influential — and just as misleading, in my opinion — is the notion that New France was doomed to be a loser in the inevitable struggle because of some sort of basic fatal flaw.

Certainly there were important differences distinguishing the French and English colonial societies in North America: differences in language, religion, political institutions, and relations between Natives and European colonists. But there was also great diversity within each of the two camps. Within the broadly delineated New France of the eighteenth century could be found the comparatively Europeanized society of Canada, with its military aristocracy; its seigneurial agrarian life; and its towns, with their diverse assortment of merchants, artisans, priests, nuns, soldiers, and officials. Île Royale, on the other hand, displayed a much more capitalist character, with fishing and trading to the fore and little trace of any feudal elements, whereas Acadia had been dominated by its free peasantry. Slavery and plantation agriculture were prominent features of life in Louisiana. And in the backcountry claimed by Louisiana, as well as Canada's *pays d'en haut*, various Aboriginal modes of existence prevailed, and the handful of French who frequented these regions had to adapt to that reality. French North America, like English North America, was not a homogeneous whole. In searching out the causes of all-out war, one might just as well point to affinities linking neighbouring sections of the rival empires Louisiana and South Carolina, Canada and New York, Île Royale and Massachusetts as attempt to find some essential cultural dichotomy.

The fact is that, through most of the colonial period, New France and English America were at peace, and when they did come to blows, it was seldom over genuinely colonial issues. Aboriginal nations such as the Mi'kmaq had basic and enduring motives for hostility toward the colonizing powers, and since the English usually posed a greater threat, they often ended up allying themselves with the French. But French Canadians had little cause, obedience to their monarch apart, for fighting New Englanders. There was always a certain amount of border skirmishing in peripheral regions of uncertain ownership, such as Newfoundland and Hudson Bay, but, by and large, the two nations colonized separate regions and had few points of friction. Historians used to believe that competition over the western fur trade drove the English and French colonizers into mortal combat, but recent research indicates that international fur trade rivalries were more a result than a cause of international hostilities; the two powers used the fur trade in an attempt to attract Native nations into their respective commercial-diplomatic orbits. Indeed, it seems quite likely that, if left to their own devices, French Canadians and Anglo-Americans would have shared the continent just as the Spanish and Portuguese shared South America, not always in peace perhaps, but without harbouring plans to destroy each other's settlements utterly.

In colonial North America, war — that is, war between English and French, though not war between colonizers and Natives — was largely a European import. Canada went to war because France went to war. Men from the Iroquoian communities of St. Lawrence, along with *troupes de la marine* and French-Canadian militia, as well as allied Natives from the *pays d'en haut*, relied mainly on guerrilla raids to harass the designated enemy to the south. As long as war was conducted mainly by North Americans, New France more than held its own; even though it was vastly outnumbered by the Anglo-Americans, authoritarian French Canada was organized for war and, more important, it could rely on Native support. Thus, the idea that defects in French colonial society preordained the defeat of 1760 are hard to credit, since Canada's military record suggests strength rather than weakness through most of the period. In a sense, that very strength itself led to the downfall, in that early French successes in the Seven Years' War helped to galvanize England and British North America into an extraordinary mobilization of forces. What sealed the doom of New France was the sudden Europeanization of the conflict in 1758. When Britain poured men, ships, and equipment into the fray, the mode of fighting changed abruptly, as did the balance of forces, and Canada's brand of frontier raiding was now of little account. In sum, New France's involvement in major war, and also its ultimate defeat, were mainly the result of European intervention; they were not determined by the shape of its colonial society.

And what of the consequences of the Conquest? Generations of Canadians, English- as well as French-speaking, have come to view this event as the central cataclysm in their country's history, a humiliating defeat which lies at the root of Quebec nationalism, and a heavy blow to the social development of French Canada which left it backward and impoverished for centuries to come. Of course, the Conquest did ultimately have far-reaching effects for Canada; without it there would never have been an English Canada, nor would there have been a binational federal state. But was French Canada humiliated by the Conquest and did it then enter a period of social disarray?

That is certainly not the way it appeared to most contemporaries in the 1760s. Then it seemed clear that England had beaten France in a war and had taken Canada as its prize. French Canadians had no reason to feel like a defeated and humbled people, and there is little indication that they did feel that way in the decades following the Conquest. There may have been some apprehension that property would be threatened, that the Catholic religion would be persecuted, or even that residents would be deported as the Acadians and the people of Île Royale had been only a few years earlier. These concerns proved groundless, however, for, with the war now at an end, Britain had no need and no desire to depopulate the colony. There were, indeed, some troublesome issues surrounding the legal system, the status of the Church, and the admission of French Canadians to public office. Moreover, some residents — mostly government officials, merchants, and military officers — quit the colony as soon as it passed into Britain's empire, though it is an exaggeration to refer to this exodus as a social "decapitation," particularly when many of the emigrants were metropolitan French who would likely have left Canada even if it had remained under the rule of France. As a colony, New France had always been dominated by European intendants, bishops, and, to a large extent, judges and merchants. After 1760 it would be ruled by a different set of outsiders who happened to be British. This did not seem remarkable to most contemporaries, for nationalism — the belief that government and governed should have the same ethnic and linguistic identity — was not then a powerful force anywhere in the world.

The idea that French Canada was a conquered nation rather than a ceded colony was the product of a very different epoch, one that began almost a century after the conclusion of the Seven Years' War. Between the Conquest and the emergence of the Myth of the Conquest stretched a long and eventful period of history filled with momentous developments in Canada and around the Atlantic world. The American Revolution, the Haitian Revolution, and the Latin American wars of independence brought European imperial rule to an end throughout most of the western hemisphere. With the French Revolution and the wars of Napoleon, *anciens régimes* crumbled and the "principle of nationality" gained adherents across Europe. French Canada felt the force of these global developments. One result was the nationalist-democratic Rebellion of 1837–38, a revolt against British rule inspired by a republican vision of national independence (not, as some have suggested, by any sort of desire to return to Bourbon rule). Only after the defeat of this insurrection, and after the predominantly French portion of Canada (Lower Canada) had been yoked politically to English-speaking parts of British North America, did chastened and more conservative elements of the French-Canadian elite begin to speak longingly of the glories of New France. Along with the idealization of the supposedly conservative and Catholic French regime went a view of French–English conflict as inveterate, enduring, and unchanging. This idea that "the English" were the enemy and that the Conquest had been a social disaster that ruined French Canada's development began to enjoy wide appeal in the second half of the nineteenth century; this was when the French were losing political influence to a rapidly expanding English Canada, and when ordinary French Canadians found their lives disrupted by a capitalism that seemed to speak only English and to benefit only anglophones. The Myth of the Conquest, the belief that the cession constituted an epoch-making tragedy with social as well as political dimensions, was a product of French Canada's social stresses in the 1860s, not the 1760s. And, as the political economy of Canadian capitalism continued to develop to the disadvantage of French Quebec, the Myth of the Conquest continued to hold sway throughout the twentieth century.

Canada in the immediate wake of the Conquest was certainly a traumatized society, but the trauma it suffered had been caused much more by the war itself than by the cession to Britain. Especially in Quebec City and its region, the physical destruction had been immense, not to mention the economic dislocation occasioned by the blockade and famine. To make matters worse, the French government's partial renunciation of its debts wrecked many colonial fortunes. Rebuilding took years. But the Conquest as such — the transfer of New France from one empire to another — struck at French-Canadian society only in limited and selective ways.

For most people, and in most aspects of existence, the advent of British rule made little difference. The habitants — which is to say, the great majority of French Canadians — continued their agrarian way of life, colonizing ever-expanding territories on the edges of the St. Lawrence valley. Basic family self-sufficiency remained central, but increasingly habitants lucky enough to possess prime wheat-growing lands grew substantial surpluses for sale overseas. Access to British imperial markets helped stimulate this development, but the trend toward export agriculture had been set long before the Conquest. Tithes and seigneurial exactions continued more or less as before, though some of the seigneurs were now English merchants and officers who had purchased seigneuries from emigrating French seigneurs. Over the decades, seigneurial rents tended to bear down more heavily on the peasantry as land became more scarce and agriculture more lucrative, but, again, the tendency under the British regime was the culmination of developments begun under the French regime; the Conquest was largely incidental.

At the top levels of French-Canadian society, the change in imperial masters posed serious problems. The clergy were no longer subsidized, nor were they integrated into the state, now officially Protestant. However, the Catholic Church weathered the storm quite nicely, quietly developing a working relationship with a succession of British governors and discovering, for the rest, the benefits of ecclesiastical independence beyond the reach of their Most Catholic Majesties of France. The *noblesse* was damaged badly by the elimination of the colonial military force and of the officers' careers it had come to depend on. The rising value of seigneurial incomes helped to cushion the blow, but nobles could no longer look to government for preferment as they had in the past. Canadian merchants were also damaged by the Conquest. Traders from Britain and the Thirteen Colonies swarmed into the St. Lawrence Valley hard on the heels of the conquering armies, bringing low-priced merchandise that undercut resident merchants. Business connections with Britain and contacts with the occupying army were at a premium now that Canada's commerce had to be redirected into a different imperial system, and so French-Canadian importers and exporters were immediately placed at a disadvantage. The fur traders of Montreal held out for a time, but, within twenty years, anglophone capitalists dominated even that branch of commerce.

Was the Conquest good or bad for women? In most essential respects, it seems to have left power relations between the sexes unchanged. French-Canadian civil law, including the rules defining marital property rights and inheritance, remained in place after an initial period of uncertainty following the cession. Visitors from overseas — British now, rather than French — still remarked on the independent and domineering character of the Canadian ladies. There were certainly major realignments of gender ideology in the nineteenth century, as public life was, with increasing insistence, declared off limits to women. This occurred long after the Conquest, however, and the change clearly mirrored widespread international trends, discernible in France itself, as well as in England and English-speaking North America.

The Iroquois, Huron, and other Natives resident in the St. Lawrence colony certainly suffered as a result of the Conquest; or, to put it more accurately, the conclusion of French–English conflict reduced the Natives' value as military auxiliaries and gave them less bargaining power and room to manoeuvre. Officials under the British regime wished to retain the allegiance of the local Aboriginal population, particularly as war once again loomed: against the United States and France. After the 1820s, peace seemed more assured and Iroquois assistance less necessary, and subsidies meant to reward allegiance were phased out. Encroachment on their land base at Kahnawaké and Oka undermined the Natives' agrarian economy, just at a time when government tribute was disappearing. Many men sought external income working in the northwest fur trade and the forest industry, but impoverishment was the fate of these Native communities in the post-Conquest era.

In the *pays d'en haut*, war's end brought a painful transition as options suddenly closed down for the Aboriginal nations of the west. The Seven Years' War had kept American settlers and land speculators at bay, but soon they were pouring over the Appalachians in spite of Britain's efforts to reserve the territory to Amerindians. Moreover, the British military, after dislodging the French from Detroit and other posts in the region, settled in as an army of occupation in spite of Native protests. They also cut off "presents," the tribute previously offered as a token of alliance. The overall refusal of the British to play the role of a good alliance "father" provoked the reconstitution of an anti-British alliance of many western tribes which, under Pontiac's leadership, came close to driving the British out of the region. One enduring legacy of the period of French ascendancy in the *pays d'en haut* was the tradition of Pan-Indian alliances. Creating unity out of these culturally diverse and politically fragmented groups was exceedingly difficult, but, from Pontiac's time until the early nineteenth century, a series of concerted efforts did help slow the Anglo-American onslaught. The fact that the British, now embroiled in conflict with their colonists, were prevailed on to take up aspects of Onontio's role was certainly a factor, but the impulse to resist came largely from the Natives themselves.

New France did indeed disappear, both in its narrow "Canadian" sense and in its wider, continental meaning, encompassing the *pays d'en haut* and the scattered enclaves of French settlement. After the Conquest, the Maritime region took on a distinctly British character. The residents of Île Royale were all deported, though with less brutality than the Acadian removal a few years earlier. Soon Yankee settlers from New England spread through the region, followed by British immigrants and Loyalist refugees; when Acadians began to straggle back years later, they found themselves geographically, culturally, and politically marginalized. In Louisiana, the French and African elements of colonial society, along with the institution of slavery, persisted under Spain's rule. The arrival of Acadian refugees to colonize the bayous of the lower Mississippi only reinforced the French quality of the colony. Under Napoleon, France repossessed Louisiana, then promptly sold it to the young American republic. Society was thoroughly Americanized in the nineteenth century, though French and Creole ways subsisted as picturesque folkloric vestiges.

If we were to seek for the legacy of New France, we might find it, at the most superficial level, in the French place-names — Coeur d'Alene, Terre Haute, Port Mouton — strewn across North America and regularly mispronounced by the current inhabitants. It might also be found in the various pockets in Canada and the United States where French is still spoken. More significantly, of course, the Canadian settlement along the banks of the St. Lawrence established frameworks — language, customs, law — for the development of modern Quebec (not that one would wish to portray French Quebec as a mere survival left over from the French regime; contemporary Quebec has been shaped by its colonial past no more and no less than Connecticut or Ontario). There is a third aspect to the legacy of New France, broader in scope and more profound in its implications than the other two mentioned so far: that is its role as a critical part of the colonial history of North America generally.

The thrust of this book [*The People of New France*] has been to present the people of New France as participants in a momentous and multidimensional process of colonization, one in which mere "Frenchness" is only part of the story. In the seventeenth and eighteenth centuries,

Catholic immigrants from France, working often in close relations with Natives, blacks, and Protestants, reconstituted a version of European society on the banks of the St. Lawrence. The settler society of "Canada" spawned smaller French colonies, none of them homogeneously French, in the Great Lakes, the Mississippi, and the Maritimes. Through the process of expansion, the French collided with, traded with, fought, wooed, and allied themselves with dozens of Aboriginal peoples, from the Arctic to the Gulf of Mexico. This was one element, though a crucially important one, of the broad process of colonization which also involved other Natives of North America, as well as English, Spanish, and Dutch settlers, and enslaved Africans. In that it constituted, not simply a community of transplanted Europeans, but a complicated pattern of Native–European interaction over a vast terrain, New France shaped the destinies of a continent.

Topic Seven

The Impact of the American Revolution on the Maritime Colonies

Loyalist immigrants travelling to settle in Canada. Reconstruction by C.W. Jefferys.

Ironically, Britain's success in expelling France from North America contributed to its own expulsion from the Thirteen Colonies only 15 years later. In the minds of many American colonists, the removal of the French threat from Quebec and Louisbourg ended the need for Britain in North America. This realization, along with a growing sense of nationalism among the Thirteen Colonies, led to the demand for greater self-government. Britain's attempt to tax the colonies finally led to open rebellion. The first armed clash at Lexington, Massachusetts, in mid-April 1775, officially began the American Revolution.

The Nova Scotians had to make a difficult decision: to support Britain, join the American cause, or remain neutral. Three-quarters of Nova Scotia's roughly 20 000 settlers in 1775 were New Englanders with strong economic and family ties with the New England colonies. This being the case, why did they choose to remain loyal to the Crown? George A. Rawlyk offers an explanation for their loyalty in "The American Revolution and Nova Scotia Reconsidered."

During the American Revolution, thousands of American farmers, craftsmen, and small merchants, as well as large landowners and government officials, sided with the Crown. After Britain's defeat, about 80 000 of these United Empire Loyalists chose, or were forced, to depart with the British garrisons, and more than half of them settled in two of the remaining British colonies to the north, Nova Scotia and Quebec. Approximately 30 000 went to Nova Scotia, almost doubling the size of the existing population; about 5000 came to the St. Lawrence Valley, doubling, perhaps even tripling, the English-speaking population there, from 4 or 5 percent to 10 or 15 percent of the total population; and nearly 10 000 settled in the western portion of the Province of Quebec, which became Upper Canada in 1791. The Loyalist migration led to the founding of two new colonies, New Brunswick and Upper Canada. In "The Family in Exile: Loyalist Social Values after the Revolution," Ann Gorman Condon examines the personal bonds and ideals that characterized the first two generations of Loyalist families in Nova Scotia and New Brunswick. How did the exile experience help to produce a special Loyalist culture?

For a good overview of this period, consult the relevant chapters in Philip A. Buckner and John G. Reid, eds., *The Atlantic Region to Confederation: A History* (Toronto: University of Toronto Press, 1994); see, in particular, the essay by J.M. Bumsted, "1763–1783: Resettlement and Rebellion," pp. 156–83.

The classic account of Nova Scotia's response to the revolutionary struggle in the Thirteen Colonies is John Bartlet Brebner's *Neutral Yankees of Nova Scotia* (Toronto: McClelland and Stewart, 1969 [1937]). For a history of Nova Scotia–New England relations, see George Rawlyk, *Nova Scotia's Massachusetts: A Study of Massachusetts–Nova Scotia Relations, 1630 to 1784* (Montreal/Kingston: McGill-Queen's University Press, 1973). Also useful are *Revolution Rejected, 1775–1776*, ed. George A. Rawlyk (Scarborough, ON: Prentice-Hall, 1968), and the essays in three collections of articles by Margaret Conrad: *They Planted Well: New England Planters in Maritime Canada* (Fredericton: Acadiensis Press, 1988); *Making Adjustments: Change and Continuity in Planter Nova Scotia, 1759–1800* (Fredericton: Acadiensis Press, 1991); and *Intimate Relations: Family and Community in Planter Nova Scotia, 1759–1800* (Fredericton: Acadiensis Press, 1995). She has also edited, with Barry Moody, *Planter Links: Community and Culture in Colonial Nova Scotia* (Fredericton: Acadiensis Press, 2001).

J.M. Bumsted's *Henry Alline* (Toronto: University of Toronto Press, 1971) reviews the career of the leader of an important religious revival in Nova Scotia during the years of the American Revolution. George A. Rawlyk examines the evolution of radical evangelicalism after the American Revolution in *The Canada Fire: Radical Evangelicalism in British North America, 1775–1812* (Montreal/Kingston: McGill-Queen's University Press, 1994).

The anthology *The United Empire Loyalists*, ed. L.S.F. Upton (Toronto: Copp Clark, 1967) provides a general overview. Three general studies of the Loyalists are Wallace Brown and Hereward Senior, *Victorious in Defeat: The Loyalists in Canada* (Toronto: Methuen, 1984);

Christopher Moore, *The Loyalists: Revolution, Exile, Settlement* (Toronto: McClelland and Stewart, 1994); and Ann Gorman Condon, *The Envy of the American States: The Loyalist Dream for New Brunswick* (Fredericton: New Ireland Press, 1984). Barry K. Wilson has written a biography of the most reviled Loyalist in the United States, *Benedict Arnold: A Traitor in our Midst* (Montreal/Kingston: McGill-Queen's University Press, 2000). Arnold spent six years in St. John's after the Revolution.

Neil MacKinnon reviews the impact of the Loyalists on Nova Scotia in *The Unfriendly Soil: The Loyalist Experience in Nova Scotia, 1783–1791* (Montreal/Kingston: McGill-Queen's University Press, 1986). On the background of the American Loyalists, see W.H. Nelson, *The American Tory* (Toronto: Oxford, 1961). For information on Black Loyalists who came to Nova Scotia after the American Revolution, see James W. St. G. Walker's *The Black Loyalists: The Search for a Promised Land in Nova Scotia and Sierra Leone, 1783–1870* (Toronto: University of Toronto Press, 1992 [1976, Longman Group and Dalhousie University Press]).

Robert S. Allen has compiled a useful bibliography, *Loyalist Literature: An Annotated Bibliographical Guide to the Writings on the Loyalists of the American Revolution* (Toronto: Dundurn Press, 1982). For books and articles produced after 1981, consult Bruce Bowden, "The Bicentennial Legacy — A Second Loyalist Revival," *Ontario History* 77 (1985): 65–74. On the Loyalist tradition in Ontario, see Norman Knowles, *Inventing the Loyalists: The Ontario Loyalist Tradition and the Creation of Usable Pasts* (Toronto: University of Toronto Press, 1997).

WEBLINKS

Newfoundland and the American Revolutionary War, 1775–1783
http://www.heritage.nf.ca/exploration/amer_rev.html

A detailed examination of the impact of the American Revolution on Newfoundland and Labrador.

Black Loyalists
http://collections.ic.gc.ca/blackloyalists

A digital collection describing the experiences of Black Loyalists who came to Canada following the American Revolution. Digitized journal entries, letters, and additional documents make up the collection.

Edward Winslow Letters
http://atlanticportal.hil.unb.ca/acva/en/winslow/index.php

A searchable database of letters and diaries written by the Loyalist Winslow family who settled in Nova Scotia after the American Revolution.

Post-War Settlement Documents
http://www.royalprovincial.com/genealogy/settle/settle.shtml

Transcriptions of land grant warrants and other documents regarding Loyalists settling in the Maritimes and Upper Canada after the American Revolution.

Loyalist Settlement
http://www.canadiana.org/citm/themes/pioneers/pioneers4_e.html

Digitized legal documents and correspondence of Loyalist settlers.

United Empire Loyalists
http://www.uelac.org/index.html

As the website of the United Empire Loyalists' Association of Canada, the site contains Loyalist histories and links to Loyalist print resources.

Article Fifteen

The American Revolution and Nova Scotia Reconsidered

George A. Rawlyk

On the eve of the American Revolution, Nova Scotia was little more than a political expression for a number of widely scattered and isolated communities. These stretched from Halifax to Maugerville on the St. John River and to the tiny outpost of Passamaquoddy on the St. Croix. At the end of the Seven Years' War many land-hungry settlers from Rhode Island, New Hampshire, Massachusetts, and Connecticut pushed up into the fertile regions bordering the Bay of Fundy which had been abandoned by the Acadians when they were expelled from the peninsula in 1755. In 1775 Nova Scotia had a population of only approximately 20 000 inhabitants,[1] three-quarters of whom were New Englanders with strong economic, cultural, and family ties with their former homeland.[2]

In spite of the fact that Nova Scotia was virtually New England's northeastern frontier and was peopled by a majority of recently arrived New Englanders,[3] the colony refused in 1775 and 1776 to join in attempting to shatter the framework of the British colonial system. Instead, most of the inhabitants, especially the New Englanders, endeavoured to pursue a policy of neutrality, even though their moral support was firmly behind the "rebels." It is interesting to note that this policy of neutrality was exactly the same policy that the New Englanders severely condemned when it had been adopted by the Acadians two decades earlier. However, toward the end of the Revolution, the sympathies of the neutral New Englanders, largely as the result of serious depredations committed by American privateers throughout Nova Scotia from 1777 to 1782, shifted towards Great Britain.[4]

Why did Nova Scotia not join the Thirteen Colonies in attempting to break away from Britain in 1775 and 1776? Three distinct schools of thought have emerged in the effort to answer this question. First, the proponents of the "Halifax-merchant" school have stressed that the influential Halifax merchants were directly responsible for keeping Nova Scotia loyal to the Crown.[5] The merchants, believing that the Revolution was a Heaven-sent opportunity to supplant the New England colonies in the West Indian trade, and also that in the long run their colony would gain more than it would lose in retaining political and economic ties with Britain, were able to impose their will upon the other inhabitants. This is indeed an interesting interpretation, but one without any real foundation, since in 1775 the population of Halifax was only 1800 and the influence of the Halifax merchants was largely confined to the area of the Bedford Basin.[6] It is clear that their economic ties with Britain were strong, but it is just as clear that they were in no effective position to impose their will upon the other Nova Scotians,

Source: George A. Rawlyk, "The American Revolution and Nova Scotia Reconsidered," *Dalhousie Review* 43, 3 (Autumn 1963): 379–394. Reprinted by permission.

who in actual fact reacted violently to the merchant clique that was attempting to manipulate the economic and political life of the colony.

Second, W.B. Kerr, who has written far more about Nova Scotia during the Revolutionary period than any other historian, has strongly argued that as early as 1765 it was inevitable that Nova Scotia would remain loyal to George III. Kerr maintains that there was an almost total absence of "national sentiment"[7] among the New Englanders of Nova Scotia and that, because of this lack of "nationalism,"[8] there was very little popular support for the revolutionary cause in Nova Scotia.[9] It appears that Kerr has clearly underestimated the general significance of the widespread sympathy for revolutionary principles. This feeling was prevalent throughout Nova Scotia, with the notable exception of Halifax, in 1775 and 1776. Moreover, he has failed to draw sufficient attention to the profound impact that the isolation of most of the Nova Scotian settlements and the British control of the North Atlantic had upon seriously weakening the indigenous Revolutionary movement.

Third, J.B. Brebner, in his excellent work, *The Neutral Yankees of Nova Scotia*, has asserted that the Revolutionary movement failed in Nova Scotia because "the sympathizers with rebellion among the outlying populace could make no headway because their friends in the rebellious Colonies had no navy and because they themselves could not assemble from the scattered settlements an effective force for unassisted revolt."[10] Brebner's is certainly the most satisfactory answer to the original question regarding Nova Scotia and the Revolution. A careful and critical examination of events in the Chignecto region of Nova Scotia in the years 1775 and 1776 will not only serve to prove the validity of Brebner's thesis, but will also cast a considerable amount of light upon the relations between Nova Scotia and the colonies to the south during a most critical period.

The Isthmus of Chignecto provided the stage upon which a somewhat inconsequential scene from the American Revolutionary drama was played. The Eddy Rebellion of 1776 had most of the characteristics of a tragic comedy; a glorious failure, it was nevertheless accompanied by death and destruction.

The Chignecto Isthmus is a narrow neck of land joining the peninsula of Nova Scotia to the North American mainland. Roughly ten miles in width and twenty in length, the Isthmus is bordered on the northeast by Baie Verte, on the southwest by the Cumberland Basin, and on the northwest and southeast by the Sackville and Amherst Ridges, respectively. J.C. Webster, one of New Brunswick's outstanding historians, has asserted that "no area of its [Chignecto's] size anywhere in America has a greater or more varied wealth of historical memories and traditions."[11] There is much evidence to support Webster's sweeping generalization.

The vacuum created by the expulsion of the majority of the Acadians from the fertile Isthmus in 1755 was quickly filled at the end of the Seven Years' War by settlers from New England.[12] Unlike the Acadians, these men energetically began to clear and to cultivate the ridge lands, which had a heavy forest cover.[13] Only after many frustrating failures were the New Englanders able to master marsh agriculture.[14] From 1772 to 1775 they sullenly observed the arrival of over 500 Yorkshire immigrants seeking "a better livelihood"[15] in the New World. These newcomers had been recruited by the aggressive lieutenant governor of Nova Scotia, Michael Francklin.[16]

Thus in 1775 the general Chignecto Isthmus region contained three important elements within its population. The New Englanders were the most numerous, but the Yorkshiremen were not too far behind. Together these two groups numbered 220 families.[17] The third element was the Acadian; there were 30 Acadian families, most of the members of which worked on the land belonging to the English-speaking farmers.[18]

There was considerable friction and ill-feeling between the New Englanders and the newcomers from the north of England on the one hand, and between the former and the Halifax government on the other. Most of the New Englanders detested their new neighbours, not only because the Yorkshiremen had settled on land that the New Englanders had long coveted and considered to be rightfully theirs, but also because the outlook of the Englishmen was almost diametrically opposite to that of the Americans. The Yorkshiremen were Methodists closely tied to the mother country and all she represented, while the New Englanders were Congregationalists who had been greatly influenced by the North American environment and whose ties with the mother country were extremely tenuous. The old world was in conflict with the new on this narrow neck of land.

The New Englanders, moreover, were greatly dissatisfied with the Halifax government. Had not Francklin encouraged the Yorkshiremen to settle in the Isthmus? Furthermore, the New Englanders reacted violently to the fact that a small clique of Halifax merchants controlled the legislative and executive functions of government,[19] stubbornly refusing to grant to the New Englanders the right of "township form of government," which Governor Lawrence had promised them in 1758 and 1759.[20]

A spark was needed to set the kindling discontent ablaze. The American Revolution provided the spark, but the fire was quickly and easily extinguished before it could spread and result in any serious damage.

The centre of organized activity against Nova Scotia during the first years of the Revolution was the tiny lumbering outpost of Machias, a few miles west of the St. Croix River.[21] Most of the inhabitants wanted to grow rich by sacking the prosperous Nova Scotian settlements, particularly Halifax. These freebooters, these eighteenth-century filibusters, unsuccessfully endeavoured to hide their real, selfish motive beneath a veneer of concern for Revolutionary principles.

In the summer of 1775 they proposed to General Washington to invade Nova Scotia if supported by a force of 1000 soldiers and four armed vessels.[22] When Washington was asked to act upon this bold plan in August, he tactfully refused; all available men and supplies were needed for the proposed Quebec invasion. His reasoned arguments justifying his refusal are of considerable consequence since they explain why Washington refused to mount any kind of offensive against Nova Scotia in 1775 and 1776:

> As to the Expedition proposed against Nova Scotia by the Inhabitants of Machias, I cannot but applaud their Spirit and Zeal; but, after considering the Reasons offered for it, there are Several objections . . . which seem to me unanswerable. I apprehend such an Enterprise inconsistent with the General Principal upon which the Colonies have proceeded. That Province has not acceded, it is true, to the Measures of Congress; and therefore, they have been excluded from all Commercial Intercourse with the other Colonies; But they have not Commenced Hostilities against them, nor are any to be apprehended. To attack *them*, therefore, is a Measure of Conquest, rather than Defence, and may be attended with very dangerous consequences. It might, perhaps, be easy, with the force proposed, to make an Incursion into the Province and overawe those of the Inhabitants who are Inimical to our cause; and, for a short time prevent the Supplying the Enemy with Provisions; but the same Force must continue to produce any lasting Effects. As to the furnishing Vessels of Force, you, Gentlemen, will anticipate me, in pointing out our weakness and the Enemy's Strength at Sea. There would be great Danger that, with the best preparation we could make, they would fall an easy prey either to the Men of War of that Station [Halifax] or some who would be detach'd from Boston.[23]

Washington was no doubt right in the long run, but the inhabitants of Machias almost intuitively realized that in the summer of 1775 Nova Scotia was ripe for plucking from the British colonial tree. American economic pressure had resulted in a serious recession,[24] Governor Legge was alienating leading elements of the population, and the exploits of the Revolution had captured the imagination of the New Englanders.[25] In addition, there were only 36 British regulars guarding Halifax,[26] and Legge, who seriously believed that the New Englanders "were rebels to the man," sadly observed that "the fortifications [of Halifax] were in a dilapidated state, the batteries . . . dismantled, the gun-carriages decayed, the guns on the ground."[27] If the men from Machias had had their way, the invading force would have been enthusiastically welcomed and openly supported by the vast majority of "Yankees" and would have easily gained control of the colony. However, the lack of suitable land communications between the various settlements in Nova Scotia, as well as between Nova Scotia and the other colonies, together with the British control of the Atlantic, would have probably forced the American troops to abandon Nova Scotia after a brief occupation. Washington's refusal to attack Nova Scotia when it was ripe for conquest and the arrival of military reinforcements in Halifax in October[28] virtually made certain that the colony would remain within the framework of the British colonial system during the war years.

In the summer months an indigenous revolutionary movement came into being in the Chignecto region.[29] It was led by John Allan, a Scot who had been won over to the American revolutionary cause, and Jonathan Eddy, who had left Massachusetts to settle in the Isthmus after the Seven Years' War. Sam Rogers, Zebulon Rowe, Obadiah Ayer, and William Howe, among others, all respected and prosperous New Englanders, supported Allan and Eddy. These men were greatly encouraged by the successful sacking in August of Fort Frederick, a tiny British military outpost at the mouth of the Saint John River, by a small Machias force,[30] and also by the bold pronouncement of the inhabitants of Maugerville in favour of the Revolution. The Maugerville settlers declared that they were willing "to submit ourselves to the government of the Massachusetts Bay and that we are ready with our lives and fortunes to share with them the event of the present struggle for liberty, however God in his providence may order it."[31]

Towards the end of November, Allan, Eddy, and their not insignificant following were given an excellent opportunity to precipitate a crisis that could have conceivably led to a successful rebellion. The long-simmering discontent with the government authorities finally boiled over when the assembly, controlled by the small Halifax merchant clique with strong commercial ties with Britain, passed two acts, one to call out a fifth of the militia, the other to impose a tax for its support.[32] Almost immediately the two bills were loudly denounced throughout the colony, but especially in the Chignecto region. Allan and Eddy, instead of quickly harnessing the deep dissatisfaction within the framework of armed rebellion, decided to widen first the popular basis of their support by sending a rather mildly worded yet firm protest against the two bills to Governor Legge. In the protest, which was eventually signed by almost 250 inhabitants including many Yorkshiremen, the Chignecto settlers objected to the new tax and to the possibility of being forced to "march into different parts in arms against their friends and relations."[33] Allan and Eddy had succeeded in gaining much popular support for their attack upon the Halifax government, but at the moment when they attempted to use this support to emulate the example of the colonies in revolt, Legge suddenly pulled the rug from under their unsuspecting feet. Realizing the seriousness of the discontent as reflected in the Chignecto petition, the governor promptly suspended the two contentious acts. In so doing, Legge had removed the catalyst from the potential revolutionary situation not only in the Isthmus but throughout Nova Scotia.

Failing to grasp the significance of Legge's clever manoeuvre, Allan and Eddy decided during the first weeks of January 1776, that the time was propitious for fomenting an insurrection. Nothing could have been further from the truth. Having won the support of the Acadians, but the equally enthusiastic disapprobation of the Yorkshiremen, Allan and Eddy decided that before taking any further steps on the road to rebellion it was first imperative to sound out carefully the general feeling of the mass of New Englanders towards the proposed vague plan.

The two leaders were genuinely shocked to discover that the vast majority of New Englanders, even though they "would have welcomed an army of invasion,"[34] stubbornly refused to support the planned insurrection. Ground between the millstones of contending forces, most of the Chignecto New Englanders, as well as those throughout the colony, had decided to walk the tightrope of neutrality until it was clear that a strong rebel invading force would be able to gain effective control of Nova Scotia. Allan and Eddy were forced to alter drastically their proposed policy; they decided to petition General Washington and the Continental Congress to send an "army of liberation" to Nova Scotia. The Machias plan of August 1775 had been resurrected.

Jonathan Eddy, with a band of fourteen men, had set out in February from Chignecto to persuade Washington and the Continental Congress to invade Nova Scotia. On March 27, Eddy met with the American general at Cambridge.[35] Washington carefully considered Eddy's often illogical arguments, but believing that the British forces that had abandoned Boston[36] ten days earlier were now in Halifax, the general informed the ambassador that "in the present uncertain state of things . . . a much more considerable force [than Eddy had even requested] would be of no avail."[37] Washington reaffirmed the policy he had first enunciated on hearing of the Machias plan in August of the preceding year.[38] The disillusioned Eddy next went to the Continental Congress in Philadelphia, but as he expected, here too his urgent appeal fell on unresponsive ears.[39] After his return to the Isthmus in May it was decided that, as a last resort, the government of Massachusetts should be approached for military aid. The persistent Eddy, accompanied by Howe, Rogers, and Rowe, immediately set sail for Boston.

During the months of January and February the Halifax government had been strangely indifferent to developments in the Chignecto Isthmus. The loyalist leaders, Charles Dixon and the Rev. John Eagleson, had bombarded the governor and his Executive Council with frantic letters.[40] A delegation had been sent to General Washington by the New Englanders;[41] and on hearing a rumour that the American army had captured Bunker Hill, the supporters of Allan and Eddy had procured "a chaise and six horses, postillion and a flag of liberty, and drove about the isthmus, proclaiming the news and blessings of liberty."[42] Dixon and Eagleson demanded immediate government action. In March the Executive Council resolved "that the lieutenant-governor [Francklin] be desired to proceed, as soon as possible to [Chignecto] . . . and there make a strict inquiry into the behavior and conduct of the inhabitants, and to make report thereof to the governor; also, that he will apprehend all persons, who, on due proof, shall be found guilty of any rebellious and treasonable transactions."[43] Francklin, however, was able to accomplish absolutely nothing. It was not until June that the government exerted some semblance of authority on the troubled Isthmus. This delay was at least partly the result of the recall of Legge in May and his replacement by Lieutenant-Colonel Arbuthnot.[44] In June, 200 Royal Fencibles[45] under the command of Lieutenant-Colonel Joseph Gorham were sent to occupy Fort Cumberland, which had been abandoned by the British eight years earlier.[46] Fort Cumberland, the reconstructed French Fort Beauséjour, was strategically located at the extreme southern tip of the Fort Cumberland Ridge which, together with the Fort Lawrence Ridge, cuts through the Chignecto marshlands until it almost touches the waters of the Bay of Fundy. Gorham found the fort in a state of serious disrepair. He reported that "the face of the Bastions, Curtains, etc., by being so long exposed to the heavy rains and frost were bent down to such a slope that one might with ease ascend any part of the fort."[47] Gorham set about repairing the fort, and he went out of his way to overlook what he considered to be the harmless activities of the energetic American sympathizers. He hoped that a simple show of strength would completely undermine the position held by the Eddy–Allan faction.

It was not until July that the Halifax authorities, at last convinced of the seriousness of the revolutionary movement in the Isthmus, considered it necessary to strike against the leaders of the "American Party." A proclamation was issued offering a reward of £200 for the capture of

Eddy and £100 for Allan, Howe, and Rogers.[48] On hearing that he was a man with a price on his head, Allan decided to join his friends in Massachusetts and left a committee in charge of "the revolutionary interests."[49]

Eddy was unsuccessful in his attempt to persuade the General Court of Massachusetts to send a military expedition "supplied with some necessaries, as provisions and ammunition . . . [to] destroy those [Nova Scotian] forts and relieve our brethren and friends."[50] Nevertheless, he had not entirely failed. He was promised sufficient ammunition and supplies to equip properly whatever force he himself could muster. Eddy immediately rushed off to Machias, where he knew there was a group of men still vitally interested in attacking Nova Scotia. By carefully playing on their cupidity, Eddy was able to recruit 28 men from Machias.[51] On August 11, just as the invading army was embarking, Allan arrived. Fully aware of the weakness of the revolutionary movement on the Isthmus, Allan endeavoured in vain to dissuade Eddy from carrying out his rash and hopeless plan. Eddy refused to come to grips with the hard facts of reality; he hoped that his force would build up like a giant snowball at Passamaquoddy and Maugerville and that the Chignecto New Englanders would eagerly rally to his banner. He seemed to believe that it would be only a matter of time before his liberating army would force the British to abandon "New England's Outpost."[52]

At Passamaquoddy, a few miles to the east of Machias, Eddy added seven new recruits and then sailed to Maugerville in three whale boats.[53] At the settlement on the upper Saint John River he found the inhabitants "almost universally to be hearty in the cause,"[54] but was able to enlist only 27 settlers and 16 Indians.[55] Eddy's liberating army, now numbering some 80 men, returned to the mouth of the Saint John River to await the arrival of the promised ammunition and supplies from Boston.[56] There was an unexpected prolonged delay, and the force was unable to move eastward until the last week of October. On October 29, Eddy's men easily captured fourteen of Gorham's troops who were stationed at the military outpost of Shepody, to the south of present-day Moncton.[57] The invaders[58] then swung sharply to the north and made their way up the Petitcodiac and Memramcook rivers to the Acadian settlement of Memramcook, where Eddy had no trouble whatsoever in persuading a number of Acadians to support him.[59] From Memramcook, on November 5, Eddy and his men marched eastward toward their immediate objective — Fort Cumberland.[60]

The supporters of Allan and Eddy on the Isthmus loudly "expressed their Uneasiness at seeing so few [invaders] . . . and those unprovided with Artillery."[61] They vehemently argued that, taking everything into consideration, there was no possible chance of success. Even if Fort Cumberland were captured, and this was highly unlikely, British reinforcements would readily rout Eddy's motley collection of undisciplined freebooters, Indians, and Acadians. Eddy was forced to resort to outright intimidation and to false promises in order to win the unenthusiastic support of his friends. His policy was objectively described by his associate Allan:

> That they [Chignecto New Englanders] had supply'd the Enemys of America which had much displeased the States. That the Congress doubted their integrity, that if they would not rouse themselves and oppose the British power in that province [Nova Scotia] they would be looked upon as enemys and should the country be reduced by the States they would be treated as conquered people and that if they did not Incline to do something he [Eddy] would return and report them to the States. But if they would now assert their rights publickly against the King's Govt, he was then Come to help them and in Fifteen days Expected a reinforcement of a large body of men.[62]

These reinforcements existed only in Eddy's active imagination.

Only 50 New Englanders, against their better judgement, rallied to Eddy's banner, and they were joined a short time later by 27 men from the Cobequid region of Nova Scotia.[63]

The invading army now numbered roughly 180 men.[64] Eddy must be given a considerable amount of credit for using his relatively small force to gain virtual control of the entire Chignecto Isthmus, except, of course, for Fort Cumberland. Most of the Yorkshiremen, fearing the destruction of their property if they supported Gorham, quickly surrendered their guns and ammunition to the invaders.[65] It should be noted that well over half of the New Englanders supported neither Eddy nor Gorham, but instead carefully pursued a policy of neutrality.

Eddy was not a demagogue, nor was he a megalomaniac. He was convinced that all ties with Britain should be severed, and his fanatical enthusiasm for the revolutionary cause seriously dulled his already undeveloped sense of military strategy. In spite of fantastic rumours regarding the size of Eddy's invading force which spread like wildfire throughout Nova Scotia during the months of October and November, the inhabitants could not be aroused from their lethargic neutrality.

As early as August, Gorham had heard of Eddy's invasion plans, but it was not until the beginning of November that he learned that Eddy was in the Chignecto region.[66] With fewer than 200 troops at his command[67] and believing that Eddy had at least 500 men,[68] Gorham was of the opinion that he was in no position to attack the invaders.[69] Therefore he felt that the only alternative was to adopt a defensive policy and to wait for reinforcements from Halifax. This was the right policy at the right time.[70]

During the early morning hours of November 7, Eddy's forces experienced their only real victory in the futile Chignecto campaign. Taking advantage of a thick fog which had settled over the coastal region, Zebulon Rowe and a handful of men thirsting for excitement and possible loot set out to capture a sloop filled with supplies for the Fort Cumberland troops.[71] Because of the low tide the sloop lay on the broad mud flats to the southwest of the fort. Eddy's description of this most humorous incident of the rebellion makes fascinating reading:

> After a Difficult March, they arrived opposite the Sloop; on board of which was a Guard of 1 Sergt and 12 men, who had they fir'd at our People, must have alarmed the Garrison in such a Manner as to have brought them on their Backs. However, our men rushed Resolutely towards the sloop up to their Knees in Mud, which made such a Noise as to alarm the Centry, who hailed them and immediately called the Sergt of the Guard. The Sergt on coming up, Ordered his Men to fire, but was immediately told by Mr. Row[e] that if they fired one Gun, Every Man of Them should be put to Death; which so frightened the poor Devils that they surrendered without firing a Shot, although our People Could not board her without the Assistance of the Conquered, who let down Ropes to our Men to get up by.[72]

As the working parties from the fort arrived to unload the sloop, they too were easily captured.[73] Altogether 34 of Gorham's troops, including Captain Barron, Engineer of the Garrison, and the Chaplain, the bibulous Rev. Eagleson, were seized by Rowe's detachment.[74] The captured sloop was sailed away at high tide in the direction of the Missiquash River, but not before the Royal Fencibles "fired several cannon shots"[75] at the brazen enemy.

Only two attempts were made to capture Fort Cumberland, one on November 13[76] and the other nine days later.[77] Both were miserable failures. Before Eddy could organize a third attempt, British reinforcements arrived.

On November 27 and November 28, the British relieving force, consisting of two companies of Marines and one company of the Royal Highlanders, finally landed at Fort Cumberland.[78] The relieving force had sailed from Halifax and Windsor.[79] On the 28th Gorham ordered Major Batt, an officer who had accompanied the reinforcements, to lead an attack on Eddy's camp, one mile north of the fort.[80] At five-thirty in the morning of the 29th, Batt marched out of Fort Cumberland with 170 troops, hoping to surprise the "rebels."[81] If it had not been for an alert young Negro drummer who furiously beat the alarm when he sighted the enemy,[82] Eddy's men would have been slaughtered in their sleep. Wiping sleep from their eyes, Eddy's confused followers ran into the neighbouring woods in search of cover.[83] In the skirmish that followed only seven "rebels" and four British soldiers were killed.[84] Seeing the hopelessness of the situation, Eddy ordered his men to retreat westwards "to the St. John River . . . and there make a stand."[85] Batt refused to pursue the "rebels"; instead he had his men put to the torch every home and barn belonging to those inhabitants of the Isthmus who had openly supported Eddy.[86] The billowing dark clouds of smoke could be seen by the defeated invaders as they fled in panic towards Memramcook.[87]

Eddy's rash attempt to capture Fort Cumberland failed not only because he lacked artillery, but also because his men were poorly trained, undisciplined, and badly led. With British control of the North Atlantic firmly established, with Washington's refusal to support the invasion, and with the great majority of Nova Scotians desperately trying to be neutral, Eddy's task was hopeless. Even though the Eddy Rebellion, by any broad strategic standards, was quite insignificant in the larger revolutionary context, it is of some importance as an illustration of the fact that in 1775 and 1776, under their superficial neutrality, the New Englanders tacitly supported the revolutionary movement. Moreover, the Eddy Rebellion helps to indicate how effectively British naval power and the isolated nature of the settlements of Nova Scotia had "neutralized the New England migrants."[88]

From 1777 to 1782 almost every Nova Scotian coastal settlement (with the notable exception of Halifax) from Tatamagouche on Northumberland Strait to the Saint John River was ravaged by American privateers.[89] As a result of these freebooting forays many New Englanders in Nova Scotia, who had originally been rather sympathetic to the Revolution, became increasingly hostile to their brethren to the south. In 1775 and 1776 most of the Nova Scotians "divided betwixt natural affection to our nearest relations, and good Faith and Friendship to our King and Country,"[90] had decided to walk the tightrope of neutrality even though they appeared to lean precariously in the direction of their "nearest relations." By the closing years of the conflict, however, as the "Neutral Yankees" reached the end of their hazardous journey, they had begun to lean towards the opposite extreme, toward the King.

What real impact did the Revolution have upon the inhabitants of Nova Scotia? Of course most of them resolved to adopt a policy of neutrality; many suffered because of the depredations of the American privateers; while a few, especially the Halifax merchants, grew rich from the usual profits of war. But was there nothing else? M.W. Armstrong has convincingly argued that probably the most important impact of the Revolution upon Nova Scotia was in precipitating the "Great Awakening of Nova Scotia."[91] In addition, Armstrong has emphasized that the "Great Awakening" encouraged the development of neutrality:

> Indeed, the Great Awakening itself may be considered to have been a retreat from the grim realities of the world to the safety and pleasantly exciting warmth of the revival meeting, and to profits and rewards of another character . . . an escape from fear and divided loyalties . . . an assertion of democratic ideals and a determination to maintain them, the Great Awakening gave self-respect and satisfaction to people whose economic and political position was both humiliating and distressing.[92]

The prophet and evangelist of the spiritual awakening was Henry Alline, who, when he was twelve, had moved from Rhode Island to Falmouth, Nova Scotia.[93] An uneducated farmer, Alline had experienced an unusual "Conversion,"[94] and in 1776 he began to preach an emotional Christian message that has been described as being a combination of "Calvinism,

Antinomianism, and Enthusiasm."[95] The flames of religious revival[96] swept up the Minas Basin in 1777, across the Bay of Fundy in 1779, and to the South Shore in 1781.[97] All Protestant churches in Nova Scotia were in one way or another affected by the "Great Awakening," and largely as a direct result the evangelical wing of the various Protestant churches was able to dominate Maritime religious life throughout the nineteenth century.

British sea power, the isolated nature of the settlements, the refusal of Washington to mount an offensive against Nova Scotia, and perhaps the religious revival, all combined to keep the "Yankees" neutral during the Revolution.

NOTES

1. W.B. Kerr, "Nova Scotia in the Critical Years, 1775–6," *Dalhousie Review* (April 1932): 97.
2. S.D. Clarke, *Movements of Political Protest in Canada, 1640–1840* (Toronto, 1959), 63.
3. It should be borne in mind that there was a significant German-speaking population in the Lunenburg region and that there were pockets of Highland Scots, Yorkshiremen, Acadians, and Scots-Irish scattered throughout the peninsula of Nova Scotia. Most of these settlers (a few Acadians and Scots-Irish are the exception to the rule) also remained neutral during the Revolution even though their sympathies lay with the Crown.
4. J.B. Brebner, *The Neutral Yankees of Nova Scotia* (New York, 1937), 329–37.
5. V. Barnes, "Francis Legge, Governor of Loyalist Nova Scotia, 1773–1776," *New England Quarterly* (July 1931): 420–47. See also a convincing criticism of this view in W.B. Kerr, "The Merchants of Nova Scotia and the American Revolution," *Canadian Historical Review* (March 1932): 21–34.
6. A.L. Burt, *The United States, Great Britain, and British North America* (Toronto, 1940), 13.
7. W.B. Kerr, *The Maritime Provinces of British North America and the American Revolution* (Sackville, n.d.), 59.
8. Kerr, *The Maritime Provinces*, 60.
9. Kerr, *The Maritime Provinces*, 53–60.
10. Brebner, *Neutral Yankees of Nova Scotia*, 352.
11. J.C. Webster, *The Forts of Chignecto* (Sackville, 1930), 5.
12. W.C. Milner, *History of Sackville, New Brunswick* (Sackville, 1955), 14–21.
13. B.J. Bird, "Settlement Patterns in Maritime Canada, 1687–1876," *The Geographic Review* (July 1955): 398–99.
14. Bird, "Settlement Patterns," 398–99.
15. W.C. Milner, "Records of Chignecto," *Collections of the Nova Scotia Historical Society*, vol. 15 (Halifax, 1911), 41–45.
16. Milner, "Records of Chignecto," 40.
17. Kerr, *The Maritime Provinces*, 68.
18. Kerr, *The Maritime Provinces*, 68.
19. J.M. Beck, *The Government of Nova Scotia* (Toronto, 1957), 22–25.
20. D.C. Harvey, "The Struggle for the New England Form of Township Government in Nova Scotia," Canadian Historical Association, *Report* (1933), 18 [hereafter CHAR].
21. D.C. Harvey, "Machias and the Invasion of Nova Scotia," CHAR (1932), 17.
22. J.C. Fitzpatrick, ed., *The Writings of George Washington* (Washington, 1931), 3: 415.
23. Fitzpatrick, ed., *Writings of George Washington* 3: 415–16.
24. The Petition of the Chignecto Inhabitants, December 23, 1775, *Nova Scotia Archives*, A94, 330–38.
25. Kerr, "Nova Scotia in the Critical Years 1775–6," 98.
26. Governor Legge to the Secretary of State, July 31, 1775, *Canadian Archives Report for 1894* (Ottawa, 1895), 334 [hereafter CAR, 1894].
27. E.P. Weaver, "Nova Scotia and New England during the Revolution," *American Historical Review* (October 1904), 63.
28. B. Murdoch, *A History of Nova Scotia* (Halifax, 1860), 2: 554.
29. Kerr, *The Maritime Provinces*, 69.
30. Kerr, *The Maritime Provinces*, 63.
31. Quoted in F. Kidder, *Military Operations in Eastern Maine and Nova Scotia during the Revolution* (Albany, 1867), 64.
32. Kerr, *The Maritime Provinces*, 70.

33. The Petition of Chignecto Inhabitants, *Nova Scotia Archives*, A94, 330–38.
34. Quoted in Kerr, *The Maritime Provinces*, 73.
35. Fitzpatrick, ed., *Writings of George Washington* 4: 437.
36. H. Peckham, *The War for Independence* (Chicago, 1959), 32.
37. Fitzpatrick, ed., *Writings of George Washington* 4: 438.
38. Fitzpatrick, ed., *Writings of George Washington* 4: 438.
39. Kerr, *The Maritime Provinces*, 73.
40. See *CAR, 1894*, 345.
41. *CAR, 1894*, 345.
42. Kerr, *The Maritime Provinces*, 74.
43. Quoted in Murdoch, *History of Nova Scotia* 2: 568.
44. In the administrative shuffle Francklin was demoted to Indian Agent.
45. The Royal Fencibles were mostly recruited from the Loyalists in the Thirteen Colonies.
46. W.B. Kerr, "The American Invasion of Nova Scotia, 1776–7," *Canadian Defense Quarterly* (July 1936): 434.
47. Gorham's Journal, *CAR, 1894*, 360.
48. Kerr, *The Maritime Provinces*, 78.
49. Kidder, *Military Operations*, 12.
50. Petition of Jonathan Eddy, Aug. 28, 1776, in P. Force, ed., *American Archives*, 5th series (Washington, 1851), 2: 734.
51. *American Archives* 2: 734.
52. Kidder, *Military Operations*, 12.
53. Gorham's Journal, 355.
54. Quoted in Harvey, "Machias and the Invasion of Nova Scotia," 21.
55. Kerr, "The American Invasion," 434.
56. Kerr, "The American Invasion," 435.
57. Kerr, "The American Invasion," 435.
58. The description of the Rebellion is to be found in Gorham's Journal, *CAR, 1894*, 355–57, 359–65, and in Eddy's Journal, in Harvey, "Machias and the Invasion of Nova Scotia," 22–24.
59. Eddy's Journal, 22.
60. Eddy's Journal, 22.
61. Eddy's Journal, 22.
62. Allan's Journal, in Harvey, "Machias and the Invasion of Nova Scotia," 24.
63. Kerr, "The American Invasion," 435.
64. Eddy's Journal, 23.
65. Kerr, "The American Invasion," 436.
66. Gorham's Journal, 355.
67. Gorham's Journal, 360.
68. Gorham's Journal, 356.
69. Gorham's Journal, 360.
70. For the opposite point of view see Kerr, "The American Invasion," 441: "A well-directed sortie could at any time have broken up Eddy's camp."
71. Eddy's Journal, 22.
72. Eddy's Journal, 22.
73. Eddy's Journal, 22–23.
74. Eddy's Journal, 22–23.
75. Eddy's Journal, 23; Gorham's Journal, 356.
76. Gorham's Journal, 361–62.
77. Gorham's Journal, 361–62.
78. Gorham's Journal, 362.
79. Gorham's Journal, 362. This point must be emphasized especially, after examining Stanley's inaccurate reference to an overland march. See G.F.G. Stanley, *Canada's Soldiers, 1605–1954* (Toronto, 1954), 118.
80. Gorham's Journal, 362.
81. Gorham's Journal, 362.
82. C.E. Kemp, "Folk-Lore About Old Fort Beauséjour," *Acadiensis* (October 1908): 301–302. Also see Kerr, "The American Invasion," 440.
83. Gorham's Journal, 362.
84. Kerr, "The American Invasion," 441.

85. Eddy's Journal, 23.
86. Gorham's Journal, 362.
87. The contest for present-day western New Brunswick continued until the end of the Revolutionary War. In the summer of 1777 Allan's invading force of some 100 men from Machias was compelled to retreat overland from the St. John Valley toward the St. Croix when confronted by a strong British military expedition led by Major Gilford Studholme and Francklin. For the remainder of the war Allan unsuccessfully attempted to persuade the St. John River Indians to join the Revolutionary cause.
88. Brebner, *The Neutral Yankees*, 353.
89. Brebner, *The Neutral Yankees*, 324–35.
90. Petition of the Inhabitants of Yarmouth, Dec. 8, 1775. Quoted in Brebner, *The Neutral Yankees*, 291.
91. M.W. Armstrong, "Neutrality and Religion in Revolutionary Nova Scotia," *New England Quarterly* (Mar. 1946): 50–61.
92. Armstrong, "Neutrality and Religion," 57, 58, 60.
93. Armstrong, "Neutrality and Religion," 55.
94. See W. James, *The Varieties of Religious Experience* (New York, 1958), 134–35: "My sins seemed to be laid open; so that I thought that every one I saw knew them, and sometimes I was almost ready to acknowledge many things, which I thought they knew; yea sometimes it seemed to me as if every one was pointing me out as the most guilty wretch upon earth."
95. Quoted in Armstrong, "Neutrality and Religion," 58.
96. The following is Alline's description of the Liverpool revival of 1776: "We had blessed days, the Lord was reviving his work of grace. Many under a load of sin cried out, what shall we do to be saved? and the saints seemed much revived, came out and witnessed for God. In a short time some more souls were born to Christ, they came out and declared what God had done for their souls and what a blessed change had taken place in that town." Quoted in Armstrong, "Neutrality and Religion," 55–56.
97. Armstrong, "Neutrality and Religion," 55.

Article Sixteen

The Family in Exile: Loyalist Social Values after the Revolution

Ann Gorman Condon

"All happy families are alike but an unhappy family is unhappy after its own fashion." Thus begins Leo Tolstoy's *Anna Karenina*, that extraordinary fictional journey into the private lives of the Russian aristocracy in the nineteenth century.[1] While modern anthropologists might gasp at Tolstoy's willingness to make such sweeping generalizations about the family, no one can deny his success in creating a vivid world of intimacy and intrigue, devotion and deceit, noble suffering and base humiliation, climaxing, of course, in the necessary self-destruction of its flawed heroine, followed by a ringing affirmation of traditional, and very Christian, family values.

Culturally, Tsarist Russia was a far different place than colonial Canada, but they did, for a short while, have one thing in common: an official ruling class. Until the mid-nineteenth century, the British North American provinces were ruled by a group of privileged officers who

Source: Ann Gorman Condon, "The Family in Exile: Loyalist Social Values after the Revolution," *Intimate Relations: Family and Community in Planter, Nova Scotia, 1759–1800*, ed. Margaret Conrad (Fredericton: Acadiensis Press, 1995), pp. 42–53. Reprinted by permission.

held their powers independently of the people they governed and reinforced their authority by elaborate social codes and extensive family connections. Indeed, so powerful and so notorious were these sets of provincial oligarchs that they are known pejoratively even to this day in the former colony of Upper Canada, now Ontario, as "The Family Compact."

Alas, thus far Canada's period of gentry rule has inspired no Tolstoyan masterpiece, no insider account of the intimate life, passions, and pairings of this select group. In fact, it is both remarkable and regrettable that, for all the many treatises on the political operations of the Family Company, we have so few accounts of its internal dynamics: its elaborate network of filiations and obligations, its shared aspirations and anxieties, and the mechanisms by which it ensured the transmission not only of property and power from generation to generation, but of a distinctive code of values.[2]

Using the new methodologies developed by family historians and the wealth of personal letters left by prominent Loyalist families (which extend in some cases through four generations), I have begun a research project aimed at discovering the personal bonds and ideals which united these people over such a long stretch of time. Eventually, I will include representative family writings from five of the British North American colonies, spread over three generations. I have started with the Maritime provinces because the Loyalist style of cultural leadership was established here so very quickly after their arrival in the 1780s and is so well chronicled in their letters to each other.

This essay represents the "first fruits" of my work, my first attempt to identify patterns and figures in this very complex material, based mainly on the Jarvis Papers and Robinson Papers in the New Brunswick Museum and the Bliss Papers in the Public Archives of Nova Scotia. Unfortunately, editorial constraints will not permit me to explore the wealth of material in these letters fully, but let me at least hint at the tone and atmosphere of family life among the Loyalist grandees by quoting three sets of love letters from prominent Loyalists to their wives.

My first example is a letter from Edward Winslow, the unfailingly gallant, but perpetually impoverished, Massachusetts Loyalist, to his wife Mary. The two had married before the Revolutionary War and she accompanied him on his circuitous flight pattern after 1775 — from Boston, to Halifax, to New York City, to Annapolis, Nova Scotia, and finally, ten years later, to their permanent abode in Kingsclear, New Brunswick. Throughout this long hegira, Mary managed the family household, which at times included the first eight of their eleven children, Edward's elderly parents, and his two spinster sisters. The letter I quote was written in 1784, while Edward was in Halifax, looking, as always, for a profitable job, and apparently aware that his lonely, overburdened wife could use some cheering up. Winslow starts off with trumpets blaring:

> what do I care whether it's the fashion for men to write long letters to their wives or not. . . .
> In matters where my own feelings are concerned I will not be shackled by any of the rules
> which bind the generality of mankind. . . . I cannot enjoy a pleasure equal to that of writing
> to you, and that's sufficient for writing. If other men do not experience the same sensation
> they have not the same degree of affection.

He then launches into a hilarious description of the fashionable ladies of Halifax and, with mock pity, bemoans the fact that the

> immensity of False-Tops False Curls, monstrous Caps. Grease, Filth of various kinds, Jewels,
> painted paper and trinkets, hide and deform heads of Hair that in their natural state are really
> beautiful. Rouge & other dirt cover cheeks and faces that without would be tolerable, whilst
> the unfortunate neck and breasts remain open to the inclemency of the weather & the view
> of the World.

But his Mary, he notes, is the exact opposite: "From 16 years old to the present time you have literally set your Cap at no creature on earth but me. Regardless of Fashion you have only endeavoured by uniform cleanliness to make yourself desirable in my eyes." After declaring his continuing love for her, Winslow closes by saying he still hopes that she will be able once more to enter the world of fashion and elegance.[3]

My second example is a series of letters from Beverley Robinson, the dashing young military officer from New York. Beverley had married Nancy Barclay during the war, and he proved, in New Brunswick, to be a bit of a martinet. Even though Nancy had abandoned a comfortable home in New York City for a refugee farm on the Nashwaaksis River, and had borne eleven children during their marriage, Beverley cannot resist chastising her for "laziness" and negligence. In one 1799 letter, he gave her elaborate instructions on the proper way to cool down and curry horses, and then proceeded to remind her to wrap his doughnuts securely so they will remain moist. The last batch were so dry he could not eat them![4]

Yet the petty irritations of married life did not undermine Beverley's devotion to his wife. For example, when he heard that Nancy was worried about losing her attractiveness now that she was forced to wear spectacles, Robinson rushed to reassure her with this stunning declaration:

> my present feelings have nothing to do with the respectability of your appearance, no madam my imagination is not confined to the age of 45 but wanders back to those days of yore when you was all youth and beauty I all ardour and affection . . . you are and shall be my beloved and adored mistress and as such only I will cherish the recollection of you.[5]

A year later, on their twenty-second wedding anniversary, Beverley acknowledged, with exquisite sensitivity, that although many changes had taken place since "the day that gave my Nancy to me, I can truly say that she is dearer to me now than when I received her with the rapture of a Bridegroom."[6]

My final example concerns Jonathan Bliss. A crusty, 47-year-old bachelor when he came to New Brunswick, Bliss had spent the Revolutionary War in England, enjoying, to the full, the pleasures of London and Bristol. He came to New Brunswick for the sake of a job, but candidly admitted that he was too old, too spoiled by England to appreciate such a new country, however promising.[7] Bliss performed his duties as attorney general in a minimal sort of way and amused himself by writing political poetry. In 1789, after much deliberation, he decided to take a wife. He returned to his American home in Massachusetts and married the daughter of the richest man in Worcester County. She was Mary Worthington, a woman in her late 20s, and thus a full 20 years younger than Bliss. Her letters to her husband make it clear that she embodied the ideal of female grace and submissiveness so cherished by people in the eighteenth century.[8]

Unexpectedly, passionately, Jonathan Bliss fell in love with his young wife. She and the four sons she bore became the enchanted centre of his life. In his letters to Mary, this aging, cynical lawyer resorted to baby talk. He confessed to her that she had made him the "happiest man in New Brunswick"— but ruined him for living alone. Mary was more deferential and demure in her responses to this older man, but she did assure Bliss that his companionship supplied all the love and support she once drew from family and friends. When Mary died in 1799 delivering their fifth child, Bliss was crushed. He would never remarry, and for both Jonathan and their sons, her memory would profoundly shape their ideals of womanhood and of happiness.[9]

It seems to me that, on the surface at least, these are remarkable letters — delicate, witty, warmly demonstrative. They suggest deep mutual concern and enduring affection, the ideal of "companionate marriage" which Lawrence Stone has described so forcefully for the English gentry of the eighteenth century and which Bernard Bailyn finds so powerfully at work within the family of Thomas Hutchinson in colonial Massachusetts. It is an ideal, according to

Richard Sennett, which calls for detachment and careful control in public roles, but a warm, expressive, supportive behaviour among one's intimates.[10]

Yet how are we, citizens of the late twentieth century, living as we do in the "Age of Deconstruction," to interpret these letters? Do we take them at face value? Or do we look for evasions, masks, and ambiguities which subvert and undermine the highly polished surface? These are some of the questions I am pursuing through the thousands of Loyalist family letters still available in our public archives. My goal is to uncover the inner workings of power and inti-macy among the people known universally in Canadian history as The Family Compact. As for the all-important question of interpretation, my strategy is to pursue a dual track: to try to appre-ciate at full value the depth of feeling and mutual dependency radiating through these letters, and at the same time to recognize that these statements were also calculated performances, sur-vival measures and personal defences against an undeserved fate and a relentlessly cruel world.[11]

Rather than digress into methodology, I would like to use the balance of this essay to describe the three major conclusions which I have reached at this stage in my research. I hope this will provide a concrete sense of the richness of the material contained in these Loyalists' letters, as well as practical examples of my interpretive strategy.

First, it seems abundantly clear from the written sources that, for the Loyalist refugees, the family was the most important institution in their lives. Despite occasional attempts by histo-rians (including myself) to embroider Loyalist life during their years in the Maritime provinces, the fact remains that these colonial gentry found their new physical environment forbidding and its public life totally lacking in beauty or grandeur. Even those Loyalists who came with money, servants, and prestigious public posts found their new homes strange and alienating.[12]

Since there was little hope of returning to America, and neither their Christian beliefs nor their self-respect would permit them to give in to despair, these displaced people threw their energies into their immediate families — the one area of life they could control and also the one area capable of positive response. Within the day-to-day life of their families, within the houses so carefully constructed and tastefully furnished, they could reenact their days of glory. They could organize little entertainments for friends according to the remembered standards of colonial Boston and New York; they could dress in silks and velvets and dancing shoes; they could exchange gossip and wit and observe the courtesies of a world far removed from the fron-tier. In such ways, private life became far more important than the crude tedium of public affairs.

Second, the fact that the Loyalists were exiles, not simply immigrants, had important psy-chological repercussions. The mentality of exile has been described many times by novelists and essayists in our century. Indeed, exile has come to be the salient fact of modern existence. Put simply, exiles are rootless, mutilated people, who live two lives simultaneously: first, their ordinary life which they find dull, even repulsive; and second, their imagined life — their dreams, memories, and feelings of nostalgia, which are full of warmth, vitality, and success. In a remarkable essay, "The Mind of Winter," the literary critic Edward Said notes how many out-standing chess players, novelists, poets, and adventurers in the twentieth century are exiles — people to whom the imaginary life is much more important than the real world.[13]

The personal letters of the Loyalists provide multiple diverse glimpses into the imaginary world which they cherished during long exile in the Maritimes. And what were its contents? The answer is obvious: it was filled with remembered moments of glory and power in colonial America! It was the world painted so magnificently by John Singleton Copley and described most recently by Richard Bushman.[14] It was a world of refinement, taste, and elegance — a world where men were so confident of their authority in both society and the family that they chose to display the feminine side of their nature in their portraits. Hence the silk stockings, ruffled shirts, and velvet suits worn by Copley's subjects. Hence the private, domestic backdrops of sinuously carved furniture and bookcases full of the bound books which signified a man of taste. Their wives' appearance complemented the men's. Although their dresses and jewels were dazzling, their faces were those of the hostess — gentle, attentive, welcoming. Despite their elaborate garb, there was nothing worldly about these women. They were domestic creatures — decorative, dependent, nurturing of husbands and guests. Their pride came from domestic accomplishment — a piece of needlework, a fine table, an appealing bowl of fruit. Their personal world did not extend beyond the front door.[15]

These prescribed male and female roles were reenacted in their letters as they doubtless were in the actual homes of the Loyalists. In fact, the extraordinary charm and grace of the Loyalist letters were quite deliberate, expressing affirmations of their cultural ideals. Although fewer in number, the women's letters were as lively and extroverted as the men's. And they were cheerful, often deliberately so, for it was clearly against the common code for either men or women to complain about their fate. Unfortunately, we have no extant letters written by Edward Winslow's wife, Mary. We do know that she was very upset when her husband decided to send their son Murray, aged 12, to military school in England. This could suggest that she had already experienced too many separations in her life. Otherwise, she seems to have borne her fate bravely and silently.[16]

Few letters from Beverley Robinson's wife, Nancy, have survived, but from her husband's comments it seems that she fell into a depression after moving with her eleven children to the howling wilderness. The fascinating response to her melancholy was that several members of her family — not only her husband, but her mother, her son, and her brother — began writing letters urging Nancy to carry on and bear her burdens stoically.[17]

Jonathan Bliss's wife, Mary, wrote letters regularly to her family and her husband, many of which survive. They are marked by delicate sensitivity and a humorous vein of self-mockery. Clearly, Mary, too, went through a difficult emotional period during at least one New Brunswick winter. After admitting to her sister that she felt a certain loneliness while her husband was away on business, Mary blamed herself for her low spirits — not her four young children, nor her absent husband, nor the piercing cold. She ended this confessional letter by telling her sister not to worry, for she had just written out two pages of resolutions to improve herself and now felt much better![18]

It is notable that all letters from Loyalist women to men contained an apology for the "stupidity" of their letters, ascribed usually either to their allegedly poor handwriting or to the scattered nature of their thoughts. Although the letters themselves do not bear out this harsh judgement, it seems to have been an unwritten rule among these Loyalists that women must openly and repeatedly acknowledge their inferiority to men. Some historians call this trait "learned helplessness," but I find it more significant. Although they were encouraged to tease and flirt with the men of their circle, like other eighteenth-century women, Loyalist women did defer to male superiority — men's education and worldly knowledge. This seems to have been fundamental to the marriage bargain, an essential part of the reciprocal, complementary roles they performed as husband and wife. In accepting this deference, men implicitly agreed to protect and cherish such "stupid" but lovable creatures.

Third, the letters suggest that Loyalist children were deeply affected by their parents' history, and the most talented devoted a significant portion of their lives to redeeming their parents' fate by achieving great distinction in their professional lives. The impact of Loyalist values on their *redeemer children* is without doubt the most important finding of my research thus far. These children were raised with enormous affection and care, but also with firm discipline and fond expectations. Children were expected to carry the torch — maintain the codes of manner and dress and use their talents to bring honour to family.[19] Among the numerous examples available, consider the case of Henry Bliss. Perhaps the most talented of all the Loyalist sons,

Bliss was educated at King's College, Nova Scotia, and the Inner Temple in London. He emerged laden with academic prizes, good looks, and acclaimed charm. Bliss chose to settle in London, where he painstakingly established a reputation as a distinguished lawyer, ran for Parliament, and, in his private moments wrote at least seven historical dramas in iambic pentameter, exalting Loyalist principles. Although he considered these verse plays to be the most important aspect of his productive life, they were anachronistic to English tastes and failed utterly to win Bliss any notice, much less any commercial success. Admittedly discouraged, Bliss nonetheless continued writing such plays to the end of his life, in order to affirm the parental code and his own unrealized sense of destiny.[20]

The lives of Edward and Maria Jarvis illustrate a similar pattern of frustrated idealism. He was the English-educated son of Loyalist merchant Munson Jarvis and she, the daughter of a prominent medical man in Saint John. Soon after their marriage they lived for four years in the British colony of Malta, where Edward held an appointment as a law officer, and they both enjoyed the elaborate social life of the colony's rulers. Eventually, Edward's appointment as Chief Justice of Prince Edward Island permitted the Jarvises and their growing family to return to North America. They were dismayed, however, by the dull, "bumpkin" life on the island. In consequence, the two expended both their health and their limited fortune building a grand house —"Mount Edward"— near Charlottetown and giving heroic entertainments in order to expose the local population to the best British standards. Maria's exertions produced a heart condition, and she died soon after the house was finished. The disconsolate Edward remained heavily in debt for the rest of his life, and confessed to his brother that he was so short of funds he felt he could not comment on his children's choice of marriage partners, even though he disapproved! Such were the links between financial power and patriarchal authority.[21]

A variation on second-generation experience was that of William Bliss, son of Jonathan and brother to Henry. After English legal training, William returned to Halifax to marry the richest bride in that city, Sarah Ann Armstrong, the adopted daughter of his father's childhood friend, Loyalist Sampson Salter Blowers. Within a decade William's connections enabled him to get appointed to the Nova Scotia Supreme Court. But despite this great honour, his very comfortable life, and apparently happy family, William worried ceaselessly in his letters to his brothers that he had sold out, taken the easy road, instead of seeking fame by pursuing the law in London or risking his all on a literary career.[22]

The preoccupation of these Loyalist children with their parents' world — their lifelong efforts to redeem and vindicate the parental sacrifice — meant that they, too, lived a great deal of their existence in the "floating world" of the imagination. Unlike the sons of ordinary immigrants, they had difficulty sinking roots in the local Canadian soil, committing themselves to the realities of time and place. In 1825 Henry Bliss recognized the disadvantages of this outlook and told William that he was considering returning to New Brunswick and marrying a local beauty:

> To marry a local girl will give me some connexion in the country, some friends. I mean some common interests with others; and I shall find somebody to sympathize with me, or seem to do it. That is just what our family has always wanted. We have been alone and unconnected with all the society in which we lived; and had any of us stumbled how the world would have trod on us! But then our situation . . . had its advantages — for when their daughters whored, or their sons got drunk, it touched not us. . . . I sometimes regret that Father did not take a different side, or that the side he did take was not more successful in the American Revolution. We should now have been great Yankees at Boston — full of money and self conceit. . . . But then I might never have seen Kean . . . nor the inside of the Louvre . . . nor the Pont du Gard, nor so much of this beautiful Earth. No I am well content with my destiny. How can people doubt that God is good?[23]

This introspective, ambivalent letter, written at the age of 27, perfectly captures the dilemma of second-generation Loyalists — their cosmopolitan outlook, coupled with a severe, often crippling detachment from ordinary life. Only with the third generation do we find Loyalist heirs rooting themselves in the local soil, identifying with its landscape and people, including even the Protestant dissenting sects, who once represented the antithesis of all that the Loyalist gentry stood for.[24] Moreover, their obsession with Loyalist sacrifice lessened. It is true that genealogy became a hobby with the third generation, as did commemorating their ancestors in local churches and cemeteries, but such activities were not an unpaid debt, haunting their waking hours. As well, obsession with family life diminished. Relations between husbands and wives of the third generation were far more relaxed and informal, but also more separate. Husbands spent much of their leisure time in clubs or hunting camps or militia musters. This apparent preference for the exclusive company of males was a new development, an assertion of a type of "rugged" masculine identity which their grandfathers deliberately avoided.[25] Likewise, the third generation of Loyalist wives and mothers became more civic minded, more involved in such reform movements as temperance, public health, and religious education. Their children were increasingly sent off early to boarding school, where the girls were permitted to study an academic curriculum and even aspire to university by the end of the century, while the boys' training emphasized military drill from school days onward.[26]

As an inevitable part of this evolution, Loyalist elegance, Loyalist exclusivity, and Loyalist intensity gradually dissolved. Although their grandchildren certainly respected their ancestors, they themselves had become Canadians and Victorians. In the words of the great conservative historian William L. Morton, grace had been transformed into respectability.[27]

Thus the special Loyalist culture — the special circumstances produced by the exile experience — seems to have lasted two generations at most. What we need to define is how it shaped, and perhaps even transformed, English Canada in general and Planter society in particular. It is a striking fact that the rampant individualism that seized American culture in the nineteenth century — the exaltation of success, of the loner, the wilderness, and even of violence — never took hold of nineteenth-century Canadian culture.[28] On the contrary, group loyalties to the community and the family, a cordial acceptance of the complementarity of the sexes, a strong emphasis on public duty, as well as an equal insistence on the sheer joy of human companionship were the values which the Loyalists brought with them from colonial America and kept vividly alive through most of the nineteenth century. Philosophically, these exiles were Aristotelians rather than Platonists, Arcadians rather than Utopians. Surely their dominance for 75 years left a residue which requires definition. Indeed, it seems singularly unfortunate that the ruling historical metaphor for the Loyalist contribution to Canadian culture is Northrop Frye's "the garrison mentality." Without denying the elements of arrogance and paranoia in the Loyalist personality, we must also recognize the social virtues of wit, learning, style, and profound human solidarity. Sustained exploration of their private papers may bring both the positive and negative aspects of the Loyalist legacy into proper balance.

NOTES

1. Leo Tolstoy, *Anna Karenina*, trans. Rosemary Edmunds (London, 1954), 13.
2. The *Jalna* series of Mazo de la Roche is, I believe, the closest fictional attempt to re-create the private life of Ontario's landed gentry, but, unlike Tolstoy's novel, the *Jalna* novels are set in the period after the gentry's fall from political power and are essentially a romantic rejection of modern industrial Canada, not a depiction of the gentry in its years of power. More salient are several recent scholarly studies of Loyalist women. Especially noteworthy are Katherine McKenna, "Options for Elite Women in Early Upper Canadian Society: The Case of the Powell Family," in *Historical Essays on Upper Canada: New Perspectives*, ed. J.K. Johnson and Bruce

G. Wilson (Ottawa, 1989), 401–24, and her recently published book, *A Life of Propriety: Anne Murray Powell and Her Family* (Montreal/Kingston, 1994), as well as Janice Potter-MacKinnon, *While Women Only Wept: Loyalist Refugee Women in Eastern Ontario* (Montreal/Kingston, 1993). Also valuable are three doctoral studies: Robin Burns, "The First Elite of Toronto: An Examination of the Genesis, Consolidation, and Duration of Power in an Emerging Colonial Society" (Ph.D. thesis, University of Western Ontario, 1975); Robert L. Fraser, "Like Eden in Her Summer Dress: Gentry, Economy and Society, Upper Canada, 1812–1840" (Ph.D. thesis, University of Toronto, 1979); Beatrice Spence Ross, "Adaptation in Exile: Loyalist Women in Nova Scotia after the American Revolution" (Ph.D. thesis, Cornell University, 1981). My study, *The Envy of the American States: The Loyalist Dream for New Brunswick* (Fredericton, 1984) deals briefly with family life.

3. Edward Winslow to his Wife, W.O. Raymond, ed., *The Winslow Papers* (Saint John, 1901), 225–27.

4. Beverley Robinson to Nancy Robinson, 21 November 1799, Robinson Family Papers, New Brunswick Museum.

5. Ibid., 11 November 1799.

6. Ibid., 20 January 1800.

7. Jonathan Bliss to S.S. Blowers, 19 September 1786, Bliss Family Papers, Public Archives of Nova Scotia [PANS].

8. Phillip Buckner, "Jonathan Bliss," *Dictionary of Canadian Biography,* VI (Toronto, 1987), 74–6. Thomas Vincent, "The Image and Function of Women in the Poetry of Affection in Eighteenth Century Maritime Canada," in *Making Adjustments: Change and Continuity in Planter Nova Scotia, 1759–1800,* ed. Margaret Conrad (Fredericton, 1991), 234–46.

9. Jno. Bliss to Mary Bliss, 4 June 1792, and Mary Bliss to Jno. Bliss, 23 July 1792, Bliss Papers, PANS. The story of the devotion of the Bliss men to Mary Worthington Bliss has never been written, but can be traced through the family papers.

10. Lawrence Stone, *The Family, Sex and Marriage in England, 1500–1800* (New York, 1977); Bernard Bailyn, *The Ordeal of Thomas Hutchinson* (Cambridge, MA, 1974); Richard Sennett, *The Fall of Public Man* (New York, 1977), 98–107. For a fine survey of recent scholarship on the family in Europe and North America, see Tamara K. Hareven, "The History of the Family and the Complexity of Social Change," *American Historical Review* 96 (1991): 95–124.

11. In developing my interpretive approach I have been especially influenced by the work of the French philosopher Paul Ricouer. For an explanation of this methodology see my "The Celestial World of Jonathan Odell: Symbolic Unities within a Disparate Artifact Collection," in *Living in a Material World: Canadian and American Approaches to Material Culture,* ed. Gerald L. Pocius (St. John's, 1992), 192–226. I find the recent effort by Edward Said to develop a "contrapuntal" approach to historical experience an equally rich, if less systematic, attempt to capture both the pure and impure elements of literary texts within a single conceptual framework. See *Culture and Imperialism* (New York, 1993).

12. Neil MacKinnon captures this estrangement especially well in *This Unfriendly Soil: The Loyalist Experience in Nova Scotia, 1783–1791* (Kingston, 1986).

13. Edward Said, "The Mind of Winter: Reflections on Life in Exile," *Harper's* 269 (1984): 49–55. For a subtle exploration of the imaginary worlds of exiled writers Joseph Conrad and Vladimir Nabokov, among others, see Michael Seidel, *Exile and the Narrative Imagination* (New Haven, 1987).

14. Richard L. Bushman, *The Refinement of America: Persons, Houses, Cities* (New York, 1992).

15. Margaret Doody, "Vibrations," *London Review of Books,* 5 August 1993, 13–14.

16. Edward Winslow to his wife Mary, 15 September 84, *Winslow Papers.*

17. Beverley Robinson, Jr., to Anna Robinson, 29 October [1799?] and Thomas Barclay to Beverley Robinson, 1 November 1799, Robinson Papers.

18. Mary Bliss to Frances Ames, 13 February 1797, Bliss Papers, PANS.

19. The best book on parent–child relations for this period is Philip G. Greven, *The Protestant Temperament: Patterns of Child-Rearing, Religious Experience and the Self in Early America* (New York, 1977). Equally insightful is a three-generation study of Virginia families within almost the same time frame as this essay on Loyalist families: Jan Lewis, *The Pursuit of Happiness: Family and Values in Jefferson's Virginia* (New York, 1985).

20. Bertis Sutton, "The Expression of Second-Generation Loyalist Sentiment in the Verse Dramas of Henry Bliss," *Nova Scotia Historical Review* 13, 1 (1993): 43–77.

21. Anna Maria Jarvis to Caroline Boyd, 6 March 1832; E.J. Jarvis to William Jarvis, 4 August 1835 and 30 January 1837; E.J. Jarvis to Mrs. William Jarvis, 21 September 1849, Jarvis Papers, New Brunswick Museum. J.M. Bumsted and H.T. Holman, "Edward James Jarvis," *Dictionary of Canadian Biography,* VIII (Toronto, 1985), 428–30.

22. William Bliss to Henry Bliss, 18 May 1828, Bliss Papers, PANS.

23. Henry Bliss to William Bliss, Marseilles, 7 January 1825, Bliss Papers, PANS.
24. See, for example, Ann Gorman Condon, ed., "'The Young Robin Hood Society': A Political Satire by Edward Winslow," *Acadiensis* 15 (1986): 120–43.
25. W.L. Morton, "Victorian Canada," in *The Shield of Achilles: Aspects of Canada in the Victorian Age,* ed. W.L. Morton (Toronto, 1968), 311–33. For the equivalent development in the United States, see E. Anthony Rotundo, *American Manhood: Transformations in Masculinity from the Revolution to the Modern Era* (New York, 1993).
26. These impressionistic findings are based on my reading of the letters of William Jarvis, Jr., and his two wives and children in the 1860s and 1870s, Jarvis Papers.
27. Morton, "Victorian Canada."
28. Alexis de Toqueville was the first to recognize these traits, in volume II of his *Democracy in America* (New York, 1957). For modern interpretations, see Richard Slotkin's trilogy: *Regeneration through Violence: The Mythology of the American Frontier, 1600–1860* (New York, 1973); *The Fatal Environment: The Myth of the Frontier in the Age of Industrialization, 1800–1890* (New York, 1985); and *Gunfighter Nation: The Mythology of the Frontier in Twentieth Century America* (New York, 1992). For the Canadian comparison, see Marcia B. Kline, *Beyond the Land Itself: Views of Nature in Canada and the United States* (Cambridge, MA, 1970).

Topic Eight

Upper Canada and the War of 1812

Notice published in Quebec City, 29 June 1812, ordering all persons of
American citizenship to leave the city immediately, or face arrest.

With the Constitutional Act of 1791, Upper Canada emerged as a new British colony, composed largely of Loyalists escaping from the newly independent Thirteen Colonies. The Loyalists, however, dropped in three decades from a majority to minority status. On account of the large-scale American (non-Loyalist) migration, the Americans by 1812 outnumbered the Loyalists and recent British immigrants by four to one in the colony's population of roughly 75 000. The War of 1812 pressured the American immigrants to choose sides. Not all Upper Canadians were prepared to support Britain, as E. Jane Errington points out in "Reluctant Warriors: British North Americans and the War of 1812." With such initial indifference to the British cause, how did England ultimately successfully defend the colony? What role did the First Nations play in the Great Lakes theatre of war? Robert D. Allen examines that question in "His Majesty's Indian Allies: Native Peoples, the British Crown and the War of 1812."

Women also played a role in the Upper Canadian theatre of war, the most famous being Laura Secord. But has the role of Secord been exaggerated in later accounts? In her essay, "'Of Slender Frame and Delicate Appearance': The Placing of Laura Secord in the Narratives of Canadian Loyalist History," Cecilia Morgan examines Secord's image in the literature of the late 19th and early 20th centuries. She concludes that Canadian historians transformed her into a larger-than-life figure by focusing on her loyalty and patriotism.

Although a growing literature now exists on Upper Canada, the best introductory text remains Gerald M. Craig's *Upper Canada: The Formative Years, 1784–1841* (Toronto: McClelland and Stewart, 1963). Important sources on the Loyalists who settled in the new colony include Bruce Wilson, *As She Began: An Illustrated Introduction to Loyalist Ontario* (Toronto: Dundurn Press, 1981); James J. Talman, ed., *Loyalist Narratives from Upper Canada* (Toronto: Champlain Society, 1946); and Janice Potter-MacKinnon, *While the Women Only Wept: Loyalist Refugee Women in Eastern Ontario* (Montreal/Kingston: McGill-Queen's University Press, 1993). Mrs. Simcoe's diary is an invaluable primary text for the early social history of the province; John Ross Robertson's fully annotated edition of the diary appeared under the title *The Diary of Mrs. John Graves Simcoe, Wife of the First Lieutenant-Governor of the Province of Upper Canada, 1792–6* (Toronto: Coles Publishing, 1973 [1911]). Mary Quayle Innis edited an abridged version, entitled *Mrs. Simcoe's Diary* (Toronto: Macmillan, 1965).

Currently, a great deal is being published on the economic and political history of Upper Canada. Economic issues are introduced in Chapter 6 ("Upper Canada") of Kenneth Norrie and Douglas Owram's *A History of the Canadian Economy*, 2nd ed. (Toronto: Harcourt Brace, 1996), pp. 115–45, and, in greater depth, in Douglas McCalla's "The 'Loyalist' Economy of Upper Canada," *Histoire Sociale/Social History* 16, 32 (November 1983): 279–304, as well as in his *Planting the Province: The Economic History of Upper Canada, 1784–1870*, Ontario Historical Studies Series (Toronto: University of Toronto Press, 1993). For the early history of the ideology of Upper Canada politics, see Jane Errington, *The Lion, the Eagle and Upper Canada: A Developing Colonial Ideology* (Montreal/Kingston: McGill-Queen's University Press, 1987), and David Mills, *The Idea of Loyalty in Upper Canada, 1784–1850* (Montreal/ Kingston: McGill-Queen's University Press, 1988).

For background on the First Nations in Upper Canada, consult Charles M. Johnston, ed., *The Valley of the Six Nations: A Collection of Documents on the Indian Lands of the Grand River* (Toronto: Champlain Society, 1964); Peter Schmalz, *The Ojibwa of Southern Ontario* (Toronto: University of Toronto Press, 1991); Janet Chute, *The Legacy of Shingwakanse: A Century of Native Leadership* (Toronto: University of Toronto Press, 1998); and Donald B. Smith, *Sacred Feathers: The Reverend Peter Jones (Kahkewaquonaby) and the Mississauga Indians* (Toronto: University of Toronto Press, 1987). Daniel G. Hill's *The Freedom-Seekers: Blacks in Early Canada* (Agincourt, ON: Book Society of Canada, 1981) is a popular summary of the history of Blacks in Upper Canada and in British North America in general.

Pierre Berton has written two popular accounts of the War of 1812: *The Invasion of Canada, 1812–1813* (Toronto: McClelland and Stewart, 1980), and *Flames across the Border, 1813–1814* (Toronto: McClelland and Stewart, 1981). A more recent study is Wesley B. Turner's *The War of 1812: The War That Both Sides Won* (2nd ed., Toronto: Dundurn Press, 2000). A more detailed treatment is Victor Suthren, *The War of 1812* (Toronto: McClelland and Stewart, 1999). George F.G. Stanley's *The War of 1812: Land Operations* (Toronto: Macmillan, 1983) provides the best review of the war's military history. In *The Iroquois in the War of 1812* (Toronto: University of Toronto Press, 1998), Carl Benn looks at the Six Nations' involvement. The best biography of one of the greatest First Nations leaders of all times is John Sugden's *Tecumseh: A Life* (New York: Henry Holt and Company, 1997). George Sheppard examines the social fabric of Upper Canadian society at the time of the War of 1812 in *Plunder, Profit and Paroles: A Social History of the War of 1812 in Upper Canada* (Montreal/Kingston: McGill-Queen's University Press, 1994). David S. Heidler and Jeanne T. Heidler have edited *Encyclopedia of the War of 1812* (Santa Barbara, CA: ABC-CLIO, 1997).

Alison Prentice et al., *Canadian Women: A History*, 2nd ed. (Toronto: Harcourt Brace, 1996) examines changes in the lives of British North American women in the late 18th and early 19th centuries. See as well Jane Errington, *Wives and Mothers, School Mistresses and Scullery Maids: Working Women in Upper Canada, 1790–1840* (Montreal/Kingston: McGill-Queen's University Press, 1995); and Cecilia Morgan, *Public Men and Virtuous Women: The Gendered Languages of Religion and Politics in Upper Canada, 1791–1850* (Toronto: University of Toronto Press, 1996). Colin M. Coates and Cecilia Morgan's *Heroines and History: Madeline de Verchères and Laura Secord* (Toronto: University of Toronto Press, 2001) compares the images of these two "heroines" in early Canadian historical writing.

WEBLINKS

The War of 1812
http://www.archives.gov.on.ca/english/exhibits/1812/index.html

A virtual exhibit on the War of 1812 by the Government of Ontario. Contains details on participants, battlegrounds, and many digitized primary source documents.

The Treaty of Ghent
http://www.dfait-maeci.gc.ca/department/history/keydocs/keydocs_details-en.asp?intDocumentId=3

The 1814 peace Treaty of Ghent, which ended the War of 1812 between Great Britain and the United States.

Context of the War of 1812
http://www.galafilm.com/1812/e/index.html

This website contains many documents and images concerning the participants in the War of 1812.

Peace and Conflict: The War of 1812
http://www.histori.ca/peace/page.do?pageID=336

Journal entries, speeches, images, and maps relating to the participants in the War of 1812.

War of 1812 Articles
http://www.warof1812.ca/1812art.htm

Many articles containing excerpts from journals and letters of participants in the War of 1812. The site also contains battle reports and biographies.

Negotiations
http://www.galafilm.com/1812/e/people/iroq_negos.html

The account of John Norton, or Teyoninhokarawen, of negotiations between Iroquois in both Canada and the United States during, and after, the War of 1812. Norton's full account is available in the Champlain Society database.

Article Seventeen

Reluctant Warriors: British North Americans and the War of 1812

E. Jane Errington

Come all ye bold Canadians,
I'd have you lend an ear,
Unto a short ditty
Which will your spirits cheer.
Concerning an engagement
We had at Detroit town,
The pride of those Yankee boys,
So bravely we took down.[1]

So began one of the few Canadian ballads from the War of 1812. It tells the story of the glorious Canadian victory at Detroit, of how "our brave commander, Sir Isaac Brock" together with a handful of eager, undaunted Canadian boys forced the Yankees to surrender.

Those Yankee hearts began to ache,
Their blood it did run cold,
To see us marching forward
So courageous and so bold.
Their general sent a flag to us,
For quarter he did call,
Saying "Stay your hand, brave British boys,"
"I fear you'll slay us all."

Source: E. Jane Errington, "Reluctant Warriors: British North Americans and the War of 1812," *The Sixty Years' War for the Great Lakes, 1754–1814*, eds. David Curtis Skaggs and Larry L. Nelson (East Lansing: Michigan State University Press, 2001): 325–336. Reprinted by permission.

The ballad, like many others of its kind, extolled the glorious victory of a heroic and patriotic people. And the sentiments expressed in this particular campfire song have become, if only unconsciously, part of the Canadian legacy of the War of 1812. In popular culture, the War of 1812 is often characterized as the first real test of the new peoples and of their earlier decision to remain loyal to the Empire and the British King during the first American civil war, or what is more commonly termed the Revolution. In 1812, the story goes, Canadians, and particularly Upper Canadians, gallantly fought for their homes, their communities, their colony, and their King. They fought for peace, and to preserve a way of life that was inherently more "civilized" than that of the enemy from the south. The Canadian victory, first at Detroit and then of the war itself, both confirmed the justness of their cause and illustrated that Upper Canadians were willing and eager combatants who had remained true to their loyalist heritage.

But as we know, how governments and popular culture remember and extol a conflict often bears little resemblance to the nature of the war itself or the attitudes of its participants. In the case in point here, all that fought in the War of 1812 claimed and continue to claim victory. For U.S. songwriters, veterans and their families, politicians, and even historians, the War of 1812 was the second War of Independence. It confirmed the righteousness of the Revolution and illustrated the ability of the new republic and its people to defend themselves against all odds. For Upper Canadians in 1815 and throughout the nineteenth and into the early twentieth centuries, the war represented the beginning of nationhood. It illustrated the strength of a nation in arms and the innate patriotism and loyalty of the Canadian people. And for the British of course, the War of 1812, if ever mentioned, was a minor, if regrettable, campaign in their contest with Napoleon.

Yet when Stephen Miles, editor of the Kingston *Gazette,* reported in late June 1812 that the United States and Great Britain and, thus, its British colonies in North America were now officially at war, his readers, although not particularly surprised, were nonetheless dismayed.[2] Since before the turn of the century, many Upper Canadians had lived in fear that they would be forced to take up arms against friends, family, and neighbors to the south. And, for twenty years, local residents had done all they could to avoid what most considered would be an "unnatural" conflict. But it had been to no avail. Miles' announcement, and General Isaac Brock's call to arms and hasty march to Detroit brought an end to years of speculation and trepidation. Upper Canadians in 1812 did not want war. Those who in the post war period came to be characterized as "brave Canadian boys" were, in 1812, very reluctant warriors. Few, if any, were willing, as the ballad related to "go along with Brock . . . without further adieu." Indeed, throughout the three years of war, as had been the case since the colony had been created, colonial leaders lived with the knowledge that some, if not most, Upper Canadians were not only reluctant, but would refuse to fight at all. Even worse it was feared, some would join the invading forces or welcome them with open arms.

The roots of this reluctance, or what one historian has characterized as wide spread indifference, can be traced back to the time before the creation of the colony.[3] The American Revolution, it is frequently asserted, created not one nation but two. In 1783–84, as Americans debated how best to govern themselves, approximately ten thousand former residents of the old thirteen colonies began to make their way north to the British colony of Quebec.[4] This heterogeneous group of "Loyalists" was bitter and felt betrayed. They were the losers in that momentous civil war over the future of their homes; and, harassed and persecuted by neighbors and republican officials, they were now political refugees — forced to leave their homes and most of their possessions and seek asylum, as one loyalist later remembered "in the howling wilderness."[5] For some at least, their flight north across the St. Lawrence or lower Great Lakes was a confirmation of their continued allegiance to the king and to a way of life that ensured order, stability and personal liberty, (not licentiousness as they believed was now being encouraged in the new republic).[6] Yet these British loyalists were, by birth and inclination, also Americans. Although they were still British subjects, "home" was North America; and it was with this land and these people, not with the rolling hills of the British Isles, with whom they identified.

It is therefore not surprising, as one commentator noted, that, soon after the Revolution, "passions mutually subsided" on both sides of the border.[7] In 1792, local officials of the newly formed colony of Upper Canada invited American settlers to cross the border and take up land and establish businesses. With reportedly little or no "attachment to the King of Great Britain" or consciousness of the international border, thousands of restless pioneers came north, as many of their neighbors went west, to find land, to find employment, and generally to grasp new opportunities for themselves and their children.[8] By 1810, it is estimated that "loyalist element was scarcely noticeable amongst the diversity of people" who had flooded into the colony after about 1792.[9] Just before the War of 1812, Upper Canada was, demographically at least, an American colony.[10]

The geographic realities, which facilitated the movement of American pioneer farmers north, also encouraged Upper Canadians to look and travel south. Although poor and in many cases nonexistent roads and other means of communication isolated individual Upper Canadian communities from each other, the St. Lawrence River and the lower Great Lakes provided easy access north and south. Until well into the 1830s, residents of New York and the New England states were Upper Canadians' closest and most accessible neighbors. Visitors, mail, news, and information from Europe, from the United States, and even from the most eastern sections of British North America traveled fastest and most efficiently to and from Upper Canada by way of New York, Boston, or Philadelphia.[11]

The bonds forged by geography were strengthened in the early years by strong personal and professional ties, north and south. Despite the turmoil and, for some loyalists, the legacy of bitterness left by the Revolution, Upper Canadians and Americans "were still interesting objects to each other."[12] For almost all Upper Canadians before the War of 1812, the United States was their former home and remained the home of relatives and friends. A French traveler, La Rochefoucault-Liancourt noted as early as 1795, that though some "American Loyalists . . . still harbour enmity and hatred against their native land and countrymen . . . these sentiments [were] daily decreasing" and were "not shared by the far greater number of emigrants who arrive from the United States, Nova Scotia and New Brunswick."[13] Within a short time, it was reported that "the most social harmony" existed between "gentleman on the American side and those on the British side" of the border.[14] Leading loyalists like Richard Cartwright of Kingston regularly visited their old homes in the United States; merchants, traders, and farmers engaged in lucrative economic relations with associates across the border; Upper Canadians entertained American visitors in their homes; a growing number attended camp meetings and met at quarterly sessions led by itinerant American preachers; some Upper Canadian children went south to school; and a few residents, taking advantage of the regular ferry services, which by 1800 linked Kingston and Niagara and their closest American communities, crossed the border to shop or take a cure.[15] Being a resident of this British colony did not mean that even the most loyal subjects rejected their close association with their old homes. Indeed, throughout the first twenty-five years of colonial development, most Upper Canadians considered themselves part of a North American community, which spanned the border.

Upper Canada was officially and administratively a British colony, however. To gain land and vote, settlers had to swear an oath of allegiance to the British crown and, twice annually, adult men had to muster for militia training. Moreover, there is no question that for colonial leaders, including British office holders sent by London, like Lieutenant Governors Simcoe and Gore and General Sir Isaac Brock, and members of the indigenous elite, like

Richard Cartwright of Kingston, allegiance to the Empire and to the principles enshrined in the British Constitution also helped to define who and what they were.

Some historians have suggested that for these men, being Upper Canadian meant being anti-American; and that throughout the first generation of colonial development, these Upper Canadians rejected all things emanating from south of the Great Lakes. Thus, it is implied, Upper Canadians in 1812 were willing and, in fact, eager to defend their place in the Empire. Certainly, many leading Upper Canadians, like the Reverend John Strachan of York, were scornful of the republic and its lack of order and justice. And in 1812, many went out of their way to express their willingness to take up arms in defense of their homes. However, even the most conservative and patriotic Upper Canadians could not and did not try to deny the importance of geography and shared interests with neighbors to the south.

As they began to lay the political and economic foundations of the new British colony, the Upper Canadian elite could not help but be conscious of how similar the colony was to communities south of the frontier. Upper Canadians and Americans, particularly in New York and New England, shared not only a land and people, they also shared many common concerns of settlement and of future development. Most Upper Canadians were pioneer farmers and their daily struggle for survival — clearing the bush, building homes, planting and harvesting — was a re-creation of events being pursued south of the border. As a number of commentators noted, there was little to distinguish the backwoods of Upper Canada from the frontier of the United States.[16] Upper Canadians of all economic and political stripes drew frequently on American models when considering, for example, how to build roads, till the soil, establish banks, or foster local markets. Although Upper Canada was a British province, many consciously acknowledged that the United States had much to offer residents in the new colony.

Even in political affairs, colonial leaders did not reject all things American. Although they feared the insidious influence of republicanism and democracy and often predicted the political disintegration of the United States, men like John Strachan and Richard Cartwright believed that many Americans shared their concerns. In particular, they applauded the Federalists of New England and New York for their stance in support of order against unbridled democracy. And Upper Canadians recognized that, like themselves, the Federalists wanted to maintain and increase commerce and contact across the border. Between 1800 and 1812, and indeed, throughout the years of war, leading Upper Canadians made fine distinctions between those they viewed as "good" American citizens and the policies of the American government; and they were sympathetic to the plight of those Americans who, like themselves, were suffering under the policies of rapacious republicanism.[17]

Thus, for most Upper Canadians, allegiance to Great Britain usually did not automatically conflict with their continuing sense of being part of a North American community. There were times, however, when Upper Canadians were forced to recognize the apparent contradiction of their position. The colony had been created, after all, not by amicable cooperation but out of bitter confrontation between Great Britain and the United States. Moreover, although geographic proximity encouraged a sense of community that spanned the lakes, it also provided the continuing potential for local tensions, as well as the possibility that the Great Lakes–St. Lawrence basin might once again be the theater of armed conflict between the two nations.

Between 1791 and 1812, Upper Canadians worked hard to re-establish and cement amicable relations along what was still a largely unmarked and porous border. Both prudence and personal inclination encouraged this. Most Upper Canadians lived, it must be remembered, within a few miles of the expanding and dynamic republic. More importantly, close personal and economic associations with friends and family members south of the Great Lakes would be harmed and perhaps irrevocably severed if the two governments were at odds.

It was not surprising, therefore, that just before the turn of the century, one settler in Niagara suggested that residents of the area gather together for various sporting events, to supplement the already existing "intercourse of economic, friendship and sociability between the people of the province and those in the neighbouring part of the United States."[18] Upper Canadians applauded when the American garrison showed the colony's flag and played the "British Grenadiers" on the occasion of the king's birthday. "Such acts of civility" should be encouraged, many Upper Canadians believed.[19] Upper Canadians, too, should show "a spirit of mutually liberality, candour and forbearance," for only "by preserving harmony and promoting good neighbourhood" could "friends of both nations . . . respectively increase their national prosperity."[20]

Colonial leaders also pointedly condemned those counterfeiters, smugglers, criminals, and deserting British soldiers who used the border to avoid apprehension. "National difficulties," as one commentator terms it, erupted frequently as a result of "the mutual incursions and acts of jurisdiction and other interferences of the subject of one government within the known and acknowledged limits of the other."[21] Such acts were to be "deprecated" and Upper Canadians were cautioned to avoid "becoming habituated to mutual prejudices, jealousies, reflections, reproaches and all that process of national alienation which had, in the progress of ages, rendered the British and the French so inveterate in their hostility as to call each other natural enemies."[22]

At the same time, it is clear that many Upper Canadians never really recognized that a border existed at all — and they not only traveled back and forth at will, but after 1800 when customs duties were established, regularly avoided paying duties on trade goods. Smuggling seems to have been one of the most lucrative and accepted (if not respectable) means of doing business and it was eagerly supported on both sides of the border.[23] In the summer, "crafts of all sorts and sizes crowded the River St. Lawrence."[24] In the winter, ice conditions permitting, sleighs laden with goods made the journey. One U.S. customs officer at Sackets Harbor reported in 1809, at the height of the Embargo, "all the force I can raise is not sufficient to stop them." The smugglers "appear determined to evade the law at the risk of their lives." Indeed, he concluded, fearfully, "my life and the lives of my deputies are threatened daily; what will be the fate of us God only knows."[25]

Many Upper Canadians and Americans obviously benefited from smuggling; the embargo of 1808 and the War of 1812 only enhanced their profits. For officials on both sides of the border, however, the extensive smuggling threatened to disrupt peaceful relations between their governments. Therefore, some in the colony (a number of whom were undoubtedly losing business to the smugglers) called on Upper Canadians to stop evading the law. In the fall of 1810, for example, residents of Kingston and officials on the south shore of Lake Ontario organized a cooperative effort to apprehend smugglers. "Such instances of the reciprocation of acts of justices and liberality," one contributor to the Kingston *Gazette* remarked with approval, "were much more conducive to mutual prosperity than a state of legislative counteraction and hostility."[26] Everyone, it was believed, had a responsibility to encourage "the preservation of peace" between Upper Canada and the United States.[27]

The periodic problems that erupted along the border were, for the most part, local concerns. And various individual attempts to encourage civility and goodwill in the years before the War of 1812 seemed to be successful. Yet, it was always evident that harmony on the Great Lakes frontier did not ensure peace between the governments of the United States and Great Britain. For, although open warfare between Great Britain and the United States had ended in 1784, the Treaty of Paris had not stopped the two nations from jockeying for position on the western frontier.

In July 1794, Upper Canadians read excerpts from an Albany paper that the United States intended a "total conquest" of the west and "a reduction of the interior posts of the Upper

Provinces."[28] First, American officials began to stop all boats and goods from entering Upper Canada from the south. Then, General "Mad" Anthony Wayne and a contingent of troops began to advance on British forts inside the young republic. What had sparked these actions was the U.S. government's belief that British officials were actively encouraging the Native nations of the northwest to raid American frontier settlements. Moreover, Great Britain was refusing to relinquish forts in the west. Upper Canadians watched apprehensively as imperial officials responded and most expected that war would be declared immediately. It was with considerable relief that leading colonists learned of the success of John Jay's mission to London.[29]

It was soon evident that the resolution of this controversy in 1795 did not really resolve the differences between the two governments. Between 1796 and 1800, Upper Canadians watched with interest and some concern as American neutrality was buffeted by the combined pressure of war in Europe and internal political divisions. Thomas Jefferson's victory in 1800 brought renewed fears that the United States would join France in its campaign against Great Britain. And, although those fears appeared for a time to be unfounded, the *Chesapeake* Affair in 1807 threatened once again to bring war to the Great Lakes frontier. Despite calls by Upper Canadians and Federalists in the United States for restraint, the American government sounded the alarm and made preparations for war. Upper Canadian leaders had little alternative but to call the colony to arms.

The most pressing concern of colonial leaders in 1807 and 1808, as it would be in 1812, was that the majority of Upper Canadians would be at best, reluctant combatants. Indeed, it was feared that many might refuse to fight at all. Most residents had no political or emotional attachment to the king or the British Empire. Moreover, most had only recently arrived from the United States.

Colonial leaders did what they could to cope with the situation. In a speech to the local militia in December 1807, Richard Cartwright explained to assembled men that it was the American government, and the Republicans, "that blind and misguided party," who were threatening to plunge the continent into war. The "most enlightened and patriotic citizens" of the United States realized that war would harm American commerce and "ultimately the existence of their independence." By defending themselves, Cartwright intimated, Upper Canadians were defending not only their homes, but also the interests of many of their friends and neighbors in the United States. As the official government gazette, the *Upper Canada Gazette* reported, "one congressman had even written to the present that 'we are doing no good. I fear we are about to plunge the nation into the most dreadful calamities, unnecessarily and wantonly.'"[30]

For the next four years, the Upper Canadian elites waged a pointed and increasingly assertive propaganda campaign to try to convince their readers that, if and when war broke out, settlers could and should defend their new homes against the forces of tyranny (and republicanism). By doing so, it was explicitly stated, they would be remaining true to their old homes and beliefs. Most Upper Canadians appear to have ignored such entreaties. And although international tensions continued to threaten local peace, residents continued to move back and forth across the border, and till their fields and trade.

Even in January and February 1812, when General Isaac Brock, the president of the colony, warned that although "we wish and hope for peace" war was probably at no great distance and "it was our duty to be prepared"[31] most turned a deaf ear. The members of the House of Assembly refused to pass measures to require militiamen to forswear allegiance to any foreign country; and Brock's request to suspend the writ of habeas corpus was denied. As George Sheppard has commented in his groundbreaking work, *Plunder, Profits and Paroles,* "The colonists were firm in their belief that they were not responsible for the deteriorating relationship between Britain and the United States."[32] And one colonist suggested, in a letter in a provincial newspaper that "if your [the United States] quarrel is with Britain, go and avenge yourselves on her own shores."[33]

Colonial leaders and Imperial officials were, not surprisingly, alarmed. For the next four months, the propaganda campaign to convince Upper Canadians to take up arms if need be, intensified. But, when editor Stephen Miles of Kingston announced that war had been declared in June 1812, life continued as usual for most Upper Canadians; individuals, goods, and news continued to flow across the border. More to the point, most settlers resisted calls to muster and train. Even when Brock instituted changes to the Militia Act that granted volunteers exemptions from statute labor, jury duty and personal arrest for small debts, militia quotas were rarely met. It is clear in June and July 1812, that most Upper Canadians were still reluctant to go to war. And Brock and others feared that "the great mass of people" would either flee back to their old homes or "join the American government" and work for the overthrow of the British in North America.[34]

Even once actual fighting began, the war seemed to have little direct impact on the lives of most Upper Canadians. It was only in the western portions of the colony that residents suffered property damage, men were injured and died of their wounds or disease, and families were left bereft. And although many of the militiamen in the Niagara region called out in late June and early July seemed to be willing to defend their own homes and businesses, the incident of desertion was high. Moreover, Brock predicted that "most would leave anyway once the harvest began."[35] As George Sheppard has observed, colonists' indifference to the war was striking and it was not restricted to only the "recent arrivals from the United States."[36] Both Loyalists and late Loyalists, farmers, craftsmen, and politicians tried to avoid service.

As the war dragged on, many Upper Canadians even began to resist providing supplies and support to the British cause. Although there is no question that some Upper Canadians directly benefited from the war, many others did not. Militia duty took men away from the fields and their shops; the prices of goods and services increased dramatically; and the British forces often confiscated livestock, grain and other goods when they could not purchase them. In parts of the province, Upper Canadians watched, seemingly helpless, as their farms were razed to the ground by enemy forces; war widows were often frustrated when they turned to colonial officials for financial assistance.

For most Upper Canadians, the actual conflict did little to break down their reluctance to take up arms. And for many, being thrust into the maelstrom of battle only served to foster a resentment of their own government as well as that of the enemy. As Sheppard has concluded, "while a few colonists assisted the British forces, the majority resorted to desertion or paroles to avoid serving."[37]

> Come all ye bold Canadians,
> Enlisted in the cause,
> To defend your country,
> And to maintain your laws,
> Being all united,
> This is the song we'll sing;
> Success unto Great Britain,
> And God save the King.

It seems more than questionable that these words were truly sung by Canadians during the first months of the War of 1812. In June and July 1812, as had been the case for the previous twenty-five or so years, Upper Canadians did all they could to avoid war. Geography, personal inclination, commerce, and, to some degree, politics all encouraged these British colonists to consider themselves part of a community, which spanned the Great Lakes and the St. Lawrence basin. To find that, despite all their best efforts, war was being thrust upon them, was daunting and many, no doubt, resented this intrusion onto their lives. It is not surprising that Upper Canadians were reluctant warriors in 1812. It was only after the war was over and that memory had dimmed that these reluctant warriors could become "bold Canadians."

NOTES

1. "The Bold Canadian: A Ballad of the War of 1812," taken from Morris Zaslow, ed., *The Defended Border* (Toronto: Macmillan Co. of Canada, 1964), 303–4.

2. Kingston *Gazette,* 30 June 1812, taken from the *Albany Gazette*. Miles began, "it is pretty clearly ascertained that war with the United States is no longer to be avoided."

3. George Sheppard, *Plunder, Profits and Paroles: A Social History of the War of 1812 in Upper Canada* (Montreal and Kingston: McGill–Queen's University Press, 1994).

4. Certainly, estimates vary from 6,000 to 10,000.

5. [Richard Cartwright], *Letters from an American Loyalist in Upper-Canada*, Letter X, (Halifax, Nova Scotia: 1810).

6. See among others, Janice Potter, *The Liberty We Seek: Loyalist Ideology in Colonial New York and Massachusetts* (Cambridge, Mass: Harvard University Press, 1983) for a detailed discussion of loyalist ideology.

7. Francóis-Aléxandre-Fréderic, duc de La Rochefoucault-Liancourt, *Travels in Canada* (1795; Reprint, Toronto: William Renwick Riddell, 1917), 44.

8. Ibid., 36. See also John Maud, *Visit to the Falls of Niagara in 1800* (London: Longmans, Rees, Orme, Brown and Green, 1826), 60.

9. Michael Smith, *A Geographical View of British Possessions in North America* (Philadelphia: P. Mauro, 1813), 82.

10. See among others, Smith, *A Geographical View,* 61, for estimates of population in the colony in 1810.

11. See Stephen Roberts, "Imperial Policy, Provincial Administration and Defences of Canada" (Ph.D. thesis, Oxford University, 1975); John Lambert, *Travels Through Canada and the United States* (London: C. Cradock and W. Joy, 1814); John Melish, *Travels Through the United States of America* (Belfast: Jos. Smyth, 1818).

12. Robert Gourlay, *General Introduction to Statistical Account of Upper Canada* (London: Simpkin and Marshall, 1822), 115.

13. Ibid., 74.

14. D'Arcy Boulton, *A Sketch of His Majesty's Province of Upper Canada* (London, 1805; Reprint, Toronto: Baxter, 1961), 32.

15. See travelers' accounts already cited and numerous references in the local papers, including *Upper Canada Gazette,* 19 April 1797; 25 September 1817; 10 February 1820; 23 June 1825. It is known that Richard Cartwright, a prominent resident of Kingston, regularly made trips south after 1800. See Cartwright, see among others, Smith, *A Geographical View,* 61, for estimates of population in the colony in 1810. Papers, Q.U.A. So too did Joel Stone, Solomon Jones Papers, Q.U.A. and Robert Hamilton (Bruce Wilson, *The Enterprises of Robert Hamilton* [Ottawa: Carleton University Press, 1984]) to name only a few.

16. Ralph Brown, *Mirror for Americans* (New York: American Geographical Society, 1903) and travel accounts previously noted.

17. I have developed these ideas extensively in *The Lion, The Eagle and Upper Canada: A Developing Colonial Ideology* (Kingston and Montreal: McGill–Queen's University Press, 1987, 1995).

18. *Upper Canada Gazette,* 31 May 1799.

19. Ibid., 27 January 1798.

20. Kingston *Gazette,* 25 September 1810.

21. Ibid., 11 October 1810.

22. Ibid., 25 September 1810.

23. In addition to numerous references in the local newspapers, for the most part condemning the practice, and in travel accounts, governments on both sides of the border were forced to try to cope with the issue. See A.L. Burt, *The United States, Great Britain and British North America* (New York: Russell and Russell, 1961); Alexander C. Flick, ed., *The History of the State of New York,* 10 vols. (New York: Columbia University Press, 1933–37).

24. Matilda Ridout, Lady Edgar, *General Brock* (Toronto: Oxford University Press, 1926), 109.
25. Report of Hart Massey, 14 March 1809, quoted in Flick, *The History of the State of New York*, 5:199.
26. Kingston *Gazette*, 2 October 1810; 6 November 1810.
27. Ibid., 6 November 1810; 11 October 1810.
28. *Upper Canada Gazette*, 10 July 1794.
29. See Burt, *The United States*, for discussion of the rising tensions before the war; and Errington, *Lion and the Eagle*, chapter 4, for a more complete discussion of Upper Canadian reaction to this.
30. *Upper Canada Gazette*, 15 October 1808.
31. Reported in the Kingston *Gazette*, 28 January 1812.
32. Sheppard, *Plunder*, 37.
33. Quoted in ibid., 36.
34. Melish, *Travels*, 485. See also discussion in Errington, *Lion and the Eagle*, chapter 4, and Sheppard, *Plunder*.
35. Sheppard, *Plunder*, 47.
36. Ibid., 74.
37. Ibid., 98.

Article Eighteen

His Majesty's Indian Allies: Native Peoples, the British Crown and the War of 1812

Robert S. Allen

The appointment of William Johnson in 1755 as His Britannic Majesty's "Sole Agent for and Superintendent of the Affairs of our faithful subjects and allies, the six united Nations of Indians and their Confederates in the Northern Parts of North America," created a formal, imperial and centralized Indian Department to direct the affairs of Native peoples on behalf of the British Crown.[1] Prior to the pivotal influence of the regime of Sir William Johnson (1755–74), Indian affairs in colonial America had been marked by a long, vexing and generally rudderless period of imperial "salutary neglect." Inter-colonial land rivalries and wrangling disunity had only further complicated British–Indian relations which fluctuated between the benign and the intolerable. But by the 1750s, the looming

Portrait of Sir William Johnson from Augustus C. Buell, *Sir William Johnson* (New York, 1903). Courtesy, Clarke Historical Library, Central Michigan University.

and final conflict with France for paramountcy in North America turned British vacillation into resolve. The appointment by royal commission of a single Crown official for the administration and management of Indian Affairs was therefore a sensible and long overdue imperial initiative. Finally, after one hundred and fifty years of permanent British settlement along the eastern shores of the "new world" a formal and centralized policy for the indigenous or Native peoples had emanated from Britain. The cohesive vehicle for implementing the policy directives was the

Source: Robert S. Allen, "His Majesty's Indian Allies: Native Peoples, the British Crown and the War of 1812," *Michigan Historical Review*, 14 (Fall 1988):1–24. Reprinted by permission.

British Indian Department, the forerunner of the present Department of Indian and Northern Affairs Canada. Until the end of the War of 1812, the fundamental and motivating tenet of the policy was to court and maintain the allegiance of the Native peoples to the royal cause. As a result, and especially in the post-1774 years against the common enemy (the Americans), an enduring and symbiotic relationship evolved between the Native peoples and the British Crown which was rooted in the mutual need and desire for "protection and survival."[2] British Indian policy from 1774 to 1815 was thus geared to ensure the preservation and defense of Canada through the military use and assistance of "His Majesty's Indian Allies."[3]

The Native peoples were not duped by this British scheme, and demonstrated an equal shrewdness in manipulating Crown officials in order to preserve traditional tribal lands and culture. Yet the fundamental and significant difference was that the British manipulated successfully. Perhaps the Indians faced a hopeless task in attempting to stem the tide of the frontier. Nonetheless, the results were conclusive, for while the Iroquois lost their ancient castles along the Finger Lakes of Upper New York, and later the tribes of the Ohio Valley were forsaken, the British, by securing invaluable Indian assistance, defeated the French and then, more particularly, defended successfully the Crown's interest in British North America from the American invaders of 1812.

The success of British Indian policy during the pre-War of 1812 years can be demonstrated by detailing a few examples. Throughout the Seven Years' War, for instance, Johnson managed to retain the loyalty of the Mohawk and others of the Six Nations Confederacy of Iroquois in the conflict between Britain and France for imperial supremacy in North America. His nominal victory at the battle of Lake George in September 1755 against the French regulars of Baron Dieskau, held the wavering Iroquois neutral for nearly three years, in spite of subsequent French successes at Fort Bull and Oswego in 1756, Fort William Henry in 1757, and Ticonderoga in 1758. But a British resurgence, exemplified by a smashing victory of Johnson's loyal Iroquois at the battle of La Belle Famille near Fort Niagara in July 1759 against a French relief column, coupled with the fall of Quebec two months later, ended French imperial ambitions in North America.[4]

In April 1775, less than a year after the death of Sir William Johnson, the 'shots heard round the world' at Lexington and Concord initiated a cruel and bitter civil war and rebellion in colonial America. Once again, the military support of Native peoples was vital to the Crown's vested interest in America. British Indian policy was successful during these years in large measure because of the several tribes that had long opposed the intrusion into their lands of their hereditary foe, the American backwoodsman. Native peoples were thus thrown into a natural military alliance with the British Crown, and against the common enemy.

Yet at the peace negotiations of 1783, British plenipotentiaries "sold the Indians to Congress" and transferred sovereignty of all Indian-held lands south of the Great Lakes and west of the Mississippi River, to the new United States — the first abandonment.[5] The warriors were "thunderstruck."[6] They had not lost their war nor their land. Indeed in June and August 1782, the Indians had won two successive and decisive victories at Sandusky and Blue Licks against the Americans. In the latter engagement, the legendary Daniel Boone of Kentucky was among the routed.[7] Following some hasty rethinking, prompted by the fear of Indian reprisals, the British decided to retain the eastern posts; and the warriors, now encouraged and supplied by His Majesty's government, continued to struggle to preserve and defend aboriginal lands. After years of conflict, tribal resistance in the Ohio Valley finally collapsed at the battle of Fallen Timbers in August 1794. At this critical moment, the British at nearby Fort Miami, despite the most avowed promises to the contrary, slammed shut the gates of the fort, and assumed a lofty position of splendid isolation.[8] The formalization of the Jay Treaty with the American republic soon after stipulated in part the removal of the British from the western post by June 1796. Joseph Brant, the Mohawk chief and Loyalist, tersely summarized the situation by stating that "this is the second time the poor Indians have been left in the lurch."[9]

British Indian policy between 1775 and 1796 had been effective and coldly calculating. The new Loyalist settlements north of the lakes and rivers at Amherstburg, Sandwich, Newark, Quinte and along the upper St. Lawrence, protected as they had been for thirteen years by a convenient Indian barrier, prospered and gained a measure of security, while to the south, warriors fought and died, not to preserve and defend British Canada, but in a vain attempt to retain ancient tribal lands.[10]

Between 1796 and 1807 the influence and prestige of the British Indian Department waned to insignificance as the Indians were no longer needed as military allies. During these quiet years, expenditures were drastically reduced, and the department was re-organized. In a "Plan for the Future Government of the Indian Department" in June 1796, the position of Superintendent of Indian Affairs was established for each of the replacement forts in Upper Canada.[11] As a result, for instance, Matthew Elliott was appointed superintendent for the new British post at Amherstburg. Although the traditional military role of the department had reached a nadir at this time, the superintendents were nonetheless instructed to "use the utmost diligence to preserve and promote friendship between the troops and Indians . . . and to maintain harmony at the King's (new) posts."[12] The wisdom of attempting to maintain the chain of friendship alliance proved prophetic. The "Chesapeake Affair" of June 1807 and the bellicose reaction by an aroused American public for a redemption of national honor produced a fear of invasion in the weakly defended settlement of the Canadas. In particular, the position of Upper Canada was precarious because the defensive strategy devised by the British, already heavily burdened with the Napoleonic war, was to preserve the fortress of Quebec and subordinate all other considerations. Once again, the future security, and even survival, of Upper Canada was to be largely dependent on the allegiance and fighting qualities of His Majesty's Indian Allies. As a result, the British Indian Department was quickly restored to a respectful position of prominence as it was to play an integral role in combating this new danger.

During the winter of 1807–08, Sir James Craig, the captain general and governor-in-chief of British North America, developed a policy for the frontier which was to guide the conduct of the British Indian Department for the next three hectic years. Craig reasoned that in the event of a war, the Indians would not be idle, and if the British did not use them, they undoubtedly would be "employed against us."[13] Therefore, the Indians must be conciliated, but their chiefs must be persuaded not to engage in a premature attack on the Americans. Thus, cautioned Craig, the officers of the Indian Department should avoid making any commitment with them at least in public. In a dispatch to a worried Francis Gore, the lieutenant governor of Upper Canada, Craig noted the "long lasting ties" between the King and the tribes, and suggested that provisions be supplied to the Indians to enable them to protect themselves against the Americans who "obviously desired to take their country."[14] Craig ordered that "the officers of the Indian Department must be diligent and active, the communications must be constant, these topics must be held up to them not merely in Great Councils and public assemblies, they should be privately urged to some of their leading men, with whom endeavours should be used to lead them to a confidence with us."[15]

The dual Indian policy of Craig, one public and one private, was very reminiscent of the immediate post-1783 efforts. As before, the British Indian Department was to renew the old courtship rituals, and secure Indian loyalty to the King, and thus preserve British imperial and territorial jurisdiction in Upper Canada by confounding the expansionist ambitions of the United States. Gore was enthusiastic about the plan and sent William Claus, the deputy superintendent general of Indian Affairs, to the British post of Amherstburg, the key Indian center in the province, where he was to assemble the chiefs, "consult privately" with them and remind them of the "Artful and Clandestine manner, in which the Americans have obtained possession of their lands, and of their obvious intention of ultimately possessing themselves of the whole and driving the Indians out of the Country."[16] However, the officers of the department were reminded to dissuade the tribes from any warlike action until or unless Britain should be at war with the United States.

In the spring of 1808 several Indian bands began to assemble at Amherstburg to hear the British speak in council. For the officers of the Indian Department, the implementation of Craig's policy required delicate and intricate negotiations, particularly since "the Indian Nations owing to the long continuance of Peace have been neglected by us, and from the considerable curtailments made in the Presents to those People it appears, that the retaining of their attachment to the King's Interests has not of late years been thought an object worthy of serious consideration."[17] As a consequence, William Claus, Matthew Elliott and others worked diligently to regain the affections of the Indians. In one council, a Shawnee contingent under Captain Johnny, Blackbeard, and the Buffalo, was told that the King was trying to maintain peace with the Americans, but if he failed, the Indians could expect to hear from the British and together they would regain the country taken from them by the Americans. Heartened by this news, Indian warriors and chiefs, including the influential Shawnee leader Tecumseh who, like Pontiac and Joseph Brant before him, dreamed of a united Indian confederacy, gathered in increasing numbers at Amherstburg to meet with the British. Although the innocuous public councils were conducted with great decorum, formality, and military pomp, the private communications with select chiefs (the backroom politics of the day) were where the real strategy was formulated and entrenched. Yet, in spite of the different Indian Nations collecting on the Wabash to preserve their country from any encroachments, the tribes remained somewhat wary of promised British support. In fact, Major-General Isaac Brock noted that "before we can expect an active co-operation on the part of the Indians the reduction of Detroit and Michilimackinac must convince that people, who conceive themselves to have been sacrificed in 1794, to our policy, that we are earnestly engaged in the war."[18] In spite of these justifiable Indian concerns, the efforts of the British Indian Department in renewing the chain of friendship at Amherstburg was an unqualified success.

For the next two years tribal delegates constantly visited the British at Amherstburg to pledge their support to the King and to receive gifts and provisions in return. The department, receiving no instructions to the contrary, continued to win and maintain the allegiance of the various tribes. By the summer of 1810, Indian frustration and anger at American encroachments on their lands and British Indian Department inspiration, combined to make the Indian appetite for war increasingly difficult to control. In July, a Sauk and Fox delegation arrived at Amherstburg and requested clothing, kettles, muskets, shot, and powder. In council, Elliott urged the Indians to "keep your eyes fixed on me; my tomahawk is now up; be you ready, but do not strike until I give the signal."[19] This speech exhilarated the tribes who were now most enthusiastic about the prospects of a new British–Indian alliance against the common enemy. In November, 2,000 Shawnee, Sauk, Winnebago, Ottawa, and Potawatomi gathered at Amherstburg for a grand council. Tecumseh acted as spokesman for the tribes and informed the British that "we are now determined to defend it [their land] ourselves, and after raising you on your feet leave you behind but expecting you will push forward towards us what may be necessary to supply our wants."[20]

The officers of the British Indian Department were astounded by these words. Elliott wrote Claus stating that "our Neighbours are on the eve of an Indian War, and I have no doubt that the Confederacy is almost general."[21] The November council had placed the British in a difficult and embarrassing position. The policy of 1808 had been too successful. Now the great

Fort McKay, painting by Peter Rindisbacher, circa 1821. (Courtesy of the McCord Museum of Canadian History, Montreal, M1378.)

problem for the department was to prevent the overzealous Indians from attacking the Americans before the official declaration of war between Great Britain and the United States. In a desperate attempt to reverse policy, the department was instructed to dissuade tribes from their projected plan of hostility. The chiefs were to understand clearly that they "must not expect any assistance" from the British.[22] By the summer of 1811 the officers of the Indian Department were striving frantically to stall the Indian war by attempting to convince various influential chiefs that the time was not ripe. But the Indians' desire for war was unshakable and sporadic raids commenced against the American settlements along the Wabash River. The Americans deduced that British intrigue and instigation was behind the revival of Indian resistance and Indian–American and Anglo-American relations rapidly deteriorated. Following the battle of Tippecanoe on 7 November 1811 in which "British muskets were found on the battlefield," the Americans charged that "the whole of the Indians on this frontier have been completely armed and equipped out of the king's stores" at Amherstburg.[23] A war between the Indians, Americans and British now appeared certain.

For several months, prior to Tippecanoe, the British Indian Department had made genuine efforts to prevent an Indian war, but the vacillation of policy and the long delays in communicating often different instructions had hampered the effectiveness of the department and confused the visiting chiefs. The only alternative was the renewal of the traditional friendship and military alliance as revived in 1808. Therefore, throughout the spring of 1812, following the latest instructions of using "your utmost endeavours to promote His Majesty's Indian Interest in general," the British Indian Department secretly prepared the tribes for war.[24] By June of 1812 when the United States finally declared war on Great Britain and proceeded to invade Upper Canada, the British Indian Department, probably relieved at receiving the news, was waiting at Amherstburg with an impatient host of Indian warriors for the commencement of military action.

Nowhere was the success of the long-standing and evolving British Indian policy better demonstrated than during the War of 1812. From the moment hostilities commenced, the fighting efforts of His Majesty's Indian Allies were generally successful, particularly during the first few critical summer months of 1812, as evidenced by a series of Indian inspired victories at such places as Michilimackinac and along the Detroit River at Brownston, Maguaga (Monguagon) and Detroit.[25] The Native leaders came from many tribes and regions of the Great Lakes. Roundhead, Walk-in-the-Water and Split Log were Wyandot, formerly known as the Huron of Detroit; Main Poc was a Potawatomi; Newyash, an Ottawa; Tomah, a Menonomee; Black Hawk, a Sauk from the upper Mississippi; and there were many others. Yet Tecumseh, a Shawnee, emerged as the individual of dominant authority and influence among the tribes.[26] Subsequently glamorized in poetry and prose by non-native writers, especially Canadian, Tecumseh possessed no particular love nor loyalty to Canada.[27] His sole interest was to establish a strong pan-Indian movement and resist the Americans who were coveting the traditional lands of the Native peoples. Thus during the War of 1812, the warriors used the necessary convenience of a formal military alliance with the British, flung themselves against the common enemy, and in the process fought magnificently, if unwittingly, in the defense of the British Crown in Canada. In January 1813, Roundhead, with Wyandot and others of His Majesty's Indian Allies, spearheaded a smashing and bloody British–Indian victory over the Americans at the River Raisin (Frenchtown), now Monroe, Michigan.[28] The killing of some Americans wounded after the battle by warriors, an event neither unique nor rare for both sides in the annals of frontier warfare in America, merely heightened the intensity and determination of the combatants. Near Fort Meigs along the Maumee River in May, Tecumseh caught a reinforcement of Kentucky volunteers in the woods, and virtually slaughtered them. Yet, at Fort Stephenson along the Sandusky River in August, the warriors decided to assume the role of spectators, and watched British regulars destroy themselves in futile charges against the formidable enemy defenses.[29]

But with the American naval victory at Put-in-Bay on Lake Erie in September 1813, the British position at Fort Malden (Amherstburg) became untenable. The tactical decision to withdraw from the region, owing to the fact that the Americans now controlled Lake Erie and could play havoc with British logistics, especially provisioning, was vehemently opposed by the chiefs and warriors, who remembered 1783 and 1794. To the Native peoples, the British departure was also a symbolic abandonment of Indian territorial interests, and thus represented a third betrayal. A few days later on 5 October 1813, at Moravian Town on the Thames River, representatives of many tribes — Shawnee, Ottawa, Ojibwa, Potawatomi, Wyandot (those who hadn't defected), Delaware, Sauk, Fox, Winnebago and even some Creek from the South, stood grimly with Tecumseh; and possibly feeling that courage and defiance were their only remaining true allies, faced for a final time the ever advancing ancient enemy. The battle was brief and furious. The 41st Regiment of Foot (later the Welch Regiment), physically exhausted after fourteen months of almost continuous and arduous campaigning against much superior forces, at least in numbers, uncharacteristically broke ranks after firing two ragged volleys, and surrendered or dispersed.[30] His Majesty's Indian Allies, positioned in the swamps and woods to the right of the British position, continued to contest the battle for a time, before stubbornly, but in good order, giving way. Tecumseh was slain; and with him ended the dream of a united Indian resistance against the territorial ambitions of the United States in the lower Great Lakes region.[31]

Although His Majesty's Indian Allies faded from the scene along the Detroit front, following the Battle of the Thames, what ended in one area had just begun in another. This second front — the Northwest — merits some considerable attention, for important events took place there which are too little known, and which could have altered dramatically the future geographic boundaries of Canada and the United States. Again, His Majesty's Indian Allies were prominent.

British paramountcy in the upper Mississippi and the Northwest depended on the military allegiance of the Indian tribes of that vast region. The British and Indian capture of Michilimackinac; and the Potawatomi massacre of Fort Dearborn (Chicago) in the summer of 1812 had "opened the northern hive" of Indians against the Americans.[32] Equally important, the zealous activities of the officers of the British Indian Department and several prominent Canadian fur traders in courting and maintaining the alliance with the tribes had resulted in a "British" domination in the Northwest which remained unchallenged until the late spring of 1814.[33]

In May of that year, an American force from St. Louis under General William Clark, governor of Missouri Territory, ascended the Mississippi and, meeting only token resistance from the Sauk and Fox, took possession of Prairie du Chien. After constructing a stockade which he named Fort Shelby and content with his success, Clark returned to St. Louis. He left a small garrison of about seventy men under Lieutenant Joseph Perkins of the Twenty-Fourth United States Infantry to guard the village and the new post. The news of the American presence in the upper Mississippi stung the British commandant at Michilimackinac, Lieutenant Colonel Robert McDouall. He reacted immediately by dispatching a force "to dislodge the American General from his new conquest, and make him relinquish the immense tract of country he had seized upon in consequence and which brought him into the very heart of that occupied by our friendly Indians." Although his own position was weak, McDouall was fully cognizant of the critical threat posed by the Americans at Prairie du Chien to British military hegemony and Canadian fur trade interests in the Northwest. If the enemy was not removed from the area "there was an end to our connection with the Indians . . . tribe after tribe would be graned [sic] over or subdued, and thus would be destroyed the only barrier which protects the Great trading establishments of the North West and the Hudson's Bay Company."[34]

In late June, an expedition under Lt. Col. William McKay was dispatched to Prairie du Chien. They were joined en route by voyageurs, Green Bay militia, and a horde of Indians. McKay was singularly unimpressed with the tribal allies and commented upon his arrival in front of Fort Shelby that his contingent had swelled to 650 men, of whom 120 were Canadian Volunteers, Michigan Fencibles, and officers of the Indian Department, the remainder Indians who proved to be "perfectly useless."[35] The small American fort containing two blockhouses and six pieces of cannon was situated on a hill overlooking the village. A large gunboat, the *Governor Clark*, was anchored in the middle of the Mississippi River. This floating blockhouse, immune from the effects of musket fire, mounted fourteen cannon and had a crew of eighty men. It was constructed so that the men on board could row swiftly in any direction. The unexpected appearance of McKay and his mixed force on Sunday, 17 July, caught the Americans by surprise. It was a pleasant day and the officers were preparing to take a pleasure ride and enjoy an outing in the country. After a dramatic exchange of notes, Perkins concluded by stating that he preferred to defend to the last man rather than surrender. This produced a three hour barrage against the fort and gunboat. The Americans returned the fire. The *Governor Clark*, leaking and taking casualties, withdrew down river. For the next two days McKay conducted siege operations. Two breastworks were constructed, and "a constant but perfectly useless" musket fire was maintained against the fort. Some of the Indians "behaved in a most villanous manner" and plundered the inhabitants in the village. On 19 July, McKay "resolved to accomplish something more decisive," and marched his troops into the recently completed works and prepared red hot shot for the cannon. The Americans, seeing "that a severe assault of some kind was about to be made, raised the white flag." By the terms of the capitulation, McKay took possession of the fort, several pieces of cannon, military and camp equipment, and a large quantity of ammunition and foodstuffs. The surrendered garrison was permitted to retire unmolested in boats down river to St. Louis. McKay was pleased with the Michigan Fencibles who "behaved with great courage, coolness and regularity," and "tho in the midst of a hot fire not a man was even wounded." Indeed, purred McKay, "all acted with that courage and activity so becoming Canadian Militia or Volunteers."[36]

Two days after the success at Fort Shelby, the Indians, whose military prowess had been so recently maligned by McKay, won a crushing victory over the Americans at Rock Island rapids, a few miles south of Prairie du Chien. This American force of about 120 regulars and rangers under the command of Major John Campbell, and unaware of the recent developments, was arriving in six keelboats to reinforce the garrison at Fort Shelby. Near the Indian villages scattered along the banks of the Rock River, about 400 Sauk, Fox and Kickapoo attacked and severely mauled the relief column. The Indians fought with a fierce intensity and, desperate to protect their villages and property, "the women even jumped on board with hoes and some breaking heads, others breaking casks, some trying to cut holes in her bottom to sink her, and others setting fire to her decks."[37] After fifty Americans were killed and wounded in the engagement. Joined by the timely arrival of the *Governor Clark*, Campbell and his remnant made a precipitate retreat to St. Louis. A jubilant McKay reported that "this is perhaps one of the most brilliant actions fought by Indians only since the commencement of the war."[38]

The twin victories at Prairie du Chien and the Rock Island Rapids in July, coupled with the successful defense of Michilimackinac in August, reasserted and confirmed British superiority in the Northwest. In the Upper Mississippi, McKay crowned his success in a symbolic sense by modestly renaming Fort Shelby, Fort McKay. He then promptly retired to his quarters for he had developed "a swelling on the right side of the head" and "a violent fever." In fact he was suffering from a severe case of the mumps. He soon recovered and departed for Michilimackinac.

His successor at Fort McKay was Captain Thomas Gummersall (Tige) Anderson, the commander of the Mississippi Volunteers. As post commandant, Anderson strengthened Fort McKay and built a northeast blockhouse. He worried about the poor harvest that year, and because of the want of provisions, he ordered the Mississippi Volunteers to help the local farmers in getting in the grain. The troops were also kept occupied performing daily garrison duties. There were few diversions, except for excessive rum drinking and watching the occasional exciting spectacle of inter-tribal lacrosse in which several participants usually "got sore wounds from the ball and the hurl stick."[39]

In late summer a second and larger American expedition of 350 men and eight gunboats under the command of Major Zachary Taylor, future president of the United States, was launched against the Indian villages along the Rock River. About 1,200 Sauk, Fox, Kickapoo, Winnebago, and Sioux under the leadership of Black Hawk, the Sauk and "zealous partisan of the British case," assembled to meet the American threat. Fully aware of these events, Anderson dispatched Duncan Graham of the Indian Department and thirty men, and James Keating of the Royal Artillery with two swivel-guns and a 3 pounder to bolster Indian courage. In the early morning of 5 September, the Indians and Canadians attacked Taylor's flotilla at Rock Island. The accuracy of the guns under Keating which was "base enough to knock the Splinters into the men's faces" in the gunboats, and the confidence of the Indians who "raised a yell and commenced firing on us in every direction," convinced Taylor of the futility of attempting to destroy the Indian villages and corn fields, and of pushing north to Prairie du Chien.[40] With the Indians in pursuit for nearly three miles, the Americans retreated down river. They had suffered about fifteen killed and wounded. Indian casualties were considered negligible. At the entrance of the Des Moines River, Taylor built Fort Johnson. In October, this last vestige of an American presence in the upper Mississippi was burned, and the garrison retired to St. Louis. No further military efforts were made against Rock Island or Prairie du Chien.

By the late autumn at Fort McKay, rations were becoming scarce. To alleviate the food shortage, Anderson discharged the Green Bay militia and sent them home. The remaining troops received corn one day, flour and pork the next. Of greater concern was the increasing number of Indian families who were camping around Prairie du Chien awaiting the arrival of the annual supplies from the Indian Department. These problems remained unsolved when Anderson was finally relieved of his temporary command on 30 November 1814. His dedication and abilities were proven, and he remained at Fort McKay in local command of the Michigan Fencibles. Andrew Bulger, a Newfoundlander, took command of Fort McKay on this last day of November, his twenty-fifth birthday.[41] The situation was both dangerous and delicate as the new commandant had inherited the twin problems of garrison discontent and tribal irritation at the scarcity of provisions. The troops were bored and insolent. They were now existing mainly on a scanty allowance of bread and a ration of "wild meat" when available. Determined to preserve order, Bulger began to instill a sense of pride and discipline in his men. This goal was achieved in early January 1815, when he quickly suppressed a near mutiny among the Michigan Fencibles and flogged the three worst offenders. Thereafter the corps assumed a more steadfast military bearing.[42]

In addition, Bulger was instructed to "cultivate a good understanding" with the Indian tribes and maintain their allegiance to the British. Throughout the winter of 1814–15, his duties were "as unceasing as they were arduous," and he succeeded in gaining the continued affection of the Indians by visiting several of their villages.[43] Unfortunately he also became embroiled in a bitter feud with Robert Dickson, Agent and Superintendent to the Western Indians, over the control and feeding of the Indian allies. Dickson had been prominent in the fur trade for thirty years before the war, and he was the senior officer of the British Indian Department in the Northwest. He was married to a Sioux woman and was genuinely concerned at the destitute condition of the Indians, apart from their military value. Relations between the two men became increasingly strained over specific areas of responsibility. Dickson insisted that supplies to the Indians must be increased and he showed a bias in feeding the Sioux bands. Bulger endeavored "to promote a fair, equal and judicious distribution" of provisions and gifts to the Indian families, and he refused to allow the Indian Department to usurp his authority or that of the British army.[44] He reported to McDouall that the conduct of Dickson had placed the garrison and other western Indian allies in danger of further starvation. The feud became petty and degenerated into name-calling. McDouall fully supported Bulger, and in one letter he referred to Dickson as that "insidious, intriguing, dangerous, yet despicable character."[45] This nastiness was terminated when McDouall finally ordered that "the Indian Department on the Mississippi is subject to and entirely under the orders of Captain Bulger."[46] In April 1815 Dickson was ordered to Michilimackinac. This whole episode, coupled with the boredom and isolation of Prairie du Chien, so disgusted Duncan Graham that "was there not favourable appearances to the termination of this drudgery," he reckoned that "he would throw up instantly." The disconsolate Graham proved prophetic when he wrote:

> Here we are posted since last fall, without news from any quarter, and destitute of provisions, sociability, harmony or good understanding. Not even a glass of grog, nor a pipe of tobacco, to pass away the time, and if a brief period don't bring a change for the better, I much dread the united Irishmen's wish will befall this place which god forbid it should — a bad Winter, a worse Spring, a bloody Summer, and no King.[47]

In fact official news of peace reached Prairie du Chien in the late spring of 1815. Strong war-parties to threaten St. Louis, and "keep the Americans at home to defend that place" had already been dispatched. In these raids the Indians "took more scalps within the last six weeks than they did during the whole of the preceding spring and summer upon this frontier."[48] Bulger immediately recalled the warriors. As the basis of the peace treaty was status quo ante bellum, the "mutual restoration of all forts" became a priority. At Michilimackinac, McDouall was "penetrated with grief at the restoration of this fine Island, a fortress built by Nature for herself." He was "equally mortified at giving up Fort McKay to the Americans," but there was no alternative but compliance. The crestfallen McDouall concluded by observing that "our negotiators as usual, have been egregiously duped . . . they have shown themselves profoundly ignorant of the concerns of this part of the Empire."[49] At Fort McKay on 23 May, Bulger assembled the chiefs for a grand council and explained the terms of the peace. Black Hawk, that "whole hearted man and unflinching warrior, cried like a child saying our Great Mother [Great Britain] has thus concluded, and further talk is useless." Two days later, after distributing presents to the tribes and leaving them "above want," His Majesty's troops gathered their possessions, burned the fort and departed the upper Mississippi forever. Of particular note during this period of the so-called 'British' occupation of Prairie du Chien, was that all three post commanders and most of the garrison, were Canadians.[50]

Figure 18.1 Western Upper Canada and the Northwest, 1796–1818.

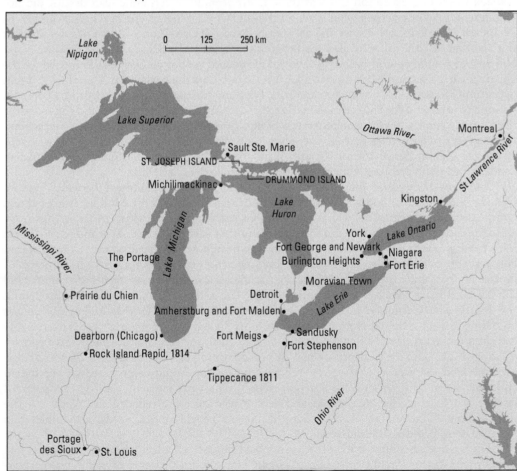

Source: From Robert S. Allen, *"The British Indian Department and the Frontier in North America, 1755–1830,"* Canadian Historic Sites/Lieux historiques canadiens No. 14. Used with permission.

In the Northwest, the War of 1812 was a very different matter than the one played out along the Detroit. When the United States went to war in June 1812 to redress national honor and capture Canada, an early territorial ambition which anticipated the American vision of manifest destiny for the continent, the key consideration for Upper Canada was defense. The concept of 'Manifest Destiny,' replete with spiritual and religious connotations, was used by the United States to justify that westward sweeping movement in which successive Indian frontiers were conquered and pacified. It was God's will, apparently, that Americans must dominate and control North America. The suggestion that the United States usurped a large part of the continent by purchase, war and theft, is too harsh. But, an argument could be made that the zealous young republic dispossessed tribe after tribe during the long epic years of 'Westward Ho:' and it did so by taking thousands upon thousands of hectares or acres of unceded Indian lands, to which no consideration, recognition nor acknowledgement was given that these indigenous peoples might have at least the benefit of the right of prior occupancy or aboriginal title, as they had enjoyed the use and occupancy of their lands since time immemorial.

Manifest Destiny proved most successful for the expansionist ambitions of the United States, except, of course, in the case of Canada during the War of 1812. The failure to take Canada was a rare exception through these many years in which American destiny did not manifest. Yet Americans were mollified, for they did win the Indian war in the War of 1812, as Tecumseh's Confederacy was irretrievably crushed and the Great Lakes Indian frontier secured. But the War of 1812 also provided the prospects for a little Canadian manifest destiny. In the Northwest, a number of prominent Canadian fur traders, supported by the Indian tribes of the upper Great Lakes and Mississippi Valley, also viewed, in their way, the War of 1812 as an opportunity to grasp and consolidate territory. For these two groups, the war became a common struggle to achieve a possible permanent British hegemony in that hinterland and thus preserve the fur trade and the traditional Indian way of life against American expansion and settlement. His Majesty's Indian Allies and the Canadians won their war but lost the peace, and with it, a chance to grab at destiny; for at Ghent, British negotiators sacrificed Indian and Canadian ambitions in the Northwest for a renewed Anglo-American cordiality.

The post-1815 years indeed produced an "Era of Good Feelings" between Britain, Canada and America, and a number of councils took place at Fort McKay, Amherstburg, Drummond Island and other Indian Department posts in which British officials "distinctly and explicitly" informed the assembled warriors that His Majesty's government would no longer assist nor countenance the tribes in any hostile actions against the United States. Further, the warriors were counselled to bury the hatchet, plant corn and be content. "I rubbed my eyes and cleared my ears, before I could believe what I saw or heard" commented the die-hard Black Hawk.[51] His response typified the reaction of Native peoples throughout the Northwest. Certainly, a dramatic and permanent shift in British Indian policy was unfolding. Indeed, the old glorious days of military "pomp and ceremony" were irretrievably lost. In a few years new strategy would evolve to civilize and Christianize the Native peoples residing in Canada, by "collecting them in villages (reserves)," and inducing them to cultivate the land. As well, education and religious instruction would be provided for the Indian children, along with general medical expenses.[52] Thus was born in Canada the paternal reserve system, and the once proud and defiant warriors were reduced to "Wards" of the state — from "Warriors to Wards." For the Native peoples, hoes, seeds, and bibles had replaced shot, powder, and muskets.

Throughout the long period of British–Indian military alliances, the Native peoples had been caught in the grip of two forces, an empire and a frontier, neither of which was particularly distinguished for mercy, and both of which were eventually destined to resolve their differences by other methods than costly Indian wars. Repeatedly during these critical years for the tribes inhabiting the Great Lakes region, the warriors attached themselves to the British in each fight against the Americans, as the Native peoples tried to salvage some remnants of their traditional lands and cultural values, as the original people. In the War of 1812, the warriors lashed out in one final desperate defense of the old order. But, from the beginning of contact, Native peoples in America and Canada could only delay or retard, but not stem, the tide of these technologically dominant and ever intruding newcomers. The Indian struggle was made even more difficult by rampant tribal factionalism which (then as now) broke the spirit of Indian unity and harmony; and made the pretense of the existence of an Indian state or home-land, the merest of fictions. A final deathblow for Indian interests was that in the grand theater of international diplomacy, Native peoples were considered expendable. By the end of the War of 1812, His Majesty's Indian Allies were no longer needed nor desired by the British in Canada. Nonetheless, Native peoples retained an affection and loyalty to the British Crown. This continued attachment stemmed in part from periodic bouts of British fairness and justice toward them, as best evidenced by the Royal Proclamation of 1763 in which the crown estab-lished a formal procedure for purchasing the Indian interest in their traditional lands; and to the fact that the warriors and British soldiers had fought side by side over many years, as friends and comrades-in-arms. Yet, during a lengthy summer council in 1818, a sage old chief rose and addressed the assembled. He knew full well that all was lost for his generation, and concluded the speech to British Crown officials with a simple truth:

> You are very kind when you want us to fight for you but when that Service is performed, "the Store door be shut against us."[53]

His observation reflected the "End of an Era."[54]

NOTES

This essay was originally presented at the symposium, *War on the Great Lakes: Canada and the United States in the War of 1812*, at Monroe County Community College, January 1987.

1. Royal Commission of Sir William Johnson, Court of St. James, 11 March 1761, *Documents Relative to the Colonial History of the State of New-York*, eds. E.B. O'Callaghan and B. Fernow, 15 vols. (Albany: Weed, Parsons and Co., 1856–87) 7: 458–9. The official titles varied slightly in wording from April 1755. The 1761 version is the most complete in descriptive detail.
2. This theme to the Royal Proclamation of 1763 is detailed in Jack Stagg, "Protection and Survival: Anglo-Indian Relations 1748–1763 — Britain and the Northern Colonies" (Ph.D. dissertation, University of Cantab., 1984).
3. This theme is developed by Robert S. Allen, "His Majesty's Indian Alliances: British Indian Policy in the Defence of Canada, 1774–1815: (Ph.D. dissertation, University of Wales, forthcoming).
4. For La Belle Famille, see Brian Leigh Dunnigan, *Siege — 1759: The Campaign Against Niagara* (Youngstown, N.Y.: Old Fort Niagara Association, 1986), 69–80; and for a general account of the French and Indian War which combines history and literature, Francis Parkman, *Montcalm and Wolfe* (1884; reprint, New York: Collier, 1962).
5. See, National Archives of Canada (hereafter NAC), Ottawa, Haldimand papers, MG21, B100: 157.
6. Haldimand to Thomas Townshend (later Lord Sydney), 23 October 1782, ibid., MG21, B55:233. For an assess-ment of the critical 1782–83 period on the American frontier, Colin G. Calloway, "Suspicion and Self-Interest: British-Indian Relations and the Peace of Paris," *The Historian* 48 (1985): 41–60.
7. Milo M. Quaife, "The Ohio Campaigns of 1782," *Mississippi Valley Historical Review* (Now *Journal of American History*) 18 (1931).
8. Maj. William Campbell to Lt. Col. R.G. England, Fort Miami, 20 August 1794, *The Correspondence of Lieut. Governor John Graves Simcoe, with Allied Documents relating to his administration of the government of Upper Canada*, ed., E.A. Cruikshank, 5 vols. (Toronto: Ontario Historical Society, 1923–31), 2: 396.

9. Joseph Brant to Joseph Chew, *Michigan Pioneer and Historical Society Collections* 20 vols. (Lansing, MI: Michigan Pioneer and Historical Society, 1892), 434–35, (hereafter MPHC).

10. For Loyalist settlement in Canada, see *The Loyal Americans: The Military Role of the Loyalist Provincial Corps and Their Settlement in British North America, 1775–1784,* ed. Robert S. Allen (Ottawa: National Museums of Canada, 1983).

11. For a general account of the British Indian Department, see Robert S. Allen, "The British Indian Department and the Frontier in North America, 1755–1830," Canadian Historical Sites: Occasional Papers in Archaeology and History 14 (1975); hereafter "British Indian Department." For a specific account of a senior Indian Department official, see Reginald Horsman, *Matthew Elliott: British Indian Agent* (Detroit: Wayne State University, 1964).

12. Alexander McKee to Lord Dorchester, Detroit, 7 June 1796, PAC, RG8 (Military), C Series, 249.

13. Craig to Gore, Quebec, 6 December 1807, NAC, Report on Canadian Archives for 1896 (Ottawa, 1897): 31, note B.

14. Craig to Gore, Quebec, 28 December 1807, MPHC 25 (1984): 232–3.

15. Ibid.

16. Gore to Claus, York, 29 January 1808, enclosing "Secret Instructions," NAC, RG10 (Indian Affairs), 11. For a brief account of British intrigue among the tribes, see Reginald Horsman, "British Indian Policy in the Northwest, 1807–1812," *Mississippi Valley Historical Review* 45 (1958): 51–66.

17. Craig to Gore, Quebec, 10 March 1808, MPHC 25 (1894): 239–40.

18. Brock to Sir George Prevost, Captain General and Governor-in-Chief of British North America, York, 2 December 1811, *The Life and Correspondence of Major-General Sir Isaac Brock, K.B.,* ed. F.B. Tupper (London: Simpkin and Marshall, 1847), 123–30.

19. Elliott to Claus, Amherstburg, 9 July 1810, MPHC 25 (1894): 269–70.

20. Speech of Tecumseh to Major Taylor, Fort Malden (Amherstburg), 15 November 1810, MPHC 25 (1894): 275–7. For an account of Tecumseh's motivation, see Charles H. Goltz, "Tecumseh and the Northwest Indian Confederacy" (Ph.D. dissertation, Western Ontario, 1973).

21. Elliott to Claus, Amherstburg, 16 November 1810, MPHC 25 (1894): 277–8.

22. Craig to Gore, Quebec, 2 February 1811, MPHC 25 (1894): 280–1.

23. From the *Scioto Gazette* (Chillicothe, Ohio), 27 November 1811, and the *Western Intelligencer* (Worthington, Ohio), 25 December 1811.

24. "Instructions for the Good Government of the Indian Department," received by Sir George Prevost, Quebec, 1 May 1812, MPHC 25 (1894): 295–304.

25. General details of these events can be gleaned from George F.G. Stanley, *The War of 1812: Land Operations* (Ottawa: National Museums of Canada, 1983), 83–117 and Pierre Berton, *The Invasion of Canada, 1812–1813* (Toronto: McClelland and Stewart, 1980), 101–88. Personal accounts of these events can be read in *Richardson's War of 1812,* ed. Alexander C. Casselman (Toronto: Historical Publishing Col., 1902) and *War on Detroit: The Chronicles of Thomas Vercheres de Boucherville and the Capitulation by an Ohio Volunteer,* ed. Milo M. Quaife (Chicago: Lakeside Press, 1940).

26. A recent biography is R. David Edmunds, *Tecumseh and the Quest for Indian Leadership* (Boston: Little, Brown and Company, 1984).

27. Some Canadian examples include John Richardson (1828), Charles Mair (1886) and Bliss Carman (1918). An American version is provided by R. David Edmunds, "The Thin Red Line: Tecumseh, the Prophet, and Shawnee Resistance," *Timeline* 4 (December 1987/January 1988): 2–19.

28. For full details, see Dennis M. Au, *War on the Raisin: A Narrative Account of the War of 1812 in the River Raisin Settlement, Michigan Territory* (Monroe, MI: Monroe Country Historical Commission, 1981).

29. These events can be followed in *Richardson's War of 1812,* 148–88; Stanley, *The Way of 1812,* 148–61; and Pierre Berton, *Flames Across the Border 1813–1814* (Toronto: McClelland and Stewart, 1981), 101–47.

30. Two personal accounts of the 41st Regiment of Foot (later the Welch Regiment) during the War of 1812 are "The War in Canada," by an unidentified officer, property of The Welch Regiment Museum (Cardiff), hand-written and unpublished, n.d.; and "A Common Soldier's Account (Shadrach Byfield)," *Recollections of the War of 1812* (1828–1854; reprint Toronto: Baxter Publishing Company, 1964), 1–107.

31. See John Sugden, *Tecumseh's Last Stand* (Norman: University of Oklahoma Press, 1985).

32. See "John Kinzie's Narrative of the Fort Dearborn Massacre," ed. Mentor L. Williams, *Journal of the Illinois State Historical Society* 46 (Winter 1953): 343–62.

33. The portion of this article dealing with the War of 1812 in the Northwest has been largely excerpted from Robert S. Allen, "Canadians on the Upper Mississippi: The Capture and Occupation of Prairie du Chien during the War of 1812," *Military Collector and Historian* (Fall 1979): 118–23; for general accounts see Alex R. Gilpin,

The War of 1812 in the Old Northwest (Toronto: Ryerson Press, 1958) and G.F.G. Stanley, "British Operations in the American Northwest, 1812–15," *Journal of the Society for Army Historical Research* 22 (1943): 91–106.

34. McDouall to Lt. Gen. Gordon Drummond, Michilimackinac, 16 July 1814, *MPHC* 15 (1890): 611.
35. McKay to McDouall, Prairie du Chien, Fort McKay, 27 July 1814, *MPHC* 15 (1890): 623.
36. Ibid.
37. McKay Report, Supplement, 29 July 1814, ibid.
38. Ibid.
39. Captain Thomas G. Anderson, "Anderson's Journal at Fort McKay, 1814," *Wisconsin Historical Collections* 9 (1882): 207–61.
40. The battle at Rock Island is described in Milo M. Quaife, "An Artilleryman of Old Fort Mackinac," *Burton Historical Collection Leaflet* No. 6 (1928): 39–40.
41. Andrew Bulger, *An Autobiographical sketch of the services of the late Captain Andrew Bulger of the Royal Newfoundland Fencible Regiment* (Bangalore, India: Regimental Press, 2nd Bt., 10th Regiment, 1865).
42. Brian Leigh Dunnigan, "The Michigan Fencibles," *Michigan History* 57 (Winter 1973): 277–95.
43. McDouall to Bulger, Instructions, Michilimackinac, 29 October 1814, NAC, MG19, E5 (Bulger Papers), 1.
44. Ibid.
45. McDouall to Bulger, Michilimackinac, 20 February 1815, ibid.
46. Ibid.
47. Graham to John Lawe, Prairie du Chien, 14 March 1815, *Wisconsin Historical Collections* 10 (1883–85): 131.
48. Andrew Bulger, *An Autobiographical sketch*, 21; *Kingston Gazette* (Kingston, Upper Canada), 29 April 1815.
49. McDouall to Bulger, Michilimackinac, 5 May 1815, MAC, RG8 (Military), C Series, 688.
50. Allen, "Canadians on the Upper Mississippi," 118.
51. Black Hawk Speech, Indian Council, Drummond Island, 7 July 1818, NAC, MG19, F29 (William McKay).
52. This theme is developed by John F. Leslie, "Commissions of Inquiry into Indian affairs in the Canadas, 1828–1858: Evolving a corporate memory for the Indian Department" (M.A. dissertation, Carleton, 1984).
53. Ocaita (Ottawa Chief) to William McKay (Deputy Superintendent and Agent of the British Indian Department) 7 July 1818, NAC, MG19, F29 (William McKay).
54. Allen, "British Indian Department," chapter entitled "The End of an Era," 86–93.

Article Nineteen

"Of Slender Frame and Delicate Appearance": The Placing of Laura Secord in the Narratives of Canadian Loyalist History

Cecilia Morgan

To most present-day Canadians, Laura Secord is best known as the figurehead of a candy company, her image that of a young, attractive woman wearing a low-cut ruffled white gown.[1] Some may even harbour a vague memory from their high-school courses in Canadian history of her walk in 1813 from Queenston to Beaver Dams, to warn British troops of an impending American attack. From the mid-nineteenth century, the story of that walk has been told by a number of Canadian historians of the War of 1812 in Upper Canada. Its military implications in assisting the British during the War of 1812 have been the subject of some rather heated

Source: Cecilia Morgan, "'Of Slender Frame and Delicate Appearance': The Placing of Laura Secord in the Narratives of Canadian Loyalist History," *Journal of the Canadian Historical Association*, New Series, vol. 5 (1994): 195–212.

debate. Did Laura Secord actually make a valuable contribution to the war? Did her news arrive in time and was it acted upon? However, another and as yet little-discussed issue is the way in which late-nineteenth- and early-twentieth-century historians attempted to transform Secord into a heroine, a symbol of female loyalty and patriotism in this period's narratives of Loyalist history.

As historian Benedict Anderson argues, the formation of modern national identities has involved more than the delineation of geographically defined boundaries and narrow political definitions of citizenship. Nations, Anderson tells us, are "imagined political communities," created by their citizens through a number of political and cultural institutions and practices: shared languages, newspapers, museums, and the census. Furthermore, as Anderson (and others) have emphasized, it is also within narratives of "the nation's" history that these imagined communities are formed and national identities are created.[2] To the promoters of late-nineteenth-century Canadian nationalism and imperialism, such narratives were of critical importance in understanding Canada's link to Britain and British political, social, and cultural traditions. As Carl Berger argues in *The Sense of Power*, "history in its broadest cultural sense was the medium in which [these traditions were] expressed and history was the final and ultimate argument for imperial unity."[3] Those who wrote these historical narratives also worked diligently to create national heroes who symbolized loyalty and the preservation of the imperial link. Historians interested in early-nineteenth-century Ontario history found that a cast of such figures lay conveniently close to hand: Major-General Sir Isaac Brock and the Upper Canadian militia, the colony's saviours during the American invasion of 1812.

But Brock and the militia were not the only significant figures to be commemorated and celebrated, for it was during this period that Laura Secord became one of the most significant female symbols of Canadian nationalism. As feminist historians have pointed out, the formation of imagined national communities has been frequently, if not inevitably, differentiated by gender. While Anderson's work has been extremely influential on historian's understanding of national identities, he fails to recognize "that women and men may imagine such communities, identify with nationalist movements, and participate in state formations in very different ways."[4] And, in their use of iconography, monuments, or written narratives of the nation's history, proponents of nationalism have frequently relied on gender-specific symbols and imagery.[5] Yet in these textual and visual representations of nationalities, gender as an analytic category has also varied according to its context and has been influenced by other categories and relationships, particularly those of race, class, religion, and sexuality. By looking at the process whereby Secord became a national heroine and at the narratives that were written about Secord's walk, we can further our understanding of the links between gender, race, and imperialism in late-nineteenth-century Canadian nationalism and feminism.[6]

Secord became part of the narratives of Loyalist self-sacrifice and duty to country and Crown primarily — although not solely — because of the attempts of women historians and writers who, from the 1880s on, strove to incorporate women into Canadian history and to dislodge the masculine emphasis of the nineteenth-century Loyalist myths of suffering and sacrifice. Women such as Sarah Curzon, the feminist writer, historian, and temperance advocate, insisted that white Canadian women, past and present, had something of value to offer the nation and empire and that their contribution as women to the record of Canadian history be acknowledged and valued. Secord, she (and others like her) argued, was not outside the narrative of Canadian history and she (and other women) therefore had a place in shaping the "imagined communities" of Canadian nationalist and imperialist discourse. Unlike that of other, potentially unruly and disruptive, women in Canadian history, Laura Secord's image could be more easily domesticated to accord with late-Victorian notions of white, middle-class femininity.[7] It could also be moulded by feminists to argue for a greater recognition of the importance of such femininity to Canadian society. Moreover, Laura Secord was not an isolated figure. Ranged behind and about her was a whole gallery of women in Canadian history, from Madeleine de Verchères of New France to the anonymous, archetypal pioneer woman of the backwoods of Upper Canada; women, these "amateur" historians insisted, who were historical figures as worthy of study as their male contemporaries.[8]

Before discussing the writing of Laura Secord into Loyalist history, however, it is crucial to outline the gendered nature of the nineteenth-century narratives of the War of 1812. Historians who have studied Upper Canadian politics have duly noted that assertions of loyalty and sacrifice during the war became the basis for many claims on the Upper Canadian state, in the competition for land and patronage appointments and for compensation for war losses.[9] Donald Akenson, for example, has pointed to the way in which claims to loyal duty during the war were used in attempts to justify the access of some residents to certain material benefits. Such claims were also made to legitimate the exclusion of others from such rewards.[10] Yet what has not been included in these historians' analysis of sacrifice in the war as a bargaining chip in the struggle for material gains in Upper Canada is the gendered nature of the narratives that were used. In Upper Canadians' commemorations of the War of 1812, the important sacrifices for Country and monarch were made by Upper Canadian men, frequently in their capacity as members of the militia who risked life and limb to protect women and children, homes and hearths, from the brutal rampages of hordes of bloodthirsty Americans. During the war, and in its aftermath, women's contributions to the defence of the colony were either downplayed or ignored, in favour of the image of the helpless Upper Canadian wife and mother who entrusted her own and her children's safety to the gallant militia and British troops.[11]

Personifying the whole, of course, was the masculine figure of Isaac Brock, the British commander who made the ultimate sacrifice for the colony when he died at the Battle at Queenston Heights in 1812. Brock provided those who shaped the history of the war with a dualistic image of nationalism, one that managed to celebrate both Upper Canadian identity and colonial loyalty to Britain. He was also a Christ-like figure, a man who had given both his troops and the colony beneficent paternal guidance and wisdom but who had not spared himself from the physical dangers of war — physical dangers that really only threatened men in the military. Those who contributed to the glorification of Brock claimed that he had provided an invaluable means whereby the colonists might resist the enemy's encroachments. Brock had inspired Upper Canadian men, who might emulate his deed of manly patriotism, and he had reassured Upper Canadian women that, come what may, they could look to their husbands, fathers, sons, and brothers for protection.[12]

This kind of narrative, which emphasized masculine suffering, sacrifice, and achievements, was not unique to that of the War of 1812. As Janice Potter-MacKinnon argues, the history of Upper Canadian Loyalism focused on male military service and the political identification of male Loyalists with the British Crown and constitution:

> Well into the twentieth century, loyalty was a male concept in that it was associated with political decision-making — a sphere from which women were excluded. The same can be said of the idea that the Loyalists bequeathed conservative values and British institutions to later generations of Canadians: women have had no role in fashioning political values and institutions. The notion that the Loyalists were the founders of a nation had obvious and unequivocal gender implications. The amateur historian William Caniff was right when he equated the "founders" with the "fathers."[13]

Admittedly there was no automatic and essential connection between military activities and masculinity in Canadian history for, as Colin Coates has pointed out, the woman warrior tradition was not unknown to nineteenth-century Canada.[14] But specific female images (or images of femininity in general) as symbols of loyalty and patriotism in Upper Canada are almost completely lacking in the discourses of the period, and they display a general reluctance to admit that women could have contributed to the war effort as civilians.[15] This silence about women and the feminine — except as helpless victims to which the masculine bravery of Upper Canadian men was inextricably linked — was quite the opposite of the discourses of the French Revolution, with their glorification of Marianne; the American Patriot's figure of the republican mother; or even the more conservative use of the British figure of Britannia.[16]

The earliest efforts to call attention to Secord's contribution to the war were made by her husband James, by her son, and by Laura herself. In a petition written February 25, 1820, and addressed to Lieutenant Governor Sir Peregrine Maitland, James Secord requested a licence to quarry stone in the Queenston military reserve. After mentioning his own wartime service — he had served as a captain in the militia — his wounds, and the plundering of his home by American troops, Secord claimed that "his wife embraced an opportunity of rendering some service, at the risk of her own life, in going thru the Enemies' Lines to communicate information to a Detachment of His Majesty's Troops at the Beaver Dam in the month of June 1813."[17] A second, similar petition was turned down in 1827 but Maitland did propose that Laura apply for the job of looking after Brock's monument. It is not clear whether Maitland was aware of the gendered and nationalist symbolism of a Canadian woman caretaking the memory of a British general; he did, however, have "a favourable opinion of the character and claims of Mr. Secord and his wife."[18] However, Maitland's successor, Sir John Colborne, was apparently not as well-disposed toward the family and the job went to Theresa Nichol, the widow of militia Colonel Robert Nichol.[19]

When James died in 1841, Laura submitted two petitions to Governor Sydenham: one that asked that her son be given his father's post as customs' collector and another that asked for a pension. Both cited her poverty, her lack of support since her husband's death, and her need to support her daughters and grandchildren. While her petitions used the language of female dependency noted by Potter-MacKinnon in Loyalist women's submissions, they also featured her service to her country in 1813 and her new position as the head of a household.[20] Her son Charles's article, published in an 1845 edition of the Anglican paper, *The Church*, publicized her walk, calling attention to his mother's service to her country and the British Crown.[21] Eight years later Laura Secord wrote her own account of her trek to warn the British Lieutenant James Fitzgibbon, in a piece that appeared in the *Anglo American Magazine* as part of a larger narrative of the war. While this article would be used and cited by others from the 1880s on, it was written in a straightforward manner, with few of the rhetorical flourishes or personal details that would characterize later accounts. And, while Secord concluded her story with the observation that she now wondered "how I could have gone through so much fatigue, with the fortitude to accomplish it," she did not stress her need to overcome physical frailty in reaching Fitzgibbon.[22]

Secord achieved some success in her campaign for some financial recognition on the part of the state in 1860, when she presented her story to the Prince of Wales during his tour of British North America. She was also the only woman whose name appeared on an address presented by the surviving veterans of the Battle of Queenston Heights to the Prince, in a ceremony attended by five hundred visitors and at which a memorial stone was laid on the site where Brock fell. Her "patriotic services," claimed the *Niagara Mail* in 1861, were "handsomely rewarded" by the prince with an award of £100.[23] One of her more recent biographies argues that the prince "provided the magic touch that transformed the 'widow of the late James Secord' into the heroine, Laura Secord."[24]

However, Secord did not become a heroine overnight. Her own efforts to draw attention to the service she had rendered to her country should not be seen as attempts to create a cult for herself, but rather as part of the Upper Canadian patronage game, in which loyal service to Crown and country was the way to obtain material rewards.[25] Furthermore, she died in 1868, almost twenty years before her popularity began to spread. Still, references to Secord had begun to appear in a few mid-nineteenth-century accounts of the War of 1812. For example, the American historian Benson J. Lossing's *The Pictorial Field-Book of the War of 1812* devoted a page to Secord and the Battle of Beaver Dams. The page's caption read "British Troops saved by a Heroine," and Laura's own written account was the voice that supplied Lossing with his information.[26] The Canadian historian and government official, William F. Coffin, elaborated on her story by adding the cow — which, he claimed, she had milked in order to convince the American sentry to let her pass. While some regard Coffin's account as yet another example of a romantically inclined nineteenth-century historian playing fast and loose with the facts, his placing of Secord in a context of pioneer domesticity foreshadowed subsequent stories appearing two decades later.[27] Secord thus was not rescued from complete obscurity by Curzon and others in the 1880s and '90s; she was, however, given a much more prominent place in their narratives of the war and Upper Canadian loyalty.

Sarah A. Curzon has become known in Canadian women's history as a British-born suffrage activist and a founding member of the Toronto Women's Literary Society (which would later become the Canadian Woman's Suffrage Association) and the editor of a women's page in the prohibition paper, the *Canada Citizen*. But she was also an avid promoter of Canadian history and was one of the co-founders of the Women's Canadian Historical Society of Toronto (WCHS) in 1885, along with Mary Agnes Fitzgibbon, a granddaughter of Lieutenant James Fitzgibbon. Furthermore, Curzon and Fitzgibbon were supporters of Canada's "imperial connection" to Britain, a link which they believed would benefit Canada both economically and culturally.[28] Emma Currie was another major contributor to the campaign to memorialize Secord. Indeed, her book, *The Story of Laura Secord and Canadian Reminiscences*, was published in 1900 as a fundraiser for a monument to the "heroine" of Upper Canada. Currie lived in St. Catharines, helped found the Woman's Literary Club in that city in 1892, and would later join the Imperial Order of the Daughters of the Empire (IODE). She too was a supporter of the Women's Christian Temperance Union and women's suffrage.[29]

But these women were not alone in their crusade to win recognition for Secord. Other Canadian nationalist writers like Charles Mair, Agnes Maule Machar, and William Kirby praised Secord's bravery in their poetry and prose,[30] while local historical societies and those who purported to be "national" historians, such as Ernest Cruikshank, also published papers that focused on the Battle of Beaver Dams and acknowledged Secord's role in it.[31] Much of their work, as well as that of Curzon and Currie, was part of late-Victorian Canadian imperialist discourse, which perceived the past as the repository of those principles (loyalty to Britain, respect for law and order, and the capacity for democratic government) that would guide the nation into the twentieth century.[32] As Berger has argued, the local history societies that spread in the 1880s and 1890s were part of this "conservative frame of mind" in which loyalism, nationalism, and history were inextricably linked.[33]

Tributes in ink comprised the bulk of this material but they were not the only efforts to memorialize Secord. As Currie's book indicates, printed material might be used to raise funds and spread awareness in order to create more long-lasting, substantive reminders, such as monuments and statues. On June 6, 1887, W. Fenwick, a grammar school principal in Drummondville, wrote to the *Toronto World and Mail* asking for better care for the Lundy's Lane graveyard, a national monument to be erected to honour those who had died there, and a separate monument to Laura Secord. Curzon joined in a letter-writing campaign, calling for the women of Canada to take up the matter, and petitions were presented to the Ontario legislature. When these were unsuccessful, the Lundy's Lane and Ontario Historical Societies mounted fundraising drives for the monument, sending out circulars asking Canadian women and children to contribute 10¢ and 1¢ respectively to the cause.[34] A competition for the sculpture was held and won by a Miss Mildred Peel, an artist and sculptor who also would paint the portrait of Secord hung in 1905 in the Ontario legislature.[35] After fourteen years of campaigning, the monument was unveiled June 22, 1901, at Lundy's Lane. In 1911, the Women's Institute of Queenston and St. David's felt that the village of Queenston (site of the Secord home during the War of 1812) had not done enough to honour Secord's memory and built a Memorial Hall as part of Laura Secord school. The gesture that ensconced her name in popular culture came in 1913, when Frank O'Connor chose Secord as the emblem for his new chain of candy stores.[36]

While it was not suggested that celebrating Secord's contribution was the sole responsibility of Canadian womanhood, many aspects of this campaign were shaped by deeply gendered notions and assumptions about both past and present. The idea that women might have a special interest in supporting the subscription drive, for example, or petitioning the legislature, linked perceptions of both womanhood and nationalism, drawing on the underlying assumptions of self-sacrifice and unselfishness that lay at the heart of both identities.[37] Groups such as the WCHS, with their "unselfish patriotism," were exactly what the country needed, Kirby told Mary Agnes Fitzgibbon upon being made an honorary member of the society, adding "let the women be right and the country will be might!"[38] Moreover, while male writers and historians certainly expressed an interest in Secord, it is important not to overlook the significance of the participation of Anglo-Celtic, middle- and upper-middle-class women in the writing of Canadian history, a task they frequently undertook as members of local historical societies. Such women scrutinized historical records in order to find their foremothers (in both the literal and metaphorical sense).[39] However, they also were fascinated with the entire "pioneer" period of Canadian history, both French and English, and with both male and female figures in this context. For the most part, women members of historical societies researched and presented papers on as many generals and male explorers as they did "heroines."[40]

There was, however, a difference in their treatment of the latter. They insisted that Canadian women's contributions to nation building be valued, even though they had not achieved the fame and recognition of their male counterparts. To be sure, they did not offer alternative narratives of early Canadian history and tended to place political and military developments at its centre. Nevertheless, they sought to widen the parameters of male historians' definitions of these events in order to demonstrate their far-reaching effects on all Canadian society. In the meetings of organizations such as Canadian Women's Historical Societies of Toronto and Ottawa, papers were given on topics such as "Early British Canadian Heroines" or "Reminiscences" of pioneer women.[41] Women such as Harriet Prudis, who was active in the London and Middlesex Historical Society during this period, believed that while the history of the pioneer women of the London area

> records no daring deed . . . nor historic tramp, like that of Laura Secord, yet every life is a record of such patient endurance of privations, such brave battling with danger, such a wonderful gift for resourceful adaptability, that the simplest story of the old days must bear, within itself, the sterling elements of romance. While they took no part in the national or political happenings of the day, it may be interesting to us, and to those who come after us, to hear from their own lips how these public events affected their simple lives.[42]

Their efforts were shared by male novelists and historians who not only glorified Secord but also wished to rescue other Canadian women of her era and ilk from obscurity.[43] However, as more than one honorary member of the WCHS told Fitzgibbon, Canadian women should have a special desire to preserve records of their past. According to Mair, "the sacred domestic instincts of Canadian womanhood will not suffer in the least degree, but will rather be refreshed and strengthened" by the Society's "rescuing from destruction the scattered and perishable records of Ontario's old, and, in many respects, romantic home life."[44] The collection of material concerning this latter area, Mair and others felt, should be the special work of Canadian women.[45]

The extent to which this relegation of the "social" realm to women historians sets a precedent for future developments, whereby "romantic home life" was perceived as both the preserve of women and the realm of the trivial and anecdotal is not entirely clear.[46] Certainly it does not appear to have been Mair's intention that these areas be perceived as trivial or unworthy of male historians' attention, while women such as Mary Agnes Fitzgibbon were as eager to research battles and collect military memorabilia as they were concerned with "primitive clothing, food cookery, amusements, and observances of festivals attending births and wedlock or the Charivari."[47] Yet it was probably no coincidence that the first historian to seriously challenge the military value of Secord's walk was the male academic W.S. Wallace, who in 1930 raised a furor among public supporters of Secord with questions concerning the use of historical evidence in documenting her walk.[48]

This, then, was the context in which Laura Secord became an increasingly popular symbol of Canadian patriotism: one of feminism, history, patriotism, and imperialism. While many of these histories were, as Berger has pointed out, local and might seem incredibly parochial in their scope, their authors saw locally based stories as having a much wider emotional and moral significance in the narratives of the nation.[49] Hence, narratives of Secord's contribution to the War of 1812 and to the colonial link with the British Empire were marked by the interplay of locality, nationality, and gender. First, Laura and James Secord's backgrounds were explored and their genealogies traced, in order to place them within the Loyalist tradition of suffering and sacrifice. For those writers who were concerned with strict historical accuracy, such a task was considerably easier for the Secords than for Laura's family, the Ingersolls. James's male ancestors had fought in the Revolutionary War for the British Crown and the many military ranks occupied by the Secord men were duly listed and acclaimed. Moreover, the Secords could claim a history of both allegiance to the British Crown and a desire for the protection of the British constitution; they were descended from Huguenots who arrived in New York from LaRochelle in the late seventeenth century.[50]

But it was not only the Secord men who had served their country and suffered hardships. The Loyalist legacy inherited by both Laura and James had, it was pointed out, been marked by gender differences. As Curzon told her audiences, James Secord's arrival in Canada had been as a three-year-old refugee, part of his mother's "flight through the wilderness, with four other homeless women and many children, to escape the fury of a band of ruffians who called themselves the "sons of Liberty." After enduring frightful hardships for nearly a month, they finally arrived at Fort Niagara almost naked and starving." Curzon went on to comment that these were by no means "uncommon experiences." Frequently, she pointed out, Loyalist men had to flee "for their lives" and leave their women and children behind (as well as their "goods, chattels, estates, and money"). Their loved ones were then left to endure the terrors of the wilderness

> unprotected and unsupported, save by that deep faith in God and love to King and country which, with their personal devotion to their husbands, made of them heroines whose story of unparalleled devotion, hardships patiently borne, motherhood honourably sustained, industry and thrift perseveringly followed, enterprise successfully prosecuted, principle unwaveringly upheld, and tenderness never surpassed, has yet to be written, and whose share in the making of this nation remains to be equally honored with that of the men who bled and fought for its liberties.[51]

Unfortunately for Laura's popularizers, the Ingersoll family did not fit as neatly into the Loyalist tradition. Her father, Thomas, had fought against the British in 1776 and had seen his 1793 land grant cancelled as a result of British efforts to curb large-scale immigration of American settlers into Upper Canada.[52] As J.H. Ingersoll observed in 1926, Laura's inability to claim the United Empire Loyalist pedigree "has been commented upon." However, some historians argued that Thomas Ingersoll came to Upper Canada at Lieutenant Governor Simcoe's request.[53] For those poets and novelists who felt free to create Laura's loyalism in a more imaginative manner, her patriotism was traced to a long-standing childhood attachment to Britain. They insisted that she chose Canada freely and was not forced to come to the country as a refugee.[54] Moreover, despite these historians' fascination with lines of blood and birth, they were equally determined to demonstrate that the former could be transcended by environment and force of personality. The loyal society of Upper Canada and the strength of Laura's own commitment to Britain were important reminders to the Canadian public that a sense of imperial duty could overcome other relationships and flourish in the colonial context.[55]

Accordingly, these historians argued, it should come as no surprise that both Laura and her husband felt obliged to perform their patriotic duty when American officers were overheard planning an attack on the British forces of Lieutenant Fitzgibbon.[56] However, James was still suffering from wounds sustained at the Battle of Queenston Heights and it therefore fell to Laura — over her husband's objections and concern for her safety — to walk the twenty miles from Queenston to warn the British troops at Beaver Dams. (Here the linear chronology of the narratives was frequently interrupted to explain out that Laura had come to his aid after the battle when, finding him badly wounded and in danger of being beaten to death by "common" American soldiers, she had attempted to shield him with her own body from their rifle butts — further evidence that Laura was no stranger to wifely and patriotic duty.[57])

Laura's journey took on wider dimensions and greater significance in the hands of her commemorators. It was no longer just a walk to warn the British but, with its elements of venturing into the unknown, physical sacrifice, and devotion to the British values of order and democracy, came to symbolize the entire "pioneer womanish experience in Canadian history.[58] Leaving the cozy domesticity and safety of her home, the company of her wounded husband and children, Secord had ventured out into the Upper Canadian wilderness with its swamps and underbrush in which threatening creatures, such as rattlesnakes, bears, and wolves, might lurk.[59] And even when Sarah Curzon's 1887 play permitted Laura to deliver several monologues on the loveliness of the June woodland, the tranquillity of the forest was disrupted by the howling of wolves.[60]

But most serious of all, in the majority of accounts, was the threat of the "Indians" she might meet on the way. If Secord's commitment to Canada and Britain had previously been presented in cultural terms, ones that could be encouraged by the colonial tie and that might transcend race, it was at this point that her significance as a symbol of white Canadian womanhood was clearest. While her feminine fragility had been the subject of comment throughout the stories, and while her racial background might have been the underlying subtext for this fragility, it was in the discussions of the threat of Native warriors that her gender became most clearly racialized.[61] Unlike the contemporary racist and cultural stereotypes of threatening Black male sexuality used in American lynching campaigns, however, her fears were not of sexual violence by Native men — at least not explicitly — but of the tactics supposedly used by Native men in warfare, scalping being the most obvious.[62]

To be sure, some stories mentioned that Secord had had to stay clear of open roads and paths "for fear of Indians *and* white marauders" (emphasis mine).[63] But even those who downplayed her fear of a chance encounter with an "Indian" during her journey were scrupulous in their description of her fright upon encountering Mohawks outside the British camp. Secord herself had stated that she had stumbled across the Mohawks' camp and that they had shouted "woman" at her, making her "tremble" and giving her an "awful feeling." It was only with difficulty, she said, that she convinced them to take her to Fitzgibbon.[64] As this meeting with the Natives was retold, they became more menacing and inspired even greater fear in Secord. In these accounts, at this penultimate stage in her journey she stepped on a twig that snapped and startled an Indian encampment. Quite suddenly Secord was surrounded by them, "the chief throws up his tomahawk to strike, regarding the intruder as a spy."[65] In some narratives, he shouted at her "woman! What does woman want!" Only by her courage in springing to his arm is the woman saved, and an opportunity snatched to "assure him of her loyalty."[66]

Moved by pity and admiration, the chief gave her a guide, and at length she reached Fitzgibbon, delivered and verified her message —"and *faints*."[67] Fitzgibbon then went off to fight the Battle of Beaver Dams, armed with the knowledge that Secord had brought him and managed to successfully rout the American forces. In a number of narratives, this victory was frequently achieved by using the threat of unleashed Indian savagery when the Americans were reluctant to surrender.[68] While the battle was being fought, Secord was moved to a nearby house, where she slept off her walk, and then returned to the safety of her home and family. She told her family about her achievement but, motivated by fear for their security (as American troops continued to occupy the Niagara area) as well as by her own modesty and self-denial, she did not look for any recognition or reward. Such honours came first to Fitzgibbon.[69]

Women such as Curzon and Currie might see Secord's contribution as natural and unsurprising (given her devotion to her country) but they also were keenly aware that their mission of commemoration necessitated that their work appeal to a popular audience. These narratives were imbued with their authors' concerns with the relations of gender, class, and race and the way in which they perceived these identities to structure both Canadian society and history. For one, Secord's "natural" feminine fragility was a major theme of their writings. As a white woman of good birth and descent, she was not physically suited to undertake the hardships involved in her walk (although, paradoxically, as a typical "pioneer woman" she was able to undertake the hardships of raising a family and looking after a household in a recently settled area.) Her delicacy and slight build, first mentioned by Fitzgibbon in his own testimony of her walk, was frequently stressed by those who commemorated her.[70] Her physical frailty could be contrasted with the manly size and strength of soldiers such as Fitzgibbon and Brock.[71] Nevertheless, the seeming physical immutability of gender was not an insurmountable barrier to her patriotic duty to country and empire. The claims of the latter transcended corporeal limitations. Even her maternal duties, understood by both conservatives and many feminists in late-nineteenth-century Canada to be the core of womanly identity, could be put aside or even reformulated in order to answer her country's needs.[72] While her supporters did not make explicit their motives in stressing her frailty, it is possible to see it as a subtext to counter medical and scientific arguments about female physical deficiencies that made women, particularly white, middle-class woman, unfit for political participation and higher education.[73]

Furthermore, there were other ways to make Secord both appealing and a reflection of their own conceptions of "Canadian womanhood," and many historians treated her as an icon of respectable white heterosexual femininity. Anecdotes supposedly told by her family were often added to the end of the narratives of her walk — especially those written by women — and these emphasized her love of children, her kindness and charity toward the elderly, and her very feminine love of finery and gaiety (making her daughters' satin slippers, for example, and her participation as a young woman in balls given by the Secords at Newark). Indeed, they went so far as to discuss the clothing that she wore on her walk. Her daughter Harriet told Currie that she and her sisters saw their mother leave that morning wearing "a flowered print gown, I think it was brown with orange flowers, at least a yellow tint."[74] Elizabeth Thompson, who was active within the Ontario Historical Society and was also a member of the IODE, also wrote that Secord wore a print dress, adding a "cottage bonnet tied under her chin . . . bal-briggan stockings, with red silk clocks on the sides, and low shoes with buckles"— both of which were lost during the walk.[75]

For her most active supporters, the walk of Laura Secord meant that certain women could be written into the record of loyalty and patriotic duty in Canadian history, and female hero-ines could gain recognition for the deed they had committed. In the eyes of these historians, such recognition had heretofore been withheld simply because of these figures' gender, for in every other significant feature — their racial and ethnic identities, for example — they were no different than their male counterparts. But such additions to the narrative were intended to be just that: additions, not serious disruptions of the story's focus on the ultimate triumph of British institutions and the imperial tie in Canada. Like her walk, Secord herself was con-structed in many ways as the archetypical "British" pioneer woman of Loyalist history, remem-bered for her willingness to struggle, sacrifice, and thus contribute to "nation building." These historians also suggested that patriotic duties and loyalty to the state did not automatically con-stitute a major threat to late-nineteenth-century concepts of masculinity and femininity. Secord could undertake such duties, but still had to be defined by her relations to husband and children, home and family. She did not, it was clear, take up arms herself, nor did she use her contribution to win recognition for her own gain.

In the context of late-nineteenth- and early-twentieth-century debates about gender rela-tions in Canadian society, Secord was a persuasive symbol of how certain women might breach the division between "private" and "public," the family and the state, and do so for entirely unselfish and patriotic reasons. The narratives of Laura Secord's walk helped shape an image of Canadian womanhood in the past that provided additional justification and inspiration for turn-of-the-century Canadian feminists. These women could invoke memory and tradition when calling for their own inclusion in the "imagined community" of the Canadian nation of the late nineteenth century.[76] Furthermore, for those such as Curzon who were eager to widen their frame of national reference, Secord's legacy could be part of an imperialist discourse, linking gender, race, nation, and empire in both the past and the present.

NOTES

Much of the research and writing of this paper was conducted with the financial assistance of Canada Employment. I would also like to thank Colin Coates, Marian Valverde, and the *Journal*'s anonymous readers for their much-appreciated suggestions and encouragement. The members of the gender, history, and national identities study group have provided invaluable comments and support: Lykke de la Cour, Paul Deslandes, Stephen Heathorn, Maureen McCarthy, and Tori Smith.

1. A Dorian Gray–like image that, as the company has enjoyed pointing out, becomes younger with the passage of time. See the advertisement, "There must be something in the chocolate," *The Globe and Mail*, November 25, 1992, A14.

2. This term has been an invaluable methodological tool in thinking about the narratives of Secord. See Benedict Anderson, *Imagined Communities: Reflections on the Origin and Spread of Nationalism*, rev. ed. (London and New York, 1991). See also Eric Hobsbawm and Terence Ranger, eds., *The Invention of Tradition* (New York, 1983). Like Anderson's work, however, this collection does not address the complex relationships of gender, nation-alism, and the "invented traditions" it analyzes.

3. Carl Berger, *The Sense of Power: Studies in the Ideas of Canadian Imperialism 1867–1914* (Toronto, 1970), 78.

4. Catherine Hall, Jane Lewis, Keith McClelland, and Jane Rendall, "Introduction," *Gender and History: Special Issue on Gender, Nationalisms, and National Identities* 5, 2 (Summer 1993): 159–64.

5. Recent work by historians of Indian nationalism explores the use of female images, particularly that of the nation as mother. See, for example, Samita Sen, "Motherhood and Mother Craft: Gender and Nationalism in

Bengal," *Gender and History: Special Issue on Gender, Nationalisms and National Identities*, 231–43. See also the essays in *History Workshop Journal Special Issue: Colonial and Post-Colonial History* 36 (Autumn 1993), and Mrinalini Sinha, "Reading *Mother India*: Empire, Nation, and the Female Voice," *Journal of Women's History* 6, 2 (Summer 1994): 6–44.

6. One of the few Canadian historians to point to these connections has been George Ingram, in "The Story of Laura Secord Revisited," *Ontario History* 57, 2 (June 1965): 85–97. Other works tackling these questions have looked at such areas as social reform. See Angus McLaren, *Our Own Master Race: Eugenics in Canada, 1885–1945* (Toronto, 1990), and Mariana Valverde, *The Age of Light, Soap, and Water: Moral Reform in English Canada 1885–1925* (Toronto, 1991).

7. For a heroine who was not so easily domesticated, see Colin M. Coates, "Commemorating the Woman Warrior of New France: Madeleine de Verchères, 1696–1930," paper presented to the 72nd Annual Conference of the Canadian Historical Association, Ottawa, June 1993; also Marina Warner, *Joan of Arc: The Image of Female Heroism* (London, 1981).

8. See, for example, the *Transactions* of both the Women's Canadian Historical Society of Ottawa and those of the Women's Canadian Historical Society of Toronto, from the 1890s to the 1920s.

9. David Mills, *The Idea of Loyalty in Upper Canada, 1784–1850* (Montreal and Kingston, 1988).

10. Donald H. Akenson, *The Irish in Ontario: A Study in Rural History* (Montreal and Kingston, 1984), 134.

11. See Cecilia Morgan, "Languages of Gender in Upper Canadian Politics and Religion, 1791–1850" (Ph.D. thesis, University of Toronto, 1993), ch. II. It is interesting that, while the militia myth has been challenged by many historians, its gendered nature has received very little attention. See, for example, the most recent study of the War of 1812, George Sheppard's *Plunder, Profit, and Paroles: A Social History of the War of 1812 in Upper Canada* (Montreal and Kingston, 1994).

12. Morgan, 56–60; see also Keith Walden, "Isaac Brock: Man and Myth: A Study of the Militia Myth of the War of 1812 in Upper Canada 1812–1912" (M.A. thesis, Queen's University, 1971).

13. Janice Potter-Mackinnon, *While the Women Only Wept: Loyalist Refugee Women in Eastern Ontario* (Montreal and Kingston, 1993), 158.

14. Coates, "Commemorating the Heroine of New France."

15. Morgan, ch. II.

16. On the French Revolution, see Maurice Agulhon, *Marianne into Battle: Republican Imagery and Symbolism in France, 1789–1880*, trans. Janet Lloyd (Cambridge, 1981). For republican motherhood, see Linda Kerber, "The Republican Mother: Female Political Imagination in the Early Republic," in *Women of the Republic: Intellect and Ideology in Revolutionary America* (Chapter Hill, 1980); for Britannia, see Madge Dresser, "Britannia," in Raphael Samuel (ed.), *Patriotism, the Making and Unmaking of British National Identity*, vol. 3; *National Fictions*, ed. Raphael Samuel (London, 1989), 26–49.

17. The petition is reprinted in Ruth McKenzie's *Laura Secord: The Legend and the Lady* (Toronto, 1971), 74–5. To date, McKenzie's book is the most thorough and best-researched popular account of the development of the Secord legend.

18. Ibid., 76.

19. Ibid., 76–77; also Sheppard, 221.

20. McKenzie, 84–85.

21. Ibid., 49ff.

22. Ibid., 91–92; also in Benson J. Lossing, *The Pictorial Field-Book of the War of 1812* (New York, 1869), 621.

23. McKenzie, 102.

24. Ibid., 103–4.

25. For an analysis of patronage in nineteenth-century Ontario, see S.J.R. Noel, *Patrons, Clients, Brokers: Ontario Society and Politics 1791–1896* (Toronto, 1990).

26. Lossing, 621.

27. William F. Coffin, *1812: The War, and Its Moral: A Canadian Chronicle* (Montreal, 1864), 148.

28. See Sarah A. Curzon, *Laura Secord, the Heroine of 1812: A Drama and Other Poems* (Toronto, 1887). For biographical sketches of Curzon and Fitzgibbon, see Henry James Morgan, *The Canadian Men and Women of the Time: A Hand-Book of Canadian Biography* (Toronto, 1898 and 1912), 235–36 and 400. Curzon's work is briefly discussed in Carol Bacchi's *Liberation Deferred? The Ideas of the English-Canadian Suffragists, 1877–1918* (Toronto, 1981), 26–27 and 44, but Bacchi's frame of reference does not take in Curzon's (or other suffragists') interest in history as an important cultural aspect of their maternal feminism and imperialism.

29. Morgan, 1912, 288–89; see also Mrs. G.M. Armstrong, *The First Eight Years of the Women's Literary Club of St. Catharines, 1892–1972* (n.p., 1972); Emma A. Currie, *The Story of Laura Secord and Canadian Reminiscences* (St. Catharines, 1913).

30. Charles Mair, "A Ballad for Brave Women," in *Tecumseh: A Drama and Canadian Poems* (Toronto, 1901), 147; William Kirby, *Annals of Niagara*, ed. and intro. by Lorne Pierce (Toronto, 1927 [1896]), 209–10. Kirby had been Currie's childhood tutor in Niagara and both she and Curzon continued to look to him for advice, support, and recognition (Archives of Ontario [AO]), MS 542, William Kirby Correspondence, Reel 1, Curzon and Currie to Kirby, 1887–1906. Kirby and Mair were made honorary members of the WCHS (AO, MU 7837-7838, Series A, WCHS papers, Correspondence File 1, William Kirby to Mary Agnes Fitzgibbon, April 11, 1896, Charles Mair to Fitzgibbon, May 8, 1896). For Machar, see "Laura Secord," in her *Lays of the True North and Other Poems* (Toronto, 1887), 35. See also Ruth Compton Brouwer, "Moral Nationalism in Victorian Canada: The Case of Agnes Machar," *Journal of Canadian Studies* 20, 1 (Spring 1985): 90–108.

31. See, for example, "The Heroine of the Beaver Dams," *Canadian Antiquarian and Numismatic Journal* 8 (Montreal, 1879): 135–36. Many thanks to Colin Coates for this reference. See also Ernest Cruikshank, *The Fight in the Beechwoods* (Drummondville: Lundy's Lane Historical Society, 1889), 1, 13–14, 19.

32. Berger, 89–90.

33. Ibid., 95–96.

34. Janet Carnochan, "Laura Secord Monument at Lundy's Lane," *Transactions of the Niagara Historical Society* (Niagara, 1913), 11–18.

35. Carnochan, 13.

36. McKenzie, 118–19.

37. Marilyn Lake has made a similar argument about Australian nationalist discourse during World War One. See her "Mission Impossible: How Men Gave Birth to the Australian Nation — Nationalism, Gender and Other Seminal Acts," *Gender and History. Special Issue on Motherhood, Race and the State in the Twentieth Century* 4, 3 (Autumn 1992): 305–22, particularly 307. For the theme of self-sacrifice in Canadian nationalism, see Berger, 217. The links between the discourses of late-Victorian, white, bourgeois femininity and that of Canadian racial policy have been explored by Valverde in *The Age of Light, Soap, and Water*, in the contexts of moral reform, the white slavery panic, and immigration policies. See also Bacchi, *Liberation Deferred?*, ch. 7. For gender and imperialism in the British and American contexts, see Vron Ware, *Beyond the Pale: White Women, Racism and History* (London and New York, 1992). The seminal article on imperialism and British womanhood is Anna Davin, "Imperialism and Motherhood," *History Workshop Journal* 5 (Spring 1978): 9–65.

38. WCHS papers, MU 7837-7838, Series A, Correspondence File 1, Kirby to Fitzgibbon, April 14, 1896.

39. See, for example, Mrs. J.R. Hill, "Early British Canadian Heroines," *Women's Canadian Historical Society of Ottawa Transactions*, 10 (1928): 93–98; Harriet Prudis, "Reminiscences of Mrs. Gilbert Ponte," *London and Middlesex Historical Society Transactions* (1902, pub. 1907): 62–64.

40. Harriet Prudis, "The 100th Regiment," *L & M H S Transactions*, V (1912–1913), n.p.; Agnes Dunbar Chamberlin, "The Colored Citizens of Toronto," *WCHS of Toronto Transactions*, 8 (1908): 9–15; also the biography of Brock by Lady Edgar, one of the first presidents of the WCHS [*Life of General Brock* (Toronto, 1904)].

41. See note 37 above.

42. Prudis, 62.

43. See Ernest Green, "Some Canadian Women of 1812–14," *WCHS of Ottawa Transactions* 9 (1925): 98–109.

44. WCHS papers, MU 7837-7838, Series A, Correspondence File 1, Mair to Fitzgibbon, May 8, 1896.

45. Ibid.; see also WCHS papers, MU 7837-7838, Series A, Correspondence File 1, John H. to Fitzgibbon, May 6, 1896.

46. As Linda Kerber argues, it was precisely this relegation that women's historians of the 1960s and '70s had to confront in their attempts to lift women's lives from the "realm of the trivial and anecdotal." See her "Separate Spheres, Female Worlds, Woman's Place: The Rhetoric of Women's History," *The Journal of American History* 75, 1 (June 1988): 9–39, esp. 37.

47. Mair to Fitzgibbon, May 8, 1896.

48. W.S. Wallace, *The Story of Laura Secord* (Toronto, 1932). For a response to Wallace, see "What Laura Secord Did," *Dunnville Weekly Chronicle*, 35 (1932), reprinted from Toronto *Saturday Night*, June 22, 1932.

49. Berger, 96. As M. Brook Taylor has pointed out about the work of nineteenth-century writers such as John Charles Dent, Francis Hincks, and Charles Lindsey, "National historians were essentially Upper Canadian historians in masquerade." See his *Promoters, Patriots, and Partisans: Historiography in Nineteenth-Century Canada* (Toronto, 1989), 231.

50. Currie, 21–33.

51. Curzon, *The Story of Laura Secord, 1813* (Lundy's Lane Historical Society, July 25, 1891), 6–7.

52. See Gerald M. Craig, *Upper Canada: The Formative Years 1784–1841* (Toronto, 1963), 49, for a discussion of this shift in policy. McKenzie also argues that Ingersoll did not fulfill his settlement obligations (29). See also Currie, 38–39.

53. J.H. Ingersoll, "The Ancestry of Laura Secord," *Ontario Historical Society* (1926): 361–63. See also Elizabeth Thompson, "Laura Ingersoll Secord," 1. Others argued that Ingersoll was urged by Joseph Brant to come to Upper Canada (Ingersoll, 363). The Brant connection was developed most fully and romantically by John Price-Brown in *Laura the Undaunted: A Canadian Historical Romance* (Toronto, 1930). It has also been pointed out that Price-Brown picked up the story, "invented out of whole cloth" by Curzon, that Tecumseh had fallen in love with one of Secord's daughters. See Dennis Duffy, *Gardens, Covenants, Exiles: Loyalism in the Literature of Upper Canada/Ontario* (Toronto, 1982), 61. In Price-Brown's account, Tecumseh proposes just before he is killed; Laura, however, disapproves of the match (259–69).

54. Price-Brown, 16–17, 180–82.

55. Just as French Canadians could overcome other ties (see Berger, 138–39).

56. Thompson, 2; Currie, 48; Ingersoll, 362.

57. Price-Brown's "fictional" account is the most colourful, since one of the American officers who did not intervene to save the Secords was a former suitor of Laura's, whom she had rejected in favour of James and Canada (252–55). See also Currrie, 53–54.

58. Norman Knowles, in his study of late-nineteenth-century Ontario commemorations of Loyalism, argues that pioneer and rural myths subsumed those of Loyalism ("Inventing the Loyalists: The Ontario Loyalist Tradition and the Creation of a Usable Past, 1784–1924," Ph.D. thesis, York University 1990). To date, my research on women commemorators indicates that, for them, both Loyalism (particularly people, places, and artifacts having to do with 1812) and the "pioneer past" were closely intertwined; both were of great significance and inspirational power in their interpretations of the past. See Elizabeth Thompson, *The Pioneer Woman: A Canadian Character Type* (Montreal and Kingston, 1991) for a study of this archetype in the fiction of Canadian authors Catherine Parr Trail, Sara Jeanette Duncan, Ralph Connor, and Margaret Laurence.

59. The most extensive description is in Curzon's *The Story of Laura Secord*, 11–12.

60. Curzon, *Laura Secord: The Heroine of the War of 1812*, 39–47.

61. While examining a very different period and genre of writing, I have found Carroll Smith-Rosenberg's "Captured Subjects/Savage Others: Violently Engendering the New American" to be extremely helpful in understanding the construction of white womanhood in the North American context. See *Gender and History* 5, 2 (Summer 1993): 177–95. See also Vron Ware, "Moments of Danger: Race, Gender, and Memories of Empire," *History and Theory* (1992): 116–37.

62. See Ware, "To Make the Facts Known," in *Beyond the Pale* for a discussion of lynching and the feminist campaign against it. Smith-Rosenberg points to a similar treatment of Native men in Mary Rowlandson's seventeenth-century captivity narrative (183–84). While the two examples should not be conflated, this issue does call for further analysis.

63. Cruikshank, 13.

64. Secord in Thompson, 4–5.

65. See, for example, Blanche Hume, *Laura Secord* (Toronto, 1928), 1. This book was part of a Ryerson Canadian History Readers series, endorsed by the IODE and the provincial Department of Education.

66. Ibid., 15.

67. Curzon, *The Story of Laura Secord*, 13.

68. See, for example, Cruikshank, 18.

69. Currie, 52–53. Fitzgibbon supposedly took full credit for the victory, ignoring both Secord's and the Caughnawaga Mohawks' roles (McKenzie, 66–67). He later became a colonel in the York militia and was rewarded for his role in putting down the 1837 rebellion with a £1000 grant (89–90).

70. Fitzgibbon in Thompson, 6.

71. Hume, 4.

72. For example, in Curzon's play Secord is asked by her sister-in-law, the Widow Secord, if her children will not "blame" her should she come to harm. She replies that "children can see the right at one quick glance," suggesting that their mother's maternal care and authority is bound to her patriotism and loyalty (34).

73. See Wendy Mitchinson, *The Nature of Their Bodies: Women and Their Doctors in Victorian Canada* (Toronto, 1991), esp. "The Frailty of Women."

74. Currie, 71.

75. Thompson, 3. Balbriggan was a type of fine, unbleached, knitted cotton hosiery material.

76. See Hobsbawm and Ranger, "Introduction: Inventing Tradition," particularly their argument that invented traditions are often shaped and deployed by those who wish to either legitimate particular institutions or relations of authority or to inculcate certain beliefs or values (9). In this case I would argue that the Secord tradition served very similar purposes, although it was used both to legitimate and, for certain groups of women, to subvert.

Topic Nine

The Rebellions of 1837 in the Canadas

Soldiers with artillery open fire on the St. Eustache Roman Catholic church, which was occupied by Patriotes. Lithograph by N. Hartnell, based on a drawing by Lord Charles Beauclerk.

The rebellions in the Canadas followed a long period of constitutional strife. In Lower Canada the appointed executive and legislative councils were predominantly English speaking, while the Assembly was almost entirely French speaking. In 1837, Louis-Joseph Papineau, an articulate bilingual lawyer, led a number of the Lower Canadian reformers into open revolt against the entrenched conservative elite who retained control of the provincial revenue. Was the insurrection of 1837 in Lower Canada strongly supported? In his essay, "From Folklore to Revolution: Charivaris and the Lower Canadian Rebellion of 1837," Allan Greer suggests that the charivari, a French-Canadian ritual, allowed supporters of popular rights a way to show their opposition to British rule. By wearing charivari masks and carrying noise-makers, French Canadians could safely voice their opposition to British officials while keeping their identities concealed.

Colin Read reviews parallel developments to the immediate west in "The Rebellion of 1837 in Upper Canada." Here a small group of radical reformers under William Lyon Mackenzie took up arms to secure what they felt were needed constitutional liberties. But their efforts were short lived. Why was the Rebellion of 1837 in Upper Canada so quickly suppressed while in Lower Canada it proved much more serious and lasted much longer? What do these articles reveal about the causes of the rebellions of 1837 in the two Canadas?

Fernand Ouellet's *Lower Canada, 1791–1840* (Toronto: McClelland and Stewart, 1980) is essential for any understanding of the Lower Canadian rebellion. Helen Taft Manning's *The Revolt of French Canada, 1800–1835* (Toronto: Macmillan, 1962), an older study, covers the constitutional struggle. A popular account is Joseph Schull's *Rebellion* (Toronto: Macmillan, 1971). Ramsay Cook has edited a valuable collection of essays on the background to the rebellion entitled *Constitutionalism and Nationalism in Lower Canada* (Toronto: University of Toronto Press, 1969). For the agricultural situation in the 1830s, see R.M. McInnis, "A Reconsideration of the State of Agriculture in Lower Canada in the First Half of the Nineteenth Century," in *Canadian Papers in Rural History*, ed. Donald H. Akenson, vol. 3 (Gananoque, ON: Langdale Press, 1982), pp. 9–49, and Allan Greer's important study *Peasant, Lord and Merchant: Rural Society in Three Quebec Parishes, 1740–1840* (Toronto: University of Toronto Press, 1985). Greer offers a new analysis of the events of 1837 in *The Patriots and the People: The Rebellion of 1837 in Rural Lower Canada* (Toronto: University of Toronto Press, 1993), and in "1837–38 Rebellion Reconsidered," *Canadian Historical Review* 76 (1995): 1–18. In *Les Rébellions de Canada 1837–1838* (Montréal: Éditions du Boréal Express, 1983), historian Jean-Paul Bernard provides a summary of the various interpretations of the Lower Canadian uprisings. Jack Verney has written a biography of E.B. O'Callaghan, one of the Patriotes' great English-speaking allies, entitled *O'Callaghan: The Making and Unmaking of a Rebel* (Ottawa: Carleton University Press, 1994).

Elinor Kyte Senior reviews the military history of the rebellions in *Redcoats and Patriotes: The Rebellions in Lower Canada, 1837–38* (Stittsville, ON: Canada's Wings, 1985).

In Upper Canada the central figure of the Rebellion was William Lyon Mackenzie, the subject of *The Firebrand* (Toronto: Clarke Irwin, 1956), a lively biography by William Kilbourn. F.H. Armstrong and Ronald J. Stagg's article on Mackenzie in volume 9 of the *Dictionary of Canadian Biography* should also be consulted. On the background to the troubles in Upper Canada, see the documentary collection by Colin Read and Ronald J. Stagg, *The Rebellion of 1837 in Upper Canada* (Toronto: Champlain Society, 1985). Carol Wilton has written an important study on *Popular Politics and Political Culture in Upper Canada, 1800–1850* (Montreal/Kingston: McGill-Queen's University Press, 2000).

For the impact of the rebellions of 1837/38 in Lower Canada see Jacques Monet, *The Last Cannon Shot: A Study of French-Canadian Nationalism, 1837–1850* (Toronto: University of Toronto Press, 1969), and Maurice Séguin, *L'idée d'indépendance au Québec: Génèse et historique*

(Trois-Rivières: Le Boréal Express Limitée, 1968). Chester New's *Lord Durham's Mission to Canada* (Toronto: McClelland and Stewart, 1963 [1929]) continues to provide insight into Durham's important mission and report. For an overview of subsequent developments in the 1840s, see J.M.S. Careless, *The Union of the Canadas: The Growth of Canadian Institutions, 1841–1857* (Toronto: McClelland and Stewart, 1967).

WEBLINKS

1837–1839: Rebellion
http://www.canadiana.org/citm/themes/constitution/constitution10_e.html

Digitized legal documents that dealt with the rebellions and Lord Durham's arrival in Canada.

Report of Lord Durham
http://www2.marianopolis.edu/quebechistory/docs/durham

A copy of Lord Durham's report.

The Rebellion Years — Documents
http://northernblue.ca/hconline/chapters/5/5docs.php

Digitized commentary written by key figures in the rebellions about the rebellions and their aftermath.

Upper Canada Rebellion 1837: The End
http://www.sg-chem.net/UC1838

Biographies and letters of leading actors in the Rebellion of 1837 in Upper Canada — includes both "Family Compact" members and rebels.

Rebellion Events in Upper Canada
http://northernblue.ca/hconline/chapters/5/5upper.php

Digitized documents and pictures relating to the 1837 Rebellion in Upper Canada. Included is William Lyon Mackenzie's rebellion proclamation.

Documents of the Rebellions of 1837 and 1838
http://www.canadiana.org/citm/specifique/rebellions_e.html

This site contains digitized primary source documents about the times before, during, and after the 1837/1838 rebellions. Included are Louis-Joseph Papineau and his colleague's Ninety-two Resolutions and the Rebellion Losses Bill of 1849.

Article Twenty

From Folklore to Revolution: Charivaris and the Lower Canadian Rebellion of 1837

Allan Greer

We have given this Charivari
Because it is our right.
(from a Basque popular play)[1]

For those interested in the connections between politics and popular culture, the charivari holds a peculiar fascination. Originally an aggressive ritual directed against marital deviants, the charivari came in France to be used for overtly political purposes. 'The charivari', Charles Tilly has observed, 'deserves special attention because it illustrates the displacement of an established form of collective action from its home territory to new ground; during the first half of the nineteenth century French people often used the charivari and related routines to state positions on national politics.'[2] But the French were not the only people who deployed the charivari form for political purposes in the first half of the nineteenth century; a broadly similar development occurred at about the same time in the former French colony of Canada. Indeed, the transition was much more abrupt in North America than in Europe. The French-Canadian charivari had long been notable for its traditionalism as to form, object and occasion, but suddenly in 1837, when Lower Canada (now the province of Quebec) was rocked by a revolutionary upheaval, this folkloric ritual made a dramatic appearance as an important vehicle for mobilizing the population against the colonial government. Enlisted not simply to 'state positions' or register 'protests', the charivari form was actually used to destroy elements of the existing state structure and even to prefigure a new regime. This was displacement with a vengeance!

On the surface, there was little in the Canadian charivari custom in the years before the Rebellion of 1837 that foreshadowed its future political role. To British visitors of the early nineteenth century, it seemed a picturesque but essentially harmless practice, something that could be written up in travel books to enliven the standard account of vast forests and magnificent waterfalls. The following description was based on a charivari that occurred at Quebec City in 1817:

> Here is a curious custom, which is common through the provinces, of paying a visit to any old gentleman, who marries a young wife. The young men assemble at some friends house, and disguise themselves as satyrs, negroes, sailors, old men, Catholic priests, etc., etc. Having provided a coffin, and large paper lanthorns, in the evening they sally out. The coffin is placed on the shoulder of four of the men, and the lanthorns are lighted and placed at the top of poles; followed by a motley group, they proceed towards the dwelling of the new married couple, *performing* discordantly on drums, fifes, horns, and tin pots, amidst the shouts of the populace. When they arrive at the house of the offender against, and hardy invader of, the laws of love and nature, the coffin is placed down, and a mock service is begun to be said over the supposed body. In this stage of the affair, if Benedict invites them into his house and entertains them,

Source: Allan Greer, "From Folklore to Revolution: Charivaris and the Lower Canadian Rebellion of 1837," *Social History*, 15, 1 (January 1990): 25–43.

he hears no more of it. If he keeps his doors shut, they return night after night, every time with a fresh ludicrous composition, as *his courtship*, or *will*, which is read over with emphasis, by one of the frolicking party, who frequently pauses, whilst they salute the ears of the persecuted mortal with their music and shouting. This course is generally repeated till they tire him out, and he commutes with them by giving, perhaps, five pounds towards the frolic, and five pounds for the poor.[3]

Though this all seemed 'curious' to an Englishman, a charivari along these lines would not have looked strange to a tourist from France. The mocking, carnivalesque tone of the proceedings, the nocturnal setting, the loud and raucous noise, the masks and costumes of the participants and the elaborate, insistently public, street procession all recall French practices dating back to the Middle Ages.[4] Similarly the occasion of charivaris, following a wedding, particularly that of an ill-assorted couple, matches the customs of Canada's original mother-country. There were differences, however. French customs, in this as in other matters, varied greatly from region to region. Moreover, practices seem to have evolved over the years so that, even before the emergence of the fully political charivari in the nineteenth century, charivari-type harassment, sometimes associated with other customs, was often directed against all kinds of unpopular figures such as corrupt officials, submissive husbands or promiscuous women. The colonial ritual, by contrast, seems quite uniform and consistent, from the seventeenth century to the nineteenth and from one end of Lower Canada to the other. More faithful than their European cousins to early modern models, the French of Canada always directed charivaris at newly married couples only. This seems to be one of those areas in which a European overseas settlement functioned as a sort of 'cultural museum' in which customs were distilled, purified and preserved, even as they changed drastically or disappeared in the old country.[5] Such resolute orthodoxy prior to the Rebellion makes the politicization of the charivari in 1837 all the more surprising. What was there about this 'curious custom'— annoying but hardly subversive in appearance — that lent itself to a situation of acute political strife?

Although the charivari was a custom characteristic of a pre-industrial society, it would be a mistake, in my view, to regard it as simply a throwback, an expression of a 'primal ethic', hostile to market relations and punitive in its reaction to nonconformist behaviour.[6] In its Canadian guise, at least, the ritual was not part of any larger pattern of collective regulation of marriage and domestic life through public demonstrations. There was no French-Canadian equivalent of the *azouade* ('donkey-ride') or 'skimmington', humiliating punishments inflicted in early modern France and England on submissive husbands, scolding wives and other deviants.[7] Neither did drunks and women accused of pre-marital sex have reason to fear a charivari, as was the case in some areas of Germany and the US South. Here it was the marital match itself that was at issue, not the content of domestic life. Prior to 1837, Canadian charivaris always followed a wedding and, in every case I have examined, the marriage was a 'mismatch': either the groom was much older than the bride or vice versa, or else one of the partners had been previously married. Several accounts also mention a social mismatch accompanying the disparity in age or marital status. There was, for example, Monsieur Bellet, the target of the Quebec City charivari described above. A prominent merchant of the town, this sixty-seven-year-old widower had married his young servant girl. Just as typical was the charivari directed against a 'widow lady of considerable fortune' who wed 'a young gentleman of the Commissariat Department'.[8]

Widowers marrying again were never the exclusive, or even the primary target of Canadian charivaris. Indeed, weddings joining widows and bachelors were far more likely to trigger a demonstration than the remarriage of men. Moreover, people of all ages and both sexes took part in the festivities, though men appropriated the starring roles. A bishop's ordinance condemning a Quebec charivari in 1683 makes explicit reference to the participation of 'a large number of persons of both sexes'.[9] In Renaissance France, by way of contrast, charivaris were commonly the work of village youth societies and they were directed specifically against mature widowers or outsiders who deprived local young men of a potential mate. This has led some anthropologically minded scholars to analyse the ritual and the payment exacted from the victim in terms of a specifically male intervention in the 'marriage market',[10] but, in French Canada, charivari does not seem to have arisen from any protectionist impulses of bachelordom.

Why then, if not to regulate the local supply of brides, were ill-assorted marriages singled out for persecution? Writing of Old Régime France, André Burgière suggests that charivari directed at widows and widowers stemmed from ancient Catholic misgivings about remarriage. The traditionalist crowd thus took it upon itself to enforce restrictions long abandoned by the clergy. As a result, the church emerged as the earliest and most consistent opponent of charivari, for the ritual represented a clear assault on its current marital regulations.[11] In seeking links between the mentality underlying charivari and the outlook of the official church, Burgière opens a promising line of enquiry. Yet it seems to me that the connections may have been much closer than he realizes — at least they were in French Canada. Priests and bishops had reservations, not only about remarriages, but also about the other mismatches that provoked charivaris. Moreover, these were not ancient objections discarded by the clergy centuries before they were taken up by the mob; they were concerns that found expression even in the nineteenth century. The marital ideology of the charivari, I would argue, was not an anachronism and it was not essentially in contradiction with clerical views.

As far as the church was concerned, the wedding ceremony was a sacrament and therefore it could only be approached in a special spiritual state. The *Rituel* of the diocese of Quebec, a sort of priests' manual published in 1703 but still widely used more than a century later, insisted that prospective brides and grooms must 'have a genuinely pure intent, looking to marriage only for the glory of God and their own sanctification, and not for the satisfaction of their cupidity, their ambition, their greed and their shameful passions'. The fiancés, of course, had to take confession before the nuptials and curés [priests] were expected to impress upon them the true nature of marriage:

> Curés will inform the faithful that the purpose of this sacrament is to give to married persons the grace which they require to help and comfort one another, to live together in sanctity, and to contribute to the edification of the Church, not only by bringing forth legitimate children, but also by taking care to provide for their spiritual regeneration and a truly Christian education. *They will above all point out to those who wish to marry that persons who wed out of sensuality, seeking in marriage only sensual pleasure, or out of avarice, endeavouring only to establish a temporal fortune, commit a great sin, because they profane this sacrament,* and, in using something holy to satisfy their passions, they offend against the grace that Our Lord has attached to it.[12]

To marry for money or out of mere sexual appetite was not just morally reprehensible then, it was a serious sin for it defiled the holy sacrament of marriage.

This was all very well at the theoretical level, but how was a priest to detect such impure motives and prevent them from profaning the wedding rite? Unless candidates for matrimony made a direct confession of greed or lust, he could never be sure about their spiritual state. To refuse to marry anyone about whom he harboured suspicions would be to court disasters of all sorts (lay hostility, unsanctioned cohabitation, recourse to Protestant ministers . . .); furthermore, secular law would not allow refusal without good cause. In practice then, the effort to ensure the purity of marriage consisted mainly of general exhortations to this effect and personal discussions, in the confessional and elsewhere, with candidates for wedlock. Naturally, a curé would give particular attention to couples whose external circumstances seemed suspicious. When a young woman married an old widower it might just be that she was after his money and that he, for his part, had more than a moderate share of lust in his heart. Thus we find a conscientious Canadian priest writing to his bishop for advice in the case of a rich widow of his parish who wished to marry a bachelor half her age. Legally, 'you may not refuse to celebrate an ill-assorted marriage,' answered the bishop, but, 'in your capacity as confessor, you should refuse absolution to anyone who wishes to marry only in order to get rich.'[13] Disparities of age and wealth were not objectionable in themselves, but they did alert vigilant clergymen to the possibility of sinful motives. By the same token, the determination of a widow or widower to remarry, while perfectly acceptable in itself, could also raise questions. Here was someone who had already established a family and who perhaps had children. Were they marrying again for the right reasons or were they simply looking for a new sex partner? Just to be on the safe side, the priestly manual cited above therefore specified a supplement to the wedding ceremony for second marriages that consisted mainly of Psalms 127 and 128, with their heavy emphasis on wives like fruitful vines and husbands with quivers full of children.

A priest had to marry an 'ill-assorted' couple even if he harboured doubts about the purity of their intentions, but the crowd in the street might react differently to the outward signals of impurity, giving loud and dramatic voice to widely held suspicions. The charivari might then be seen as a symbolic accusation of defiling a sacred rite. This surely is why a wink-and-nudge sexual jocularity, not to say downright obscenity, formed a central theme of most charivaris. Admittedly, sexual allusions were a feature of other carnival-type festivities but it seems to me that, beyond the general cheekiness, there was a specific and personal change of illicit lust implied in the charivari. It is important to emphasize, however, that it was not 'immorality' as such that was being chastised. Recall that, in French Canada, charivaris were not directed against adulterers, spouse beaters and the like. Nor, as far as I can tell, were couples of roughly the same age ever persecuted by crowds who cited other grounds for believing they were marrying out of sensuality or avarice. The immediate purpose of charivari was not to correct immorality or even to guard the sanctity of marriage against 'real' impurity. It amounted, rather, to a ritualistic response to the *signs* of desecration, a public rebuke filled with accusations of lasciviousness, that aired suspicions shared by clergy and laity alike.

But more was involved than a simple clearing of the air; charivari was also, as many commentators have pointed out, a punitive procedure. Victims were punished through both humiliation and monetary exaction, two penal techniques favoured by the church and the criminal courts of the period. Public shaming was, of course, a central feature of any charivari, inseparable from the noisy charge of desecration. It recalled the *amende honorable*, a practice common under the French regime when criminals had to go through the town wearing only a shirt and stopping occasionally to beg God's forgiveness.[14] The ecclesiastical version of the *amende honorable*, much milder than that prescribed by the judiciary, involved a public confession of sin, for example by couples who had engaged in premarital sex.[15] Like these practices of church and state, charivari penalized people by making a public spectacle of their faults. The *amende honorable* was more than simply a penal technique, however. In the forms deployed by both priests and judges the wayward subject had to become a penitent, confessing his sin and participating in his own correction. The charivari, too, as I shall argue below, involved an important penitential element. But, before leaving the subject of the punitive aspects of charivari, let us look at the monetary penalties that, along with public shaming, were designed to make the ceremony an unpleasant experience for its victims.

Considerable emphasis was placed, by Lower Canadian crowds at least, on the payment of what amounted to a charivari fine. The sums involved were often quite substantial — fifty pounds, to take one example from Montreal[16]— though the exact amount varied from case to case, depending, it seems, on the subject's ability to pay. The level of the fine was indeed the subject of elaborate and prolonged negotiation. Usually some respected local figure was employed as a mediator during the daytime intervals between the raucous visitations and he would try to establish the terms of peace and then, later, he might see that the funds were disposed of according to the agreed-upon arrangement. Meanwhile, as negotiations proceeded by day, at night the air still rang with increasingly annoying demonstrations calculated to break down the resistance and loosen the purse-strings of the unfortunate victims. The proceeds of a charivari were normally divided fifty-fifty, with half the fine going to the participants to pay for their 'expenses' (i.e., celebratory drinks in the tavern) while the other half was contributed to an organized charity or distributed directly to the local poor.

This use of fines was another way in which a charivari insisted on its own legitimacy by aping the methods of constituted authority. Under the British regime as well as the French, magistrates generally kept a specified share of any fines and ordered the balance to be turned over to a parish vestry, a hospital, or to government coffers. The church also collected monetary penalties, notably from couples seeking permission to marry in spite of the impediment of consanguinity. A bishop usually issued a dispensation only on payment of a substantial fee, set, it appears, according to the petitioner's financial resources as reported by the parish priest. By the early nineteenth century — a time when charivaris were particularly frequent — money from this source had come to constitute a major element in the revenues of the diocese of Quebec. Even though the funds were applied to good Catholic charities, the practice aroused serious concern in the Vatican.[17] Like the clergy, the charivari crowds were probably actuated to some degree by purely economic considerations: all indications are that merchants and other relatively wealthy individuals were singled out for persecution.

Besides functioning as a penalty and as a means of soaking the rich, the charivari fine played a third and equally important role. It acted as a token of agreement signifying the re-establishment of peace between the targets and the perpetrators of ritual attack. In offering money, the newly married couple signified, however, reluctantly, their submission to the judgement of their neighbours. Moreover, this forced gift implied a recognition — purely at the level of outward acts, of course — of the legitimacy of the charivari itself. The subjects were needled, nagged, annoyed and threatened until they made a gesture signifying acceptance of the charivari, until they themselves became participants in the proceedings. When victims treated the ceremony with disdain, when they refused to sue for peace or, worse still, when they called on the 'forces of order' to stop the demonstration, the invariable result was that the charivari intensified. From the crowd's point of view, the offence was then compounded for, in addition to soiling the wedding rites, the subjects had also challenged its own authority to right the wrong. This is why charivaris could go on and on — sometimes for three weeks or a month — and with escalating intensity; when couples were stubborn in their refusal to pay, the custom itself became the issue and the struggle therefore raged all the more fiercely.

As soon as the fine had changed hands, however, the harassment stopped. The money served then as a token for the crowd as well as for the victim and it placed the former under an obligation to drop hostilities. A village notary at Terrebonne watched (and probably participated in) a charivari against a sixty-eight-year-old widow who married a bachelor, and cooper by trade, aged fifty. As recorded in the notary's diary, the demonstration went on for five days, escalating on each successive night:

> such that, in order to have peace, our young couple were forced to employ a mediator to discuss terms with these gentlemen. After intense negotiations an agreement was finally concluded this morning and it was settled that for three pounds, of which one pound to pay the expenses of the charivari and the rest to be distributed to the local poor, the newlyweds may in future indulge peacefully in all the pleasures of their union.[18]

There may have been some hard feelings in the wake of a charivari, but there is no indication that, under normal circumstances, they would have been lasting. We hear, on the contrary, of a young man of Montreal who married a widow in 1833; exactly a year after his charivari he was elected for the first time as local representative to the colonial assembly.[19] Certainly there is no reason to think that Canadian charivari victims were 'permanently marked' as were, according to E. P. Thompson, the targets of the less restrained sort of 'rough music' dished up in the English-speaking world.[20] But then, accusation and punishment were only part of the ritual of charivari; these were but preliminaries to the treaty of peace and reconciliation, marked by the presentation of expiatory coin.

We have moved, in discussing the charivari fine, from the area of punishment to the realm of reconciliation. Except where the crowd was defeated or thwarted in its aims, the thrust of its actions seems to have been to bring about, willy-nilly, the reintegration into the community of wayward members suspected of desecration. Nowhere in the French-Canadian record prior to 1837 does one find relentless persecution, or any apparent desire to expel or eliminate a 'cancerous element' by means of charivari. This was hardly a lay version of excommunication, then; the more apt analogy would be to less absolute ecclesiastical sanctions, corrective measures such as the fine or the *amende honorable* that required sinners to make their submission to a higher authority in order to gain readmittance to the fold.

Aiming as it did to reintegrate 'deviants' rather than to expel them, the charivari was not the expression of pure hostility; on the other hand, it was hardly a friendly or anodyne operation. It took resistance for granted and was designed to overcome that resistance. And when opposition, from the charivari subject or from a third party, was serious, ugly scenes could ensue. The night watch of Montreal tried to break up a charivari in 1821 and even managed to arrest a few isolated revellers, but the crowd soon counter-attacked, beating up the constables on the scene and besieging their headquarters until the prisoners were released.[21] A man was killed in the same city two years later when the charivari victim fired on the crowd assembled outside his windows; the mob tore down his house in retaliation.[22] Episodes of this sort provided grist to the mill of middle-class reformers anxious to suppress the 'barbarous custom' of charivari.[23] Yet to regard such violent conflict as simply an instance of the clash of popular turbulence and bourgeois order is to miss some crucial characteristics of the charivari as practised in Lower Canada.[24] Far from being spontaneous or anarchic, these were fairly organized demonstrations, carefully prepared in advance. More to the point, charivaris, though filled with bluffs and threats to their targets, were quite restrained. Real violence occurred only when the crowd came under actual attack. From the outside, the Montreal riots of 1821 and 1823 look like folkloric customs that got 'out of hand', but really all that separated them from a 'normal' charivari was the active challenge mounted, in one case by the police, in the other by the bridegroom. The crowd's insistence on its own authority and on its right — indeed its duty — to carry out its mandate was a common feature of all charivaris.

The pre-1837 charivari was not in any clear sense oppositional. Whereas themes of social and political criticism were very much a part of charivari and carnivalesque entertainments in Renaissance Europe,[25] in French-Canada, despite the presence of anti-clerical overtones and such 'ritual inversion' symbolism as cross-dressing, subversive messages were quite muted. Indeed, one might well consider the charivari a 'conservative' ceremony (in so far as the vocabulary of political doctrine has any meaning in this context). Not only did it ape the procedures of priests and magistrates, it functioned as a complementary form of social control, helping to chasten deviants of a very particular sort in strictly limited circumstances. Its ultimate point of reference, moreover, was the orthodox teachings of Catholicism. Intervening when the purity of the marital sacrament was in jeopardy, the charivari crowd acted so as to restore harmony and equilibrium, in the relationship between individuals and the community as well as in that linking God and humanity.

Thus, even though many authorities — and in particular the clergy — objected to the tumultuous street demonstrations, these must be recognized as indicative of a hegemonic relationship. People staging a charivari were giving proof of their active attachment to ideological principles justifying a social order in which they, for the most part, occupied subordinate positions. At the same time they were, of course, insisting on their own right to regulate certain specific aspects of the life of the community. This was scarcely a revolutionary position totally at odds with ruling-class precepts; neither bishops nor governors valued passive obedience. The ideal of the 'loyal subject' or of the 'faithful Catholic' implied a positive commitment and allowed for a good deal of direct popular initiative. Nevertheless, in spite of consensus at the level of general principles, there was conflict when magistrates and priests tried to suppress this particular form of public demonstration.

Charivari presumed a sort of 'people power' of the street as one of the constituents of the larger political-ecclesiastical order. It was, then, 'democratic' in a literal sense. This was a combative democracy, one which had to be defended against the repressive measures of officialdom. It was nevertheless a subordinate democracy, an exercise of popular power which assumed the existence of non-popular authority in a well-regulated community. But what if the community was not well regulated and the government no longer legitimate? This was the situation during the revolutionary crisis of 1837 when the colonial regime lost the capacity to rule with the consent of the governed. At that juncture, when attempts were made to base authority on popular sovereignty, the charivari form came to serve as a very useful vehicle for pressing the claims of the embryonic new order. This instrument of popular governance within the state (and church) became a weapon of revolt against the state.

The Lower Canadian crisis of 1837, which culminated in armed insurrection in November and December of that year, grew out of the campaign for colonial autonomy and democratic reform led by the middle-class radicals of the 'Patriot party'.[26] Thanks mainly to the consistent electoral support of the bulk of the French-Canadian population, these liberal politicians managed to control the provincial legislative assembly. Opposed to the Patriots was a coalition of merchants, government officials and settlers from the British Isles who tended to dominate all the other branches of the colonial state, including the executive, the judiciary and the non-elective legislative chamber. Acute political conflict had brought the machinery of representative government to a grinding halt by 1836. Finally, the imperial government intervened in the following spring, hoping to end the impasse by issuing a clear refusal to Patriot demands for constitutional reform and depriving the assembly of its financial powers. The result was a storm of protest that lasted through the summer of 1837, with great public rallies, calls for a boycott of British imports and vague talk by Patriot leaders about a re-enactment of the American Revolution at some point in the future. The constant theme of radical rhetoric was that the British measures against the assembly had made colonial rule in Lower Canada illegal and illegitimate. Apart from stirring up popular indignation, however, the Patriots made no serious efforts to prepare for a war which they still believed to be many years away. Events moved towards a showdown more quickly than predicted, though, as the mobilization of the populace, particularly the inhabitants of the Montreal District, provoked repressive counter-measures which in turn led to further resistance.

As the conflict intensified in June and July, noisy demonstrations, often carried out at night by disguised bands, became common. In August newspapers began to report ritual attacks against government partisans that they did not hesitate to call 'charivaris' (victims and attackers also used this term) and that did indeed seem to be closely modelled on the popular custom. This was the first appearance of political charivaris in Lower Canada and it came in two quite distinct phases. The first phase, from August to mid-October, seems to have been rather more spontaneous and popular in origin whereas, during the second phase (late October–early November 1837), the co-ordinating role of the Patriot bourgeois leadership became more apparent and charivaris were used for more clearly strategic purposes.

In the late summer and early fall of 1837 there were reports from several villages that a masked party gathered by night outside the home of a prominent Tory and 'gave him a serenade whose chords were scarcely soothing to the ears'.[27] These demonstrations resemble the politicized charivaris that became common in France under the July monarchy; indeed, they may have been inspired by European models, although I have no evidence of a direct connection. Certainly the negative serenades fit into established Canadian charivari traditions that were, of course, a French import of an earlier century; the link with native custom appears particularly in the choice of specific targets during this first phase of political charivaris. Masked revellers did not attack such obvious objects as officials or soldiers.[28] Nor did they direct their serenades against members of the English-speaking minority, even though many of the latter manifested a paranoid counter-nationalism that made them violent defenders of the British Empire. Anti-Patriot anglophones might be ostracized by their neighbours or they might find the tails and manes of their horses cut off. (This last form of harassment could certainly be placed under the broad heading of the carnivalesque, for it was a kind of symbolic castration designed to make the animal's owner a laughing-stock when he rode it in public.)[29] However, attacks modelled much more closely on the charivari were reserved, in the early fall of 1837, for French-Canadian partisans of the government, and particularly for individuals who had until recently taken part in the Patriot movement but had 'deserted the cause of the nation' when revolution loomed on the horizon. Members of the group — whether defined linguistically or in terms of political allegiance — who had broken ranks during an emergency when petty differences had to be forgotten, these 'turncoats', were perfect targets for a treatment, the charivari, which had always served, not to attack 'outsiders', but to reprove and punish the familiar deviant. Essentially expressions of hostility, these early political charivaris did not demand anything in particular of their victims, but they did probably have the effect of curbing the activities of influential French-Canadians who might have been inclined to speak out in favour of the government.[30]

Political charivaris of a special sort came to play a much more important role at a later stage of the confrontation, that is, in the two months preceding the military denouement of late November 1837. The central development of this period — one which led inexorably to the armed clash — was the breakdown of local administration in the countryside of western Lower Canada. While it awaited the arrival of additional troops from neighbouring colonies in the summer of 1837, the government had tried to stem the tide of agitation by banning 'seditious assemblies', but it found that proclamations to this effect were simply ignored. Particularly in the heavily populated Montreal District, long a Patriot hotbed, giant rallies succeeded one another and often it was the justices of the peace and militia captains, upon whom the colonial authorities depended to enforce their writ, who were organizing them. The governor reacted to this flagrant defiance by dismissing 'disloyal' magistrates and officers. Denouncing this move as further proof of British tyranny, Patriots who held the Queen's commission but who had been overlooked in the purge made a great show of resigning. Beginning in October, meetings were held in many parishes to set up new local administrations and, in the ensuing elections, the 'martyred' officers were usually reinstated. A parallel local government, based on popular sovereignty and completely divorced from the colonial regime, was then taking shape. On 23–4 October a great public meeting held at the village of St. Charles to establish a federation of six counties south of Montreal gave official Patriot approval to these unco-ordinated local initiatives and urged all good citizens to imitate them.

Local government in Canada had always been rather rudimentary and subordinate to the central authorities in Quebec City. (The child of absolutism, Canada was ruled by colonial regimes — first the French, later the British — whose preoccupations were largely military and who dispensed with direct taxation and therefore with the communal institutions that could be so troublesome to western European monarchies.) By the time of the Rebellion, justices of the peace and militia captains, whose responsibilities were more of a police than of a military nature, were the only important public authorities, apart from priests, in the rural parishes of Lower Canada. They were all appointed by the governor but they were definitely members of the communities they administered. Indeed, the inhabitants found various ways of 'domesticating' officials who appeared in theory to be the agents of an external power. Each captain, for example, was presented with a 'maypole', a tall tree trunk decorated with flags and banners and planted in the ground in front of his house, in an elaborate ceremony that implied popular ratification of the governor's choice. In the fall of 1837 many maypoles became 'liberty poles' and, to mark the transformation, a sign reading 'elected by the people' was attached to a captain's mast.[31]

But what about officers and magistrates who declined to resign? There were many loyalists who tried to maintain their positions, even in areas where the population was overwhelmingly hostile to the government. From the Patriot point of view, these hold-outs were the willing agents of despotism and rebels against the emergent local regimes. At a more practical level, they appeared as potentially dangerous spies and fifth-columnists at a time when war with Great Britain looked less and less remote. The issue of the Queen's commissions therefore served to personalize the struggle by identifying important enemies and bringing great constitutional conflicts down to the local level. Accordingly, loyalist officers and magistrates in massively Patriot communities came under great pressure to resign. Some suffered the fate of Captain Louis Bessette, a prosperous inhabitant whose evening meal was disturbed by the sound of axes biting into wood. Going out to investigate, he found a band of men with blackened faces in the process of chopping down his maypole. The mast crashed to the ground and a great cheer went up from the party; the house was then besieged by the noisy, stone-throwing crowd until Bessette agreed to turn over his commission.[32] The cutting down of captains' maypoles was a favourite gesture in 1837 and one rich in symbolic meaning. If the mast had originally been planted as a phallic token of respect for a patriarchal figure, Bessette's experience was, then, one of symbolic castration. At another level, however, this action should be seen as revoking the popular ratification of the captain's appointment that the maypole embodied. 'You are no longer our captain,' was the clear message addressed to Louis Bessette.

Whether accompanied by the severing of maypoles or not (and, of course, many of the magistrates and officers who held commissions were not militia captains), the charivari form was the preferred mechanism in the countryside south of Montreal for forcing refractory office-holders to resign. National origin and previous political commitments were now (October–November) no longer a consideration. Anyone who continued to hold office was subject to attack. Dudley Flowers of St. Valentin was the victim of one typical charivari, which he described two weeks later in a judicial deposition:

> I am a Lieutenant in the Militia. On the twenty seventh day of October last in the afternoon the following persons viz. C.H.O. Côté, Olivier Hébert, L.M. Decoigne, Julien Gagnon, Amable Lamoureux and Jacob Bouchard, came to my house and demanded my commission as such Lieutenant to which I made answer that I would give it up to none but the governor of the Province. Doctor Côté said that if I did not give up my commission I would be sorry for it — to which Gagnon added, 'Si vous ne voulez pas vivre en haine avec nous autres rendez votre commission.' Upon this they went away. About eleven o'clock in the night of the same day the same persons returned — at least I have every reason to believe that they were the same persons. . . . They began yelling in the most frightful manner. They threw stones at my house and broke the greatest part of my windows. A large stone passed very near one of my

children and would have killed him if it had struck him. Julien Gagnon who had seen my barn full of oats when he came in the day time told me that I should not have to thresh them unless I gave up my commission and also said that my grain, my house and outhouses would be burnt. I saw one of the mob go with a firebrand to my barn with the intention as I verily believe of setting fire to it. But it was in a damp state from the recent rain and the fire would not take.

On the night of the following day (28th October last) it might be about ten o'clock a masked mob, composed of about thirty or forty persons attacked my house in a similar manner . . .

On the following day (Sunday) about seven in the evening, some sixty or seventy individuals attacked my house a third time in the same manner and with the same threats as on the former occasions but if possible with much more violence, beating kettles and pans, blowing horns, calling me a rebel, saying it would be the last time they would come as they would finish me in half an hour. They had in a short time with stones and other missiles broken in part of the roof of my house and boasted that it would soon be demolished. Fearing that such must inevitably be the case, I opened the door and told them that if four or five of their party would come in and give their names I would give them up my commission. Four or five of them did come in, disguised in the most hideous manner but refused to give their names. Finding that my life was actually in danger if I refused to comply with their requests, I handed them my commission. There were about fifteen of the last mentioned mob masked . . .

The same persons have declared in my presence that they were determined to compel in the same manner all persons holding commissions from her Majesty to surrender them. One of these individuals told me boastingly that they had obtained no less than sixty-two commissions in one day. I firmly believe that if Doctor Côté and some of the ringleaders were taken up and punished it would have the effect of alarming the others and keeping them quiet.[33]

Many of the features of the 'traditional' charivari were present in this episode: the nocturnal setting, the 'hideous' disguises, the raucous serenade of blaring horns, banging pots and shouted insults. Even the lieutenant's initial encounter with the Patriot delegation recalled the negotiating process by which charivari fines were normally set: the talks were businesslike, superficially friendly but with an undertone of menace, and they were held in daylight, in an atmosphere that contrasted sharply with that of the charivari itself. Flowers resisted for some time the summons to resign but, following the examples of an ordinary charivari crowd faced with a stubborn old widower, his attackers simply intensified their efforts, bringing more supporters and threatening ever more ferocious punishment on each successive evening. There were differences too, of course, notably in the stone-throwing and the overt threats of serious violence.

That the Patriots should have had recourse to the charivari custom at this juncture is not surprising. A coercive practice in which the aggressors' identities were concealed had obvious attraction at a time when arrest was still a real danger. This anonymity probably also served an equally important psychological purpose for the participants, that of overcoming inhibitions against aggressive behaviour. Indeed, the entire ritualistic package of charivari surely had this function. After all, Dudley Flowers was apparently a long-time resident of the community and he knew his attackers personally; even though he was a political enemy, the lieutenant was also a neighbour and therefore someone with whom it was important to maintain peaceful, though not necessarily cordial, relations. To turn on him with overt hostility would be to go against ingrained habits; masks and a familiar ritual may have made easier the transformation of neighbourly Jekylls into frightening Hydes.

The charivari custom offered more than simply an antidote to fears and uncertainties, however. The turning over of a sum of money was the central event of a traditional charivari and much of the pageantry was designed to extort this gift from an unwilling giver. What a perfect vehicle for forcing loyalists to resign or, more precisely, to 'turn over their commissions' as the Patriot mobs usually put it. The political charivaris of this second stage of the drama of 1837 were rather blunt in declaring their intention to overcome opposition to their demands, and low-level violence, consisting mainly of stone-throwing, was common. Men like Dudley Flowers, who resisted the initial attack, were likely to have their windows broken. Captain Bessette suffered more damage than any of the other charivari victims; after chopping down his maypole, the attacking party forced its way into his house and, calling for his resignation with a deafening roar, the intruders pounded out a rhythm with sticks and clubs until his table, windows and stovepipe had been smashed to bits. Now this toll of broken glass and damaged roofs, though severe by the standards of ordinary pre-Rebellion charivaris, seems quite light considering the context of serious political crisis. Even more striking is the complete absence of personal injuries. When one places this record against the cracked heads and burned houses that resulted from, for example, the anti-Irish riots of contemporary New England and New Brunswick — not to mention the destruction wrought by crowd action in revolutionary episodes comparable to 1837 — the restraining influence of the charivari form becomes all the more apparent.[34]

Of course Dudley Flowers was not impressed with the relative mildness of the treatment he received: he truly thought his life and his property were in real and immediate peril and, though he was no coward, he was frightened enough to abandon his home and flee with his family to the city shortly after the events reported in his deposition. This is because the charivari, 'political' or otherwise, was designed to be frightening, particularly in the eyes of those who resisted its edicts. Before 1837, coffins and skull-and-crossbones designs hinted at deadly intentions but, during the Rebellion, the threats were much more explicit. Crowds attacked stubborn magistrates and officers with talk of arson and murder. Who could be sure they were simply bluffing when, as was often the case, masked revellers were seen carrying guns as well as firebrands? Lieutenant Flowers felt he had had a lucky escape and that only the damp weather had saved his barnful of grain from the Patriot torches. He might have been less worried had he known how many other loyalists had been similarly threatened, without one single building ever being fired. The fact that he did believe himself to be in serious danger shows just how well the charivari served its theatrical purposes in the fall of 1837, when dozens of local officials capitulated to the Patriot mobs.

So far I have been discussing the way in which the charivari form was applied during the campaign of late October–early November for wholly novel political purposes. Yet, beyond the surface resemblances, there were also elements of continuity with the past in the basic function of the ritual. For example, the extortion of royal commissions seems to have been more than simply a means of destroying the government presence in the countryside; it also had meaning in the context of the specific relationship between an individual and the community of which he was a member. In other words, this forced gift played a role analogous to that of the ordinary charivari fine in signifying the giver's submission to the authority of the collectivity. But now the community as a whole and the Patriot cause were identified. Accordingly, some charivari victims were forced to shout 'Vive la liberté!' or to cheer for Papineau, the Patriot chief, as further proof of recognition of the incipient new regime. In accepting the victim's commission, the crowd gave its implicit assurance (sometimes it was clearly stated) that the charivari was at an end.[35]

There was a sense, then, in which a non-resigning officer such as Dudley Flowers was treated as a sinner, a contaminating influence in a community otherwise true to new civic ideals. The charivari worked so as to force him into a position of a penitent who had to purchase his reintegration into the fold at the price of a militia commission. Thus the admonition addressed to Lieutenant Flowers by Julien Gagnon during the preliminary visit to his home: resign your position, 'if you do not wish to live in a state of hatred with us.' No one expected him to become a militant Patriot overnight, but he was being offered an opportunity to make peace with his offended neighbours. It is important to emphasize that, just as conventional charivaris were aimed not against general immorality but against a specific affront to the wedding ceremony, so Flowers was targeted for a specific offence rather than some general nonconformity. Though government supporters at the time, not to mention later historians, saw the Rebellion of 1837 as stemming from a xenophobic French-Canadian hostility to English-speaking fellow-citizens, no one reproached Dudley on national or religious grounds. His 'crime' was not in professing Protestantism, in speaking English, or even in believing in the Queen's majesty, but simply in retaining a commission at a time when all good citizens had a duty to resign. The atonement required of this wayward soul was just as specific and limited as the 'sin' itself. He had merely to make a gesture — that of turning over his commission — that signified a renunciation of former 'treason' and an acceptance of the authority of the Patriot crowd. The emphasis was on the outward act indicating a transfer of allegiance without any further surrender of personal autonomy. This was made clear to another loyalist militia officer, who proclaimed to the fifty blackened faces shouting for his resignation 'that if they compelled him to give up his commissions they could not change his principles'; that is alright, came the sarcastic reply, we do not wish to alter your religion.[36]

The boast reported by Dudley Flowers of sixty-two political charivaris in his region alone may have been exaggerated but the basic point that, within a few weeks, dozens of resignations had been secured by this means is undeniable. By the second week of November there was, to all intents and purposes, no official government presence in most of the populous rural parishes of the District of Montreal, and an elective magistracy and militia were beginning to operate in its place. In such a situation the government naturally had recourse to its now reinforced military forces to enforce its own claim to sovereignty. The British expeditions that ventured out from Montreal were surprised at the resistance offered by the inhabitants, hastily organized through the revolutionized militia companies. The initial armed encounter at St. Denis (23 November) was, in fact, a Patriot victory but, since the insurgent military effort was localized, fragmented and defensive, the troops soon crushed their amateur opponents. What followed, in many localities, was a series of very unritualistic punitive actions; loyalists then had the satisfaction of watching flames race through the homes of neighbours who had so recently issued empty threats of arson. Turmoil continued for over a year, in Upper Canada (Ontario) as well as Lower Canada, while Patriot refugees in the northern states tried to enlist American support. But, by the end of the decade, the republican movement had been effectively destroyed.

French-Canada in particular was permanently marked by this defeat. The middle-class professionals who had once been at the centre of the Patriot movement hastily jettisoned their alliance with the artisans and peasants in the rush to make their peace with established authority. Police forces, public school systems and elaborate bureaucracies reinforced the colonial state, while the Catholic clergy saw its power and influence grow by leaps and bounds. Changes of this sort helped to contain social conflict in the mid-nineteenth century, but they hardly eliminated it. Lower Canada was actually a much more violent place and a more deeply divided society after 1840 than it had been before the Rebellion. Strikes by canal and railroad navvies heralded the advent of capitalism, but more typical of the age were essentially retrograde upheavals such as the Gavazzi riots which pitted Montreal's Catholics and Protestants against one another in 1853.[37] Lacking 'enlightened' allies and politically 'progressive' outlets for their resentment, plebeian rioters vented their anger on one another.

Not surprisingly, the French-Canadian charivari of these bitter mid-century decades was quite different from the ritual of the pre-Rebellion period. A recent study focusing on the

Trois-Rivières region, 1850–80, indicates that charivari was no longer linked exclusively to marriage and the sanctity of the wedding rites.[38] Belatedly following the lead of other countries, Lower Canadians turned the charivari into an all-purpose weapon for chastising moral transgressions and punishing nonconformists. Sexual deviants, drunkards and converts to Protestantism now joined mismatched couples as common targets of noisy demonstrations. Moreover, the attacks were much more vicious than they had been during the insurrection or earlier. Barns were burned, and men were stripped, beaten and thrown in the river. And no longer did a victim have to resist for a crowd to be provoked into violence: the first notice one villager had of his charivari came in the form of a whip lashing across his face. There was less emphasis than in the past on monetary exaction for many mobs sought, not a token of surrender, but the expulsion from the community of an offensive neighbour. In the changed circumstances of the post-Rebellion era, then, the charivari form was deployed in radically new and decidedly more cruel ways.

It seems significant that the most violent and intolerant phase in the history of the French-Canadian charivari occurred at a time of comparative weakness for the 'labouring classes'. When the rough music was at its roughest, it was also at its most politically impotent. Along with other forms of plebeian hellraising, charivari shocked the bourgeoisie, but did little to curb the growth of elite power after 1840. In fact, the Canadian state never again faced a challenge as serious as that mounted to the sound of blaring horns and banging pots at the time of the Rebellion.

For such an orthodox and mild-mannered custom, the traditional French-Canadian charivari had proved remarkably effective as a vehicle of revolt. Of course the Patriots were soundly beaten. This is hardly surprising, given the relative strength of the parties in conflict: a small colony with no external allies faced the premier imperial power on earth at a time when the latter was not distracted by serious difficulties at home or abroad. The wonder is that the inhabitants of Lower Canada were able to cripple colonial rule to the extent that they did in the fall of 1837. This is where the politicized charivari form made a crucial contribution. Serving at first, as in contemporary France, as a medium of complaint and protest, it was soon deployed as the central element in a campaign to destroy government power in the countryside and to assert a practical sort of popular sovereignty. This was a truly revolutionary role for a venerable ritual, even if the ensuing debacle did expose the military and diplomatic weaknesses of the Patriot movement.

The charivari was well suited for its insurrectional mission in a number of practical ways. The very fact, first of all, that it was a custom of collective action made it an important cultural resource when groups of people had to be assembled and organized. Since collective institutions and traditions were rather weak in French Canada, recourse to the charivari was all the more natural. Additionally, and more specifically, charivari was a more useful device under the circumstances because of the way it concealed the identity of aggressors. Above all, the traditional focus on extortion lent itself to Patriot strategies in the fall of 1837, as did the larger drama of forcing wayward individuals to make a gesture of renunciation and submission. Charivari had always been coercive, but only in a very discriminating way. Its techniques were therefore well adapted to the delicate task of exacting a particular type of obedience from certain recalcitrant individuals, all without bloodshed.

In addition to its strictly tactical role, the charivari form functioned as a framework within which the villagers of Lower Canada grappled with the moral and philosophical problems of revolt. Linked to widely held and long-standing beliefs concerning relations between the individual, the community and the cosmic order, the custom was deeply rooted in dominant political and religious ideologies. At the same time, it embodied an implicit assertion of popular rights to a share of public authority. Here was a democratic germ, and one whose claims to legitimacy were formidable. Thus, when the crisis of colonial rule came, a law-abiding peasantry that brought out its charivari masks and noise-makers in order to depose local officials could feel it was doing the right thing in the right way.

NOTES

Research for the paper was funded by the Social Sciences and Humanities Research Council. Wally Seccombe, David Levine, Patrick Manning and Michael Wayne were kind enough to read an earlier draft of this article and to give me helpful criticism, while André Lachance, Serge Gagnon and Jean-Marie Fecteau brought archival materials to my attention. My sincere thanks to all of them.

1. Violet Alford, 'Rough music or charivari', *Folklore*, LXX (December 1959), 508.
2. Charles Tilly, *The Contentious French* (Cambridge, Mass., 1986), 30. Other works dealing with the political use of the charivari form under the July monarchy include: Félix Ponteil, "Le ministre des finances Georges Humann et les émeutes anti-fiscales en 1841', *Revue Historique*, LXXIX (1947), 332; Rolande Bonnain-Moerdyk and Donald Moerdyk, 'A propos du charivari, discours bourgeois et coutume populaire', *Annales: économies, sociétés, civilisations* (hereafter AESC), 29e année (May–June 1974), 693–704; Yves-Marie Bercé, *Fête et révolte: des mentalités populaires du XVIe au XVIIIe siècle* (Paris, 1976), 43–4; Maurice Agulhon, *La République au village: les populations du Var de la Révolution à la Ile République* (Paris, 1979), 266.
3. John Palmer, *Journal of Travels in the United States of North America and in Lower Canada performed in the year 1817* (1818), 227–8. On this particular charivari, see also, 'Un charivari à la Québec', *Bulletin des Recherches historiques* (Lévis), XLIV (Aug. 1938), 242–3; *Le Canadien* (Quebec), 10 Oct. 1817. Travel accounts describing other charivaris are cited in Bryan D. Palmer, 'Discordant Music: charivaris and white-capping in nineteenth-century North America', *Labour-le travail*, III (1978), 6–62.
4. Among the works dealing with the charivaris of early modern France, see Arnold Van Gennep, *Manuel de folklore français contemporain*, 4 vols (Paris, 1937–49), II, 614–28; Roger Vaultier, *Le folklore pendant la guerre de Cent Ans d'après les lettres de remission du trésor des chartes* (Paris, 1965); Natalie Z. Davis, 'The reasons of misrule' in *Society and Culture in Early Modern France* (Stanford, 1975), 97–123; Claude Gauvard and Altan Gokalp, 'Les conduites de bruit et leur signification à la fin du Moyen Age: le charivari', AESC, 29e année (May–June 1974), 693–704; Jacques LeGoff and Jean-Claude Schmitt (eds). *Le Charivari* (Paris, 1981).
5. Emmanuel Le Roy Ladurie is convinced that French folktales recorded in contemporary Quebec display archaic characteristics not present in European versions since the eighteenth century. See *Love, Death and Money in the Pays d'Oc,* trans. Alan Sheridan (Harmondsworth, 1984), 271–2, 437–9.
6. This phrase comes from Bertram Wyatt-Brown, *Southern Honor: Ethics and Behavior in the Old South* (New York, 1982), 435–61. More subtle versions of the same view can be found in Edward Shorter, *The Making of the Modern Family* (New York, 1975), 46–7 and Peter Burke, *Popular Culture in Early Modern Europe* (New York, 1978), 200.
7. In addition to the works cited in the previous note, see E. P. Thompson, '"Rough Music": le charivari anglais', AESC 27e année (March–April 1972), 285–312; Martin Ingram, 'Ridings, rough music and the "Reform of Popular Culture" in early modern England', *Past and Present*, CV (Nov. 1984), 79–113; Christian Desplat, *Charivaris en Gascogne: la 'morale des peuples' du XVIe au XXe siècle* (Paris, 1982).
8. Edward Allen Talbot, *Five Years' Residence in the Canadas: including a Tour through part of the United States of America, in the year 1823* (1824), 300.
9. *Rituel du diocèse de Québec, publié par l'ordre de Monseigneur l'évêque de Québec* (Paris, 1703), 363.
10. Of course, by the eighteenth century, the French charivari was no longer (if it ever was) a specialized weapon to be used only against widowers who 'stole' potential wives from the young men of a locality.
11. André Burgière, 'Pratique du charivari et répression religieuse dans la France d'ancien régime' in LeGoff and Schmitt, *op. cit.,* 190–1.
12. *Rituel du diocèse de Québec,* 347, 329 (my translation and my emphasis). Cf. Jean-Louis Flandrin, *Families in Former Times: Kinship, Household and Sexuality,* trans. Richard Southern (Cambridge, 1979), 161–4.
13. Serge Gagnon, 'Amours interdites et misères conjugales dans le Québec rural de la fin du XVIIIe siècle jusque vers 1830 (l'arbitrage des prêtres)' in François Lebrun and Normand Séguin (eds), *Sociétés villageoises et rapports villes-campagnes au Québec et dans la France de l'ouest, XVIIe–XXe siècles* (Trois-Rivières, 1987), 323 (my translation). This case occurred in 1810.

14. André Lachance, *La justice criminelle du roi au Canada au XVIIIe siècle: tribunaux et officiers* (Québec, 1978), 113–15.

15. Gagnon, *op. cit.*, 324.

16. Talbot, *op. cit.*, 303.

17. Gagnon, *op. cit.*, 317.

18. Public Archives of Canada (hereafter PAC), MG24, I109, diary of F.-H. Séguin, 73. My translation does not do justice to the *double entendre* of the final phrase of the original, which suggests both full rights of possession in the legal jargon familiar to our notary-diarist and sexual fulfilment: *'les nouveaux mariés pourront à l'avenir se livrer paisiblement à toutes les jouissances de leur union.'*

19. Robert-Lionel Séguin, *Les divertissements en Nouvelle-France* (Ottawa, 1968), 73.

20. Thompson, *op. cit.*, 290.

21. Talbott, *op. cit.*, 302–3.

22. Palmer, *op. cit.*, 28–9; Archives nationales du Québec, depot de Montréal, P1000/49–1102, émeute de juin 1823 à Montréal; Bibliothèque nationale du Québec, Montréal, journal of Romuald Trudeau, 1 June 1823.

23. Though the magistrates of Montreal did issue a local ordinance prohibiting charivaris in the 1820s, there was never any provincial legislation, like that in place in France from the time of the Revolution, that was clearly directed against the custom. On the eve of the Rebellion, the legislative council of Lower Canada did consider a bill 'to repress the abuses consequent upon the assembling together of large numbers of persons under pretext of Charivaris': *Journals of the Legislative Council of the Province of Lower Canada*, vol. 25, 194 (26 Jan. 1836). On parallel campaigns to combat 'vagrancy', rationalize poor relief and regulate taverns, see Jean-Marie Fecteau's important thesis, 'La pauvreté, le crime, l'état: Essai sur l'économie politique du contrôle social au Québec, 1791–1840' (these de doctorat de 3e cycle, Université de Paris VII, 1983).

24. Palmer, *op. cit.*

25. Davis, *op. cit.*, Burke, *op. cit.*, 199–204; Emmanual Le Roy Ladurie, *Carnival in Romans*, trans. Mary Feeney (New York, 1979), esp. 301–2, 316.

26. Among the more important works on the Rebellion and the political developments leading to it, see Gérard Filteau, *Histoire des patriotes: L'explosion du nationalisme*, 3 vols. (Montreal, 1938–42); S. D. Clark, *Movements of Political Protest in Canada, 1640–1840* (Toronto, 1959), 259–330; Fernand Ouellet, *Lower Canada 1791–1840: Social Change and Nationalism* (Toronto, 1980); Jean-Paul Bernard, *Les Rébellions de 1837–1838: Les patriotes du Bas-Canada dans la mémoire collective et chez les historiens* (Montréal, 1983); Elinor Kyte Senior, *Redcoats and Patriotes: The Rebellions in Lower Canada 1837–38* (Ottawa, 1985).

27. *La Minerve* (Montreal), 10 Aug. 1837 (my translation). See also *Le Populaire* (Montreal), 27 Sept. 1837; 2, 9 and 16 Oct. 1837; *Montreal Gazette*, 30 Sept. 1837.

28. There was one exception to this pattern. A crowd that had turned out to greet the Patriot leader Louis-Joseph Papineau at St. Hyacinthe, learning that the commander of British forces happened also to be staying in the town, gathered round the house where the latter was staying for a noisy vigil punctuated by catcalls and anti-government slogans.

29. Archives nationales du Québec, documents relatifs aux événements de 1837–1838 (hereafter ANQ, 1837), deposition of Robert Hall, 15 July 1837. This practice, previously unknown in French-Canada as far as I can tell, may have been picked up from British immigrants. On animal mutilation of this sort in England, see Ingram, *op. cit.*, 87.

30. This insistence on a certain unanimity on fundamental issues, and the concomitant punitive approach to dissenters, is quite common in most societies under emergency conditions such as revolution or war. See, for example, Rhys Isaac, 'Dramatizing the ideology of revolution: popular mobilization in Virginia, 1774 to 1776', *William and Mary Quarterly*, third series, XXXIII (July 1976), 357–85.

31. Robert Christie, *A History of the Late Province of Lower Canada, Parliamentary and Political, from the Commencement to the Close of its Existence as a Separate Province*, 6 vols. (Montreal, 1866), v. 32–3. On French maypole customs and the transformation of the maypole into the liberty pole at the time of the Revolution, see Van Gennep, *Manuel de Folklore*, vol. 1, part 4, 1516–75; Mona Ozouf, *La fête révolutionnaire 1789–1799* (Paris, 1976), 280–316; Le Roy Ladurie, *Carnival in Romans*, 296–7; Jean Boutier, 'Jacqueries en pays croquant: les révoltes paysannes en Aquitaine (décembre 1789–mars 1790)', AESC, 34e année (July–Aug. 1979), 764–5.

32. ANQ, 1837, no. 257, deposition of Louis Bessette, 5 Nov. 1837.

33. ANQ, 1837, no. 146, deposition of Dudley Flowers, 3 Nov. 1837. For accounts of similar charivaris, see the following depositions: *ibid.*, no. 75 (Isaac Coote, 10 Feb. 1838); no. 109 (Louis-Marc Decoigne, 17 Feb. 1838); no. 122 (Pierre Gamelin, 9 Nov. 1837); no. 90 (David Vitty, Rickinson Outtret, Robert Boys and Thomas Henry, 5 Nov. 1837); no. 103 (Nelson Mott, 6 Dec. 1837); no. 128 (C. H. Lindsay, 8 Nov. 1837); no. 87

(Antoine Bruneau, 17 Dec. 1837); no. 314 (Jean-Baptiste Casavant, 12 Nov. 1837); no. 115 (François St-Denis, 7 Nov. 1837); no. 318 (Benjamin Goulet, 20 Nov. 1837); no. 516 (Orange Tyler, 16 Nov. 1837); no. 3557 (W. U. Chaffers, 9 Nov. 1937); no. 158 (Ambroise Bédard, 10 Nov. 1837); PAC, RG4, A1, 524: 11 (Loop Odell, 17 Nov. 1837). Additional information appears in *Le Populaire*, 5 Nov. 1837; *L'Ami du Peuple* (Montréal), 8 Nov. 1837; PAC, RG9, 1A1, vol. 48, James McGillvary to David McCallum, 26 Nov. 1837; Archives du diocèse de St-Jean-de-Québec, H. L. Amiot to Mgr. Bourget, St Cyprien, 16 Nov. 1837.

34. Ray Billington, *The Protestant Crusade 1800–1860: A Study of the Origins of American Nativism* (New York, 1938); Scott W. See, "The Orange order and social violence in mid-nineteenth century Saint John', *Acadiensis*, XIII (Autumn 1983), 68–92. See also Sean Wilentz, *Chants Democratic: New York City and the Rise of the American Working Class, 1788–1850* (New York, 1984), 264–5.

35. There may have been an exception to this rule in Dudley Flowers's case, for a man approached him a few days after he had surrendered his commission and told him he must sign a copy of the resolutions passed at the St Charles meeting, failing which he would receive another visitation that night. Understandably intimidated, the lieutenant hastily packed up his family and left the parish, and so it is impossible to know whether an attack really was planned. It seems likely that his visitor was an isolated individual playing a cruel joke since all the other charivari accounts indicate that hostilities ceased once the commission changed hands.

36. PAC, RG4, A1, vol. 524, no. 11, deposition of Loop Odell, 17 Nov. 1837. This point needs to be qualified in the light of one isolated but glaring counter-example. In the parish of St. Valentin, a French-Canadian convert to Protestantism was visited one night in mid-October by a party that 'made ludicrous noises with horns, bells, pans and other things'; after asking him if he was a Patriot, the attackers 'required that he should renounce his religion and go back to the Roman Catholic religion' (ANQ, 1837, no. 135, deposition of Eloi Babin, 13 Nov. 1837). Though scarcely an issue in other parts of Lower Canada, religion was a source of controversy in this one locality where a group of Swiss missionaries was active. Local inhabitants tended to view the mission as an instrument of the government party, for it accepted money from the Montreal merchants and refused to take part in the Patriot campaigns of 1837. See René Hardy, 'La rebellion de 1837–1838 et l'essor du protestantisme canadien-français', *Revue d'histoire de l'Amérique française*, XXIX (Sept. 1975), 180–1.

37. Elinor Kyte Senior, *British Regulars in Montreal: An Imperial Garrison, 1832–1854* (Montréal, 1981), 109–33; Michael S. Cross, '"The Laws are like Cobwebs": popular resistance to authority in mid-nineteenth century British North America' in Peter Waite, Sandra Oxner and Thomas Barnes (eds.), *Law in a Colonial Society: The Nova Scotia Experience* (Toronto, 1984), 110–12.

38. René Hardy, 'Le charivari dans la sociabilité rurale' (unpublished paper).

Article Twenty-One

The Rebellion of 1837 in Upper Canada

Colin Read

The years 1837–38 in Upper Canada saw rebellions break out at Toronto and near Brantford, saw the borders of the province violated time and again by raids launched from the United States, saw rebel pitted against loyalist, reformer against tory, and neighbour against neighbour. Little wonder, then, that the Rebellion era has long been of interest to historians and general public alike and has formed the stuff of legend in Canadian history. Undeniably, the Rebellion was an important, if uncharacteristic, event in the life of a province (Ontario) whose politics have usually been marked by tranquillity, even somnolence, rather than by violence and strife.

Source: Colin Read, "The Rebellion of 1837 in Upper Canada," *The Canadian Historical Association Historical Booklet* No. 46 (Ottawa: Canadian Historical Association, 1988), 2–24.

1. THE CONSERVATIVE DESIGN

The political roots of the unrest that beset the province in the 1830s can be traced back to 1791. In the aftermath of the American Revolution, some seven thousand refugees — United Empire Loyalists — poured into the old province of Quebec. Most settled westward from Montreal — the greater part along the St. Lawrence River and on the north shore of Lake Ontario, a few around Niagara and Detroit. These western Loyalists sought a government separate from that of Quebec, one free from francophone influence. Their reward was the Constitutional Act of 1791 and the creation of Upper Canada.

The act gave the new province a framework of government. Upper Canada was to have a lieutenant governor, answerable to the governor general at Quebec and, ultimately, to the British imperial government. In this position, he came to exercise wide powers, among them appointing the executive and legislative councillors. These were important people. The members of the executive council helped frame and implement administrative policies; those of the legislative council initiated legislation and revised or rejected legislation originating from the assembly. The last body, although elected on a broad property franchise, had severely restricted powers. The framers of the Constitutional Act had, like others, searched history for lessons, and one of the things they found, or thought they found, was that the democratic assemblies of the rebelling Thirteen Colonies, by being overly strong, had caused the American Revolution. To prevent a similar occurrence, they limited the powers of the people of Upper Canada. Not only could the legislation of the assembly be rejected by the legislative council, but it could also be turned back by the lieutenant governor or the British government. With its powers so circumscribed, the assembly was in danger of being little more than a debating society. The prospect would not have upset the architects of this governmental system unduly. To them, if the common people, through the assembly, did not have the decisive voice in governmental affairs, that was only just, since they were but one of three elements of society, and an element whose political rights in England and the colonies were of more recent vintage than those of the Crown or the aristocracy.

The new government, then, was to be a balanced one, blending the elements of King (the lieutenant governor), Lords (the two appointed councils), and Commons (the assembly). No one element would be able to run roughshod over the rights of the others. Instead, the interests of all would be served by a system designed to produce stability, harmony, and orderly growth, rather than the revolution, strife, and chaos which advocates of such a balanced constitution saw in its new republican rival to the south.

Vested interests soon began to accumulate within the governmental structure of Upper Canada, particularly as local government also rested heavily on the appointive rather than elective principle. True, almost from the first, leading Loyalists found themselves sharing power with able, more recently arrived immigrants. Yet there were always those who felt themselves well qualified, but who found the doors of office closed to them. The lucky appointees clung to the offices they had and often acquired more, trying to ensure in the process that relatives and friends inherited or collected their share. The tendency for a few to consolidate power and influence by accumulating offices was exacerbated by the fact that lieutenant governors came and went with some regularity and that the newly arrived ones turned to those office-holders crowded about them for advice. These, of course, normally took the opportunity to promote their own interests and those of like-minded men and to represent those interests and their views as those of all well-disposed citizens in the province. The extent to which the governors were in the pockets of their advisers should not be overstated, however. The former had their instructions from London and were often far from ready to let local officials pursue courses different from those prescribed at the seat of the Empire. On balance, however, the officials of the colony were extremely influential. Those occupying the central positions of power at the capital, York (renamed Toronto in 1834), are known to history as the "Family Compact." Perhaps the term is unfortunate, implying as it does a concentration of power at the centre that ignores in some measure the local bases and sources of influence of its members. Perhaps, too, the term is inaccurate in suggesting that all those members were personally interrelated, but that term does convey the essentially closed and oligarchic structure of power in the province.

Within the "compact," a capable, talented individual like John Beverley Robinson, a son of Loyalist parents who had as his patron John Strachan, from 1812 the rector of York and later archdeacon of the province, could collect a bewildering array of offices. Robinson became first acting attorney general, next, solicitor general, then attorney general, and finally chief justice, finding time along the way to sit in the assembly, become speaker of the legislative council, and president of the executive council. As well, in the Upper Canada of the period, he could see his brother Peter become a member of the executive and legislative councils, as well as of the assembly, and Commissioner of Crown Lands, and his brother William become a member of the assembly and a Commissioner of the Welland Canal Company.

Besides power, office brought money and land as payment, but often not enough of the former to satisfy rising expectations. Many an official complained of being short of cash. Yet the Robinsons and other like them did not starve — far from it — and were mindful of the fact that they enjoyed certain material privileges — fine houses, handsome carriages, or elegant clothes perhaps. Nevertheless, a John Beverley Robinson believed that his lot in life was a relatively hard one. He burned candles late into the night worrying over the affairs of state and the concerns of men — not for him the easy joys of long evenings of idle talk in the ale house. And what might a Robinson worry about as the tallow melted?

He might well worry about the security of the colony. Upper Canada had been founded by men and women who fled the Revolution in the Thirteen Colonies. After them came immigrants from Britain, but there came, too, settlers pushing up from the United States, some claiming to be "late Loyalists," others making no claims except upon the province's good farm land. These last particularly were people to be watched and watched carefully in an age of revolution.

When the Americans revolted, had they not been helped in their bloody cause by the French, who then paid for their sin against God and Britain by being convulsed with revolution themselves? Indeed, the French had become so infected with the revolutionary virus that they attempted to spread the contagion abroad by force of arms. Inevitably, Britain, the one power true to God's law in the eyes of the Loyalists, stood as the great counterrevolutionary agent of the age of the French Revolutionary and Napoleonic Wars. Not surprisingly (to a Robinson), Britain and her colonies were attacked by a perfidious United States bent on helping her old ally, France.

The War of 1812 had, in fact, several causes, not the least of which was a long-standing controversy over maritime rights. Equally, there were Americans who coveted Upper Canada, and, unfortunately, the events of the war demonstrated that a significant portion of the province's approximately one hundred thousand inhabitants were either indifferent or hostile to the British cause. Had it not been for the British regulars in the colony and their Indian allies, Upper Canada would surely have fallen to the Americans. How to purge the province of this lamentable pro-American element was clearly a major question, then, for Robinson and his circle.

They found the answer, or so they thought, in the decision to exclude incoming American immigrants from the province. A long and bitter controversy, the "Alien Question," ensued in which Robinson played a leading role, a controversy ending only in 1828 with Americans *already resident* in the province being able, after meeting certain residence requirements, to take the oath of allegiance and secure full civil rights and privileges. But the episode left a bitter legacy, as well as several unanswered questions, behind it. Similarly divisive and inconclusive were the major controversies over the privileges of the Church of England.

Robinson devoutly believed that the fledgling British colony of Upper Canada required an official or established church to provide through sound religion vital social cement to knit the community together in harmony. The Constitutional Act was interpreted as setting aside one-seventh of all the unsurveyed land in the province for the Church of England, the supposed "Protestant" church referred to in the act. These clergy reserves, and the Crown reserves, also one-seventh of the unsurveyed lands, were scattered throughout the townships, angering many residents who perceived them as impediments to economic and social development, since they generally were settled more slowly than surrounding lots. The clergy reserves, of course, angered many in the diverse Upper Canada religious community who were not members of the Church of England. Various Presbyterians, in particular, clamoured for a share of reserve revenues, but were unsuccessful in their demands in the pre-Rebellion period. Certain voluntaryists, who believed that churches should not be financed by the government but from the purses of their followers, argued that all these revenues should be devoted to secular purposes. The reserves thus became the most obvious symbol of the many privileges of the Church of England in the colony, a symbol John Beverley Robinson was determined to protect.

Robinson had a particular mind-set. He, and others like him, wished to see an organic, hierarchical community created in Upper Canada, one based on a balanced constitution and an established church. They wished also to stress the necessity of loyalty to Great Britain on a continent housing the predatory democracy and the licentious "mobocrats" of the United States. Here, the War of 1812 was a touchstone for them, demonstrating for everyone and for all time the essentially unprincipled and opportunistic policies of the revolutionary republic to the south. In short, tories or office-holders or Loyalists such as Robinson had both a garrison mentality and a conservative vision, seeing Upper Canada as a beleaguered outpost and a beacon of British civilization on a continent which had unleashed the evils of revolution on the world.

Some have suggested that Robinson and those like him in Upper Canada sought to create a gentility of themselves, to become the holders of great landed estates which they could pass on intact to their heirs and hence establish, like the British aristocracy, families which would give tone and direction to society. The application of this term should not be taken to indicate that the views of a Robinson were exclusively agrarian. They were not. Certainly he, and others like him, would not have welcomed the smokestacks of industry in the young province, but they were willing to acknowledge that a healthy commercial sector was vital to both the economy and society of the colony. Hence they put their weight behind such enterprises as the Bank of Upper Canada, established 1819, and the Welland Canal Company, created 1824. In sum, the Robinsons of the province were in favour of economic development that was supportive of an essentially agrarian society. This is one factor helping explain why the leaders of the tories, or conservatives as they liked to style themselves, attracted widespread support to the province, particularly in the towns and in the old Loyalist settlements in the eastern parts of the colony. The influx of Britons after the end of the Napoleonic Wars, especially the half-pay officers pensioned from the British army and navy, added significantly to that support.

2. THE GROWTH OF OPPOSITION

The conservative vision was not shared by everyone, however. The structure and operation of government, the privileges of the Church of England, the Crown and clergy reserves, the attempted exclusion of American settlers, the favouring of certain business enterprises — all these had their critics. So, too, did the rampant land speculation made possible by the province's lax policies, the inadequate sums devoted to primary education, and so on. In fact, a full catalogue of the accumulated grievances of all the inhabitants would have been an enormously long one.

Inevitably, opposition voices began to vocalize their objections to these perceived grievances. A small grouping of such individuals appeared before the War of 1812. Then in 1817 Robert Gourlay, a Scot and a would-be colonizer, arrived in the province. He canvassed the settlers' discontents and became convinced that the provincial government was monumentally derelict in its duty to the ordinary folk. He launched an extra-parliamentary protest movement, but was expelled from Upper Canada by officials appalled at both his methods and his message.

In the 1820s the conservative government's critics in the assembly began to coalesce as an identifiable group, but their organization was rather loose and their electoral success by no means assured. The conservatives carried the elections of 1820 and 1824, but lost to the reformers in 1828. These, in turn, lost to their opponents in 1830, but then won the election of 1834. One of the few constants in this changing scene was that the urban ridings of the province — Cornwall, Brockville, Kingston, York (Toronto), Hamilton, Niagara, (London became a separate riding only in 1836) — had an almost unblemished tory record. For their part, the reformers proved to be particularly strong north of Toronto and in the peninsula west of Lake Ontario and north of Lake Erie.

Despite their internal disagreements, most reformers could agree that the present governmental regime was too oligarchic and that the Robinsons of the world had too much power and privilege. The reformers' general desire to diffuse power and diminish privilege was made more intense by developments elsewhere. The year 1830 saw a series of revolts, albeit unsuccessful ones, against the established order in continental Europe. The movement for change was such that not even counter-revolutionary Britain was unaffected. There the Reform Bill of 1832 saw a significant widening of the parliamentary franchise. And 1832 also saw in the United States the re-election of President "Andy" Jackson, who had made a name for himself as the defender of the common man against those entrenched interests which would threaten the continuing vitality of the American experiment in democracy. To the Upper Canadian reformers, then, internal and external considerations suggested the necessity, and the expediency, of protesting things as they were, of opposing the tories.

A simple tory-reform dichotomy, however, obscures the fact that neither the tories nor the reformers were monolithic. The tories could agree on certain essentials, but could wage fierce internal fights. The reformers could agree that things needed changing, but could not always agree on the nature or degree of those changes. For instance, in the late 1820s and on into the 1830s, some talked at length about the needs for responsible government. What exactly did they mean? To a W.W. or a Robert Baldwin, this concept required the executive councillors to have the confidence of the assembly. If they lost that confidence (or voting majority), they should resign. Beneath this apparently simple premise lay another: that relatively closely knit political parties with reasonably coherent programmes were emerging, since party structure was necessary to gather and maintain voting majorities. Responsible government would be party government. In any case, the Baldwinite version of reform would clearly give the assembly far more control over the executive than it had had before. The Baldwins, father William Warren and son Robert, were eminently respectable Anglo-Irish immigrants, urban professionals who could, and who did, argue that their proposal was perfectly consistent with recent British practice. They came to be regarded as the leaders of the moderate reformers.

One reformer who was not moderate was William Lyon Mackenzie. A Lowland Scot, he had come to Upper Canada in 1820, working for three years as a merchant, then founding a newspaper (the *Colonial Advocate*) in 1824. First elected to the assembly in 1828, he was repeatedly expelled from it in the early 1830s for allegedly libelling its conservative members, but he eventually emerged from the ordeal as a martyr. He advocated a variety of solutions for the province's ills, including responsible government, but "Little Mac," as he was fondly called by admirers, was increasingly inclined towards more radical American electoral and democratic models. In the assembly elected in 1834 he chaired a grievance committee. Its report, issued the succeeding year, was largely his. Its sweeping indictment of the provincial government led the Colonial Office in London to remove Lieutenant-Governor Colborne who, whatever his deficiencies, had been following instructions to calm political passions by conferring more appointments on reformers around the province.

The man the Colonial Office chose to pour oil on troubled waters was Francis Bond Head, a sometime adventurer and author, and Senior Assistant Poor Law Commissioner of Kent County, England. His appointment has puzzled many historians, but it may be that the British thought his appointment justified by his reputation as a tried-and-true reformer and by his administrative experience in Kent. The former might appease the irate reformers of the province; the latter might prove valuable as increasing numbers of poor British immigrants came to the colony.

After arriving in Upper Canada in January of 1836, the new governor attempted to win over the reformers by admitting two of them, Robert Baldwin and Dr. John Rolph of Norfolk, into his executive council. Baldwin was able to persuade all the councillors to sign a memorandum insisting that Head confer with them on all items of executive business and declaring that he must accept their advice on certain vital issues. Head refused to agree and, when the councillors in turn refused to withdraw their document as he insisted they should, he appointed a new council, composed entirely of tories.

The assembly tried to bring Head to his knees by paralysing the government. It stopped passing grants of money. The governor retaliated by withholding assent from money bills already passed and by dissolving the assembly and calling a new election. Governors had been partisan in election campaigns before, but never as much as Head in 1836. He branded his opponents disloyal, suggesting they were conniving with dangerous external enemies. No one need have asked who. Government bureaucrats took their lead from him, contriving to hurry land patents conferring the right to vote to known tories. In the election itself, returning officers sometimes refused to let reformers vote. Just how widespread such incidents were cannot be known, but they did occur and likely affected some results. They are scarcely enough in themselves, however, to explain the tory avalanche that buried the reformers. The tories took over twice as many seats as their opponents. The electoral pendulum, long in motion, had swung back once again to the tories.

The reformers did not see it quite this way. Many were convinced that electoral fraud had cheated them of victory. Charles Duncombe, a reformer from Oxford County, took a petition alleging as much to the British government. The petition was referred back to the new assembly, where it received short shrift from a committee appointed to investigate its charges.

In these circumstances some defeated reformers, such as moderates Robert Baldwin and Marshall Spring Bidwell, lapsed into silence. But Mackenzie, his fiery temper suggested by the red wig he wore, refused to take defeat, his own or that of his comrades, quietly. Having established a new paper, *The Constitution*, on a significant date, the fourth of July 1836, he used it to ring out new complaints and to toll the long list of old ones. He noted particularly the many troubles besetting what he regarded as his constituency, the farmers of the province.

3. ECONOMIC DISCONTENTS

The farmers, the backbone of the economy, were beginning to suffer hard times. In 1836 crop harvests about the province, particularly potatoes and wheat, were unusually small. This was reflected in prices. In 1835 wheat had generally sold in Upper Canada for its customary four shillings per bushel, but in 1836 the substandard harvest drove the price upward. By October a bushel sold for over six shillings. And prices continued to climb on into 1837 before dipping in the second half of that year.

The precipitous rise in wheat prices hurt many. Townsfolk and farmers who did not grow enough wheat to meet their own needs had to pay higher prices. Those farmers whose crops failed, or failed to meet expectations, found the situation difficult, even ruinous, particularly those who were newly established and who had gone into debt to buy land. Those, though, whose crops did not fail, benefited from higher prices.

At the same time that the province was wracked by agricultural distress, it suffered from an international tightening of credit which followed a long period of economic expansion in the United States and Great Britain. The commercial economy of the province was based on a great chain of credit which stretched from British wholesaler to Upper Canadian retailer to local farmer, and back again. All were locked in an interdependent relationship in this credit system, and when one member was squeezed the others felt the pinch. British wholesalers, themselves pushed, demanded payment of their accounts from the colonial merchants who, in turn, sought their money from farmer creditors. Little wonder that by 1837 cash was in short supply and that interest rates on the money available were climbing.

The Upper Canadian banks, affected by the currency shortage, particularly of "hard money" or coins which had, so it seemed, a more secure value than paper money, pressed the government for relief in the form of permission to suspend withdrawals of hard currency by depositors. The legislature met in June and July of 1837 to consider the request, deciding that the three chartered banks in the colony would have to apply individually for such permission. In the event, the Commercial Band asked for and was granted the right to suspend specie (or hard money) in September 1837, permission that was extended to the other two — the Gore Bank and the Bank of Upper Canada — the following March.

4. THE MOVEMENT TO REBELLION

This general economic downturn added fuel to existing political discontent. Mackenzie, for one, was prepared to heap blame on Sir Francis Bond Head and his circle; increasingly, he made the British government a target too. It had faced great difficulties from much more determined reformers in Lower Canada and had seen fit in March 1837 to establish government by decree there. On July 19 an exasperated Mackenzie, pointing out in *The Constitution* the similarity between the grievances of the province's reformers and those of the American revolutionaries, suggested that the reformers organize political unions, which might, coincidentally, "be easily transferred . . . to military purposes." Political unions had been known before in the province, having been created in emulation of those in Britain that helped produce the great Reform Bill of 1832. In fact, there was in 1837 one in existence in Toronto, formed in October 1836. At the end of July 1837 it, too, called for more unions, as well as the establishment of a close working relationship with reformers in the two Canadas, cemented by a common convention. Reformers about the province heeded the cries from Toronto, though less so than is usually thought. They created two hundred unions, Mackenzie was to claim, and this has generally been believed. The real figure was but a fraction of that, perhaps one-tenth, certainly no more than one-eighth.

The union movement was strongest in the Home District, about Toronto, and in the London District to the west (see map on the next page). Occasionally, the movement brought on brawls between rival gangs of tories and reformers, as at Vaughan and Bayham. Nonetheless,

Figure 21.1 Upper Canada at the Time of the Rebellion

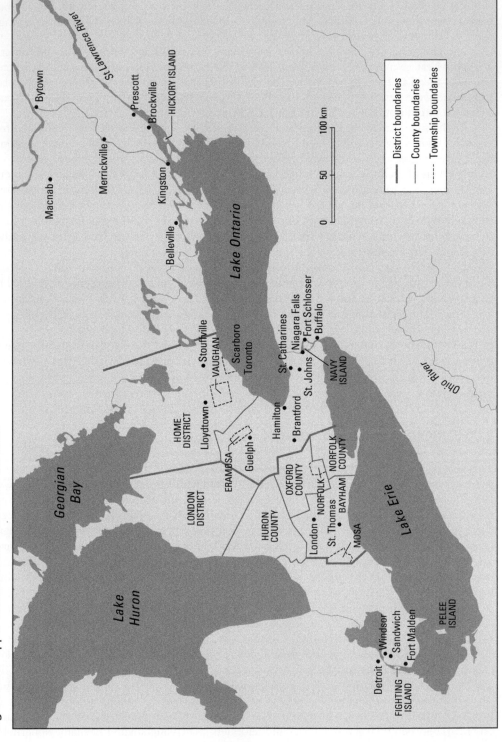

the general run of meetings was reasonably peaceful. Seldom did they involve military training. Despite Mackenzie's dark hints, their primary purpose was, as Mackenzie himself put it in *The Constitution* of 13 September, "Agitation! agitation! agitation!"— all this to culminate in a great reform convention. So certain was Governor Head that nothing serious was afoot that he acceded to the request of Sir John Colborne, now the commander of the British forces in the Canadas, to send as many men as he could spare from the one British regiment in the province to Lower Canada, to aid the authorities as the situation there worsened. In a show of bravado, he sent them all.

Mackenzie decided some time that autumn to escalate agitation into rebellion, first speaking with some ten other reformers in late October, telling them that, now that the soldiers had been withdrawn, it was time to strike. A quick blow would rally thousands. The meeting broke up when one reformer, Dr. T. D. Morrison, denounced the whole thing as treason, but Mackenzie continued plotting, eventually bringing John Rolph and Morrison himself into the fold. The conspirators agreed to send Jesse Lloyd, founder of Lloydtown, to Lower Canada to seek information about the intentions of the radical reformers there. Though the radicals of the two Canadas were to achieve very little in the way of coordination and cooperation, this did not stop Mackenzie from claiming in the following weeks that the two were acting in close concert. Eventually he agreed with a small coterie of radicals north of Toronto to raise the standard of revolt and the capital on 7 December. Toronto taken, Rolph would be proclaimed head of a provisional government.

5. REBELLION

Though he published a proposed constitution for an independent Upper Canada based on American models on 15 November, "Mac" did precious little the rest of that month to organize a large-scale revolt. Not till December did he really bestir himself. He dashed off a circular on the first, calling on the people to rise in arms, and at Stoverville (Stouffville) on the second he informed a gathering that Lower Canada had fallen to rebels there. In fact, rebellion had broken out there and the *patriotes* had won the initial battle at St. Denis on 23 November. Thereafter, however, their fortunes declined — something Mackenzie did not yet know. He may have believed, as he told the Stoverville audience, that victory was simply a matter of marching.

On Sunday, 3 December, Mackenzie received a message from Rolph in Toronto to the effect that the government had learned what was afoot and was about to arrest the ringleaders of the plot. He urged a rising on the fourth before the authorities could act. The doctor was skittish, Mackenzie decided. Unfortunately, Rolph's message circulated to others and men did begin to muster on the Monday. "Little Mac," though he wanted to, could not stop the premature movement.

Monday saw men gathering at Montgomery's Tavern, just north of Toronto. Their mustering did not pass unnoticed. Seven alarmed men, loyal to the government, tried to breach their lines to warn the capital. One, Colonel Moodie, was shot from his horse, later dying in agony. Three of his comrades were taken but the remaining three did break through. Mackenzie, who had arrived on the scene, and two companions captured two Torontonians, alderman John Powell and wharf owner Archibald MacDonell, who had ridden out to see if the rumours circulating of revolt were true. After this capture, one of Moodie's escaped comrades rode past, shouting that Moodie had been shot. Powell drew a concealed pistol and killed Anthony Anderson, one of the few rebels with any military expertise. Powell then spurred his way south, bringing news of the rising to a sleeping lieutenant governor, who had been warned several times in the recent past about the dangerous drift of events by Colonel James FitzGibbon, Clerk of the Assembly, but who had foolishly ignored the warnings.

Now a chastened Head had to organize things quickly. Since the regulars were out of the province, he knew that the militia would have to be the main line of defence. On paper it consisted of all male citizens aged sixteen to sixty, but in reality it was badly organized and trained. Hence in Toronto, rather than relying solely on the militia, Head and the authorities issued a general call for volunteers, a procedure they were to follow at other times in the months to come. And rather than relying on just citizens of Toronto, they appealed to those to both the east and west for aid.

"Little Mac" and the five hundred or so rebels who had gathered by Tuesday morning wasted the precious advantage they had. The government was off-guard, unprepared, but still they dithered. When Mackenzie finally did lead his men south, the marching rebels met a party carrying a flag of truce headed by none other than Dr. John Rolph, who had been asked to deal with the insurrectionists by a lieutenant governor unaware of his involvement in the rising. Rolph's two companions were Robert Baldwin and Hugh Carmichael, reformers both. The flag brought the rebels an offer of amnesty if they dispersed. Mackenzie wanted it in writing. When Head was asked for this, better apprised of the strength of the enemy, which was much less than originally thought, he refused. At some point in these proceedings, Rolph advised Mackenzie to ignore Head's offer and to take the city, but again the rebel chieftain delayed.

That evening Mackenzie bestirred himself, but could persuade only part of his men to follow him into Toronto. Their advance was stalled, however, by a small loyal outpost which opened fire and then fled. That night the capital was reinforced by sixty or seventy men led by Allan MacNab, Speaker of the Assembly, an influential tory who championed his own, and the town of Hamilton's, interests in the assembly. A few others came in from Scarborough Township. This helped prompt the ever-cautious Rolph to yet another change of direction. He sent a message to Mackenzie advising him to disband his force. He slipped away after learning that "Mac" and his lieutenants had declined his advice, deciding instead to launch their attack on Thursday, 7 December, the day originally planned.

Wednesday passed in rather desultory fashion, with both rebels and loyalists receiving reinforcements. The former, however, suffered some desertions; so their number, some four hundred by Thursday, compared very poorly with the loyalists' fifteen hundred. The man who was to command the rebel forces, Anthony Van Egmond, at last arrived from the far-off Huron Tract, sensibly advising the insurgents to withdraw, but Mackenzie would have none of it. His followers, most so poorly armed that only about two hundred could actually fight, waited as the government forces, led by Colonel FitzGibbon, marched upon them. The battle was a rout. A triumphant Head ordered the burning of Montgomery's Tavern, the rebels' headquarters. The home of prominent radical David Gibson was also torched. Fleeing rebels were hunted down and brought before Head, who freed them. He offered rewards, however, for the leaders, most of whom escaped, "Little Mac" included. A few, Van Egmond among them, were not so lucky, with Van Egmond, in his mid-sixties, soon dying from the cold and damp of his jail cell.

Beyond Toronto, the first news of the Rebellion was generally that the rebels had been successful. This was the report that reached the Brantford area on the sixth or seventh of December. It was accompanied by the "news" that the authorities, to forestall further revolt, were about to arrest various locally prominent radicals, Charles Duncombe and Eliakin Malcolm among them. These two, aided by others, immediately set about organizing resistance, telling their followers that now was the time to take advantage of the "fall" of Toronto to end oppression. With considerable success, they spread their efforts westward to the St. Thomas area and beyond. In the township of Norwich, for example, Duncombe mobilized some two hundred men, Malcolm secured about one hundred south of Brantford in Oakland and vicinity, while others elsewhere rallied another two hundred. By 13 December Duncombe thus had some five hundred rebels gathered at Oakland. They were to march to join Mackenzie's "victorious" forces in Toronto. Unfortunately for them, they were about to be surrounded by irate loyalists.

Officials at Toronto, once revolt had broken out there, expected trouble in the west which had a reputation for radicalism. Allan MacNab, having helped disperse Mackenzie's men, was ordered westward with five hundred volunteers. The western loyalists mustered too. Consequently, on the thirteenth, government supporters, including one hundred warriors from the Six Nations' Reserve near Brantford, were about to fall upon Duncombe's force from all points of the compass. Learning this, Duncombe, on the evening of the thirteenth, had his men retreat from Oakland to Norwich, then disperse. MacNab's force swept into the rebel encampment at Oakland early on the fourteenth to find it deserted. In the days that followed, MacNab's men rounded up the rebels, capturing several hundred, but none of the ringleaders.

6. CAUSES OF THE REBELLION

The twin revolts in Upper Canada over, many wondered why the rebels had taken up arms. Of course, as has been seen, the accumulated political grievances of the reformers had played a major part, as had short-term economic distress. So too had the factor of personality. Clearly Mackenzie had persuaded, or duped, men into rebelling. And circumstance had played its part. Had the rumours of rebel success not been so rift and communications so bad, Duncombe and his band would never have shouldered weapons. But had there been something else, some deeper structural economic or social problem little acknowledged by contemporaries but whose influence, insidious and pervasive, was at work nonetheless? Several historians have speculated that such was indeed the case.

About Toronto and in the west, rebels had rallied from forty-one townships. These were primarily agricultural in character and were relatively long settled, just the sort, it has been suggested, where farmers had contracted debts to merchants and bankers in purchasing farms, stock, and machinery. Doubtless, such debts had been contracted and doubtless many incurring them had been caught in the credit squeeze of 1837 described earlier. But was farm debt a real long-term problem, or more importantly considered a long-term problem? This was not likely the case, particularly since many farmers must have looked kindly upon the credit system, in normal times at least, knowing that without it they could not have farmed. Usually, credit was beneficent, not malevolent. The evidence suggests rather that those locales which produced rebels, far from being economically depressed, were prosperous and, hence, that the notion that deep-rooted economic distress was at the root of rebellion must be discarded. For one thing, contemporaries noted the relative prosperity of the insurgent areas. For another, one hard indicator of prosperity, population growth, bears out their comments. That indicator, though, warrants some discussion.

The rebel areas of the province grew in the thirties at a faster rate than did the non-rebel areas. Some will ask: had the former grown too quickly, had the flood of British immigrants coming into Upper Canada created intense social pressures which spread discontent, then disaffection? This question has two dimensions; the first relates to Toronto, the second to the rural rebel areas.

As indicated, large numbers of immigrants crossed the Atlantic to the Canadas in the 1830s. Over 50,000 arrived at Quebec in each of the two peak years of the decade, 1831 and 1832, most passing on to Upper Canada. Some were paupers, a greater number temporarily poor because of the expenses of the voyage, and these together posed a serious financial threat to the limited resources of public charity and private philanthropy. A portion too, especially in the cholera year of 1832, carried contagious diseases and threatened the health of all. The various threats posed by the immigrants were perceived most readily at Toronto, the great jumping off point to the interior. The kinds of tensions created in Toronto by the arrival of so many so quickly were severe, it has been suggested, and form an essential backdrop for a sophisticated understanding of the real causes of the Rebellion, not just in Toronto but around the province. This general line of argument obscures two salient points. The first is that Toronto's growth lagged somewhat behind that of the province as a whole. The capital's population was 9,252 in 1834, the year of its incorporation, 9,765 in 1835, 9,654 in 1836, and 10,871 in 1837, a growth rate over the period of 17.5 per cent, compared to the provincial average of 23.6 per cent. To repeat a point made earlier: Toronto was a jumping off point for the interior. Most of the thousands arriving in the city moved on, and did not remain to cause untold problems. The second point is an equally obvious one. Toronto was not the province. Even if one can demonstrate that the city suffered severe social tensions on the eve of the Rebellion because of the immigrant influx, one should not assume that those tensions obtained throughout the entire colony.

Can we then argue that as the immigrants spread through the province they created severe demographic pressures in certain areas, the rebel areas, by occupying land so rapidly that farmers already there were unable to acquire more, either for themselves or for their sons, creating economic and social discontent and thus fruitful ground for rebellion? Not likely: the one study we have for the Home District, the region along Lake Ontario centred on Toronto and stretching back to Georgian Bay, of the pattern of land acquisition, based on the granting of land patents (legal titles), concludes that the general disappearance of land there from the market came only in the 1840s. An even more detailed study of a smaller section of that region, the later Peel County, to the west of Toronto, identifies the critical years demographically as being later still. As for the rebel townships in the west, they certainly were capable of absorbing more people than they contained in the Rebellion era. In 1837 the rural sections of those predominantly rural townships had 30,910 people, or 20.9 per square mile. In 1851 the corresponding figures were 69,038 and 46.7, and in 1871, 82,692 and 55.9.

Certainly these rebel areas were capable in 1837 of absorbing more people, as was the province at large. While most Upper Canadians might not have wanted the diseased, the poverty-stricken, or even just the overly pretentious, they generally welcomed new immigrants, knowing that most brought at least a little money that could be spent locally, to the benefit of merchant and farmer alike. As the immigrants settled and succeeded, they benefitted all, particularly their neighbours, whose property values increased as settlement grew. Within reasonable limits, the more people, the better. Though it may be true, as has been suggested by numerous historians, that a deep demographic crisis existed in the Lower Canada of the 1830s, such was not the case in Upper Canada.

What of the rebels themselves? Even if they came from prosperous regions, were they perhaps economically disadvantaged members of those regions? Evidently not. Occupationally, the insurgents can be grouped into three broad categories: farmers; labourers; and innkeepers, merchants, craftsmen, professionals, and the like. Here, it seems reasonable to suggest that they represented an occupational cross-section of their agrarian society, though indeed some observers have been surprised at the number of doctors caught up in the revolt, perhaps a dozen or so, and of professionals generally. The numbers of those professionals, however, were so small as to render unconvincing for the Upper Canadian rebellion the argument advanced by Fernand Ouellet for the Lower Canadian one: that it was led by liberal professionals who sought to advance their own particular class interests by generalizing them to all the discontented and disadvantaged of their society. Beyond occupational levels, it is worth noting that most of the Upper Canadian rebels were married, and averaged just over thirty years of age. The accumulated facts thus suggest that the rebels were, for the most part, well-settled members of a reasonably prosperous agrarian society.

Other characteristics of the insurgents are significant. The available statistical data show that they were mainly North American, interlaced with significant numbers of Britons, as many as one-third of those about Toronto and one-fifth of those in the west. Those rebels who had religious affiliations tended to be drawn from "non-established" denominations or sects — Episcopal Methodists, Congregationalists, Baptists, even pacifist Quakers. They bore antipathy towards the privileges of the Church of England in the colony and the pretensions of the other "established" or would-be "established" churches, notably the Church of Scotland and the Church of Rome.

The rebels' reasons for taking up arms, therefore, were complex. There is no single cause or grand overriding explanation. A North American orientation which resented a distant power and a colonial system of government, short-term economic dislocation, or more individual motivation, whether family loyalties or personal friendships and animosities, all played a part. So too did specific political grievances as well as the general reform perception that the world was ordered too much in the interests of the few, too little in the interests of the many. Nor should one forget that few rebels understood the real military situation in the Canadas, having been convinced by a Mackenzie or a Duncombe that successful rebellion was simply a matter of marching.

7. REPERCUSSIONS

The news of revolt carried quickly over the province. In the east the populace, already frightened by the outbreak of rebellion in the lower province, mustered promptly to defend the upper one, though there were exceptions. Notably, the Laird of MacNab, a feudal Highland chieftain who ruled a domain high up the Ottawa Valley, found it impossible to rally his settlers, who were perhaps more disgusted with him than they were with the provincial government. Magistrates in Merrickville on the Rideau doubted the loyalty of some who belonged to the local political union and arrested them, holding trials. Along the St. Lawrence members of the Brockville political union were also arrested. Panic reigned for a time at Kingston as some believed that the radicals might try to attack the town, now that the garrison at Fort Henry had been removed to Lower Canada. Arms were despatched to the local authorities at Belleville, who were similarly convinced that widespread treason was afoot there. They rounded up a score or so of the local settlers.

To the west of Toronto, Hamilton officials were also convinced by the existence of political unions that treason was widespread. Like-minded officials regarded meetings in Eramosa township near Guelph, in the Short Hills back of St. Catharines, and in and about London with great suspicion. But only in Mosa Township to the west of London were there men prepared to rally to the rebel cause. These mustered, thinking that Duncombe was successful or was about to be. Learning the truth of the matter, they scattered to the winds. Most of those arrested outside of the rebel areas had met simply to discuss what to do: to be neutral or to form defensive associations against supposedly hostile tory forces. Perhaps the dominant note in the colony, however, was one of loyalty as men in every area rushed to the defence of the Crown, mostly out of conviction but in some cases out of expediency as settlers felt the necessity of demonstrating their allegiance to, and affection for, the British connection.

Demonstrations of loyalty were made the more essential by the fact that Mackenzie had fled to Buffalo and set about organizing a force to invade Upper Canada. On 13 December he led a few men over to Navy Island in the Niagara River, just above the falls, from whence he issued a grandiloquent proclamation urging Upper Canadians to throw off their yoke of oppression and declaring the establishment of a provisional government. His small force, commanded by an American, Rensaeller Van Rensaeller, was opposed by militiamen who rushed to the frontier. In late December, thirty-five of these provided the most startling and controversial incident of the entire Upper Canada Rebellion.

The thirty-five rowed over to Fort Schlosser on the American shore, where, at 2 a.m. on 30 December, they boarded a small steamer, *The Caroline*, which had been supplying Navy Island. They killed one of those on board, and cut the vessel loose from its moorings. Catching the current, it raced toward the falls, but, legend to the contrary, ran aground and then broke up, rather than plunging intact over the abyss. The episode, however, did plunge British-Canadian-American relations to a new low for the postwar period as many citizens of the republic were outraged at the violation of their soil and their waters and the killing of one of their countrymen. Sympathy for Mackenzie and his cause — the Patriot cause, as it became known — skyrocketed in the United States. This did translate into a number of volunteers to help those on Navy Island, but not enough for them to be able to overcome the several thousand facing them on the Canadian shore. Consequently, they abandoned the island, the last withdrawing on 14 January. But this did not end the Patriot raids. The furore over *The Caroline* helped ensure that. Most American recruits to the Patriot cause probably hoped to free a country they thought enslaved, as well as to secure revenge. Some others, unemployed in the hard times of the mid-thirties, were as much concerned with the prospect of improving their own position as with helping others. Booty beckoned. Whatever the motivation, the numbers of Patriots were ever small, though their secret organizations and elaborate rituals spread the opposite impression.

The first Patriot raid of the new year occurred along the Detroit River in early January. Some three hundred men, although contemporary estimates put the number as high as two thousand, gathered before seizing a schooner, *The Anne*, at Detroit. Using her and various small craft, they sailed south. On 8 January *The Anne* appeared before Fort Malden, firing on the town, sailing off when a steamer with a hundred militiamen from Windsor came in view. The next day, *The Anne* ventured out again, but the thirty or so on board ran her aground just south of Fort Malden, falling prisoner to the militiamen mustered to oppose them. Despite the inglorious end to this escapade, other Patriots carried on the struggle.

On 23 February several hundred occupied Fighting Island in the Detroit River but were driven off on the 25th by a force from Sandwich — 500 militiamen and British Regulars, the latter part of those rushed back to the province following the suppression of the Lower Canadian Rebellion. In the east, in the last week of February, about 200 patriots crossed over from the American shore to Hickory Island in the St. Lawrence, preparatory to an attack on Kingston, but retreated on learning of massive loyalist preparations to repel them. Near month's end, the western part of the province was again the focus of the Patriots' attention when approximately 400 raiders crossed the Lake Erie ice from the Sandusky peninsula and landed on Pelee Island. Not until 3 March did 350 British regulars, militiamen, and Indian volunteers reach the island and drive them off.

All of these abortive attacks caused great concern in a province recently convulsed by rebellion and very much obsessed with the invasions of the War of 1812. The government, which found its jails full of Mackenzie and Duncombe rebels, took extraordinary steps to deal with the Patriot threat. It passed acts forbidding armed drilling and permitting magistrates to seize arms they deemed dangerous to the public peace. Captured Patriots could be tried by court martial.

Other legislation concerned not the Patriots and the Patriot raids, but the rebels and the Rebellion period. The government enacted legislation exempting loyalists from prosecution for actions taken to put down the Rebellion. As for captured rebels, they could be held without bail and writs of *habeas corpus* in their cases not returned for thirty days. Those who admitted their guilt could petition the lieutenant governor for pardon, but pardon might involve any number of penalties, including transportation to a penal colony. In fact, of the 262 prisoners in the province eventually indicted for their parts in the rebellion, 181 petitioned under this statute. Fortunately, most were not transported and, in fact, were free by the end of the summer of 1838.

Three petitioners, including Samuel Lount and Peter Matthews in Toronto, were denied pardons, their crimes being considered too great. They were among the fifty-three tried that spring in the normal court system of the colony for treason — twelve in Toronto, twenty-six in Hamilton, and fifteen in London. Lount and Matthews were peculiarly unfortunate. Found guilty, they were condemned to die and were hanged on 12 April, despite many appeals for clemency on their behalf. Thirty-one of those tried were far more fortunate. Found not guilty, they were released. The remaining twenty were judged guilty but did not share Lount and Matthews' fate, being subjected to a variety of lesser punishments, the most severe of which was transportation to Australia.

The treatment of the prisoners, particularly the two hangings, became a cause of great grievance with many reformers. These, however, were ill placed to help those for whom they agitated. In the assembly itself four reformers — accused traitors Charles Duncombe of Oxford, John Rolph of Norfolk, William Benjamin Wells of Grenville, and David Gibson of the first riding of York — were unseated. As for the reform press, it was clearly in retreat. A few of the remaining papers were occasionally emboldened to protest harassment of the reform populace, which occurred more often and more severely in the Home District than elsewhere, but on the whole the climate of opinion was such that none dared to be too critical of the governing or its self-proclaimed agents.

These conditions helped persuade the Patriots that they must persist in their activities. Early on the morning of 30 May in the St. Lawrence, a small band rousted the passengers of the Upper Canadian-owned steamship, the *Sir Robert Peel*, and sank her. In June thirty-two men slipped across the Niagara frontier from the United States and, joined by about seventy locals, robbed a few houses on the night of 20 June, then attacked an inn housing thirteen militia cavalrymen. These they captured, then released before fleeing themselves. Several raiders were taken and tried. One was hanged, three sent to penitentiary, and seventeen sentenced to transportation. These severe punishments were enacted in part to dissuade the Patriots from further activities. The Patriots did relent for a time, but only a time.

On 11–12 November, 150–180 raiders landed from two schooners near Prescott and took up position in a windmill. Attacked on the thirteenth by about 500 militiamen and regulars, they drove them back. The attackers returned on the sixteenth, their numbers doubled, and carried the day, but only after a bloody battle. And still the Patriots persisted.

Early on the night of 2 December, some 150 crossed the Detroit River above Windsor. They attacked a militia barracks containing twenty men or so, killing several. They then met and murdered two others before being confronted by approximately 300 more, who put them to flight. Twenty-five patriots died in battle and five who had been taken captive were shot summarily on the orders of Colonel John Prince, "a Prince by nature as he is by name," or so one elated tory thought.

The Patriots captured at Windsor and Prescott were treated even more harshly than their predecessors, being tried before court martials, not civil courts. No fewer than *seventeen* were hanged. This helped persuade the Patriots to cease their activities. Though border outrages did continue for a year or more, these were all relatively minor as the Patriot movement, after a year of effort without a single significant success to its credit and many of its most devoted adherents dead or in jail, ran out of steam.

8. CONCLUSIONS

Even though the Upper Canadian Rebellion, which led to the Patriot raids, was a failure, it generally has been viewed as an ultimate success by historians, who have typically considered it an important, if somewhat faltering, step forward in the province's political evolution. Their argument is that the Canadian Rebellions forced the British government to rethink its colonial policy, which it signified in Upper Canada by replacing the inept Francis Bond Head as lieutenant governor, though it rather unfortunately chose the rigid Sir George Arthur as his replacement, and by charging Lord Durham to investigate the causes of the Rebellion in the upper, as well as in the lower, province and to make appropriate recommendations. Durham, who visited Upper Canada only briefly in the summer of 1838, blamed the outbreak of rebellion there mostly on the Family Compact's rigid control of government. Improve the governmental system, he concluded, and generally all would be well. It is said that his famous report, released in 1839 after he had resigned his post, proposed to improve that system by granting responsible government to the two Canadas after they had been united. Hence the Rebellion, the argument goes, led to the granting of responsible government. This overlooks several salient facts: Durham did not use the term "responsible government" in his report, though the phrase appeared in the margins of the printed version. He spoke of "self government" rather than "responsible government." More significantly, responsible government was not soon granted by a British government worried about the loyalty of Canada's colonists, some of whom had lately been in arms. Responsible government came only have a long parliamentary struggle in the 1840s, being formally achieved in 1848, shortly *after* it had been won in Nova Scotia, which had not suffered a rebellion.

The Rebellion and the succeeding Patriot raids had several unfortunate repercussions. Despite the effects of British garrison expenditures, the economic depression in place before the Rebellion deepened. The dislocations caused by unrest added to the unfortunate effects of the continuing shortage of specie and sub-standard harvests. Emigration increased from the colony, not just of rebels and their families, but of those fearing political and social turmoil. Significantly, population loss was greatest in the rebel areas. While the population of the province as a whole grew from 396,719 in 1837 to 406,842 in 1839, it increased microscopically in the rebel townships, from 104,341 to just 104,955. In fact, the number in those townships in 1839 had declined from the 105,271 of the previous year. Immigration and natural increase were more than offset by those who fled the turmoil. Across the province those who left sold farms, and property generally, at distress prices.

Some, of course, were not free to leave. As the table on the next page shows, over one thousand men found themselves jailed for their parts, real or supposed, in the Rebellion and the Patriot raids. Fortunately, most were imprisoned for relatively short periods, but some were not. Over one hundred were sent to the penal colonies. Twenty climbed the gallows. One wonders what they would have replied had they been asked if the Rebellion had been for good or ill.

While perhaps one can appreciate the courage or conviction of those who resorted to arms, one must be aware that their actions, directly or indirectly, added to the catalogue of human suffering. This was one occasion when violent protest did not succeed. It did, however, serve to strengthen the resolve of conservatives like John Beverley Robinson to stand on guard for the colony, sure as they were that, had the Rebellion succeeded, the young province would soon have been absorbed by the United States — a reasonable assumption. If so, then the compact

Table 21.1   Legal Dispositions of the State Prisoners

	Rebels		Patriots	
	#	%	#	%
Imprisoned	706	93.1	156	57.1
Transported	24	3.2	99	36.3
Banished	26	3.4	—	—
Executed	2	0.3	18	6.6
Totals	758	100.0	273	100.0

tories represented a position not so alien to Canada's successful national development as earlier generations of pro-reform historians alleged.

Of course, the rebels have their admirers, who find comfort in the reflection that the rebels, springing from the ranks of the reformers, articulated very real grievances and their protests eventually helped produce many needed changes. And the rebels, in taking up arms, dramatically demonstrated the courage of their convictions in resisting perceived oppression. Such considerations provide a much more solid historical apology for the insurgents of 1837 than earlier conclusions that the Rebellion in Upper Canada led directly to the granting of responsible government, a notion where wishful thinking rather than historical reality is clearly father to the thought.

Topic Ten

Social History of British North America

A Methodist minister, Rev. John Burwash, poses with his choir in this photo. The photo was likely taken in the 1860s.

The social history of settlement in British North America in the early and mid-19th century is really a collection of separate regional stories. Two French-speaking populations existed — the French Canadians in the St. Lawrence Valley and the Acadians in New Brunswick. English-speaking communities had been established in the Maritime colonies and in Newfoundland, as well as in the St. Lawrence Valley and in Upper Canada.

Willeen Keough's "The Riddle of Peggy Mountain: Regulation of Irish Women's Sexuality on the Southern Avalon, 1750–1860," reviews the intrusion of middle-class ideals of female domesticity and respectability into Newfoundland society. But did these middle-class values replace Irish plebian culture on the southern Avalon? In the mid-19th century proponents of the new values of middle-class society were increasingly women themselves. Alison Prentice outlines the female entry into teaching in her important article, "The Feminization of Teaching in British North America and Canada 1845–1875." Why did females come to dominate in the teaching school by the late 19th century? In the popular world a number of the clergy also had educational roles. In "Dry Patriotism: The Chiniquy Crusade," Jan Noel reviews the early career of Father Charles Chiniquy. How was he able to briefly make the temperance movement so popular in the St. Lawrence Valley?

In *A History of Newfoundland and Labrador* (Toronto: McGraw-Hill, 1980), Frederick W. Rowe deals with early settlement in Newfoundland. Several specialized articles on the early history of Newfoundland appear in *Early European Settlement and Exploration in Atlantic Canada*, ed. G.M. Story (St. John's: Memorial University, 1982). Gordon Rothney gives a short summary of Newfoundland's history in his booklet *Newfoundland: A History*, Canadian Historical Association, Historical Booklet no. 10 (Ottawa: CHA, 1964). For the First Nations history in Newfoundland, see Ingeborg Marshall, *A History and Ethnography of the Beothuk* (Montreal/ Kingston: McGill-Queen's University Press, 1996). An important study is by Jerry Bannister, *The Rule of the Admirals: Law, Custom and Naval Government in Newfoundland, 1699–1832* (Toronto: University of Toronto Press, 2003).

For an understanding of the social history of the Maritime region in the mid-19th century, consult Phillip A. Buckner and John G. Reid, eds., *The Atlantic Region to Confederation: A History* (Toronto: University of Toronto Press, 1994); and W.S. MacNutt, *The Atlantic Provinces, 1712–1857* (Toronto: McClelland and Stewart, 1965). MacNutt has also written *New Brunswick, A History: 1784–1867* (Toronto: Macmillan, 1963). Douglas Baldwin has written a popular history of Prince Edward Island, *Land of the Red Soil* (Charlottetown: Ragweed Press, 1990). *Separate Spheres: Women's Worlds in the Nineteenth-Century Maritimes,* eds. Janet Guildford and Suzanne Morton (Fredericton: Acadiensis Press, 1994) looks at the history of women in the Maritimes. In "The Relief of the Unemployed Poor in Saint John, Halifax, and St. John's," *Acadiensis* 5, 1 (1975): 32–53, Judith Fingard reviews the early system of poor relief, a topic often ignored.

The best overview of the Canadas remains J.M.S. Careless's *The Union of the Canadas: The Growth of Canadian Institutions, 1841–1857* (Toronto: McClelland and Stewart, 1967). R. Cole Harris provides a survey of Quebec and Ontario in the study he authored with John Warkentin, *Canada before Confederation: A Study in Historical Geography* (Toronto: Oxford University Press, 1974), pp. 65–109 and 110–68, respectively. On Canada West see J.K. Johnson's *Historical Essays on Upper Canada* (Toronto: McClelland and Stewart, 1975) and his second collection of articles under the same title, edited with Bruce G. Wilson (vol. 2; Ottawa: Carleton University Press, 1989). Also of value is *Patterns of the Past: Interpreting Ontario's History*, eds. Roger Hall, William Westfall, and Laurel Sefton MacDowell (Toronto: Dundurn Press, 1988).

A number of valuable social histories of the Canadas in the mid-19th century now exist. They include David Gagan, *Hopeful Travellers: Families, Land and Social Change in Mid-Victorian Peel County, Canada West*, Ontario Historical Studies Series (Toronto: University of Toronto Press,

1981); Michael Katz, *The People of Hamilton, Canada West: Family and Class in a Mid Nineteenth Century City* (Cambridge, MA: Harvard University Press, 1975); and Jack Little, *Crofters and Habitants: Settler Society, Economy, and Culture in a Quebec Township, 1848–1881* (Montreal/ Kingston: McGill-Queen's University Press, 1991). For a survey of life in rural Canada East, consult Serge Courville and Normand Séguin, *Rural Life in Nineteenth-Century Quebec*, Canadian Historical Association, Historical Booklet no. 47 (Ottawa: CHA, 1989). Jan Noel reviews the temperance movement in British North America in *Canada Dry: Temperance Crusades before Confederation* (Toronto: University of Toronto Press, 1995).

Alison Prentice et al., *Canadian Women: A History*, 2nd ed. (Toronto: Harcourt Brace, 1996) provides a review of Canadian women's lives in the mid-19th century. Micheline Dumont et al., *Quebec Women: A History*, trans. R. Gannon and R. Gill (Toronto: Women's Press, 1987) summarizes developments in Canada East during the same period. Three of the most perceptive contemporary witnesses of Upper Canada or Canada West are women: Catharine Parr Traill, Susanna Moodie, and Anna Jameson. Their writings are available in abridged editions in McClelland and Stewart's New Canadian Library Series: Traill's *The Backwoods of Canada* (1836) and *The Canadian Settler's Guide* (1854), Moodie's *Roughing It in the Bush* (1852), and Jameson's *Winter Studies and Summer Rambles in Canada* (1838). Marian Fowler's *The Embroidered Tent: Five Gentlewomen in Early Canada* (Toronto: House of Anansi, 1982) contains sketches of these women's lives.

WEBLINKS

Education in Ontario
http://www.archives.gov.on.ca/english/exhibits/education/index.html

This site describes the history of elementary and secondary education in Ontario from 1807 onward. It also contains many digitized primary source documents.

Slavery Debate in Nova Scotia
http://gateway.uvic.ca/spcoll/digit/slavery_opinion/index.html

A digitized document from 1802 debating the legality of a single case of slavery in Nova Scotia at the time.

Hygiene
http://www.civilization.ca/educat/oracle/modules/jphardy/page01_e.html

A study of societal changes in personal hygiene over the decades in British North America.

Human Rights in Ontario
http://www.archives.gov.on.ca/english/exhibits/humnrits/index.html

This virtual exhibit contains digitized historical documents and photographs from the Archives of Ontario about the evolving recognition of human rights in the province.

Postal Reform
http://www.civilization.ca/educat/oracle/modules/jwillis/page01_e.html

A history of postal reform in British North America in the early 19th century.

Article Twenty-Two

The Riddle of Peggy Mountain: Regulation of Irish Women's Sexuality on the Southern Avalon, 1750–1860

Willeen Keough

A striking scene from the life of an Irish-Newfoundland woman, Peggy Mountain, emerges in the court records of the southern Avalon and the diary of a local magistrate. In early December 1834, Peggy brought her husband, Michael, before the local magistrates at Ferryland for desertion. She was pregnant and the court ordered that Michael support Peggy and the expected baby during the winter; arrangements would be made with a Patrick Welsh to take her into his home at Michael's expense. Michael initially indicated his willingness to comply "as well as his ability would allow", but the very next day, he reneged on his promise "by order of [Catholic parish priest] Father [Timothy] Browne". Michael held his ground, even when the magistrates ordered that he be put in jail for contempt and kept on bread and water for a month. Meanwhile, Peggy was temporarily placed at a local public house, but Father Browne, "under threat of the highest nature he could inflict", ordered her removed and, as there was no other accommodation available, the justices housed her in the local jail. Magistrate Robert Carter, Jr., was taken aback by the activities of Father Browne and wrote in his diary: "The Priest is inveterate against a poor unfortunate female under his displeasure and against whom he appears to direct his greatest malice and enmity. . . . How such conduct will end let time decide." Matters came to a head rather quickly. Peggy was very ill and the jailer reported that there were no coals for heating her cell. The priest did not relent and continued to speak out against Peggy in the chapel and wrote an open letter against her that was read publicly at the jailhouse. In the meantime, the local magistrates arranged for a Mrs. Cahill to attend Peggy in the jail. Peggy finally gave birth to a daughter on a night so cold that the ink froze in Carter's office and the bread froze in his storeroom. The child survived only a few hours. Peggy was then moved to Mrs. Cahill's house, but again, the priest ordered that she be removed. Finally, magistrate Carter himself took her in. Several days later, Peggy left for St. John's in the *Water Lily* and slipped quietly out of the annals of the southern Avalon.[1]

This episode raises many questions. Why was the priest so angry at Peggy? Did he blame her for the breakdown of the marriage? Did he suspect that the coming child was not her husband's? What threat did he perceive in Peggy's continuing presence in the community? Although the historical record does not provide the specific reason for the shaming and ostracizing of Peggy Mountain, it seems that Father Browne's anxiety over "aberrant" female sexuality was central to the issue. Especially intriguing is the sharp contrast between the responses of the local magistrates and the priest to Peggy Mountain's circumstances, for they represent two important mechanisms for patrolling the boundaries of female sexuality — the legal system and formal religion.[2]

Feminist scholarship has argued that an important indicator of patriarchal domination is the degree to which a society seeks to regulate women's bodies in terms of marriage, sexuality and reproduction.[3] As Newfoundland was a British fishing station/colony in the period under

Source: Willeen Keough, "The Riddle of Peggy Mountain: Regulation of Irish Women's Sexuality on the Southern Avalon, 1750–1860," *Acadiensis*, 31, 2 (Spring 2002): 38–70.

study, hegemonic discourses on female sexuality in contemporary Britain provide context for the discussion as the extent of their infiltration in the local context is tested. By the 18th century, the British legal tradition was a patriarchal regime that relegated women's bodies to the control of fathers or husbands. Concerns about patrilineal inheritance and the legitimacy of heirs lent particular urgency to the protection of the chastity value of wives and daughters. At the same time, Enlightenment thought was challenging the association of sinfulness with sexuality that had been the legacy of 17th-century Puritanism. Yet men and women did not have equal access to the sexual freedom of the age. Uncontrolled female sexuality was seen as a threat, not only to property and legitimacy, but also to the very foundation of the social order itself. Female sexuality was, therefore, channeled into marriage and motherhood, while the division between public (rational, active, individualist, masculine) and private (emotional, passive, dependent, feminine) domains was underscored.

These discourses grew within the context of late-18th- and early-19th-century evangelicalism as it shaped middle-class ideals of female domesticity, fragility, passivity and dependence. Female sexuality was further constrained as middle-class ideology fashioned a dichotomized construction of woman as either frail, asexual vessel, embodied in the respectable wife and mother, or temptress Eve, embodied in the prostitute. Separate sphere ideology intensified. Women who occupied "public" spaces or who demonstrated a capacity for social or economic independence, even physical hardiness, were increasingly seen as deviant. Overt female sexuality was particularly problematic for it "disturbed the public/private division of space along gender lines so essential to the male spectator's mental mapping of the civic order".[4] As the 19th century unfolded, legal, medical and scientific discourses continued to embellish the construction of woman as "the unruly body", consumed by her "sex", problematic by her very biological nature and requiring increased monitoring and regulation.

These discourses on female sexuality and respectability were infiltrating 18th- and 19th-century Newfoundland through its British legal regime and an emerging local middle class of administrators, churchmen and merchants, many of whom maintained strong ties with Britain.[5] On the island, gender ideology was tempered by the exigencies of colonial policy as it was articulated by central authorities in St. John's. And this ideology also assumed ethnic undertones as the Irish population in Newfoundland increased. From the mid-1700s onward, as Irish servants increasingly replaced English labour in the fishery and as an Irish-Newfoundland trade in passengers and provisions expanded, Irish migration to the island swelled.[6]

British authorities in Newfoundland watched the growing number of Irish migrants with levels of concern ranging from wariness to near hysteria. Official correspondence and proclamations for the period articulated several common themes about the Irish population. The authorities claimed that the Irish were a "disaffected", "treacherous" people who would prove to be Britain's "greatest Enemy" in times of war. They bred prodigiously and were already overtaking the local English-Protestant population in numbers. Officials claimed these "Wicked & Idle People", who were prone to excessive drink and disorderly behaviour, terrorized "His Majesty's loyal Protestant subjects" and were responsible for most of the crime that occurred over the winter. Thus, a battery of orders and regulations attempted to limit the numbers of Irish remaining on the island after the fishing season was over.[7]

Three important contextual elements framed the perspective of visiting British authorities towards the Irish in Newfoundland. First, their attitudes reflected contemporary English perceptions of difference between the Anglo-Saxon and Gaelic "races". Second, most of the Irish in Newfoundland were Catholics, and were therefore subject to a penal regime similar to that which existed in Ireland and Great Britain at the time. Third, Britain was ambivalent about permanent settlement in Newfoundland until the early 1800s. For centuries, British authorities had viewed Newfoundland as a fishing station rather than a colony, and had struggled to promote the migratory fishery, at the expense of a resident sector, in order to preserve the hub of the industry in the West of England and to maintain Britain's nursery for seamen. Nonetheless, British authorities in Newfoundland expressed more concern about the Irish remaining on the island than the English, and official discourse constructed "Irishness" as inherently feckless, intemperate, disloyal and unruly. The Irish were a "problem" group that required constant regulation and surveillance.

Part of this official discourse focused on an image of the Irish woman immigrant as a vagrant and a whore. This fits within a broader context in which British authorities discouraged the presence of all women in Newfoundland. The very characteristics that made women essential to colonial ventures on the mainland — their stabilizing effect, their essential role in forming a permanent population — posed a threat to British enterprise in Newfoundland, as a resident fishery would weaken the migratory sector. As Capt. Francis Wheler, a naval officer in Newfoundland, reassured the home government in 1684: "Soe longe as there comes noe women they are not fixed".[8] While official policy discouraged women migrants in general, authorities in St. John's highlighted the undesirability of Irish women in particular. Official documents of the period portray Irish women immigrants as degenerate, unproductive and dangerous to the social and moral order. Central authorities argued that these women caused "much disorder and Disturbance against the Peace" and inevitably became a charge on the more respectable inhabitants of the island. Many "devious", single Irish women, they said, arrived in Newfoundland pregnant and disguised their condition until they had hired themselves out to unsuspecting employers. Running through the records was a subtext that once Irish women were permitted to remain, all the elements for reproducing this undesirable ethnic group would be in place. The Irish woman immigrant, then, was a particular "problem" for local authorities, requiring special regulation of her own. In particular, the single Irish female servant required monitoring, for her social and economic independence from a patriarchal family context and her potential sexual agency flouted a growing middle-class feminine ideal that embodied domesticity, economic dependence and sexual passivity. Still, early governors were not without solutions to the "problem". In 1764, Hugh Palliser ordered that no Irish women be landed in Newfoundland without their providing security that they were well behaved and would not become a charge on the inhabitants. Thirteen years later, John Montague ordered that the transportation of Irish women servants to Newfoundland cease altogether.[9]

Despite these characterizations and orders, employers continued to hire male and female Irish servants for service in the fishery and domestic work, particularly in Conception Bay, St. John's and on the southern Avalon. The Irish presence increased and took on more permanence as the migratory fishery, plagued by almost continuous years of warfare, declined and the resident fishery expanded, in both proportionate and absolute terms. Along the southern Avalon, Irish men and women formed fishing households and hired servants of their own. Away from the watchful eyes of visiting governors, an Irish planter society took root in most harbours.[10] It was reinforced through increasing Irish migration through the close of the 18th century and into the early decades of the 19th century.

How did hegemonic constructions of womanhood, and particularly Irish womanhood, play out on the southern Avalon, where community formation was still in its early stages among an essentially plebeian Irish population and where gender relations were still contested terrain? How were they interpreted by the local middle class and received within the essentially plebeian Irish community of the area? On the southern Avalon, the plebeian community was comprised primarily of fishing servants, washerwomen, seamstresses, midwives, artisans, small-scale boat-keepers and planters, and by the 19th century, numerous "independent" fishing families (in as much as they could be independent from their merchant suppliers). The plebeian community shared a common consciousness and exerted political pressure on occasion — either in the form of the "mob" in direct collective actions or as the menacing presence behind anonymous actions and threats. They were not a working class for they lacked class consciousness. But they did have a distinct and vigorous plebeian culture, with its own rituals, its own patterns of work and leisure, and its own world view. Their social superiors were the local merchants or merchants' agents, vessel owners and masters, Anglican clergy and more substantial boatkeepers and planters, who were part of an emerging middle class in Newfoundland in the late 18th and early 19th centuries. They functioned as quasi-patricians with their control of employment opportunities, relief, supply and credit, and administrative and magisterial functions. Although tied to the plebs through interdependence in the fishery, this group maintained social distance through religious affiliation and exclusive patterns of socializing and marriage.[11]

The ways that Irish womanhood was constructed by these distinct yet interdependent groups may provide a key to unlocking the riddle of Peggy Mountain. In Britain, the working class adopted and refashioned middle-class feminine ideals during the 19th century to support their own bid for respectability in the Chartist movement and to satisfy the male-centred agenda of trade unionism. Furthermore, the British middle class encouraged this development of a working-class respectability — one that imitated middle-class ideals while maintaining sufficient difference to preserve class boundaries. In rural Britain and Ireland, as well, women were impelled into domesticity by a powerful combination of proscriptive ideology and the marginalization and devaluation of women's labour in agriculture and cottage industries. But did similar processes occur on the southern Avalon? Or were there tensions between hegemonic rhetoric and the realities of Irish-Newfoundland women's lives that delayed the intrusion of such feminine ideals into plebeian culture? And did a lack of consistency between the attitudes of secular and religious authorities in the area towards Irish female respectability further attenuate the encroachment?

In order to answer such questions, it is first necessary to examine Irish women within the context of the plebeian culture of the southern Avalon. Within this population, women acquired significant status and authority in family and community as they assumed vital social and economic roles during immigration and early settlement.[12]

With increasing numbers of women moving to the southern Avalon and elsewhere in Newfoundland, the fears of the British government were confirmed. Once women came, the population became fixed. Given the transient nature of employment in the Newfoundland fishery, male fishing servants commonly found employment in different areas from year to year, moving in and out of districts, and between harbours within a district, as work opportunities shifted. In time, the presence of women tied them to particular communities. On the southern Avalon, some Irish fishermen were joined by wives or fiancées from the home country or married women from the small, established English planter group. Increasingly, however, they found wives among single or widowed Irish immigrant women and, by the turn of the century, among an expanding group of local first- and second-generation Irish-Newfoundland women. Matrilineal bridges often factored in the clustering of families in particular coves and harbours, while matrilocal/uxorilocal residence patterns played an intrinsic role in community formation, as many couples established themselves on land already occupied by the wife or apportioned from or adjacent to the family property of the wife.

The Irish did not establish separate communities on the southern Avalon but intermingled with English planter families and servants already in the area. The result was the almost total assimilation of the old English planter society into the Irish-Catholic ethnic group. In the late 17th century, there had been a strong English-Protestant planter presence on the shore; a century later, the population was almost totally Catholic (Figure 22.1).[13] This shift corresponded with the influx of Irish into the area, but it was not just the net result of Irish in-migration and English out-migration. Parish records and anecdotal evidence

Figure 22.1 Over-wintering Population, Southern Avalon, 1735–1857

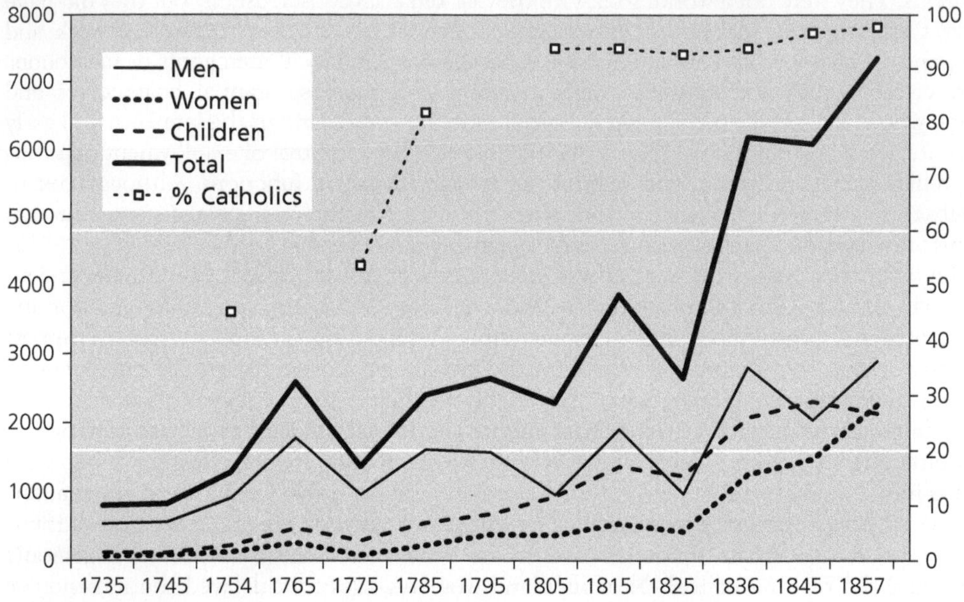

Source: Governor's Annual Returns of the Fisheries and Inhabitants at Newfoundland, 1735–1825, CO 194; Newfoundland Population Returns, 1836, 1845, 1857.

provided by Catholic and Anglican clergy indicate that intermarriage, conversion and assimilation worked in conjunction with Irish immigration to produce this change. Indeed, a sense of fatalism pervaded the records of the Society for the Propagation of the Gospel as the Anglican clergy bemoaned the loss of "the multitude into the strange pastures" of Catholicism.[14] The Catholic clergy, by contrast, noted with mounting satisfaction the numbers of Protestants converting from "the flock of the stranger" to "the bosom of Christianity".[15] The English Protestants were not moving out; they were merely shifting religious allegiances. This was particularly true within plebeian culture, where families with English surnames such as Glynn, Williams, Yard, Carew, Maddox and Martin were steadily incorporated into a growing and maturing Irish-Catholic population. Irish women played a vital part in the process, as potential spouses or cohabiting partners of not only incoming Irish-Catholic migrants but also English-Protestant men. By the turn of the 19th century, much of the population of the southern Avalon, particularly within plebeian culture, was Irish or partly Irish. A beleaguered English-Protestant group, composed mostly of middle-class mercantile and administrative families, retreated and turned inwards on itself, occasionally recruiting marriage partners from St. John's or England to maintain its homogeneity.[16]

Plebeian women in the study area were an intrinsic part of the economic life of their fledgling communities. They played a vital role in subsistence production for their households. In addition, women ran public houses, looked after boarders, provided nursing services and took in paid washing and sewing — mostly catering to single, male, fishing servants. Women were "shipped" as servants to merchant, administrative and planter families, and while the majority were recruited as domestic servants, a smaller number worked as fishing servants, heading, splitting, salting and drying fish as part of shore crews.[17] Regardless of the type of service, and whether "shipped" by oral agreement or written contract known as a "shipping paper", the law looked upon these arrangements as formal contracts and required both servants and employers to fulfill their obligations under the agreements.[18] The existence of this system of contractual employment, recognized by law, conjures up an image of the Irish woman servant that was far more purposeful than the impoverished, immoral woman of the 18th-century governors' proclamations.

Some women, primarily widows, were fishing employers and operated fishing premises in their own right.[19] A greater number ran fishing plantations with their husbands or common-law partners,[20] with the responsibility for boarding fishing servants and dieters (winter servants working only for room and board) added to their other household and subsistence duties. And increasingly, plebeian women became shore crews for the family production unit in the fishery, replacing the hired, transient, primarily male servants who had been the backbone of the traditional planter fishery.[21] On shore, they performed the crucial work of salting and drying fish, a process that required careful attention and good judgment to ensure the quality of the cure. Along the southern Avalon, the momentum for the shift to the household unit began as early as the 1780s — again, that period when the Irish were arriving in ever increasing numbers.[22] The post-war recession that followed the Napoleonic Wars saw the final demise of the older system of waged labour. War-time inflation carried over into post-war wages and provisions but fish prices plummeted. Planters, unable to offset their losses, either went bankrupt or turned increasingly to family labour to meet production needs. With the old planter fishery in its death throes and the resident fishery in crisis, women stepped into the breach and took the place of male fishing servants on the stages and flakes, producing saltfish for market. Their presence at these public sites of economic production and their vital and recognized contribution to the process was an important source of power for these women, even into the 20th century.[23] This was terrain worth retaining, and even when fishing families hired servant girls, it was not to replace the women of the house in outdoor work, but to assume household tasks in order to "free" their mistresses to contribute to more important family enterprises.

Further evidence of women's participation in the public, economic sphere is provided by mercantile records, which suggest that women were a vital part of the exchange economy of the area.[24] Significant numbers performed some independent form of economic activity and held accounts in their own names as *femmes sole* [*femmes soles* referred to spinsters, widows, divorced women, or married women entirely independent of their husbands as regards property], regardless of marital status.[25] Some were heads of households that produced saltfish and oil for market. Many more sold pigs, fowl, eggs and oakum. They earned wages haying, tending gardens or making fish on merchants' flakes. They also did washing and sewing for local single fishing servants and middle-class customers. Many combined their paid services in a package of economic coping strategies that helped families make ends meet. Women's work for a mercantile firm was credited to their accounts. Work for other people in the community was "contra'd" against the accounts of their customers; in other words, a balancing entry was made in the merchant's ledger, giving the woman credit and her customer a debit entry. Some women had credit balances or received a small amount of cash when they "settled up" in the fall. Some even had their profits applied towards the debts of male relatives. Many others had debit balances, but so did most men in the community — a chronic symptom of the truck system that underpinned the resident fishery. Merchants carried these debts forward and rarely wrote them off, suggesting confidence in the women's earning abilities. Of course, men's names headed the accounts more frequently than women's, for merchants would have been mindful of the repercussions of coverture[26] in relation to debt, but legal principle and accounting practice masked the full extent of women's participation in the exchange economy. Women's labour in family work units contributed to the production of fish and oil credited to accounts of fathers or husbands.

Women used many of the goods appearing under the names of male household heads for household production, expending labour and producing goods that were assigned no market value and therefore were not included in formal business ledgers of the day. Furthermore, merchant books did not record female networks of informal trade — the exchange of eggs for butter, for example, or milk for wool — which helped women keep their families clothed and fed.[27]

Religion in both orthodox and informal observance was another important source of informal female power within the Irish community of the southern Avalon, particularly before the encroachment of ultramontanism and the devotional revolution of the mid to late 19th century. There is evidence that Catholic women in Newfoundland performed religious rites and assumed religious authority in the century before these intrusions. Bishop Michael Fleming complained to his superiors that prior to the establishing of Catholic missions in the late 18th century: "The holy sacrament of Matrimony, debased into a sort of 'civil contract', was administered by captains of boats, by police, by magistrates and frequently by women. The Sacrament of Baptism was equally profaned".[28] Fleming was also dismayed that midwives had assumed the authority to dispense with church fasts for pregnant women. Dean Cleary's "Notebook" refers to women at St. Mary's taking "the sacred fire from the altar to burn a house"— perhaps a rite of exorcism of some sort, but certainly an act with ritualistic overtones.[29] According to the oral tradition, women primarily kept the faith alive before the priests' arrival by observing Catholic rituals and teaching children their prayers. Indeed, as one informant stated and most others implied: "If it was left to the men, sure there'd be no religion at all".[30] These references suggest that women played an important custodial role in relation to the Catholic religion in the period of early settlement. Furthermore, female figures were prominent in the Irish-Catholic hagiolatry of the area. To this day, the Virgin Mary, St. Brigid and "Good St. Anne" are a powerful triumvirate. On the southern Avalon, as in Ireland, there was an alternative pre-Christian religious system operating in tandem with, and sometimes overlapping, formal Catholic practice. This melange of ancient beliefs and customary practices made up a very real part of the mental landscape of the Irish community, and women were important navigators of this terrain. Women made and blessed the bread that had special powers to keep fairies from stealing their children; the same bread could help people who were "fairy-struck"— lost in the woods or back-meadows — find their way home. Women anointed their homes with holy water and blessed candle wax to protect their families from dangers such as thunder and lightning. Women read tea leaves and told fortunes. They ritually washed and dressed the dead, "sat up" with corpses at wakes to guard their spirits overnight, smoked the "God be merciful" pipes,[31] and keened at gravesides to mourn the departed and mark their passage into the next life. Certain women had special healing powers — the ability to stop blood with a prayer, for example. A widow's curse, by contrast, had the power to do great harm. The bibe, the equivalent of the Irish banshee, was a female figure, as was the "old hag" who gave many a poor soul a sleepless night.[32] And places like Mrs. Denine's Hill, Peggy's Hollow and Old Woman's Pond (named for the women who had died there) had magical qualities that could cause horses to stop in their tracks and grown men to lose their way.[33] Thus, in both formal and informal practice, Irish women acted as mediators of the natural and supernatural worlds and, by extension, played a vital role in reinforcing the identity of the ethno-religious group in the area.

Court records for the area reveal that plebeian women also featured in numerous collective actions and individual interventions to protect personal, family and community interests during the period — deploying power through verbal threats and physical confrontations that did not fit middle-class ideals of femininity.[34] The women of the Berrigan family, for instance, were an important force in the family's struggle to hold fast to their fishing "room"[35] on the south side of Renews harbour in the late 1830s and early 1840s. John Saunders, a local merchant and JP [justice of the peace], made repeated attempts to take possession of their premises (likely for rent arrears or non-payment of debt), but his efforts met with persistent resistance from the family, including the Berrigan women. In 1838 and 1842, family members were charged with violently assaulting two different deputy sheriffs as the officers tried to remove them from the property. Finally, in 1843, the Berrigans were found guilty of intimidating and assaulting John Saunders himself, as he tried to take possession of the fishing room. There were variations in terms of the family members involved in each case, but Bridget and Alice (daughters, sisters, or relatives by marriage) were involved in two of the three incidents, while the family matriarch, Anastatia, was present every time.[36] These women's participation was not unusual within the historical context of this fishing-based economy. As essential members of their household production unit, the Berrigan women were defending a family enterprise in which they felt they had an equal stake, using compelling means to protect their source of livelihood in the face of perceived injustice at the hands of their supplying merchant and the formal legal system.

Indeed, plebeian women on the southern Avalon were not reluctant to use physical violence in sorting out their daily affairs. In assault cases brought before the southern Avalon courts during the period, women were aggressors almost as often as they were victims (by a proportion of 86:100). Of the 111 complaints involving women during the period, 50 were laid against male assailants of female victims, but 61 involved female aggressors.[37] Furthermore, these women assailants were not particular about the sex of their victims: 32 were women and 28 were men (with child victims in the remaining case). All the female aggressors were of the plebeian community. Most episodes involved the use of threatening language and/or common assault with a variety of motivations, including defence of personal or family reputation, employment disputes over wages or ill treatment, defence of family business, enforcement of community standards and defence of individual or family property. The physical assertiveness of these women and the court's matter-of-fact handling of these cases suggest that women's violence was no more shocking to the community than men's. Gender relations within the plebeian community were fluid and these women felt they had the right to carve out territory for themselves and their families in the public sphere.[38]

Of course, there were 50 cases involving plebeian women victims of male violence. These ranged from complaints of threatening language and ill treatment to more serious charges of physical and sexual assaults. In feminist scholarship, male violence against women — actual or potential — has been cited as a mechanism of patriarchal control. Yet it is evident that on the southern Avalon, the use of physical violence was not gender-specific; this was not a context characterized primarily by male aggressors and female victims. Clearly too, plebeian women felt that it was their prerogative to take their abusers to court. They perceived themselves as individuals with rights which should be protected by the legal system, and they were not deterred by notions of female respectability and self-sacrifice from asserting their claims to justice in a public forum.

Irish plebeian womanhood on the southern Avalon was not engulfed by the constraints of separate sphere ideology or constructions of passivity, fragility and dependence. Nor was it easily channeled into formal marriage — a key site for the control of female sexuality within the English common-law tradition and middle-class ideology. In marriage, a woman was accessible to male sexual needs and could fulfill her destiny as reproducer of the race; yet her sexuality could be safely constrained within the roles of respectable wife and mother. Indeed, a woman's entire person was subsumed in the identity of her husband within marriage. As *feme covert*, she could not own property, enter into contracts without her husband's approval, sue or be sued. And her husband had a regulatory interest in her body and sole rights to her services, both domestic and sexual (the latter, again, reflecting anxiety over the legitimacy of heirs).

While formal marriage was institutionalized as the proper means of ordering society, within the predominantly Irish plebeian community of the southern Avalon, informal marriages and

Figure 22.2 Over-wintering Population in Districts of Ferryland, Trepassey and St. Mary's, 1735–1857

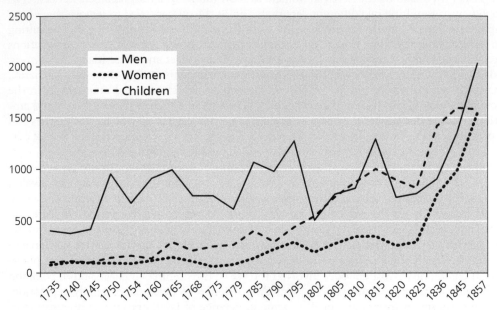

Source: Governor's Annual Returns of the Fisheries and Inhabitants at Newfoundland, 1735–1825, CO 194; Newfoundland Population Returns, 1836, 1845, 1857.

common-law relationships were tolerated and seen as legitimate.[39] Given the different understanding of gender that had evolved in Gaelic Ireland — one in which traditions of transhumance, communal property and partible inheritance contrasted with English preoccupations with private property and patrilineal inheritance — this is, perhaps, not surprising. Within the Irish tradition, the chastity requirement for wives and daughters was muted, and informal marriages and divorces, illegitimacy and close degrees of consanguineous marriage were tolerated. Irish traditions differed from English norms of sexual behaviour.[40]

In 1789, Father Thomas Ewer, the Catholic priest stationed at the new Catholic mission in Ferryland, complained of the irregularity of marital arrangements in his parish.[41] What Ewer was observing were frequent incidents of common-law relationships and informal marriages, separations and divorces in the area, part of a marital regime that kept fairly loose reins on female sexuality and, in effect, provided freedom for number of women from the repercussions of coverture. It is difficult to determine the extent of such relationships on the southern Avalon, given the lack of parish records, particularly before the 1820s. However, the 1800 nominal census of 166 family groupings in Ferryland district suggests the existence of as many as 33 such relationships (20 per cent of the total), either then or in the recent past.[42] References to common-law relationships also appeared occasionally in court hearings and governors' correspondence.[43] Such arrangements were accepted by the local population, especially when children were cared for in stable family relationships and did not become a charge on the community.

Irish plebeian women who entered into formal marriages on the southern Avalon were not readily constrained either, given their vital role as co-producers in family economies. In this, they were similar to their counterparts in rural Ireland, or certainly 18th-century rural Ireland, where women gained status from their role as co-producers in a mixed farming and domestic textile economy.[44] Within both contexts, married women exercised considerable autonomy in running their households and also had significant influence over matters outside home. While a façade of patriarchal authority was usually maintained in both cultures, male decision-making was frequently directed by women behind the scenes. Clarkson describes this family power structure in Ireland as a "matriarchal management behind a patriarchal exterior".[45] The oral tradition on the southern Avalon has a more homespun equivalent: "She made the cannon-balls, and he fired them".

In general, then, middle-class constructs of female respectability and anxieties about regulating female sexuality did not easily insinuate themselves into Irish plebeian culture on the southern Avalon. Women's essential role in community formation, powerful position in an alternative belief system, deployment of informal power in community life, and essential roles in subsistence production and the fishery mitigated against the adaptation of middle-class ideologies that did not fit local realities. Furthermore, because the southern Avalon remained a pre-industrial society into the 20th century, plebeian women's status did not undergo the erosion experienced by their counterparts in the industrializing British Isles. In rural Ireland, the marginalization of women from agricultural work and the collapse of the domestic textile industry and the "potato culture"[46] in the early 19th century led to a depreciation of women's worth, both as producers and reproducers. Similarly, in England, the masculinization of farm labour and dairying and the mechanization and industrialization of cottage industries led to the devaluation of women's labour.[47] On the southern Avalon, however, women's status as essential co-producers in the fishing economy, as well as reproducers of family work units within that economy, remained intact and forestalled any masculinist project within plebeian culture to circumscribe their lives.

If members of the local middle class were going to attempt to introduce feminine ideals into the fishing community, then this was the network of plebeian gender relations with which they must contend. And one of the forums in which they might have made efforts to rein in Irish womanhood on the southern Avalon was the local court system. Throughout the 16th and 17th centuries, justice in Newfoundland had been a makeshift affair, dispensed by fishing admirals — the captains of the first fishing vessels to reach every harbour at the start of the fishing season. This system, with a right to appeal decisions to the visiting naval commodore, was given legislative sanction in 1699. In 1729, in grudging acknowledgement of the overwintering population, the naval governor at Newfoundland was permitted to appoint justices of the peace and surrogates to hear fishery disputes in the absence of fishing admirals and seasonal governors. As the century progressed, the legal regime in Newfoundland expanded to include customs officers (1739) and courts of vice-admiralty (1744), oyer and terminer (1750) and common pleas (1789). In 1791, a court of civil jurisdiction was introduced and its jurisdiction was broadened to include criminal matters the following year. But the face of the law most frequently encountered by the plebeian community on the southern Avalon was that of the local, middle-class magistrate. Magistrates were appointed from among the principal merchants and inhabitants of the area and, throughout the study period, they were overwhelmingly members of the mercantile community, although several Anglican clergymen and a resident doctor also sat for brief periods.[48]

Feminist scholarship has argued that within the British legal tradition, the court system — a regime dominated by male legislators, judges, lawyers and juries — was one of the chief mechanisms for regulating female sexuality.[49] Women did, however, have varying degrees of agency within this framework, depending on specific historical contexts. On the southern Avalon, plebeian women were a vital part of local court life, as civil litigants, as complainants and defendants in criminal matters, as witnesses and petitioners and as parties in estate matters. Indeed, the courtroom was more often a site of their empowerment than their oppression. Women's visibility in the court system and their reception by magistrates suggests that the legal milieu, at least at the local level, may not have been as inhospitable as it was in other jurisdictions.[50] Court cases dealing directly with issues of female sexuality in the southern Avalon reveal a laissez-faire attitude on the part of local magistrates in monitoring plebeian womanhood.[51]

Seduction law in the 18th and early 19th century fit comfortably with constructions of female sexuality as passive and of women as virtual possessions. This civil action, which was based on the English common-law principle that a master could sue for the loss of a servant's services due to injury, could be taken only by a woman's legal guardian (usually, the father). Damages were evaluated in terms of *the guardian's* loss of a daughter's or ward's domestic services during pregnancy and lying-in, not in terms of *her* pain and suffering or reduced social and economic expectations.[52]

The seduction action was not uncommon in other jurisdictions. It is intriguing, then, that only one case survives in the court records for the southern Avalon. On 4 October 1827, Catharine Delahunty, a widow, complained that James H. Carter had seduced her daughter, Ellen, and asked for £100 compensation for the loss of Ellen's services. Ellen appeared at the trial as a witness and told the court that for the past year, Carter had persistently courted her attention, first by offering her work, knitting socks and cutting "sounds"[53] on the stage head, and then by suggesting assignations in the woods to cut firewood. The couple had gone on several woodcutting expeditions and, eventually, Ellen had become pregnant. Her mother claimed that Ellen had been unable to carry out her duties from the seventh month of her pregnancy onwards, that her recuperation from childbirth had been slow and that her capacity to work thereafter had been reduced as a result. Ellen's sister, Catharine Kelly, appeared as a witness for the defence, claiming that she had recently had to warn Ellen against "walking with Robert Brine . . . a married man". Catharine countered with character witness Martin Conway, who swore that he had "never seen Ellen Delahunty conduct herself differently from what well behaved Girls in her situation in life do". The effort by the defendant to present Ellen as an "unchaste" woman would not have disproved Catharine's suit, as the action was for compensation for loss of household services; however, he may have been hoping to lower the award for "damaged goods". Certainly, the £30 recommended by the jury was far less than the £100 compensation sought by Catharine; but this was still a substantial amount of money, and a significant award for this particular court.[54] Indeed, given that seduction suits generally garnered higher awards than paternity suits and given that James Carter was a member of a wealthy, middle-class family in Ferryland, Catharine and Ellen demonstrated a fair degree of legal savvy in proceeding in this manner. Certainly, no local awards under the bastardy law approached £30 during the period.

Still, the bastardy action provided another option for pregnant women who wished to make reluctant fathers live up to their paternal responsibilities. Unlike the seduction suit, the bastardy action was taken by the woman herself. On the southern Avalon, bastardy suits were more common than seduction actions, suggesting a degree of female agency in the courts. Still, there were only nine bastardy cases for the period. Women may have had other informal community mechanisms to bring to bear on reluctant fathers, or, perhaps, single mothers on the southern Avalon had social and economic opportunities, such as a reasonable expectation of work, future marriage or family support, that minimized the need for bastardy actions. Still, it is significant that nine women were willing to take public, political action by bringing the alleged fathers of their children to court. By using the court system in this way, these women acted as autonomous legal entities rather than legal dependents.

The results of their actions are known in only six of the nine cases. In all six, support for the child was ordered, and in half of these cases, the mothers were also awarded lying-in expenses. In early April 1791, for example, Catherine Oudle (also, Audle), a single woman of Ferryland, appeared before the magistrates and named John Murray, Sr., a fisherman at Ferryland, as the father of her unborn child. When Catherine gave birth to a boy on 22 April, Murray was ordered to pay the following support and expenses:

> the sum of ten shillings . . . toward the Laying in of the s^d. Catherine Audle & ye maintenance of ye s^d Child, to the time of making this Order . . . the sum of two shillings weekly & ever[y] week from this present time for the maintenance of the s^d Child — so long as the Child shall be chargeable to the s^d. Harbour . . . [or alternatively] weekly & ever[y] week ye sum of two shillings & sixpence, in Case the s^d. Catherine Audle shall not Nurse or take Care of the Child herself.[55]

Similarly, when Manus Butler admitted to fathering Elizabeth Carney's child, the court was thorough in its support order for £9.19.6, detailing expenses for a midwife's attendance (£1.1.0), nursing services for a childbed illness suffered by Elizabeth (£2.2.0) and the nursing and clothing of the child from its birth to the court hearing (£6.16.6). In addition, the court ordered 3s.6d. per week continuing maintenance for the child.[56]

There is no indication that either the mother's character or her sexual history was called into question in any of the cases examined. Furthermore, the mother's word seemed sufficient to establish paternity, although in three of the nine cases, the fathers also admitted the claim. In four of the cases, the purported fathers had left the district, usually before the claim was made. In one case, more dramatically, a reluctant father, William Walsh, ran from the courtroom and later successfully resisted arrest by brandishing a knife at the two constables dispatched to fetch him back. Walsh was not apprehended, but several of his companions were later fined for helping him escape.[57] Indeed, the magistrates took pains to track down absconding fathers or, if unsuccessful, to attach any wages remaining in the hands of employers in the district. Of course, the court was primarily acting to ensure that mother and child not become a charge on the community. But the bastardy law provided women with some access to financial assistance and the opportunity to act as independent agents in the court. Furthermore, local magistrates were receptive to their claims and made reasonable efforts to have fathers acknowledge their responsibilities.[58]

Infanticide and concealment of birth cases were also potential terrain for patrolling female sexuality. The vast majority of defendants in these cases in British and colonial courts shared a similar profile. They tended to be young, unmarried, plebeian or working-class women, especially servants. Most, already caught in difficult socio-economic circumstances, acted out of fear of the social disgrace and reduced employment prospects that unwed motherhood would bring. Courts were generally reluctant to prosecute and juries were generally reluctant to convict on infanticide charges; the lesser charge of concealment was more commonly employed with success, although even in such cases, the courts were often sensitive to the desperation and limited options that motivated the mothers' actions.[59]

Remarkably, no cases of infanticide or concealment of birth survive in the court records for the southern Avalon. It is unlikely that the local court would have turned a blind eye to such matters. Given that illegitimacy did not carry a heavy stigma within the Irish plebeian tradition of the southern Avalon in this period, family or community support probably cushioned the hardship of illegitimate births. Single, plebeian mothers may have been in a relatively strong position to survive socially and economically. Furthermore, they had access to the court system to seek financial assistance from reluctant fathers and reason to expect successful results. Thus, the fear of unwed motherhood was, perhaps, not as keenly felt on the southern Avalon as elsewhere.

The manifestation of female sexuality which most induced patriarchal anxieties about the moral order was prostitution. More than any other woman, the prostitute, with her blatant sexual agency, flouted middle-class constructions of female passivity and threatened the rationality and self-control that defined middle-class masculinity. Furthermore, by conducting her business in public, she transgressed the careful ordering of separate spheres. Yet, ironically, courts in British jurisdictions often treated prostitutes with a degree of tolerance, seeing them as a necessary social evil; they serviced male lust in ways that were beyond the capacity of "respectable" wives and mothers. Only the most outrageous examples received the full brunt of the legal system.[60]

No evidence of charges against women for prostitution or the catch-all vagrancy survives among the court records of the southern Avalon. On the surface, this seems to suggest that local constables and magistrates were little concerned about women of "ill repute". The court did, however, take action against female complainants who were deemed to be threats to the moral order in two sexual assault cases. In 1773 Mary Keating accused Stephen Kennely of attempting to rape her. He had come into her house, she claimed, and "sat upon the Bed after her husband went out . . . [and] treated her in a barbarous and cruel manner wanting to get his will of her". Kennely would have killed her, Mary claimed, had not one John McGraugh prevented him. Various "principal Inhabitants" of Ferryland testified, however, that the Keating house was a "disorderly house" where they entertained "riotous friends"; the defendant, Kennely, by contrast, was represented as "a man of an Honest Character". Based on these character profiles, the magistrates ordered that Mary and her husband be "turned out of the country".[61] The court took similar action against Catharine Power of Renews, a woman notorious for her drunken and promiscuous behaviour, when she complained in 1806 that William Deringwater (also, Drinkwater) had sexually assaulted her in her home. The court, however, was not convinced by the "unsoported solitary deposition" of this "woman of infamous character". Furthermore, a defence witness swore that he had put Catherine to bed intoxicated earlier in the evening and three others testified that Deringwater had been at his own home at the time of the alleged assault. The court acquitted the defendant and ordered that the plaintiff, Catharine, be sent back to Ireland at the first opportunity.[62]

The most intriguing aspect of these two cases is the order for removal of the complainant. Local courts issued sentences of transportation to the home country with some regularity in cases involving property crimes, especially in the 18th and early 19th centuries. However, in terms of breaches of the peace or crimes against the person, magistrates generally ordered deportation only in the most extreme cases of violence or riotous behaviour. The banishment of Mary Keating and Catherine Power suggests that the behaviour of these women of "infamous character" was similarly seen as an extreme threat to the moral and social order. Despite a generally relaxed attitude towards the conduct of plebeian women, the middle-class magistrates of the southern Avalon did set some boundaries for their sexual behaviour.

Incidents of rape and other forms of male violence against women are indicators of unequal power relations between men and women. It is notable that only eight cases involving complaints of rape or assault with intent to commit rape survive in the local court records for the period. Of course, such incidents were likely under-reported. However, women's ability to fend for themselves in physical confrontations may have acted as a deterrent to sexual assault. Of the eight reported cases, three resulted in guilty verdicts and three were dismissed. In another, the defendant was cleared of the rape charge but found guilty of a common assault. Any record of the disposition of the remaining case has not survived. This middling conviction rate might initially suggest an ambivalent attitude towards the crime on the part of the southern Avalon magistrates. In the cases resulting in convictions, however, the magistrates and juries appeared responsive to the women complainants. Corroboration was not essential to proving the charge, for in only one of the three cases — the attempted rape of Mary Jenkins — did the complainant provide a supporting witness. In the Jenkins matter, the main offender absconded and could not be punished, but two of his companions were convicted as accessories and ordered to pay fines (£1 each) and compensation to the victim (£2 each), an unusual resolution of an assault case for this particular court. Even the witness for the complainant, a timid shoemaker who had been present in the house at the time of the attempted rape, was fined for not rendering assistance.[63] In the other two cases ending in convictions (in 1829 and 1841), the defendants were given prison terms of 12 months and one month, respectively.[64] Both attacks, but particularly the violence of the 1829 assault, attracted sentences beyond the court's standard correctives of small fines and orders to keep the peace.

In many jurisdictions, the treatment of female sexuality as a precipitating factor in sexual assault made rape trials an ordeal for victims. Using "a model of female sexuality as *agent provocateur*, temptress or seductress",[65] justices and defence lawyers often minutely examined the sexual, moral and social history of the complainant and her previous relationship with the accused to determine how she had "contributed to her own downfall". On the southern Avalon, however, the former character of the woman complainant was called into question in only two cases — the alleged assaults of Mary Keating and Catharine Power — reflecting the persistent attitude in the justice system that women of "ill repute could not be raped". Yet only in the case of Mary Keating did the court make its finding solely on the basis of the previous characters of the parties involved.

The British legal system could also monitor female sexuality by protecting the husband's right to consortium. Because a husband had the right to control his wife's body, he had several legal recourses if denied her sexual services. He could seek a court order to have his wife return to the matrimonial bed. He could also initiate various court actions against a third party and demand compensation for loss of consortium: criminal conversation (having sexual relations with the wife), enticement (encouraging the wife to leave her husband) and harbouring (providing the wife with refuge after she had run away).

There are only two brief references to loss of consortium matters on the southern Avalon during the study period. A court order in the 1773 records for Ferryland district directed Simon Pendergrass to pay Edward Farrel £5 in compensation for having had "criminal correspondence" with Farrel's wife, a relationship that had apparently been going on "for some time".[66] The second matter was fleetingly referred to in the letterbooks of the colonial secretary's office in St. John's. In October 1760, Governor James Webb ordered William Jackson, JP of the district of Trepassey, "to take up and send hereunder custody one Clement O'Neal, who has carried with him ye Wife of Josh. Fitzpatrick as Likewise all his Moveable Effects".[67]

While details are sketchy, the two cases appear to have been handled in different ways, possibly reflecting a difference in attitude between the authorities involved. The Ferryland court seems to have dealt fairly leniently with the former case: it ordered a small payment to compensate the plaintiff, Farrel, for a rather long-term encroachment on his proprietary rights. The second order, which the governor issued after a hearing at St. John's, had a more ominous and punitive tone. O'Neal was to be arrested and his effects attached. The order implied that Mrs. Fitzpatrick was to return to the matrimonial home. While the evidence is meagre, it is possible that the local magistrates had a more lenient attitude towards the issue of consortium than authorities more removed from local circumstances. Nonetheless, the scarcity of consortium cases fits with the prevalence of informal marital arrangements, the acceptance of informal separation and divorce, and the lack of pre-occupation with primogeniture[68] and legitimacy in the southern Avalon — all elements of a marriage regime that kept relatively loose control over female sexuality.

The southern district court records for the period reveal only four cases involving domestic violence against women. Although such incidents, as with rape, were likely under-reported, the low numbers may have been a further indicator of plebeian women's significant status within their families and their ability to hold their own in physical struggles. The magistrates on the southern Avalon appeared to be responsive to the woman complainant in each of the reported cases. In two matters, the alleged abusers were made to enter into peace bonds and ordered to return for trial; unfortunately, the judgments in these two cases were either not recorded or have not survived. The other two cases resulted in what were essentially court orders for separation and maintenance. There was no indication in the records that the magistrates, in their handling of the four cases, made any effort to encourage the complainants to return to their husbands.

Indeed, in a 1791 matter involving extreme domestic violence, the court moved quickly to protect wife and children and remove them from the abusive situation. Margarett Hanahan (also, Hanrahan) complained on 31 January that upon returning home the previous evening, she had discovered her husband, Thomas, trying to suffocate their youngest child and that he had later "ill-used" and flogged their older child with a bough "to oblidge it to make water". When Margarett had tried to interfere, Thomas had threatened her with a hatchet. The court observed the marks of violence on wife and children and sentenced Thomas to 39 lashes on the bare back as well as imprisonment until he could provide security for a peace bond. The magistrates also granted Margarett's request to be separated from her husband. And two and a half months later, the court ordered the husband to leave the district. This was, effectively, an order for divorce — more than 175 years before the Supreme Court of Newfoundland had jurisdiction to grant divorces.[69] Given the flexibility of the local marital regime, Margarett was certainly free to move into another, informal family arrangement; indeed, by 1800, she and her two children were living with John Ellis at Ferryland.[70]

None of the women involved in these southern Avalon cases was forced to remain in abusive marriages and none was found to have deserted and forfeited all rights to maintenance and child custody. Furthermore, the outcome of *Hanahan v. Hanahan* indicated the court's willingness to punish excessively violent husbands in kind. This contrasted with 18th- and 19th-century cases in England and Planter Nova Scotia, for example, in which courts generally dealt leniently with wifebeaters and encouraged women to return to abusive situations for the sake of preserving the marriage, regardless of the violence of the assault. This was an approach which frequently placed battered women in even great danger and which certainly discouraged the reporting of domestic violence.[71]

While Newfoundland courts did not obtain jurisdiction over matrimonial causes until 1847 or the power to grant divorces until 1867, magistrates did exercise a *de facto* jurisdiction in granting separations and support for deserted spouses and children. On this basis, they heard at least seven matrimonial cases during the study period, including the case of *Mountain v. Mountain*. One was initiated by a husband who had been turned out of the matrimonial home — an intriguing case in its own right, as the wife was ordered to pay him £3, "which was to be in full of all Demands he shall pretend to have on the House of Goods in Consideration that he has a Child to maintain".[72] The remaining six were initiated by wives and again the local magistrates were pragmatic and responsive to the women involved, sanctioning *de facto* separations and awarding maintenance for wives and children, whether it had been the wife or the husband who had left the matrimonial home. It does not appear that magistrates applied pressure on wives to reconcile with their husbands in any of these cases.

As well, women who had separated from their husbands were not expected to live the remainder of their lives in sexual denial or forfeit all rights to child custody and support. For example, after Mary Dunn's successful suit in 1791 for child maintenance from her estranged husband, Timothy, she began to cohabit with a William Hennecy, with no indication in the records that she thereby forfeited her right to child support.[73] Similarly, Ann St. Croix of St. Mary's was not penalized for her post-separation relationship with another man. On 16 October 1821, Ann brought her husband, Benjamin St. Croix, to court for neglect and ill treatment and sought an order for support for herself and their seven children. Ann was only 33 years old and much younger than her 77-year-old husband, a fact that the court clerk obviously felt worthy of note as he underscored their ages twice in the court records. The unhappy couple had already been living apart since 1819 and the court recognized this *de facto* separation. It also ordered Benjamin to give up the use of his house and garden to Ann and the children, to pay her £6 at the end of the current fishing season and to pay £5 annually for the future support of the children, who were to remain in Ann's care.[74] Ann may have already moved into another, informal marital relationship with Edward Power, a fisherman of St. Mary's. Whether this was the case, or whether her new-found freedom from Benjamin had simply put her in a celebratory mood is unclear, but on 17 July 1822, almost nine months to the day after her court-sanctioned separation from her husband, Ann gave birth to a male child who, she claimed, had been fathered by Power. That October, she went back to court to seek support for the child from her new paramour, but he had already left the area and was not expected to return. Nonetheless, the court ordered that the balance of his wages with his current employer, £4.15.4, be retained for the support of the child and that from this amount, 40s. be paid for lying-in expenses and 3s. per week for support until the wages were depleted.[75] Furthermore, there was no hint of moral judgment about Ann's extra-marital relationship with Power, and she did not jeopardize her original claim for child custody or support from her former husband, St. Croix.

The wife's character during the marriage was also not at issue in the awarding of support. On 13 August 1804, for example, Mary Kearney of Trepassey told the court that her husband, Andrew, had "turned her to Door" about 15 months earlier and that she had since been supported by her brother. Andrew testified that since the marriage, Mary had "behaved very Ill frequently getting drunk and totally neglecting her household affairs". Furthermore, six months after the nuptials, Mary had given birth to a male child who, according to Andrew, was not his. Yet, despite Andrew's claims concerning his wife's slatternliness and sexual immorality, the court granted Mary maintenance of 3s. per week for life, provided that she had no children by any other man. Furthermore, Mary obtained this order despite having some alternative means of support (her brother); thus, the court was acting not out of concern that Mary would become a charge on the community, but in recognition of her right to maintenance from her husband who had turned her out of the matrimonial home.[76]

What is most striking in the court life of the southern district is its relatively benign treatment of female sexuality when compared with other jurisdictions in Britain, Canada, and even Newfoundland. Christopher English has offered some explanations for the court's pragmatism in its dealings with both men and women. He notes that the *Judicature Acts* of 1791, 1792 and 1809 provided that English law be received in Newfoundland only "so far as the same can be applied".[77] The local magistrates were men with stakes in the community, he argues, who dispensed justice based on an understanding of local issues and a familiarity with local inhabitants; if they thought English law was deficient or inappropriate for Newfoundland situations, they simply made new law. These are useful insights into how the legal regime manifested itself "on the ground" in many outports during the period.

However, local magistrates and administrators (most wore a double cap) on the southern Avalon were also part of the emerging middle class with its middle-class ideals of femininity. Certainly, the behaviour of women within their own class was carefully monitored. Although there were some 18th-century women of the local gentry who led public and independent lives, most women of this class were retiring into genteel domesticity by the turn of the following century. Wives and daughters socialized only with other middle-class families in the area or in St. John's (some also wintered with relatives in England). They married members of their own class. They did no physical labour on flakes or in fields; rather, their work entailed rearing children and supervising domestic servants. They did not appear personally in the court house. In matters that did involve them, such as probate or debt collection, they were usually represented by men from their own circle. Certainly, their names did not appear in any of the cases involving assault, bastardy, slander, rape or domestic violence. (This is not to suggest that such incidents did not occur among the middle class, but merely that they were not played out in public.) Totally absent in the area were the types of activities that gave middle-class women elsewhere a "respectable" admittance into the public sphere — church fund-raising and philanthropic work, for example, or involvement in anti-slavery and temperance movements. These women's lives were increasingly circumscribed by the parameters of gender ideology; indeed the gentility and respectability of these women helped to maintain class boundaries in small fishing communities where contact between middle-class and plebeian men was more frequent and social distance therefore less clearly demarcated.[78]

Yet, while middle-class contemporaries in Britain were trying to encourage a modified form of respectability among the working class — one that involved a refashioned construction of female respectability — middle-class magistrates and administrators on the southern Avalon had reason to hesitate in imposing restrictions on plebeian women. These men were primarily either merchants or agents, or connected by kinship or marriage to local mercantile families that made their money by supplying local fishing families in return for their fish and oil. And the resident fishery had become overwhelmingly dependent on household production in which the labour of plebeian women, work that took place in public spaces on stage head and flake, was essential. In addition, these women, in their various economic capacities, were also an intrinsic part of the exchange economy and the truck system — the supply and credit practices which underwrote the resident fishery. The working woman was not a "social problem"; she was an economic necessity. It was, thus, not in the interests of local magistrates to encourage the withdrawal of plebeian women into the respectability of the private sphere.[79]

The other key player in Peggy Mountain's drama was the Catholic Church. Why was the response of the priest to Peggy's situation so different from that of the magistrates? The answer may lie with the relationship between Irish plebeian women and the Catholic authorities. Father Browne also had a stake in the local community; he too was familiar with local circumstances and personalities, as he had been at the mission in Ferryland for 20 years. Yet he did not try to accommodate Peggy as did the local magistrates. Rather, he hounded Peggy out of the district because of her "deviant" sexual behaviour. It might be tempting to explain the matter simply in terms of a clash between secular and religious authorities over jurisdiction in arbitrating local disputes. Yet this model of tension must be qualified. Browne did not regularly intervene in other matters before the court. Indeed, he often socialized with Carter and other local merchants and magistrates, and would himself be shunned and stripped of his priestly faculties by his bishop in 1841 on a litany of charges, including his too frequent and conspicuous fraternizing with the local Protestant "Ascendancy".[80] If this was a turf war, it was fought on the grounds of female respectability, for the tension in the episode appears to have emanated from Browne's dissenting views on the regulation of Irish-Newfoundland womanhood.

Certainly, Father Brownes' reaction was not out of line with church efforts to monitor female sexuality. When Catholic clergy were finally permitted to operate openly in

Newfoundland after 1784, priests were overwhelmed by the numbers of informal family arrangements in their new missions. In Father Ewer's 1789 report on Ferryland district, it was the indecency of women's having multiple partners that became the particular focus of paternalistic concern (or, perhaps, blame), as he noted:

> The magistrates had for custom here, to marry, divorce & remarry again different times, & this was sometimes done without their knowledge, so that there are women living here with their 4th husband each man alive & form different familys in repute. I would wish to know if these mariages are but simple contracts confirmed & disolved by law, or the sacrament of matrimony received validly by the contracting partys. If the latter it will be attended with much confusion in this place, with the ruin of many familys & I fear the total suppression of us all as acting against the government.[81]

British authorities in Newfoundland acknowledged the validity of some local marriage practices, given the lack of access to formal marriage rites in the period.[82] But the Catholic church, which had grown away from its Celtic-Christian roots by the late 18th century, was not so sanguine and, while realizing that it must tread carefully around local regulations, was determined to untie such bonds that yet "remain[ed] to be separated from adultery".[83] With the priests, then, came a concerted effort to bring women into formalized marriages within the precepts of the church. Parish records after 1820 suggest the priests enjoyed increasing success and, as a result of their efforts, the options of cohabitation and informal separation and divorce disappeared.

The dichotomized construction of woman as respectable wife and mother or temptress Eve, was also part of church discourse. Thus, with the priests came the practice of "churching" women after childbirth. This was a perfunctory, shady ritual, usually a few prayers mumbled at the back door of the priest's residence over a woman who had to be "purified" for the "sin" of conceiving a child. With the priests also came a more systematic shaming of adulterous wives and unwed mothers, reflecting a double sexual standard that laid the "sin" of pre- and extramarital sexual relationships overwhelmingly at the feet of "unchaste" women. Particularly in terms of illegitimacy, mothers were punished more harshly than fathers, suffering public humiliation, even ostracism, as they were denounced from the altar and denied (either for a limited period of public penance, or indefinitely) churching and the sacraments.[84] Here, then, was a reinforcement of the chastity requirement of middle-class ideology.

Church efforts to control "unruly" womanhood gained momentum after Bishop Michael Fleming assumed office in the 1830s. The desire to monitor female virtue was the primary motivation in Fleming's decision to bring the Presentation nuns to Newfoundland from Galway in 1833. In his 1837 report to Propaganda Fide, he expressed his abhorrence of the way in which "the children of both sexes should be moved together pell-mell" in the island's schools and portrayed their intermingling as "dangerous" and "impeding any improvement of morals".[85] In a later letter to Father O'Connell, he explained his urgency in sponsoring the sisters' mission, even at considerable personal cost. It was crucial, Fleming felt, that young Newfoundland women be removed from mixed schools in order to protect "that delicacy of feeling and refinement of sentiment which form the ornament and grace of their sex". In separate schools, the nuns could "fix . . . [their] character in virtue and innocence", prepare them for motherhood and domesticity and lead them to their destiny as moral guardians of their families. A curriculum that included knitting, netting and plain and fancy needlework would ease the transition from work on flakes and in gardens to pursuits more properly reflecting womanly respectability. And "solidly instructed in the Divine precepts of the Gospel", they would abandon the ancient customary practices that were an alternate source of female power, a power that competed with the church's own authority in the spiritual realm.[86]

The Presentation sisters did not actually arrive in communities on the southern Avalon until the 1850s and 1860s. But the effort to rein in unruly womanhood had begun with the arrival of sanctioned Catholicism, and was articulated as early as Father Ewer's 1789 expression of concern about women's living arrangements. Furthermore, the endeavour intensified as the 19th century unfolded. And while a conflict existed for local magistrates between ideology and economic reality, there was no such conflict for the church in the pursuit of its civilizing mission on the southern Avalon. Within the framework of Catholic orthodoxy, the denial of female sexuality, the celebration of selfless motherhood, and the increasing pressure on women to transform their homes into spiritual havens, removed from the outside world, were impelling women to retire into domesticity and respectability. These pressures would intensify as the repercussions of the devotional revolution in the Irish Catholic church of the later 19th century were felt through the regular recruitment of religious personnel from Ireland.[87]

Still, church constructions of femininity met with resistance from the plebeian community because they clashed with the realities of plebeian women's lives. But some inroads were being made by the 1830s. Father Browne's success in driving Peggy Mountain out of Ferryland suggests a widening of the wedge. A further indicator was the virtual withdrawal of Irish plebeian women from the courts on matters specifically related to female sexuality. Although they continued to appear in the records on matters such as debt, wages, common assault and property, their willingness to pursue matters such as sexual assault, domestic violence, bastardy, separation and maintenance seemed negligible after the 1830s. Only four such cases survive in the records — one sexual assault (1841), one case of domestic violence (1843) and two bastardy suits (both 1854) — despite a growing population. Women were increasingly reluctant, then, to air these matters in public, a reluctance that can be linked more readily to church attributions of shame and guilt to female sexuality than to magisterial hostility. Increasingly wary of public court actions, Irish women were left with the weaker options of either handling these matters privately, or not pursuing them at all.

During the last half of the 18th and the first half of the 19th century, middle-class ideals of female domesticity and respectability infiltrated Newfoundland society through its English legal regime and an emerging local middle class of administrators, churchmen and merchants. These middle-class constructs of female respectability did not, however, easily insinuate themselves into Irish plebeian culture on the southern Avalon, where women played a significant role in community formation, held property, inhabited public spaces such as court house and stage head, had a joint custodial control of culture and a powerful place in an alternative belief system that ran in tandem with formal Catholicism, and played vital roles in subsistence and in the production of saltfish for the marketplace. Furthermore, while local administrators and magistrates on the southern Avalon, such as Carter, were part of the emerging middle class with its middle-class ideals, and certainly they carefully monitored the behaviour of women within their own class, they had reason to pause in trying to impose restrictions on plebeian women. As members of local mercantile networks they were dependent on the presence of plebeian women in the public economic domain. These local magistrates therefore had a collective interest in forestalling the equation between plebeian female respectability, and the private sphere. The Catholic clergy, by contrast, saw the regulation of "unruly" womanhood as part of their civilizing mission in Newfoundland and pursued this goal with increasing zeal as the 19th century progressed. While church ideals of femininity conflicted with plebeian realities, their efforts were already making inroads as the *Water Lily* slipped its moorings at Ferryland and carried Peggy Mountain into historical obscurity.

NOTES

1. The term "Irish women" in this article includes both Irish immigrant women and Irish-Newfoundland women in the multi-generational ethnic group of the area, unless the context specifies women in Ireland. The term "southern Avalon" incorporates the area from Bay Bulls to Dog Point in St. Mary's Bay on the Avalon Peninsula of Newfoundland. The case summary derived from *Peggy Mountain v. Michael Mountain*, 23, 29, 30 December 1834, 2, 12, 19 January, 23 February 1835, Ferryland, box 1, ff. 57–60, 64, GN 5/4/C/1; Robert Carter Diary, 30, 31 December 1834, 1, 5, 12 January, 14, 15, 16, 19, 20, 21, 23, 28 March, 6, 9 May 1835, MG 920, Provincial Archives of Newfoundland and Labrador [PANL]. The writer gratefully acknowledges the financial assistance of the Social Sciences and Humanities Research Council of Canada and the Institute of Social and Economic Research, Memorial University.

2. I have borrowed this concept from Susan M. Edwards who discusses "the patrolling of the boundaries of thought on the nature of the sexuality of women", in *Female Sexuality and the Law: A Study of Constructs of Female Sexuality as They Inform Statute and Legal Procedure* (Oxford, 1981), p. 173.

3. The literature upon which the following discussion is based includes: Constance Backhouse, *Petticoats and Prejudice: Women and Law in Nineteenth-Century Canada* (Toronto, 1991); Linda Cullum and Maeve Board, "A Woman's Lot: Women and Law in Newfoundland from Early Settlement to the Twentieth Century", in Linda Kealey, ed., *Pursuing Equality: Historical Perspectives on Women in Newfoundland and Labrador* (St. John's, 1993), pp. 66–162; Joy Damousi, *Depraved and Disorderly: Female Convicts, Sexuality and Gender in Colonial Australia* (Cambridge, 1997); Anna Clark, *The Struggle for the Breeches: Gender and the Making of the British Working Class* (Berkeley, 1995); Lenore Davidoff, "Regarding Some 'Old Husbands' Tales': Public and Private in Feminist History", in *Worlds Between: Historical Perspectives on Gender and Class* (Cambridge, 1995), pp. 227–76; Davidoff and Catherine Hall, *Family Fortunes: Men and Women of the English Middle Class, 1780–1850* (Chicago, 1987); Edwards, *Female Sexuality*; Theodore Koditschek, "The Gendering of the British Working Class", *Gender and History*, 9, 2 (August 1997), pp. 333–63; Lynda Nead, *Myths of Sexuality: Representations of Women in Victorian Britain* (Oxford and New York, 1988); Roy Porter, "Mixed Feelings: The Enlightenment and Sexuality in Eighteenth-Century Britain", in Paul-Gabriel Bouc, ed., *Sexuality in Eighteenth-Century Britain* (Manchester, 1982), pp. 1–27; Jane Rendall, *Women in an Industrializing Society: England, 1750–1880* (Oxford, 1990); Sonya O. Rose, *Limited Livelihoods: Gender and Class in Nineteenth Century England* (Berkeley, 1992); G.S. Rousseau and Roy Porter, "Introduction," in Rousseau and Porter, eds., *Sexual Underworlds of the Enlightenment* (Chapel Hill, 1988), pp. 1–24; Carol Smart, "Disruptive Bodies and Unruly Sex: the Regulation of Reproduction and Sexuality in the Nineteenth Century", in Carol Smart, ed., *Regulating Womanhood: Historical Essays on Marriage, Motherhood and Sexuality* (London and New York, 1992), pp. 7–32.

4. Judith Walkowitz, *City of Dreadful Delight: Narratives of Sexual Danger in Late-Victorian London* (Chicago, 1992), p. 23.

5. Up to the early decades of the 19th century, most of this group were Anglo-Protestant and many returned to Britain after stays of varying lengths on the island. Those who remained kept their strong family, commercial and/or professional connections with Britain. There was a smaller Irish mercantile element in Newfoundland as well but, while this group achieved increasing prominence in St. John's in the 19th century, Irish merchant-planters on the southern Avalon (again, predominantly a Protestant group) had wound up their interests in the area by the late 18th century.

6. For information on Irish immigration to Newfoundland in general, see the scholarship of John J. Mannion, including: "Introduction", in John J. Mannion, ed., *The Peopling of Newfoundland: Essays in Historical Geography* (St. John's, 1977), pp. 5–9; Mannion, "Tracing the Irish: A Geographical Guide", *The Newfoundland Ancestor*, 9, 1 (Spring 1993), pp. 4–18.

7. See, for example, Remarks of Naval Officer Cummins in relation to Newfoundland [c. 1705], Colonial Office [CO] 194/3/424-5. See also Capt. Van Brugh to Commissioners for Trade, 6 November 1738 (transcribed from CO 194/10/93), Subseries 04-056/01, f. 25-B-2-1; Governor Cadre Smith to Commissioners for Trade, 1742, Governor Byng to Commissioners for Trade, 1743 (from CO 194/11/41), Sub-series 04-057/02, f. 25-A-27-56, 04/058, Keith Matthews Collection, Coll. 24, box 9, Maritime History Archives [MHA]; Order, Governor Hugh Palliser, 2 June 1767, GN 2/1/A, 4/41–44/1764; Order, Palliser, 31 October 1764, GN 2/1/A, 3/272-3/1764; Order, Governor John Byron, 29 September 1769, GN 2/1/A, 4/201/1869; Order, Byron, 31 October 1770, GN 2/1/A, 4/285/1770; Order, Governor Molinoux Shuldham, 24 June 1772 GN 2/1/A, 5/60/1772; Order, Shuldham, 13 July 1772, GN 2/1/A, 5/102/1772; Order, Shuldham, 12 October 1773, GN 2/1/A, 5/143/1772; Order, Governor Robert Duff, 12 July 1775, GN 2/1/A, 6/17/1775; Orders (2), Duff, 16 October 1775, GN 2/1/A, 6/100–1/1775; Circular Letter, Governor John Montague to the Magistrates of the various districts

in Newfoundland, 6 October 1777, GN 2/1/A, 7/33–35/1777; Order, Montague, 3 October 1778, GN 2/1/A, 7/70, 1778; Proclamation and Public Notice, Governor Mark Milbanke, 13 October 1789, GN 2/1/A, 12/38–41/1789; Milbanke to James O Donel (Catholic Prefect-Apostolic, later Bishop, at Newfoundland), 2 November 1790, GN 2/1/A, 12/102/1790; Public Notice, Governor Richard King, 19 September 1792, GN 2/1/A, 12/157/1792; Proclamation, Governor William Waldegrave and covering correspondence to the Magistrates of Newfoundland, 27 September 1798, GN 2/1/A, 14/282-7/1798; Proclamations (2), Governor John Gambier, 18 September 1802, GN 2/1/A, 16/282–87/1802, PANL.

8. W. Gordon Handcock, *'Soe longe as there comes noe women': Origins of English Settlement in Newfoundland* (St. John, 1989), p. 32.

9. Order, Govenor Hugh Palliser, 2 July 1764, 3/232/1764, GN 2/1/A; Order, Governor John Montague, 10 October 1777, 7/35-6/1777, GN 2/1/A, PANL. See also Capt. James Story, "An account of what fishing ships, Sack Ships, Planters & boat keepers from Trepasse to Bonavist & from thence to faire Island the Northward part of Newfoundland", 1 September 1681, 16-D-1-006, MHA; Order of Hugh Palliser in *Pendergrass v. Blakener*, 2 October 1766, GN 2/1/A, 4/23/1766, PANL.

10. In Newfoundland, a "planter" was a resident, as opposed to migratory, proprietor of fishing premises.

11. I draw from E.P. Thompson's conceptualization of 18th-century English society in *Customs in Common* (London, 1991), chapter 2.

12. The following sections derive from a much fuller discussion by the writer in Willeen Keough, "The Slender Thread: Irish Women on the Southern Avalon, 1750–1860", Ph.D. thesis, Memorial University, 2001. See especially chapters 2–7.

13. On the 17th-century planters, see Sir John Berry, "A list of ye Planters Names with an acct. of their Concerns from Cape de Race to Cape Bonavista", 12 September 1675 (from CO 1/35 [17ii], 149v-156), 16-C-2-035, Keith Matthews Collection, MHA; Capt. Story, "An account", 16-D-1-006, MHA; Berry Census, 1675, 1677 (from CO 1), GN 2/39/A, PANL. Figure 22.1 presents data from 1735 to 1857 in roughly ten-year intervals. As the figures for 1755 were not available, figures for 1754 were used. The data on the number of Catholics in the population for 1765 and 1795 were not reliable.

14. Bishop Aubrey Spencer to Rev. A. M. Campbell, 22 June 1842, G series, vol. 1, ff. 9-10, MG 598, SPG, PANL. See also from the same collection: Petition of the Inhabitants of Bay Bulls for a Clergyman, 19 October 1773, C series, box 1, f. 56; Rev. John Dingle to Rev. Doctor Morris, Secretary to the SPG, 22 November 1801, C series, box 1A/18, f. 180; "Report on the Diocese of Newfoundland, Mission of Ferryland, 1845", E series, n.f.; Bishop Edward Field to Rev. Ernest Hawkins, November 1845, G series, vol. 1, f. 159, PANL.

15. "The State of the Catholic Religion in Newfoundland Reviewed in Two Letters by Monsignor Fleming to P. John Spratt", 1836, p. 91, Bishop Michael Anthony Fleming Papers, 103/26, Roman Catholic Archives, St. John's [RCASJ]. See also from the same collection, Fleming, *Report of the Catholic Mission in Newfoundland in North America,* submitted to the Cardinal Prefect of Propaganda Fide (Rome, 1837), p. 39. See also Father Thomas Ewer to Archbishop Troy of Dublin, 20 September 1796, in Cyril Byrne, ed., *Gentlemen-Bishops and Faction Fighters: The Letters of Bishops O Donel, Lambert, Scallan and Other Irish Missionaries* (St. John's, 1984), pp. 140–2.

16. A limited number of English surnames — largely of local mercantile and administrative families — predominate surviving Anglican parish records for the area, with a healthy addition of English surnames from the middle class of St. John's and, less frequently, England itself. Baptismal records for Ferryland district provide an occupational profile of Anglican fathers for the period between 1823 and 1855: three clergymen; 19 merchants or merchant/planters; two merchants/sub-collectors of customs; one merchant/naval lieutenant; seven masters of merchant vessels; one master of merchant vessel/merchant; one master of merchant vessel/planter; three planters; one mercantile agent; one gentleman; four carpenters; one sail-maker; one blacksmith; one labourer/mason; one labourer; 12 fishermen; three not given. Intriguingly, no fishermen fathers were listed before the mid 1830s and 10 appeared only in the 1840s and 1850s. See Church of England Parish Records — Petty Harbour Parish, box 2, Baptisms, Ferryland District, PANL.

17. Numerous examples of women in these various occupations can be found in the court records for the districts of Ferryland and Trepassey-St. Mary's. See GN 5/1/C/1, 5/2/C/1-4, 8; GN 5/4/C/1, 8, PANL; 340.9 N45, Provincial Reference Library, St. John's [PRL]. Examples also appear in mercantile records for the area, particularly Sweetman Collection (records of Saunders and Sweetman, a firm operating out of Placentia with dealers in St. Mary's Bay, including portions of the study area), MG 49 and Collection of Alan F. Goodridge and Son (a firm operating out of Renews), MH 473, PANL.

18. The writer's database of court cases contains 25 employment disputes involving women in the area. In nine of these cases, formal shipping agreements were actually referenced and/or produced. See *Jane Costeloe v. Bridget Whealon,* 3 August 1795, 340.9 N45, n.f., PRL; Brigus South, "Dwyer, Anstice", re: *Anstice Dwyer v. Cornelius Kelly,* 27 October 1797, John Mannion Name File (private collection, St. John's). See also *Frida*

Tobin v. Mary Bony, 29 September 1818, St. Mary's, ff. 47-8; *Catherine Lancrop v. John Doody, Jr.*, 29 September 1818, St. Mary's f. 52, GN 5/4/C/1; *Margret Neile v. John and James Munn*, 2 November 1818, Ferryland, f. 62, GN/5/1/C/1; *Elizabeth Cullen v. James Shortall*, c. 26 September 1787, Ferryland, box 1, f. 43, GN 5/4/C/1; *Jane Austin v. Robert Brennan*, 25 September 1843, *Margaret Dunphy v. Nicholas Power*, 14 September 1846, *Ellen Leary v. John Butler*, 5 October 1848, Ferryland, Box 2, n.f., GN 5/4/C/1, PANL. The terms of all agreements, formal or informal, oral or written, were generally upheld by the court.

19. For example, in 1773, Mary Shea was granted a fishing room on the northwest side of Ferryland harbour "to quietly and peaceably possess the same so long as you shall enjoy it to the advantage of the Fishery". See Grant of a Fishing Room to Mary Shea, 15 September 1773, n.f., 340.9 N45, PRL. In 1775, Alice Thomas of Renews was sued by her fishing servants for their wages. See *Lawrence Dunn & J. Whealon v. Alice Thomas*, 5 October 1775, 340.9 N45, PRL. Catharine Clements of Renews was the proprietor of a fishing premises and fishing employer in Renews in the 1780s and 1790s. See Petition of James Rows, Renews [c. 14 August 1784], Order, Governor John Campbell, 27 August 1784, GN 2/1/A, 10/49-51/1784, PANL; *Catharine Clements v. James Rouse*, 31 August 1785, n.f., 340.9 N45, PRL. In 1794, Jane Holly was one of several boatkeepers in Ferryland district entangled in a dispute between a former and current supplier. See *Thomas Gibbs & Co. v. William Knox, John Rice, & Henry Studdy*, 11 August 1794, Ferryland, box 1, n.f., GN 5/4/C/1, PANL. In the 1820s, Ann Ryan was renting a fishing room and premises in Caplin Bay — including stages, flakes, beaches, dwelling house, gardens and lands — from Philip Tree for £6 per annum. See Philip Tree, Mortgage to John Teague, 29 November 1823, Ferryland, ff. 97-8, GN 5/1/C/1, PANL. The mercantile records of Sweetman's and Goodridge's also contain various accounts for fish and oil from households headed by women. See MG 49 and MG 473, PANL, respectively.

20. In this discussion, the term "common-law", when applied to a relationship between a man and a woman, indicates that the couple were not married by a religious, civil, or informal ceremony, but were cohabiting and having a sexual relationship as if they were husband and wife. Common-law relationships had no legal status during the study period and were deemed a "civil inconvenience" by central authorities because they deviated from a moral order that bolstered a patriarchal system of property inheritance. See Cullum and Baird, "A Woman's Lot", p. 119.

21. Smaller numbers of fishing servants continued to be hired, but mostly to supplement household labour.

22. The Governors' annual returns in the CO 194 series contain a section on the personnel involved in the resident fishery. The "momentum" referred to here is demonstrated by dramatically declining numbers of hired servants in relation to an ever-increasing planter group (masters, mistresses and children).

23. The vital role of women in the traditional fishery has also been discussed by other writers, including Ellen Antler, "Women's Work in Newfoundland Fishing Families", *Atlantis*, 2, 2, (1977), pp. 106–13; Sean Cadigan, *Hope and Deception in Conception Bay: Merchant-Settler Relations in Newfoundland, 1785–1855* (Toronto, 1995); Hilda Chaulk Murray, *More Than Fifty Percent: Women's Life in a Newfoundland Outport, 1900–1950* (St. John's, 1979); Marilyn Porter, "'She was Skipper of the Shore Crew': Notes on the History of the Sexual Division of Labour in Newfoundland", in Carmelita McGrath, Barbara Neis and Marilyn Porter, eds., *Their Lives and Times: Women in Newfoundland and Labrador: A Collage* (St. John's, 1995), pp. 33–47.

24. See Sweetman Collection (various loose materials), boxes 2, 3, MG 49; Goodridge Collection, 1839, 1841 ledgers, MG 473, PANL. In addition, merchants' and boatkeepers' accounts, including entries involving women's services, were occasionally brought forward as evidence in court cases relating to matters such as debt and balances owing on servants' wages. See GN 5, PANL; 340.9 N45, PRL.

25. The Sweetman records are piecemeal over an extended period, but the Goodridge records are intact for 1839 and 1841 and indicate that 60 women in Renews (adult female population of approximately 150) held separate accounts in those two years. They were surely not all widowed or single women.

26. Coverture was the principle at English common law whereby a married woman's legal identity was absorbed into that of her husband.

27. For other discussions of women's participation in exchange economies, see Johanna Miller Lewis, "Women and Economic Freedom in the North Carolina Backcountry", in Larry D. Eldridge, ed., *Women and Freedom in Early America* (New York and London, 1997), pp. 191–208; Elizabeth Mancke, "At the Counter of the General Store: Women and the Economy in Eighteenth-Century Horton, Nova Scotia", in Margaret Conrad, ed., *Intimate Relations: Family and Community in Planter Nova Scotia, 1759-1800* (Fredericton, 1995), pp. 167–81.

28. "Two Letters", p. 90, Fleming Papers, 103/26, RCASJ. Until Governor John Campbell issued a Declaration of Liberty of Conscience in 1784, the Catholic religion operated underground, with a handful of priests travelling incognito from harbour to harbour.

29. Dean Patrick Cleary [parish priest, Witless Bay], "A Note of Church History [1784–1850]", p. 28, Fleming Papers, 103/32, RCASJ.

30. Information from the oral tradition derives from a series of interviews conducted from 1999 to 2001 with 21 informants, male and female, from seven communities in the study area. For further discussion of the methodology, see Keough, "Slender Thread", chapter 1.

31. These were communal pipes, shared by those at the wake-house. After a smoker drew in the smoke, he or she exhaled it with the invocation "God be merciful".

32. The "hag" was a supernatural creature who came in the night and sat on the chest of her prey in an effort to impede or stop the victim's breathing. The visitation evoked a choking sensation and left the sufferer in a semi-conscious state from which s/he could only be wakened by calling his or her name backwards. Not all variations of the "hag" actually involved a female apparition; sometimes she manifested herself more diffusely in the form of a bad nightmare from which the sufferer could not wake, or a feeling of paralysis that kept the victim pinned to the bed. Still, such unfortunates were said to be "hag-rode" or "hag-ridden"— rendered insensible by the powers of this terrifying female phantasm.

33. Information on informal religious beliefs and practices in the study area comes from the oral tradition. See Willeen Keough: "The Old 'Hag' Meets Saint Brigid: Irish Women and the Intersection of Belief Systems on the Southern Avalon, Newfoundland", *An Nasc*, 13 (Spring 2001), pp. 12–25. There is a literature on the derivative system in Ireland which includes J.S. Connolly, *Priests and People in Pre-Famine Ireland, 1780–1845* (Dublin, 1982); George Casey, "Irish Culture in Newfoundland", in Cyril J. Byrne and Margaret Harry, eds., *Talamh En Eisc: Canadian and Irish Essays* (Halifax, 1986), pp. 203–27; W.G. Wood-Martin, *Traces of the Elder Faiths of Ireland*, vol. 2 ([1902] Port Washington and London, 1970). The oral tradition is particularly helpful in reconstructing the early spiritual life of the community. Many of these practices survived in the area well into the 20th century and there is no evidence to suggest that they skipped generations after migration, only to be revised later.

34. Similar incidents involving plebeian women of Conception Bay and Prince Edward Island have been reported by Sean Cadigan and Rusty Bittermann, respectively. See Cadigan, *Hope and Deception*, chapter 4; Bittermann, "Women and the Escheat Movement: The Politics of Everyday Life on Prince Edward Island", in Janet Guildford and Suzanne Morton, eds., *Separate Spheres: Women's Worlds in the 19th-Century Maritimes* (Fredericton, 1994), pp. 23–38.

35. The term "room" refers to fishing premises, including stages, "flakes" (structures for drying fish), sheds, wharves and fish stores for the landing, processing and storing of fish, as well as "cookrooms" for the accommodation of crews.

36. *John W. Saunders v. Thomas Berrigan*, 3, 5 November 1836, 1835–47 journal, ff. 62, 64-5, GN 5/2/C/3; *J.W. Saunders Esqr v. Thomas Berrigan*, Writ No. 8, Action in Ejectment, issued 25 September for return 1 November 1836, GN 5/2/C/4; *Regina v. Anastatia Berrigan & others*, 3, 20 September 1838, Ferryland, box 1, n.f., GN 5/4/C/1; *Regina v. William Berrigan, Anastatia Berrigan, Bridget Berrigan, and Alice Berrigan*, 31 December 1842, 31 January, 23 February 1843, *Regina c. James Gearing, Sr., Benjamin Wilcox, Edward Berrigan, Anastatia Berrigan, Thomas Berrigan, Sr., and Thomas Berrigan, Jr.*, 13, 14, 20, 27 June 1843, *Regina v. Thomas Berrigan, Jr.*, 5 February 1844, Ferryland, box 2, n.f., GN 5/4/C/1, PANL.

37. See Keough, "Slender Thread", chapters 5 and 6. In gauging the significance of the number of complaints found, several factors should be kept in mind. While court records for the southern Avalon are available from 1773 onwards, these records predominantly represent post-1780s cases; references to earlier cases appear only sporadically in governors' correspondence. The court records are, themselves, incomplete as no concerted effort to preserve the records was made until the late 20th century. As evidenced by various temporal gaps, many records have been lost due to neglect. And while a system evolved whereby matters were entered under several headings — such as causes, writs, minutes and judgments — rarely are the full set of records for any given case available. Furthermore, the cases examined here relate almost exclusively to the districts of Ferryland and Trepassy-St. Mary's. Roughly half the study area, the section from Bay Bulls to Toad's Cove, fell within the court boundaries of the central court district, and unfortunately, an examination of the records for that district (which included all cases in the capital, St. John's) was beyond the scope of this study. With the exception of occasional references from governors' correspondence, this subarea was not represented in my court case database. Finally, the number of adult women in the population of the area for which records have been examined thoroughly was quite small until the second quarter of the 19th century. Only by the 1830s did it exceed 400 (Figure 22.2). In Figure 22.2, data for the closest year is used when data for the five-year interval is not available. There was no 1740 census return for St. Mary's, but numbers would have been fairly low at this point. Numbers of servants were over-reported in 1836 for individual communities of the Ferryland district. There was obviously an overlap in reporting some residents as both masters/mistresses and servants, for their combined number exceeds total population figures and combined totals of religious denominations for the district. The number used here is from the Abstract at the end of the census which contains a separate total for servants that

does tally with the other totals. No separate summer/winter breakdown appears in the census data for 1836, 1845 and 1847. In 1845 a total of 211 servants was reported for the Ferryland district and 141 for 1857. As these individuals are not differentiated by gender, they are not accounted for in this figure. Age categories also shifted in 1857, with the most significant change in terms of this figure being the shift from an "under 14" category to an "under ten" category.

38. These findings differ significantly from Judith Norton's in her examination of assault cases in the Planter townships of Nova Scotia in the first 50 years of settlement. Norton notes: "Women were particularly vulnerable in early Nova Scotia. In the 45 recorded incidents of abuse or assault identified in the early court records, 20 of the victims and five of the assailants were females". See Norton, "The Dark Side of Planter Life: Reported Cases of Domestic Violence", in Conrad, ed., *Intimate Relations*, pp. 182–9, particularly p. 185.

39. This was true of plebeian and working-class communities in the British Isles as well. See, for example, Clarke, *Struggle for the Breeches*; Connolly, *Priests and People*; Stephen Parker, *Informal Marriage, Cohabitation and the Law 1750–1989* (New York, 1990); Rendall, *Women in Industrializing Society*.

40. Kathleen M. Brown discusses the differences in systems of knowledge about gender between England and Gaelic Ireland in *Good Wives, Nasty Wenches, and Anxious Patriarchs: Gender, Race, and Power in Colonial Virginia* (Chapel Hill, 1994), pp. 33–7. The Irish system was eroded over time, however, by the incursions of English law and culture and an increasingly centralized and patriarchal Catholic church.

41. Father Ewer to Archbishop Troy, Dublin, 30 November 1789, in Byrne, ed., *Gentlemen-Bishops*, pp. 77–9.

42. This number may underestimate the phenomenon, for the census-taker, magistrate Robert Carter (father of Robert Carter, Jr.), would likely not have questioned claims of marital status unless he was personally aware of a couple's circumstances. See Pole Papers, 1799–1800, MG 205, PANL. For a more detailed analysis, see Keough, "Slender Thread", Appendix D.

43. As part of the process of obtaining a grant in 1750 to Pigeon's Plantation in Ferryland, for example, Elizabeth Gobbet, who had lived with Elias Pigeon before his death, had to swear to the court at Ferryland that she was not currently married to John Allen, but that they were "only keeping company together." See GN 2/1/A, 1/115, 136, 141/1750; Carter-Benger-Nason Collection, MG247, PANL. In 1759, Henry Ticker petitioned the Governor for title to a plantation of his deceased mother in Ferryland; the property was currently in the possession of Thomas Power, with whom his mother had been living "in the state of incontinency without being married to him". See Order of Governor Richard Edwards to the fishing admirals and magistrates of Ferryland, 13 October 1759, GN 2/1/A, 3/44-5/1759, PANL. In 1787, Hannah (Carney) and William Mcdaniel admitted to the local court that they were not actually married but living common law. See *Catherine Weston v. Hannah & William Mcdaniel*, 8 March 1787, Ferryland, box 1, ff. 25-6, GN 5/4/C/1, PANL. In 1802, Mary Stokes of St. Mary's sued William Kearney for her deceased mother's possessions because William and her mother had not been married but merely living "in adultery". See *Mary Stokes v. William Kearney*, 30 September 1802, St. Mary's, n.f., 340.9 N45, PRL.

44. Rural Irish women performed domestic tasks as well as heavy agricultural work in the fields. They also gathered seaweed for fertilizer and food, carried peat for fuel, kept livestock, sold eggs and distilled and sold spirits. In addition, they generated what was often the family's only cash income through their work in cottage woollen and linen industries. For a discussion of women's status in rural Ireland and the decline in that status by the early 19th century, see L.A. Clarkson, "Love, Labour and Life: Women in Carrick-on-Suir in the Late Eighteenth Century", *Irish Economic and Social History*, 20 (1993), pp. 18–34; Mary Daly, "Women in the Irish Workforce from Pre-industrial to Modern Times", *Saothar*, 7 (1981), pp. 74–82; Hasia R. Diner, *Erin's Daughters in America: Irish Immigrant Women in the Nineteenth Century* (Baltimore, 1983); David Fitzpatrick, "The Modernisation of the Irish Female", in Patrick O'Flanagan, Paul Ferguson and Kevin Whelan, eds., *Rural Ireland: Modernisation v. Change, 1600–1900* (Cork, 1987), pp. 162–8; Dierdre Mageean, "To Be Matched or to Move: Irish Women's Prospects in Munster", in Christiane Harzig, ed., *Peasant Maids — City Women: From the European Countryside to Urban America* (Ithaca, 1997), pp. 57–97; Janet A. Nolan, *Ourselves Alone: Women's Emigration from Ireland, 1885-1920* (Lexington, Kentucky, 1989).

45. Clarkson, "Love, Labour and Life", p. 30.

46. "Potato culture" refers not just to horticultural practices, but a whole cycle of dependence on the potato that developed among almost half Ireland's population in the decades before the great famine — a cycle marked by early marriage, high fertility rates and subdivision of the land to accommodate growing numbers, resulting in even greater dependence on the potato to sustain following generations.

47. See, for example, Leonore Davidoff, "The Role of Gender in the 'First Industrial Nation': Farming and the Countryside in England, 1780–1850", in *Worlds Between*, pp. 180–205; Koditschek, "Gendering of the British Working Class"; Rendall, *Women in Industrializing Society*; Deborah Valenze, *The First Industrial Woman* (New York and Oxford, 1995).

48. On the Newfoundland justice system in general, see Christopher English and Christopher P. Curran, "A Cautious Beginning: The Court of Civil Jurisdiction, 1791", *Silk Robes and Sou'westers: The Supreme Court 1791–1991* (St. John's, 1991); English, "The Reception of Law in Ferryland District, Newfoundland, 1786–1812", paper presented to a joint session of the Canadian Law and Society Association and the Canadian Historical Association, Brock University, 2 June 1996; English, "From Fishing Schooner to Colony: The Legal Development of Newfoundland, 1791–1832", in Louis A. Knafla and Susan W.S. Bunnie, eds., *Law, Society, and the State: Essays in Modern Legal History* (Toronto, Buffalo, London, 1995), pp. 73–98. The observations on southern Avalon magistrates are drawn from GN5, PANL; 340.9 N45, PRL. See also Keough, "Slender Thread", chapters 6, 8, 9, Appendix A.

49. Backhouse, *Petticoats and Prejudice*; Cullum and Baird, "A Woman's Lot"; Karen Dubinsky, "'Maidenly Girls' or 'Designing Women?': The Crime of Seduction in Turn-of-the-Century Ontario", in Franca Iacovetta and Mariana Valverde, eds., *Gender Conflicts: New Essays in Women's History* (Toronto, 1992), pp. 27–66; Edwards, *Female Sexuality*.

50. Despite the incomplete nature of the court records for the area, the writer's database on civil and criminal cases and estate matters involving women on the southern Avalon includes more than 500 entries for the period. For other writings on the presence of Newfoundland women in the court system, see Trudi D. Johnson, "Matrimonial Property Law in Newfoundland to the End of the Nineteenth Century", Ph.D. thesis, Memorial University, 1998; Krista Simon, "A Case Study in the Reception of Law in Newfoundland: Assessing Women's Participation in the Courts of Placentia District, 1757–1823", Honours dissertation, Memorial University, 1999.

51. The reader is urged not to clump the following cases together in a total that will have little significance. We cannot read the same meaning into a woman's being charged with prostitution, for example, and a woman's taking her husband to court for abuse or desertion. Furthermore, in many of the following categories (e.g., seduction, infanticide, prostitution, loss of consortium and rape), low numbers are positive indicators of women's status. The significant participation of Irish-Newfoundland women in the court system is demonstrated in the previous note. Also indicative of women's status and authority were the informal mechanisms they used to obtain justice within their communities. See Keough, "Slender Thread", chapter 5 and 6.

52. Backhouse, *Petticoats and Prejudice*; Dubinsky, "'Maidenly Girls'".

53. The "sound" was the air-bladder that ran along the inside of the backbone of the cod fish and controlled its buoyancy. It was removed during the splitting process, salted and eaten as a local delicacy.

54. Fishermen's wages in the area, for example, generally ranged from £20 to £30 per season in the late 1820s. Case details appear in *Catharine Delahunty v. James H. Carter*, 4 October 1827, Ferryland, box 1, ff. 142-5, GN 5/2/C/1, PANL.

55. *Catherine Oudle (or Audle) v. John Murray, Sr.*, 3 or 4 (both dates appear in the record), 25 April 1791, Ferryland, box 1, n.f., GN 5/4/C/1, PANL.

56. *Elizabeth Carney v. Manus Butler*, 16, 23 May 1791, Ferryland, box 1, n.f., GN 5/4/C/1, PANL.

57. *Margaret Mackey v. William Walsh*, 29 April, 9 May 1836, 15 February 1837, Ferryland, box 1, ff. 86-8, 95, GN 5/4/C/1, PANL.

58. After Newfoundland achieved representative government in 1833, one of its earliest pieces of legislation was *4 William 4, Cap. 7, An Act to provide for the Maintenance of Bastard Children* (1834). By its terms, a woman about to have an illegitimate child would swear to its paternity before a justice of the peace, and the purported father was to provide security for maintenance of the child or, in default, be jailed. If he felt that he had been wrongly charged or if the complainant was a woman of "ill-fame" or a "whore", then he could appeal the claim in the next quarter sessions. In addition, magistrates had discretionary powers to require either the mother or the father to provide security of £20 for the child's care. Ultimately, then, both mother and father were deemed financially responsible for the child. Of the nine cases examined on the southern Avalon, five were heard before the passage of this Act and four after its enactment. However, in these cases, the mother's character was never challenged or made an issue.

59. See, for example, Backhouse, *Petticoats and Prejudice*; Carol Berkin and Leslie Horowitz, eds., *Women's Voices, Women's Lives: Documents in Early American History* (Boston, 1998); Cullum and Baird, "A Woman's Lot"; Allyson N. May, "'She at First Denied It': Infanticide Trials at the Old Bailey", in Valerie Frith, ed., *Women & History: Voices of Early Modern England* (Toronto, 1995), pp. 19–49.

60. Backhouse, *Petticoats and Prejudice*; Edwards, *Female Sexuality*; Randolph Trumbach, "Modern Prostitution and Gender in *Fanny Hill*: Libertine and Domesticated Fantasy", in Rousseau and Porter, eds., *Sexual Underworlds*, pp. 69–85.

61. *Mary Keating v. Stephen Kennedy*, 14 September 1773, n.f., 340.9 N45, PRL.

62. *Catharine Power at the Suit of the Crown v. William Deringwater, alias Drinkwater*, 20 September 1806, Ferryland, box 1, n.f., GN 5/4/C/1, PANL.

63. *Re: Mary Jenkins*, 24 February 1794 (this is the date that appears in the records, but the year was more likely 1795, for the record falls between matters heard 17 November 1794 and 20 May 1795), Ferryland, box 1, n.f., GN 5/4/C/1, PANL.

64. *Rex v. Timothy Callahan*, 21 August 1829, Ferryland, box 1, f. 2, GN 5/4/C/1; *Rex v. Timothy Callahan*, 29 October 1830, Ferryland, box 1, ff. 227, 229-30, GN 5/2/C/1; *Mary Place v. John Higgins*, 17 February 1841, Ferryland, box 2, n.f., GN 5/4/C/1, PANL.

65. Edwards, *Female Sexuality*, p. 50. See also Backhouse, *Petticoats and Prejudice*; Cullum and Baird, "A Woman's Lot"; Dubinsky, "'Maidenly Girls'".

66. Order re: Simon Pendergrass, 8 October 1774, n.f., 340.9 N45, PRL.

67. Order, Governor James Webb to William Jackson, JP, District of Trepassey, 6 October 1760, GN 2/1/A, 3/115/1760, PANL.

68. Testimentary practices on the southern Avalon demonstrated a disposition to "share and share alike" both real and personal property among all children, with the exception of primary fishing premises, which were generally bequeathed to sons. See Keough, "Slender Thread", chapter 7; Johnson, "Matrimonial Property Law".

69. *Margarett Hanahan v. Thomas Hanahan*, 31 January, 1 February, 11 April 1791, Ferryland, box 1, n.f., GN 5/4/C/1, PANL. Christopher English discusses this case and interprets the judgment as a "virtual divorce" in "The Reception of Law", pp. 40–2.

70. Pole Papers, 1799–1800, MG 205, PANL. This option was also pursued by other separated or deserted women in the area.

71. See, for example, Anna Clarke, "Humanity or Justice? Wifebeating and the Law in the Eighteenth and Nineteenth Centuries", in Smart, ed., *Regulating Womanhood*, pp. 187–206; Margaret R. Hunt, "'The Great Danger She Had Reason to Believe She Was In': Wife-beating in the Eighteenth Century", in Frith, ed., *Women & History*, pp. 81–102; Norton, "The Dark Side", pp. 183–4; Mary Lyndon Shanley, *Feminism, Marriage, and the Law in Victorian England, 1850–1895* (Princeton, 1989).

72. *Re: Petition of Philip Moloy*, 27 August 1750, GN 2/1/A, 1/115,1750, PANL. There is no mention of whether the child in question was a child of the marriage.

73. *May Dunn v. Timothy Dunn*, 14 March 1791, Ferryland, box 1, n.f., GN/5/4/C/1, PANL. See also Pole Papers, 1799-1800, MG 205, PANL.

74. *Ann St. Croix v. Benjamin St. Croix*, 16 October 1821, St. Mary's, f. 111, GN 5/4/C/1, PANL.

75. *Ann St. Croix v. Edward Power*, 17 July 1822, St. Mary's, ff. 130-1, GN 5/4/C/1, PANL.

76. *Mary Kearney v. Andrew Kearney*, 13 August 1804, N.F., 340.9 N45, PRL.

77. English, "Reception of Law", p. 44.

78. The experiences of middle-class women on the southern Avalon are discussed in Keough, "The Slender Thread", chapter 9.

79. In this regard, resident magistrates may have been more pragmatic and utilitarian than governors, chief justices and visiting surrogates who were not directly involved in the fishery. This may, to some extent, explain the contrast in my observations of the southern Avalon and those of Cadigan in relation to the court's perception of women's "place" in Conception Bay. See Cadigan, *Hope and Deception* and "Whipping Them into Shape: State Refinement of Patriarchy Among Conception Bay Fishing Families, 1787–1825", in McGrath, Neis and Porter, eds., *Their Lives and Times*, pp. 48–59. Cadigan observes a much greater effort by courts in Conception Bay to impose standards of female respectability and domesticity than I have found on the southern Avalon. However, he assumes an unproblematic transplanting of patriarchy from the Old World to the New — untempered by migration and early settlement experiences — and views women's status as secondary within a patriarchal family structure that was reinforced by the formal legal system and male "discipline . . . by the fist". See Cadigan, *Hope and Deception*, pp. 64–82. Such findings do not mesh with the southern Avalon data. Cadigan's study area, though, contained a different ethnic mix of English and Irish, and economic diversification was greater in Conception Bay with the development of the North Shore, Labrador, and seal fisheries and various related trades. It is possible that these contrasting developments resulted in different gender relations within fishing households in the two areas.

80. Other charges against Browne included neglect of his pastoral duties and the appropriation of church property for his family's benefit. See Bishop Fleming to Cardinal Franconio, Prefect of Propaganda Fide, 23 September 1842, Fleming Papers, 103/17/7, RCASJ. Various entries throughout the Robert Carter Diary also indicate that Browne was very much a part of Carter's social circle.

81. Father Ewer to Archbishop Troy, 30 November 1789, in Byrne, ed., *Gentleman-Bishops*, pp. 77–9. Prefect Apostolic James O Donel had already expressed similar concerns to Leonardo Antonelli, Cardinal Prefect of Propaganda Fide. See O Donel to Antonelli, c. December 1785, in Byrne, ed., *Gentlemen-Bishops*, p. 55. The clergy were also worried about the closeness of consanguinity in Newfoundland marriages. See Bishop Thomas

Scallan to Cardinal Francesco Luigi Fontano, Prefect of Propaganda Fide, 6 October 1822, in Byrne, ed., *Gentlemen-Bishops*, pp. 329–33.

82. While marriage according to the rites of the Church of England was the legal standard in Britain through much of the period, in Newfoundland, marriages solemnized by Catholic clergy were acknowledged, and those performed by laymen, such as justices of the peace, were permitted in the absence of authorized clergy. By 1824 statute, Catholic clergy were put on equal footing with Anglican clergy in terms of celebrating marriage, and in 1833 authority to celebrate marriage was also extended to Dissenter ministers. For a discussion of early marriage law in Newfoundland, see Johnson, "Matrimonial Property Law", pp. 120–32.

83. O Donel to Antonelli, C. December 1785, in Byrne, *Gentlemen-Bishops*, p. 55.

84. The information on churching and shaming comes from the oral tradition of the area. Connolly notes that in Ireland, similarly, the greatest disgrace for illegitimacy was borne by the mother and, to a lesser extent, the child. See Connolly, *Priests and People*, pp. 188–9.

85. Fleming, *Report* [1837], pp. 3–4, RCASJ.

86. Michael Anthony Fleming, "Letter on the State of Religion in Newfoundland", 11 January 1844, addressed to the Very Rev. Dr. A. O'Connell, Dublin (Dublin, 1844), p. 18. See too Frank Galgay, Michael McCarthy, Sr. Teresina Bruce and Sr. Magdalen O'Brien, *A Pilgrimage of Faith: A History of the Southern Shore from Bay Bulls to St. Shott's*, Frank Galgay, ed. (St. John's, 1983), chapter 9.

87. Because the Catholic population at Newfoundland was predominantly Irish, a strong link was naturally forged with the Irish-Catholic church. From the latter 18th century through the 19th century, Irish orders monopolized the spiritual stewardship of the island's Catholic congregation: Irish Augustinian friars and Irish Franciscan Recollet priests spearheaded this ministry; Presentation Sisters from Galway and the Sisters of Mercy from Dublin arrived in the colony in 1833 and 1842, respectively, to educate Catholic girls; the Irish Christian Brothers came out to teach Catholic boys in 1875. Although these orders eventually admitted native Newfoundlanders, generations would pass before a substantial complement could be drawn locally. Furthermore, there was an early perception that local people would not make "proper" priests, nuns, or brothers. Recruitment of personnel from Ireland was therefore significant even into the 20th century. See Byrne, ed., *Gentlemen-Bishops*; Arthur P. Monahan, "Canada", in Patrick J. Corish, ed., *A History of Irish Catholicism* (Dublin, 1971), pp. 1–34; Michael F. Howley, *Ecclesiastical History of Newfoundland* (Boston, 1888); Sister M. Williamina Hogan, *Pathways of Mercy in Newfoundland, 1842–1984* (St. John's, 1986); Paul O'Neill, *Upon This Rock: The Story of the Roman Catholic Church in Newfoundland and Labrador* (St John's, 1984); C.F.C. O'Toole, *Challenged: The Story of Edmund Rice and the Christian Brothers in North America Since 1825* (Bristol, 1975).

Article Twenty-Three

The Feminization of Teaching in British North America and Canada 1845–1875

Alison Prentice

According to Solomon Denton, the local school inspector for the country of York in New Brunswick, many districts in his area were having trouble keeping schools open in 1856. There were many reasons, but a striking and not uncommon one mentioned by Denton was the failure in certain places to agree "as to what Teacher to employ." The problem, the inspector said, was that "one party wishes for a female, while the other insists upon a male Teacher; the end is, that they engage neither."[1]

Though most such disputes probably ended less drastically, it is nevertheless clear that the same debate was taking place in many parts of British North America in the middle years of

Source: Alison Prentice, "The Feminization of Teaching in British North America and Canada 1845–1875," *Histoire Sociale/Social History*, 8, no. 15 (May 1975): 5–20. Reprinted by permission.

the nineteenth century. Yet by the end of the century the question of whether to employ a male or a female teacher had become academic, for in most places in Canada, almost the only elementary school teachers available for hire were women. What had happened between 1856 and 1900 to bring about this significant change?

The answer, as in most historical questions, is a complex one, which at once goes beyond either educational or feminine history alone, to a consideration of a series of interrelated developments in the roles played by schools, teachers and women, and in the ideology concerning them, during this formative period in Canadian history. Perhaps the first point that has to be made by way of introduction is the negative one that the "feminization of teaching" does not refer to the entry of women into a role that they had never occupied before. Women had taught school before the middle of the nineteenth century in British North America; what they did not do, in most regions, is teach publicly to any great extent, that is, in large schools outside the home. Our first concern, then, is the making of elementary school teaching into an occupation that was conducted chiefly in non-domestic surroundings.

Though this may seem an obvious point it requires some discussion, largely because the movement of elementary instruction out of the home and into the larger environment of the school has been misunderstood by historians in the past. Students of educational history are now becoming increasingly aware, however, of both how momentous the movement was in the totality of western social history,[2] and how rapidly the alteration sometimes occurred in particular places during times of intense economic and social change.[3] Equally important too is the growing recognition that the movement of formal elementary instruction into institutions known in Canada as public schools, its extension to greater numbers of children, and, over more years in the lives of individual children, does not mean that, prior to this movement, most children went totally uninstructed. Many, on the contrary, we believe, were exposed to considerable "schooling" in the earlier decades of the century, and many of their teachers, furthermore, were women. How many, in both cases, it is probably impossible to know, for useful statistics did not begin to be gathered before the creation of centralized educational administrations, which, in central and eastern British North America, took place at mid-century. But we do know that before the 1840s there were, in the populated regions, a great many small private schools, that is schools run in their own households or rooms, by both men and women, and sometimes by married couples.[4] Male teachers were no doubt in the majority in most provinces before the 1840s, and it is also true that the "public" school of that era, or the school that was too large to accommodate in one's home, was probably almost exclusively the preserve of the schoolmaster rather than the schoolmistress. The feminization of teaching which took place in the second half of the nineteenth century was thus, in the first place, a movement of women into *public* school teaching, at a time when elementary education itself was gradually moving out of the household and into the ever growing public institutions that would eventually almost monopolize the name of "schools."[5]

The second and better known aspect of our subject is the fact that in the third quarter of the century in most of British North America and Canada, women became a majority among common or elementary school teachers. Less well known is the fact that this change was closely related to two contemporary educational movements: the first, a campaign to promote the grading of school children, and, as a result, to promote the consolidation of small schools into larger schools and school systems, especially in urban areas; and the second, a passionate campaign to raise the status of teaching as a profession.

The first of these movements, the physical separation of children into classes or grades within each school or school system, was undertaken largely in the name of efficiency. The chief goal was an efficient division of labour, with the more experienced teachers taking the advanced grades and the less well trained, engaged at lower rates of pay, taking the younger children or beginners. The end result of organizing schools in this way, it was claimed, was that larger numbers of pupils could thus be more cheaply and effectively taught.[6] At the same time, however, higher salaries were energetically pursued by schoolmen of the same era, as an essential part of their campaign to make the teaching profession respectable and to induce well qualified people to remain in it as a lifetime career.[7] Clearly the two goals were to some extent incompatible, as cheapness was promoted on the one hand and higher salaries and respectable careers were touted on the other. The gradual introduction of more and more female teachers at least partially solved the problem, for the employment of growing numbers of women in the lower ranks of expanded teaching staffs made it possible for school administrators to pursue both goals at once. Relatively higher salaries could be made available for male superintendents, inspectors, principal teachers and headmasters, yet money saved at the same time by engaging women at low salaries to teach the lower grades.[8]

As the dilemma reported by school inspector Denton illustrates, all of this could not have taken place without considerable discussion of the pros and cons of admitting women to public school teaching in the first place. Was it respectable for women to teach outside the home? More pertinent to school authorities was the question of feminine ability. Were women capable of governing large numbers of pupils in the not always comfortable environment of the public school? These questions were raised again and again among educators and laymen. The idea of a predominantly feminine elementary teaching force was one which only gradually gained acceptance in British North America.

The feminization of teaching was made possible by three conditions. One was the eventual acceptance and promotion of the idea by leading educational administrators and propagandists of the day. Another and probably more basic condition was the growing tendency on the part of money-conscious school trustees to see women as having an increasingly useful role to play in their rapidly expanding schools and school systems.[9] Between 1845 and 1875, relatively more and more women were hired, and by the latter date they had become the majority among common or elementary school teachers in most provinces. Equally basic to all of this was, of course, the interest in and acceptance of their changing role by the women themselves, and the society that financed and used the schools.

What was the reaction of the educational administrators, a new and increasingly powerful breed during our period, to the proliferation of women teachers in the common schools? The most pressing issue as far as most of them were concerned was the question of discipline. The relative "mental ability" of females was a consideration with some concerned educators, but most nineteenth century critics of "female teaching" were far more worried about how school children could be governed by women.[10] Supporters of women in the schools also felt that the question was a crucial one. Edmund Hillyer Duval, who was principal of the Provincial Training School for teachers in St. John, New Brunswick, put forward what was to become a leading argument for feminization, when he claimed in 1855 that women might actually be better than men at schoolroom discipline. The supposition that females were "not so capable of maintaining government in Schools," he said, was a sentiment with which he could not concur, since he believed that they usually maintained "as efficient order" as did their male colleagues, and "often by gentler means." Duval pointed out that this opinion was supported by evidence not only from the province of New Brunswick, but also from England and from the New England states.[11]

If the question of school government was the chief debating point, the question of cost was the more telling factor. For Duval, and for many other school authorities, the main reason for engaging female teachers was less their real or imagined qualifications, than the fact that they could be obtained relatively cheaply.[12] That this was the essential motive emerges from the literary as well as the statistical records of Upper and Lower Canada, New Brunswick and Nova Scotia. Over and over again local as well as provincial officials explained that female teachers were not only as good as male teachers but could be had "at a saving of 50 per cent."[13]

J.B. Meilleur, who was the first Chief Superintendent of Schools for Lower Canada, reported as early as 1850 that the number of schools taught by females already slightly exceeded, in that province, "the half of the whole number of Schools." The reason, he explained, was simply that the service of female teachers could be obtained more cheaply than those of males.[14]

At first this fact was clearly received by educators with mixed feelings, and criticism of the iniquitously low salaries paid by many school trustees was the stock in trade of educational officials in every province. According to one critic, a school inspector for the New Brunswick counties of Sunbury, York, Carleton and Victoria, writing in 1867, the result of women accepting low salaries was that many of the best qualified men left the teaching profession.[15] In Nova Scotia, ambivalence regarding female teachers came out in expressions of official concern about seasonal alterations on school personnel. Two provincial superintendents of schools, J. William Dawson in 1851 and Alexander Forrester in 1859, deplored the constant changing, "from males to females, and from females to males, every half year — the males teaching in winter and the females in summer." The practice, which was widespread in other provinces, was considered "in every way injurious to the cause of education." In 1851, the argument went that a good teacher, of whatever sex, should be retained. But in 1859, by referring to the ideal teacher in the masculine gender throughout his report, Alexander Forrester left no doubt about which sex he wished to see more permanently established in the schools.[16]

Forrester's views may have softened somewhat by the late 1860's, but by 1871 Nova Scotia's new Superintendent of Schools, J.B. Calkin, expressed grave misgivings once again about what he called the increasing "disproportion in numbers" between male and female teachers. Convinced that the cause was "the unreasonable desire of many sections to have cheap Schools," Calkin believed that the inevitable result of the trend would be a deterioration in education, as few women either reached the higher ranks of the profession, or were capable of taking charge of the more advanced pupils.[17]

In Upper Canada the Chief Superintendency was retained for more than a quarter of a century by one man, the dynamic Methodist propagandist, Egerton Ryerson. Political to the core, Ryerson's approach to the question of female teaching was circumspect. He stated as early as 1848 that women teachers should be "encouraged" and even went so far as to say that it might well be an "advantage" to employ females to instruct younger pupils,[18] but not until 1865 did he go into the matter fully and even then his statement was less than a complete commitment. In the annual superintendent's report for that year, official support was given to the view that females were as good as male teachers in some areas. Ryerson said he agreed with American educationists that females were "best adapted to teach small children, having, as a general rule, most heart, most tender feelings, most assiduity, and, in the order of Providence, the qualities best suited for the care, instruction and government of infancy and childhood." At the same time, however, he insisted that as many male teachers were "as painstaking to instruct, encourage, govern, and secure the attention of little children" as females. Clearly in 1865, Ryerson was still reluctant to commit himself to the view that women were in some areas superior to men. But by the following year the Chief Superintendent had capitulated. Women, the 1866 report announced, *were* best suited to teach the young; therefore the fact that proportionally more and more women teachers were to be found in the common schools of Upper Canada, was to be considered progress in the right direction.[19]

Ryerson's new opinion was cited in at least two provinces shortly after this as important evidence that the trend to feminization was a desirable one. In New Brunswick, where the reception of female teachers was still far from enthusiastic, it was nevertheless pointed out in the School Superintendent's Report for 1867 that many sister provinces did not share New Brunswick's aversion to female teachers, and that in Upper Canada, moreover, official opinion regarded "the increase of these Teachers as a circumstance favourable to the diffusion of good elementary instruction."[20] In British Columbia, official opinion allowed itself true enthusiasm. Quoting *verbatim* much of what Ryerson had said on female teaching, British Columbia's Superintendent of Education claimed in 1872 that it was "generally conceded" that most women teachers possessed "greater aptitude for communicating knowledge," and were "usually better disciplinarians, especially among younger children, than males." Woman's mission, he went on to say, was "predominantly that of an educator."[21]

Thus in the three decades between 1845 and 1875, chief superintendents in at least three provinces had joined J.B. Meilleur of Quebec in accepting female teachers in public schools. Their acceptance, however, was clearly qualified by the tendency, in at least two cases, to stress women's special suitability to instruct the very young. And in Nova Scotia, J.B. Calkin still refused to adopt the new stance.

Whatever their private or public opinions on the subject, however, educational administrators were having, by the late 1860s, to face the truth that the feminization of the teaching force was fast becoming a reality. In the case of Upper Canada, Ryerson's 1866 statement anticipated by only three years the point at which women teachers in fact became the majority in the province, for this occurred in 1869. A look at comparative data for the provinces of Lower Canada, Nova Scotia and New Brunswick reveals slightly different patterns of feminization in each, but that only Lower Canada departed radically from the experience of her sister provinces. Her departure was in having a majority of female teachers two decades earlier, reaching this state as early as 1850, and in the rapid movement of women to a position of numerical dominance (Table 23.1). No province could match Lower Canada in this respect, but slowly in the other three provinces feminization was clearly taking place. Most similar to each other were the provinces of Upper Canada and Nova Scotia, which despite the far greater total number of teachers employed in the former, exhibited almost identically changing sex ratios

Table 23.1   Sex Ratios among Common or Public School Teachers in Lower and Upper Canada, Nova Scotia and New Brunswick, 1851–1871

		Lower Canada		Upper Canada		Nova Scotia		New Brunswick	
		No.	%	No.	%	No.	%	No.	%
1851	males	—	—	2,251	77.8	662	80.2	—	—
	females	—	—	726	22.2	163	19.8	—	—
1856	males	892	32.2	2,622	71.1	—	—	485	56.0
	females	1,877	67.8	1,067	28.9	—	—	381	44.0
1861	males	1,270	29.9	3,031	69.9	649	69.6	—	—
	females	2,980	70.1	1,305	30.1	283	30.4	—	—
1866	males	—	—	2,925	61.1	603	62.6	422	52.5
	females	—	—	1,864	38.9	361	37.4	382	47.5
1871	males	1,115	21.8	2,641	49.8	806	52.6	402	44.2
	females	4,005	78.2	2,665	50.2	726	47.4	507	55.8

Females already a majority according to the Annual Report for 1850.

Source: From the *Annual Reports* of the Superintendents of Public or Common Schools for the various provinces, and the *Nova Scotia Journal of Education*, No. 19 (July 1868).

over the two decades. In New Brunswick, the transition appears to have been less dramatic, but there too, the balance was gradually shifting.

If the provincial superintendents were accepting a trend, it should be pointed out that there were also a number of ways in which they were actually promoting it. The first and most obvious encouragement given to female teachers was the opening of the early normal schools to women. In Upper Canada, male students were in the majority when women were first admitted to the provincial Normal School soon after it opened in the 1840s, and remained in this position throughout the 1850s, but by the end of the 1860s female students became numerically dominant, reflecting their position in the profession as a whole.[22] In Quebec too, sex ratios among Normal School students seemed to reflect the provincial situation, with women in the majority at McGill Normal School when it opened in 1857, and becoming the majority provincially as soon as Laval opened its new normal school to women in the session of 1857–58.[23] In some cases, prospective women teachers received special consideration. In Upper Canada, for example, they continued to be admitted to the Normal School at the age of sixteen when the minimum age for men was raised to eighteen. According to the instructions of the Chief Superintendent of Schools in that province, also, restrictions on the employment of aliens in the 1840s were not, after 1847, to be applied to women teachers. Finally, regulations of the Upper Canadian Council of Public Instruction for 1850 exempted women who were applying for first and second class teaching certificates from examination in a small number of specified areas.[24] In Lower Canada, in 1852, female teachers were to be examined by School Inspectors, but were excused from the usual examinations before Boards of Examiners.[25]

The insidious feature of such concessions of course was that they helped to ensure both the lower pay and status of many female teachers. Yet it is also true, as has been suggested, that low pay and status were probably a condition of female employment in the first place. In New Brunswick, the Chief Superintendent associated the introduction of increasing numbers of women teachers into the schools, in 1865, with two factors: the low wages offered by rural trustees on the one hand, and the classifying and grading of schools in villages and towns on the other. In the latter case, he judged, "nearly three-fourths of all the teaching could be most economically and satisfactorily performed by females."[26]

The association between feminization and the expansion of graded schools in the urban centres can be seen when the sex ratios among the teachers of Toronto and Halifax are compared with the provincial ratios of Upper Canada and Nova Scotia, respectively (Table 23.2). While feminization took place more slowly and a little later in Halifax than in Toronto, by 1861 in Toronto and 1871 in Halifax, women outnumbered their male colleagues in the neighbourhood of two to one. In Ontario and Nova Scotia, however, the proportion of women teachers remained far lower, with only a slight majority in Ontario by 1871 and remaining still a minority in Nova Scotia in that year. Thus in both provinces, the chief urban centres were very much in advance in the process of feminization. A comparison of the city of St. John and the province of New Brunswick in 1871 gives similar results, with 52 female to 19 male teachers reported for the city, or a ratio of 73.2 percent to 26.8 percent, and a total of 507 female to 402 male teachers in the province as a whole, creating a much closer ratio of 55.8 percent to 44.2 percent.[27]

That the more rapid feminization of urban centres reflected the development of graded school systems and professional hierarchies within the school emerges clearly from a look at salary scales in Toronto and Halifax. In the former, a hierarchical pattern was in evidence as early as 1858 in the non-Catholic schools of the city. Headed by a superintendent whose annual salary was $1,200 and six headmasters who were paid $700 each, the city's teachers were ranked according to function, training and sex, and were paid accordingly, with two male assistants at $520, four headmistresses at $400, seven variously titled female teachers at $320, six female assistants at $280, seven other female assistants (usually titled junior) at $240 and three female monitor teachers at $170 each.[28]

Table 23.2   Sex Ratios of Common or Public School Teachers in Urban and Provincial Settings

		1851		1861		1871	
		No.	%	No.	%	No.	%
Toronto	male	12	75.0	20	33.0	—	—
	female	4	25.0	41	67.0	—	—
Upper Canada	male	2,551	77.8	3,031	69.9	—	—
	female	726	22.2	1,305	30.1	—	—
Halifax	male	9	64.3	12	48.0	27	34.6
	female	5	35.7	13	52.0	51	65.4
Nova Scotia	male	662	80.2	649	69.6	806	52.6
	female	163	19.8	283	30.4	726	47.4

Source: From the *Annual Reports* of the Superintendents of Common or Public Schools, Upper Canada and Nova Scotia, 1851–1871, and the *Reports of the Board of School Commissioners for the City of Halifax*.

The city schools of Halifax were organized in a similar way. Seven male principals earned an annual salary of between $600 and $800 each, while the two female principals were paid between $400 and $500; although the thirteen first class male teachers made between $400 and $600 a year, the annual salaries of the forty-three first class female teachers ranged from $250 to $400 — and so on down the line (Table 23.3). In one school which employed only first class teachers, all but one of the men earned $600 a year and the principal $800, while none of the women were paid more than an annual salary of $360 (Table 23.4).

In 1850 a trustee from Hamilton, Upper Canada, listed the benefits of centralized graded school systems as follows: (1) the attraction of more children into the school system because higher classes could be provided; (2) an improvement in the status of teachers; and (3) provision for the instruction of larger numbers of children at less cost.[29] The trustee did not elaborate further, but as has already been suggested in a general way, the second and third goals could only be achieved at the same time through the creation of hierarchies based on sex, with male teachers receiving higher salaries as principal and teachers of the upper grades, while females taught the lower grades at lower rates of pay.

In Toronto between 1851 and 1861, the relative salaries of female teachers, compared to those of their male colleagues, declined and the decline was dramatic, from 69.9 percent to 41.4 percent. In the province of Upper Canada as a whole, where hierarchical patterns had not yet made as great an impact, relative female salaries also dropped, but only from 60.3 percent to 50.1 percent.[30] It is interesting to observe that during this decade the relative salaries of female teachers who boarded with their employers, or "boarded around" as the expression went, actually went up from 67 percent to 71.4 percent of the salaries of male teachers who boarded around. Only salaries "without board" worsened in comparison with men's salaries, suggesting that in Upper Canada the old rural communities where the teacher was an itinerant who boarded with the local inhabitants, treated male and female teachers more equally than the urban centres that were coming into being.[31]

This did not hold true for New Brunswick, however, where in 1855, at least, male teachers were paid on average, semi-annually £26.16.2 without board, compared to the £20.19.8½ paid to women. Their salaries were thus closer, with women earning about 78 percent on the

Table 23.3   Teachers Employed in the Public Schools of Halifax, 1870

		Number with this Status	Salary Range
Principals	male	7	$600–$800
	female	2	400–500
First Class Teachers	male	13	400–600
	female	43	250–400
Second Class Teachers	male	4	360–400
	female	2	160–300
Third Class Teachers	male	2	160–320
	female	2	160–240
Not classified	male	2	300–700
	female	0	

Source: "List of Teachers Employed in the Public Schools," *Report of the Board of School Commissioners for the City of Halifax for Year 1870*, pp. 33–36.

Table 23.4   Teachers of the Albro Street School, Halifax, 1870

Principal	Mr. McLoughlan	1st class	$800 per annum
Teachers	Mr. Sterns	1st class	600 ″ ″
	Mr. Daker	1st class	600
	Mr. Smith	1st class	600
	Mr. McLean	1st class	600
	Mr. Artz	1st class	440
	Miss Graham	1st class	360
	Miss McCloskey	1st class	330
	Miss M.L. Johns	1st class	330
	Mrs. Payne	1st class	330
	Miss Caldwell	1st class	250

Source: "List of Teachers Employed in the Public Schools," *Report of the Board of School Commissioners for the City of Halifax for the Year 1870*, p. 34.

average of what was earned by men, than were the salaries of male and female teachers who boarded around, at £17.8.3½ and £10.13.5¼ respectively, for in the latter case women earned only 61 percent of what was earned by men.[32] It would be interesting if statistics could be found to show how the New Brunswick pattern developed during the decades that followed, or what the pattern was in other provinces for teachers who boarded, compared with those who did not. Statistics comparing urban and provincial salaries generally for the Maritime provinces and Lower Canada would also illuminate the results that we have for Upper Canada and Toronto, and Nova Scotia and Halifax, cited above.

Certainly there is no doubt that in the city of Halifax, hierarchical patterns not only were emerging, but were deliberately based on sex. A directive attached to the Halifax salary list, published in 1870, noted that from that date salaries in the city were to be rationalized so that eventually teachers in all schools would be paid on the same scale, at first appointment. The scale provided that first and second class male teachers would start at $400 and $350 respectively, while first and second class females would begin at $250 and $200.[33]

In the light of these differences, why were women willing to take on the job of teaching in city schools? Part of the answer to this question is of course the shortage of employment available to women other than domestic work. But one must add to this, first of all, the very desire to work outside the home, as the household became less and less the centre of industry and as the domestic employment which had for so long claimed large numbers of women clearly began to lose whatever attraction it may have had. Evidence from Upper Canada in the 1840s suggests, indeed, that to some observers there was little to choose between domestic service and teaching in the early years. The two occupations were frequently compared, and in tones of considerable disparagement, with some holding that female teachers were on the same (low) social and educational level as "spinsters and household servants," while others noted that teachers in general were no better than the "lowest menials."[34]

If domestic work and teaching commended similar wages in the 1840s, any improvement, however little, in the salaries or status of the latter would be bound to make teaching seem an attractive possibility. The salaries of female teachers in Halifax and Toronto, furthermore, were so much higher than the provincial averages for teachers in Nova Scotia and Upper Canada, that they must have held a special allure for women coming from outside these cities, in spite of the fact that they compared so poorly with the salaries of urban male teachers. For many women, then, even the lowest ranks of city school hierarchies may have provided opportunities for respectable independence, and as time went on, both a higher status and higher wages than had been available to them in the past.

Whether it amounted to the rationalization of what had already happened, or a prediction of things to come, the portrayal of women as ideally suited to the instruction and government of the very young must also have had an impact on prospective teachers. In the inspirational text for teachers published by Alexander Forrester in 1867 when he was Chief Superintendent of Schools in Nova Scotia, the author noted that while formerly, "female teaching" had been "confined to private families, or private schools, or matrons' village schools," it had now become prevalent in public schools in both the old world and the new. The superintendent was not anxious to discuss the prejudices that existed against women teachers, but to make a point regarding their "qualifications and position." It was sufficient, he claimed to note, that "both by the law of nature and revelation," there was "a position of subordination and of dependence" assigned to women, and that thus there ought to be "situations in educational establishments better adapted to the one sex than the other." Accordingly, it was generally admitted that the infant and primary departments were "best fitted for the female," while "the head masterships, and the more advanced sections" ought to be reserved for the male teachers in schools.[35]

If elementary school teaching, even at comparatively low rates of pay, nevertheless opened up opportunities to work outside the home for women who, before, had largely devoted their lives to the domestic sphere, and if the propaganda and discussion of the period also helped to steer women into subordinate positions in urban school systems, a third force helped to ensure that they would remain in the lower ranks. This was the reputation, deserved or otherwise, that women had for retiring from the profession after a few years, just as experience was "beginning to make them really efficient" as the Superintendent of Schools for New Brunswick put it. The problem, in this administrator's view, was that their places were then filled by "younger and less experienced recruits from the Training School," the ultimate effect of which was to lower the reputation of all female teachers, whether they were experienced or not.[36] Men too, however, were accused of treating the profession as temporary employment, undertaken only for quick money during bad times, and there seems, at this stage of the research, no way of knowing whether or not the tendency was really more pronounced among women. For our purposes it remains sufficient to know that at least one influential superintendent thought this to be the case, for, once again, the spread of such opinions was bound to suggest to women as well as to their male colleagues that the lower salaries for female teachers were justified.

So far this essay has cited the views of men on the subject of women teachers. What were the opinions of the women themselves? As might be expected, statements by women teachers are hard to come by, but the few that are to be found suggest that, if the majority accepted their low status and low pay, some women at least were far from satisfied with their position.

Elizabeth Ann Inglis, a teacher who wrote complaining of her lot to the Chief Superintendent of Schools for Upper Canada in 1849, blamed her male colleagues and their poor opinion of women for the low status of female teachers. Although, according to Inglis, some of her school trustee employers had candidly admitted that her work was superior to that of most men, her salary, in the course of a ten-year career, had never reflected this fact.[37]

A "female teacher" writing anonymously for the *Journal of Education for the Province of Nova Scotia* several decades later, also felt that instruction by women was "undervalued." Basing her opinion on what she believed to be woman's dominant role as educator within the home, this teacher claimed for women superiority not just as instructors of the very young, but of all ages of children, typing them "natural educators." Female teachers were, in far larger proportion than men, "suited to the work, and from a consciousness of their adaptation to it" continued "to teach and love the profession, while by far the greater number of males, conscious of their want of adaptation to the work they have assumed" left the profession "for something more congenial." The fact that women received less pay for the same labour was, in the view of this writer, "a sad commentary" on the chivalry and gallantry of male Nova Scotians. Although women's claim to equal pay for equal work was the chief message that the *Journal*'s anonymous correspondent wished to convey, she also wanted to see women promoted to positions of leadership in the schools. In her view, it could only be to the benefit of schools in Nova Scotia if, in some cases, "active, energetic female teachers were placed over them."[38]

It could be said that the leap to leadership had already been made, for there were of course female principals in public schools where the school population was divided according to sex. Thus two of the public schools in the city of Halifax boasted women teachers at the top by 1870.[39] But mixed schools rarely if ever had female principals in the 1870s. Furthermore, it was not really until the end of the century that Canadian women teachers felt secure enough in the profession to speak out strongly on the subject of their inequality.

A paper called "The Financial Outlook of the Women Teachers of Montreal," which was published in 1893 by Miss E. Binmore in *The Education Record of the Province of Quebec*, is in sharp contrast with the muted and anonymous statement of "a Female Teacher" and outlines provocative views on the gradually evolving position of women in the teaching profession. At first, according to Binmore, women had worked, as in any new field, virtually "on sufferance," for trustees who could not afford to pay the usual salaries, because opportunities for female employment were only gradually thrown open, and because there were always more women seeking work than there were positions. In the long run, however, "efficiency and success" would always be recognized and women paid accordingly. In the light of this situation, the author felt that it was especially regrettable that the city of Montreal had failed either to promote women to principalships or to remunerate them adequately, and that in this respect the city lagged far behind other cities on the continent. Citing a recent petition of Montreal women teachers on the subject of their exploitation, Binmore noted that salaries for women were so low and board and room so high in certain localities of the city, that some of the teachers concerned were unable to pay for basic necessities like clothing or medical care; nor could they afford books, church contributions or further education.[40]

Though the author of this 1893 discussion felt it was necessary to disassociate herself from some of the more radical opinions on women current in her period, her analysis of the role of women in teaching nevertheless went far beyond the defensive positions taken by either Elizabeth Ann Inglis in 1849 or the anonymous "Female Teacher" in 1871. The abilities of women teachers are not even discussed; Binmore obviously took them for granted. Equal rights for these teachers were demanded openly and a paper printed, in the author's own name, in a widely circulated educational journal. Another small point that should be noted is that the expressions "female teacher" or "female teaching" do not appear in Binmore's paper. "Woman teacher," furthermore, was deliberately chosen instead of "lady teacher," for, as the author explained, not only had the word "lady" lost much of its original meaning, it also, insofar as it retained that meaning, implied membership in a leisured class. Binmore did not believe that teaching in Montreal in the 1890s amounted to leisure; it was for equal work that she was demanding equal pay for women.

The position of women teachers in the decades between 1845 and 1875 would not have permitted such a strong expression of women's rights or needs. Only just emerging from the world of domestic and private instruction into the world of the public schools, women faced much prejudice. Prejudice was caused by fear of female competition generally, or in particular that women teachers, by accepting low salaries, degraded the profession and drove out competent men. It was caused by the genuine belief that women were constitutionally ill adapted to the public classroom, because the disciplinary and organizational demands of the public school were too great. Prejudice also arose from the belief that many women did not intend to make a life-time career of teaching.

Such prejudice was overcome by admitting women to teaching as assistants, as instructors of the younger children and lower grades, and portraying them as essentially dependent on the guidance of male principals and head teachers. Both women and men were encouraged in this by the perpetuation of the myths that the special mission of women was the instruction of the very young, and that nature dictated their dependent status on the one hand, and the male's position of leadership on the other. Prejudice was also overcome by the fundamental fact that women teachers cost less. Expanding school systems could often hire two female teachers for the price of one male; male teachers at the same time could claim, as a result of the employment of women, the salaries and status that so many school promoters felt was their due and an essential aspect of educational reform.

The entry of large numbers of women into public school teaching was thus accepted because their position in the schools was generally a subordinate one. Their move into public teaching facilitated — and was facilitated by — the emergence of the public school itself, and in urban centres, of large, graded public school systems, in which hierarchical professional patterns were feasible. To the extent that this pattern persisted and spread, and to the extent that school children absorbed messages from the organization of the institutions in which they were educated, Canadian children were exposed to a powerful image of woman's inferior position in society. One must not discount, moreover, the impact on the women themselves. The experience of public school teaching, the experience of its discipline and of its hierarchical organization, became the experience of large numbers of Canadian women by the end of the nineteenth century.

NOTES

An earlier version of this paper was read at the Tenth Annual Conference, Canadian Association for American Studies, "Women in North America," University of Ottawa, October 1974.

1. *Report of the Superintendent of Education for New Brunswick for the Year 1856*, p. 71.
2. Although parts of his thesis have been challenged, the most dramatic general account of this change remains that of Philippe Ariès, *Centuries of Childhood: A Social History of Family Life* (New York: Random House, Vintage Books, 1962), trans. by Robert Baldick.
3. For a Canadian example of a sudden increase in the average ages and number of children attending school in a particular locality, see Michael B. Katz, "Who Went to School?" *History of Education Quarterly*, 12 (Fall 1972).
4. The variety of schooling in Upper Canada is described in R.D. Gidney, "Elementary Education in Upper Canada: A Reassessment," *Ontario History*, 65 (September 1973).
5. In the absence of statistics it is impossible to estimate the number of women teaching in non-domestic schools before the mid 1840's. Early official encouragement to the idea of employing females may be found in Dr. Charles Duncombe's Report on Education to the Legislature of Upper Canada (1836) and in the Nova Scotia Board of Education's "Rules and Regulations for the guidance and government of the several Boards of Commissioners . . . " (1841). J. Donald Wilson, "The Teacher in Early Ontario," in F.A. Armstrong, H.A. Stevenson and J.D. Wilson, eds., *Aspects of Nineteenth Century Ontario* (Toronto: University of Toronto Press, 1974), pp. 223 and 229; and School Papers, Halifax City 1808–1845, RG 14, No. 30, Public Archives of Nova Scotia.
6. This point is examined more fully in my doctoral dissertation, "The School Promoters: Education and Social Class in Mid-Nineteenth Century Upper Canada," (University of Toronto, 1974).
7. "The School Promoters," chapter 8.
8. *Ibid.*, pp. 298–310.
9. In "The Education of Females in Mid-Nineteenth Century Ontario," (to be published in *Histoire sociale — Social History* in November 1975), Ian Davey notes the extent to which the expansion of schooling was associated in that province with an increase in the enrolment of girls. But I have found no evidence of school authorities relating the hiring of more female teachers to this trend. On the other hand, the two factors were associated in early rural schools in the common practice of hiring women to replace the male teachers during the summer, when there were undoubtedly fewer male students at school, and in reference to the need for female teachers if girls were to be educated in separate classrooms or separate schools, from boys. On the latter point, see *Remarks on the State of Education in Canada by "L"* (Montreal, 1848), pp. 129–130.
10. *Report of the Superintendent of Education for Upper Canada for the Year 1858*, Appendix A, p. 5; "The School Promoters," p. 299.
11. *Report of the Superintendent of Education for New Brunswick for the Year 1855*, p. 35.
12. *Ibid.*
13. *Report of the Superintendent of Education for Upper Canada for the Year 1860*, Appendix A, p. 190; *Report . . . for Ontario for the Year 1869*, Appendix D, p. 86.
14. Province of Canada, *Journals of the Legislative Assembly, 1851*, Volume 10, Appendix 2, K.K. "Report on Education in Lower Canada, 1849–50." In *Les Instituteurs laïques au Canada Français, 1836–1900* (Québec: Les Presses de L'Université de Laval, 1965), André Labarrère-Paulé notes that the first Lower Canadian statistics giving the sex of teachers appeared in the annual education report for 1853–54, when there were already 1,404 female teachers compared to 808 males or a ratio of 63.5% to 36.5% (p. 179). *Les Instituteurs laïques* traces the gradual increase in the number of women teaching in Quebec schools to the end of the nineteenth century, but, as the title suggests, is essentially concerned with the history of the French Canadian male lay teacher. In the context of the search of this group for professional status and better pay, the feminization of teaching is portrayed as no less than a disaster. For example, with respect to the mid-1850s, Labarrère-Paulé asks: "La profession d'instituteurs va-t-elle au Bas-Canada dès sa naissance devenir la proie des infirmes, des incapables et des femmes? Va-t-elles tomber en quenouille?" (p. 181). The church, he states, favoured feminization: "Les jeunes filles sont plus maniables. Leur incompétence même est un gage de tranquilité" (p. 459). Because of clerical influence and feminization, Labarrère-Paulé concludes, the early promise of a competent male teaching profession was virtually crushed by the end of the nineteenth century.
15. *Report of the Superintendent of Education for New Brunswick for the Year 1867*, p. 34.
16. *Report of the Superintendent of Education for Nova Scotia for the Year 1851*, p. 29; *Report . . . for Nova Scotia for the Year 1858*, p. 253.

17. *Report of the Superintendent of Education for Nova Scotia for the Year 1871*, p. xii. The evidence for a change in Forrester's attitude is to be found in his 1867 *Teacher's Text-Book* (Halifax: 1867), pp. 565–66. For another negative statement from the 1870's, see the *Journal of Education for the Province of Nova Scotia*, No. 48 (April 1873), p. 18.

18. Egerton Ryerson to Mr. Benjamin Jacobs, 1 February, 1848, Education Papers (Record Group 2), C 1, Letterbook D, p. 151, Public Archives of Ontario; "Proceedings of the Board of Education of Upper Canada, 29 February, 1848," J.G. Hodgins, ed., *Documentary History of Education in Upper Canada* (Toronto: Warwick Bros. & Ritter, 1894–1910), 7: 726.

19. *Report of the Superintendent of Education for Upper Canada for the Year 1865*, Part I, p. 7; *Report . . . for the Year 1866*, Part I, pp. 4–5.

20. *Report of the Superintendent of Education for New Brunswick for the Year 1867*, p. 8.

21. *Report of the Superintendent of Schools for British Columbia for the Year ending July 31st, 1873*, p. 7.

22. *Report of the Superintendent of Education for Ontario for the Year 1869*, Part II, Table K.

23. *Report of the Superintendent of Education for Lower Canada for the Year 1858*, Normal School Reports. On the interest of women in the McGill Normal School, see Donna Ronnish, "The Development of Higher Education for Women at McGill University from 1857 to 1899 with Special Reference to the Role of Sir John William Dawson," (M.A. Thesis, McGill University, 1972), pp. 15–19.

24. "The School Promoters," pp. 301 and 305.

25. Province of Canada, *Journals of the Legislative Assembly, 1852–53*, Volume 2, No. 4, Appendix J.J., "Report of the Superintendent of Education for Lower Canada for 1852."

26. *Report of the Superintendent of Education for New Brunswick for the Year 1865*, p. 9.

27. *Report . . . for New Brunswick for the Year 1871*.

28. *Report of the Past History, and Present Condition, of the Common or Public Schools of the City of Toronto* (Toronto: 1859), pp. 108–25.

29. D. Legge to Egerton Ryerson, 31 October, 1850, Education Records, (RG 2) C-6-C, Public Archives of Ontario.

30. "The School Promoters," p. 307.

31. *Ibid.*, pp. 304–05.

32. *Report of the Superintendent of Education for New Brunswick for the Year 1855*.

33. *Report of the Board of School Commissioners for the City of Halifax for the Year 1870*, p. 33.

34. W.H. Landon, *Report of the Superintendent of Schools for the Brock District* (Woodstock: 1848), pp. 3–4; The Colborne Memorial, 1848, RG 2 C-6-C, pp. 3–4, Public Archives of Ontario.

35. *The Teachers' Text-Book*, (Halifax: 1867) pp. 565–66.

36. *Report of the Superintendent of Education for New Brunswick for the Year 1867*, pp. 8–9.

37. Elizabeth Ann Inglis to Egerton Ryerson, 29 December, 1849, RG 2 C-6-C, Public Archives of Ontario.

38. "Female Teaching," *Journal of Education for the Province of Nova Scotia*, No. 36 (April 1871), p. 559.

39. *Report of the Board of School Commissioners for the City of Halifax for the Year 1870*, p. 559.

40. Miss E. Binmore, "The Financial Outlook of the Women Teachers of Montreal," *The Educational Record of the Province of Quebec*, 13 (March, 1893), pp. 69–74.

Article Twenty-Four

Dry Patriotism: The Chiniquy Crusade

Jan Noel

Between 1848 and 1851 thousands of French-speaking Catholics in the Province of Canada came forward in their parish churches to take the temperance pledge. As word of this conversion reached non-Catholics across North America, the reaction was one of pure astonishment. For several decades evangelical Protestants had laboured long and hard to eradicate drunkenness;

Source: Jan Noel, "Dry Patriotism: The Chiniquy Crusade," *Canadian Historical Review*, 71, 2 (1990): 189–207. Reprinted by permission of University of Toronto Press Incorporated (www.utpjournals.com).

and now a Catholic priest was securing more converts in a single day than these earlier workers had won with years of steady effort. Contemporaries shook their heads and laid it down to the eloquent charm of Father Charles Chiniquy. This idea has stood the test of time; the full-length biography of Chiniquy published by Canadian historian Marcel Trudel in 1955 attributed the priest's vast influence to 'honeyed flattery' and other excesses of his oratory.[1]

When we move beyond personal qualities to examine Chiniquy in the context of his times, however, it appears that his popularity was not a product of eloquence alone. The man's impact was greater than this exclusive emphasis on his speaking ability would suggest. One function of charismatic leaders is to mediate between old and new authority,[2] to usher in a changing of the guard. Chiniquy was part of a much broader process in which a whole people took a turn to the right, rejecting radical politics and turning instead to ecclesiastical leadership in time of change. Since former anti-clericals became ardent admirers of the church-led temperance crusade, it seems quite possible that this startling success played a part in establishing the Catholic church as arbiter of social questions in French Canada. Because the church retained this decisive influence for a full century, Chiniquy's contribution to its prestige at a crucial time was more important than his fleeting effect on the consumption of alcohol.

The greater submissiveness of French Canadians after 1840 is in little doubt, not just on the question of drinking but in a general receptivity to the teachings of their church. Historians have noted the transformation of French-Canadian society in the dozen years following the rebellions of 1837–8.[3] Before the rebellions the *parti patriote,* led by the flaming orator Louis-Joseph Papineau, commanded both the Assembly and the popular imagination. Besides objecting to British rule, these leaders also acted in opposition to their own clergy, who acquiesced in that role. Many *patriotes,* inspired by liberal currents in Europe and America, opposed church control in such vital areas as education and tithing. Before the 1830s ended, thousands of people joined the uprising which the *patriotes* led. In the decade that followed, though, the church recovered the popularity it had lost, and a new fervour arose among the people.

There were many signs of Catholic renewal. The clergy grew in number and offered an unprecedented variety of institutions and services. Processions and pilgrimages proliferated, and streets were renamed in honour of saints. The hierarchy began to force an alliance with elected politicians, and an agreement with the Reform party on an education bill was one important outcome. Impressed with this new vigour in an old institution, influential individuals began to endorse its efforts. Etienne Parent, longtime editor of *Le Canadien* and French Canada's leading intellectual, abandoned his former scepticism to support an activist social Catholicism which envisioned priests as national leaders. Another intellectual and former patriote, François-Xavier Garneau, held out slightly longer. A critical attitude towards the clergy surfaced in the first volume of his *Histoire du Canada* in 1845. By the time the third volume appeared four years later, Garneau, after weathering much criticism, was ready to concede that religion and nationality were inseparable. It took some time for the changed climate to affect everyone. Enthusiastic converts to secular liberalism did not relinquish their ideas without resistance, and it was not until Confederation that conservative Catholic influences really stifled liberal expression.[4] By 1850, however, it was clear which way the wind was blowing.

In the midst of this reorientation of French-Canadian society, the temperance movement enjoyed its years of greatest success. The movement appears to have made its own contribution to the church's newfound prestige. It created a large, enthusiastic body of supporters for the clergy's vision of moral reform. It also propelled a priest into the position of national hero. Cutting down on drinking was a surprisingly popular idea that enhanced the status of Father Chiniquy and other priests who championed it.

A distinctive feature of the French-Canadian temperance leadership was the near absence of 'self-made men,' the evangelical businessmen and labour aristocrats who were prominent in other places with strong temperance movements such as the United States, English Canada, and northern England. Perhaps because of the relative scarcity of French-Canadian entrepreneurs, the initiative remained largely in the hands of the priests. Nor does temperance seem to correlate as closely as it did in America and Britain with industrialization,[5] since the movement peaked before Montreal's industrial transformation of the 1850s and, in any case, enjoyed more enduring success in rural parishes than in urban ones. Priestly monopoly of leadership also meant that women played a less active role in French-Canadian temperance campaigns than they did elsewhere.[6]

Two distinctive currents accounted for anti-drink sentiment in French Canada. The first was a desire for a more progressive society on the part of the left-leaning professionals, the group associated with rebellion in the 1830s and in subsequent decades with the *rouge* political group and with the Institut canadien. The other current stemmed from the program for an uncompromisingly Catholic state presented by ultramontane clergymen from the 1840s on through the nineteenth century. This concurrence on temperance is noteworthy in light of the fact that the more usual stance of liberals and ultramontanes was poles apart, with swords drawn.

Part of the reason temperance could appeal to both liberals and conservatives was that drinking had become a serious problem among the predominantly French-speaking population concentrated in Lower Canada (or, as it was renamed in 1841, Canada East). The habitant had kept much of his French culture intact after the British takeover in 1760, but he had the misfortune to adopt the drinking habits of his British and American cousins. Although Governor Murray had reported in 1762 that the newly conquered population was a sober one,[7] things changed with the influx of cheap rum from the British West Indies. When British traders who had recently settled in the country discovered that rum was one of the few trade items which the relatively self-sufficient farmers were willing to buy, they made the substance available in quantity. By the 1790s travellers were reporting that the French Canadians were heavy drinkers.[8] To add to the already abundant supply, local production of alcohol also increased in the early nineteenth century; and the introduction of a steam process for distilling made domestic liquor cheap as well. In 1807 *Le Canadien* expressed alarm that the taste for spirits 'has spread markedly in this country.'[9]

Everywhere reasons arose for taking a glass — or four. As the towns grew, sanitation problems increased, and Montrealers began to doctor their dubious water with brandy before drinking it. Towns also suffered from a lack of recreation facilities, and drinking was one of the few amusements available to the lower classes. This is not to imply that their 'betters' were more temperate. Gentlemen saw no disgrace in bibulous banquets and late-night carousing, and moralists began to attribute the decline of many seigneurs' sons to drink.[10] The bitter climate also invited heavy use of the liquor now so freely available; outdoor labourers, carters, and farmers came to consider alcohol a necessary warmer and stimulant. According to both clerical and lay observers, drinking reached its height in many parishes in the 1830s. Indeed, when French-Canadian temperance groups began to appear after 1837, one society's idea of reform was to restrict members to six small glasses of liquor a day.[11] Forces were in the making, though, to curb this convivial lifestyle.

Particularly keen on transforming French Canada was a cluster of ultramontane clergy who believed the church should play a decisive role in both the social and political spheres. Their leader was Ignace Bourget, who became bishop of Montreal in 1840. Often viewed as a reactionary, Bourget was in some ways a most effective social reformer. He laid the groundwork for a system of local schools by recruiting large numbers of clergy to teach in them. When concern arose that too many French Canadians were emigrating to New England, he helped to arrange settlement in the Eastern Townships and other regions where farmland was still available. As local farm folk and Irish immigrants poured into Montreal, Bourget's clergy created a whole range of magdalene homes and orphanages, hospitals, and asylums, and a school for the deaf founded on the most up-to-date principles.

Responding dynamically to the grave concerns of the day, the ultramontane wing of the church had not yet assumed its classic conservative, or *bleu,* coloration. Bishop Bourget was in many ways a thoroughly modern man of the 1840s. He identified more with the reforming middle classes than the comfortable aristocracy. He seemed to find the nostrums of Samuel Smiles congenial; like Protestant reformers, he encouraged prudence and thrift. He declared idleness the mother of all vice. He urged college directors to place less emphasis on Latin and more on preparing the young for farming and trade. Along with practical education, he encouraged workers' savings banks and insurance schemes.[12]

Another modernizing feature of the bishop's program was temperance. Despite the movement's American origins, Bourget did not dismiss it as a Protestant cause the way his predecessor, Bishop Lartigue, had done. On the contrary, he was convinced that drunkenness was the 'mal capital de ce pays,'[13] that drinking on Saints' days was a prime cause of sexual immorality and domestic strife, and that it was possible to change such customs. Indeed, he supported radical change. By 1845 the prelate had accepted another conclusion Protestant temperance leaders had reached: that total abstinence was the only way to prevent backsliding in a world where there was such constant temptation to overindulge in drink. Like the Protestants, Bourget upheld the extreme measure as a charity the strong should undertake to help other, weaker souls who were unable to drink a little without drinking a lot.[14] Bourget was a key figure in mid-century temperance efforts in French Canada, which would begin with a religious revival in 1840 and reach a crescendo in the Chiniquy crusade of 1848–51.

Although a few temperance societies modelled on those in Catholic Ireland appeared around Quebec City in 1838, French-Canadian temperance did not reach a wide audience until Bishop Bourget invited a hellfire-and-damnation preacher from France to conduct a series of parish revival meetings in 1840–1.[15] Tactics such as darkening the church and recreating the sounds of hell so vividly that women and children were warned to stay away helped touch off a *reveil religieux* in some sixty parishes from Gaspé to Bytown. Many lapsed Catholics used the occasion to return to the sacraments, and a number of parishes erected large public crosses to symbolize their newfound fervour.

To help sustain penitents now resolved on sober virtue, temperance societies were set up at the time of the *reveil.* The response, though not overwhelming, was positive. At the close of sessions held in September 1840 at the parish of Notre-Dame de Québec, a great crowd of men and women, including prominent citizens and people from surrounding parishes, joined the new temperance organization. There was also a favourable response at Trois-Rivières. But Montrealers, who were not noted for obedience to the clergy and who lived in a distilling centre, were not so enthusiastic. The town's elite demurred, and the women did not join. Unlike Quebeckers, few Montrealers pledged total abstinence; but several thousand men did promise greater moderation — and men, as the heavier drinkers, were the major focus of temperance work in French Canada.[16] Montreal's journal *L'Aurore* called upon the principal citizens to support the society, urging that it was not, as many supposed, only for drunkards. Still, most of the early members were drawn from the lower classes, who were willing to brave such prejudice.[17]

Overall, the *reveil* gave impetus to reform. Several priests began to circulate to preach temperance, and in 1844 it was reported that there were 75,000 Catholic temperance society members in Canada East.[18] They seem to have had some impact on drinking habits, too. Archbishop Joseph Signay of Quebec congratulated his people on a marked increase in sobriety. Individual rumsellers noted a drop in buyers, and there was a decline in imports of the hard liquor these early societies condemned. While there was no dramatic change in custom, it appears that a number of people in the region around Quebec City did reduce their consumption of alcohol.[19]

Involved in Quebec temperance work from its beginning was a small, dark-eyed priest named Charles Chiniquy. The son of a Kamouraska notary, Chiniquy had lost both parents early in life. He had been encouraged by a friendly local priest to enter the seminary, and after ordination he began his priestly career as a chaplain at the Quebec Marine Hospital. There he had worked with Dr James Douglas,[20] a Scottish-born temperance advocate, and had begun to read English-language temperance literature. Before long, Chiniquy was convinced that many of the ills he saw at the hospital could be traced to drink. He and several other priests had begun preaching temperance some months before the religious revival got underway.[21] Their hopes had been raised by the temperance work of Father Theobold Matthew in Ireland, a campaign which was said to be creating a moral revolution among his people. After founding a temperance society in his own Beauport parish in 1839, Father Chiniquy perceived such a dramatic new commitment to morality and to schooling that he had a temperance column erected in order to record for future generations the miraculous transformation of the people of Beauport. This ceremony was no trifling affair. It included seven choirs of women in snowy robes, an equestrian contingent, a sea of banners, dozens of ecclesiastics, and 10,000 chanting parishioners, all marching in procession to immortalize Chiniquy's accomplishment.[22] The little Quebec suburb was perhaps a modest stage for this maestro; but his day would come.

As the 1840s progressed, French Canada was to face increasing difficulties. Appalling misery and growing fears of crime accompanied the influx of Irish famine immigrants after 1847; meanwhile, French Canadians migrated in swelling numbers to the United States. Respected figures in the community would join Chiniquy in relating the problem of drink to poverty and crime, and to French Canada's ability to survive in the midst of the rapidly advancing anglophone communities in North America. While the religious revivalists had presented temperance as a path to personal salvation, the emphasis during the second half of the decade would shift to drying up the vale of tears here below.

This more worldly wave of temperance sentiment had some radical associations — most notably Judge Mondelet. Serving first in the circuit and then in the superior court at Montreal, Charles Mondelet was one of the few laymen in French Canada to become a leader in the temperance cause. He was a man of independent mind whom one historian has called a follower of Voltaire.[23] No party man, he had broken with the *patriotes* in the 1830s over what he considered their extremism; yet he acted as defence counsel for those same *patriotes* when they were imprisoned in 1837. In 1838 he too suffered arrest. In the following decade he published his *Letters on Elementary and Practical Education* which heavily influenced the provincial Education Act of 1841. Mondelet had not taken the clerical path to temperance beliefs; his conversion was probably due not to the *reveil* but to the influence of his father, a coroner who had long maintained that drink was largely responsible for crime.[24] On good terms with the city's young liberals, the judge was invited to address the Institut canadien on a variety of subjects during its peak of popularity in the late 1840s. There he dispensed modernizing advice: to rise early, eat and drink moderately, and keep busy; to educate women, that they might raise the moral tone of the whole household; to make tomorrow's society a rational one by keeping the young away from suspicious nursemaids.[25] When Mondelet became a temperance activist around 1845, he introduced a secular and *rouge* strain into what had hitherto been a religious movement among French Canadians.

Mondelet presented alarming evidence to the public. He had determined that drink was a contributing factor in seven-eighths of all crimes committed. Releasing to the press examples gathered during his years on the bench, he claimed that case after case had shown that excessive use of drink occasioned violence, arson, and theft. His hand was strengthened when both his fellow judge, J.S. McCord, and the city jailor also acknowledged a strong correlation between drunkenness and crime. Mondelet further insisted that young criminals were learning their skills in taverns — veritable academies of crime, which drained off the money which should have been spent on education of a more wholesome kind.[26] The judge insisted that the wealthy, as well as the poor, were guilty, and he supported the point by publicizing the drunken misconduct of seigneurs' sons, including the death by *delirium tremens* of a young gentleman at Longueuil. The outspoken judge predicted that a sober population would wear a dramatically different character. Arson, suicide, and drunken accidents would become rare occurrences; public health and conduct would improve. The desire for education and self-improvement would become general and would lead Canada to new prosperity. In Mondelet's view, eliminating alcohol would bring about 'a complete revolution in human affairs.'[27]

When the felonies and tragedies were tallied, it seemed that curbing drink might be a progressive step. Mondelet's ideas appear to have found favour with the young intelligentsia, and discipline became more fashionable than dissipation. *L'Avenir*, the journal of the left-wing intellectuals, exhorted its readers to pass the long winter evenings in study and other forms of self-improvement. Young French-Canadian leaders, the influential journalist Etienne Parent proudly noted in 1848, no longer fell prey to the dissipated habits that had claimed so many of their elders.[28] Many other reformers became convinced that temperance was vital. The editor of the *Lower Canadian Agricultural Journal*, for instance, said sobriety would improve farming in the most basic way, by making the farmer more vigorous.[29] School Superintendent J.B. Meilleur, who had long advocated levying higher liquor taxes as a source of school funding, approved for use in the schools a temperance manual which had been written by Chiniquy.[30] Political radicals such as T.S. Brown and Wolfred Nelson also endorsed the campaign against drink. Brown, who had led *patriote* forces at Saint Charles, became a platform speaker on temperance, presenting 'King Alcohol' as the great oppressor of the poor.[31]

By the late 1840s, when Judge Mondelet called for the abolition of taverns, others were sufficiently alarmed about Montreal's growing crime and misery to agree. *La Revue canadienne* argued that for *les grands maux* one needed *les grands remèdes*. Since it was intemperance that filled the streets with ragged beggars and the jails with criminals, then '*down with licenses for taverns,* which for the most part are infamous hangouts for brigands . . . down with these useless places full of idlers and sluggards who are the terror and the dread, the shame and despair of the towns and villages.'[32]

Another cause of great concern was the growing number of French Canadians who were emigrating to the United States. Here, again, there were those who posited drink as a contributing factor. A legislative committee appointed to enquire into French-Canadian migration singled out intemperance as a leading cause, finding that lumberjacks who frittered away their wages on wild living had no savings to fall back on when periodic slumps hit the timber trade. Thus, unemployed lumbermen were forced to emigrate. The committee also unearthed cases of farmers compounding the chronic problems of scarce land and capital by drinking themselves into such heavy debt that they had to sell out and leave.[33]

As such testimony mounted, those who worried about French Canada's future began to see drink as a menace. The Quebec Committee on Reform and Progress passed temperance resolutions, and the Montreal Institut canadien chose Father Chiniquy as the appropriate lecturer for the subject of 'National Industry and Economy.' Hector Langevin, then at the beginning of his long political career, declared that drunkenness had become so serious that it had replaced assimilation as the great national peril: 'This small people has grown . . . its language and customs will not perish. But an even greater danger threatens it; this time it doesn't concern Anglicization; it's the canker of intemperance that is devouring it, ravishing the dignity of the rational man.'[34] By the second half of the 1840s, temperance had sufficiently strong endorsement to become a French-Canadian national crusade. The little curé's hour had come.

Father Chiniquy's message can be summed up in one sentence: the national survival of French Canadians depends upon temperance. Avoiding the polarizing political issues of the rebellion era, Chiniquy focused on social and economic modernization that the people must undertake together. In the crisis atmosphere of the late 1840s he offered simple, timely relief. Giving up drink might be unpleasant, but it was preferable to the decay and disappearance of a people. By linking sobriety to patriotism, Chiniquy was able to unite religious and secular temperance supporters and to create a mass temperance fervour which had no parallel elsewhere in British North America.

When he gathered a broad segment of the laity behind him in a national campaign, Chiniquy was exercising the expanded priestly leadership which lay at the heart of the ultramontane programme. For, despite the fact that he was well regarded by liberal nationalists, he was an ultramontane Catholic who championed an extension of church authority. He publicly proclaimed the rights of the church and the duty to submit to the pope. With the ultramontane's disregard for the dividing line between religion and politics, Chiniquy pronounced in favour of the Reformers in parliament in a way even their leader, Louis-Hippolyte La Fontaine, considered improper.[35] When the developing rift between Bishop Bourget and some of the more anticlerical *rouges* forced Chiniquy to choose a side late in his campaign, he was to declare that 'all that which relates to virtue, order, justice and law is the domain of the priest, know that well.'[36] His visits to hundreds of parishes reinforced this authority on the local level. When he took his leave, a delegation of the local notables frequently came to thank him for changing their lives. He responded with unequivocal advice about where people were to turn in future difficulties. They must, as he told the people of St Geneviève in the spring of 1849, 'follow their good curé's wide counsel.'[37] This is not to argue that everyone who heard such advice took heed, but it certainly did the church no harm that the most popular hero of the decade endorsed its claims. While the austere bishop worked away in Montreal laying the solid foundations of the ultramontane state (whose symbolic capitol was the imposing new Dorchester Street cathedral modelled on St. Peter's in Rome), the flamboyant lieutenant was out riding the highways and byways winning recruits for that state. The temperance pledge might perhaps be regarded as a pledge of allegiance.

The evangelist began visiting parishes in the Montreal diocese to preach temperance in the early months of 1848.[38] After hearing his orations, hundreds, and sometimes thousands, in parish after parish stepped forward and pledged never again to drink. In the first eighteen months of campaigning, Chiniquy visited 110 localities and persuaded 200,000 men, women, and children to take the pledge. He generated much excitement because, to a considerably greater extent than during the earlier campaign, there clearly was a mass renunciation of alcohol. Believing, as nineteenth-century temperance converts tended to do, that a dry world would be much brighter, the people became collectively optimistic. For once, they were the ones in the vanguard of progress. They said Chiniquy reminded them of the *patriotes* and they called him the new Papineau — for like the rebel hero, he offered them a vision of a radically better future. As the crusade progressed along the dusty backroads of Canada East, it swelled to a triumphal march. Whole parishes turned out to greet the temperance priest with flags and marching bands, militia musters and cannonades. They quickly bought up 10,000 copies of his temperance manual, and they proudly hung his picture on their walls.

Chiniquy continued to campaign through 1850 and most of 1851, towards the end preaching in the Quebec diocese as well. Largely due to the excitement that he generated, even parishes he did not visit hastened to take the pledge from other, lesser known itinerant preachers. By 1850, 400,000 teetotallers,[39] which amounted to nearly half the population of Canada East and a clear majority of the francophone population, had been won.

Those who attribute this striking upsurge to Chiniquy's eloquence are not entirely mistaken. There was some real substance to his message, but there was also plenty of style. The young priest combined his timely nationalism with a platform manner that was almost irresistible. Editors seldom reprinted his speeches, and when they did, they paired them with apologies, complaining that they were unable to capture his effect.[40] Part of this sprang from the suspense he built up by using stage effects, such as sudden unexpected appearances which led to rumours that he had arrived by miracle. When he strode out to face his audience, Chiniquy used his diminutive frame to maximum effect. People sometimes felt he was overrated when they first saw him, for he had the sad, sheepish look of a loser. But he approached the altar so solemnly that the crowd suddenly sensed a greater force than his own slight person at work. One observer reported that during the course of his sermons he seemed to transform himself from a lamb into a lion. At the climax he raised a large golden crucifix the pope had given him and asked various groups in the audience to strike down the Goliath of drink. He ended on an exultant note, urging mothers to dry their tears, and children and pastors to rejoice, together the parish was going to strike a blow on their behalf. Chiniquy's performances moved people to weep.[41]

The curé did not mince words with his audiences. Out in the country parishes, he spoke about farm life and daily concerns, a departure from the usual formal sermon style. Farm families, shaken by several decades of agrarian crisis, were worried about competition from British and American immigrants who seemed to till the soil so successfully. 'How you complain,' he told the people who packed into the village churches, 'of the newcomers who seem to be invading our land, of the contemptuous way they treat you.'[42] Immigrants had already acquired the best town properties, ancient families were being driven from their seigneuries by the creditor's whip. 'Your turn is coming,' Chiniquy warned his audiences: 'Yes, it is with a heart full of inexpressible sadness that I tell you: before many years, if a prompt and universal change doesn't take place among you, you will be driven from your houses, and your children will remain there in the capacity of servants and slaves.'[43] God had deliberately sent the English, Scots, Irish, and Americans to punish Canada. The immigrants were not to blame, for their methods were entirely honourable: frugality, hard work, and a commitment to educating their children. It was almost a foregone conclusion that the French Canadians would lose their lands to these more disciplined people unless they were willing to give up the ruinous addiction that left them sluggish and disorganized.

Chiniquy called town audiences, too, to embark on a new age of industry: 'We ought not to bring from Europe what we can get at home. We have been upwards of two hundred years in Canada and we manufacture nothing, not even a pin or a button. I have been ashamed while travelling in the United States, and seeing their extensive manufactures, to think that we are yet in our cradles. Last year I heard a party of gentlemen on board a steamboat conversing about some *great progress*, which turned out to be the establishment of a manufactory of *tobacco pipes!* We suffer from a want of nationality, a want of union, a want of energy.'[44] Sober, schooled, and enterprising, French Canada would at least, the preacher promised, hold its own among the advanced countries of the world.

One of Bishop Bourget's aims in establishing temperance societies was to replace the political clubs of the Rebellion era, to align the people with the curé rather than the tavern Dantons.[45] There is plenty of evidence that Chiniquy did indeed sway the group it was hardest for the clergy to sway: Papineau's followers. Mondelet had already convinced a number of liberals that a sober people might have considerably fewer social problems, but the populist priest moved reform out of the realm of theory. He actually persuaded the thirsty thousands to stop drinking; he seemed able to reverse longstanding customs in a way few would have predicted possible. In 1848 *L'Avenir* singled out Chiniquy as a priest moved by reason and love of country, a philanthropist who would relieve the people's distress by making them thrifty and sober. Public accolades for his work arrived from Mondelet and his friends, with the judge presenting Chiniquy with a gold medal before a crowd of some 8000 people in a ceremony at Longueuil. One convert in the parish of St Caesaire who combined hatred for the political union with English Canada with love for Chiniquy expressed the utopianism of the hour: 'The Union destroyed with time, and drunkenness gone, Lower Canada will be at the door of all the happiness we could wish for here below.'[46]

When Chiniquy rode into the former rebel stronghold of St Eustache in March 1849, the clerical victory seemed nearly complete. No rebels now, the people lined up to take the pledge. Thanking their visitor afterwards, the villagers compared themselves to the ancient Israelites. In what was perhaps an allusion to the rebellion or to Governor Colborne's repression afterwards, they lamented that 'the walls of the temple had risen up against them.'[47] They blamed it on their worship of a false god, the golden calf of drink. Now 'Moses'— Chiniquy — had come to lead them into the promised land. There, with God's help and their curé's approval, they would find a new life. Any lingering doubts about their public submissiveness to bishop and governor were laid to rest in their spokesman's final ringing declaration: 'Peace on earth to all men!' The sheep may have converted to the stern new moral order during the *reveil*. Chiniquy was now performing the harder task; he was bringing in the goats.

Not only were priests and patriotes reconciled; class distinctions too, were temporarily blurred. Earlier temperance campaigns, in French Canada and elsewhere, had drawn most of their support from the working classes; Chiniquy brought people of influence into the fold as well. By the autumn of 1848, *rouge* and ultramontane newspapers agreed that he had won over 'all of the most respectable inhabitants of the country' and 'all of French Canada's most eminent people.'[48] Mayors and other local notables came out to greet him; they chaired meetings which passed resolutions seeking tighter restrictions on the sale of drink.

Even Protestants recognized the campaign as an unprecedented success. The Rev. William Taylor, a longtime leader in the English-Canadian temperance movement, at a huge rally held in Montreal, congratulated the priestly orator for his remarkable accomplishment. Also impressed was the parliament of the Province of Canada, which awarded Chiniquy an honorarium of £500 for outstanding service to the country and passed restrictive tavern legislation which he had helped to draft.

The fact was that French Canada had become quite startlingly dry. The 400,000 pledge-takers of 1848–51 had clearly stopped, or at least greatly reduced, their intake of alcohol. Taverns, which often closed when Chiniquy came to town, stayed shut after he left. By the autumn of 1848, forty parishes and townships in the Montreal district had closed their drinking places. By the next summer, seventy-five parishes across Canada East were dry. By June 1849, nearly all the distilleries had suspended their operations,[49] and scores of puncheons had been returned by country merchants who had no buyers. Molson's, the largest distillery in the province, which had weathered earlier temperance campaigns without any serious inconvenience, reported a loss of £15,000 in 1849.[50] When the Chiniquy crusade got underway, imports of alcohol sank to the lowest point in decades. Domestic production also hit bottom as the campaign crested in 1849–50. By 1850, Chiniquy had apparently succeeded in turning a society long known for its joie-de-vivre into the most bone-dry temperance stronghold in North America.

Table 24.1   Canada East Distilleries

Year	Gallons produced
1847	645,386
1848	317,840
1849	246,920
1850	79,914

Source: Ouellet, *Histoire*, II, 617

Yet trouble was stirring. By September 1851 Bishop Bourget had received so much disturbing information about his prize preacher that he could delay action no longer. He had just received a woman's testimony — later affirmed under oath — that Chiniquy had attempted to seduce her. This was all the more worrisome because there was solid evidence that Chiniquy had done the same thing several years earlier. He had made overtures to a woman in the parish of St Pascal during a week of temperance preaching there in 1846 — only to be thwarted by the local curé who, notified by the woman, had appeared in her stead at the appointed place of rendezvous. This incident, never publicized, had been whitewashed; Father Brassard, a longtime friend of Chiniquy's, had convinced Bourget that the conduct ascribed had not been serious enough to warrant taking action against the promising young preacher. Evidence continued to mount, however, that Chiniquy was making advances to women he met in the course of his travels. By 28 September 1851 Bourget had heard enough. He wrote a letter ordering his troublesome hero to cease all pastoral work in the Montreal diocese.[51]

Thus it was that in October 1851 Chiniquy boarded a westbound train and went to work as a missionary to French-Canadian settlers in Illinois. Within five years he incurred the wrath of the bishop of the Chicago diocese when he became the subject of allegations of sexual misconduct and disobedience to his superiors. Excommunicated from the Catholic church in 1856, he converted to Presbyterianism, married, and returned to Canada. He carved out a second career for himself, becoming a world-renowned writer and lecturer against the Catholic church. To the end he retained a fiery tongue which he used to inflame the hearts of men.

The most dramatic effects of the Chiniquy crusade did not last. While the orator's disgrace was not generally known, his absence was sufficient cause for a rapid plunge in enthusiasm. Tavern-keepers began setting up shop again when Chiniquy's campaign ground to a halt in the autumn of 1851. By 1852 Bourget was lamenting that enemies of temperance were attacking 'de tous côtés, et avec fureur.'[52] Liquor consumption began to climb again. In 1853 brewer-distiller Thomas Molson wrote to a friend that the temperance movement had relaxed and plans were underway for expansion of his Montreal distilling operation.[53] It is true that many of Chiniquy's rural converts continued to shun alcohol, and pockets of teetotal farmers in Quebec remained for decades afterwards. But in the towns, particularly, many people returned to their old ways.[54]

Chiniquy's more significant contribution was probably that of mediating between old and new authority. Canadians of the 1830s had witnessed the failure of the radical and often anti-clerical *patriotes*. In the following decade the people had responded by turning their backs on radical politics and finding their hero in a temperance priest who championed the authority of the church. Chiniquy's devoutly Catholic phase did not last very long, but it seems quite possible that, as historians uncover more material on popular religious attitudes, we may find the dry crusade helped consolidate the new, enduring power of the church.

Chiniquy had clearly secured a firm hold on the popular imagination; he had, as one contemporary put it, built 'an altar in the heart of every *Canadien*.'[55] The church was slow to dethrone the popular idol even after he gave offense. Hoping to avoid scandal, Bishop Bourget kept silent about the priest's sexual misdemeanours, and the full story did not come out until the publication of Marcel Trudel's biography of Chiniquy in 1955 — more than a century after his expulsion from the Montreal diocese. Upset by Chiniquy's attacks on the Catholic church after his departure, the hierarchy did forbid the populace to attend a series of inflammatory lectures he gave on a return visit to Canada East in 1859; but the crowds simply could not stay away. Fifty years after his brilliant temperance crusade, an enormous contingent of French Canadians joined his funeral procession when he went to his final resting place in Montreal's Côte des Neiges Cemetery. Another fifty years had passed when Professor Trudel observed in his biography of Chiniquy: 'Certainly, in our French Canadian society, one speaks constantly of Chiniquy, he has even become with us an immense figure of legend.'[56]

The mischievous Father Chiniquy turned well-established categories on their head in his own day as in our own. The preacher of the dull virtue of sobriety became the stuff of legend; the priest who would all too soon leave the church became a great Catholic *patriote* in the public mind. By means of his *tour de force* of 1848–51, Chiniquy in all likelihood helped to forge the new and lasting image of the church as guardian of the national destiny. His work embodied the new Catholicism championed by Bishop Bourget and Etienne Parent. Losing the stigma of a reactionary, anti-nationalist force, the church re-emerged as the patriotic champion of reform. Today, when the legends have lost their listeners and the church is a shadow of its former self, perhaps Chiniquy can still surprise us, forcing us to re-examine a nineteenth-century society that has often been regarded as a paragon of Catholic isolationism. The popularity of the temperance movement, with its Protestant origins and its emphasis on Weberian virtues such as thrift, prudence, and industry, suggests a surprising eagerness on the part of French Canadians to come to an accommodation with an anglophone continent. In the 1840s Chiniquy's promises of *survivance* won support for virtues more commonly associated with the Anglo-American, Protestant side of Canada's heritage. Hoping to save itself, little Rome-on-the-St Lawrence crooked its knee to Samuel Smiles.

NOTES

For helpful advice on this manuscript at various stages, a note of thanks to J.M.S. Careless, Cheryl Krasnick-Warsh, Douglas McCalla, Roberto Perin, Wynton Semple, Susan Trofimenkoff, and Sylvia Van Kirk.

1. M. Trudel, *Chiniquy* (Trois-Rivières 1955), 47
2. On this subject see the discussion by Charles Taylor in T. Hockin, ed., *Apex of Power: The Prime Minister and Political Leadership in Canada* (Scarborough, Ont. 1971), 112.
3. Jacques Monet observed that French-Canadian nationalism 'became ultramontane' in the 1840s; 'French Canadian Nationalism and the Challenge of Ultramontanism,' Canadian Historical Association, *Historical Papers*, 1966, 41. Fernand Ouellet remarked upon a 'révolution psychologique' among the bourgeoisie in the same period; *Histoire économique et sociale du Québec 1760–1850* (Montréal 1971), 591. On the growing influence of the church during this period see also Michel Brunet, L'Eglise catholique du Bas-Canada et le partage du pouvoir à l'heure d'une nouvelle donne (1837–1854),' Canadian Historical Association, *Annual Papers*, 1969, 37–51; and P. Hurtubise, ed., *Le laic dans l'Eglise canadienne française de 1830 à nos jours* (Montreal 1972), 4.
4. F. Ouellet, 'Nationalisme canadien-francais et laïcisme au XIXe siècle,' in J.P. Bernard, *Les idéologies québécoises au 19e siècle* (Montreal 1973), 55. On the changing position of F.-X. Garneau see *Dictionary of Canadian Biography*, vol. IX, 'Garneau, François-Xavier.'
5. For a cogent analysis of up-and-coming commercial-industrial centres as seats of temperance sentiment see Ian Tyrell, *Sobering Up* (Westport, CT 1979). In Canada West the movement enjoyed greater longevity in rural districts than in urban areas, just as occurred in Canada East; but Toronto remained a temperance stronghold during the second half of the nineteenth century in a way that Montreal did not. J. Noel, 'Dry Millennium: Temperance and a New Social Order in Mid-19th Century Canada and Red River (PHD thesis, University of Toronto, 1987), chap. 6.
6. Although women joined French-Canadian temperance societies, the president of each local society was almost always the curé, and temperance orators were drawn almost exclusively from the male clergy. This stood in contrast to English-speaking communities in the Canadas, where in the 1840s women were active in fundraising, preparing temperance ceremonies, and selling the *Canadian Temperance Advocate* door-to-door. Like American women, English Canadians began founding separate female temperance societies in the 1840s and appearing as platform speakers in the following decade. See Noel, 'Dry Millennium,' chap. 4. The subordinate role of women in French-Canadian temperance is seen in the Société de la Croix, which became the leading temperance organization in the 1850s after Chiniquy's departure. Women and children were not permitted to join this society as individuals; if the *paterfamilias* joined, the whole family was automatically enrolled. See Alexis Mailloux, *La Société de Tempérance dite Société de la Croix* (Québec 1848), 5.

7. G. Malchelosse, 'Ah! mon grand-pèr', comme il buvait!' *Cahiers des Dix*, 8 (1943): 142.

8. See, for example, Malchelosse, 'Ah!' 142; Gerald Craig, ed., *Early Travellers in the Canadas* (Westport, CT 1955), 8. On the expanding trade in rum with the habitants see Allan Greer, *Peasant, Lord, and Merchant* (Toronto 1985), 157–9, 284–5 n47. Greer writes that rum, imported at low prices from New England and the British West Indies, 'appears to have been the most important vehicle of growth' in the trade of Anglo-American merchants in Quebec. 'It quickly became the liquor of mass consumption in the Canadian countryside after the Conquest . . . [and] the habitants . . . soon gained a reputation as drinkers.' Greer explains that peasants, like native peoples, had 'a limited capacity to absorb imported commodities. Hence the recourse to liquor with its . . . property of creating an escalating demand.'

9. *Le Canadien*, 15 août 1807. On the growing domestic production see H.A. Innis and A.R.M. Lower, eds., *Select Documents in Canadian Economic History, 1783–1885* (Toronto 1933), I, 65; F. Ouellet, *Eléments d'histoire sociale du Bas-Canada* (Montréal 1971), 85; G. Hildebrand, 'Les débuts du mouvement de tempérance dans le Bas-Canada 1828–1840' (MA thesis, McGill University, 1975), 16.

10. On seigneurial and upper-class drinking see *Canada Temperance Advocate* (CTA), Sept. 1836; Malchelosse, 'Ah!' 146–7; and Jane Brierley, ed., *A Man of Sentiment: The Memoirs of Philippe-Joseph Aubert de Gaspé* (Montréal 1988), 69, 120, 211, 250, 263, 380. Urban drinking practices are noted in W.H. Parker, 'The Towns of Lower Canada in the 1830s,' in R.P. Beckinsale, eds., *Urbanization and its Problems* (New York 1968), 400, 416.

11. Camille Roy, 'Panégyrique de Messire Edouard Quertier,' *Les leçons de notre histoire* (Québec 1929), 272. On drink as a protection against the elements see Hildebrand, 'Les Débuts,' 20; *Les mélanges religieux* (MR), 6 juil. 1849, 8 jan. 1850; *Journal of the Legislative Assembly of (the Province of) Canada* (JLAC), 1849, app. zzz. On the excesses of the 1830s see Hugolin Lemay, *Bibliographie de la tempérance* (Québec 1910), 25; Innis and Lower, *Select Documents*, 11, 256; and D. Levack, *Un pionier de l'abstinence totale: Mgr. Ignace Bourget, 1799–1885* (Montréal 1945), 10.

12. On Bishop's Bourget's reforms see J. Grisé, *Les conciles provinciaux de Québec et L'Eglise canadienne (1851–1886)* (Montréal 1979), 52; Leon Pouliot, *Monseigneur Bourget et son temps*, III (Montréal 1972), 144–6; *Mandements, lettres pastorales, circulaires et autres documents publiés dans le diocèse de Montréal depuis son érection jusqu'à l'année 1868* (Montréal, 1887), 11, 194; *Dictionary of Canadian Biography*, XI, 'Bourget, Ignace,' and X, "Bethelet, Antoine-Olivier.'

13. Hurtubise, ed., *Le laïc*, 33–4; *Mandements, lettres pastorales*, jan. 1849, 11, 188.

14. For the bishop of Montreal's endorsement of total abstinence see *Mandements, lettres pastorales*, jan. 1842, 1, 197.

15. N.-E. Dionne, *Monseigneur de Forbin-Janson: Sa vie, son oeuvre en Canada* (Québec 1895), discusses this episode, as does Louis Rousseau, 'Les missions populaires de 1840–42: acteurs principaux et conséquences,' Société canadienne de l'Eglise catholique, *Sessions d'étude* 53 (1986): 7–21. For reports of the rapid growth of temperance societies in Quebec after the bishop's visit see *Le Canadien*, 20 déc. 1840 and 15 jan. 1841; J.S. Buckingham, *Canada, Nova Scotia and New Brunswick and the Other British Provinces in North America, with a Plan of National Colonization* (London 1843), 261. The support in the Trois-Rivières district, which grew to 10,000 temperance society members by April 1841, is reported in MR, 30 mars 1841, and *Le Canadien*, 9 avril 1841.

16. Although the stories in Chiniquy's temperance manuals suggest that ordinary farm wives (and not just disreputable women in the towns) drank, the hierarchy identified intemperance as a male vice, MR, 12 mars 1844.

17. *L'Aurore*, 8 jan. 1841; MR, 18 juil. 1843. On the preference for moderation over total abstinence see MR, 19 and 22 jan. 1841.

18. C. Chiniquy, *Manuel ou règlements de la Société de Tempérance* (Québec 1844), 125.

19. Lemay, *Bibliographie*, 22, reports Archbishop Signay's remarks. Further evidence of the decline in hard liquor consumption is found in Ouellet, *Histoire*, 617; and NA, MG 28, III, 18, vol. 239, Robin, Jones and Whitman Company Correspondence, 1841–3, letter of clerk Elias de la Parelle from Caraquet, 24 Aug. 1841: 'A number of the folks here have joined the Temperance Society and the remainder will do so very shortly; so that we will not require rum next season.'

20. James Douglas (1800–1886), who established a medical practice in Quebec City in 1826, subsequently directed the Marine and Emigrant Hospital and co-founded the city's first mental asylum at Beauport. Physicians played a considerable role in temperance reform. The nineteenth-century movement traced its intellectual origins to the Philadelphia surgeon Dr Benjamin Rush, who demonstrated that many mental and physical illnesses could be traced to the heavy drinking of the day. Though doctors frequently prescribed alcohol, a number of them endorsed the teetotal movement. This was much more true of the United States than of Britain, where the temperance movement was often perceived as an attack on the medical establishment. A number of leading Lower Canadian physicians endorsed Chiniquy's temperance manual and the then-controversial notion that teetotalism would not be injurious to one's health.

21. Early workers in the field included Father Pierre Beaumont of St Jean Chrysôstome parish and Father B. Durocher of Château Richler, as well as Father Dufrene of St Gervais. *Bulletin des recherches historiques* 3 (1987): 12, 44–5; G. Lemoine, *L'association Catholique de Tempérance de la Paroisse de Beauport* (Québec 1843), 7.

22. *Le Canadien's* description of the event is reprinted in Victor Levy-Beaulieu, *Manuel de la petit littérature du Québec* (Montréal 1974), 103.

23. Marcel Trudel, *L'influence de Voltaire au Canada* (Montréal 1945), 159.

24. CTA, July 1836. The strong correlation between drinking and crime was pointed out by a number of judges, grand juries, and prison officials, as well as by the Parliamentary Inquiry into Intemperance in 1849. See J. Noel, 'Temperance Evangelism: Drink, Religion and Reform in the Province of Canada (MA thesis, University of Ottawa, 1978), chap. 4. The mid-nineteenth-century prohibition drive in the United States has been character-ized as a response to the spectre of pauperism and urban crime. Tyrell, *Sobering Up*, 216. Canada's Maritime regions have been particularly well served with illuminating discussions of the interrelation between criminality and alcohol abuse. See Judith Fingard, *The Dark Side of Life in Victorian Halifax* (Halifax 1980), and Peter McGahan, *Crime and Policing in Maritime Canada* (Fredericton, NB 1988).

25. *L'Avenir*, 31 déc. 1847, 12 fév. 1848

26. CTA, 1 Feb. 1845; MR, 22 Oct. 1847; JLAC, 1849, app. zzz

27. MR, 24 Oct. 1848

28. Parent's comments are found in J. Huston, comp., *Le répertoire national* (Montréal 1893), IV, 81. *L'Avenir's* call for self-improvement is found in the 16 octobre 1847 issue.

29. *Lower Canada Agricultural Journal*, Sept. 1848.

30. MR, 3 mai 1849; Charles Chiniquy, *Manuel de la Société de Tempérance dedié à la jeunesse canadienne* (Montréal 1847), preface; *Dictionary of Canadian Biography*, X, 'Meilleur, Jean Baptiste.'

31. *Speech of T.S. Brown, Esquire, at the Union Tent, I.[ndependent] O.[rder] of R.[achabites] Soirée, March 23, 1848* (Montréal 1848), 3–5; Chiniquy, *Manuel des Sociétés de Tempérance dedié à la jeunesse du Canada* (Montréal 1849), 85.

32. Cited in MR, 2 nov. 1847

33. MR, 4 déc, 1849

34. Chiniquy, *Manuel* (1849), 8

35. P. Sylvain, 'Quelques aspects de l'antagonisme libérale-ultramontane' in Bernard, *Les ideologies québécoises*, 135; Trudel, *Chiniquy*, 301

36. *La Minerve*, 21 juin 1849

37. Ibid., 7 mai 1849

38. There are accounts of the Chiniquy crusade in Trudel, *Chiniquy*, 87–130, and in P. Berton, *My Country* (Toronto 1977), chap. 8.

39. MR, 6 sept. 1850; G. Carrière, 'L'Eglise canadienne vers 1841,' *Revue de l'Université d'Ottawa* 24 (1954): 72

40. MR, 10 Oct. 1848

41. This description is drawn from MR, 30 mars 1849; CTA, 1 May 1849; Trudel, *Chiniquy*, 94.

42. Chiniquy, *Manuel* (1849), 143–4

43. Ibid.

44. CTA, 1 May 1849

45. Brunet, 'L'Eglise,' 92

46. MR, 2 juin 1848. *L'Avenir*, 6 sept. 1848, applauded Chiniquy's patriotism.

47. MR, 30 mars 1849

48. *L'Avenir*, 6 sept. 1848; MR, 8 sept. 1848

49. MR, 19, 26 sept. 1848, 1 juin 1849; see also JLAC, 1849, app. zzz; CTA, 1 Jan. 1849.

50. M. Denison, *The Barley and the Stream: The Molson Story* (Toronto 1955), 119, 195, 207

51. Chiniquy's amorous adventures are traced in Trudel, *Chiniquy*, 66ff, 126–35.

52. *Mandements, lettres pastorales* 19 mars 1852, II, 293

53. Denison, *Barley*, 234

54. JLAC, 1859, vol. 17, no. 5, app. 43; JLAC, 1856, vol. 14, no 6, app. 62; J. Douglas, *Journals and Reminiscences of James Douglas M.D., Edited by His Son* (New York 1910), 211; A. Mailloux, *Essai sur le luxe et la vanité des parures* (Ste Anne de la Pocatière, Québec 1867), 129. Post-Confederation temperance drives seemed to rein-force this early pattern; in 1917 it was reported that 'rural Quebec was and is, aridly dry, the City of Montreal was and is soaking, sopping wet.' Ben Spence, *Quebec and the Liquor Problem* (np, nd [1917]), 33.

55. Trudel, *Chiniquy*, 216

56. Ibid., 308

Topic Eleven

Labour in British North America

Lieutenant Colonel By supervises the construction of the locks in Ottawa, originally called Bytown. Twentieth-century painting by C.W. Jefferys.

British North America in the mid-19th century remained predominantly rural and agricultural. In the United Canadas, for example, out of a population of roughly two million, only 135 000 — approximately 8 percent — lived in the three major urban centres of Montreal (60 000), Quebec City (45 000), and Toronto (roughly 30 000). In Atlantic British North America the population remained overwhelmingly rural as well. Earlier in the 19th century the fur trade remained an important aspect of the British North American economy, and it still was in the North West, but by the mid-19th century agriculture and the forest industries predominated, while in Atlantic British North America, fisheries and shipbuilding remained equally important.

Carolyn Podruchny looks at labour relations in the fur trade in the early period in "Unfair Masters and Rascally Servants? Labour Relations among Bourgeois, Clerks and Voyageurs in the Montreal Fur Trade, 1780–1821." She describes how class, ethnic, and cultural differences contributed to create a paternalist labour system. How did masters, according to Podruchny, command and maintain their authority, particularly when labour was scarce? What tensions arose in the master and servant relationship? In her article, "Class Conflict on the Canals of Upper Canada in the 1840s," Ruth Bleasdale examines the economic basis of disturbances in the construction period. How did class contribute to the labour unrest? What do Podruchny's and Bleasdale's articles tell us about class differences in the late 18th and early 19th centuries in British North America?

General accounts of Canadian labour in British North America include Bryan D. Palmer, *Working-Class Experience: The Rise and Reconstitution of Canadian Labour, 1800–1980* (Toronto: Butterworth and Co., 1983); and W.J.C. Cherwinski and G.S. Kealey, eds. *Lectures in Canadian Labour and Working-Class History* (St. John's, Newfoundland: Committee on Canadian Labour History, 1985). For the fur trade period, see Edith I. Burley, *Servants of the Honourable Company: Work, Discipline, and Conflict in the Hudson's Bay Company, 1770–1879* (Toronto: Oxford University Press, 1997). Carolyn Podruchny has also written "Baptizing Novices: Ritual Moments among French Canadian Voyageurs in the Montreal Fur Trade, 1780–1821," *Canadian Historical Review*, 83, 2 (June 2002): 165–95. John N. Jackson looks at the canals in the Niagara Peninsula of Canada West in *The Welland Canals and Their Communities: Engineering, Industrial, and Urban Transformation* (Toronto: University of Toronto Press, 1997).

For an overview of economic developments in British North America in the mid-nineteenth century, see the chapters entitled "Wood, Banks, and Wholesalers: New Specialties, 1800–1849" and "The Steam Revolution" in Michael Bliss's *Northern Enterprise: Five Centuries of Canadian Business* (Toronto: McClelland and Stewart, 1987), pp. 129–92. John A. Dickinson and Brian Young examine the economic history of mid-19th-century Canada East in *A Short History of Quebec*, 3rd ed. (Montreal: McGill-Queen's University Press, 2003), while Douglas McCalla does the same for Canada West in *Planting the Province: The Economic History of Upper Canada, 1784–1870*, Ontario Historical Studies Series (Toronto: University of Toronto Press, 1993).

Four important studies of British North American city life in the 19th century with reference to labour are David T. Ruddel's *Quebec City, 1765–1832: The Evolution of a Colonial Town* (Ottawa: National Museums of Canada, 1987), J.M.S. Careless's *Toronto to 1918: An Illustrated History* (Toronto: Lorimer, 1984); John C. Weaver's *Hamilton: An Illustrated History* (Toronto: Lorimer, 1982); and T.W. Acheson, *Saint John: The Making of a Colonial Urban Community* (Toronto: University of Toronto Press, 1985).

For references to labour in general works of the history of Atlantic British North America in the mid-19th century, see Phillip A. Buckner and John G. Reid, eds., *The Atlantic Region to Confederation: A History* (Toronto: University of Toronto Press, 1994); and W.S. MacNutt, *The Atlantic Provinces, 1712–1857* (Toronto: McClelland and Stewart, 1965). *Separate Spheres: Women's Worlds in the Nineteenth-Century Maritimes*, eds. Janet Guildford and Suzanne Morton (Fredericton: Acadiensis Press, 1994) looks at the history of women in the Maritimes.

WEBLINKS

Fort Langley

http://www.pc.gc.ca/lhn-nhs/bc/langley/index_e.asp

Fort Langley was part of the Hudson's Bay Company's network of fur trading posts on the Pacific Coast. This site describes the history of the fort and the workers who were employed there.

The Métis in Alberta

http://www.albertasource.ca/metis/eng/beginnings/beginnings_fur_era.htm

This site has many resources on the history of Métis in Alberta, including their employment by the North West Company and the Hudson's Bay Company.

The Rideau Canal

http://www.pc.gc.ca/lhn-nhs/on/rideau/index_e.asp

The Rideau Canal is a National Historic Site of Canada. This website about the canal has interactive maps and an illustrated history of its construction and operations.

The St. Lawrence River Canals Vessel

http://www.hhpl.on.ca/GreatLakes/Documents/Gilmore/default.asp

This website contains a copy of a lengthy paper about a vessel designed specifically for the St. Lawrence River Canals, called a "Canaller." It describes in great detail both the vessel and the canals it was designed to travel through.

St. Peters Canal

http://www.pc.gc.ca/lhn-nhs/ns/stpeters/index_e.asp

The St. Peters Canal is a prominent canal in Nova Scotia, and links to the Atlantic Ocean. This site has a detailed description of its history.

Article Twenty-Five

Unfair Masters and Rascally Servants? Labour Relations among Bourgeois, Clerks, and Voyageurs in the Montréal Fur Trade, 1780–1821

Carolyn Podruchny

The history of working peoples in the fur trade has recently become a subject of concentrated interest.[1] The publication of Edith Burley's *Servants of the Honourable Country*, which explores the master and servant relationship between Orkney workers and Hudson's Bay Company

Source: Carolyn Podruchny, "Unfair Masters and Rascally Servants? Labour Relations Among Bourgeois, Clerks and Voyageurs in the Montréal Fur Trade, 1780–1821," *Labour/Le Travail*, 43 (Spring 1999): 43–70. Reprinted by permission.

(HBC) officers stands as an important development in focussing attention squarely on the workers themselves, and demonstrates the extent of their power through insubordination and resistance.[2] A general pattern of master and servant relations existed among most fur trade companies and their labour forces which was similar to other 18th-century labour contexts. Servants signed a contract for several years, agreeing to be obedient and loyal to their master in exchange for food, shelter, and wages.[3] However, labour relations were highly influenced by local conditions. The personality of individual masters, the availability of food resources, the difficulty of work, and the cultural conventions of the labour force all affected the nature of the master-servant relationship. As many fur trade scholars have contended, there was never just one fur trade: it varied tremendously in different contexts.[4] The same can be said of labour relations in the fur trade. Process and flexibility were dominant characteristics in the relationships between masters and servants.

French Canadian *voyageurs*[5] working in various Montréal-based fur trade companies developed a distinct culture which emerged in the early 18th century and lasted to the mid-19th century. During the most active period of the Montréal trade, the labour force grew from 500 men in the 1780s to over 2000 by the time the North West Company (NWC) merged with the HBC in 1821. As voyageurs travelled from their homes in Lower Canada to the Native interior, they underwent continuous transformations in identity and their culture came to be shaped by liminality.[6] Voyageur culture was also structured by masculinity. The cluster of values that permeated voyageur culture and became markers of the ideal man included being tough, daring, risk-taking, hard-working, jovial, and carefree.[7] The voyageurs made direct links between their work and their gendered identity as men. This was a means in which to ground themselves in their passage out of French Canadian society as adolescents, and into the adult world of the exotic and dangerous *pays d'en haut* or "Indian country" where they had to become courageous and tough adventurers. Their masculine identity was influenced by their French Canadian peasant and Catholic upbringing, the Native peoples they met in the interior, and of course the hegemonic rule of their masters. Although many voyageurs became freemen (independently trading and living off the land[8] and joined Native families or emerging métis communities,[9] their occupational culture remained distinct from these groups. Voyageur culture was also different from that of other labour forces, such as the Kahnawake Iroquois, and Orcadians. The men from these groups did not often work together, and language barriers prevented close communication.

As the fur trade in North America varied tremendously during its long history and expansive presence, it is not surprising that its paternalistic structure also varied tremendously.[10] Patterns between regions and among different companies changed over time. Fur trade historian Jennifer Brown contends that the managers of Montréal companies had greater difficulty in controlling their servants than did the HBC officers. The more fortunate HBC officers would rely on the London committee to lay down the standard rules of conduct which served as a basis for governing their men's behaviour. The Montréal companies not only lacked this central disciplining influence, but they also had further obstacles with which to contend. Discipline was not easy to administer while voyageurs traded *en derouine* (out on their own among Native peoples), or on long journeys requiring their support and assistance. Brown goes on to assert that not only were Montréal masters outnumbered by French Canadian voyageurs, but:

> they also generally lacked the vertical social integration that helped to hold the Hudson's Bay men together. Differences of status, without the mitigating prospect of promotion, and of ethnic background meant that relations between the two groups were often characterized more by opposition, bargaining, and counter-bargaining, than by solidarity. In addition, the French Canadians could draw on a long tradition of independent behaviour, social and sexual, in the Indian country.[11]

The particular form of paternalism in the post-Conquest Montréal fur trade was shaped by the high degree of control exercised by voyageurs in the labour system. Flexibility in contracts, frequent labour shortages, and continual re-postings gave the voyageurs bargaining power. Voyageurs' power was also augmented by isolation which increased their masters' dependence on them.

Burley challenges Brown's characterization of the HBC workforce as more rigidly controlled and less independent than the French Canadian voyageurs. She contends the Orcadians opposed and bargained with their masters like the voyageurs.[12] Although the culture of voyageurs was distinct from other fur trade labourers, all engaged in similar types of resistance and agency. These correlations are worth serious note, but the fractured nature of the sources prevents scholars from arguing convincingly that voyageurs were either more or less independent and 'rascally' than other fur trade labourers. The partners and clerks in the NWC did not keep detailed or consistent reports of their activities at fur trade posts, and they commented less on the behaviour of their men. It is thus difficult to compare quantitatively the extent to which voyageurs and other fur trade labourers resisted the rule of their masters. This paper instead focuses on the nature and patterns of voyageur and master relations, providing comparisons with other fur trade labourers where possible.

After the 1763 conquest of New France, the fur trade operating out of Montréal reorganized under the direction of Scottish, English, American, and a few French Canadian managers who called themselves *bourgeois*.[13] These companies, which eventually merged into the NWC, hired French Canadian men mainly from parishes around Montréal and Trois Rivières to transport goods and furs from Montréal to the North American interior during the summer months. They were also hired to work year-round at the company posts and handled trading with Native peoples. There is no question that the job of voyageurs was difficult. They performed near miraculous feats of transporting goods and furs over immense distances and undertook challenging canoe routes. Work at the interior posts was easier than that on the summer canoe brigades, but voyageurs were responsible for a tremendous range of duties, which included construction, artisan crafts, hunting, fishing, and trading. Threats to voyageurs' well-being, including starvation and physically debilitating overwork, came mostly from the harsh environment, but hostile Native peoples and cruel masters could contribute to the misery. Despite the harsh working and living conditions, voyageurs developed a reputation as strong, capable, and cheerful, although sometimes unreliable, servants. The writings of the bourgeois and clerks working in the trade reveal a deep admiration for their skill and effectiveness as workers, and a tolerance for petty theft and minor insolence.[14] This article concerns itself with two questions: why did voyageurs put up with their tough lot without overt revolt, and what was the substance of the relationship between voyageurs and their masters? Because voyageurs were primarily non-literate and left little record of their experiences, we must rely on the writings of a diverse group of literate outsiders, including the powerful fur trade partners, lowly clerks, and assorted travellers to the north-west interior. A close and extensive examination reveals a complex network of accommodation and resistance in the master and servant relationship. This article maps out some patterns in the period from 1780 to 1821, which was the height of competition between trade companies and the expansion into the interior.

The Montréal fur trade labour system was organized around indentured servitude, paternalism, and cultural hegemony. The fur trade managers and clerks acted as paternal masters directing the labour of voyageurs. Voyageurs signed a legal contract, or *engagement*, which established the framework for the paternal relationship. The principal tenet of the contract dictated that servants obey their masters in exchange for board and wages. Voyageurs and their masters, however, interpreted the contract differently in particular contexts. Their diverging and situational "readings" of the legal contract led to the emergence of a "social contract" which constituted the actual working relationship between the two groups. The "social contract" was expressed in the customs which came to characterize the fur trade workplace and the dialogue between servants and masters over acceptable working conditions. Masters tried to enforce obedience, loyalty, and hard work among voyageurs, while the voyageurs struggled to ensure that their working conditions were fair and comfortable, and that masters fully met their paternal obligations. Voyageurs exercised relative cultural autonomy on the job, and often controlled the workpace and scope of their duties. Their masters, however, maintained ultimate authority by exercising their right to hire and fire voyageurs and by successfully profiting in the trade.

Although masters and servants can be understood as constituting two loose but distinct "classes" within the fur trade, it is important to be aware of the ranges within each class in terms of power, authority, and duty. Some masters were junior clerks, bound in a paternal relationship with senior clerks and partners. These clerks were paid a smaller annual salary than senior bourgeois, and did not hold shares in the partnerships which made up the Montréal fur trading companies. Partners were granted voting privileges in business meetings, in addition to their company shares and higher salaries.[15] Engagés also had varying status. At the bottom were seasonally employed summer men, referred to as mangeurs du lard, or Porkeaters, who paddled between Montréal and the Great Lakes. Wintering engagés, or hommes du nord, who paddled canoes to and worked at the interior posts, scorned these greenhorns. Within the canoe, paddlers called middlemen or milieu, were subject to the authority of the foreman and steersman, or devant and gouvernail, who usually acted as canoe and brigade leaders. Some estimates suggest that these bouts could earn from one third to five times as much as paddlers.[16] Interpreters and guides, paid usually twice or three times as much as other engagés, also assumed more authority by their greater wealth and knowledge.[17]

Although the ethnic divisions did not entirely follow occupational lines, the Montréal bourgeois became more and more British after the 1763 Conquest, while the voyageurs were primarily French Canadians. British discrimination against French Canadians, and fellow-feeling among voyageurs contributed to the social distance between masters and servants. Voyageurs lived within a different cultural ethos than that of the bourgeois, one which emphasized independence, strength, courage, and cultural adaptation rather than profit, obedience, and cultural supremacy. These different frames of reference distanced voyageurs from their masters, and frequently impeded harmonious workplace relations. Despite the range of roles within each group, the division between bourgeois and voyageur, or master and servant, served as a basic social organization of the fur trade.[18] Class, ethnic, and cultural difference operated in conjunction to create a paternalistic and hegemonic labour system.

Masters and servants accepted their positions as rulers and ruled. Voyageurs could challenge the substance and boundaries of their jobs and loyalty to their masters without contesting the fundamental power dynamics. Voyageurs' acceptance of their masters' domination was based on a deeply held belief in the legitimacy of paternalism. Voyageurs certainly became discontented, resisted their masters' authority, and sometimes revolted, but it was outside of their conception of the world to challenge the hegemonic culture.[19] Thus, the structure of cultural hegemony was not inconsistent with the presence of labour strife. Although voyageurs participated in the formulation of the master and servant relationship, they challenged the terms of their employment and contracts without fundamentally challenging their position in the power relationship. Voyageurs, clerks and bourgeois engaged in a dialogue of accommodation and confrontation as a means of constructing a workable relationship.[20] To assert the power and agency of the voyageurs does not deny the framework of subordination; rather it looks within it. Hegemony did not envelop the lives of the voyageurs and prevent them from defending their own modes of work, play, and rituals. Hegemony offered, in the words of E.P. Thompson, writing of the 18th-century English plebeians, a "bare architecture of a structure of relations of domination and subordination, but within that architectural tracery many different scenes could be set and different dramas enacted."[21]

What "scenes of rule" were enacted in the north-west fur trade? The mutuality intrinsic to paternalism and hegemony governed social relations and made up the substance of the "social contract" between the bourgeois and voyageurs in the north west. Each party accepted their roles and responsibilities in the master and servant relationship, but they pressed the boundaries, and tried to shape the relationship to best suit their desires and needs. The difficulty masters encountered in enforcing authority, and the precariousness of survival meant they had to be particularly responsive to their servants. Part of hegemony involved appearances.[22] Masters often engaged in self-consciousness public theatre, while voyageurs offered their own form of counter-theatre. Through this means of communication masters and servants came to accept common ideas of the way things should work. The formula laid out in the labour contracts served as the crux from which both parties tried to digress. In the "social contract," or "ritual theatre," masters attempted to evade their provision of welfare, and the voyageurs tried to ease the strain of their work and to control aspects of the workplace. A dialogue of resistance and accommodation kept the paternalistic relationship fluid and flexible, which was crucial to its resilience. Paternalistic hegemony was constantly being negotiated and, in the fur trade, management authority never came close to being absolute or ubiquitous.

Because the NWC and XY Company (the second most significant of the Montréal companies, hereafter XYC) were co-proprietorships, contracts were made in the names of the various firms or individuals comprising the shareholders and joint partnerships. No engagements were issued specifically in the name of the NWC or XYC, as all of the outfitting was carried out by shareholder partners and firms.[23] The labour contracts of all partnerships, both within and outside of the NWC, however, were remarkably similar. Contracts reveal voyageurs' names, parishes of origin, destinations in the north west, job positions, lengths of term, and salaries. The language of most contracts underscored the paternal nature of the relationship, requiring voyageurs to obey their masters, to work responsibly and carefully, to be honest and well-behaved, to aid the bourgeois in making a profit, and to remain in the service. For example, a contract form for the firm McTavish, McGillivrays & Co., and Pierre de Rocheblave, Ecuïer, clearly instructs the *engagé*:

> to take good and proper care, while on routes, and to return to the said places, the merchandise, provisions, furs, utensils, and all the things necessary for the voyage; to serve, obey and to faithfully carry out all [orders] of the same Bourgeois, or all others who represent the Bourgeois, which are required by the present contract, he lawfully and honestly commands, to make his profit, avoid misfortune, warn him if you know of danger; and generally do all that a good and loyal servant must and is obliged to do, without doing any particular trading; do not leave or quit the said service, under the pain carried by the laws of this Province, and the loss of your wages.[24]

Masters were bound to pay the voyageurs' wages and provide them with equipment. The substance of the equipment, and the provision of food and welfare for the *engagé*, were rarely specified in contracts, and thus provided one of the few places for obvious negotiation between the masters and servants.[25] Custom came to dictate that equipment consisted of one blanket, one shirt, and one pair of trousers.[26]

In order to enforce the terms of the legal contracts, bourgeois tried to regulate their servants through legal and state sanctions. In January 1778, an official of the NWC sent a memorandum to Governor Guy Carleton asking him "that it be published before the Traders and their Servants that the latter must strictly conform to their agreements, which should absolutely be in writing or printed, and before witnesses if possible, as many disputes arise from want of order in this particular." The memorandum goes on to ask that men be held to pay their debts with money or service and that traders hiring men already engaged to another company should purchase their contracts.[27] Lower Canadian law eventually recognized the legality of notarial fur trade contracts, and a 1796 ordinance forbade *engagés* to transgress the terms or desert the service.[28] In Lower Canada, the legislature empowered Justices of the Peace (JPs) to create and oversee the rules and regulations for master and servant relations.[29]

Bourgeois on occasion turned to the law to enforce the terms of the contract. Voyageurs were charged with breaking contracts, mainly for deserting, rather than for insolence or disobedience.[30] The files of the Court of Quarter Sessions in the District of Montréal reveal a range of cases: voyageurs accepted wages from one employer while already working for another, they obtained advance wages without appearing for the job, and they deserted the service.[31] Cases of voyageur desertion and theft can also be found in the records of the Montréal civil court.[32] In 1803, the British government passed the Canada Jurisdiction Act by which criminal offenses committed in the "Indian territories" could be tried in Lower Canada, and the five JPs named were all prominent fur trade bourgeois, although the court's power remained limited.[33] It is difficult to determine the effectiveness of court action to control workers, especially since prosecution rates have not survived in most of the records. Presumably the bourgeois would not continue to press charges if their efforts did not pay off. Yet pressing charges against voyageurs did not seem to deter them from continuing to desert, cheat contract terms, and steal from their employers.

Other efforts to control workers included cooperation between companies to limit contract-jumping and blacklisting deserters. In 1800 NWC officer William McGillivray wrote to Thomas Forsyth of Forsyth, Ogilvy and McKenzie:

> I agree with you that protecting Deserters would be a dangerous Practice and very pernicious to the Trade and fully sensible of this when any Man belonging to People opposed to the North West Company have happened to come to our Forts, we have told the Master of such to come for them and that they should not be in any way wise prevented from taking them back.

McGillivray assured Forsyth that he was not protecting one of their deserters and had told his master to come and claim him. He went on to discuss the case of the NWC *engagé*, Poudriés, who was allowed to return to Montréal because of ill health on the understanding that he was to pay his debt in Montréal or return to the north west to serve out his time. McGillivray explained that when the NWC discovered that Poudriés engaged himself to Forsyth, Ogilvy & McKenzie they attempted to arrest him. McGillivray accused Forsyth of protecting him, and requested that he be returned to NWC service or that his debt be paid, continuing:

> With regard to paying advances made to Men I wish to be explicit, we have alwise made it a practice and will continue so to do to pay every shilling that Men whom we hire may acknowledge to their former Master such Men being free on the Ground. We hire no Men who owe their Descent considering this a principle not to be deviated from in determining to adhere strictly to it we cannot allow others to treat us in a different manner — if a Man was Free at the Point au Chapeau we do not consider him at liberty to hire until he has gone to it.[34]

McGillivray decided to purchase voyageurs' engagements from their previous masters rather than paying their wages, and warned other fur trade companies against hiring any deserters.[35] The other fur trade companies soon followed suit.[36]

Voyageurs occasionally took their employing masters to court, most often to sue for wages.[37] Cases of this kind were widespread in all sorts of labour contracts in New France and Lower Canada, so it is not surprising that voyageurs followed suit. However, servants were not usually successful in claiming wages for jobs which they had deserted, or where they had disobeyed their masters.[38] The colonial government and legal system supported fur trade labour contracts, but the contracts were difficult to enforce because of the limits of the policing and justice systems in the north west. Masters thus relied more on the "social contract" which they were constantly negotiating with their servants.

Masters and voyageurs had different views of their "social contract," which frequently resulted in rocky negotiations. They agreed that servants were supposed to obey their masters' requirements to trade successfully in exchange for fair board and wages. Their divergent readings of "the deal" were based on different ideas of what was fair. Establishing a mutual understanding of obligations was easier if servants respected their masters. Servants respected those masters who they regarded as tough but evenhanded.

How did masters command and maintain their authority? In many historic circumstances, masters turned to physical might or the law as a principal vehicle for hegemony. But at the height of fur trade competition, the arm of the law was short and the high value of labour discouraged masters from physically intimidating their workers. Masters relied on paternalistic authority as an accepted ideology to justify and bolster their might. The ideology was expressed in the "theatre of daily rule."[39] Bourgeois and clerks imposed their authority believing that they were superior and were obliged to control their inferior servants. Masters also contributed to a dominant public discourse of their superiority, or enacted the "theatre of rule" in material ways. They ensured their access to more and better food, fancier clothing, and better sleeping conditions than voyageurs.[40] Further in the interior, away from the larger fur trade administrative centres, bourgeois and clerks had to rely on inexpensive symbols and actions to enforce their authority. Carefully maintained social isolation, differential work roles, control over scarce resources, reputation, and ability all symbolized masters' authority.[41]

Differentiation in work roles was very apparent in travel. Bourgeois were usually passengers aboard canoes, and only helped their men paddle and portage in cases of extreme jeopardy. At times the rituals of travel situated bourgeois at the head of a great procession. In his reminiscences of a fur trading career, Alexander Ross described how the light canoe, used for transporting men and mail quickly through the interior, clearly positioned the bourgeois as a social superior:

> The bourgeois is carried on board his canoe upon the back of some sturdy fellow generally appointed for this purpose. He seats himself on a convenient mattress, somewhat low in the centre of his canoe; his gun by his side, his little cherubs fondling around him, and his faithful spaniel lying at his feet. No sooner is he at his ease, than his pipe is presented by his attendant, and he then begins smoking, while his silken banner undulates over the stern of his painted vessel.[42]

HBC surveyor Philip Turnor, both envied and criticized that the NWC

> give Men which never saw an Indian One Hundred Pounds pr Annum, his Feather Bed carried in the Canoe, his Tent which is exceedingly good, pitched for him, his Bed made and he and his girl carried in and out of the Canoe and when in the Canoe never touches a Paddle unless for his own pleasure all of these indulgences.[43]

At posts, bourgeois and clerks did not participate in the vigorous round of activities which kept the post functioning smoothly, such as constructing and maintaining houses, building furniture, sleighs and canoes, gathering firewood, hunting, and preparing food. Rather, these masters kept accounts, managed the wares and provisions, and initiated trade with Native peoples.

Bourgeois and clerks were encouraged to keep a distance from their labourers. Junior clerks in particular, whose authority in isolated wintering posts was threatened by experienced labourers, had to establish firm lines of control. When the NWC clerk George Gordon was still a novice, he received advice from a senior clerk, George Moffatt, to be independent, confident, very involved in the trade, and

> Mixt. <u>very seldom</u> with the Men, rather retire within yourself, than make them your companions.— I do not wish to insinuate that you should be haughty — the contrary — affability with them at times, may get You esteme, while the observance of a proper distance, will command you respect, and procure from them ready obedience to your orders.[44]

In 1807, John McDonald of Garth was sent out as a novice to take over the NWC's Red River Department which was notorious for its corruption and difficult men. A French Canadian interpreter, who had long been in the district managing to secure great authority among voyageurs and Native peoples, had to be reminded by McDonald: "you are to act under me, you have no business to think, it is for me to do so and not for you, you are to obey."[45]

Probably the greatest challenges the bourgeois and clerks faced in asserting authority and controlling workers came from the circumstance of the fur trade itself — the great distances along fur trade routes and between posts, and the difficulties of transportation and communication. The arduous job of traversing an unfamiliar and inhospitable terrain led to frequent accidents. The incomplete nature of the sources obscures any measurement of mortality rates, but the writings of the bourgeois are filled with literally hundreds of cases of trading parties losing their way along routes, injuring themselves or perishing in canoeing accidents, being attacked by bears, and starving, to name a few of the mishaps.[46]

Masters and voyageurs dealt with the danger which infused the fur trade in a particular way. Both social groups idealized strength, toughness, and fortitude. Voyageurs competed with each other to perform awesome feats of dexterity and endurance.[47] They played rough and risk-taking games and tried to push themselves beyond their limits. In doing so, they tried to distract themselves from, and desensitize themselves to the risks inherent in fur trading and the deaths, accidents, and illnesses around them. Rather than being overwhelmed by the danger and tragedy, they made a virtue of necessity and flaunted their indifference. By incorporating manly violence and aggression into daily life, in their competitions and brawling, men could toughen themselves for the challenges of their jobs.[48] For example, in August of 1794, the Athabasca brigade raced the Fort George brigade from the south side to the north side of Lake Winnipeg. Duncan McGillivray, in charge of the Fort George crew, explained that

> The Athabasca Men piqued themselves on a Superiority they were supposed to have over the other bands of the North for expeditions marching [canoeing], and ridiculed our men *a la façon du Nord* for pretending to dispute a point that universally decided in *their* favor.

Despite the fact that the Fort George crew was more heavily loaded than the Athabasca crew, the two groups were evenly matched. They pressed on for 48 hours before agreeing to call a truce and set up camp on shore. Not surprisingly, McGillivray was delighted with their progress.[49] During a return trip to Montréal in 1815, John McDonald's crew of Canadians raced McGillivray's crew of Iroquois all day. The Canadians allowed the Iroquois to pull ahead at the start of the day, but they raced past them in the evening.[50]

Bourgeois encouraged the 'rugged' ethos of the voyageurs, which conveniently suited their agenda for quick, efficient, and profitable fur trade operations.[51] In some instances, bourgeois had to remind voyageurs of their manly pride in skill and endurance. During a particularly difficult journey, Alexander Mackenzie began to hear murmurs of discontent. The desire to turn back increased when one of the canoes was lost in a stretch of rapids. In order to encourage them to continue, Mackenzie

> brought to their recollection, that I did not deceive them, and that they were made acquainted with the difficulties and dangers they must expect to encounter, before they engaged to accompany me. I also urged the honour of conquering disasters, and the disgrace that would attend them on their return home, without having attained the object of the expedition. Nor did I fail to mention the courage and resolution which was the peculiar boast of the North men; and that I depended on them, at that moment, for the maintenance of their character. . . . my harangue produced the desired effect, and a very general assent appeared to go wherever I should lead the way.[52]

Whether or not Mackenzie's "harangue produced the desired effect," it seems clear that both bourgeois and voyageurs valued the strength and courage required to paddle farther into the north west.

Accommodation among voyageurs, clerks and bourgeois made up part of the master and servant relationship. They worked closely for long periods of time, often shared living quarters, and faced many calamities and adventures together. As many disputes were caused by shortages of provisions, the surest way in which bourgeois and clerks could ensure loyalty was to provide plenty of good food for their men. Bourgeois and clerks fostered accommodation by meeting other paternal duties, such as attempting to protect their men from dangers in the workplace, providing medicines, and treating men with respect. Masters also solidified their hegemony through generosity and kindness, reminiscent of a kind of feudal largesse. Extra rations of alcohol and food, known as *regales*, were provided on significant occasions, such as settling accounts and signing new engagements.[53] Routine "rewards," such as the customary provision of drams at portages, were also incorporated into the more tedious aspects of fur trade work.[54] Sometimes masters' generosity was self-interested. When McKay gave his men moose skin to make themselves shoes, mittens, and blankets to last them through the winter, he warned them that "we have a strong opposition to contend with this year" and that they must be ready to go at a moment's notice.[55] His gifts no doubt consolidated his authority, but they also helped the voyageurs to perform their duties more effectively.

Despite these points of accommodation, harmony in the workplace was continually under stress as voyageur resistance to master authority characterized labour relations in the fur trade. Voyageurs' discontents focused on such unsuitable working and living conditions as poor rations, or unreasonable demands by masters. Voyageurs turned to strategies such as complaining to their bourgeois and attempting to bargain for better working conditions to highlight their concerns and initiate change. Like the Orcadians working for the HBC, individual action was a more common form of worker resistance than was organized collective protest.[56]

Complaining by the voyageurs became a form of "counter-theatre," which contested bourgeois hegemonic prerogatives. Just as the bourgeois often asserted their hegemony in a theatrical style, especially with canoe processions, the voyageurs also asserted their presence by "a theatre of threat and sedition."[57] In one illuminating example in the summer of 1804, while trying to travel through low water and marshes, Duncan Cameron's men ceaselessly complained about the miserable conditions and difficulty of the work. They cursed themselves as "Blockheads" for coming to "this Infernal Part of the Country", as they called it, damning the mud, damning the lack of clean water to quench their thirst, and damning the first person who chose that route. Cameron tried to be patient and cheerful with them, as he knew that complaining was their custom.[58] Voyageurs sometimes chose to limit the theatre of resistance to a small, and perhaps more effective scale by complaining to their bourgeois in private, so that they would not appear weak in front of the other men. During a difficult trip from Kaministiquia to Pembina, Alexander Henry the Younger commented that little or nothing was said during the day when the men had "a certain shame or bashfulness about complaining openly," but at night everyone came to complain about bad canoes, ineffective co-workers, and shortages of gum, wattap, and grease.[59] Often voyageurs restricted their complaining in front of their bourgeois to avoid losing favour. If they approached the bourgeois or clerk individually with strategic concerns, their demands were more likely to be met than if they openly abused their masters for unspecified grievances.[60]

When labour was scarce, men often bargained for better wages, both individually and in groups. In a large and organized show of resistance in the summer of 1803, men at Kaministiquia refused to work unless they received a higher salary.[61] However, these types of group efforts to increase wages were more rare than the relatively common occurrence of men trying to individually bargain for better remuneration or conditions. Daniel Sutherland of the XYC instructed his recruiting agent in Montréal, St. Valur Mailloux, to refuse demands made by a couple of *engagés* for higher wages, and to appease the men with small presents. One *engagé* named Cartier caused turmoil by telling the XYC wintering partners that Mailloux was hiring men at significantly higher wages and by asking them for his pay to be increased to that amount. Sutherland became angry with Mailloux, warning him "Always [offer more to] oarsman and steersman, but never exceed the price that I told you for going and coming [paid to the paddlers].[62] Voyageurs could refuse to do tasks outside the normal range of their duties without extra pay as a means of increasing their wages.[63] They also frequently demanded better working conditions. Most often their concerns centred on safety, and they could refuse to take unreasonable risks.[64] Men with valued skills and knowledge, such as interpreters and guides, were in the best position to bargain for better working conditions and more pay.[65] Because fur trade labour was frequently scarce, and the mortality rate was high, skilled men were valued. Masters often overlooked servant transgressions and met servant demands in an effort to maintain their services.

Voyageurs also attempted to deceive their masters by pretending to be ill, or by lying about resources and Native peoples in the area to evade work. It is difficult to judge the extent to which voyageurs tried to trick their masters, especially when they were successful. However, hints of this practice, and suspicions of bourgeois and clerks emerge frequently in fur trade journals, suggesting that the practice was widespread. In December 1818, stationed near the Dauphin River, George Nelson became frustrated with one of his men, Welles, who frequently sneaked in "holiday" time by travelling slowly or claiming to be lost.[66] Less suspecting bourgeois probably did not catch the "dirty tricks" more careful voyageurs played on them regularly. Some masters, however, questioned their men's dubious actions and sent out "spies" to ensure that voyageurs were working honestly.[67] Other deceptions were of a more serious nature. Alexander Mackenzie was suspicious that his interpreters were not telling prospective Native trading partners what Mackenzie intended, which could have serious repercussions for the trade.[68]

When efforts to deceive their masters were frustrated, voyageurs could become sullen and indolent, working slowly and ineffectively, and even openly defying bourgeois orders. In one case in the fall of 1800, while trying to set out from Fort Chipewyan, James Porter had to threaten to seize the wages of a man who refused to embark. When the voyageur reluctantly complied he swore that the devil should take him for submitting to the bourgeois.[69] More serious breaches of the master and servant contract included stealing provisions from cargo. Though Edward Umphreville kept up a constant watch of the merchandise in his canoes, a father and son managed to steal a 9 gallon keg of mixed liquor.[70] George Nelson described the pilfering of provisions as routine.[71] Men also sometimes stole provisions to give extra food to their girlfriends or wives.[72] For the Orcadians working in the HBC service, Burley characterizes this type of counter-theatre — working ineffectively and deceiving masters — as both a neglect of duty and as an attempt to control the work process.[73] The same applies to the voyageurs.

One area of particular unease between voyageurs and masters was the issue of voyageurs freetrading with Native peoples. Unlike the HBC, the Montréal fur trading companies did not prohibit voyageurs from trading with Native peoples on the side to augment their income; some masters even expected them to do so as long as they did not abuse the privilege.[74] However, masters were often upset to find their men trading with Native peoples, because they wanted to concentrate the profit into their company's hands, and considered freetrading as "contrary to the established rules of the trade and the general practice among the natives."[75] In an 1803 trial over trading jurisdiction, John Charles Stuart, a NWC clerk, testified that when any men brought skins from the wintering grounds for the purpose of trading on their private account, "it was by a Special Favour" granted by their bourgeois, supported in the clause "Part de pactons" in their contracts. Although the practice was customary, the bourgeois retained the right to grant or refuse it.[76] After the 1804 merger of the XYC and NWC, the bourgeois decided to restrict private trade to increase profitability in the newly reformed company. Any man caught with more than two buffalo robes or two dressed skins, or one of each, would be fined 50 livres NW currency, and any employee caught trafficking with "petty traders or Montréal men" would forfeit his wages. The bourgeois were able to enforce this new restriction because the merger had created a surplus of men, so that employment became tenuous, and many voyageurs were concerned that their contracts would not be renewed.[77] In the minutes of the 1806 annual meeting, NWC partners agreed to ban men from bringing furs out of the interior in order to discourage petty trading.[78]

Voyageurs sometimes moved out of the "counter-theatre of daily resistance" to engage in "swift, direct action" against their masters' rule. Deserting the service was an outright breach of the master and servant contract.[79] Desertion should not be viewed as the single and straight-forward phenomenon of voyageurs quitting their jobs. Rather, voyageurs deserted for a variety of purposes. Temporary desertions could provide a form of vacation, a ploy for renegotiating terms of employment, and a means of shopping for a better job. Men deserted when they were ill and needed time to recuperate.[80] Men also deserted when they thought their lives might be in danger, as was the case in March 1805, when servants of both the NWC and XYC ran off from the fishery at Lac La Pluie because they feared the Native people there wanted to kill them.[81] Voyageurs felt they could desert because they had a clear notion of their rights as workers which was instilled by the reciprocal obligations of paternalism. This may be one of the more significant differences between Orcadians working for the HBC and the voyageurs. Orcadians did not desert very often because of the lack of "desirable places to go." Orcadians would most often desert to NWC posts, while voyageurs more often became freemen, joined Native families, or returned to the St. Lawrence valley.[82]

As part of the continual negotiation of the master and servant "social contract," bourgeois and clerks responded to voyageurs' counter-theatre with intense performances of authority. They disciplined their men for transgressions of the master and servant contract, and sought to encourage voyageur obedience. Servant privileges, such as the provision of regales or sale of liquor might be curtailed or denied.[83] Bourgeois and clerks also frequently humiliated and intimidated their men. In one case during a journey to the Peace River in summer 1793, Alexander Mackenzie was confronted with a man who refused to embark in the canoe. He wrote:

> This being the first example of absolute disobedience which had yet appeared during the course
> of our expedition, I should not have passed it over without taking some very severe means to
> prevent a repetition of it; but as he had the general character of a simple fellow, among his

companions, and had been frightened out of what little sense he possessed, by our late dangers, I rather preferred to consider him as an object of ridicule and contempt for his pusillanimous behaviour; though, in fact, he was a very useful, active, and laborious man.[84]

He also confronted the chief canoe maker during the same trip about his laziness and bad attitude. Mackenzie described the man as mortified at being singled out.[85] This kind of ritualized public shaming reinforced masculine ideals of effectiveness and skill. On an expedition to the Missouri in 1805, one of Larocque's men wished to remain with Charles McKenzie's party. Larocque became angry and told the man his courage failed him like an old woman, which threw the man into a violent fit of anger.[86] On occasion, a voyageur could be whipped for delinquency,[87] and bourgeois and clerks sometimes used the fear of starvation as a means of asserting authority over their men.[88]

In cases of severe dereliction, bourgeois could take the liberty of firing their employees.[89] In some cases, voyageurs were happy to be let go because they desired to become freemen. Nelson fired Joseph Constant, for example, for his "fits of ill humour without cause and Constant went on to become a prosperous independent trader."[90] However, it was a very serious matter when voyageurs decided to quit. Bourgeois and clerks made efforts to recoup deserters, and could punish them with confinement.[91]

The usual difficulties of the weather, accidents, and the constant challenge of the strenuous work could lead to high levels of stress and to anxieties among bourgeois, clerks, and voyageurs. Voyageurs' blunders, lost and broken equipment, and voyageur insolence often exacerbated tensions.[92] Alexander Henry the Younger grew frustrated with one of his men named Desmarrais for not protecting the buffalo he shot from wolves. He grumbled:

> My servant is such a careless, indolent fellow that I cannot trust the storehouse to his care. I made to-day a complete overhaul, and found everything in the greatest confusion; I had no idea matters were so bad as I found them. . . . Like most of his countrymen, he is much more interested for himself than for his employer.[93]

On rare occasions violence punctuated the generalized tension of master-servant relations in the fur trade. Mutual resentments could lead to brawls between the masters and servants.[94]

More typically tensions in the master and servant relationship were expressed in nastiness and unfairness, rather than violence. Motivated by the desire to save money and gain the maximum benefit from their workers, bourgeois pushed their men to work hard, which could result in ill will. Most serious cases of ill will and injustice concerned bourgeois selling goods to voyageurs at inflated prices and encouraging voyageurs to go into debt as soon as they entered fur trade service. It is difficult to find many instances of "bad faith" in bourgeois writing, as they would not likely dwell on their cruelty as masters, nor reveal their unfair tricks. However, travellers, critics of fur trade companies, and disgruntled employees provide clues. The French Duke de La Rouchefoucault Liancourt, travelling through North America in the late eighteenth century, commented that the NWC encouraged vice among their men by paying them in merchandise, especially luxuries and rum, so that none of them ever earned a decent wage.[95] Lord Selkirk, certainly no fan of the NWC, criticized the bourgeois further for exploiting their men, pointing out that *engagés* often left their French Canadian families in distress, and were unable to provide for them because the cost of goods in the interior was double or triple the price in Lower Canada, and men were usually paid in goods rather than cash. The NWC saved further costs on men's wages by encouraging addiction to alcohol, and then paying wages in rum at inflated prices. The Company placed no ceiling on its men's credit, so that many of them fell deeply into debt.[96]

Despite Selkirk's obvious bias against the NWC, he was not alone in his misgiving about Montréal fur trade company labour practices. As a new clerk in the XYC, George Nelson was instructed to provide any trade goods his men might ask for, and to encourage them to take up their wages in any of the trade goods on board the canoe. Nelson was initially uneasy with this mode of dealing,

> for thought I what is there more unnatural, than to try to get the wages a poor man for a few quarts of rum, some flour & sugar, a few half fathoms of tobacco, & but verly little Goods who comes to pass a few of his best years in this rascally & unnatural Country to try to get a little money so as to settle himself happily among the rest of his friends and relations.

Eventually Nelson came to justify his participation in this system of exploitation because he felt that the men would ruin themselves anyway, and that most of them were disobedient "black-guards" for whom slavery was too good.[97] Nelson was also surprised that these men could live such a carefree existence while deeply in debt and with few material possessions.[98] His comment reveals one of the deep cultural fissures between masters and servants.

Voyageur responses to the cruelty of bourgeois and clerks could reach intense heights in the ongoing counter-theatre of resistance. Ill will between servants and masters could impede work. Sometimes the tensions were so strong that voyageurs refused to share the fruits of their hunting and fishing with their masters.[99] The more outrageous instances of masters abusing servants could lead to collective resistance among the voyageurs in the form of strikes or mass desertion. When a voyageur named Joseph Leveillé was condemned by the Montréal Quarter Sessions to the pillory for having accepted the wages of two rival fur-trading firms in 1794, a riot ensued. A group made up largely of voyageurs hurled the pillory into the St. Lawrence River and threatened to storm the prison. The prisoner was eventually released and no one was punished for the incident.[100] Voyageurs seemed to have developed a reputation for mob belligerence in Lower Canada. Attorney general Jonathan Sewell warned in a 1795 letter to Lieutenant Colonial Beckworth that officers in Lower Canada should be given greater discretionary power to counter the "riotous inclinations" of the people, especially of the "lawless band" of voyageurs.[101]

Instances of mass riots or collective resistance were not unknown in New France and Lower Canada. However, the small population, diffuse work settings, and not too unreasonable seigneurial dues usually restricted expressions of discontent to individual desertions or localized conflicts.[102] Yet, the instances of collective action could have created a precedent and memory for future mass protest.[103] On occasion voyageurs deserted en masse during cargo transports or exploration missions. In these cases men worked closely in large groups doing essentially the same difficult and dangerous tasks. Communication, the development of a common attitude to work, and camaraderie fostered a collective consciousness and encouraged collective action. In the summer of 1794 a Montréal brigade at Lac La Pluie attempted to strike for higher wages. Duncan McGillivray explained:

> A few discontented persons in their Band, wishing to do as much mischief as possible assembled their companions together several times on the Voyage Outward & represented to them how much their Interest suffered by the passive obedience to the will of their masters, when their utility to the Company, might insure them not only of better treatment, but of any other conditions which they would prescribe with Spirit & Resolution.

When they arrived at Lac La Pluie the brigade demanded higher wages and threatened to return to Montréal without the cargo. The bourgeois initially prevailed upon a few of the men to abandon the strike. Soon after most of the men went back to work, and the ringleaders were sent to Montréal in disgrace.[104]

Efforts at collective action in the north west did not always end in failure. In his third expedition to the Missouri Country in fall 1805 and winter 1806, Charles McKenzie's crew of four men deserted. They had been lodged with Black Cat, a chief in a Mandan Village, who summoned McKenzie to his tent to inform McKenzie of their desertion. The men had traded away all of the property to Native people and intended to do the same with McKenzie's property, but Black Cat secured it. When McKenzie declared he would punish his men, Black Cat warned that the Native people would defend the voyageurs. When McKenzie tried to persuade the men to return to service, they would not yield.[105] Men who spent their winters in the *pays d'en haut* became a skilled and highly valued labour force and felt entitled to fair working conditions; they were not afraid to work together to pressure the bourgeois.[106]

Despite the occasions of mass actions, voyageurs more often acted individually than collectively. Their most powerful bargaining tool in labour relations was the option of desertion. The decision to desert could be caused by any number of poor working conditions, such as bad food, an unfair master, and difficult journeys. Voyageurs used desertion often as a means of improving their working conditions rather than quitting their jobs. Although bourgeois took voyageurs to court for deserting their contracts, the measure had little effect as voyageurs continued to desert anyway. The option to desert acted as a safety valve, relieving pressure from the master and servant relationship. If voyageurs were very unhappy with their master, they could leave work for another company, return to Lower Canada, or become freemen. This safety valve worked against a collective voyageur consciousness. Collective action was also hindered because voyageurs valued independence.[107] They left farms where feudal relationships prevailed to enter into contracted servitude, but part of the pull to the north west may have been the promise of a more independent way of life than that on the Lower Canadian farm. Voyageurs idealized freemen and many chose this path, becoming independent hunters and petty traders, living primarily off the land with their Native families.[108]

Some permanent deserters maintained a casual relationship with fur trading companies, serving the occasional limited contract, or selling furs and provisions. One man, Brunet, was forced to desert because his Native wife insisted on it. He rejoined the company under a freer contract. His wife began again to pressure him to desert the company and live with her Native relatives.[109] Another man named Vivier decided to quit his contract in November 1798 because he could not stand living with Native people, as he was ordered to do by his bourgeois, John Thomson:

> he says that he cannot live any longer with them & that all the devils in Hell cannot make him return, & that he prefers marching all Winter from one Fort to another rather than Live any Longer with them.

Thompson refused to give him provisions or equipment because in the fall he had provided him with enough to pass the winter. Thomson was frustrated with his behaviour all season, as he had refused to return to the fort when ordered. Vivier had become so disenchanted with the trade that he offered his wife and child to another Voyageur, so he could return to Lower Canada, but his wife protested. Thomson finally agreed to provide him with ammunition, tobacco and an axe on credit, and Vivier left the post. It is unclear whether he remained with his Native family. A month and a half later Vivier returned to the post, and appeared to take up work again.[110] Voyageurs may have returned to work for fur trade companies because they could not find enough to eat, or desired the protection that a post provided. Fear of starvation and the dangers of the north west may have discouraged voyageurs from deserting in the first place. In one case, Alexander Henry the Younger came across a pond where André Garreau, a NWC deserter, had been killed in 1801 with five Mandans by a Swiss party.[111]

Although it is difficult to quantify the occurrence of turbulence and accommodation in the relations between masters and servants, negotiations over acceptable labour conditions dominated the north-west fur trade. Masters controlled the workforce by ensuring that all men immediately became indebted to their company, and by being the sole providers of European goods in the interior. Masters also capitalized on the risk-taking and tough masculine ethos to encourage a profitable work place. However, their best way to maintain order was to impress their men with their personal authority which was garnered by a strong manner, bravery, and effectiveness. Formal symbols, such as dress, ritual celebrations, access to better provisions, and a lighter work load reminded voyageurs of the superior status and power of their bourgeois. This "theatre of daily rule" helped to lay out the balance of the hegemonic structure of paternal authority. Masters also turned to the courts to prosecute their men for breaches of contract, and attempted to cooperate with other companies to regulate the workforce, but these methods were far from successful in controlling their voyageurs. The "social contract" overshadowed the legal contract between masters and servants, establishing an effective working relationship that was key to ensuring a well-functioning trade and high profits.

In turn, voyageurs asserted their cultural autonomy and resisted master authority. Their "counter-theatre" shaped the working environment. Voyageurs generally had very high performance standards for work, which were bolstered by masculine ideals of strength, endurance, and risk-taking. Nonetheless, voyageurs created a space to continually challenge the expectations of their masters, in part through their complaining. They also set their own pace, demanded adequate and even generous diets, refused to work in bad weather, and frequently worked to rule. When masters made unreasonable demands or failed to provide adequate provisions, voyageurs responded by working more slowly, becoming insolent, and occasionally freetrading and stealing provisions. More extreme expressions of discontent included turning to the Lower Canadian courts for justice, but, like the bourgeois and clerks, voyageurs found that their demands were better met by challenging the social, rather than the legal, contract. Their strongest bargaining tool proved to be deserting the service, which they sometimes did *en masse*. Overall, voyageurs acted more individually than collectively, as the option to desert the service acted more as a safety valve against the development of a collective voyageur consciousness.

The master and servant relationship was thus a fragile balance, constantly being negotiated. Ruling-class domination was an on-going process where the degree of legitimation was always uneven and the creation of counterhegemonies remained a live option. E.P. Thompson's emphasis on theatre and the symbolic expression of hegemony ring true for the voyageurs and bourgeois, whose power struggles were as often about respect and authority as about decent wages and provisions.[112] The difficult working conditions, regular fear of starvation, and absence of a police force positioned labour mediation in the forefront of the trade and strengthened the symbolic power of the "theatre of daily rule." The "social contract" between the masters and servants overshadowed their legal contract, and determined the day-to-day relations between the two groups. Frequently, accommodation allowed the fur trade to run smoothly, and voyageurs and bosses cooperated, especially in the face of extreme threats. Yet just as often, labour disputes and power struggles characterized the trade.

PARDEVANT les Témoins, soussignés ; fut présent

lequel s'est volontairement engagé et s'engage par ces présentes à Messrs. WILLIAM M'GILLIVRAY, SIMON M'GILLIVRAY, ARCHIBALD NORMAN M'LEOD, THOMAS THAIN, et HENRY MACKENZIE, de Montréal, Négocians et Associés, sous le nom de M'TAVISH, M'GILLIVRAYS & Co. et PIERRE DE ROCHEBLAVE, Ecuïer, à ce present et acceptant pour hiverner pendant l'espace de

en qualité de

avoir bien et duement soin, pendant les routes, et étant rendu aux dits lieux, des Marchandises, Vivres, Pelleteries, Ustensiles, et de toutes les choses nécessaires pour le voyage ; servir, obéir, et exécuter fidèlement tout ce que les dits Sieurs Bourgeois, ou tout autre représentant leurs personnes, auxquels ils pourraient transporter le présent engagement, lui commanderont de licite et honnête, faire leur profit, éviter leur dommage, les en avertir s'il vient à sa connaissance ; et généralement tout ce qu'un bon et fidèle engagé doit et est obligé de faire, sans pouvoir faire aucune traite particulière ; s'absenter ni quitter le dit service, sous les peines portées par les loix de cette Province, et de perdre ses gages. Cet engagement ainsi fait pour et moyennant la somme de

argent de Grand Portage,

avec un équipement,

qu'ils promettent et s'obligent de bailler et payer au dit engagé, un mois après son retour à Montréal, où le présent engagement finira, au bout des dits   années. Car Ainsi, &c. Promettant, &c. Obligeant, &c. Renonçant, &c. FAIT ET PASSE' à

et ont signé à l'exception du dit engagé, qui ayant déclaré ne le savoir faire, de ce enquis, a fait sa marque ordinaire, après lecture faite.

TEMOINS.

Source: "*Engagement* or contract signed by servants entering into service for fur trade partnership McTavish, McGillivrays & Co. and Pierre de Rocheblave." *Winnipeg, Provincial Archives of Manitoba, Fort William Collection,* MG1 CI 33.

NOTES

I wish to thank the Social Sciences and Humanities Research Council of Canada, the Imperial Order of the Daughters of the Empire, and the History Department of the University of Toronto for financial assistance during the research and writing of this article. I would also like to thank Allan Greer, Ian Radforth, Sylvia Van Kirk, Catherine Carstairs, and Eva Plach for their helpful comments on earlier drafts of this article.

1. Some broader studies of labour and capital in early Canadian history briefly mention fur trade workers, such as H. Clare Pentland, *Labour and Capital in Canada, 1650–1860* (Toronto: James Lorimer & Co., 1981), 30–3; and Bryan D. Palmer, *Working-Class Experience: Rethinking the History of Canadian Labour, 1800–1991* (Toronto: McClelland & Stewart 1992); 35–6. European labourers first received significant examination by Jennifer S.H. Brown, *Strangers in Blood: Fur Trade Families in Indian Country* (Vancouver: University of British Columbia Press 1980). Native labourers have been subject to some examination by Carol M. Judd, "Native Labour and Social Stratification in the Hudson's Bay Company's Northern Department, 1770–1870," *Canadian Review of Sociology and Anthropology*, 17, 4 (November 1980) 305–14.

2. Edith Burley, *Servants of the Honourable Company: Work, Discipline, and Conflict in the Hudson's Bay Company, 1770–1879* (Toronto, New York and Oxford: Oxford University Press 1997); Philip Goldring first began to compile information on labourers in *Papers on the Labour System of the Hudson's Bay Company, 1821–1900*, Volume I, Manuscript Report Series, no. 362, Parks Canada, (Ottawa: Ministry of Supply and Services 1979). Also see Ron C. Bourgeault, "The Indian, the Métis and the Fur Trade: Class, Sexism and Racism in the Transition from 'Communism' to Capitalism," *Studies in Political Economy: A Socialist Review*, 12 (Fall 1983), 45–80 and Glen Makahonuk, "Wage-Labour in the Northwest Fur Trade Economy, 1760–1849," *Saskatchewan History*, 41 (Winter 1988), 1–17.

3. For a brief report of master and servant law in a colonial setting see Douglas Hay and Paul Craven, "Master and Servant in England and the Empire: A Comparative Study," *Labour/Le Travail*, 31 (Spring 1993), 175–84.

4. Daniel Francis and Toby Morantz, *Partners in Furs: A History of the Fur Trade in Eastern James Bay, 1600–1870* (Montréal and Kingston: McGill-Queen's University Press), 167.

5. Louise Dechêne uses the term *voyageur* to identify the small-scale independent fur traders, working alone or in small groups, with some financial backing from merchants, from the late 17th century to the mid-18th century. Louise Dechêne, *Habitants and Merchants in Seventeenth-Century Montréal*, trans. Liana Vardi, (Montréal: McGill-Queen's University Press 1992), 94. Later, the term came to be used more widely to refer to contracted labourers, or *engagés*. I use the term *voyageur* interchangeably with *engagé*, servant, and worker.

6. The term "liminal" is used by cultural anthropologists to mean interstitial, implying both margins and thresholds, and a transitional state. The concept was first suggested by Arnold van Gennep in his work *The Rites of Passage*, trans. by Monika B. Vizedom and Gabrielle L. Caffee, (London: Routledge and Kegan Paul 1909). The concept was further developed by Victor Turner, *The Ritual Process: Structure and Anti-Structure* (Chicago: Aldine, 1969), 94–5 and *Blazing the Trail: Way Marks in the Exploration of Symbols* (Tucson: University of Arizona Press 1992), 48–51. For a theoretical discussion and cross cultural comparisons of *communitas* or the development of community in liminal spaces see Turner, *The Ritual Process*, 96–7, 125–30 and *Blazing the Trail*, 58–61.

7. My understanding of masculinity as a category for historical analysis is informed by Joan Scott, "Gender: A Useful Category of Historical Analysis," *American Historical Review*, 91, (December 1986), 1053–75 and R.W. Connell, *Masculinities* (Berkeley and Los Angeles: University of California Press 1995), 67–92.

8. John E. Foster, "Wintering, the Outsider Adult Male and the Ethnogenesis of the Western Plains Métis," *Prairie Forum*, 19, 1 (Spring 1994), 1–13.

9. See Jacqueline Peterson and Jennifer S.H. Brown, eds., *The New Peoples: Being and Becoming Métis in North America* (Winnipeg: University of Manitoba Press 1985) and Gerhard J. Ens, *Homeland to Hinterland: The Changing Worlds of the Red River Métis in the Nineteenth Century* (Toronto: University of Toronto Press 1997).

10. See Palmer, *Working-Class Experience*, 41–51.

11. Brown, *Strangers in Blood*, 88.

12. Burley, *Servants of the Honourable Company*, 15–16.

13. The term "bourgeois" was used in 18th and 19th-century Canada to refer to the Montréal fur trade merchants and managers, which included company partners and all but the most junior clerks.

14. For a representative example see W. Kaye Lamb, ed., *Sixteen Years in Indian Country: The Journal of Daniel Williams Harmon, 1800–1816* (Toronto: The MacMillan Company of Canada 1957), 197–98.

15. Toronto, Ontario Archives (hereafter OA), North West Company Collection (hereafter NWCC), MU 2199, Box 4, No. 1 (Photostat of original), "An Account of the Athabasca Indians by a Partner of the North West

Company, 1795," revised 4 May 1840 (Forms part of the manuscript entitled "Some Account of the North West Company," by Roderick McKenzie, director of the North West Company. Original at McGill Rare Books (hereafter MRB), Masson Collection (hereafter MC), C.18, Microfilm reel #22. Photostat can also be found at National Archives of Canada (hereafter NAC), MC, MG19 C1, Vol. 55, Microfilm reel #C-15640); 51.

16. George Heriot, *Travels Through the Canadas, Containing a Description of the Picturesque Scenery on Some of the Rivers and Lakes; with an Account of the Productions, Commerce, and Inhabitants of those Provinces* (Philadelphia: M. Carey 1813), 254; and MRB, MC, C.27, Microfilm reel #13, Roderick McKenzie, Letters Inward [all the letters are from W. Ferdinand Wentzel, Forks, McKenzie River], 1807–1824, pp. 3, 23.

17. "An Account of the Athabasca Indians by a Partner of the North West Company, 1795," pp. 51; and Alexander Mackenzie, Esq., "A General History of the Fur Trade from Canada to the North-West," *Voyages from Montréal on the River St. Laurence through the Continent of North America to the Frozen and Pacific Oceans in the Years 1789 and 1793 with a Preliminary Account of the Rise, Progress, and Present State of the Fur Trade of that Country* (London: R. Nobel, Old Bailey, 1801), 34.

18. Brown, *Strangers in Blood* 35, 45–8. Also see E.P. Thompson's discussion of "patricians" and "plebs" in *Customs in Common: Studies in Traditional Popular Culture* (New York: The New Press 1993), 16–17.

19. For a discussion on cultural hegemony and the consent of the masses to be ruled, see T.J. Jackson Lears, "The Concept of Cultural Hegemony: Problems and Possibilities," *American Historical Review*, 90 (June 1985), 567–593.

20. Edith Burley also found that the relationship between masters and servants in the HBC was constantly subject to negotiation. Burley, *Servants of the Honourable Company*, 110–11.

21. Thompson, *Customs in Common*, 85–6.

22. This is suggested by Thompson, *Customs in Common*, 45–6.

23. Lawrence M. Lande, *The Development of the Voyageur Contract (1686–1821)* (Montréal: McLennan Library, McGill University 1989), 41.

24. Winnipeg, Provincial Archives of Manitoba (hereafter PAM), Fort William Collection (hereafter FWC), MG1 C1; fo. 33, contract form for McTavish, McGillivrays & Co. My translation.

25. For examples see Joseph Defont's 1809 contract with the North West Company, PAM, FWC, MG1 C1, fo. 32-1 and the contract of Louis Santier of St. Eustache with Parker, Gerrard, Ogilvy, & Co. as a *milieu* to transport goods between Montréal and Michilimackinac, 21 Avril [sic] 1802, NAC, MG19 A51.

26. Mackenzie, "A General History," 34.

27. NAC, Haldimand Papers, "Memorandum for Sir Guy Carleton," 20 January 1778, cited by Harold Adams Innis, *The Fur Trade in Canada* (Toronto: University of Toronto Press 1956, first published in 1930), 221.

28. *Ordinances and Acts of Quebec and Lower Canada*, 36 George III, chpt. 10, 7 May 1796.

29. Grace Laing Hogg and Gwen Shulman, "Wage Disputes and the Courts in Montreal, 1816–1835," in Donald Fyson, Colin M. Coates and Kathryn Harvey, eds., *Class, Gender and the Law in Eighteenth- and Nineteenth-Century Quebec: Sources and Perspectives* (Montréal: Montréal History Group, 1993), 129.

30. For one example see Montréal, McCord Museum of Canadian History, North West Company Papers, M17607, M17614, Deposition of Basil Dubois, 21 June 1798, and Complaint of Samuel Gerrard, of the firm of Parker, Gerrard and Ogilvie against Basil Dubois.

31. Montréal, Archives nationales de Québec, depot de Montréal (hereafter ANQM), Court of Quarter Sessions of the District of Montréal, TL32 S1 SS1, Robert Aird vs. Joseph Boucher, 1 April 1785, JP Pierre Foretier; Atkinson Patterson vs. Jean-Baptiste Desloriers dit Laplante, 21 April 1798, JP Thomas Forsyth; and Angus Sharrest for McGillivray & Co. vs. Joseph Papin of St. Sulpice, 14 June 1810, JP J-M Mondelet. These cases were compiled by Don Fyson as part of a one in five sample of the whole series.

32. ANQM, Cours des plaidoyers communs du district de Montréal (hereafter CPCM), Cour du samedi (matières civiles superieurs), TL16 S4/00005, pp. 37, 27 mars 1784, JPs Hertelle De Rouville and Edward Southouse; and TL16 S4/00002, no page numbers, 2 Avril 1778, JPs Hertelle De Rouville and Edward Southouse.

33. The JPs were William McGillivray, Duncan McGillivray, Sir Alexander Mackenzie, Roderick McKenzie, and John Ogilvy. Marjorie Wilkins Campbell, *The North West Company* (Toronto: MacMillan Company of Canada 1957), 136–7.

34. NAC, North West Company Letterbook, 1798–1800 (hereafter NWCL), MG19 B1, vol. 1, pp. 131, William McGillivray to Thomas Forsyth, Esq., Grand Portage, 30 June 1800.

35. NAC, NWCL, MG19 B1, vol. 1, pp. 152–3, William McGillivray to McTavish, Frobisher and Company, Grand Portage, 28 July 1800.

36. NAC, Letterbook of Sir Alexander McKenzie and Company, kept by Daniel Sutherland (hereafter LAMC), pp. 40, D. Sutherland to Henry Harou, 15 May 1803.

37. ANQM, CPCM, Cour du vendredi (matières civiles inferieurs), TL16 S3/00001, pp. 41, 314–25, 3 juillet 1770 and 3 juillet 1778, JPs Hertelle De Rouville and Edward Southouse; and TL16 S3/00008, no page numbers, 13

janvier 1786, JPs Hertelle De Rouville and Edward Southouse, 6 octobre 1786 (followed by several other entries later in the month), JPs John Fraser, Edward Southouse and Hertelle De Rouville, and 27 octobre 1786, JPs Edward Southouse and Hertelle De Roubille; and Eliot Coues, ed. *New Light on the Early History of the Greater Northwest: The Manuscript Journals of Alexander Henry* (Minneapolis: Ross and Haines, 1897), vol. 2, 860-1, Sunday, 27 March 1814.

38. Hogg and Shulman, "Wage Disputes and the Courts in Montréal" 128, 132, 135–40, 141–3.

39. Thompson, *Customs in Common*, 43, 45–6.

40. Elizabeth Vibert, *Traders' Tales: Narratives of Cultural Encounters in the Columbia Plateau, 1807–1846* (Norman and London: University of Oklahoma Press 1997), 110–12.

41. James Scott Hamilton, "Fur Trade Social Inequality and the Role of Non-Verbal Communication," Ph.D. Thesis, Simon Fraser University, 1990, 138, 261–3.

42. Alexander Ross, *Fur Hunters of the Far West; A Narrative of Adventures in Oregon and the Rocky Mountains* (London: Smith, Elder and Co. 1855), 1: 301–2.

43. J. B. Tyrrell, ed. *Journals of Samuel Hearne and Philip Turnor* (Toronto: Champlain Society 1934), Journall III, "A Journal of the most remarkable Transactions and Occurences from York Fort to Cumberland House, and from said House to York Fort from 9th Septr 1778 to 15th Septr 1779 by Mr Philip Turnor," 15 July 1779, 252.

44. OA, George Gordon Papers, MU 1146G, Moffatt, Fort William, to George Gordon, Monontagué, 25 July 1809. See also Hamilton, "Fur Trade Social Inequality," 135–6. Burley found a similar pattern in the HBC, Burley, *Servants of the Honourable Company*, 122–3.

45. NAC, Autobiographical Notes of John McDonald of Garth, 1791–1815, written in 1859, photostat, MG19 A17, pp. 119–21. The original can be found at MRB, MS 406, and a typescript can be found at the OA, MU 1763.

46. For a few examples of becoming lost see MRB, MC, C.8, microfilm reel #14, Alexander McKenzie, Journal of Great Bear Lake, 18–26 June 1806, pp. 20; MRB, MC, Journal of John MacDonell, Assiniboines-Rivière qu'Appelle, 1793–95, Thursday, 13 March 1794 and Monday, 8 December 1794, pp. 11, 22; and OA, Company of Temiscamingue, Microfilm #MS65, Donald McKay, Journal from January 1805 to June 1806, Thursday, 12 September 1805, pp. 32 (I added page numbers). For examples of canoeing accidents see NAC, MC, MG19 C1, vol. 1, microfilm reel #C-15638, Charles Chaboillez, "Journal for the Year 1797," Wednesday, 16, 19 and 31 August 1797, pp. 4, 6; NAC, MC, MG19 C1, Vol. 4, Microfilm reel #C-15638, William McGillivray, "Rat River Fort Near Rivière Malique . . . ," 9 September 1789 to 13 June 1790 (written transcript precedes original on reel, both badly damaged), pp. 73–4; and NAC, MC, MG19 C1, Vol. 8, Microfilm reel #C-15638, W. Ferdinand Wentzel, "A Journal kept at the Grand River, Winter 1804 & 1805," 9 October 1804, pp. 9. On bear attacks see Toronto, Metropolitan Reference Library, Baldwin Room (hereafter MRL BR), S13, George Nelson's Journal "No. 7", describing the Lake Winnipeg district in 1812, written as a reminiscence, pp. 283–4; NAC, MG19 A17, Autobiographical Notes of John McDonald of Garth, 1791–1815, written in 1859 (Photostat), pp. 54–5, 65–6; and "First Journal of Simon Fraser from April 12th to July 18th, 1806," Appendix B, *Public Archives Report for 1929*, pp. 109–45, (transcript from a copy at University of California at Berkeley, Bancroft Collection, Vol. 4; originals at the Provincial Archives of British Columbia), Sunday 13 July 1806, pp. 143–4. On starvation see MRB, MC, C.24, Microfilm reel #2, Archibald Norman McLeod, Journal kept at Alexandria, 1800, Thursday, 19 February 1801, pp. 22; NAC, MG19 A14, Microfilm reel #M-130, John Stuart, Journal kept at North West Company Rocky Mountain House, 1805–6 (original at Provincial Archives of British Columbia), Saturday, 1 February 1806, pp. 20; and MRL BR, S13, George Nelson's Journal "No. 5," June 1807–October 1809, written as a reminiscence, dated 7 February 1851, pp. 209–10.

47. Coues, ed., *New Light*, 1: 11 August 1800, pp. 30–1; MRL BR, S13, George Nelson's diary of events on a journey from Cumberland House to Fort William, part in code, 3 June–11 July 1822 (notes taken from a transcription made by Sylvia Van Kirk); Tuesday, 9 July 1822; *ibid.*, Nelson's diary of events on a journey from Fort William to Cumberland House, 21 July–22 August 1822 (notes taken from a transcription made by Sylvia Van Kirk); Monday, 19 August 1822; and Alexander Ross, *Fur Hunters of the Far West; A Narrative of Adventures in Oregon and the Rocky Mountains,* (London: Smith, Elder and Co. 1855), II: 236–7.

48. Elliot J. Gorn describes this pattern as well in "Gouge and Bite, Pull hair and Scratch: The Social Significance of Fighting in the Southern Backcountry," *American Historical Review*, 90 (Feb. 1985), 18–43.

49. Arthur S. Morton, ed., *The Journal of Duncan McGillivray of the North West Company at Fort George on the Saskatchewan, 1794–5* (Toronto: The MacMillan Company of Canada Limited 1929), 11.

50. NAC, Autobiographical Notes of John McDonald of Garth, 215.

51. In a different case, Gunther Peck found that middle class commentators condemned miners' penchant for risk-taking in late 19th century Nevada. Gunther Peck, "Manly Gambles: The Politics of Risk on the Comstock Lode, 1860–1880," *Journal of Social History*, 26 (Summer 1993), 701–23.

52. See entries Friday, 31 May 1793 and Thursday, 13 June 1793, Mackenzie, *Voyages from Montréal*, 285, 295–6, 322–6.

53. For examples see Coues, ed., *New Light*, vol. 1, 10, 243, 23 July 1800, and 6 May 1804; Lamb, ed., *Sixteen Years*, 105, Sunday, 19 July 1807; and Ross Cox, *Adventures on the Columbia River* (New York: J. & J. Harper 1832), 304–5, 19 September 1817.

54. For examples see NAC, MC, MG19 C1, vol. 1, microfilm reel #C-15638, pp. 3, Friday, 11 August 1797, Charles Chaboillez, "Journal for the Year 1797"; NAC, MC, MG19 C1, Vol. 9, Microfilm reel #C1-5638, pp. 16, Unidentified North West Company Wintering Partner, "Journal for 1805 & 6, Cross Lake," Sunday, 10 November 1805; MRB, MC, C.1, microfilm reel #55, pp. 66, Duncan Cameron, "The Nipigon Country," with extracts from his journal in the Nipigon, 1804–5, (also found in the OA, Photostat, MU 2198 Box 3, Item 3; and in triplicate typescript, MU 2200, Box 5 (a-c)); and Mackenzie, *Voyages from Montréal*, 325, Thursday, 13 June 1793.

55. Approximately 20 June 1807, described in TRML, BR, S13, pp. 186, George Nelson's Journal "No. 5," June 1807–October 1809, written as a reminiscence, dated 7 February 1851.

56. Burley, *Servants of the Honourable Company*, 118–20.

57. E.P. Thompson, *Customs in Common*, 67.

58. Cameron, "The Nipigon Country," 38–39.

59. Coues, ed., *New Light*, 1: 247–8, 28 July 1804.

60. A blacksmith named Philip earned the wrath of his bourgeois, McKay, when he abused him both behind his back and to his face. Nelson, Journal "No. 5", 2 (labelled pp. 186). George Nelson felt pressured by the continual complaints made by his men about their rations. He worried that his men were spreading discontent among each other and preferred them to approach him directly with their concerns. Nelson, "A Daily Memoranda," pp. 8, Friday, 10 February 1815.

61. Mentioned in Coues, ed., *New Light*, 1: 247, 1 July 1804.

62. NAC, LAMC, 1802-9, vol. 1, MG19 A7, pp. 18–19, 25–6, D. Sutherland to Monsr. St. Valur Mailloux, Montréal, 10 November 1802, 29 November 1802, and 20 December 1802, (originals in the Seminaire de Quebec). My translation.

63. For one example of men demanding their pay be doubled for extra duties see Chaboillez, "Journal for the Year 1797," 49, Tuesday, 20 March 1798.

64. MRB, MC, C.27, Microfilm reel #13, pp. 2, Athabasca Department, Great Slave Lake, W.F. Wentzel to Roderick McKenzie, Letters Inward, 1807–1824, 5 April 1819.

65. NAC, MC, MG19 C1, vol. 3, microfilm reel #C-15638, pp. 8–15, François-Antoine Larocque, "Missouri Journal, Winter 1804–5"; and Nelson, "A Daily Memoranda," pp. 30–2, Saturday, 8 April 1815.

66. See entries Monday, 2 November 1818, and from Tuesday, 1 December 1818 to Wednesday, 30 December 1818, OA, MU 842, pp. 10–11, 18–23, Diary of George Nelson, in the service of the North West Company at Tête au Brochet, 1818–19.

67. NAC, MC, MG19 C1, Vol. 15, Microfilm reel #C-15638, pp. 7, Fragment of a journal, attributed to W. Ferdinand Wentzel, kept during an expedition from 13 June to 20 August 1800, Friday, 26 June 1800.

68. MRB, MC, C.8, microfilm reel #14, pp. 125, Alexander Mackenzie, Journal of Great Bear Lake, March 1806.

69. On trip from Athabasca to the McKenzie River, NAC, MC, MG19 C1, Vol. 6, Microfilm reel #C-15638, pp. 50, James Porter, Journal kept at Slave Lake, 18 February 1800 to 14 February 1801, 29 September 1800. Porter quotes the man as saying "Si Je avait Point des gages que le Diable ma aport si vous ma Soucier Embarker." See also John Thomson, who records that this man, named Bernier, gave further trouble to Porter on the trip. Thompson's interpretation of Bernier's swearing is "swearing the Devel myte take him if he had stirred a Step." See entries Monday, 29 September 1800 to Saturday, 4 September 1800, MRB, MC, C.26, Microfilm reel #15, pp. 1–2, John Thompson, "Journal, Mackenzies River alias Rocky Mountain, 1800–1."

70. OA, NWCC, MU 2199, pp. 8, Photostat of original, Edward Umfreville, "Journal of a Passage in a Canoe from Pais Plat in Lake Superior to Portage de L'Isle in Rivière Ouinipique," June to July 1784, Wednesday 23, June 1784. Forms part of the manuscript entitled, "Some Account of the North West Company," by Roderick McKenzie, director of the North West Company. Typescripts can be found also in the OA, NWCC, MU 2200, Box 5, Nos. 2 (a), (b), and (c). Photostats and typescripts can also be found in NAC, MC, Vol. 44, Microfilm reel #C-15640; the MRB, MC, C.17; and the MHS, P1571. For other examples of theft see MRB, MC, C.24, Microfilm reel #2, pp. 5, Archibald Norman McLeod, Journal kept at Alexandria, 1800, Friday, 28 November 1800; OA, Angus Mackintosh Papers; MU 1956, Box 4, pp. 2–3, Journal from Michilimackinac to Montréal via the French River, summer 1813. 16 July 1813; and NAC, MC19 C1, Vol. 2, microfilm reel #C-15638, pp. 10, Michel Curot, "Journal, Folle Avoine, Riviere Jaune, Pour 1803 & 1804," Lundi, 11 October 1803.

71. TMRL, BR, S13, pp. 9, George Nelson's Journal "No. 1," written as a reminiscence, describing a journey from Montréal to Grand Portage, and at Folle Avoine, 27 April 1802–April 1803 (a typescript can also be found in the George Nelson Papers of the TMRL, BR).

72. Coues, ed., *New Light*, 1: 25, 6 August 139–44.

73. Burley, *Servants of the Honourable Company*, 139–44.

74. Mackenzie, "A General History," 34. On the HBC prohibition of private trading see Burley, *Servants of the Honourable Company*, 139–44. However, Burley suggests that the lack of reporting on this offense may indicate that the officers tacitly allowed their men to do so (144–52).

75. Described by Ross, *Fur Hunters*, 1: 159.

76. MHS, GLNP, Folder 7, P791, pp. 2, NWC Letters, 1798–1816, Dominique Rousseau and Joseph Bailey v. Duncan McGillivray, (originals from the Judicial Archives of Montréal).

77. Campbell, *The North West Company*, 155.

78. Wallace, W. Stewart, ed., *Documents Relating to the North West Company* (Toronto: Champlain Society 1934), Minutes of the Meetings of the NWC at Grand Portage and Fort William, 1801–07, with Supplementary Agreements (originals in Montréal, Sulpician Library, Baby Collection), 216, 15 July 1806.

79. For an example see MRB, MC, C.7, microfilm reel $4, pp. 4, Journal of John MacDonell, Assiniboines-Riviere qu'Appelle, 1793–95, (typescript copy in NAC, MC, MG 19 C 1, vol. 54, microfilm reel#C-15640), 5 December 1793 to 6 December 1793.

80. McLeod, Journal kept at Alexandria, pp. 40, Saturday, 30 May 1801; and "The Diary of John Macdonell" in Charles M. Gates, ed., *Five Fur Traders of the Northwest* (St. Paul: Minnesota Historical Society 1965), 72, 1 June 1793.

81. "The Diary of Hugh Faries" in Gates, ed., *Five Fur Traders*, 233–34, Monday, 25 March 1805.

82. Burley, *Servants of the Honourable Company*, 153–4.

83. For example, see McLeod, Journal kept at Alexandria, 15, Friday, 2 January 1801.

84. Mackenzie, *Voyages from Montréal*, 329, Saturday, 15 June 1793.

85. *passim*, pp. 373–4, Saturday, 29 June 1793.

86. MRB, MC, C.12, Microfilm reel #6, pp. 41, Charles McKenzie, "Some Account of the Missouri Indians in the years 1804, 5, 6 & 7," addressed to Roderick McKenzie, 1809. Photostat and typescript copies can be found in NAC, MC, MG19 C1, Vol. 59, Microfilm reel #C-15640 and OA, NWCC, MU2204, Vol. 3 and MU2200 Box 5–4 (a), and the account is published by W. Raymond Wood and Thomas D. Thiessen, eds., *Early Fur Trade on the Northern Plains: Canadian Traders Among the Mandan and Hidatsa Indians, 1738–1818; The narratives of John Macdonell, David Thompson, François-Antoine Larocque, and Charles McKenzie* (Norman: University of Oklahoma Press 1985).

87. For one example see McLeod, Journal kept at Alexandria, Saturday, 22 November 1800.

88. Nelson, Journal No. 1, pp. 43, Saturday, 17 November 1809.

89. Nelson, "A Daily Memoranda," 8, Friday, 10 February 1815; and "The Diary of Hugh Faries," pp. 235, Tuesday, 2 April 1805.

90. TMRL, BR, S13, pp. 14–15, George Nelson's Coded Journal, 17 April–20 October 1821, entitled "A continuation of My Journal at Moose Lake," (notes made by Sylvia Van Kirk), Thursday, 10 May 1821. Constant had been threatening to desert the service for years, and he did make arrangements with another bourgeois, William Connolly, to leave the service. *ibid.*, Thursdays, 10 and 24 May 1821, pp. 14–15, 20.

91. "The Diary of Hugh Faries," pp. 206, Sunday, 26 August 1804.

92. Coues, ed., *New Light*, 1: 114, 9 October 1800.

93. *passim*, pp. 99–100, 18–19 September 1800.

94. Cox, *Adventures*, 166–7.

95. *Voyages dans l'Amerique par la Rouchefoucould Liancourt*, Vol. II, 225, Paris, An. 7; cited by Thomas Douglas, Earl of Selkirk, *A Sketch of the British Fur Trade in North America; with Observations Relative to the North-West Company of Montréal*, 2nd edition (London: James Ridgway 1816), 36–7.

96. Selkirk, *A Sketch of the British Fur Trade*, 32–47.

97. Nelson, Journal, 13 July 1803–25 June 1804, 1–2, 34, Friday, 15 July 1803.

98. TMRL, BR, S13, pp. 7–9, George Nelson, Tête au Brochet, to his parents, 8 December 1811.

99. Nelson, "A Daily Memoranda", pp. 17–18, 40–1, Thursday, 9 March 1815, Tuesday, 23 May 1815 and Wednesday, 24 May 1815.

100. NAC, 'Civil Secretary's Letter Books, 1788–1829', RG7, G15C, vol. 2, CO42, vol. 100, Sheriff Edward Gray to Attorney General James Monk, 9 June 1794; J. Reid to same, 12 June 1794; T.A. Coffin to James McGill, 21 July 1794; cited by F. Murray Greenwood, *Legacies of Fear: Law and Politics in Quebec in the Era of the French Revolution* (Toronto: University of Toronto Press 1993), 80, 285.

101. NAC, Jonathan Sewell Papers, MG23 GII10, Volume 9, pp. 4613–4, Jonathan Sewell to Lieutenant Colonel Beckworth, 28 July 1795. Donald Fyson brought this reference to my attention.

102. Terence Crowley, "'Thunder Gusts': Popular Disturbances in Early French Canada," *Canadian Historical Association Historical Papers* (1979), 11–31; and Jean-Pierre Hardy et David-Thiery Ruddel, *Les Apprentis Artisans à Québec, 1660–1815* (Québec: Les Presses de L'Université du Québec 1977), 74–80.

103. Jean-Pierre Wallot, *Un Québec qui Bougeait: trame socio-politique du Québec au tournant du XIXe siècle* (Montréal: Boréal 1973), 266–7.

104. Morton, ed., *The Journal of Duncan McGillivray,* 6–7.

105. Charles McKenzie, "Some Account of the Missouri Indians," 72, 77–8.

106. MRB, MC, C.5, Microfilm reel #5, abridged version on Microfilm reel #6, pp. 75, 79, Alexander Henry the Younger, travels in the Red River Department, 1806, Saturday, 26 July 1806 and Thursday, 7 August 1806.

107. Alexander Ross, *Fur Hunters of the Far West; A Narrative of Adventures in the Oregon and Rocky Mountains,* 2 vols. (London: Smith, Elder and Co. 1855), II: 236–237.

108. Toronto; Metropolitan Reference Library; Baldwin Room; S13; George Nelson, Tête au Brochet, to his parents, 8 December 1811; pp. 9–11; and Ross, *Fur Hunters of the Far West,* 1: 291–93.

109. Nelson, Journal, 13 July 1803–25 June 1804, pp. 22–3, Monday, 31 January 1804, Monday, 14 February 1804, Tuesday, 15 February 1804, and Thursday 17 February 1804.

110. NAC, MC, MG19 C1, Vol. 7, Microfilm reel #C-15638, pp. 19–24, John Thomson, "A Journal kept at Grand Marais ou Rivière Rouge, 1798," Sunday, 18 November 1798, Monday, 19 November 1798, Tuesday, 20 November 1798, and Friday, 4 January 1799.

111. Henry, Travels in the Red River Department, pp. 50, Wednesday, 23 July 1806.

112. Thompson, *Customs in Common,* 74–5.

Article Twenty-Six

Class Conflict on the Canals of Upper Canada in the 1840s

Ruth Bleasdale

Irish labourers on the St. Lawrence canal system in the 1840s appeared to confirm the stereotype of the Irish Celt — irrational, emotionally unstable, and lacking in self-control. Clustered around construction sites in almost exclusively Irish communities, they engaged in violent confrontations with each other, local inhabitants, employers, and law enforcement agencies. Observers of these confrontations accepted as axiomatic the stereotype of violent Paddy, irreconcilable to Anglo-Saxon norms of rational behaviour, and government reports, private letters, and newspaper articles characterized the canallers as "persons predisposed to tumult even without cause."[1] As one of the contractors on the Lachine Canal put it: "they are a turbulent and discontented people that nothing can satisfy for any length of time, and who never will be kept to work peaceably unless overawed by some force for which they have respect."[2]

Yet men attempting to control the disturbances along the canals perceived an economic basis to these disturbances which directly challenged ethnocentric interpretations of the canallers' behaviour. In the letters and reports of government officials and law enforcement agents on the canal works in Upper Canada the violence of the labourers appears not as the

Source: Ruth Bleasdale, "Class Conflict on the Canals of Upper Canada in the 1840s," *Labour/Le Travail,* 7 (Spring 1981), 9–39. Reprinted by permission.

excesses of an unruly nationality clinging to old behaviour patterns, but as a rational response to economic conditions in the new world. The Irish labourers' common ethno-culture did play a part in shaping their response to these conditions, defining acceptable standards of behaviour, and providing shared traditions and experiences which facilitated united protest. But the objective basis of the social disorder along the canals was, primarily, class conflict. With important exceptions, the canallers' collective action constituted a bitter resistance to the position which they were forced to assume in the society of British North America.

Southern Irish immigrants flooding into the Canadas during the 1840s became part of a developing capitalist labour market, a reserve pool of unskilled labourers who had little choice but to enter and remain in the labour force.[3] Most southern Irish arrived in the new world destitute. "Labouring paupers" was how the immigration agent at Quebec described them.[4] They had little hope of establishing themselves on the land. By the 1840s the land granting and settlement policies of government and private companies had combined to put land beyond the reach of such poor immigrants. Settlement even on free grants in the backwoods was "virtually impossible without capital."[5] The only option open to most southern Irish was to accept whatever wage labour they could find.

Many found work in the lumbering, shipping, and shipbuilding industries, and in the developing urban centres, where they clustered in casual and manual occupations. But the British North American economy could not absorb the massive immigration of unskilled Irish.[6] Although the cholera epidemics of 1832 and 1834 and the commercial crisis of 1837 had led to a decline in immigration and a shortage of labour by 1838, a labour surplus rapidly developed in the opening years of the 1840s, as southern Irish arrived in record numbers.[7] Added to this influx of labourers from across the Atlantic was a migration of Irish labourers north across the American border. During the 1830s the movement of labourers across the border had usually been in the opposite direction, a large proportion of Irish immigrants at Quebec proceeding to the United States in search of employment on public works projects. But the economic panic of 1837 had put a stop to "practically every form of public work" in that country, and further stoppages in 1842 sent 1000s of Irish labourers into the Canadas looking for work. Some new immigrants at Quebec still travelled through to the United States despite the dismal prospects of employment in that country; Pentland concludes, however, that the net flow into Canada from the United States in the years 1842–43 was 2,500.[8] Large-scale migration of the unskilled south across the American border revived in the latter half of the decade, but the labour market continued to be over-supplied by destitute Irish immigrants fleeing famine in their homeland.[9]

The public works in progress along the Welland Canal and the St. Lawrence River attracted a large proportion of the unemployed Irish throughout the decade. The Emigration Committee for the Niagara District Council complained that construction sites along the Welland operated "as beacon lights to the whole redundant and transient population of not only British America, but of the United States."[10] From the St. Lawrence Canals came similar reports of great numbers of "strange labourers" constantly descending on the canals. Even with little work left in the early months of 1847, labourers were still pouring into the area around the Williamsburg Canals. Chief Engineer J.B. Mills asked the Board of Works what could be done with all the labourers.[11]

Many did secure work for a season or a few years. The massive canal construction programme undertaken by the government of the Canadas during the 1840s created a demand for as many as 10,000 unskilled labourers at one time in Upper Canada alone. The work was labour intensive, relying on the manpower of gangs of labourers. While mechanical inventions such as the steam-excavator in the Welland's Deep Cut played a small role in the construction process, unskilled labourers executed most aspects of the work, digging, puddling, hauling, and quarrying.[12] The Cornwall Canal needed 1,000 labourers during peak construction seasons in 1842 and 1843; the Williamsburg Canals required as many as 2,000 between 1844 and 1847; while the improvements to the Welland employed between 3,000 and 4,000 labourers from 1842 to 1845, their numbers tapering off in the latter half of the decade.[13]

Despite this heavy demand, there were never enough jobs for the numbers who flocked to canal construction sites. Winter brought unemployment of desperate proportions. While some work continued on the Cornwall and Williamsburg Canals and on the Welland to a greater extent, the number of labourers who could be employed profitably was severely limited. Of the 5,000 along the Welland in January 1844, over 3,000 could not find jobs, and those at work could put in but a few days out of the month because of the weather.[14] Even during the spring and summer months, the number of unemployed in the area might exceed the number employed if work on one section came to an end or if work was suspended for the navigation season.[15]

Only a small number of those unable to get work on the canals appear to have found jobs on farms in the area. Despite the pressing demand for farm labourers and servants during the 1840s, the peasant background of the southern Irish had not equipped them to meet this demand, and many farmers in Upper Canada consequently professed reluctance to employ Irish immigrants.[16] The Niagara District Council's 1843 enquiry into emigration and the labour needs of the district noted that farmers were not employing the labourers along the canal because they did not know "the improved system of British agriculture." Four years later the emigration committee for the same district gave a similar reason as to why farmers would not hire the immigrants squatting along the Welland Canal: "from the peculiar notions which they entertain, from the habits which they have formed, and from their ignorance of the manner in which the duties of farm labourers and servants are performed in this country, they are quite unprofitable in either capacity."[17] In the last half of the decade, fear that famine immigrants carried disease acted as a further barrier to employment of the Irish on farms.[18]

Despite their inability to find work the unemployed congregated along the canal banks. As construction commenced on the Welland, canal Superintendent Samuel Power endeavoured to explain why the surplus labourers would not move on: "the majority are so destitute that they are unable to go. The remainder are unwilling as there is not elsewhere any hope of employment." Four years later the situation had not changed. The Niagara District Council concluded that even if there had been somewhere for the unemployed to go, they were too indigent to travel.[19] Instead they squatted along the public works, throwing together shanties from pilfered materials — the fence rails of farmers and boards from abandoned properties.[20]

These shanties of the unemployed became a part of all construction sites. Their occupants maintained themselves by stealing from local merchants, farmers, and townspeople. According to government and newspaper reports, pilfering became the order of the day along public works projects, the unemployed stealing any portable commodity — food, fence rails, firewood, money, and livestock.[21] While reports deplored this criminal activity, observers agreed that it was their extreme poverty which "impelled these poor, unfortunate beings to criminal acts."[22] The *St. Catharines Journal*, a newspaper generally unsympathetic to the canallers, described the condition of the unemployed in the winter of 1844:

> . . . the greatest distress imaginable has been, and still is, existing throughout the entire line of the Welland Canal, in consequence of the vast accumulation of unemployed labourers. . . . There are, at this moment, many hundreds of men, women, and children, apparently in the last stages of starvation; and instead . . . of any relief for them . . . in the spring, . . . more than one half of those who are now employed *must* be discharged. . . . This is no exaggerated state-ment; it falls below the reality, and which requires to be seen, in all its appalling features to entitle any description of it to belief.[23]

Such descriptions appear frequently enough in the letters of government officials to indicate that the *Journal* was not indulging in sensational reporting. The actual numbers of those on the verge of starvation might fluctuate — two years earlier 4,000 unemployed labourers, not a few hundred, had been "reduced to a state of absolute starvation."[24] But the threat of starvation was an ever-present part of life in the canal zones.

Upper Canada lacked a system of public relief which might have mitigated the suffering of the unemployed and their families. Only gradually between 1792 and 1867 was there a "piecemeal assumption of public responsibility for those in need" and not until the mid-1840s did the province begin to operate on the principle of public support.[25] Even had the principle of public relief been operative, the Niagara, Johnston, and Eastern District lacked the resources to provide a relief programme such as that offered by Montreal to unemployed labourers on the Lachine Canal.[26] Nor was private charity a solution to the endemic poverty of the unemployed. When thousands of destitute immigrants first arrived in St. Catharines seeking employment on the Welland Canal in the spring of 1842, many citizens in the area came to their aid. But as the *St. Catharines Journal* pointed out in similar circumstances two years later: "Those living in the vicinity of the Canal [had] not the means of supporting the famishing scores who [were] hourly thronging their dwellings, begging for a morsel to save the life of a starving child."[27]

The suffering of the unemployed shocked private individuals and government officials such as William Merritt who led a fund-raising campaign for the starving and charged the Board of Works that it was "bound to provide provisions, in some way."[28] The crime of the unemployed became an even greater concern as desperate men violated private property in their attempts to stay alive. But for the Board of Works and its contractors the surplus labourers around the canals provided a readily exploitable pool of unskilled labour. From this pool, contractors drew labourers as they needed them — for a few days, weeks, or a season — always confident that the supply would exceed the demand. The men they set to work were often far from the brawny navvies celebrated in the folklore of the day. Weakened by days and months without adequate food, at times on the verge of starvation, labourers were reported to stagger under the weight of their shovels when first set to work.[29]

Contractors offered temporary relief from the threat of starvation; but they offered little more. The typical contractor paid wages which were consistently higher than those of farm labourers in the area of construction sites. But for their back-breaking, dangerous labour and a summer work day of 14 hours, navvies received only the average of slightly above average daily wage for unskilled labour in the Canadas.[30] Since individual contractors set wage rates, wages varied from canal to canal and from section to section on the same canal; however, they usually hovered around the 2s6d which Pentland suggests was the average rate for unskilled labour during the decade. On the Cornwall and Williamsburg Canals wages fluctuated between 2s and 3s, and if on the Welland Canal labourers in some seasons forced an increase to 4s, wages usually dropped back to 2s6d at the onset of winter, when contractors justified lower wages on the grounds that labourers worked fewer hours.[31]

These wage levels were barely adequate to sustain life, according to an 1842 government investigation into riots on the Beauharnois Canal. Many of those who testified at the hearings — foremen, engineers, magistrates, and clergymen — maintained that along the St. Lawrence labourers could not live on 2s6d per day. A conservative estimate gave the cost of food alone for a single labourer for one day at 1s3d, suggesting that at the going rate a labourer could only feed himself and his wife, not to mention children, and then only on days when he was employed.[32] Under the best of circumstances, with work being pushed ahead during the summer months, this would only mean 20 days out of the month. In winter, if he was lucky enough to get work on the canals, he could not expect to put in more than ten days in a good month.[33] Inadequate as his wages were, the labourer could not even be certain of receiving them. After a few months in a contractor's employ, labourers might discover that they had worked for nothing, the contractor running out of funds before he could pay his men. Other contractors, living under the threat of bankruptcy, forced labourers to wait months on end for their wages. These long intervals between pay days reduced labourers to desperate circumstances. Simply to stay alive, they entered into transactions with cutthroat speculators, running up long accounts at stores or "selling their time at a sacrifice," handing over the title to their wages in return for ready cash or credit. Such practices cost labourers as much as 13 per cent interest, pushing them steadily downward in a spiral of debt and dependency.[34]

Labourers might become indebted to one of the "petty hucksters who swarmed around public works, charging whatever they could get," or to one of the country storekeepers who took advantage of an influx of labourers to extract exorbitant prices.[35] Or frequently the contractor who could not find the money to pay wages found the means to stock a company store and make a profit by extending credit for grossly overpriced provisions. Although contractors claimed they set up their stores as a convenience to the labourers, a government investigation concluded that in actual fact, stores were "known to be a source of great profit on which all the contractors calculated."[36] Many contractors ensured a profit from the sale of provisions by paying wages in credit tickets redeemable only at the company store. This system of truck payment was so widespread along the canals and so open to abuse[37] that the Board of Works introduced into the contracts a clause stipulating that wages must be paid in cash. The Board's real attitude toward truck, however, was more ambivalent than this clause suggests. Its 1843 Report to the Legislature argued that "truck payment" was in many cases "rather to be controlled than wholly put down."[38] It did not put a stop to store pay, and according to its officials on construction sites it did not control it very well either.[39] The result was that many canallers worked for nothing more than the provisions doled out by their employer. They did not see cash. Few could have left the public works with more than they had had when they arrived. Many were probably in debt to the company store when their term of work ended.

The combination of low wages, payment in truck, and long waits between pay days kept canallers in poverty and insecurity, barely able to secure necessities during seasons of steady employment, unable to fortify themselves against seasons of sporadic work and the inevitable long periods when there was no work at all. Government commissions and individual reports detail the misery of the labourers' existence. Drummond, member of the Legislature for Quebec, had served on the Commission investigating conditions along the Beauharnois. During debate in the House, his anger at the "grinding oppression" which he had witnessed flared into a bitter denunciation of "sleek" contractors who had "risen into a state of great wealth by the labour, the sweat, the want and woe" of their labourers. He charged the government with having betrayed and abused the immigrant labourers:

> They were to have found continued employment, and been enabled to acquire means to purchase property of their own. They expected to meet with good treatment and what treatment had they met with?— With treatment worse than African slaves, with treatment against which no human being could bear up.[40]

Drummond was backed up by Montreal MP Doctor Neilson, whose experience as medical attendant to the Lachine labourers prompted a less passionate, but no less devastating appraisal:

> Their wants were of the direst kind. He [Dr. Neilson] had frequently to prescribe for them, not medicine, nor the ordinary nourishments recommended by the profession, but the commonest necessaries of life; he daily found them destitute of these necessaries, and he was, therefore, most strongly of opinion that the system under which they were employed, and which afforded them such a wretched existence ought to be fully enquired into.[41]

Conditions were equally bad on canals further up the St. Lawrence system. Work did not guarantee adequate food even on the Welland, which offered the highest wages.[42] David Thorburn, Magistrate for the Niagara District, wondered how the labourers could survive, as he watched them hit by a drop in wages and a simultaneous increase in food prices, struggling to feed their families, unable to provide "a sufficiency of food — even of potatoes."[43]

Work did not guarantee adequate housing either. A few contractors live up to the commitment to provide reasonable and "suitable accommodation," constructing barrack-like shanties along the works for the labourers and their families.[44] But as Pentland has pointed out, the bunkhouse, "a sign of some responsibility of the employer for his men," was a development of the latter half of the nineteenth century.[45] The typical contractor of the 1840s left his employees to find whatever housing they could. Since only a very small percentage of canallers found room and board among the local inhabitants, most built their own temporary accommodation, borrowing and stealing materials in the neighbourhood to construct huts and shacks, similar to the shanties thrown up by the unemployed.[46] A canaller usually shared accommodation with other canallers either in the barrack-like structures provided by the contractors or in the huts they erected themselves. Of the 163 shanties built by labourers at Broad Creek on the Welland, only 29 were single family dwellings. The rest were occupied by one, two, or three families with their various numbers of boarders. These dwellings formed a congested shanty town typical of the shanty towns which sprang up along the canals, and reminiscent of squalid Corktown, home of labourers on the Rideau Canal in the 1820s and 1830s.[47]

For the brief period of their existence, these shanty towns along the canals became close-knit, homogeneous working-class communities, in which the bonds of living together reinforced and overlapped the bonds formed in the workplace. Canallers shared day to day social interaction and leisure activities, drinking together at the "grog" shops which sprang up to service the labourers and lying out on the hillsides on summer nights.[48] And they shared the daily struggle to subsist, the material poverty and insecurity, the wretched conditions, and the threat of starvation.

Bound together by their experiences along the canals, the Irish labourers were also united by what they brought from Ireland — a common culture shaped by ethnicity. Canaller communities were not simply homogeneous working-class communities, but Irish working-class communities, ethnic enclaves, in which the valued norms, traditions, and practices of the southern Irish ethno-culture thrived. Central to this culture was a communal organization which emphasized mutuality and fraternity, primarily within family and kinship networks.[49] While the persistence of kinship relationships amongst the canallers cannot be measured, many labourers lived with women and children in family units. In the winter of 1844, 1300 "diggers" brought 700 women and 1200 children to live along the Welland between Dalhousie and Allanburg; and at Broad Creek in the summer of 1842, the Board of Works enumerated 250 families amongst the 797 men and 561 women and children. Shanty towns around the Cornwall and Williamsburg Canals also housed many women and children who had followed the labourers from Ireland or across the Canadian-American border, maintaining the strong family structure characteristic of southern Ireland.[50]

Given the Irish pattern of migrating and emigrating in extended families, kinship networks may also have been reproduced on the canals. The fact that both newly arrived immigrants and labourers from the United States were from the limited region of Munster and Connaught increases the probability that canallers were bound together by strong, persisting kinship ties. But whether or not the labourers were bound by blood they brought to the construction sites traditions of co-operation and mutual aid in the workplace. As peasants in Munster and Connaught, they had held land individually, but had worked it co-operatively. When forced into wage labour to supplement the yields from their tiny holdings, the pattern of work again had been co-operative — friends, relatives, and neighbours forming harvesting or construction gangs which travelled and worked together throughout the British Isles.[51]

The clearest evidence of cultural unity and continuity along the canals was the labourers' commitment to the Roman Catholic faith. In contrast with the Irish Catholic labourers in the Ottawa Valley lumbering industry whom Cross found to be irreligious, canal labourers took their religion seriously enough to build shanty chapels for worship along the canals and to contribute to the construction of a new cathedral in St. Catharines. A stone tablet on the St. Catharines cathedral commemorates "the Irish working on the Welland Canal [who] built this monument to faith and piety" but who, in their eagerness to be part of the opening services, crowded into the churchyard 2,000 strong, destroying graves and markers in the process.[52]

Canallers were prepared to defend their faith in active conflict with Orangemen. Each July 12th brought violent clashes between Orangemen commemorating the Battle of the Boyne, and Roman Catholic labourers infuriated at the celebration of an event which had produced the hated penal code. The entire canaller community rallied to participate in anti-Orange demonstrations. In 1844 all the canallers along the Welland, organized under leaders and joined by friends from public works projects in Buffalo, marched to confront Toronto Orangemen and their families on an excursion to Niagara Falls.[53] Similarly, all labourers on the Welland were encouraged to participate in an 1849 demonstration. A labourer with a large family who was reluctant to march on the Orangemen at Slabtown was ordered to join his fellows or leave the canal. He should have left the canal. Instead he went along to Slabtown and was shot in the head.[54]

The canallers also demonstrated a continued identification with the cause of Irish nationalism and the struggle for repeal of the legislative union of Britain and Ireland. They participated in the agitation for repeal which spread throughout the British Isles and North America in 1843.[55] Lachine Canal labourers joined Irishmen in Montreal to call for an end to Ireland's colonial status; and labourers on the Welland met at Thorold to offer "their sympathy and assistance to their brethren at home in their struggle for the attainment of their just rights."[56] On the Williamsburg Canals, labourers also met together in support of Irish nationalism and Daniel O'Connell, the "Liberator" of Ireland. A local tavern keeper who interrupted a pro-O'Connell celebration by asking the canallers to move their bonfire away from his tavern lived in fear they would be back to burn the tavern down.[57]

Strong, persisting ethno-cultural bonds united the canallers, at times in active conflict with the dominant Protestant Anglo-Saxon culture. But their ethno-culture was also a source of bitter division. A long-standing feud between natives of Munster County and those from Connaught County divided the labourers into two hostile factions. The origin of the feud is obscure. It may have developed during confrontations in the eighteenth and nineteenth centuries between striking agricultural labourers of one county and black leg labourers transported across county lines. Or possibly it dated as far back as the rivalries of the old kingdoms of medieval Ireland.[58] Whatever its origin, the feud had become an integral part of the culture which southern Irish labourers carried to construction projects throughout Britain and North America.[59]

The feud did not simply flare up now and then over an insult or dispute between men who otherwise mingled freely. Feuding was part of the way in which canallers organized their lives, membership in a faction dictating both working and living arrangements. Men of one faction usually worked with members of the same faction. At times Cork and Connaught did work together under one contractor on the same section of work, particularly during the first few seasons of construction on the Welland when contractors hired labourers regardless of faction. But contractors quickly learned to honour the workers' preference with work with members of their faction, if only for the peace of the work.[60] Members of the same faction usually lived together also, cut off from the other faction in their separate Cork or Connaught community. Members of these communities offered each other material assistance in weathering difficult times. During summer and fall 1842 when half the Connaughtmen along the Broad Creek were ill with malaria, those Connaughtmen who were able to work "shared their miserable pittance," and provided necessities and medicine for the sick labourers and their dependants.[61] During the same season, the Connaughtmen also pooled their resources to retain a lawyer to defend 17 faction members in prison awaiting trial.[62]

The other side of this communal help and support, however, was suspicion of outsiders and intense hostility towards members of the rival factions. Hostility frequently erupted into violent confrontations between the factions. These confrontations were not a ritualized reminder of past skirmishes, but battles in deadly earnest, involving severe beatings and loss of life. The brutality of the encounters between Cork and Connaught led the St. Catharines Journal to denounce the participants as "strange and mad belligerent factions — brothers and countrymen, thirsting like savages for each other's blood — horribly infatuated."[63] Most participants in these skirmishes were heavily armed with "guns, pistols, swords, piles, or poles, pitch forks, scythes," many of which were procured from local inhabitants or the militia stores. In preparation for their revenge on the Corkmen, in one of their more spectacular thefts, Connaughtmen on the Welland actually took possession of blacksmith shops and materials to manufacture pikes and halberds.[64] Usually they simply accosted citizens in the streets or raided them at night.[65]

Armed conflict between the factions could reduce the canal areas to virtual war zones for weeks on end, "parties of armed men, 200 or 300 in number constantly assembling and parading," planning attack and counter-attack, at times fighting it out on the streets of St. Catharines and smaller centres around the Williamsburg Canals.[66] As Power explained to military authorities in the Niagara District: "one riot is the parent of many others, for after one of their factional fights the friends of the worsted party rally from all quarters to avenge the defeat."[67]

The fighting of two drunken men might precipitate a clash between the factions.[68] But men who reported to the Board of Works concerning factional fights were unanimous in concluding that the underlying cause of feuding was the massive and chronic unemployment in the canal areas. David Thorburn, magistrate for the Niagara District, explained: "The first moving cause that excites to the trouble is the want of work, if not employed they are devising schemes to procure it, such as driving away the party who are fewest in number who are not of their country. . . ."[69] Another magistrate for the Niagara District agreed that "the want of employment to procure bread" was the "principal root" of all the troubles; and Captain Wetherall, appointed to investigate the unrest along the canals, reached the same conclusion: "Strife to obtain work takes place between the two great sectional parties of Cork and Connaught. . . . The sole object of these combinations is to obtain work for themselves, by driving off the other party."[70] These observers appreciated the fact that the feud was a deep-seated hostility rooted in the southern Irish culture. They also believed that the Irish were given to letting their hostilities erupt into open conflict. Nonetheless, they were convinced that the problems associated with the feud, the open conflict and disruption of the work, would disappear if the problem of unemployment were solved.

This was the argument put forward by the labourers themselves at a meeting called by James Buchanan, ex-consul at New York and a respected member of the Irish community in North America. Buchanan posted notices along the Welland asking the "Sons of Erin" to meet with him to "reconcile and heal the divisions of [his] countrymen in Canada."[71] Corkmen refused to attend since the Connaughtmen's priest was helping to organize the meeting. But the Connaughtman sent delegates to meet privately with Buchanan and assembled for a public meeting at Thorold. After listening to patriotic speeches and admonitions to peace and order, the Connaughtmen laid down their terms for an end to factional fights: "give us work to earn a living, we cannot starve, the Corkmen have all the work, give us a share of it."[72]

Thus, along the canals the feud of Cork and Connaught became the vehicle through which an excess of labourers fought for a limited number of jobs. In this respect, the feud was similar to other conflicts between hostile subgroups of workers competing in an over-stocked labour market. In the unskilled labour market of the Canadas, competition was frequently between French Canadians and Irish labourers. Along the canals, in the dockyards, and particularly in the Ottawa Valley lumbering industry, the two ethnic groups engaged in a violent conflict for work, at times as intense and brutal as the conflict of Cork and Connaught.[73]

Similar ethnic clashes occurred between Anglo-Saxon and Irish Celtic labourers competing in the unskilled labour market in Britain. Long-standing animosities between these two groups have led historians to emphasize the xenophobic nature of such confrontations.[74] But in an analysis of navvies on the railways of northern England, J.B. Treble argues that these superficially ethnic clashes were actually rooted in economic conditions which fostered fears that one group was undercutting or taking the jobs of the other group. Treble concludes that however deep the racial or cultural animosities between groups of labourers, "the historian would ignore at his peril economic motivation, admittedly narrowly conceived in terms of personal advantage, but for that very reason immensely strong."[75] Like the conflict between Irish and French and Irish and Anglo-Saxon labourers, the factional fights became part of a general process of fragmentation and subgrouping which John Foster sees developing during the nineteenth century in response to industrialization. By bringing hostile groups into competition with each other, the process militated against united action and the growth of a broad working-class consciousness.[76] The feud was one variation in this broader pattern of division and conflict amongst workers.

Yet the feud and the bitter fight for work did not preclude united action in pursuit of common economic goals. In a few instances the factions joined together to demand the creation of jobs. During the first summer of construction on the Welland thousands of labourers and their families repeatedly paraded the streets of St. Catharines with placards demanding "Bread or Work," at one point breaking into stores, mills, and a schooner. In a petition to the people of Upper Canada, they warned that they would not "fall sacrifice to starvation:" "we were encouraged by contractors to build cantees [sic] on said work; now can't afford 1 meals victuals . . . we all Irishmen; employment or devastation."[77] Setting aside their sectional differences and uniting as "Irish labourers," Cork and Connaught co-operated to ensure that no one took the few hundred jobs offered by the Board of Works. Posters along the canal threatened "death and vengeance to any who should dare to work until employment was given to the whole." Bands of labourers patrolled the works, driving off any who tried to take a job.[78] By bringing all construction to a halt the labourers forced the Superintendent of the Welland to create more work. Going beyond the limits of his authority, Power immediately let the contract for locks three to six to George Barnett, and began pressuring contractors to increase their manpower.[79] But as construction expanded the canallers began a scramble for the available jobs until the struggle for work was no longer a conflict between labourers and the Board of Works, but a conflict between Cork and Connaught, each faction attempting to secure employment for its members.[80]

The following summer unemployed labourers on the Welland again united to demand the creation of jobs. This was a season of particularly high and prolonged unemployment. In addition to the usual numbers of unemployed flooding into the area, 3,000 labourers discharged from the feeder and the Broad Creek branches in the early spring had to wait over three months for work to commence on the section from Allanburgh to Port Colborne. Incensed by the Board of Works' apparent indifference to their plight, the unemployed pressured officials until in mid-July Power again acted independently of the Board, authorizing contractors to begin work immediately.[81] Anticipating the Board's censure, Power justified his actions as necessary to the protection of the work and the preservation of the peace: "However easy it may be for those who are at a distance to speculate on the propriety of delaying the work until precise instructions may arrive, it is very difficult for me, surrounded by men infuriated by hunger, to persist in a course which must drive them to despair."[82] The jobs opened up by Power could employ only half of those seeking work, but that was sufficient to crack the canallers' united front and revive the sectional conflict.[83] In general, Cork and Connaught appear to have united to demand jobs only during periods when there was virtually no work available, and consequently no advantage to competing amongst themselves.

It was in their attempts to secure adequate wages that the canallers most clearly demonstrated their ability to unite around economic issues. During frequent strikes along the canals the antagonistic relationship between the two factions was subordinated to the labourers' common hostility towards their employers, so that in relation to the contractors the canallers stood united. A Board of Works investigation into one of the larger strikes on the Welland Canal found Cork and Connaught peacefully united in a work stoppage. Concerning the strike of 1,000 labourers below Marshville, the Board's agent, Dr. Jarrow, reported that the labourers at the Junction had gone along the line and found both factions "generally ready and willing" to join in an attempt to get higher wages:

> No breach of the peace took place, nor can I find a tangible threat to have been issued. . . . Several men have been at work for the last two days on many of the jobs. . . . Those who have returned to work are not interfered with in the least degree. Contractors do not seem to apprehend the least breach of the peace. . . . The workmen seem well organized and determined not to render themselves liable to justice . . . Both the Cork and Connaught men are at work on different jobs below Marshville, and they seem to have joined in the Strick [sic] and I have not been able to find that their party feelings have the least connection with it.[84]

This was not an isolated instance of unity between the factions. Many strikes were small, involving only the men under one contractor, who usually belonged to the same faction; however, on the Welland in particular, Cork and Connaught joined in large strikes. Unity may have been fragile, but the overriding pattern that emerges during strikes is one of co-operation between the factions.[85] Not only did the factions unite in large strikes, but during a small strike involving only members of one faction, the other faction usually did not act as strike-breakers, taking the jobs abandoned by the strikers. What little information there is on strike-breaking concerns striking labourers confronting members of their own faction who tried to continue work, suggesting that the decision to work during a strike was not based on factional loyalties or hostilities.[86] Thus, most strikers did not become extensions of the bitter conflict for work. Rather strikes brought labourers together to pursue common economic interests. The instances in which Cork and Connaught united provide dramatic evidence of the ability of these economic interests to overcome an antipathy deeply rooted in the canallers' culture.

Canallers frequently combined in work stoppages demanding the payment of overdue wages. More often their strikes centred on the issue of wage rates. In a report concerning labour unrest on the canals of Upper and Lower Canada, Captain Wetherall concluded: "the question of what constitutes a fair wage is the chief cause from which all the bitter fruit comes." The priest among labourers on the Williamsburg agreed with Wetherall, going so far as to suggest that if the rate of wages could be settled once and for all troops and police would not be required for the canal areas. Similarly, Thorburn ranked wage rates with unemployment as a major cause of labour disturbances on the Welland.[87]

Since officials often reported "many" or "a few" strikes without indicating how many, the level of strike activity can only be suggested. Contractors expected, and usually faced, strikes in the late fall when they tried to impose the seasonal reduction in wage rates.[88] Strikes demanding an increase in wages were harder to predict, but more frequent. Each spring and summer on the Cornwall, Welland, and Williamsburg Canals work stoppages disrupted construction. Even in winter those labourers fortunate enough to continue working attempted to push up wages through strikes.[89] The degree of success which canallers enjoyed in their strikes cannot be determined from the fragmentary and scattered references to work stoppages. It is clear, however, that they forced contractors to pay wages above the level for unskilled, manual labour in general, and above the 2s or 2s6d which the Board of Works considered the most labourers on public works could expect.[90] On the Cornwall and Williamsburg Canals, strikes secured and maintained modest increases to as high as 3s and 3s6d.[91] Gains were much greater on the Welland. As early as winter 1843 labourers had driven wages to what Power claimed was the highest rate being offered on the continent.[92] While Power's statement cannot be accepted at face value, wages on the Welland may well have been the highest for manual labour in the Canadas, and in the northeastern United States where jobs were scarce and wages depressed. Strikes on the Welland forced wages even higher during 1843 and 1844, until the Board of Works calculated that labourers on the Welland were receiving at least 30 per cent more than the men on all the other works under its superintendence.[93]

How did the canallers, a fluid labour force engaged in casual, seasonal labour, achieve the solidarity and commitment necessary to successful strike action during a period of massive unemployment? Work stoppages protesting non-payment of wages may have been simply spontaneous reactions to a highly visible injustice, requiring little formal organization, more in the nature of protests than organized strikes. But the strikes through which canallers aggressively forced up wages or prevented contractors from lowering wages, required a greater degree of organization and long-term commitment. Labourers might be on strike for weeks, during which time they would become desperate for food.

In a variety of ways, the canallers' shared ethno-culture contributed to their successful strike action. Strikers found unity in the fact that they were "all Irishmen," in the same way that the unemployed identified with each other as "Irishmen" in their united demands for work. In the only well-documented strike by canallers, the Lachine strike of 1843, the labourers themselves stated this clearly. Corkmen and Connaughtmen issued joint petitions warning employers and would-be strike-breakers that they were not simply all canallers, they were "all Irishmen" whose purpose and solidarity would not be subverted.[94] Membership in a common ethnic community provided concrete aid in organized united action. At least in summer 1844 on the Welland, leadership in anti-Orange demonstrations overlapped with leadership in labour organization. During this season of frequent strikes, as many as 1,000 labourers assembled for mass meetings.[95] The authorities could not discover exactly what transpired at these meetings, since admittance was restricted to those who knew the password; a military officer, however, was able to observe one meeting at a distance. Ensign Gaele reported witnessing a collective decision-making process in which those present discussed, voted on, and passed resolutions. He drew particular attention to the participation of a man "who appeared to be their leader," a well-spoken individual of great influence, the same individual who had ridden at the head of the canallers on their march to intercept the Orangemen at Niagara Falls.[96] The situation on one canal during one season cannot support generalizations concerning organization on all canals throughout the 1840s. It does, however, suggest one way in which unity around ethno-cultural issues facilitated unity in economic struggles, by providing an established leadership.

Of more significance to the canallers' strike activity was the vehicle of organization provided by their ethno-culture. Like other groups of Irish labourers, most notably the Molly Maguires of the Pennsylvania coal fields, canallers found that the secret societies which flourished in nineteenth-century Ireland were well-adapted to labour organization in the new world.[97] At a time when those most active in strikes were subject to prosecution and immediate dismissal, oath-bound societies offered protection from the law and the reprisals of employers. The government investigation into disturbances on the Beauharnois found sufficient evidence to conclude that secret societies were the means by which the canallers organized their strikes. But it was unable to break through the labourers' secrecy and uncover details concerning the actual operation of the societies.[98] Similarly, Rev. McDonagh, despite his intimate knowledge of the canallers' personal lives, could only offer the authorities the names of two societies operating along the Welland, the Shamrock and Hibernian Societies. He could provide no information as to how they functioned, whether there were a number of small societies or a few large ones, whether all labourers or only a segment of the canallers belonged to them. And he "couldn't break them."[99]

The oaths which swore labourers to secrecy also bound them to be faithful to each other, ensuring solidarity and commitment in united action, and enforcing sanctions against any who betrayed his fellows. In addition, societies operated through an efficient chain of communication and command which allowed for tactics to be carefully formulated and executed.[100] Navvies did not develop a formal trade union. Consequently, in comparison with the activities of workers in the few trade unions of the 1820s, 1830s, and 1840s in British North America, the direct action of the Irish labourers appears "ad hoc."[101] But the fact that the navvies' organization was impenetrable to authorities and remains invisible to historians should not lead to the error of an "ad hoc" categorization. Although clandestine, secret societies were noted for the efficiency, even sophistication, of their organization,[102] and although not institutionalized within the formal, structured labour movement, they were the means of organizing sustained resistance, not spontaneous outbreaks of protest. Organization within secret societies, rather than within a formal trade union, also meant that canallers did not reach out to establish formal ties with other segments of the working class. As a result, they have left no concrete evidence of having identified the interests of their group with the interests of the larger working class, no clear demonstration that they perceived themselves as participating in a broader working-class struggle. But while their method of organization ruled out formal linking and expression of solidarity with the protest of other groups of workers, secret societies testified to the Irish labourers' link with a long tradition of militant opposition to employers in the old world. The secret societies which flourished in Dublin throughout the first half of the nineteenth century were feared by moderates in the Irish nationalist movement, because of their aggressive pursuit of working-class interests. During the same period, the agrarian secret societies of the southern Irish countryside primarily organized agricultural labourers and cottiers around issues such as rising conacre rents and potato prices. Although the ruling class of Britain and Ireland insisted that agrarian societies were essentially sectarian, these societies were, in fact, the instruments of class action, class action which at times united Protestant and Catholic labourers in a common cause.[103]

This cultural legacy of united opposition was invaluable to the canal labourers in their attempts to achieve higher wages. During their years of conflict with landlords and employers, the peasant labourers of southern Ireland acquired a belief system and values necessary to effective united action in the work place. Their belief system probably did not include a political critique of society which called for fundamental change in the relationship between capital and labour. Although Chartist and Irish nationalist leaders worked closely in the mid-nineteenth century, none of the varied radical strains of Chartism made significant advances in Ireland, which suggests that Irish labourers may not have seen themselves as members of a broader class whose interests were irreconcilable to the interests of capital.[104] But if theory had not given them a framework within which to understand the conflict of capital and labour, experience had created in them a deep-seated suspicion of employers and a sensitivity to exploitation. They brought to the new world the belief that their interests were in conflict with the employers' interest. Wetherall tried to explain their outlook to the Board of Works:

> They look on a Contractor as they view the "Middle Man" of their own Country, as a grasping, money making person, who has made a good bargain with the Board of Works for labour to be performed; and they see, or imagine they see, an attempt to improve that bargain at their expense . . . such is the feeling of the people, that they cannot divest themselves of the feeling that they are being imposed on if the contractor has an interest in the transaction.[105]

In the labourers' own words, posted along the works during the Lachine strike: "Are we to be tyrannized by Contractors . . . surrender/To No Contractors who wants to live by the sweat of our Brow."[106]

Irish labourers also brought to the new world a willingness to defy the law and, if necessary, use force to achieve their ends. Years of repression and discrimination had fostered what Kenneth Duncan has characterized as "a tradition of violence and terrorism, outside the law and in defiance of all authority."[107] In Britain the Irish labourers' willingness to challenge the law and the authorities had earned them a reputation for militance in the union movements, at the same time that it had infused a revolutionary impulse into Chartism.[108] In the Canadas, this same willingness marked their strike activity.

Newspapers and government officials usually reported the strikes along the canals as "rioting" or "riotous conduct," the uncontrollable excesses of an ethnic group addicted to senseless violence.[109] Yet far from being excessive and indiscriminate, the canallers' use of violence was restrained and calculated. Force or the threat of force was a legitimate tactic to be used if necessary. Some strikes involved little, if any, violence. Although he claimed to have looked very hard, Dr. Jarrow could find no instances of "outrage" during the first week of the Marshville strike, a strike involving 1,500 labourers along the Welland. In another large strike on the Welland the following summer, the *St. Catharines Journal* reported that there were no riotous disturbances.[110] When strikers did use force it was calculated to achieve a specific end. Organized bands of strikers patrolling the canal with bludgeons were effective in keeping strikebreakers at home.[111] Similarly, when labourers turned their violence on contractors and foremen, the result was not only the winning of a strike but also a remarkable degree of job control.[112] After only one season on the Williamsburg Canals, labourers had thoroughly intimidated contractors. One did not dare go near his work. Another the labourers "set at defiance" and worked as they pleased.[113] Canallers also attacked the canals, but these were not instances of senseless vandalism. Power viewed what he called "extraordinary accidents" as one way in which labourers pressured for redress of specific grievances.[114] On the Welland a related pressure tactic was interfering with the navigation. During the strike of approximately 1,500 labourers in summer 1844, captains of boats were afraid to pass through because they feared rude attacks on their passengers. Such fears appear to have been well founded. The previous winter, 200 canallers had attacked an American schooner, broken open the hatches, and driven the crew from the vessel, seriously injuring the captain and a crew member. Soldiers were required to keep "at bay the blood-thirsty assailants" while the crew reboarded their vessel.[115]

The canallers' willingness to resort to violence and defy authority antagonized large segments of the population who lamented the transplanting to the new world of outrages "characteristic only of Tipperary."[116] But despite the protestations of newspapers and private individuals that the canallers' use of force was inappropriate to the new world, the Irish labourers' militant tradition was well-suited to labour relations and power relations in the Canadas. The canallers' experience with the government and law enforcement agencies could only have reinforced what the past had taught — that the laws and the authorities did not operate in the interests of workers, particularly Irish Catholic workers. In their strikes, canallers confronted not just their employers, but the united opposition of the government, courts, and state law enforcement officers.

The government's opposition to strikes was based on the conviction that labourers should not attempt to influence wage rates. To government officials such as J.B. Mills of the Williamsburg Canal, the repeated strikes along the canals added up to a general "state of insubordination among the labourers," an "evil" which jeopardized the entire Public Works programme. Reports of the Board of Works condemned strikers for throwing construction schedules and cost estimates into chaos, and applauded contractors for their "indefatigable and praiseworthy exertions" in meeting turnouts and other difficulties with their labourers.[117] Leaving no doubt as to its attitude toward demands for higher wages, the Board worked closely with contractors in their attempts to prevent and break strikes. On their own initiative, contractors met together to determine joint strategies for handling turnouts and holding the line against wage increases.[118] The Board of Works went one step further, bringing contractors and law enforcement officers together to devise stratagems for labour control, and assuming the responsibility for co-ordinating and funding these stratagems.[119] Contractors and the Board joined forces in a comprehensive system of blacklisting which threatened participants in strikes. Operating on the assumption that the majority of the "well-disposed" were being provoked by a few rabble-rousers, contractors immediately dismissed ringleaders. Even during a peaceful strike such as the one at Marshville, in winter 1843, contractors discharged "those most active."[120] For its part the Board of Works collected and circulated along the canals descriptions of men like "Patrick Mitchell, a troublesome character" who "created insubordination amongst labourers" wherever he went.[121] Once blacklisted, men like Mitchell had little hope of employment on the public works in Canada.

Many labourers thus barred from public works projects also spent time in jail as part of the Board's attempt to suppress disturbances. Although British law gave workers the right to combine to withdraw their services in disputes over wages and hours, employers and the courts did not always honour this right. When the Board of Works' chief advisor on labour unrest argued that the Board should suppress the "illegal" combinations on the Welland and Williamsburg Canals, he was expressing an opinion widely held in British North America and an opinion shared by many officials involved in controlling labour unrest on the Public Works.[122] While opinion was divided over the rights of workers, there was general agreement that employers had the right to continue their operations during a strike, the course of action usually chosen by contractors, who seldom opted to negotiate with strikers. Workers who interfered with this right, by intimidating strike-breakers or contractors or generally obstructing the work, invited criminal charges. Since the charge of intimidation and obstruction was capable of broad interpretation, including anything from bludgeoning a contractor to talking to strike-breakers, this provision of the law gave contractors and the Board considerable scope for prosecuting strikers.[123]

To supplement existing labour laws, the Board of Works secured passage of the 1845 Act for the Preservation of the Peace near Public Works, the first in a long series of regulatory acts directed solely at controlling canal and railway labourers throughout the nineteenth century.[124] The Act provided for the registration of all firearms on branches of the Public Works specified by the Executive. The Board of Works had already failed in earlier attempts to disarm labourers on projects under its supervision. An 1843 plan to induce canallers on the Beauharnois to surrender their weapons was discarded "partly because there [was] not legal basis for keeping them." The following year a similar system on the Welland was also abandoned as illegal. Magistrates who had asked labourers to give up their weapons and to "swear on the Holy Evangelist that they had no gun, firearm, or offensive weapon," were indicted.[125] The 1845 Public Works Act put the force of the law and the power of the state behind gun control.

Most members of the Assembly accepted the registration of firearms along the canals as unavoidable under circumstances which "the existing law was not sufficient to meet."[126] A few members joined Aylwin of Quebec City in denouncing the measure as a dangerous over-reaction to a situation of the government's own making, "an Act of proscription, an Act which brought back the violent times of the word Annals of Ireland."[127] A more sizeable group shared Lafontaine's reservations that the bill might be used as a general disarming measure against any citizen residing near the canals. But the Attorney General's assurances that the disarming clause would apply "only to actual labourers on the public works," secured for the Bill an easy passage.[128] Even a member like Drummond, one of the few to defend canallers' interests in the House, ended up supporting the disarming clause on the grounds that it would contribute to the canallers' welfare by preventing them from committing the acts of violence to which contractors and hunger drove them. Drummond managed to convince himself that disarming the labourers would not infringe on their rights. He believed that all men had the right to keep arms for the protection of their property. But the canallers had no property to protect —"they were too poor to acquire any." Therefore they had neither the need, nor the right to possess weapons.[129]

In addition to disarming the labourers, the Public Works Act empowered the Executive to station mounted police forces on the public works.[130] Under the Act, Captain Wetherall secured an armed constabulary of 22 officers to preserve order among the labourers on the Williamsburg Canals. The Board of Works had already established its own constabulary on the Welland, two years prior to the legislation of 1845. Throughout 1843 and 1844 the Welland force fluctuated between 10 and 20, diminishing after 1845 as the number of labourers on the canals decreased. At a time when even the larger communities in Upper Canada, along with most communities in North America, still relied on only a few constables working under the direction of a magistrate, the size of these police forces testifies to the Board's commitment to labour control.[131] While the forces fulfilled various functions, in the eyes of the Board of Works their primary purpose was to ensure completion of the works within the scheduled time. Even protection of contractors from higher wages was not in itself sufficient reason for increasing the size of one of the forces. When Power asked for accommodation for a Superintendent of Police at the Junction, the Board answered that the old entrance lock was the only place where a strong force was necessary, since no combination of labourers for wages on the other works could delay the opening of the navigation, "the paramount object in view." A later communication expressed more forcefully the Board's general approach to funding police forces, stating that the only circumstances under which the expense of keeping the peace could be justified were that if it were not kept up the canals would not be "available to the trade."[132]

Despite this apparently strict criteria for funding police, the Board usually intervened to protect strike-breakers, probably because any strike threatened to delay opening of the navigation in the long, if not the short, term. Indeed, in their 1843 Report to the legislature, the Commissioners argued that it was part of their responsibility to help contractors meet deadlines by providing adequate protection to those labourers willing to work during a strike.[133] In meeting this responsibility the Board at times hired as many as 16 extra men on a temporary basis. When it was a question of getting the canals open for navigation the government appears to have been willing to go to almost any lengths to continue the work. In the winter of 1845, the Governor-General gave Power the authority to hire whatever number of constables it would take to ensure completion of construction by spring.[134]

Canal police forces worked closely with existing law enforcement agencies, since the common law required the magistrates to give direction in matters "relating to the arrest of suspected or guilty persons," and generally to ensure that the police acted within the law.[135] But Wetherall's investigation into the conduct of the Welland Canal force revealed that magistrates did not always keep constables from abusing their powers: "The constables oft exceed their authority, cause irritation, and receive violent opposition, by their illegal and ill-judged manner of attempting to make arrests." In one instance, the constables' behaviour had resulted in a member of the force being wounded. In another, an action had been commenced for false imprisonment. Wetherall also drew attention to complaints that the police force was composed of Orangemen, at least one of whom had acted improperly in "publicly abusing the Roman Catholic Religion — damning the Pope — etc., etc."[136]

The Williamsburg Canal force also came under attack for its provocative behaviour. Inhabitants of Williamsburg Township petitioned the Governor-General concerning the conduct of Captain James Macdonald and his men during a circus at Mariatown:

> The police attended on said day where in course of the evening through the misconduct of the police on their duty two persons have been maltreated and abused cut with swords and stabbed, taken prisoners and escorted to the police office that all this abuse was committed by having the constables in a state of intoxication on their duty when the Magistrate who commanded them was so drunk that he fell out of a cart. A pretty representative is Mr. MacDonald.[137]

The Roman Catholic priest on the Williamsburg Canal joined in denouncing the police force, warning the labourers: "They are like a parcel of wolves and roaring mad lions seeking the opportunity of shooting you like dogs and all they want is the chance in the name of God leave those public works."[138]

Of invaluable assistance to the constables and magistrates were the Roman Catholic priests, hired by the Board of Works as part of the police establishment, and stationed amongst canallers. Referred to as "moral" or "spiritual" agents, they were in reality police agents, paid out of the Board's police budget, and commissioned to preserve "peace and order" by employing the ultimate threat — hell.[139] They were of limited value in controlling Orange/Green confrontations. They were actually suspected of encouraging them.[140] Their effectiveness in stopping factional fights was also limited, at least on the Welland where the Reverend McDonagh was suspected of harbouring sectional sentiments.[141] Their most important function was to prevent or break strikes. Intimate involvement in the canallers' daily lives equipped them as informers concerning possible labour unrest.[142] When canallers struck, authorities could rely on priests to admonish labourers to give up their "illegal" combinations and return to work, to show "that the Gospel has a more salutary effect than bayonets."[143] Priests were not insensitive to the suffering of their charges, and to its immediate cause. McDonagh repeatedly argued the canallers' case with government officials, contractors, and civil and military authorities.[144] On the Williamsburg Canals, the Reverend Clarke's criticism of the treatment of labourers became such an embarrassment to the government that he was shipped back to Ireland, supposedly for health reasons.[145] But at the same time that priests were protesting conditions along the canals, they were devoting most of their energy to subverting the protest of their parishioners. McDonagh fulfilled this function so successfully that the Superintendent on the Welland Canal told the Board he knew of "no one whose services could have been so efficient."[146]

By supplementing existing laws and enforcement agencies, the government was able to bring an extraordinary degree of civil power against the canal labourers. Even an expanded civil power, however, was inadequate to control the canallers and the military became the real defenders of the peace in the canal areas. As early as the first summer of construction on the Welland, the Governor-General asked the Commander of the Forces to station the Royal Canadian Rifles in three locations along the Welland, 60 men at St. Catharines, 60 at Thorold, and 30 at Port Maitland. In addition, a detachment of the coloured Incorporated Militia attached to the Fifty Lincoln Militia was stationed at Port Robinson. Aid was also available from the Royal Canadian Rifles permanently stationed at Chippewa.[147] From these headquarters, troops marched to trouble spots for a few hours, days, or weeks. Longer postings necessitated temporary barracks such as those constructed at Broad Creek and Marshville in fall 1842.[148] No troops were posted on either the Cornwall or Williamsburg Canals, despite the requests of contractors and inhabitants. Detachments in the vicinity, however, were readily available for temporary postings.[149]

With a long tradition of military intervention in civil disturbances both in Great Britain and British North America, the use of troops was a natural response to the inadequacies of the civil powers.[150] Troops were important for quickly ending disturbances and stopping the escalation of dangerous situations such as an Orange/Green clash or a confrontation between labourers and contractors.[151] The use of troops carried the risk that men might be shot needlessly. As Aylwin told the Legislature:

> If the constable exceed his duty there is a certain remedy; he may perhaps throw a man in prison; but if that man be innocent he will afterwards be restored to his family; when however, the military are called out the soldier is obliged to do his duty, and men are shot down who perhaps . . . are quite as unwilling to break the peace as any man in the world.

Such had been the case during a confrontation on the Beauharnois Canal. Troops were called in and "bloody murders were committed." Labourers were "shot, and cut down, and driven into the water and drowned."[152] On the canals of Upper Canada, however, the military does not appear to have charged or opened fire on canallers. No matter how great their numbers or how well they were armed, canallers usually disbanded with the arrival of troops and the reading of the Riot Act.

Detachments were even more valuable as a preventive force. Before special detachments were posted along the Welland, the Governor-General explicitly instructed magistrates to use the troops in a preventive capacity, calling them out if "there should be any reason to fear a breach of the Peace, with which the civil power would be inadequate to deal."[153] Magistrates gave the broadest possible interpretation to the phrase "any reason to fear" and repeatedly called in the military when there had been merely verbal threats of trouble. When a large number of unemployed labourers appeared "ripe for mischief," when strikers seemed likely to harass the strike-breakers, magistrates requisitioned troops.[154]

Magistrates used the troops to such an extent that they provoked the only real opposition to military intervention in civil affairs — opposition from the military itself. Both on-the-spot commanders and high-ranking military officials complained that troops were being "harassed" by the magistrates, that the requisitions for aid were "extremely irregular," and that the troops were marching about the frontier on the whim of alarmists.[155] The expense of keeping four or five detachments on the march does not appear to have been a factor in the dispute over the use of troops, since the civil authorities met the cost of deploying troops in civil disturbances. The British Treasury continued to pay for salaries, provisions, and stores, but the Board of Works accepted responsibility for constructing barracks and for providing transportation and temporary accommodation at trouble spots when necessary.[156] The only point at issue appears to have been the unorthodox and unnecessary use of detachments.

This dispute was the only disharmony in the co-operation between civil and military authorities and even it had little effect on the actual operation of the system of control. At the height of the dispute, commanding officers still answered virtually all requisitions, although in a few instances they withdrew their men immediately if they felt their services were not required.[157] After the Provincial Secretary ruled that commanders must respond to all requisitions, whatever the circumstances, even the grumbling stopped.[158] Particularly on the Welland, regular troops were kept constantly patrolling the canal areas in apprehension of disturbances, "looking for trouble," as Colonel Elliott put it.[159]

With special laws, special police forces, and a military willing, if not eager to help, the government of the Canadas marshalled the coercive power of the state against labourers on the public works. Yet the government failed to suppress labour unrest and to prevent successful strike action. Many officials and contractors accepted this failure as proof of the Celt's ungovernable disposition. Invoking the Irish stereotype to explain the disorder along the canals, they ignored their own role in promoting unrest and obscured the class dimension of the canallers' behaviour. They also misinterpreted the nature of the relationship between the canallers' ethno-culture and their collective action. What the southern Irish brought to the new world was not a propensity for violence and rioting, but a culture shaped by class relations in the old world. Class tensions, inseparably interwoven with racial hatred and discrimination, had created in the southern Irish suspicion and hatred of employers, distrust of the laws and the authorities, and a willingness to violate the law to achieve their ends. This bitter cultural legacy shaped the Irish labourers' resistance to conditions in the Canadas and gave a distinctive form to class conflict on the canals.

NOTES

I would like to thank Don Avery and Wayne Roberts for their comments on earlier drafts of this paper.

1. Public Archives of Canada, Record Group 11, Department of Public Works: 5, Canals (hereafter cited RG11-5), Welland Canal Letterbook, Samuel Power to Thomas Begly, Chairman of Board of Works (hereafter cited WCLB), Power to Begly, 12 August 1842.

2. Public Archives of Canada, Record Group 8, British Military and Naval Records I, C Series, Vol. 60, Canals (hereafter cited C Series, Vol. 60), Bethune to MacDonald, 31 March 1843.

3. H.C. Pentland, "Development of a Capitalistic Labour Market in Canada," *Canadian Journal of Economics and Political Science*, 25 (1959), 450–61.

4. A.C. Buchanan, Parliamentary Papers, 1842, No. 373, cited in W.F. Adams, *Ireland and the Irish Emigration to the New World* (Connecticut 1932).

5. Gary Teeple, "Land, Labour, and Capital in Pre-Confederation Canada," in Teeple, ed., *Capitalism and the National Question in Canada* (Toronto 1972), Leo A. Johnson, "Land Policy, Population Growth and Social Structure in the Home District, 1793–1851," *Ontario History* 63 (1971), 41–60. Both Teeple and Johnson attach particular significance to the ideas of Edward Gibbon Wakefield who advocated a prohibitive price on land to force immigrants into the labour force. V.C. Fowke, "The Myth of the Self Sufficient Canadian Pioneer," *Transactions of the Royal Society of Canada*, 56 (1962).

6. R.T. Naylor, "The Rise and Fall of the Third Commercial Empire of the St. Lawrence," in Gary Teeple, ed., *Capitalism and the National Question in Canada* (Toronto 1972), 1–13; Teeple, "Land, Labour, and Capital," 57–62.

7. H.C. Pentland, "Labour and the Development of Industrial Capitalism in Canada," Ph.D. thesis, University of Toronto, 1960, 239. In the fall of 1840, contractors in the Chambly Canal could not procure labourers even at what the government considered "most extravagant rates." Canada, *Journals of the Legislative Assembly, 1841*, Appendix D. W.F. Adams, *Ireland and the Irish Emigration* and Helen I. Cowan, *British Emigration to British North America: The First Hundred Years* (Toronto 1961).

8. Pentland, "Labour and Industrial Capitalism" 273. See also: Frances Morehouse, "The Irish Migration of the 'Forties,'" *American Historical Review*, 33 (1927–28), 579–92.

9. The best treatment of famine immigrants in British North America is Kenneth Duncan, "Irish Famine Immigration and the Social Structure of Canada West," *Canadian Review of Sociology and Anthropology* (1965), 19–40.

10. Report of the Niagara District Council, *Niagara Chronicle*, 4 August 1847.

11. RG11-5, Vol. 390, file 93, Williamsburg Canals, Estimates and Returns, 1844–58, Public Notice of the Board of Works issued by Begly, 26 February 1844; RG11-5, Vol. 390, file 94, Police Protection and the Williamsburg Canals, Mills to Begly, 16 February 1847.

12. J.P. Merritt, *Biography of the Hon. W.H. Merritt* (St. Catharines 1875), 310. Concerning the construction industry in Britain, Gosta E. Sandstrom has argued that the very existence of an easily exploitable labour pool

deferred mechanization, relieving state and private management "of the need for constructive thinking." Gosta E. Sandstrom, *The History of Tunnelling* (London 1963). For a discussion of the relationship between labour supply and the development of mechanization in the mid-nineteenth century see Raphael Samuel, "The Workshop of the World: Steam Power and Hand Technology in mid-Victorian Britain," *History Workshop*, 3 (1977), 6–72. Labourers on North American canals in the 1840s were still performing basically the same tasks their counterparts had performed half a century earlier during the canal age in Europe. For a description of these tasks see: Anthony Burton, *The Canal Builders* (London 1972). Alvin Harlow describes a variety of new inventions used on the Erie Canal, which might have made their way to the canals of the Canadas. These ranged from a sharp-edged shovel for cutting roots to a stump-puller operated by seven men and a team of horses or oxen. Alvin Harlow, *Old Towpaths: The Story of the American Canal Era* (New York 1964), 53.

13. John P. Heisler, *The Canals of Canada*, National Historic Sites Service, Manuscript Report Number 64, December 1971, 220–1, 224–5, 226–7.

14. RG11-5, Vol. 407, file 113, Thorburn to Daly, 10 January 1844.

15. *Ibid.*, Thorburn to Murdock, 18 August 1842; RG11-5, WCLB, Samuel Power to A. Thomas Begly, Chairman of Board of Works, Power to Begly, 20 March 1843; *Ibid.*, Power to Begley, 17 July 1843.

16. Duncan, "Irish Famine Immigration," 25–6. For a discussion of the application of the improved system of British agriculture to Upper Canada see: Kenneth Kelly, "The Transfer of British Ideas on Improved Farming to Ontario During the First Half of the Nineteenth Century," *Ontario History*, 63 (1971), 103–11.

17. *St. Catharines Journal*, 31 August 1843; *Niagara Chronicle*, 4 August 1847.

18. Duncan, "Irish Famine Immigration," 26.

19. RG11-5, WCLB, Power to Begly, 8 April 1843; *Niagara Chronicle*, 4 August 1847.

20. RG11-5, Vol. 390, file 94, Hiel to Begly, 16 February 1847.

21. RG11-5, Vol. 390, file 93, Public Notice Board of Works, 26 February 1844; *Legislative Journals*, 1844–45, Appendix Y, Report of Mills, 20 January 1845; *Ibid.*, Mills to Begly, 21 January 1845; *Ibid.*, Jarvis to Daily, 28 October 1845.

22. *Niagara Chronicle*, 4 August 1847.

23. *St. Catharines Journal*, 16 February 1844.

24. Petition of Constantine Lee and John Williams Baynes to Sir Charles Bagot, cited in Dean Harris, *The Catholic Church in the Niagara Peninsula* (Toronto 1895), 255. Lee was the Roman Catholic priest for St. Catharines, Baynes the community's Presbyterian minister. See also: RG11-5, Vol. 389, file 89, Correspondence of Samuel Keefer, 1843–51, Superintendent of Welland Canal, 1849–52, Keefer to Begly, 1 February 1843; RG11-5, Vol. 407, file 114, McDonagh to Killaly, 2 May 1843; Vol. 407, file 113, Thorburn to Daly, 10 January 1844; RG11-5, Vol. 381, file 56, John Rigney, Superintendent Cornwall Canal, 1841–44, Godfrey to Begly, 22 April 1843; *Ibid.*, Godfrey to Begly, 8 June 1843.

25. Richard Splane, *Social Welfare in Ontario 1791–1893* (Toronto 1965), 68–9, 74.

26. *St. Catharines Journal*, 26 January 1844.

27. *St. Catharines Journal*, 16 February 1844.

28. Harris, *The Catholic Church in the Niagara Peninsula*, 255; RG11-5, Vol. 388, file 87, Correspondence of General Killaly, 1841-45, Welland Canal, Merritt to Killaly, 12 August 1842.

29. RG11-5, Vol. 389, file 89, Keefer to Begly, 1 February 1843. Terry Coleman discusses the stereotype of the navvy on construction sites in the British Isles in his chapter, "King of Labourers," Terry Coleman, *The Railway Navvies: A History of the Men Who Made the Railways* (London 1965), ch. 12.

30. Farm labourers' wages appear in RG5-B21, Emigration Records, 1840–44, Information to Immigrants, April 1843, for Brockville, Chippewa, Cornwall, Fort Erie, Indiana, Niagara, Port Colborne, Prescott, Queenston, Smith's Falls; *Ibid.* For the Information of Emigrants of the Labouring Classes, December 1840, the Johnston District. Wages were not consistently higher in the area round any one of the canals. Newspapers also contain references to wage levels for farm labourers. Only newspapers appear to have paid much attention to the serious accidents on construction sites. Navvies crushed by stones, kicked by horses, and drowned in the locks made good copy. Work on the canals under consideration did not involve tunnelling, by far the most hazardous aspect of the navvy's work. But the malaria-producing mosquito which thrived on many canal construction sites in North America made up for this. In October 1842 Dr. John Jarrow reported to the Board of Works that "scarcely an individual" from among the over 800 men who had been on the Broad Creek works would escape the "lake fever." Three-quarters of the labourers' wives and children were already sick. Very few of those under two would recover. RG11-5, Vol. 407, file 104, Welland Canal Protection 1842–50, Memorandum of Dr. John Jarrow to the Board of Works, 1 October 1842.

31. H.C. Pentland, "Labour and the Development of Industrial Capitalism in Canada," 232. Pentland underlines the difficulty in making valid generalizations because of "considerable variation from time to time and from

place to place." All wages have been translated into Sterling, using the conversion rate of 22s.2 3/4 d. Currency per £ Sterling, published in Canada, RG5-B21, Quarter Return of Prices in the Province of Canada in the Quarter Ending 31 October 1844. The variation in wages along the canals was determined through the frequent references to wage levels in the records of the Department of Public Works and newspaper articles. Wages fluctuated within the same range on the Lachine and Beauharnois Canals in Canada East. H.C. Pentland, "The Lachine Strike of 1843," *Canadian Historical Review* 29 (1948), 255–77; *Legislative Journals*, 1843, Appendix T, Report of the Commissioners appointed to inquire into the Disturbances upon the line of the Beauharnois Canal, during the summer of 1843. *Legislative Journals*, 1843, Appendix Q; *Ibid.*, 1845, Appendix AA.

32. Given that labourers at Beauharnois used company stores and received store pay as did many canallers in Upper Canada, and considering the fairly constant price of foodstuffs along the St. Lawrence system, the find-ings of the Beauharnois Commission can be applied to labourers on the Cornwall, Welland, and Williamsburg Canals. *Legislative Journals*, 1843, Appendix T; RG5-B21, Information to Immigrants, April 1843; *Ibid.*, For the Information of Emigrants of the Labouring Classes, December 1840, the Johnston District; *Ibid.*, Quarterly Return of Prices for the City of Montreal in the Quarter ended 31st October 1844.

33. These figures represent averages of the estimated number of days worked during each month on the Cornwall, Welland, and Williamsburg Canals.

34. WCLB, Power to Begly, April 1842; *Ibid.*, Power to Begly, 10 March 1843; Welland Canal Commission, folder 8 (hereafter cited WCC-8), Begly to Power, 24 January 1844; RG11-5, Vol. 390, file 94, Killaly to Begly, 26 March 1846; Vol. 381, file 56, Godfrey to Begly, 8 June 1843; Vol. 389, file 89, Keefer to Begly, 2 May 1848; RG11-5, Vol. 388, file 88, Correspondence of Hamilton Killaly, Assistant Engineer on Welland Canal, 1842–57, Keefer to Begly, 14 March 1849. Frequently the government withheld money from contractors, making it impossible for them to pay their labourers. The government also took its time paying labourers employed directly by the Board of Works.

35. *Legislative Journals*, 1843, Appendix Q; WCLB, Power to Begly, 1 October 1842.

36. C Series, Vol. 60, Memorandum of Captain Wetherall, 3 April 1843.

37. *Legislative Journals*, 1843, Appendix Q. WCLB, Power to Begly, 1 February 1944. Power draws attention to the public outcry, but does not elaborate.

38. *Legislative Journals*, 1843, Appendix Q.

39. RG11-5, Vol. 388, file 87, Correspondence of Hamilton Killaly, 1841–55, McDonagh to Killaly, 25 January 1843; WCLB, Power to Sherwood and Company, 1 February 1844; Vol. 390, file 94, Wetherall to Killaly, 2 March 1844.

40. Elizabeth Nish, ed., *Debates of the Legislative Assembly of United Canada*, Vol. IV, 1844–45, Lewis Thomas Drummond, 1460.

41. *Ibid.*, Wilfred Nelson, 1511.

42. The cost of living does not appear to have fluctuated significantly from canal to canal. See note 32.

43. RG11-5, Vol. 407, file 113, Thorburn to Daly, 19 January 1844.

44. RG11-5, Vol. 388, file 87, Articles of Agreement between the Board of Works and Lewis Schiclaw, 1 April 1845. See Ruth Bleasdale, "Irish Labourers on the Canals of Upper Canada in the 1840's," M.A. thesis, University of Western Ontario, 1975, 34–7.

45. Pentland, "The Lachine Strike of 1843," 259.

46. Bleasdale, "Irish Labourers on the Canals," 36–7.

47. RG11-5, Vol. 407, file 104, Memorandum of Dr. Jarrow, 1 October 1842. A.H. Ross, *Ottawa, Past and Present* (Toronto 1927), 109.

48. WCLB, Power to Begly, 17 January 1845; RG11-5, Vol. 390, file 93, Mills to Begly, 26 June 1845; RG11-5, Vol. 389, file 90, Miscellaneous, 1842–51, Keefer to Robinson, 1 March 1842.

49. Conrad Arensberg, *The Irish Countryman* (New York 1950), 66–8.

50. *St. Catharines Journal*, 16 February 1844; RG11-5, Col. 407, file 104, Memorandum of Dr. Jarrow, 1 October 1842.

51. T.C. Foster, *Letters on the Condition of the People of Ireland* (London 1847); J.G. Kohl, *Travels in Ireland* (London 1844); K.H. Connell, *The Population of Ireland, 1760–1845* (Oxford 1950).

52. Michael Cross, "The Dark Druidicial Groves," Ph.D. thesis, University of Toronto, 1968, 470; Harris, *The Catholic Church in the Niagara Peninsula*, 262–4; *St. Catharines Journal*, 25 August 1843; Harris, *The Catholic Church in the Niagara Peninsula*.

53. C Series, Vol. 60, Merritt to Daly, 21 September 1844; C. Series, Vol. 60, Elliott to Young, 23 July 1844.

54. C Series, Vol. 317, MacDonald to Daly, 14 July 1849.

55. Adams, *Ireland and Irish Emigration*, 89.

56. *St. Catharines Journal*, 24 August 1843.

57. *Legislative Journals*, 1844–45, Appendix Y, Gibbs to Higginson, 6 January 1845.

58. T.D. Williams, *Secret Societies in Ireland* (Dublin 1973), 31.

59. E.P. Thompson, *The Making of the English Working Class* (Middlesex 1972).

60. By commencement of the second season of construction, employers followed William Hamilton Merritt's suggestion to employ only Corkmen on the upper section and only Connaughtmen on the lower section of the Welland Canal. On the Williamsburg Canals also the factions laboured on different sections of the work.

61. WCLB, Power to Begly, 25 August 1843.

62. RG11-5, Vol. 407, file 104, Robinson to Begly, 19 October 1842.

63. *St. Catharines Journal*, 7 July 1842.

64. RG11-5, Vol. 407, file 113, Thorburn to Daly, 10 January 1844; Vol. 407, file 104, Hobson to Daly, 20 January 1844; Vol. 407, file 113, Thorburn to Daly, 17 January 1844.

65. *Ibid.*, Thorburn to Daly, 10 January 1844; *Legislative Journals*, 1844–45, Appendix Y, Jarvis to Daly, 28 October 1844.

66. *Ibid.*, Appendix Y, Killaly to Daly, 5 November 1844; RG11-5, Vol. 389, file 89, Power to Begly, 17 January 1845; Vol. 407, file 113, Thorburn to Daly, 10 January 1844; *St. Catharines Journal*, 7 July 1843; *Brockville Recorder*, 8 August 1844.

67. WCLB, Power to Elliott, 28 December 1843.

68. RG11-5, Vol. 407, file 113, Thorburn to Daly, 10 January 1844.

69. *Ibid.*

70. RG11-5, Vol. 407, file 104, Hobson to Daly, 20 January 1844. *Ibid.*, Wetherall to Killaly, 26 March 1844.

71. RG11-5, Vol. 407, file 113, Public Notice to the Sons of Erin, Engaged on the Welland Canal, who are known as Corkmen and Connaughtmen, 12 January 1844.

72. WCC-6, Thorburn to Daly, 19 January 1844.

73. Pentland, "The Lachine Strike of 1843;" J.I. Cooper, "The Quebec Ship Labourers' Dark Druidicial Groves;" Michael Cross, "The Shiners' War: Social Violence in the Ottawa Valley in the 1830's," *Canadian Historical Review* 54 (1973), 1–26.

74. E.L. Tapin, *Liverpool Dockers and Seamen, 1870–1890* (Hull 1974).

75. J.H. Treble, "Irish Navvies in the North of England, 1830–50," *Transport History* 6 (1973), 227–47.

76. Foster's comparative study of class consciousness in three nineteenth-century towns rests on an analysis of varying degrees of fragmentation and sub-group identification. For an argument see: John Foster, "Nineteenth-Century Towns — A Class Dimension," in H.J. Dyos, ed., *The Study of Urban History* (London 1968), 281–99. See also John Foster, *Class Struggle and the Industrial Revolution: Early Industrial Capitalism in Three English Towns* (London 1974), and Neville Kirk, "Class and Fragmentation: Some Aspects of Working-Class Life in South-East Lancashire and North-East Cheshire, 1850–1870," Ph.D. thesis, University of Pittsburgh, 1974. Kirk endeavours to explain the decline of class consciousness in mid-nineteenth century England in terms of the fragmentation of the working class into subgroups, emphasizing the widening gap between "respectable" and "non-respectable" workers, and the bitter conflict between Roman Catholic Irish and other segments of the workforce.

77. Petition of Lee and Baynes, cited in Harris, *The Catholic Church*, 255. RH11-5, Vol. 407, file 113, Thorburn to Murdock, 18 August 1842; *St. Catharines Journal*, 11 August 1842; Vol. 388, file 87, Petition presented to Reverend Lee, 1 August 1842.

78. *St. Catharines Journal*, 11 August 1842.

79. WCLB, Power to Begly, 12 August 1842.

80. *St. Catharines Journal*, 11 August 1842; WCLB, Power to Begly, 15 August 1842.

81. Welland Canal Commission, folder 6 (hereafter cited WCC-6), Power to Begly, 14 February 1843; WCLB, Power to Begly, 20 March 1843; *Ibid.*, Power to Begly, 17 July 1843.

82. *Ibid.*, Power to Begly, 1 August 1843. The following winter, Thorburn praised Power for his attempts to ease unemployment by ensuring that contractors hired as many labourers as possible. RG11-5, Vol. 407, file 113, Thorburn to Daly, 19 January 1844. Of course Power may have been motivated equally be a desire to push the work ahead.

83. WCLB, Power to Begly, 25 August 1843.

84. RG11-5, Vol. 407, file 104, Jarrow to Merritt, 6 January 1843.

85. Pentland describes the betrayal of one faction by the other in one of the large strikes on the Lachine. Pentland, "The Lachine Strike."

86. For example: RG11-5, Vol. 407, file 104, Cotton and Row to Wheeler, 26 August 1846.

87. C Series, Vol. 60, Memorandum of Wetherall to the Board of Works, 3 April 1843; Vol. 90, file 94, Clarke to Killaly, 6 March 1845; RG11-5, Vol. 407, file 113, Thorburn to Daly, 10 January 1844.

88. See for example: *Legislative Journals*, 1844–45, Appendix Y, Jarvis to Begly, RG11-5, Vol. 390, file 93, Mills to Killaly, November 1844; *Ibid.*, Mills to Killaly, 29 November 1845.

89. *Legislative Journals*, 1843, Appendix Q; *Legislative Journals*, 1844–45, Appendix AA; RG11-5, Vol. 381, file 56, Godfrey to Begly, 26 March 1844; Vol. 390, file 94, Wetherall to Killaly, 2 March 1844; Vol. 389, file 89, Power to Begly, 4 March 1845.

90. *Legislative Journals*, 1843, Appendix Q; *Legislative Journals*, 1844–45, Appendix AA.

91. *St. Catharines Journal*, 7 June 1844; RG11-5, Vol. 381, file 56, Godfrey to Begly, 9 April 1844.

92. RG11-5, WCLB, Power to Begly, 10 March, 1843.

93. WCLB, Power to Begly, 17 July 1843; *St. Catharines Journal*, 16 November 1843; WCC-7, Power to Begly, 7 December 1843; *Legislative Journals*, 1844–45, Appendix AA.

94. *Montreal Transcript*, 28 March 1843, cited in Pentland, "The Lachine Strike," 266.

95. According to the *St. Catharines Journal*, 20 September 1844, there were four major strikes between 1 April and 20 July.

96. C Series, Vol. 60, Gaele to Elliott, 23 July 1844; *Ibid.*, Elliott to Young, 23 July 1844.

97. For an analysis of secret societies in Ireland see Williams, *Secret Societies in Ireland*. For a study of the Molly Maguires see Anthony Bimba, *The Molly Maguires* (New York 1932).

98. *Legislative Journals*, 1843, Appendix T.

99. RG11-5, Vol. 407, file 113, Thorburn to Daly, 10 January 1844.

100. Williams, *Secret Societies in Ireland*, 31.

101. Stephen Langdon, "The Emergence of the Canadian Working Class Movement, 1845–75," *Journal of Canadian Studies*, 8 (1973), 3–4.

102. Williams, *Secret Societies in Ireland*, 31.

103. *Ibid.*, 7, 25–7.

104. Rachel O'Higgins, "The Irish Influence in the Chartist Movement," *Past and Present*, 20 (1961), 83–96.

105. C Series, Vol. 60, Wetherall to Board of Works, 3 April 1843.

106. Montreal Transcript, 28 March 1843.

107. Duncan, "Irish Famine Immigration."

108. O'Higgins, "Irish in Chartist Movement," 83–6.

109. *St. Catharines Journal*, 31 August 1843; *Niagara Chronicle*, 10 July 1844; for further examples of the sensational manner in which newspapers reported labour disturbances see: *St. Catharines Journal*, 16 November 1843, 14 December 1843, 21 December 1843, 17 May 1844, 2 August 1844, 16 August 1844, 20 September 1844; *Niagara Chronicle*, 20 February 1845; *Brockville Recorder*, 7 September 1843, 21 December 1843, 21 March 1844, 8 August 1844; *Cornwall Observer*, 8 December 1842, 9 January 1845.

110. RG11-5, Vol. 407, file 104, Jarrow to Merritt, 6 January 1843; *St. Catharines Journal*, 28 June 1844.

111. RG11-5, Vol. 407, file 113, Thorburn to Daly, 10 January 1844; C Series, Vol. 60, testimony of James McCloud, sworn before Justices Kerr and Turney, 14 September 1844.

112. *Legislative Journals*, Jarvis to Daly, 28 October 1844; WCLB, Power to Begly, 3 January 1844.

113. *Legislative Journals*, Jarvis to Daly, 28 October 1844.

114. WCLB, Power to Begly, 14 February 1843.

115. RG11-5, Vol. 407, file 113, Thorburn to Begly, 1 July 1844; *Cornwall Observer*, 8 December 1842. See also: WCLB, Power to Begly, April 1842.

116. *Cornwall Observer*, 9 January 1845.

117. RG11-5, Vol. 390, file 93, Mills to Killaly, 29 November 1845; *Ibid.*, Mills to Killaly, November 1844; *Legislative Journals*, 1845, Appendix AA.

118. RG11-5, Vol. 407, file 113, Thorburn to Daly, 10 January 1844; Vol. 407, file 113, Thorburn to Daly, 17 January 1844.

119. RG11-5, Vol. 407, file 113, Thorburn to Daly, 10 January 1844.

120. RG11-5, Vol. 407, file 104, Jarrow to Merritt, 6 January 1843.

121. WCC-7, Power to Begly, 10 February 1843; *Ibid.*, Begly to Power, 8 April 1843; WCC-8, Begly to Power, 3 September 1845.

122. A.W.R. Carrothers, *Collective Bargaining Law in Canada* (Toronto 1965), 13–15. C Series, Vol. 60, Wetherall to Board of Works, 3 April 1843; *Legislative Journals*, 1843, Appendix T. Also see Pentland, "The Lachine Strike," for a discussion of the conflicting opinions concerning combinations and strikes.

123. Carrothers, *Collective Bargaining Law*, 14; Henry Pelling, *A History of British Trade Unions* (Middlesex 1973), 31–2.

124. Act for the better preservation of the Peace and the prevention of riots and violent outrages at and near public works while in the progress of construction, 8 Vic.c.6.

125. Pentland, "Labour and the Development of Industrial Capitalism," 413; RG11-5, January 1844; WCLB, Power to contractors, 16 January 1844; Vol. 407, file 104, Wetherall to Killaly, 26 March 1844.

126. *Legislative Debates,* 1844–45, Attorney General James Smith, 1443.

127. *Ibid.,* Thomas Aylwin, 1459.

128. *Ibid.,* Louis Hippolyte Lafontaine, 1505; *Ibid.,* Attorney General James Smith, 1515–17.

129. *Ibid.,* Lewis Thomas Drummond, 1516–17.

130. *Ibid.,* Drummond, 1515.

131. WCLB, Bonnalie to Begly, 12 March 1844; RG11-5, Vol. 388, file 89, Power to Begly, 11 February 1846; *Ibid.,* Power to Begly, 17 January 1847; RG-8, C Series, Vol. 60, Daly to Taylor, 17 May 1845; RG11-5, Vol. 390, file 94, Hill to Begly, 16 February 1847; *Ibid.,* Hill to Begly, 21 June 1847. Both forces continued until the great bulk of the work on their respective canals was finished, the Welland Canal constabulary until 31 December 1849, that on the Williamsburg Canals until 31 October 1847, the month that the last of the canals was opened.

132. WCC-8, Begly to Power, 2 December 1845; *Ibid.,* Begly to Power, 27 December 1845.

133. *Legislative Journals,* 1843, Appendix Q.

134. WCLB, Power to Begly, 3 March 1845; *Ibid.,* Power to Begly, 14 February 1845.

135. Leon Radzinowicz, *A History of the Criminal Law and Its Administration from 1750,* Vol. III (London 1948), 284.

136. RG11-5, Vol. 407, file 104, Wetherall to Killaly, 26 March 1844.

137. RG-5, C1, Provincial Secretary's Office, Canada West, Vol. 161, #11,362, Memorial of Inhabitants of Mariatown to Lord Metcalf Governor General.

138. *Ibid.,* Vol. 164, #11,611, MacDonald to Daly, 12 September 1845.

139. Report of a Committee of the Executive Council, 31 July 1844, cited in Pentland, "Labour and Industrial Capitalism," 432. The Board of Works also employed moral agents on the Beauharnois and Lachine Canals in Lower Canada. Pentland, "Labour and Industrial Capitalism," 414, Reverend McDonagh received £200 per annum for his services on the Welland Canal.

140. C Series, Vol. 317, MacDonald to Begly, 14 July 1849.

141. RG11-5, Vol. 407, file 104, Wetherall to Killaly, 26 March 1844.

142. *Ibid.,* Vol. 279, #2,195, Extract from Report of the Committee of the Executive Council, 25 October 1849; Vol. 407, file 114, McDonagh to Killaly, 2 May 1843; Vol. 407, file 104, Hobson to Daly, 20 January 1844.

143. RG11-5, Vol. 407, file 114, McDonagh to Killaly, 2 May 1843; Vol. 90, file 94, Clarke to Killaly, 6 March 1845; Vol. 90, file 94, Wetherall to Killaly, 2 March 1844; Vol. 388, file 87, McDonagh to Killaly, 25 January 1843; Vol. 407, file 113, Thorburn to Daly, 10 January 1844; Vol. 407, file 104, Killaly to Begly, 10 October 1849.

144. *Ibid.,* McDonagh to Killaly, 25 January 1843; Vol. 407, file 114, McDonagh to Killaly, 2 May 1843; Vol. 407, file 104, Wetherall to Killaly, 26 March 1844.

145. PSO CW, Vol. 164, #11,611, MacDonald to Daly, 12 September 1845.

146. RG11-5, Vol. 407, file 104, Killaly to Begly, 10 October 1849.

147. C Series, Vol. 60, Daly to Armstrong, 19 August 1842; *Ibid.,* Morris to Taylor, 19 August 1842; WCLB, MacDonald to Begly, 18 April 1843; C Series, Vol. 60, requisition to Fitzwilliam, 12 July 1844.

148. RG11-5, Vol. 407, file 104, Robinson to Begly, 1 October 1842.

149. RG11-5, Vol. 379, file 44, Magistrates of the Eastern District to Begly, 31 August 1842; *Journals of the Legislative Assembly,* 1844–45, Appendix Y, 8 January 1845; Dundas; RG11-5, Vol. 407, file 113, Thorburn to Murdock, 18 August 1842.

150. Radzinowicz, *A History of the Criminal Law,* Vol. IV, 115–39.

151. See for example WCLB, Power to Begly, 3 January 1844; Vol. 407, file 104, Hobson to Daly, 20 January 1844.

152. *Legislative Debates,* 1844–45, Thomas Aylwin, 1456.

153. RG11-5, Vol. 407, file 113, Thorburn to Murdock, 18 August 1842.

154. WCLB, Power to Elliott, 3 January 1844; C Series, MacDonald to Col. Elliott, 2 April 1844; *Ibid.,* Merritt to Daly, 21 September 1844; PSO CW, Vol. 100, #4956, Milne to Bagot, 21 December 1842.

155. C Series, Vol. 60, Armstrong to Browning, Military Secretary, 11 January 1844; *Ibid.,* Temporary Commander of Canada West to Elliott, 16 July 1844.

156. *Ibid.,* Wm. Fielder to Taylor, 8 September 1843; Vol. 379, file 44, Harvey to Killaly, 30 August 1842.

157. RG11-5, Vol. 379, file 44, Tuscore to Killaly, 5 September 1842; WCLB, Power to Elliott, 3 January 1844; *Ibid.,* Power to Elliott, 28 December 1843.

158. C Series, Vol. 60, Elliott to Cox and Gaele, 30 September 1844.

159. *Ibid.,* Temporary Commander of Canada West to Elliott, 16 July 1844.

Topic Twelve

Communities in British North America

Celebrations such as this were important events in the social life of early settlers. This work is by J.C. Stadler from *Minutes of the Canadians:* an aquatint, 1807, after a watercolour by Heriot.

The following three articles look at communities in British North America before Confederation. In "Gender Ideology and Black Women as Community-Builders in Ontario, 1850–70," Shirley J. Yee finds similarities between what Black women did and what "women in North America had always done for the benefit of their families and communities." But at the same time, "their experiences reflected the particular historical experiences of Blacks: coping with racism among whites and with the internal struggles among Black emigration leaders." How did the African-Canadian experience compare with that of the First Nations in the Canadas? Did oppression help to form cohesive African-Canadian communities?

The Atlantic region was ethnically diverse from the beginning, largely as a result of immigration patterns. Ethnic, religious, and cultural diversity within the dominant society often led to tension and conflict in the region. In the mid-19th century, violence broke out between the Irish Protestants and Irish Catholics in Saint John. The tensions arose when a large influx of poor Irish Catholics, fleeing the potato famine that swept Ireland in the 1840s, supplanted the predominantly Protestant population, established in the early 19th century. In reaction to this "unwelcome" immigration, the ranks of the nativist Protestant Orange Order swelled. The Orangemen precipitated one of the most violent riots in Canadian history in Saint John on July 12, 1849. Scott W. See reconstructs the context of the riot and explains its significance in "The Orange Order and Social Violence in Mid-Nineteenth-Century Saint John." How did the Orange Lodge contribute to the deteriorating relationship between the initially harmonious relationship between the Protestant and Catholic Irish in New Brunswick?

In "Reciprocal Work Bees and the Meaning of Neighbourhood," Catharine Anne Wilson examines a popular phenomenon in rural communities in Canada West. She focuses in particular on the significance of work bees in constructing communities and neighbourhoods. What role did "bees" play in building viable communities in Canada West? Was the formation of communities incorporating disparate religious and cultural groups more successful in rural areas than in the cities and towns of British North America?

The literature on communities in British North America is growing. The essential work remains Paul Robert Magocsi, ed., *Encyclopedia of Canada's Peoples* (Toronto: University of Toronto Press, 1999). Jan Noel has edited a useful collection of essays, *Race and Gender in the Northern Colonies* (Toronto: Canadian Scholars' Press Inc., 2000). The literature on the Irish in British North America is also growing. The list of important studies includes Donald Harman Akenson, *The Irish in Ontario: A Study in Rural History* (Montreal: McGill-Queen's University Press, 1984); Bruce S. Elliott, *Irish Migrants in the Canadas: A New Approach* (Montreal: McGill-Queen's University Press, 1988); and Cecil J. Houston and William J. Smyth, *The Sash Canada Wore: A Historical Geography of the Orange Order in Canada* (Toronto: University of Toronto Press, 1980; Milton, ON: Global Heritage Press, 1999). Sherry Olson and Patricia Thornton have written on the urban Catholic Irish, "The Challenge of the Irish Catholic Community in Nineteenth-Century Montreal," *Histoire sociale/Social History*, 35 (2002): 321–62.

Aboriginal Ontario, eds. E.S. Rogers and Donald B. Smith (Toronto: Dundurn Press, 1994), provides an overview of the First Nations in 19th-century Upper Canada/Canada West. A general review of the changes in Native communities is provided by Elizabeth Graham in *Medicine Man to Missionary: Missionaries as Agents of Change among the Indians of Southern Ontario, 1784–1867* (Toronto: Peter Martin Associates, 1975). For Aboriginal developments in Canada East, see Daniel Francis, *A History of the Native Peoples of Quebec, 1760–1867* (Ottawa: Indian Affairs and Northern Development, 1983). For information on the Mi'kmaq population in Maritime British North America see L.F.S. Upton, *Micmacs and Colonists: Indian–White Relations in the Maritimes, 1713–1867* (Vancouver: University of British Columbia Press, 1979);

and Harald E.L. Prins, *The Mi'kmaq: Resistance, Accommodation, and Cultural Survival* (Fort Worth, TX: Holt, Rinehart and Winston, 1996). Daniel N. Paul provides a Mi'kmaq perspective in *We Were Not the Savages* (Halifax: Fernwood Publishing, 2000).

Several chapters in Robin W. Winks's *The Blacks in Canada* (Montreal/Kingston: McGill-Queen's University Press, 1971) deal with the arrival and the lives of Black immigrants in the Canadas. Allen P. Stouffer looks at the antislavery movement in Canada West in *The Light of Nature and the Law of God* (Montreal/Kingston: McGill-Queen's University Press, 1992). In "Black Parents Speak: Education in Mid-Nineteenth Century Canada West," *Ontario History* 89, 4 (December 1997): 269–84, Claudette Knight looks at the question of schooling for African Canadians. Additional articles on African-Canadian women appear in Peggy Bristow et al., *"We're Rooted Here and They Can't Pull Us Up": Essays in African Canadian Women's History* (Toronto: University of Toronto Press, 1994). Richard Menkis examines attitudes toward Jews in his "Antisemitism and Anti-Judaism in Pre-Confederation Canada," in *Antisemitism in Canada: History and Interpretation*, ed. Alan Davies (Waterloo: Wilfrid Laurier University Press, 1992), pp. 11–38.

For an understanding of communities in Canada consult the following general works: Peter A. Baskerville, *Ontario: Image, Identity, and Power* (Don Mills, ON: Oxford University Press, 2002); and John Dickinson and Brian Young, *A Short History of Quebec*, 3rd ed. (Montreal: McGill-Queen's University Press, 2003). For Atlantic British North America consult Phillip A. Buckner and John G. Reid, eds., *The Atlantic Region to Confederation: A History* (Toronto: University of Toronto Press, 1994); Margaret R. Conroad and James K. Hiller, *Atlantic Canada: A Region in the Making* (Don Mills, ON: Oxford University Press, 2001), and W.S. MacNutt, *The Atlantic Provinces, 1712–1857* (Toronto: McClelland and Stewart, 1965). A specific study is "The Moral Economy of the Commons: Ecology and Equity in the Newfoundland Cod Fishery, 1815–1855," *Labour/Le Travail*, 43 (Spring 1999): 9–42.

WEBLINKS

The Freedom Trail
http://www.freedomtrail.ca/home.html

Biographies, stories, and images of immigrants to Canada who arrived from the Underground Railroad and settled in the communities of the Niagara Region of Ontario.

Black History in Guelph and Wellington County
http://guelph.ca/museum/BlackHistory/index.htm

A virtual exhibit about the African-Canadian people and settlements in Guelph and in Wellington County in Ontario.

Ontario Black History Society Archives
http://collections.ic.gc.ca/obho

Stories, oral histories, and other resources about the people who founded, lived, and are living in African-Canadian settlements in Ontario.

Religious and Ethnic Tolerance in Toronto
http://collections.ic.gc.ca/toronto/immig.html

This site describes the sometimes conflicting, sometimes harmonious, relationships between different religious and ethnic groups in the Toronto area from times before European contact to the late 20th century.

Atlantic Communities
http://www.collectionscanada.ca/05/050408_e.html

Photographs by French photographer Paul-Émile Miot of people and communities in
Newfoundland and Cape Breton Island in the mid-1800s.

Urban Life in Montreal
http://www.mccord-museum.qc.ca/en/keys/virtualexhibits/twolenses/

This site compares photos taken by a photographer in Montreal in the 1860s to those taken of
the same places a century later.

Article Twenty-Seven

Gender Ideology and Black Women as Community-Builders in Ontario, 1850–70

Shirley J. Yee

Elizabeth Jackson Shadd Shreve was known to Blacks in Buxton, Ontario, as an energetic
Christian woman who "travelled about, on horseback, through the bush, and over roads almost
impassable at times, ministering to the sick, collecting and delivering food and clothing for the
needy, and preaching the Gospel."[1] Anecdotal references to individual Black women, such as
the one above, tell a great deal about the material and spiritual contributions Black Canadian
women made to their communities. Although scholars of Canadian women's history have long
acknowledged the need to develop the diverse histories of racial minorities in Canada, they
have just begun to uncover the richness of Black Canadian women's historical experiences.[2]

The purpose of this essay is to explore the possibilities for developing a collective history
of Black women in Canada, beginning with southern Ontario in the mid-nineteenth century,
a critical place and time in the history of Black Canadian settlement. Black Canadian women's
experiences as community-builders challenged simplistic notions of "true" womanhood as
they struggled to survive and construct family and community institutions, such as churches,
schools, and benevolent organizations.

The status of early Black migrants to Canada varied. Some had been born free, others had
been freed by their masters or had escaped. Some travelled alone, others in small groups. In some
cases, whole Black church congregations moved to Canada.[3] They set up communities at principal stops on the Underground Railroad: Chatham, Windsor, Amherstburg, and Sandwich.
Some had brought with them enough capital to begin farms or businesses. The vast majority,
however, were escaped slaves who had arrived destitute, a transient population in want of the
basic necessities of life: food, clothing, shelter, and employment.[4] In 1850 Black educator and
abolitionist Mary Bibb wrote that hundreds of fugitive slaves arrived in Sandwich every day.[5]

Between the 1830s and 1850s a number of factors facilitated the resettlement of Blacks in
Canada: Britain's formal abolition of slavery in the empire in 1833, the enforcement of hitherto

Source: Shirley J. Yee, "Gender Ideology and Black Women as Community-Builders in Ontario, 1850–70," *Canadian
Historical Review* 75, 1 (1994): 53–73. Reprinted by permission of University of Toronto Press Incorporated.

dormant Black codes in the northern United States, and the Fugitive Slave Act of 1850.[6] These events exacerbated growing frustration with white-led abolitionism, which had, since the 1830s, struggled unsuccessfully to abolish slavery and racism. Black leaders who supported separatism from white organizations sought to nurture the development of independent Black communities both in and outside the United States. Convinced that there was little hope for eliminating racial oppression in the United States, Blacks who already supported voluntary Black emigration to Great Britain, Canada, Mexico, and Africa stepped up their campaigns after 1850.[7]

The mobility of Black immigrants and the myths and legends that have enshrouded the Underground Railroad have made it difficult to pin down accurate population statistics on Canadian Blacks. Eyewitness accounts often exaggerated the number of Blacks who actually made it to Canada. Manuscript census reports, beginning with the first Canadian census in 1851, provide official data on Black women, children, and men.[8] Impressionistic accounts by visitors to Canada, muster rolls, letters, newspapers, and church membership records provide population estimates as well as information about daily life. Such sources reveal that until the 1860s, Black men outnumbered Black women who migrated to Canada.[9] Women were often pregnant and/or encumbered with young children, which made the trek slow and more dangerous than if men travelled alone or with other adults. Samuel Gridley Howe, agent for the United States Freedman's Inquiry Commission, noted in the 1850s that "the refugees were mostly men; and to this day, the males are most numerous, because women cannot so easily escape."[10] By 1850 the sex ratio of Black immigrants had begun to even out. The Canadian census counted 2502 Black males and 2167 Black females in Upper Canada in 1851, by then called Canada West. Unofficial accounts recorded significant increases in the total Black population during the next two years. In 1851 and 1852, approximately 25 000 to 30 000 Blacks resided in Canada.[11] Throughout the decade, the numbers of Blacks increased. Canadian historian Fred Landon estimated that between 1850 and 1860, the Black population grew from 40 000 to 60 000.[12] But, despite the steady flow of Blacks to Canada, they made up a small percentage of the total population.[13]

Whites sometimes exhibited hostility toward Black newcomers. Name calling, occasional riots, and public school segregation illustrated the persistence of race prejudice in North America and dismayed those Blacks who had believed in Canada as a haven for the oppressed. A white man from Chatham asserted matter-of-factly that even though the laws "know nothing about creed, color, or nationality," Blacks would always be considered inferior "because their color distinguishes them."[14] In a circular letter addressed to citizens of both Canada and the United States, Mary Ann Shadd Cary, a strong proponent of emigration, noted bitterly that it was an "indisputable fact" that the rights and privileges of Blacks under the British Crown had been "very much infringed upon through prejudice of *color*."[15] In 1861 U.S.–born Black abolitionist William Wells Brown, who had sung Canada's praises in September of that year, wrote: "The more I see of Canada, the more I am convinced of the deeprooted hatred of the Negro, here."[16]

Women as well as men testified that the only reason they stayed in Canada was that British law protected them from enslavement and ostensibly provided them with legal rights as British citizens. One woman told Howe in the 1850s that although she endured more insults in St. Catharines than in her former home in New York state, "the colored people [in Canada] have their rights before the law." Another woman added, "If it were not for the Queen's law, we would be mobbed here, and we could not stay in this house." A Black man in Toronto observed that race prejudice in Canada was "equally strong as on the other side," and that the law was "the only thing that sustains us in this country."[17]

Nevertheless, Black women and men struggled to build a community. Upon arrival in Canada, they sought livelihoods. Underground Railroad connections were helpful for finding housing and jobs. Elizabeth Shadd (Williams Shreve) wrote to her sister Mary Ann Shadd Cary from Wilmington, Delaware, in the 1850s, asking her to house temporarily an escaped slave from Baltimore, a Mrs. Veasy. Shadd asked her sister to find work for Veasy, describing her as "a good seamster" who could earn a living "by her needle [sic]." She assured her sister that Veasy would not sponge off the Cary family, for she was an "industress [sic] working woman and a very pleasant agreeable boddy."[18]

In Canada, employment opportunities for Black men and women resembled those in the United States. In both countries, Black women, married and unmarried, contributed to the economic survival of their families. Typically, Black men worked as farmers and labourers, although they sometimes found employment as waiters, barbers, cooks, teamsters, mechanics, plasterers, tobacconists, tavern keepers, ministers, and sailors. Opportunities for Black women tended to be limited to domestic-related work such as servants, nurses, housekeepers, milliners, tailoresses, and spinsters, a common term for seamstress.[19] Educated women found school-teaching a meagre but essential source of income. Such occupations were typical for most wage-earning women in Canada during this period. For Black women, such work was no different from what they had done in the United States as slaves or as free Blacks.

Some expanded their domestic skills by establishing small businesses, such as boarding houses, restaurants, and hat and seamstress shops.[20] A few Black women who ran businesses helped build family fortunes, establishing their families as the social and financial elite of the Canadian Black community. Such was the case of the Duval family of Collingwood, Ontario. During the 1860s Mrs. Duval ran a dressmaking shop out of her home, while her husband, Pleasant, operated a successful barbershop and soft-drink parlour.[21]

While some free Blacks prospered, most struggled to eke out a living. Yet many still believed that Canada was a better place than the United States. A former slave woman reported: "Rents and provision are dear here, and it takes all I can to support myself and children. I could have one of my children well-brought up and taken care of . . . but I cannot have my child go there [the United States] on account of the laws, which would not protect her: but had I to struggle much harder than at present, I would prefer it to being a slave."[22]

The limited types of paid employment available to most Black women in Canada reflected their status as poor immigrant women. As women, in particular, such wage-earning opportunities clearly reflected prevailing gender/race ideologies, which relegated them to unskilled domestic-related labour. Other aspects of Black women's lives were less clear on the subject of gender roles and illustrate contradictions between dominant expectations and reality. The daily realities of women's lives often confounded the simplistic set of notions of "true" womanhood. Expectations of piety, purity, domesticity, and submissiveness had been widely disseminated in gift books, female magazines, newspapers, schools, and churches in the United States and Canada beginning in the 1820s.[23] Respectable women were supposed to be frail and dependent on men, and to shun physical labour. For urban middle-class white women, to whom this model was supposed to apply, such expectations were unrealistic, given their supervisory duties in the household and their social responsibilities. This model was even less realistic for working-class and poor women who toiled at low-paying, low-status jobs for long hours, seven days a week, in addition to caring for their own families.

Testimony by former slave women reveals that an appreciation for being treated like a lady coexisted with pride in the backbreaking physical labour in which they engaged in order to build homesteads. Mrs. John Little, who had escaped with her husband from Virginia and settled in Queen's Bush, proudly noted: "The best of the merchants and clerks pay me as much attention as though I were a white woman: I am as politely accosted as any woman would wish to be." Given the existence of anti-Black sentiment that many Blacks described, such kindness was probably a relief and provided hope that life would indeed improve in Canada. But, at the same time that she appreciated such treatment, Mrs. Little apparently did not adopt the full list of qualifications that supposedly accompanied "true womanhood." Clearly, she did not make any pretences to frailty and submissiveness, for she took pride in being able to work alongside her husband in the physical construction of their homestead. On the long journey to Canada, she had learned "bushwacking" and farming, which enabled her to clear the land "so that we could have a home and plenty to live on."[24] Such participation in the establishment of homes and farms was not a new experience for most migrating Black women. Those who had been slaves had long been accustomed to hard, heavy labour. As John Little noted: "My wife worked right along with me . . . for we were raised slaves, the women accustomed to work, and undoubtedly the same spirit comes with us here: I did not realize it then; but now I see she was a brave woman."[25]

The harsh realities of frontier life tended to blur gender roles.[26] Black women who made the trek to Canada, whether alone or in groups, encountered many of the same hardships as native-born or immigrant white women who made similar journeys. Conditions often dictated that women take on so-called male tasks in order to survive. In this context, the comments of John Little and his wife make sense. As former slaves whose work often was undifferentiated according to sex and as free Blacks who struggled to establish homesteads, women contributed to the construction of the home and farm while, at the same time, they expressed satisfaction for being treated well.

In Canada as in the United States, the Black community appeared torn over how to position itself with regard to dominant sex role ideology. On the one hand, the creation of patriarchal households held a particular historical significance for free Blacks. At the very least it was a rejection of slavery, in which masters held the ultimate power to determine sex roles for the benefit of the slaveholding economy.[27] Slave fathers had been violated both physically and figuratively by the slave master, whose "laws" affected the formation of all social relations, including community among the slaves. As historians of U.S. slavery have aptly pointed out, resistance by both male and female slaves manifested itself in the creation of strong bonds between blood and nonblood kin who struggled to forge social roles among themselves that bore little resemblance to the roles dictated by the master.[28] To slave women, whose bodies had been violated as breeders and as sexual objects, advocating dominant codes of morals and manners flew in the face of equally dominant stereotypes of Black women as domineering and morally degraded.

The adoption of dominant standards of "true" manhood and womanhood, therefore, illustrated prevailing conceptions of "freedom" in nineteenth-century North America, in which men were dominant and women subordinate. Black immigrants to Canada brought with them these assumptions of "proper" gender roles. At the same time, economics helped determine whether husbands/fathers could be sole breadwinners and women the dependent caretakers of the household. Prosperous Black families had the means to create this "ideal" family structure. Yet the predominance of the working class and poor within the free Black community made it exceedingly difficult for most families to attain this ideal. It was not uncommon for free Black families to view husbands/fathers as heads of household whether or not they were sole providers.

Regardless of economic circumstances, participation in community activities was considered a part of Black women's social responsibility and illustrates the strength and adaptability of gender ideologies among migrating Blacks. The career of writer, teacher, and editor Mary Ann Shadd Cary illustrates the struggle over such expectations in the Canadian Black community. Cary was an outspoken supporter of the emigrationist movement to Canada who became one of her generation's most controversial Black women activists. Born in October 1823 in Wilmington, Delaware, she was the eldest of Abraham and Harriet Parnell Shadd's thirteen children. The Shadds were one of the leading free Black abolitionist families that had established roots in both the United States and Canada. Mary Ann's abolitionist training at home was augmented by her education at a private Quaker school in West Chester, Pennsylvania.[29] In the winter of 1851 she arrived in the village of Windsor, where she had accepted a teaching position from the American Missionary Association to run a school for fugitive slaves. Within a year, she was immersed in various community activities and in the accompanying internal political struggles over such issues as education and mutual aid.

Much of her early writings extolled the virtues of Canada, before disillusion set in by the mid-1850s. In 1852 she published a pamphlet entitled "A Plea for Emigration, or Notes on Canada West," in which she promoted Canada as a prime site for Black resettlement.[30] She expressed her allegiance to British Canada in the prospectus she wrote for the Black Canadian newspaper, the *Provincial Freeman*. In the essay she supported the editors' right "to express emphatic condemnation of all projects having for their object in a great or remote degree the subversion of the principles of the British Constitution, or of British rule in the Provinces."[31]

Her commitment to the development of the Black communities in Canada earned the respect of her activist colleagues, but her directness and willingness to criticize even the most esteemed Black male leaders threatened her reputation as a "lady." As one person observed, Shadd enjoyed "the confidence of the entire Canadian population of Windsor," but that the wives of her opponents "respect her as much as they fear her."[32] Her well-publicized feud with Henry and Mary Bibb over whether to seek public support for fugitive schools led Henry Bibb to write: "Miss Shadd has said and writes many things we think will add nothing to her credit as a lady."[33]

Throughout her career, Shadd challenged expectations of "proper" female behaviour. She was an outspoken woman during a time when women were supposed to be demure and submissive to men. Her career illustrates that while Black women's participation in community-building may have been considered an acceptable extension of women's domestic responsibility beyond the private household, those who did so found themselves in a delicate balancing act.

Within this context, Black women often worked with Black men in building institutions that were critical to daily life. Black women's involvement in the establishment of churches, schools, and mutual aid societies reflected a long legacy of cooperation between Black men and women. The construction of churches was one of the first activities in which Blacks engaged on arrival in Canada. An examination of women's role in the Black churches can provide a glimpse of their daily lives, although it cannot tell the whole story, since not all Blacks joined exclusively Black churches.

The Black churches in Canada, as in the United States, served not only the spiritual needs of their congregations, but also functioned as the hubs of political and social activities. It was through the churches that Blacks often organized on behalf of improved schooling, benevolence, and social reform. The Methodist, Methodist Episcopal, and Baptist denominations were the most common among Black newcomers.[34] In 1851 the Board of the Baptist Missionary Convention counted 80 000 Black members of the Baptist Church in Canada West.[35] Black religious leaders in the United States attempted to keep abreast of the activities of their Canadian brethren. As early as 1843 the Connecticut preacher J.W.C. Pennington reported that 444 African Methodist Episcopal churches had been established in Canada.[36] The Methodist church was also strong among Blacks. In Chatham, a bustling farming, mercantile, and shipping town on the Underground Railroad, most Blacks belonged to the eastern or western branch of the Methodist church.

In addition to filling membership rolls, Black women helped in the construction of church edifices. Much of this work took place at night, after the day's work, and was divided by sex. A group of Black women in the British Methodist Episcopal congregation in Windsor, for example, carried water from the Detroit River for mortar, while the men mixed the mortar, held the torches, and constructed the building.[37] Women were also responsible for providing food at church functions and raising money to maintain the building, pay the ministers' salaries, and finance various church projects.[38] They played a central role in organizing the annual First of August celebrations to commemorate the abolition of slavery in the British empire. This holiday also served as an opportunity to point a shameful finger at Fourth of July celebrations in the United States, which honoured independence at the same time that it condoned slavery.[39]

Women also helped shape church policy. In the First Calvinistic Baptist Church in Toronto, women constituted nearly half of the committee that, in 1855, petitioned the provincial parliament to defeat a bill that would have reduced church property rights and intervened in the internal management of the churches.[40] The formation of the Baptist Sunday (also called Sabbath School) Committee and the Women's Home Missionary Society exemplified Black women's participation in the institutional development of the Black Canadian churches and its evangelical role in Canadian society. Both organizations were part of the Amherstburg Baptist Association, founded in 1841 as the Amherstburg Baptist Association for Coloured People. The purpose of the association was to unify Black Baptist churches in Michigan and Ontario in response to the racism they confronted in white churches in both the United States and Canada.[41] The establishment and maintenance of Sabbath schools was an important component of the association's work in religious education, and was overseen by the Baptist Sunday School Committee, formed in 1871.

Black churchwomen participated on several levels of the church hierarchy. As superintendent of the Sabbath schools, Elizabeth J. Shadd Shreve often delivered the committee's report at the annual association conventions. The association also encouraged the expansion of Sunday school facilities. In 1876, for example, the organization collected funds for the development of a Sabbath school library at the affiliate church in Shrewsbury, Ontario.[42] The female members organized fundraising events in order to carry out their charge "to promote the Gospel of Christ, to aid the weak churches and contribute to the Baptist Missionary Convention of Ontario." Black women's participation in fundraising for the Black Baptist churches was not new, for the association had from time to time called upon the women to raise contributions, decades before the formal establishment of the society.[43]

The formation of the Women's Home Missionary Society was a significant part of Black women's individual and collective activism within Canada's Black Baptist churches. It represented a move to consolidate women's activism within the association and to assign permanently to the women the task of keeping the association solvent and developing its missionary work into the twentieth century. The means by which members achieved the goals of the society were in keeping with traditional ways in which women, irrespective of race, participated in the maintenance of their churches.

Black women's efforts to build and sustain schools for Black Canadians also represented a long history of community activism that had its roots in northern free Black communities in the United States.[44] Black women who pursued teaching in the Canadian settlements during the mid-nineteenth century reflected occupational trends among both Blacks and whites in North America. Teaching was an occupation in transition. Throughout the century, women began replacing men in low-paying elementary school positions, while men, mostly white, moved into higher-paying administrative work within the schools. For women, teaching served multiple purposes. First, it was one of their only sources of income, besides agricultural or domestic work. Second, it fulfilled expectations of women as nurturers of the next generation.[45] Among whites, public acceptance of women teachers came slowly, while in the Black communities in Canada and the United States, teaching had long been a respectable occupation for women.

The demand for education in the Black settlements in Canada was high and writers for the rival Black newspapers, *Provincial Freeman* and the *Voice of the Fugitive*, called for more teachers and schools. In Black society, education held a symbolic as well as practical importance. To many Blacks, education was the key to freedom, a privilege denied in slavery. It served as a way to combat charges of racial inferiority and would produce a generation of skilled men and women who would, leaders hoped, foster the development of a self-reliant community. To this end, men and women with even the most rudimentary education were expected to contribute to the advancement of schooling for Blacks.[46] Mary Ann Shadd once noted that she and other teachers of fugitives wanted to instill "confidence, intelligence, [and] independence," instead of "ignorance [and] servility."[47]

Some schools followed prevailing gender conventions by segregating students by sex. Spokesmen for the Buxton Mission boasted in 1856 of the existence of two schools, one for women, the other for men. Although both sexes received lessons in religion, the curriculum reflected contemporary models of male and female education. While young men took classes in "the common branches" of an English education, which included Latin, Greek, and mathematics, young women were taught domestic skills, particularly "plain sewing." Women could pursue a teaching career if they were willing to pay for additional courses in the "higher branches of female education."[48] Most schools for Black Canadians, however, were not as elaborate as the Buxton Mission School. Typically, teachers operated one-room school houses or taught classes in their own homes to both sexes.

It was not unusual for Black educators in the settlements to bring with them a background in abolitionist work. Mary Ann Shadd, Mary Miles Bibb, and Amelia Freeman Shadd had been active in the movement before migrating to Canada. Mary Miles Bibb was a school-teacher and abolitionist from Boston, Massachusetts. She and her husband, Henry, were fervent emigrationists who helped establish the Black community in Sandwich, Ontario, in 1850. Henry Bibb once described his "beloved wife" as "a bosom friend, a help-meet, loving companion in all the social, moral, and religious relations of life."[49] Mary Bibb's activism also existed apart from her husband's activism. While he published the *Voice of the Fugitive*, she helped him direct the controversial Refugee Home Society at the same time that she struggled to maintain her private school, which suffered constantly from inadequate funding, supplies, and heat.[50]

During the late 1850s, Mary Ann Shadd Cary co-taught a school with her sister-in-law, Amelia Freeman Shadd, in addition to taking over the editorship of the *Provincial Freeman* in 1853. Her marriage to Thomas F. Cary in 1856 did not prevent her continued participation in these activities. While her husband stayed in Toronto to take care of his business, she moved to Chatham to teach, edit, and care for their growing family.[51] When her responsibilities became overwhelming, Shadd relied on her family for assistance. Her sisters, Amelia C. and Sarah M. Shadd, sometimes substituted for her at the school and helped care for the young Cary children.[52]

Amelia Freeman Shadd was the daughter of American Black activist Martin H. Freeman.[53] Her marriage to Isaac Shadd, a younger brother of Mary Ann and Elizabeth Shadd, represented the union of two respected Black activist families who had worked closely in the emigration movement. Like the Shadd children, Amelia Freeman had been a part of Black activist circles since childhood. Educated at Oberlin College, she taught in Pittsburgh before relocating to Canada. Observers held her in high esteem. Mary Ann Shadd described her as an "energetic Christian woman" who was "zealous in her duties as a moral and religious instructor." One Black writer called Amelia Freeman Shadd a "woman of great forebearance and integrity."[54]

Although Black leaders enthusiastically promoted education as an essential part of community-building, they faced a variety of obstacles to sustaining schools. Most teachers struggled to keep their schools open. Attendance was frequently sporadic, teaching materials were outdated and in short supply, and school buildings were poorly heated and shabby. Even at successful Buxton, attendance rates at the day school fell because of a shortage of female teachers.[55] Benjamin Drew commented on the poverty-stricken conditions of the Black schools in Amherstburg, noting that the teacher was "much troubled by the frequent absences of the pupils, and the miserable tattered and worn-out condition of the books." Although he praised her efforts in the face of such dire prospects, he was pessimistic about the future of education for Blacks, describing the school as "one more dreary chapter to the pursuit of knowledge under difficulties."[56] Economic hardship was constant throughout the 1850s and sometimes forced community leaders to hold fundraisers to help their teachers.[57]

Problems with funding and irregular attendance in the Black schools were not very different from the difficulties white schools faced in Canada before compulsory education in 1871. Canadian officials as well as American observers, however, acknowledged that racial discrimination shaped school policy in many Canadian towns. The fact that British law provided common schools for all did not mean that it guaranteed social equality. Even influential white Canadians who supported Black education could do nothing about efforts by white parents to keep their children separated from Blacks.[58] It was not uncommon for towns to build separate schools for Black and white children and, in at least one instance, the district school was abolished rather than allow Blacks to attend. Often, there were not enough schools for Blacks and the Black schools that did exist were usually inferior to the white schools. Mary Ann Shadd protested the "large and handsome school houses" built for white children compared with the "single miserable contracted wooden building" for Black pupils.[59] The unending struggle for equal education in Canada contributed to increasing disenchantment with the mythical land of Canada. Shadd described the history of education for Blacks in the counties of Kent, Essex, and Lambton as "a chapter of wrong, ignorance and prejudice" that reflected badly on "the *British name.*"

Not only did Blacks have to confront prejudice and discriminatory policies from without, they also had to contend with differences within the Black community. Black women participated actively in the internal politics of the community. One of the most heated debates among Black leaders concerned the funding of schools and racial segregation. Although a strong advocate of Black initiative and self-reliance, Mary Ann Shadd was "utterly opposed" to segregation "under any circumstances." Whether imposed by white society, in the form of segregation laws and customs, or as a result of Black initiative, through the formation of Black organizations, made no difference to Shadd. Both situations, she argued, prevented the possibility of eliminating racism. She encouraged Blacks to avoid racial segregation at all costs and to create institutions that made no distinctions based on race.

Shadd apparently practised what she preached. Before moving to Canada, she had joined in an African Methodist church in the United States for a brief time, but left the congregation because of its "distinctive character."[60] In 1851 she opened a school in her home for children "of all complexions." In that year she wrote to George Whipple, secretary of the American Missionary Association, expressing emphatic opposition to "the Spirit of Caste," stating that "whatever excuse may be offered in the states for exclusive institutions, I am convinced that in this country, and in this particular region (the most opposed to emigration of colored people I have seen), none could be offered with a shadow of reason."[61] She remained unshakable on this point, and, eight years later, opened a school with Amelia Freeman Shadd, advertised as a "School for All!"[62] Shadd's position, however, was based more upon principle than reality, for apparently only Black children attended her school. In 1855 Benjamin Drew recorded the existence of one interracial school, taught by Mary Bibb.[63]

The issue of segregation was tied to funding and placed Mary Ann Shadd at loggerheads with Mary and Henry Bibb. What began as a disagreement over policy quickly disintegrated into a highly publicized personal feud that lasted until Henry Bibb's death in 1854.[64] According to Shadd, the principle of self-help should be the guiding force for sustaining the schools in the Black settlements, and the community should not rely on the Canadian government for assistance. The Bibbs took a different position on the school issue. Although they, too, would have liked self-sustaining schools, experience had taught them that such a policy was untenable, given the destitute condition of fugitive slaves in Canada. In 1851 a disheartened Mary Bibb reported that the schools could not continue to exist without outside help. In fact, the private school that Bibb had opened out of her home in 1851 failed after about a year owing to lack of adequate financial support, after which she earned money as a seamstress.[65] By the time Shadd arrived on the scene in 1851, the Bibbs had decided to petition the Canadian government for assistance.

Under the Separate Schools Act of 1850, the Canadian government had officially recognized the existence of segregated schools. Thus, segregated "government" and private schools coexisted for Black Canadians, but neither was funded adequately. In 1853 Mary Bibb taught at a government school, while Shadd persisted in her push for self-sustaining private schools that made no racial distinctions. Like Mary Bibb, however, Shadd encountered attendance problems and severe material shortages.[66] After Shadd found that most Black parents were unable to pay the tuition, she embarked upon fundraising trips to the United States. Unsuccessful attempts to raise money for her school led Shadd to accept assistance from the American Missionary Association.[67]

Shadd became embroiled in the larger question of fundraising in the Canadian Black communities. The solicitation of funds, whether for the upkeep of schools and salaries for teachers or for providing food and clothing for fugitive slaves, was the subject of intense debate between those Blacks who saw such donations as a reflection of Christian charity and those who viewed the practice as ripe for corruption and undermining to the struggle for self-reliance.[68] Black benevolent associations in Canada, in which women played an integral part, were established in order to promote self-reliance. As in the United States, the creation of these organizations resulted both from the exclusion of Blacks from white societies and from the desire to serve the particular needs of the community. Most were founded by Blacks, but at least one was established by a white woman, Ellen Abbott, for the benefit of poor Black women. Abbott, a domestic servant who emigrated to Canada in 1835, was married to a free Black man.[69]

The structure of the organizations were similar to their counterparts in the United States. Many functioned under the auspices of the church, while others were auxiliaries to male fraternal associations. Some were segregated by race, others by sex, and a few welcomed men and women of both races. For Black women, as for white women, benevolent societies were avenues through which they could participate in public activities. Typically, women were assigned the task of raising money for their churches and schools, and clothing impoverished members of their community.

Perhaps the best-known Black Canadian benevolent organizations were the "true bands." In 1855 Benjamin Drew counted fourteen of these organizations in Canada West. The goal of the bands was to foster independence by raising money to improve schools, providing temporary assistance to needy Black families, and caring for the sick. A clear connection existed between the bands and the Black churches. The True Band of Chatham, Ontario, for example, pledged to "unify all churches and prevent division." Finally, the members of this band also saw the organization as a mechanism for self-government by intervening in disputes among its members.[70]

Like the true bands, the Provincial Union Association espoused a broad agenda. It had included women since its inception in 1854. The union, as it was commonly called, was spearheaded by supporters of the *Provincial Freeman* and encompassed many of the ideas

Mary Ann Shadd had advocated, such as the development of interracial cooperation in an effort "to promote harmony — not based on complexional differences among her Majesty's subjects" by removing "the stain of slavery from the face of the earth — and check its progress in America by all legitimate means." Coalition-building was central to the agenda, but members of the union also promoted self-reliance through education in "literary, scientific and mechanical" fields and the maintenance of a newspaper that provided a vehicle to voice the concerns of Black Canadians. The union also pledged to support the *Provincial Freeman* and the association's 35 agents from the Black communities in Toronto, Chatham, Hamilton, Dresden, London, and Amherstburg. In order to accomplish these goals, a mechanism for fundraising was established through the formation of a fourteen-member Ladies Committee, which accepted the responsibility of organizing annual fairs in cities where auxiliaries could be formed. Mary Ann Shadd was assigned the task of organizing local female auxiliaries.[71]

In addition to participating with Black men in community organizations, Black women sometimes formed all-female associations. The Mutual Improvement Society, established by the Colored Ladies of Windsor, for example, promoted adult education for Black residents. Mary Bibb served as president of the society. Other female organizations were designed explicitly to help fugitive slaves, such as the Ladies Coloured Fugitive Association, the Ladies Freedman's Aid Society, the Queen Victoria Benevolent Society, and the Toronto Ladies' Association for the Relief of Destitute Colored Fugitives.[72]

Black women's participation in charitable societies in Canada exemplified an important type of unpaid female labour that was an essential part of community-building during the mid-nineteenth century. Such societies served an important function by bringing together the concerns of Black communities for economic self-reliance and improved education.

The reconstruction of familiar institutions in Black settlements in Ontario during the 1850s and 1860s illustrates the gendered dimensions of community-building and the important role women played in transplanting community in a new land. Black women in Canada did what women in North America had always done for the benefit of their families and community — they earned and raised money, taught school, organized relief organizations for the needy, and helped construct and sustain their churches. At the same time, their experiences reflected the particular historical experiences of Blacks: coping with racism among whites and with the internal struggles among Black emigration leaders.

As immigrants, Black women pioneers to Canada shared certain experiences with native-born and white women as well as with Black men. Black and white immigrants had viewed Canada as a land of opportunity, and they experienced the joys and frustrations of transplanting familiar values, customs, and institutions to a new environment while, at the same time, hoping to become accepted in Canadian society. Many Blacks soon tempered such idealism, however, as they came to realize that social attitudes and institutionalized racism in Canada differed little from those in the United States.

The extensiveness of Black women's activism raises questions about the degree to which dominant notions of "true womanhood" held true among Blacks, in particular, and for U.S. and Canadian society, in general, at least in the form set forth in the prescriptive literature. As they worked with and sometimes apart from Black men to sustain their new communities, Black Canadian women continually blurred the line between public and private and tailored their own notions of "true" womanhood to the realities they faced in daily life.

Clearly, a tension existed between the dominant ideal and reality. Expectations of women's "natural" duty to the nurturance of a moral home and community existed in the Canadian Black communities as they had among Blacks in the United States. On both sides of the border, the adoption of patriarchal structures that ironically symbolized freedom also illustrated the pervasiveness of sex role ideology. The implementation of such structures, however, was interrupted by the intimate role Black women played in the social, economic, and political dimensions of Black life. Through their public activism, Black women maintained the interconnectedness of family and community, the private and the public — between which there was little distinction. Perhaps the greatest irony in this process of community-building was that however much Black women blurred the lines between the public and the private, they simultaneously constructed institutions — family, schools, churches, benevolent societies — that were founded on the ideology of separate spheres.

NOTES

1. D.S. Shreve et al., *Pathfinders of Liberty and Truth: A History of the Amherstburg Regular Missionary Baptist Association, Its Auxiliaries and Churches* (Merlin, ON: n.p. 1940), 63; Dorothy Shadd Shreve, *The AfricCanadian Church: A Stabilizer* (Jordan Station, ON: Paideia Press 1983); see also James K. Lewis, "Religious Nature of the Early Negro Migration to Canada and the Amherstburg Baptist Association," *Ontario History* 58 (June 1966): 117–33.

2. Gail Cuthbert Brandt, "Postmodern Patchwork: Some Recent Trends in the Writing of Women's History in Canada," *Canadian Historical Review* 72 (Dec. 1991): 468; Joan Sangster, "New Departures in Canadian Women's History," *Journal of Canadian Studies* 23 (Spring/Summer 1988): 235; Adrienne Shadd, "Three Hundred Years of Black Women in Canada, circa 1700–1980," *Tiger Lily* 1, 2 (1987): 4–13; and Afua Cooper, "In Search of Mary Bibb, Black Woman Teacher in Nineteenth Century Canada West," *Ontario History* 83 (Dec. 1991): 39–54. Other recent historiographical essays on Canadian women include Margaret Andres, "Attitudes in Canadian Women's History, 1945–1975," *Journal of Canadian Studies* 12 (Summer 1977): 69–78; Margaret Conrad, "The Rebirth of Canada's Past: A Decade of Women's History," *Journal of Canadian Studies* 23 (Spring/Summer 1988): 234–41; Eliane Leslau Silverman, "Writing Canadian Women's History, 1979–1981: An Historiographical Analysis," *Canadian Historical Review* 63 (Dec. 1982): 513–33; and Sylvia Van Kirk, ed., "Canadian Women's History: Teaching and Research," special issue of *Resources for Feminist Research/Documentation de la recherché feministe* (July 1979): 5–13. For general surveys and anthologies on Canadian women's history see Susan Mann Trofimenkoff and Alison Prentice, eds., *The Neglected Majority: Essays in Canadian Women's History*, 2 vols. (Toronto: McClelland and Stewart 1977, 1985); Veronica Strong-Boag and Anita Clair Fellman, eds., *Rethinking Canada: The Promise of Canadian Women's History* (Toronto: Copp Clark 1986); Micheline Dumont et al., *Quebec Women: A History* (Toronto: Women's Press 1987), and Alison Prentice et al., *Canadian Women: A History* (Toronto: Harcourt Brace 1988).

3. William Pease and Jane Pease, *Black Utopia: Negro Communal Experiments in America* (Madison: State Historical Society of Wisconsin 1963), 8.

4. Edith G. Firth, ed., *The Town of York, 1815–1834: A Further Collection of Documents of Early Toronto* (Toronto: Champlain Society for the Government of Ontario 1966), 333–34; Daniel G. Hill, "Negroes in Toronto, 1793–1865," *Ontario History* 15 (1963): 76–7, and Daniel G. Hill, *The Freedom Seekers* (Concord, ON: Irwin Publishing 1981), 168; R. Douglas Francis, et al., *Origins: Canadian History to Confederation* (Toronto: Holt, Rinehart and Winston 1988), 155–56, 302; Fred Landon, "Amherstburg, Terminus of the Underground Railroad," *Journal of Negro History* 10 (Jan. 1925), 2.

5. Sandwich, ON, Gerrit Smith Papers, Mary Bibb to Gerrit Smith, 8 Nov. 1850, in Black Abolitionist Papers (BAP), reel 6.

6. Black codes varied, from state to state, but generally restricted Black immigration and denied Blacks the right to petition, vote, sit on juries, or testify against white persons. The Fugitive Slave Act made it a federal crime to aid fugitive slaves. See *Statutes at Large*, 31st Cong., 1st sess., 463–65, 1850; Leon Litwack, *North of Slavery: The Negro in the Free States, 1790–1860* (Chicago: University of Chicago Press 1961), 69–72, 74–75; Fred Landon, "The Negro Migration to Canada after the Passing of the Fugitive Slave Act," *Journal of Negro History* 5 (Oct. 1920): 22–36.

7. Pease and Pease, *Black Utopia*, 5; Floyd J. Miller, *The Search for a Black Nationality, 1787–1863* (Urbana: University of Illinois Press 1979), 104–33; Headley Tulloch, *Black Canadians: A Long Line of Fighters* (Toronto: NC Press 1975), 82–3; Robin Winks, *The Blacks in Canada* (New Haven: Yale University Press 1971), 63–64; M.R. Delany, "Official Report of the Niger Valley Exploring Party," in M.R. Delany and Robert Campbell, *Search for a Place: Black Separatism and Africa, 1860* (1860; reprint, Ann Arbor: University of Michigan Press

1969), 27–147, and *The Condition, Elevation, Emigration, and Destiny of the Colored People of the United States* (1852; reprint, New York: Arno Press 1968), 174–75.

8. The category "People of Color, Mulattoes and Indians" on the enumeration sheets enabled census takers to identify a person's race. They marked the space if an individual was included in one of the above groups and left it unmarked if the person was white.

9. University of Western Ontario (UWO), Mary Ann Shadd Cary (MASC) Papers, series A, *Provincial Freeman,* Jan. (185? torn), E. Williams to Mary Ann Shadd Cary, Wilmington, Del., 18 Jan. 1852.

10. Samuel G. Howe, *Report to the Freedman's Inquiry Commission, 1864* (New York: Arno Press 1969).

11. Census of Canada, 1851, cited in John K.A. Farrell, "Schemes for the Transplanting of Refugee American Negroes from Upper Canada in the 1840s," *Ontario History* 52 (1960): 245, and the *Voice of the Fugitive,* May 1851, 2; Benjamin Drew, *Northside View of Slavery or the Refugee: or the Narrative of Fugitive Slaves in Canada* (Boston 1856), v.

12. Landon, "The Negro Migration to Canada," 22.

13. For example, 40 Blacks out of a total population of 3000 resided in the village of Galt. In larger commercial centres such as Toronto, London, St. Catharines, and Chatham, the Black population ranged in the hundreds, but still constituted a relatively small percentage of the total. In the largest town on Drew's list, Toronto, there were approximately 1000 Blacks out of a total population of 47 000. See Drew, *Northside View,* 14, 17–18, 94, 118, 136, 147, 234, 291, 308, 322, 341, 348, 367, 378; Howe, *Report,* 44.

14. Howe, *Report,* 44.

15. Howard University, Moorland-Spinarn Research Center, MASC Papers, Mary Ann Shadd Cary, circular, n.d.

16. William Wells Brown, "The Colored People of Canada," in *The Black Abolitionist Papers,* vol. 2, ed. C. Peter Ripley (Chapel Hill: University of North Carolina Press 1986), 466; Howe, *Report,* 46; *Pine and Palm,* 30 Nov. 1861, in BAP, reel 13.

17. Howe, *Report,* 45.

18. UWO, MASC Papers, series A, E. Williams to Mary Ann Shadd Cary, Wilmington, Del, 18 Jan. 1852.

19. Much of Black women's wage-earning work probably went undocumented, for census takers typically marked the occupation of men, but left the space blank for most women. *Census of Canada,* Town of Chatham, Ontario, 1861.

20. Drew, *Northside View,* 173; Prentice et al., *Canadian Women,* 82.

21. Hill, "Negroes in Toronto," 167, 171–73, and 175–77.

22. Drew, *Northside View,* 44.

23. See Barbara Welter, "The Cult of True Womanhood, 1820–1860," *American Quarterly* 18 (Summer 1966): 151–74; James O. Horton, "Freedom's Yoke: Gender Conventions among Antebellum Free Blacks," *Feminist Studies* 12 (Spring 1986): 51–76; Shirley J. Yee, *Black Women Abolitionists: A Study in Activism, 1828–60* (Knoxville: University of Tennessee Press 1992), 44–56; and Prentice et al., *Canadian Women,* 83–84.

24. Drew, *Northside View,* 233.

25. Ibid., 218.

26. See John Mack Faragher, *Women and Men on the Overland Trail* (New Haven: Yale University Press 1979); Julie Roy Jeffrey, *Frontier Women: The Trans-Mississippi West, 1840–1880* (New York: Hill & Wang 1979); and Susanna Moodie, *Roughing It in the Bush* (Toronto: McClelland & Stewart 1962).

27. Gerda Lerner, ed., *Black Women in White America* (New York: Vintage Books 1972), 15–42; Jacqueline Jones, *Labor of Love, Labor of Sorrow* (New York: Basic Books 1985), 11–43.

28. See Eugene D. Genovese, *Roll, Jordan, Roll: The World the Slaves Made* (New York: Vintage Books 1972), and John Blassingame, *Slave Community* (New York: Oxford University Press 1974).

29. Abraham Shadd (b. 1801) was a delegate to the American Anti-Slavery Convention, and in 1859 was elected as the first Black representative in Raleigh Township, Ontario. See Dorothy Sterling, ed., *We Are Your Sisters: Black Women in the Nineteenth Century* (New York: W.W. Norton 1984), 164–6; Winks, *The Blacks in Canada,* 215.

30. *Provincial Freeman,* 25 March 1854; *Voice of the Fugitive,* 3 June 1852; Mary Ann Shadd, "A Plea for Emigration, or Notes on Canada West" (Detroit 1852).

31. Shadd worked with the Rev. Samuel Ringgold Ward, who founded the *Provincial Freeman* in 1853. It was Shadd, however, who apparently gave the paper its name. UWO, MASC Papers, Mary Ann Shadd to Samuel Ward, n.d.

32. Windsor, American Missionary Association Collection, Ontario Black History Society, box 2, envelope 4, Alexander MacArthur to George Whipple, 22 Dec. 1852.

33. *Voice of the Fugitive,* 15 July 1851.

34. The census of 1861 reveals that Blacks were affiliated with a variety of denominations. For example, in three enumeration districts in the town of Chatham, the following denominations were represented: Methodist,

Baptist, Church of England, Roman Catholic, Disciple, Congregational, Episcopal, Church of Scotland, Shaker, and Quaker. *Census of Canada*, Town of Chatham, 1861.

35. *Voice of the Fugitive*, 4 Nov. 1851. This number may have been exaggerated. The Canadian census counted 45 353 Baptists in 1851. *Census of the Canadas*, 1851.

36. Speech by J.W.C. Pennington, delivered at Freemasons' Hall, London, England, 14 June 1843, in *Black Abolitionist Papers*, vol. 1, ed. C. Peter Ripley (Chapel Hill 1985), 110. Pennington may have overestimated the actual numbers of Black churches.

37. Hill, "Negroes in Toronto," 138.

38. *Voice of the Fugitive*, 30 July 1851; Hill, "Negroes in Toronto," 142.

39. *Voice of the Fugitive*, 16 and 30 July 1851; *Provincial Freeman*, 15 Aug. 1857.

40. *Provincial Freeman*, 3 Nov. 1855.

41. Amherstburg Baptist Association (ABA), minutes, 8 Oct. 1841; Shreve, *The AfricCanadian Church*, 47, 52–53.

42. ABA Sabbath School convention, minutes, 14–16 Sept. 1876.

43. McMaster Divinity College, Canadian Baptist Archives, ABA, minutes, 18 Aug. 1849, 14 Sept. 1871; Shreve et al., Pathfinders, 63.

44. For a general history of Black education in the United States see Carleton Mabee, *Black Education in New York State from Colonial Times to Modern Times* (New York: Syracuse University Press 1979).

45. Alison Prentice, "The Feminization of Teaching," in Prentice and Trofimenkoff, eds., *The Neglected Majority*, 50–54.

46. William Still to the *Provincial Freeman*, 11 Nov. 1854.

47. Mary Ann Shadd Cary (1858?), in BAP.

48. "Sixth Annual Report of the Buxton Mission," 16 June 1856, in *The Ecclesiastical and Missionary Record* 12 (July 1856): 139.

49. Henry Bibb, *Narrative of the Life and Adventures of Henry Bibb* (1850), 190–91.

50. Pease and Pease, *Black Utopia*, 113–22; Winks, *The Blacks in Canada*, 205–8; *Voice of the Fugitive*, 13 Aug. 1851.

51. Cary may have owned the first ice company in Toronto and later owned a bathhouse and several barbershops. In 1854 he was one of the 35 men appointed as officers for the Provincial Union Association, a local benevolent association to aid destitute Blacks. Hill, "Negroes in Toronto," 168; *Provincial Freeman*, 19 Aug. 1854; UWO, MASC Papers, Thomas F. Cary to Mary Ann Shadd Cary, 11 June 1851.

52. Amelia Cisco Shadd was the sixth Shadd child, born 25 Oct. 1831, and Sarah Matilda Shadd was the ninth, born 1 Nov. 1839. UWO, Shadd Family Papers; "Record of the Shadd Family in America," 1905; Amelia Shadd to David T. Williamson, 25 July 1854, Toronto, in BAP; Mary Ann Shadd Cary to George Whipple, 3 Nov. 1859, in BAP; Sterling, ed., *We Are Your Sisters*, 174.

53. Martin H. Freeman was vice-president of Allegheny Institute and later president of Avery College.

54. Mary Ann Shadd to George Whipple, 3 Nov. 1859, in BAP; *Weekly Anglo-African*, 5 April 1862, in BAP.

55. "Eighth Annual report of the Buxton Mission," 21 June 1858, in *Ecclesiastical and Missionary Record*, 14 Aug. 1858, 120; *Voice of the Fugitive*, 26 March 1851.

56. Drew, *Northside View*, 348; Jason H. Silverman and Donna J. Gillie, "'The Pursuit of Knowledge under Difficulties': Education and the Fugitive Slave in Canada," *Ontario History* 74 (June 1982): 98, 101.

57. Mental Feasts, gatherings that featured poetry, readings, lectures, and choral concerts, were popular fundraising events in the United States and Canadian Black communities. *Provincial Freeman*, 3 and 10 Jan. 1857, in BAP.

58. Egerton Ryerson, the superintendent of schools for Canada West, could only offer an apology to the Blacks of Amherstburg, one he claimed was "at variance with the principle and spirit of British Institutions." Egerton Ryerson to Isaac Rice and Robert Pedan, 5 March 1846, in Silverman and Gillie, "Pursuit of Knowledge," 98.

59. Silverman and Gillie, "Pursuit of Knowledge," 96; *Pine and Palm*, 30 Nov. 1861, in BAP; *Provincial Freeman*, 26 July 1856.

60. *Provincial Freeman*, 12 July 1856; Mary Ann Shadd Cary to George Whipple, 23 Nov. 1851, in BAP.

61. Mary Ann Shadd to George Whipple, 23 Nov. 1851, in BAP.

62. *Provincial Freeman*, 28 Jan. 1859.

63. Drew, *Northside View*, 321–22; *Voice of the Fugitive*, 17 June 1852, in BAP; Mary Ann Shadd to George Whipple, Boston, 3 Nov. 1859, in BAP.

64. Mary Ann Shadd to George Whipple, 28 Dec. 1852 and 21 July 1852, in BAP; Sterling, ed., *We Are Your Sisters*, 169.

65. Mary E. Bibb, "Schools among the Refugees," *Anti-Slavery Bugle*, 12 April 1851, BAP; Cooper, "The Search for Mary Bibb," 47.

66. Cooper, "Search," 71; Mary Ann Shadd to Executive Committee–AMA, Windsor, 3 April 1852, in BAP.

67. Mary Ann Shadd to George Whipple, 7 Feb. 1853 and 21 June 1859, in BAP.
68. Winks, *The Blacks in Canada*, 158–59, 206–7.
69. Prentice et al., *Canadian Women*, 104.
70. Drew, *Northside View*, 236–37.
71. *Provincial Freeman*, 19 Aug. 1854; *Voice of the Fugitive*, 13 Jan. 1855, 19 Aug. 1854.
72. Hill, "Negroes in Toronto," 179, and Drew, *Northside View*, 238.

Article Twenty-Eight

The Orange Order and Social Violence in Mid-Nineteenth-Century Saint John

Scott W. See

In March 1839, the St. Patrick's, St. George's and St. Andrew's societies held a joint meeting in Saint John, New Brunswick. Delegates noted and condemned the Protestant–Catholic confrontations that appeared to be endemic in Boston and other unfortunate American cities. In a spirit of congeniality, they applauded themselves on the good fortune of living in a British colony free of such acrimonious religious strife. Generous toasts were proposed to young Queen Victoria, Lieutenant Governor Sir John Harvey, and, most effusively, to each other.[1] A short eight years later, after Saint John and neighbouring Portland had experienced a series of bloody riots involving Protestant Orangemen and Irish Catholics, those sentiments would be recalled with bitter irony. Sarcastic comparisons would then be drawn between Saint John and New Orleans, a tumultuous city with a reputation for collective violence.[2]

What happened to shatter the calm, and why would the toasts of 1839 turn out to be so farcical in the light of events during the 1840s? Why would Saint John and Portland, relatively stable communities that escaped major incidents of social violence prior to the 1840s, become ethno-religious battlegrounds involving natives and immigrants?[3] The growth of Irish Catholic immigration to Saint John and Portland before mid-century was accompanied by the expansion of the Orange Order as an institutionalized nativist response to those unwelcome settlers. Confrontations between the two groups began with relatively mild clashes in the late 1830s and culminated in the great riots of 1847 and 1849. The Ireland-based Orange Order, fuelled originally by British garrison troops and Irish Protestant immigrants, attracted significant numbers of native New Brunswickers and non-Irish immigrants because of its anti-Catholic and racist appeal. By mid-century it functioned as a nativist organization whose purpose was to defend Protestantism and British institutions against Irish Catholic encroachment. The clashes in Saint John and Portland were not primarily the result of transplanted rivalries between Protestant and Catholic Irish immigrants, as was commonly believed by contemporaries and historians.[4] Rather they represented both a vehement rejection of certain immigrants because of cultural and religious differences and a symbolic struggle to protect Protestant jobs against competitive Irish Catholic famine victims during a decade of severe economic hardship. Thus as Irish Catholic immigration burgeoned, so did the nativist Orange Order.

Source: Scott W. See, "The Orange Order and Social Violence in Mid-Nineteenth Century Saint John," *Acadiensis* 13, 1 (Autumn 1983): 68–92. Reprinted by permission.

Saint John was New Brunswick's most populous city in the nineteenth century.[5] Settled by Loyalists in 1783 and incorporated two years later, it rapidly developed into the province's primary port for the export of staple timber goods and the import of manufactured products and foodstuffs. Lying in its northern shadow was the shipbuilding and mill town of Portland, now annexed into greater Saint John. The localities were connected by several roads, the busiest thoroughfare being a dilapidated bridge spanning an inlet on the harbour's northern extremity.[6] Both communities bustled in mid-century; along the narrow streets and wharves sailors rubbed shoulders with tradesmen, merchants, lawyers, mill workers, and itinerant labourers. Moreover, both gained their economic focus almost entirely from New Brunswick's timber staple. Sawn lumber and deals were shipped to the British Isles from their wharves, while numerous sawmills and shipyards dotted their skylines. In turn, the two communities received the bulk of New Brunswick's imports, including immigrants.[7]

Despite their industriousness, Saint John and Portland had fallen on hard times in the 1840s. Indeed all of New Brunswick suffered from the worst sustained downturn since the colony's inception.[8] Several factors accounted for this. First, the colony had enjoyed decades of timber trading privileges with Great Britain due to a combination of preference subsidies and high tariffs for foreign imports. But starting in 1842, England began to shift toward a policy of free trade in an attempt to curtail its soaring deficits. Subsequently it lowered or dropped its foreign tariffs and increased colonial duties. News of England's policy change created chaos in New Brunswick. Fears of the ramifications of such a move led to a decade of lost confidence among investors and merchants. Although New Brunswick would experience a slight recovery in 1844, due primarily to speculation that Great Britain's railroad fever would stimulate the timber trade, the decade would be marked by high unemployment, rising commodity prices, commercial bankruptcies, and legislative indebtedness.[9] Second, a worldwide glut of lumber and overexploitation of New Brunswick's forests caused a severe export slump.[10] Later in the decade, moreover, hundreds of workers were displaced as the province's sawmills abandoned labour-intensive operations in favour of steam-driven machinery.[11] These factors combined to create a decade of commercial distress that crippled Saint John and Portland, especially in the years 1842–43 and 1845–49.

During this decade of financial hardship, these communities experienced dramatic changes in immigrant patterns. Prior to the 1840s, both were relatively homogeneous. Indeed New Brunswick in general consisted primarily of the descendants of Loyalists and pre–Revolutionary War New England settlers, plus a moderate number of immigrants from England, Scotland, and Ireland. The only significant non-Protestants were the Acadians, who populated the northern and eastern shores and the northwestern interior. Moreover, the immigrant flow throughout the 1830s was strikingly consistent; for example, 1832 and 1841 differed in raw totals by only twelve.[12] This fairly uniform influx brought an increasingly large proportion of Irish, a trend that would continue to mid-century.[13]

Prior to the 1840s the majority of these Irishmen came from the Protestant northern counties. Most were of Scots or English ancestry, reflecting the British colonization of Ireland. They were artisans and tenant farmers with modest savings who sought a better life within the British colonial system. Most importantly, they shared cultural and ideological views with the native New Brunswickers and other British emigrants they encountered. They adhered to Protestantism and supported the English constitutional and political domination of Ireland. Thus they made a relatively smooth transition to their new lives in New Brunswick.[14]

During the 1830s, however, emigrant patterns within Ireland shifted and thereby profoundly altered the demographic face of New Brunswick. The more skilled, financially solvent Protestant Irishmen from northern counties began to be replaced by more destitute Catholics from Ireland's poorer southern and western regions. The percentage of Irish Catholics who emigrated to New

Brunswick before 1840 was small, yet ever-increasing. The trickle became a flood as a tragic potato famine decimated Ireland's staple crop from 1845 to 1848.[15] New Brunswick's immigration rate would increase yearly by at least 150 percent from 1843 until 1847, when the Irish famine tide finally crested. For the mid-1840s, the province would receive virtually all of its immigrants from the Catholic districts of Ireland. For example, of the 9765 immigrants arriving in 1846, 99.4 percent were from Ireland. Of these, 87 percent landed in Saint John, clearly underscoring the city's role as the province's chief immigration port. The overwhelming majority were poor Catholic agricultural labourers.[16] New Brunswick in the 1840s, and particularly Saint John, was bombarded with thousands of non-Anglo-Saxon Protestants.

The influx of Irish Catholics dramatically altered the ethno-religious faces of Saint John and Portland. Although perhaps half of the incoming Irish used the ports as temporary shelters, earning enough at manual labour along the docks for the fare on a coastal vessel heading for the United States, thousands of the poor agrarian peasants remained.[17] By mid-century, more than one-third of the residents of Saint John and Portland were born in Ireland. More profoundly, Catholicism mushroomed. Roman Catholics were as large as any Protestant sect in Saint John by the mid-1840s; when the 1861 census appeared, the first to include religious data, both localities had populations almost 40 percent Catholic. Since the Acadians, who were New Brunswick's only other substantial Catholic population, were practically nonexistent in the Saint John region during mid-century, Irishmen accounted almost entirely for the high Catholic population.[18]

The Irish Catholics settled primarily in two sections of Saint John and Portland. They clustered in overcrowded squalor in York Point, a district of northwestern Saint John bounded roughly by Union Street to the south, George's Street to the east, Portland Parish to the north, and the bay to the west.[19] In Portland, they huddled in the busy wharf area on the harbour's northern shore. The two districts, connected by the "Portland Bridge," grew into twin ethno-religious ghettos during the 1840s.[20] They were so strongly identified with Irish Catholics that they would play host to virtually all of the major episodes of social violence between Orangemen and Irishmen during the decade.

The influx of thousands of Celtic Catholics into the Protestant Anglo-Saxon bastions of Saint John and Portland triggered a nativist response among the more entrenched residents. A useful paradigm for interpreting nativism was pioneered by John Higham, and while his model concerned American movements, it applies equally well for any nativist response. Higham's nativism was the "intense opposition to an internal minority on the ground of its foreign . . . connections," or a "defensive type of nationalism." Though Higham cautioned that the word "nativism," of nineteenth-century derivation, has become pejorative, his definition provides a valuable intellectual foundation for analyzing people's reaction to immigrants.[21] In the context of the British colonial experience, nativists tended less to focus on place of birth than to draw inspiration from the virtues of Protestantism and British institutions.[22] From this perspective, the local response to incoming Irish Catholics may clearly be considered as a nativist response. Protestants who wanted to discourage Catholic settlement and block further immigration began to channel their energies into an institutionalized counteroffensive during the 1840s. As Saint John's *Loyalist and Conservative Advocate* explained:

> The necessity . . . for Protestant organization in this Province, arose not more from the many murderous attacks committed upon quiet and unoffending Protestants, by Catholic ruffians, than from the dreary prospect which the future presented. The facts were these: several thousands of immigrants were annually landing upon our shores; they were nearly all Catholics, nearly all ignorant and bigotted, nearly all paupers, many of them depraved . . . What have we to expect but murder, rapine, and anarchy? Let us ask, then, should not Protestants unite? Should they not organize?[23]

The call to battle was dutifully answered by an organization with a history of responding to similar entreaties in Ireland and England — the Loyal Orange Order.

The Orange Order became the vanguard of nativism in mid-nineteenth-century New Brunswick, yet the organization was neither new nor unique to the province. After a violent birth in Loughgall, Ireland, in 1795, Orangeism quickly spread throughout Northern Ireland and England. As a fraternal body tracing its roots to a feuding tradition between Protestant and Catholic weavers and farmers, the Orange Order paid ideological homage to the British Crown and Protestantism. Group cohesion was provided by a system of secret rituals, an internal hierarchy of five "degrees" and the public celebration of symbolic holidays such as 12 July, the anniversary of the victory of the Prince of Orange (King William III) over Catholic King James II at the Battle of the Boyne in 1690. In the early nineteenth century the Orange Order was firmly entrenched in the British Isles, where its members fervently combated the growth of Jacobinism and Roman Catholicism.[24]

Given the ideological foundations of the Orange Order, it transferred well within the British Empire. British garrison troops who joined the organization while stationed in Ireland carried warrants for new lodges when they transferred to new posts. Irish Protestant immigrants who settled in England and British North America also brought Orange warrants as part of their "cultural baggage." By the early nineteenth century, British regulars in Halifax and Montreal were holding formal Orange meetings. Lodges mushroomed as they found support among Loyalists and the swelling ranks of Irish Protestant immigrants. In 1830 a Grand Orange Lodge, headquartered in Upper Canada, obtained permission from Ireland to issue lodge warrants for all of British North America except New Brunswick.[25]

New Brunswick's organized lodges, dating from the turn of the century, clearly reflected a similar pattern of garrison troop and Irish immigrant conveyance. The earliest known lodge, formed among soldiers of the 74th Regiment in Saint John, met regularly by 1818. Six years later they obtained an official Irish warrant.[26] After several abortive efforts to establish civilian lodges in the mid-1820s, Orangeism became rooted among Saint John's Irish Protestants in 1831. Initial growth was sluggish. Fifteen local, or "primary," lodges existed by 1838, representing ten in Saint John and Portland. Membership tended to be small, with some lodges having only a handful of regular participants. Even the establishment of a provincial Grand Orange Lodge in 1837–38, under the mastership of James McNichol, failed to generate widespread growth and attract significant numbers. With the advent of the 1840s, New Brunswick's Orange Lodges, particularly in Saint John and Portland, were staffed primarily by small numbers of recent Irish Protestant immigrants and British troops.[27]

A catalyst appeared in the 1840s to spur growth in the fledgling organization. The rising tide of famine immigration brought concerned Protestants to the organization's doorstep, seeking action and viable solutions to the Irish Catholic "menace." By the close of 1844, when the transition from Protestant to Catholic emigrant was well underway in Ireland, New Brunswick had 27 lodges. Of these, ten were less than a year old. As Irish Catholics arrived and filtered throughout the province, Orange Lodges burgeoned to lead the counteroffensive. Buttressed by a network of primary, county, district, and provincial lodges, Orangeism swept up the St. John River Valley hard on the heels of the Catholic immigrants. Mid-century found 123 primary lodges across the province, representing a five-year growth of 455 percent.[28] Together with its smaller Nova Scotia affiliates, New Brunswick's Orange Order boasted an estimated 10 000 members. Yet despite its impressive expansion, the Orange Order's seat of power and membership base remained firmly rooted in Saint John and Portland.[29]

The traditional membership pools did not account for the explosive growth of Orangeism. Irish Protestant immigration dropped dramatically during the 1840s, becoming negligible by mid-century. Moreover, Britain reduced its garrison troops because of budgetary constraints.

What, then, explained the Orange Order's meteoric rise? How did the organization broaden its attraction to ensure its survival? The answers were to be found in the Order's ideological appeal to native New Brunswickers and non-Irish Protestant immigrants.

Evidence of Orange membership in the 1840s clearly proved that initiates came from various cultural groups and classes. While the organization may have been rooted among British garrison troops and Irish Protestant settlers, it succeeded only because it found a willing supply of Loyalist and New England descendants and non-Irish immigrants who shared its philosophical tenets. In other words, to tell the story of Orangeism in mid-nineteenth-century New Brunswick is to trace the growth of an indigenous social movement. At least half of all identified Orangemen in mid-century were born in New Brunswick. They came from all walks of life, including legislators, barristers, magistrates, doctors, ministers, farmers, artisans, and unskilled labourers. Motivated primarily by locally defined problems and prejudices, many New Brunswick natives and immigrants found the Orange Order both philosophically and socially attractive.[30]

In the Saint John region, some natives participated in Orange activities when lodges first appeared in the early nineteenth century. Indeed, several of the nascent city lodges drew their membership exclusively from transplanted New Englanders and Loyalists from America's mid-Atlantic and southern regions.[31] When the provincial Grand Orange Lodge organized in 1844, prestigious native Saint John residents were there. They included W.H. Needham, a justice of the peace, H. Boyd Kinnear, a lawyer, and Thomas W. Peters, Jr., a city official. Each would assume an Orange leadership role at some point in his career.[32] During the period of intensified social violence, in 1845–49, Saint John and Portland residents embraced the Orange Order because of its campaign to protect Protestantism and British hegemony against the bewildering and oftentimes frightening effects of Irish Catholic immigration.[33] For example, Portland's Wellington Lodge welcomed its largest initiate group since its inception in the meeting following the great Orange–Catholic riot of 12 July 1849.[34]

Membership lists also illuminated the Orange Order's effective appeal to native-born in Saint John and Portland. Data gleaned from official lodge returns, trial transcripts, Orange histories, and newspapers yielded the names of 84 active Orange members in the late 1840s. When matched against the available 1851 manuscript census returns from Saint John County, they showed significant native involvement in Orangeism: 56 percent were not Irish-born, including 43 percent native and 13 percent other Protestant immigrants.[35] Moreover, the entrenchment of Irish Protestants in the Orange Order was evident because 80 percent of them had emigrated to New Brunswick prior to 1840. The occupational range already noted for provincial Orangemen was corroborated by the Saint John evidence, though a higher proportion of members could be classified as skilled or unskilled labourers. Finally, the portrait of Saint John Orangemen revealed a youthful organization: almost three-quarters of those traced were less than 40 years old in 1851.[36] Clearly, the Orange Order in Saint John and Portland in mid-century represented a mixture of native-born and Protestant immigrants.

The essential ideological glue of the Orange Order was unquestioning loyalty to the Crown and an emphatic rejection of Roman Catholicism. With these concepts codified in the initiation oaths, Orangeism guaranteed itself a philosophical continuum that transcended the divergent social appeals and emphases of individual primary lodges.[37] In New Brunswick, lodges exercised a great deal of independence. Several accepted only temperate men; others attracted members by offering burial insurance plans; still more touted their commitment to charitable endeavours.[38] New Brunswick's Orange Lodges had disparate social and functional appeals, and many men gathered under the symbolic Orange banner. Except in the rare case where evidence exists, individual motives for joining the organization are a matter for speculation.

Nevertheless, the philosophies and goals of Orangemen may be justifiably construed from organizational rhetoric and collective behaviour.

Orange rhetoric in the 1840s strikingly resembled the propaganda campaigns carried out by American and British nativists during the same period. New Brunswick Orangemen charted an elaborate counteroffensive to combat Irish Catholic immigration and permanent settlement. The organization's views were stated succinctly in two documents from the late 1840s. In a welcoming address to Lieutenant Governor Edmund Head, Orangemen explained:

> Our chief objects are the union of Protestants of the several denominations, to counteract the encroachments of all men, sects or parties, who may at any time attempt the subversion of the Constitution, or the severance of these Colonies from the British Empire; to bind Protestants to the strict observance of the Laws, and to strengthen the bonds of the local authorities, by the knowledge that there is ever a band of loyal men ready in case of emergency, to obey their commands, and assist them in the maintenance of order.[39]

Thomas Hill, the zealous Orange editor of the *Loyalist and Conservative Advocate*, was more direct in his appraisal of the fraternity:

> Orangeism had its origins in the *necessity* of the case; it has spread in this Province, also from *necessity*, for had not the country been infested with gangs of lawless ruffians, whose numerous riots, and murderous deeds compelled Protestants to organize for mutual defence, Orangeism would have been scarcely known. And whenever the *Cause* shall disappear, Orangeism may retrograde.[40]

Underscored in the above quotations was the unique philosophical framework which Orangemen operated within: unquestioning loyalty, exclusive Protestantism, and the threat to carry out their policies with vigilante force.

New Brunswick's Orangemen, in an effort to check the Irish Catholic invasion, fought a rhetorical battle on several fronts. The overarching goal was to maintain the colony as a Protestant and British bulwark against Catholicism. The Orange Order directly appealed to all Protestants who feared that the ethno-religious supremacy enjoyed by Anglo-Saxons would be permanently undermined or destroyed by the swelling numbers of Celtic Irishmen. Orangemen even advocated the repeal of legislation giving Catholics the franchise and the right to serve in the legislature.[41]

Anti-Catholic diatribes grew in part from a papal conspiracy myth that enjoyed a North American vogue in the mid-nineteenth century.[42] New Brunswick's Orangemen claimed the famine immigration was but a skirmish in a global battle, masterminded in the Vatican, to expunge Protestantism from the earth. A Saint John editor who supported Orangeism warned that "A great, perhaps a final, conflict is at hand between Protestant Truth and Popery leagued with Infidelity."[43] Orangemen embarked on a propaganda campaign to educate Protestants about the Pope's despotic control over Catholics — in church, in the home, in the workplace, and on the hustings. Only by removing the insidious network of priests, Orangemen argued, could papal control over the "uncivilized minds" of the Irish Catholics in New Brunswick be broken.[44]

Another vital weapon in the Orangemen's arsenal rested upon the assumption that the Celtic Irish were inherently an unruly and violent race. The stereotype had a measure of truth. As a subjugated people under English rule, Irish Catholics often resorted to disruptive tactics to achieve their goals.[45] As poor Irish Catholics crowded into squalid quarters in York Point and Portland, Orangemen bandied stereotypes of the Celtic propensity for strong drink and villainy. After all, they argued, "no one can deny that the lower orders of the Roman Catholic Irish are a quarrelsome, headstrong, turbulent, fierce, vindictive people."[46] Petty crime did increase dramatically as Saint John and Portland absorbed thousands of the famine immigrants, but it is more plausible to suggest that factors such as overcrowding, poverty, and hunger were more responsible for creating a crucible for crime than were cultural idiosyncrasies.[47] Tragically, Orangemen painted all Catholics with the same nativist brush. Though even the most scurrilous propagandists recognized that not all immigrants participated in this orgy of crime, they nevertheless called for Orange vigilantism in York Point and Portland. Moreover, they suggested dispersing the immigrants among loyal Protestants. The theory was that such a dilution would facilitate social control and the assimilation of those immigrants who chose to remain. For the Orangemen of mid-nineteenth-century Saint John, every Celtic Irishman was a potential criminal.[48]

New Brunswick's Orange rhetoric was also laced with racism, mirroring the contemporary British philosophy of Anglo-Saxon superiority.[49] Ethnicity was mingled with class as Orangemen railed against the "ignorant Mickie" hordes who formed a substandard "class of people." The destitution of famine immigrants as they disembarked in Saint John, and the squalor of their ghettos in York Point and Portland, appeared to corroborate Orange assertions of Celtic inferiority. Here was positive proof that the Protestant Anglo-Saxon must remain firmly in legislative and judicial control in order to assure the colony's peaceful survival.[50] The more zealous Orange propagandists, believing that assimilation was a bankrupt concept, called for the deportation of all Celtic Catholics. One might as well, they argued, "attempt to change the colour of the Leopard's spots, or to 'wash the Ethiope white,' as to attempt to tame and civilize the wild, turbulent, irritable, savage, treacherous and hardened natives of the Cities and Mountains of Connaught and Munster."[51] The editors of the *Loyalist and Conservative Advocate*, the *Weekly Chronicle*, and the *Christian Visitor*, all either Orange members or openly sympathetic to the organization's policies, regularly exposed their readers to racist editorials, Irish jokes, and vignettes pointing out the subhuman proclivities of the Celtic immigrant. Through their efforts, the argument of Anglo-Saxon racial superiority fell convincingly upon the ears of native Protestants who feared the demise of peace, order, and good government in New Brunswick.[52]

Yet another focal point for Orange propagandists was the tangible threat that the poor Irish Catholic immigrants represented a formidable and willing pool of cheap labourers.[53] The famine victims, thrust into the severely depressed economy of the 1840s, were greeted as pariahs by Saint John's working classes. The destitute Irish Catholics eagerly accepted the most demanding and lowest-paying jobs, which in a healthy economic environment would be vacant. But during the "hungry forties," unemployed native labourers were forced to compete with the immigrants for these undesirable jobs.[54] In an attempt to combat the debilitating effects of immigrant competition, such as a general lowering of wage scales, Orangemen sounded the call for economic segregation. They suggested that Protestant merchants and employers should hire and do business only with coreligionists. By ostracizing Roman Catholic labourers, Orangemen hoped to persuade entrenched immigrants to leave, and to discourage incoming Catholics from settling in the community.[55]

While Saint John's Orangemen fought a rigorous rhetorical battle, perhaps their most effective campaigns involved physical engagements with Irish Catholics. Indeed, collective social violence grew in direct proportion to the rising levels of famine immigration and Orange membership during the 1840s. In the aftermath of each confrontation, Orangemen enjoyed even greater Protestant support from natives and immigrants alike. The number of local lodges and engorged memberships at mid-century were tributes to the Orange Order's successful appeal. The persuasive rhetorical campaigns may have won converts, but the bloody riots gave concerned Protestants tangible "proof" of the Irish Catholics' uncivilized behaviour.

The first clearly identifiable incident of collective violence between Orangemen and Catholics in Saint John occurred on 12 July 1837. Small Catholic crowds forced entry into two merchants' stores and attempted to burn them.[56] In later years such incendiarism was eclipsed by more traditional rioting. The spring of 1841 found Irish Catholics clashing with Orangemen in the streets of Saint John. At issue was an Orange commemorative arch erected to celebrate the visit of a dignitary.[57] Catholics reacted similarly the following year on 12 July, when a crowd of several hundred gathered outside a Saint John home flying the Union Jack festooned with orange ribbons. Their jeers and taunts brought Orange reinforcements from across the city; by evening a general riot prompted Mayor William Black to swear in 150 special constables. The all-Protestant volunteer squad arrested several Irish Catholics, most of whom were ultimately found guilty of rioting.[58] Although these early disturbances paled when compared to subsequent riots, they established important patterns that would be repeated throughout the decade. While Irish Catholics would be deservedly or incorrectly labelled the aggressors, the Orangemen would invariably be perceived as the defenders of Saint John's Protestant and Loyalist traditions. Moreover, an exclusively Protestant constabulary and judiciary would consistently arrest and convict only Irish Catholics for disturbing the peace.

The next three years, coinciding with the first substantial waves of Irish Catholic immigrants and the attendant surge of Orangeism, brought several important episodes of social violence. The Twelfth of July in 1843 witnessed clashes between religious crowds in Saint John and Portland, though an official Orange procession was not held.[59] A more serious incident occurred in March of the following year. Squire Manks, Worshipful Master of the recently established Wellington Orange Lodge, shot and mortally wounded a Catholic Irishman during a dispute at York Point. Angry residents poured into the streets and demanded revenge. Rather than being arrested, however, Manks was placed into protective custody and expeditiously exonerated by an examining board of city magistrates. The verdict was self-defence.[60] The year closed with sporadic riots from Christmas until after New Year's. Crowds of up to 300 Irish Catholics roamed throughout York Point and Portland's wharf district, attacking Orangemen and their property. The Orangemen enthusiastically reciprocated. Two companies of British regulars finally succeeded in quashing the disturbances, but not before one Catholic had died and dozens more from both sides had received serious injuries. Although uninvolved residents bemoaned the apparent state of anarchy, the rioting was neither indiscriminate nor uncontrolled. Catholics and Orangemen carefully picked fights only with "certain . . . obnoxious individuals."[61]

The tensions of the winter of 1844–45 culminated in a St. Patrick's Day riot that eclipsed all earlier Orange–Catholic conflicts in its violence. On 17 March 1845, Portland Orangemen fired without provocation upon a group of Catholic revellers. The incident touched off a wave of reprisals. By nightfall general rioting between Orangemen and Irish Catholics had spread throughout the wharf district and York Point. The fighting was most intense at the foot of Fort Howe Hill in Portland.[62] The rioters dispersed when British troops positioned an artillery piece near Portland's wharves. The ploy was at best symbolic, for the concentrated fighting abated in the evening when the well-armed Orangemen gained a measure of control over the streets. The riot killed at least one Catholic, although several bodies were probably secreted away for private burials. The tally of wounded was correspondingly high, with dozens of combatants being hurt seriously enough to warrant medical attention.[63] The examinations and trials in the riot's aftermath followed the patterns established in 1842. Although authorities arrested several Orangemen, including two suspected of murder, Saint John's all-Protestant Grand Jury preemptively threw out their bills before the cases could be brought to trial. Instead the jury returned bills for several Irish Catholic rioters, two of whom were ultimately found guilty and sentenced. The swift vindication of Orangemen by the Grand Jury, despite an abundance of damaging testimony, illustrated the reluctance of Protestant authorities to condemn Orange violence and their continuing propensity to convict only Irish Catholics.[64]

Saint John and Portland escaped collective social violence for the next two years, but the hiatus did nothing to diminish enmity or foster peaceful linkages between Orangemen and Irish Catholics. The latter abstained from public displays on the St. Patrick's Days of 1846 and 1847. Orangemen quietly observed 12 July in their lodges in 1845; the following year they took a steamer to Gagetown for a procession with their brethren from Queens, Kings, and York Counties.[65] For 1847's Twelfth of July, when famine immigration was reaching its zenith, city Orangemen invited neighbouring brethren and staged the largest procession since the organization's inception. On 14 July a Saint John newspaper trumpeted the now familiar requiem for the Orange holiday: "Dreadful Riot! The Disaffected District [York Point] Again in Arms — Shots Fired — Several Persons Dreadfully Wounded — the Military Called Out."[66] The two-year truce had yielded only larger numbers of Catholic immigrants and nativist Orangemen, and a more sophisticated network for the combatants in both groups to utilize in battle.

The Twelfth of July started quietly enough in 1847, but as Saint John's and Portland's Orangemen began to make their way to their lodges, crowds of wary Irish Catholics spilled into the streets. One of the larger Portland lodges, probably Wellington, entertained the amateur band from the local Mechanics' Institute. All of the band members were Orangemen. In the early evening, the group led a procession of Orangemen and onlookers through the streets of Portland, across the bridge, and into the heart of the Roman Catholic ghetto at York Point.[67] The tunes they played, like most Orange favourites, were clearly offensive to Irish Catholics.[68] At the foot of Dock Street, the crowd attacked the procession with sticks and bricks, smashing many of the band's instruments and forcing the revellers to flee back across the Portland Bridge. Gathering reinforcements and firearms from their lodges and homes, the undaunted Orangemen quickly returned to their enemy's stronghold.[69]

The Irish Catholic crowd, which by now had grown to several hundred, also made use of the respite and collected weapons in the event of a reappearance of the humiliated band members and Orangemen. The buttressed Orange legions did attempt to revive the procession and music when they reached York Point. A battle was inevitable. Volleys of shots from both parties shattered the summer air, leaving scores of wounded lying in the streets along the procession route. The melee continued throughout the evening, with most of the bloodshed occurring along Dock and Mill Streets and the bridge. At midnight detachments of the 33rd Regiment, dispatched at the mayor's request, converged upon York Point only to find the streets deserted. Rather than chance an engagement with the military, both sides ceased hostilities.[70] Aided by the darkness, the Irish Catholics escaped capture and returned to their homes. The constabulary failed to make any arrests after the riot, and the Grand Jury issued no warrants.[71]

Assessment of the riot's severity is hampered due to the secretive removal of the dead and wounded by both parties, particularly the Irish Catholics. Official tallies included only one Catholic killed and several seriously wounded, but everyone involved knew that many had died during the encounter.[72] The significance of the conflict, however, emerged unclouded in the following months. Both sides were organized, well stocked with weapons, and clearly prepared to kill for their beliefs. Catholics had gathered hours before the Orange procession had entered York Point; they were motivated by a desire to "defend" their "territory." Orangemen consciously provoked the enemy by twice marching in procession and playing obnoxious songs through the most Catholic district of Saint John. An undeniable linkage also emerged between the Orange Order and the Mechanics' Institute, which was symbolic of the nativist attraction that Orangeism had to the economically beleaguered Protestant workers facing stiff competition from famine immigrants. Finally, the riot underscored the Orange belief in vigilante justice. The procession's return to York Point represented a "heroic" action to remove a dangerous Catholic "mob" from Saint John's thoroughfares. According to Orange sympathizers, the anemic state of the city's constabulary justified the vigilantism.[73] In retrospect, the riot of 1847 illuminated the entrenchment of social violence as a perennial method of interaction between Orangemen and Catholics.[74]

A year of bloody skirmishes was the riot's true legacy, for neither side had emerged with a clearcut victory on the Twelfth. A wave of assaults and murders swept Saint John and Portland during the weeks that followed; Orange and Catholic vengeance was the motive for all of them.[75] A sensational series of witness examinations after the murder of a suspected Orangeman in September brought religious antipathy to a fever pitch. Dozens of testimonials exposed paramilitary networks operated by militant Orangemen and Catholics. Personal revenge on a small scale appeared to be the favourite tactic of the weaker and outnumbered Catholics. Orangemen, enjoying the support of a Protestant majority, preferred a collective vigilantism whereby they dispensed extralegal justice while acting as an unofficial watchdog of the Irish lower orders.[76] By the year's end, it was apparent that the Orange–Catholic struggle had not diminished. Both sides habitually armed themselves if they ventured into unfriendly districts; each tried desperately to identify its most virulent enemies, and in many cases, both were prepared to kill for their causes.

The religious conflict of the 1840s peaked two years later in Saint John's worst riot of the nineteenth century. The city was quiet in 1848, much as it had been in 1846, because local Orangemen travelled to Fredericton to participate in a massive demonstration.[77] But as the Twelfth approached in 1849, Saint John's Orangemen advertised for the first time their plans for hosting provincial brethren and sponsoring an elaborate procession.[78] Motivated by vivid memories of the inconclusive 1847 conflict, Orangemen and Irish Catholics grimly prepared themselves for battle. On the eve of the holiday, Mayor Robert D. Wilmot met with local Orange officials and asked them to voluntarily abandon their plans to march. But the Orangemen, well-versed on their rights, rejected the suggestion because no provincial statute gave civilian officials the authority to ban public processions.[79] The march, they insisted, would proceed as planned.

With a measure of fatalism, Saint John prepared for the occasion. While Orangemen from Carleton, York, Kings, and Queens Counties were boarding steamers and carriages for Saint John, Irish Catholics were buying arms and ammunition. Shopkeepers along Prince William Street, King Street, and Market Square boarded their windows and decided to declare the day a business holiday.[80] Early on the morning of the Twelfth, hundreds of Orangemen from Saint John and Portland collected at Nethery's Hotel on Church Street and marched to a nearby wharf to greet the Carleton ferry. Among the disembarking brethren was Joseph Corum, the Senior Deputy Grand Master of the New Brunswick Grand Lodge. As the procession leader, Corum would have the honour of representing King William by riding a white horse. The Orangemen came heavily armed with pistols, muskets, and sabres. After assuming a military file, they began the march to the Portland suburb of Indiantown, where they would meet the steamer bringing reinforcements from the northern counties. Their planned route would take them through both Irish Catholic bastions — York Point and Portland's wharf district.[81]

Upon reaching York Point they encountered a large pine arch, symbolically green, which spanned the foot of Mill Street. Several hundred jeering Irish Catholics clustered near the arch's supporting poles; they implored the Orangemen to continue. Outnumbered for the moment, the Orangemen accepted the humiliation and dipped their banners as they passed under the arch. While a few stones were hurled at the Orangemen, and they responded with warning shots, no fighting broke out.[82] Without further incident, the procession reached Indiantown, where it gratefully welcomed scores of reinforcements. Among the newcomers was another pivotal Orange leader. George Anderson, a Presbyterian grocer and primary lodge master, was a veteran of several disturbances in his home town of Fredericton. Anderson, bedecked with a sword that indicated his rank, assumed a position next to Corum at the column's head. The procession now numbered approximately 600 people. The men were heavily armed, the majority carrying muskets on shoulder straps. A few clutched axes that would be used to destroy the green bough when they returned to York Point. Finally, a wagon filled with weapons and supplies took up a station at the rear of the procession. As the Orangemen made their way back to York Point, Portland inhabitants observed that the procession resembled a confident army about to engage in battle.[83]

In the meantime, authorities attempted to alleviate the growing tensions with three separate plans, all of which would ultimately fail to prevent a conflict. Mayor Wilmot's first scheme was to defuse the powder keg by removing the pine arch and dispersing the Catholic crowd in York Point. Wilmot, accompanied by a magistrate and a constable, was physically rebuffed in this endeavour by a cohesive, territorially minded crowd that chanted "Stay off our ground!" He then dispatched Jacob Allan, the Portland police magistrate, to intercept the Orangemen before they reached York Point.[84] Allan asked Corum and Anderson to bypass the Catholic district by using the longer Valley Road on their approach to Saint John. After conferring with their followers, the leaders rejected Allan's suggestion. Their men had suffered humiliation during the morning's passage under the Catholic arch; now they insisted on "Death or Victory."[85] Wilmot borrowed the third and final plan from Saint John's history of dealing with riots. At his request, 60 British soldiers stationed themselves in Market Square to prevent general rioting. While the choice of location would do nothing to prevent a conflict, for Market Square lay to the south of York Point and the Orangemen would enter from the north over the Portland Bridge, it would serve to contain the battle within the Catholic ghetto. The detachment's failure to position itself between the advancing Orangemen and the offensive arch, when it had ample time to do so, raised questions about the sincerity of the authorities' attempts to prevent bloodshed.[86]

General rioting broke out along Mill Street before the procession arrived at the bough. The Catholic crowd now numbered approximately 500, and like the Orangemen, many had armed themselves with muskets. Reports of who fired the first shots varied, but roofers working on a Mill Street building agreed that Orangemen opened fire after being met with a volley of stones and brickbats.[87] Several Catholics lay wounded or dying after the barrage, and then their guns answered the Orangemen's. A heated battle ensued. Men and women along Mill Street threw anything they could at the better-armed Orange contingent. Some engaged in fistfights with individuals they were able to pull from the Orange ranks. Corum struggled to free himself after a handful of Irishmen grabbed his horse's tether. A dozen Catholics captured the wagon filled with arms and gave its driver a sound thrashing. Hundreds of shots were fired, and at least twelve combatants lost their lives. The Irish Catholics suffered most of the casualties. After several minutes of furious fighting, the Orangemen emerged from York Point. As they headed for the safety of the troops, their procession was still intact.[88]

The British garrison, after remaining stationary in Market Square throughout the heat of the battle, went into action as soon as the Orangemen left the Irish Catholic ghetto. Without firing a shot, the soldiers marched past the procession and positioned themselves on Dock Street to seal off the Catholic district. This manoeuvre effectively doused what remained of the conflict.[89] It also gave the Orangemen the opportunity to continue their procession unmolested, for any Catholics wishing to leave York Point in pursuit would have to contend first with the soldiers. The Orangemen, heady with their successful assault on the enemy's territory, proceeded through Market and King Squares and made a circle through the city's centre. Only when they entered Market Square again, with the intention of parading through York Point for the third time, were the troops commanded to impede their progress. Being satisfied with their efforts, the

Orangemen agreed to disband. With the Orange threat finally removed, the Irish Catholics waiting in York Point also dispersed. The great Saint John riot of 1849 was over.[90]

The riot's judicial aftermath followed patterns well established by 1849, although there was one notable exception. At Lieutenant Governor Edmund Head's insistence, the Saint John Grand Jury served warrants on Orange participants as well as the Catholics. This attempt at impartiality was severely undermined, however, by a prejudiced investigative team that included the prominent Orangeman W.H. Needham.[91] Ultimately, all but five of the bills against Orangemen, including those for Corum, Anderson, and eighteen others, were dropped before the defendants reached trial. The five Orangemen who actually stood in the dock were swiftly declared innocent by a jury that remained seated. Much to the prosecution's dismay, the jury ignored recent provincial legislation that clearly outlawed armed public processions.[92] For the Irish Catholics, on the other hand, the judicial pattern of the 1840s remained intact. Of the 24 implicated, six were tried on assault charges, one for attempted murder, and four for unlawful assembly. Two were eventually found guilty, including the alleged "ringleader" who led the defence of the green arch. John Haggerty, immigrant labourer and father of three, would spend his sixty-third birthday in the provincial penitentiary while serving his one-year sentence for assault.[93]

The 1849 riot signalled an end to collective social conflict between Orangemen and Catholics, although small skirmishes would continue for years.[94] Various factors brought about this extended truce, the most important being the hegemony established by Orangemen in Saint John and Portland. In a sense, Orangemen had won the battle of the 1840s. The Irish Catholics' attempts to check the growth of Orangeism with counter-demonstrations had failed. They undeniably suffered the most casualties in the course of the riots. Moreover, a fusion between all levels of authority and the Orange Order had taken place. Orangemen, constables, and British soldiers had combined to contain every major disturbance within the Irish Catholic ghettos of York Point and Portland. The Orange Order became an acceptable accomplice for the maintenance of social control. A double standard had clearly emerged: authorities found Orange vigilantism preferable to "mob rule" by the Irish Catholic "lower orders."[95] During the 1840s Orangemen served as constables, magistrates, and legislative representatives. Excepting one active magistrate in Saint John, the Irish Catholics were excluded from power. This inequity profoundly shaped law enforcement during the riots and trials. No Catholic would be allowed to sit on juries; moreover, only Irish Catholics would be found guilty of rioting offences. Even when Orangemen stood in the dock, such as after the York Point riot of 1849, they were expeditiously exonerated.[96] Ethnicity and religion targeted the Irish Catholics for suppression during the 1840s; meanwhile Orangeism developed into an unofficial arm of social control to protect the Protestant majority.

New Brunswick's improved economic environment after mid-century contributed to the demise of collective conflict by alleviating some of the fierce competition between immigrants and natives. The "Hungry Forties" had indeed been more than a historical cliché to many colonists. A sustained depression had brought scarcities of goods, food, and services. Natives had competed with Irish Catholic immigrants for limited jobs, a factor that had contributed to the rapid growth of Orangeism. Economic variables alone did not cause the Orange–Green riots, but they certainly helped to account for a foundation of social tension.[97] As the province successfully weathered the English transition to free trade in the 1850s, investment capital increased and jobs became more available.[98] Thus Orangemen found one of the key elements of their rhetorical campaign against Irish Catholics undermined. Ultimately, fuller employment fostered better relations between Protestant and Catholic workers.

Another factor in the disappearance of perennial disturbances between Protestants and Catholics was the Orange Order's discontinuance of 12 July processions while it fought for provincial incorporation. Saint John and Portland Orangemen wisely decided not to risk any negative publicity that might accompany collective violence with Irish Catholics while the bill was being debated in the New Brunswick legislature. The process lasted 25 years, but eventually the tradeoff of abstention for legitimacy proved fruitful.[99] Not until after the bill finally passed in 1875, in the midst of the emotional separate schools issue, would Orangemen again take to Saint John's streets to display their fervent brand of loyalty and Protestantism.[100]

Finally, a drastic reduction in the number of Irish Catholic immigrants after 1848 helped to subdue the nativist impulse. The tide of famine immigrants had dropped as precipitously as it had risen. Improving conditions in Ireland accounted for a general reduction in emigrants, especially from the poorer Catholic counties. In addition, a discriminatory immigration policy, instituted at the behest of Lieutenant Governors Sir William Colebrooke and Sir Edmund Head, curtailed Catholic immigration while it increased the number of more desirable Protestant settlers from the British Isles.[101] The results were striking: between 1851 and 1861 the percentages of Irish compared to the total immigration population dropped dramatically in both Saint John and Portland. This decrease also reflected the continuing out-migration of transient Catholics to the "Boston States" and to other British North American provinces.[102] Finally, it indicated the beginnings of a process of acculturation; the sons and daughters of Catholic and Protestant immigrants would be listed as New Brunswickers in the 1861 census. The "soldiers" of the 1840s — both Orange and Green — would be supplanted by generations to whom the violent experiences of the "Hungry Forties" would be historical anecdotes.

The Orange Order was New Brunswick's institutionalized nativist response to Irish Catholic immigration during the 1840s. Prior to this decade, the organization was a small and mostly invisible fraternal order dominated by Irish Protestant immigrants and British garrison troops. As Irish Catholic famine victims poured into Saint John and Portland during the 1840s, however, Protestant natives and non-Irish-born immigrants joined the Orange Order. Orangemen spearheaded a rhetorical campaign to combat the famine immigration, using anti-Catholic and racist propaganda to discourage the Irish from settling permanently in the city. Additionally, the Orange Order increasingly acted as a paramilitary vigilante group that freely engaged in riots with bellicose Irish Catholics. The combination of nativist rhetoric and a mutual willingness to engage in armed conflict provided a decade of collective social violence that culminated in the tragic riot of 12 July 1849. Thus Saint John and Portland, like several eastern seaboard cities in the United States, experienced a strong nativist impulse and several destructive episodes of social violence.

NOTES

1. *Weekly Chronicle* (Saint John), 22 March 1839.
2. *Morning News* (Saint John), 24 September 1847.
3. For this study, social violence is defined as "assault upon an individual or his property solely or primarily because of his membership in a social category." See Allen D. Grimshaw, "Interpreting Collective Violence: An Argument for the Importance of Social Structure," in *Collective Violence*, ed. James F. Short, Jr., and Marvin E. Wolfgang (Chicago, 1972), pp. 12, 18–20.
4. Sir Edmund Head to Lord Grey, 15 July 1849, Colonial Office Series [CO] 188, Public Record Office [PRO], London; *Royal Gazette* (Frederiction), 19 September 1849; D.R. Jack, *Centennial Prize Essay on the History of the City and County of St. John* (Saint John, 1883), pp. 136–37; Reverend J.W. Millidge, "Reminiscences of St. John from 1849 to 1860," *New Brunswick Historical Society Collections*, Vol. IV (1919), pp. 8, 127.
5. Its mid-century population stood at 23 000, making one in every 8.5 New Brunswickers a Saint John resident. Portland, with 8500 inhabitants, was roughly one-third the size of Saint John. See New Brunswick Census, 1851, Provincial Archives of New Brunswick [PANB].
6. Presentment of the Saint John Grand Jury, 27 October 1847, Minutes, Saint John General Sessions, PANB.

7. *Morning News*, 8, 11 September 1843; Abraham Gesner, *New Brunswick; with Notes for Emigrants* (London, 1847), pp. 122–24; Reverend W.C. Atkinson, *A Historical and Statistical Account of New Brunswick, B.N.A. with Advice to Emigrants* (Edinburgh, 1844), pp. 28–29, 36–37.

8. The 1840s was a particularly depressed decade, but as Graeme Wynn eloquently pointed out, the colony was already a veteran of the nineteenth century boom and bust "bandalore": in 1819, 1825, and 1837, New Brunswick suffered trade depressions due to financial downturns and the erosion of speculation capital in Great Britain: *Timber Colony: A Historical Geography of Early Nineteenth Century New Brunswick* (Toronto, 1981), pp. 3–33, 43–53. See also P.D. McClelland, "The New Brunswick Economy in the Nineteenth Century," *Journal of Economic History*, 25 (December 1965): 686–90.

9. W.S. MacNutt, *New Brunswick, a History, 1784–1867* (Toronto, 1963), pp. 283–84, 296; MacNutt, "New Brunswick's Age of Harmony: The Administration of Sir John Harvey," *Canadian Historical Review*, 32 (June 1951): 123–24; D.G.G. Kerr, *Sir Edmund Head: The Scholarly Governor* (Toronto, 1954), pp. 39–54; Wynn, *Timber Colony*, pp. 43–44, 51–53.

10. *Colonial Advocate* (Saint John), 14 July 1845; MacNutt, *New Brunswick*, p. 285; Wynn, *Timber Colony*, pp. 51–53.

11. *New Brunswick Reporter* (Fredericton), 13 October 1848, 24 August 1849; *Morning News*, 28 May 1849; Wynn, *Timber Colony*, pp. 150–55; MacNutt, *New Brunswick*, p. 310.

12. Immigration Returns, New Brunswick Blue Books, 1832–50, Public Archives of Canada [PAC]; "Report on Trade and Navigation," *Journal of the House of Assembly of New Brunswick*, 1866.

13. Only in 1853, after the famine abated in Ireland, would English immigrants once again become the largest group. See New Brunswick Census, 1851; "Report on Trade and Navigation," *Journal of the House of Assembly of New Brunswick*, 1866; William F. Ganong, *A Monograph of the Origins of Settlements in the Province of New Brunswick* (Ottawa, 1904), pp. 90–120.

14. Cecil Woodham-Smith, *The Great Hunger: Ireland 1845–9* (London, 1962), pp. 206–9; Lawrence J. McCaffrey, *The Irish Diaspora in America* (Bloomington, IN, 1976), pp. 59–62; William Forbes Adams, *Ireland and Irish Emigration to the New World* (New York, 1932); Donald Akenson, ed., *Canadian Papers in Rural History*, vol. III (Gananoque, ON, 1981), pp. 219–21.

15. Woodham-Smith, *Great Hunger*, pp. 29, 206–13; John I. Cooper, "Irish Immigration and the Canadian Church before the Middle of the Nineteenth Century," *Journal of the Canadian Church Historical Society*, 2 (May 1955): 13–4; Adams, *Ireland and Irish Emigration*; McCaffrey, *Irish Diaspora*, pp. 59–62; Oliver MacDonagh, "Irish Emigration to the United States of America and the British Colonies During the Famine," in *The Great Famine: Studies in Irish History 1845–52*, ed. R. Dudley Edwards and T. Desmond Williams (Dublin, 1956), pp. 332–39.

16. Immigration Returns, New Brunswick Blue Books, PAC; M.H. Perley's Report on 1846 Emigration, in William Colebrooke to Grey, 29 December 1846, CO 188.

17. Ibid.; *Royal Gazette*, 17 March, 7 July 1847; *Saint John Herald*, 12 November 1845; James Hannay, *History of New Brunswick* (Saint John, 1909), vol. II, p. 70: MacDonagh, "Irish Emigration," pp. 368–73; Adams, *Ireland and Irish Emigration*, p. 234; Woodham-Smith, *Great Hunger*, pp. 209–10.

18. New Brunswick Census, 1851, 1861; *Morning News*, 8, 11 September 1843; Alexander Monro, *New Brunswick; with a Brief Outline of Nova Scotia, and Prince Edward Island* (Halifax, 1855), p. 125; James S. Buckingham, *Canada, Nova Scotia, New Brunswick, and the Other British Provinces in North America* (London, 1843), pp. 409–10.

19. Kings Ward, which included all of York Point and was roughly equal in size to the other Saint John wards, had twice the population of any ward in the 1851 New Brunswick Census. For descriptions of York Point, see Grand Jury Reports, 16 December 1848, Minutes, Saint John General Sessions, PANB, and D.H. Waterbury, "Retrospective Ramble Over Historic St. John," *New Brunswick Historical Society Collections*, vol. IV (1919), pp. 86–88.

20. Colebrooke to Grey, 28 January 1848, CO 188; Gesner, *New Brunswick*, p. 124.

21. John Higham, *Strangers in the Land: Patterns of American Nativism 1860–1925* (New Brunswick, NJ, 1955), pp. 3–4; Higham, "Another Look at Nativism," *Catholic Historical Review* 44 (July 1958): 148–50.

22. For examples of Canadian nativist studies, see Howard Palmer, *Land of the Second Chance: A History of Ethnic Groups in Southern Alberta* (Lethbridge, 1971); Palmer, "Nativism and Ethnic Tolerance in Alberta: 1920–1972," Ph.D. thesis, York University, 1974; Simon Evans, "Spatial Bias in the Incidence of Nativism: Opposition to Hutterite Expansion in Alberta," *Canadian Ethnic Studies* 6, 1–2 (1974): 1–16.

23. *Loyalist and Conservative Advocate* (Saint John), 13 August 1847. See also issues from 20, 27 August 1847.

24. For histories of the Orange Order, see Hereward Senior, *Orangeism in Ireland and Britain 1765–1836* (London, 1966), especially pp. 4–21, 194–206; Senior, "The Early Orange Order 1795–1870," in *Secret Societies in Ireland*, ed. T. Desmond Williams (Dublin, 1973); Peter Gibbon, "The Origins of the Orange Order and the United Irishmen," *Economy and Society* 1 (1972): 134–63.

25. Canadian Orange Order histories include Cecil Houston and W.J. Smyth, *The Sash Canada Wore: A Historical Geography of the Orange Order in Canada* (Toronto, 1980); Hereward Senior, *Orangeism: The Canadian Phase* (Toronto, 1972); Senior, "The Genesis of Canadian Orangeism," *Ontario History* 60 (June 1968): 13–29.

26. James McNichol's report, *Loyal Orange Association Report, 1886* (Toronto, 1886); *Sentinel*, 3 July 1930; J. Edward Steele, comp., *History and Directory of the Provincial Grand Orange Lodge and Primary Lodges of New Brunswick* (Saint John, 1934), p. 11.

27. Miscellaneous Orange documents, courtesy of Professor Peter Toner, University of New Brunswick at Saint John; James McNichol's report, *Loyal Orange Association Report, 1886*; Steele, *History of the Orange Lodges of New Brunswick*, pp. 11, 17–21; Houston and Smyth, *The Sash Canada Wore*, pp. 69–70.

28. Lodge returns, in *Minutes of the Grand Orange Lodge of New Brunswick* [various publishers, 1846–55]; *Annual Reports of the Grand Orange Lodge of the Loyal Orange Association of B.N.A.* [various publishers, 1846–50]; *New Brunswick Reporter*, 10 May 1850; *Loyalist*, 8 June 1848; *Carleton Sentinel* (Woodstock), 15 July 1854; *Sentinel*, 3 July 1930; Steele, *History of the Orange Lodges of New Brunswick*, pp. 11–13, 37–39, 53–55, 59.

29. Because Nova Scotia's lodges, which received their warrants directly from New Brunswick, were only two years old in mid-century, the vast majority of the 10 000 members resided in New Brunswick. See "Minutes of the Grand Orange Lodge of New Brunswick and Nova Scotia," in *Weekly Chronicle*, 6 July 1849; Orange Order documents, Peter Toner; *Minutes of the Grand Orange Lodge of New Brunswick, 1846–50; Sentinel*, 3 July 1930.

30. Correspondence from John Earle in *Annual Report of the Grand Orange Lodge of the Loyal Orange Association of B.N.A.*, 1851; *New Brunswick Reporter*, 26 April 1850; Head to Grey, 7 September 1847, CO 188; *New Brunswick Courier* (Saint John), 25 July 1840; Steele, *History of the Orange Lodge of New Brunswick*, p. 11.

31. Houston and Smyth, *The Sash Canada Wore*, pp. 70–2; Steele, *History of the Orange Lodges of New Brunswick*, pp. 115–8.

32. "Minutes of the Organizational Meeting of the Grand Orange Lodge of New Brunswick, 1844," in Steele, *History of the Orange Lodges of New Brunswick*, p. 11; New Brunswick Census, 1851.

33. James Brown letters to *New Brunswick Reporter*, 28 April, 5, 12 May 1848; *Morning News*, 18 July 1849; John Earle's correspondence, in *Annual Report of the Grand Orange Lodge of the Loyal Orange Association of B.N.A.*, 1851.

34. Minute book, Wellington Orange Lodge, Portland, New Brunswick Museum [NBM], Saint John.

35. 1851 manuscript census returns from Saint John County are incomplete. Returns from only four of the city's wards are extant: Kings, Dukes, Sydney, and Queens. Records from Portland Parish and Carleton are missing.

36. Returns for Saint John County, New Brunswick Manuscript Census, 1851, PANB; Orange documents, including dispensations and lodge returns, Peter Toner; *Minutes of the Grand Orange Lodge of New Brunswick, 1846–55*; Evidence, Saint John Riot Trials, Documents, New Brunswick Executive Council Records, PANB; New Brunswick Supreme Court Documents, PANB. The newspapers consulted were the *Loyalist*, *Weekly Chronicle*, and *Morning News* for the 1840s, as well as the *Daily Sun* (Saint John), 13 July 1897, and Steele, *History of the Orange Lodges of New Brunswick*.

37. *Laws and Ordinances of the Orange Association of British North America* (Toronto, 1840), p. 11; *The Orange Question Treated by Sir Francis Hincks and the London "Times"* (Montreal, 1877).

38. For example, Portland's Wellington Lodge attempted to combat negative publicity after a decade of social violence by declaring itself a "benefit" organization in 1851. See Minute Book, Wellington Orange Lodge, NBM. See also *Rules and Regulations of the Orange Institution of British North America* (Toronto, 1838), p. 5; Steele, *History of the Orange Lodges of New Brunswick*.

39. *Morning News*, 24 January 1849; *Headquarters* (Fredericton), 24 January 1849.

40. *Loyalist*, 1 October 1847.

41. *Minutes of the Grand Orange Lodge of New Brunswick, 1852*; Rev. Gilbert Spurr's address to Orangemen, in *Loyalist*, 15 October 1847; Head to Grey, 26 July 1848, CO 188; *New Brunswick Reporter*, 26 October 1849; *Carleton Sentinel*, 2 July 1850; *Weekly Chronicle*, 15 July 1842, 4 February 1848; *Christian Visitor* (Saint John), 8 March 1848; Steele, *History of the Orange Lodges of New Brunswick*, pp. 13–15, 21.

42. For discussions of the papal conspiracy theory in North America, see S.M. Lipset and Earl Raab, *The Politics of Unreason* (New York, 1970), pp. 47–59, David B. Davis, "Some Themes of Counter-Subversion: An Analysis of Anti-Masonic, Anti-Catholic, and Anti-Mormon Literature," *Mississippi Valley Historical Review* 47 (September 1960): 205–7, Higham, *Strangers in the Land*, pp. 5–6.

43. *Church Witness* (Saint John), 21 September 1853.

44. *Minutes of the Grand Orange Lodge of New Brunswick, 1846–55*, particularly S.H. Gilbert's sermon in 1854; Grand Orange Lodge of New Brunswick's address to Queen Victoria, in Head to Grey, 28 April 1851, CO 188; *New Brunswick Reporter*, 9 April 1850; *Carleton Sentinel*, 16 July 1850; *New Brunswick Reporter*, 1 October 1847; *Weekly Chronicle*, 31 August 1849, 18 July 1851; *Loyalist*, 24 September 1847; *Church Witness*, 16 July, 13 August 1851, 6 July 1853.

45. Adams, *Ireland and Irish Emigration*, pp. 363–4; Carl Wittke, *The Irish in America* (Baton Rouge, LA, 1956), pp. 46–7; Kenneth Duncan, "Irish Famine Immigration and the Social Structure of Canada West," *Canadian Review of Sociology and Anthropology* 11 (February 1965): 33, 39.

46. *Loyalist*, 6 April 1848.

47. Alexander McHarg Diary, NBM; *Morning News*, 8 January, 8 December 1841, 6 January, 14 June 1843, 5 January 1848; *Weekly Chronicle*, 5 January, 28 June 1844, 26 November 1847; *Queen vs. David Nice*, New Brunswick Supreme Court Documents, PANB.

48. *Loyalist*, 30 March 1848; *New Brunswick Reporter*, 20 April 1850; *New Brunswick Assembly Debates*, 8 March 1850, PANB; *Morning News*, 24 January 1849; *Loyalist*, 16 July, 15, 28 October, 4 November 1847; *New Brunswick Reporter*, 19 November 1847, 15 March 1850; *Morning News*, 11 August 1847.

49. For excellent studies of racism in the British Isles, see L.P. Curtis, Jr., *Anglo-Saxons and Celts: A Study of Anti-Irish Prejudice in Victorian England* (Bridgeport, CT, 1968), pp. 8–9, 24–26, and *Apes and Angels: The Irishman in Victorian Caricature* (Devon, England, 1971), passim.

50. *Weekly Chronicle*, 31 August, 28 September 1849; *Loyalist*, 24 September 1847.

51. *Loyalist*, 1 October, 11 November 1847.

52. *New Brunswick Reporter*, 10 May 1850; *Loyalist*, 16 July, 17 September, 15 October 1847; *Weekly Chronicle*, 29 July 1842.

53. The theme of competition between immigrant labourers and nativists in North America is explored in Oscar Handlin, *Boston's Immigrants* (Cambridge, MA, 1959), pp. 180–87, Higham, *Strangers in the Land*, p. 57, Adams, *Ireland and Irish Emigration*, p. 353.

54. M.H. Perley's Report on 1846 Emigration, in Colebrooke to Grey, 29 December 1846, CO 188; *Royal Gazette*, 17 March, 7 July 1847; Wynn, *Timber Colony*, pp. 155–56; Kathryn Johnston, "The History of St. John, 1837–1867: Civic and Economic," Honours thesis, Mount Allison University, 1953, pp. 24–28.

55. *Loyalist*, 24 March 1845, 17 September, 28 October, 4 November, 9, 23 December 1847; *New Brunswick Reporter*, 10 September 1847; *New Brunswick Reporter*, 19 November 1847.

56. Joseph Brown to R.F. Hazen, 11 July 1837, R.F. Hazen Papers, NBM; *Weekly Chronicle*, 14 July 1837.

57. *New Brunswick Reporter*, 26 April, 10 May 1850.

58. *Morning News*, 13 July, 5 August 1842; *Weekly Chronicle*, 15 July, 12 August 1842; *New Brunswick Courier*, 16 July, 13, 27 August 1842; Minutes, Saint John General Sessions, 9, 10, 17 December 1842, 25 March 1843, PANB; *Sentinel*, 29 October 1891.

59. *New Brunswick Reporter*, 26 April 1850.

60. Mayor Lauchlan Donaldson to Alfred Reade, 8 March 1844, New Brunswick Supreme Court Documents, PANB; McHarg Diary; *Morning News*, 5 April 1844.

61. *Weekly Chronicle*, 3 January 1845; *Morning News*, 3 January 1845; *Headquarters*, 8 January 1845; McHarg Diary.

62. Donaldson to Reade, 29 March 1845, Saint John Grand Jury to Colebrooke, 27 March 1845, "Riots and Disasters," New Brunswick Executive Council Records [Executive Council Records], PANB; *Loyalist*, 24 March 1845; *Weekly Chronicle*, 21 March 1845.

63. Minutes, New Brunswick Executive Council, 7 April 1845, PANB; Report of Doctors Robert and William Bayard, 17 March 1845, "Riots and Disasters," Executive Council Records; McHarg Diary; *Weekly Chronicle*, 21 March 1845; *Morning News*, 19 March 1845; *Observer* (Saint John), 18 March 1845; *New Brunswick Reporter*, 21 March 1845; *New Brunswick Courier*, 22 March 1845; *Loyalist*, 24 March 1845.

64. Minutes, Saint John General Sessions, 20, 22, 26 March, 14 June 1845; Donaldson to Reade, 22 March 1845, "Riots and Disasters," Executive Council Records; *New Brunswick Courier*, 5 July 1845; *Saint John Herald*, 2 July 1845.

65. *Minutes of the Grand Orange Lodge of New Brunswick*, 1847; *Weekly Chronicle*, 17 July 1846.

66. *Morning News*, 14 July 1847.

67. Orange supporters tried to disassociate the Orange Order, the Mechanics' Institute Band, and the crowd that followed the procession. The *Loyalist*, 16 July 1847, claimed that the band had nothing to do with the Orange procession, while Clarence Ward made the dubious assertion that the Orange entourage consisted of "children." See "Old Times in St. John—1847," *Saint John Globe*, 1 April 1911, p. 8. Yet an article in the *Orange Sentinel*, 29 October 1891, proudly revealed that all the band members were Orangemen.

68. For examples of these songs, see *The Sentinel Orange and Patriotic Song Book* (Toronto, 1930?), and R. McBride, ed., *The Canadian Orange Minstrel for 1860, Contains Nine New and Original Songs, Mostly All of Them Showing Some Wrong that Affects the Order or the True Course of Protestant Loyalty to the British Crown* (London, 1860). Note particularly "Croppies Lie Down," a nineteenth-century favourite of Orangemen in Europe and North America.

69. *New Brunswick Courier*, 17 July 1847; *Morning News*, 14 July 1847; *Loyalist*, 16 July 1847; *Sentinel*, 29 October 1891; McHarg Diary.

70. *Morning News*, 14 July 1847; Colebrooke to Grey, 30 July 1847, Documents, Executive Council Records, PANB; McHarg Diary; *New Brunswick Courier*, 17 July 1847; *Loyalist*, 16 July 1847; Ward, "Old Times in St. John — 1847."

71. *New Brunswick Courier*, 7 August 1847.

72. Colebrooke to Grey, 30 July 1847, CO 188; *Morning News*, 14 July 1847.

73. *Loyalist*, 16 July 1847; Ward, "Old Times in St. John — 1847."

74. One newspaper referred to it as a "civil war": *Morning News*, 14 July 1847.

75. *New Brunswick Courier*, 24 July 1847; *Morning News*, 14, 21, 23, 28 July 1847; *Loyalist*, 23 July 1847; *Weekly Chronicle*, 30 July 1847.

76. *Queen vs. Dennis McGovern*, 7–17 September 1847, New Brunswick Supreme Court Documents, PANB. Note especially the testimonies of Thomas Clark, James Clark, Ezekiel Downey, and Edward McDermott. See also *Morning News*, 24 January 1848; *Weekly Chronicle*, 10 September 1847; *New Brunswick Courier*, 11 September 1847; *Loyalist*, 10 September 1847; *Morning News*, 8 September 1847.

77. *Weekly Chronicle*, 14 July 1848. Fredericton's Orangemen invited provincial brethren to celebrate the anniversary of their successful 1847 battle with Irish Catholics: *New Brunswick Reporter*, 10 May 1850.

78. *Weekly Chronicle*, 6 July 1849.

79. Head to Grey, 15 July 1849, CO 188. The question of the legality of public processions, especially armed ones, would become a hotly debated topic in the House of Assembly after the riot, yet no restrictive legislation would emerge from the debate.

80. Testimonies of Thomas Paddock and Francis Jones, "Riots and Disasters," Executive Council Records; *New Brunswick Reporter*, 13 July 1848; Head to Grey, 15 July 1849, CO 188.

81. *Morning News*, 13 July 1849; *New-Brunswicker* (Saint John), 14 July 1849; *New Brunswick Courier*, 14 July 1849; Testimonies of Francis Jones, George Noble, Jacob Allan, Charles Boyd, Squire Manks, and George McKelvey, "Riots and Disasters," Executive Council Records; Head to Grey, 15 July 1849, CO 188.

82. Testimonies of Josiah Wetmore, Jeremiah McCarthy, George Nobel, and Jacob Allan, "Riots and Disasters," Executive Council Records; Head to Grey, 15 July 1849, CO 188; *Sentinel*, 3 July 1930.

83. Testimonies of Jacob Allan, George Mason, Samuel Dalton, Samuel Gordon, and Francis Jones, "Riots and Disasters," Executive Council Records; Head to Grey, 15 July 1849, CO 188; *Weekly Chronicle*, 13 July 1849; *New Brunswicker*, 14 July 1849; *Sentinel*, 3 July 1930.

84. Head to Grey, 15 July 1849, CO 188; Testimonies of James Gilbert, Henry Gilbert, John Nixon, John Fitzpatrick, Joseph Wetmore, and James Clark, "Riots and Disasters," Executive Council Records.

85. Testimonies of Jacob Allan, Francis Jones, and Squire Manks, "Riots and Disasters," Executive Council Records; Head to Grey, 15 July 1849, CO 188; *Sentinel*, 29 October 1891, 3 July 1930.

86. Head to Grey, 15 July 1849, CO 188; Jacob Allan testimony, "Riots and Disasters," Executive Council Records; *Morning News*, 13 July 1849; *Temperance Telegraph* (Saint John), 19 July 1849.

87. Testimonies of James McKenzie, William Smith, Francis Wilson, and Francis Jones, "Riots and Disasters," Executive Council Records; *Temperance Telegraph*, 19 July 1849; *Weekly Chronicle*, 13 July 1849; *Morning News*, 13 July 1849.

88. Testimonies of Squire Manks, James McKenzie, William Smith, Francis Wilson, and Jeremiah Smith, "Riots and Disasters," Executive Council Records; *Morning News*, 13 July 1849; *Christian Visitor*, 14 July 1849; *Weekly Chronicle*, 13 July 1849.

89. Head to Grey, 15 July 1849, CO 188; Charles Boyd testimony, "Riots and Disasters," Executive Council Records; *Morning News*, 13 July 1849; *New-Brunswicker*, 14 July 1849; *Weekly Chronicle*, 13 July 1849.

90. Testimonies of Charles Boyd and Jacob Allan, "Riots and Disasters," Executive Council Records; *Morning News*, 13 July 1849; Head to Grey, 15 July 1849, CO 188.

91. Head to Grey, 15 July 1849, CO 188; *Morning News*, 23 July 1849; *New Brunswick Courier*, 21 July 1849.

92. William B. Kinnear to Head, extract, 6 September 1849, in Head to Grey, 7 September 1849, CO 188; Recognizances, July–September 1849, "Riots and Disasters," Executive Council Records; Documents, Saint John Justice Court, 1849, PANB; Inquests, 1849, New Brunswick Supreme Court Documents, PANB; 12 Victoria, c. 29, 1849, *New Brunswick Statutes*, 1849; *Morning News*, 30 July 1849; *New Brunswick Courier*, 21, 28 July 1849; *Temperance Telegraph*, 23 August 1849.

93. Documents, Saint John Justice Court, 1849; Kinnear to Head, extract, 6 September 1849, in Head to Grey, 7 September 1849, CO 188; John Haggerty petition to Head, September 1849, in Judicial Documents, Executive Council Records; *Weekly Chronicle*, 24 August 1849; *New Brunswick Courier*, 18, 25 August 1849.

94. *New Brunswick Courier*, 19 July 1851, 16, 23, 30 July, 6, 13 August 1853; *Weekly Chronicle*, 18 July 1851; *Morning News*, 15, 20 July 1853; *New Brunswick Reporter*, 15, 22 July 1853; *Freeman* (Saint John), 14 July 1855; McHarg Diary.

95. *Loyalist*, 30 March 1848; *New Brunswick Reporter*, 20 April 1850. Irish immigrants in the United States experienced a similar double standard: see Theodore M. Hammett, "Two Mobs of Jacksonian Boston: Ideology and Interest," *Journal of American History* 62 (March 1976): 866–7.

96. Documents, Saint John Justice Court, 1849; "Riots and Disasters," Executive Council Records.

97. W.W. Rostow explored the linkages between social unrest and economic downturns in *British Economy of the Nineteenth Century* (Oxford, 1948), pp. 123–25.

98. Wynn, *Timber Colony*, pp. 84–86, 166–67; MacNutt, *New Brunswick*, p. 329; James R. Rice, "A History of Organized Labour in Saint John, New Brunswick, 1813–1890," M.A. thesis, University of New Brunswick, 1968, pp. 33–34.

99. *Journal of the House of Assembly of New Brunswick*, 1850–1, 1853–4, 1857–60, 1867, 1872–5; 38 Victoria, c. 54, 1875, *Statutes of New Brunswick*, 1875.

100. Saint John's Orangemen sponsored a massive procession on the first Twelfth of July following the bill's assent. See *Freeman*, 13, 15, 18 July 1876; *Morning News*, 14, 17 July 1876.

101. Colebrooke to Grey, 30 July 1847, Head to Grey, 15 July 1849, CO 188; Colebrooke Correspondence, 1847, Head Correspondence, 1849, PANB.

102. New Brunswick Census, 1851, 1861; Immigration Returns, New Brunswick Blue Books, 1850–5, PAC; "Report on Trade and Navigation," *Journal of the House of Assembly of New Brunswick*, 1866.

Article Twenty-Nine

Reciprocal Work Bees and the Meaning of Neighbourhood

Catharine Anne Wilson

The reciprocal work 'bee' deserves to be understood as a vital and characteristic element of nineteenth-century rural Ontario. It was as much a part of Ontario folk culture as the potlatch was for West Coast Natives, and much more common than the charivari.[1] The bee was an integral part of the farm economy and an important social resource. Through reciprocal work, individual farm families who lacked self-sufficiency in labour and skills were given a measure of insurance against hard times while they established and maintained a workable farm unit. The bee was also a key component in the structuring, operation, and definition of neighbourhood.

The study of reciprocal work bees takes us directly into the construct and concept of neighbourhood. Neighbourhood is not generally understood as part of the larger social system, but tends to be treated peripherally in relation to such categories as class, ethnicity, and gender, if it is not ignored entirely.[2] As such, a disjunction exists between the family unit and the wider world. By examining the structure and process of reciprocal work bees, we reach a deeper understanding of the relationship between the individual, the family, and the larger social order. Neighbourhood, however, is a nebulous idea. Most commonly it is recognized as comprising people at a certain time who live near each other. In this article it goes beyond this spatial and temporal definition to include interaction, process, and a sense of belonging.[3] In the nineteenth century, neighbourhood was not just the people who lived near you but the basis

Source: Catharine Anne Wilson, "Reciprocal Work Bees and the Meaning of Neighbourhood," *Canadian Historical Review*, 82(3) (2001): 431–64. © University of Toronto Press Incorporated.

for economic activity, social support, and the organization of day-to-day living. Though some settlements may have been made up of independent and isolated families that kept to themselves, or tightly knit groups united by ethnicity and religion, others used the bee to develop highly effective networks of interaction. At the bee, people from diverse cultural backgrounds came together and were incorporated according to their genealogy, wealth, age, gender, and skills. Thus the bee helped to create a structural and cognitive order in the neighbourhood. Like the potlatch, it was not only an economic and social exchange but also a process through which shared values and a collective identity were created and communicated. Like the charivari, the bee was a mechanism of social integration identifying those who belonged and those who did not. As such, neighbourhood might, but did not necessarily, include the generosity and kindness that came with 'neighbourliness.'

This study offers a different perspective of the bee. Too often it has been eulogized as the epitomy of the selfless communal ideal. Whether seen through the eyes of storytellers and journalists who lament the passing of the 'old rural values' of community, kindliness, and generosity or academics with their own laments, the bee has come to symbolize and celebrate the good old days of neighborliness in an age of growing individualism and commercialism. Rural sociologists and anthropologists, often coming from a background of the urban/folk continuum, view the decline of cooperative labour as part of the larger process of modernization and individualization of society. Marxist historians view reciprocal labour as evidence of the moral economy and the antithesis to capitalistic farming systems. Feminist historians depict cooperative labour such as the quilting bee as part of the female world of support, equality, mutual dependency, and deep affection — values not duly appreciated in a male culture of independence and competition.[4] By examining how the bee actually functioned in an economic and social sense in the nineteenth century, we can better understand how the rural neighbourhood emerged, how informal labour markets were part of the social whole, and how the bee fit into the broader culture of Ontario. The bee was not the simple embodiment of a selfless communal ideal; it was a complex and sometimes paradoxical phenomenon that played an important role in a rural society of private property and social hierarchy.

'BUSY AS BEES'

What settlers called a 'bee' was a neighbourly gathering where people worked together industriously with the bustle of bees in a hive.[5] Bees occurred with regularity and frequency throughout the calendar year in early Ontario. In the spring, bees were called for raising houses and barns, shearing sheep, picking the burrs from fleece, ploughing and dragging the land for planting, and piling logs to clear the land. In the hot, dry days of summer, farm folk gathered together at bees to clear water courses, mow and cradle hay, shell peas, and cut grain. Once the busy harvest season slowed down, a new round of bees began. There were bees for spreading manure, husking corn, ploughing fields, picking and peeling apples, and hunting squirrels and pigeons. Fanning and threshing bees were often held in the barn in the winter months. This was also the time when neighbourhoods turned their energies to processing clothing and food. Bees for butchering livestock, plucking fowl, spinning wool, and sewing quilts and carpets enlivened the long winter months, and sawing and chopping bees kept the family warm and ready for the next round of clearing and building in the spring.[6]

Though bees were not daily or even universal events, many farm families found their year liberally sprinkled with such occasions. The fall could be a particularly busy beeing time. In a period of ten days in September 1869, the Michie family of Reach Township went to a cradling bee, a raking bee, a threshing bee, a quilting bee, a dunging bee, and two binding bees.[7] On occasion, double-bees were held, where, for example, the men might have a chopping bee while the women quilted, or a quilting during the day was followed by a paring bee in the evening. Indeed, Susanna Moodie, who was no fan of such occasions, complained that 'people in the woods have a craze for giving and going to bees, and run to them with as much eagerness as a peasant runs to a racecourse or a fair.'[8] This was particularly true of the early settlement days when clearing and building were at their height. Then 'the call of the woodman, the falling timber, the merry "Yo-heave" of the Raising Bee, could . . . be heard on every side,' and the fires from logging bees lit up the whole sky at night.[9] As settlement moved inland, so too did beeing activity. Well into the twentieth century, barn-raising bees were still being held in Temiskaming District, 'Ontario's New Frontier.'[10] By then, in the older more established parts of the province, bees, in general, were declining in number. The logging and raising bees of the early settlement days had given over to threshing and silo-filling bees of a more intensive mixed-farming system. Bees, therefore, were an integral part of the farming year and the social calendar for many Ontario farm families well into the twentieth century.

'THE STILL BEE GATHERS NO HONEY': THE ECONOMICS OF THE BEE

Reciprocal work was typical of all agricultural communities, but especially frontier areas where land was readily available and capital and labour were in short supply. In early Ontario, few settlers had cash with which to hire labourers. With land readily available, labourers were costly and hard to come by, especially in the backwoods.[11] Most families, particularly those with young children, were simply unable to perform all the tasks themselves without assistance from neighbours. This was especially true of chopping, logging, and building, which required special skills and immense physical strength. As cultivated acreages increased, it was also true for certain periods of the year such as harvest time, when work demands reached their peak and time was of the essence. By holding a bee, individual farming families who were not self-sufficient in terms of meeting the demands of peak labour periods in the year or possessing all the skills and equipment required to establish a home and farm could attain those ends. The bee was, in effect, an informal labour exchange, part of the hidden economy overlooked by census takers and economic historians. It was a forum for labour in a variety of ways. It served to concentrate labour for those events requiring large numbers. It provided families with extra labour in emergencies that might never be fully repaid. But, most often, it simply redistributed labour over time so that families had more at certain times in the year, in their personal settlement history, or in their life course, a debt that was then fully repaid at a later date.

The beeing phenomenon, therefore, was an essential part of the farm economy. Through reciprocal labour, the farm family was able to create capital. It was also better able to cope with risks. With a low standard of living, no insurance, and the possibility of sudden and unexpected calamities, it was essential to be on good terms with your neighbours. This was especially true in newly settled areas where population was highly dispersed and kin networks were not yet established. If your barn burnt, your fields were flooded, or your husband was killed, you needed to be able to rely on reciprocal aid rather than face these disasters on your own. If you were not part of this neighbourhood exchange system, the backwoods could be a frightening, risky, even hostile place.[12]

Certain jobs required the calling of a bee for reasons of economy and efficiency. Clearing land — chopping, logging, burning and fencing — could be done by hired labour before mid-century for £3–£4 currency per acre.[13] Most settlers, cash poor, knew this cost was an imprudent way to spend what little money they had. The goal was to clear enough land as soon as possible for a self-sustaining farm (about 30 to 50 cleared acres). Achieving this aim on one's own was a task that took nearly a lifetime, as the average clearing rate was 1.23–1.55 acres a year.[14] By the time a man was ready to plant the first acre he had cleared, it had already begun to grow over with weeds. Settlers were anxious to meet the cleared acreage required of settlement duties (5 cleared acres in the first year), make their farm self-sustaining and get their field crops by early September. Besides being time-consuming, clearing the land was extremely strenuous and dangerous work requiring considerable but rare skill with the axe. It was almost imperative to call a bee for hoisting and manoeuvring the heavy logs into piles to burn. In a single day, a bee of twenty men with five yoke of oxen could log 5 acres (a whole field), the cost being plenty of whiskey, some simple food, and work in return.[15] Likewise, erecting log buildings was a job requiring the strength and skill of more than one or two people. Time was of the essence, for families needed shelter from the cold, and barns needed to be ready to house crops and livestock come the fall. It took about sixteen men and four yoke of oxen to hoist up and connect the heavy logs of a house or barn. According to the Emigration Questionnaire conducted in 1840–1, to hire labour to erect a simple one-room log hut cost from £4–£15 currency. Such a price was prohibitive for most settlers. As respondents from the Canada Company District and Bathurst pointed out, the usual custom was for neighbours to call a bee, which cost only meat and drink estimated to be about £2 currency.[16]

Other bees were called because the chores were time-consuming and monotonous and needed to be accomplished with greater speed than one family could muster. Harvesting provided one such example. Winter wheat ripened just before barley and often overlapped with it, making the harvest a particularly busy time. Labourers were hard to find, and to hire a harvester cost five to six shillings currency per day.[17] By inviting eight neighbours to a threshing bee, 250 bushels could be hauled in while good weather prevailed, then threshed and made ready for market.[18] Once fanning mills and then threshing machines began being hired by the hour or the day, households could maximize their financial investment by calling a bee to bring back loads of grain as quickly as possible. Bees also made more efficient use of time in the production of household goods. Ill-prepared for the onslaught of winter, new settlers knitted and wove yarn to keep large families warm outside in the bracing cold and cozy inside when the fires grew low. Sewing, knitting, and spinning in the volumes required was tedious, time-consuming, and labour-intensive work best done in the daylight. These hours, however, were just when children and chores demanded attention. As much as 60 yards of linen could be manufactured at one bee, seventeen scanes [skeins] of woollen yarn spun, or an entire quilt quilted.[19] Moreover, some jobs, such as husking corn or peeling apples, were simply so mind-numbing and irksome that the competitive spirit and sociability of the bee were needed to spur people to work to their full potential. At these bees, partying and working were easily and happily combined.

Disasters such as illness, irregular rains, late occupancy of a farm, or enforced absence often meant that a backlog of work accumulated. Bees might be called to help a sick neighbour harvest a crop or cut a winter supply of wood.[20] This kind of bee was a form of charity and was functionally distinct from the more routine annual work bees. Belonging to a regular circle of reciprocal labour was a source of insurance. There was considerable security in knowing that many people owed you favours and that you could call upon them in time of need.

In this manner, reciprocal work furthered the economic growth of individual families, the community, and the province. As Doug McCalla asserts in his economic history of Upper Canada: 'If the provincial economy must be summarized in terms of a single, pre-eminent product, the farms themselves were its chief accomplishments.'[21] Clearing land and erecting farm buildings were the most important elements in this extensive growth and capital creation. In the process of creating farms, reciprocal work bees made families structurally dependent on their neighbours. Such patterns of dependence may have created neighbourhoods that were self-sufficient even when individual farmers were not.[22] Furthermore, bees helped to create the basic physical infrastructure of community life, as they were frequently called to erect mills, churches, and schools.[23]

Bees were also an important part of the exchange economy of early Ontario. A tendency exists for scholars of nineteenth-century Ontario to place too much emphasis on wheat exports and, thus, the importance of cash in the economy. The economy was much more complex, involving a system of exchange that included not only cash but also the barter of goods that the family produced and the credit that settlers extended to neighbours and received in return. Indeed, anything that 'earned credit in the local economy . . . would help to sustain farm making.'[24] Certainly the giving and receiving of labour as found in the custom of bees was a part of this exchange system.

Like most significant interaction, an accounting process was at work. It may have been subtle and hidden beneath the rhetoric of neighbourliness, but it was present nevertheless. Participation was part of an exchange of labour, skills, equipment, information, hospitality, and good will. Reciprocal work operated much like a bank, in which all made their deposits and were then entitled to make their withdrawals or acquire small loans. One could even attain personal credit for the contributions made by ancestors or close relatives. It was possible to borrow and then abscond, but most settled families probably contributed and received in equal quantities. Was beeing, however, viewed by the participants as a business transaction or, in an attempt to make sense of this phenomenon, are we projecting our twentieth-century capitalist values on the past? The farm diaries do not clarify the mentality at work. On the one hand, the researcher senses that farmers who did not trust a mental system of checks and balances began their diaries as a way of keeping track of bees and other forms of reciprocal labour. Bees were frequently recorded and clearly identified as such. Walter Beatty, near Brockville, carefully noted the participant, the location, and the type of bee his family attended. For example, on 18 September 1849 his entry reads, 'Jock goes to George Toes Dung Bee.' Return labour was just as carefully accounted. For example, on 24 May 1849 he wrote, 'Thomas Davis sent his horses and son to Plow.'[25] When W.F. Munro gave advice to farmers on calculating their costs in the backwoods, he reminded them to 'take into account the "bees."'[26] It was clearly not as strict an accounting, however, as we might expect. When costs were itemized, they were rarely given in monetary terms, but were generally a day's work for a day's work. But the rule had to be flexible. Inequalities were bound to exist — someone would have a bigger field to harvest, a smaller pile of wood to chop. A family raising a frame barn and having seventy people at the bee would not be expected to attend seventy bees in return. The major players might be repaid with labour, the skilled framer paid cash, and the others paid with the feast and frolic that followed. Clearly they did not have a strict accounting, but it was understood that the same effort would be returned and, in the end, a redistribution of skills, equipment, labour, and hospitality would occur.[27]

Reciprocal work, therefore, played an integral role in the exchange economy, assisting individual farm families to establish a workable farm unit and insure against hard times. In this manner, it contributed to the extensive growth of the larger provincial economy.

'HE THAT HANDLES HONEY SHALL FEEL IT CLING TO HIS FINGERS': THE INFLUENCE OF ASSOCIATION

Beyond contributing to the economic structure of neighbourhood, the bee was a social resource. In the early settlement period, with a scarcity of religious and educational institutions and with kin networks stretching back generations, this factor was especially important. The need to cooperate brought people of diverse backgrounds and potentially divisive lines of affiliation together. The bee provided the mechanism for social integration and bonding. Each and every individual raising or quilting can be viewed as an interaction episode where patterns of association and meaning were confirmed and sometimes initiated or reshaped.[28] By participating and abiding by the rules as they were understood, people of various ages, classes, genders, skills, and experiences were incorporated into the group.

A code of behaviour developed regarding communal labour that extended beyond a mere accounting system to encompass social relations. Those giving advice to new settlers urged them to take heed that every favour conferred required a return favour. As Catharine Parr Traill, a leading authority on life in the backwoods, told her readers, "It is, in fact regarded in the light of a debt of honour, you cannot be forced to attend a bee in return, but no one that can does refuse, unless from urgent reasons; and if you do not find it possible to attend in person you may send a substitute in a servant or in cattle, if you have a yoke.' Though this might be an inconvenience, this 'debt of gratitude ought to be cheerfully repaid.'[29] This generalized reciprocity, 'I'll help you with something later,' implied a certain degree of trust and closeness. The request to return the effort at another bee could be met in three ways: accept it, discharge the debt later, and reinforce the bonds; accept to return the favour in another form, maybe discharge the debt, and reinforce the bonds; or refuse to attend, renege on your repayment, and risk breaking the social bond. Few risked exclusion from the system altogether because alienating your neighbours could be costly financially and socially.[30]

Because of this obligatory reciprocity, work groups could become highly stable among a core of persistent farmers, or even last for a generation or more.[31] It was unlikely that all labour obligations would be repaid in the same season, but they might linger for years, cementing and lengthening the lines of obligation, especially among people who shared the same values of hard work, neighbourliness, and trust. The stability of the group was essential to mutual aid. As such, the self-interest of individual families conjoined with the shared interest of the neighbourhood.

Constant social contact and mutual dependency did not necessarily imply deep affection, as work groups could be torn asunder by a serious accident or quarrels between families. Tensions simmering beneath the surface of neighbourhood life frequently erupted at bees, especially those where whiskey was liberally served. Patrick Dunigan, for example, who had accused a neighbour of stealing his valuable oak tree, was stripped and tortured with hot irons by his neighbours at a bee. Hatred between Patrick Farrell and James Donnelly Sr over possession of 50 acres culminated at a bee in June 1857 when Donnelly killed Farrell with a handspike.[32] Such violence, even verbal disagreements, acquired significance in the rumour mill. Someone drunk, disorderly, uncooperative, or insulting was clearly breaking the code of neighbourliness and was a nuisance, if not a serious liability, to completing the job efficiently and without incident. Such behaviour not only threatened life and property but also jeopardized the working relationship of the group. That person was apt to be ostracized.

In this manner, the bee was a way of asserting community identity and belonging: one either adhered to the shared values of hard work and neighbourliness and belonged or was left out. For example, two young Englishmen who considered themselves above assisting at a logging bee in Douro Township in the 1830s were ridiculed with laughter.[33] In another case, Thomas Niblock, who had gained the reputation of not paying his debts on time and disparaging his neighbours' company, was not included in the beeing circle in Delaware and had to hire men to help him clear and harvest.[34] So important was a 'neighbourly' attitude that responsible, cheerful, and generous effort even took precedence over the actual quality of the work done. The neighbourly quilter was still asked to a quilting even if her stitches were uneven. Sloppy work could always be ripped out and replaced at a later date; a fissure of friendly relations was more difficult, time-consuming, and costly to repair.[35]

Besides the cheerful repayment of labour, hospitality was an integral part of the exchange and one of the most valued virtues of the social code. Just what constituted appropriate, neighbourly hospitality changed over time. In the early days of sparse settlement and rough ways, hospitality took the form of simple food, entertainment, and plenty of whiskey. Whiskey, in particular, was the measure of hospitality. Commentators were quick to point out in the 1820s that you simply could not raise a barn without it.[36] Generally it took sixteen men to raise a building, and five gallons of whiskey was the recommended store to have on hand.[37] An inexperienced grog-boss, as at Moodie's bee, inadvertently wreaked havoc by being too generous too early in the day. Susanna Moodie's 'vicious and drunken' guests stayed on after the logging bee with their 'unhallowed revelry, profane songs and blasphemous swearing,' and left her to pick up the broken glasses, cups, and strewn remnants of the feast. Not surprisingly, Susanna condemned bees as being 'noisy, riotous drunken meetings, often terminating in violent quarrels, sometimes even bloodshed.'[38] Concern over accidents, quarrels, expense of provisions, and damage to property occasioned by such drinking brought about a contest between the whiskey supporters on the one side and the evangelicals and temperance advocates on the other in many communities. Evangelicals and temperance advocates met with considerable resistance in their attempt to redefine traditional patterns of hospitality as sinful. For example, a Waterdown man wishing to raise a sawmill without whiskey had to send to the Indian mission on the Credit before he could obtain willing men.[39] In another case, men turned out to a raising in Missouri Township, but once the foundation was laid, refused to raise the barn unless whiskey was served. When no whiskey appeared, the men left.[40] At times resistance could take a nasty turn. For example, when Thomas Brown, who had previously been part of a gang of young men who caroused at any bee within riding distance, took the pledge, he became a target of ridicule. When he next attended a bee and refused to drink, whiskey was forcibly poured down his throat and he was beaten.[41] By the 1870s, however, as the farming population became more established, older, and respectable, and as evangelicalism gained converts, strong drink was either not offered or limited to moderate amounts after the job was done.[42] Though hospitality continued to be a vital component of the exchange, elaborate meals and entertainment replaced generous quantities of whiskey.

By reciprocating in the appropriate fashion through hospitality and labour, people demonstrated their support for reciprocal labour and the shared values that supported it. In so doing, they became or continued to be part of the neighbourhood. This process of incorporation worked to integrate newcomers and established settlers, young and old, rich and poor, women and men not as equals, but with clearly defined identities within the larger group. Though Catharine Parr Traill viewed the coming together of the educated gentleman, the poor artisan, the soldier, the independent settler, and the labourer in one common cause as the 'equalizing system of America,' it was neither so romantic nor so revolutionary. Although the bee publicly identified people as belonging, it also established, confirmed, and renegotiated their status in the rural hierarchy, whether that standing was based on experience, skills, age, class, or gender.

Bees constituted a rite of passage for new settlers, a time when they were incorporated into the group values and understandings that could make them into useful and valued members of the neighbourhood. Reciprocal labour tied new and established families together. On the one hand, established farmers who expanded their operations needed additional labour. On the other hand, new settlers relied on more experienced settlers for their skill, equipment, advice, and any older children they could spare.[43] When Mr. Sinclair arrived in Howard Township (Kent Co.) in the 1830s, for example, he had a neighbour accompany him to summon the locals to his raising. As newcomer, he had no outstanding favours to call upon, no reputation established as a trustworthy and hard worker, and therefore needed William Anderson to provide an introduction. With no house of his own, and his wife sick with lake fever, Sinclair had to rely on another neighbour to assist in preparing for the feast and festivities that followed. In repaying all these favours in the customary way, the Sinclair family could establish its claim to membership in the neighbourhood and the rights and responsibilities that status conferred.[44]

The bee, like the farm operation itself, incorporated people of all ages into its service while publicly acknowledging their status within the group. The very young and the very old, for example, were relegated to the sidelines to watch, cheer, and pass judgment. Those able to participate in the work were given responsibilities according to their perceived capabilities and talents. It was standard practice, for example, for dangerous, strenuous work, such as raising or logging, to get experienced young men. Though an older man might shout the orders to 'heave ho,' only someone with a 'steady head and active body' could go out on a beam.[45] On several occasions while raising barns, seasoned men had let a bent slip and someone had been killed.[46] Novices, therefore, had to be kept away from dangerous work. In John Geikie's account of a logging bee at his father's farm in the 1830s or 1840s, John and his brother (who were under fifteen years of age) were allowed only to watch on the sidelines and do the 'lighter parts of the business.' They lopped off branches, made piles of brush, brought the men pails of water, and kept the animals out of danger of falling trees. The men did the chopping and the 'wild work' of rolling the logs together.[47] As power saws and threshing machines were introduced later in the century, the specialized knowledge required to run the machines and ownership of this technology reinforced the age-based hierarchy. Boys, or men past their prime, were limited to carrying the logs and pitching blocks at the sawing bee, or pitching grain at the threshing bee. Only experienced, active men in their prime could take their place next to the saw blade or the threshing machine. When a worker was considered to be too old to be trusted with the serious or dangerous work, the meaning of his aging was publicly recognized, his status altered, and he was relegated to the sidelines.[48]

The bee also incorporated people of different classes. Gentlemen farmers such as the Langtons, the Stricklands, and the Moodies invited the educated gentleman, the independent settler, the tenant farmer, and the poor labourer alike to join together in common cause. That such a meeting of classes and temporary laying aside of differences was invariably cause for comment suggests that people were well aware of the social hierarchy. After raising their house in 1833, Traill concluded that, 'In spite of the difference of rank among those that assisted at the bee, the greatest possible harmony prevailed.'[49] Such patterns of dependence cutting across classes did not lessen inequality. As scholars studying festive labour in primitive societies have observed, the exchange was not always between equals and was, in fact, a way of reinforcing or establishing one's place in the social hierarchy.[50]

Gentlemen farmers admitted that bees, especially raisings, were essential and unavoidable. They participated in reciprocal labour, but took pains when possible to distance themselves from the lower classes and express their superiority. Both could be achieved in a number of ways. Usually the host was the work boss when a bee was convened, but where inequality between the host and workers was great, the host hired a foreman. John Thomson, a retired half-pay officer who held several properties in the Orillia area, did so when he ordered his hired hand to invite neighbours and Natives, procure supplies, and conduct the raising. It was only when workers threatened to leave because of rain and poor preparation that Thomson got involved and set about cajoling and flattering them to stay for another day.[51]

A typical way to use the bee to express one's place in the social hierarchy was through conspicuous giving — to serve a lavish feast and throw a better party than most participants could afford. Settlers expected the well-to-do to throw a good bee. To live in a commodious frame house and serve your guests only pork and peas outside was not meeting the code of hospitality. It was a challenge for most settlers to acquire and prepare enough simple fare for their guests, given the primitive storage and cooking facilities of early settlement life, but they were all expected to do their best, even if it turned out to be a very modest affair. At the Sinclairs' raising in 1831, for example, the men sat on the beams, ate bread, butter, and meat, and drank water and whiskey. They had no plates, only their pocket knives.[52] In contrast, the Stewarts, gentlemen farmers in Douro Township, threw a splendid affair at their raising. The guests sat down in the kitchen and parlour to a feast of roast pig, boiled and roast mutton, fish pie, mutton pie, ham, potatoes and a variety of vegetables, followed by puddings and tarts. In the afternoon, when rain broke up the work, tea and cakes were served. Guests were entertained by a pianist throughout the afternoon, danced to fiddle music throughout the evening, and, at eleven, sat down to another feast of a wide variety of meat, desserts, and decanters of currant cordial. Dancing continued thereafter, and everyone was bedded down for the night under buffalo robes and bear skins. At the end of it all, Frances Stewart was able to look back in satisfaction and conclude, 'Altogether it looked very respectable.'[53] The Stewarts had succeeded in meeting their guests and their own expectations of fitting hospitality, given their station in life, and had confirmed their position of superiority in the neighbourhood.

On such occasions it was expected that the host would at least temporarily cast aside class differences and condescend to rub shoulders with his workers. Such had been expected of the landed class in the Old World at festive occasions.[54] It was the host's way of demonstrating his good will, mutual respect, generosity of spirit, and appreciation towards workers. These were integral parts of the concept of hospitality and necessary components of a continuing social relationship. When a well-to-do host was not forthcoming, guests might demand festivities fitting his station. For example, when an owner of 500 acres called a raising, but hadn't planned any entertainment, a large group of young women cornered him during the proceedings and forced him to consider how the evening should be spent.[55] When the host succumbed, dancing and games were organized. Likewise, after rain postponed John Thomson's raising, he and two gentlemen friends retired to his dining room while the remaining workers were relegated to the kitchen for the rest of the day. This division caused 'some envious feelings among certain yankiefied personages' of what Thomson called the 'no-Gent' class. To keep the workers satisfied and willing to stay overnight, Thomson and his friends had to be 'mixed up among them' as they did all they could 'to do away with any bad impression.'[56] Thereafter, Thomson resumed his distance.

In the months that followed, Thomson, like other gentlemen, paid his return labour not by attending what was deemed an 'odious gathering,' but by sending his hired hands or a yoke of oxen.[57] The gentleman class participated in reciprocal labour only as long as it was necessary. As an ex-settler flatly stated, 'A gentleman . . . has no business with it — the idle riff-raff are they who will surely come, getting drunk, eating up all your pork and flour, and fighting like Irishmen.'[58] John Langton considered establishing a gentleman's logging association to avoid the bees altogether, and Moodie simply stopped going or even sending anyone or anything in his place.[59] Clearly the bee was not the democratizing agent it was sometimes characterized to be.

The bee incorporated people of different age, background, and gender. The view of farm men as commercialists working alone for exchange and profit, while women worked together building neighbourhood and kin ties, needs further examination.[60] The study of bees suggests that both men and women were part of the world of mutuality. Reciprocal work has generally been viewed from the separate spheres of ideology. A tendency exists to see logging, raising, and threshing bees as purely male events, and as examples of a 'male community' from which women were excluded.[61] In contrast, feminist scholars have viewed quiltings and other forms of female reciprocity as part of a 'female community' of empathy, spirituality, support, and non-hierarchical arrangements.[62] Scholars now recognize, however, that gender is best understood as a relational system. Through the interaction of men and women, the meaning of gender is created, reinforced, and transformed. More attention is now given to the construction of gender in everyday experience and in settings where men and women operate together. Scholars of rural communities recognize that, unlike urban men and women, who were increasingly defined by their differences from one another, rural men and women continued to share many of 'the tasks which produced their income and sustained their families.'[63] Bees viewed as interaction episodes are exceptionally good opportunities to examine men and women working together, because this form of reciprocal work rarely occurred without the participation of both sexes.

Men were the principal actors in reciprocal labour that involved physical strength and danger. They also exchanged labour among themselves. Women were the principal actors in reciprocal labour that involved the preparation of clothing and food. They also exchanged labour among themselves. Rarely did men and women exchange labour with each other. Beyond these significant differences there was much commonality. Both men and women were involved in bees for the capital development of their farming operation (cleared fields, buildings, household goods), for market (grain, fowl, cloth), and for basic family sustenance (food and clothing). A successful bee — where work was done well, no incidents occurred, and guests were pleased with the hospitality — required the participation of both men and women. Their work, responsibilities, and space intersected at various points throughout the event. Even though they were main actors in different kinds of bees, men and women shared the values and experiences of diligence, skill, competition, hierarchical working structures, and neighbourliness. Gender, nevertheless, was an essential variable in understanding their lives.

Logging bees were substantively about men and the rituals of manliness. The loggers formed gangs in different parts of the field and competed to see who would finish logging their section first. It was very strenuous work shifting and heaping logs. In the hottest days of summer, the hours were dreadfully long, the logs terribly heavy, the work tiring and dirty, the grog foul tasting and plentiful. It took physical stamina to last the day. It took bravery to run the risk of breaking a leg or losing one's life. And it took a great deal of self-control to keep a clear head. As Munro explained in *Backwoods Life*, logging was what 'tries a men's mettle.'[64] Just to participate as a main actor (one who rolled and piled the logs) was a mark of one's prowess. Being allowed to drive the oxen marked the beginning of manhood, and, by participating and observing, boys soon learned what was expected of them once they graduated to the status of main actors. Strength, speed, and energy were all valued, and skill was deeply appreciated and critically evaluated. Lives were at stake. Save for the skill of a good axeman, a tree might fall on man or beast. Men gained and lost reputations at these events as the strongest, the fastest, or the most skilful. Such identities were created in the heat of work and confirmed in the competitive sports that often followed. As Geikie recounted after attending a logging bee in Bidport Township in the 1830s, there was much bragging about chopping prowess, much comparison between men regarding their skills, and much laughing at those who had accidents or used inferior equipment.[65] Heavy drinking, smoking, and fights were part of the equation too, though the 'rough back countryman' style of manhood exhibited by Monaghan, who attended Moodie's bee on a hot July day in 1834 'in his glory, prepared to work or fight,' gradually lost favour to the more morally upright male who was esteemed for his strength, skill, stamina — and his self-restraint.[66]

Women played a supporting role at bees where men held centre stage and were a valued audience. As anthropologists who study spectacles argue, the role of spectator is not passive or neutral, as spectacles require exchange between actors and audience.[67] At barn raisings, for example women cheered the men on as they competed to see which team raised their side first. As Russel Clifton recalled from his barn-raising youth, he was often one of the first lads to ride up with the bent, and 'usually there was some girl among the women that I hoped would worry about my falling.'[68] Even at logging bees, the dirtiest and roughest events of all, women might participate as spectators. For example, Anne Langton and her kitchen helpers walked down and took 'a view of the black and busy scene' at their logging.[69] At hunting bees, women swarmed the fields, supporting their teams by bringing the hunters provisions and relieving them of their game.[70] In the exchange, men and women confirmed their own and each other's gendered identities. To defy these identities was to court disapproval.[71]

Even more important than their valued role as spectators was women's role in preparing and executing the feast and festivities; these were essential components of any successful bee, the first instalment in the pay-back system, and an integral part in developing the farm.[72] Women were indispensable in this capacity. If a family could not supply enough female labour itself, additional women were hired or, more commonly, neighbouring women gave their labour, crockery, cooking utensils, and, on occasion, their kitchens, with the understanding that they would receive help in return.[73] It was hard work. For most women, even with help, it took two or three days to prepare the house and food, in order to set out what was considered 'a respectable table' and to make room for the dancing or games that followed. Great activity then ensued on the day of the event, with cooking, keeping the fires going, serving food, minding children, and being the cheerful hostess.[74] Once the festivities were over, the clean-up began.

In a sense, the role of actor and spectator were reversed at the feast, as the hostess took centre stage. As fictional accounts portrayed it, 'supper was the great event to which all things moved at bees.'[75] Considerable pressure existed for women to perform. Isabella Bishop concluded in *The Englishwoman in America* (1856) that the 'good humour of her guests depends on the quantity and quality of her viands.'[76] Being hostess to a bee gave women a rare occasion to exhibit themselves, their skills, and their homes. Though men might eat with a 'take what you have and you won't want fashion,' they nevertheless took stock of the meal. In their accounts of bees, men carefully and, if the host, proudly itemized the menu and often evaluated the hostess. Wilkie, for example, after attending a chopping bee, noted that Mrs Wegg 'provident dame had busied herself to some purpose.'[77] Women, however, were the most exacting critics when it came to the meal. As men competed with and assessed each other while logging, women evaluated each other at the feast. As Stan Cross recalled of his parents barn raising, senior women eagerly offered their assistance so that they could 'see first-hand how my mother, who was one of their peers, would approach such an undertaking especially with three babies in tow.'[78] So great was the competition and the pressure to prepare a fine feast that M. E. Graham, in an article entitled 'Food for Bees,' urged Ontario farm women not to give themselves 'dyspepsia preparing bountiful, fancy and varied threshing feasts.' She went on to say, 'I know for truth that we simply cook that we may equal or excel the other women in the neighbourhood.'[79] A lot was at stake, for the quality of the hospitality could determine the family's reputation and its continuing membership in the ring of reciprocity. It was only after the feast and the festivities were over and the guests had gone away happy that the host and hostess could relax and congratulate themselves on having held a successful event.

The quilting was the female counterpart of the male logging bee. As men were the central actors at a logging bee and women played a supporting role, the reverse was true of quiltings. It was an event organized and held by and for women which combined work with socializing. For days the hostess prepared the house and the food for the event, made arrangements for the children, and pieced scraps together to form the top of the quilt. Whereas a general call might be sent out for a barn raising, women were individually invited to a quilting. The guests would secure the top, wool, and backing to a frame, quilt it, and remove it from the frame, ready for use, in the same day. To be invited to a quilting generally meant you were not only a member of a particular social circle but also accomplished in sewing skills. Whereas men were esteemed for their strength, stamina, and bravery, women were praised for their detail and dexterity. The good seamstress sewed fast, short, even stitches and wasted no thread. The hostess was evaluated on her hospitality, and the artistry and skill exhibited by her quilt top. As experienced men took the lead at loggings, experienced women took the lead at quiltings and were known as the 'queen bees.' Young girls learned how to sew from their mothers and grandmothers on doll quilts. Once they were experienced enough, they would be invited to participate in their first bee. In this manner, quilting skills were passed down through the generations, reaffirming the female role and female connectedness.[80]

Usually we think of the quilting bee as a female-only affair, but in the nineteenth century, though women held centre stage, men played significant supporting roles. When young women were present, the hostess, who controlled the social space of the marriage market, invited young men too.[81] A.C. Currie, a young bachelor in Niagara, got invited to several quilting bees over the winter of 1841. Sometimes he had two a week.[82] While the women sat around the quilting frame, the men, under the supervision of the queen bees, would sit on the sidelines and aid by threading needles, chatting, and flirting. As spectators, they were to appreciate the women's domestic skills and social charms; as supporting actors, they were to mingle with the young women at the 'frolic' of charades, dancing, singing, and flirtations that usually followed. Such flirtations at apple paring and corn husking bees, where men and women participated as equals, took priority over the actual work accomplished, at least in the retelling. At paring bees, men might peel apples and throw them to the women, who cored, quartered, and strung them. Once the old folks retired for the evening, the young people kissed, danced, and played all sorts of games. Wilkie excitedly recounted his experiences at such a bee when, alone in a moonlit room, amid much whispering and gentle tittering, a game of forfeit ensued and he found himself holding a 'bonnie lass' on each knee.[83] In this manner, bees provided an opportunity for courtship under the supervision of the community.

At the bee, one's identity was confirmed within the neighbourhood. Though people might work together in harmony like bees in a hive, they took their place within a non-egalitarian and differentiated group. While initiating, reshaping, and conforming patterns of association between individuals, the bee also served a variety of functions for the neighbourhood as a whole. One contemporary deemed it to be 'the fete, the club, the ball, the town-hall, the labour convention of the whole community.'[84]

'THE BEE-LINE'

Another layer of understanding about the operation of neighbourhood emerges when we stop in time and space and analyze one family's beeing experience over a number of years. Besides confirming the economic and social importance of bees, the action-structure of one family and its neighbourhood in a spatial and interactive sense is revealed. We are able to describe how several overlapping 'working' networks existed at once. This layering is in part a reflection of the second point revealed by this method of analysis. As the entire family was drawn into beeing, the main actors brought their own social networks and social space to bear on the beeing network that developed, so that each family had its own patterns of exchange that were peculiar to them. We can see the neighbourhood not only as a static diagram of interaction but also as a dynamic process that was perpetuated, recreated, and modified as the main actors changed.

Lucy Middaugh of Mountain Township (Dundas Country) was nearly sixty-two years of age when she made her first entry on 1 May 1884 into the diary that has been used for this analysis.[85] Over the next four years she kept a daily account of the social and economic activities of the household. Lucy was known by her friends for possessing an unusual 'ability in the affairs of domestic life' and for practising 'a thrift and economy which was indeed commendable.'[86] Certainly her diary reflects an economy with words, but such a terse style was not unusual in the era. Her diary recording was not a journey of self-discovery, but a simple record of events — usually one-line entries — of the lives of her family and neighbourhood. Bees and other events — births, deaths, visits — were recorded as a matter of fact, not described or evaluated.

Two generations before Lucy, the Middaughs had come to Canada in 1778 from New York state and settled in Matilda Township in Dundas County. As lots in the front townships filled up, the next generation pushed north into the neighbouring township of Mountain. Lucy's father-in-law purchased lot 2, concession 6, in Mountain Township in 1824. In 1845 he died and left the farm and a one-storey frame house to his son John and his new wife, Lucy. By the time Lucy started making entries in her diary, most of her eleven children had grown up. Over the diary years, Lucy's household contained her husband, John, who was suffering from dropsy and would die two years into the diary, and her second son, Charles, age thirty-seven, and his wife, Min, who ran the farm and remained childless. Besides the old and young couples, Lucy's twenty-three-year-old daughter, Tory, was at home, as was her twenty-year-old son, Ezra, who temporarily returned home from California for nearly two years. Their farm and community were well beyond the pioneer stage and were typical of the established farming community of that era. They had 250 acres, of which 230 were improved. They raised a wide variety of field crops and livestock, had five stables, and several horse-drawn vehicles.[87] Situated midway on the Clark Road, between the villages of South Mountain and South Gower, they were surrounded by other farm families in similar circumstances. Like other farms, reciprocal labour was important to the Middaugh household. Of the six people in the house only old John, owing to his illness, was not an active participant at bees. Other members regularly exchanged labour with neighbours and went to an average of eight bees a year. After family members had attended five bees in one month in the fall of 1884, Lucy dryly commented, 'more Bees than Honey.' But the Middaughs had been going to bees for decades, even generations, and, by the 1880s, it was an integral part of their household economy and a key component in the structuring, operation, and definition of their neighbourhood.

The Middaughs partook of bees at what might be considered three tiers of networks defined according to the intensity of the relationship — such as the degree of interaction, visiting, and swapping labour. Those in the first tier were their immediate neighbours — the Beggs, Clarks, Christies, and VanAllens. All were established families who had resided on the road for two or three generations and were cultivating over 80 acres.[88] They were households at the same stage in the life cycle who had kitchens full of grown children to spare for labour. These were the kind of families most apt to continue to engage in reciprocal labour long after the exigencies of early settlement were over.[89] Indeed, a tradition of reciprocity that had been established by the older generations at least forty years earlier was now being continued by the younger generation. The VanAllens, Christies, Beggs, and Clarks had all exchanged labour with each other in the 1840s. In fact, the VanAllens' and Clarks' relationship with the Middaughs extended back to 1803, when the original settlers had arrived in Matilda Township.[90] Old Lucy still visited the Christies, but most of the coming and going both for work and for socializing was now between the younger generation. Hardly a day went by that family life wasn't punctuated by a visit to the neighbours, someone coming to help Charles, or Lucy visiting the sick.

In this first tier of beeing, physical distance, not kin, was the overriding cohesive ingredient. Elizabeth Clark was John Middaugh's sister, and their children worked together as

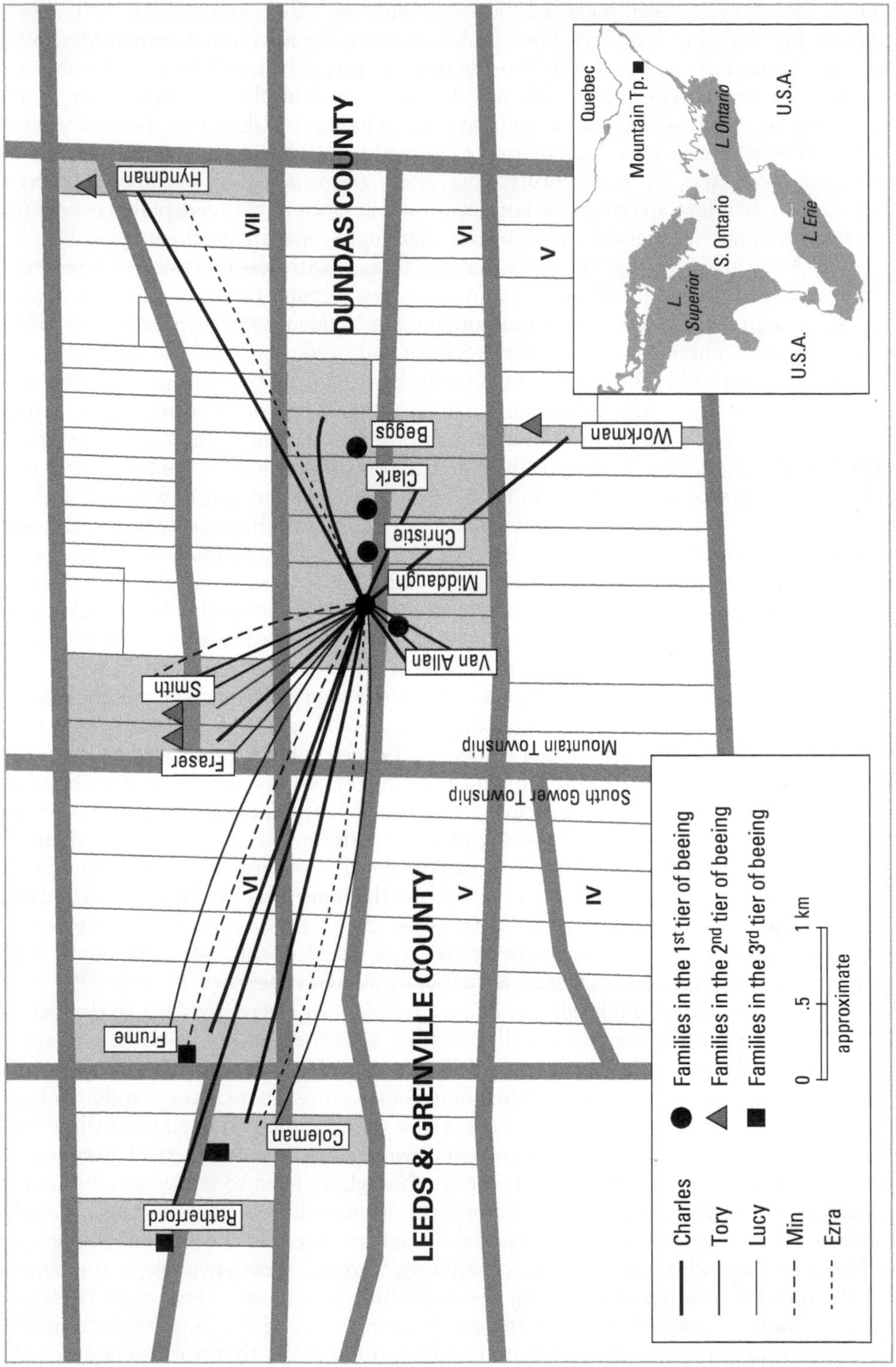

Figure 29.1 The Beeing Networks of the Middaugh Family, Mountain Township, Dundas County, 1884–8

cousins. No kin relationship existed, however, with the other families, nor were they bound together by religion or ethnicity. The VanAllens across the road were German Methodists like the Middaughs, but the Beggs and Christies next door were Irish and Scottish Presbyterians. A mixture of propinquity — being able to drive horses and machinery without expending too much time or energy — and trust born from years of living next door tied these people together in mutual dependency. As in other parts of the world, neighbourhood was the primary unit for reciprocal work and, by mid-century, that often meant all those on a concession line.[91] Propinquity, therefore, overrode the connections of kin that might have pulled people together and the differences of religion and ethnicity that might have driven them apart.

The Middaughs' neighbourhood extended, though with less intensity, to a second tier of families whose homes could be reached by travelling through the fields. The Smiths and the Frasers, though located one concession north of the Middaughs, abutted onto the back of the Middaugh farm. Three generations of the Smiths had lived there, and the original settlers had done business with old John Middaugh as far back as 1828. The current generation had several young women of Tory's age and they did much visiting. The Frasers were long-time friends of Lucy and John. Their families had known each other as far back as 1803, and Tory was friends with their daughter. The Workmans lived on the concession south of the Middaughs and were old friends. This second tier also included Alex Hyndman and his family, who had settled in the area before 1829 and were the furthest away at 5 kilometres to the northeast. As Alex had married Lucy's daughter, and he and Charles were of similar age and interests, much generalized helping and sharing occurred between the two families. The economically vital beeing group was, therefore, coterminous with farms on either side and those reachable by walking through the fields — in short, the geographic neighbourhood. It extended beyond this immediate group in the first and second tier to include only close relatives such as the Hyndmans.

Beyond the second tier of beeing was a third tier that really must not be included within the regular and economically vital group of reciprocal labour or the neighourhood. The Middaughs were occasionally invited to bees at the Colemans, Frumes, and Ratherfords, who lived farther away to the northwest in the Township of South Gower, about an hour away by horse and buggy. As less visiting occurred with these families, the social connections are less clear. The Frumes, German Methodists, may have known the Middaughs in their Matilda Township days, and the Ratherfords had worked for old John in the 1850s. Indeed, this third tier suggests that bees sometimes extended beyond the immediate neighbourhood and provided the opportunity to meet new people. In this case, they were quilting and paring bees, which were often used for the courting opportunities they afforded, and, not surprisingly, it was the young, unmarried, Tory and Ezra who were usually invited or sent.

Though the entire Middaugh family, save for old John, were involved in the beeing network, not everyone participated equally. Charles, as household head and heir to the family farm, was arguably the most important participant, who had the most to gain or lose. He participated in raisings, wood bees, and ploughing bees at farms where a longstanding relationship existed dating back to his grandfather's era. These were families who had lived there for over a generation, were neighbours or relatives, and within the first two tiers of networks. It was important to send the most able member and household head to show commitment to and respect for these primary working relationships. In attending the bees himself, Charles also confirmed his status within the family and the neighbourhood. In contrast, his younger, unmarried brother Ezra, who was home temporarily with no real roots anymore in the community, went to only two raisings and a paring bee, something Charles would not even be expected to attend. Charles, therefore, was very important in maintaining the family's place in the local social and economic network and in maintaining the stability that was essential for effective reciprocal labour to function.

One is struck, however, by how important women were as principal actors too — and not just in supplying food for the festivities. Over the diary years, Charles and Ezra attended a combined total of fourteen bees, while the women in the house — Tory, Min, and Lucy — attended a combined total of sixteen bees. As the woman in charge of the household, Min found time to attend only four bees. Lucy, though still winning first prizes at the fair for her quilts, attended only two quilting bees, where she had women her age for company. Her neighbourhood role had become one of visiting the sick on behalf of the family. Tory, however, was central to the beeing network and nearly as important as Charles. She attended quiltings, parings, rag-rug bees, and a raising — that one at her sister's place. She rarely went to the Beggs, a neighbouring household of five young men. Instead, her activity was focused on neighbours with young women her age, friends, co-religionists, and relatives further away. Here the difference with Charles ended, as Tory travelled just as far and as often as Charles as family representative. As long as Tory lived at home, then, she made a valuable contribution to the family and the neighbourhood. While Charles seems to have maintained the essential, immediate, and long-term connections necessary to his and the family's future on the farm, Tory contributed to these ties and expanded the family's contacts in neighbouring townships. This network was important for the marriage market and for those children who would have to move beyond the farm to make new homes. Both Charles and Tory partook of the world of mutuality, working in groups that used and strengthened the ties born of geography and genealogy. Their 'working' neighbourhood, built on generations of relationships, also helped shape their future opportunities.

This analysis of the Middaugh family's beeing experience reveals the complexity of the configurations of neighbourhood and the agency of its actors. Overlapping 'working' neighbourhoods had existed for generations and were modified as the main actors changed. The persistence of the beeing network over the generations was, in part, because these families were social equals with similar demands on their labour supply. In this way a relative degree of equality was built into the exchange. Immediate neighbours of long-standing acquaintance made up the core of the working group, with relatives being important, though less so. Individual members of the family participated, and they all played a particular role according to their position within the family, their perceived future in the community, and their commitment to it.

'TO BEE OR NOT TO BEE'

What the bee actually meant to participants can only be judged from their actions and the evaluations they have left. Contemporary accounts repeatedly revealed that if a bee functioned well — the job got done, money was saved, people had fun and knew their place — the communal effort was applauded. Participants, however, were well aware of the exchange system that underlay this event and were reluctant to depict reciprocal work as selfless behaviour.[92] They knew that the communal and the individual ethic were in operation. While selfish ambition and the man who did not do his share were clearly frowned upon, individual gain had an acknowledged place in the system. The barn raising, for example, was a momentous achievement in an individual family's measure of material success. It symbolized not only their reasons for emigrating and their years of saving and planning but also their material wealth, social improvement, and independence. Indeed, private property and individual ownership were never in question. Though people agreed to share their labour, tools, and time, it was always clear whose field had been logged, whose cattle would use the newly raised barn, and who could sleep under the quilt. Most participants would have been baffled to find twentieth-century

writers casting the bee as the embodiment of the selfless communal ideal and the polar opposite of the capitalistic spirit of individualism and material gain. Instead, most farm families
understood that work was a commodity and also a means to foster neighbourly relations. Their
lively networks of reciprocal labour fostered both individual prosperity and mutual reliance.
This social reality flies in the face of a number of dichotomies that have been developed by
scholars, such as use versus exchange, sufficiency versus commercialization, and the moral
economy versus the market economy.[93] That reciprocal work often resulted in a warm sense of
generosity, belonging, and security within a larger community was an important by-product
deeply appreciated by people at the time and lamented later when lost. When given the opportunity to be released from the constraints of scarce labour and capital, however, many people
chose to leave the obligations and inconvenience of cooperative work behind for other ways
over which they had greater control.

The main complaints levelled against bees had to do with managing people. Cooperation
is not easy. As with any kind of communal work, industrious workers had to share with the idle,
and individual decisions were constrained by the decisions of the group. One common complaint was that it was difficult to control the workers. Some came with the attitude that the
host was lucky to have them and they drank and ate heartily while leaving little in the way of
quality workmanship. Farmers felt they had more control over their workers and the quality of
work if they hired labourers. Furthermore, bees could be costly if the work was shoddy, yet the
host was bound to feast and entertain the workers. After her logging bee had gone wrong,
Susanna Moodie went out of her way to declare, 'I am certain, in our case, had we hired with
the money expended in providing for the bee, two or three industrious, hard-working men, we
should have got through twice as much work, and have had it done well, and have been the
gainers in the end.'[94] The main disadvantage with the bee was being called upon at an inconvenient time for return work. Just when a farmer needed to see or harvest his own fields, he was
called upon by others to work theirs.[95]

Given the difficulties in managing people, it is not surprising that once other viable alternatives arose, bees declined. Bees persisted in remote areas where hired labour was hard to find
and the price of labour was high. They also continued to operate in situations such as the
Middaughs' where persistent farm families of similar status had a tradition of reciprocal work
firmly established. In other populous and longer settled areas, however, where farmers were
expanding their operations and entering into a cash economy, it was more convenient to hire
workers, and the cash payment — an immediate reciprocity — took into consideration the
quality and quantity of the work done.[96] Farmers were then free of the obligations of reciprocal
labour and could attend to their own farms — and according to their own schedule. The
growing availability of cash and hired labour removed the necessity of relying on bees.

Technology was not as central as some have argued in the decline of bees.[97] The introduction at mid-century of patented iron apple peelers, the self-raking reaper, and, later, cross-
cut saws reduced the need for bees by cutting the time and labour needed in processing
apples, harvesting, and sawing.[98] Some of the new technology, such as threshing machines
in the 1880s and later silo-filling equipment, did not alter the tradition of collective work,
but was often cooperatively owned and operated. Threshing bees and silo-filling bees continued well into the twentieth century. Only after the First World War, with the introduction of combines and tractors, was one man able to do the work that had previously taken a
neighbourhood.[99]

The need for bees also declined with the rise of more formal strategies for security and new
forms of entertainment. Insurance companies offering compensation for damage done by fire,
fraternal orders offering sickness and death benefits, and eventually the welfare state all played
their part in reducing the effect of hard times and families' reliance on traditional networks of

neighbourhood support.[100] Furthermore, bees now competed with lodge meetings, Sunday school picnics, school concerts, and agricultural fairs for the visiting and courtship opportunities they provided.

As the economics, technology, and social aspects of farm life changed, bees slowly became a thing of the past.

CONCLUSION

Though often idealized as the epitome of the selfless communal ideal, participants in bees behaved as though there was no inherent or insurmountable conflict between individual and communal goals. Both men and women participated in reciprocal labour using the ties born of geography and genealogy to build their resources, increase their own productivity, and shape their future opportunities. Through this sharing, many individual farm families were able to acquire the extra labour, skills, and equipment necessary for capital improvements, so that profitable farming could proceed. Such structural dependence on neighbours reduced the risk of life in the backwoods. Many people found that, through reciprocal work, they could succeed individually and that it was in their own material and social interest to be neighbourly. The network of labour exchange, in effect, produced individual prosperity and mutual reliance. In the process, neighbourhoods were created that could be defined by their spatial dimension, membership, shared values, and collective identity. Such neighbourhoods were dynamic entities, with fluid patterns of interaction particular to each family and responsive to the social networks and social space that individual participants brought to bear on the network as it developed. Finally, though the bee facilitated neighbourhood and often neighbourliness, it did so in a way that incorporated differences in class, age, gender, and skill and acknowledged the importance of private property and social hierarchy.

NOTES

1. Bryan D. Palmer. 'Discordant Music: Charivaris and Whitecapping in Nineteenth Century North America,' *Labour–Le Travail* 3 (1978): 5–62; Allan Greer, 'From Folklore to Revolution: Charivaris and the Lower Canadian Rebellion of 1837,' and Tina Loo, 'Dan Cramer's Potlatch,' both in Tina Loo and Lorna R. McLean, eds., *Historical Perspectives on Law and Society in Canada* (Mississauga: Copp Clark Longman 1994), 35–55, 219–53; and Pauline Greenhill, 'Welcome and Unwelcome Visitors: Shivarees and the Political Economy of Rural-Urban Interaction in Southern Ontario,' *Journal of Ritual Studies* 3, 1 (1989).

2. Studies such as those done by Bradbury, Parr, and Marks come close to examining neighbourhood, but still link families only with the larger urban area and economy and bypass the neighbourhood as a unit of analysis. See Bettina Bradbury, *Working Families: Age, Gender and Daily Survival in Industrializing Montreal* (Toronto: McClelland & Stewart 1993); Joy Parr, *The Gender of Breadwinners* (Toronto: University of Toronto Press 1990); and Lynne Marks, *Revivals and Roller Rinks: Religion, Leisure, and Identity in Late-Nineteenth-Century Small-Town Ontario* (Toronto: University of Toronto Press 1996). So far the study of neighbourhood has been the preserve of sociologists. For example, for the study of neighbourhood helping exchanges in modern Toronto, see Barry Wellman, 'The Community Question,' *American Journal of Sociology* 84 (1979): 1201–31.

3. A vast literature exists on community. For the most recent overview of this literature in a Canadian context, see John Walsh and Stephen High. 'Re-thinking the Concept of Community,' *Histoire Sociale* 23 (Nov. 1999): 255–73. In what follows I have borrowed my approach from economists, ethnographers, and cultural historians. Many of my ideas coalesced in the community studies seminar I co-taught as part of the Tri-University Doctoral Program. Although I cannot benefit from direct questioning and observation of those actually involved in bees, some of the sources left provide something similar to the ethnographer's notebook in that they record people doing things. I have interpreted these actions as statements. The most reliable evidence for rendering the facts are diaries and farm accounts. Bees were carefully recorded as a way of keeping accounts of work owing and as

noteworthy social events. Settlers' guides often presented the 'how-to' of holding a bee because of its necessity in the backwoods and because of its central importance as an entry point into community life. Somewhat less reliable, but still very valuable, are the numerous travellers' accounts, memoirs, and late nineteenth-century settlement histories. Bees appear in these sources with regularity as they were memorable events. These stories are usually based on the author's direct memory of events, what they heard from others, or what they thought possible.

4. For an example of an anthropologist, see Solon T. Kimball, 'Rural Social Organization and Co-operative Labour,' *American Journal of Sociology* 55 (1949): 38–49; for a Marxist interpretation, see James A. Henretta, 'Families and Farms: *Mentalité* in Pre-industrial America,' *William and Mary Quarterly*, series 3, 35, 4 (1978): 3–32; and for a feminist interpretation, see Marjorie Kaethler and Susan D. Shantz, *Quilts of Waterloo County* (Waterloo: Johanns Graphics 1990), and Nancy Grey Osterud, *Bonds of Community: The Lives of Farm Women in 19th Century New York* (Ithaca: Cornell University Press 1991).

5. Samuel Strickland, *Twenty-Seven Years in Canada West*, vol. 1 (1853: Edmonton: Hurtig Publishers 1972), 35; Martin Doyle, *Hints on Emigration to Upper Canada* (Dublin: Curry 1832), 61; and George Easton, *Travels in America* (Glasgow: John S. Marr & Sons 1871), 89. John MacDougall noted that the term was not derived from the work habits of bees, but from a word from Ancient Saxon days when danger brought people together for defence, *Rural Life in Canada* (1913; Toronto: University of Toronto Press 1973), 132. Such forms of reciprocal labour were part of an established tradition from the Old World. Peasants in Norway, Ireland, Scotland, and elsewhere had long used reciprocal work to erect buildings, harvest produce, and create cloth. In South America a distinction was drawn between exchange labour and festive labour. Charles Erasmus, 'Culture Structure and Process: The Occurrence and Disappearance of Reciprocal Farm Labor,' *Southwestern Journal of Anthropology* 12 (1956): 445–6. Exchange labour usually included about ten people who regularly exchanged a day's work for a day's work. Festive labour could include more than one hundred people. The obligation to reciprocate was not so great, but the host was to provide extraordinary food and festivities. No such clear distinction was drawn by settlers in Ontario. Both the big barn raisings that drew large numbers and the smaller occasions when groups of neighbours regularly got together to exchange labour were called bees.

6. Queen's University Archives, Walter Beatty papers, Walter Beatty Diary, 1838–92, box 3057: ibid., Ewan Ross Papers, John MacGregor Diary, 1877–83, series 3, binder 94, no. 2504; ibid., Ewan Ross papers, James Cameron Diaries, 1854–1902, series 3, binders 25–33, no. 2504; Lucy Middaugh Diary, 1884–87, private possession of Jean Wilson; John Tigert Diaries, 1888–1902, private possession of Tigert family; Joseph Abbott Diary, 1819, reprinted in his *Emigrant to North America* (Montreal: Lovell & Gibson 1843); and James O'Mara, 'The Seasonal Round of Gentry Farmers in Early Ontario,' *Canadian Papers in Rural History* 2 (1980): 103–12.

7. Cited in W.H. Graham, *Greenbank* (Peterborough, Ont.: Broadview Press 1988), 249

8. Susanna Moodie, *Roughing It in the Bush* (1852: Toronto: McClelland & Stewart 1962), 156

9. James M. Young, *Reminiscences of the Early History of Galt and the Settlement of Dumfries* (Toronto: Hunter, Rose & Co. 1880, 43; and Strickland, *Twenty-Seven Years*, 1: 97

10. 'A New Ontario Raising,' *Farmer's Advocate* 47 (8 Feb. 1912): 222

11. For the most comprehensive study of rural labour in nineteenth-century Ontario, see Terry Crowley, 'Rural Labour,' in Paul Craven, ed., *Labouring Lives: Work and Workers in Nineteenth-Century Ontario* (Toronto: University of Toronto Press 1995), 13–102. For frontier labour, see Daniel Vickers, 'Working the Fields in a Developing Economy: Essex County, Mass., 1630–1675,' in Stephen Innes, ed., *Work and Labor in Early America* (Chapel Hill: University of North Carolina Press 1988), 60.

12. Immigrant guidebook writers were well aware of the necessity of reducing risk in the backwoods and urged their readers to take part in bees. See William Hutton, *Canada: Its Present Condition, Prospects and Resources Fully Described for the Information of Intending Emigrants* (London 1854), 42–3; Catharine Parr Traill, *The Backwoods of Canada* (1836; Toronto: McClelland & Stewart 1929), 121; and Easton, *Travels in America*, 90–3, 168.

13. National Archives of Canada (NA), Emigration Questionnaire, 1840–1, RG 1, B21, vol. 1; Doyle, *Hints on Emigration*, 48, 65; Abbott, *The Emigrant to North America*, 113; Easton, *Travels in America*, 90; Traill, *Backwoods of Canada*, 52–3; George Henry Hume, *Canada as It Is* (New York: Stodart 1832), 13, 135; and Alexander Carlisle Buchanan Sr, *Emigration Practically Considered* (London: Colburn 1828), 5.

14. Peter Russell, 'Upper Canada: A Poor Man's Country? Some Statistical Evidence,' *Canadian Papers in Rural History* 3 (1982): 136, 144

15. W.F. Munro, *The Backwoods' Life* (1869; Shelburne: The Free Press 1919), 55; John C. Geikie, ed., *Adventures in Canada: Or Life in the Woods* (Philadelphia: Porter & Coates 1882), 40; and Strickland, *Twenty-Seven Years*, 1: 97

16. Barns usually cost a bit less. For the cost of hiring labour for such purposes, see Emigration Questionnaire, 1840–1; Edward Allan Talbot, *Five Years' Residence in the Canadas* (London: Longman, Hurst, Rees, Orme, Brown & Green 1824), 189–90; and Hutton, *Canada, 78*. For the cost and popularity of holding a bee, see Emigration Questionnaire; see also Frederick Widder, *Information for Intending Emigrants of All Classes to Upper Canada* (Toronto: Scobie & Balfour 1850), 4; and University of Guelph Archives, Dougall Family Papers, 1844–69, Henry Dougall to Brother, 26 July 1852.

17. Emigration Questionnaire; Hutton, *Canada,* 11; Doyle, *Hints on Emigration, 49*

18. Isabella L. Bishop, *The Englishwoman in America* (London: W. Clowes & Sons 1856), 202–3, 206

19. MacGregor Diary, 15 Nov. 1878; and Canniff Haight, *Country Life in Canada Fifty Years Ago* (Toronto: Hunter, Rose & Co. 1885), 214

20. Louis Tivy, *Your Loving Anna: Letters from the Ontario Frontier* (Toronto: University of Toronto Press 1972), 87

21. Doug McCalla, *Planting the Province: The Economic History of Upper Canada, 1784–1870* (Toronto: University of Toronto Press 1993), 243. Starting in 1819, the value of cleared land was considered to be five times that of uncultivated land. Ibid., 28–9, 69–70. 106.

22. McCalla makes this point regarding credit, *Planting the Province,* 69.

23. Young, *Reminicences,* 88–9; Thomas Need, *Six Years in the Bush* (London: Simplein, Marshall & Co. 1838), 96

24. McCalla, *Planting the Province,* 82, 146

25. Beatty Diary; see also Tigert Diary and Middaugh Diary. Some anthropologists have interpreted the potlatch as a system of credit or a return on the interest-bearing investment. Loo, 'Dan Crammer's Potlatch,' 231.

26. Munro, *Backwoods Life,* 38

27. A day's work for a day's work was generally the custom throughout North and South America. See Basil Hall, *Travels in North America, in the Years 1827–1828* (Edinburgh: Cadell & Co. 1829), 311–12; and Erasmus, 'Culture Structure and Process,' 445. For what happened when inequalities existed, see Erasmus, 'Culture Structure,' 447; and Kimball, 'Rural Social Organization,' 42. See also Peter G. Mewett, 'Associational Categories and the Social Location of Relationships in a Lewis Crofting Community,' in Anthony P. Cohen, ed., *Belonging* (Manchester: Manchester University Press 1982), 103. Mewett distinguishes between balanced reciprocity (return work at the same type of job) and generalized reciprocity (just helping out with anything later), 112–13.

28. I first came across the use of 'interaction episode' as an analytical tool in Rhys Isaac's *The Transformation of Virginia* (Chapel Hill: University of North Carolina Press 1982), chap. 'A Discourse on the Method.' My thanks to Richard Reid for drawing my attention to this work. The concept is borrowed from ethnographers and begins with the premise that society is not primarily a material entity, but must be understood as the dynamic product of the activities of its members, a product that is shaped by the images participants have of their own and other's performances. Interaction episodes or dramatic events such as the bee are like knots of encounter in the ongoing social life and are suspended in the threads of continuing relationships. The visual image is like knots in lacework. By studying the converging threads and their nodal events we can better understand the structure, action, and meaning of society. Another useful model is to view the interaction episode as a stage play.

29. Traill, *Backwoods of Canada,* 122

30. Contemporary writers urged new settlers to repay the favour: Hall, *Travels,* 312; Talbot, *Five Years' Residence,* 69; Doyle, *Hints of Emigration,* 45. See also Paul Voisey, *Vulcan: The Making of a Prairie Community* (Toronto: University of Toronto Press 1988), 147; and Jane Marie Pederson, *Between Memory and Reality: Family and Community in Rural Wisconsin, 1870–1970* (Madison: University of Wisconsin Press 1992), 154.

31. Kimball, 'Rural Social Organization,' 47; Erasmus, 'Culture Structure and Process,' 447; and Anthony Buckley, 'Neighbourliness — Myth and History,' *Oral History* II.I (1983); 49

32. *Globe,* 10 Sept. 1880, 6, and 6 Feb. 1880, I. For other examples, see Ray Fazakas, *The Donnelly Album* (Toronto: Macmillan of Canada 1977), 10–14. For a similar tension between a local social order that stressed harmony and the undercurrent of violence brought on by frontier conditions, see Susan Lewthwaite, 'Violence, Law, and Community in Rural Upper Canada,' in Jim Phillips, Tina Loo, and Susan Lewthwaite, eds., *Essays in the History of Canadian Law* (Toronto: University of Toronto Press 1994), 353–86. Successful work groups could manage disputes by avoiding direct confrontation; they resorted to gossip instead. To avoid recriminations they made the host responsible for decisions involving risk. See Mewett, 'Associational Categories,' 112, 116.

33. James Logan, *Notes of a Journal Through Canada* (Edinburgh: Fraser & Co. 1838), 46

34. NA, Niblock Letters, MG 24, 180, microfilm A-304. Thomas Niblock to Edward Niblock, 27 Jan. 1850. For those who broke the code and were considered divergent or outsiders, see Kimball, 'Rural Social Organization,' 41; and Conrad M. Arensberg and Solon T. Kimball, *Family and Community in Ireland* (Cambridge Mass: Harvard University Press 1948), chap. 12.

35. Interview with quilters at a quilting bee, Martin House, Doon Village, 1 July 1996

36. Thomas Brush Brown, *Autobiography of Thomas Brush Brown* (1804–1894) (private printing by Isabel Grace Wilson, 1967, available at the Oxford County Library), 17–18. For the importance of whiskey and hospitality, see also David Wilkie, *Sketches of a Summer Trip to New York and the Canadas* (Edinburgh: J. Anderson Jr & A. Hill 1837), 173, 176–7; Hall, *Travels*, 2: 311; Young, *Reminiscences*, 61; Strickland, *Twenty-Seven Years* 1: 37; and William Thompson, *A Tradesman's Travels in the United States and Canada the Years 1840, 41 and 42* (Edinburgh: Oliver & Boyd 1842), 103.

37. Patrick Shirreff, *A Tour Through North America* (Edinburgh: Oliver 7 Boyd 1835), 125. For the usual amount of whiskey per man, see Rev. T. Sockett, ed., *Emigration: Letters from Sussex Emigrants* (London: Phillips, Petworth and Longman & Co. 1833), 28; and Centennial Museum, Judicial Records, Peterboro County, Peterborough, MG.8-2V, Inquest of Charles Danford, Smith Township, Accession No. 71-007, box 5, 1876, no. 30.

38. Moodie, *Roughing It*, 156–62; and also Wilkie, *Sketches*, 176; Patrick Shirreff, *A Tour*, 125

39. Emily Weaver, *Story of the Counties of Ontario* [Toronto: Bell & Cockburn 1913], 165; and Pederson, *Between Memory and Reality*, 142, 217, 219

40. Brown, *Autobiography*, 25

41. Ibid., 23–4

42. Charles Marshall, *The Canadian Dominion* (London: Longmans, Green 1871), 63; see also Easton, *Travels in America*, 169.

43. Doyle, *Hints on Emigration*, 60–1

44. Alexander Sinclair, *Pioneer Reminiscences* (Toronto: Warwick Bros & Rutter 1898), 11–12

45. Frances Browne Stewart, *Our Forest Home* (1889; Montreal Gazette Printing 1902), 174, 177; and *Canada Farmer* 2, 9 (15 Nov. 1870)

46. Trent University Archives, Court Records of the United Counties of Northumberland & Durham, Coroners' Inquests, Inquest of James Hill, 84-020, Series E, box 49; and Judicial Records Peterboro County, Inquest of Charles Danford. A bent was made of two posts connected with a beam. It was laid on the foundation and then raised to form the frame of the barn.

47. Geikie, *Adventure in Canada*, 40–4, 47–8; see also Logan, *Notes of a Journey*, 45.

48. Jim Brown, 'Memories of Work Bees,' *Up the Gatineau!* 21 (1995): 9; and Royce MacGillivray, *The Slopes of the Andes: Four Essays on the Rural Myth in Ontario* (Belleville: Mika Publishing 1990), 90

49. Traill, *The Backwoods*, 135; see also Moodie, *Roughing It*, 156 and Logan, *Notes of a Journey*, 46.

50. Erasmus, 'Culture Structure and Process,' 458

51. Archives of Ontario, John Thomson Diary, MU-846, Part 2, 22–4 April 1834. This was done elsewhere as well; see Erasmus 'Culture Structure and Process,' 448.

52. Sinclair, *Pioneer Reminiscences*, 12; see also Wilkie, *Sketches*, 177; and Strickland, *Twenty-Seven Years*, 35–6.

53. Stewart, *Our Forest Home*, 174–6

54. Catharine Anne Wilson, *A New Lease on Life* (Montreal and Kingston, McGill- Queen's University Press 1994), 110

55. *Canada Farmer* 2, 9 (15 Nov. 1870)

56. Thomson Diary, 22–4 April 1834

57. For example, see Thomson Diary, July, Oct and Nov. 1833, and June 1834. John Langton and Moodie sent their hired men to bees also. Anne Langton, *A Gentlewoman in Upper Canada* (Toronto: Clarke Irwin 1964), 167; and Moodie, *Roughing It*, 162.

58. Ex-Settler, *Canada in the Years 1832, 1833, and 1834* (Dublin: Hardy 1835), 115

59. Langton, *A Gentlewoman* 166; and Moodie, *Roughing It*, 162

60. Nancy Osterud goes further than most historians in understanding the rural family and community as gendered relationships. While she acknowledges that men participated in cooperative work, she still tends to see men as part of the commercial world and argues that women were the ones who sustained cooperative relations. In fact, she goes as far as to argue that women advocated a model of interdependence as an alternative to male dominance and capitalist social relations. She states that women used mutuality as a strategy of empowerment. Osterud, *Bonds of Community*

61. John Mack Faragher, *Women and Men on the Overland Trail* (New Haven: Yale University Press 1979), 112 and 116

62. Carroll Smith-Rosenberg, 'The Female World of Love and Ritual: Relations between Women in Nineteenth-Century America.' *Journal of Women in Culture and Society* 1, 1 (1875): 1–29; Kaethler and Shantz, *Quilts of Waterloo County*, 12; Ruth Schwarts Cowan, *More Work for Mother* (New York: Basic Book Publishers 1983), 112.

63. For gender as a relational system, see Joan W. Scott, 'Women's History,' in Peter Burke, ed., *New Perspectives on Historical Writing* (University Park: Pennsylvania State University Press 1995); and for rural communities, see Pederson, *Between Memory and Reality*; Osterud, *Bonds of Community*; and Royden Loewen, *Family, Church, and*

Market: The Mennonite Community in the Old and the New Worlds, 1850–1930 (Toronto: University of Toronto Press 1993).

64. Munro, *Backwoods Life,* 55

65. Geikie, *Adventures in Canada,* 41–3

66. Moodie, *Roughing It,* 158; and for similar accounts of logging bees, see Logan, *Notes on a Journey,* 45; William Johnston, *Pioneers of Blanchard* (Toronto: William Briggs 1899), 188–9, 227; and Wilkie, *Sketches* 174–5. See also Mark Carnes and C. Griffen, eds., *Meanings for Manhood* (Chicago: University of Chicago Press 1990); and Pederson, *Between Memory and Reality,* 142–3.

67. Bonnie Huskins, 'The Ceremonial Space of Women: Public Processing in Victorian Saint John and Halifax,' in Janet Guildford and Susanne Morton, eds., *Separate Sphere: Women's Worlds in the 19th-Century Maritimes* (Fredericton: Acadiensis Press 1994), 147

68. Cited in West Oxford Women's Institute, *The Axe and the Wheel: A History of West Oxford Township* (Tillsonburg: Otter Publishing 1974), 17

69. Langton, *A Gentlewoman,* 94

70. Abbott, *The Emigrant,* 42

71. An extreme, but nonetheless suggestive, case occurred in 1918 when a young Quebec girl dressed in male attire participated in a log-driving bee, and, when exposed, was sentenced to two years at the Portsmouth Penitentiary in Kingston. Original 11 June 1918, reprinted in the *Toronto Star,* 19 May 1992.

72. Elizabeth Jane Errington, *Wives and Mothers, School Mistresses and Scullery Maids: Working Women in Upper Canada, 1790–1840* (Montreal and Kingston: McGill-Queen's University Press 1995), 96

73. Catharine Parr Traill, *The Female Emigrant's Guide and Hints on Canadian Housekeeping* (Toronto: MacLear 1854), 40; Sinclair, *Pioneer Reminiscences,* 12; Geikie, *Adventures in Canada,* 44

74. Munro, *Backwoods' Life,* 55; Stewart, *Our Forest Home,* 172–6; Wilkie, *Sketches,* 176–8; Bishop, *The Englishwoman,* 205–6; Tivy, *Your Loving Anna,* 89

75. Ralph Connor, *The Man from Glengarry* (Toronto: The Westminster Co 1901), 211.

76. Bishop, *The Englishwoman,* 205–6

77. Wilkie, *Sketches,* 176

78. Stan Cross, 'The Raising,' *Up the Gatineau!* 21 (1995): 7

79. M.E. Graham, 'Food for Bees,' *The Farming World* 18 (11 Sept. 1900): 104

80. Strickland, *Twenty-Seven Years,* 2: 295–6; Thompson, *Tradesman's Travel,* 37; and for a wood-picking bee that was similarly arranged, see Munro, *Backwoods' Life.* 57.

81. Peter Ward, 'Courtship and Social Space in Nineteenth-Century English Canada,' *Canadian Historical Review* 68 1 (1987): 35–62.

82. University of Western Ontario, Regional Collection, William Leslie Papers, box 4178, A.C. Currie to Richard Leslie, 25 December 1841; and see also Strickland, *Twenty-Seven Years,* 2: 296; Munro, *Backwoods' Life,* 57; and Thompson, *Tradesman's Travels,* 37.

83. Wilkie, *Sketches,* 182–6; and see also Haight, *Country Life,* 67–8; Geikie, *Adventures in Canada,* 326–7; Traill, *Female Emigrant's Guide,* 75; and Gavin Hamilton Green, *The Old Log House* (Goderick: Signal-Star Press 1948), 109.

84. Marshall, *Canadian Dominion,* 62

85. Middaugh Diary. The people mentioned in the diary have all been matched with the 1871 manuscript census; *Historical Atlas of the Counties of Leeds and Grenville* (1861; Belleville: Mika Publishing 1973); and *Illustrated Historical Atlas of Stormont Dundas and Glengarry Counties, Ontario* (1879; Belleville: Mike Silk Screening 1972). I would like to thank my mother, Mrs Jean Wilson, the great-grandaughter of Lucy, for treasuring our family heirlooms and assisting me in reconstructing the family relationships. The value of using farm women's diaries is amply revealed in Laurel Ulrich's Pulitzer Prize–winning book *A Midwife's Tale: The Life of Martha Ballard, Based on Her Diary, 1785–1812* (New York: Vintage Books 1990); Royden Loewen, '"The Children, the Cows, My Dear Man and My Sister": The Transplanted Lives of Mennonite Farm Women,' *Canadian Historical Review* 73, 3 (1992): 344–73; and Ward, 'Courtship and Social Space,' 35–62.

86. Obituary of Lucy Middaugh, in the private possession of Mrs. Jean Wilson

87. 1871 Agricultural Census for Mountain Township

88. Ibid.; Land Registry Abstract for Concession 6, Mountain Township; St Andrew's United Church, Hallville, Ontario Centennial Anniversary 1834–1934 brochure

89. Munro talks about the importance of grown children in his *Backwoods' Life,* 56. See also Erasmus, 'Culture Structure and Process,' 456; Kimball, 'Rural Social Organization,' 41; and Buckley, 'Neighbourliness,' 50. Fay E. Dudden, in another contest, notes that it was often the neighbourhood youth that was shared. *Serving Women: Household Service in Nineteenth-Century America* (Middletown, Conn.: Wesleyan University Press 1983), chap. 1.

90. Farm/store ledger of John Middaugh, 1816–1850s, in private possession of Mrs Jean Wilson; and J. Smith Carter, *The Story of Dundas* (1905; Belleville: Mika Publishing 1973), 449–63

91. Mewett, 'Association Categories,' 110–11; Munro, *Backwoods' Life,* 219; and Sinclair, *Pioneer Reminiscences,* 11

92. Doyle, *Hints on Emigtation,* 61–2; and Traill, *The Backwoods,* 122

93. See Stephen Innes for his insightful discussion of the need for greater caution when using such dichotomies to describe the past. 'John Smith's Vision,' in Stephen Innes, ed., *Work and Labour in Early America,* 36–40

94. Moodie, *Roughing It,* 13; see also the Diary of William Proudfoot, 12 June 1833, cited in Edwin Guillet, *Pioneer Days in Upper Canada* (1933; Toronto: University of Toronto Press 1975), 127; and Ex-Settler, *Canada,* 115

95. John J.E. Linton, *The Life of a Backwoodsman; or, Particulars of the Emigrant's Situation in Settling on the Wild Land of Canada* (London: Marchant Singer & Co. 1843), 14; Langton, *Gentlewoman,* 155, 166; *Canada Farmer* 2, 12 (12 Dec. 1870); Traill, *Backwoods,* 122. For a scholarly discussion of the problems associated with bees or other forms of cooperative work, see Erasmus, 'Culture Structure and Process,' 456–61; Cowan, *More Work for Mother,* 117; Pederson, *Between Memory and Reality,* 149.

96. Traill, *Backwoods,* 121; and Strickland, *Twenty-Seven years,* I: 37

97. Kimball, in 'Rural Social Organization,' 42, places significant weight on technology as a factor in the decline of cooperative labour. Erasmus disagrees, placing more emphasis on the growth of a money economy and on more intensive agriculture that makes cooperative work inconvenient and inefficient in terms of the costs and quality of work done. 'Culture Structure and Process,' 456. See also Pederson, *Between Memory and Reality,* 154–5.

98. *Farmer's Advocate* 59 (10 April 1924); 548; McCalla, *Planing the Province,* 225; and Lois Russell, *Everyday Life in Colonial Canada* (London: B.T. Batsford 1973), 90

99. Pederson, *Between Memory and Reality,* 151–4

100. McCalla, *Planting the Province,* 161; Mewett, 'Associational Categories,' and James F. Taylor Calnan, '"A Home Not Made with Hands": National Voluntary Associations and Local Community in Prince Edward County, Ontario, at the Turn of the 20th Century' (PhD dissertation, University of Guelph 1999).

Rupert's Land and the Red River Colony

An ox pulls a Red River cart through a prairie community in this mid-19th-century painting by W.G.R. Hind.

By the mid-19th century, a new and distinct society emerged in the Red River Colony at the junction of the Red and the Assiniboine rivers in Rupert's Land, the vast area of the North American continent controlled by the Hudson's Bay Company. In particular, a distinct society had formed at the junction of the Red and Assiniboine rivers, known as the Red River colony. By 1850, the colony had a population of more than 5000 mixed-bloods and several hundred non-Native settlers. Of the mixed-blood population, roughly half were English-speaking Métis, or "Country-born," the descendants of the British fur traders and their Native wives. The other half were French-speaking Métis, the descendants of the early French fur traders and their Native wives.

Did these two groups create a cohesive society, or did they coexist in a state of friction? In "The Flock Divided: Factions and Feuds at Red River" Frits Pannekoek argues that religion split the colony into two hostile factions. Fellow historian Irene M. Spry reaches the opposite conclusion in "The Métis and Mixed Bloods of Rupert's Land before 1870." She argues that the two groups of mixed bloods were united by their common First Nations heritage. Any division that existed was class-based, relating to the occupational differences between the farmers and the hunters or plains traders.

The early chapters of Gerald Friesen's *The Canadian Prairies: A History* (Toronto: University of Toronto Press, 1984) offer a good overview of the history of Rupert's Land. Sarah Carter's *Aboriginal People and Colonizers of Western Canada to 1900* (Toronto: University of Toronto Press, 1999) is also very useful. A valuable new collection of essays is Theodore Binema, Gerhard J. Ens, and R.C. Macleod, eds., *From Rupert's Land to Canada* (Edmonton: University of Alberta Press, 2001).

D.N. Sprague looks at the Red River Colony in the mid-19th century in his introduction to *The Genealogy of the First Métis Nation: The Development and Dispersal of the Red River Settlement, 1820–1900* (Winnipeg: Pemmican Publishers, 1983), compiled by D.N. Sprague and R.P. Frye. Frits Pannekoek provides a full study of Red River society in *A Snug Little Flock: The Social Origins of the Riel Resistance, 1869–70* (Winnipeg: Watson and Dwyer, 1991). J.R. Miller reviews the secondary literature on the Red River Colony in "From Riel to the Métis," *Canadian Historical Review* 69 (1988): 1–20. This study complements Frits Pannekoek's "The Historiography of the Red River Settlement, 1830–1868," *Prairie Forum* 6 (1981): 75–85. Important essays on the Métis appear in Jennifer S. Brown and Jacqueline Peterson, eds., *The New Peoples: Being and Becoming Métis in North America* (Winnipeg: University of Manitoba Press, 1985). Gerhard Ens provides an interesting insight into Red River society in "Dispossession or Adaptation? Migration and Persistence of the Red River Métis, 1835–1890," Canadian Historical Association, *Historical Papers* (1988): 120–44; and in his book, *Homeland to Hinterland: The Changing Worlds of the Red River Métis in the Nineteenth Century* (Toronto: University of Toronto Press, 1996). A recent local study is Robert J. Coutts, *The Road to the Rapids: Nineteenth Century Church and Society at St. Andrew's Parish, Red River* (Calgary: University of Calgary Press, 2000). J. Barkwell Lawrence, Leah Dorion, and Darren R. Prefontaine have edited an interesting collection of papers on the Métis, entitled *Métis Legacy* (Winnipeg: Pemmican Publications, 2001).

Excellent maps of the Red River and all of Rupert's Land appear in Richard Ruggles, *A Country So Interesting: The Hudson's Bay Company and Two Centuries of Mapping, 1670–1870* (Montreal/Kingston: McGill-Queen's University Press, 1991).

Dale R. Russell provides a detailed review of the location of First Nations' groups on the territory that is now the Prairie provinces in *Eighteenth-Century Western Cree and Their Neighbours* (Hull, PQ: Canadian Museum of Civilization, 1991). As a supplement to this monograph, see James G.E. Smith's "The Western Woods Cree: Anthropological Myth and

Historical Reality," *American Ethnologist* 14 (1987): 434–48. Interesting excerpts from early travellers' accounts of what is now Western Canada appear in Germaine Warkentin's edited work, *Canadian Exploration Literature: An Anthology* (Toronto: Oxford University Press, 1993). Hugh A. Dempsey's two biographies, *Crowfoot* (Edmonton: Hurtig, 1972) and *Big Bear* (Vancouver: Douglas and McIntyre, 1984), introduce the Plains Indians in the mid-19th century; see also his *The Amazing Death of Calf Shirt and Other Blackfoot Stories: Three Hundred Years of Blackfoot History* (Saskatoon: Fifth House, 1994). A recent study of Big Bear's First Nation is John S. Milloy's *The Plains Cree: Trade, Diplomacy and War, 1790 to 1870* (Winnipeg: University of Manitoba Press, 1989). The Blackfoot experience is reviewed by John Ewers in *The Blackfeet: Raiders in the Northwestern Plains* (Norman, OK: University of Oklahoma Press, 1958). Laura Peers looks at the Western Ojibwa in *The Ojibwa of Western Canada: 1780–1870* (Winnipeg: University of Manitoba Press, 1994).

A comparative description of two 19th-century families, one from the Red River Colony and one from Prince Edward Island, is provided by J.M. Bumsted and Wendy Owen in "The Victorian Family in Canada in Historical Perspective: The Ross Family of Red River and the Jarvis Family of Prince Edward Island," *Manitoba History* 13 (1987): 12–18.

WEBLINKS

Champlain Society
http://link.library.utoronto.ca/champlain/search.cfm?lang=eng

The digital collections of the Champlain Society contain several important European accounts of Rupert's Land and the Red River Colony. Browse the database by subject, and select for example, "Manitoba — History," "Northwest, Canadian — History — Sources," or "Selkirk, Thomas Douglas, Earl of, 1771–1820 — Diaries."

Red River Settlement Papers
http://www.nosracines.ca/e/toc.asp?id=1180

Digitized collection of published letters, dispatches, and other documents from the early Red River Settlement, published in 1819.

Red River Journal
http://www.canadiana.org/ECO/ItemRecord/41912?id=a2008919b6c6abaa

A digitized journal depicting life at the Red River Colony during the years 1820–1823.

Red River Settlement Council Minutes
http://www.mhs.mb.ca/docs/pageant/24/minutes1837.shtml

Recorded minutes of a Council meeting held at Fort Garry, Red River Settlement, on 16 June 1837.

The Red River
http://www.ccge.org/ccge/english/Resources/rivers/tr_rivers_redRiver.asp

A website by the Canadian Council for Geographic Education about the Red River.

Article Thirty

The Flock Divided: Factions and Feuds at Red River

Frits Pannekoek

The settlement of Red River changed in the late 1850s and early 1860s. From a relatively quiet backwater, it became the confluence of the northward frontier of the American Republic and the western frontier of the Canadian colonies. In 1858 there were only a few buildings outside Upper Fort Garry at the forks of the Red and Assiniboine, but within ten years there was a drugstore, grist mill, gun shop, harness shop, bookstore, butcher shop, tinsmith, photography studio, carriage shop, two saloons, and a newspaper office. Steamboats, the *Anson Northup* (1859) and the *International* (1862), even attempted, although without great success, to navigate between Moorhead in Dakota and Red River.

Much of this change was due to a major influx of Canadian and American immigrants. Even before the immigration, however, Red River was changing of its own accord. During the six years before 1849, 1232 new people were added to the colony. This growth was internal, rather than the result of immigration, since only 28 families arrived in Red River between 1849 and 1856. This increase placed a substantial burden on the means of livelihood: the river lot and the hunt. Because the family lands could no longer be divided indefinitely among the numerous sons, as had been the tradition, many moved to the plains along the Assiniboine River. Others moved to the United States or into the western interior along the Saskatchewan River at places such as Victoria in what is now Alberta and Prince Albert in present-day Saskatchewan.

There were four major groups in the Red River settlement. The most significant were those of mixed-blood heritage. In 1871 the total population was 11 400. Of these, 5740 were Métis or Catholic French/Cree-speaking mixed-bloods. These lived in the parishes south and immediately west of the junctions of the Red and Assiniboine rivers. The 4080 Protestant and English-speaking mixed-bloods lived in the parishes largely north of the junction of the two rivers and after 1854 around Portage la Prairie. It has been argued by some that the Indian blood tied these two groups together as one family. While that would seem commonsense, in fact there was little unity between the two groups during the Riel Resistance. Indeed, the English-speaking Protestant mixed-bloods, who proudly called themselves Halfbreeds, were at odds with Riel. Why? It would seem that the two groups should be of single mind. When the events in the decade preceding the resistance are examined closely, the influence of the Reverend Griffiths Owen Corbett in creating a split between the Halfbreeds and Métis is evident. This bizarre clergyman with his petty politics and religious bigotry managed to effectively divide the mixed-blood community into its Protestant and Catholic halves. Coincidentally he reinforced the Halfbreeds' anti-Hudson's Bay Company and pro-imperial sentiments. When Riel attempted to appeal to the mixed bloods for unity in 1869 he would fail. Corbett had been too effective. The Canadians, with their anti-Catholicism and imperial bombast, would find supporters in the Halfbreed parishes of Red River.

Source: This article, taken from Frits Pannekoek's *A Snug Little Flock: The Social Origins of the Riel Resistance, 1869–70* (Winnipeg: Watson and Dwyer, 1991), pp. 143–70; originally appeared in *The Beaver* 70, 6 (December 1990–January 1991). Reprinted by permission.

In the 1850s, at the same time that there were significant demographic and social changes in Red River, both Canada and Great Britain began to show a peculiar interest in the future of Rupert's Land. Red River, of course, chased every rumour of change and there were as many factions as there were alternatives. In the early 1860s Crown Colony status seemed most likely. The Duke of Newcastle, colonial secretary from 1859 to 1864, favoured the creation of a Crown Colony in Rupert's Land as a connecting link between Canada and British Columbia, all of which would eventually comprise a British North American federation. He was supported in his stand by substantial Canadian and British railroad and financial interests. But Red River was only vaguely aware of what was happening in the Colonial Office and at Hudson's Bay House, London. As rumour increased of imperial support for the Crown Colony status after 1859, it seemed apparent to Red River that change of some sort was inevitable. The settlement hoped that it would be immediate. No firm plan was offered, however, by either the Canadian government, the imperial government, or the Company. Confusion remained the only political certainty.

The agitation for change in Red River's political status started in 1856–57 in Canada and filtered through to Red River via the *Globe,* the Toronto newspaper read by many of the informed and literate. James Ross, Halfbreed son of Alexander Ross, historian and former sheriff, expressed the prevailing sentiments:

> We ought to have a flood of immigration to infuse new life, new ideas, and destroy all our old associations with the past, *i.e.,* in so far as it hinders our progress for the future — regular transformation will sharpen our intellects, fill our minds with new projects and give life and vigour to all our thoughts, words and actions.

The first petition for change came in June of 1856 from the Protestant clergy. Their demands were moderate, including only restrictions on the importing of alcohol and the introduction of the elective principle in the Council of Assiniboia. They did not wish the removal of the Councillors, only that vacancies be filled by election, and that the settlement be divided for that purpose into districts.

No serious pro-Canadian agitation developed until a few months later. On 26 February, William Dawson of the Dawson-Hind expedition, sent by the Canadian government to assess the fertility of the Assiniboine-Saskatchewan country, gave a lecture, "Canada Past and Present." Interest was high and the governor, the clergy, and some of the Company's active and retired gentlemen attended. There was, however, no open political movement at the parish level. Interest turned into open agitation only when William Kennedy returned to Red River on 7 February 1857 after a number of years of anti-Company agitation in Upper Canada. Like his relative Alexander Kennedy Isbister, who had been instrumental in the presentation of the 1847 petition to the imperial parliament, he was an embittered ex–Hudson's Bay Company employee.

From March to May, a number of meetings organized by Kennedy were held in the Kildonan school house and in the neighbouring Halfbreed parishes. An elder of the Presbyterian Church, Kennedy ingratiated himself with the Kildonan settlers, especially Donald Gunn, one of its leading members, and Rev. John Black, who had strong Canadian sympathies. The Company was severely criticized and annexation to Canada advocated. When Governor F.G. Johnson, who had succeeded Adam Thom as recorder, attended one of the first March meetings, he was requested to leave. As a result of the meetings the younger settlers displayed their open sympathy with Kennedy and signed his petition for union with Canada. The older settlers, still believing that a certain deference was due the Company, hesitated to make a decision.

In May, Kennedy convinced some in Red River—the exact parishes cannot now be known, but probably they were those between the Upper and Lower Forts—to elect five members, including himself and Isbister, to serve in the provincial legislature of Canada. Kennedy for his part had allowed reports to spread that he was a representative of Canada. While he publicly denied these reports, he left the vague impression that he had to do so because he was a secret agent. The five members were actually sent off, but Kennedy had second thoughts about the legality of the proceedings. He chose to recall the delegates when he heard that Captain John Palliser was arriving at the head of the British expedition to the North-West and that he might have some concrete instructions for Red River's future.

This spelled the effective end of Kennedy's agitation. By the winter of 1858–59, the semblance of unity that momentarily had existed in Red River disintegrated under the force of new pressures. Rev. G.O. Corbett, arriving in the spring of 1858, was the cause.

Corbett, of the Church of England, was a contentious and difficult individual, spending much of his life quarrelling with his bishops, the Hudson's Bay Company, his fellow clergymen, and the Colonial and Continental Church Society, which sponsored him. While not a charismatic leader, he was something of a gadfly with strong convictions about the rights of Englishmen, and even stronger convictions that these rights were being denied to the Halfbreeds by the tyranny of the Hudson's Bay Company and the Church of Rome. A popular and effective speaker, his views fell on the fertile ground of the political and social unrest in the late 1850s and early 1860s. Corbett aroused the Halfbreeds and directed their energies against both the Company and the Catholics, convincing them that their future lay within a Protestant Crown Colony firmly affixed to the British Empire. Crown Colony status seemed to guarantee an extension of the full rights and privileges of the British constitution and offered a fellowship of English-speaking people, under the loose British nationalism with which the empire had always anointed its subjects.

When in 1862 Corbett found himself the centre of an unsavoury scandal and defended himself by identifying it as a Company plot to discredit him and his movement for Crown Colony status, feelings grew so intense that Red River split into two factions. The pro-Company group, who believed Corbett guilty, included strangely enough the Métis, who disliked his anti-Catholicism. The anti-Company group, who were the most fervent Crown Colony advocates, believed him innocent, and were composed principally of the Protestant English-speaking Halfbreeds. In the end the two groups verged on open war.

Rev. G.O. Corbett despised the Catholics, considered them barbarians, and used the newspaper to propagandize his sentiments. In a community torn by dissent and rife with status tensions, Corbett's anti-Catholicism was absorbed as eagerly as his anti-Company rhetoric. He taught the Halfbreeds that because they were Protestant they were superior to the Catholic Métis of Red River.

Corbett felt that the British liberties of Red River, a Protestant colony of a Protestant queen, were succumbing to the tyranny of the Church of Rome. Corbett, seeing, as he imagined, too many examples of the growing power of the papal "anti-Christ," felt it his duty to warn of the dangerous consequences. His greatest concern was William Mactavish, the governor of Assiniboia. Mactavish had married a Catholic daughter of Andrew McDermot in Saint-Boniface cathedral, and in the following years baptized his children into the Catholic faith. All of Protestant Red River had considered the marriage an insult to Bishop Anderson of the Church of England, who had apparently expected to conduct the ceremony. Corbett was convinced that, with the governor a virtual Catholic, and with seven Catholics against seven Protestants on the Council of Assiniboia, "the balance of power [was] with the Pope of Rome."

When an official report of the legislative proceedings of the Council of Assiniboia referred to the Catholic bishop as "Lord Bishop," Corbett had what he considered proof. Legally only Bishop Anderson, who wanted no part in the controversy and who unsuccessfully cautioned Corbett to moderate his stand, was entitled to the title. Only Anderson had been appointed by "Her Most Gracious Sovereign the Queen." Corbett considered use of the title for Bishop Taché both "insidious" and "unconstitutional." When the Council of Assiniboia continued its folly by passing a law forbidding all government activity on Catholic holidays, there was no longer any doubt in Corbett's mind — Red River had fallen to the pope.

These religious tensions that had split the society asunder tended to centre on the settlement along the Assiniboine River, but their impact was felt throughout the whole of Red River. The *Nor'Wester* newspaper was particularly effective in ensuring that the controversies of the 1860s would continue to exacerbate social, religious, and racial divisions. Every imagined slight was well publicized and exaggerated. In 1860, for example, a heated battle waged between Henry Cook, a Halfbreed Anglican schoolmaster, and François Bruneau, one of the principal Métis, over the quality of Protestant and Catholic education. So virulent did Protestant sentiment become that James Ross, rather moderate in his anti-Catholicism and at times a restraining influence on Corbett, fearing a loss of Protestant business, refused on first request to publish an obituary and eulogy for Sister Valade, one of the first and most venerated sisters at Saint-Boniface. When in August 1861 Ross dared to publish an article suggesting that the Halfbreeds were superior to the Métis, the elder Riel visited Ross and "il lui a chanté une chanson, la chanson du juge Thom." In other words Riel threatened Ross's life, just as he had done years earlier to Adam Thom, the first recorder of Rupert's Land, who had voiced similar bigotries.

An understanding of these religious divisions is critical to the understanding of the crises which faced Red River as Corbett commenced his agitation for Crown Colony status in 1858. In December of 1858 Corbett and his cohort, Reverend John Chapman of St. Andrew's parish, the Company's chaplain, circulated their first petition advocating Crown Colony status. Corbett believed that annexation to Canada would place Red River "altogether in the hands of a subordinate power." He felt that if Red River were a Crown Colony, it would become the civil and commercial hub of the west, with its own elected assembly — a feature that was central to all of Corbett's arguments. He believed that "whatever advantages Canada enjoys, apart from her natural position, she derives these from her connection with England as Crown Colony." He damned the Company for its alleged inability to maintain law and order and its obstruction of material progress. Both would be remedied, he believed, when Rupert's Land assumed its rightful place in the empire as a Crown Colony.

Donald Gunn, William Kennedy, and James Ross, the leaders of the Canadian party, vigorously opposed Corbett and circulated a counter-petition advocating annexation to Canada. At this point, William Kennedy and James Ross, both Halfbreeds with strong British-Canadian connections, still felt Canada offered the best future — and Crown Colony status would offer continued domination by the Company. Both petitions were sent to the House of Lords, where they were ignored.

Corbett's agitation for political change assumed an even wider and more popular basis in the early 1860s. On 30 October 1862 the Council of Assiniboia petitioned the British government for troops in the face of a rumoured Sioux attack, a feared American invasion, and the growing local disaffection. The Council's petition made the rounds of Kildonan, Headingley, and St. Paul's parishes, gathering some 1183 signatures. As the petition was circulating, Rev. G.O. Corbett; Rev. John Chapman, the former Company chaplain; and James Ross, who joined Corbett's party when it became apparent that Canada was no longer interested in annexation, circulated a counter-petition condemning the Council of Assiniboia and the Company, and requesting Crown Colony status. Ross also refused to publish the Council's petition in his newspaper, the *Nor'Wester*. The counter-petitioners claimed that troops were not so much needed as a more efficient government. There was considerable confusion as to who supported which petition, since many attempted to delete their signatures from the Council's petition in order to support the counter-petition. The Company, as a disciplinary action, deprived Ross of his public offices of sheriff, governor of the gaol, and postmaster. Both petitions were ultimately sent to the Colonial office, where they too were ignored.

The Council's petition was seen by the aroused Halfbreeds as a plot to crush their efforts to throw off the yoke of the Hudson's Bay Company. Consequently, when the lurid details of Corbett's presumed attempts to induce the miscarriage of his illegitimate child by Maria Thomas struck like a thunderbolt from nowhere, his protested innocence and his accusations of a Company conspiracy appeared completely credible to the Halfbreeds. After all, earlier that winter Maria had been persuaded in front of a magistrate to deny the rumours of an affair. The denial had been acceptable, but when Corbett was jailed on the abortion charges and refused bail, in spite of precedent for granting such a request, the Halfbreeds were certain that the Company had resurrected a charge which had no substance and which had already been dismissed. Many were convinced that Maria Thomas's father, having pressed the charges, and Thomas Sinclair, the magistrate, were in the Company's pay. In effect, the question became not one of Corbett's guilt or innocence, but rather one of support for, or opposition to, the Company's supposed tyranny.

Corbett was charged with violation of 24 and 25 Victoria ch. 100, passed in 1861. It states that:

> Whosoever, with intent to procure the miscarriage of any woman, whether she be, or not be with child, shall unlawfully administer to her or cause to be taken by her, any poison or noxious thing, or shall unlawfully use an instrument or other means whatsoever with the like intent, shall be guilty of felony, and, being convicted thereof, shall be liable at the discretion of the Court to be kept in penal servitude for life, or for any term not less than three years, or to be imprisoned for any term not exceeding two years, with or without hard labour, and with or without solitary confinement.

In his charge to the jury on the ninth day of the Corbett trial, which was published on 12 May 1863 in the *Nor'Wester*, Recorder Black felt that he ought to elaborate on the law:

> I may state that the law regarding this crime has within the last 35 years, undergone various changes. At one time the law made a distinction between acts in which the attempt was made on a woman quick with child and one not quick with child. Previous to the passing of the statute under which the prisoner is indicted that which regulates this offence made it material whether or not the woman was pregnant. By a subsequent statute 7 Wm. IV, and Vic. ch. 85, that distinction was done away with, and there were some slight differences and alterations, which were embodied in the statute under which the prisoner is indicted.

The outcome of the case was not the result of this new "mass" concern with abortion that swept America and Great Britain in the 1850s through to the 1880s. Prior to the 1850s and 1860s life was construed to begin with "quickening" or "stirring in the womb," and abortion before "quickening" was not a felony. Corbett attempted to abort Maria Thomas's and his alleged child after the fourth month. The scurrilous *Nor'Wester* indicated that Corbett, whom they supported, had been unjustly accused of "murder." Nevertheless the abortion was not successful, and despite Maria Thomas's explicit testimony, Corbett was jailed for six months, an extremely light sentence given the damning evidence.

The trial commenced on Thursday, 19 February 1863, continued for nine days, and heard 61 witnesses. Rev. John Chapman described the shocking trial to the secretaries of the Church Missionary Society:

> What a spectacle . . . Mr. Corbett in one box & Maria Thomas a young girl of 16 years in the witness box, with her babe in her arms which she declares is Mr. Corbett's and whose embryo life he is charged with attempting to destroy by means of medicine, instruments &c.

The Bishop appointed Archdeacon James Hunter to conduct an independent church investigation and, before the court made its own decision, he pronounced Corbett guilty as charged. The court then followed suit. Corbett refused to recognize the jurisdiction of the Court of Assiniboia, or to accept its decision, and continued his accusations of a conspiracy on the part of the Company and the Church of England. For the rest of his life, he insisted upon his innocence and he was supported in his view by many in Red River. Some indeed were prepared to resort to arms.

The first incident occurred at nine o'clock on the morning of Saturday, 6 December 1862. In response to the denial of bail for Corbett, 150 to 200 persons, principally from Headingley but with groups from St. James, St. John's, St. Paul's, and St. Andrew's, arrived at Fort Garry. Governor Alexander Grant Dallas, Simpson's unpopular successor from the Pacific coast, favoured a hard line, but when riot was threatened he allowed Corbett to address the crowd. Corbett, for his part, encouraged all to continue their fight for justice. Finally James Ross and ten to twelve of the more respected members of the crowd persuaded Dallas that he would have to allow bail or suffer the consequences.

The second instance of mob rule occurred during the third month of Corbett's six-month sentence. On 14 April the Halfbreeds submitted a petition signed by 552 of their number, requesting a pardon for Corbett. Six days later, after Dallas had refused to consider their pleas, Corbett was freed by force. The governor responded by arresting James Stewart, the mixed-blood schoolmaster of St. James parish school and a ringleader in the agitation.

Governor Dallas, suspecting a plot to free Stewart, called upon 25 Métis and 25 Halfbreeds to defend the prison. Only five of the Halfbreeds would serve; the Métis, who had no use for "Corps Bête" as they called the anti-Catholic Corbett, appeared in full force. At ten o'clock on the morning of 22 April, 27 protesters, headed by William Hallett and James Ross, demanded an interview with Dallas. When Dallas refused to meet the insurgents, Ross sent a petition demanding the liberation of Stewart, the cessation of all discussion over the Corbett affair, and the removal of Sheriff McKenney, a supporter of the Company, who had replaced Ross. Dallas again refused, and Ross rode into the prison compound and liberated Stewart. It is evident that had Dallas not forbidden a violent confrontation, the Métis would have used force to stop Ross, which in turn would have triggered *une guerre civile* between Protestant and Catholic Red River. Fortunately, most of the 25 Métis were from Saint-Boniface and under the control of the moderate François Bruneau. Had *les hivernants*, the Métis boatmen and tripmen living at Cheval Blanc and Saint-Norbert, been involved, as had been initially intended, blood would most certainly have been shed. The "winterers" were hardly as charitable as their brethren at Saint-Boniface and after a long season of winter confinement would have been ready to flex their muscles in a Red River spring in order to teach the insolent Protestants a lesson. Consequently nothing was done to recapture Stewart.

The situation had deteriorated to such an extent that late in May, one month after the Corbett escape, John Bourke, who had been involved in all three acts of defiance, and James Stewart went so far as to attempt the organization of a "provisional government." It is probable that Corbett himself was involved. Stewart suggested that Headingley, St. James, and Portage la Prairie should secede from Red River and form an independent colony subordinate only to the Crown. Ultimately the proposal failed to gain sufficient support, and the conspirators, who lacked apparent organizational ability, gave up the plan.

Within the colony generally the jail breaks were followed by an increased questioning of Red River's traditional leaders. Even after suspension by both the bishop and the Colonial and Continental Church Society, Corbett returned to Headingley, where he assumed his clerical duties. The bishop sent replacements, including William Henry Taylor from the neighbouring parish, but the congregation locked the church doors and refused admittance to any clergyman save Corbett. In a ludicrous climax to the issue, John Chapman, formerly Corbett's ally, finally forced the door and preached to an empty church. The bishop then ordered Corbett to leave Rupert's Land by 1 September 1863, but even in this he was defied and Corbett remained in the settlement until the following June.

In the neighbouring parish of St. James the persecution of the pro-Corbett group was equally vigorous if somewhat less successful. While James Stewart was allowed to teach for two months following his escape, Rev. William Henry Taylor, on poor terms with Stewart because of an earlier dispute over the location of the school, hired a replacement with the bishop's approval. Stewart then opened a private school where the great majority sent their children, forcing Taylor to close his. Taylor never regained his popularity.

The parishes along the Red River were also affected by the upheaval. Not only did many refuse to attend church services, but Archdeacon James Hunter was attacked for his investigations into the Corbett case. John Tait, a carpenter and miller from St. Andrew's parish, circulated a number of vicious rumours against Hunter to prove that any untruth could find support in Red River. Consequently, he reasoned, Corbett was probably just as easily innocent as guilty. Bishop Anderson urged Hunter to sue but a court case was avoided when Tait signed an apology that was read from St. Andrew's pulpit, and paid Hunter £100. Hunter announced that he would distribute the sum among Tait's daughters and when he failed to do so, Tait sued but lost.

As a result of the gossip and ill-feeling generated by the Corbett and related affairs, both Bishop Anderson and Archdeacon Hunter, his presumed successor, resigned their positions. Hunter commented that "the storm is pitiless, *a systematic blackening of the characters of all*. No one can live in this land with this adversary, and my prophecy is that in two years there will not be four clergymen on the two rivers."

His prediction possessed a degree of truth and by 1867 all of the most prominent clergymen had left Red River: Anderson in 1864, Hunter in 1865, and Chapman and Taylor in 1867. Their numbers were further reduced by William Cockran's death in 1864.

By 1865, then, the Halfbreeds had achieved a degree of confidence about their own identity, largely through Corbett's influence. They were to liberate Red River from the two tyrannies of the Hudson's Bay Company and the Roman Church. With Red River a Crown Colony, they would then follow Corbett, a thoroughly Protestant Englishman. They would have the balance of power. In the first decades of the history of the settlement, identity had been based on race, and rank in the Company. With Corbett's agitation acting as a catalyst, racial ties were weakened. They did not see themselves as English-speaking Protestant versions of the Métis. They did not identify with the Métis Nation. They were not petty settlers in a squalid little Company settlement in the isolated and frigid heart of British North America. They were not poverty-stricken coloured parishioners of the white-missionary–dominated Church of England. They were Protestant subjects of Her Most Britannic Majesty's Empire, an empire upon which the sun never set.

Article Thirty-One

The Métis and Mixed-Bloods of Rupert's Land before 1870

Irene M. Spry

Were the English-speaking mixed-bloods and French-speaking métis of what is now western Canada separate and mutually hostile groups? Or were they friendly and closely linked with each other? Frits Pannekoek contends that the *country-born* (as he terms the English-speaking mixed-bloods)[1] and the métis of Red River Settlement "were at odds years before the [Riel] resistance, and the origins of that hatred lay in the nature of Red River society." He concludes: "In fact, upon closer examination of the origins of Métis–Country-born hatred, it becomes apparent that the first Riel resistance was in part caused and certainly exacerbated not by racial and religious antagonisms introduced by the Canadians, but rather by a sectarian and racial conflict with roots deep in Red River's past."[2]

This view of the divisions within Red River Settlement is directly contrary to what a métis, Louis Goulet, remembered. Writing of 1867, when his family returned to Red River from the far western plains, he recollected:

> Something was missing in the Red River Colony: There wasn't the same feeling of unity and friendship that had always been felt among those people of different races and religions. And he [his father] wasn't the only one unhappy with the way things were going.
>
> The old-timers seemed to feel a strange mood in the air. Newcomers, especially the ones from Ontario, were eagerly sowing racial and religious conflict, banding together to fan the flames of discord between different groups in the Red River Settlement. These émigrés from Ontario, all of them Orangemen, looked as if their one dream in life was to make war on the Hudson's Bay Company, the Catholic Church and anyone who spoke French. . . . The latest arrivals were looking to be masters of everything, everywhere.[3]

Continuing tradition among twentieth-century English-speaking descendants of the Selkirk settlers supports Louis Goulet. As Miss Janet Bannerman of Old Kildonan recalled, "The relations between the French-speaking families and the rest of us in Red River were always of friendliness and goodwill. In the very earliest and hardest days of the settlement that friendship was established upon a lasting foundation by the French-Canadians and the métis who showed warmhearted kindness to the poor Scottish people when the lack of food at the Forks compelled them to go down to the buffalo hunters' headquarters at the mouth of the Pembina river in the winter time."[4] This, in turn, is consistent with Miss Anne Henderson's memories of walks, when she was a child early in this century, with her grandfather, who introduced her to all the friends he met, many of whom were French-speaking.[5] Similarly, George Sanderson, Jr., writing of his boyhood in Portage la Prairie, mentioned among his chums the "Pochas" [Poitras] and "Demers" [Desmarais] boys.[6]

Very little evidence of conflict, let alone "hatred," has come to light except in the clerical sources on which Pannekoek's conclusion seems in large measure to be based. Such sources, it

Source: Irene M. Spry, "The Métis and Mixed-Bloods of Rupert's Land before 1870," *The New Peoples: Being and Becoming Métis in North America,* eds. Jacqueline Peterson and Jennifer S.H. Brown (Winnipeg: University of Manitoba Press, 1985). Reprinted by permission.

is submitted, must be used with great reserve. Independent evidence is needed to test the testimony of writers who were concerned to convert the adherents of rival dogmas and to protect their own flocks from counter-conversion. Hostility between Catholic and Protestant divines was a byword in Rupert's Land.[7] Such antagonism as there may have been between French- and English-speaking communities was, indeed, largely sectarian, but it does not seem to have been racial in origin.

A preliminary survey of such nonclerical evidence as is available concerning the nature of the relationships of the natives of the country of Indian and French and Indian and other white descent[8] suggests that, far from being mutually hostile, métis and mixed-bloods were, as W.L. Morton put it, linked by "ties of blood and of long association on hunt and trip."[9]

Alexander Ross's celebrated statement may, perhaps, be taken with a pinch or two of salt, but it must at least be considered:

> We have now seen all the different classes of which this infant colony was composed brought together. The better to advance each other's interest, as well as for mutual support, all sects and creeds associated together indiscriminately, and were united like members of the same family, in peace, charity, and good fellowship. This state of things lasted till the Churchmen began to feel uneasy, and the Catholics grew jealous; so that projects were set on foot to sep- arate the tares from the wheat. . . .
>
> Party spirit and political strife has been gaining ground ever since. The Canadians became jealous of the Scotch, the half-breeds of both; and their separate interests as agricul- turalists, voyageurs, or hunters, had little tendency to unite them. At length, indeed, the Canadians and half-breeds came to a good understanding with each other; leaving then but two parties, the Scotch and the French. Between these, although there is, and always has been, a fair show of mutual good feeling, anything like cordiality in a common sentiment seemed impossible; and they remain, till this day, politically divided.[10]

Significantly, Ross said nothing about the mixed-bloods as a separate group, except as he described where each community lived; on the contrary, in his book *The Red River Settlement*, he noted a number of apparent affinities among and cooperation between métis and mixed- bloods. Thus, in his account of talk among Rupert's Landers, Ross mentioned their "narrations." These were "made up of an almost unintelligible jargon of the English, French and Indian lan- guages."[11] This suggests at least some mingling of the English- and French-speaking elements in the population of mixed descent, an impression borne out by a traveller's observation con- cerning a cart train south of Red River Settlement: "In the 'polyglot jabber'" of the métis drivers "he heard 'fine broad Scotch,' a scattering of Gaelic and Irish brogue, and a plentiful mixture of 'rapidly uttered French *patois*.'"[12] Another traveller in the Red River Valley in 1864 joined a cart train under the command of Antoine Gingras, who "knew English" as well as French, though his drivers spoke only Indian and French.[13] J.G. Kohl in the 1850s recorded a bilingual statement by a métis: "Où je reste? Je ne peux pas te le dire. Je suis Voyageur — je suis Chicot, monsieur. Je reste partout. Mon grand-père était Voyageur: il est mort en voyage. Mon père était Voyageur: il est mort en voyage. Je mourrai aussi en voyage, et un autre Chicot prendra ma place. Such is our course of life."[14]

Louis Goulet, in describing the Frog Lake massacre, mentioned that he and his friends, André Nault and Dolphis Nolin, conversed in English mixed with a little French when they were held by the Cree.[15] He noted, too, that a French-speaking métis of Scottish descent, Johnny Pritchard, was interpreter to Tom Quinn. Presumably this meant that he could speak English.[16] A granddaughter of Norbert Welsh (an Irish-French métis), in enumerating the lan- guages that her grandfather had at his command, ended the list with "and, of course, English."[17]

Similarly, some mixed-bloods spoke French — people such as Charles Thomas, who was in charge of the Hudson's Bay Company post at Reindeer Lake when Father Taché visited it in 1847.[18] "Big Jim" McKay, later to become the Honourable James McKay of Deer Lodge, whose father came from Sutherlandshire, spoke French,[19] as did members of another family of McKays, the "Little Bearskin" McKays, William McKay, his brother John ("Jerry") McNab Ballenden McKay, and his son Thomas.[20] Joseph Finlayson, one of the Roderick Finlayson family, also wrote and spoke French fluently.[21] It would appear, therefore, that many métis and mixed-bloods, at least among the elite, spoke both French and English, as well as one or more of the Indian languages, in which tongues those who did not speak both French and English could and did communicate. The English-speaking pioneer settlers of Portage la Prairie, for instance, were fluent in Cree, which "enabled them to associate freely with the French Half-breeds" of White Horse Plain, among whom most of them could claim cousins.[22]

No doubt the métis and mixed-bloods of Rupert's Land spoke this diversity of languages at least in part because they were the descendants of a rich diversity of ancestors. Their maternal forebears included Cree, Ojibwa, and Chipewyan, as well as French Canadians and Scots; their paternal ancestry included not only French and English, but also Orcadian, Scots, Irish, Shetland, and other European strains, notably the Danish ancestry of the numerous progeny of Peter Erasmus, Sr.[23] Baptiste Bruce, for instance, the guide with Dr. John Rae's Arctic expedition of 1848–49, claimed Highland and French as well as Indian descent.[24] Alick Fisher's mother was a métis.[25] Baptiste Robillard, a former guide with the Cumberland boat brigade, was accompanied out on the plains by a son-in-law, John Simpson, said to be the natural son of Thomas Simpson, the ill-fated Arctic explorer.[26] A long roster of names like Baptiste Kennedy attests to the complex mixture of origins among the métis. Among the mixed-bloods, similarly, there were many with French ancestry. "Big Jim" McKay had French antecedents through his mother, who was a Gladu(e).[27] Joe McKay, a "Little Bearskin," married one of the Poitras girls.[28] George Sanderson had two French grandmothers and a niece named Desmarais.[29]

It would be interesting to have a count of all mixed marriages, both *à la façon du pays* (according to the custom of the country) and those solemnized by the clergy. The fragmentary nature of the documentary record makes this impossible, but, even without such comprehensive information, it is evident that many marriages spanned the alleged gulf between the mixed-blood and métis groups. Among the marriages recorded in the Protestant parishes of Red River Settlement, a number involved couples with French and non-French names. It cannot, of course, be assumed that having a Scottish name meant that an individual was a mixed-blood, nor that all métis had French names. Some whose fathers came from Scotland or the Orkneys grew up speaking French and were assimilated to the culture of a French-speaking, Catholic métis mother, as in the case of the Bruce and Dease families.[30] In other cases, seemingly non-French marriages had in them a strong French element, as in the case of James McKay's marriage to Margaret Rowand[31] and Jeanette [Janet] Tate's marriage to Alex Birston.[32] Moreover, dominance in a family of French, Catholic culture did not necessarily exclude non-French influences any more than a dominant non-French culture excluded French or Catholic influences.

A further complication in an attempt to analyze marriages listed in the parish registers is that not all the apparently French–non-French marriages were between métis and mixed-bloods of whatever descent. At least a dozen Swiss–Swiss and a half-dozen French–French (or, more likely, Canadien–Canadienne) unions have been identified. Further, an apparently métis–mixed-blood marriage may turn out to be a Canadian–Scottish marriage. This adds uncertainty to the relevance of seeming cross-marriages to the question of métis–mixed-blood relationships. Norman Kittson, for example, who came from Quebec, married a daughter of Narcisse Marion, also from Quebec.[33]

Unfortunately, it has not been possible to analyze marriages in the Indian settlement, although some of the settlers there, such as Joseph Cook and his children,[34] were of mixed origin. Nor has it been possible to include data from the French-Catholic parishes. The fire that destroyed St. Boniface cathedral in 1860 destroyed most of the early formal records. There is, however, a list in the Provincial Archives of British Columbia of men married by the Catholic missionaries from the time of their arrival in 1818 to February 15, 1831.[35] Among the almost three hundred names listed, nearly twenty are non-French: mostly McDonnells, McLeods, and the like. Undoubtedly, some of their descendants had been assimilated to the culture of métis mothers, though the wives' names are not given.

Other scattered records that survive show that non-French names were, in some instances, changed to a spelling better suited to French pronunciation than the original spelling was. For example, "Sayer" became "Serre"[36] and "McKay" became "Macaille."[37] Similarly, French spelling was sometimes anglicized. Thus, the descendants of Michel Reine (Rayne and other variants), from Strasbourg, became "Wren."[38]

Despite all these gaps and ambiguities, the records in the Hudson's Bay Company and church registers of what appear to be cross-marriages between métis and mixed-bloods in the Protestant parishes of Red River Settlement from 1820 to 1841[39] are of considerable interest (see Table 31.1).

The spelling of names in these records varies from one to another and even from index to entry. It is, moreover, phonetic in character, and in many cases difficult to make out. Some marriage entries in the parish registers differ from those in the company registers and some either do not appear in the latter or are illegible. The usage adopted by the Provincial Archives of Manitoba in its index has therefore been followed.

Some of the men whose names appear in this list may have come from Europe. Certainly men from the Orkneys, Scotland, England, and elsewhere married women of mixed Indian–French ancestry, such as Hugh Gibson from the Orkneys, who married Angélique Chalifoux; Francis Heron and Henry Hallet, Sr., from England, who married Isabella Chalifoux and Catherine Dansee, respectively; meanwhile, Louis Gagnon from France married Jane McKay. John Wasuloski, probably a de Meuron, married Justine Fournier. George Saunderson (Sr.), from Scotland, married Lisset Lagimonère (Lagimodière), both of whose parents came from Quebec. There are other uncertainties in the list, but, imperfect as it is, it suggests that some 30 marriages among a total of 450, probably 5 percent or more, were marriages of men and women with French names to men and women with non-French names. This surely indicates that the métis and mixed-blood communities cannot have been rigidly isolated from each other. Indeed, the Reverend William Cockran bears witness to a French element in the mixture of origins among his parishioners at St. Andrews: In 92 families there were 39 European males and one female. The rest were "Orkney, English, Scotch, French, Welsh, Norwegian, Negro, and Jewish half-breeds."[40]

The Company's register of marriages for 1841 to 1851[41] shows proportionately fewer apparent cross-marriages, only some nine or ten out of a total of more than four hundred, but even this must have meant that there was a certain amount of going and coming between the métis and mixed-blood groups.

Further, marriages recorded in the parish registers were only those formally solemnized by the clergy. Unregistered marriages, *à la façon du pays,* may well have involved a greater proportion of cross-marriages, since the clergy were not, in general, sympathetic to members of their own congregation marrying into a rival sect. Fragmentary evidence of marriages which do not appear to be listed in the official registers has come to light. A paper on James McKay mentions two such cross-marriages: John Rowand to Julie Demarais; Angus McKay to Virginia Boulette.[42] John Moar married Matilda Morrisseau at Lac Seul in 1859.[43] Angus Harper married Peggy La Pierre at Oxford House in 1830,[44] and Joseph Everette married Nancy McKay in 1846.[45] The financial records for Red River Settlement mention one Louise McLeod, widow of Baptiste Larocque.[46] Nancy McKenzie, the discarded country wife of Chief Factor J.G. McTavish, married Pierre Leblanc.[47] One of the Carrière sisters of St. Boniface married Roger Marion (son of Narcisse Marion), while the other became Mrs. Henry Donald Macdonald.[48]

That Protestant anglophones and Catholic francophones did, indeed, associate with each other is made still more clear by reminiscences recorded in W.J. Healy's *Women of Red River*. Father Louis-François Laflèche used to visit the Sinclair house to play the piano there and to exchange music with the Sinclair girls. Everybody in the Settlement seems to have gone to St. Boniface cathedral to hear Sister Lagrave play the organ built by Dr. Duncan, medical officer of the Sixth Regiment of Foot[49] and "Christmas midnight mass at St. Boniface cathedral was always attended by many parties from across the river."[50]

On the St. Boniface side of the river, the Narcisse Marion home was a centre of hospitality that included English-speaking Protestants. Mrs. Henry Donald Macdonald (née Angélique Carrière) related that it was a "great house for dances. . . . Many of the Kildonan people and the other people across the river used to come to our parties, and we went to theirs. We knew them all."[51] Indeed, it was Narcisse Marion who hospitably received the Reverend John Black when he arrived to become the first Presbyterian minister in the Colony, and arranged for him to be taken across the river to the home of the leading Presbyterian, Sheriff Alexander Ross.[52]

Not only did colonists from the different parishes go to each other's parties, but also their children mixed with each other at school. Miss Janet Bannerman recalled that there were several children from well-to-do French-speaking families at her first school, St. John's parochial school. Among them she remembered Joseph and Marguerite Leclair, Emile Bouvette, Ambroise Fisher, Henri Laronde, and Baptiste Beauchemin.[53] By the same token, some anglophone children went to school in St. Boniface, notably James McKay's three children.[54]

Mrs. W.R. Black, granddaughter of Kate and Alexander Sutherland of Kildonan, rounded off her recollections in this way: "I have said so much about the Riels and the Lagimodières because they and the other French-speaking families who were our neighbours are associated with my earliest memories almost as much as the English-speaking families of Red River." Her father, John Sutherland, built a new house across the river after the flood of 1852 swept away the original Sutherland house at Point Douglas. The whole family spoke French as well as English and John Sutherland became a confidant of his French-speaking neighbours and a link between them and the Kildonan settlers.[55]

Business transactions also linked the French- and English-speaking communities: grain from the Carrières' farm at St. Boniface was taken to Robert Tait's mill to be ground;[56] Moise Goulet, a noted plains trader, when illness forced him to retire, sold his whole outfit to A.G.B. Bannatyne;[57] Norbert Welsh, another prominent trader of Irish and Quebec descent, after a disillusioning transaction with "Bobbie" (Robert) Tait, took charge of Bannatyne's cart trains en route to St. Paul and, when he set up in business for himself, dealt with Bannatyne.[58] On January 1, 1846, Peter Garrioch went to see his friend Pascal Berlan[d], about getting some buffalo for him, in company with Peter Pruden and two others.[59] Frederick Bird was apprenticed to a Catholic blacksmith named Bovette.[60]

Although the evidence is scanty, it would appear that métis and mixed-bloods joined together in the great Red River buffalo hunt. Alexander Ross records that in 1840 the captain of the hunt was one Jean-Baptiste Wilkie, "an English half-breed brought up among the French,"

Table 31.1   Apparent Marriages between Métis and Mixed-Bloods

Entry Number	Cross-Marriage, with Date and Reference Number
13	Michael Lambere to Peggy (January 25, 1821 SJM[a] 1820–1835)
18	George Saunderson to Lisset Lajimonière (March 30, 1821 SJM 1820–1835)
23	William Dickson to Justine Pacquette (June 9, 1821 SJM 1820–1835)
36	John Warring to Lydia Fournier (November 11, 1821 SJM 1820–1835)
37	Martin Norte to Catherine Treathey (November 11, 1821 SJM 1820–1835)
58	Joshua Halero to Françoise Laurain (November 18, 1823 SJM 1820–1835)
82	Henry Hallet, Jr., to Catherine Parenteau (October 18, 1824 SJM 1820–1835)
83	David Sandison to Louisa Giboche (October 19, 1824 SJM 1820–1835)
111	John Anderson to Mary (Murray?) [Desmarais] (January 31, 1826 SJM 1820–1835)
122	William Mackay to Julia Chalifoux (August 13, 1826 SJM 1820–1835)
124	James Swain to Margaret Racette (October 3, 1826 SJM 1820–1835)
125	William Birston to Hazelique Marchand (December 8, 1826 SJM 1820–1835)
129	William Bruce to Frances Andre (1827 SJM 1820–1835)
134	Andrew Spence to Susette L'Eunay (October 30, 1827 SJM 1820–1835)
167	George Kipling to Isabella Landrie (November 19, 1828 SJM 1820–1835)
176	Peter Pruden to Josette (Susette) Gothvier (May 7, 1829 SJM 1820–1835)
177	James Monkman to Nancy Shaboyee (May 12, 1829 SJM 1820–1835)

Entry Number	Cross-Marriage, with Date and Reference Number
194	Pierre St. Pierre to Susannah Short (February 8, 1830 SJM 1820–1835)
202	Francis Desmarais to Harriet Spence (date and reference number missing)
212	John Batish Shurdan to Mary Lewis (January 6, 1831 SJM 1820–1835)
215	Aimable Hogue to Margarette Taylor (March 24, 1831 SJM 1820–1835)
221	Hugh Cameron to Mary Jordan (October 26, 1831 SJM 1820–1835)
236	John Aimable McKay to Lizette La Vallee (March 12, 1832 SJM 1820–1835)
253	Charles Desmarais to Harriet Favel (February 7, 1833 SJM 1820–1835)
272	William Spence to Loraine Truche (March 6, 1834 SJM 1820–1835)
287	James Swain to Josette Couteau (January 7, 1835 SJM 1820–1835)
289	William Sutherland to Suzette Truche (December 26, 1834 SJM 1835–1854)
308	James McNab to Sarah Michael (January 21, 1836 SJM 1835–1854)
331	John Swain to Mary Alerie (January 18, 1837 SJM 1835–1854)
332	Baptiste De Champ to Margaret Johnston (January 19, 1837 SAM[b] 1835–1860)
376	Baptist DeMarais to Sophia Erasmus (December 28, 1837 SJM 1835–1860)
390	Andrew Dennet to Mary Martinois (September 25, 1838 SAM 1835–1860)
434	Peter Warren Dease to Elizabeth Chouinard (August 3, 1840 SAM 1835–1860)

Source: Provincial Archives of Manitoba; HBCA, E.4/1b; parish registers for St. John's and St. Andrew's (Church of England Index to Parish Registers, 1820–1900).
[a]sjm — St. John's Marriages
[b]sam — St. Andrew's Marriages

while one of Wilkie's captains was a member of the Hallett family.[61] Ross himself travelled with the hunt that year; the late Miss Sybil Inkster once spoke to me of her relatives going to the buffalo hunt; and Henry Erasmus "accompanied the buffalo hunters on trips to the prairies after meat," of which he got a full share, even though he did not actually take part in the hunt itself.[62] The Reverend John Smithurst wrote in June 1840 that most of his parishioners (all Anglicans) had gone either on the buffalo hunt or with the boat brigades.[63] In June 1845, Peter Garrioch was with the buffalo hunt, which certainly numbered métis families among those in the one hundred tents. Of these, Garrioch mentioned Francis Lauze [Lauzon] and Morin.[64] George Sa[u]nderson, Jr., gives a lively description of the way in which francophone boys were trained to hunt buffalo. He appears to have watched these proceedings. He states explicitly that the "Pochas" [Poitras] family were on one hunt in which his family took part.[65]

Besides the buffalo hunt, the major occupation of the mixed-bloods and métis was freighting, in boat brigades to York Factory and up the Saskatchewan; in the Red River cart trains to the south, to St. Peter's and St. Paul, and west by the Carlton Trail and other traditional overland routes; and in winter with dog trains carrying the winter packet or other urgent freight.

Scattered data about the personnel of boat brigades suggest a mixture of racial origins. In the Hudson's Bay Company's account books the names of some of the tripmen who received advances are listed, especially in the case of advances made at York Factory. The record of advances at York in the summers of 1826 and 1830, for example, gives a mingle-mangle of French and non-French names: In 1826, ten men with French names and four with non-French names received advances. Five others with French names and one uncertain did not have accounts.[66] In 1830, ten French names appear, with four names that originated in the United Kingdom, two mixed names (François Whitford and François Bruce), and one Indian name.[67] It is possible, though not documented, that the crew of each boat was separated on the basis of French or non-French origin.

Information about the personnel of the cart brigades is also limited, but suggests a similar mixture. The *Daily Minnesotan* for July 22, 1854, stated that "Messrs. Kittson, Rolette, Caviller, Grant and others had arrived at Traverse des Sioux with nearly two hundred carts." The same journal published a letter on September 13, 1858, stating that the Sioux had killed two men on the plains, "Busquer" [Louis Bosquet], in charge of Henry Fisher's carts, and John Beads.[68] *The St. Paul Daily Pioneer* reported on July 12, 1870, that the *St. Cloud Times* had recorded 70 arrivals of Red River carts since July 9. They belonged to Gingras and Bannatyne.[69] The voyageurs' signatures to a Hudson's Bay Company contract to make the journey from Fort Garry to St. Peter's in 1850 included nine French names and seven Orcadian and other non-French names.[70]

Only one document has been found containing information about mixed personnel travelling in winter with dog trains. The party left from Île-à-la-Crosse, not from Red River, but it may be significant: Samuel McKenzie, writing on January 15, 1867, noted that "Peter Linklater and Michel Bouvier go with the North Packet to Carlton accompanied by Baptiste Payette and James Wilson."[71] A party was sent from Red River Settlement in 1832 to bring back a herd of sheep from the United States. It too was mixed, having had in it, besides Scots, a French Canadian, and an Irishman, two French half-breeds and two young English half-breeds.[72]

Some information is available about the voyageurs and hunters who accompanied the increasingly numerous expeditions engaged in exploration, surveying, and other official missions in the nineteenth century, to say nothing of pleasure parties travelling on the western plains in "search of adventure and heavy game."[73] John Rae's Arctic searching expedition of 1848–49, for example, included, besides Canadians and Shetlanders, Baptiste Bruce, the guide already mentioned, Baptiste Emelin [Hamelin], Baptiste Fredrique, Xavier Laplante [Antoine Plante],

William Sabiston, and Edmund Stevenson, all natives of the country, and so, presumably, of mixed-blood or métis origin. The natives in his team in 1850–51 were John Fidler, John Hébert dit Fabien (not from Red River), Charles Kennedy, Alexandre Laliberté dit Lachouette, Peter Linklater, Baptiste Marcellais, Baptiste Peltier, and Samuel Sinclair, who was probably a native of the country. However, none of the Rupert's Landers with Rae's 1853–54 expedition had a French name. They were Jacob Beads; John Beads, Jr.; Henry Fidler; and James Johnstone.[74]

Palliser's expedition set out from Red River in 1856 with the following men, besides James Beads, the expedition's servant: John Ferguson, first guide; Henry Hallet[t], second guide; Pierre Beauchamp; Samuel Ballenden[dine]; George Daniel; Baptiste Degrace; Perre Falcon; Amable Hogue; Donald Matheson; [Antoine] Morin; John Foulds; George Morrison; Charles Racette; John Ross; John Simpson; Thomas Sinclair; Robert Sutherland; George Taylor; Joseph Vermette; and Pascal.[75] At least some of Palliser's "Red River contingent" in 1858 were of French origin: among the Red River men who stayed with him at Fort Edmonton during the winter of 1858–59 were Pierre Beauchamp and Baptiste La Graisse, while Chief Factor W.J. Christie, who, on behalf of Palliser, paid off those who returned to Red River, called out "*assez*" to each man when he had taken all the trade goods to which his wage entitled him. Others, such as Todd and Ballenden, were of at least partly non-French origin.[76] In the fall of 1858, James Beads returned from Edmonton to Red River, on hearing that his brother had been killed by the Sioux. When Beads came back in the spring of 1859 he brought with him the redoubtable hunter Jean-Baptiste Vital[le].[77]

When Henry Youle Hind set off in 1858 for the western plains, his party included "six Cree half-breeds, a native of Red River of Scotch descent [John Ferguson?], one Blackfoot half-breed, one Ojibway half-breed, and one French Canadian." It is noticeable that, with one exception, he did not consider the European derivation of the "half-breeds" of sufficient importance to be mentioned.[78]

The Boundary Survey of 1872–76 recruited a troop of native scouts styled "the 49th Rangers," under the command of William Hallett. The deputy commander's name was McDonald, and the names of the three sub-leaders were Gosselin, Lafournais, and Gaddy. The rank and file, too, included men of both French and Scottish or other descent.[79]

Records of sportsmen travelling in the west for pleasure do not always give the names of their voyageurs and hunters, but Hudson's Bay Company accounts show that the Comte de la Guiche had in his employment John Ferguson, Alexis Goulait, and Goulait's son,[80] in June 1851, when he left Red River on a trip to the Rocky Mountains. Lord Dunmore's party set out on August 22, 1862, with Jim McKay (spelled Mackay by Dunmore) as hunter-in-chief, Baptiste Valet as hunter, James Whitford, Pierre (?) and (?) De Charme as buffalo hunters and drivers, and Joe Macdonald as hunter, cook, and driver.[81]

None of this suggests any sharp segregation between Red River mixed-bloods and métis. Indeed, Palliser, describing the expedition's great buffalo hunt in 1858 in the neighbourhood of modern Irricana, Alberta, commented: "The run was magnificent, and there was considerable emulation between my Saskatchewan and my Red River men,"[82] a comment that indicates some solidarity of the group from Red River, regardless of descent, vis-à-vis the group from Lac Ste. Anne; elsewhere, however, Palliser commented on what seemed to him a remarkable difference in energy and progressiveness between the Canadian and French and the Scottish "half-breeds."[83]

Other mixed ventures include the party of emigrants from Red River to the Columbia River, which in 1841 made the extraordinary journey across the plains and through the mountains under James Sinclair's leadership. Its members numbered among them an almost equal balance of men with names suggesting French and non-French origin, all of them speaking either French or English. Table 31.2 shows the list of men in the original agreement between

Table 31.2 Emigrants from Red River Settlement to the Columbia River, in the James Sinclair Party, 1841

François Jacques	James Birston
Julien Bernier	John Cunningham
Baptiste Oreille or Rhelle	Alexander Birston
Pierre Larocque	Archibald Spence
Louis Larocque	François Gagnon
Pierre St. Germain	Joseph Klyne
John Spence	James Flett
Henry Buxton	John Tate
Gonzaque Zastre	Horatio Nelson Calder
William Flett	Toussaint Joyal
Charles McKay	[David Flett]

Source: HBCA, B.235/d/82, p. 56; A.12/7, fo. 392d (agreement between emigrants to the Columbia River and Hudson's Bay Company, dated 31 May 1841); William J. Betts, "From Red River to the Columbia," *The Beaver* (Spring 1971): 50–55.

the emigrants and the Company. Cash advances were made to all but three of these men and to two not listed in the agreement: David Flett and Pierre Larocque, Jr.[84] John Flett is not in either list, but other evidence makes it clear that he was with the party.[85]

In contrast, none (or, at most, one)[86] of the second group of Red River emigrants to the Columbia, who, again under James Sinclair's leadership, went in 1854 to Walla Walla (Washington), seems to have had a French name, at least according to the list given by John V. Campbell, Sinclair's brother-in-law, who, as a lad, was a member of the party.[87]

Of greater importance than evidence of mixed parties freighting, travelling, and emigrating from Red River Settlement is the story of the joint mixed-blood–métis struggle against the claim of the Hudson's Bay Company to the exclusive right to trade in furs in Rupert's Land and, until the License to Trade lapsed in 1859, in the Indian territories beyond. W.L. Morton tells this story admirably in his introduction to *Eden Colvile's Letters, 1849–52*.[88] With a brief lull, while the Sixth Regiment of Foot were stationed at Red River from 1846 to 1848, the mixed-blood–métis population of Red River Settlement agitated throughout the 1840s for recognition of their "rights," as natives of the country, to take part in the fur trade and for redress of other grievances. The Sayer trial in 1849 established that, in practice, the joyful shout of the métis, "Le commerce est libre," was justified, but the natives of Rupert's Land still wanted a voice in the government of the colony.

Evidence in Peter Garrioch's diary of métis–mixed-blood friendship and fraternization has already been cited. Garrioch also makes it clear that the men who banded together in 1845 to resist the imposition by the Council of Assiniboia of an import duty on goods brought in from American territory were of diverse origins: Canadian, Irish, métis, and mixed-blood. Besides Peter Garrioch, they were Peter Hayden, Alexis Goulet, St. Germain (which Garrioch spelled Chagerma), Dominique Ducharme, Henry Cook, and Charles Laroque.[89]

On August 29, 1845, a larger group of mixed-blood and métis traders submitted a list of questions to Governor and Chief Factor Alexander Christie concerning their rights (see Table 31.3).[90] In another version of this list of signatures, given by Alexander Begg in his *History of the North-West,* four of these names are omitted: Pierre Laverdure, Edward Harmon [or Harman], James Monkman, and Edward [Antoine] Desjarlais, Sr.[91] Two others were added: Adal Trottier and Charles Hole [possible Houle]. Again, this is a not uneven mixture of métis and mixed-bloods.

In 1846, two parallel petitions, one in French and one in English, were drafted at a meeting held on February 26 in Andrew McDermot's house. The petitions contained demands for free trade and representative government. James Sinclair carried both of them to England, where Alexander K. Isbister submitted them to the imperial government.[92] As W.L. Morton noted: "The settlement was an Anglo-French colony, a European-Indian community, and the métis, excluded from public office like the English half-breeds, were only demanding that the

Table 31.3   Signatories to the Letter to Governor C.F. Alexander Christie, dated 29 August 1845

James Sinclair	Peter Garrioch
Baptiste Laroque	Jack Spence
Thomas Logan	Alexis Goulait [Goulet]
Pierre Laverdure	Antoine Morin
Joseph Monkman	William McMillan
Baptiste Wilkie	Louis Letendre [dit Batoche]
Baptiste Farman (Famian)	Robert Montour
Edward Harman	Jack Anderson
John Dease	James Monkman
Henry Cook	Antoine Desjarlais, Snr.
William Bird	Thomas McDermot
John Vincent	

Source: HBCA, D.5/15, fos. 139a–139b; PAM MGZ 135, "Red River Correspondence"; Alexander Begg, *History of the North-West,* 3 vols. (Toronto: Hunter, Rose and Co., 1894–95), 1: 261–62. Begg omits Montour but adds Adel Trottier and Charles Hole.

institutions of the Colony should reflect its ethnic composition. In so doing they spoke for the English half-breeds as well as for themselves, as they were to do again in 1869."[93] As well, "English half-breeds" such as James Sinclair spoke for their métis associates — as, for instance, in the Sayer trial, at which Sinclair represented the four métis defendants and their armed colleagues who had surrounded the court house.[94]

The younger generation of mixed-bloods and métis was frustrated and restless. The demand for representation on the council and for a free trade in furs was a demand for an outlet for ambition, energy, and enterprise.[95]

The métis organized a "council of the nation" and pressed upon Sir George Simpson still another petition when he arrived in the Settlement in June 1849. Sent with a covering letter from Sinclair, dated June 14, 1849, this petition was signed by William McMalen [McMillan], Louis Rielle [Riel Sr.], Pascal Berland, Baptiste Fairjeu, Baptiste Laroque, Antoine Morein, Louis Letendre, Solomon Amelin, and Urbain Delorme.[96] A letter presented to Simpson when he was again in Red River Settlement in the summer of 1850 was signed by William McMillan, Solomon Amelin, Louis Riel, and eighteen others. They demanded that Recorder Thom should go and that they should have representation on the Council "chosen from our nation by ourselves."[97]

Yet another petition in 1851 reached the Company via the Aborigines' Protection Society and the Colonial Office asking "that Red River be granted British liberty, a Governor appointed by the Crown, a judge similarly appointed and able to speak English and French, power in the Governor to appoint Councillors in an emergency, the dismissal of Councillors who had forfeited public confidence or been subservient to the Company, and the removal of Thom to some other British colony." The 540 signatures were attested by five leading métis.[98]

These data, fragmentary and incomplete as they are, cannot be conclusive, but, as far as they go, they do suggest an intermingling of mixed-bloods and métis, fellow feeling and cooperation between the two groups, not separation or hostility. This impression is strengthened by yet another petition sent in 1857 to the Legislature of Canada "from Donald McBeath and others[,] inhabitants and Natives of the Settlement situated on the Red River, in the Assiniboine Country. . . ."[99]

This petition was promulgated by a mixed-blood, "Captain" William Kennedy, of Arctic fame, who visited Red River in 1857 as an emissary of Canadian commercial interests. It bore the signatures of 119 men with French names or known to be French-speaking, as well as fourteen more who may have been of French origin, and two with mixed names, out of a total of 511, including a number with Indian or probably Indian names. Though not all the apparently French signatures were those of métis — that of Narcisse Marion, for example — the francophone roster is considerable. This is surprising, since, according to Alvin C. Gluek, Jr., the Catholic clergy had discouraged their parishioners from signing the petition.[100]

As late as 1869–70, a contemporary observer, Walter Traill, commented: "The natives [of Red River Settlement], both English and French, though not resenting the newcomers from the newly formed Dominion, wonder why it is that they . . . should be slighted by Canadians who are coming to rule them." And again: "If the Canadian Government . . . had recognized the natives, both English and French, both would have given their loyal support."[101]

"Hostility" reported by rival clerics, if it existed, may well have reflected deference to the missionaries' wishes and pressures. However, at least one missionary, that turbulent priest Father G.-A. Belcourt, cooperated closely with Sinclair and Isbister. Besides Sinclair, Thomas McDermot, John Anderson, and Peter Garrioch attended the meeting on February 26, 1846, at which Belcourt presided, speaking in French. It appears that they were the only English-speaking people at this meeting.[102]

An observation made by Eugene Bourgeau, botanical collector with the Palliser expedition, is further evidence of mutual métis–mixed-blood friendship. A compatriot, Ernest St. C. Cosson, the eminent French botanist, said of Bourgeau: "Par l'influence que lui donnait sa double qualité de Français et de catholique, il se concilia l'amitié de ces peuplades [the natives of the West], qui ont gardé le souvenir de notre domination, comprennent notre langue, et sont restées fidèles aux principaux dogmes de notre religion."[103] [*Editor's Translation:* Because of the influence he has as both a Frenchman and a Catholic, he has won the friendship of these natives of the west, who remember our rule, understand our language, and have remained loyal to the principal beliefs of our religion.] This was the man whose account of the Sunday services held by Palliser (a staunch Protestant) led Charles Gay to write in *Le Tour du Monde:* "Touchant accord que celui de ces croyances si diverses, ailleurs si fécondes en antagonismes et en rivalités, se confondant, au pied des montagnes rocheuses, dans une même bonne foi et dans une commune simplicité!"[104] [*Editor's Translation:* Religious beliefs, so full of divergences leading to conflicts and rivalries, came together, at the foot of the Rocky mountains, into a common good faith and simplicity.]

Palliser, too, noted this harmony. The métis Catholics from Lac Ste. Anne asked leave "to attend Divine worship," despite the fact that the prayers read for the Red River men, who "belonged to the Church of England," were from that Church's service. Palliser, therefore, through an interpreter, "conducted the lessons and half the prayers in Cree." He mentioned "this circumstance to show the respectful tendency and absence of bigotry of these men, in their appreciation of Divine service."[105]

If, then, even religious differences did not go very deep, were there important cleavages in Red River society? The answer must surely be yes. There were two fundamental divisions,[106] but these were not divisions between métis and mixed-blood.

The first was a division between the well-educated and well-to-do gentry, the officers and retired officers of the Hudson's Bay Company and those of their progeny who had achieved respectability, the clergy, and the prosperous merchants, in contrast to the mass of unlettered, unpropertied natives of the country — the "engagés" of the Hudson's Bay Company and of the Nor'Westers before them and their descendants. James Sinclair, for example, was recognized as a "gentleman"; he was a close friend of his British-born son-in-law, Dr. William Cowan, an officer of the Hudson's Bay Company, as well as of his brother, Chief Factor William Sinclair II, and even of Sir George Simpson, despite his battles with the Company.[107] This set him apart from the ordinary tripmen, whom he employed on his freighting ventures. The gap was one occasioned by ambition, affluence, education, and social status as against poverty and the inferior status of employees or, at best, of hunters, petty traders, or small farmers.

The second was the division between the professional farmer and the hunter and plains trader, between the sedentary population and those to whom the freedom of a wandering life out on the plains was more important than economic security and material comfort. This was the irreconcilable cleavage, so convincingly analyzed in George F.G. Stanley's classic, *The Birth of Western Canada,*[108] and described in Goulet's, Welsh's, and Sanderson's reminiscences.

As Jennifer Brown concludes in *Strangers in Blood,* the "half-breed" descendants of the men of both the North West and Hudson's Bay Companies "combined to define and defend common interests and finally to take military action in the Rebellions of 1869 and 1885."[109] Western Canada, as we know it today, was indeed born of conflict, conflict not between métis and mixed-blood, but between a wandering, free life and settlement; a conflict between agriculturalists, especially the flood of newcomers in search of landed property and wealth, and the old way of life that both métis and mixed-bloods had had in common with their Indian cousins, a way of life based on adjustment to the natural environment and the shared use of the free gifts of nature. That way of life was doomed with the coming of surveyors, fences, police, organized government, settlers, and private rights of property in real estate and natural resources.[110] With it went the prosperity and independence of all but a small elite of métis and mixed-bloods alike.

NOTES

1. Here the term *mixed-blood* is used (in spite of its biological ineptitude) instead of Pannekoek's term *country-born* to denote anglophone Rupert's Landers of hybrid Indian and white ancestry. After all, the children of Jean-Baptiste and Julie Lagimodière and those of Kate and Alexander Sutherland and other Selkirk settlers were country-born even though they had no Indian ancestry. A possible alternative might be to use *métis* with a qualifying adjective, as Alexander Morris did: "The *Metis* who were present at the [North West] Angle [of the Lake of the Woods] and who, with one accord, whether of French or English origin." (*The Treaties of Canada with the Indians of Manitoba and the North-West Territories* [Toronto: Belfords, Clarke and Co., 1880], 51). Similarly, Isaac Cowie wrote of one man being an Irish and another a French Métis in his book, *The Company of Adventurers: A Narrative of Seven Years in the Service of the Hudson's Bay Company* (Toronto: William Briggs, 1913), 191, and George F.G. Stanley of "English Métis" in "Indian Raid at Lac la Biche," *Alberta History* 24 (Summer 1976) 3: 25. It seems simpler, however, to use *mixed-blood* for the anglophones of mixed ancestry as a reasonably close equivalent of *métis* for the francophones of mixed descent.

2. Frits Pannekoek, "The Rev. Griffiths Owen Corbett and the Red River Civil War of 1869–70," *Canadian Historical Review* 57 (June 1976) 2: 134.

3. Guillaume Charette, *Vanishing Spaces: Memoirs of Louis Goulet* (Winnipeg: Éditions Bois-Brulés, 1980; translated by Ray Ellenwood, from the original French edition, *L'Espace de Louis Goulet,* 1976), 59.

4. W.J. Healy, *Women of Red River* (Winnipeg: Russell, Lang and Co. Ltd., 1923), 88.

5. Personal conversation, Winnipeg, May 22, 1973.

6. George William Sanderson, "'Through Memories [*sic*] Windows' as Told to Mary Sophia Desmarais, by her Uncle, George William Sanderson (1846–1936)," 2, Provincial Archives of Manitoba (hereinafter cited as PAM) MGI/A107.

7. John Palliser wrote from Edmonton of "the black looks of the hostile divines. I understand that sometimes hostilities have proceeded further than mere looks." (HBCA, D.5/49, 1859 [2], fos. 245–46). I am grateful to the Hudson's Bay Company for kind permission to use material in its archives. The Rev. John Smithurst wrote in his journal: "We see the eagle of Rome watching to seize as its prey these precious souls." (PAC, MG19, E6, vol. 2, June 12, 1841). Father A.G. Morice, in his *Histoire de l'Église catholique dans l'Ouest canadien* (St. Boniface et Montréal: Granger Frères, 1915), 1:216, commented on the arrival of the Methodist missionaries that they "allaient se mesurer plutôt avec les enseignements de la Robe Noire et les pratiques religieuses que ses néophytes tenaient d'elles, qu'avec les ténèbres épaisses et l'immoralité révoltante dans lesquelles croupissaient encore plusieurs des nations barbares du Canada central" (i.e., western Canada). There are many similar passages throughout the work.

8. Since the European origins of mixed-bloods included Highland and Lowland Scottish, Orcadian, Shetland, Swiss, Danish, and other strains, as well as French, the commonly used description, *English,* scarcely seems appropriate.

9. W.L. Morton, ed., *Alexander Begg's Red River Journal and Other Papers Relative to the Red River Resistance of 1869–1870* (Toronto: Champlain Society, 1956), 12.

10. Alexander Ross, *The Red River Settlement* (London: Smith, Elder and Co., 1856; reprinted Edmonton: Hurtig, 1972), 80–81. References are to the Hurtig reprint.

11. Ibid., 79.

12. Cited in Rhoda R. Gilman, Carolyn Gilman, and Deborah M. Stultz, *The Red River Trails: Oxcart Routes between St. Paul and the Selkirk Settlement, 1820–1870* (St. Paul: Minnesota Historical Society, 1979), 14. This "polyglot jabber" was, no doubt, Bungay, which the late Mrs. J.L. Doupe told me was widely used when she was a child in Winnipeg.

13. J.A. Gilfillan, "A Trip through the Red River Valley in 1864," *North Dakota Historical Quarterly* 1 (October 1926 to July 1927) 4: 37–40.

14. J.G. Kohl, *Kitchi-Gami: Wanderings round Lake Superior,* trans. Lascelles Wraxall (London: Chapman and Hall, 1860; reprinted Minneapolis: Ross and Haines, 1956), 260. I am indebted to Jacqueline Peterson for this reference.

15. Charette, *Vanishing Spaces,* 119.

16. Ibid., 116.

17. Television broadcast, Ontario TV, 1981. "The Last Buffalo Hunter," featuring Norbert Welsh.

18. Barbara Benoit, "The Mission at Île-à-la-Crosse," *The Beaver* (Winter 1980): 46.

19. Inkster papers, typescript account of the career of "The Honourable James McKay — Deer Lodge," 1 and 5, PAM. See also Allan Turner, "James McKay," *Dictionary of Canadian Biography,* ed. Francess G. Halpenny and

Jean Hamlin, 11 vols. (Toronto: University of Toronto Press, 1972) 10: 473–75; N. Jaye Goossen, "A Wearer of Moccasins: The Honourable James McKay of Deer Lodge," annotated typescript published in substance in *The Beaver* (Autumn 1978): 44–53; and Mary McCarthy Ferguson, *The Honourable James McKay of Deer Lodge* (Winnipeg: published by the author, 1972).

20. Cowie, *Company of Adventurers*, 191–92.

21. Ibid., 192.

22. A.C. Garrioch, *The Correction Line* (Winnipeg: Stovel Co. Ltd., 1933), 200–1. I am indebted to Mr. Brian Gallagher for this reference.

23. Irene M. Spry, "A Note on Peter Erasmus's Family Background" and "Family Tree," in Peter Erasmus, *Buffalo Days and Nights* (Calgary: Glenbow-Alberta Institute, 1976), 303–5, 324–28, and end papers.

24. E.E. Rich, ed., *John Rae's Correspondence with the Hudson's Bay Company on Arctic Exploration, 1844–1855* (London: Hudson's Bay Record Society [HBRS], 1953), 353–54.

25. Cowie, *Company of Adventurers*, 220.

26. Ibid., 348. It is possible that Cowie was mistaken; Sir George Simpson also had a son called John.

27. Inkster Papers, "James McKay," 1, PAM.

28. Mary Weekes, *The Last Buffalo Hunter, As Told by Norbert Welsh* (New York: Thomas Nelson and Sons, 1939; Toronto: Macmillan of Canada, 1945), 23.

29. Sanderson, "Memories," title and p. 8, and list of marriages, Table 1, p. 101, PAM, MGI/A107.

30. Lionel Dorge, "The Métis and Canadian Councillors of Assiniboia," *The Beaver* (Summer, Autumn, and Winter 1974), especially Part 3, 56–57. Douglas N. Sprague, in his research on Sir John A. Macdonald and the métis, has analyzed cross-marriages on the basis of the 1870 census, from which he has been able to trace all marriages back for three generations.

31. Goossen, "James McKay," 47.

32. Charles A. Throssell wrote the following note on January 20, 1966: "John Tate — Who's [sic] only daughter, Jeanette, married Alex Burston about 1830. . . . They were both of French Canadian descent." This note was sent by Alex Burston's daughter, Mrs. Mary Burston Throssell, to Mr. William J. Betts of Bremerton, Washington. He very kindly sent me a copy on November 14, 1971. An entry in St. John's parish register states that Alex Burston [Birston] married Janet Tate on June 28, 1832, No. 237, St. John's Marriage Register, 1820–1835.

33. W.L. Morton, Introduction in E.E. Rich, ed., *London Correspondence inward from Eden Colvile, 1849–1852* (London: HBRS, 1956), xiv, l, 246.

34. HBCA, E.4/1b, also recorded in PAM, Parish records. Some cross-marriages are recorded in the Indian church register of marriages, such as that of Sally Erasmus to Antoine Kennedy, December 23, 1847 (no. 57d), HBCA E.4/2.

35. Provincial Archives of British Columbia (hereinafter cited as PABC), Add Mss 345, File 135.

36. Les Archives de la Société historique de St. Boniface has the record of the marriage of "Guillaume Serre," alias William Sayer. I am indebted to Lionel Dorge for a copy of this record.

37. Dorge, "Métis and Canadian Councillors," Part 3, 57.

38. PABC, Wren Family papers; Spry, "Note on Family Background," in Erasmus, *Buffalo Days and Nights*.

39. HBCA, E.4/1b and 2, and PAM microfilm of parish registers. There are some discrepancies between these two sets of records. Marriages of Barbara Gibson and Isabella Spence to James Louis have been omitted because James Louis was the son of a mulatto from New England, not, as might be supposed, of French extraction. A record of the marriage of Margaret Louis [or Lewis] is omitted for the same reason (HBCA, E.4/1b, fo. 221, and A.38/8, fo. 36). I am indebted to the keeper of the Hudson's Bay Company Archives for this information. Nancy Budd's marriage to Michel Reine is also omitted because he was from Strasbourg.

40. John E. Foster, "Missionaries, Mixed-bloods and the Fur Trade: Four Letters of the Rev. William Cockran, Red River Settlement, 1830–1833," *Western Canadian Journal of Anthropology* 3 (1972) 1: 110 and 112.

41. HBCA, E.4/2.

42. Goossen, "James McKay," 48.

43. The marriage contract is reproduced in Sylvia Van Kirk, *"Many Tender Ties": Women in Fur-Trade Society, 1670–1870* (Winnipeg: Watson and Dwyer Publishing Ltd., 1980), 118.

44. Ibid., 117–19.

45. HBCA, B.239/Z/39, fo. 22.

46. HBCA, B.235/c/1, fo. 248d.

47. Van Kirk, *"Many Tender Ties,"* 188.

48. Healy, *Women of Red River*, 119.

49. Ibid., 34–35.
50. Ibid., 208.
51. Ibid., 119.
52. Ibid., 68.
53. Ibid., 87.
54. Ferguson, *James McKay*, 60.
55. Healy, *Women of Red River*, 59 and 61.
56. Ibid., 119.
57. Charette, *Vanishing Spaces*, 70.
58. Weekes, *Last Buffalo Hunter*, 35–45, 57, 60–72, and 201–2.
59. Garrioch Journal, January 1, 1846, PAM.
60. Sanderson, "Memories," 12, PAM, MGI/A107.
61. Ross, *Red River Settlement*, 248 and 271.
62. Erasmus, *Buffalo Days and Nights*, 6.
63. PAC, MG19 E6, vol. 2, journal entry for June 21, 1840.
64. Garrioch Journal, June 10 and 16, October 1 and 2, 1845, PAM.
65. Sanderson, "Memories," 3, PAM, MG9/A107.
66. HBCA, B.235/d/26, fo. 2d, 1826.

John Ashburn
J. Bts [*sic*] Boisvert (no account)
Alexis Bonamis dit Lesperence
Rennes Cardinal (no account)
Antoine Deschamps (no account)
Antoine Dagenais
Leon Dupuis
Toussaint Joyal
Louis La Rive
Jacques Le'Tang (no account)

Louis Lapierre dit Brilliant
François Laframboise (no account)
William Malcolm
Simon Martin (no account)
Pierre Papin
Medard Poitras
David Scott
Jacques St. Denis
David Sandison
Louis Thyfault [*sic*]

67. HBCA, B.235/d/44, 1830.

François Savoyard
Carriole Lagrasse
Pierre Savoyard
James Birston
Antoine Lambert
Alex Carrier
François Whitford
François Bruce
Matouche

Henry House [Howse?]
Joseph Savoyard
Richd Favel
Bte Boyer
George Kipling
Charles Larocque
Amable Lafort
Joseph Delorme

Cowie wrote that Baptiste Kennedy was a guide in a brigade with steersmen from Red River Settlement named Cameron, Spence, Cunningham, and William Prince, an Indian (*Company of Adventurers*, 117).
68. Minnesota Historical Society, St. Paul.
69. St. Paul Public Library, Minnesota.
70. PABC, Add Mss 345, vol. 2, file 70.
71. HBCA, B.27/c/1, fo. 20.
72. Robert Campbell, "A Journey to Kentucky for Sheep: From the Journal of Robert Campbell, 1832–1833," *North Dakota Historical Quarterly* 1 (October 1926 to July 1927) 1: 36.
73. A phrase used by Palliser of the two friends who joined him on his expedition, Captain Arthur Brisco and William Roland Mitchell (Irene M. Spry, ed., *The Papers of the Palliser Expedition* [Toronto: Champlain Society, 1968], 338–39).
74. Rich, ed., *John Rae's Correspondence*, 350–78.
75. Spry, ed., *Palliser Papers*, 37 n.1.
76. Ibid., 340–41.
77. Ibid., 403.
78. *North-West Territory: Report on the Assiniboine and Saskatchewan Exploring Expedition* (Toronto: John Lovell, 1859), 39.
79. John E. Parsons, *West on the 49th Parallel* (New York: William Morrow and Co., 1963), 53.

80. HBCA, B.235/a/15, Upper Fort Garry Journal, June 16, 1851.

81. "Log of the Wanderers on the Prairies in Search of Buffalo Bear Deer &c in 1862," ms. in the possession of Lord Dunmore.

82. Spry, ed., *Palliser Papers*, 258.

83. Ibid., 169.

84. HBCA, A.12/7, fo. 392d. Agreement between emigrants to the Columbia River and Hudson's Bay Company, dated May 31, 1841, and HBCA, B.235/d/82, fo. 30. 56. cash paid to emigrants. Whether there were two Pierre Larocques is not clear. The accounts list Pierre Larocque Jr., the agreement simply Pierre Larocque.

85. William J. Betts, "From Red River to the Columbia," *The Beaver* (Spring 1971): 50–55, reproduces John Flett's own account of the journey.

86. Toussaint Joyal may have been with the second group of emigrants.

87. John V. Campbell, "The Sinclair Party — An Emigration Overland along the Old Hudson's Bay Company Route from Manitoba to the Spokane Country in 1854," *Washington Historical Quarterly* 8 (July 1916): 187–201.

88. See also Irene M. Spry, "Free Men and Free Trade," unpublished paper submitted to the Canadian Historical Association meeting held in Saskatoon in 1979, and "The 'Private Adventurers' of Rupert's Land," in John E. Foster, ed., *The Developing West: Essays on Canadian History in Honor of Lewis H. Thomas* (Edmonton: University of Alberta Press, 1983), 49–70.

89. Garrioch Journal, March 1 and 9, 1845, PAM. See also E.H. Oliver, *The Canadian North-West: Its Early Development and Legislative Records*, vol. 1 (Ottawa: Government Printing Bureau, 1914), 315, which lists Charles Laurance, Dominique Ducharme, Peter Garrioch, Henry Cook, Peter Hayden, and Alexis Goulait as petitioners to the Council. It does not include St. Germain.

90. Christie to Simpson, September 5, 1845, enclosing the letter from Sinclair et al. dated August 29, 1845, HBCA, D.5/15, fos. 139a, 139b. Sinclair's letter is reproduced in Lewis G. Thomas, ed., *The Prairie West to 1905* (Toronto: Oxford University Press, 1975), 56–57, with Christie's reply, 58–59. No source is given and the spelling of some of the names is different from that in the copy enclosed by Christie. Another copy of the letter is in PAM, RRS/RRC, 1845–47.

91. Alexander Begg, *History of the North-West*, 3 vols. (Toronto: Hunter, Rose, 1894–95), 261–62.

92. *Correspondence Relating to the Red River Settlement and The Hudson's Bay Company*, British Parliamentary Papers, vol. 18, 1849, Colonies, Canada (Shannon: Irish Universities Press, 1969).

93. Morton, Introduction in Rich, ed., *Eden Colvile's Letters*, lxxxix.

94. A good account of the trial and of the role of Sinclair and Garrioch is given in Morton, Introduction in Rich, ed., *Eden Colvile's Letters*, lxxxii–lxxxvi, and another in Roy St. George Stubbs, *Four Recorders of Rupert's Land* (Winnipeg: Peguis Publishers, 1967), 26–29.

95. Morton, Introduction in Rich, ed., *Eden Colvile's Letters*, lxxxix.

96. Ibid., citing HBCA, D.5/25, June 2, 1849, enclosed in Sinclair to Simpson, June 14, 1849.

97. Ibid., p.c., citing HBCA, D.5/28, June 1, 1850; HBCA, A.13/4, fos. 519–20; and A.12/5, Simpson, July 5, 1850.

98. Ibid., pp. cvii–cviii, citing HBCA, A.13/5, enclosure in a letter from F. Peel, C.O., to Pelly, dated December 30, 1851. Attempts to find the signatures in HBCA, the Public Record Office, London, England, and the Archives of the Aborigines' Protection Society, Rhodes House, Oxford, England, have failed, so it has not been possible to discover the origins of the signatories.

99. The original petition with all the signatures is in PAC, RG 14-C-I, vol. 64, petition no. 1176, received and filed May 22, 1857. Oddly, the signature of Roderick Kennedy is not among the 511 signatures attached to the petition, though he presented it to the Legislature, and his name is the only one given in the Select Committee version. It was printed in *The Toronto Globe* for June 12, 1857, and as Appendix 15 of the *Report of the Select Committee of the House of Commons on the Hudson's Bay Company, 1857*.

100. Alvin C. Gluek, Jr., *Minnesota and the Manifest Destiny of the Canadian Northwest* (Toronto: University of Toronto Press, 1965), 123–25.

101. Mae Atwood, ed., *In Rupert's Land: Memoirs of the Walter Traill* (Toronto: McClelland and Stewart, 1970), 204 and 208. Sanderson wrote of the Rising when he was captured by Riel's men, when he was with the Portage party: "I was not afraid of the French half-breeds . . . I knew Riel and many of his adherents, in fact I was related to some of his leaders" (PAM, MG9/A107, Part 2, 1).

102. Garrioch Journal, February 26, 1846, PAM.

103. *Bulletin de la Société botanique de France* vol. 13, 1866, liv, cited in Spry, ed., *Palliser Papers*, xxviii n. 5. The number of the volume is given incorrectly in this citation.

104. "Le Capitaine Palliser et l'Exploration des Montagnes Rocheuses, 1857–1859," *Le Tour du Monde: Nouveau Journal des Voyages* (Paris: 1861), 287, cited in Spry, ed., *Palliser Papers,* xxviii.

105. Spry, ed., *Palliser Papers,* 238 n.5.

106. A third cleavage might be identified, namely, the generation gap between the children and grandchildren of the well-established Principal Settlers of the colony and their aging precursors. See Morton, Introduction in Rich, ed., *Eden Colvile's Letters,* 1xxxix.

107. This impression is derived from a wide range of material by and concerning both James Sinclair and William Sinclair II, including Journal of Dr. William Cowan, PAC, MG19 E8.

108. George F.G. Stanley, *The Birth of Western Canada* (Toronto: University of Toronto Press, 1960; 1963; reprinted from the original edition, Longmans, Green and Co. Ltd., 1936).

109. Jennifer S.H. Brown, *Strangers in Blood: Fur Trade Company Families in Indian Country* (Vancouver and London: University of British Columbia Press, 1980), 173.

110. Irene M. Spry, "The Tragedy of the Loss of the Commons in Western Canada," in *As Long as the Sun Shines and Water Flows: A Reader in Canadian Native Studies,* ed. Ian A.L. Getty and Antoine S. Lussier (Vancouver: University of British Columbia Press, 1983), 203–28.

Topic Fourteen

The Pacific Coast

These men were members of the first elected assembly of the colony of Vancouver Island, which met in 1856.

In the early 19th century, North West Company traders, operating out of Montreal, reached the Fraser and Columbia River basins. Subsequently, the Hudson's Bay Company, after its union with the North West Company in 1821, extended fur-trading operations from Fort Vancouver on the Columbia (opposite present-day Portland, Oregon) all along the north Pacific coast, including the area of the present-day American states of Washington and Oregon. The extension of the boundary between present-day Canada and the United States along the 49th parallel to the Pacific coast in 1846, however, forced the Hudson's Bay Company to leave Fort Vancouver. It established its new commercial headquarters at Victoria, on Vancouver Island. This new society was initially a cultural mix of First Nations and Europeans before it became predominantly non–Native. Sylvia Van Kirk looks at five interracial families in "Tracing the Fortunes of Five Founding Families of Victoria," an article that complements her essay in Topic Two on Indian women in fur trade society. Why did female descendants of prominent fur trade families adjust more successfully to the new British American society than their male counterparts?

In 1858, the discovery of gold on the Fraser River opened up the mainland. Britain organized the separate colony of British Columbia that same year, to secure British control. James Douglas, the governor of Vancouver Island, became governor of the new mainland colony as well, establishing British institutions and making New Westminster the new capital. In 1866, the two colonies were united to become the colony of British Columbia. In "Hardy Backwoodsmen, Wholesome Women, and Steady Families: Immigration and the Construction of a White Society in Colonial British Columbia, 1849–1871," Adele Parry describes the ideal immigrants sought for the new settler society of British Columbia. Why did the attempt to establish the desired "stable settler society of the imperialists' dreams," fail to materialize?

The maritime fur trade is reviewed in Robin Fisher's *Contact and Conflict: Indian–European Relations in British Columbia, 1774–1890*, 2nd ed. (Vancouver: University of British Columbia Press, 1992), and James R. Gibson's *Otter Skins, Boston Ships, and China Goods: The Maritime Fur Trade of the Northwest Coast, 1785–1841* (Montreal/Kingston: McGill-Queen's University Press, 1992). R. Cole Harris's *The Resettlement of British Columbia* (Vancouver: University of British Columbia Press, 1996) reviews First Nations and newcomer interchanges. The impact of disease is examined in Robert Boyd, *The Coming of the Spirit of Pestilence: Introduced Infectious Diseases and Population Decline among Northwest Coast Indians 1774–1874* (Vancouver: University of British Columbia Press, 1999). A *Stol:lo Coast Salish Historical Atlas*, ed. Keith Thor Carlson (Vancouver: Douglas & McIntyre, 2001) provides an extraordinary review of the history of the Stol:lo people of the lower Fraser River in southwestern British Columbia, and northwestern Washington. For the early history of the Hudson's Bay Company on the Columbia, and along the Pacific Coast, see Dorothy Nafus Morrison's *Outpost: John McLoughlin and the Far Northwest* (Portland, Oregon: Oregon Historical Society Press, 1999, 2004).

Margaret A. Ormsby has written a valuable introduction to *Fort Victoria Letters, 1846–51* (Winnipeg: Hudson's Bay Record Society, 1979), edited by Hartwell Bowsfield. *The Fort Langley Journals, 1827–30*, ed. Morag MacLachlan (Vancouver: University of British Columbia Press, 1998) contain rich ethnographic information. In "The Colonization of Vancouver Island, 1849–1858," *B.C. Studies* 96 (Winter 1992–93): 3–40, Richard Mackie reviews the colony's first decade, and in *Trading beyond the Mountains: The British Fur Trade on the Pacific, 1793–1843* (Vancouver: University of British Columbia Press, 1996), he examines the precolonial period. Clarence G. Karr looks at James Douglas, the early governor, in "James Douglas: The Gold Governor in the Context of His Times," in *The Company on the Coast*, ed. E. Blanche Norcross (Nanaimo: Nanaimo Historical Society, 1983): 56–78. Very valuable for an understanding of lives of both James and Amelia Douglas is their joint biography by John Adams, *Old Square-Toes and His Lady* (Victoria, BC: Horsdal & Schubart Publishers Limited, 2001). On the history of coal mining in the early settlement period, see Lynne Bowen's *Three Dollar Dreams* (Lantzville, BC: Oolichan Books, 1987) and John Douglas Belshaw's "Mining Technique and Social Division on Vancouver Island, 1848–1900," *British Journal of Canadian Studies* 1 (1986): 45–65. Tina Loo recounts the history of law and order in British Columbia in *Making Law, Order, and Authority in British Columbia, 1821–1871* (Toronto: University of Toronto Press, 1994). Adele Perry expands upon the themes of her article in *On the Edge of Empire: Gender, Race and the Making of British Columbia 1849–1871* (Toronto: University of Toronto Press, 2001).

The standard, but now rather dated, history of the area is Margaret Ormsby's *British Columbia: A History* (Toronto: Macmillan, 1958). It should be supplemented by Jean Barman, *The West beyond the West: A History of British Columbia*, rev. ed. (Toronto: University of Toronto Press, 1996) and Hugh J.M. Johnston, ed., *The Pacific Province: A History of British Columbia* (Vancouver: Douglas and McIntyre, 1996). *British Columbia: Historical Readings*, eds. W. Peter Ward and Robert A.J. McDonald (Vancouver: Douglas and McIntyre, 1981) contains several valuable essays on early British Columbia history. A valuable well-illustrated account of the province's entire history is Patricia E. Roy and John Herd Thompson's *British Columbia: Land of Promises* (Don Mills, ON: Oxford University Press, 2005).

WEBLINKS

Pacific Explorations
http://www.library.ubc.ca/prdla/explore.html

A database of primary-source records of early voyages of exploration of the Pacific Coast.

The Colonization of Vancouver Island
http://www.canadiana.org/ECO/mtq?id=7a8668f9e0&doc=61818

A digitized copy of correspondence from the chair of the Hudson's Bay Company with regard to the colonization of Vancouver Island.

The Oregon Treaty, 1846
http://www.ccrh.org/comm/river/docs/ortreaty.htm

Text of the Oregon Treaty of 1846 between the United States and the United Kingdom.

1862 Smallpox Epidemic in Victoria
http://web.uvic.ca/vv/student/smallpox

This site details the historical events of the 1862 smallpox epidemic in Victoria, and the reactions of people with religious, medical, and governmental backgrounds to it.

Historical Censuses of Vancouver Island
http://history.mala.bc.ca

Personal directories, property registries, and censuses for communities on Vancouver Island from about the time of Confederation to several decades afterwards.

Queen Victoria's Victoria
http://web.uvic.ca/vv/

This website describes with vivid pictures and detail daily life in the city of Victoria, during the reign of its namesake.

British Columbia Landscapes
http://www.royalbcmuseum.bc.ca/exhibits/journeys/english/index.html

An interactive site detailing the widely varying environments of the province of British Columbia. Such challenging physical geography had great influence on settling patterns.

Article Thirty-Two

Tracing the Fortunes of Five Founding Families of Victoria

Sylvia Van Kirk

A recent popular history of Victoria is entitled *More English Than the English*.[1] While this might symbolize the ethnic aspiration of this city, it obscures the actual mixed-race origins of many of its founding families. Only recently has there been much pride or interest in the fact that among the most prominent of Victoria's founders were families who were also of First Nations origin. This article explores why this was so by looking at the processes of colonization experienced by five Hudson's Bay Company/Native families who were comprised of some of the earliest principal settlers of Victoria. A look at a map of the settlement in 1858 (Map 32.1) illustrates the dominant position of the family properties of James Douglas, William H. McNeill, John Work, John Tod, and Charles Ross. These men had all been officers of the Hudson's Bay Company (HBC): all had Native wives, but of different First Nations origin. Although all these officers had toyed with the idea of retiring to Britain or eastern Canada, they chose to settle at Fort Victoria, the heart of the new Crown Colony of Vancouver Island (created in 1849). Coming from the elite of the fur trade hierarchy, these men had the wherewithal to purchase the expensive estates made available by the HBC. In Victoria, they hoped to maintain their social and economic standing by becoming part of the landed gentry, the elite class in the Wakefieldian colonization scheme that aimed to replicate an essentially British social hierarchy.[2]

For these men, Victoria offered the prospect of settling their families in "civilized" yet geographically familiar surroundings, where it was hoped that they would secure a place as part of the colonial elite. Being of mixed race, however, these families confronted particular challenges in adapting to this cultural frontier. Recent studies of prevailing colonial discourses reveal that the new settler society was intent on reproducing White British "civilization"—a project in which miscegenation was increasingly feared and denigrated. According to one commentator, the progeny of mixed unions were "a bad lot," being weak both "morally and intellectually."[3] With Aboriginal ancestry quickly becoming a source of shame, Native mothers and children

Source: *BC Studies* 115/116 (Autumn/Winter 1997/98): 149–79.

Map 32.1   Victoria, 1858 (drawn from Official District Map)

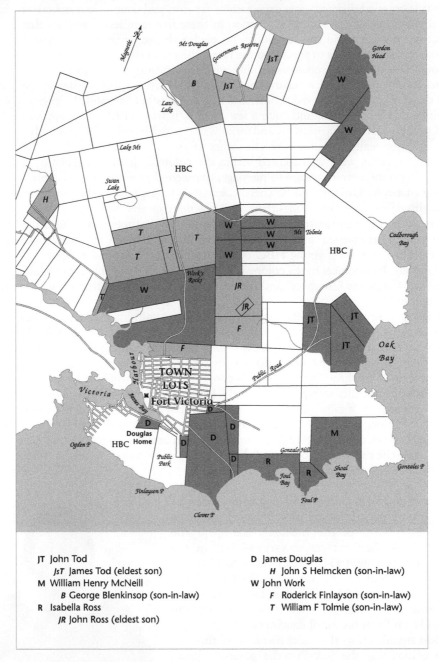

JT John Tod
  JsT James Tod (eldest son)
M William Henry McNeill
  B George Blenkinsop (son-in-law)
R Isabella Ross
  JR John Ross (eldest son)

D James Douglas
  H John S Helmcken (son-in-law)
W John Work
  F Roderick Finlayson (son-in-law)
  T William F Tolmie (son-in-law)

were subject to growing pressure to acculturate to the fathers' British heritage. Assimilation can be seen as a strategy adopted by these families in an effort to maintain class status, which could be undermined by the racist attitudes of incoming colonists. Especially for the second generation, there was little room for a middle ground; these children could not build an identity that acknowledged the duality of their heritage.

Little attention has been paid to the fact that this process of acculturation was gendered and that it entailed different role expectations for sons and daughters, respectively. In examining the fortunes of the second generation in these five families, it appears that a complex interaction of gender and class dynamics, coupled with the particular demographics of early Victoria, enabled the girls to transcend the racist climate of the colony more successfully than the boys. The sons had considerable difficulty in securing the status of gentlemen; none enhanced, and most failed to maintain, the families' fortunes. Racial stereotypes helped to blight the sons' prospects, as did deficiencies in colonial schooling and the vagaries of pioneer agriculture. If they married, and quite a few did not, it was (with one exception) to Métis or Indian women. Both occupationally and socially, the mixed-blood sons, even in these elite families, could not really compete with the influx of aspiring young Englishmen. Many of the daughters, however, were well secured within the colonial elite. Paradoxically, although the daughters' options were restricted to marriage, the second generation was highly successful in fulfilling that role. Unlike their brothers, colonial demographics worked to the advantage of the daughters; in the early decades there were few marriageable immigrant women who could compete with the acculturated daughters of former HBC officers. All the daughters of the second generation married: almost all married White men. Their marriage patterns evolved from marrying promising young HBC officers to marrying colonial officials and incoming White settlers. Newcomers to the colony were soon aware of the influence of what was dubbed the "Family Company Compact" and the advantage that could accrue from marrying "*a big wigs* daughter."[4]

A fascinating window on the experiences of these families and the process of acculturation is provided by the rich collection of portraits in the British Columbia Archives and Records Service (now BC Archives). As several commentators have observed, photographs are, themselves, valuable historical documents that have not received enough serious study from historians.[5] In these families, photos convey in ways that words cannot the process of acculturation, especially as experienced by the Native wives. Most of the photos have come to the archives as part of family albums and collections. Whether the originals were small *cartes de visite* or cabinet portraits, they illuminate social networks and family aspirations. In the second generation, the scarcity of sons' portraits may in itself be a significant indicator of social failure, while the numerous portraits of the daughters underscore their successful assimilation to British material culture.

In order to appreciate the social challenges faced by these families, it is necessary to sketch their fur trade background.[6] Most of the husbands had spent the better part of their careers at various posts in the Columbia Department (Map 32.2). They had initially married according to the fur trade "custom of the country" and produced large families. Family size varied between seven and thirteen children, with the sex ratio weighted heavily in favour of daughters.

Most significant to the social hierarchy of this new British colony was the fact that the governor, James Douglas, was an HBC officer who had a part-Cree wife, Amelia (Plates 32.1 and 32.2). As the daughter of Chief Factor William Connolly and Miyo Nipiy, her marriage at Fort St. James in 1828 was typical of the pattern of young officers marrying the daughters of their superiors.

Plate 32.1 BC Archives, A-2833.

Map 32.2   Select Posts of the Columbia District of the HBC

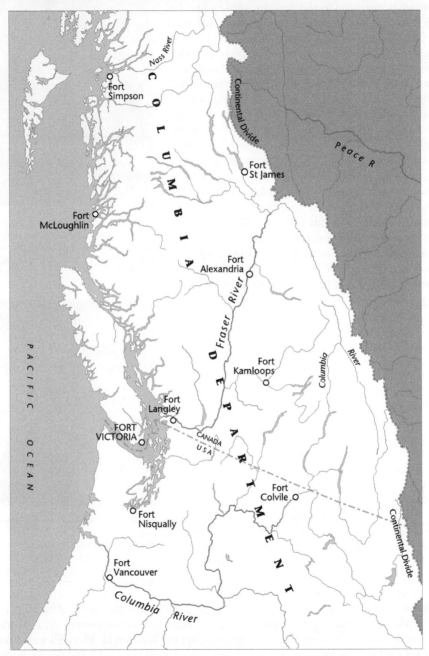

The Douglases soon moved to Fort Vancouver, where most of their thirteen children were born. Unlike the other families, the mortality rate in the Douglas family was high. When they moved to Fort Victoria in 1849, there were only four surviving daughters, two boys and five girls having died very young. Another son and daughter born in the early 1850s completed the family. Douglas bought up several hundred acres of choice land in Victoria, which he parlayed into considerable wealth, and he was among the first to build a substantial home outside the fort. In 1863, when he was knighted for his services to the colony, his wife became Lady Douglas.

One of Douglas's colleagues who had high hopes for the opportunities Victoria promised his large family was Chief Factor John Work. His Métis wife, Josette Legacé, the daughter of a French-Canadian father and a Spokane mother, had grown up at posts on the Columbia River. Married in 1826, the Works spent many years much farther north at Fort Simpson before retiring to Victoria in 1850 with a family of three boys and eight girls. John Work became the largest landowner in early Victoria, his Hillside Farm encompassing over 1000 acres. Although he died in 1861, his wife survived him by 35 years (Plate 32.3).

The untimely death of a father could seriously affect the fortunes of an HBC family. Charles Ross only lived long enough to see Fort Victoria built in 1844, but he left his widow able to buy her own estate of 145 acres on Ross Bay. Like Josette Work, Isabella Ross (Plate 32.4) was the daughter of a French-Canadian engagé but, like Amelia Douglas, she was born far from Victoria. Her mother was Ojibway; Isabella had grown up in the Great Lakes region and was married at Rainy Lake in 1822. Most of her children, six boys and four girls, were born west of the Rockies and all lived to adulthood.

Although often referred to as "Indian," the wives of these men were all of mixed descent. Although these marriages cut across class and ethnicity, they are, nonetheless, representative of fur trade endogamy. The wives' fathers were connected to the HBC, and the women themselves grew up within or near various fur trade posts. All these marriages were long-lasting monogamous unions, the country marriages eventually being confirmed by church rites whenever clergymen became available. The Douglases and the Rosses had church marriages at Fort Vancouver in 1838, and the Works had one upon their arrival at Fort Victoria in 1849.

In the other two families, the McNeills and the Tods, the marriages harkened back to the long-established pattern of officers contracting alliances with high-ranking First Nations women whose connections were useful to advancing their husbands' respective commercial positions. Captain William H. McNeill was a Bostonian who first entered the Pacific coast trade in competition with the HBC. His first wife, known as Mathilda, was a Kaigani Haida chief, an alliance which undoubtedly helped to make him such a successful trader that the HBC went to some lengths to lure him into its service in the early 1830s. This union produced twelve children, with seven girls and three boys surviving to adulthood. Mathilda died in 1850, shortly after the birth of the youngest children (twin girls), and McNeill soon settled his motherless family in Victoria. Upon his later retirement in 1863,

Plate 32.2 Portrait of Amelia, Lady Douglas. This plate and Plate 32.1 show Lady Douglas's acculturation to the role of governor's wife over a decade, c. 1858 to 1872. BC Archives, A-01679.

Plate 32.3 Mrs. John Work and her two youngest children. Original: *Carte de visite.* Photographer: S.A. Spencer. BC Archives, A-01825.

he brought a second wife, a high-ranking Nishga woman named Neshaki, to live on his 200-acre estate, which encompassed much of south Oak Bay.

Chief Trader John Tod had a more checkered marital experience than did most of his contemporaries. By his first short-lived country marriage to a mixed-blood woman, Tod had a son (James) who eventually settled in Victoria. Through an ill-fated marriage to an English woman in the late 1830s, he had a daughter, but his second wife, having gone mad, was placed in an asylum in England. Tod then returned to the Columbia District, where he took his last country wife around 1843. Sophia Lolo was the daughter of a prominent chief at Fort Kamloops (Jean-Baptiste Lolo dit St. Paul) and his Shuswap wife (Plate 32.5). In 1850, Tod settled with Sophia and a growing family, ultimately five boys and two girls, on a 100-acre estate in Oak Bay.

In these families, the patriarchal role exercised by the British fathers was greater than usual because of their own cultural bias. In fur trade society, Native wives brought their husbands valuable knowledge with regard to trade and even survival. There is also ample evidence that they were devoted mothers and exercised a strong influence within the family circle. When McNeill's Haida wife died in 1850, he took the unusual step of lamenting his loss to Governor Simpson: "My poor Wife . . . had been a good and faithful partner to me for twenty years and we had twelve children together . . . the deceased was a most kind mother to her children, and *no* Woman could have done her duty better, although an Indian."[7] Moving though it is, this quotation underscores McNeill's ambivalence toward his wife's Native background. Like the other patriarchs in this study, he was to be an active agent in the colonization of his own family.

HBC officers never seem to have questioned the desirability of acculturating their families to British norms and customs. Though their private correspondence is filled with paternal concern for the welfare of their children, this was posited in terms of negating the latter's Indianness. It was never suggested that the children's First Nations heritage should be actively incorporated into their upbringing. At the fur trade posts, fathers sought to Anglicize their wives and children, introducing them to the basics of English literacy and to Christian obser-

Plate 32.4 Isabella Ross in her widow's weeds. Photographer, probably S.A. Spencer. BC Archives, 7049 A-1280.

Plate 32.5 Sophia Lolo, wife of John Tod. Photograph may have been taken on the occasion of the Tods' church marriage in 1863. Photographer: S.A. Spencer. BC Archives, A-01483.

vances such as Bible reading and prayers. Material acculturation also started at the posts, as is illustrated in Plate 32.6, a fascinating 1865 portrait of Sophia Lolo's parents and two younger sisters. Here the traditional costume of the mother is contrasted to the partially anglicized dress of the daughters. Tartan dresses and shawls, worn with First Nations leggings and moccasins, became the typical costume for women at the HBC forts in the early nineteenth century.[8]

Plate 32.6 Jean-Baptiste Lolo dit St. Paul, his wife and two daughters. Taken by Charles Gentile in 1865 at Fort Kamloops. BC Archives, 2007 A-950.

Fathers worried about their children growing up at isolated posts without "proper education or example." In 1834, John Work wrote to his retired colleague Edward Ermatinger: "I have now here four fine little girls, had I them a little brushed up with education, and a little knowledge of the world, they would scarcely be known to be Indians."[9] Thus fur trade officers were eager to place their children at the first school established at Fort Vancouver in the 1830s; after that venture failed, Douglas and Work both placed their daughters with American missionaries in the Willamette Valley.[10] To provide the requisite education for enabling sons to secure a position in the HBC or to take up some other profession was a problem. To send sons (or daughters) away to eastern Canada or Great Britain was a risky and expensive business, even if they were entrusted to the care of relatives or friends.

These concerns much occupied Charles Ross, who had kept his large family under his wing until he received a promotion upon moving to Fort Victoria. In the fall of 1843 he sent his three teenaged children (two sons and a daughter) off to England for an education. Colleagues were aghast at the expense, but Ross had hopes that his offspring would do well with his nephew in London. A touching letter written to his "honoured Father" by eighteen-year-old Walter indicates that he had found a good placement as a wool merchant's clerk and that his brother and sister were "much improved in their learning." Ross never received this letter, however, having died the previous year, and relatives were soon expressing their dissatisfaction with his children, whom they found "extremely indocile and addicted to habits incompatible with a residence in this country."[11] The three children were sent back to their mother in Victoria in the fall of 1845. Further light is shed on father–son relationships and on the difficulties of educating sons by looking at the efforts of Edward Ermatinger who, after retiring to St. Thomas (Ontario), acted as a "surrogate father" for sons of colleagues such as John Tod. In 1841, Tod sent James, his eldest son, east to Ermatinger where, in spite of social conflict, James gained agricultural skills that helped him to manage his own property later in Victoria.[12]

In colonial Victoria, where the norms of their husbands' culture were dominant, the role of Native mothers in socializing their children was circumscribed. The fathers' prescriptions were now supported by new agents of colonization: the church and the school. All these families adhered to the Church of England, which helped to affirm their elite status. Their marriages were sanctioned by church rite, and the wives and children were baptized and became active members of the Anglican congregation that formed around the Reverend Edward Cridge after his arrival in 1855.[13] Christian education was deemed of the utmost importance, and schooling specifically for the children of the elite was set up with the arrival of the first Anglican missionaries, Robert and Emma Staines. The five families in question dominated the Fort Victoria school register in the early 1850s; out of 30 pupils listed, there were four Douglases, five Works, three McNeills, three Rosses, and two Tods.[14] Boarding children at this school was expensive (fifteen pounds per annum), so it was frustrating to fathers subscribing to this school when their hopes, especially for their boys, were disappointed. By all accounts Mrs. Staines and her successors were much more successful with the girls' education than was her husband with the boys' education. The girls were being groomed for marriage; their education emphasized dress, deportment, and ladylike accomplishments such as music, singing, drawing, and languages.[15] The boys, on the other hand, did not really get the more demanding education, either practical or classical, that their role expectations demanded. Staines was evidently not up to the job and attempted to control his teenage charges by meting out severe corporal punishment.[16] Life at this school stood in painful contrast to the more carefree and close familial life most of these children had previously known. Although the boys' school had improved considerably by the early 1860s, the differential impact of this early colonial education appears to have been a significant factor in shaping the next generation.

In colonial Victoria racism intensified, generating invidious comparisons. It irked some incoming settlers that Native families should rank so high in the social hierarchy. Visitors and even working-class British immigrants pronounced society in the new colony deficient because some of its leading officials were married to Native women. Shortly after her arrival from England in 1854, Annie Deans wrote home disparagingly of Douglas: a man who had spent his life among North American Indians and got one for a wife could scarcely know anything about governing an English colony.[17] While there is ample evidence that the daughters of these HBC families featured in the early society of Victoria, they could be subject to unflattering evaluation. Charles Wilson, a British army officer, recounting the round of balls and other social activities he attended in the early 1860s, observed: "Most of the young ladies are half breeds & have quite as many of the propensities of the savage as of the civilized being."[18] Among these families, such remarks increased attempts to hide Native backgrounds and to adopt all the trappings of British fashion and mores.

These social tensions were poignantly revealed in the Douglas family which, because of its position, was subject to particular scrutiny. Initially, Amelia Douglas kept in the social background, partly because she did not speak English very well. The social calendar was kept by her daughters and a Douglas niece from Britain, but as the contrasting portraits indicate (compare Plate 32.1 and 32.2), Lady Douglas became increasingly comfortable in her role as the governor's wife. Douglas wrote proudly of his wife after a New Year's levee in the early 1870s: "Darling good Mamma was nicely got up and won all hearts with her kindness and geniality."[19] When Lady Franklin visited Victoria in 1861, she was curious to meet the "Indian" wife of the governor. She found Amelia to have "a gentle, simple & kindly manner" and was fascinated that her Native features were less pronounced than were those in some of her daughters.[20]

Plate 32.7, the earliest known picture of the Douglas daughters, shows them in completely Anglicized, if modest, daytime apparel; other portraits reveal that their costumes soon reflected the latest European styles. The weddings of the four Douglas daughters, which occurred between 1852 and 1862, became increasingly elaborate affairs. When Agnes married Arthur Bushby, a well-born young British civil servant, a guest observed that it was a gorgeous wedding, "the ladies coming out in style."[21] But nothing in early Victoria capped the wedding of the youngest daughter, Martha, who, after being "finished in England," married another colonial official, Dennis Harris, in 1878. Plate 32.8 features the bride and numerous attendants in elaborate imported gowns; many of Victoria's notables are among the guests. The now-widowed Lady Douglas is prominent at the right edge of the photo, while the

Plate 32.7 An early 1850s photograph of the Miss Douglases. Left to right are Agnes, Jane, and Alice. Taken outside at Fort Victoria. BC Archives, A-02836.

Plate 32.8 The wedding of Martha Douglas to Dennis Harris, 1878. Taken on the veranda of the Douglas home by Hannah Maynard. BC Archives, A-01236. Next page, detail of wedding party.

Douglas heir, James Jr., is cavalierly reclining at his sister's feet.

In the mid-1860s Governor Douglas had decided to send his teenaged son to England for further education (Plate 32.9). Douglas's ensuing correspondence provides detailed insight into his aspirations for his son:

> I had one main object in sending [James] to England which was, to give him a sound and good education, that he might . . . be qualified, through his own exertions to occupy a respectable position in society, and perhaps take a distinguished part, in the legislation of his Native country . . . he was to come here, and assist in the management of my property which with his political avocations, would furnish employment enough, and emolument greater than any other profession he might engage in.[22]

But young James was to cause his father much anguish from disappointment when he displayed little intellectual progress to mortification when he appeared about to fall into bad company and pawned the farewell gifts from his parents. James Jr. eventually returned to the colony to do his father's bidding, and in 1878 he married a White woman, Mary Elliott, daughter of a colonial politician. But contemporary observers emphasized that young Douglas was not a patch on his father.[23] Whatever promise he had was cut short by his death in 1883 at the age of 32. Family affairs in the second generation of the Douglas family were largely managed by the prominent White sons-in-law, especially Dr. J.S. Helmcken, who had married the eldest daughter, Cecilia.

Among the most socially successful families in early Victoria were the Works. Hillside House (Plate 32.10), renowned for its hospitality, was much frequented by military officers and prominent settlers. Charles Wilson's description of a New Year's celebration in 1861 appears to have been typical: "There were about 30 at dinner — such a display of fish, flesh and fowl and pastry as is seldom seen. We danced until 12 & then all hands sat down to a sumptuous supper and then set to

Plate 32.9 A formal portrait of the governor's son, James Douglas, Jr. BC Archives, A-01240.

work dancing again until a very late hour." "The Works," this young officer enthused, "are about the kindest people I ever came across."[24] Mrs. Work seems to have been very much part of this scene and earned the admiration of all who met her. Even the American historian Hubert H. Bancroft acknowledged that "the Indian wife, in body and mind, was strong and elastic as steel."[25] By the time Bancroft met her in 1878, Josette had been a widow for over fifteen years, but as her portrait (Plate 32.11) indicates, she had become the epitome of the Victorian matron. At a glance, she could be taken for Queen Victoria herself! When she died at an advanced age in 1896, she was eulogized for "her usefulness in pioneer work and many good deeds."[26]

Plate 32.10 The Work family home, Hillside House, built in the HBC style in the early 1850s. Note Mrs. Work, now widowed, is in the centre of the family group. BC Archives, A-05578.

In no family were the fortunes of sons and daughters so sharply contrasted as they were in the Work family. John Tod, who was much interested in the welfare of his colleague's family, observed in 1864: "It is rather remarkable that so numerous a family of daughters should have turned out so well, their exemplary good conduct having gained the universal esteem and respect of their neighbours, and the only two Sons, who survived their father, should have displayed characters the very reverse!"[27] At the time of their father's death in 1861, most of the daughters had already married, the two eldest long since to HBC officers Roderick Finlayson and W.F. Tolmie, respectively, both of whom were to number among Victoria's most prominent citizens. The sons, however, were still young. At age 22, John Jr. proved quite incapable of taking on the role of head of household; friends worried that he would bring ruin on the family with his intemperate and extravagant habits.[28] Whatever his faults, his mother was prepared to overlook her son's failings and he lived out his life with her, helping to manage a diminished Hillside Farm. David, the

Plate 32.11 Josette Work as "Queen Victoria." Cabinet Portrait. Photographer S.A. Spencer. BC Archives, A-01836.

younger son (Plate 32.3), eventually secured employment as a clerk in the HBC store in Victoria, but for some reason Tod thought him a despicable character. Neither David nor John Jr.

Plate 32.12 "Rock Bay," the home of Roderick and Sarah (Work) Finlayson. BC Archives, 31163 B-2262.

married, dying at the ages of 49 and 32, respectively. Again leadership in this family passed to the British sons-in-law. The opulent lifestyle enjoyed by several of the Work daughters in the late nineteenth century is seen in Plate 32.12. In building his mansion at Rock Bay, Roderick Finlayson was the first person to import California redwood; his wife Sarah developed an active interest in gardening, becoming renowned for her Oriental poppies.[29]

It is interesting to speculate what would have happened to the Ross family had the father lived to preside over the Victoria years. Charles Ross's eldest sons had come of age before the settlement period, and he had sought to prepare them for placement in the HBC. Governor Simpson had apparently assisted in securing a position for John, the eldest son. After his father's death, John continued in the HBC service at Fort Victoria, and tried to assume the role of head of the family. His brothers, who had been returned from England, were taken into the HBC's farming operations at Fort Nisqually, leaving the younger sons to continue their education in Victoria and to help their mother develop her estate. In 1858 John Ross had expanded the family holdings in Victoria by purchasing a 200-acre farm called Oaklands, but with his premature death several years later this asset was quickly liquidated.[30] By this time, unfortunately, the younger sons had gained a reputation as "bad boys," running into debt and being in trouble with the law for disorderly conduct.[31]

Family problems were compounded when the widow herself married again in 1863 to a young fortune hunter from Canada, Lucius Simon O'Brien.[32] The new stepfather was soon at odds with the sons, going so far as to charge Alexander several times with assault. Ross was never convicted, but relations deteriorated so badly that his mother wanted to separate from her new husband. While O'Brien had been prepared to overlook race in marrying the landed widow, once his plans went awry, he played to racist stereotypes in a vicious manner, publishing the following notice in the Victoria *Daily Chronicle* in April 1864:

> Whereas My Wife, Isabella, has left my bed and board because I will not support her drunken sons, nor allow her to keep drunk herself, and have a lot of drunken squaws about her, this is to forbid all persons, harbouring her, or trusting her on my account, as I will pay no debts she may contract.[33]

A few days later, the youngest son, William, attempted to come to his mother's defence and charged that O'Brien was trying to swindle the family:

> His every act since his marriage has been to try to get everything from my mother, and turn us (the children) out of the house; selling all he could lay his hands on, and by his conduct, turn my mother out of her own house. Will you do me and my mother the simple justice to publish this, as such a statement as O'Brien has made is calculated to injure her and myself.[34]

When the family then began proceedings against O'Brien to prove that he was actually a bigamist, he apparently decided to seek his fortune up-island, where he came to an untimely end a few years later.[35]

This was not the end of Ross family trials, however. In 1866, after numerous brushes with the law, sons Francis and William were convicted of robbing a Chinese man and were sentenced to five years at hard labour. This harsh fate aroused public sympathy and a widely supported petition to the governor asked for their release, claiming that their health was suffering. Sir James Douglas testified that he had known their "most respectable parents" and that these young men were not the blackguards they were made out to be.[36] After serving about two years, the Ross boys were released on condition of their banishment from the colony.

Although the younger Ross daughters attended the balls given by the officers of the British navy in the 1850s, they never attained the status they desired. Thomas Hankin observed that although they were very fine-looking girls, "they had a great deal of Indian blood in them and were supposed to be only on the edge of society."[37] Of all the daughters in the five families under discussion, the Ross daughters were the only ones who married mixed-bloods. The eldest married Charles Wren, a Métis who had emigrated from Red River to Oregon; after her death in 1859, he married her younger sister.[38] Flora, the youngest Ross daughter, married Paul K. Hubbs in 1859, an American settler who was described as "a white Indian," but within a decade this marriage had dissolved.[39] Flora Ross went on to become the only woman in this study to have her own occupation, becoming Matron of the Asylum at New Westminister. Plate 32.13, a portrait of Flora Ross taken in the 1890s, makes a statement about the social respectability she had achieved in her own right.

By the early 1870s, the Victoria Rosses had had to sell off a good deal of their property. The remaining son, Alexander, settled down and married in 1868 but was reduced to being a labourer on the neighbouring Pemberton estate where he died suddenly of a heart attack in 1876.[40] The widow Ross, until her death in 885, was maintained by her daughter Flora in a small house on the grounds of the convent of the Sisters of St. Ann.[41] A desire for respectability and a disavowal of any Native heritage is manifest in Plate 32.14, an astonishing family portrait of the one surviving Ross son who, after some years in Victoria, settled in Washington State. While this picture strikes contemporary viewers as amusing, this was not its intent. It symbolizes Charles Jr.'s ethnic identification with his Highland Scots father. The poignancy of this picture becomes apparent

Plate 32.13 Flora, the youngest daughter of Charles and Isabella Ross. Taken in New Westminister in 1896. Note the 1890s fashions. BC Archives, 7052 A-022445.

when one knows the family history and realizes that Charles Jr.'s wife, Catherine Toma, was a Nisqually from the Puget Sound Region.[42]

Scottish affectations are also evident in the McNeill family. Like his contemporaries, the elder McNeill tried to place his sons in the HBC, but the 1850s were a time of hardening attitudes toward taking sons into junior officer ranks. One son, Harry, was apparently an efficient trader at Fort Simpson but resented not being given the rank of clerk. He went on to disobey his father over a romantic entanglement with a Native woman and quit the service, joining his brothers in Victoria in the mid-1850s.[43] While the younger McNeill boys did not gain the notoriety of the Rosses, they did seem to have trouble settling down in Victoria, appearing in police records as having been charged with disorderly conduct. Sons Harry and Alfred apparently sought better prospects on the mainland. Harry was an effective overseer of Native work crews that were clearing the way for the Collins Overland Telegraph in the mid-1860s, but he returned to Victoria where he died in 1872 at the age of 38.[44] Alfred is listed as a farmer in the Yale District in the 1881 census, but, curiously, he is omitted from his father's will of 1876. Only Captain McNeill's eldest son and namesake seems to have given him any satisfaction.

Plate 32.15, one of the few portraits of second-generation males that has survived, conveys the younger McNeill's gentlemanly aspirations. His wedding in June 1853 to Mary Macauley, the mixed-blood daughter of the bailiff of one of the HBC farms, underscores this couple's ethnic orientation. It was a "proper and grand wedding," which included a procession around the village led by a piper in full Scottish regalia.[45] The younger McNeill had been employed as master of the mail boat (which ran a regular route between Victoria and the Puget Sound in the 1840s) and as part of several exploratory expeditions to the mainland before he settled down to farm his father's estate. He died in 1889 at the age of 57 as a result of injuries suffered in a buggy accident.[46]

Plate 32.14 A Highland chieftain? Charles Ross Jr. with his Native wife and family. The origin of this picture is not known, but it was given to the BC Archives by a descendant. Note the fur rug on the floor. BC Archives, 97185 H-4646.

Plate 32.15 William Henry McNeill, Jr., eldest son of Captain McNeill and his Haida wife, known as Mathilda. Note velvet lapels on his coat and plaid tie. BC Archives, G-03236.

Although he maintained a certain respectability, it appears that William Jr. did not achieve the social status of his sisters. Plate 32.16 is most intriguing, for it reflects the surviving McNeill sisters' acculturation and also makes a significant statement about kin ties. All the sisters are dressed in elaborate but sombre Victorian gowns, which indicates that this photo may have been taken around the time of their father's death in 1875. Standing at the back are the youngest and still-unmarried twins Rebecca and Harriet; dominant on the right is the matriarchal eldest sister Lucy. Her marriage to HBC officer Hamilton Moffat in 1856 underscored the social networking among the women in these families, for her bridesmaids were Jane Douglas and Mary Work.[47] The other McNeill sisters were all considered to have married well. In 1864, Fanny married bank clerk James Judson Young, who became provincial secretary. Both the twins married Englishmen; in 1879 Rebecca married Thomas Elwyn, who had served as gold commissioner, and in 1889 Harriet married John Jane, who had been a Royal Engineer.

Of all members of these five families, the record is most sparse with regard to John Tod's Shuswap wife and their children. Apart from vital statistics, Plate 32.5 is the most informative surviving clue about Sophia Lola and how she adapted to life in Victoria. This picture, which may

Plate 32.16 Five surviving daughters of Captain W.H. McNeill and his Haida wife, c. 1875. Standing are the twins, Rebecca (l) and Harriet (r); seated (l to r) are Fanny, Mathilda (holding a family photograph album now in the BC Archives), and Lucy. Photographer: Hannah Maynard. BC Archives, F-09960.

have been taken at the time of her church marriage in 1863, invites various readings, but it seems to indicate an ambivalence about the constraints of Victorian dress and customs. Unlike their mother, the Tod daughters mixed with other fur traders' families in Victoria society. Mary, the eldest, married American settler J.S. Bowker in 1864, while the younger sister married a successful merchant, J.S. Drummond.[48]

The Tod sons did not find suitable wives, and the 1881 census finds all five, ranging in ages from 24 to 36, still under the family roof working the farm. The eldest son and namesake, John Jr., failed to secure the family estate; after an ill-fated venture as a saloon-keeper, he left for the States. The second son, Alexander, showed promise as a farmer and stock raiser but died of consumption in 1889, as had a younger brother before him. A good deal of the Tod estate passed into the hands of the Bowker son-in-law, but by the 1890s the original family house had been purchased by strangers. Only James, Tod's eldest son by his first marriage, enjoyed any real success as a farmer. Tod had bought James his own farm when he arrived from the east; reputedly a man of prodigious strength, the younger Tod developed an extensive property known as Spring Bank Farm, which he passed on to two of his sons.[49] In 1857 James married one of the Macauley daughters, making him a brother-in-law of William McNeill Jr.

The wives and children in these elite HBC/Native families were subject to a process of acculturation designated to negate their Native heritage. To a considerable degree this was successful. Generally, the Native wives adapted remarkably well to being mistresses of substantial colonial households. The second generation, having the benefits of considerable education, was far removed from its Aboriginal roots. Yet there was no guarantee that the stigma of Native blood could truly be transcended. Indeed, racist attitudes intensified in the late nineteenth century, and miscegenation was held to be undesirable. These attitudes are painfully underscored in the public denunciation of some of Victoria's founding families by the American historian, Hubert Howe Bancroft.

In the late spring of 1878, Bancroft spent a month in Victoria collecting reminiscences and records for his mammoth history of the Pacific northwest. Anxious to meet the retired HBC officers who had played such an important role in the development of the region, he was gratified by the hospitality and generous assistance of former traders and/or their descendants.[50] One can only imagine, then, the dismay that these families must have felt to find their Native heritage so excoriated in the pages of the awaited *History of the Northwest Coast* when it appeared in 1886. In a highly personal passage, in which some of Victoria's leading citizens were named, Bancroft ruminates on "the fur trader's curse":

> It has always seemed to me that the heaviest penalty the servants of the Hudson's Bay Company were obliged to pay for the wealth and authority advancement gave them, was the wives they were expected to marry and the progeny they should rear . . . I could never understand how such men as John McLoughlin, *James Douglas*, Ogden, *Finlayson, Work* and *Tolmie* and the rest could endure the thought of having their name and honors descend to a degenerate posterity. Surely they were possessed of sufficient intelligence to know that by giving their children Indian or half-breed mothers, their own old Scotch, Irish or English blood would in them be greatly debased, and hence they were doing all concerned a great wrong. Perish all the Hudson's Bay Company thrice over, I would say, . . . sooner than bring into being offspring subject to such a curse.[51]

Bancroft's lament was implicitly gendered. He was decrying the sons: those who had failed to carry on the family name with any success. But, as we have seen, miscegenation was not the problem — the differing experience of sons and daughters gives the lie to Bancroft's assertion. The dynamics of class and race, it should be emphasized, have a gendered impact. Males were required to move in a more public occupational and social world than were their female counterparts, and racial stereotyping, which emphasized deficiencies as inherent, worked strongly against them. Among the boys, what might have passed as rowdy youthful behaviour among other elite males was associated with dissolute Native character and resulted in their being subjected to harsh discipline. Many were not well trained to play the roles that their fathers had hoped for them. Indeed, their fathers themselves may have colluded in racist stereotyping, expressing doubts about their sons' ability to succeed and favouring White suitors for their daughters.[52] Given the gender demographics of colonial Victoria, the sons in these families were soon outnumbered by well-educated, ambitious young Englishmen with whom they had to compete both occupationally and socially. In early Victoria, these sons are conspicuous by their almost complete absence from the social record. They must have resented the competition from the young British gentlemen who monopolized the affections of their sisters. Significantly, in the second generation there was no intermarriage among these families.

Unlike their brothers, whose success and failures would be judged in the public sphere, the daughters' success and failures would occur in the private sphere of marriage. Here colonial demographics worked to the advantage of the daughters; in the early decades there were few marriageable immigrant women who could compete with these elite "daughters of the country." For the most part, the fathers' wealth and position and the daughters' personal success in equipping themselves to play the roles expected of British middle-class wives and mothers were sufficient to overcome racial prejudice. This fact accounts for the astonishing marriage rate of 100 percent for the daughters of the second generation. Their marriages to incoming White colonists served, of course, to dilute Native ancestry even further.[53]

Plate 32.17 Tolmie family group, taken in front of their veranda at Cloverdale in 1878. Mother and father are seated, flanked by three sons, standing, and enclosing the youngest children, symbolizing family solidarity. (Man seated apart left is a family friend.) BC Archives, 16040 G-4990.

The spread of attitudes such as Bancroft's contributed to the process of distancing and denial experienced by many descendants of the five founding families of Victoria. Family narratives and obituaries increasingly highlighted the pioneering role of these fathers; if the mothers were mentioned at all, there was no reference to their being Native. When Simon Fraser Tolmie, who became premier of the province, fondly reminisced about growing up at Cloverdale (Plate 32.17), the family estate, he hardly mentioned his mother and omitted all reference to his remarkable Work grandmother.[54] In his family narrative of 1924, Donald H. McNeill was at pains to emphasize that his grandfather had been the first White settler of south Oak Bay but did not acknowledge that he was descended from high-ranking Haida and Tongass women.[55] Popular writers also ignored the Native heritage of these families. A 1928 volume about the early women of Vancouver Island includes a whole chapter entitled "The Wives of the First Landowners"; although it focuses on the Work women, the reader would be hard pressed to know that they were of Native descent.[56]

And so the Native origin of some of Victoria's founding families was obscured for decades. The reclamation of this part of these family histories not only adds to the richness of the city's history, but also illuminates the complex intersection of the dynamics of race, class, and gender.

NOTES

This article originated as a presentation to an invited symposium on cultural borderlands at Princeton University in March 1995. I benefited greatly from the comments of participants, especially Natalie Zemon Davis. Revisions of this work were stimulated by the responses to versions given at First Nations House at the University of Toronto, my seminar on Aboriginal/non-Aboriginal relations, and several conferences. My research assistant in Victoria, Christopher Hanna, has been an invaluable aid, and I am grateful to Adele Perry, Ted Chamberlin, Jean Barman, John Adams, Charlene Porsild, Bettina Bradbury, Jack Gregg, Jennifer Brown, and Shirley Wishart for their interest and comments. The staff of the British Columbia Archives were ever helpful, especially Kathryn Bridge, with her expertise in photographs. Many thanks also to Cole Harris for his careful, thoughtful editing and to Eric Leinberger for drawing the maps. All the photographs are published with the permission of the BC Archives.

1. Terry Reksten, *"More English Than the English": A Very Social History of Victoria* (Victoria: Orca, 1986).
2. For an excellent discussion of the ideology behind the colonization scheme for Vancouver Island, see Richard Mackie, "The Colonization of Vancouver Island, 1849–58," *BC Studies* 96 (Winter 1992–93): 3–40. According to Mackie, "the rank structures of the company and the colony merged. The Family Company Compact made the transition from a fur trade elite to a colonial elite through its control of land and political power" (31–32).
3. BC Archives, E/B/A1 5.2, Alexander Allan, "Cariboo & the Mines of British Columbia" (1878); see also Adele Perry, "'The Prevailing Vice': Mixed-Race Relationships and Colonial Discourse in British Columbia, 1858–1871" (Ph.D. thesis, Department of History, York University, 1977), ch. 3. For a more general study of the growing fear of miscegenation in the nineteenth-century Anglo-American context, see Robert Young, *Colonial Desire: Hybridity in Theory, Culture and Race* (London: Routledge 1995).
4. Margaret Ormsby, ed., *Fort Victoria Letters, 1846–1851* (Winnipeg: Hudson's Bay Records Society, 1979), vol. 32, LX.
5. For a useful discussion of the importance of photographs as historical documents and the challenges involved in reading them, see J. Robert Davison, "Turning a Blind Eye: The Historian's Use of Photographs," *BC Studies* 52 (Winter 1981–82): 16–38; Elizabeth Heyert, *The Glass-House Years: Victorian Portrait Photography, 1839–70* (London: George Prior, 1978); and Alan Thomas, *The Expanding Eye: Photography and the Nineteenth-Century Mind* (London: Croom Helm, 1978).
6. The following synopsis of the origins of these five families is derived mainly from Sylvia Van Kirk, *"Many Tender Ties": Women in Fur Trade Society in Western Canada, 1670–1870* (Winnipeg: Watson and Dwyer, 1980).
7. Hudson's Bay Company Archives (hereafter HBCA), D.5/30, Simpson Correspondence Inward, McNeill to Simpson, 5 March 1851.
8. BC Archives, Edward Ermatinger Correspondence, John Work to Ermatinger, Fort Simpson, 13 December 1834. See also "Five Letters of Charles Ross, 1842–844," *British Columbia Historical Quarterly* 7 (April 1943): 109.
9. For a discussion of Native women's evolving fashions at the fur trade posts, see Van Kirk, *"Many Tender Ties,"* 99–103.
10. For the difficulties with the school at Fort Vancouver, see Thomas Jessett, ed., *Reports and Letters of Herbert Beaver, 1836–38* (Portland: Champoeg Press, 1959).
11. BC Archives, Charles Ross Clipping File, Walter to Father, 1 March 1845; HBCA, A.10/19 and 20, Walter P. Ross and Mary Tait to HBC Secretary, 13 June and 7 August 1845.
12. Jennifer Brown, *Strangers in Blood: Fur Trade Company Families in Indian Country* (Vancouver: UBC Press, 1980), 185–90.
13. BC Archives, Reminiscences of Bishop Edward Cridge. In 1875, most of the old HBC families followed Cridge to his Reformed Episcopal Church, formed after his break with Bishop George Hills.
14. BC Archives, ADD. MSS. 1774, School Register, Fort Victoria, 1850–52.
15. Dorothy Blakey Smith, ed., *The Reminiscences of Doctor John Sebastian Helmcken* (Vancouver: UBC Press, 1975), 120; Dorothy B. Smith, ed., *Lady Franklin Visits the Pacific Northwest* (Victoria: Provincial Archives of British Columbia, 1974), II, 34–35.
16. BC Archives, ADD. MSS. 1912, Memoirs of James Anderson, vol. 9, 158–76.
17. BC Archives, E/B/D343, Annie Deans Correspondence, 29 February 1854.

18. George Stanley, ed., *Mapping the Frontier; Charles Wilson's Diary of the Survey of the 49th Parallel, 1858–1862* (Toronto: Macmillan, 1970), 28, 45, 87–88.

19. Marion B. Smith, "The Lady Nobody Knows," *British Columbia: A Centennial Anthology* (Toronto: McClelland and Stewart, 1958), 479.

20. Smith, *Lady Franklin Visits*, 12, 22–23.

21. Wilson, *Mapping the Frontier*, 175.

22. BC Archives, B/40/2A, Douglas Private Letter-Book, 1867–79, to A.G. Dallas, 23 July 1867.

23. Hubert Howe Bancroft, *Literary Industries* (San Francisco: History Co., 1890), 534.

24. Wilson, *Mapping the Frontier*, 135.

25. Bancroft, *Literary Industries*, 534.

26. Nellie de Bertrand Lugrin, *The Pioneer Women of Vancouver Island, 1843–1866* (Victoria: Women's Canadian Club of Victoria, 1928), 64.

27. BC Archives, Ermatinger Correspondence, John Tod to Ermatinger, 1 June 1864.

28. Ibid., 15 March 1864 and 12 November 1868.

29. Reksten, "More English Than the English," 82–84.

30. *British Colonist*, 14 December 1863 and 8 February 1864.

31. *British Colonist*, 30 April 1859, 2 and 20, and 21 May 1862, 3. See also several entries in the charge books of the Victoria Police Department from 1858 to 1860 in BC Archives.

32. BC Archives, Records of Christ Church Cathedral, Marriage Register, 29 June 1863. O'Brien is identified as the eldest son of Dr. Lucius O'Brien of Quebec, C.E.

33. *Daily Chronicle*, 30 April 1864. See also *British Colonist*, 26 August 1863, 3; 1 September 1863, 3; 27 September 1864, 3; and *Daily Chronicle*, 1 September 1863.

34. *Daily Chronicle*, 4 May 1864.

35. BC Archives, Vancouver Island, Supreme Court, Cause Books, 616–17; Colonial Correspondence, John Morley, file 1,170, Inquest into the Death of Lucius O'Brien, 1866.

36. BC Archives, Colonial Correspondence, file 1,352, petitions (1866).

37. BC Archives, Philip Hankin Reminiscences, 166.

38. BC Archives, Wren Family Papers, Will of Charles Wren, 6 February 1864.

39. BC Archives, Christ Church Cathedral, Marriage Register, 6 December 1859; Gordon Keith, ed., *The James Francis Tullock Diary, 1876–1910* (Portland: Binford and Mort, 1978), 16.

40. *British Colonist*, 23 September 1876, 3.

41. *Daily Chronicle*, 24 April 1885; BC Archives, Wren Family Papers, Carrie to Isabella, 17 August 1880.

42. BC Archives, Charles Ross Clipping File, Biographical Notes. For further discussion on the Ross family in Washington State, see Cecelia Svinth Carpenter, *Fort Nisqually: A Documented History of Indian and British Interaction* (Tacoma: Tahoma Research Service, 1986). Carpenter is a descendant of Charles and Catherine Ross.

43. BC Archives, McNeill Letterbook, 18 October 1855; Helen Meilleur, *A Pour of Rain: Stories from a West Coast Fort* (Victoria: Sono Nis, 1980), 207.

44. Meilleur, *A Pour of Rain*, 208; British Columbia, Division of Vital Statistics, Death Certificate of Henry McNeill.

45. Smith, *Helmcken Reminiscences*, 153–54.

46. BC Archives, Donald McNeill, Personal Record, 1924; *British Colonist*, 31 October 1889.

47. BC Archives, Lucy Moffat Clipping File.

48. James K. Nesbitt, "The Diary of Martha Cheney Ella, 1853–56," *British Columbia Historical Quarterly* 13, Pt. 1 (April 1949): 91–112; and Part 2 (July–October 1949): passim.

49. For biographical information on the Tod family, see Robert Belyk, *John Tod: Rebel in the Ranks* (Victoria: Horsdal & Schubart, 1995).

50. Bancroft, *Literary Industries*, 530–39.

51. Hubert Howe Bancroft, *History of the Northwest Coast* (San Francisco: History Co., 1886), vol. 2, 650–51. I have italicized all the officers who settled in Victoria. My attention was first drawn to this quote when reading Janet Campbell Hale's fascinating autobiography, *Bloodlines: Odyssey of a Native Daughter* (New York: Random House, 1993). Bancroft's thoughts on miscegenation reflect the growing prejudice in the United States, especially after the American Civil War, as discussed in Young, *Colonial Desire*.

52. For further discussion of fathers' ruminations on the failings of their mixed-blood sons, see Brown, *Strangers in Blood*, 188–89: John Tod wrote to Ermatinger, "Well have you observed that all attempts to make gentlemen of them have hitherto proved a failure. The fact is there is something radically wrong about them all."

53. Although a detailed analysis of the third generation of these families is beyond the scope of this study, it should be observed that the sharply divergent patterns of the second generation do not hold into the third generation. Sons in the female lines of such families as the Helmckens, the Finlaysons, and the Tolmies did distinguish themselves in various branches of Victoria's professional and political life in the later nineteenth century. However, by this time, both in terms of blood and socialization, there was little of their Native ancestry left. On the other hand, the marriage rate of the daughters was not nearly as high as it was during the previous generation — a trend that requires further investigation.

54. See. S.F. Tolmie, "My Father: William Fraser Tolmie, 1812–1886," *British Columbia Historical Quarterly* 1 (October 1937): 227–40.

55. Ibid. 46, Donald McNeill, Personal Record, 1924.

56. Lugrin, *Pioneer Women of Vancouver Island*, ch. 5.

Article Thirty-Three

Hardy Backwoodsmen, Wholesome Women, and Steady Families: Immigration and the Construction of a White Society in Colonial British Columbia, 1849–1871

Adele Perry

Who was in and who was out? One of the primary ways which mid-nineteenth-century British Columbians negotiated inclusions and exclusions was through the practice and discourse of immigration. Immigration derived its social and political significance from its double ability to dispossess local peoples and establish a settler-society in their stead. The settler society this process sought to build was explicitly racialized and deeply gendered. In seeking "hardy backwoodsmen", colonial promoters encouraged men committed to hard work, steadiness, and rural life; in demanding "wholesome women", they sought women who would simultaneously serve as beacons of imperial society and constrain the excesses of white men; in courting "steady families", they pursued stable units that would exemplify the virtues of the same-race, nuclear family. Together, "hardy backwoodsmen, wholesome women and steady families" were constructed as the immigrants able to transform British Columbia into the stable settler society of imperialists' dreams.

Studies of the flow of people between Europe and the Americas in the "Great Migration Era" have tended to leave a blind spot, namely their disinterest in interrogating the politicized character of nineteenth-century "new world" migration.[1] When people left Europe for the Americas or Australia, they did not simply move into large, empty spaces. Instead, they participated in a process of colonization in which Aboriginal dispossession and settler migration were irreparably linked. As Daiva Staisulis and Nira Yuval-Davis argue, migration is one of the chief ways in which settler societies constitute themselves.[2] For individuals and families, migration was probably motivated primarily by straightforward social and economic needs, but the overarching

Source: "Hardy Backwoodsmen, Wholesome Women, and Steady Families: Immigration and the Construction of a White Society in Colonial British Columbia, 1849–1871," *Histoire sociale/Social History*, 33 (November 2000): 343–360. Reprinted by permission.

structure of imperialism transformed these needs into imperial acts.[3] Immigration sometimes troubled and sometimes nourished the politics of empire. In either case, it cannot be separated from them.

A better acknowledgement of the connections between migration and imperialism necessitates a return to an older phase in the writing of Canadian history, albeit with newly critical eyes. The past two decades have witnessed an increasing emphasis on the social experience of immigrant peoples to Canada. Historians have rejected earlier studies in which "immigration was acknowledged as a key ingredient in transcontinental nation-building but the immigrants were largely ignored or relegated to cameo appearances".[4] They have embraced the vantage point of the immigrant instead of the policy-maker and analysed how these people, like women and the working class, were active agents who shaped their own history. This historiographic shift is premised on a needed critique of histories that artificially isolate the powerful from both the cause and effect of their authority. An unintended and less useful consequence of changing historiographic imperatives has been to detach the process of migration from its larger political context. Instead of treating the political and social history of immigration as distinct processes, historians need to reckon with the profound ties that connect the politician with the peasant and the policy-maker with the people.

Acknowledging these ties is crucial to understanding white settler colonies like British Columbia. The significance of immigration in colonial contexts derives from its central position in the very business of imperialism. Settler societies aim simultaneously to dispossess Aboriginal peoples and to replace them with relatively homogeneous settler populations, and immigration is one of the tools that has allowed them to do so. Colonies of settlement are distinguished from other kinds of colonies chiefly by their reproductive and gendered character. That colonizers *settle* implies more than residence. It denotes a reproductive regime dependent on the presence of settler women who literally reproduce the colony. Immigration must therefore provide more than non-Aboriginal bodies. Ideally, it must provide the right kind of bodies, those suited to building a white settler colony.

These connections between immigration, empire, and gender came together in mid-nineteenth-century British Columbia in an especially revealing way. Its society was the product of three sometimes conflicting imperial intentions: the fur trade, the gold rush, and the British tradition of settler colonies. North America's northern Pacific coast and the Columbia Plateau were densely populated by linguistically, culturally, and politically diverse First Nations people reliant on foraging, hunting, and fishing. The Hudson's Bay Company (HBC) began trading with local peoples in the late eighteenth century, and formal colonial authority was established in 1849 when Vancouver Island was made a British colony.

The discovery of gold on the mainland's Fraser River in 1858 precipitated the creation of a mainland colony called British Columbia. It was, according to imperial opinion, destined to be a major colony of settlement. "[N]ever did a colony in its infancy present a more satisfactory appearance," remarked one Anglican cleric. By 1866 and 1867, however, "those who once entertained most extravagant expectations began to despond."[5] Imperial downsizing followed despondency. In 1866 the two colonies were merged, retaining the name of British Columbia, and in July 1871 British Columbia joined Canada as a province, bringing the colonial period to a close.

These shifts in political form reflected widespread disappointment in British Columbia's performance as a settler colony. "The high tide of immigration expected never reached the Colony," explained Governor Frederick Seymour, "and the ebb proved much stronger than anticipated."[6] To be sure, the population expanded: there were fewer than 1,000 settlers in 1855 and over 10,000 in 1871. But the settler population never rivalled the Aboriginal one, which, despite massive depopulation wrought by smallpox, likely hovered around the 45,000 mark in the early 1870s.[7]

Settler British Columbia did not grow as quickly as imperial observers hoped it would, nor did it grow in the way they had hoped. The periphery, like the metropole, defied pretences of ethnic and racial homogeneity.[8] For a supposed white settler colony, British Columbia was not very white: Chinese, African-American, Latino, and Kanaka (Hawaiian) settlers were a significant presence. Jews and continental Europeans pressed operative definitions of whiteness, and Americans unsettled the colony's claims to Britishness. In 1861 the local official for Douglas, a small gold-rush town on the mainland, enumerated 97 Chinese, 40 Americans, 20 Mexicans, 17 Europeans, and 6 "coloured" people. They dwelled amongst "About 700 Natives".[9] It would have been difficult to find in one place a greater mixture of different nationalities," wrote German mathematician Carl Friesach after visiting Yale, another small mining town. "Americans were undoubtably [sic] in the majority — California, especially had sent a large contingent. Then followed Germans, French, and Chinese. Next came Italians, Spaniards, Poles, etc.," he noted.[10]

The special plurality that characterized resource towns helped shape the entire colony. American missionary Matthew Macfie found Victoria, the capital city, a small and alarmingly cosmopolitan place in the early 1860s:

> Though containing at present an average of only 5,000 or 6,000 inhabitants, one cannot pass along the principal thoroughfares without meeting representatives of almost every tribe and nationality under heaven. Within a limited space may be seen — of Europeans, Russians, Austrians, Poles, Hungarians, Italians, Danes, Swedes, French, Germans, Spaniards, Swiss, Scotch, English and Irish; of Africans, Negroes from the United States and the West Indies; of Asiatics, Lascars and Chinamen; of Americans, Indians, Mexicans, Chilanoes, and citizens of the North American Republic; and of Polynesians, Malays from the Sandwich Islands [Hawaii].[11]

Macfie's fevered attempt to classify this population perhaps speaks more to his own discomfort with the mutability of racial boundaries, but it is not surprising that this discomfort was triggered in British Columbia. The diversity fostered by the gold rushes of the early colonial days diminished but never disappeared. When British Columbia entered Canadian confederation in 1871, its settler society was constituted, according to one probably conservative count, by 8,576 whites, 1,548 Chinese, and 462 Africans.[12]

That British Columbia's settlers were overwhelmingly male further suggested its failure to fit the norms of a white settler colony. While the female proportion ebbed and flowed over the colonial period, it never exceeded a high of 35 per cent of the white society and reached lows of 5 per cent.[13] Imperial discourse that accorded white women a special role as harbingers of empire rendered this demographic problem a political one. A popular emigration guide by "A Returned Digger", like so many others, despaired of what to do with a society so lacking in women. "The great curse of the colony", he explained, "is the absence of women. I doubt if there was one women to a hundred men twelve months ago. I am quite sure that now, when I am writing, there must be at least two hundred men to every woman."[14] In colonial discourse, the continuing demographic dominance of First Nations people, the plurality of settler society, and its prevailing masculinity became irreparably intertwined, a three-part symbol of British Columbia's departure from dominant social norms and expectations.

Colonial promoters — a term I apply to a loose collection of journalists, politicians, officials, missionaries, and self-appointed do-gooders — looked to immigration to address the smallness, diversity, and masculinity of settler British Columbia and to render it a prosperous and respectable settler colony. They attributed the colony's lamentable imperial performance to the sparseness of its settler society. The *British Columbian* newspaper argued that the colony's poor showing stemmed from its underpopulation, "because we have only a mere handful of population, a few thousand people living upon one another".[15] The colony lacked white population of nearly every description. The Victoria press noted,

> If we enter our churches, they want worshippers; our school houses want scholars; our streets and highways want pedestrians and vehicles; our merchants want trade; our traders want customers; our steamboats want passengers and freight; our workshops want workmen; our fertile valleys want farmers; our gold and silver mines want miners; in short, the two Colonies want population.[16]

While the colony had resources, wrote the *Cariboo Sentinel*, "without a population a country may remain forever a barren wilderness, dotted here and there with a few fisherman's huts and a few miners' and lumberman's cabins, and known only to the world as an inhospitable and poverty-stricken place."[17]

If colonial promoters suggested that British Columbia's ills stemmed from the sparseness of the white population, they had a related and almost boundless faith in the political potential of white bodies to make it a successful colonial enterprise. Even the most shameless boosters, however, recognized that British Columbia's distance from centres of white population meant that active state intervention was required for mass immigration to occur. If they wanted a white population, they would have to work for it, bidding it to come hither, assisting its passage, and supporting it on arrival. "To have our country filled up we must not only assist people to reach our shores, but we must show them the way to earn a living after they get here," wrote the *Colonist* in 1866.[18] The intervention of both the local and colonial state was required. "What right has the most remote of the British Colonies to expect immigration without even *asking for it*," agreed the New Westminster press, "to say nothing of *assisting* it?"[19]

Colonial promoters' demands for immigration were part and parcel of a programme of asserting white supremacy in British Columbia. Himani Bannerji has recently dubbed immigration a "euphemistic expression for racist labour and citizenship policies".[20] In colonial British Columbia the process worked to exclude First Nations migrants and to minimize nonwhite settlers. It was difficult, although hardly impossible, to argue for the removal of First Nations with local and obvious territorial claims. Those from distant territories were easy targets for settlers committed to visions of racial segregation. The city of Victoria worked hard to control and limit the presence of the so-called Northern Tribes — people from the coastal societies of the Nisga'a, Hieltsuk, Nexalk, Kwakwaka'wakw, Tlingit, and especially the wealthy and powerful Haida and Tsimshian — who made annual spring visits to Victoria for trade, wage work, and festivity. In 1859 a police constable found 2,235 Northern peoples, the bulk of them probably Haida and Tsimshian, living on the outskirts of Victoria.[21] As annually as they arrived, local burghers demanded their eviction. The language they used to stigmatize Northern peoples invoked the overlapping discourses of morality, criminality, and gender that have often been used to identify and marginalize immigrant groups. "Vagrancy, filth, disease, drunkenness, larceny, maiming, murder, prostitution, in a multiplied form, are the invariable results of an annual visit from the Northern Tribes," raged the *Colonist*. "We unhesitantly declare for stopping the immigration."[22]

Those who defended the rights of Northern peoples to visit Victoria — and, by implication, their status as legitimate immigrants and thus colonial citizens — relied on another staple of immigration discourse, namely the argument that the Northern peoples' presence, however unpalatable, was sweetened by their cheap labour. When settlers demanded that Northern peoples be forcibly evicted, missionary William Duncan argued that "the driving-away policy is contrary to the interests of our Colony, which needs at least the labor of the Indians". He referred to those who doubted the local need for Aboriginal labour to "the kitchens and nurseries, the fields and gardens around Victoria".[23] Governor James Douglas proposed schemes of moral and social regulation as an alternative to eviction, arguing that Northern peoples' willingness to serve as a colonial labour force made them valuable to whites. "[I]t is hardly creditable to the civilization of the nineteenth century, that so especial an element of health, as labour of the cheapest description, should be, in a manner, banished from the Colony," he explained.[24]

The sweat and toil of the Northern peoples ultimately failed to buy them a legitimate role in settler Victoria. Those who wanted racial segregation of colonial space were bolstered and legitimated by the apocalyptic smallpox epidemic of 1862, when Northern peoples were repeatedly and forcibly evicted from Victoria, a process later condoned and organized by public health legislation.[25] A brand of settler imperialism premised on the removal and containment of local peoples ultimately won out over the version that positioned them as subservient labourers for the ruling minority. Historians need to broaden our understanding of migration to account for the plurality and movement of the so-called old world and to make room for the migrations of Aboriginal North America. Doing so complicates our analysis of migration and lays bare the extent to which immigration functioned as a mechanism of inclusion and exclusion.

That this process worked to include whites and exclude others is confirmed by the experience of settlers of Asian and African extraction. Douglas — himself an archetypal hybrid figure, hailing from a "creole" mother and a Scottish father and having married the half-Cree Amelia Connolly — encouraged the migration of mainly middle-class African Americans associated with the Pioneer Society of San Francisco in 1858. Other settlers did not share his enthusiasm. Despite the African Americans' apparent fit with the colony's putative values of hard work, Protestantism, and respectability, their sizable presence in Victoria was regarded by many white people as a problem. Whether Victoria would replicate or challenge American-style segregation in her churches, theatres, and saloons was a significant item of debate until the black population began to disperse in the mid-1860s.[26]

It was Chinese immigration that created the most ambivalence among British Columbia's white commentators. Representations of Chinese men celebrated industriousness and sometimes located them on the colonists' side of the local imperial divide. The Grand Jury of Cayoosh (later Lillooet) told the Governor in 1860 that Chinese settlers were a benefit to white traders and the government alike. The jury further requested that the state acknowledge the Chinese as settlers, asking that they "afford them every due protection to prevent their being driven away, wither by attacks from Indians or otherwise".[27]

More often Chinese men were positioned as undesirable immigrants who would imperil rather than bolster colonialism. The *Cariboo Sentinel* argued that Chinese men should not be colonists for a variety of reasons, all indicating their fundamental difference and many invoking explicitly gendered images. The Chinese, the newspaper argued, were "aliens not merely in nationality, but in habits, religion"; they never became "good citizens" or served on juries or fire companies; they never married or settled outside China and were "more apt to create immorality than otherwise"; they dealt "entirely with their own countrymen"; they hoarded their money and evaded taxes; and, lastly, they were, ironically for immigrants, "inimical to immigration".[28] No restrictions were imposed on Chinese immigration, although colonists debated ways — prominent among them being a miner's licence fee levied on Chinese men alone — designed to regulate their place within settler society."[29] Such discussions anticipated the highly organized, pervasive, and vociferous attacks on Chinese people that began later in the nineteenth century and continue to shape contemporary life and politics.[30]

The role of immigration to colonial British Columbia was thus an explicitly racial one. The "'bone, muscle, and intellect,' that is required here", explained the Victoria press plainly, "differs materially from the Indian or the African. It is Caucasian — Anglo-Saxon bone, muscle, and intellect we want."[31] Class, and the politics of respectability that so often went with it, also helped determine who would be included and who excluded. Not all white people were created equal. British Columbia's colonial promoters did not want convicts, although one, tellingly, was willing to tolerate juvenile offenders as long as they were placed on First Nations settlements.[32]

When the Colonial Office inquired about the emigration of distressed Lancashire mill operatives, local officials were similarly unreceptive. Douglas replied that "this Colony offers but a poor field for destitute immigrants", warning that "instead of improving their condition, it is to be feared, that by emigrating in great numbers to this Colony, they would only be involved in a more hopeless state of distress and poverty".[33] British Columbia's officials were ultimately as fearful of organized immigration's class implications — of the shovelling out of paupers — as were others in British North America.

Immigration to this settler colony was an issue of race and class, and also very much one of gender. British Columbia's colonial failure was linked, in critics' minds, not only to the smallness and diversity of the settler society but also to the failure of increasingly hegemonic gender norms to take root there. British Columbia was home to a small, highly mobile handful of settler men living amongst a large Aboriginal society. This particular demography fostered a rough, vibrant homosocial culture created by and for young men and the widespread practice of white-Aboriginal domestic and conjugal relationships. Immigration was sought as a corrective for both. When promoters called for immigration, they called for a process that would address the society's perceived gendered deficiencies as well as its racial peculiarities.

Three gendered images dominated discussions of immigration. First, the hardy backwoodsman — a steady, hard-working man willing to meet the difficulties of colonial life and permanently settle in British Columbia — shaped discussions of men and migration. The hypothetical hardy backwoodsman was constructed in contrast to the rough gold miners who so pervaded the colony. British Columbia had two major gold rushes — the Fraser River Gold Rush of 1858 and the Cariboo Gold Rush of 1862–1863 — and a host of smaller ones. Waves of young, footloose men disillusioned with the false promises of capitalist, industrial society were attracted by each strike of gold. Prevailing discourse understood these men as wandering, immoral, and anti-social. George Grant, secretary of a surveying party, argued that the gold rushes brought "not an emigration of sober, steady householders, whose aim was to establish homes, and live by their own industry, but of fever-hearted adventurers from all parts of the world,— men without a country and without a home".[34]

Miners' inadequacies as colonists became axiomatic in popular colonial discourse. "It must be admitted that a very considerable section of our population is composed of adventurers, who, having been attracted to our shores by our gold, feel little or no interest in the permanent success of the Colony," wrote the *British Columbian*.[35] For British Columbia to fulfil its imperial potential, hardy backwoodsmen would have to replace the wandering miners. In 1859 Douglas told the Colonial Office, "The mining population are proverbially migratory and unsettled in their habits, seldom engaging in any other than their own absorbing pursuits, and therefore, it is he who tills the soil, the industrious farmer, who must clear the forest, bring the land into cultivation, and build up the permanent interests and prosperity of the Colony."[36]

The hardy backwoodsman stood in contrast not only to the wandering miner but to another masculine drain on the colonial enterprise, the "croaker". This term, along with grumbler, was applied to men deemed unable to weather the difficulties of colonial lie. Whether an erstwhile son of wealth or an urban loafer, the croaker was flummoxed by the realities of pioneering and proceeded to complain instead of work. Gilbert Malcolm Sproat, a sawmill owner, magistrate, amateur anthropologist, and promoter of immigration, described the croakers:

> [C]ertain persons came into the country who had a strong desire to make a living without taking off their coats — a desire which could not be gratified. The friends of these persons at home sent them money, which they put into silly investments. They rode to the diggings, and road [sic] back again. They hung, like mendicants, round the doors of the Government offices. They croaked in the streets, spent their time idly in bar-rooms, and finally disappeared.[37]

Here, the language of class is put to work in the service of gender and race: the croaker is idle and delicate, bearing the mark of both femininity and bourgeois laxity. The local press argued a similar position. Some settlers, one paper argued, "only remain to croak and whine for a season, and eventually, like sickly lambs or untimely fruit, unequal to the task of combatting [sic] and overcoming the hardships and privations incident to all new countries, drop off to their native land".[38] The test of manliness these "sickly lambs" fail is thus generated by the specificities of the colonial context.

This was a test that the hardy backwoodsman passed. Just as they repelled the weak, colonies were thought to attract the most manly of British men who stood in contrast not only to their less rugged fellows, but to the indigenous men they alternately feminized or feared.[39] "As a rule," commented the local press, "it is the most energetic, hardy, manly, self reliant of her sons who first people her Colonies."[40] Ideal male immigrants were hard-working, disciplined, and predisposed to rural life. The new colony, argued a supporter in 1860, "does not want the idle, the profligate, and sickly".[41] The hardy backwoodsman embraced diligent labour, especially agricultural labour, just as the gold miner rejected it. His single state meant that he was able to devote himself fully to labour, to define himself as an entirely economic being. One much-reprinted emigration guide advised, "A family is a burden till a man is established."[42]

The discourse of the hardy backwoodsman both reflected and masked single men's economic significance to a colony materially tied to resource extraction. Despite the significance of Aboriginal people to British Columbia's wage-labour force, employers persisted in seeking non-Native miners and farmers and believed, in keeping with the Anglo-American world, that only men could fulfil these roles. That a work force of single men was literally reproduced elsewhere spared the colony the costs of maintaining and creating labour in the next generation.[43] Labour-force politics reinforced the prevailing gendered patterns of immigration and ensured that single men formed the overwhelming majority of independent immigrants. They also comprised a surprising percentage of assisted ones. Between 1849 and 1852 the HBC imported over 400 people, 250 of whom were adult men mainly destined to labour on Island farms.[44] The search for hardy backwoodsmen persisted throughout the colonial period. A proposed 1864 Vancouver Island scheme put "farm labourers" alongside "unmarried female domestic servants" and "married couples" as people whose passages should be subsidized.[45]

Yet single men, hardy or otherwise, constituted an ambivalent force for colonial promoters. Sproat thought that their tendency to wander made them a waste of public funds.[46] More fundamentally, imperial regimes were consistently troubled by the large numbers of working-class men assigned responsibility for practically enforcing them [the rules of the colony].[47] White soldiers, miners, and farmers frequently failed to meet standards of racial distance and superiority set by imperial masters. Racial concerns about young, footloose men in colonial contexts were also gendered concerns. Colonial promoters were disturbed by how regularly white men formed relationships and families with local women. Settler men who opted to remain single were also a worry. Increasingly in the mid-nineteenth century the domestic family was constructed as a necessary component of adult life. To be rendered a responsible colonial citizen who was appropriately distanced from local peoples, the hardy backwoodsman needed a wholesome woman.

The scarcity of white women in British Columbia became, along with the smallness of the settler population, axiomatic for the colony's condition. As I have argued elsewhere, white women were constructed as "fair ones of a purer caste"[48] with three related roles in the local colonial project. White women would first compel white men to reject the rough homosocial culture of the backwoods in favour of normative standards of masculinity, respectability, and permanence. "Women! women! women! are the great want," wrote aristocrat Harry Verney from London. "The normal state is man with a help meet for him, and if something is not soon done, either by the Imperial or Colonial Government, or by some philanthropists at home, I know not what will become of us. Poor man goes sadly down hill if he remains long without the supporting influence of women."[49] White women were considered to be men's collective better half, as the only force capable of ensuring their proper behaviour. Such a discourse accorded them a role, albeit a limited one, as agents in both imperialism and immigration.

White women would secondly address shortages in the local labour market and relieve overpopulation in Britain. That the supposed need for domestic servants and wives in British Columbia neatly matched fears of "surplus women" in Britain gave calls for female immigration a special efficacy. A female immigration to British Columbia, wrote one observer, "would be as great a boon to the colony as I am sure it would be to many of the underpaid, under-fed, and over-worked women who drag out a weary existence in the dismal back streets and alleys of the metropolis".[50] Immigration was thus invoked as a mechanism for simultaneously resolving the different crises of gender that troubled the metropole and the periphery.

White women's third service to the colonial project was the explicitly racial one of discouraging mixed-race sexual, domestic, and conjugal relationships. As white men's "natural" objects of desire, they would draw men away from the temptations of Aboriginal women and, in doing so, shore up the colonial project as a whole. "That many of the native women are cleanly, industrious, and faithful, we do not pretend to deny," wrote New Westminster's *Mainland Guardian*, "but, we regret to to [sic] say, they are the exceptions. With the increase of our white female population, we look for new life in our agricultural pursuits and we hope that every inducement will be offered to healthy industrious women, who are desirous of finding good husbands and comfortable homes, in this province, to come out to us."[51] This discourse was premised on the construction of white women as uplifting and on the representation of First Nations women as base and threatening that circulated throughout colonial British Columbia.

In these ways, the discourse of wholesome women emphasized the political utility of ordinary, working-class women above those who held an official role in the colonial project like missionaries' or officials' wives. Their contribution lay not in independent action, but rather in their ability to transform plebeian men. Such a discourse imbued women migrants with an agency less often acknowledged in historiography. At any rate, the sheer ideological weight of the conviction that a society lacking white women could not be a moral or even adequate one provided the motivation necessary to orchestrate immigration schemes in 1862, 1863, and 1870. Organized as joint efforts of the local elite, missionaries, and British feminists, these immigration campaigns are remembered in popular lore as the "brideships", as colony- (and, later, nation-) building enterprises. Together, the *Tynemouth*, *Robert Lowe*, and *Alpha* carried roughly a hundred women, largely teenagers from working-class and sometimes indigent backgrounds. They were putatively destined to be domestic servants, but popular discourse ensured that their real destiny lay in the marriage market. As wives of miners and farmers, colonial promoters hoped, these wholesome women would render British Columbia's fragile colonial project a stable one.[52]

The young working-class women produced by these female immigration schemes ultimately unsettled the colonial project rather than securing it. Instead of behaving as beacons of imperial rectitude, the immigrants acted like the young, working-class women that they were. Colonial promoters were deeply disappointed. By the close of the colonial period, their faith in the political usefulness of white female migration was profoundly shaken. In 1872 Sproat looked back on his experience with three separate female immigration efforts, commenting, "How to send single women to Victoria safely across the continent, and through San Francisco, is a problem which I cheerfully hand over for solution to those who are more experienced in the management of that sex than I am."[53] The fundamental problem with white female migration, he argued, was that *single* women were necessarily a moral problem. "The very delicate and difficult question of introducing single unmarried women into British Columbia might be partly solved by sending out a few, in charge of the heads of families — the women being from the same district as the families, and thus having an addition[al] guard for their self-respect," he argued.[54]

Wholesome women, much like hardy backwoodsmen, challenged the colonial project at the same time as they bolstered it. The enthusiasm for white female migration was always tempered and eventually overwhelmed by the conviction that single women, like men, were a dangerous population that could only be properly contained by families. After the disasters of the assisted female migration efforts of 1862 and 1863, the "steady family" gained a special cachet in pro-immigration discourse that would only increase after the 20 servant-women transported on the *Alpha* in 1870 proved, like their predecessors, a disappointment to those who so sought their importation. The Female Immigration Board that oversaw this scheme recommended that the colonial government abandon the project of female immigration and shift its monies and attentions to the "assisted passages of Families, and relatives of Farmers, Mechanics, and others settled in this Colony".[55] In pledging their support for the importation of families, and not single women, members of the board endorsed the stable family as the best kind of immigration for the colony.

They were not alone in suggesting that same-race domestic families would be the best base for a settler society and thus the best immigrants. Families simultaneously constrained young women and encouraged men to be permanent and diligent settlers. The *Victoria Press* argued, "The very class which we want above all others is the married agriculturist — the man whose social circumstances will bring him to the soil, and make him a permanent as well as productive inhabitant."[56] Sproat agreed, writing that "the married farmer with modest means, and accustomed to work in the fields, is the best kind of immigrant for British Columbia".[57] The HBC supported family migration when it imported 36 married colliers to work Nanaimo's coalfields.[58] That the Colonial Office shared this familial ideal is suggested by its willingness to pay for the passage of the wives and families of the Royal Engineers, the soldier-settlers sent to enforce British claims to the mainland.[59] On rare occasions the colonial government subsidized the migration of individual families,[60] but more often used land law to buttress domestic family formation. In Vancouver Island, nuclear family formation was encouraged by laws that gave white men an additional 50 acres of free land if they were married and 10 more acres for each child under the age of 10.[61]

The overlap between immigration discourse and immigration practice was usually indirect. These demands for hardy backwoodsmen, wholesome women, and steady families were rarely parlayed into concrete action. Immigration was what colonial pundits always wanted and never got. In referring to immigrants as "mythical beings", politician John Sebastian Helmcken astutely recognized the somewhat hypnotic role immigration played in colonial discourse.[62] The mythic rather than actual character of immigration to colonial British Columbia was not for lack of heated rhetoric or wild scheming. Colonial promoters held mass meetings, struck committees, wrote passionate letters, and developed plans for using immigration to secure their imperial fortunes.[63] With the exception of the 20 servant women carried on the *Alpha* in 1870, however, the colonial government's immigration efforts were largely confined to the cheap and discursive: they subsidized mail, explored territory, printed essays, and hired lecturers to regale the masses of various urban centres. In 1861, for instance, British Columbia created an exhibit for the World's Fair designed to prove to "struggling, hard worked Englishmen how easily a livelihood may be earned here".[64]

The modesty of these efforts deeply disappointed those who considered immigration key to imperial success. They complained bitterly about the local government's apparent inability to organize immigration. In 1864 the mainland press commented that, excepting "fifty pounds paid to a parson at Lillooet for an Essay," the colony had "not yet expended a single dollar" on immigration.[65] Five years later, the same newspaper despaired that there was not one person responsible for immigration "[a]mongst the army of officials who absorb the revenue of the Colony."[66]

If British Columbia's local government was unable, its imperial masters were unwilling. The Colonial Office argued that, given its location, British Columbia could only reasonably expect emigrants from the Australasian colonies, not from Britain, and repeatedly announced that it had no intention of ever assisting emigration to the colony.[67] When pestered to subsidize steam communication, Colonial Office staff made it clear that they lacked the requisite political will. "When this Country was supposed to be overpeopled, there was the appearance of a domestic object in schemes for using the proceeds of English taxes to encourage emigration. But that state of things has long ceased to exist," one noted.[68] Domestic issues like overpopulation fuelled the various assisted emigration schemes of the 1830s and 1840s and would again motivate major emigration schemes in the *fin de siècle*. These efforts ground to a near halt when popular economic fortunes bettered and events like New Zealand's Maori Wars and the Indian Rebellion of 1857 challenged British faith in the imperial project.

Whether in London, Victoria, or New Westminster, many doubted British Columbia's ability to attract settlers, but only a few challenged its need for a large white population. In 1861 the *Victoria Press* argued that mass immigration was an impractical goal cooked up by those unaccustomed to colonial labour, race politics, and labour relations. "It may suit a number of lackadaisical beings who are entirely unfitted for Colonial, or in fact any practical useful life, to be enabled to obtain, by a superabundant supply of immigrants, civilized *servants* at the same price they now pay for Indians," the press wrote.[69] Yet those who questioned the merits of feasibility of mass white immigration never captured the mainstream of public discourse. Ultimately, British Columbia's apparent inability to attract white and especially British immigrants served not as a reason for challenging the viability of colonialism, but rather as a rationale for the colony's entry into Canadian confederation.[70] If British Columbia could not use immigration to become a stable settler colony in its own right, it would try to do so as a Canadian province. That British Columbia finally registered a white majority in the first census taken after confederation suggests that this strategy was effective. With continuing depopulation of First Nations and the arrival of the transcontinental railroad in 1866 — that tangible technology of both capital and nation and conveyor of migrants *par excellence*— British Columbia would begin to look increasingly like a textbook white settler colony, but it would continue to be haunted by a spectre of hybridity that was, in the final analysis, more nurtured by immigration than vanquished by it.

British Columbia's colonial pundits spilled much ink on the topic of immigration. They did so because immigration was central to their effort to transform British Columbia into a white settler colony. For them, immigration was a mechanism of inclusion and exclusion, one that would marginalize First Nations people, minimize non-white settlers, and nurture white migration. It would do so in explicitly gendered ways that reflected the importance of gender to the construction of a settler society. In newspapers, government reports, and colonial circles, they called for the immigration of white, preferably British immigrants who would fit into three gendered models: the hardy backwoodsman, the wholesome woman, and the steady family. This discourse reflected a minority's aspirations rather than a society's social experience. However constant and blustery the pro-immigration discourse, British Columbia's settler society would continue to be small, dominated by men, and relatively diverse until the Canadian Pacific Railroad integrated the province into more continental patterns of demography and settlement. Immigration was indeed a tool for negotiating exclusions and inclusions, but not always in predictable ways.

NOTES

Adele Perry is assistant professor in the Department of History at St. Paul's College, University of Manitoba. This article is drawn from her forthcoming *On the Edge of Empire: Gender, Race, and the Making of British-Columbia, 1849–1871* (Toronto: University of Toronto Press, 2000). She would like to thank the organizers of the conference "Recasting European and Canadian History" for their contributions to this paper.

1. See, for instance, Bernard Bailyn, *The Peopling of British North America: An Introduction* (New York: Knopf, 1986). For a revealing example, see the explicit definition of Ontario's Leeds and Landsdowne townships as "empty" in Donald Harman Akenson, *The Irish in Ontario: A Study in Rural History* (Montreal and Kingston: McGill-Queen's University Press, 1984), p. 55.

2. Daiva Staisulis and Nira Yuval-Davis, "Introduction: Beyond Dichotomies — Gender, Race, Ethnicity and Class in Settler Societies", in Staisulis and Yuval-Davis, eds., *Unsettling Settler Societies: Articulations of Gender, Race, Ethnicity and Class* (London: Sage, 1995).

3. On this point in a later period, see Stephen Constantine, "Introduction: Empire Migration and Imperial Harmony", in Constantine, ed., *Emigrants and Empire: British Settlement in the Dominions Between the Wars* (Manchester: Manchester University Press, 1990). See also Rita S. Kranidis, ed., *Imperial Objects: Essays on Victorian Women's Emigration and the Unauthorized Imperial Experience* (New York: Twanye, 1998).

4. On this shift, see Franca Iacovetta, "Manly Militants, Cohesive Communities, and Defiant Domestics: Writing About Immigrants in Canadian Historical Scholarship", *Labour/Le Travail*, vol. 36 (Fall 1995), p. 221. Also see Iacovetta with Paula Draper and Robert Vantresca, "Preface", in Iacovetta, Draper, and Vantresca, eds., *A Nation of Immigrants: Women, Workers, and Communities in Canadian History, 1840s–1960s* (Toronto: University of Toronto Press, 1998).

5. Henry Wright, *Nineteenth Annual Report of the Missions of the Church of England in British Columbia for the Year 1877* (London: Rivingtons, 1878), pp. 16–17.

6. British Columbia Archives (hereafter BCA), GR 1486, mflm B–1442, Great Britain, Colonial Office, British Columbia Original Correspondence (hereafter CO 60), CO 60/32, Frederick Seymour to Duke of Buckingham and Chandos, March 17, 1868.

7. All population figures from colonial British Columbia are at best guesses. These are from British Columbia, *Report of the Hon. H. L. Langevin, C.B., Minister of Public Works* (Ottawa: I. B. Taylor, 1872), p. 22; and Edward Mallandaine, *First Victoria Directory, Third [Fourth] Issues, and British Columbia Guide* (Victoria: Mallandaine, 1871), pp. 94–95. Also see R. Cole Harris and John Warkentin, *Canada Before Confederation: A Study in Historical Geography* (Ottawa: Carleton University Press, 1991), chap. 7.

8. Antoinette Burton, *At the Heart of Empire: Indians and the Colonial Encounter in Late-Victorian Britain* (Berkeley: University of California Press, 1998).

9. BCA, "Colonial Correspondence", GR 1372, mflm B–1330, file 620/16, John Bowles Gaggin to W. A. G. Young, April 3, 1861.

10. Carl Friesach, "Extracts from *Ein Ausflug nach Britisch-Columbien im Jahre 1858*", in E. E. Delavault and Isabel McInnes, trans., "Two Narratives of the Fraser River Gold Rush", *British Columbia Historical Quarterly*, vol. 1 (July 1941), p. 227.

11. Matthew Macfie, *Vancouver Island and British Columbia: Their History, Resources and Prospects* (London: Longman, Green, Longman, Roberts & Green, 1865), pp. 378–379.

12. British Columbia, *Report of the Hon. H. L. Langevin*, p. 22.

13. On this, see Adele Perry, *On the Edge of Empire: Gender, Race, and the Making of British Columbia, 1849–1871* (Toronto: University of Toronto Press, 2000), chap. 1.

14. A Returned Digger, *The Newly Discovered Gold Fields of British Columbia* (London: Darton and Hodge, 1862, 8th ed.), p. 7.

15. "Our Great Want", *British Columbian*, January 9, 1869.

16. "Our Wants", *British Colonist*, June 5, 1861.

17. "Emigration", *Cariboo Sentinel*, June 18, 1868.

18. "Assisted Immigration", *British Colonist*, December 11, 1866.

19. "Population, Population", *British Columbian*, May 29, 1869.

20. Himani Bannerji, *On the Dark Side of the Nation: Essays on Multiculturalism, Nationalism and Gender* (Toronto: Canadian Scholars' Press, 2000), p. 4.

21. "Our Indian Population", *Weekly Victoria Gazette*, April 28, 1859.

22. "Invasion of the Northern Indians", *British Colonist*, April 18, 1861.

23. William Duncan, "The Indian Question", *British Colonist*, July 4, 1861. On Aboriginal wage labour, see John Lutz, "After the Fur Trade: Aboriginal Wage Labour in Nineteenth-Century British Columbia", *Journal of the Canadian Historical Association* (1992), pp. 69–94.

24. National Archives of Canada (hereafter NAC), Great Britain, Colonial Office Correspondence, Vancouver Island (hereafter CO 305), CO 305/10, mflm B–238, James Douglas to Sir Edward Bulwer Lytton, May 25, 1859.

25. See Perry, *On the Edge*, chap. 5.

26. For an argument for black migration to Vancouver Island, see Mary A. Shadd, *A Plea for Emigration; or, Notes of Canada West, in its Moral, Social, and Political Aspect With Suggestions Respecting Mexico, West Indies, and Vancouver's Island, for the Information of Colored Emigrants* [Detroit: George W. Pattison, 1842], pp. 43–44. On black people in Victoria society, see Irene Genevieve Marie Zaffaroni, "The Great Chain of Being: Racism and Imperialism in Colonial Victoria, 1858–1871" (MA thesis, University of Victoria, 1987), chap. 4; Crawford Killian, *Go Do Some Great Thing: The Black Pioneers of British Columbia* (Vancouver: Douglas and McIntyre, 1978).

27. NAC, CO 60/8, MG 11, mflm B–83, "Address of the Grand Jury at Cayoosh to Governor Douglas", in James Douglas to Duke of Newcastle, October 9, 1860.

28. "Our Chinese Population", *Cariboo Sentinel*, May 16, 1867.

29. See, for an explanation of why they were impracticable, NAC, CO 63/3, mflm B–1489, "Speech of His Honor the Officer Administering the Government at the Opening of the Legislative Council", *British Columbia Government Gazette*.

30. On this, see Kay Anderson, *Vancouver Chinatown: Racial Discourse in Canada, 1875–1980* (Montreal and Kingston: McGill-Queen's University Press, 1991); Patricia E. Roy, *A White Man's Province: British Columbia Politicians and Chinese and Japanese Immigrants, 1858–1914* (Vancouver: University of British Columbia Press, 1989).

31. "Indian vs. White Labor", *British Colonist*, February 19, 1861.

32. "Convict Labor", *British Columbian*, January 11, 1865; "Juvenile Offenders — Colonization", *British Columbian*, May 30, 1869.

33. NAC, CO 305/20, MG 11, mflm B–244, and CO 60/16, MG 11, mflm B–89, James Douglas to the Duke of Newcastle, July 14, 1863.

34. George M. Grant, *Ocean to Ocean: Sandford Fleming's Expedition Through Canada in 1872* (Toronto: James Campbell & Son, 1873), p. 308. Also see Adele Perry, "Bachelors in the Backwoods: White Man and Homosocial Culture in Up-Country British Columbia, 1858–1871", in R. W. Sandwell, ed., *Beyond City Limits: Rural History in British Columbia* (Vancouver: University of British Columbia Press, 1998).

35. "Arterial Highways", *British Columbian*, January 2, 1862.

36. NAC, CO 60/4, MG 11, mflm B–80, James Douglas to Edward Bulwer Lytton, July 11, 1859.

37. Gilbert Malcolm Sproat, *British Columbia: Information for Emigrants* (London: Agent General for the Province, 1873), p. 4.

38. "The Soil of British Columbia", *British Columbian*, February 3, 1863.

39. On masculinity and colonization, see Mrinalini Sinha, *Colonial Masculinity: The "Manly Englishman" and the "Effeminate Bengali" in the Late Nineteenth Century* (Manchester: Manchester University Press, 1995); Elizabeth Vibert, *Traders' Tales: Narratives of Cultural Encounters on the Plateau, 1807–1846* (Norman: University of Oklahoma Press, 1997).

40. "The Colonial Policy of Great Britain", *British Colonist*, May 2, 1863.

41. "Testimonial to D. G. F. MacDonald, Esq., C.E.", *Weekly Victoria Gazette*, January 30, 1860.

42. A Returned Digger, *The Newly Discovered Gold Fields*, p. 8.

43. This is dealt with, to some extent, in Alicja Muszynski, *Cheap Wage Labour: Race and Gender in the Fisheries of British Columbia* (Montreal and Kingston: McGill-Queen's University Press, 1996). Muszynski, however, discusses the economics of the single male immigrant as unique to Chinese men, when in fact most non-Natives lacked co-resident families.

44. University of British Columbia Library (hereafter UBCL), CO 305/3, mflm R288, A. Colville to John Packington, November 24, 1852, p. 1.

45. British Library, BS 72/1, "England, Emigration Commissioners", *Colonization Circular*, no. 25, 1866 (London, Groombridge and Sons), p. 8.

46. BCA, Add Mss 257, file 3, Gilbert Malcolm Sproat to Lieutenant Governor, "Memo re European Immigration into B.C.", November 3, 1871.

47. See, for instance, Kenneth Ballhatchet, *Race, Sex and Class under the Raj: Imperial Attitudes and Policies and their Critics, 1783–1905* (London: Werdenfeld and Nicholson, 1980), chap. 5.

48. One of the Disappointed, untitled piece in the *British Columbian*, June 7, 1862, Adele Perry, "'Fair Ones of a Purer Caste': White Women and Colonialism in Nineteenth-Century British Columbia", *Feminist Studies*, vol. 23, no. 3 (Fall 1997), pp. 501–524.

49. "Sir Harry Verney Upon British Columbia", *British Columbian*, August 20, 1862.

50. A. D. G., "British Columbia: To the Editor of the Times", *London Times*, January 1, 1862.

51. "Immigration", *Mainland Guardian*, February 9, 1871.

52. See Perry, *On the Edge*, chaps. 6–7, for an analysis of female immigration to British Columbia.

53. BCA, GR 419, box 10, file 1872/1, British Columbia, Attorney General, "Documents", G. M. S., "Memorandum on Immigration, Oct. 1972", pp. 95–96.

54. BCA, GR 419, box 10, file 1872/1, "Attorney General Documents", G. M. Sproat, "Memorandum of a few Suggestions for opening the business of emigration to British Columbia, referred to as Memo C, in a letter of G. M. Sproat to the Honourable the Provincial Secretary, dated 29th August 1972", pp. 4–5.

55. BCA, GR 1372, mflm B–1314, file 995/23, "Colonial Correspondence", Wm. Pearse, John Robson, W. J. MacDonald to Colonial Secretary, July 12, 1870; E. G. A. "The Immigration Board", *British Colonist*, June 24, 1870.

56. "The Overland Route", *Victoria Press*, March 16, 1862.

57. BCA, GR 419, box 10, file 1872/1, British Columbia, "Papers Related to Immigration, 1972", G. M. S., "Memorandum on Immigration, Oct. 1872".

58. BCA, add mss E/BM91A, Andrew Muir, "Private Diary", November 9, 1848–August 5, 1850 [transcript]; Add Mss A/C/20.1/N15, James Douglas — Joseph William McKay, "Nanaimo Correspondence, August 1852–September 1853" [transcript].

59. NAC, MG 11, CO 609/9, mflm B–83, G. C. Lewis to James Douglas, August 11, 1860, draft reply, in James Douglas to the Duke of Newcastle, May 12, 1860.

60. See, for instance, James E. Hendrickson, ed., *Journals of the Colonial Legislatures of the Colonies of Vancouver Island and British Columbia, 1851–1871*, vol. 1: *Journals of the Council Executive Council, and Legislative Council of Vancouver Island, 1851–1866* (Victoria: Provincial Archives of British Columbia, 1980), pp. 133–134.

61. "The New Land proclamation for Vancouver Island", *British Colonist*, March 8, 1861; "Salt Spring Island", *Victoria Press*, November 10, 1861; Macfie, *Vancouver Island and British Columbia,* p. 205.

62. "Legislative Council", *British Colonist*, February 4, 1869.

63. See examples in Hendrickson, ed., *Journals of the Colonial Legislatures*, vol. 2: *Journals of the House of Assembly, Vancouver Island, 1856–1863*, vol. 3: *Journals of the House of Assembly, Vancouver Island, 1863–1866*, and vol. 4: *Journals of the Executive Council, 1864–1871, and of the Legislative Council, 1864–1866, of British Columbia.*

64. "Industrial Exhibition Circular", *British Columbian*, May 30, 1861.

65. "Emigration", *British Columbian*, June 15, 1864.

66. "What Shall We Do With Them?", *British Columbian*, June 4, 1869.

67. NAC, MG 11, CO 60/5, mflm B–81, T. W. C. Murdoch and Frederic Rogers to Herman Merivale, April 28, 1859; mflm 69.303, Great Britain, House of Commons, Parliamentary Papers, vol. 38 (1863), no. 403, "Emigration: Number of Emigrants who left the United Kingdom for the *United States, British North America, the several colonies of Australia, South Africa,* and other Places respectively: distinguishing, as far as practicable, the Native Country of the Emigrants, 1860–1863", mflm 69.303, p. 7.

68. NAC, MG 11, CO 60/14, mflm B–87, H. M. [Herman Merivale], April 8, note *en verso* in T. W. C. Murdoch to Frederic Rogers, March 31, 1862.

69. "The Immigration Bubble", *Victoria Press*, July 27, 1861.

70. BCA, GR 1486, CO 60/29, mflm B–1440, Frederick Seymour to Duke of Buckingham and Chandos, September 24, 1867.

Topic Fifteen
Confederation

LA CONFEDERATION!!!

This political cartoon was drawn in 1864 for *La Scie* by Quebec cartoonist
Jean-Baptiste Côté. Côté portrays Quebec as a lamb about to be swallowed.
Upper Canada Reform leader George Brown is riding the seven-headed
Confederation monster, and Lower Canada Conservative leader George-
Étienne Cartier is one of the two men wafting incense. Both men supported
Confederation.

Union of the British North American colonies had been considered as far back as 1790. A renewed interest arose in the 1850s, when increasing tensions between British North America and the United States and the emerging political deadlock in the Canadas made the option of a larger colonial union attractive. At neither time, however, were the conditions right for union.

The opportunity for Canadian and Maritime politicians to bring about Confederation came only in the mid-1860s. The details of union were worked out at two important conferences in 1864. At the Charlottetown conference, in September, the delegates agreed in principle on a number of important features of the eventual federation, including the principle of regional representation in the upper house (Senate) and that of "representation by population" in the lower house (House of Commons). They also agreed on the division of powers between the federal and the provincial governments. A second conference at Quebec, in October, finalized these understandings in the Seventy-Two Resolutions, the basis for the British North America Act. Between 1864 and 1867, the politicians worked to convince their respective colonial assemblies to adopt Confederation.

The idea of Confederation was strongly opposed in Canada East. In "Confederation and Quebec," a chapter from his book *The French-Canadian Idea of Confederation, 1864–1900,* 2nd ed., Arthur I. Silver points out that French Canadians in the St. Lawrence Valley judged the proposal mainly in terms of its potential impact on French-Canadian nationalism. Whereas the *bleus* (under George-Étienne Cartier) were convinced that the proposed union guaranteed the autonomy of Quebec — in Silver's words, "in the promotion and embodiment of the French-Canadian nationality"— the *rouges* (under Antoine Dorion) remained unconvinced, and opposed the scheme. Why ultimately, did a narrow majority of the French-speaking members of the assembly of the Union of the Canadas agree to union? What similarities and differences existed between the position of the Upper Canadian Reformers and that of the French Canadians on Confederation?

Confederation was seen in Canada West as a solution to the perennial problem of political deadlock in the Canadas, and enjoyed widespread support. In a chapter of his book, "Confederation: The Untold Story," in *Getting It Wrong: How Canadians Forgot Their Past and Imperilled Confederation,* Paul Romney argues that Upper Canadian Reformers embraced Canadian federation as a way of securing autonomy within the existing Union of the Canadas, and, after 1867, Ontario's position within a larger Canadian nation. What arguments did Upper Canadian reformers put forward to argue in favour of Confederation? What was the decisive factor in convincing Canada West to support the project?

Many excellent books exist on the subject of British North American federation. Good starting points include Donald Creighton's *The Road to Confederation* (Toronto: Macmillan, 1964), W.L. Morton's *The Critical Years, 1857–1873* (Toronto: McClelland and Stewart, 1968), and Christopher Moore's *1867: How the Fathers Made a Deal* (Toronto: McClelland & Stewart, 1997). A lively account of the Confederation movement in the Canadas and the Atlantic region is P.B. Waite's *The Life and Times of Confederation, 1864–1867* (Toronto: University of Toronto Press, 1962). P.B. Waite has edited the original debates in the United Canadas in *The Confederation Debates in the Province of Canada, 1865* (Toronto: University of Toronto Press, 1967). Janet Ajzenstat, et al., *Canada's Founding Debates* (Don Mills, ON: Stoddart Publishing, 1999), is also an important work. *Confederation,* edited by Ramsay Cook (Toronto: University of Toronto Press, 1967), contains important articles on the subject, including the essay on New Brunswick by Alfred G. Bailey entitled "The Basis and Persistence of Opposition to Confederation in New Brunswick" and George F.G. Stanley's "Act or Pact: Another Look at Confederation." Ged Martin has edited an interesting collection, *The Causes of Canadian Confederation* (Fredericton: Acadiensis Press, 1990), one of the highlights being his own essay, "The Case Against Canadian Confederation," pp. 19–49. Martin has also published *Britain and the Origins of Canadian Confederation* (Vancouver: University of British Columbia Press, 1995). J.M.S. Careless's *Brown of the Globe*, vol. 2 (Toronto: Macmillan, 1963), and Donald Creighton's *John A. Macdonald*, vol. 1, *The Young Politician* (Toronto: Macmillan, 1952), review the ideas and the important role of these leading figures in the Confederation movement.

For an account of Canada East's response, see Marcel Bellavance, *Le Québec et la Confédération: Un choix libre? Le clergé et la constitution de 1867* (Sillery, PQ: Septentrion, 1992). An older treatment of the same subject is Jean-Charles Bonenfant, *The French Canadians and the Birth of Confederation*, Canadian Historical Association, Historical Booklet no. 21 (Ottawa: CHA, 1966).

In the Atlantic region, Confederation met with a mixed response. In New Brunswick, a pro-Confederation government was initially defeated, and subsequently reelected. In Nova Scotia, Charles Tupper, leader of the Confederation forces, refused even to bring the issue to a vote in the provincial assembly. On the reaction of the Maritime colonies to British North American Confederation, see Phillip A. Buckner, "The 1860s: An End and a Beginning," in *The Atlantic Region to Confederation: A History*, ed. Phillip A. Buckner and John G. Reid (Toronto: University of Toronto Press, 1994), pp. 360–86.

WEBLINKS

Approaching Confederation
http://www.canadiana.org/citm/themes/constitution/constitution12_e.html

A collection of documents from 1850 to 1867, detailing the letters and early resolutions that were precursors to the successful Union of British North America.

Confederation: Quebec
http://www.collectionscanada.ca/confederation/023001-2140-e.html

This site richly describes the historical context of the province of Quebec at the time of Confederation.

Confederation Rejected: Newfoundland
http://www.heritage.nf.ca/law/debate.html

An account of the debate and ultimate rejection of Confederation in Newfoundland.

Joseph Howe
http://www.gov.ns.ca/legislature/Facts/Howebio.html

A biography of Joseph Howe. Includes digitized letters by Howe, among other resources.

Quebec Resolutions, 1864
http://www.archives.gov.on.ca/english/centennial/12_quebec_resolutions.htm

A digitized page of the Quebec Resolutions, 1864.

Confederation Documents
http://www.collectionscanada.ca/confederation/023001-2600-e.html

Dozens of digitized documents that demonstrate the unique issues faced by all provinces and territories that entered Confederation.

Article Thirty-Four

Confederation and Quebec

A.I. Silver

When French Lower Canadians were called on to judge the proposed confederation of British North American provinces, the first thing they wanted to know was what effect it would have on their own nationality. Before deciding whether or not they approved, they wanted to hear "what guarantees will be offered for the future of the French-Canadian nationality, to which we are attached above all else."[1] From Richelieu's Rouge MPP to Quebec's Catholic-Conservative *Courrier du Canada*, everyone promised to judge the work of the Great Coalition according to the same criterion.[2] Even Montreal's *La Minerve*, known to be George-Étienne Cartier's own organ, promised to make its judgement from a national point of view:

> If the plan seems to us to safeguard Lower Canada's special interests, its religion and its nationality, we'll give it our support; if not, we'll fight it with all our strength.[3]

But this quotation reminds us that concern for the French-Canadian nationality had geographical implications, that Canadians in the 1860s generally considered French Canada and Lower Canada to be equivalent. When French Canadians spoke of their *patrie*, their homeland, they were invariably referring to Quebec. Even the word *Canada*, as they used it, usually referred to the lower province, or, even more specifically, to the valley of the St. Lawrence, that ancient home of French civilization in America, whose special status went back to the seventeenth century. Thus, when Cartier sang "O Canada! mon pays! mes amours!" he was referring to the "majestic course of the Saint-Laurent";[4] and Cartier's protégé, Benjamin Sulte, versifying like his patron, also found French Canada's "Patrie . . . on the banks of the Saint-Laurent."[5]

Throughout the discussion of Confederation, between 1864 and 1867, there ran the assumption that French Canada was a geographical as well as an ethnic entity, forming, as the *Revue Canadienne* pointed out optimistically, "the most considerable, the most homogeneous, and the most regularly constituted population group" in the whole Confederation.[6] *La Minerve*, which, as has been seen, characterized Lower Canada by a religion and a nationality, referred also to a "Franco-Canadian nationality, which really exists today on the banks of the St. Lawrence, and which has affirmed itself more than once."[7] Nor was the equation of Lower Canada with French Canada only a pro-Confederationist notion. The editors of the *Union Nationale* also maintained that the way to defend the French-Canadian nationality was to defend the rights of Lower Canada.[8]

It followed from this equation that provincial autonomy was to be sought in the proposed constitution as a key safeguard of the interests of French Canada. "We must never forget," asserted the *Gazette de Sorel*, "that French Canadians need more reassurance than the other provinces for their civil and religious immunities." But since French Canada was a province, its immunities were to be protected by provincial autonomy; hence, "this point is important above all for Lower Canada."[9]

Source: A.I. Silver, "Confederation and Quebec," *The French-Canadian Idea of Confederation, 1864–1900*, 2nd ed. (Toronto: University of Toronto Press, 1997), pp. 33–50. Reprinted by permission of University of Toronto Press Incorporated.

On this key issue, French Canadians felt themselves to have different interests from those of other British North Americans. Thus, Cartier's organ:

> The English . . . have nothing to fear from the central government, and their first concern is to ensure its proper functioning. This is what they base their hopes upon, and the need for strong local governments only takes second place in their minds.
>
> The French press, on the contrary, feels that guarantees for the particular autonomy of our nationality must come before all else in the federal constitution. It sees the whole system as based on these very guarantees.[10]

Le Courrier de St-Hyacinthe agreed that "we do not have the same ideas as our compatriots of British origin concerning the powers which are to be given to the central government. . . . We cannot consent to the loss of our national autonomy."[11] The Rouges also saw opposition between French- and English-Canadian interests. It was because of this opposition, they commented pessimistically, that George Brown had been able to reveal details of the Quebec Resolutions in Toronto, to the evident satisfaction of Upper Canadians, while in Lower Canada the ministers refused to make any information public.[12]

New Brunswick's governor, A.H. Gordon, in whose house Cartier had been a guest after the Charlottetown Conference, also saw an opposition between English- and French-Canadian aspirations. He reported to the Colonial Secretary that while the former seemed to expect a very centralized union, "'federal union' in the mouth of a Lower Canadian means the independence of his Province from all English or Protestant influences."[13]

This was, indeed, what it seemed to mean to the French-Canadian press. Thus:

> We want a confederation in which the federal principle will be applied in its fullest sense — one which will give the central power control only over general questions in no way affecting the interests of each separate section, while leaving to the local legislatures everything which concerns our particular interests.[14]

A confederation would be a fine thing, but only "if it limited as much as possible the rights of the federal government, to general matters, and left complete independence to the local governments."[15] As early as 1858, French-Canadian advocates of a British North American confederation had argued that "it would certainly be necessary to give the separate [provincial] legislatures the greatest possible share of power," and even that the federal government should have its powers only "by virtue of a perpetual but limited concession from the different provinces."[16]

While most papers did not go so far as to support the provincial sovereignty which that last implied,[17] they did opt for coordinate sovereignty:

> The federal power will be sovereign, no doubt, but it will have power only over certain general questions clearly defined by the constitution.
>
> This is the only plan of confederation which Lower Canada can accept. . . . The two levels of government must both be sovereign, each within its jurisdiction as clearly defined by the constitution.[18]

What, after all, could be simpler than that each power, federal or provincial, should have complete control of its own field?

> Isn't that perfectly possible without having the local legislatures derive their powers from the central legislature or vice versa? Isn't it possible for each of these bodies to have perfect independence within the scope of its own jurisdiction, neither one being able to invade the jurisdiction of the other?[19]

To be sure, the fathers of Confederation were aware that French Canadians would reject complete centralization. John A. Macdonald told the Assembly that though he would have preferred a legislative union, he realized it would be unacceptable to French Canadians. Nevertheless, he felt the Quebec Resolutions did not provide for a real federalism, but would "give to the General Government the strength of a legislative and administrative union." They represented "the happy medium" between a legislative and a federal union, which, while providing guarantees for those who feared the former, would also give "us the strength of a Legislative union."[20] In short, he appeared to understand the Quebec scheme to provide for the closest thing possible to a legislative union, saving certain guarantees for the French Canadians' "language, nationality, and religion."

This interpretation was hotly rejected by French Canadians of both parties, including those who spoke for Macdonald's partner, Cartier:

> Whatever guarantees may be offered here, Lower Canada will never consent to allowing its particular interests to be regulated by the inhabitants of the other provinces. . . . We want a solid constitution . . . but we demand above all perfect freedom and authority for the provinces to run their own internal affairs.[21]

Let there be no mistake about it: anything close to a legislative union "cannot and will not be accepted by the French-Canadian population." A centralized union would be fatal to the French-Canadian nationality.[22] The *Courrier de St-Hyacinthe,* in fact, summed up the whole French-Canadian position when it said:

> But whatever guarantees they decide to offer us, we cannot accept any union other than a federal union based on the well-understood principles of confederations.[23]

In taking this view, French Canadians were led to reject another position adopted by John A. Macdonald: that the United States example proved the necessity of a strong central government. He argued that the Civil War had occurred there because the individual states had too much power under the American constitution — power which had given the federation too much centrifugal thrust. To avoid this, British North America must have a dominant central authority.[24]

In French Canada, even *La Minerve* considered Macdonald's reasoning to be nonsensical. "We believe that this is a specious argument. The United States have a strongly centralized government, which is even capable of acting despotically, as we can see every day." If you gave a central government too much power over too many localities, it would inevitably antagonize some of them.

> This is precisely what happened in the United States, where the war was caused not by the excessive power of the local governments, but by the central government, whose tyrannical actions came into direct opposition to the particular interests of a considerable part of the confederation.[25]

Le Journal de Québec agreed wholeheartedly. The causes of the American Civil War were to be sought, not in the powers of the states, but in "the awful tyranny which the central government of the United States imposes on the state authorities, by taking them over and stealing their most inalienable powers."[26]

There was agreement between Bleus and Rouges that the autonomy of a French-Canadian Lower Canada was the chief thing to be sought in any new constitution. Accordingly, the

Confederation discussion revolved around whether or not the Quebec plan achieved that aim. As far as the opposition was concerned, it did not. The Rouges maintained that this was an "anglicizing bill,"[27] the latest in a line of attempts to bring about the "annihilation of the French race in Canada," and thus realize Lord Durham's wicked plans.[28] And it would achieve this goal because it was not really a confederation at all, but a legislative union in disguise, a mere extension of the Union of 1840.[29] "It is in vain," cried C.-S. Cherrier at a Rouge-sponsored rally, "that they try to disguise it under the name of confederation. . . . This *quasi* legislative union is just a step toward a complete and absolute legislative union."[30]

The evidence of Confederation's wickedness could be seen by its opponents on every hand. Did it not involve representation by population — the dreaded "rep by pop" which French Canadians had resisted so vigorously till now?[31] And were not English Canadians proclaiming that centralization was to be the chief characteristic of the new regime? The Canadian legislature had even ordered the translation and publication of Alpheus Todd's essay on the provincial governments — an essay which included the remark that these would be "subject to the legal power of the federal parliament."[32] Indeed, argued the Rouges, it was hardly worthwhile for Quebec to have such an elaborate, two-chamber parliament as was proposed, since, as Todd made clear, the federal legislature "will be able to quash and annul all its decisions."[33]

The Quebec Resolutions themselves indicated that Todd was right, that the provincial powers would be scarcely more than a mirage:

> Mind you, according to everything we hear from Quebec, the prevailing idea in the confer-
> ence is to give the central government the widest powers and to leave the local governments
> only a sort of municipal jurisdiction.[34]

Le Pays had been afraid of this from the time the Great Coalition had announced its programme. "Without finances, without power to undertake major public works, the local legislature will hardly be anything other than a big municipal council where only petty matters will be discussed."[35] When the Quebec Conference had ended, opposition papers still had the same impression: "In short, the general parliament will have supreme control over the local legislatures."[36] Even provincial control of education was an illusion, since the governor general at Ottawa could veto any provincial legislation in the field.[37]

Finally, English-Canadian talk of creating a new nationality only strengthened Rouge fears that Confederation meant centralization and assimilation. When the legislature refused to pass A.-A. Dorion's resolution of January 1865, that Canadians neither desired nor sought to create a new nationality, his brother's newspaper became convinced that it was all over for Lower Canada and its French-Canadian nationality.[38]

In answering all these opposition arguments, the Bleus certainly did not attempt to defend the notion of a strong or dominant central government. But, they maintained, that was not at all what British North America was going to get. Lower Canada, liberated from the forced Union of 1840, would become a distinct and autonomous province in a loose and decentralized Confederation — that was the real truth of the matter.

The defenders of Confederation refuted the opposition's arguments one after another. Did the Rouges speak of rep by pop? Why, any schoolboy ought to see the difference between rep by pop, which the Bleus had opposed as long as the legislative union remained, and a "confederation which would give us, first of all, local legislatures for the protection of our sectional interests, and then a federal legislature in which the most populous province would have a majority *only in the lower house*."[39] As long as there was only a single legislature for the two Canadas, rep by pop would have put "our civil law and religious institutions at the mercy of the fanatics." But Confederation would eliminate that danger by creating a separate province of Quebec with its own distinct government:

> We have a system of government which puts under the exclusive control of Lower Canada those questions which we did not want the fanatical partisans of Mr. Brown to deal with. . . .
>
> Since we have this guarantee, what difference does it make to us whether or not Upper Canada has more representatives than we in the Commons? Since the Commons will be concerned only with general questions of interest to all provinces and not at all with the particular affairs of Lower Canada, it's all the same to us, as a nationality, whether or not Upper Canada has more representation.[40]

This was central to the Bleu picture of Confederation: all questions affecting the French-Canadian nationality as such would be dealt with at Quebec City, and Ottawa would be "powerless, if it should want to invade the territory reserved for the administration of the local governments."[41] As for the questions to be dealt with at Ottawa, they might divide men as Liberals and Conservatives, but not as French and English Canadians. "In the [federal] Parliament," said Hector Langevin, "there will be no questions of race, nationality, religion or locality, as this Legislature will only be charged with the settlement of the great general questions which will interest alike the whole Confederacy and not one locality only."[42] Cartier made the same point when he said that "in the questions which will be submitted to the Federal parliament, there will be no more danger to the rights and privileges of the French Canadians than to those of the Scotch, English, or Irish."[43] Or, as his organ, *La Minerve*, put it, Ottawa would have jurisdiction only over those matters "in which the interests of everyone, French Canadians, English, or Scotch, are identical."[44] For the rest — for everything which concerned the French Canadians *as* French Canadians — for the protection and promotion of their national interests and institutions, they would have their own province with their own parliament and their own government.

And what a parliament! and what a government! Why, the very fact that Quebec was to have a bicameral legislature was proof of the importance they were to have. "In giving ourselves a complete government," argued the Bleus, "we affirm the fact of our existence as a separate nationality, as a complete society, endowed with a perfect system of organization."[45] Indeed, the very fact that Ontario's legislature was to have only one house while Quebec's had two served to underline the distinctiveness, the separateness, and the autonomy of the French-Canadian province:

> It is very much in our interest for our local legislature to have enough importance and dignity to gain respect for its decisions. . . . For us, French Canadians, who are only entering Confederation on the condition of having our own legislature as a guarantee of our autonomy, it is vital for that legislature not to be just a simple council whose deliberations won't carry any weight. . . .
>
> The deeper we can make the demarcation line between ourselves and the other provinces, the more guarantee we'll have for the conservation of our special character as a people.[46]

Here was the very heart and essence of the pro-Confederation argument in French Lower Canada: the Union of the Canadas was to be broken up, and the French Canadians were to take possession of a province of their own — a province with an enormous degree of autonomy. In fact, *separation* (from Upper Canada) and *independence* (of Quebec within its jurisdictions) were the main themes of Bleu propaganda. "As a distinct and separate nationality," said *La Minerve*, "we form a state within the state. We enjoy the full exercise of our rights and the formal recognition of our national independence."[47]

The provinces, in this view, were to be the political manifestations of distinct nationalities. This was the line taken in 1858 by J.-C. Taché, when he wrote that in the provincial institutions, "the national and religious elements will be able to develop their societies freely, and the separate populations realize . . . their aspirations and their dispositions." And it was widely understood that Taché had played a vital role in influencing the course of the Quebec Conference.[48] Cartier himself had told that conference that a federal rather than a unitary system was necessary, "because these provinces are peopled by different nations and by peoples of different religions."[49] It was in this light that *La Minerve* saw the Quebec programme as establishing "distinctly that all questions having to do with our religion or our nationality will be under the jurisdiction of our local legislature."[50] All the pro-Confederation propagandists were agreed that "the future of our race, the preservation of everything which makes up our national character, will depend directly on the local legislature."[51] It was the Lower Canadian ministers who had insisted, at the Quebec Conference, that education, civil, and religious institutions should be under provincial jurisdiction, in order that Quebec should have the power to take charge of the French-Canadian national future.[52] Indeed, that power extended well beyond civil and religious institutions. It included the "ownership and control of all their lands, mines, and minerals; the control of all their municipal affairs"[53]— everything "which is dearest and most precious to us"[54]— all power, in fact, necessary to promote the national life of French Canada.

All these powers were to be entrusted to the government of a province in which French Canadians would form "almost the whole" of the population, and in which everyone would have to speak French to take part in public life.[55] Yes, Confederation, by breaking up the union of the two Canadas, would make the French Canadians a majority in their own land,[56] so that "our beautiful French language will be the only one spoken in the Parliament of the Province of Quebec."[57]

What was more, the control which French Canadians would exercise over their wide fields of jurisdiction would be an absolute control, and "all right of interference in these matters is formally denied to the federal government."[58] The Bleus, in fact, claimed to have succeeded in obtaining a system of coordinate sovereignty. "Each of these governments," they explained, "will be given absolute powers for the questions within its jurisdiction, and each will be equally sovereign in its own sphere of action."[59] Some over-enthusiastic advocates of the new regime even claimed that the provinces alone would be sovereign, "the powers of the federal government being considered only as a concession of specifically designated rights."[60] But even the moderate majority was firm in maintaining that the provinces would be in no way inferior or subordinate to the federal government, that they would be at least its equal, and that each government would be sovereign and untouchable in its own sphere of action:

> In the plan of the Quebec conference there is no delegation of power either from above or from below, because the provinces, not being independent states, receive their powers, as does the federal authority, from the imperial parliament.[61]

Politicians and journalists expressed this same view, in the legislature as well as in print. Thus, Joseph Blanchet told the Assembly: "I consider that under the present plan of confederation the local legislatures are sovereign with regard to the powers accorded to them, that is to say in local affairs."[62]

It may be that French-Canadian Confederationists went further than they ought to have done in interpreting the Quebec Resolutions the way they did. Part of the reason for this may have been ignorance. A Bleu backbencher like C.B. de Niverville of Trois-Rivières could admit in the legislative debates that he had not read the resolutions, and what's more, that his ignorance of the English language had prevented him from following much of the debate. In this very situation he saw — or thought he saw — an argument for Confederation. For as he understood it, the new arrangement would remove French-Canadian affairs from an arena where men such as he were at a disadvantage, and place them before a group of French-speaking legislators:

> Indeed, what sort of liberty do we have, we who do not understand the English language? We have the liberty to keep quiet, to listen, and to try to understand! [Hear! hear! and prolonged laughter.] Under Confederation, the Upper Canadians will speak their language and the Lower Canadians will speak theirs, just as today; only, when a man finds that his compatriots form the great majority in the assembly in which he sits, he'll have more hope of hearing his language spoken, and as they do today, members will speak the language of the majority.[63]

Such an argument seems virtually to have ignored the very existence of the federal parliament, or at least of the authority it would have over French Canadians.

The case of de Niverville may have been extreme, but it was certainly not the only case of Bleus interpreting the Confederation plan in such a way as to maximize the powers of the provinces and minimize those of Ottawa far beyond anything we have been accustomed to. The federal power to raise taxes "by any mode or system of taxation" was interpreted so as to exclude the right of direct taxation.[64] The federal veto power was represented not as a right to interfere with provincial legislation, but only as an obligation upon Ottawa to act as "guardian of the constitution" by keeping clear the distinction between federal and provincial jurisdictions.[65]

But more important than any of these *specific* arguments was the wide-ranging exuberance of pro-Confederation propaganda. Here was a source of rhetoric that seemed to be promising that Confederation would give French Canadians virtual independence. Quebec was "completely separated from Upper Canada and has a complete governmental organization to administer *all its local affairs* on its own."[66] In the legislative council, E.-P. Taché interrupted his English-language speech on Confederation to tell his French-Canadian followers in French: "If a Federal Union were obtained, it would be tantamount to a separation of the provinces, and Lower Canada would thereby preserve its autonomy together with all the institutions it held so dear."[67] This could not be too often repeated: "The first, and one of the principal clauses of the constitution is the one that brings about the repeal of the Union, so long requested by the Rouges, and separates Lower Canada from Upper Canada."[68] What patriotic French Canadian could fail to be moved by what the fathers of Confederation had achieved?

> We've been separated from Upper Canada, we're called the Province of Quebec, we have a French-Canadian governor . . . we're going to have our own government and our own legislature, where everything will be done by and for French Canadians, and in French. You'd have to be a renegade . . . not to be moved to tears, not to feel your heart pound with an indescribable joy and a deserved pride at the thought of these glorious results of the patriotism and unquenchable energy of our statesmen, of our political leaders, who . . . have turned us over into our own hands, who have restored to us our complete autonomy and entrusted the sacred heritage of our national traditions to a government chosen from among us and composed of our own people.[69]

This sort of exaggerated rhetoric invited an obvious response from the opposition. If you really are serious about separation from Upper Canada, they asked, if you really do want to obtain autonomy for French Lower Canada, then why not go the whole way? Why not break up the old union altogether, instead of joining this confederation? "Everyone is agreed that only the repeal of the union would give us the independence of action needed for the future of Lower Canadians."[70] If necessary, some sort of commercial association would be sufficient to satisfy Upper Canada in return for political separation.[71]

The Confederationists answered this, not by saying that Quebec's independence was an undesirable goal, not by saying that French Canadians wanted to join together with English Canadians to form a Canadian nation, but by claiming that complete independence was simply not practicable:

> The idea of making Lower Canada an independent State . . . has appealed to all of us as schoolboys; but we don't believe that any serious adult has taken it up so far. . . . We simply cannot do everything on our own.[72]

This was, perhaps, a temporary condition, and it was to be hoped that one day Quebec *would* be in a position to make good her independence. Yes, French Canada "can and must one day aspire to become a nation";[73] for the moment, however, "we are too young for absolute independence."[74] Of course, whoever says "we are too young" implies that one day we shall be old enough — and Confederation, in the meanwhile, would preserve and prepare French Quebec for that day of destiny.[75]

One obvious reason why complete independence was not a realistic goal for the present was that Lower Canada was still part of the British Empire, and imperial approval, without which no constitutional change was possible, could not be obtained in the face of intense English-Canadian opposition.[76] But beyond that, it should be clear that an independent Quebec would inevitably be gobbled up by the United States. "We would be on our own, and our obvious weakness would put us at the mercy of a stronger neighbour."[77] French Canadians must understand, therefore, that, "unless we hurry up and head with all sails set toward Confederation, the current will carry us rapidly toward annexation."[78]

The weakness of an independent Quebec would be both military and economic. The first of these weaknesses could hardly be more apparent to Quebeckers than it was in the mid-1860s, for just as the Anglo-American frictions created by the Civil War were impressing upon them the dangers arising from American hostility, the desire of British politicians to disengage themselves from colonial defence responsibilities was causing Canadians to think as never before of their own defences. Intercolonial cooperation seemed a natural response to the situation:

> No-one could deny that the annexation of the British colonies, either by their consent or by force, is intended and desired by the northern states; it is a no less evident truth that, as things stand today, we could resist their armies with help from Europe; but that on their own, without a political union, without a strong common organization, the colonies could, in the foreseeable future, sustain such a combat — that is something which no-one would dare to maintain.[79]

It was in these circumstances that the Confederation project presented itself. Only weeks after the end of the Quebec Conference, the St. Alban's raid brought the fear of imminent war with the United States. Yet at the same time, recent British military reports on colonial defence made Quebeckers wonder how much help they could expect if war broke out. "We must not place unlimited hopes on the support of the mother-country in case of war with our neighbours. Circumstances more powerful than the will of men could render such confidence illusory."[80] Yet the prospect for the separate British North American colonies without British support was bleak: "separate from each other, we'd be sure to be invaded and crushed one after the other."[81] Not only would Confederation give Quebec the advantage of a joint defence organization with the other colonies, but also, by this very fact, it would make Britain willing to give more help in case of war than she would have been willing to give to the isolated and inefficient defence effort of a separate Quebec.[82]

Quebec's economic weakness could be seen already in the flood of emigration directed toward the United States. Clearly, French Lower Canada's economy was not able, on its own, to support all its population. To keep her people at home, the province must cooperate with others to create opportunities. As French Canadians went to seek manufacturing jobs in New England, manufacturing must be established in Lower Canada;[83] by 1867, Quebec papers were appealing to outside capital to set up mills in the province.[84] Long before, Hector Langevin, in a prize-winning essay, had looked to the development of the St. Lawrence transportation system to check emigration by providing jobs in commercial enterprises.[85] But the St. Lawrence was an interprovincial organization — even more in the era of railroads than in that of the canal.[86]

Thus, the need for economic viability dictated some form of central authority and prevented Quebec's independence from being complete:

> The more provinces there are gathered together, the greater will be the revenues, the more major works and improvements will be undertaken and consequently, the more prosperity there will be. What Lower Canada was unable to do on its own, we have done together with Upper Canada; and what the two Canadas have been unable to do together will be done by the confederation, because it will have markets and sea ports which we have not had.[87]

The British North American provinces had been endowed with resources enough. If they worked together to develop them, they could enjoy abundance, material progress, and even economic power.[88] But if they failed to cooperate, if they remained separate and isolated, then their economies would be weak, and inevitably they would become dependent on the United States, the prosperous neighbour to the south. "But we know that where there is economic dependence there will also be political dependence."[89]

There were strong reasons, then, why Quebec's independence could not be complete, why the nationalist longing for separateness had to compromise with the practical need for viability. But if some form of association with the rest of British North America was necessary, the degree of unification must be the minimum required to make Quebec viable. In the spring of 1867, on his way home from London, where he had helped write the BNA Act, Cartier told a welcoming crowd at a station-stop in the Eastern Townships that his main preoccupation had always been to protect the French-Canadian nationality, language, and institutions. "That is why I was careful to make sure that the federal government would receive only that amount of power which was strictly necessary to serve the general interests of the Confederation."[90] This meant, as E.-P. Taché had explained in 1864, that Ottawa would have enough power "to do away with some of the internal hindrances to trade, and to unite the Provinces for mutual defence," but that the provinces would remain the agencies to which the "majority of the people" would look for the protection of their "rights and privileges" and "liberties."[91]

Perhaps this arrangement was not *ideal*; perhaps, even, Confederation was only "the least bad thing in a very bad world."[92] The French-Canadian leaders, after all, had not been alone at the constitutional conferences, and French Canada's own needs and aspirations had had to be reconciled with "our condition of colonial dependence and the heterogeneous elements which make up our population."[93]

Nevertheless, it had to be admitted that, despite Rouge protestations to the contrary, the old union could not have continued longer,[94] that the only alternative to Confederation would have been rep by pop,[95] and that, whatever degree of central authority there might be in the confederation, the patriotism of French-Canadian leaders could be relied on to promote the interests of their nationality, just as their patriotism had already won so much for French Canada in the making of the confederation.[96]

And what, then, in the final analysis, had they won? According to Bleu propaganda, Confederation was to be seen as an "alliance" or "association" of nations, each in its own autonomous province, and cooperating for the common welfare.[97] And this "alliance with your neighbours,"[98] this *federal alliance among several peoples*,"[99] was to be regulated by the terms of a treaty or pact drawn up freely among them. Even the imperial authorities, according to Cartier, in preparing and passing the British North America Act, had accepted that they were only giving the official stamp of approval to an interprovincial compact. "They understood . . . that the Quebec plan was an agreement among the colonies, which had to be respected, and they respected it."[100] Confederation had, thus, been achieved because four separate colonies had formed "a pact" among themselves.[101]

And in the federal alliance thus formed, Quebec was to be the French-Canadian country, working together with the others on common projects, but always autonomous in the promotion and embodiment of the French-Canadian nationality. "Our ambitions," wrote a Bleu editor, "will not centre on the federal government, but will have their natural focus in our local legislature; this we regard as fundamental for ourselves."[102] This was, no doubt, an exaggerated position, like the statement of de Niverville in the Canadian legislature, but what it exaggerated was the general tendency of the Confederationist propaganda. It underlined the Quebec-centredness of French Canada's approach to Confederation, and the degree to which French Quebec's separateness and autonomy were central to French-Canadian acceptance of the new regime.

NOTES

1. *La Gazette de Sorel*, 23 June 1864.
2. Perrault quoted in the *Gazette de Sorel*, 3 Sept. 1864; *Le Courrier du Canada*, 24 June 1864.
3. *La Minerve*, 9 Sept. 1864. After the Quebec Resolutions were known, journalists, politicians, and clergy still claimed to judge them by the same criterion. See, e.g., *Le Journal de Québec*, 24 Dec. 1864; Joseph Cauchon, *L'Union des provinces de l'Amérique britannique du Nord* (Québec: Côté, 1865), 19, 41; *Nouvelle constitution du Canada* (Ottawa: Le Canada, 1867), 59.
4. Most relevantly quoted in Auguste Achintre and J.B. Labelle, *Cantate: La Confédération* (n.p., n.d.), 4. Cartier, indeed, saw French Canada as geographically defined. J.-C. Bonenfant claims that while he fought for the French Canadians, "seuls à ses yeux comptent ceux qui habitent le Bas-Canada." See Bonenfant's article "Le Canada et les hommes politiques de 1867," in the *RHAF* 21, 32 (1967): 579–80. At the 1855 funeral of Ludger Duvernay, the founder of the Saint-Jean-Baptiste Society, Cartier had warned that every nationality, including French Canada, must possess an "élément territorial" in order to survive. See Joseph Tassé, ed., *Discours de Sir Georges Cartier* (Montréal: Senécal et Fils, 1893), 95. Cartier also used the very expression "French Canada" in a geographical sense, meaning Lower Canada. See, e.g., Tassé, *Discours*, 83.
5. *La Revue Canadienne* 1 (1864): 696.
6. Ibid., 4 (1867): 477.
7. *La Minerve*, 25 Sept. 1865.
8. *L'Union Nationale*, 3 Sept. 1864. All of these quotations, of course, are merely variations of Louis-François Laflèche's statement (in *Quelques considérations sur les rapports de la société civile avec la religion et la famille* (Trois-Rivières, 1866), 43, "Les Canadiens-français sont réellement une nation; la vallée du St-Laurent est leur patrie."
9. *La Gazette de Sorel*, 14 Jan. 1865; also, *La Minerve*, 10 and 14 Sept. 1864.
10. *La Minerve*, 14 Sept. 1864.
11. *Le Courrier de St-Hyacinthe*, 23 Sept. 1864; also *Le Journal de Québec*, 4 July 1867.
12. *Le Pays*, 8 Nov. 1864.
13. In G.P. Browne, ed., *Documents on the Confederation of British North America* (Toronto: McClelland and Stewart, 1969), 42–43; also, 47, 49, 168 for Gordon's other assertions on the matter.
14. *Le Courrier de St-Hyacinthe*, 2 Sept. 1864.
15. *La Gazette de Sorel*, 30 July 1864.
16. J.-C. Taché, *Des Provinces de l'Amérique du Nord et d'une union fédérale* (Québec: Brousseau, 1858), 147, 148.

17. Some did support provincial sovereignty, however — at least at times. See, e.g., *La Gazette de Sorel*, 27 Aug. 1864.

18. *Le Courrier de St-Hyacinthe*, 2 Sept. 1864; also, 28 Oct. 1864.

19. *Le Journal de Québec*, 1 Sept. 1864; also, 6 Sept. 1864; *Le Courrier du Canada*, 30 Sept. 1864, and 10 Oct. 1864.

20. In P.B. Waite, ed., *The Confederation Debates in the Province of Canada, 1865* (Toronto: McClelland and Stewart, 1963), 40, 41, 43. Macdonald's belief that he had obtained something more centralized than a federation is dramatically expressed in his well-known letter of 19 Dec. 1864 to M.C. Cameron (PAC, Macdonald papers), in which he predicts that within a lifetime, "both local Parliaments and Governments [will be] absorbed in the General power."

21. *La Minerve*, 15 Oct. 1864. See also *Le Courrier de St-Hyacinthe*, 2 Sept. 1864.

22. *Le Courrier du Canada*, 16 Sept. 1864.

23. *Le Courrier de St-Hyacinthe*, 18 Oct. 1864. See also *Le Pays*, 13 Oct. 1864; *L'Ordre*, 14 Oct. 1864; *Contre-poison: La Confédération c'est le salut du Bas-Canada* (Montréal: Senécal, 1867), 9.

24. The argument is stated clearly and briefly in the letter to M.C. Cameron mentioned above. See also Donald Creighton, *John A. Macdonald*, 2 vols. (Toronto: Macmillan, 1966), 1: 369, 375–76, 378–80; P.B. Waite, "The Quebec Resolutions and the *Courrier du Canada*, 1864–1865," in the *CHR* 40, 4 (Dec. 1959): 294; etc., etc.

25. *La Minerve*, 15 Oct. 1864.

26. *Le Journal de Québec*, 27 Aug. 1864. See also Cauchon, *L'Union des provinces*, 39. *Le Courrier du Canada*, far from seeing the U.S. constitution as embodying the error of excessive decentralization, found it an apt model for the Quebec Conference to follow. See J.-C. Bonenfant, "L'Idée que les Canadiens-français de 1864 pouvaient avoir du fédéralisme," in *Culture* 25 (1964): 316. Some Rouges, notably Médéric Lanctôt in *L'Union Nationale*, went so far as to maintain that it would be more desirable for Lower Canada to join the U.S. than the British North American Union, precisely because it would have more autonomy as an American state.

27. *Le Pays*, 27 Mar. 1867.

28. Ibid., 2 Apr. 1867; also, 23 July 1864; and *La Confédération couronnement de dix années de mauvaise administration* (Montréal: Le Pays, 1867), 5.

29. *La Confédération couronnement*, 5, 8; *Le Pays*, 12 Nov. 1864, 9 Feb. 1865, 2 Apr. 1867.

30. C.-S. Cherrier, et al., *Discours sur la Confédération* (Montréal: Lanctot, Bouthillier et Thompson, 1865), 13.

31. *Le Pays*, 23 and 28 June, 14 July, 8 Nov. 1864; *L'Ordre*, 27 June 1864; *L'Union Nationale*, 8 Nov. 1864; *Confédération couronnement*, 13.

32. Alpheus Todd, *Quelques considérations sur la formation des Gouvernements locaux du Haut et du Bas-Canada . . .* (Ottawa: Hunter, Rose et Lemieux, 1866), 5.

33. *Le Pays*, 28 July 1866; also, 27 Sept. 1864, and 19 July 1866.

34. *Le Pays*, 25 Oct. 1864.

35. Ibid., 23 July 1864; also, *L'Ordre*, 22 July 1864.

36. *L'Union Nationale*, 11 Nov. 1864; also, 3 Sept. 1864; *Le Pays*, 14 and 23 July 1864.

37. *L'Ordre*, 14 Nov. 1864.

38. *Le Défricheur*, 25 Jan. 1865. All these fears which inspired the opposition also provoked doubts in the minds of some people who were otherwise supporters of the government. "Nous avons toujours dit," remarked *Le Canadien*, on 3 Aug. 1866, "que dans le plan de confédération actuel, on n'avait pas laissé assez de pouvoir aux gouvernements locaux et trop au gouvernement général." See also, e.g., 3 Feb. 1865.

39. *Le Journal de Québec*, 5 July 1864.

40. *Réponses aux censeurs de la Confédération* (St-Hyacinthe: Le Courrier, 1867), 47–49.

41. *La Minerve*, 20 Sept. 1864; also, *Le Courrier du Canada*, 11 July 1864.

42. *Parliamentary Debates on the Subject of the Confederation of the British North American Provinces* (Ottawa, 1865), 368.

43. Ibid., 54–55.

44. *La Minerve*, 15 Oct. 1864.

45. Ibid., 17 July 1866.

46. *Le Journal des Trois-Rivières*, 24 July 1866. Also, *Le Courrier de St-Hyacinthe*, 10 July 1866.

47. *La Minerve*, 1 July 1867; also, 2 July 1867: "[Comme] nation dans la nation, nous devons veiller à notre autonomie propre."

48. Taché, *Des Provinces*, 151: "Les éléments nationaux et religieux pourront à l'aise opérer leurs mouvements de civilisation, et les populations séparées donner cours . . . à leurs aspirations et à leurs tendances." During the Confederation Debates, Joseph Blanchet claimed that the Quebec Resolutions were, essentially, the very

scheme which Taché had presented in his 1858 pamphlet (p. 457 of the Ottawa edition of the debates). Joseph Tassé asserted in 1885 that Taché had acted as special adviser to the Canadian ministers at the Quebec Conference. (See J.-C. Bonenfant, "L'Idée que les Canadiens," 314.) And Taché's son told an interviewer in 1935 that his father (whose uncle, Sir E.-P. Taché, had repeatedly recommended the nephew's scheme to the conference) had several times been called into the sessions, "vraisemblablement pour donner des explications sur son projet." See Louis Taché, "Sir Etienne-Pascal Taché et la Confédération canadienne," in the *Revue de l'Université d'Ottawa* 5 (1935): 24.

49. In Browne, *Documents*, 128.

50. *La Minerve*, 30 Dec. 1864. See also *Le Journal de Québec*, 24 Dec. 1864.

51. *Le Courrier de St-Hyacinthe*, 28 Oct. 1864; also, 23 Sept. and 22 Nov. 1864.

52. *Le Courrier du Canada*, 7 Nov. 1864. See also 11 Nov. 1864.

53. *Le Courrier du Canada*, 13 Mar. 1867; also, 28 June 1867.

54. *La Minerve*, 1 July 1867; also, 2 July 1867; and the speech of Sir Narcisse Belleau in the *Confederation Debates* (Waite edition), 29.

55. *Le Courrier de St-Hyacinthe*, 10 July 1866.

56. Cauchon, *L'Union*, 45.

57. *Contre-poison*, 20. See also *Réponses aux censeurs*, 48.

58. *Contre-poison*, 20; also, *Le Journal de Québec*, 15 Nov. 1864, and 24 Dec. 1864; Cauchon, *L'Union*, 45–46; *L'Union des Cantons de l'Est* (Arthabaskaville), 4 July 1867; Governor Gordon in Browne, *Documents*, 75; Bishop Larocque in *Nouvelle constitution*, 75.

59. *Le Courrier de St-Hyacinthe*, 28 Oct. 1864.

60. E.-P. Taché, quoted in Bonenfant, "L'Idée que les Canadiens," 315.

61. Joseph Cauchon, *Discours . . . sur la question de la Confédération* (n.p., n.d.), 8: "les provinces, n'étant pas des états indépendants, reçoivent, avec l'autorité supérieure, leurs organisations politiques du Parlement de l'Empire. Il n'y a que des attributs distincts pour l'une et pour les autres." See also Cauchon, *L'Union*, 40, 52; *Le Courrier du Canada*, 7 Nov. 1864, and Waite, "Quebec Resolutions," 299–300.

62. Joseph Blanchet in *Débats parlementaires sur la question de la Confédération des provinces de l'Amérique Britannique du Nord* (Ottawa: Hunter, Rose et Lemieux, 1865), 551.

63. Ibid., 949.

64. *L'Union des Cantons de l'Est*, 12 Sept. 1867. This argument about direct taxation will not be as unfamiliar to historians as to other payers of federal income tax.

65. *La Minerve*, 3 Dec. 1864; also, 11 Nov. 1864; *Le Courrier de St-Hyacinthe*, 22 Nov. 1864; *Le Courrier du Canada*, 7 Nov. 1864.

66. *Contre-poison*, 13.

67. *Confederation Debates* (Waite edition), 22.

68. *Contre-poison*, 11. Episcopal statements recommended Confederation on the same basis. Bishop Baillargeon of Tloa, who administered the diocese of Quebec, noted in his pastoral letter that, although there would be a central government, Confederation would, nevertheless, comprise four distinct provinces. "C'est ainsi que le Bas-Canada, désormais séparé du Haut, formera sous le nouveau régime une province séparée qui sera nommé 'la Province de Québec'" (in *Nouvelle constitution*, 53).

69. *Contre-poison*, 3.

70. *L'Union Nationale*, 3 Sept. 1864; also, *Confédération couronnement*, 5.

71. *L'Union Nationale*, 7 Nov. 1864. Even the pro-Conservative *Gazette de Sorel* admitted, on 23 June 1864, that it had always preferred a straightforward breakup of the union as the best solution for French Canada. Also, 30 July 1864.

72. *La Minerve*, 5 Jan. 1865.

73. *Le Journal de Québec*, 17 Dec. 1864.

74. *Le Pionnier de Sherbrooke*, 9 Mar. 1867.

75. See Cauchon, *L'Union*, 29.

76. *La Minerve*, 28 Sept. 1864.

77. *Le Courrier de St-Hyacinthe*, 25 Nov. 1864; also, *Le Courrier du Canada*, 10 Oct. 1864.

78. Cauchon, *L'Union*, 25. Cartier put the same alternative to the legislative assembly, when he said: "The matter resolved itself into this, either we must obtain British American Confederation or be absorbed in an American Confederation." (*Confederation Debates*, Waite edition, 50.) See also *La Minerve*, 13 Jan. 1865; and *Nouvelle constitution*, 60, 66–67, 78ff.; *La Revue Canadienne* 2 (1865): 116, on Confederation as an alternative to "le gouffre et le néant de la république voisine."

79. *La Revue Canadienne* 2 (1865): 159.

80. *La Minerve*, 7 Dec. 1864. The danger of war with the U.S. was announced not only by *La Minerve* in December 1864, but also by *Le Courrier du Canada*, 26 Nov. 1866, and *La Gazette de Sorel*, 19 Nov. 1864, while the need to prepare for British disengagement was urged by the *Journal de Québec*, 17 Dec. 1864, and *Le Courrier du Canada*, 5 Oct. 1864.

81. Cauchon, *L'Union*, 32. See also Jules Fournier, *Le Canada: Son présent et son avenir* (Montréal: *La Minerve*, 1865), 4.

82. *Contre-poison*, 8.

83. *L'Union Nationale*, 19 July 1866.

84. *L'Union des Cantons de l'Est*, 3 Jan. 1867.

85. Hector Langevin, *Le Canada, ses institutions, ressources, produits, manufactures, etc., etc., etc.* (Québec: Lovell et Lamoureux, 1855), 96.

86. *L'Union des Cantons de l'Est*, 8 Aug. 1867.

87. *Contre-poison*, 48–49.

88. Taché, *Des provinces*, 10–11; *Le Courrier de St-Hyacinthe*, 23 July 1867; *Réponses aux censeurs*, 3–4; Achintre and Labelle, *Cantate*, 2–3, 8; Cauchon, *L'Union*, 3; Henry Lacroix, *Opuscule sur le présent et l'avenir du Canada* (Montréal: Senécal, 1867).

89. *La Revue Canadienne* 2 (1865): 103. See also Fournier, *Le Canada*, 2–3, who argued that as long as Canada was economically dependent on overseas trade, she would be politically at the mercy of the U.S., unless she had her own all-British rail link with an ice-free port in New Brunswick or Nova Scotia. See also Cauchon, *L'Union*, 34–35.

90. *L'Union des Cantons de l'Est*, 23 May 1867.

91. Taché was speaking at the Quebec Conference. In Browne, *Documents*, 127–28.

92. Quoted in Waite, "Quebec Resolutions," 297. See *Le Courrier du Canada*, 11 Nov. 1864.

93. *Le Courrier de St-Hyacinthe*, 22 Nov. 1864. The opposition tried to stress the weakness and isolation of the French-Canadian delegates to the constitutional conferences as a reproach to them. E.g., *Le Pays*, 13 Oct. 1864. But Confederationists thought it only reasonable to take realities into account. E.g., *La Minerve*, 25 Feb. 1865; *La Gazette de Sorel*, 1 Sept. 1866.

94. *La Gazette de Sorel*, 23 June and 23 July 1864, 14 Jan. 1865; *Le Courrier du Canada*, 24 June 1864; *Le Courrier de St-Hyacinthe*, 8 Nov. 1864; *L'Union des Cantons de l'Est*, 4 Apr. 1864; *La Minerve*, 9 Sept. and 30 Dec. 1864; *Le Journal de Québec*, 15 Dec. 1864; Cauchon, *L'Union*, 19; *Contre-poison*, 7; the pastoral letters of Bishops Cooke and Larocque, in *Nouvelle constitution*, 58–59, 68.

95. *La Minerve*, 28 Dec. 1864; *La Gazette de Sorel*, 30 July 1864; Louis-François Laflèche and Bishop Baillargeon, quoted in Walter Ullmann, "The Quebec Bishops and Confederation," in the *CHR* 44, 3 (Sept. 1963), reprinted in G.R. Cook, ed., *Confederation* (Toronto: University of Toronto Press, 1967), 53, 56, 66.

96. *Le Courrier du Canada*, 22 June 1864; Bishops Baillargeon and Cooke in *Nouvelle constitution*, 54–55, 60; E.C. Parent to J.I. Tarte, Ottawa, 4 Sept. 1866, in PAC, Tarte papers (MG 27, 11, D16). Just as they had promoted French-Canadian interests at the constitutional conferences, Quebec's 65 MPs would watch over French Quebec's interests at Ottawa. For they would be sent to Ottawa as representatives of Quebec, the French-Canadian province, and their responsibility would be toward that province and its autonomy. See Bonenfant, "L'Idée que les Canadiens," 317; *Le Courrier de St-Hyacinthe*, 22 July 1864.

97. *La Gazette de Sorel*, 25 Feb. 1865; *La Minerve*, 1 July 1867. It was perfectly clear, of course, what Quebec's nationality was considered to be. It was French-Canadian. But what nationalities were to be attributed to the other provinces was never certain. French Canadians were aware of distinctions among the English, Scottish, and Irish nationalities, and they may have seen the other provinces as having unique national characters determined by their respective blends of these various elements. But they were always vague on this point. Cartier, however, did suggest a similar distribution of religious characteristics when he said (in the legislative debate on the Quebec resolutions) that Ontario would be Protestant, Quebec Catholic, and the Maritimes pretty evenly divided between the two denominations (e.g., in Tassé, *Discours*, 422).

98. *L'Union des Cantons de l'Est*, 4 July 1867.

99. *Contre-poison*, 8; also, 10.

100. *L'Union des Cantons de l'Est*, 23 May 1867.

101. *Le Journal de Québec*, 4 July 1867. See also the Bishop of St-Hyacinthe, in *Nouvelle constitution*, 65. J.-C. Taché had assumed, in 1858, that a confederation would necessarily be brought about by an intercolonial pact. See his *Des provinces*, 139.

102. *Le Courrier de St-Hyacinthe*, 10 July 1866. We shall find this point of view adopted not infrequently by French-Quebec journalists in the first decades after Confederation.

Article Thirty-Five

Confederation: The Untold Story

Paul Romney

In 1859 Upper Canadian Reformers embraced the idea of Canadian federation, somewhat gingerly, as a way of securing the autonomy which they had expected from responsible government but which the union of 1841 had denied them. Some of them also expressed enthusiasm for a broader scheme, which George Brown called confederation: the political union of British North America as a whole. But no one advocated confederation as a substitute for Upper Canadian autonomy; no one argued that local autonomy was worth sacrificing to achieve the wider union.

This fact is important because, less than five years later, both Canadian federation and British North American confederation suddenly entered the realm of political reality. In June 1864 Brown and George Cartier, leader of the *bleus,* agreed to pursue federation. At once John A. Macdonald scrambled aboard the bandwagon and reached for the reins, committing himself to federation as long as the others would pursue its implementation within a wider union if possible. In September 1864, at Charlottetown, the Canadian leaders persuaded their counterparts in the Maritime colonies to consider such a union, and a month later they all worked it out in detail in conference at Quebec. Not all the colonies pursued the scheme to its conclusion, but in 1867 a British statute, the British North America Act, 'federally united' the colonies of Canada, New Brunswick, and Nova Scotia. As part of that scheme, Canada was divided into two provinces, Ontario and Quebec, corresponding to Upper and Lower Canada (they could not keep their old names, since Canada was to be the name of the union as a whole). So it was that, five years after that, in his speech at Woodstock to the voters of North Oxford, Oliver Mowat could hail Canadian confederation as the long-delayed realization of Upper Canada's aspirations to self-government.

It is crucial to remember that Confederation originated in an agreement to federalize United Canada, because the implications of its origin have too often been forgotten. Historians have seen Confederation as the fruition of a succession of proposals for British North American union dating back to the eighteenth century, ignoring the feature that distinguished this particular scheme: its origin in the need to gratify the yearning of French Canadians and Upper Canadians alike to be masters in their own house. English-Canadian writers in particular treated Confederation as essentially an exercise in nation-building. They degraded the federal structure of the new union into a secondary feature, designed chiefly to accommodate the cultural peculiarity of French Canadians; but they asserted that Canadian federalism was meant to be much more centralized than the classic model, as epitomized by the United States.[1]

In this chapter I redress this old-established and largely unrecognized tendency to exaggerate the nation-building aspect of Confederation. In considering the founders' expressions of centralizing zeal, I pay closer attention than previous writers to the historical context that evoked their words. I also challenge a story that has long been fundamental to the centralist idea of Canada: the notion that the Quebec conference decided to reverse the American

Source: Paul Romney, "Confederation: The Untold Story," in *Getting It Wrong: How Canadians Forgot Their Past and Imperilled Confederation* (Toronto: University of Toronto Press, 1999): 87–108, 299–301. Reprinted by permission of University of Toronto Press Incorporated.

pattern of federalism by assigning what is called the residuary legislative power to the 'general' (i.e., federal) government rather than to the 'local' (provincial) governments. The chapter closes with a look at the Upper Canadian Reformers' assessment of what had been achieved, expressed at a party convention in Toronto in June 1867.

Without doubt the Quebec scheme was far more centralized than the federation the Reformers had discussed in 1859. The federal legislature received much more power than the bare minimum that the convention had been willing to concede, including several powers lacked by the U.S. Congress. The Quebec conference also departed from the American pattern in another way that defeated the assumptions of 1859: it refused to assign the residuary power to the local governments. The U.S. constitution defined the powers of Congress only, leaving the residue of legislative power to the states. This arrangement was generally taken as evidence that the individual states had retained their original sovereignty and were therefore constitutionally superior to the federal government. Under the Quebec scheme, by that measure, the local governments would *not* outrank the general.

In the executive sphere, too, the Quebec resolutions gave the general government important powers lacked by its American counterpart. The governor general (acting through his ministers, of course) was empowered to appoint all judges above the rank of magistrate and given sole charge of the colonial militia, the equivalent of the state-controlled National Guard in the United States. Not only that, he would wield over the provinces certain powers until then exercised in London. He could disallow provincial legislation within a year of its enactment. He would also appoint the provincial lieutenant-governors, who could themselves veto legislation at the time of enactment or reserve it for review by the general government. These powers appeared to give the general government the same pre-eminence within Confederation as the British government enjoyed within the empire.

Such provisions created the appearance of a dominant central power, and that impression was enhanced by the frankness with which advocates of confederation celebrated the nation-building aspect of the enterprise. They proclaimed their intention to found a new nationality, which would turn British North Americans into something more than mere 'colonists.' Instead of being half a dozen inconsiderable colonies, said George Brown, they would rise at once to the position of a great and powerful state. John Hamilton Gray of Prince Edward Island foretold the day when they would take their places among the first nations of the world. D'Arcy McGee dreamed famously of an end to hyphenated Canadianism, of a day when 'Canadians' pure and simple formed 'one great nationality, bound, like the shield of Achilles, by the blue rim of the ocean.' John A. Macdonald, George Cartier, Charles Tupper, and Alexander Galt spoke to similarly exalted effect.[2]

Besides these paeans to wider union, there were many testimonies to the Fathers' centralizing intent. With civil war raging in the United States, the promoters of Confederation took care to assure British Americans that the proposed constitution was free of the flaws that seemed to have contributed to the American débacle. Macdonald declared that the Quebec resolutions encompassed 'a powerful Central Government, a Central Legislature, and a decentralized system of minor legislatures for local purposes,' giving the former 'all the great subjects of legislation . . . all the powers which are incident to sovereignty.' A clamour of voices belittled the proposed local governments as subordinate, minor, inferior, and municipal. The powers of the federal government would in reality be unlimited, objected Louis-August Olivier of Montreal. Provincial parliaments would be left to legislate on dog taxes and the running at large of swine, grumbled Prince Edward Islander George Coles. Most telling was the testimony of Antoine-Aimé Dorion, the *rouge* leader who had joined George Brown to form the abortive Liberal ministry of 1858. At that time, he said, he (Dorion) had advocated 'a real confederation, giving the largest powers to the local governments, and merely a delegated authority to the General Government.' The present proposal reversed that arrangement, as well as reaching beyond the province of Canada — a scheme that he had always opposed.[3]

While Dorion clung to his earlier views, those of Brown, his former ally, seemed to have changed dramatically. Even before the preliminary conference at Charlottetown in September 1864 — even before talk had finally turned from Canadian federation to British North American confederation — Brown's newspaper was announcing that the 'sovereign' power, including the legislative residue, would be vested in the general government, while the local governments would wield only 'definite and expressly delegated' authority. According to the *Globe*, the Americans had got it the wrong way round when they made their federal government the creature or delegate of the states. In the Canadian federation, the local governments would belong to the federal government. The local governments should be constructed on the simplest and cheapest model, as befitted their modest status.[4]

At Quebec, Brown himself pressed this last idea on an unreceptive conference. The local governments, he said, 'should not be expensive, and should not take up political matters.' He wanted the local executive and legislature to be directly elected for a term of three years. The legislature should consist of a single chamber and should exercise its authority subject to a lieutenant-governor appointed by the general government. When other delegates balked at this proposal, he reminded them how trivial were the matters they had agreed at Charlottetown to leave to the local governments.[5]

To the centralist scholars of the 1920s and 1930s, all these voices from the 1860s proved that the Fathers had intended to create a dominant federal government. Some historians came to hear something else in them as well. Brown's words in particular, supplemented by those of future prime minister Alexander Mackenzie, were evidence that the Upper Canadian Reformers had subscribed fully to the centralist scheme and that their subsequent championing of provincial rights was a renegade act. True, there were no self-incriminating statements from Oliver Mowat, who had become a judge right after the Quebec conference and played no part in the ensuing controversy, but silence did not exempt him from blame. In an influential work on the provincial-rights controversy, one of Donald Creighton's students would argue that Mowat's failure to contradict his colleagues invited 'at least a presumption' that he acquiesced in their views, even if privately he disagreed with them. This argument prepared the ground for Creighton himself to arraign Mowat as a liar and traitor — fit companion in this for the Liberal Lucifer, Mackenzie King.[6]

But was Brown really quite the centralizer in 1864 that modern historians have supposed? When you look at what he said in the light of the Upper Canadian Reform tradition, or in the immediate context in which he said it, some of it appears less centralist than first appears. Take his zest for the nation-building aspect of Confederation. There had been a lot of talk about British American 'nationality' at the 1859 convention, and Brown had contributed his share. The mere fact that he talked up the same line after the Quebec conference does not make him any more of a centralist then than five years earlier.

Nor does his and the *Globe's* tendency to compare the local governments to municipalities in itself contradict his earlier position. To twentieth-century writers it signified that the local governments were to be inferior and even trivial, and some of his contemporaries made the same assumption. That is what the municipal analogy meant to them. But that is not necessarily what it meant to Upper Canadian Reformers. To Reformers, municipal government was the best sort, because it meant local control. One of the first big measures of the LaFontaine-Baldwin government was the Municipal Corporations Act of 1849, which set up a completely elective system of local government in Upper Canada right down to the township and village level. The success of this system influenced Reform thinking on the subject of federation.

Listen again, then, to Mr. Nickerson of Norfolk County, who was so ready in 1859 to spill his blood to resist enslavement by Lower Canada: 'He approved of Federation. They had that principle already in their township and county municipalities, and had it not wrought most admirably and successfully? (Hear, hear.) . . . The two provinces would have their own Legislature to transact their own local business, and there would be a general body to transact *any little business of a general nature,* affecting the whole Federation.'[7] To Reformers like Nickerson, speaking of the new local governments as municipal was by no means to belittle them. If anything, it was to emphasize their efficacy as organs of local autonomy.

Unlike Nickerson (and Brown himself) in 1859, however, five years later Brown and his paper apparently *did* use the municipal example to belittle the new local governments, not merely to explain them. Like municipalities, the local governments would be 'subordinate.' Their powers would be 'delegated.' Their jurisdiction would be 'insignificant.' Yes, Brown and the *Globe* said all that. But why did they say it, and what else did they say? In order to understand what they meant, we need to consider their words in a wider context.

Brown was a leading member of the coalition formed in June 1864 to pursue the policy of Canadian federation. For two years, the province had had a weak government committed to a last effort to make the constitution of 1840 work properly. Its western leader was John Sandfield Macdonald, Brown's main rival for the Reform leadership. Brown and his closest friends stood aloof, promising only provisional support and watching carefully, although William McDougall broke ranks and asserted his independence by joining the cabinet. Sandfield Macdonald's eastern counterpart was Louis-Victor Sicotte, a moderate whose position between George Cartier's *bleus* and Antoine Dorion's *rouges* sometimes earned him the epithet *mauve*. Sicotte boosted his strength in Lower Canada by persuading Dorion to join the government.

This arrangement crumbled within a year. Dorion quit over fiscal policy; Upper Canadian Reformers were offended by the passage of a bill to strengthen the Roman Catholic separate schools, despite the opposition of most Upper Canadian members. Sandfield Macdonald was forced to dump Sicotte in favour of Dorion as his eastern co-premier and to take Mowat into the cabinet as a guarantee of his future adherence to Reform principles. The new government went to the polls in July 1863, but the election only sharpened sectional tensions, since the Reformers won a big majority and the *rouges* suffered an equally sweeping defeat. The government succumbed to a vote of confidence as soon as it met the new legislature, in March 1864. The Conservatives resumed office, only to be defeated in their turn three months later. Canadian politics was deadlocked, at least in the short run, since a new election offered little likelihood of any fundamental change of forces. Not only that, but with politics so polarized, and Upper Canada continuing to gain in population on the lower province, representation by population began to seem inevitable. Suddenly federation — Brown's favourite policy since 1859 — seemed to offer the only alternative.

Seemed so to Cartier at any rate; to John A. Macdonald perhaps it was less promising. A master coalition-builder, he needed more room to manoeuvre than a polarized politics afforded. So far the constitution of 1840 had served him well. If it must be changed, he preferred to widen the field of play by bringing in the other British American colonies. This had, after all, been his party's policy since 1858, though less (as we saw) because Canadian Conservatives liked the idea than because it offered an imposing, but satisfactorily impracticable alternative to Dorion's policy of federalizing United Canada. Now it seemed more feasible, and Brown thought it a fine idea as long as the new arrangement provided genuine autonomy for Upper Canada and representation by population in the federal legislature. The result was the Great Coalition — a government led by Cartier, Brown, and Macdonald under the nominal premiership of a *bleu* elder statesman, Sir Étienne-Paschal Taché.[8]

In the early weeks of the Great Coalition, the chief opponents of its policy in Upper Canada were people who feared that federal government must be weak government. Naturally, the *Globe* tried to reassure them by emphasizing those aspects of the scheme that made for a strong central authority. Even then, though, it took pains to assure its readers that the local governments would enjoy genuine autonomy. The general government would be sovereign, in the sense that it would possess the residuary legislative power and the local governments only specified powers; but this federal sovereignty would not mean very much in practice. It was largely a formal device, designed to establish the point that the federation was indissoluble; reversing the American model would quash any idea that member governments could opt out when they felt like it. Sovereignty need not give the general government a very wide range of duties and would not give it the slightest power to interfere with local functions.[9]

The *Globe* had to amplify these assurances at the end of August. Lower Canadians had been keeping an eye on the only paper owned by a minister. They did not have a comprehensive system of local government as Upper Canada did, and to them the municipal analogy did indeed signify triviality and weakness. The succession of editorials harping on the strength of the central government, and describing the local powers as *delegated*, made them fear that federation would pose a threat to French Canada. The *Globe* told them not to worry. The local governments would not be subject to the general government in the way that municipalities were subject to the province that created them. No: their authority would derive from the British Crown and Parliament, and 'Congress' (the general legislature) would have no power to interfere with it. 'Such legislation would be beyond the control of the central power, set apart from it, untouchable by it.'

We must remember that the point of federation was to depoliticize the contentious issues that had led to sectional deadlock in United Canada. The *Globe* maintained that this could be done just as effectively by allocating specific powers to the local governments as by awarding them the residuary power, with its connotations of sovereignty. When the paper spoke of *delegated* powers, it meant law-making powers that were expressly defined rather than residuary. It did not mean that those powers would be granted to the local legislatures by the general legislature, which could therefore resume them as it saw fit.

So federal 'sovereignty' would not in itself pose a threat to provincial autonomy. Having established that, the *Globe* went on to argue that what really mattered was the actual distribution of power. 'The real sovereignty under a federal form of government rests with the body which has the largest share of power . . . The central power might be nominally supreme, but yet it might delegate to the local bodies such extensive jurisdiction as to deprive itself of all weight in the country.' The crucial thing was to write a constitution that gave the local legislatures ample power and confined the federal authority — call it sovereign or not — to matters of general interest.[10]

Well! Haven't we just caught the *Globe* with its foot in its mouth? Less than three weeks later, after Charlottetown, Brown's paper was reporting that almost all the important subjects of legislation would be allotted to the general government. At Quebec, as we saw, Brown himself would press for simple local governments on the ground that the powers provisionally assigned to them at Charlottetown were insignificant. On top of that, as summer turned to autumn, the scope of local autonomy appeared to be shrinking in other ways. The *Globe* began talking about a lieutenant-governor — possibly one appointed by the central government — armed with a veto over local legislation.[11] After the Quebec conference, there was also the federal disallowance power to explain away. It is easy to understand why French-speaking critics in particular condemned the Quebec scheme as a legislative union in all but name.[12]

Clearly Brown believed that the federal government would be the leading political forum after Confederation. The strategy in 1864 was to identify certain thorny questions and localize them, thereby relieving the polarization that had deadlocked union politics. But this does not mean that the local legislatures were not to enjoy genuine autonomy. Far from it: local autonomy was essential to the goal of sanitizing Canadian politics. More important, though, it was implicit in the founders' decision to base Confederation on the constitution of the British empire. Even in the 1820s, before the advent of responsible government, William and Robert Baldwin and the Letter on Responsible Government had insisted on the sovereignty of the colonial legislature as a matter of inherent right. With the maturing of the colonial system in British North America, local autonomy had become a political reality. Whatever they had once been, the governor's authority to reserve or veto colonial legislation, and the imperial government's authority to disallow it, had shrunk to the merest contingent power, to be wielded only in the last resort.

Robert Baldwin Sullivan had tried to define the limits of responsible government in 1844. The governor general, he suggested, would be justified in ignoring his ministers if they advised him to appoint a rebel in arms to command the militia. Obviously, this was an extreme contingency and a very unlikely one. Such an example implied that, short of such extremity, the governor was obliged to act on his ministers' advice and correspondingly to give his assent to the acts of his legislature. One of the Reformers' complaints against Governor General Metcalfe in 1844 concerned his decision to reserve for imperial review a government bill, duly passed by the legislature, that banned secret societies such as the Orange Order. Metcalfe's action was incontestably *legal*— the Act of Union vested that power in his office — but the Reformers condemned it as a breach of the conventions of responsible government. Accordingly, the great symbol of the final triumph of responsible government in Canada was the refusal of a later governor, Lord Elgin, to reserve another controversial measure, the Lower Canada Rebellion Losses Act of 1849, which entitled victims of military action during the rebellion to compensation.[13]

This brings us to Donald Creighton's accusation that Oliver Mowat lied about the Quebec agreement, for the charge relates in part to the issue of federal control of provincial legislation. One of the leading episodes in the provincial-rights controversy was Ottawa's repeated disallowance between 1881 and 1885 of an Ontario measure called the Rivers and Streams Act. This and similar episodes persuaded Mowat and other provincial premiers that the federal veto should be abolished. In a newspaper interview in 1887, Mowat recalled the discussion of the disallowance proposal at Quebec. Delegates had granted the power because some of them feared that the federal government would be too weak without it. It was generally understood, though, that the power would be subject to the same constitutional constraints as the imperial veto.[14]

The record of the Quebec conference contains not a word to contradict Mowat's statement, and the resolutions, if anything, confirm it. The fiftieth declares that any bill of the general Parliament may be reserved 'in the usual manner' for imperial review and that local bills may be reserved 'in like manner' for review by the federal government. The next resolution states that bills of the general Parliament shall be subject to disallowance by Her Majesty like those of the existing colonies and that local bills shall be subject 'in like manner' to disallowance by the governor general. Nor was this mere verbiage. So clearly was it understood that the two powers were to be analogous that A.-A. Dorion made a point of criticizing the assumption. Unlike the British government, he argued, the proposed federal government would be embroiled in colonial party politics and would inevitably succumb to the temptation to use the veto for party-political purposes. The controversy over the Rivers and Streams Act proved his criticism to be prescient, but the criticism itself only confirms what Mowat said later about the founders' conception of the veto.[15]

Twentieth-century centralists were well aware that Confederation was based on the imperial constitution, but they invariably saw this as evidence of the founders' intention to set up a dominant central government. They knew about the advent of responsible government, and they all thought it a good thing; but for some reason, when they came to think about Confederation, they forgot about it. In Creighton's story, for instance, British Americans, anxious to avoid the fatal flaws of American federalism, found the answer in 'another rather informal federal system, with which they were all perfectly familiar and which they infinitely preferred to the American. This was, of course, the Old Colonial System of the second British Empire, with its sovereign Imperial Parliament and its dependent colonial legislatures.' Yet by Creighton's own account, some fifty pages earlier, the Old Colonial System had expired in the 1840s, when the British government conceded responsible government to the North American colonies.[16] Why should the Fathers of Confederation have had that obsolete system in mind in designing the Canadian constitution, rather than the new system with which they were in fact 'all perfectly familiar' in 1864? Creighton did not even consider the question.

For the Upper Canadian Reformers at least, we need only read the *Globe* to prove Creighton wrong. In an editorial entitled 'English Ideas of Federation,' it cited the British empire as an example of the way in which local self-government could render the central power stronger, not weaker — only it was the *new* imperial system that showed this, not Creighton's Old Colonial System. So long as the British colonies were governed from Downing Street, declared the *Globe*, 'they were always discontented, and complaints were constant, sometimes ending in rebellion, and always injurious to the authority of the parent State. When local self-government was granted all this ceased, and the colonies are now more loyal to the mother country than the mother country is loyal to the colonies.[17]

This article is especially pertinent, because it was written to reassure people who feared that federal union must be weaker than legislative union. It did not propose to resolve that difficulty by putting the local governments under the political constraints of the Old Colonial System. It proposed to do so by granting them the freedoms of the new system. Accordingly, the *Globe* dismissed the idea that the Quebec scheme was a legislative union in disguise: the conference had done too much to preserve the autonomy of the provinces, and given the local legislatures too much real power, for that charge to hold. The *Globe's* argument conformed to Brown's own remarks at Quebec, where he insisted that the specified local powers were ample to maintain local autonomy.[18]

Certainly disallowance made no difference. The *Globe* compared it not to the imperial veto but to something still less threatening: the Crown's power in Britain to refuse assent to bills passed by Parliament. That power, though still existing in law, had atrophied long since. According to the *Globe*, the central government's veto would no more destroy the federal character of the constitution than the defunct royal veto could destroy the 'popular' character of the British constitution. It had been created to guard against the chance that local legislatures might abuse their autonomy by passing laws that were unjust to local minorities, but the federal government would not dare to exercise it unless the local government were clearly in the wrong. Any indiscretion in its use would probably cause an outcry that would sweep it into oblivion.[19]

It looks then as though Brown and his supporters were not quite the zealous centralists in 1864 that some twentieth-century writers made them out to be. They did intend to make the federal government stronger than its American counterpart seemed to be. And they did hope to lay the basis of a new nationality — even Mowat, in one of his few recorded remarks at Quebec, approved of that idea.[20] But they did not mean to subject the local governments to a dominating federal overlordship or to award them merely municipal powers and status. Their first priority was to relieve Upper Canada of the 'baneful domination' (Mowat's words in 1859) of Lower Canada. In fact, the whole confederation movement sprang from Brown's timely proposal, in March 1864, to resolve United Canada's political deadlock by moving towards a federal union. He consented to pursue a wider union, or confederation, only on condition that, if it did not happen, Canadian federation would proceed regardless. But even if the wider project did go ahead, experience convinced the Reformers that it could succeed only if based on a genuine local autonomy, designed to remove vexatious local issues from the sphere of 'national' politics.

To Reformers in particular, the *new* imperial system offered a promising model for the new nationality. It had made a reality of the ideal of local self-government that had inspired them since the 1820s. It also presented a spectacle of multinational cohesion that the Old Colonial System, with its political constraints and restrictive trade regulations, never had. Looking back, we may well think that that cohesion owed less to the structure of the imperial constitution than to the massive flow of British population and investment to the North American colonies after 1850. Still, in the 1860s that constitutional machinery seemed an effective means of combining local autonomy with the minimum of political cohesion required to dissuade the member provinces from thinking that they had joined a club that they could leave whenever they liked. The federal appointment of lieutenant-governors, the formal powers of that office, the federal power of disallowance — these were not instruments of federal dominance but symbols of the new national unity.

The same is true of the residuary legislative power. When Reformers such as Brown proposed to define the local powers and leave the remainder to the central legislature, they did not mean to create a powerful engine of federal legislative domination. On the contrary, their intention was to shore up the new federal power, lest it be too feeble, by investing it with a symbolic sovereignty. The *Globe* said repeatedly that, in terms of actual power, it did not matter whether you specified the powers of the local government or those of the general government. Local autonomy would be guaranteed by the amplitude of the authority assigned to the local governments by the fact that it was conferred by the British Parliament.

Besides, the Fathers of Confederation did not assign the residue to Ottawa after all. True, it is generally accepted that they reversed the American pattern by assigning the residuary power to the federal instead of the local governments and that they did so in order to create a highly centralized federation, in which the central government would predominate. The evidence seems strong. The Canadian government was committed to that plan from the start. Both John A. Macdonald and the *Globe* advocated it strongly. It may actually have been adopted at the Charlottetown conference, although the only people who said so were those who favoured the plan. At Quebec, when certain delegates denied that the question had been settled at Charlottetown and insisted on reopening it in any case, their bid to allocate the residue to the local governments was defeated. And in 1872 one of the delegates, John Hamilton Gray of New Brunswick, published a book in which he stated that the conference had reversed the American scheme.[21]

When, therefore, Donald Creighton stated that the Fathers of Confederation had 'unanimously resolved that general or residuary powers were to lie, not with the local, but with the general legislature,'[22] he was stating common knowledge. *But common knowledge was incorrect — the Fathers had done nothing of the sort.* Instead, having unanimously declined to assign the residue to the local governments, they had split it in two. They had devised a list of itemized powers for each government and rounded off each list with a catch-all category. That for the 'General Parliament' stated: 'And *Generally* respecting all matters of a general character, not especially and exclusively reserved for the Local Governments and Legislatures.' And that for the 'Local Legislatures' stated: 'And *generally* all matters of a private or local nature, not assigned to the General Parliament.'[23] In short, 'general' powers were assigned to *both* legislatures.

John A. Macdonald claimed nothing more when he explained the Quebec resolutions to the provincial legislative assembly at the opening of its debate on the subject in February 1865. At one point he declared: 'We have expressly declared that all subjects of general interest not distinctly and exclusively conferred upon the local governments and local legislatures, shall be conferred upon the General Government and Legislature.' Later he quoted that declaration verbatim, as I have above. Both times he presented this arrangement as the delegates' answer to what they had perceived as the great weakness of the American system. He never claimed that they had assigned the residue to the general legislature. Neither did Charles Tupper, premier of Nova Scotia. Presenting the Quebec scheme to the house of assembly, Tupper explained that it remedied the weakness of the American system by defining the powers of both the general and the local legislatures rather than those of the former alone. He did not even mention what it did about the residue.[24]

In the course of the Canadian debate on confederation, where these details were discussed more thoroughly than in the other provinces, two MPPs asserted that the Quebec scheme reversed the American pattern, but this was just one of many misconceptions that found expression in the legislature.[25] Most Canadian politicians regarded the American system as flawed in that the states had bestowed specific powers on Congress, reserving the residue for themselves. That arrangement had fostered ideas of state sovereignty, including the notion that individual states could nullify federal laws within their territory or even secede from the union. It was natural to see a reversal of the American pattern in the arrangement devised at Quebec to avoid this error. If there was anything more than this to Gray's statement in 1872, it may have been an urge to believe that the position that he himself had advocated at Quebec had prevailed.

In 1872, through, Gray, like later generations, was seeing the Quebec Resolutions through the prism of the British North America (BNA) Act. The circumstances under which this momentous document was drafted, early in 1867, are still unclear, but they bear the marks of a determined effort on the part of British officials to overbear the colonial will and centralize the scheme of confederation. Drafting was delayed for nearly two years by opposition to the Quebec scheme in the Maritime provinces. Newfoundland and Prince Edward Island stayed out, and it was only in December 1866 that plenipotentiaries from Nova Scotia and New Brunswick met a Canadian delegation in London to work out a revision of the scheme, on the basis of which their provinces might join the impending Canadian federation. The London resolutions retained the division of the legislative residue as agreed at Quebec, and the conference inserted that arrangement in its draft bill based on the resolutions. Then the British got into the act. In the first parliamentary draft of the confederation bill the local residuary power disappeared, while the federal residue was moved to the head of the section dealing with the powers of the federal parliament and presented in the terms with which we are familiar from the final act. It invested parliament with the power to make laws for the 'peace, order, and good government' of the 'United Colony' in relation to all matters not exclusively confided to the local legislatures and went on to enumerate certain federal powers 'for greater Certainty, but not so as to restrict the Generality of the foregoing Terms of this section.' The local residue gave way to a clause referring to matters that the general parliament might from time to time, as it saw fit, transfer to the local jurisdiction.[26]

It was Creighton's guess that these changes reflected the influence of the governor general, Lord Monck, and the Colonial Office ministers, all of whom shared Macdonald's centralizing zeal. If so, they had a field day: this draft also designated the local heads of government as 'superintendents' instead of lieutenant-governors. School districts have superintendents: this was municipalization with a vengeance. In a lyrical account of these proceedings, Creighton described how the North American delegates, when they met to discuss the British draft, gratefully accepted the new, improved federal residuary clause but felt obliged to reject the superintendents, 'perhaps with some regret.' I wonder how much regret Hector-Louis Langevin felt: his letters from London complain of having to watch Macdonald like a hawk in order to stop him from using his rapport with the British to make centralizing changes on the sly. Creighton makes no mention of this, although he does report Langevin's departure on a pious pilgrimage to Rome.[27]

Nor does Creighton mention the local residuary clause. Of course, he never admitted its existence. But to those who do notice its presence in the Quebec and London resolutions, its vicissitudes in those early weeks of 1867 are a matter of great interest. As draft succeeded draft, it flickered like a candle in a draft. The second official draft omitted both the original clause and its substitute. The third restored it. The fourth replaced it again with the substitute. Only with the final bill, which duly became law as the BNA Act, did it finally reclaim its place in the scheme as 'generally all matters of a merely local or private nature in the province.'[28]

In its final form, the BNA Act granted the Canadian Parliament the power to make laws for the 'peace, order, and good government of Canada' in relation to everything not confided to the local legislatures. This made it possible to say not only that the residuary power had been vested in the federal government but that the federal power was *wholly* residuary — it comprised everything that was not specifically allotted to the provinces. Twentieth-century nationalists were to make much of this arrangement. . . . But there is a huge difference between a power that comprises everything but certain exceptions (the specified powers of the local legislatures) and one that excludes not only those powers but an extra, indefinite category consisting of everything else that is 'local' rather than 'general.' In the first case, a judge would have to look at the defined local powers and decide if a disputed subject belongs there or in the federal residue. In the second case, even if a subject did not come within the defined local powers, he might have to make a judgment as to its nature. He might have to decide whether, under the circumstances, it is essentially 'general' or 'local.'

It is impossible to make a judgment of that sort without considering the question of local autonomy. Twentieth-century critics were to blast the Judicial Committee of the Privy Council for taking account of provincial autonomy in their decisions,[29] but it is hard to see that the committee was wrong in principle to do so. The Fathers of Confederation had imposed the task on it by establishing indefinite categories of 'general' and 'local' legislative powers.[30] More than that: by basing the Canadian constitution on the imperial model, they hinted at a broad conception of local autonomy, much like that enjoyed by the self-governing colonies. Whatever else the Quebec resolutions, the London resolutions, and the BNA Act may say, they certainly make no mention of the Old Colonial System, which Donald Creighton said was the basis for Confederation.

Oliver Mowat's greatest contribution to the shaping of Canada lay in his steering the Judicial Committee towards this genuinely federal view of Confederation. He may have done so for good or for ill, but his doing so was no betrayal of any commitment made by him and his political associates at Confederation. George Brown and his supporters never endorsed any other view of Confederation than was contained in the Quebec resolutions; neither did the legislature of United Canada approve anything else.

In June 1867, six hundred Upper Canadian Reformers met in convention in Toronto. The event was billed as a reprise of what the circular of invitation called 'the great Convention of 1859.' The circular recalled how 570 prominent and influential men, from all sections of Upper

Canada, had then reached conclusions that had changed the course of Upper Canadian history. Their proposals for constitutional reform had at last been implemented with the almost unanimous assent (it said) of the people of Canada, Nova Scotia, and New Brunswick.

One purpose of the new gathering was to celebrate that great victory; another was to prepare to exploit it. The Dominion of Canada would come into being on July the first, and federal and provincial elections must soon be held. Reformers must now achieve the political reforms for which constitutional reform had been merely a prerequisite. That depended on victory at the polls. A convention would help to reconcile Reformers who might have become temporarily estranged during the arduous struggle for the new constitution. It would breathe new vigour into the Reform cause.[31]

Victory had taken its toll. By arousing and channelling discontent with the constitution of 1840, the Reform party under George Brown had launched the political process that had culminated in Confederation; but it was the conservatives who stood to benefit from it. As in 1859, the Reformers were in disarray. The worst damage had been sustained at the start. The pursuit of federation in 1864 had estranged them from their Lower Canadian allies under Dorion. Brown and two colleagues (Mowat and McDougall), obliged to enter into coalition with the Conservatives as the price of reform, had had to do so as three liberals in a cabinet of twelve. To a man of Brown's nice conscience, political cohabitation with John A. Macdonald was a purgatory, and by the end of 1865 he had had enough. Confederation was assured by then, despite the defection of Prince Edward Island and Newfoundland and continuing opposition in Nova Scotia and New Brunswick. Brown quarreled with Alexander Galt over what he saw as Galt's bungling of tariff reciprocity negotiations with the United States. Outvoted on the issue in cabinet, Brown resigned.

Another reformer replaced him, and the coalition continued. But the following summer Brown took umbrage at Galt's budget, which he thought favoured Montreal financial interests and penalized those of Toronto and western Upper Canada. When he tried to whip up opposition in the legislature, he found himself deserted by almost the entire Reform caucus, with McDougall in the lead. Brown devoted himself to personal affairs, responding coolly when Lord Monck suggested that he take part in the Canadian delegation to the London conference. As a result, by 1867 many Upper Canadians were tending to associate Confederation with John A. Macdonald and the Conservatives, rather than with Brown and the Reformers. That tendency could only be strengthened by Macdonald's appointment as prime minister of the Dominion — an appointment earned by his congeniality to British officials but officially ascribed to his seniority as an executive councillor.[32]

For Brown and his supporters, Confederation promised a new beginning. Under the BNA Act, Ontario's local affairs would be a matter for Ontarians alone. At Ottawa, thanks to the principle of representation by population, the province would supply eighty-two MPs out of 181, with the prospect of a still larger share after the next census. But the party must be united and the voters reminded of what it stood for. The problem was no longer the caucus as a whole: after its initial repudiation of Brown over the budget, most of its members had returned to the fold. But Macdonald had cleverly moved to perpetuate Reform divisions by proposing to continue the coalition. He had secured the adherence of the three Upper Canadian Reform ministers by appointing them to the federal cabinet. One leading purpose of the Reform convention was to discredit and isolate the renegades.

The convention was boosted by the failure of the renegades' preemptive strike. The three Reform ministers called a meeting of Reform legislators in Toronto. Few attended, and only three MPPs and a clutch of legislative councillors were willing to remain in coalition. Brown and company improved on this advantage by nominating William Patrick to the chair of the convention. Patrick, a businessman and Methodist lay preacher, presented himself as 'a

Reformer of the old stamp.' As a Baldwinite he had supported the Liberal Conservative coalition of 1854, but after a year or two he had quit in disgust. More recently, he had been associated with John Sandfield Macdonald, and earlier in 1867 he had been mentioned in the press as a possible supporter of John A.'s coalition.[33]

Patrick symbolized the futility of the coalitionist cause by his very presence, and he could speak with authority on the 'immorality' of coalitions and the virtue and necessity of political parties. He also symbolized the continuity of Reform politics. Though long a resident of Prescott, on the St. Lawrence River, he had grown up in Toronto when it was still a town called Muddy York and had been related by marriage to Thomas Morrison, a leading collaborator of William Lyon Mackenzie's. He commenced his duties as chairman by reminiscing about the York election of 1828, when Dr. Morrison had stood against John Beverley Robinson with the backing of Robert Baldwin and R.B. Sullivan. He recalled 'young Sullivan' running to and fro in his shirtsleeves at the hustings, marshalling support for the Reform candidate. By the end of his speech, few in the audience could doubt that the true Reform tradition reposed with them that day in the Toronto Music Hall.[34]

Led by Patrick, a series of speakers descanted on the themes announced in the circular of invitation. They celebrated Confederation as a triumph for the principles of 1859. The BNA Act contained defects, to be sure — the Senate was non-elective, for instance, and the House of Commons subject to re-election only at five-year intervals. Nevertheless, the act had delivered the two essential requirements: representation by population and local control of local affairs. Only by abandoning coalition and returning to party politics, however, could Upper Canadians reap the benefits.

Two features of the discussion were especially portentous. First of all, Confederation was celebrated almost entirely as a realization of Upper Canadian autonomy.[35] One resolution looked forward to transcontinental expansion, but on the whole there was less grand talk about transcontinental nationality now than in 1859, when it had seemed only a distant prospect. This was natural, since most Reformers had embraced Confederation chiefly as a means to ending the union with Lower Canada, but it foreshadowed the zeal with which Reformers would defend Ontario's autonomy within the new union. The second portent was the delegates' attitude to the man who was to be their great enemy in the struggle for provincial rights, John A. Macdonald. In 1859, speakers had flayed Tories in general for subjugating the province to the Lower Canadian yoke, but they had not named names. This time they singled out Macdonald.

Brown led the way. He did not try to hide his chagrin at the prospect that his great enemy, the chief agent of Lower Canadian domination, might receive credit for the victory, and reap the fruits of the victory, for which Reformers had sacrificed so much. The gangling Scot spoke feelingly of the 'degradation' of being obliged, as the price of Upper Canadian liberty, to enter into coalition in 1864. No men had ever entered government with such sore hearts as he and Mowat on that occasion, and the day he got out of that business was the happiest of his life. After such sacrifices, and such a victory, were they now to 'make terms with the enemy'? Were they to 'renew the hateful compact' and make Macdonald prime minister?[36]

The prospect of Macdonald as prime minister coloured the delegates' hostility to coalition. Coalition was bad in any case, because a strong, watchful opposition was essential to good government, and corruption flourished in its absence. But coalition with Macdonald was like supping with the devil, and coalition under Macdonald's leadership was worse still. Alexander Mackenzie recalled that he had opposed coalition in 1864 as 'an extremely dangerous experiment,' fearing that some Reformers would end up 'not merely coalesced but fused with the Tories.' His fears had been justified, but he had been outvoted in caucus by those who felt that Macdonald was so treacherous that he must be watched from inside the cabinet. Then, however, Macdonald had not been prime minister. At first Sir Étienne Taché had headed the government. On his death, Brown had vetoed Macdonald's succession (as well as that of Cartier, the *bleu* leader) and secured the appointment of a lesser *bleu*, Sir Narcisse Belleau. Mackenzie contrasted Brown's principled defence of Reform interests in 1864 and 1865 with the craven alacrity with which McDougall and his fellow-renegades were not reaching for office under the arch-enemy of Reform.[37]

Macdonald was the enemy: the enemy of Reform, the enemy of the people — perhaps something worse. William McDougall's plight reminded one delegate of a picture of a simple young man who had just been checkmated in a chess game with the great enemy of mankind. The speaker laughingly denied any intention of comparing Macdonald to the enemy of mankind or McDougall to a simple young man, but he believed that the latter had sold himself for $8,000 a year. This was the only explicit reference to Satan, but several speakers depicted Macdonald as a figure of diabolical cunning. One spoke of William Howland, another Reform collaborator, as an honest man who had got caught in one of Macdonald's 'clever political tricks.' The collaborators were bewitched, suggested Brown; Macdonald, a very 'astute' man and a skilled manipulator, had thrown 'the glamour' over their eyes. Even the one delegate to speak up for coalition appealed to these fears. They were told, he noted, that Macdonald was crafty and cunning and that he had kept up the coalition in order to split the Reformers. Why play into his hands, then? Why meet cunning with foolishness?[38]

The temper of the meeting was thrown into sharp relief by the speeches of Howland and McDougall. They attended only after receiving special invitations by a vote of the convention. Howland's speech was conciliatory and McDougall's combative, but they conveyed the same message. There was nothing wrong with coalition in a good cause. They had agreed to enter the federal cabinet out of consideration for the four Maritime members, all Reformers, who would otherwise be outnumbered by Tories. With the Maritimers, the Upper Canadian collaborators would make seven Reformers in a cabinet of thirteen. This would prevent Macdonald from using the patronage of the Intercolonial Railway, which the BNA Act required to be built between Halifax and Quebec, to establish a Conservative hegemony.

Such were their excuses, but what really mattered was the challenge they posed to their fellow-Reformers' deepest convictions. Howland chided the delegates for thinking only of Upper Canada and not of their fellow-colonists, particularly the Maritime Reformers. When invited to join the federal cabinet, said McDougall, they had felt bound to look at the question 'not only from a party point of view, but from an Upper Canada and also a British North American point of view.' He flouted the Reformers' propensity to identify Upper Canada with themselves: Upper Canadians as a whole, Tories as well as Reformers, had been disadvantaged by the constitution of 1840. Not only that, but Tories as well as Reformers had worked and taken risks for Confederation. In a deliberate rebuff to Brown's claims to the chief credit for the achievement, he paid pointed tribute to Macdonald's hard and devoted labour for the cause.[39]

These were fighting words. To dispute the identity of Upper Canada and Reform was to challenge the Reformers' self-conception as the people's champions against Tory oppression. To say that Tories and Reformers alike had suffered under the old constitution was to scorn the belief that Tories had used it to rule Upper Canada against the wishes of the people. To offer Macdonald even qualified praise was to prove that you had sold out to a man who was the people's enemy, if not the enemy of mankind. Maybe McDougall had forgotten how to talk to Reformers, but more probably he didn't care. His reputation within the party had never recovered from his accepting office under Sandfield Macdonald in 1862. He was really addressing himself to the electors, not the convention.

At any rate, inside the Music Hall his words fell on deaf ears. Brown jeered at the notion that a seven-to-six majority (even if all seven were Reformers, which he doubted) could stop an astute operator like Macdonald, armed with prime ministerial powers and the patronage of the Intercolonial, from having his way in cabinet. And what was to happen at the provincial elections? Were Reformers to surrender Ontario to the Tories for the sake of having McDougall and company in cabinet in Ottawa for a few weeks, until Macdonald should choose to dismiss them? Seconding his leader, Alexander Mackenzie tarred the Maritime Reformers with the collaborationist brush. They would have done better to work with Reformers in Upper and Lower Canada to install a Reform government in Ottawa. They should certainly not have accepted office without consulting their Canadian counterparts, especially in a cabinet that excluded Dorion and the *rouges*. (Here he eulogized the *rouge* leader.) And what had the people of Upper Canada done, that they should be sacrificed at the shrine of the Maritime so-called Reformers?[40]

Refusing to be sacrificed, the convention rejected coalition all but unanimously. Led by Brown, the Reformers bid vigorously for the fruits of Confederation at the federal and provincial elections. The Reform vote split sufficiently to give Macdonald a majority of federal seats in Ontario as well as power in Ottawa, while his provincial collaborator Sandfield Macdonald was able to form a coalition ministry in Toronto. In 1871, however, Sandfield Macdonald would be ousted, and two years later Alexander Mackenzie would replace John A. Macdonald as prime minister of Canada.

NOTES

1. I recount the rise of the centralist interpretation in chapter 11 [of this book, Paul Romney, *Getting It Wrong: How Canadians Forgot Their Past and Imperilled Confederation* (Toronto: University of Toronto Press, 1999)].
2. All quoted in F.R. Scott, *Essays on the Constitution: Aspects of Canadian Law and Politics* (Toronto, 1977) 5–7.
3. Coles quoted in ibid., 22; *Parliamentary Debates on the Subject of the Confederation of the British North American Provinces* (Quebec, 1865), 176 (Olivier); 250 (Dorion); 1002 (Macdonald).
4. *Globe*, 1 Aug., 8 Aug, 17 Sept., and 4 Oct. 1864.
5. G.P. Browne, ed., *Documents on the Confederation of British North America* (Toronto, 1969), 113–15. See also Careless, *Brown of the Globe*, II, 167–9.
6. J.C. Morrison, 'Sir Oliver Mowat and the Development of Provincial Rights in Ontario,' in *Three History Theses* (Toronto, 1961), 6; and see above, 9.
7. *Globe*, 15 Nov. 1859 (emphasis added). See also ibid., 11 Nov. (Burr).
8. Careless, *Brown of the Globe*, I, 257, 283–5; II, 61–135; Hodgins, *John Sandfield Macdonald*, 45–74; Ged Martin, *Britain and the Origins of Canadian Confederation, 1837–1867* (Basingstoke, 1995), 47–55.
9. Ibid., 1 Aug. 1864.
10. Ibid., 30 Aug. 1864; see also 3 Sept., 16 Sept., and 21 Sept. 1864.
11. Ibid., 4 Oct. 1864.
12. See, among others, the speeches of Antoine and Eric Dorion, Louis-August Olivier, Henri Joly, and Joseph Perrault.
13. Legion, *Letters on Responsible Government*, 128; Careless, *Union of the Canadas*, 82, 123–6.
14. *Globe*, 4 July 1887; Christopher Armstrong, *The Politics of Federalism: Ontario's Relations with the Federal Government, 1867–1942* (Toronto, 1981), 25–30.
15. *Debates on . . . Confederation*, 258.
16. Donald Creighton, *Dominion of the North: A History of Canada* (1944: rev. ed., Toronto, 1957), 253–62, 306.
17. *Globe*, 17 Sept. 1864.
18. Browne, ed., *Documents*, 120.
19. *Globe*, 10 and 25 Nov. 1864.
20. Browne, *Documents*, 120.
21. Ibid., 42, 81–3, 122–5; John Hamilton Gray, *Confederation; or, the Political and Parliamentary History of Canada, from the Conference at Quebec, in October, 1864, to the Admission of British Columbia, in July, 1871*, vol. I (Toronto, 1872), 44–5, 55–7.
22. Creighton, *Dominion of the North*, 311.
23. Browne, *Documents*, 157–61 (emphasis added).

24. *Debates on . . . Confederation*, 33, 41; *Debates and Proceedings of the House of Assembly . . . of the Province of Nova Scotia, 1864* (Halifax, NS, 1864), 207.
25. *Debates on . . . Confederation*, 404 (Rose), 807 (Walsh).
26. Ibid., 221–4, 237–41, 256–60.
27. Donald Creighton, *The Road to Confederation: The Emergence of Canada, 1863–1867* (Boston, 1965), 418–19; Andrée Desilets, *Hector Louis Langevin: un père de la confédération canadienne (1826–1906)* (Québec, 1969), 164–7. See also Alfred D. DeCelles, 'Sir Georges Étienne Cartier,' in DeCelles, *Papineau, Cartier*, rev. by W.L. Grant, The Makers of Canada Series, vol. 5 (London, 1926), 102–3.
28. Browne, *Documents*, 275, 293, 326; W.P.M. Kennedy, *The Constitution of Canada: An Introduction to Its Development and Law* (Oxford, 1922), 437–9.
29. *Report Pursuant to Resolution of the Senate . . . Relating to the Enactment of the British North America Act, 1867* (Ottawa, 1939) (hereafter O'Connor Report), annex 1, 47; Scott, *Essays on the Constitution*, 35–48.
30. This is certainly what Brown, for one, had in mind: Browne, ed., *Documents*, 123.
31. *Globe*, 28 June 1867.
32. Careless, *Brown of the Globe*, II, 187–239.
33. Ibid., 239–047; on Patrick, see *DCB*, XI, 676–7.
34. *Globe*, 28 June 1867; on Morrison, see *DCB*, VIII, 642–4.
35. *Globe*, 28 June 1867 (Circular of invitation, Brown [2nd and 3rd speeches], Blake, Irving); ibid., 29 June (Crooks, Pardee).
36. Ibid.; 28 June (Brown [3rd speech]).
37. Ibid.; Careless, *Brown of the Globe*, II, 199–203. On Belleau, see *DCB*, XII, 86–7.
38. *Globe*, 28 June (Brown [3rd and 4th speeches], A. Mackenzie, Spohn, Gillespie, Gordon).
39. Ibid.
40. Ibid. (Brown [4th speech], A. Mackenzie).

CONTRIBUTORS

Robert S. Allen (1942–1997) was the Deputy Chief, Claims and Historical Research Centre, Department of Indian and Northern Affairs.

Ruth Bleasdale teaches history at Dalhousie University in Halifax, Nova Scotia.

Ann Gorman Condon (1936–2001) taught Canadian history at the University of New Brunswick in Fredericton.

John A. Dickinson teaches Canadian history in the History Department at the Université de Montréal.

Heather Rollason Driscoll is the director of operations for the Office of the Vice-President, Governmental and Institutional Relations at the University of Toronto.

W.J. Eccles (1917–1998) taught Canadian history at the University of Toronto.

E. Jane Errington is a professor of history at the Royal Military College of Canada in Kingston, Ontario.

Elizabeth A. Fenn teaches history at George Washington University, Washington, D.C.

Allan Greer teaches Canadian history at the University of Toronto.

Naomi Griffiths taught Canadian history at Carleton University in Ottawa. She is now retired.

José Igartua teaches history at l'Université du Québec in Montréal.

Willeen Keough teaches history at Simon Fraser University in Burnaby, British Columbia.

André Lachance taught history at the Université de Sherbrooke, Québec, and is now retired.

D. Peter MacLeod is the author of *The Canadian Iroquois and the Seven Years' War* (Toronto: Dundurn Press, 1996).

Elizabeth Mancke teaches in the Department of History at the University of Akron in Ohio.

Cecilia Morgan teaches in the Department of Theory and Policy Studies in Education at the Ontario Institute for Studies in Education at the University of Toronto.

Jan Noel teaches Canadian history at the University of Toronto, Erindale campus.

Frits Pannekoek is president of Athabasca University in Alberta.

Adele Perry holds the Canada Research Chair in Western Canadian Social History at the University of Manitoba.

Carolyn Podruchny teaches Canadian history at York University in Toronto.

Alison Prentice is Professor Emerita, University of Toronto.

Harald E.I. Prins teaches anthropology at Kansas State University at Manhattanville, Kansas.

George A. Rawlyk (1935–1995) taught Canadian history at Queen's University, Kingston, Ontario.

Colin Read teaches Canadian history at Huron College, at the University of Western Ontario, London, Ontario.

Paul Romney has taught at the Center for Canadian Studies in the School of Advanced International Studies, John Hopkins University, and currently works as a freelance writer.

Sylvie Savoie teaches in the Département d'histoire et de sciences politiques at the Université de Sherbrooke, Sherbrooke, Québec.

Scott W. See teaches Canadian history at the University of Maine, in Orono.

Arthur I. Silver teaches Canadian history at the University of Toronto.

Irene M. Spry (1907–1998) was Economics Professor Emerita at the University of Ottawa.

Bruce G. Trigger teaches in the Department of Anthropology at McGill University in Montréal.

Sylvia Van Kirk taught Canadian history at the University of Toronto, and is now Professor Emerita.

Wendy C. Wickwire teaches history in the Department of History at the University of Victoria.

Catharine Anne Wilson teaches Canadian history at the University of Guelph in Guelph, Ontario.

Shirley J. Yee teaches Women's Studies at the University of Washington, in Seattle.

PHOTO CREDITS

INDEX

Abbott, Ellen, 442
Aborigines' Protection Society, 508
Abortion, 494
Abstinence, 375
Acadians, 239, 449
  clothing, 139–140
  demographic expansion,
    136–137
  deportation, 134
  deputies, 150, 151, 155
  disputes, 140
  economy, 137–138, 139
  families, 137, 139, 140
  first settlement, 135
  health, 140–141
  in Louisiana, 232
  military service issue, 156, 157
  neutrality, 135–136
  qualified oath, 147
  refusal to swear allegiance to
    British, 145, 150–151, 153–154
  religion, 141, 146
  smuggling, 141
  social mores, 141
  standard of living, 138–139, 140
  survey of lands, 151
  trade, 141
Acculturation, of fur trade families,
  520, 523–525, 530–532
Act for the Preservation of the Peace
  near Public Works, 421–422
Act of Union, 572
Adair, James, 172
Adams, Abigail, 172, 173
Adultery, 118, 123–125
Ainslie, Thomas, 206
Akenson, Donald, 283
Aldridge, Christopher, 152
Alerie, Mary, 503
Allan, Jacob, 457
Allan, John, 241–242, 243
Allied Tribes of British Columbia, 50
Alline, Henry, 245
Alpha, 544, 545
Amantacha, Louis, 101
Amende honorable, 124, 301, 303
American Civil War, 556
American Missionary Association,
  438, 442

American Revolution, 175–178,
  180–181, 314
  See also Eddy Rebellion of 1776
Amherst, Jeffery, 160, 167–168, 179,
  181, 206
Amherstburg Baptist Association for
  Coloured People, 439
Amhurstberg grand council, 271–272
Andaerraehaan, 102
Andaonhaan, 102
Anderson, Anthony, 321
Anderson, Benedict, 282
Anderson, Bishop, 491, 496
Anderson, George, 456, 457, 458
Anderson, John, 502
Anderson, Thomas Gummersall
  (Tige), 275, 276
Anderson, William, 470
Andre, Frances, 502
Anglo American Magazine, 284
Anne (Queen of England), 145, 154
The Anne, 326
Annontaguelté (Mohawk chief), 99
Antko, Lucy, 49
Arbuthnot, Mariot, 242
Ariés, Philippe, 112
Armstrong, Lawrence, 150, 152,
  153, 155, 156, 157, 158
Armstrong, M.W., 245
Armstrong, Sarah Ann, 253
Arthur, Sir George, 328
Assimilation
  and class status, 519–537
  Confederation and, 557
  of English-Protestant planters,
    337–338
  Royal Proclamation of 1763
    and, 213
  See also Acculturation
Aubuchon, Marie Josephe, 113
L'Aurore, 375
Avalon. *See* Newfoundland
Ayer, Obadiah, 241
Aylwin, Thomas, 422
Azouade ("donkey ride"), 299

Baieuville, Bailly de, 120
Bailyn, Bernard, 250
Baldwin, Robert, 317, 318, 572, 578

Baldwin, William Warren, 317, 572
Ballendendine, Samuel, 505
Bancroft, Hubert Howe, 527, 533
Bank of England, 85
Bank of Upper Canada, 316, 319
Bannatyne, A.G.B., 501
Bannerji, Himani, 540
Bannerman, Janet, 497, 501
Baptist Sunday School
  Committee, 439
Barbeau, Marius, 48
Barclay, Nancy. *See* Robinson, Nancy
Barnes, Thomas, 150
Barnett, George, 416
Barn-raising bees, 466, 479
Barter system, reciprocal work bees
  and, 468
Bartlett, Josiah, 177
Bastardy action, 344–345, 352
Batt, Major, 244, 245
Battle of Beaver Dams, 284, 285, 289
Battle of Blue Licks, 269
Battle of Carillon, 194, 196
Battle of Fallen Timber, 269
Battle of Lake George, 191, 269
Battle of Quebec, 206–213, 228
  battlefield tactics, 209–211
  British objective, 208, 227
  Montcalm's decision to attack,
    210–211
  popular view of, 206
  positioning of British troops,
    209–210, 211
  strength of French troops, 209
Battle of Queenston Heights, 283
Battle of Sandusky, 269
Battle of Ste. Foye, 195
Battle of the Boyne, 414, 450
Battle of the Thames, 273
Battle of Tippecanoe, 272
Baynton, Wharton, and Morgan, 220
Beads, Jacob, 505
Beads, James, 505
Beads, John, 504
Beads, John, Jr., 505
Beale, Governor, 64, 68
Béarn regiment, 206
Beatty, Walter, 468
Beauchamp, Pierre, 505

Beauharnois, Charles de la
    Boische, 106
Beauharnois Canal, 411, 419, 424
Beebe, Lewis, 176
Bees, work, 464–486
    accounting of work done, 468
    age-based hierarchy, 471
    as charity, 467
    class relations, 471–472
    code of behaviour, 469
    decline of, 480–481
    economic role of, 466–468
    gendered division of labour, 466,
        472–474
    gender relations, 474–475, 479
    hospitality, 470, 471–472, 474
    and local social networks,
        475–479
    obligatory reciprocity, 469–470
    problem of managing people, 480
    as rite of passage, 470–471
    social role of, 468–475
    types of, 465–466
Begg, Alexander, 507
Begg family (Dundas County),
    476, 478
Belcourt, G.-A., 508
Benevolent associations, 442–443
Bennett, Joseph, 156
Berger, Carl, 282, 287
Berland, Pascal, 501
Berrigan family, 340–341
Bessette, 306
Bibb, Henry, 348, 441, 442
Bibb, Mary Miles, 348, 434, 440,
    441, 442, 443
Bidwell, Marshall Spring, 318
Bigamy, 124–125
Binmore, E., 369–370
Biological warfare
    allegations of, 167–170, 173–178
    British and, 180–181
    ethics of, 178–181
    French and, 179–180
    Native allegations of, 174–175
    Spanish and, 179
Bird, Frederick, 501
Bird, James, 68
Birston, Alex, 499
Birston, William, 502
Black, Hawk, 277, 278
Black, John, 491, 501
Black, W.R., 501
Blackbeard (Shawnee), 271
Blackbird, Andrew, 174
Black Cat (Mandan chief), 400
Black churches, 438–439

Black codes, 435
Black experience
    American Revolutionary War,
        175, 177
    in British Columbia, 541
    community-building, 443
    dominant sex role ideology and,
        436–437, 438, 439, 443–444
    emigration from U.S., 434–435
    employment and economic
        activities, 436–437
    internal community politics,
        441–443
    militia, 423
    racial prejudice in Canada,
        435–436
    smallpox, 175, 177
    women pioneers, 434–447
Black Hawk, 273, 275
Blacklisting, 421
Blanchet, Joseph, 559
Bleu, and Confederation, 558–560
Bliss, Henry, 252–253
Bliss, Jonathan, 250
Bliss, Mary, 250, 252
Bliss, William, 253
Blowers, Sampson Salter, 253
Board of the Baptist Missionary
    Convention, 548
Board of Trade, 146, 148, 154, 157, 158
Board of Works, 411, 412, 413,
    416, 421
Boas, Franz, 48, 49, 50, 57
Boat brigades. See Canoe brigades
Bolivar, Santiago, 47
Boone, Daniel, 269
Bosher, John F., 112
Bosquet, Louis, 504
Bostwick, Henry, 218
Bouat, François-Marie, 105
Bouchard, Jacob, 306
Boucher, Marie, 118
Bougainville, Louis-Antoine de, 210
Boulette, Virginia, 501
Boundary Survey of 1772–76, 505
Bouquet, Henry, 168, 170, 179
Bourgeau, Eugene, 508–509
Bourgeois, 389
    authority and social distance,
        393–394
    See also Master–servant
        relationship
Bourget, Ignace, 374–375, 378,
    381, 382
Bourke, John, 495
Bouvette, Emile, 501
Bouvier, Michel, 504

Bowker, J.S., 532
Brant, Joseph, 269
Brassard, Father, 381
Brébeuf, Jean de, 32, 39, 99
Brebner, J.B., 134, 149, 239
Breslay, René-Charles de, 104
"Brideships," 544
Brine, Robert, 344
Britain
    assimilation of French, 213
    Native alliance in War of 1812,
        270–272
    Native policy, 269–273, 278–280
British Columbia
    and Confederation, 546
    diversity, 539, 541
    female population, 539
    promotion for white settlers,
        537–550
    united with Vancouver Island, 538
British Indian Department,
    268–269, 270–272, 274
British North America (BNA) Act,
    567, 576, 577, 578
Brock, Sir Isaac, 260, 265, 266,
    271, 283
Brown, George, 555, 567, 568, 569,
    570, 573, 576, 577, 578
Brown, Jennifer, 77, 81, 388, 509
Brown, Thomas, 470
Brown, T.S., 377
Brown, William Wells, 435
Browne, Timothy, 334, 352
Bruce, Baptiste, 499
Bruce, François, 504
Bruce, William, 502
Brûlé, Etienne, 28, 31, 101
Bruneau, François, 493, 495
Brunet, Michel, 214
Bubonic plague, 171
Buchanan, James, 415
Buffalo hunt, 501, 504, 505
Buffalo (Shawnee), 271
Bulger, Andrew, 276, 277
Burley, Edith, 387, 389, 397
Bushby, Arthur, 526
Bushman, Richard, 251
Butler, Manus, 345
Buttes à Neveu, 209–210, 211

Cachouintioui (Seneca chief), 98
Caen, Emery de, 100
Calkin, J.B., 363, 364
Cameron, Duncan, 395
Cameron, Hugh, 503
Campbell, Maj. John, 275
Campbell, John V., 506

Campion, Étienne, 217

Canada East. *See* Lower
Canada/Canada East

Canada Jurisdiction Act, 392

Canadian Volunteers, 274

Canadian Woman's Suffrage
Association, 284

Canadian Women's Historical
Society of Ottawa, 286

Canadian Women's Historical
Society of Toronto, 286

Le Canadien, 373, 374

Canal construction
construction process, 409–410
contractors, 411, 412, 420
labour market conditions, 409–410
labour needs, 410
living conditions, 410, 413
suppression of labour unrest,
421–425
truck payment, 412
violence, 415–416, 420
wages, 411

Canal police force, 422–423

Canoe brigades, 389, 504

Captain Johnny (Shawnee), 271

Carleton, Sir Guy, 176, 213, 220,
222, 391

Carlton Trail, 504

Carmichael, Hugh, 322

Carney, Elizabeth, 345

The Caroline, 326

Caron, Jean-Baptiste, 125

Carrière, Angélique, 501

Cart brigades, 504

Carter, James H., 344

Carter, Robert, Jr., 334

Cartier, George-Étienne, 554, 555,
556, 558, 562, 568

Cartier, Jacques, 27

Cartwright, Richard, 262, 263, 265

Cary, Mary Ann Shadd. *See* Shadd,
Mary Ann

Cary, Thomas F., 440

Catholic Church
Conquest and, 231
and female "respectability,"
350–351
and marriage, 114
and marriage of "ill-sorted"
couples, 300–301
and patriotic reform, 373,
377–378, 379, 382
prestige and influence of, 309, 373
ultramontanism, 373

Catin, Catherine, 126

Caulfeild, Thomas, 148

Chalifoux, Angélique, 500

Chalifoux, Isabella, 500

Chalifoux, Julia, 502

Chalifoux, Therisa, 89

Champlain, Samuel de, 28, 29, 32, 100

Chapman, John, 493, 495, 496

Charbonneau, Hubert, 112

Charismatic leaders, 373

Charity, 411, 467

Charivaris, 298–313
European form, 298
fines, 301–302
French Canadian form, 298–300
hegemony, 304
marital ideology of, 300–301
of mid-nineteenth century, 310
politicized form, 304–311
public shaming, 302
purpose of, 301, 310
reconciliation, 303
social control, 126, 303–304
targets, 299–300, 305–309
violence, 303, 306–307, 308, 310

Charlevoix, Jean, 30

Charlevoix, Pierre-François-Xavier
de, 174

Charly, Louis Saint-Ange, 217

Chartier, Pierre, 126

Chartism, 337, 419

Chauvignerie, Sieur de, 106, 107

Chesapeake Affair, 265, 270

Chickasaw, 193

Chinese immigration, 541

Chiniquy, Charles, 373, 376, 377–382

Chiniquy crusade, 372–384

Chinn, Edward, 218

Chipewyan, 64

Chippewa, 174

Cholera, 171

Chouinard, Elizabeth, 503

Christie, Alexander, 507

Christie, W.J., 505

Christie family (Dundas County),
476, 478

Church Missionary Society, 495

Church of England, 315, 316

The Church, 284

Clark, A.H., 138, 139, 141

Clark, Elizabeth, 476

Clark, William, 274

Clarke, John, 68

Clarke, Reverend, 423

Clark family (Dundas County), 476

Clarkson, L.A., 343

Class
and collective action, 416–420
and ideal immigrants, 541–545

and labour militancy, 418–420
marriage as social distinction of,
85, 87, 88–89
and mixed marriages, 518–537
reciprocal work bees, 471–472
and "respectable womanhood,"
335, 349–352
Tories, 314–316

Claus, William, 270

Cleary, Dean, 340

Clemenceau, Etienne, 104

Clergy reserves, 316

Clifton, Russel, 473

Coates, Colin, 283

Cocking, Matthew, 84

Cockran, William, 500

Coffin, William F., 284

Colbert, Jean-Baptiste, 104

Colbourne, Sir John,
284, 380

Colebrooke, Sir William, 459

Colen, Joseph, 72

Coles, George, 568

Collins Overland Telegraph, 531

Colonial Advocate, 317

Colonial and Continental Church
Society, 492, 496

Colored Ladies of Windsor, 443

Column formation, 211

Commercial Bank, 319

Compagnie des Indes, 215

Concealment of birth cases, 345

Confederation
British Columbia and, 546
political deadlock in United
Canada, 570, 574
Quebec and, 554–566

Confederation debate
American constitution, 556,
569, 575
Bleu interpretation of proposed
union, 558–563
division of powers, 559–560,
568–569
fears of centralization and
assimilation, 557
federal veto power, 560, 568,
572, 573
provincial (local) autonomy,
554–556, 558–560,
571–576
provincial powers, 559
representation by population, 557
residuary legislative power, 568,
574–576
Rouges, 557
self-government, 573

Connolly, Amelia. *See* Douglas, Lady Amelia
Connolly, William, 52
Conquest
  and agrarian way of life, 231
  and Catholic Church, 231
  and merchants, 231
  and Native peoples, 231–232
  and nobles, 231
  and Quebec nationalism, 229–231
  Seven Years' War, 227–228
  and women, 231
Consortium, 347
Constant, Joseph, 398
Constitutional Act of 1791, 314
The Constitution newspaper, 318, 319, 321
Continental Congress, 242
Conway, Martin, 344
Cook, Henry, 493, 507
Cook, Joseph, 500
Copley, John Singleton, 251
Corbett, Griffiths Owen, 490, 492–496
Cork/Connaught sectional section conflict, 414–416
Corktown, 413
Corn
  horticulture, 10–11
  trade in, 28–29
Cornwall Canal, 410, 411, 418
Cornwallis, Charles, 177
Corporal punishment, 101, 104
Cortés, Hernán, 179
Corum, Joseph, 456, 457, 458
Cosby, Alexander, 152, 158
Cosson, Ernest St. C., 508
Côté, C.H.O, 306
Council of Assiniboia, 491, 493, 494, 507
Coureurs de bois, 29, 31, 32
Le Courrier du Canada, 554
Le Courrier du St-Hyacinthe, 555, 556
Courtship, and social networks, 475
Couteau, Josette, 503
Coutume de Paris, 114
Cowan, William, 509
Craig, Sir James, 270
Cree, 64, 195
Creighton, Donald, 214, 569, 572, 573, 574, 575
Cridge, Edward, 525
Crime, drink and, 376
Criminal conversation, 347
Croghan, George, 168, 220, 221
Cross, Michael, 414

Cross, Stan, 474
Crown reserves, 316
Cruikshank, Ernest, 285
Cumberland House, 85
Curzon, Sarah A., 282, 284–285, 287, 288
Custody, and child support, 349

Daigle, Jean, 134
D'Ailleboust, Charles, 99, 103
Dakota, 195
Dallas, Alexander Grant, 495
Daniel, George, 505
Dansee, Catherine, 500
D'Artigny, Rouer, 126
Darragon, Marie-Madeleine, 121
Davis, Thomas, 468
Davis-Yuval, Nira, 537
Dawson, J. William, 363
Dawson, William, 491
Deans, Annie, 525
Dease, Peter Warren, 503
"Decapitation" thesis, 223–224, 230
De Champ, Baptiste, 503
Dechêne, Louise, 112, 119
Decoigne, L.M., 306
Degrace, Baptiste, 505
Delahunty, Catharine, 344
Delahunty, Ellen, 344
Delaunay, Henry, 126
Delière, Julien, 121
DeMarais, Baptist, 503
Demarais, Francis, 503
Demarais, Julie, 501
Dennet, Andrew, 503
Denton, Solomon, 360
Deringwater, William, 346
Desertion, 392, 397, 399, 400
Desjarlais, Edward, Sr., 507
Desmarais, Charles, 503
Desmarais, Mary, 502
Détailly, Jacques, 105
Devant, 390
Dickson, Robert, 276
Dickson, William, 502
Diderot, 114, 116
Dièreville, Sieur de, 137
Dieskau, Jean-Armand, Baron de, 269
Direct taxation, 560
Disallowance, power of. *See* Veto power
Dismissal, for dereliction of duty, 396, 398
Divorce, 348–349
Dixon, Charles, 242
Dobie, Richard, 218
Doll (Inuit women), 83–84

Donkin, Robert, 180
Donnelly, James, Sr., 469
Dorion, A.-A., 557, 568, 569, 572
Douart, Jacques, 39, 101–103
Doucett, John, 153–154, 158
Douglas, Agnes (Mrs. Arthur Bushby), 526
Douglas, Lady Amelia, 520, 522, 525, 526, 541
Douglas, Cecilia (Mrs. J.S. Helmcken), 527
Douglas, James (Quebec doctor), 376
Douglas, Sir James, 518, 520–522, 524, 525, 527, 530, 540, 541, 542
Douglas, James, Jr., 527
Douglas, Jane, 532
Douglas, Martha (Mrs. Dennis Harris), 526
Douglas, Thomas. *See* Selkirk, Lord
Douglass, William, 171
Drew, Benjamin, 441, 442
Drinking habits
  and disrupted family life, 118
  at work bees, 469–470
Drouin, Pierre, 126
Drummond, J.S., 532
Drummond, Lewis Thomas, 412
Ducharme, Dominique, 507
Dumesnil family, 125
Duncan, Kenneth, 420
Duncan, William, 540
Duncombe, Charles, 322, 323, 325, 327
Dunigan, Patrick, 469
Dunmore, John Murray, Earl of, 175, 177
Dunmore, Lord, 505
Dunn, Mary, 348–349
Dunn, Timothy, 349
Dupas, Pierre, 104
Dupont, Jean-Claude, 140
Duval, Edmund Hillyer, 363
Duval, Françoise, 119
Duval family (Collingwood), 125
Duval family (New France), 436

Eagleson, John, 242, 244
Eccles, William John, 98
Ecuyer, Simeon, 168, 169
Eddy, Jonathan, 241–242, 243, 244, 245
Eddy Rebellion of 1776, 239–248
  British naval power and, 245
  Chignecto region, 239–240, 241
  defeated, 244–245
  insurgents, 243–244
  refusal of Americans to attack Nova Scotia, 240, 242, 243

Edgar, William, 218, 221
Education
   and acculturation, 524, 525, 527
   adult, 443
   Black schools, 441–442
   gendered curriculum, 440, 525
   graded school system, 361–362,
     365–366
   normal schools, 365
   segregation, 442
Education Act of 1841, 376
*The Education Record of the Province
   of Quebec*, 369
Elgin, James Bruce, Earl of, 572
Elliott, Colonel, 424
Elliott, Mary, 527
Elliott, Matthew, 271
Elwyn, Thomas, 532
Emigration Committee for the
   Niagara District Council, 409
Engagés, 390
   See also Voyageurs
English, Christopher, 349
English Test Act of 1673, 146
Enticement, 347
Erasmus, Henry, 504
Erasmus, Peter, Sr., 499
Erasmus, Sophia, 503
Ermatinger, Edward, 524
Ermatinger, Lawrence, 218
Ethier, Marie-Josephe, 121
Ethiopian Regiment, 175, 177
Everette, Joseph, 501
Ewers, Thomas, 342, 351, 352

Faber, Jeanne Duplessis, 120
Fabien. *See* Hébert, John
Falcon, Perre, 505
Families
   Acadians, 137, 139, 140
   domestic violence, 115–116,
     118–121, 348, 352
   interference in marital
     relationships, 122
   intervention to stop domestic
     violence, 120
   and privacy, 120–121
   reputation and honour of,
     125–126
   Victoria fur trade families,
     518–537
Family Compact, 315
Farge, Arlette, 125
Farrell, Patrick, 469
Favel, Harriet, 503
Federalists, American, 265
Feltman, William, 178

Fenimore, James, 174
Fenwick, W., 285
Ferguson, John, 505
Ferrière, C. de, 114, 116
Fidler, Henry, 505
Fidler, John, 505
Fifty Lincoln Militia, 423
Finlay, James, 218
Finlayson, Joseph, 499
Finlayson, Roderick, 499, 528, 529
First Calvinistic Baptist Church, 439
First Nations
   Anglo–Native relations, 146,
     150, 153, 158, 159, 160,
     268–270, 278–279
   authority, concepts of, 98–100
   belief systems, 4–5
   blood feuds, 26–27
   and Christian missionaries, 30,
     32, 33–34, 36–38
   collective responsibility for
     deviance, 99–100
   Conquest and, 231
   contact narratives, 47–60
   diet, 10–11
   dreams of united First Nations
     confederacy, 232, 271, 273
   earliest encounters with
     Europeans, 17–18
   French alliance, 27–31, 35–36,
     39, 189
   and French justice, 103–107
   horticulture, 10–11, 28–29, 40
   infanticide, 71
   intertribal trade, 11, 25–26
   intertribal trade rivalry, 29,
     35–36, 38–39, 40
   loss of unceded lands, 269
   Manifest Destiny and, 278
   map making, 15–17
   of Maritime provinces, 4–22,
     146, 153, 158, 159, 160
   mission communities, 105, 108
   Native place-names, 14–15
   Northern Tribes of Pacific
     Coast, 540
   prophets, 50
   reserve system, 278
   resistance against land
     encroachment, 232
   seasonal migration, 10
   and Seven Years' War,
     188–202, 269
   smallpox, 33–35, 101, 168–170,
     174–175, 191–193, 195–197
   sovereignty, concepts of, 98–100
   and War of 1812, 268–281

First Nations women
   agriculture, 26, 40
   autonomy and influence of, 67–70
   country wives, 64–76
   diet, 71
   fecundity of, 70–71
   as guides and consultants, 67
   as interpreters, 67
   labour, 10
   marital relations, 71–72
   and protection of fur traders,
     68–69
   as "social brokers," 66
   "turning off," 72, 84
   violence against, 72–73
   and white fur traders, 65–70
Fisher, Alick, 499
Fisher, Henry, 504
Fishing admirals, 343
FitzGibbon, James, 284, 289, 322
Fitzgibbon, Mary Agnes, 285,
   286, 287
Flandrin, Jean-Louise, 119
Fleming, Michael, 340, 351
Flett, David, 506
Flowers, Dudley, 306–307, 308, 309
Forrester, Alexander, 363, 368
Forsyth, Ogilvy and McKenzie, 392
Forsyth, Thomas, 392
Fort Beauséjour, 159, 160, 242
Fort Cumberland, 242, 244
Fort Dearborn, 274
Fort Detroit, 195
Fort Duquesne, 192
Fort Frederick, 241
Fort Frontenac, 194, 215
Fort Johnson, 275
Fort La Baye, 194
Fort Lawrence, 159
Fort Malden, 272
Fort McKay, 275, 276, 277
Fort Michilimakinac, 195
Fort Niagara, 192, 215
Fort Oswego, 196
Fort Ouyatanon, 195
Fort Pitt, 167–170
Fort Presqu'ile, 192
Fort St. Joseph, 194, 195
Fort Shelby, 274–275
Fort Stephenson, 272
Fort William Henry, 175, 192, 196
41st Regiment of Foot, 273
Foster, John, 416
Foulds, John, 505
Fournier, Justine, 500
Fournier, Lydia, 502
Fox nation, 193, 271, 275

Franchère, Gabriel, 66
Francklin, Michael, 239, 242
Franklin, Lady Jane, 525
Fraser, Simon, 47–58
Fraser family (Dundas County), 478
Fredrique, Baptiste, 504
Freeman, Amelia. *See* Shadd,
    Amelia Freeman
Freeman, Martin H., 440
Frémont, Catherine, 113
French, John, 66, 80
Frobisher, Benjamin, 218, 219, 221
Frontenac, Louis de Baude de, 40, 99
Fugitive Slave Act of 1850, 435
Fundraising, *vs.* self-reliance,
    442–443
Fur trade
    alliances with Native peoples,
        65, 83
    country marriages, 84, 85, 89,
        499, 500, 520, 522–523
    coureurs de bois, 29, 31, 32, 215
    differentiation in work roles, 393
    Dutch trade, 29, 30
    and French authority and
        sovereignty, 106
    imperial wars and, 229
    Louisiana traders, 220
    Montréal companies, 388
    Montréal labour system,
        389–390
    Native women, role of, 67, 82–83
    occupational lines and status, 390
    open competition, 217–219
    partners, 390
    perceptions of status of Native
        women, 69–70, 71
    structure of French trade,
        215–217
    War of 1812 and, 274
    See also Hudson's Bay Company;
        North West Company
        (NWC)

Gaele, Ensign, 418
Gage, Thomas, 169, 179, 218
Gagnon, Julien, 306, 307, 308
Gagnon, Louis, 500
Galbraith, John, 88
Galt, Alexander, 568, 577
Gamble, William, 158
Gareau, Léonard, 103
Garneau, François-Xavier, 373
Garnier, Michelle, 105
Garreau, André, 400
Garrioch, Peter, 501, 504, 506
Gay, Charles, 509

Gazette de Sorel, 554
Geikie, John, 471, 473
Gender
    adultery, 123–125
    and black experience, 339,
        436–437, 438, 443–444
    Catholic orthodoxy and,
        350–352
    conceptions of "Canadian
        womanhood," 288–290
    female political symbols, 284
    and Loyalist culture, 249–250, 252
    middle-class ideology, 335,
        349–350
    and mixed marriages, 518–537
    nationalism and, 283–284,
        286–287, 289–290
    pay gap, 362–363, 366–368
    reciprocal work bees, 466,
        472–475, 479
    segregated schools, 351, 440
    voyageur identity, 388
Gendron, Geneviève, 125
Gendron, Marie-Anne, 125
George I, 154
Giboche, Louisa, 502
Gibson, David, 322, 327
Gibson, Hugh, 500
Gingras, Antoine, 498
Globe newspaper, 491, 569, 571,
    573, 574
Gluek, Alvin C., Jr., 508
Gluskap, 4
Godet, Dominique, 217
Gold rushes, 542
Gordon, A.H., 555
Gordon, George, 394
Gore, Sir Francis, 262, 270
Gore Bank, 319
Gorham, Joseph, 242, 244
Gossip, and self-regulation, 125–126
Gothvier, Josette (Susette), 502
Goulait, Alexis, 505
Goulet, Alexis, 507
Goulet, Louis, 497, 498
Goulet, Moise, 501
Gouriaux family, 125
Gourlay, Robert, 317
Gouvernail, 390
Governor Clark, 274
Governor general, 314
    office, 568, 569, 571
Graham, Andrew, 64, 84
Graham, Duncan, 275
Graham, M.E., 474
Grant, George, 542
Grant, William, 218

Gray, John Hamilton, 567, 568, 574
"Great Awakening," 235–246
Green Bay militia, 274, 275
Greene, Jack, 151
Grey, Charles, 180
Grieco, Sara Matthews, 123
Grier, James, 172
Grotius, Hugo, 179, 180
Grover, William, 81
Guiche, Compte de la, 505
Gun control, 421–422
Gunn, Donald, 491, 493

Hache, Robert, 104
Haggerty, John, 458
Haida, 540
Halero, Joshua, 502
Halfbreeds. *See* Mixed-bloods
Halifax
    building of, 148, 149
    merchants of, 238–239, 240, 241
    smallpox, 175
"Halifax-merchant" school, 238
Hallet, Henry, Jr., 502
Hallet, Henry, Sr., 500, 505
Hallet family, 504
Hallett, William, 495, 505
Hamelin, Baptiste, 504
Hanahan, Margaret, 341,
    346–347, 348
Hanahan, Thomas, 341,
    346–347, 348
Hancock, John, 176
Hankin, Thomas, 530
Harbouring, 347
Harmon, Edward, 507
Harper, Angus, 501
Harris, Dennis, 526
Harvey, Sir John, 447
Hayden, Peter, 507
Head, Sir Edmund, 452, 458
Head, Sir Francis Bond, 318, 319,
    322, 328
Heagerty, John J., 175
Healy, W.J., 501
"Heathen people," accepted rules of
    warfare on, 179
Hébert, John, 505
Hébert, Olivier, 306
Hegemony, 304, 390–391
Helmcken, J.S., 527, 545
Henderson, Anne, 497
Hennecy, William, 349
Henripin, Jacques, 112
Henry, Alexander, 217, 218, 221
Henry, Alexander (the younger), 66,
    396, 398, 400

Henry, John Joseph, 176
Heron, Francis, 500
Hicks, Gershom, 169
Hieltsuk, 540
Higham, John, 449
Hill, Jonathon D., 49
Hill, Thomas, 452
Hill-Tout, Charles, 48
Hind, Youle, 505
Hocquart, Gilles, 124
Hogue, Aimable, 503, 505
Hole, Charles, 507
Hommes du nord, 390
Hôpital Général de Québec, 124
Hospitality, and social relationships,
     470, 471–472, 474
House, Henry, 65
How, Edward, 152
Howe, Samuel Gridley, 435
Howe, William, 241, 243
Howland, William, 579
Hudson's Bay Company, 505
     amalgamation with NWC, 77, 86
     chief factor, 80
     council, post, 81
     financial crisis, 85
     governor (field), 79
     governor (London), 79
     imported labour, 545
     labour relations, 387, 388–389
     London Committee, 79
     mixed marriages, 518, 520
     Nor'Westers, competition with,
          84–85
     Orcadian servants, 79, 84
     patriarchal structure, 78–81
     policy regarding women, 81–82
     rules of conduct, 388
     second, to chief factor, 81
     trade monopoly, 506
     Victoria fur trade families,
          518–537
     See also Fur trade
Huet, Father, 100
Hunt, George T., 24, 40
Hunter, James, 495, 496
Hunting bees, 474
Huron, 195
     anti-missionary feeling, 33–34, 37
     Christian converts, 36–37
     confederacy, 24–25
     exchange in people, 27, 28, 32
     intertribal trade system, 25–26
     rivalry with Iroquois, 29, 35–36,
          38–39
     trade relations with French,
          27–31

Huronia, 25
     destruction of, 39–41
     epidemics, 33–35
     missionaries in, 30, 31–34, 40
Hyndman, Alex, 478

Ignace, Joseph, 156
Illegitimacy, 345, 351
Immigration
     American settlers, 262–263
     British working-class women,
          543–545
     Colonial Office and, 542, 546
     "hardy backwoodsman" ideal,
          542–543
     Newfoundland, 336–338
     promotion for white settlers,
          537–550
     to Upper Canada (1830s),
          323–324
     Yorkshire, 239–240
Imperial Order of the Daughters of
     the Empire (IODE), 285, 289
Incorporated Militia, 423
Indian Rights Association, 48, 49, 50
Infanticide, 71, 345
Ingersoll, J.H., 288
Ingersoll, Thomas, 288
Inglis, Elizabeth Ann, 168
Inkster, Sybil, 504
Innis, H.A., 216
Inoculation, 172–173
Intercolonial Railway, 579
Interior Tribes of British Columbia,
     48, 49, 50
Irish immigrants
     British perceptions of, 335–336
     canallers, 408–430
     communal organization,
          413–414, 415
     and economic competition, 416
     famine immigration, 449, 450
     nationalism, 414
     Orange/Green confrontations,
          414, 423, 453–458
     plebian women, 334–360
     secret societies, 418–419
     sectional conflicts, 413–416
     unemployment, 409,
          410–411, 416
     worker resistance, 419–420
Iroquois, 27, 193, 269
Isbister, Alexander Kennedy, 491,
     492, 507
Jackson, Andrew, 317
Jacobs, Ferdinand, 84
Jamaica, British conquest of, 146

James II, 450
Jane, John, 532
Jarrow, John, 417, 420
Jarvis, Edward, 253
Jarvis, Maria, 253
Jarvis, Munson, 253
Jay Treaty, 269
Jefferson, Thomas, 172, 176, 265
Jenkins, Mary, 347
Jenner, Edward, 170
Jenness, Diamond, 48
Jesuit Relations, 99
Jesuits, 26, 30, 31–34, 36–37, 38,
     39, 99
Johnson, F.G., 491
Johnson, Sir William, 169, 174, 218,
     220, 221, 268, 269
Johnston, Margaret, 503
Johnstone, James, 505
Jordan, Mary, 503
Joubert, Jean-Baptiste, 125
Le Journal de Québec, 556
*Journal of Education for the Province
     of Nova Scotia*, 369
Judicature Acts, 349
Judicial Committee of the Privy
     Council, 576
Judson, James, 532

Kearney, Andrew, 349
Kearney, Mary, 349
Keating, James, 275
Keating, Mary, 346
Kelly, Catharine, 344
Kelsey, Henry, 80
Kennedy, Baptiste, 499
Kennedy, Charles, 505
Kennedy, William, 491–492, 493, 508
Kennely, Stephen, 346
Kerr, W.B., 239
Ketakamigwa, 4
Ketchiniweskwe (great spirit), 4
Kickapoo nation, 275
Killibuck (Delaware nation), 169
King, Mackenzie, 569
Kingston *Gazette*, 264
Kinnear, H. Boyd, 451
Kipling, George, 502
Kirby, William, 285
Kirke, David, 101
Kirkness, Andrew, 72
Kittson, Norman, 500
Knight, James, 80
Knox, John, 211
Kohl, J.G., 498
Kwakwaka'wakw, 540
Kwalos, 50–51

Labour
    as commodity, 480
    engagement contracts, 391
    Montréal fur trade system,
        389–390
    spontaneous protests, 418
    strikes, 399, 417, 418, 420
    surplus, 409–410
    wages of canallers, 411
    work bees, 466–468
    See also Master–servant
        relationship
Lachouette. *See* Laliberté, Alexandre
Ladies Coloured Fugitive
    Association, 443
Ladies Freedman's Aid Society, 443
Lady Calpo, 66
Laflèche, Louis-François, 501
LaFontaine, Louis Hippolyte, 378, 421
LaFontaine-Baldwin government, 569
La Forière (Montagnais chief), 100
La Galissonière, Roland-Michel
    Barrin de, 98
Lagimonère, Lisset, 500, 502
La Graisse, Baptiste, 505
Lagrave, Sister, 501
Laird of MacNab, 325
Lalemant, Gabriel, 39
Lalemant, Hierosme, 99
Laliberté, Alexandre, 505
Lamallice, Madam, 67
Lambere, Michael, 502
Lamoureux, Amble, 306
Landon, Fred, 435
Landrie, Isabella, 502
Landry, Claude, 137
Landry, René, 137
Langevin, Hector, 377, 558, 576
Langston, Anne, 474
Langston, John, 472
La Pierre, Peggy, 501
Laplante, Xavier. *See* Plante,
    Antoine
La Roche Daillon, Joseph de, 31
La Rochefoucault-Liancourt, 262
Larocque, Baptiste, 501
Larocque, Pierre, Jr., 506
Laroque, Charles, 507
La Rouchefoucault Liancourt,
    Duke de, 398
Lartigue, Bishop, 375
Launay, Nicolas de, 121
Laurain, Françoise, 502
Laura Secord Memorial Hall, 286
Laura Secord school, 286
Lauzon, Francis, 504
Laval, François de Montmorency, 113

La Vallee, Lizette, 503
Laverdure, Pierre, 507
Lawrence, Charles, 160, 240
Leblanc, Charles, 126
Leblanc, Pierre, 501
LeBorgne, Emmanuel, 137
Le Caron, Joseph, 100, 102
Léchelle, Jean, 217
Lechmere, Thomas, 158
Leclair, Joseph, 501
Leclair, Marguerite, 501
Leeuwenhoek, Anthony van, 171
Legge, Francis, 240, 242
Le Jeune, Paul, 101
Lemoine Monière, Alexis, 217
Leslie, Alexander, 178, 181
Le Tessier, Julienne, 124
L'Eunay, Susette, 502
Leveillé, Joseph, 399
Lévis, François Gaston, Chevalier
    de, 206, 209, 210, 211
Lewis, Andrew, 169
Lewis, Mary, 503
L'Huillier Chevalier, François, 217
Lieutenant governor, 314
Line formation, 211
Linklater, Peter, 504, 505
Livingston, Robert, 178
Lloyd, Jesse, 321
Logging bees, 473, 474
Lolo, Jean-Baptiste, 523
Lolo, Sophia (Mrs. John Tod), 523, 532
London and Middlesex Historical
    Society, 286
Longueil, Charles Le Moyne de,
    179–180
Lossing, Benson J., 285
Lottin, Alain, 117, 119, 122
Louisbourg, 155, 160, 228
Louisiana
    Acadian refugees, 232
    French traders from, 220
Louis XIV, 104, 145
Lount, Samuel, 327
Lower Canada Agricultural Journal, 377
Lower Canada/Canada East
    drinking habits, 374
    emigration to United States, 376
    female teachers, 362, 364, 365
    temperance movement, 372–384
Lower Canada Rebellion Losses Act
    of 1849, 572
Loyalist and Conservative Advocate, 449
Loyalists, 314
    and English-Canadian
        nationalism, 283–284,
        286–287, 287–288, 289–290

    exile mentality, 251–252
    gender relations, 249–251, 252
    grandchildren of, 254
    redeemer children of, 252–254
    ties with United States, 261–262
Lundy's Lane Society, 286

MacArthur Douglas, 206
Macauley, Mary (Mrs. William
    Henry McNeill, Jr.), 532
Macdonald, Henry Donald, 501
Macdonald, James, 423
Macdonald, Joe, 505
Macdonald, John A., 556, 567, 568,
    570, 574, 575, 577, 578, 579, 580
Macdonald, John Sandfield, 570, 580
MacDonell, Archibald, 321
Machar, Agnes Maule, 285
Mackay, William, 502
Mackenzie, Alexander (explorer),
    395, 396, 397
Mackenzie, Alexander (future prime
    minister), 569, 578, 580
Mackenzie, William Lyon, 317,
    318, 319
MacLean, Charles, 85
MacLeod, Peter, 174
MacNab, Allan, 322, 323
Mactavish, William, 492
Maillet, Geneviève, 124
Mainguy, Jean-Julien, 124
Main Poc, 273
Mair, Charles, 285, 287
Maisonneuve, Paul de Chomedey, 103
Maitland, Sir Peregrine, 284
Malaria, 171
Malartic, comte de, 206
Malcolm, Eliakin, 322
Mamaltree (Delaware nation), 168
Manifest Destiny, 278
Manks, Squire, 454
Marcellais, Baptiste, 505
Marchand, Hazelique, 502
Mareuil, Father de, 174
Mariet, Joseph, 104
Marion, Narcisse, 501, 508
Marion, Roger, 501
Maritime provinces
    Conquest and, 232
    and Quebec Resolutions, 575
    See also New Brunswick;
        Nova Scotia
Marriages
    à la façon du pays (country mar-
        riages), 84, 85, 89, 124, 499,
        500, 520, 522–523
    Catholic clergy and, 351

common-law relationships, 124–125, 341–342, 349
fur trade, 64–76, 83–84, 520, 522–523
"ill-sorted," 300–301
Loyalist, 249–250, 252
Métis cross-marriages, 498–503
Orcadian servants, 83
plebian Irish women, 341–343
Victoria fur trade families, 518–537
Marshville strike, 420
Martinois, Mary, 503
Mascerene, Paul, 135, 150, 151, 152
Massachusetts Bay Company, 78
Massignon, Geneviève, 140
Master–servant relationship, 387–408
authority in, 393–394, 401
clerks, 390
collective resistance, 399–400
complaining as "counter-theatre," 395–396
court action to control workers, 392
disciplinary measures, 397–398
hegemony in, 390–391
paternalism, 389–390
resistance and accommodation in, 391, 395–396
"social contract," 393, 397
"theatre of resistance," 395–397, 401
unfair labour practices, 398–399
Mather, Cotton, 172
Matheson, Donald, 505
Matthews, Peter, 327
Maypole, and popular ratification, 306
McBeath, Donald, 508
McCalla, Doug, 467
McCarthy, Mary, 209
McConnell, Michael, 169
McDermot, Andrew, 492, 507
McDonagh, Reverend, 419, 423
McDonald, John, 394
McDouall, Robert, 274, 276, 277
McDougall, William, 570, 577, 579, 580
McGee, D'Arcy, 567, 568
McGill, James, 219
McGillivray, Duncan, 394, 399
McGillivray, William, 392
McIlwraith, Thomas, 48
McKay, Angus, 501
McKay, James "Big Jim," 499, 505
McKay, Jane, 500
McKay, Joe, 499

McKay, John Aimable, 503
McKay, John ("Jerry") NcNab Ballenden, 499
McKay, Nancy, 501
McKay, Thomas, 499
McKay, Lt. Col. William, 274
McKay, William (mixed blood), 499
McKellar, Patrick, 211
McKenney, Sheriff, 495
McKenzie, Charles, 398
McKenzie, Nancy, 501
McKenzie, Samuel, 504
McLeod, Louise, 501
McMillan, William, 508
McNab, James, 503
McNeill, Alfred, 531
McNeill, Donald H., 534
McNeill, Fanny (Mrs. James Judson), 532
McNeill, Harriet (Mrs. John Jane), 532
McNeill, Harry, 531
McNeill, Lucy (Mrs. Hamilton Moffat), 532
McNeill, Mathilda, 522
McNeill, Rebecca (Mrs. Thomas Elwyn), 532
McNeill, William H., 518, 522–523
McNeill, William Henry, Jr., 531, 532
McNichol, James, 450
McTavish, Catherine, 88
McTavish, John George, 86, 87, 88, 501
McTavish, McGillivrays & Co., 391
M'Cullough, John, 169
Mechanics' Institute, 455
Meilleur, J.B., 363, 364, 377
Mellanson, Peter, 154
Menominee nation, 193, 194
Menonomee nation, 273
Merritt, William, 411
Metcalf, Sir Charles, 572
Methodism, Black churches, 438–439
Métis
buffalo hunt, 501, 504, 505
business, 501
cooperation and fraternization with mixed-bloods, 497–514
and Corbett affair, 492, 495
cross-marriages, 499–503
language, 498
and political representation, 507–508
religious tolerance, 509
and trading rights, 506–507
Michael, Sarah, 503

Michie family, 465–466
Michigan Fencibles, 274, 276
Middaugh, Charles, 476, 478, 479
Middaugh, Ezra, 476
Middaugh, John, 476
Middaugh, Lucy, 475–476, 479
Middaugh, Min, 476, 479
Middaugh, Tory, 476, 479
Middlekauff, Robert, 181
Middlemen (milieu), 390
Miles, Robert, 87
Miles, Stephen, 266
Militia Act, 266
Mills, J.B., 409, 421
La Minerve, 554, 555, 556, 558
Miquelon, Dale B., 214
Mitchell, Sam, 56, 57
Mixed-bloods
acculturation of, 520, 523–525, 530–532
buffalo hunt, 501, 504, 505
business, 501
and Corbett affair, 492, 495
cross-marriages, 499–503
language, 499
pro-Canadian agitation, 491–492, 493
and sectarianism, 490–496
Miyo Nipiy, 520
Moar, John, 501
Moffat, Hamilton, 532
Moffatt, George, 394
Mohawk, 29, 30, 269
Molly Maguire, 418
Molson, 381
Molson, Thomas, 381
Monck, Lord, 575
Mondelet, Charles, 376–377, 379
Monkman, James, 502, 507
Montague, John, 336
Montague, Mary Montague, 172
Montcalm, Louis Joseph, Marquis de, 197, 206, 207, 210, 211, 212
Montgay, Captain, 206
Montgomery, Field-Marshal Viscount, of Alamein, 206
Montgomery's Tavern, 321, 322
Montmagny, Charles Hault de, 34
Montreal merchants, 213–227
British competitors, 218–219
British military's mistrust of, 220–221
"decapitation" interpretation, 223–224
economic displacement of, 213–215
French competitors, 218

Montreal merchants (Contd.)
  under French regime, 215–217
  investment in fur trade, 216–217
  political representation, 221–223
Montreuil, Pierre-André Gohin, Comte de, 206
Moodie, Colonel, 321
Moodie, Susanna, 466, 470, 472, 480
Morin, Antoine, 505
Morris, Charles, 137
Morrison, George, 505
Morrison, T.D., 321
Morrison, Thomas, 578
Morrisseau, Matilda, 501
Morton, W.L., 254, 498, 506
Mountain, Peggy, 334
Mowat, Oliver, 552, 567, 576, 577
Mundurucú, 69
Municipal Corporations Act of 1849, 569
Munro, W.F., 468, 473
Murray, David, 48
Murray, James, 211, 213, 218, 374
Mutual Improvement Society, 443

Nafrechou, Isaac, 104
Nationalism
  English-Canadian, 283–284, 286–287, 289–290
  and Myth of the Conquest, 230–231
  Quebec, 229–230
Nativism, 447, 449–450, 459
Nault, André, 498
Naval Stores Act, 146, 153
NcNeal, Hector, 176
Needham, W.H., 451, 458
Neighbourhood
  community identity and belonging, 469
  concept of, 464–465
Neilson, Wilfred, 412
Nelson, George, 66, 68, 396, 398, 399
Nelson, Wolfred, 377
Neshaki (Mrs. W.H. McNeill), 523
New Brunswick
  famine immigration, 449, 450
  female teachers, 362, 363
  "Hungry Forties," 448, 458
  nativism, 447, 449–450, 459
Newfoundland
  fishing admirals, 343
  Irish immigration, 335–336
  magistrates, 343, 349
  migratory fishery, 336
  plebian community, 334–360
  social superiors, 337

New France
  capital offences, 104, 105
  and destruction of Huronia, 40–41
  drunkenness, 105–106
  and intertribal rivalries, 29, 35–36, 38–39, 40
  justice, 98–111
  marital separation, 112–130
  marriage in, 113–115
  murder, 99, 100, 103
  Native alliances, 27–31, 35–40, 102, 106–107
  property rights, 114–115
  Seven Years' War and, 227–228
  social control, 125–126
Newyash, 273
Niagara District Council, 409, 410
Niagara Mail, 284
Niblock, Thomas, 469
Nichol, Robert, 284
Nichol, Theresa, 284
Nicholson, Francis, 145, 148, 154
Nicks, John, 83
Nisga'a, 540
Niverville, C.B. de, 559–560
Nlaka'pamux, contact narratives, 47–60
NokanekautkEn, 51
Nolin, Dolphis, 498
Normal schools, 365
Norte, Martin, 502
North West Company (NWC), 217, 388, 391, 398–399
Nor'Wester newspaper, 493, 494
Nor'Westers, 72, 84–84
Nova Scotia
  Acadian refusal to swear allegiance, 145, 150–151, 153–154
  and American Revolution, 238–248
  boundary survey, 159
  British attempts to elicit Acadian allegiance, 150–151, 154–157
  Chignecto Isthmus region, 239–240
  civilian government, 148–150, 151–152
  Eddy Rebellion of 1776, 239–248
  female teachers, 362, 363, 365
  judicial functions, 150
  lack of Protestant subjects, 147, 148, 153

Native peoples, 146, 153, 158, 159, 160
New England settlers, 160, 238–240
  raids by American privateers, 245
  religious revival, 235–246
  underfunding by metropolitan government, 149, 153, 157–158
  Yorkshire immigrants, 239, 244

Oakes, Forrest, 218, 219
O'Brien, Lucius Simon, 529–530
O'Connell, Daniel, 414
O'Connell, Father, 351
O'Connor, Frank, 286
Ojibwa/Ojibway, 64, 175, 273
Olivier, Louis-August, 568
Ontario Historical Society, 286, 289
Orange Order
  anti-Catholicism, 449, 452
  and Irish Catholic immigration, 452–453
  membership, 451
  and nativism, 447, 449–450, 459
  Orange/Green confrontations, 423, 453–458
  origins, 450
  and Protestantism, 450, 452
  racism, 453
  and social violence, 447–464
  vigilantism, 452, 453, 458
Orcadian employees, Hudson's Bay Company, 79, 83
Orkney labourers, 79, 83
Ostracism, and social control, 99
Ottawa nation, 174, 192–193, 194, 271, 273
Ouche, Alic, 100
Oudle, Catherine, 345
Ouellet, Fernand, 214, 324

Pacquette, Justine, 502
Page, John, 172
Palliser, Hugh, 336
Palliser, John, 492, 505, 509
Papineau, Louis-Joseph, 373
Parent, Etienne, 373, 377, 382
Parenteau, Catherine, 502
Parkman, Francis, 214
parti patriote, 304, 309, 321, 373
Pascal, 505
Paternalism, 389
  mutuality and, 391
  and social organization of fur trade, 390

and "theatre of daily rule,"
393–395, 401
"theatre of resistance, 395–397, 401
Paternity suits, 344–345, 352
Paterson, Alexander, 218
Patriarchal family, 78
Patrick, William, 577–578
Patriot raids, 326, 327–328
Patronage, 219–221, 285
Payette, Baptiste, 504
Payette, Jean-Baptiste, 126
Peel, Mildred, 286
Peltier, Baptiste, 505
Pennington, J.W.C., 438
Pentland, H.C., 409, 411, 413
Perkins, Joseph, 274
Peters, Thomas W., Jr., 451
Petit-Boismorel, Françoise, 120
Petroglyphs, 17
Philipps, Erasmus James, 156
Philipps, Richard, 137, 147, 148,
152, 153, 155, 156, 160
Philips, Louis, 53–54, 56
Phyn and Ellice, 218, 220
Pieau, Pierre du, 104
Pioneer Society of San Francisco, 541
Pitt, William, 227
Plains of Abraham. *See* Battle
of Quebec
Plante, Antoine, 504
Poitras family, 504
Police force, public works, 422–423
Political parties, emergence of, 317
Pomeroy, Seth, 179
Pontiac's Rebellion, 160, 168,
217, 232
Pontleroy, Major, 208
Porkeaters (*mangeurs du lard*), 389
Porteous, John, 218
Potawatomi, 174, 193, 271
Potawatomi nation, 273
Potter-MacKinnon, Janice, 283
Potts, John, 84
Poudret, Antoine, Jr., 126
Powell, John, 321
Power, Catharine, 346, 349
Power, Samuel, 410, 415, 416, 417,
418, 420, 422
Presentation nuns, 351, 352
Prince, John, 327
Pritchard, Johnny, 498
Property rights, and separation,
114–115
Prostitution, 346
Provincial Freeman, 438, 440, 442, 443
Provincial Training School for
teachers (St. John), 362

Provincial Union Association,
442–443
Pruden, Peter, 501, 502
Prudis, Harriet, 286
Public relief, 411
Public shaming, 99, 126, 302, 398
Puritanism, and sexuality, 335

Quarantine, 172
Quebec
British naval blocade, 227–228
and Confederation, 554–566
independence option, 561–562
smallpox outbreak, 176–177
Quebec Act, 160
Quebec Committee on Reform and
Progress, 377
Quebec Conference, 559
Quebec Gazette, 218, 222
Quebec Marine Hospital, 375
Quebec Resolutions, 555, 556, 557,
559, 568
Queen Victoria Benevolent
Society, 443
Quilting bees, 466, 474–475
Quinn, Tom, 498
Quitrents, 147, 157–158

Race, racism
intermarriage, 542, 544
marginalization of Aboriginal
peoples, 534, 537–538,
540–541, 542, 544, 546
Orangeism, 453
and people of mixed ancestry,
518–537
and social hierarchy, 518–537
stereotyping, 520, 533
Racette, Charles, 505
Racette, Margaret, 502
Rae, John, 499, 504
Ragueneau, Father, 102
Ramezay, J.-B.-N.-R., Sieur de, 106,
107, 208
Rape. *See* Sexual assault
Rebellion of 1837–38
Brantford area, 322–323
Catholic Church, 309
causes, 323–325
economic downturn, 318–319
insurgents, 324–325, 327
Lower Canada, 304, 309, 321
middle-class professionals, 309
outcomes, 328–329
Patriot raids, 326, 327–328
political charivaris, 304–311
political unions, 319

popular discontent, 316–318
reformers, 317
and responsible government,
328–329
Toronto, 321–322
Upper Canada, 313–329
Recollet, 30
Red River settlement
anti-Hudson's Bay Company
sentiments in, 492, 493
creation of, 85
and Crown Colony status, 491,
493, 496
relations between Métis and
mixed-bloods, 497–514
religious tensions, 490,
492–496, 498
social divisions, 509
social groupings, 490
Reform Bill of 1832, 317
Reform party, 373, 576–580
Reine, Michel, 500
Relief of Destitute Colored
Fugitives, 443
Religious revival, 235–246
Rensaeller, Rensaeller Van, 326
Reparation ceremony, 102–103
Reparation payments, 26, 99, 100, 102
Representation by population ("rep
by pop"), 557, 562, 570, 577
Reserve system, 278
Residuary power, 568, 574–576
Responsible government, 317,
328, 573
La Revue canadienne, 377
Rich, E.E., 214
Richardson, John, 70
Rideau Canal, 413
Riel, Louis, Sr., 493, 508
Rivers and Streams Act, 572
Robert Lowe, 544
Roberts, Simon, 99
Robertson, Colin, 89
Robillard, Baptiste, 499
Robinson, Beverley, 250
Robinson, John Beverley, 315, 578
Robinson, Nancy, 250, 252
Robinson, Peter, 315
Robinson, William, 315
Rocheblave, Pierre de, 391
Roger, Joseph, 126
Rogers, Sam, 241, 243
Rolph, John, 321, 327
Ross, Alexander, 65, 393, 491, 498,
501, 504, 530
Ross, Charles, 518, 524, 529
Ross, Charles, Jr., 530–531

Ross, Flora, 530
Ross, Francis, 530
Ross, Isabella, 522, 529, 530
Ross, James, 491, 493, 494, 495
Ross, John, 505, 529
Ross, Walter, 524
Ross, William, 530
Rouges, and Confederation debate, 555, 557
Roundhead, 273
Rowand, John, 501
Rowand, Margaret, 499
Rowe, Zebulon, 241
Roy, Pierre, 124
Royal Artillery, 275
Royal Canadian Rifles, 423–424
Royal Fencibles, 242, 244
Royal Proclamation of 1763, 213
Ryerson, Egerton, 363

Sabiston, William, 505
Said, Edward, 251
St. Alban's raid, 561
St. Catharines Journal, 410, 411, 415
St. Croix, Ann, 349
St. Germain, 507
St. Paul. *See* Lolo, Jean-Baptiste
St. Pierre, Pierre, 503
Saint-Vallier, Jean Baptiste de la Croix-Chevrières de, 115
Sanderson, George, Jr., 497, 499
Sandison, David, 502
Sapir, Edward, 48
Sauk nation, 271, 273, 274, 275
Saunders, John, 340
Saunders, Vice-Admiral, 208
Saunderson, George, Jr., 504
Saunderson, George, Sr., 500, 502
"Savage people," accepted rules of warfare on, 179
Sayer trial, 506
Secord, Charles, 284
Secord, Harriet, 289
Secord, James, 283, 287, 288
Secord, Laura
    commemoration of, 281–294
    and ideals of "Canadian womanhood," 282–283, 288–290
    and Loyalist tradition, 287–288
    patronage, 284–285
    racialized gender, 281–288
Secret societies, 418–419
Seduction suits, 344
Séguin, Robert-Lionel, 124, 125
Self-help, self-reliance, 442
Selkirk, Lord, 85, 398

SEmalitsa, 51–52, 53, 57
Sennett, Richard, 251
Separate Schools Act (1850), 442
Separation
    decisions rendered, 122–123
    grievances of women, 117–121
    grounds for, 115–117
    and legal capacity of women, 114
    in New France, 112–130
    types of application for, 116
Sergeant, Henry, 81
Seven Years' War, 232
    allegations of biological warfare, 167–170
    Britain and, 227–229
    and fall of New France, 227–228
    smallpox, 174–175
Sewell, Jonathan, 399
Sexual assault, 346–347, 352
Seymour, Frederick, 538
Shaboyee, Nancy, 502
Shad, Isaac, 440
Shadd, Abraham, 437
Shadd, Amelia Freeman, 440, 441
Shadd, Elizabeth (Williams Shreve), 436
Shadd, Harriet Parnell, 437
Shadd, Mary Ann, 435, 436, 437–438, 440, 441–442, 443
Shawnee nation, 271, 273
Sheppard, George, 265, 266
Shipboy, Thomas, 221
Shirley, William, 137
Short, Susannah, 503
Shreve, Elizabeth Jackson Shadd, 434, 439
Shurdan, John Batish, 503
Sicotte, Louis-Victor, 570
Signay, Joseph, 375
Sillon, Pierre, 124
Simcoe, John Graves, 262
Simpson, Sir George, 71, 76, 86–89, 508, 509, 529
Simpson, John, 499, 505
Simpson, Thomas, 499
Sinclair, Betsy, 86, 87
Sinclair, James, 505, 507, 508, 509
Sinclair, Samuel, 505
Sinclair, Thomas, 505
Sinclair, William, II, 509
Sinclair family, 471–472
Sioui decision (1990), 98
Sir Robert Peel, 327
Six Nations' Confederacy, 269
Six Nations' Reserve, 323
"Skimmington," 299
Slavery, 232

Smallpox
    American Revolution, 175–178
    Fort Pitt incident, 167–170
    inoculation, 172–173
    Native peoples, 168–170, 174–175, 191–193, 195–197
    quarantine, 172
    symptoms of, 170–171
    transmission of, 171–172
    Variola virus, 170
    See also Biological warfare
Smith family (Dundas County), 478
Smithurst, John, 504
Smuggling, 264
Social control
    charivaris, 126, 303–304
    Native forms of, 98–100
    public gossip and, 125–126
Society for the Propagation of the Gospel, 338
Solomons, Ezekiel, 218
Solomons, Levy, 218
Soulés, François, 177
Sparrow decision (1987), 87
Spence, Andrew, 502
Spence, Harriet, 503
Spence, William, 503
Split Log, 273
Sproat, Gilbert Malcolm, 542, 543, 545
Stacey, C.P., 208–209, 211
Staines, Emma, 525
Staines, Robert, 525
Staisulis, Daiva, 537
Stanley, George F.G., 190, 509
Stevens, Wayne E., 214
Stevenson, Edmund, 505
Stewart, Frances, 472
Stewart, James, 495, 496
Stone, Lawrence, 250
Stoverville (Stouffville), Rebellion of 1837–38, 321
Strachan, John, 263, 315
Strike-breaking, 422, 424
Strikes, 399, 417, 418, 420
Strong-Boag, Veronica, 77
Stuart, John Charles, 397
Sullivan, Robert Baldwin, 572, 578
Sulte, Benjamin, 554
Sutherland, Alexander, 501
Sutherland, Daniel, 396
Sutherland, John, 501
Sutherland, Kate, 501
Sutherland, Robert, 505
Sutherland, William, 503
Swain, James, 502, 503
Swain, John, 503

Sydenham, Charles Poulett Thomson, Baron, 284
Sylvain, Timothée, 120

Taché, Bishop, 493
Taché, Sir E.-P., 560, 562, 570, 578
Tait, John, 496
Tait, Robert, 501
Talon, Jean, 104
Tarleton, Banastre, 180
Tate, Jeanette, 499
Taylor, George, 505
Taylor, Margaret, 88
Taylor, Margarette, 503
Taylor, William, 380
Taylor, William Henry, 496
Taylor, Zachary, 275
TcexawatEn, 51
Tcexe'x, 52
Teachers, teaching
    Blacks, 437–438
    elementary school, 362–364
    feminization of teaching, 360–372
    gendered pay gap, 362–363, 365–368
    and job options for women, 368
    respectability of, 439
    women's perspective on, 369–370
Tecumseh, 271, 273
Teit, James, 48, 49–50, 51
Temperance movement
    Chiniquy crusade, 372–384
    ecclesiastical leadership and, 373, 374, 375, 378
    leadership of French-Canadian movement, 373–374
    and patriotic reform, 373, 377–378, 379, 382
    secular liberals and, 374, 376–377
Tetlenitsa, John, 50
Thacher, James, 178
Thanadelthur, 66–67
"Theatre of daily rule," 393–395, 401
"Theatre of resistance," 395–397, 401
Thibodeau, Catherine, 137
Thom, Adam, 491, 508
Thomas, Charles, 499
Thomas, Maria, 494
Thompson, David, 64, 68
Thompson, Elizabeth, 289
Thompson, E.P., 303, 391
Thomson, John (bourgeois), 400
Thomson, John (gentleman farmer), 471, 472

Thomson, William, 83
Thorburn, David, 413, 415, 417
Thucydides, 178
Tilly, Charles, 298
Tlingit, 540
Tod, James, 524–525, 532
Tod, John, 518, 524, 528
Tod, Mary (Mrs. J.S. Bowker), 532
Todd, Alpheus, 557
Todd, Isaac, 218, 219
Tolmie, Simon Fraser, 534
Tolmie, W.F., 528
Toma, Catherine (Mrs. Charles Ross, Jr.), 531
Tomah, 273
Tonaktouan, Nicolas, 104
Tories
    fear of American threat, 316
    political elite, 314–316
Toronto Ladies' Association, 443
Toronto Women's Literary Society, 284
Toronto World and Mail, 285
Traill, Catharine Parr, 470, 471
Traill, Walter, 508
Treathey, Catherine, 502
Treaty of Aix-la-Chapelle, 159
Treaty of Paris (1763), 160, 264
Treaty of Paris (1783), 160
Treaty of Utrecht, 145, 153
Treble, J.B., 416
Trelease, A.W., 35
Trent, William, 168, 169
Trigger, Bruce G., 102
Trotier Desauniers, Thomas-Ignace, 217
Trottier, Adal, 507
Troupes de la Marine, 113
Truche, Loraine, 503
Truche, Suzette, 503
Truck system
    canal construction, 412
    fur trade, 398
    Newfoundland fisheries, 339, 350
Trudel, Marcel, 112, 373, 381
True Band of Chatham, 442
True bands, 442
Tsimshian, 540
Tupper, Charles, 568, 575
Turner, Terence, 49
"turning off," 72, 84
Turnor, Philip, 393
Turtle's Heart (Delaware nation), 168
Twenty-Fourth United States Infantry, 274
Tynemouth, 544
Typhus, 171

Ultramontanism, 373
Umphreville, Edward, 396
Underground Railroad, 434, 435
Union of 1840, 557
United Empire Loyalists. See Loyalists
United States, 316
    Manifest Destiny, 278
    threat to independent Quebec, 561–562
Upper Canada
    Assembly, 314
    clergy reserves, 316
    creation of, 414
    Crown reserves, 316
    economic conditions, 318–319, 323
    election of 1836, 318
    female teachers, 362, 363, 364, 365
    immigration (1830s), 323–324
    land speculation, 316
    North American orientation of, 261–264
    political elite, 262–263, 314–316

Vaccination, 172
Valade, Marie-Josephe, 124
Valade, Sister, 493
Valet, Baptiste, 505
VanAllen family (Dundas County), 476, 478
Vancouver Island, British colony, 538
Van Egmond, Anthony, 322
Van Kirk, Sylvia, 77
Van Slyke, Cornelius, 174
Varennes, Marie-Renée Gauthier de, 120
Variola virus
    control of, 171–173
    incubation period, 170
    infection, 170–171
    smallpox, 170
    transmission of, 171–172
Vattel, Emmerich de, 178, 180
Vaudreuil, Pierre de Rigaud de, 105, 106, 191
Veco, Baptist, 156
Vendezeque, Marie, 124
Verchères, Madeleine de, 283
Vérendrye, Pierre Gauthier de la, 120
Vermette, Joseph, 505
Vernet, Nicholas, 118
Verney, Harry, 543
Vetch, Samuel, 148

Veto power
    federal, 560, 568, 572, 573
    imperial, 573
Victoria, fur trade families, 518–537
Violence
    charivaris, 303, 306–307, 308, 310
    domestic, 115–116, 118–121,
        348, 352
    drunkenness and, 105–106
    female, 340–341
    husbands right to correct and,
        118–119
    labour conflict, 420
    in master–servant
        relationships, 398
    reciprocal work bees, 469
    and "rugged" ethos, 394–395
    sectarianism, 447–463
    sectional rivalry, 415–416
    sexual assault, 346–347, 352
    wife-battering, 118–119
    against women, 72–73, 341,
        346–347, 348
Virginia Committee of Safety, 172
Voice of the Fugitive, 440
Voyageurs, 274
    better wages, demands for, 396
    complaints, 395–396
    contract-jumping, 392
    cultural liminality, 388
    desertion, 392, 397, 399, 400
    engagement contracts, 391
    freetrading, 397
    gender identity, 388
    indebtedness, 398–399
    legal action for wages, 393
    manly violence, 394–395
    neglect of duty, 396, 397
    occupational lines, 389
    theft, 396–397

Wabanaki, 4–22
    belief system, 4–5
    dress, 12–13
    habitat, 5–6
    health, 12
    map making, 15–17
    material culture, 7–8
    mode of subsistence, 8–10
    nations of, 6
    Native place-names, 14–15
    political organization, 6–7
    trade networks, 11
Walker, Thomas, 218
Walk-in-the-Water, 273
Wallace, W.S., 214, 287
Walsh, William, 345

Wampum, 99, 102
War of 1812
    British–Native relations,
        270–272
    Canadian propaganda
        campaign, 266
    Chesapeake Affair, 265
    Detroit front, 273
    impact of, 266
    indifference of Upper
        Canadians, 260–268
    Lake Erie, 273
    Laura Secord and, 288
    Native peoples and, 268–281
    Northwest front, 278
    peace treaty, terms of, 276–277
    in popular culture, 260–261
    upper Mississippi front, 274–277
War of the Austrian Succession, 159
Warren, William, 175
Warring, John, 502
Washington, George, 175, 176, 240,
    241, 242
Wasuloski, John, 500
Waxtko, 51, 52, 57
Wayne, Anthony Wayne, 265
Webster, J.C., 239
Welfare
    absence of public relief, 411
    benevolent associations, 442–443
Welland Canal, 409, 414, 416, 417,
    418, 420, 421, 423
Welland Canal Company, 316
Wells, William Benjamin, 327
Welsh, Nobert, 498, 501
West, John, 70, 71
West India Company, 114
Wetherall, Captain, 415, 417, 420,
    422, 423
Wheler, Francis, 336
Whipping, for delinquency, 398
Whipple, George, 441
Whitford, François, 504
Whitford, James, 505
Wikhegan, 15–16
Wilkie, Jean-Baptiste, 501
William III, 450
Williamsburg Canals, 409, 410, 411,
    414, 418, 420, 421, 422
Wilmot, Mayor, 457
Wilson, Charles, 525, 527
Wilson, James, 504
Winnebago, 271, 275
Winslow, Edward, 249–250, 252
Winslow, Mary, 249, 252
Wolfe, James, 206, 207, 209,
    210, 212

Woman's Literary Club, 282
Women
    alternative belief system, 340
    assisted female immigration,
        544–545
    black pioneers, 434–447
    and commemoration of Laura
        Secord, 281–294
    community activism, 438–443
    Conquest and, 231
    economic role of plebian
        women, 338–340, 343
    female violence, 340–341
    honour and reputation of,
        125–126
    interest in history, 285–286
    Irish woman immigrant, image
        of, 336
    legal capacity of, 114–115
    Loyalist, 249–250, 252
    management of family
        estates, 115
    prescribed role as wives,
        121, 252
    property rights, 114, 116–117
    and seduction suits, 344
    See also Class; First Nations
        women; Gender; Marriages;
        Teachers, teaching; Violence
Women's Canadian Historical
    Society (WCHS), 284
Women's Christian Temperance
    Union, 285
Women's Home Missionary
    Society, 439
Women's Institute of Queenston and
    St. David's, 286
Work, David, 528
Work, John, 518, 522, 524
Work, John, Jr., 528–529, 532
Work, Josette, 522, 527
Work, Mary, 532
Work, Sarah (Mrs. Roderick
    Finlayson), 529
Workman family (Dundas
    County), 478
Worthington, Mary. See Bliss, Mary
Wren, Charles, 530
Wroth, Robert, 156
Wyandot, 194
Wyandot nation, 273

XY Company, 391

Yellow fever, 171
York, Annie, 55–56, 57
York Point riot of 1849, 456–458